Ancient Near Eastern Texts
Relating to the Old Testament

TRANSLATORS AND ANNOTATORS

W. F. Albright, Johns Hopkins University
H. L. Ginsberg, Jewish Theological Seminary
Albrecht Goetze, Yale University
S. N. Kramer, University of Pennsylvania
Theophile J. Meek, University of Toronto
A. Leo Oppenheim, University of Chicago
Robert H. Pfeiffer, Harvard University
A. Sachs, Brown University
E. A. Speiser, University of Pennsylvania
Ferris J. Stephens, Yale University
John A. Wilson, University of Chicago

ANCIENT NEAR EASTERN TEXTS

RELATING TO THE OLD TESTAMENT

EDITED BY JAMES B. PRITCHARD

PRINCETON, NEW JERSEY
PRINCETON UNIVERSITY PRESS
1950

LONDON: GEOFFREY CUMBERLEGE, OXFORD UNIVERSITY PRESS

Printed in the United States of America
by Princeton University Press at Princeton, New Jersey

Contents

II. LEGAL TEXTS

III. HISTORICAL TEXTS

V. HYMNS AND PRAYERS

VI. DIDACTIC AND WISDOM LITERATURE

VII. LAMENTATIONS

VIII. SECULAR SONGS AND POEMS

IX. LETTERS

X. MISCELLANEOUS TEXTS

Introduction

THE ancient Near East, until about a century ago, had as its chief witness the text of the Hebrew Bible. Relatively insignificant was the evidence recovered from sources outside the Bible; that which had been found had not been sufficiently understood to serve as a reliable historical source. Through explorations and excavations carried on within the last century in Egypt, Mesopotamia, Asia Minor, and Syria, a wealth of new information has become available. This new light from extrabiblical texts has served not only to enlarge immeasurably the horizon for a knowledge of the ancient Near East, but it has also sharpened considerably the understanding of the content of the Bible itself. Not infrequently has an interest in biblical history and literature led those who pursued it into fields of discovery which have had far-reaching significance for humanistic studies in general. Hitherto unknown languages with considerable literatures have been the by-products of activity begun by those interested primarily in biblical research. The results of the labor of those whose interest led them beyond the narrower confines have now become the tools of all biblical scholars.

The purpose of this work is to make available to students of the ancient Near East—serious students of the Old Testament, we believe, are necessarily such—the most important extrabiblical texts in translations which represent the best understanding which present-day scholarship has achieved. Many of the relevant texts have been hitherto accessible only in obscure and highly technical journals. Some have been circulated widely in translations which represent a stage of understanding now happily superseded by more thorough study. Yet other texts included here have not hitherto been published in translation into a modern language.

This is not the first attempt of its kind. Extrabiblical sources have long been considered important for an understanding of the Hebrew Bible. Almost three centuries ago, John Spencer, Master of Corpus Christi College in Cambridge, sought to interpret the ritual laws of the Hebrews in the light of the relevant material from Egypt, Greece, and Rome.[1] As early as 1714, Hadrian Reland of Utrecht published his monumental work on Palestinian geography,[2] in which he recognized the importance of the monuments for biblical study. W. Robertson Smith[3] and Julius Wellhausen,[4] in the latter part of the nineteenth century, found in the literature of Arabia a point of vantage for a better understanding of biblical customs and institutions.

The importance of Assyriology for biblical studies was widely heralded through the spectacular announcements of George Smith. In a paper read before the Society of Biblical Archaeology on December 3, 1872, Smith gave translations from the Assyrian account of the flood and predicted that "we may expect many other discoveries throwing light on these ancient periods."[5] Two years later he described the fragments of an extrabiblical account of creation in a letter to the London *Daily Telegraph*.[6] These sensational announcements served to create interest among biblical scholars in the science of Assyriology, as well as to elicit popular support for further excavation and research. At about the same time that England was becoming aware of the significance of cuneiform studies, Eberhard Schrader published his *Die Keilinschriften und das alte Testament* (1872), a work which enjoyed the popularity of successive editions in German and an English translation.[7] Schrader's arrangement of the relevant cuneiform material was in the form of a commentary upon the canonical books. Later, H. Winckler published a textbook of the cuneiform inscriptions illustrating the biblical material; this appeared in three editions.[8]

1 *De legibus Hebraeorum ritualibus et earum rationibus* (Cambridge, 1685).

2 *Palaestina ex monumentis veteribus illustrata.*

3 *Kinship and Marriage in Early Arabia* (1885).

4 *Reste arabischen Heidentums* (1887).

5 *Transactions of the Society of Biblical Archaeology*, II (1873), 213-234.

6 March 4, 1875.

7 Second ed., 1883; 3rd ed., entirely rewritten by H. Zimmern and H. Winckler, 1903; English translation of 2nd ed. by O. C. Whitehouse, I (1885), II (1888).

8 *Keilinschriftliches Textbuch zum alten Testament* (Leipzig, 1892, 1903, 1909).

In the same year in which the third edition of Winckler's textbook appeared, Hugo Gressmann published his *Altorientalische Texte und Bilder zum alten Testamente* (1909). As general editor, Gressmann was responsible for the choice of the pictures and the accompanying descriptions; A. Ungnad and H. Ranke translated the texts. Ranke's translations of the Egyptian texts marked the first important collection of Egyptian material made with special reference to the Old Testament. Gressmann, in his general introduction to the work, emphasized the goals of objectivity and completeness. The translations should serve, he maintained, not only for comparison and illustration, but for contrast. This cooperative enterprise was successful, in that this work quickly became a standard work of reference for biblical scholars. By 1926 the discoveries of new texts and the improved understanding of old ones warranted an entirely new edition of Gressmann's *Texte und Bilder*.[9] The quantity of translations was almost doubled. Ranke translated the Egyptian texts; E. Ebeling was responsible for the Babylonian-Assyrian ones; Gressmann offered the North Semitic inscriptions and papyri; and N. Rhodokanakis translated a selection of South Arabic inscriptions. This work has remained until now as the most useful collection of extrabiblical material bearing upon the Old Testament. For the service rendered to French readers, mention should be made of Charles-F. Jean, *La littérature des Babyloniens et des Assyriens* (Paris, 1924), where many of the relevant texts are translated. A more popular treatment of the significance of the extrabiblical material appeared in A. Jeremias, *Das alte Testament im Lichte des alten Orients*, which first appeared in 1904. This book appeared in four German editions and in a two-volume translation into English.[10]

R. W. Rogers was the first to assemble and to present in English translation a collection of the cuneiform texts bearing upon the Old Testament. In 1912 there appeared his *Cuneiform Parallels to the Old Testament*, in which the available material was given in transliteration and translation; a second edition appeared in 1926. Even more widely used by English-speaking students of the Bible was G. A. Barton's *Archaeology and the Bible*, which first appeared in 1916, containing in Part II a generous selection of translations of Near Eastern texts, those from cuneiform having been translated by Barton himself. The translations were interspersed with notes calling attention to the biblical parallels. Barton revised this book periodically, bringing in new texts as they appeared; the seventh edition was published in 1937. Invaluable service has been rendered by this popular book in making widely known the epigraphic material which is of importance for biblical study. For English translations of Egyptian literature, students have been able to make use of the works of J. H. Breasted,[11] A. Erman,[12] and T. E. Peet.[13]

The embarrassing wealth of comparative material from the ancient Near East has made the task of selecting texts for the present volume a difficult one. Two criteria have been used in choosing the material. First, an attempt has been made to include those texts which have, from time to time, been cited in recognized commentaries as parallel to, or illustrative of, certain passages in the Old Testament. Frequently the appearance of a biblical name has been the criterion for inclusion. In other cases a treatment of a biblical theme by the writer of a text has occasioned the selection. In yet other instances a text has been included because it is representative of a type of literature—such as prayer, lamentation, ritual—which figures prominently in the Old Testament. In no case does the selection of a text commit the editor or the translator to a particular view with regard to the relationship of a biblical passage to extrabiblical material. Secondly, an attempt has been made in selecting texts for this volume to give representative types of literary expression from each of the linguistic and cultural areas of the ancient Near East. This standard has arisen out of a desire to give as broad an interpretation as possible to parallels. Relationships of the Israelites to their neigh-

[9] *Bilder* appeared in 1927.

[10] Second ed., 1906; 3rd ed., 1916; 4th ed., 1930; *The Old Testament in the Light of the Ancient East*, 2 vols. (London, 1911).

[11] *Ancient Records of Egypt*, I-V (Chicago, 1906-07); *Development of Religion and Thought in Ancient Egypt* (New York, 1912); *The Dawn of Conscience* (New York, 1934).

[12] *The Literature of the Ancient Egyptians*, translated into English by A. M. Blackman (London, 1927).

[13] *A Comparative Study of the Literatures of Egypt, Palestine, and Mesopotamia* (London, 1931).

bors can be seen to best advantage only when there is a fairly comprehensive picture of the neighbors. Thus there has been attempted a fair sampling of the extant literature from quarters contiguous to Palestine. This broader selection of materials serves yet another purpose: it makes the collection of use to students of other phases of the history of the ancient Near East.

While this is the largest collection of translations of texts relating to the Old Testament yet made, two practical considerations have limited our attainment of the goal of a truly representative selection. First, the accidents of discovery have frequently—to judge from past experience—presented anything but a representative sampling of the epigraphic material of a particular culture. Thus it may well be that certain types of literary expression from a given area have turned up in abundance, while other types of texts remain either entirely unrepresented, or with but few examples. In appraising any area or period one must keep in mind the real possibility that the sampling obtained from excavations may not necessarily be representative. Secondly, the availability of competent scholars, who could give useful translations of the known texts, has limited at a few points the selection offered in this volume. Certain areas are represented by only a few examples of texts because of the limitations which other duties or interests imposed on the scholars best equipped to make trustworthy translations. No compromise in the quality of translation was considered worth making in the interest of achieving the ideal of a completely representative selection. It should be noted, however, that the number of competent scholars who have contributed to this project is several times more than that of those who have engaged hitherto in such an undertaking.

Particularly baffling has been the problem of selecting Babylonian and Assyrian historical texts. Obviously the more important records of Babylonian and Assyrian kings mentioned in the Old Testament should be included—particularly those texts which describe campaigns conducted in Palestine and Syria. The reference in a text to a place or person known from the Bible often has been the criterion for inclusion. This selection with its index should place within ready reach the cuneiform texts containing geographical information about Syro-Palestine as it was recorded by the royal scribes of the invaders from Mesopotamia. While no claim is made for an exhaustive listing of the Palestinian place names in the records from Mesopotamia, one may expect to find here the more important references found in the texts preserved from each of the major periods of Mesopotamian history from the beginning down through the early part of the third century B.C.

In addition to the specifically historical material there has been included for each major period of Mesopotamian history a representative selection of historiographic documents, as illustrations of the methods employed by the chroniclers of the names of kings, the years, and the important events in history. These texts, while obviously not relevant to the content of the Old Testament, have been considered important as background material, throwing light upon the methods of ancient historical science.

While Gressmann's *Altorientalische Texte zum alten Testament* has served as a basis for discussion in the making of the present choice, the selection is a new one. The editor has had the cooperation of the contributors in this task. He, rather than they, must shoulder the final responsibility for the choice made. References are frequently given to significant discussions of the relationship of the texts to biblical passages in order that the student may form his own opinion of the relation of Israel to the surrounding world. The references in the footnotes to biblical material are intended to help the honest student, not to cajole him. It is hoped that this volume of translations, intended primarily for students of the Old Testament, will serve to give a perspective for a better understanding of the likenesses and the differences which existed between Israel and the surrounding cultures.

The arrangement of the texts is according to literary types. The advantage of this order over that followed by Gressmann was first suggested by Professor Ferris J. Stephens: the greatest number of readers will approach this work from an interest in the Old Testament rather than primarily from an interest in one of the other linguistic or cultural areas. For those whose interest is regional or linguistic, there has been compiled a second table of contents listing the texts according to languages.

The form of the presentation of each text aims at supplying the reader with the greatest amount of help within the least possible space. Brief introductions are given, as a rule, to the translations. They are calculated to supply, when available, the following information: a title which indicates something of the contents of the text, the provenience, the date of composition and of the actual writing of the particular text translated, the original or official publication, important translations, references to important discussions or commentaries, and other bibliographical references which might be useful to the reader. In some cases, where the contents of the text are very obscure, a brief note of interpretation has been added. An attempt has been made to keep the introductions brief so that as many texts as possible could be included in the volume. The introduction to the text and the annotations printed in the footnotes are the work of the translator whose name appears at the beginning of the section.

The general form of citation and of reference claims only the authority of general usage. At many points, what prevails as general usage in a particular discipline has been surrendered in the interest of consistency throughout the volume. Only in rare instances could the editor find such ancient authority for his demands as in the case of the numbering of every tenth line of poetry, a practice to be seen, for example, in certain cuneiform texts.[14] More frequently he has had to adopt a rule and adhere to it, in spite of the good-natured taunts of the contributors. In the interest of readability the text of the translation proper has been kept as free as possible from diacritics. Normalized spellings of proper names have been employed within the translations. This means, for example, that proper names from cuneiform sources have the simple *h* for the *ḫ*, to which cuneiformists are accustomed. Thus, every *h* in proper names from cuneiform texts, except those preceded by *s*, represents the *ḫ*. Also, in the normalization of proper names the *š* is rendered as *sh*. Unless some serious misunderstanding is likely to result the differences between *s* and *ṣ*, *t* and *ṭ*, are not indicated in proper names appearing in the translations. The name of the Assyrian god *Aššur* has been normalized to *Ashur*, despite the fact that this form so widely used in English publications does not indicate the doubling of the *š*. Italics within the translations have been used for two purposes: first, to designate a doubtful translation of a known text; secondly, to indicate transliterations. While this second use of italics has been the general rule, in some cases it was necessary to differentiate the languages in transliterations. Here practices prevailing in the particular discipline to which the text belongs have been followed. For example, in texts where it was necessary to indicate that the transliteration was Sumerian, letter-spaced Roman was used; italic was used for the Akkadian; small capitals were used to indicate the ideogram or the cuneiform sign. In transliterations of Akkadian words diacritics have been omitted from all determinatives (indicated by superior letters).

Square brackets have been used for restorations; round brackets (parentheses) indicate interpolations made by the translator for a better understanding of the translation. Obvious scribal omissions have been placed between triangular brackets; braces indicate instances of scribal repetition of material. In the translations from Ugaritic, half square brackets have been used to designate a text which has been partly restored.

A lacuna has been indicated by three dots; in case the lacuna comes before a final sentence dot, four dots appear. Following customary usage in some disciplines, a lacuna in which the text is wholly damaged or missing has been indicated in some translations by three dots enclosed within square brackets. The length of a long broken portion of text has sometimes been indicated by the translator with a statement within parentheses. Short breaks generally have not been indicated as to length; three dots may thus mean a break from as little as one sign or symbol to entire lines or passages. It has been assumed that readers who could make effective use of the information concerning the length of the missing portion of the text would be likely to have access to the original text or its transliteration.

References to the tablets, columns, lines of the text have been given usually in parentheses either within the translation, as in prose, or in the right-hand margin, when the form is poetry. Capital Roman numerals indicate the number of the tablet or some other well-recognized division; lower-

[14] e.g. *CT*, XIII (1901), 14-15; K 13,761 (King, *STC*, I, 164).

case Roman numerals have been used for columns; Arabic numerals indicate the line or lines. The Egyptian hieratic texts often used rubrics for emphasis or punctuation: passages in red ink, where the general context was in black ink. The translations of these texts use small-capital letters to indicate such rubrics.

It is a source of considerable pride that there have been eleven translators who have cooperated to produce this volume. Each is a specialist within the field with which he deals. The competence of the several translators is attested by the scientific literature which they have contributed upon various problems within their respective fields. In many cases the translators have had first-hand acquaintance with the texts themselves; in every case the translator has made use of the original or scientific publication of the text which he has translated. Because of the original character of this work the contributors to the volume have frequently felt it necessary to include in the footnotes matters of considerably more technical nature than the non-specialist is likely to utilize. These notes, it is hoped, will not distract the general reader. They will be of service, where they appear, to the more specialized reader in enabling him to see the grounds for some of the newer readings and translations offered in this volume.

The spirit of cooperative scholarship has been apparent throughout the four years this volume has been in preparation. On occasions it has been possible for members of the group to meet together for discussion of the various problems arising out of this collaboration. An advisory committee of three of the contributors has frequently advised the editor on problems which have arisen. The spirit of give-and-take has been evident in the willingness of each of the contributors to submit his completed manuscript to another member of the group for careful reading before publication. While each of the translators bears the sole responsibility for his work, not infrequently have criticisms given by colleagues been gratefully incorporated into the final draft.

A word should be said about the particular difficulty of finding general agreement on chronology. Each translator has been responsible for the dates found within the introductions and notes to his own contribution. Attempt has been made, however, to iron out as much of the discrepancy as possible and to offer to the reader a chronology which represents fairly widely held views.

Egyptian chronology is still in a state of flux, with major uncertainty for dates before 2500 B.C. and the possibility of minor adjustment for dates after 2000 B.C. The dates suggested in this volume are tentative and are often given in terms of the nearest round number. For example, Amen-em-het III is stated to have reigned "about 1840-1790" rather than "1839-1791, with about two years' margin of error"; the Old Kingdom is dated "about 2700-2200" rather than "about 2664-2181." For later periods there is little deviation from such standard reference works as *The Cambridge Ancient History.*

For the dates used in the section devoted to Babylonian and Assyrian historical texts, reference may be made to A. Poebel, The Assyrian King List from Khorsabad, *JNES*, II (1943), pp. 85-88. The dates as given by Poebel have been used in other places as well. Frequently references in the footnotes will direct the reader to other discussions of chronology upon which the translator has relied.

One point at which this volume differs from its predecessors is the inclusion of a sizable body of translations of Hittite texts. These are scattered widely in the various sections of the volume. Since these texts have not been widely discussed as to their relation to the Old Testament, the following paragraphs will serve as orientation for the general reader.

Almost all Hittite texts which we possess come from ruins near the Turkish village Boğazköy in the center of Anatolia. The ruins represent what is left of Hattusa, the capital of the Hittite empire which flourished between 1800 and 1200 B.C. The texts are written—according to a custom which the Hittites adopted from the inhabitants of Mesopotamia—on clay tablets in cuneiform. They once belonged to "archives" or "libraries" buried under the debris when Hattusa was destroyed about

1225 B.C. This means that all of them are older than this date. A more exact date can be assigned to those which were composed by, or in the name of, specific kings. For this reason the sequence of the kings, at least for the so-called "later Hittite kingdom" may be given here:

Arnuwandas	15th century
Tudhaliyas	15th century
Suppiluliumas, Tudhaliyas' son	about 1390-1354
Mursilis, Suppiluliumas' son	about 1353-1323
Muwatallis, Mursilis' son	about 1323-1300
Urhi-Tessub, Muwatallis' son	about 1300-1293
Hattusilis, Mursilis' son	about 1293-1270
Tudhaliyas, Hattusilis' son	about 1270-1240
Arnuwandas, Tudhaliyas' son	about 1240-1225

The Boğazköy texts, the greater number of which are preserved in the museums of Istanbul and Ankara, a smaller collection being in the Vorderasiatische Abteilung of the Staatliche Museen at Berlin, have been published in various series.[15]

For general orientation on the Hittites and the problems connected with them the reader may be referred to the following books: A. Götze, *Das Hethiter-Reich* (=*AO*, XXVII/2 [1928]); A. Götze, *Kleinasien* in *Kulturgeschichte des alten Orients* (*Handbuch der Altertumswissenschaft*, III, 1, 3) (1933); L. Delaporte, *Les Hittites* (1936); E. Cavaignac, *Le problème hittite* (1936); G. Furlani, *La religione degli Hittiti* (1936).

[15] *KBo*=*Keilschrifttexte aus Boghazköi*, I-VI (1916-21); *KUB*=*Keilschrifturkunden aus Boghazköi*, I-XXXIV (1921-44); *HT*=*Hittite Texts in the Cuneiform Character from Tablets in the British Museum* (1920); *BoTU* = *Die Boghazköi-Texte in Umschrift* (Leipzig, 1922-26); *VBoT* = *Verstreute Boghazköi-Texte* (Marburg, 1930); *IBoT*=*Istanbul arkeoloji müzelerinde bulunan Boğazköy tableteri I* and *II* (Istanbul, 1944 and 1947); *ABoT*=*Ankara arkeoloji müzesinde bulunan Boğazköy tableteri* (Istanbul, 1948).

Abbreviations

AAA *Annals of Archaeology and Anthropology* (Liverpool, 1908-).

AASOR *Annual of the American Schools of Oriental Research* (New Haven, 1920-).

ABL *Assyrian and Babylonian Letters Belonging to the Kouyunjik Collection(s) of the British Museum*, by R. F. Harper (Chicago, 1892-1914).

ABoT *Ankara arkeoloji müzesinde bulunan Boğazköy tableteri* (Istanbul, 1948).

AfK *Archiv für Keilschriftforschung* (Berlin, 1923-1925).

AfO *Archiv für Orientforschung* (Berlin, Vols. III ff., 1926-).

AJA *American Journal of Archaeology* (Concord, N. H. etc., 1885-).

AJSL *American Journal of Semitic Languages and Literatures* (Chicago, 1884-1941).

AKA See King

AKTRSch. *Die Alphabetischen Keilschrifttexte von Ras Schamra*, by H. Bauer (Berlin, 1936).

AO *Der alte Orient* (Leipzig, 1900-).

AOT *Altorientalische Texte zum alten Testament*, 2nd ed., edited by H. Gressmann (Berlin and Leipzig, 1926).

APAW *Abhandlungen der preussischen Akademie der Wissenschaften* (Berlin, 1804-).

AR See Breasted, Luckenbill

AS *Assyriological Studies*, Oriental Institute, University of Chicago (Chicago, 1931-).

ASAE *Annales du service des antiquités de l'Egypte* (1899-).

BA *Beiträge zur Assyriologie und semitischen Sprachwissenschaft* (Leipzig, 1889-).

BASOR (SS) *Bulletin of the American Schools of Oriental Research* (1919-). (*Supplementary Studies* [1945-].)

Bauer, *Assurbanipal* Th. Bauer, *Das Inschriftenwerk Assurbanipals* (Leipzig, 1933).

BAWb. See Meissner

BE *Babylonian Expedition of the University of Pennsylvania, Series A: Cuneiform Texts*, edited by H. V. Hilprecht (1893-1914).

BG *The Babylonian Genesis*, by A. Heidel (Chicago, 1942).

BIFAO *Bulletin de l'institut français d'archéologie orientale* (Cairo, 1901-).

BIN *Babylonian Inscriptions in the Collection of James B. Nies* (New Haven, 1918-).

BoTU *Die Boghazköi-Texte in Umschrift* (Leipzig, 1922 ff.).

Breasted, *AR* J. H. Breasted, *Ancient Records of Egypt*, Vols. I-V (Chicago, 1906-1907).

BrM British Museum

Camb. See Strassmaier

Cowley A. Cowley, editor, *Aramaic Papyri of the Fifth Century* B.C. (Oxford, 1923). Citations are by number of the document unless otherwise indicated.

CH Code of Hammurabi

CT *Cuneiform Texts from Babylonian Tablets, &c., in the British Museum* (London, 1896-).

Cyr. See Strassmaier

Dar. See Strassmaier

Deimel, *ŠL* A. Deimel, *Šumerisches Lexikon* (Rome, 1925-1937).

Erman, *LAE* A. Erman, *The Literature of the Ancient Egyptians* (London, 1927), a translation into English by A. M. Blackman of Erman's *Die Literatur der Aegypter* (Leipzig, 1923).

GCCI *Goucher College Cuneiform Inscriptions* (New Haven, 1923-).

GE A. Heidel, *The Gilgamesh Epic and Old Testament Parallels* (Chicago, 1946).

GETh R. Campbell Thompson, *The Epic of Gilgamish* (Oxford, 1930).

GGA *Göttingische gelehrte Anzeigen* (Göttingen, 1826-).

HGE F. M. Böhl, *Het Gilgamesj-Epos* (Amsterdam, 1941).

HSS *Harvard Semitic Series* (Cambridge, Mass., 1912-).

HT *Hittite Texts in the Cuneiform Character from Tablets in the British Museum* (London, 1920).

HUCA *Hebrew Union College Annual* (Cincinnati, 1924-).

IBoT *Istanbul arkeoloji müzelerinde bulunan Boğazköy tableteri I and II* (Istanbul, 1944 and 1947).

JA *Journal asiatique* (Paris, 1822-).

JAOS *Journal of the American Oriental Society* (New Haven, 1843-).

JBL *Journal of Biblical Literature and Exegesis* (Middletown, Conn., etc., 1881-).

JCS *Journal of Cuneiform Studies* (New Haven, 1947-).

JEA *Journal of Egyptian Archaeology* (London, 1914-).

JEOL *Jaarbericht, Vooraziatisch-Egyptisch Gezelschap "Ex Oriente Lux"* (Leyden, 1933-).

JNES *Journal of Near Eastern Studies* (Chicago, 1942-).

JPOS *Journal of the Palestine Oriental Society* (Jerusalem, 1920 ff.).

JQR *Jewish Quarterly Review* (London, etc., 1889-).

JRAS *Journal of the Royal Asiatic Society* (London, 1834-).

JSOR *Journal of the Society of Oriental Research* (Chicago, 1917-1932).

K Kuyounjik (British Museum, London).

KAH *Keilschrifttexte aus Assur historischen Inhalts*, Vol. I (*WVDOG*, XVI [1911]) edited by L. Messerschmidt, Vol. II (*WVDOG*, XXXVII [1922]) edited by O. Schroeder.

KAJ *Keilschrifttexte aus Assur juristischen Inhalts* (*WVDOG*, L [1927]) edited by E. Ebeling.

KAR *Keilschrifttexte aus Assur religiösen Inhalts*, Vol. I (*WVDOG*, XXVIII [1915-19]) edited by E. Ebeling.

KAV *Keilschrifttexte aus Assur verschiedenen Inhalts*, (*WVDOG*, XXXV [1920]) edited by O. Schroeder.

KB *Keilinschriftliche Bibliothek*, edited by E. Schrader (Berlin, 1889-1900).

KBo *Keilschrifttexte aus Boghazköi*, I-VI (*WVDOG*, XXX [1916] and XXXVI [1921]).

King, *AKA* E. A. Wallis Budge and L. W. King, *Annals of the Kings of Assyria* (London, 1902).

KUB *Keilschrifturkunden aus Boghazköi*, I-XXXIV (Berlin, 1921-1944).

LSS *Leipziger semitistische Studien* (Leipzig, 1903-).

Luckenbill, *AR* D. D. Luckenbill, *Ancient Records of Assyria and Babylonia* (Chicago, 1926-1927).

MAOG *Mitteilungen der altorientalischen Gesellschaft* (Leipzig, 1925-).

MDIK *Mitteilungen des deutschen Instituts für ägyptische Altertumskunde in Kairo* (Augsburg, Berlin, 1930-).

Meissner, *BAWb.* B. Meissner, *Beiträge zum assyrischen Wörterbuch* No. I (*Assyriological Studies*, No. 1), No. II (*Assyriological Studies*, No. 4) (Chicago, 1931, 1932).

MVAG *Mitteilungen der vorderasiatisch-aegyptischen Gesellschaft* (Berlin, 1896-).

Nbk. See Strassmaier

Nbn. See Strassmaier

NF Neue Folge.

NRV *Neubabylonische Rechts- und Verwaltungsurkunden*, by M. San Nicolò and A. Ungnad, Vol. I (Leipzig, 1935).

NS Nova series.

OECT *Oxford Editions of Cuneiform Texts*, edited by S. Langdon (Oxford, 1923 ff.).

OIP *Oriental Institute Publications*, Oriental Institute, University of Chicago (Chicago, 1924-).

OLZ *Orientalistische Literaturzeitung* (Berlin and Leipzig, 1898-).

PAPS *Proceedings of the American Philosophical Society* (Philadelphia, 1838-).

PBC *Le poème babylonien de la création*, by R. Labat (Paris, 1935).

PBS See *UM*

PEQ *Palestine Exploration Quarterly* (London, 1869-).

PSBA *Proceedings of the Society of Biblical Archaeology* (London, 1878-1918).

RA *Revue d'Assyriologie et d'archéologie orientale* (Paris, 1884-).

Rawlinson H. C. Rawlinson, *The Cuneiform Inscriptions of Western Asia* (London, 1861-1884).

RB *Revue biblique* (Paris, 1892-).

RHA *Revue hittite et asianique* (Paris, 1930-).

RHR *Revue de l'histoire des religions* (Paris, 1880-).

RSO *Rivista degli studi orientali* (Rome, 1907-).

RT *Recueil de travaux relatifs à la philologie et à l'archéologie égyptiennes et assyriennes* (Paris, 1870-1923).

Sachau E. Sachau, editor, *Aramäische Papyrus und Ostraka aus einer jüdischen Militär-Kolonie zu Elephantine* (Leipzig, 1911). Texts and plates in separate volumes. Citation by plate unless otherwise indicated.

SAOC *Studies in Ancient Oriental Civilization* (Chicago, 1931-).

Sayce-Cowley A. H. Sayce and A. E. Cowley, editors, *Aramaic Papyri Discovered at Assuan* (London, 1906). Citation by plate.

SBAW *Sitzungsberichte der bayerischen Akademie der Wissenschaften* (Munich, 1871-).

Schott, *GE* A. Schott, *Das Gilgamesch-Epos* (Leipzig, 1934).

ŠL See Deimel

SM *Sumerian Mythology*, by S. N. Kramer (Philadelphia, 1944).

SPAW *Sitzungsberichte der preussischen Akademie der Wissenschaften* (Berlin 1882-).

STC *The Seven Tablets of Creation*, by L. W. King, 2 Vols. (London, 1902).

Strassmaier, *Camb.* J. N. Strassmaier, *Inschriften von Cambyses, König von Babylon* (Leipzig, 1890).

———, *Cyr.* J. N. Strassmaier, *Inschriften von Cyrus, König von Babylon* (Leipzig, 1890).

———, *Dar.* J. N. Strassmaier, *Inschriften von Darius, König von Babylon* (Leipzig, 1893-97).

———, *Nbk.* J. N. Strassmaier, *Inschriften von Nabuchodonosor, König von Babylon* (Leipzig, 1889).

———, *Nbn.* J. N. Strassmaier, *Inschriften von Nabonidus, König von Babylon* (Leipzig, 1889).

TB Talmud Babylonicum.

TCL *Textes cunéiformes*, Musée du Louvre (Paris, 1910-).

Thompson, *EG* R. Campbell Thompson, *The Epic of Gilgamish* (London, 1928).

TRS *Textes religieux sumériens du Louvre*, by Henri de Genouillac, (Musée du Louvre, *Textes cunéiformes*, XV-XVI, [Paris, 1930]).

TSBA *Transactions of the Society of Biblical Archaeology* (London, 1872-1893).

UET *Ur Excavations, Texts: I Royal Inscriptions*, by C. J. Gadd, L. Legrain, etc. (London, 1928).

UM University Museum, University of Pennsylvania, *Publications of the Babylonian Section* (Philadelphia, 1911-).

Ungnad A. Ungnad, editor, *Aramäische Papyrus aus Elephantine* (Leipzig, 1911). Citations are by number of the document unless otherwise indicated.

Untersuch. *Untersuchungen zur Geschichte und Altertumskunde Aegyptens* (Leipzig, 1896-).

Urk. *Urkunden des ägyptischen Altertums* (Leipzig, 1903-).

VA Vorderasiatische Abteilung, Thontafelsammlung (Berlin).

VAB *Vorderasiatische Bibliothek* (Leipzig, 1907-1916).

VBoT A. Götze, *Verstreute Boghazköi-Texte* (Marburg, 1930).

VS *Vorderasiatische Schriftdenkmäler*, Berlin, Staatliche Museen (Leipzig, 1907-).

WVDOG *Wissenschaftliche Veröffentlichungen der deutschen Orient-Gesellschaft*, Berlin (Leipzig, 1900-).

WZKM *Wiener Zeitschrift für die Kunde des Morgenlandes* (Vienna, 1887-1940).

YOS *Yale Oriental Series, Babylonian Texts* (New Haven, 1915-).

ZA *Zeitschrift für Assyriologie und verwandte Gebiete* (Leipzig, 1886-).

ZAeS *Zeitschrift für ägyptische Sprache und Altertumskunde* (Leipzig, 1863-).

ZAW *Zeitschrift für die alttestamentliche Wissenschaft* (Berlin, Giessen, 1881-).

ZDMG *Zeitschrift der deutschen morgenländischen Gesellschaft* (Leipzig, 1847-).

ZDPV *Zeitschrift des deutschen Palaestina-Vereins* (Leipzig, 1878-).

I. Myths, Epics, and Legends

Egyptian Myths, Tales, and Mortuary Texts

TRANSLATOR: JOHN A. WILSON

Creation and Myths of Origins

THE CREATION BY ATUM

The following text served in the dedication ritual of a royal pyramid by recalling the first creation, when the god Atum of Heliopolis was on a primeval hillock arising out of the waters of chaos and there brought the first gods into being. In like manner, the god is now asked to bless the rising pyramid, an analogue of the hillock.

The text was carved inside the pyramids of Mer-ne-Re and Pepi II (Nefer-ka-Re) of the Sixth Dynasty (24th century B.C.), from which the following translation is made. Parts of the text were popular in later times, to promote the immortality of individuals.[1]

The hieroglyphic text appears in K. Sethe, *Die altägyptischen Pyramidentexten*, II (Leipzig, 1910), §1652-56. Extracts from the whole utterance have occasionally been translated, for example, J. H. Breasted, *Development of Religion and Thought in Ancient Egypt* (New York, 1912), 76 f.

O Atum-Kheprer, thou wast on high on the (primeval) hill; thou didst arise as the *ben*-bird of the *ben*-stone in the *Ben*-House in Heliopolis;[2] thou didst spit out what was Shu, thou didst sputter out what was Tefnut.[3] Thou didst put thy arms about them as the arms of a *ḳa*, for thy *ḳa* was in them.[4]

(So also), O Atum, put thou thy arms about King Nefer-ka-Re, about this construction work, about this pyramid, as the arms of a *ḳa*. For the *ḳa* of King Nefer-ka-Re is in it, enduring for the course of eternity. O Atum, mayest thou set thy protection over this King Nefer-ka-Re, over this his pyramid and this construction work of King Nefer-ka-Re. Mayest thou guard lest anything happen to him evilly throughout the course of eternity, as thou didst set thy protection over Shu and Tefnut.

O Great Ennead which is in Heliopolis, Atum, Shu, Tefnut, Geb, Nut, Osiris, Isis, Seth, and Nephthys,[5] whom Atum begot, spreading wide his heart (in joy) at his begetting (you) in your name of the Nine Bows,[6] may there be none of you who will separate himself from Atum, as he protects this King Nefer-ka-Re, as he protects this pyramid of King Nefer-ka-Re, as he protects this his construction work—from all gods and from all dead, and as he guards lest anything happen to him evilly throughout the course of eternity.

[1] For example, it appears in the 13th century B.C., in extracts, in Papyrus Chester Beatty IX, recto, viii 3-21 (*Hieratic Papyri in the British Museum. Third Series. Chester Beatty Gift*, ed. by A. H. Gardiner, Vol. I [London, 1935], 91).

[2] The god of Heliopolis was compounded of two phases of the sun, Atum and Khepper (later Atum and Re). The sanctuary at Heliopolis had a stone of sacred recognition. Associated with this stone was a bird, which was much later to be taken as the phoenix. This part of the texts is full of plays on words, such as *weben* "arise," and *ben*-bird, etc.

[3] The creation of Shu, god of air, and of Tefnut, goddess of moisture, was as explosive as a sneeze. cf. p. 6 below.

[4] The *ḳa* was the *alter ego*, or the guardian spirit, or—perhaps better—the vital force of a personality. Pictorially it was depicted as the sheltering arms. The creator-god Atum put his own vital force into his first creatures.

[5] The first nine gods, the Great Ennead, are here given, in their four generations: (1) Atum, the creator; (2) Shu, god of air, and Tefnut, goddess of moisture; (3) Geb, god of earth, and Nut, goddess of the sky; (4) the god Osiris and the goddess Isis; the god Seth and the goddess Nephthys. cf. p. 6 below.

[6] The Nine Bows were the nine traditional, potential enemies of Egypt. There is a play on the "Nine (Gods)" and the "Nine (Bows)" here. The magic of the spell protects against the potential enmity of these gods.

ANOTHER VERSION OF THE CREATION BY ATUM

An ancient Egyptian's title to eternal happiness was often asserted by associating him with various superhuman forces, including the greatest gods of the land. Thus he secured their invincible immortality. The following extract from the popular 17th chapter of the Book of the Dead sets the deceased Egyptian in juxtaposition with the creator-god Atum, implicitly securing renewed creation of life.

This text was used all over Egypt for many centuries. The following translation is taken from the Eighteenth to Twenty-First Dynasties version of the Book of the Dead (1500-1000 B.C.). The text goes back at least as far as the Middle Kingdom (2000 B.C.), when it was inscribed in the coffins of nobles. By the Eighteenth Dynasty, the text had been amplified with explanatory and confirmatory glosses.

The current translation of the opening lines of the 17th chapter is made from H. Grapow, *Religiöse Urḳunden* (*Urḳ.* v, Leipzig, 1915-17), 4-13, including a translation into German. Translations into English are needed for the Book of the Dead. A rendering into German will be found in G. Roeder, *Urḳunden zur Religion des alten Aegypten* (Jena, 1923), 237 ff.

Title

The beginning of exaltations and beatifications; going up and down in the necropolis; being an effective spirit in the beautiful west; being in the retinue of Osiris; being satisfied with the food of Wen-nofer.[1] The spell for coming forth[2] by day, assuming any forms that he may wish to assume, playing at the draughtboard, sitting in the arbor, and coming forth as a living soul, by *X*, after he moors.[3] It is of benefit to him who may do it on earth,[4] when the speech of the Lord of All takes place:

Speech of the Creator, with Glosses

"I am Atum when I was alone in Nun;[5] I am Re in his (first) appearances, when he began to rule that which he had made."

[1] Osiris.

[2] The magic spell which enables the dead to come forth from the tomb.

[3] At *X* are inserted the title and name of the deceased. "Moors" is a euphemism for "dies."

[4] There is a promise of benefit to any living person who recites this spell on behalf of the deceased.

[5] The waters of chaos, out of which life arose.

Who is he? This "Re, when he began to rule that which he had made" means that Re began to appear as a king, as one who was before the liftings of Shu had taken place,[6] when he was on the hill which is in Hermopolis.[7] . . .

"I am the great god who came into being by himself."

Who is he? "The great god who came into being by himself" is water; he is Nun, the father of the gods. Another version: He is Re.

"He who created his names, the Lord of the Ennead."

Who is he? He is Re, who created the names of the parts of his body. That is how these gods who follow him came into being.[8]

"I am he among the gods who cannot be repulsed."

Who is he? He is Atum, who is in his sun disc. Another version: He is Re, when he arises on the eastern horizon of heaven.[9]

"I am yesterday, while I know tomorrow."

Who is he? As for "yesterday," that is Osiris. As for "tomorrow," that is Re on that day on which the enemies of the All-Lord are annihilated and his son Horus is made ruler.[10] . . .

THE THEOLOGY OF MEMPHIS

When the First Dynasty established its capital at Memphis, it was necessary to justify the sudden emergence of this town to central importance. The Memphite god Ptah was therefore proclaimed to have been the First Principle, taking precedence over other recognized creator-gods. Mythological arguments were presented that the city of Memphis was the "place where the Two Lands are united" and that the Temple of Ptah was the "balance in which Upper and Lower Egypt have been weighed."

The extracts presented here are particularly interesting, because creation is treated in an intellectual sense, whereas other creation stories (like pp. 3-4 above) are given in purely physical terms. Here the god Ptah conceives the elements of the universe with his mind ("heart") and brings them into being by his commanding speech ("tongue"). Thus, at the beginning of Egyptian history, there was an approach to the Logos Doctrine.

The extant form of this document dates only to 700 B.C., but linguistic, philological, and geopolitical evidence is conclusive in support of its derivation from an original text more than two thousand years older.

The so-called "Shabaka Stone" is No. 498 in the British Museum. It was published by S. Sharpe, *Egyptian Inscriptions from the British Museum and Other Sources* (London, 1837), I, Pls. 36-38. The first understanding of its contents was that of J. H. Breasted, in *ZAeS*, XXXIX (1901), 39-54, followed by A. Erman, *Ein Denkmal memphitischer Theologie* (*SPAW*, 1911, 916-50). K. Sethe devoted a masterly study to its contents, *Dramatische Texte zu altägyptischen Mysterienspielen* (*Untersuch.*, x, Leipzig, 1928), followed by H. Junker, *Die Götterlehre von Memphis* (*APAW*, 1939, Nr. 23, Berlin, 1940). The present part of the text has been studied by J. H. Breasted, *The Dawn of Conscience* (New York, 1933), 29-42, and in H. Frankfort *et al., The Intellectual Adventure of Ancient Man* (Chicago, 1946), 55-60.

(1) Live the Horus: Who Prospers the Two Lands; the Two Goddesses: Who Prospers the Two Lands; the Horus of Gold: Who Prospers the Two Lands; the King of Upper and Lower Egypt: Nefer-ka-Re; the Son of Re: Sha-[ba-ka], beloved of Ptah-South-of-His-Wall, living like Re forever. His majesty copied this text anew in the House of his father Ptah-South-of-His-Wall. Now his majesty had found (it) as (something) which the ancestors had made but which was worm-eaten.[1] It was unknown from beginning to end. Then [his majesty] copied [it] anew, (so that) it is better than its state formerly, in order that his name might endure and his memorial be made to last in the House of his father Ptah-South-of-His-Wall in the course of eternity, through that which the Son of Re: [Sha-ba-ka] did for his father Ptah-tenen, so that he might be given life forever. . . .

(7) The Ennead gathered themselves to him, and he judged Horus and Seth.[2] He prevented them from quarreling (further), and he made Seth the King of Upper Egypt in the land of Upper Egypt, at the place where he was (born), *Su.* Then Geb made Horus the King of Lower Egypt in the land of Lower Egypt, at the place where his father[3] was drowned, Pezshet-Tawi. Thus Horus stood in (one) place, and Seth stood in (another) place, and they were reconciled about the Two Lands. . . .

[4](10) Words spoken (by) Geb (to) Seth: "Go to the place in which thou wert born." Seth—Upper Egypt.

Words spoken (by) Geb (to) Horus: "Go to the place in which thy father was drowned." Horus—Lower Egypt.

Words spoken (by) Geb (to) Horus and Seth: "I have judged you." Lower and Upper Egypt.

(But then it became) ill in the heart of Geb that the portion of Horus was (only) equal to the portion of Seth. So Geb gave his (entire) inheritance to Horus, that is, the son of his son, his first-born.[5] . . . (Thus) Horus stood over the (entire) land. Thus this land was united, proclaimed with the great name: "Ta-tenen, South-of-His-Wall, the Lord of Eternity."[6] The two Great Sor-

[6] Before the air-god Shu had lifted heaven apart from earth.

[7] Atum-Re began his creation upon a primeval hillock arising out of the abysmal waters, Nun. In this version this hillock is located in the ancient cult-center of Hermopolis. Any important cult-center was regarded by the Egyptians as potentially a place of creation and therefore had its own hill of creation, symbolized in its holy of holies. cf. pp. 3; 8; 31, n.10.

[8] The first utterance of a name is an act of creation. When Atum-Re named the parts of his body, his Ennead, the nine gods of his immediate family, came into being.

[9] The eternally rising sun cannot be destroyed.

[10] The "yesterday" of death is associated with Osiris, the god of the dead. The "tomorrow" of rebirth is associated with the ever-rising sun and with the accession of Horus to the rule of his father Osiris. The continuation of the text is not translated here.

[1] The original, rediscovered in the time of Sha-ba-ka, was presumably on papyrus, wood, or leather.

[2] The nine great gods attended Geb, the earth-god, for his judicial ruling on the contest between Horus and Seth for the rule of Egypt.

[3] Osiris.

[4] Here the text exhibits most clearly its form for dramatic purposes. A notation is used for speakers and for stage directions. "Seth—Upper Egypt" meant either that the priestly actor playing the part of Geb points out the direction to the actor who played Seth or that the Seth-actor was to go off to the south.

[5] Geb revised his first decision to divide and gave all of his dominion, the earth, to Horus.

[6] A form of Ptah was Ta-tenen, "the land arising" (out of the primeval waters, so that creation might take place).

ceresses grew upon his head.[7] So it was that Horus appeared as King of Upper and Lower Egypt, who united the Two Lands in Wall Nome,[8] in the place in which the Two Lands are united.

(15c) It happened that reed and papyrus were set at the great double door of the House of Ptah.[9] That means Horus and Seth, who were reconciled and united, so that they associated and their quarreling ceased in the place which they *reached*, being joined in the House of Ptah, "the Balance of the Two Lands," in which Upper and Lower Egypt have been weighed. . . .

(48) The gods who came into being as Ptah:—[10]

Ptah who is upon the Great Throne . . . ;
Ptah-Nun, the father who [begot] Atum;
Ptah-Naunet, the mother who bore Atum;
Ptah the Great, that is, the heart and tongue of the Ennead;
[Ptah] . . . who gave birth to the gods; . . .[11]

(53) There came into being as the heart and there came into being as the tongue (something) in the form of Atum. The mighty Great One is Ptah, who transmitted [*life* to all gods], as well as (to) their *ka*'s, through this heart, by which Horus became Ptah, and through this tongue, by which Thoth became Ptah.[12]

(Thus) it happened that the heart and tongue gained control over [every] (other) member of the body, by teaching that he[13] is in every body and in every mouth of all gods, all men, [all] cattle, all creeping things, and (everything) that lives, by thinking and commanding everything that he wishes.

(55) His Ennead is before him in (the form of) teeth and lips. That is (the equivalent of) the semen and hands of Atum. Whereas the Ennead of Atum came into being by his semen and his fingers, the Ennead (of Ptah), however, is the teeth and lips in this mouth, which pronounced the name of everything, from which Shu and Tefnut came forth, and which was the fashioner of the Ennead.[14]

The sight of the eyes, the hearing of the ears, and the smelling the air by the nose, they report to the heart. It is this which causes every completed (concept) to come forth, and it is the tongue which announces what the heart thinks.[15]

Thus all the gods were formed and his Ennead was completed. Indeed, all the divine order[16] really came into being through what the heart thought and the tongue commanded. Thus the *ka*-spirits were made and the *hemsut*-spirits were appointed, they who make all provisions and all nourishment, by this speech. (*Thus justice was given to*) him who does what is liked, (*and injustice to*) him who does what is disliked.[17] Thus life was given to him who has peace and death was given to him who has sin. Thus were made all work and all crafts, the action of the arms, the movement of the legs, and the activity of every member, in conformance with (this) command which the heart thought, which came forth through the tongue, and which gives value to everything.[18]

(Thus) it happened that it was said of Ptah: "He who made all and brought the gods into being." He is indeed Ta-tenen, who brought forth the gods, for everything came forth from him, nourishment and provisions, the offerings of the gods, and every good thing. Thus it was discovered and understood that his strength is greater than (that of the other) gods. And so Ptah was satisfied,[19] after he had made everything, as well as all the divine order.[20] He had formed the gods, he had made cities, he had founded nomes, he had put the gods in their shrines, (60) he had established their offerings, he had founded their shrines, he had made their bodies like that (with which) their hearts were satisfied. So the gods entered into their bodies of every (kind of) wood, of every (kind of) stone, of every (kind of) clay, or anything which might grow upon him,[21] in which they had taken form. So all the gods, as well as their *ka*'s gathered themselves to him, content and associated with the Lord of the Two Lands.

The Great Seat, which *rejoices* the heart of the gods, which is in the House of Ptah, *the mistress of all life*, is the Granary of the God,[22] through which the sustenance of the Two Lands is prepared,[23] because of the fact that Osiris drowned in his water, while Isis and Nephthys watched. They saw him and they *were distressed at* him. Horus commanded Isis and Nephthys *repeatedly* that they lay hold on Osiris and prevent his drowning. (63) They turned (their) heads in time. So they brought him to land.[24] He entered the mysterious portals in the glory of the lords of eternity, in the steps of him who

[7] The crowns of Upper and Lower Egypt.

[8] The province (nome) of Memphis was named "White Wall."

[9] The intertwining tutelary plants of Upper and Lower Egypt, the reed(?) and the papyrus, symbolize the reconciliation of the two parts of Egypt and of their gods.

[10] Or, with Junker: "who have (their) form in Ptah."

[11] Three other forms of Ptah appear in badly broken context. These forms of Ptah apply to the statement that follows. Ptah was both Nun, the abysmal waters, and his consort Naunet, and in these capacities he brought forth Atum, the creator-god of the Heliopolitan theology.

[12] Ptah thought of and created by speech the creator-god Atum ("Totality"), thus transmitting the divine power of Ptah to all other gods. The gods Horus and Thoth, a commonly associated pair, are equated with the organs of thought and speech.

[13] Ptah, as heart and tongue.

[14] A distinction is made between the act of creation by Atum through onanism (cf. p. 6 below) and the creation by Ptah through commanding speech with teeth and lips. Pronouncing a name was creative. Shu and Tefnut were the first deities to be spoken.

[15] The senses report to the heart. With this reported material, the heart conceives and releases thought, which the tongue, as a herald, puts into effective utterance.

[16] Literally, "every word of the god."

[17] Following previous translators, we supply something which seems to have dropped out of the text. The exact words are uncertain.

[18] "The dignity (or worth or reverence) of everything."

[19] Or, "so Ptah rested."

[20] cf. n.16 above.

[21] Upon Ptah, in his form of the "rising land." Note that divine images were not the gods themselves, but only places in which they might assume appearance.

[22] The determinative shows that "the God" was Ptah Ta-tenen.

[23] The temple of Ptah at Memphis was called the "Great Seat," or throne, and the granary which kept Egypt alive.

[24] The rescue of Osiris, the grain-god, from drowning is given in explanation of the position of Memphis as the granary of Egypt. In the following context, one must understand that Osiris's son was Horus and that Horus was the king of Egypt. Hence Horus was correctly located at Memphis.

shines forth on the horizon, on the ways of Re in the Great Seat. He joined with the court and associated with the gods of Ta-tenen Ptah, the lord of years.

Thus Osiris came to be in the land in the "House of the Sovereign" on the north side of this land, which he had reached. His son Horus appeared as King of Upper Egypt and appeared as King of Lower Egypt, in the embrace of his father Osiris, together with the gods who were in front of him and who were behind him.

THE REPULSING OF THE DRAGON AND THE CREATION

This text employed myth for ritual and magical recitation. In Egyptian belief the ship of the sun-god Re made a journey through the skies above by day and the skies below by night. Every night this ship faced the peril of destruction from a demon lurking in the underworld, Apophis. An important part of the ritual of Egyptian temples was the repulsing of this dragon, and thus the repulsing of the perils which might face nation or people. The following ritual is an extract from a papyrus containing a group of texts, for which the general heading is: "THE BEGINNING OF THE BOOK OF OVERTHROWING APOPHIS, THE ENEMY OF Re AND THE ENEMY OF King Wen-nofer—life, prosperity, health!—the justified, performed in the course of every day in the Temple of Amon-Re, Lord of the Thrones of the Two Lands, Presiding over Karnak."[1] The particular interest of the section given below is that it adds to these spells against Apophis a statement about creation.

The text is preserved in the Papyrus Bremner-Rhind (British Museum 10188), which may have come from Thebes. The present manuscript is dated about 310 B.C., but the text makes a deliberate attempt to preserve a language two thousand years older than that date. There is no doubt that the basic material derives from a relatively early period.

Photographic facsimiles of the papyrus were published by Budge in *Egyptian Hieratic Papyri in the British Museum. First Series* (London, 1910), Pls. I-XIX. Faulkner gave a transcription from hieratic into hieroglyphic in *The Papyrus Bremner-Rhind* (*Bibliotheca Aegyptiaca*, III, Brussels, 1933). The latest study and translation of the entire papyrus was given by Faulkner in *JEA*, XXII (1936), 121 ff.; XXIII (1937), 10 ff., 166 ff.; XXIV (1938), 41 ff.; with the section below (xxvi 21—xxviii 20) treated in XXIII, 172 ff.

For another reference to the repulsing of a monster at creation, see p. 417, n.49. For another account of the Repulsing of the Dragon, see pp. 11-12.

(xxvi 21) . . . THE BOOK OF KNOWING THE CREATIONS of Re and OF OVERTHROWING APOPHIS. THE WORDS TO BE SPOKEN.[2]

The All-Lord said, after he had come into being:

I am he who came into being as Khepri.[3] When I had come into being, being (itself) came into being, and all beings came into being after I came into being. Many were the beings which came forth from my mouth,[4] before heaven came into being, before earth came into being, before the ground and creeping things had been created in this place. I put together (some) of them in Nun as weary ones,[5] before I could find a place in which I might stand.[6] It (seemed) advantageous to me in my heart; I planned with my face; and I made (in concept) every form when I was alone, before I had spat out what was Shu, before I had sputtered out what was Tefnut,[7] and before (any) other had come into being who could act with me.

I planned in my own heart, and there came into being a multitude of forms of beings, the forms of children and the forms of their children. I was the one who copulated with my fist, I masturbated (xxvii 1) with my hand. Then I spewed with my own mouth:[8] I spat out what was Shu, and I sputtered out what was Tefnut. It was my father Nun who brought them up, and my Eye followed after them since the ages when they were distant from me.[9]

After I had come into being as the sole god, there were three gods beside me.[10] I came into being in this land, whereas Shu and Tefnut rejoiced in Nun, in which they were. They brought to me my Eye with them. After I had joined together my members, I wept over them.[11] That is how men came into being from the tears which came forth from my Eye. It was angry with me, after it returned and found that I had made another in its place, having replaced it with the Glorious Eye, which I had made. Then I advanced its place on my head,[12] and after it had ruled this entire land, *its rage fell away to its roots*, for I had replaced what had been taken away from it. I came forth from the roots,[13] and I created all creeping things and whatever lives among them. Then Shu and Tefnut brought forth (5) Geb and Nut. Then Geb and Nut brought forth Osiris, Horus Khenti-en-irti, Seth, Isis, and Nephthys from the body, one of them after another; and they brought forth their multitudes in this land.[14]

When (these gods) rich in magic spoke, it was the

[1] Papyrus Bremner-Rhind xxii 1. Wen-nofer is a name for Osiris.

[2] Capital letters show words rubricized in the manuscript. The following words are to be spoken as the magical ritual.

[3] Khepri was the morning sun-god, conceived as a scarab beetle. In the following context there is a play on the name Khepri and the word *kheper* "come into being."

[4] Creation was effected by the commanding utterance of Re.

[5] There is a play on the name Nun, the primordial waters in which creation took place, and *nenu* "the weary," usually a designation of the dead, but here those in inchoate pause.

[6] Other texts locate the creation on a primeval hillock arising out of the waters of Nun. cf. pp. 3, 4, and 8.

[7] The first two children of the creator-god were Shu, the air-god, and Tefnut, the goddess of moisture. The statement of their ejection into being contains plays on the words *ishesh* "spit" and Shu, and *tef* "sputter" and Tefnut. cf. p. 3 above.

[8] There is here a fusion of two myths, creation by self-pollution and creation by ejection from the mouth. cf. p. 5 above.

[9] Reference to another myth, in which, however, it was Shu and Tefnut who went out after the wandering Eye of Re. See H. Junker, *Die Onurislegende* (Vienna, 1917).

[10] Nun, Shu, and Tefnut.

[11] Apparently Re wept when he found that his Eye was missing from his body. He made a substitute eye, which displeased his missing Eye when it returned to him. The labored point of the context is a play on the words *remit* "tears," and *romet* "mankind," in explanation of human creation. cf. pp. 8a, n.6; 11, n.6; 366, n.17.

[12] Re appeased his wrathful Eye by making it the uraeus on his brow, the symbol of rule.

[13] An obscure or corrupt statement on the creation of vegetation. In the next sentence, the "among them" may refer to plant life.

[14] Shu and Tefnut, the children of Atum-Re, were miraculously brought into being. But their children, Geb (earth) and Nut (sky), were normally born "from the body," as were also the divine children of Geb and Nut. Thus we have the Ennead, the nine ruling gods, with Horus as an added member. cf. p. 3 above. The context now continues by pointing out how these created beings were to use their magic against the demon enemy of Re.

(very) spirit[15] of magic, for they were ordered to annihilate my enemies by the effective charms of their speech, and I sent out these who came into being from my body TO OVERTHROW THAT EVIL ENEMY.

HE IS ONE FALLEN TO THE FLAME, APOPHIS with a knife on his head. He *cannot* see, and his name is no (more) in this land. I have commanded that *a curse* be cast upon him; I have consumed his bones; I have annihilated his soul in the course of every day; I have cut his vertebrae at his neck, severed with a knife which hacked up his flesh and pierced into his hide.[16] . . . (11) . . . I have taken away his heart from its place, his seat, and his tomb. I have made him nonexistent: his name is not; his children are not; he is not and his family is not; he is not and his false-door is not;[17] he is not and his heirs are not. His egg shall not last, nor shall his seed knit together—and vice versa. His soul, his corpse, his state of glory, his shadow, and his magic are not. His bones are not, and his skin is not. He is fallen and overthrown. . . .

(xxviii 4) . . . See thou, O Re! Hear thou, O Re! Behold, I have driven away thy enemy; I have wiped him out with my feet; I have spat upon him. Re is triumphant over thee—variant reading: over his every fallen enemy.[18] . . . Drive thou away, consume thou, burn up every enemy of pharaoh—life, prosperity, health!—whether dead or living.[19] . . .

(Thus) thou shalt be in (14) thy shrine, thou shalt journey in the evening-barque, thou shalt rest in the morning-barque, thou shalt cross thy two heavens in peace,[20] thou shalt be powerful, thou shalt live, thou shalt be healthy, thou shalt make thy states of glory to endure, thou shalt drive away thy every enemy by thy command; for these have done evil against pharaoh—life, prosperity, health!—with all evil words: all men, all folk, all people, all humanity, and so on, the easterners of every desert, and every enemy of pharaoh—life, prosperity, health!—whether dead or living, WHOM I HAVE DRIVEN AWAY AND ANNIHILATED. THOU DISSOLVEST, FALLEN, APOPHIS. Re is triumphant over thee, APOPHIS—(to be repeated) FOUR TIMES. Pharaoh—life, prosperity, health!—is triumphant over his enemies—(to be repeated) four times.

THIS SPELL IS TO BE RECITED OVER APOPHIS DRAWN ON A NEW SHEET OF PAPYRUS IN GREEN COLOR AND PUT INSIDE A BOX ON WHICH HIS NAME IS SET, HE BEING TIED AND BOUND AND PUT ON THE FIRE every day, WIPED OUT WITH THY LEFT FOOT AND SPAT UPON FOUR TIMES IN THE COURSE OF every day. THOU SHALT SAY AS THOU PUTTEST HIM ON THE FIRE: "Re is triumphant over thee, O APOPHIS!"—FOUR TIMES, and "Horus is triumphant over his enemy!"—four times, and "Pharaoh—life, prosperity, health!—is triumphant over his enemies!"—four times.

NOW WHEN THOU HAST WRITTEN THESE NAMES OF EVERY MALE AND FEMALE WHO IS TO BE OVERTHROWN, (18) OF WHOM THY HEART IS AFRAID, THAT IS, EVERY ENEMY OF Pharaoh—life, prosperity, health!—whether dead or alive, and the names of their fathers, the names of their mothers, and the names of (their) children, inside the box, they are to be made in wax and put on the fire following the name of Apophis and burned up at the time when Re shows himself. Thus thou shalt do the first time at the height of the sun and (again) when Re sets in the west, when the sunlight is fleeing from the mountain. These things are in truth more advantageous to thee than any (other) procedure. It will go well with him who does them on earth or in the necropolis.[21]

[15] The Egyptian word is *ka*, the accompanying spirit or vital force of a personality.

[16] The detailed narration of the destruction of Apophis continues *ad nauseam*, including the activities of various gods in defense of Re. Extracts only are given here.

[17] Destruction involves killing and also the prohibition of maintenance offerings at the false-door of a tomb.

[18] Literally: "The voice of Re is made true against thee—another saying: against his every fallen enemy." The reciter is permitted a variant.

[19] These exorcisms against the enemy of the supreme god were deemed to be effective also against the enemies of the god-king.

[20] There was an under-heaven to correspond to the heaven above. In the preceding clauses, the two barques of the sun have been reversed: the sun should go to rest in the evening-barque, for his journey through the under-heaven.

[21] These instructions for the manual activity accompanying the recitation show that the interest of the exorcism is the application of magic against the dragon-demon to the damnation of the enemies of the pharaoh.

ALL MEN CREATED EQUAL IN OPPORTUNITY

The Middle Kingdom was a period in which social justice and the rights of the common man were emphasized. The text which follows purports to give the words of the creator-god in making all men equal in access to the basic necessities of life.

The text is inscribed on four wooden coffins from el-Bersheh in Middle Egypt and dates to the Middle Kingdom (2000 B.C.). Thus far, it is known only from that period.

The hieroglyphic text is as yet unpublished, except for the reference and translation given by J. H. Breasted, *The Dawn of Conscience* (New York, 1933), 221 f. It will be published in the volumes by A. de Buck, *The Egyptian Coffin Texts* (*OIP*). The present translation was made from photographs for Coffin B3C (Cairo Museum 28085) and B6C (Cairo 28094) and—in part—B1C (Cairo 28083). The text also appears on B1Bo (Boston Museum 20.1822-27).

Other texts below deal with creation and origins. For example, Amon as creator is presented in the text of pp. 368-369, Aton as creator in pp. 370-371. Other myths of origins deal with the founding of the city of Tanis (pp. 252-253) or the setting up of an estate of a god (pp. 31-32).

The All-Lord says in the presence of those stilled from tumult on the journey of the court:[1] "Pray, be prosperous in peace! I repeat for you four good deeds which my own heart did for me in the midst of the serpent-coil, in order to still evil.[2] I did four good deeds within the portal of the horizon.[3]

"I made the four winds that every man might breathe thereof *like his fellow* in his time. That is (one) deed thereof.

[1] In the entourage of the sun-god on the daily journey of his barque are the dead who have been released from the cares of this world.

[2] Creation is a sort of release from involvement. Here the creator-god, who is also the sun-god, has freed himself from the serpent-dragon which threatened his daily journey; see pp. 6-7 above. Apparently, the god's good deeds were the means of his release, stilling the evil of the serpent by stilling inequality in this world.

[3] That is, at dawn or at the beginning.

"I made the great inundation that the poor man might have rights therein like the great man. That is (one) deed thereof.

"I made every man like his fellow. I did not command that they do evil, (but) it was their hearts which violated what I had said.[4] That is (one) deed thereof.

"I made their hearts to cease from forgetting the West, in order that divine offerings might be given to the gods of the nomes.[5] That is (one) deed thereof.

"I brought into being the *four* gods from my sweat, while men are the tears of my eye."[6]

THEBES AS THE PLACE OF CREATION

Every important cult-center of Egypt asserted its primacy by the dogma that it was the site of creation. The following is an extract from a long hymn extolling Thebes and its god Amon-Re. It is dated shortly after the Amarna Revolution and is a renewed confirmation of Theban domination. The manuscript is dated to the reign of Ramses II (about 1301-1234 B.C.).

The hieratic text of Leyden Papyrus I 350 was published by C. Leemans, *Monumens égyptiens du musée d'antiquités des Pays-Bas à Leide* (Leyden, 1841-82), II, Pls. CLIX-CLXIII. The text was studied by A. H. Gardiner in *ZAeS*, XLII (1905), 12-42, and by A. Erman, Der Leidener Amonshymnus (*SPAW*, 1923, 62-81). It is translated in Erman, *LAE*, 293-302.

TENTH STANZA.[1]

Thebes is *normal* beyond every (other) city. The water and land were in her from the first times. (Then) (ii 11) sand came to *delimit* the fields and to create her ground on the hillock; (thus) earth came into being.[2]

Then men came into being in her, to found every city with her real name, for their name is called "city" (only) under the oversight of Thebes, the Eye of Re.[3]

Her majesty came as the Sound Eye and the Beneficial Eye,[4] to bind the land thereby together with (her) *ka*, coming to rest and alighting in Ishru in her form as Sekhmet, the Mistress of the Two Lands.[5] "How rich she is," they say about her, "in her name of Thebes!"[6] She remains sound in her name of the Sound Eye, *the eye within*, which is in his sun disc; Opposite-her-Lord, appearing and appointed in her place in her name of Appointed-of-Places, without her peer.[7] Every (other) city is under (her) shadow, to magnify themselves through Thebes. She is the *norm*.

[4] The juxtaposition of this statement of god's equalitarian creation and this statement of man's disobedience of god's command means that man—and not god—is responsible for social inequality.

[5] The pious service of local gods would provide credit for continued life in the West, the realm of the dead. This idea is related to the equalitarian statements which precede it. By the Middle Kingdom, the full and powerful afterlife, which had previously been the prerogative of kings alone, had been extended to all worthy men and might be won locally, without attachment to the royal court. "The nomes" were the Egyptian provinces.

[6] There are two puns: *fedu* "four" and *fedet* "sweat"; and *romet* "men" and *remit* "tears." cf. p. 6, n.11 above. In somewhat uncertain terms there is a relation of the creation of gods to the creation of humans, both exudations of the creator-god. The attempt is clumsy, because one pun calls for four gods, instead of the usual nine. These may be the four gods who assist the dead man on his arrival in the next world (e.g. K. Sethe, *Die altägyptischen Pyramidentexte*, II, §1456-57).

[1] The manuscript is divided into a series of numbered "houses," i.e. "chapters" or "stanzas." The present stanza is ii 10-15 of the papyrus. Each stanza begins and ends with a pun based on the number. Here the word *med* "ten" is picked up by the word *meter*, which probably means "normal" or "standard."

[2] Thus the primeval hillock, upon which creation took place, is located in Thebes. cf. pp. 3-4 above.

[3] One designation of Thebes was "The City" (biblical *No*), resulting in this curious claim that all other cities were permitted to use that title under her domination.

[4] Allusion to the myth of the restored eye of the sun-god.

[5] Ishru, near Karnak, was a cult-seat of the goddess Mut, here equated with the goddess Sekhmet.

[6] Pun: *weser* "rich" and *waset* "Thebes."

[7] "Opposite-her-Lord" (i.e. Amon) was an epithet of Thebes. "Appointed-of-Places" was the name of the Temple of Karnak.

THE ASSIGNMENT OF FUNCTIONS TO THOTH

The Egyptians, like the Hebrews, were fond of punning explanations of names and phenomena. The following text provides the explanation of a number of cosmological or mythological phenomena. The sun-god Re here assigns responsibility for the moon to the god Thoth, who thus becomes the "place-taker" for the sun, an adjutant of the gods.

The text is found on the Tut-ankh-Amon shrine, now in the Cairo Museum, and in the Theban tombs of Seti I, Ramses II, and Ramses III. It thus ranges from the middle of the 14th century to the middle of the 12th century B.C. However, its original was probably much earlier. The parallel texts are presented by Ch. Maystre in *BIFAO*, XL (1941), 93-98. The line numbers, 62-74, follow the Seti I version. There is a translation in G. Roeder, *Urkunden zur Religion des alten Aegyptens* (Jena, 1923), 147-48.

Then the majesty of this god[1] said: "Pray, summon to me Thoth!" Then he was brought immediately. Then the majesty of this god said to Thoth: "Behold ye,[2] I am here in the sky in my (proper) place. Inasmuch as I (65) shall act so that the light may shine in the Underworld and the Island of Baba,[3] thou shalt be scribe there and keep in order those who are in them,[4] *those who may perform deeds of rebellion . . . against me*, (70) the followers of *this dissatisfied being*.[5] Thou shalt be in my place, a place-taker. Thus thou shalt be called: 'Thoth, the place-taker of Re.' Moreover, (I) shall have thee tread upon those greater than thou." That is how the ibis of Thoth came into being.[6] "Moreover, I shall have thee stretch out thy hand[7] in the face of the primeval gods, who are greater than thou. *My speech is* good, if thou actest (so)." That is how the ibis of Thoth came into being.[8] "Moreover, I shall have thee encompass the two heavens with thy beauty and with thy rays." That is how the moon of Thoth came into being.[9]

[1] Re.

[2] Re's commands are for all the attendant gods.

[3] An otherwise unknown designation for a part of the Underworld. It may mean a subterranean cavern.

[4] Re cannot do full justice to the denizens of the world and to the denizens of the Underworld. Since he feels a responsibility to illumine the latter, he assigns the moon, Thoth, to be his deputy there.

[5] A corrupt passage. In the first part there may be reference to mankind's rebellion, as in the passage on the destruction of mankind, pp. 10-11. The second part may refer to the Apophis demon, the enemy of the sun-god; cf. pp. 6-7, 11-12.

[6] A play on words: *hab*: "tread upon" and *hib* "ibis" the bird sacred to Thoth.

[7] In command. The gods of primeval chaos were associated with the underworld.

[8] Another play on words: *khen* "speech" and *tekheni*, another term for the ibis.

[9] Another play on words: *ineh* "encompass" and *iah* "moon."

"Moreover, I shall have thee *go all the way around* the Hau-nebut." That is how the baboon of Thoth came into being.[10] That is how he became the vizier.[11] "Moreover, thou shalt be my place-taker, and the faces of all who see thee shall be opened through thee,[12] so that the eye of every man praises god for thee."[13]

THE PRIMEVAL ESTABLISHMENT OF ORDER

A responsibility of the creator-god Atum was to bring the world into order and to assign places and functions. The conquest of hostile forces and the delimitation of the next world are themes of the following text. Insofar as it deals with the place and functions of Osiris, it has been used as a magic spell for the preservation of the dead man, himself an Osiris.[1]

Here translated from the 175th chapter of the Book of the Dead, as in the Eighteenth Dynasty (1550-1350 B.C.) Papyrus of Ani (British Museum 10470; *The Papyrus of Ani*, ed. by E. A. W. Budge [London, 1913], III, Sheet 29).

Title

(1) SPELL FOR NOT DYING A SECOND TIME. WORDS TO BE SPOKEN BY Ani, the triumphant.

Atum's Question

"O Thoth, what is it that has happened? It is among the children of Nut.[2] They have made an uproar; they have seized upon quarreling; they have done evil deeds; they have created rebellion; they have made slaughterings; (5) they have created imprisonment. Moreover, in everything which we might do, they have made the great into the small. Give thou greatly, Thoth!" Thus spoke Atum.

Thoth's Reply

"Thou shalt not see (such) evil deeds, thou shalt not suffer, (for) their years are cut short and their months are curbed, inasmuch as the destruction of hidden things was made for them through all that thou hast done."[3]

Words of the Deceased

"I am thy palette, O Thoth, and I have offered up to thee thy inkwell. I am not among those whose hidden things should be damaged. Damage should not be done to me."[4]

WORDS SPOKEN BY the Osiris Ani (10): "O Atum, what is it? I am departing to the desert, the silent land!"[5]

Atum's Answer

"It has no water, it has no air—deep, deep, dark, dark, boundless, boundless—in which thou livest in the peace of heart of the silent land. Sexual pleasures are not enjoyed in it, (but) a blessed state[6] is given to (thee)[7] in recompense for water, air, and sexual pleasure, and peace of heart in recompense for bread and beer." Thus spoke Atum.

Protest of the Deceased

"In the sight of thy face? Indeed, I cannot bear the lack of thee![8] Every (other) god has *assumed* his place in the forefront of (the sun barque) Millions-of-Years!"

Atum's Reply

"Thy place belongs to thy son Horus"—thus spoke Atum—"Indeed, it shall be that he sends forth the great, (15) while he also shall rule thy place, and he shall inherit the throne which is in the Island of Flame.[9] It is further decreed that *a man* shall see his fellow, (so that) my face shall see *thy* face."[10]

Question of the Deceased, as Osiris

"O Atum, what is (my) duration of life?"—thus he spoke.

Atum's Answer

"Thou art (destined) for millions of millions (of years), a lifetime of millions. I have caused that *he send out* the great ones.[11] Further, I shall destroy all that I have made, and this land will return into Nun, into the floodwaters, as (in) its first state.[12] I (alone) am a survivor, together with Osiris, when I have made my form in another state, serpents which men do not know and gods do not see.[13]

"How good is what I have done for Osiris, distinct from all (other) gods! I have given (20) him the desert, the silent land, with his son Horus as heir upon his throne which is in the Island of Flame. *Further*, I have made his place in the barque of Millions-of-Years. Horus remains upon his throne, for the purpose of founding his monuments also. The soul of Seth has been sent apart from all (other) gods, because I have caused the restraint of his soul, which is in the (sun) barque, because he wishes to fear the divine body."[14]

10 Another play, *anan* "turn back," possibly "go around," and *anan* the baboon sacred to Thoth. The Hau-nebut were peoples to the north of Egypt, thus in an outer range of circuit.

11 The play on words which led to this identification has dropped out. Thoth was the vizier of the gods.

12 In the absence of the sun, men can see because of the moon.

13 Men are grateful.

---

1 The concept was originally related to the kingship, the dead pharaoh becoming Osiris, while his son and successor became Horus.

2 That is, among the partisans of Seth, who was the "son of Nut."

3 This seems to be the answer of Thoth, assuring Atum that the punishment of evil resides in the system which Atum created.

4 By identifying himself with the scribal equipment of Thoth, the deceased dissociates himself from the rebellious beings.

5 The deceased asks the creator-god to describe the land of burial.

6 *Akh*, a state of "effective being," or "beatitude."

7 Text: "to me."

8 Osiris—here in the person of the deceased—is being assigned to the region of the dead. He objects that he will not see the face of the sun there. In the reply Atum offers him compensations.

9 The place where the sun was born at dawn.

10 The last sentences uncertain, since the literal runs: "Further it is decreed that I see his fellow, my face to see the face of the lord." Atum seems to promise Osiris that they two will not be cut off from each other, even though Horus takes over the rule of his father in the upper world.

11 So literally, but uncertain of meaning and perhaps corrupt.

12 Atum's purpose in destroying his creation and returning it to primeval chaos is not stated here. It probably has to do with the same kind of a destruction of mankind as in the text of pp. 10-11 below. The point here is that Osiris, in the realm of the dead, escapes such destruction.

13 Atum, "Totality," included the gods of primeval chaos, who were depicted in serpent form.

14 Atum assures Osiris that the latter need not fear his enemy Seth, because Seth is sufficiently under the authority of the supreme god to

Words of Horus

"O my father Osiris, mayest thou do for me what thy father Re did for thee! I remain upon earth, so that I may establish my place."[15]

Words of Osiris

"My *heir* is healthy, my tomb endures; they are my adherents (still) on earth. (25) My enemies have been given into *woes*, for Selqet is binding them.[16] I am thy son, my father Re. Thou dost these things for me for the sake of life, prosperity, and health, while Horus remains upon his throne. Mayest thou cause that this my time of passing to a state of reverence may come."[17]

THE MYTHOLOGICAL ORIGIN OF CERTAIN UNCLEAN ANIMALS

The Egyptians viewed certain animals as devoted for a definite purpose and therefore taboo for other purposes, specifically as unclean for eating. The following text is a mythological explanation of a taboo against eating pork. Not all of the text is clear, but it does involve two well-known elements: the conflict of Horus and Seth for the rule, and a damage to one of Horus' eyes, which were the two heavenly luminaries.

The text first occurs in the coffins of the Middle Kingdom, from which it is here translated, and is continued into the Book of the Dead, being used for many centuries.

The hieroglyphic text is given by A. de Buck, *The Egyptian Coffin Texts*, II (*OIP*, XLIX, Chicago, 1938), Spell 157, pp. 326 ff. It later became the 112th chapter of the Book of the Dead and is studied and translated by K. Sethe *et al.* in *ZAeS* (1923), LVIII, 1 ff. One Middle Kingdom coffin, which treats Spells 157 and 158 consecutively without break, has an instruction at the end of Spell 158: "Not to be spoken while eating pork."[1]

The Efficacy of This Text

BEING DESTINED FOR FOOD IN THE NECROPOLIS. BEING FAVORED AND LOVED UPON EARTH. BEING AMONG THE FOLLOWERS OF HORUS AND HIS RETINUE. A MYSTERY WHICH ONE LEARNED IN THE HOUSE. KNOWING THE SOULS OF BUTO.[2]

The Claim of Exceptional Knowledge

O Batit of the evening, ye swamp-dwellers, ye of Mendes, ye of the Mendes nome, ye of the Butine *House of Praise*, ye of the Shade of Re *which knows not praise*, ye who *brew stoppered beer*[3]—do ye know why Buto was given to Horus? Ye do not know it, (but) I know it. It was Re who gave it to him in recompense for the injury in his eye. I know it.

The Myth

It was Re—he said to Horus: "Pray, let me see thy eye since this has happened to it."[4] Then he saw it. He said: "Pray, look at that *(black) part*, while thy hand is a covering over the sound eye which is there."[5] Then Horus looked at that *(black) part*. Then Horus said: "Now I see it quite white." That is how the oryx came into being.[6]

Then Re said: "Pray, look another time at that black pig."[7] Thereupon Horus looked at this pig. Thereupon Horus shrieked because of the state of his eye, which was stormy.[8] He said: "Behold, my eye is as (at) that first blow which Seth made against my eye!" Thereupon Horus swallowed his heart before him.[9] Then Re said: "Put ye him upon his bed until he has recovered."

It was Seth—he had assumed form against him as a black pig; thereupon he shot a blow into his eye. Then Re said: "The pig is an abomination to Horus." "Would that he might recover!" said the gods.

THAT IS HOW THE PIG BECAME AN ABOMINATION TO THE GODS, AS WELL AS THEIR FOLLOWERS, FOR HORUS' SAKE.[10] . . .

Deliverance of Mankind from Destruction

The themes of this myth are the sin of mankind, the destructive disappointment of their creator, and the deliverance of mankind from annihilation. However, the setting of the present text shows that its purpose was magical protection rather than moral teaching. On the walls of three royal tombs of the Empire, it accompanies certain charms to protect the body of the dead ruler. This implies that the former deliverance of mankind from destruction will be valid also in this individual case.

The text appears on the walls of the tombs of Seti I, Ramses II, and Ramses III at Thebes. Its date is thus 14th-12th centuries B.C., although the language used and the corrupted state of the text show that it followed an older original. The texts were published together by Ch. Maystre in *BIFAO*, XL (1941), 53-73. The line numbers below are those of the Seti I version. There is a translation in Erman, *LAE*, 47-49.

Other reference to man's rebelliousness and the god's punishment of men will be found in pp. 8-10, 417.

remain in the sun barque, where he had the important duty of fighting the Apophis demon. cf. pp. 6-7 above and pp. 11-12 below.

[15] Horus, the son and successor of the deceased, assents to the dispositions of the supreme god.

[16] Just how Selqet, a scorpion goddess, functioned is uncertain.

[17] May Horus, the successor on earth, aid in the beatification of Osiris, the deceased. In this speech, Osiris accepts the dispositions made by Atum-Re.

[1] De Buck, *op. cit.*, 362.

[2] The initial statement is rubricized. Each of the spells, Coffin Texts, Spells 154-60, carries a title, "Knowing the Souls of *X*," *X* being a cult-center or a region. These "Souls" were the reverted dead, often the ancient kings who had ruled at a cult-center. Acquaintance with such high personalities would facilitate the reception of the deceased Egyptian in the next world. cf. pp. 11-12, 33.

[3] Apparently all forces in or around Buto in the Egyptian Delta, who *should have known* the mythological history of that site.

[4] Horus's eye was injured in the fight with Seth for the rule. The destroyed and restored eye came to be identified with the moon.

[5] Following the reasoning of Sethe, an old sign for "black" has degenerated into a mere stroke, following the word for "part" or "mark." It is not clear how Horus, covering his uninjured eye, could see the injury in his wounded eye.

[6] Homonyms, *ma-hedj* "see-white" and *ma-hedj* "oryx." The oryx was a beast of Seth, and thus also unclean to Horus. The sense of the passage must be that Horus failed to see what Re saw.

[7] The words "another time" perhaps mean that Re directed Horus' attention to the same black mark, but with a more specific statement that the mark of injury looked like a pig, Seth's beast.

[8] Probably inflamed.

[9] In view of what follows, this must mean that Horus lost consciousness in Re's presence.

[10] More literally: "that is how the pig became abominated for Horus by the gods, like their followers," all rubricized. The omitted conclusion of the myth states that the pig had previously been a sacrificial animal for Horus and relates the myth about Horus to the Souls of Buto, with whom the deceased is so well acquainted.

It happened that . . . Re, the god who came into being by himself, when he was king of men and gods all together. Then mankind plotted something in the (very) presence of Re. Now then, his majesty—life, prosperity, health!—was old. His bones were of silver, his flesh of gold, and his hair of genuine lapis lazuli.

Then his majesty perceived the things which were being plotted against him by mankind. Then his majesty—life, prosperity, health! said to those who were in his retinue: "Pray, summon to me my Eye,[1] Shu, Tefnut, Geb, and Nut, as well as the fathers and mothers who were with me when I was in Nun,[2] as well as my god Nun also. He is to bring his court (5) with him. Thou shalt bring them *secretly*: let not mankind see; let not their hearts escape.[3] Thou shalt come with them to the Great House, that they may tell their plans, since *the* [*times*] *when* I came from Nun to the place in which I came into being."[4]

Then these gods were brought in, and these gods [*came*] beside him, putting their heads to the ground in the presence of his majesty, so that he might make his statement in the presence of the father of the eldest, he who made mankind, the king of people.[5] Then they said in the presence of his majesty: "Speak to us, so that we may hear it."

Then Re said to Nun: "O eldest god, in whom I came into being, O ancestor gods, behold mankind, which came into being from my Eye[6]—they have plotted things against me. Tell me what ye would do about it. Behold, I am seeking; I would not slay them until I had heard what (10) ye might say about it." Then the majesty of Nun said: "My son Re, the god greater than he who made him and mightier than they who created him, sitting upon thy throne, the fear of thee is great when thy Eye is (directed) against them who scheme against thee!" Then the majesty of Re said: "Behold, they have fled into the desert, their hearts being afraid because I *might* speak to them." Then they said in the presence of his majesty: "May thy Eye be sent, that it may *catch* for thee them who scheme with evil things. (But) the Eye is not (*sufficiently*) prominent therein to smite them for thee.[7] It should go down as Hat-Hor."

So then this goddess came and slew mankind in the desert. Then the majesty of this god said: "Welcome, Hat-Hor, who hast done for me *the deed for which I came*!" Then this goddess said: "As thou livest for me,[8] I have prevailed over mankind, and it is pleasant in my heart!" Then the majesty of Re said: "I shall prevail over them *as a king* (15) by diminishing them!"[9] That is how Sekhmet came into being, the (beer)-mash of the night, to wade in their blood from Herakleopolis.[10]

Then Re said: "Pray, summon to me swift and speedy messengers, so that they may run like the shadow of a body." Then these messengers were brought immediately. Then the majesty of this god said: "Go ye to Elephantine and bring me red ochre very abundantly."[11] Then this red ochre was brought to him. Then the majesty of this great god caused . . . , [and He-With]-the-Side-Lock who is in Heliopolis[12] ground up this red ochre. When further maidservants crushed barley to (make) beer, then this red ochre was added to this mash. Then (it) was like human blood. Then seven thousand jars of the beer were made. So then the majesty of the King of Upper and Lower Egypt: Re came, together with these gods, to see this beer.

Now when day broke for (20) the slaying of mankind by the goddess at their season of going upstream,[13] then the majesty of Re said: "How good it is! I shall protect mankind with it!" Then Re said: "Pray, carry it to the place in which she expected to slay mankind." Then the majesty of the King of Upper and Lower Egypt: Re went to work early in the depth of the night to have this sleep-maker poured out. Then the fields were filled with liquid *for* three palms,[14] through the power of the majesty of this god.

Then this goddess went at dawn, and she found this (place) flooded. Then her face (looked) beautiful therein. Then she drank, and it was good in her heart. She came (back) drunken, without having perceived mankind.

(The remainder of this story has to do with the origin of certain names and customs, such as the use of strong drink at the Feast of Hat-Hor.)

Heroic Tales—Exploits of Gods and Human Beings

THE REPULSING OF THE DRAGON

When the boat of the sun entered the western darkness at evening, it faced the peril of a serpent or dragon, which might destroy the sun; cf. pp. 6-7 above. Then it was the function of the god Seth to repel this beast, so that the sun might cross the underworld by night and be reborn in the morning. In like manner, man should survive death and be reborn.

1 The eye of the sun-god was an independent part of himself, with a complicated mythological history.

2 The abysmal waters, in which creation took place.

3 Was Re unwilling that mankind repent its rebellious purposes?

4 Uncertain. The translation assumes that Re is asking advice on the changed conditions since creation.

5 Nun.

6 Mankind originated as the tears of the creator-god. See pp. 6, 8, 366.

7 It seems to be argued that the Eye in its normal form is not adequate to the work of destruction, so that it should assume its form as Hat-Hor.

8 The introductory formula of an oath.

9 Uncertain. The translation assumes the sense that Re can rule mankind if they are fewer in number. It is also possible to translate: "I shall prevail over them. *But do not* diminish them (*any further*)." At any rate, it soon becomes clear that Re wishes the destruction to cease, whereas Hat-Hor is unwilling to halt her lustful annihilation.

10 The formula by which the origin of a name was explained. Sekhmet, "She Who Prevails," the goddess of violence, is here given as a form of Hat-Hor. Herakleopolis, "the Child of the King," seems to be in punning relation to the previous word, "*king*." "The mash of the night" is used in meaningless anticipation here, as it belongs to that part of the story which follows.

11 *Didi* was a red coloring material, but it is not certain whether it was mineral or vegetable. Red ochre has been found in the region of Elephantine, and hematite in the eastern desert.

12 An epithet of the High Priest of Re.

13 The meaning of this phrase is not clear.

14 The fields were covered with the blood-red beer, the "sleep-maker," to a height of about 9 inches.

The text is taken from Middle Kingdom coffins and survived into the Book of the Dead.

Hieroglyphic text in A. de Buck, *The Egyptian Coffin Texts*, II (*OIP*, XLIX, Chicago, 1938), Spell 160, pp. 373 ff. Later the 108th chapter of the Book of the Dead, with contributions to the 107th, 111th, and 149th chapters, studied by K. Sethe *et al.* in *ZAeS*, LIX (1924), 73 ff.

References to the repulsing of the dragon enemy of the sun-god are common in the Egyptian texts here translated: pp. 6-7, 8; 9-10; 14, n.7; 253; 263; 366; 367.

Title

NOT DYING BECAUSE OF A SNAKE. GOING IN AND OUT OF THE WESTERN DOORS OF HEAVEN. FLOURISHING UPON EARTH, ON THE PART OF A LIVING OR DEAD SOUL. KNOWING THE WESTERN SOULS.[1]

The Dragon of the West

I know that mountain of Bakhu upon which heaven rests.[2] It is of *ti-iaat*-stone, 300 rods in its length and 120 rods in its width.[3] Sobek, Lord of Bakhu, is on the east of this mountain. His temple is of carnelian.[4]

A serpent is on the brow of that mountain, thirty cubits in its length, three cubits of the front thereof being of flint.[5] I know the name of that serpent: "He Who is on the Mountain That He may Overthrow" is his name.

Now at the time of evening it shall turn its eye against Re. Then there shall come a halt among the crew and great stupefaction in the midst of the journey.[6] Then Seth shall bend himself in its direction. The speech which he says as magic:

"I stand beside thee, so that the journey may progress (again). O thou whom I have seen from afar, close thou thine eye! I *have been* blindfolded; I am the male.[7] Cover thy head, so that thou may be well and I may be well. I am the Rich-in-Magic; (it) has been given to me (to use) against thee. What is that? It is being an effective personality.[8] O thou who goest upon his belly, thy strength belongs to thy mountain; (whereas), behold me—when I go off *by myself*, thy strength (will be) with me, for I am he who lifts up strength.[9] I have come that I might despoil the earth-gods.[10] O Re, may he who is in his evening[11] be gracious to me, when we have made the circuit of heaven. (But) thou[12] art in thy fetters—that is what was commanded about thee previously."

Then Re goes to rest in life.

The Western Souls

I KNOW THE WESTERN SOULS. THEY ARE RE, SOBEK, THE LORD OF BAKHU, AND SETH, THE LORD OF LIFE.[13]

[1] The title is rubricized. As in pp. 10, 33 there is a claim to exceptional knowledge. One element about the present charm is that it protected the dead, buried in the ground, from serpents.

[2] The mountain of the far western limits of earth.

[3] Probably about 10 by 4 miles.

[4] The red of sunset? The crocodile-god Sobek was a western god.

[5] The serpent was over 50 feet long, with its front 5 feet armored in flint.

[6] The journey of the sun barque through the western skies. The gaze of the serpent is fascinating.

[7] A pun on *tjam* "blindfold" and *tjay* "male." If the passive, "have been blindfolded," is correct, Seth has taken measures against the hypnotic stare of the serpent. But a variant text gives: "I have bound thee," suggesting that we should read: "I have blindfolded (thee)."

[8] The question and answer are probably a gloss inserted for the mortuary purposes of the text. What, for the benefit of the dead man, is this magic against the destructive serpent? It is that the funerary ritual has made the dead man an *akh*, an "effective being."

[9] The serpent's effective power is not its own and may easily be carried off by Seth.

[10] Who have the forms of serpents.

[11] Re himself.

[12] The serpent.

[13] Rubricized. A few texts replace Re by Atum, who was the sun at evening. Since Seth was, according to another myth, the enemy of Osiris and thus of the dead, most texts replace Seth by "Hat-Hor, Lady of the Evening." Since the dead entered the west, an acquaintance with the powerful forces of the west and the afterworld was of use to the dead.

THE GOD AND HIS UNKNOWN NAME OF POWER

To the ancient, the name was an element of personality and of power. It might be so charged with divine potency that it could not be pronounced. Or the god might retain a name hidden for himself alone, maintaining this element of power over all other gods and men. The following myth tells how the supreme god Re had many names, one of which was hidden and was thus a source of supremacy. The goddess Isis plotted to learn this name and thus to secure power for herself. For this purpose, she employed the venom of a snake against Re. The text thus came to be employed as a conjuration against the bite of a scorpion, and this use probably accounts for the survival of the myth.

The two manuscripts have been dated to the Nineteenth Dynasty (1350-1200 B.C.). The Turin text is ascribed to Lower Egypt, the Beatty text to Thebes.

The fuller text is on a papyrus in Turin, published by F. Rossi and W. Pleyte, *Papyrus de Turin* (Leyden, 1869-76), Pls. CXXXI:12-CXXXIII:14, LXXVII plus XXXI:1-5. (Pls. LXXVII and XXXI constitute a single column.) There is also a facsimile in G. Möller, *Hieratische Lesestücke*, II (Leipzig, 1927), 30-32. Papyrus Chester Beatty XI (British Museum 10691), recto i-iv, is more fragmentary. It is published in *Hieratic Papyri in the British Museum. Third Series. Chester Beatty Gift*, ed. by A. H. Gardiner (London, 1935), 116-18, Pls. 64-65. Translated by A. Erman and H. Ranke, *Aegypten* (Tübingen, 1923), 301-04, and by G. Roeder, *Urkunden zur Religion des alten Aegypten* (Jena, 1923), 138-41.

THE SPELL OF the divine god, who came into being by himself, who made heaven, earth, water, the breath of life, fire, gods, men, small and large cattle, creeping things, birds, and fishes, the king of men and gods at one time, *(for whom) the limits (go) beyond years*, abounding in names, unknown to that (god) and unknown to this (god).

Now Isis was a clever woman. Her heart was craftier than (cxxxii 1) a million men; she was choicer than a million gods; she was more discerning than a million of the noble dead. There was nothing which she did not know in heaven and earth, like Re, who made the content of the earth. The goddess purposed in her heart to learn the name of the august god.

Now Re entered every day at the head of the crew, taking his place on the throne of the two horizons.[1] A divine old age had *slackened* his mouth. He cast his spittle upon the ground and spat it out, fallen upon the soil. Isis kneaded it for herself with her hand, together

[1] He made the daily journey between east and west in his sun barque.

with the earth on which it was. She built it up into an august snake; she made it in the form of a *sharp point.* It did not stir alive before her, (but) she left it at the crossroads past which the great god used to go according to the desire of his heart throughout (5) his Two Lands.

The august god appeared out of doors, with the gods from the palace accompanying him, so that he might stroll as on every day. The august snake bit him. The living fire came forth from his own self, and it *vanished among the grass.*[2] When the divine god could gain his voice, the noise of his majesty reached the heavens. His Ennead said: "What is it? What is it?", and his gods said: "What? What?" (But) he could not find his voice to answer about it. His lips were trembling, and all his members shuddered. The poison took possession of his flesh as the Nile takes possession *(of the land) after it.*

When the great god had composed his heart, he cried out to his retinue: "Come to me,[3] ye who came into being in my body, ye gods who came forth from me, that I may make known to you what has happened! Something painful has stabbed me. My heart does [not] recognize it, my eyes have not seen it, my hand did not make it, and I do not recognize it in all that I have made. I have not tasted a pain like unto it, and there is nothing more painful (10) than it.

"I am a noble, the son of a noble, the fluid of a god, who came into being as a god. I am a great one, the son of a great one. My father thought out my name.[4] I am abounding in names and abounding in forms. My forms exist as every god; I am called Atum and Horus-of-Praise. My father and my mother told me my name, (but) it was hidden in my body before I was born, in order that the power of a male or female magician might not be made to play against me. While I was going out of doors to see what I had made (and to) stroll in the Two Lands which I have created, something has stung me—I know not what. It is not really fire; it is not really water. My heart is on fire, my body is trembling, and all my members *have a birth of* chill.

"Let the children of the gods be brought to me, the beneficent of speech, who know their (magic) spells, whose wisdom reaches the heavens."

(cxxxiii 1) So the children of the gods came, every one of them having his mourning, (but) Isis came with her skill, her speech having the breath of life, her utterances expelling pain, and her words reviving him whose throat was constricted.[5] She said: "What is it, what is it, my divine father? What—a snake *stabbed* weakness into thee? One of thy children lifted up his head against thee? Then I shall cast it down with effective magic. I shall make it retreat at the sight of thy rays."

The holy god opened his mouth: "It is that I was going along the way, strolling in the Two Lands and the foreign countries, for my heart desired to see what I had created, when I was bitten by a snake, without seeing it. It is not really fire; it is not really water; (but) I am colder than water, I am hotter than fire. (5) My entire body is sweating, while I am shivering. My eye (is) not steadfast, and I cannot see. The heavens are *beating* upon my face as at the time of summer."

Then Isis said: "Tell me thy name, my divine father, for a person lives with whose name one recites (magic)."

"I am he who made heaven and earth, who knotted together the mountains, and created what is thereon. I am he who made the waters, so that the Heavenly Cow might come into being.[6] I am he who made the bull for the cow, so that sexual pleasures might come into being. I am he who made the heaven and the mysteries of the two horizons, so that the soul of the gods might be placed therein. I am he who opened his eyes, so that light might come into being, who closed his eyes, so that darkness might come into being, in conformance with whose command the Nile flows, (but) whose name the gods have not learned. I am he who made the hours, so that days might come into being. I am he who opened the year and created the river.[7] I am he who made the living fire, in order to bring into being (10) the work of *the palace.*[8] I am Khepri in the morning, Re at noon, and Atum who is in the evening."[9]

(But) the poison was not checked in its course, and the great god did not recover.

THEN Isis SAID to Re: "Thy name is not really among these which thou hast told me. If thou tellest it to me, the poison will come forth, for a person whose name is pronounced lives."

The poison burned with a burning. It was more powerful than flame or fire.

Then the majesty of Re said: "Let thy ears be given to me, my daughter Isis, that my name may come forth from my body into thy body. The (most) divine among the gods concealed it, so that my place might be wide in the Barque of Millions (of Years).[10] If there should take place a first time of (its) issuing [from] my heart, tell it to (thy) son Horus, after thou hast *threatened* him with an oath of the god and hast placed the god in his eyes."[11] The great god divulged his name to Isis, the Great of Magic.

"Flow forth, scorpion poison! Come forth from Re, O Eye of Horus! Come forth from the burning god (lxxvii 1) at my spell! It is I who acts; it is I who sends (the message). Come upon the ground, O mighty poison! Behold, the great god has divulged his name, and

[2] The last clause probably corrupt.

[3] Common in the sense of "Help me!"

[4] This was the hidden name, distinct from his many other names, through which names he appeared in many other gods. We should not be too much concerned with the literary formula which gives the creator-god a father and mother. They appear solely to confer his unknown name upon him.

[5] One who had suffered a bite or sting could not breathe the "breath of life."

[6] *Mehet Weret* "the Great Flood" carries the concept of the heavens as an ocean in the form of a cow, upon which the barque of the sun sailed.

[7] The creator-god made time and the marking of time, including the annual inundation.

[8] If the word be really "palace," the claim may be that Re established the kingship.

[9] Three forms of deity in which the sun crossed the sky.

[10] The sun barque was Re's place of command. It had greater scope if he possessed a secret name of power.

[11] If Re had to divulge his name, he was willing that Isis communicate it to Horus, but only on condition that Horus be laid under an oath to keep it secret.

Re is living, the poison is dead. So-and-so, the [son] of So-and-so,[12] is living, and the poison is dead, through the speech of Isis the Great, the Mistress of the Gods, who knows Re (by) his own name."

Directions for the Use of this Charm

Words to be spoken over an image of Atum and of Horus-of-Praise, a figure of Isis, and an image of Horus,[13] painted (on) the hand of him who has the sting and licked off by the man—(or) done similarly on a strip of fine linen, placed at the throat of him who has the sting. It is *the way of caring for* a scorpion poison. (Or) it may be worked up with beer or wine and drunk by the man who has a scorpion (bite). It is what kills the poison—really successful a million times.

THE CONTEST OF HORUS AND SETH FOR THE RULE

Lower Egypt and Upper Egypt are two distinct lands, but are united by contiguity, common dependence upon the Nile, and isolation from other lands. Egyptians have always been conscious of the difference between the "Two Lands," and the reconciliation of two competing areas is a recurrent theme in mythology and the dogma of rule. The commonest expression of this theme is a contest between the gods Horus and Seth to inherit the rule of Osiris, father of Horus and brother of Seth, with a final reconciliation of the two feuding gods to become a united pair.

The following tale draws from this myth for a lusty folkstory, told for entertainment rather than didactic purpose. The language, style, and treatment of the tale are colloquial—and will be so translated[1]—and the gods are depicted as petty and childish. The setting of the story is juridical, with the supreme tribunal of the gods, the Ennead,[2] attempting to settle the contest. The president of this tribunal is the sun-god Re.

The manuscript of the story was written in Thebes in the Twentieth Dynasty (12th century B.C.). The hieratic text is on Papyrus Chester Beatty I, recto i 1-xvi 8. Published with photographs, a transcription into hieroglyphic, translation and commentary by A. H. Gardiner, *The Library of A. Chester Beatty. Description of a Hieratic Papyrus with a Mythological Story, Love-Songs, and Other Miscellaneous Texts* (Oxford, 1931). Gardiner gives another transcription into hieroglyphic in *Late-Egyptian Stories* (*Bibliotheca Aegyptiaca*, 1, Brussels, 1932), 37-60.

I (i 1-ii 2)

The judging of Horus and Seth [took place], the strange of form, the greatest and mightiest of princes who (ever) were; when a [*divine*] child sat before the All-Lord, claiming the office of his father Osiris, the beautiful of appearings, [the son] of [Pt]ah, who lights up [*the west* with] his [appear]ance, while Thoth was presenting the Eye [to] the mighty prince who is in Heliopolis.[3]

Then Shu, the son of Re, said before [Atum, the] mighty [prince] who is in Heliopolis: "*Just is the Lord, strong and . . . is he,* in saying: Give the office to [Horus]!" (5) Then Thoth [said] to the [Ennead: "Right,] a million times!" Then Isis [gave] a great cry, and she rejoiced very, [very much, and she *stood*] before the All-[Lord,] and she said: "North wind, (go) to the west! Give the good news to King Wen-nofer—life, prosperity, health!"[4] [Then] Shu, the son [of Re,] said: "[*The*] presenting of the Eye is the justice of the Ennead!"

What the All-Lord [said]: "Here—what do you mean by taking action alone!" Then . . . said: "He has [taken] the name-ring of Horus, and the [White] Crown has been [put] on his head!"[5] Then the All-Lord was silent for a long [time, for] he was angry [at] the Ennead.

Then Seth, the son of Nut, said: "Have him dismissed (10) along with me, so that I may show you how my hand prevails over his hand [in the] presence of the Ennead, for nobody knows [any (other)] way [to] strip him!" Then Thoth said to him: "Shouldn't we know the guilty one? Now, should the office of Osiris be given to Seth, when [his] son Horus is standing (here in court)?"[6]

Then the Re-Har-akhti was very, very angry, for it was the wish of the Re (ii 1) to give the office to Seth, the great of strength, the son of Nut.[7] And Onuris gave a great cry before the Ennead, saying: "What are we going to do!"

II (ii 2-7)

(In their confusion, the gods appeal to a god of generation, who might—as a sort of obstetrician—advise them on the legitimacy of the two contestants. This god evades the responsibility of a decision and suggests that they might ask the ancient goddess Neith, an old crone whose lore might be decisive.)

III (ii 7-iii 7)

Then the Ennead said to Thoth in the presence of the All-Lord: "Please write a letter to Neith, the Great, the God's Mother, in the name of the All-Lord, the Bull Residing in Heliopolis." Then Thoth said: "I will do (it), yes, I will, I will!" Then he sat down to write a letter, and he said:

[12] The manuscript permits at this point the insertion of the name of a suffering Egyptian—"*X*, the son of (his mother) Y"—so that this charm might be used to cure him.

[13] The Turin papyrus (Pl. LXXVII) has a vignette showing these four gods, so that they may be copied for this use.

[1] For example, the pronoun, 2nd pers. sing., will be translated "you," instead of the "thou" which would be appropriate in a more dignified text of the classical language.

[2] The corporation of gods, originally nine (cf. pp. 3, 6 above), was no longer thought of in terms of a number. Presiding over this "Ennead" was Re, the "All-Lord." The reader should not be distressed if this presiding judge is called by some of his other phases of activity: the Re, the Re-Har-akhti, or Atum.

[3] At a time when the moon-god Thoth was offering to the sun-god Re the sacred eye, which was both an eye of heaven and a symbol of justice, the youthful Horus put in his claim to his father's rule.

[4] The north wind was the propitious wind. Osiris Wen-nofer was ruler in the west, the realm of the dead.

[5] This member of the Ennead, whose name is lost in a lacuna, regards the election of Horus to the rule as an accomplished fact: Horus' name written in the royal cartouche and the crown of Upper Egypt—Seth's province—upon his head. Re disagrees, as he favors Seth (cf. n.7 below).

[6] The advocate Thoth takes the legal position that a court of justice has a responsibility to establish the rights and wrongs of a case when a client has made a formal appeal.

[7] Re's partiality to Seth may be a result of Seth's activity in repelling the monster which nightly threatened to destroy the barque of Re (cf. pp. 11-12 above).

"The King of Upper and Lower Egypt: Re-(ii 10) Atum, the beloved of Thoth, the Lord of the Two Lands, the Heliopolitan, . . . ,[8] to this effect: This your servant spends the night in concern over Osiris and consulting the Two Lands every day, while Sobek endures forever.[9] What are we going to do for the two men who have been in the court for eighty years up to now, but (iii 1) no one is able to pass judgment on the two? Please write us what we should do!"

THEN Neith, the Great, the God's Mother, sent a letter to the Ennead, saying: "Give the office of Osiris to his son Horus! Don't do these great acts of wickedness, which are not in their place, or I shall be angry, and the sky will crash to the ground! And have the All-Lord, the Bull Residing in Heliopolis, told: Double Seth in his property; give him Anath and Astarte, your two daughters; and (5) put Horus in the place of his father Osiris."[10]

THEN the letter of Neith, the Great, the God's Mother, reached the Ennead, while they were sitting in the broad hall (named) "Horus-Foremost-of-Horns," and the letter was put in Thoth's hand. THEN Thoth read it out in the presence of the All-Lord and the entire Ennead. And they said with one voice: "This goddess is right!"

IV (iii 7-iv 3)

THEN the All-Lord was angry at Horus, and he said to him: "You are weak in your body, so this office is too much for you, you boy, with the taste of his mouth (still) bad!"[11] THEN Onuris was angry a million times, and likewise the entire Ennead, that is, the Thirty—life, prosperity, health![12] And the god Baba drew himself up, and he (iii 10) said to the Re-Har-akhti: "Your shrine is empty!"[13] THEN the Re-Har-akhti was hurt at the retort which had been made to him, and he lay down on his back, and his heart was very wretched. THEN the Ennead went out, and they gave a great cry in the face of the god Baba, and they said to him: "Get out! This crime which you have committed is very great!" And they went to their tents. THEN the great god spent a day (iv 1) lying on his back in his arbor, and his heart was very wretched, and he was alone.

NOW AFTER A LONG TIME, THEN Hat-Hor, the Lady of the Southern Sycamore, came, and she stood before her father, the All-Lord, and she uncovered her private parts before his face.[14] THEN the great god laughed at her. THEN HE got up, and he sat down with the Great Ennead, and he said to Horus and Seth: "Say your say!"

V (iv 3-v 6)

(The discussion immediately breaks down into wrangling. When Isis, the mother of Horus, intervenes on her son's behalf, Seth is furious and threatens to kill one of the gods every day. He refuses to take part in the trial while Isis is present. The gods therefore isolate themselves on "Central Island" and charge the ferryman not to transport any woman resembling Isis.)

VI (v 6-vi 2)

(Isis disguises herself and bribes the ferryman to take her over to "Central Island.")

VII (vi 2-viii 1)

(In the guise of a maiden, Isis lures Seth away from the Ennead and, by a play on words, tricks him into validating the claim of Horus.)

VIII (viii 1-6)

(Over the protest of Seth, the Ennead awards the office to Horus.)

IX (viii 6-ix 7)

(Seth succeeds in staying the award by challenging Horus to an ordeal. They become two hippopotamuses and try to stay under water for three full months, with the office to be given to the one who lasts longest under water. However, Isis complicates the contest by trying to harpoon Seth. He appeals to her sisterly feeling, and she withdraws the harpoon from his hide.)

X (ix 7-xi 1)

(Horus is angry at his mother's change of heart and cuts off her head. The Ennead permits Seth to punish Horus by removing his eyes and burying them "to illuminate the earth." Hat-Hor restores Horus's sight with drops of gazelle milk. Re appeals to the two contestants to stop quarreling. This episode must have some relation to the sun and the moon as the two eyes of Horus in his function as sky-god.)

XI (xi 1-xiii 2)

(A bawdy episode, in which Seth attempts to impugn the virility of Horus but is outwitted by Isis.)

XII (xiii 2-xiv 4)

THEN Seth made a great oath to god, saying: "The office shouldn't be given to him until he has been dismissed (from court) with me and we have built ourselves some stone ships and we have a race, the two (of us)! Then the one who beats his opponent, (xiii 5) the office of Ruler—life, prosperity, health!—shall be given to him!"

[8] Re here borrows the formal series of titles used by an Egyptian pharaoh. This translation omits the rest of these titles.

[9] Re suggests that he has to worry about Osiris, whereas Neith need not worry about her son Sobek, who does not die.

[10] In contrast to Re, the peppery old goddess begins her letter without any formal address. She has no doubt that Horus should receive his father's rule, but she recognizes that Seth merits some compensation, so that she recommends enriching him and giving him Re's two daughters. Anath and Astarte were Semitic goddesses; Seth served as an Egyptian god for foreign countries; thus the proposal had its point; cf. p. 249.

[11] N. Shiah, in *JEA*, xxiv (1938), 127 f., quotes Chinese taunts directed at youths, to the effect that their mouths still have the bad smell of undried mother's milk.

[12] The "Thirty" were the magisterial councils of Egypt. The word no longer necessitates an exact number, any more than the "Ennead" does.

[13] Sarcastic for: You are not functioning as a god any more. The name Baba is here determined with an animal sign. In K. Sethe, *Die altägyptischen Pyramidentexte*, II, §1349a, a Babui is described as "red of ear, colored of buttocks." Babui-Baba may be be a baboon, here in a monkeyish role.

[14] Hat-Hor was the goddess of love. Her role here was to cajole the supreme god out of his sulkiness and bring him back to the tribunal.

THEN Horus built himself a ship of cedar, and he plastered it with gypsum, and he launched it on the water in the evening time, without any man who was in the entire land having seen it. THEN Seth saw the ship of Horus, and he thought it was stone, and he went to the mountain, and he cut off a mountain peak, and he built himself a stone ship of 138 cubits.[15]

THEN THEY embarked in their ships in the presence of the Ennead. Then the ship of Seth sank in the water. THEN Seth changed himself into a hippopotamus, (10) so that he might cause the wreck of Horus' ship. THEN Horus took his harpoon, and he threw it at the majesty of Seth.[16] THEN the Ennead said to him: "Don't throw it at him!"

THEN HE took the water weapons, and he laid them in his ship, and he sailed downstream to Sais to speak (to) Neith, the Great, the God's Mother:[17] "Let me be judged with Seth, since we have been in the court for EIGHTY years up to now, (xiv 1) but no one is able to pass judgment on us! He has not been declared right over me, but a thousand times up to now I have been right over him every day! But he pays no attention to anything that the Ennead says. I contested with him in the broad hall (named) 'Way-of-Truths,' and I was declared right over him. I contested with him in the broad hall (named) 'Horus-Foremost-of-Horns,' and was declared right over him. I contested with him in the broad hall (named) 'Field-of-Reeds,' and I was declared right over him. I contested with him in the broad hall (named) 'the-Field-Pool,' and I was declared right over him."

And the Ennead said to Shu, the son of Re: "Horus, the son of Isis, is right in all that he has said!"[18]

XIII (xiv 5-xv 10)

So Thoth said to the All-Lord: "Have a letter sent to Osiris, so that he may pass judgment on the two boys." THEN Shu, the son of Re, SAID: "What Thoth has said to the Ennead is right a million times!" THEN the All-Lord said to Thoth: "Sit down and write a letter to Osiris, so that we may hear what he has to say." THEN Thoth sat down to complete a letter to Osiris, saying:

"The Bull: the Lion that Hunts for Himself; the Two Goddesses: Protecting the Gods and Curbing the Two Lands; the Horus of Gold: Discoverer of Mankind in the Primeval Time; the King of Upper and Lower Egypt: Bull Residing in Heliopolis—life, prosperity, health!—the Son of Ptah: Beneficial One of the Two Banks, Who Appears as Father of His Ennead, while he eats of gold and every (kind of) precious fayence—life, prosperity, health![19] Please write us what we are to do for Horus and Seth, so that we may not do something in our ignorance."

Now after (many days) after this, THEN the (10) letter reached the king, the Son of Re: Great of Overflow, Lord of Provisions.[20] Then he gave a great cry when the letter was read out before him. THEN he answered it very, very quickly to the place where the All-Lord was with the Ennead, saying:

"Why should my son Horus be cheated, since I am the one who made you strong? Now I am the one who made barley and emmer to keep the gods alive, as well as the cattle after the gods! And no (other) god or goddess at all found himself (able) to do it!"

Then the (xv 1) letter of Osiris reached the place where the Re-Har-akhti was, sitting with the Ennead in Xois at the bright(est) time.[21] Then it was read out before him and the Ennead. And the Re-Har-akhti said: "Please answer for me the letter very quickly to Osiris, and say to him about the letter: 'Suppose that you had never come into being, or suppose that you had never been born—barley and emmer would still exist!' "[22]

Then the letter of the All-Lord reached Osiris, and it was read out before him. THEN HE sent to the Re-Har-akhti again, saying:

"Very, very fine is everything that you have done, you discoverer of the Ennead as a deed (accomplished) while justice was permitted to sink down into the Underworld![23] Now look at the case again, yourself! As to (5) the land in which I am, it is filled with savage-faced messengers, and they are not afraid of any god or goddess! I can send them out, and they will bring back the heart of anyone who does wrong, and (then) they will be here with me![24] Why, what does it mean, my being here resting in the West, while every single one of you is outside? Who among them[25] is stronger than I? But see, they[25] discovered falsehood as an accomplishment. Now when Ptah, the Great, South-of-His-Wall, Lord of the Life of the Two Lands, made the sky, didn't he say to the stars which are in it: 'You shall go to rest (in) the West every night, in the place where King Osiris is'? 'And, after the gods, the people and the folk shall also go to rest in the place where you are'—so he said to me."[26]

Now after (many days) after this, the letter of Osiris reached the place where the All-Lord was with the Ennead. THEN Thoth took the letter, and he read it out

[15] Over 230 feet, a length suitable for a seagoing vessel or a ceremonial barge.

[16] In other accounts of the rivalry between Horus and Seth, Horus hunted the hippopotamus as an animal of Seth.

[17] As in episode III above, the elder goddess Neith seems to have served as an experienced advisor.

[18] It is not clear why Neith's response is unstated. Possibly Horus only threatened to appeal to her. At any rate, a response is given to Shu, as the spokesman for the Ennead.

[19] As in the letter to Neith in episode III above, this letter carries only the titles of the addresser, given in imitation of the fivefold titulary of a pharaoh. Attention might be directed to the interesting epithet of Re: "Discoverer of Mankind in the Primeval Time." Osiris (see the next note) it treated as the ruler of another realm, that of the dead.

[20] A royal name for Osiris as the god of grain.

[21] Xois in the Delta was a cult-seat of Re. "The bright time" may be high noon.

[22] Re abandons the real issue and argues Osiris's claim to have made the grain which keeps the gods alive.

[23] In the sarcastic view of Osiris, Re's preoccupation with building up his circle of gods has led him to neglect justice.

[24] Here, perhaps for the first time, the Egyptian underworld is regarded as a Hades for evildoers, from which Osiris may send out angels ("messengers") to claim evildoers.

[25] *Sic*, but read "you."

[26] Osiris's argument of superior authority is that he is the god of the dead and that stars, gods, and humans ultimately come to be under his rule.

before the Re-Har-akhti (10) and the Ennead. THEN THEY said: "Right, right in all that he has said is the (King): Great of Overflow, Lord of Provisions—life, prosperity, health!"

XIV (xv 10-xvi 8)

THEN Seth said: "Let us be taken to the Central Island, so that I may contend with him." THEN HE went to the Central Island, and Horus was conceded the right over him. THEN Atum, Lord of the Two Lands, the Heliopolitan, sent to Isis, saying: "Fetch Seth, fastened in handcuffs!" THEN Isis fetched Seth, fastened in handcuffs, he being a prisoner. THEN Atum said to him: "Why didn't you allow judgment to be passed on (the two of) you, instead of taking the office of Horus for yourself?" THEN Seth said to him: "No, my good lord! Let Horus the son of Isis, be called and given the office of (xvi 1) his father Osiris!"

THEN Horus, the son of Isis, was brought, and the White Crown was set upon his head, and he was put in the place of his father Osiris. And it was said to him: "You are the good king of Egypt; you are the good Lord—life, prosperity, health!—of Every Land up to eternity and forever!" THEN Isis gave a great cry to her son Horus, saying: "You are the good king! My heart rejoices that you light up the earth with your color!"

THEN Ptah, the Great, South-of-His-Wall, Lord of the Life of the Two Lands, said: "What is to be done for Seth? For, see, Horus has been put in the place of his father Osiris!" THEN the Re-Har-akhti said: "Let Seth, the son of Nut, be given to me, so that he may live with me and be a son to me. And he shall speak out in the sky, and men shall be afraid of him."[27]

THEN THEY (5) went to say to the Re-Har-akhti: "Horus, the son of Isis, has arisen as the Ruler—life, prosperity, health!" THEN the Re rejoiced very much, and he said to the Ennead: "You should be glad! To the ground, to the ground, for Horus, the son of Isis!" Then Isis said: "Horus has arisen as the Ruler—life, prosperity, health! The Ennead is in jubilee, and heaven is in joy!" They took wreaths when they saw Horus, the son of Isis, arisen as the great Ruler—life, prosperity, health!—of Egypt. The hearts of the Ennead were content, and the entire earth was in jubilation, when they saw Horus, the son of Isis, assigned the office of his father Osiris, Lord of Busiris.

It has come to a happy ending in Thebes, the Place *of Truth.*

ASTARTE AND THE TRIBUTE OF THE SEA

The excuse for introducing so damaged a document is that we may have here the Egyptian version of a tale current in Asia. The badly damaged papyrus gives us little certainty about the purport of the story, but it may be guessed that it told how the gods—in this case, the Egyptian gods—were freed of the obligation to pay tribute to the sea. The Phoenician goddess Astarte, whom the Egyptians of the Empire had introduced into Egypt and who here appears as the "daughter of Ptah," was instrumental in this deliverance from tribute. Any reconstruction must be treated with great reserve.

The Astarte Papyrus, formerly in the Amherst collection and now in the Morgan collection in New York, dates from the Eighteenth or Nineteenth Dynasty (1550-1200 B.C.). Photographs of the papyrus were given by P. E. Newberry, *The Amherst Papyri* (London, 1899), Pls. XIX-XXI. Photographs, a translation, and commentary were given by A. H. Gardiner in *Studies Presented to F. Ll. Griffith* (London, 1932), 74 ff. Gardiner points out a general similarity between the Astarte tale and *Enuma elish,* the Babylonian account of the creation, in which the enemy of the gods is *Ti'amat,* the sea (cf. pp. 60-72). A. H. Sayce called attention to possible Hittite parallels in *JEA,* XIX (1933), 56 ff. A transcription into hieroglyphic was given by Gardiner in *Late-Egyptian Stories* (*Bibliotheca Aegyptiaca,* I, Brussels, 1932), 76-81.

(At the visible beginning of the text all seems to be well with the gods, of whom Ptah, the Sky, and the Earth are mentioned. In what follows, it seems that the Sea claims tribute from the gods as their ruler and that the harvest-goddess Renenut delivered this.)

(i x+8) . . . [hi]s throne of Ruler—life, prosperity, health! And he . . . carried to him tribute . . . from the tribunal. Then Renenut carried [*this tribute to the Sea, as it was due to him*] as Ruler— life, prosperity, health! [*One of the gods said*]: ". . . sky. Now, behold, tribute must be brought to him, . . . (x+11) . . . his . . . , or he will carry us off as booty. . . . our own for . . ." [Then] Renenut [carried] his tribute of silver and gold, lapis lazuli, . . . *the* boxes. . . .

(At this point the Ennead of gods seems to express apprehension and ask questions. Perhaps their relations with the Sea have worsened through his added demands. Apparently they need an intermediary and pick Astarte as suitable for that purpose. It seems that Renenut sent a bird to appeal to Astarte to undertake this mission on behalf of the gods.)

(ii x+3) . . . And Renenut took a . . . Astarte. Then said [*Renenut to one of certain*] birds: "Hear what I shall say; thou shouldst not go away . . . another. Come, that thou mayest go to Astarte . . . [*and fly to*] her house and speak under [*the window of the room where*] she is sleeping and say to her: 'If [thou art awake, *hear my voice.*] If thou art asleep, I shall waken [thee. *The Ennead must send tribute to* the] Sea as Ruler over the [*Earth and as Ruler over*] (x+7) the Sky. Pray, come thou to them in this [*hour*]! . . . (x+12) . . . that thou go thyself, carrying the tribute of [the Sea] . . .'" Then Astarte wept . . .

(Astarte is apparently persuaded and undertakes the mission. She must cajole the Sea and appeal to his sympathy, perhaps because the tribute which she brings is insufficient.)

(x+17) . . . So [*she*] bore [*the tribute of*] the [*Sea. She reached the Sea,*] singing and laughing at him. [*Then the Sea*] saw Astarte sitting on the *shore* of the Sea. Then he said to her: "Wh[ence] comest [thou,] thou daughter of Ptah, thou furious and tempestuous

[27] The special attachment of Re and Seth is again indicated; cf. n.7 above. Seth was to be located, as the thunder-god, in the heavens with the sun-god; cf. pp. 27, n.23; 249.

goddess? Are (thy) sandals which (are on thy) feet *broken*, are thy clothes which are upon thee torn by the going and coming which (thou) hast made in heaven and earth?" Then [Astarte] said to him . . .

(Here a long lacuna intervenes. Astarte seems to win the desire of the Sea, without necessarily palliating his demand for tribute. Apparently the Sea sends her back to Ptah, with a request that the Ennead surrender the goddess to him. The next words may be his message to Ptah.)

(iii y-2) ". . . [the Enne]ad. If they give to me thy [*daughter*,] . . . them, what should I do against them myself?" And Astarte heard what the Sea [said] to her, and she lifted herself up to go before the Ennead, to [the] place where they were gathered. And the great ones saw her, and they stood up before her. And the lesser ones saw her, and they lay down upon their bellies. And her throne was given to her, and she sat down. And there was presented to her the . . .

(Thus Astarte was accepted as a member of the Ennead. Several lacunae follow, with brief passages of text. It seems that the Sea is unyielding in his demands for tribute, so that the gods must put their personal jewelry into the balances to make up the required weight.)

[Then] (iv y) the messenger of Ptah went to tell these words to Ptah and to Nut. Then Nut untied the beads which were at her throat. Behold, she put (them) into the scales. . . .

(v y) . . . It means [*arguing*] with the Ennead. Then he will send and demand . . . the seal of Geb . . . [*to fill*] the scales *with* it. Then . . .

(The remainder of a long tale is confined to meaningless scraps. The three brief excerpts given below show that the contest between the Ennead and the Sea continued through a number of episodes.)

(xi y) . . . and *he* will cover the ground and the mountains and . . .

(xv y) ". . . [*come*] to fight with him, because . . . seating himself calmly. He will not come to fight with us." Then Seth sat down . . .

(verso b) . . . and the Sea *left* . . .

THE STORY OF SI-NUHE

A strong love of country was a dominant characteristic of the ancient Egyptian. Though he might feel the responsibilities of empire-building, he wished the assurance that he would close his days on the banks of the Nile. That sentiment made the following story one of the most popular classics of Egyptian literature. An Egyptian official of the Middle Kingdom went into voluntary exile in Asia. He was prosperous and well established there, but he continued to long for the land of his birth. Finally he received a royal invitation to return and join the court. This was his real success in life, and this was the popular point of the story. Much of the tale is pompous and over-styled in wording and phrasing, but the central narrative is a credible account, which fits the period as we know it. If this was fiction, it was based on realities and deserves a respected place in Egyptian literature.

The story opens with the death of Amen-em-het I (about 1960 B.C.) and continues in the reign of his successor, Sen-Usert I (about 1971-1928 B.C.). Manuscripts are plentiful and run from the late Twelfth Dynasty (about 1800 B.C.) to the Twenty-First Dynasty (about 1000 B.C.). There are five papyri and at least seventeen ostraca. The most important papyri are in Berlin (3022 [the B manuscript] and 10499 [the R manuscript]), and were published by A. H. Gardiner, in *Berlin. Staatlichen Museen. Hieratische Papyrus, V. Die Erzählung des Sinuhe* . . . (Leipzig, 1909), Pls. 1-15. G. Maspero studied the texts in *Les Mémoires de Sinouhit* (*Bibliothèque d'Étude*, I, Cairo, 1908). The definitive study of the texts was made by A. H. Gardiner, *Notes on the Story of Sinuhe* (reprinted from *Recueil de travaux* . . . , Vols. XXXII-XXXVI, Paris, 1916), in which reference is given to the antecedent literature. A. M. Blackman gives a transcription of the texts into hieroglyphic in *Middle-Egyptian Stories* (*Bibliotheca Aegyptiaca*, II, Brussels, 1932), 1-41. Since Gardiner's edition, brief but usable documents have been cited by L. Borchardt in *ZAeS*, LXVI (1930), 14-15; by A. Rosenvasser in *JEA*, XX (1934), 47-50; by J. J. Clère in *JEA*, XXV (1939), 16-29; by W. C. Hayes, *Ostraka and Name Stones from the Tomb of Sen-mut* . . . (New York, 1942), Pl. XXVIII; and by G. Posener, *Catalogue des ostraca hiératiques littéraires de Deir el Médineh* (*Documents de fouilles* . . . , I, Cairo, 1934-38), I, Nos. 1011, 1045 recto. The story is translated in Erman, *LAE*, 14-29.

(R1) THE HEREDITARY PRINCE AND COUNT, Judge and District Overseer of the domains of the Sovereign in the lands of the Asiatics, real acquaintance of the king, his beloved, the Attendant Si-nuhe. He says:

I was an attendant who followed his lord, a servant of the royal harem (and of) the Hereditary Princess, the great of favor, the wife of King Sen-Usert in (the pyramid town) Khenem-sut, the daughter of King Amen-em-het (R5) in (the pyramid town) Qa-nefru, Nefru, the lady of reverence.[1]

YEAR 30, THIRD MONTH OF THE FIRST SEASON, DAY 7.[2] The god ascended to his horizon; the King of Upper and Lower Egypt: Sehetep-ib-Re was taken up to heaven and united with the sun disc. The body of the god merged with him who made him.[3] The Residence City was in silence, hearts were in mourning, the Great Double Doors were sealed shut. (R10) The courtiers (sat) head on lap, and the people were in grief.

Now his majesty had sent an army to the land of the Temeh-Libyans, with his eldest son as the commander thereof, the good god Sen-Usert, (R15) and even now he was returning and had carried off living captives of the Tehenu-Libyans and all (kinds of) cattle without number.

The courtiers of the palace sent to the western border to let the King's Son know the events which had taken place at the court. The messengers met him on the road, (R20) and they reached him in the evening time. He did not delay a moment; the falcon[4] flew away with his attendants, without letting his army know it. Now the royal children who had been following him in this

[1] Si-nuhe's service was to Nefru, the daughter of Amen-em-het I and wife of Sen-Usert I.

[2] Around 1960 B.C., the date of Amen-em-het I's death, as given here, would have fallen early in March.

[3] The pharaoh was the "Son of Re," the sun-god. At death he was taken back into the body of his creator and father.

[4] The new king Sen-Usert I. Although he had been coregent with his father for ten years, he had to go immediately to the capital before word of his father's death became widely known. See the next note.

army had been sent for, (B1) and one of them was summoned. While I was standing (near by) I heard his voice as he was speaking and I was a little way off. My heart was distraught, my arms spread out (in dismay), trembling fell upon all my limbs.[5] I removed myself *by leaps and bounds* to seek a hiding place for myself. I placed (5) myself between two bushes, in order to *cut (myself) off from* the road and its *travel.*

I set out southward, (but) I did not plan to reach this Residence City, (for) I thought that there would be civil disorder, and I did not expect to live after him. I crossed Lake Ma'aty near Sycamore, and I came to Snefru Island. I spent the day there on the *edge* of (10) the fields. I *came into the open* light, while it was (*still*) day, and I met a man standing near by. He stood in awe of me, for he was afraid. When the time of the evening meal came, I drew near to Ox-town. I crossed over in a barge without a rudder, by aid of the west wind.[6] I passed by the east of the quarry (15) above Mistress-of-the-Red-Mountain.[7] I gave (free) road to my feet going northward, and I came up to the Wall-of-the-Ruler,[8] made to oppose the Asiatics and to crush the Sand-Crossers. I took a crouching position in a bush, for fear lest the watchmen upon the wall where their day's (duty) was might see me.

I set out (20) at evening time, and when day broke I reached Peten. I halted at the Island of Kem-wer.[9] An attack of thirst overtook me. I was parched, and my throat was dusty. I said: "This is the taste of death!" (But then) I lifted up my heart and collected myself, for I had heard the sound of the lowing of cattle, (25) and I spied Asiatics. The sheikh among them, who had been in Egypt, recognized me. Then he gave me water while he boiled milk for me. I went with him to his tribe. What they did (for me) was good.

One foreign country gave me to another. I set off for Byblos and approached Qedem,[10] and spent (30) a year and a half there. Ammi-enshi[11]—he was a ruler of Upper Retenu[12]—took me and said to me: "Thou wilt do well with me, and thou wilt hear the speech of Egypt." He said this, for he knew my character, he had heard of my wisdom, and the people of Egypt who were there with him[13] had borne witness for me.

Then he said to me: (35) "Why hast thou come hither? Has something happened in the Residence City?" Then I said to him: "The King of Upper and Lower Egypt: Sehetep-ib-Re is departed to the horizon, and no one knows what might happen because of it." But I said equivocally: "I had come from an expedition to the land of Temeh, when report was made to me. My heart quailed; it carried (40) me off on the way of *flight.* (Yet) no one had gossiped about me; no one had spat in my face; not a belittling word had been heard, nor had my name been heard in the mouth of the herald. I do not know what brought me to this country. It was as though it might be a god."

Then he said to me: "Well, what will that land be like without him, that beneficent god, the fear of whom pervaded (45) foreign countries like (the fear of) Sekhmet in a year of pestilence?"[14] I spoke to him that I might answer him: "Well, of course, his son has entered into the palace and has taken the inheritance of his father. Moreover, he is a god without his peer. There is no other who surpasses him. He is a master of understanding, effective in plans and beneficent of decrees. Going forth and coming back are in conformance with (50) his command. He it was who subdued the foreign countries while his father was in his palace, and he reported to him that what had been charged to him had been carried out. . . .[15] How joyful is this land which he has ruled! (71) He is one who extends its frontiers. He will carry off the lands of the south, and he will not consider the northern countries (seriously), (for) he was made to smite the Asiatics and to crush the Sand-Crossers. Send to him! Let him know thy name! Do not utter a curse against his majesty. He will not fail to do (75) good to the country which shall be loyal to him!"

Then he said to me: "Well, really, Egypt is happy that it knows that he is flourishing. Now thou art here. Thou shalt stay with me. What I shall do for thee is good."

He set me at the head of his children. He married me to his eldest daughter. He let me choose for myself of his country, (80) of the choicest of that which was with him on his frontier with another country. It was a good land, named Yaa. Figs were in it, and grapes. It had more wine than water. Plentiful was its honey, abundant its olives. Every (kind of) fruit was on its trees. Barley was there, and emmer. There was no limit to any (kind of) cattle. (85) Moreover, great was that which accrued

[5] We are never directly told the reason for Si-nuhe's sudden fright and voluntary exile. Later both he and the king protest his innocence. He may have been legally guiltless, but the transition between kings was a dangerous time for one who was not fully identified with the new king. Si-nuhe's official loyalty was to the princess. The Instruction of King Amen-em-het (pp. 418-419 below) acquaints us with a palace conspiracy, perhaps a harem conspiracy, at or near the end of that king's reign. We must assume that Si-nuhe had adequate reason for his sudden and furtive departure and his long stay in Asia.

[6] Apparently Si-nuhe went southeast along the edge of the cultivated land, to avoid the peopled stretches of the Delta, and crossed the Nile where it is a single stream, somewhere near modern Cairo.

[7] Gebel el-Ahmar, east of Cairo.

[8] The fortresses at the eastern frontier, along the general line of the present Suez Canal. See also p. 446 below.

[9] The area of the Bitter Lakes.

[10] Semitic for "the East" generally. A vague term, either in the writer's ignorance of Asiatic geography or intentionally vague for a wide nomadic area.

[11] An Amorite name. It was unfamiliar to one Egyptian scribe, who tried to egyptianize it to "Amu's son Enshi."

[12] Highland country, probably including northern Palestine, southern and central Syria. See A. H. Gardiner, *Ancient Egyptian Onomastica* (London, 1947), I, 142* ff. Si-nuhe's Asiatic home of Yaa cannot be located any more definitely than this. It may be noted that it is agricultural, with herds, but within reasonable distance of desert hunting, and that it is close enough to some main road that Si-nuhe may entertain Egyptian couriers. Since he apparently went east from Byblos, a location in the valley between the Lebanon and Anti-lebanon is a possibility, but it would be wrong to push the evidence so closely. As it stands, the story gives a picture of Syria-Palestine in the patriarchal period.

[13] Other exiles like Si-nuhe? He is in a land of refuge from Egypt. From the nature of this land it seems unlikely that there would have been many Egyptian merchants.

[14] The goddess Sekhmet had to do with disease.

[15] This translation omits some of the fulsome praise.

to me as a result of the love of me. He made me ruler of a tribe of the choicest of his country. Bread was made for me as daily fare, wine as daily provision, cooked meat and roast fowl, beside the wild beasts of the desert, for they hunted (90) for me and laid before me, beside the catch of my (own) hounds. Many . . . were made for me, and milk in every (kind of) cooking.

I spent many years, and my children grew up to be strong men, each man as the restrainer of his (own) tribe. The messenger who went north or who went south to the Residence City (95) stopped over with me, (for) I used to make everybody stop over. I gave water to the thirsty. I put him who had strayed (back) on the road. I rescued him who had been robbed. When the Asiatics became so bold as to oppose the rulers of foreign countries,[16] I counseled their movements. This ruler of (100) (Re)tenu had me spend many years as commander of his army. Every foreign country against which I went forth, when I had made my attack on it, was driven away from its pasturage and its wells. I plundered its cattle, carried off its inhabitants, took away their food, and slew people in it (105) by my strong arm, by my bow, by my movements, and by my successful plans. I found favor in his heart, he loved me, he recognized my valor, and he placed me at the head of his children, when he saw how my arms flourished.

A mighty man of Retenu came, that he might challenge me (110) in my (own) camp. He was a hero without his peer, and he had repelled all of it.[17] He said that he would fight me, he intended to despoil me, and he planned to plunder my cattle, on the advice of his tribe. That prince discussed (it) with me, and I said: "I do not know him. Certainly I am no confederate of his, (115) so that I might move freely in his encampment. Is it the case that I have (ever) opened his *door* or overthrown his fences? (Rather), it is hostility because he sees me carrying out thy commissions. I am really like a stray bull in the midst of another herd, and a bull of (these) cattle attacks him. . . ."[18]

During the night I strung my bow and shot my arrows,[19] I gave free play to my dagger, and polished my weapons. When day broke, (Re)tenu was come. (130) It had *whipped up* its tribes and collected the countries of a (good) half of it. It had thought (only) of this fight. Then he came to me as I was waiting, (for) I had placed myself near him. Every heart burned for me; women and men groaned. Every heart was sick for me. They said: "Is there another strong man who could fight against him?" Then (*he tooḳ*) his shield, his battle-axe, (135) and his *armful of javelins. Now* after I had let his weapons issue forth, I made his arrows pass by me uselessly, one close to another. He charged me, and I shot him, my arrow sticking in his neck. He cried out and fell on his nose. (140) I felled him with his (own) battle-axe and raised my cry of victory over his back, while every Asiatic roared. I gave praise to Montu,[20] while his adherents were mourning for him. This ruler Ammi-enshi took me into his embrace. Then I carried off his goods and plundered his cattle. What he had planned to do (145) to me I did to him. I took what was in his tent and stripped his encampment. I became great thereby, I became extensive in my wealth, I became abundant in my cattle.

Thus did god to show mercy to him upon whom he had *laid blame*, whom he had led astray to another country. (But) today his heart is assuaged.[21] . . .

Now when the majesty of the King of Upper and Lower Egypt: Kheper-ka-Re, the justified,[22] was told about this situation in which I was, then his majesty kept sending (175) to me with presentations from the royal presence, that he might gladden the heart of this servant[23] like the ruler of any foreign country. The royal children in his palace let me hear their commissions.[24]

COPY OF THE DECREE WHICH WAS BROUGHT TO THIS SERVANT ABOUT BRINGING HIM (BACK) TO EGYPT.

"The Horus: Living in Births; the Two Goddesses: Living in Births; the King of Upper and Lower Egypt: Kheper-ka-Re; the Son of Re: (180) Amen-em-het,[25] living forever and ever. Royal decree to the Attendant Si-nuhe. Behold, this decree of the king is brought to thee to let thee know that:

"Thou hast traversed the foreign countries, starting from Qedem to (Re)tenu. One country gave thee to another, under the advice of thy (own) heart to thee. What hast thou done that anything should be done to thee? Thou hast not cursed, that thy word should be punished. Thou hast not spoken against the counsel of the nobles, that thy speeches should be opposed. (185) This plan (simply) carried away thy heart. It was in no heart against thee. This thy heaven which is in the palace[26] is firm and steadfast today. Her head *is covered* with the kingship of the land.[27] Her children are in the court.

"MAYEST THOU LAY UP TREASURES WHICH THEY MAY GIVE THEE; MAYEST THOU LIVE ON THEIR BOUNTY. Do thou return to Egypt, that thou mayest see the home in which thou didst grow up and kiss the ground at the Great Double Door and join with the courtiers. For today, surely, (190) thou hast begun to grow old; thou hast lost (thy) virility. Recall thou the day of burial, the passing to a revered state, when the evening is set aside for thee with ointments and wrappings from the hands of Tait.[28] A funeral procession is made for thee on the day of

[16] *Heqau-ḳhasut* probably simply "the rulers of (other) foreign countries," but it is worth noting that these Egyptian words were the probable origin of the term "Hyksos." We may have here an early reference to restless peoples who were later to participate in the invasion of Egypt. cf. pp. 229, n.9; 247, n.56.

[17] He had beaten every one of the land of Retenu.

[18] Si-nuhe goes on to state that he accepts the challenge, which has come to him because he is an outsider in the Asiatic scene.

[19] In practice.

[20] The Egyptian god of war.

[21] It is not clear how Si-nuhe expiated his sins, except by being a successful Egyptian in another country. This translation omits in the following text a poetical statement of homesickness for Egypt.

[22] Sen-Usert I. The manuscript incorrectly writes Kheper-kau-Re.

[23] "This servant" = me.

[24] They also wrote to Si-nuhe.

[25] *Sic*, but read "Sen-Usert."

[26] The Queen.

[27] She wears the insignia of rule?

[28] The goddess of weaving—here for mummy wrappings.

interment, a mummy case of gold, with head of lapis lazuli, with the heaven above thee,[29] as thou art placed upon a sledge, oxen dragging thee and singers in front of thee, when the dance (195) of the *muu* is performed at the door of thy tomb,[30] when the requirements of the offering table are summoned for thee and there is sacrifice beside thy offering stones, thy pillars being hewn of white stone in the midst of (the tombs of) the royal children. It should not be that thou shouldst die in a foreign country. Asiatics should not escort thee. Thou shouldst not be placed in a sheepskin when thy wall is made. This is (too) long to be roaming the earth. Give heed to *sickness*, that thou mayest return."[31]

THIS DECREE REACHED ME AS I WAS STANDING (200) IN THE MIDST OF MY TRIBE. It was read to me. I put myself upon my belly; I touched the ground; I scattered it upon my hair. I went about my encampment rejoicing and saying: "How can this be done for a servant whom his heart led astray to barbarous countries? But the indulgence which saved me from death is really good! Thy *ka* will let me effect the end of my body at home!"

COPY OF THE ANSWER TO THIS DECREE. THE SERVANT OF *THE PALACE* SI-NUHE (205) says:

"In very good peace! This flight which this servant made in his ignorance is known by thy *ka*, O good god, Lord of the Two Lands, whom Re loves and whom Montu, Lord of Thebes, favors! . . .[32]

"This is the prayer of this servant to his Lord, the saviour in the West: THE LORD OF PERCEPTION, WHO PERCEIVES PEOPLE, MAY HE PERCEIVE (215) in the majesty of the palace that this servant was afraid to say it. It is (still) like something (too) big to repeat.[33] . . . FURTHER, MAY THY MAJESTY COMMAND THAT THERE BE BROUGHT Maki from Qedem, (220) Khenti-iaush from Khent-*keshu*, and Menus from the lands of the Fenkhu.[34] They are *men exact* and reliable, *young men* who grew up in the love of thee—not to mention (Re)tenu: it is thine, like thy (own) hounds.

"Now this flight which the servant made, it was not planned, it was not in my heart, I had not worried about it. I do not know what severed me from (my) place. It was after (225) the manner of a dream, as if A MAN OF THE DELTA were to see himself IN ELEPHANTINE, or a man of the (northern) marshes in Nubia. I had not been afraid. No one had run after me. I had not heard a belittling word. My name had not been heard in the mouth of the herald. And yet—my body *shuddered*, my feet were *trembling*, my heart led me on, and the god who ordained this flight (230) drew me away. I was not at all stiff-backed *formerly*. A man who knows his land should be afraid, (for) Re has set the fear of thee throughout the earth, and the dread of thee in every foreign country. Whether I am at home or whether I am in this place, thou art he who covers this horizon, the sun disc rises at thy pleasure, the water in the River is drunk as thou wishest, and the air in the sky is breathed as thou biddest. This servant will hand over (235) THE VIZIERSHIP WHICH THIS SERVANT HAS EXERCISED IN THIS PLACE."[35]

Then they came for this servant. . . . I was permitted to spend a day in Yaa handing over my property to my children, my eldest son being responsible for my tribe. (240) My tribe and all my property were in his charge: my serfs, all my cattle, my fruit, and every pleasant tree of mine.

Then this servant came southward. I halted at the "Ways of Horus."[36] The commander there who was responsible for the patrol sent a message to the Residence to make (it) known. Then his majesty sent a capable overseer of peasants of the palace, with loaded ships in his train, (245) carrying presentations from the royal presence FOR THE ASIATICS WHO HAD FOLLOWED ME, ESCORTING ME TO THE "WAYS OF HORUS." I called each of them by his name.[37] Every butler was (busy) at his duties. When I started and set sail, the kneading and straining (of beer) was carried on beside me, until I had reached the town of Lisht.[38]

When day had broken, very early, they came and summoned me, ten men coming and ten men going to usher me to the palace.[39] I put my brow to the ground between the sphinxes, (250) while the royal children were waiting in a *recess* to meet me. The courtiers who usher into the audience hall set me on the way to the private chambers. I found his majesty upon the Great Throne in a *recess* of fine gold. When I was stretched out upon my belly, I knew not myself in his presence, (although) this god greeted me pleasantly. I was like a man caught in the dark: (255) my soul departed, my body was powerless, my heart was not in my body, that I might know life from death.

THEN HIS MAJESTY SAID TO ONE OF THESE COURTIERS: "Lift him up. Let him speak to me." Then his majesty said: "Behold, thou art come. Thou hast trodden the foreign countries *and made a flight*. (But now) elderliness has attacked thee; thou hast reached old age. It is no small matter that thy corpse be (properly) buried; thou shouldst not be interred by bowmen.[40] Do not, do not act thus any longer: (for) thou dost not speak (260) when thy name is pronounced!" Yet (I) was afraid to respond, and I answered it with the answer of one afraid: "What is it that my lord says to me? I should answer it, (but) there is nothing that I can do: it is really the hand of a god. It is a terror that is in my belly like that which produced the fated flight. BEHOLD,

[29] The canopy over the hearse.

[30] An old funerary dance.

[31] It may be all right to roam about when you are young, but now you must think that a sickness might carry you off and deprive you of a proper burial in Egypt.

[32] This translation omits good wishes for the king.

[33] Si-nuhe feels that his case is so delicate that he must sidle into it.

[34] Fenkhu perhaps Phoenicia. These Asiatics were recommended as reliable character witnesses or hostages or escort for Si-nuhe.

[35] He maintains the flattering fiction that he has been ruling his part of Asia on behalf of the pharaoh.

[36] The Egyptian frontier station facing Sinai, probably near modern Kantarah. cf. pp. 416, 478.

[37] He introduced the Asiatics to the Egyptians.

[38] The capital in the Faiyum. Si-nuhe traveled on a boat with its own kitchen.

[39] Ten were assigned to summon him and ten to escort him.

[40] Foreigners.

I AM BEFORE THEE. THINE IS LIFE. MAY THY MAJESTY DO AS HE PLEASES."

THEREUPON the royal children WERE ushered in. Then his majesty said to the Queen: "Here is Si-nuhe, (265) come as a Bedu, *(in) the guise of* the Asiatics." She gave a very great cry, and the royal children clamored all together. Then they said to his majesty: "It is not really he, O Sovereign, my lord!" Then his majesty said: "It is really he!" Now when they had brought with them their bead-necklaces, their rattles, and their sistra, then they presented them to his majesty. ". . . Loose the horn of thy bow and relax thy arrow! (275) Give breath to him that was stifled! Give us our goodly gift in this sheikh Si-Mehit,[41] a bowman born in Egypt. He made a flight through fear of thee; he left the land through terror of thee. (But) the face of him who beholds thy face shall not *blench*; the eye which looks at thee shall not be afraid!"

Then his majesty said: "He shall not fear. (280) He has no *title* to be in dread. He shall be a courtier among the nobles. He shall be put in the ranks of the courtiers. Proceed ye to the inner chambers of the *morning (toilet)*, in order to make his position."[42]

So I went forth from the midst of the inner chambers, with the royal children giving me their hands. (285) Thereafter we went to the Great Double Door. I was put into the house of a royal son, in which were splendid things. A cool room was in it, and images of the horizon.[43] Costly things of the Treasury were in it. Clothing of royal linen, myrrh, and prime oil of the king and of the nobles whom he loves were in every room. (290) Every butler was (busy) at his duties. Years were made to pass away from my body. I was *plucked*, and my hair was combed. A load (of dirt) was given to the desert, and my clothes (to) the Sand-Crossers. I was clad in fine linen and anointed with prime oil. I slept on a bed. I gave up the sand to them who are in it, (295) and wood oil to him who is anointed with it. I was given a house *which had a garden*, which had been in the possession of a courtier. Many *craftsmen* built it, and all its wood(work) was newly restored. Meals were brought to me from the palace three or four times a day, apart from that which the royal children gave, without ceasing a moment.

(300) There was constructed for me a pyramid-tomb of stone in the midst of the pyramid-tombs. The stone-masons who hew a pyramid-tomb took over its ground-area. The outline-draftsmen designed in it; the chief sculptors carved in it; and the overseers of works who are in the necropolis made it their concern. (305) Its necessary materials were made from all the outfittings which are placed at a tomb-shaft. Mortuary priests were given to me. There was made for me a necropolis garden, with fields in it *formerly (extending)* as far as the town, like that which is done for a chief courtier. My statue was overlaid with gold, and its skirt was of fine gold. It was his majesty who had it made. There is no poor man for whom the like has been done.

(So) I was under (310) the favor of the king's presence until the day of mooring had come.[44]

IT HAS COME (TO ITS END), FROM BEGINNING TO END AS IT HAD BEEN FOUND IN WRITING.

[41] A playful designation of Si-nuhe, on his return from Asia, as "Son of the North Wind."

[42] Si-nuhe's new rank is to be established by a change of dress in a properly designated place.

[43] Painted decorations. "Cool room" may have been either a bathroom or a cellar for preserving foods.

[44] Until the day of death. Gardiner has pointed out that the story resembles an autobiography prepared for a tomb wall, and "its nucleus may be derived from the tomb of a real Sinuhe, who led a life of adventure in Palestine and was subsequently buried at Lisht" (*Notes on the Story of Sinuhe*, 168).

THE TAKING OF JOPPA

One of the important officers in the army of the empire-builder Thut-mose III (about 1490-1436 B.C.) was a certain Thoth (or Thuti), who has left us evidence of his responsible concern for the conquest and administration of foreign countries.[1] His fame continued for some generations, as he appears as the hero in the following tale in a manuscript of the Nineteenth Dynasty (dated to about 1300 B.C.).

Papyrus Harris 500, now 10060 in the British Museum, verso i-iii. The manuscript is said to have come from Thebes. Photograph in *Facsimiles of Egyptian Hieratic Papyri in the British Museum. Second Series*, ed. by E. A. W. Budge (London, 1923), Pl. XLVII. Transcription into hieroglyphic in A. H. Gardiner, *Late-Egyptian Stories* (*Bibliotheca Aegyptiaca*, I, Brussels, 1932), 82-85. A study by H. P. Blok, *De beide Volksverhalen van Papyrus Harris 500 Verso* (Leyden, 1925) was reviewed by T. E. Peet, in *JEA*, XI (1925), 336-37. Translations by Peet, *JEA*, XI (1925), 225-27, and by Erman, *LAE*, 167-69.

The language and style are relatively colloquial Late Egyptian, so that the following translation uses "you" instead of "thou," except in address of the gods. The beginning of the story is lost. One may assume that General Thoth has been besieging the port of Joppa in Palestine and is conferring with the Prince of Joppa to arrange some kind of terms.

. . . 220(+x) mary[anu][2] *. . . them according to the number of baskets. . . .* [*replied*] to Thoth: "[*Have*] *100(+x)* [*loaves given to*] *him.* The garrison of Pharaoh—life, prosperity, health!—. . ." . . . their faces.

Now after an hour they were drunken, and Thoth said to [the Enemy of Joppa: "*I'll deliver*] myself, along with (my) wife and children, (into) your own town.[3] Have the (5) *ma*[*ryanu*] bring in [*the horses and give*] them feed, or an *apir*[4] may pass by . . . them." So they guarded the horses and gave them feed.

[1] On a gold bowl in the Louvre, Thoth is called: "the trusted man of the king in every foreign country and the islands which are in the midst of the Sea; he who fills the storehouses with lapis lazuli, silver, and gold; the Overseer of Foreign Countries; the Commander of the Army." On other materials belonging to Thoth, he is called: "the Follower of the King in Every Foreign Country"; "the trusted man of the King in God's Country," i.e. the East; "the Garrison Commander"; and "the Overseer of Northern Countries." See Sethe, *Urkunden der 18. Dynastie* (*Urk.*, IV), IV, 999-1002.

[2] Apparently the Indo-Iranian word for "nobles," used in Egyptian texts for Asiatic warriors. cf. pp. 237, n.43; 245, n.15; 246, n.28; 261; 262; and 477.

[3] The inclusion of wife and children makes it reasonable to assume that Thoth was offering to go over to the side of Joppa.

[4] The *'Apiru* were foreigners, some of whom served the Egyptians at this time. For the probable connection of the term *'Apiru* with the term appearing in cuneiform as *Ḫabiru*, the latter being the assumed origin of the word "Hebrew," see J. A. Wilson, in *AJSL*, XLIX (1933), 275-80. *Ḫabiru* was not an ethnic, and the present *'Apir* was not a Hebrew as far as we have any evidence. cf. p. 247, n.47.

And [*the Enemy of Joppa wanted to see the great staff of*] King Men-kheper-Re[5]—life, prosperity, health!—and they came and reported (this) to Thoth. Then [the Enemy of Jo]ppa said to Thoth: "I want to see the great staff of King Men-kheper-Re—life, prosperity, health!— of [which] the name is '. . . -the-Beautiful.' By the *ka* of King Men-kheper-Re—life, prosperity, health!—if you have it today, (10) . . . good, and bring it to me!"

And he did so and brought the great staff of King Men-kheper-Re, [*and he laid hold of*] his cloak, and he stood upright, and said: "Look at me, O Enemy of [Joppa! *Behold*] the King Men-kheper-Re—life, prosperity, health!—the fierce lion, the son of Sekhmet![6] Amon gave him his [*victory*]!" [And he] raised his [hand] and struck the Enemy of Joppa on the forehead. And he fell down, (ii 1) made [*prostrate*] before him. And he put him in fet[ters] . . . the leather. And he . . . pieces of metal, *which* [*he had had made to*] *punish* this Enemy of Joppa. And the piece of metal of four *nemset* (*weight*) was put on his feet.[7]

And he had the *two hundred baskets* brought which he had had made, and he had two hundred soldiers get down (5) into them. And their arms were filled (with) bonds and fetters, and they were sealed up with seals. And they were given their sandals, as well as their *carrying-poles* and *staves*.[8] And they had every good soldier carrying them, totaling five hundred men. And they were told: "When you enter the city, you are to let out your companions and lay hold on all the people who are in the city and put them in bonds (10) *immediately*."

And they went out to tell the charioteer of the Enemy of Joppa:[9] "Thus speaks your lord: 'Go and tell your mistress:[10] "Rejoice, for Seth[11] has given us Thoth, along with his wife and his children! See the *vanguard* of their tribute." (You) shall tell her about these two hundred *baskets*,' " which were filled with men with fetters and bonds.[12]

Then he went ahead of them to bring the good news to his mistress, saying: "We have captured Thoth!" And they opened the locks of the city before the soldiers. (iii 1) And they entered the city [and] let out their companions. And they laid hold [on the] city, small and great, and put them in bonds and fetters *immediately*. So the (5) mighty arm of Pharaoh—life, prosperity, health!—captured the city.

In the night Thoth wrote to Egypt, to King Men-kheper-Re—life, prosperity, health!—his lord, saying: "Rejoice, for Amon, your good father, has given you the Enemy of Joppa, along with all his people, as well as his (10) city! Send men to take them away as plunder, so that you may fill the House of your father Amon-Re, King of the Gods, with male and female slaves, who are fallen under your feet forever and ever!"

It has come to a happy ending, (written) by the *ka* of a scribe skillful with his fingers, the Scribe of the Army, . . .[13]

[5] Thut-mose III.

[6] The Egyptian goddess of war.

[7] *Nemset* might mean a weight or a clamp, to prevent the movement of the Prince of Joppa.

[8] If the translation "carrying-poles" is correct, this equipment was issued to the 500 soldiers who carried the baskets (or sacks?), and not to the 200 who were carried. The similarity of the stratagem to that in the tale of "Ali Baba and the Forty Thieves" is obvious.

[9] Probably this charioteer had driven the Prince of Joppa out to the parley and was waiting outside the Egyptian camp.

[10] The wife of the Prince of Joppa.

[11] The Egyptian god whom the Egyptians equated with gods of foreign countries.

[12] The terminal point of the quotation is uncertain. It is possible to read: "(You) shall tell her about these two hundred *baskets*, which are filled with men in fetters and bonds," i.e. delivered to Joppa as prisoners. However, the point of the deception would then be lost. More likely the phrase is a parenthesis of the storyteller: Tell her about these two hundred baskets—supposedly filled with tribute, but actually filled with Egyptian soldiers.

[13] The name of the copyist is illegible.

THE STORY OF TWO BROTHERS

This folk tale tells how a conscientious young man was falsely accused of a proposal of adultery by the wife of his elder brother, after he had actually rejected her advances. This part of the story has general similarity to the story of Joseph and Potiphar's wife. The two chief characters are brothers named Anubis and Bata. These were the names of Egyptian gods, and the tale probably does have a mythological setting. However, it served for entertainment, rather than ecclesiastical or moral purpose. The story is colloquial and is so translated.

Papyrus D'Orbiney is now British Museum 10183. Facsimiled in *Select Papyri in the Hieratic Character from the Collections of the British Museum*, II (London, 1860), Pls. IX-XIX, and in G. Möller, *Hieratische Lesestücke*, II (Leipzig, 1927), 1-20. The manuscript can be closely dated to about 1225 B.C. in the Nineteenth Dynasty. Transcription into hieroglyphic in A. H. Gardiner, *Late-Egyptian Stories* (*Bibliotheca Aegyptiaca*, I, Brussels, 1932), 9-29. Translation in Erman, *LAE*, 150-61.

Now they say that (once) there were two brothers of one mother and one father. Anubis was the name of the elder, and Bata[1] was the name of the younger. Now, as for Anubis, he [had] a house and had a wife, [and] his younger brother (lived) with him as a sort of minor. He was the one who made clothes for him and went to the fields driving his cattle. He was the one who did the plowing and who harvested for him. He was the one who did all (kinds of) work for him which are in the fields. Really, his younger [brother] was a good (grown) man. There was no one like him in the entire land. Why, the strength of a god was in him.

[Now] after many days after this,[2] his younger brother (5) [was tending] his cattle in his custom of every [day], and he [left off] (to go) to his house every evening, loaded [with] all (kinds of) plants of the field, [with] milk, with wood, and [with] every [good thing of] the fields, and he laid them in front of his [elder brother], who was sitting with his wife. And he drank and he ate, and [he *went out to sleep* in] his stable among his cattle [*by himself*].

Now when it was dawn and a second day had come, [he *prepared food*], which was cooked, and laid it before

[1] On the god Bata, see V. Vikentiev, in *JEA*, XVII (1931), 71-80.

[2] The unthinking formula of a storyteller making a transition in his narrative.

his elder brother. [And he] gave him bread for the fields. And he drove his cattle out to let them feed in the fields. He went along after his cattle, [and] they would say to him: "The grass [of] such-and-such a place is good," and he would understand whatever they said and would take them to the place (ii 1) of good grass which they wanted. So the cattle which were before him became very, very fine. They doubled their calving very, very much.

Now AT THE TIME OF plowing his [elder] brother said to him: "Get a yoke [*of oxen*] ready for us for plowing, for the fields have come out, and it is fine for plowing. Also come to the fields with seed, for we shall be busy (with) plowing [in] the morning." So he spoke to him. THEN [his] (5) younger brother did all the things which his elder brother had told him to [do].

Now WHEN IT WAS DAWN [AND A SECOND] DAY HAD COME, they went to the fields with their [seed], and they were busy [with] plowing, and [their hearts] were very, very pleased with their activity at the beginning of [their] work.

Now [AFTER] MANY [DAYS] AFTER THIS,[2] they were in the fields and ran short of seed. THEN HE sent his younger brother, saying: "Go and fetch us seed from the village." And his younger brother found the wife of his elder brother sitting and doing her hair. THEN HE said to her: "Get up and give me (some) seed, (iii 1) for my younger[3] brother is waiting for me. Don't delay!" THEN SHE said to him: "Go and open the bin and take what you want! Don't make me leave my combing unfinished!" THEN the lad went into his stable, and he took a big jar, for he wanted to carry off a lot of seed. So he loaded himself with barley and emmer and came out carrying them.

THEN SHE said to him: "How much (is it) that is on your shoulder?" [And he] said to her: (5) "THREE sacks of emmer, two sacks of barley, FIVE IN ALL, is what is on your shoulder."[4] So he spoke to her. THEN SHE [talked with] him, saying "There is [great] strength in you! Now I see your energies every day!" And she wanted to know him as one knows a man.

THEN SHE stood up and took hold of him and said to him: "Come, let's spend an [hour] sleeping (together)! This will do you good, because I shall make fine clothes for you!" THEN the lad [became] like a leopard with [great] rage at the wicked suggestion which she had made to him, and she was very, very much frightened. THEN HE argued with her, saying: "See here—you are like a mother to me, and your husband is like a father to me! Because—being older than I—he was the one who brought me up. What (iv 1) is this great crime which you have said to me? Don't say it to me again! And I won't tell it to a single person, nor will I let it out of my mouth to any man!" And he lifted up his load, and he went to the fields. THEN HE reached his elder brother, and they were busy with activity (at) their work.

Now AT THE [TIME] OF EVENING, THEN his elder brother left off (to go) to his house. And his younger brother tended his cattle, and [he] loaded himself with everything of the fields, and he took his cattle (5) in front of him, to let them sleep (in) their stable which was in the village.

But the wife of his elder brother was afraid (because of) the suggestion which she had made. THEN SHE took fat and grease,[5] and she became like one who has been criminally beaten, wanting to tell her husband: "It was your younger brother who did the beating!" And her husband left off in the evening, after his custom of every day, and he reached his house, and he found his wife lying down, terribly sick. She did not put water on his hands, after his custom, nor had she lit a light before him, and his house was in darkness, and she lay (there) vomiting. So her husband said to her: "Who has been talking with you?" Then she said to him: "Not one person has been talking with me except your (v 1) younger brother. But when he came [to] take the seed to you he found me sitting alone, and he said to me: 'Come, let's spend an hour sleeping (together)! Put on your curls!'[6] So he spoke to me. But I wouldn't listen to him: 'Aren't I your mother?—for your elder brother is like a father to you!' So I spoke to him. But he was afraid, and he beat (me), so as not to let me tell you. Now, if you let him live, I'll kill myself! Look, when he comes, *don't* [*let him speak*], for, if I accuse (him of) this wicked suggestion, he will be ready to do it *tomorrow* (*again*)!"

THEN his elder brother became (5) like a leopard, and he made his lance sharp, and he put it in his hand. THEN his elder (brother) stood behind the door (of) his stable to kill his younger brother when he came back in the evening to put his cattle in the stable.

Now when the sun was setting, he loaded himself (with) all plants of the fields, according to his custom of every day, and he came back. When the first cow came into the stable, she said to her herdsman: "Here's your elder brother waiting before you, carrying his lance to kill you! Run away from him!" THEN HE understood what his first cow had said. And (vi 1) another went in, and she said the same. So he looked under the door of his stable, and he saw the feet of [his] elder brother, as he was waiting behind the door, with his lance in his hand. So he laid his load on the ground, and he started to run away and escape. And his elder brother went after him, carrying his lance.

THEN his younger brother prayed to the Re-Har-akhti, (5) saying: "O my good lord, thou art he who judges the wicked from the just!" Thereupon the Re heard all his pleas, and the Re made a great (body of) water appear between him and his elder (brother), and it was full of crocodiles. So one of them came to be on one side and the other on the other. And his elder brother struck his hand twice because of his not killing him. THEN his younger brother called to him from the

[3] *Sic*, but read "elder."

[4] *Sic*, but read "my shoulder." He was carrying more than 11 bushels.

[5] It has been suggested that these were to make her vomit.

[6] The wig of her festive attire.

(other) side, saying: "Wait here until dawn. When the sun disc rises, I shall (vii 1) be judged with you in his presence, and he will turn the wicked over to the just, for I won't be with you ever [*again*]; I won't be in a place where you are—I shall go to the Valley of the Cedar!"[7]

Now when it was dawn and a second day had come, the Re-Har-akhti arose, and one of them saw the other. Then the lad argued with his elder brother, saying: "What do you (mean by) coming after me to kill (me) falsely, when you wouldn't listen to what I had to say? Now I am still your younger brother, and (5) you are like a father to me, and your wife is like a mother to me! Isn't it so? When I was sent to fetch us (some) seed, your wife said to me: 'Come, let's spend an hour sleeping (together)!' But, look, it is twisted for you into something else!" Then he let him know all that had happened to him and his wife. Then he swore to the Re-Har-akhti, saying "As for your killing (me) falsely, you carried your lance on the word of a filthy whore!" And he took a reed-knife, and he cut off his phallus, and he threw it into the water. And the shad swallowed (it).[8] And he (viii 1) was faint and became weak. And his elder brother's heart was very, very sad, and he stood weeping aloud for him. He could not cross over to where his younger brother was because of the crocodiles....

Then (the younger brother) went (7) off to the Valley of the Cedar, and his elder brother went off to his house, with his hand laid upon his head, and he was smeared with dust.[9] So he reached his house, and he killed his wife, and he threw her out (to) the dogs. And he sat in mourning for his younger brother....

(The story continues with a number of episodes. The gods fashion a wife for the self-exiled Bata, but she has a wandering eye, and the Valley of the Cedar does not give her enough scope. She is taken to the Egyptian court, where she contrives the destruction of her husband. However, the elder brother, Anubis, receives a magic sign, journeys to the Valley of the Cedar, and brings Bata back to life. Bata assumes various forms, follows his wife to Pharaoh's court, and thwarts her contrivings. In a magic way, she conceives a son by Bata. This son, who is Bata himself, is accepted by Pharaoh as the Crown Prince. When Pharaoh dies, he succeeds to the throne.)

Then one[10] said: "Have my chief officials brought to me, to his majesty—life, prosperity, health!—so that I may let them know all the things (xix 5) which have happened to me." Then [they] brought him his wife, and he was judged with her in their presence, and there was agreement among them.[11] And his elder brother was brought to him, and he made him crown prince in his entire land. And he (spent) thirty years as King of Egypt. And he departed from life, and his elder brother stood in his place on the day of death.

It has come to a happy ending. (Dedicated) to the *ka* of the Scribe of the Treasury Qa-gabu, of the Treasury of Pharaoh—life, prosperity, health!—(to) the Scribe Hori, and (to) the Scribe Mer-em-Opet. Done by the Scribe Inena, the master of this writing.[12] As for him who may disagree with this writing, (10) Thoth[13] will be an opponent to him.

[7] In the poem on Ramses II's battle at Kadesh on the Orontes, the Valley of the Cedar appears to be in or near the Lebanon. cf. p. 256 below. cf. *JEA*, xix (1933), 128.

[8] The mutilation was a self-imposed ordeal to support his oath to the sun-god. There was a familiar element in the swallowing of the phallus by the fish. In the Plutarch account of the Osiris myths, it is related that Seth dismembered Osiris and scattered the pieces. Then Isis went about and buried each piece as she found it. However, she could not find the phallus, which had been thrown into the river and eaten by certain fishes, which thereby became forbidden food.

[9] Thus showing his grief.

[10] A circumlocution for the Pharaoh, who was now Bata himself.

[11] As in other cases, the Egyptian avoids direct statement of the woman's condemnation to death.

[12] Qa-gabu was the master and Inena the pupil. cf. p. 259 below.

[13] The god of writing.

THE JOURNEY OF WEN-AMON TO PHOENICIA

When the Egyptian Empire disintegrated, it left a vacuum in its place for a generation or two. Egyptians, Asiatics, and Africans continued to think in terms of an authority which was no longer real. In the following tale Egypt had already become a "bruised reed" but was continuing to assert traditional expressions of dominance. The Asiatics were beginning to express their scepticism and their independence of their great neighbor to the south.

The story is almost picaresque in its atmosphere and must be classed as a narrative. Nevertheless, it deals at close range with actual individuals and situations and must have had a basis of fact, here exaggerated by the conscious and unconscious humor of the narrator. It does represent the situation in Hither Asia about 1100 B.C. more tellingly than a document of the historical-propagandistic category could do.

Wen-Amon, an official of the Temple of Amon at Karnak, tells how he was sent to Byblos on the Phoenician coast to procure lumber for the ceremonial barge of the god. Egypt had already split into small states and did not support his mission with adequate purchasing value, credentials, or armed force.

The papyrus, now in the Moscow Museum, comes from el-Hibeh in Middle Egypt and dates to the early Twenty-first Dynasty (11th century B.C.), shortly after the events it relates. A transcript of some of the hieratic text may be seen in G. Möller, *Hieratische Lesestücke*, II (Leipzig, 1927), 29. The original publication, out of his own collection, was by W. Golenischeff, in *Recueil de travaux* . . . , XXI (1899), 74-102. Transcription into hieroglyphic is in A. H. Gardiner, *Late-Egyptian Stories* (*Bibliotheca Aegyptiaca*, I, Brussels, 1932), 61-76. A. Erman published a translation in *ZAeS*, XXXVIII (1900), 1-14, and again in *LAE*, 174-85. The present translation profited by photographs of the manuscript. The text is written in the colloquial of Late-Egyptian and is so translated.

Year 5, 4th month of the 3rd season, day 16:[1] the day on which Wen-Amon, the Senior of the Forecourt of the House of Amon, [Lord of the Thrones] of the Two Lands, set out to fetch the woodwork for the great and august barque of Amon-Re, King of the Gods,

[1] The year was either that of the last of the Ramessids or of the kingless period following the twentieth dynasty. Ne-su-Ba-neb-Ded and Heri-Hor are treated as effective rulers but not given royal titles. The month dates throughout the papyrus are in obvious confusion; only a drastic revision would provide chronological sense.

which is on [the River and which is named:] "User-het-Amon." On the day when I reached Tanis, the place [where Ne-su-Ba-neb]-Ded and Ta-net-Amon were,[2] I gave them the letters of Amon-Re, King of the Gods, and they had them read in their presence. And they said: "Yes, I will do as Amon-Re, King of the Gods, our [lord], has said!" I SPENT UP TO THE 4TH MONTH OF THE 3RD SEASON in Tanis.[3] And Ne-su-Ba-neb-Ded and Ta-net-Amon sent me off with the ship captain Mengebet,[4] and I embarked on the great Syrian sea IN THE 1ST MONTH OF THE 3RD SEASON, DAY 1.

I reached Dor, a town of the Tjeker, and Beder, its prince, had 50 loaves of bread, one jug of wine, and one leg of beef brought to me.[5] And a man of my ship ran away and stole one [*vessel*] of gold, [amounting] to 5 *deben*, four jars of silver, amounting to 20 *deben*, and a sack of 11 *deben* of silver. [Total of what] he [stole]: 5 *deben* of gold and 31 *deben* of silver.[6]

I got up in the morning, and I went to the place where the Prince was, and I said to him: "I have been robbed in your harbor. Now you are the prince of this land, and you are its investigator who should look for my silver. Now about this silver—it belongs to Amon-Re, King of the Gods, the lord of the lands; it belongs to Ne-su-Ba-neb-Ded; it belongs to Heri-Hor, my lord, and the other great men of Egypt! It belongs to you; it belongs to Weret; it belongs to Mekmer; it belongs to Zakar-Baal, the Prince of Byblos!"[7]

And he said to me: "Whether you are important or whether you are eminent—look here, I do not recognize this accusation which you have made to me! Suppose it had been a thief who belonged to my land who went on your boat and stole your silver, I should have repaid it to you from my treasury, until they had found this thief of yours—whoever he may be. Now about the thief who robbed you—he belongs to you! He belongs to your ship! Spend a few days here visiting me, so that I may look for him."

I spent nine days moored (in) his harbor, and I went (to) call on him, and I said to him: "Look, you have not found my silver. [*Just let*] me [*go*] with the ship captains and with those who go (to) sea!" But he said to me: "Be quiet! . . ." . . .[8] I went out of Tyre at the break of dawn. . . . Zakar-Baal, the Prince of Byblos, . . . ship.[9] I found 30 *deben* of silver in it, and I seized upon it.[10] [And I said to *the Tjeker*: "*I have seized upon*] your silver, and it will stay with me [until] you find [my silver or the thief] who stole it! Even though *you have* not *stolen*, I shall take it. But as for you, . . ."[11] So they went away, and I enjoyed my triumph [in] a tent (on) the shore of the [sea], (in) the harbor of Byblos. And [*I hid*] Amon-of-the-Road, and I put his property inside *him*.[12]

And the [Prince] of Byblos sent to me, saying: "Get [out of my] harbor!" And I sent to him, saying: "Where *should* [*I go to*]? . . . If [*you have a ship*] to carry me, have me taken to Egypt again!" So I spent twenty-nine days in his [harbor, while] he [spent] the time sending to me every day to say: "Get out (of) my harbor!"

Now WHILE HE WAS MAKING OFFERING to his gods, the god seized one of his youths and made him possessed.[13] And he said to him: "Bring up [*the*] *god*! Bring the messenger who is carrying him! Amon is the one who sent him out! He is the one who made him come!" And while the possessed (youth) was having his frenzy on this night, I had (already) found a ship headed for Egypt and had loaded everything that I had into it. While I was watching for the darkness, thinking that when it descended I would load the god (also), so that no other eye might see him, the harbor master came to me, saying: "Wait until morning—so says the Prince." So I said to him: "Aren't you the one who spend the time coming to me every day to say: 'Get out (of) my harbor'? Aren't you saying 'Wait' tonight in order to let the ship which I have found get away—and (then) you will come again (to) say: 'Go away!'?" So he went and told it to the Prince. And the Prince sent to the captain of the ship to say: "Wait until morning—so says the Prince!"

When MORNING CAME, he sent and brought me up, but the god stayed in the tent where he was, (on) the shore of the sea. And I found him sitting (in) his upper room, with his back turned to a window, so that the waves of the great Syrian sea broke against the back of his head.[14]

So I said to him: "*May* Amon *favor you*!" But he said

[2] Ne-su-Ba-neb-Ded was the *de facto* ruler of the Delta, with Tanis as his capital. Ta-net-Amon was apparently his wife. At Thebes in Upper Egypt, the High Priest of Amon, Heri-Hor, was the *de facto* ruler. Ne-su-Ba-neb-Ded and Heri-Hor were in working relations with each other, and were shortly to become contemporary pharaohs.

[3] Irreconcilable with the date first given. See n.1.

[4] Not an Egyptian name.

[5] Dor is the town on the north coast of Palestine. The Tjeker (=Teukroi?) were one of the Sea Peoples associated with the Philistines in the great movements of the 15th to 12th centuries B.C. cf. p. 262. Their prince, Beder, considers it still necessary to show honor to an emissary from Egypt.

[6] This value—about 450 grams (1.2 lb. Troy) of gold and about 2.8 kilograms (7.5 lb. Troy) of silver—was to pay for the lumber.

[7] On the one hand, the gold and silver belong to the Egyptians who sent Wen-Amon. On the other hand, they belong to the Asiatics who would receive it. Beder thus has double responsibilities to recover them.

[8] The remainder of Beder's speech is badly broken but seems to combine reassurance and delay. Wen-Amon was apparently impatient, for the end of the broken context finds him in Tyre.

[9] Somewhere in this break or in one of those which follow there was the statement of Wen-Amon's arrival at Byblos (Gebal) on the Phoenician coast.

[10] Nearly the same amount as the silver which had been stolen from him, without account of the gold.

[11] It is by no means certain that Wen-Amon appropriated this silver from the Tjeker. However, the restoration of the Tjeker in this context helps to explain their vengeful attitude later in the story (ii 62 ff.).

[12] Or "inside it," the tent. Just as images of gods led the Egyptian armies into battle, so the emissary of the temple had an idol, a "traveling Amon," to make his mission successful. The restoration "I hid" depends in part on a later statement that Amon-of-the-Road was to be withheld from public view. The divine image would have its daily cult and therefore its cultic apparatus. If the translation above is correct, this apparatus was stored within the hollow image.

[13] "A great boy of his great boys," perhaps a court page, was seized with a prophetic frenzy. The determinative of the word "(prophetically) possessed" shows a human figure in violent motion or epileptic convulsion.

[14] Pictorially, not literally. Wen-Amon gives his vivid first view of Zakar-Baal, framed in an upper window overlooking the surf of the Mediterranean. cf. H. Schäfer, in *OLZ*, XXXII (1929), 812-19.

to me "How long, up to today, since you came from the place where Amon is?"[15] So I said to him: "Five months and one day up to now." And he said to me: "Well, you're truthful! Where is the letter of Amon which (should be) in your hand? Where is the dispatch of the High Priest of Amon which (should be) in your hand?" And I told him: "I gave them to Ne-su-Ba-neb-Ded and Ta-net-Amon." And he was very, very angry, and he said to me: "Now see—neither letters nor dispatches are in your hand! Where is the cedar ship which Ne-su-Ba-neb-Ded gave to you? Where is (55) its Syrian crew? Didn't he turn you over to this foreign ship captain to have him kill you and throw you into the sea? (Then) with whom would they have looked for the god? And you too—with whom would they have looked for you too?" So he spoke to me.[16]

BUT I SAID TO HIM: "Wasn't it an Egyptian ship? Now it is Egyptian crews which sail under Ne-su-Ba-neb-Ded! He has no Syrian crews." And he said to me: "Aren't there twenty ships here in my harbor which are in commercial relations[17] with Ne-su-Ba-neb-Ded? As to this Sidon, (ii 1) the other (place) which you have passed, aren't there fifty more ships there which are in commercial relations with Werket-El, and which are drawn up to his house?"[18] And I was silent in this great time.[19]

And he answered and said to me: "On what business have you come?" So I told him: "I have come after the woodwork for the great and august barque of Amon-Re, King of the Gods. Your father did (it), (5) your grandfather did (it), and you will do it too!" So I spoke to him. But he said to me: "To be sure, they did it! And if you give me (something) for doing it, I will do it! Why, when my people carried out this commission, Pharaoh—life, prosperity, health!—sent six ships loaded with Egyptian goods, and they unloaded them into their storehouses! You—what is it that you're bringing me—me also?" And he had the journal rolls of his fathers brought, and he had them read out in my presence, and they found a thousand *deben* of silver and all kinds of things in his scrolls.

(10) So he said to me: "If the ruler of Egypt were the lord of mine, and I were his servant also, he would not have to send silver and gold, saying: 'Carry out the commission of Amon!' There would be no carrying of a royal-gift,[20] such as they used to do for my father. As for me—me also—I am not your servant! I am not the servant of him who sent you either! If I cry out to the Lebanon, the heavens open up, and the logs are here lying (on) the shore of the sea![21] Give (15) me the sails which you have brought to carry your ships which would hold the logs for (Egypt)! Give me the ropes [which] you have brought [*to lash the cedar*] logs which I am to cut down to make you . . . which I shall make for you (as) the sails of your boats, and the *spars* will be (too) heavy and will break, and you will die in the middle of the sea![22] See, Amon gives voice in the sky, and he puts Seth near him.[23] Now Amon has (20) founded all lands. He has founded them, but he founded first the land of Egypt, from which you come; for skill came out of it, to reach the place where I am, and learning came out of it, to reach the place where I am. What are these silly trips which they have had you make?"[24]

And I said to him: "(That's) not true! What I am on are no 'silly trips' at all! There is no ship upon the River which does not belong to Amon! The sea is his, and the Lebanon is his, of which you say: 'It is mine!' It forms (25) the *nursery* for User-het-Amon, the lord of [every] ship![25] Why, he spoke—Amon-Re, King of the Gods—and said to Heri-Hor, my master: 'Send me forth!' So he had me come, carrying this great god. But see, you have made this great god spend these twenty-nine days moored (in) your harbor, although you did not know (it). Isn't he here? Isn't he the (same) as he was? You are stationed (here) to carry on the commerce of the Lebanon with Amon, its lord. As for your saying that the former kings sent silver and gold—suppose that they had life and health; (then) they would not have had such things sent! (30) (But) they had such things sent to your fathers in place of life and health![26] Now as for Amon-Re, King of the Gods—he is the lord of this life and health, and he was the lord of your fathers. They spent their lifetimes making offering to Amon. And you also—you are the servant of Amon! If you say to Amon: 'Yes, I will do (it)!' and you carry out his commission, you will live, you will be prosperous, you will be healthy, and you will be good to your entire land and your people! (But) don't wish for yourself anything belonging to Amon-Re, (King of) the Gods. Why, a lion wants his own property![27] Have your secretary brought to me, so that (35) I may send him to Ne-su-Ba-neb-Ded and Ta-net-Amon, the *officers*

15 Wen-Amon's courteous salutation is set in contrast with the business-like brusqueness of the Phoenician.

16 Zakar-Baal feels that Ne-su-Ba-neb-Ded has scarcely acted in good faith in permitting Wen-Amon to come without proper credentials. He argues that the Delta ruler had turned Wen-Amon over to a non-Egyptian sailor, so that Wen-Amon and "Amon-of-the-Road" might disappear without a trace.

17 A Semitic word for established trade contacts.

18 Werket-El (=Birkath-El?) was apparently a Phoenician merchant resident in Egypt, trading particularly with Sidon. The "drawn to his house" would mean either drawn up on the shore at his Sidonian office or towed along the waterways of Egypt.

19 Wen-Amon's wording shows his inability to answer Zakar-Baal's charge that there had been plenty of opportunity to supply him with credit and credentials.

20 A Semitic word written *m-r-ḳ*, either derived from *meleḳ* "king," or else to be emended to *beraḳah* "gift."

21 In Zakar-Baal's boast of independent power, he can make it rain logs.

22 Zakar-Baal's argument is not clear here. Perhaps: you have no proper exchange value to pay for the cedar; if I take the tackle of your ships, you will not be able to sail back to Egypt.

23 As god of thunder (see p. 17, n.27 above). In these capacities, Amon and Seth were gods of all lands, not of Egypt alone.

24 In contrasting Wen-Amon's meager mission with the glory of the Egyptian past, Zakar-Baal makes the remarkable statement that the god Amon founded (settled, first equipped) all lands, but Egypt first of all, and that skilled craftsmanship (technique) and learning (wisdom, education) had come to his land from Egypt.

25 The Lebanon is merely the "growing-place" for the sacred barque of Amon.

26 In contrast with the past, Wen-Amon has brought an actual god in "Amon-of-the-Road," so that there may be spiritual rather than material advantages for Zakar-Baal.

27 Perhaps a proverb.

whom Amon put in the north of his land, and they will have all kinds of things sent. I shall send him to them to say: 'Let it be brought until I shall go (back again) to the south, and I shall (then) have every bit of the debt still (due to you) brought to you.' " So I spoke to him.[28]

So he entrusted my letter to his messenger, and he loaded in the *ḳeel*, the bow-post, the stern-post, along with four other hewn timbers—seven in all—and he had them taken to Egypt.[29] And in the first month of the second season his messenger who had gone to Egypt came back to me in Syria. And Ne-su-Ba-neb-Ded and Ta-net-Amon sent: (40) 4 jars and 1 *ḳak-men* of gold; 5 jars of silver; 10 pieces of clothing in royal linen; 10 *ḳherd* of good Upper Egyptian linen; 500 (rolls of) finished papyrus; 500 cowhides; 500 ropes; 20 sacks of lentils; and 30 baskets of fish. And she[30] sent to me (personally): 5 pieces of clothing in good Upper Egyptian linen; 5 *ḳherd* of good Upper Egyptian linen; 1 sack of lentils; and 5 baskets of fish.

And the Prince was glad, and he detailed three hundred men and three hundred cattle, and he put supervisors at their head, to have them cut down the timber. So they cut them down, and they spent the second season lying there.[31]

In the third month of the third season they dragged them (to) the shore of the sea, and the Prince came out and stood by them. And he sent to me, (45) saying: "Come!" Now when I presented myself near him, the shadow of his lotus-blossom fell upon me. And Pen-Amon, a butler who belonged to him, cut me off, saying: "The shadow of Pharaoh— life, prosperity, health!— your lord, has fallen on you!" But he was angry at him, saying: "Let him alone!"[32]

So I presented myself near him, and he answered and said to me: "See, the commission which my fathers carried out formerly, I have carried it out (also), even though you have not done for me what your fathers would have done for me, and you too (should have done)! See, the last of your woodwork has arrived and is lying (here). Do as I wish, and come to load it in— for aren't they going to give it to you? (50) Don't come to look at the terror of the sea! If you look at the terror of the sea, you will see my own (too)![33] Why, I have not done to you what was done to the messengers of Kha-em-Waset, when they spent seventeen years in this land—they died (where) they were!"[34] And he said to his butler: "Take him and show him their *tomb* in which they are lying."

But I said to him: "Don't show it to me! As for Kha-em-Waset—they were men whom he sent to you as messengers, and he was a man himself.[35] You do not have one of his messengers (here in me), when you say: 'Go and see your companions!' Now, shouldn't you rejoice (55) and have a stela [made] for yourself and say on it: 'Amon-Re, King of the Gods, sent to me Amon-of-the-Road, his messenger—[life], prosperity, health!—and Wen-Amon, his human messenger, after the woodwork for the great and august barque of Amon-Re, King of the Gods. I cut it down. I loaded it in. I provided it (with) my ships and my crews. I caused them to reach Egypt, in order to ask fifty years of life from Amon for myself, over and above my fate.' And it shall come to pass that, after another time, a messenger may come from the land of Egypt who knows writing, and he may read your name on the stela. And you will receive water (in) the West, like the gods who are (60) here!"[36]

And he said to me: "This which you have said to me is a great testimony of words!"[37] So I said to him: "As for the many things which you have said to me, if I reach the place where the High Priest of Amon is and he sees how you have (carried out this) commission, it is your (carrying out of this) commission (which) will *draw out* something for you."

And I went (to) the shore of the sea, to the place where the timber was lying, and I spied eleven ships belonging to the Tjeker coming in from the sea, in order to say: " Arrest him! Don't let a ship of his (go) to the land of Egypt!" Then I sat down and wept. And the letter scribe of the Prince came out to me, (65) and he said to me: "What's the matter with you?" And I said to him: "Haven't you seen the birds go down to Egypt a second time?[38] Look at them— how they travel to the cool pools! (But) how long shall I be left here! Now don't you see those who are coming again to arrest me?"

So he went and told it to the Prince. And the Prince began to weep because of the words which were said to him, for they were painful. And he sent out to me his letter scribe, and he brought to me two jugs of wine and one ram. And he sent to me Ta-net-Not, an Egyptian singer who was with him,[39] saying: "Sing to him! Don't let his heart take on cares!" And he sent to me, (70) to say: "Eat and drink! Don't let your heart take on

[28] Wen-Amon proposes that Zakar-Baal appeal to Ne-su-Ba-neb-Ded to advance the payment against Wen-Amon's ultimate return to Egypt.

[29] Zakar-Baal was sufficiently trustful to advance some of the timbers for the barque of Amon.

[30] Ta-net-Amon.

[31] Seasoning in the mountains.

[32] The meaning of the butler's grim jest is lost to us. The word "lotus-blossom" has the determinative of a lotus leaf and also a hide. It probably was a sunshade of lotus design. At any rate, the shadow of something personal belonging to Zakar-Baal accidentally fell upon Wen-Amon. Zakar-Baal's butler, whose name should make him an Egyptian, steps in to cut Wen-Amon off from this shadow and maliciously says that it is the shadow of pharaoh of Egypt. Zakar-Baal curtly tells the butler not to pursue the matter. Perhaps we have to do with the blight of majesty. The butler's jest has point if the shadow of pharaoh was too intimate and holy to fall upon a commoner. Or see A. L. Oppenheim in *BASOR*, no. 107 (1947), 7-11.

[33] If you use wind or weather as excuses for delay, you will find me just as dangerous.

[34] We do not know who this Kha-em-Waset was. This was one of the names of Ramses IX, but is not here written as royal. The same pharaoh had a vizier of this name, which was quite common in Thebes at the time. At any rate, there is an implicit threat in the reference.

[35] This should rule out the possibility that Kha-em-Waset was Ramses IX, as Wen-Amon would probably not refer to a pharaoh a "a man."

[36] A libation to help maintain the dead.

[37] We cannot be sure whether the irony was conscious or unconscious.

[38] Wen-Amon had been away from Egypt for more than a year, seeing two flights of birds southward.

[39] Egyptian women who entertained or participated in cult ceremonies in Asia are known, for example, in the inscriptions on the Megiddo ivories (p. 263 below). cf. also p. 246, n.30.

cares, for tomorrow you shall hear whatever I have to say."

When morning came, he had his assembly[40] summoned, and he stood in their midst, and he said to the Tjeker: "What have you come (for)?" And they said to him: "We have come after the *blasted* ships which you are sending to Egypt with our opponents!"[41] But he said to them: "I cannot arrest the messenger of Amon inside my land. Let me send him away, and you go after him to arrest him."[42]

So he loaded me in, and he sent me away from there at the harbor of the sea. And the wind cast me on the land of (75) Alashiya.[43] And they of the town came out against me to kill me, but I *forced my way* through them to the place where Heteb, the princess of the town, was. I met her as she was going out of one house of hers and going into another of hers.

So I greeted her, and I said to the people who were standing near her: "Isn't there one of you who understands Egyptian?" And one of them said: "I understand (it)." So I said to him: "Tell my lady that I have heard, as far away as Thebes, the place where Amon is, that injustice is done in every town but justice is done in the land of Alashiya.[44] Yet injustice is done here every day!" And she said: "Why, what do you (mean) (80) by saying it?" So I told her: "If the sea is stormy and the wind casts me on the land where you are, you should not let them take me *in charge* to kill me. For I am a messenger of Amon. Look here—as for me, they will search for me all the time! As to this crew of the Prince of Byblos which they are bent on killing, won't its lord find ten crews of yours, and he also kill them?"

So she had the people summoned, and they stood (there). And she said to me: "Spend the night . . ."

(At this point the papyrus breaks off. Since the tale is told in the first person, it is fair to assume that Wen-Amon returned to Egypt to tell his story, in some measure of safety or success.)

THE LEGEND OF THE POSSESSED PRINCESS

This text is a pious forgery of the end of the pharaonic period. The priests of a temple at Karnak wished to enlarge the fame of their god, composed a circumstantial tale of his ancient success as a healer, cast the tale back into the reign of Ramses II, and installed the inscription in their temple. Ramses II had reigned in the 13th century B.C., whereas this text may have come from the 4th or 3rd century B.C. However, it drew successfully on traditional elements of Egypt's past: the far reach of the Egyptian Empire, the reputation of Egyptian physicians in other countries, and the marriage of Ramses II to the daughter of the Hittite king.

"The Bentresh Stela" was discovered near the Temple of Amon at Karnak, and is now Louvre C 284. It was published by E. Ledrain, *Les monuments égyptiens de la Bibliothèque Nationale* (Paris, 1879-81), Pls. XXXVI-XLIV. It has been translated by Breasted, *AR*, III, §429-47. See also the comments of G. Posener in *BIFAO*, XXXIV (1934), 75-81.

The Horus: Mighty Bull, Pleasing of Appearances, Enduring of Kingship like Atum; Horus of Gold: Powerful of Arm, Repelling the Nine Bows;[1] the King of Upper and Lower Egypt, Lord of the Two Lands: User-maat-Re Setep-en-Re; Son of Re, of his body: Ramses Meri-Amon, beloved of Amon-Re, Lord of the Thrones of the Two Lands, and all the Ennead of Thebes. . . .

Now his majesty was in Naharin[2] according to his custom of every year, while the princes of every foreign country were come, bowing down in peace to the glory of his majesty (from) as far away as the marshlands. Their tribute of gold, [silver], lapis lazuli, (5) turquoise, and all the woods of God's Land[3] was on their backs, each one leading his fellow.

Then the Prince of Bekhten[4] caused that his tribute be brought, and he set his eldest daughter at the head thereof, giving honor to his majesty and asking [*the breath*] from him. And the woman was exceedingly pleasing to the heart of his majesty, beyond anything. Then her name was formally fixed as: the Great King's Wife, Nefru-Re.[5] When his majesty reached Egypt, she fulfilled every function (of) King's Wife.

It happened that, in the year 23, 2nd month of the third season, day 22,[6] while his majesty was in Thebes, the Victorious, the Mistress of Cities, performing the ceremonies of his father Amon-Re, Lord of the Thrones of the Two Lands, at his beautiful Feast of Southern Opet,[7] the place of his heart's (desire) of the first times, one came to say to his majesty: "There is a messenger of the Prince of Bekhten who has come bearing much tribute for the King's Wife." Then he was introduced into the presence of his majesty with his tribute. He said, in giving honor to his majesty: "Praise to thee, O Re of the Nine Bows! *Behold*, we live through thee!" Then he spoke and kissed the ground before his majesty. He spoke again in the presence of his majesty: "I have come to thee, O sovereign, my lord, on behalf of Bint-

40 The word used is the same as Hebrew *mô'ēd*. e.g. Num. 16:2. cf. J. A. Wilson, in *JNES*, IV (1945) 245.

41 "The belabored, belabored ships which you send to Egypt by our companions of quarreling." This either means that Wen-Amon's ships should be smashed up or is an abusive term like English "blasted."

42 Zakar-Baal's apparently cynical abandonment of Wen-Amon has its jurisdictional justification, since Wen-Amon's appropriation of Tjeker property apparently took place somewhere between Tyre and Byblos.

43 Egyptian *I-r-s*, probably Cyprus.

44 Diplomatic exaggeration, rather than a quotation.

1 Although the two names which follow are those of Ramses II, the composer of this text has ignorantly used names of Thut-mose IV for the preceding names.

2 Perhaps written Naharaim here. Mesopotamia, or, for the Egyptians, the region of the Great Bend of the Euphrates.

3 The east in general, the land of the rising sun.

4 Not identifiable and perhaps legendary. This tale puts it at 17 months' journey from Egypt. It has been suggested that this might be a corrupted writing for Bactria.

5 In Ramses II's 34th year, he married the eldest daughter of the Hittite king; cf. pp. 256-258 below. The Hittite king sent his daughter at the head of abundant tribute. She pleased the king very much, and he fixed her formal name as "the King's Wife Maat-nefru-Re." The similarity of situation and name in our text is more than a coincidence. The priestly editor drew upon a remembered past.

6 The dates in this text are so carefully constructed as to appear circumstantial. See notes 11, 17, and 21 below.

7 Or "in Southern Opet," which was Luxor. This was probably Amon's "Feast of the Valley," which fell in the third season of the year.

resh,[8] the younger sister of the King's Wife Nefru-Re. Sickness has pervaded her body. Grant that thy majesty may send a wise man to see her!"

Then his majesty said: "Bring me the staff of the House of Life and the official body (10) of the Residence."[9] (They) were ushered in to him immediately. His majesty said: "*Behold,* ye have been summoned so that ye may hear this matter. Now bring me from amongst you one skilled in his heart, who can write with his fingers." So the Royal Scribe Thut-em-heb came into the presence of his majesty, and his majesty commanded that he go to Bekhten with this messenger.[10]

So the wise man arrived in Bekhten, and he found Bint-resh in the condition of one possessed of spirits. Indeed, he found an enemy with whom to contend. And the Prince of Bekhten again [sent to] his majesty, saying: "O sovereign, my lord, grant that his majesty command that a god be brought [*to contend with this spirit." This message came*] to his majesty in the year 26, 1st month of the third season, at the time of the Feast of Amon,[11] when his majesty was in Thebes.

Then his majesty repeated (it) in the presence of Khonsu-in-Thebes-Nefer-hotep,[12] saying: "O my good lord, I act again before thee on behalf of the daughter of the Prince of Bekhten." Then Khonsu-in-Thebes-Nefer-hotep was conducted to Khonsu-the-Carrier-out-of-Plans, the great god, who expels disease-demons.[13] Then his majesty said before Khonsu-in-Thebes-Nefer-hotep: "O my good lord, if thou turnest thy face toward Khonsu-(15)the-Carrier-out-of-Plans, the great god, who expels disease-demons, he will be made to go to Bekhten." (There was) very much nodding.[14] Then his majesty said: "Set thy magical protection with him, that I may make his majesty[15] go to Bekhten to save the daughter of the Prince of Bekhten." (There was) very much nodding of the head of Khonsu-in-Thebes-Nefer-hotep. Then he made magical protection for Khonsu-the-Carrier-out-of-Plans-in-Thebes four times.[16] His majesty commanded that Khonsu-the-Carrier-out-of-Plans-in-Thebes be taken to a great barque, five river-boats, and many chariots and horses (of) the west and the east.

This god arrived in Bekhten in the completion of one year and five months.[17] Then the Prince of Bekhten came, with his army and his officials, before Khonsu-the-Carrier-out-of-Plans, and he placed himself upon his belly, saying: "Thou hast come to us. Mayest thou be merciful to us, by the command of the King of Upper and Lower Egypt: User-maat-Re Setep-en-Re!" Then this god went to the place where Bint-resh was. Then he made magical protection for the daughter of the Prince of Bekhten, that she might become well immediately.

Then this spirit which was with her said in the presence of Khonsu-the-Carrier-out-of-Plans-in-Thebes: "Welcome, O great god who expels disease-demons! Bekhten is thy home, its people are thy slaves, and I am thy slave! (20) I shall go to the place from which I came, in order to set thy heart at rest about that for which thou hast come. But may thy majesty command to celebrate a holiday with me and with the Prince of Bekhten."[18] Then this god nodded to his prophet,[19] saying: "Let the Prince of Bekhten make a great offering in the presence of this spirit." Now while these things which Khonsu-the-Carrier-out-of-Plans-in-Thebes did with the spirit were (taking place), the Prince of Bekhten was waiting with his soldiers, and he was very frightened. Then he made a great offering in the presence of Khonsu-the-Carrier-out-of-Plans-in-Thebes and this spirit, the Prince of Bekhten celebrating a holiday on their behalf. Then the spirit went peacefully to the place which he wished, by the command of Khonsu-the-Carrier-out-of-Plans-in-Thebes, while the Prince of Bekhten was rejoicing very much, together with every man who was in Bekhten.

Then he schemed with his heart, saying: "I will cause this god to stay *here* in Bekhten. I will not let him go (back) to Egypt." Then this god tarried for three years and nine months in Bekhten. Then, while the Prince of Bekhten was sleeping on his bed, he saw this god coming to him, outside of his shrine. He was a falcon of gold, and he flew (up) to the sky and (off) to Egypt. And (25) he awoke in a panic. Then he said to the

[8] A name bearing the consonants of this name, but with unknown vocalization, appears in the Aramaic papyri of Persian times found at Elephantine. The present vocalization Bint—"daughter of"—may be unjustified.

[9] A. H. Gardiner, in *JEA*, xxiv (1938), 157 ff., says that the "House of Life" was "a scriptorium where books connected with religion and cognate matters were compiled." The pharaoh was summoning the best advice on a matter of religion, magic, and medicine.

[10] Egyptian physicians were held in respect in the ancient world. In the time of Darius an Egyptian doctor was sent by that king from one country to another to teach his medical and magical lore; see G. Posener, *La première domination perse en Égypte* (Cairo, 1936), 1 ff. The cuneiform documents from Boğazköy provide earlier evidence of this demand; see A. H. Sayce in the journal *Ancient Egypt*, 1922, 67-68.

[11] This is about 35 months after the date against n.6 above. The text against n.17 below will indicate that the journey from Egypt to Bekhten took 17 months. Thus the 35 months provides the time for a round trip, including Thut-em-heb's unsuccessful mission in Bekhten.

[12] "Khonsu in Thebes, Good of Peace," was the name of the chief manifestation of Khonsu and his name as a member of the Theban triad of Amon, Mut, and Khonsu.

[13] This entrepreneur Khonsu was apparently a subordinate form of Khonsu, who "did plans" to meet specific demands. One such function was the exorcism of disease, called "making distant the wanderers," or "strange intruders," or "demons of disease." He had a temple east of the great Amon enclosure at Karnak, not far from the temple of Khonsu-in-Thebes-Nefer-hotep. On his name, see *ZAeS*, LVIII (1923), 156-57.

[14] "Nodding" was the affirmative response of the oracle of the god Khonsu. The scene at the top of this stela shows this god being carried by priests in his ornate barque, in which he undoubtedly traveled to visit the other Khonsu. The oracle was given either by a visible forward bending of the image of the god or by the priestly interpretation of such signs. On the oracular role of Egyptian deities see pp. 448-449 below; A. M. Blackman, in *JEA*, XI (1925), 249-55; XII (1926), 176-85; J. Černý, in *BIFAO*, XXX (1930), 491 ff.; XXXV (1935), 41 ff.

[15] The god.

[16] "Four times" was a customary tag indicating the prescribed number of recitations to make magic effective. This shows that the "magical protection" was a conferred spiritual power, rather than such a visible element as an amulet.

[17] The journey from Egypt to Bekhten, by water and land, took 17 months.

[18] The spirit which possessed the princess bargained for formal recognition through a festival before he would leave the princess.

[19] The image of the god was accompanied and served by a priest, whose title we conventionally render "prophet." In the scene at the top of the stela, this individual is depicted censing the barque of his god, with the legend: "The name of the prophet and priest of Khonsu-the-Carrier-out-of-Plans-in-Thebes (is) Khonsu-het-neter-neb." An individual of this name is known at the very end of the Egyptian Empire: *JEA*, XXVII (1941), 70.

prophet of Khonsu-the-Carrier-out-of-Plans-in-Thebes: "This god is (still) here with us. He should go (back) to Egypt. So let his chariot go to Egypt." Then the Prince of Bekhten let this god proceed to Egypt, after he had been given very much tribute of every good thing, and very many soldiers and horses.

They arrived successfully in Thebes. Then Khonsu-the-Carrier-out-of-Plans-in-Thebes went to the House of Khonsu-in-Thebes-Nefer-hotep, to set the tribute of every good thing which the Prince of Bekhten had given him before Khonsu-in-Thebes-Nefer-hotep, (but) without his delivering everything thereof into his House.[20] Khonsu-the-Carrier-out-of-Plans-in-Thebes arrived successfully at his (own) House in the year 33, 2nd month of the second season, day 19,[21] of the King of Upper and Lower Egypt: User-maat-Re Setep-en-Re, for whom "given-life" is made, like Re forever.

THE TRADITION OF SEVEN LEAN YEARS IN EGYPT

The prosperity of Egypt depends upon the satisfactory flow of the Nile, particularly upon its annual inundation, and that river is antic and unpredictable. Ancient Egyptian texts have frequent references to hunger, "years of misery," "a year of low Nile," and so on.[1] The text which follows tells of seven years of low Niles and famine. In its present form the text derives from the Ptolemaic period (perhaps around the end of the 2nd century B.C.). However, its stated setting is the reign of Djoser of the Third Dynasty (about 28th century B.C.). It states the reasons why a stretch of Nile land south of Elephantine had been devoted to Khnum, god of Elephantine. It is a question whether it is a priestly forgery of some late period, justifying their claim to territorial privileges, or whether it correctly recounts an actual grant of land more than 2,500 years earlier. This question cannot be answered in final terms.[2] We can only affirm that Egypt had a tradition of seven lean years, which, by a contractual arrangement between pharaoh and a god, were to be followed by years of plenty.

The inscription is carved on a rock on the island of Siheil near the First Cataract. It was published by H. K. Brugsch, *Die biblischen sieben Jahre der Hungersnoth* (Leipzig, 1891), and by J. Vandier, *La famine dans l'Égypte ancienne* (Cairo, 1936), 132-39. Photographs were also used for the following translation.

Other heroic tales given below are the Story of Apophis and Seqnen-Re (pp. 231-232) and various exaggerated accounts of pharaonic powers and prowess, as in the Marriage Stela (pp. 257-258) and Israel Stela (pp. 376-378).

20 The chief Khonsu did not receive all the "tribute." The entrepreneur Khonsu retained his commission.

21 The sojourn in Bekhten had been 45 months. According to n.17 above, the round trip might take 34 months. The resultant 79 months is within 2 months of the 81 months between the present date and that against n.11 above.

1 These texts have been gathered in Vandier, *op.cit.* For example, on his p. 105, he gives a previously unpublished text from the First Intermediate Period (23rd-21st century B.C.), from a tomb some distance south of Thebes. "When the entire Upper Egypt was dying because of hunger, with every man eating his (own) children, I never allowed death to occur from hunger in this nome. I gave a loan of grain to Upper Egypt. . . . Moreover, I kept alive the domain of Elephantine and kept alive Iat-negen in these years, after the towns of Hefat and Hor-mer had been satisfied." He took care of his home districts first.

2 Vandier, *op.cit.*, 40-42, reviews the arguments for dating the writing of the text to Ptolemy X Soter II on the basis of much older documents.

Year 18 of the Horus: Netjer-er-khet; the King of Upper and Lower Egypt: Netjer-er-khet; the Two Goddesses: Netjer-er-khet; the Horus of Gold: Djoser, *and under* the Count, Mayor, *Royal Acquaintance,* and Overseer of Nubians in Elephantine, Madir. There was brought to him[3] this royal decree:

To let thee know. I was in distress on the Great Throne, and those who are in the palace were in heart's affliction from a very great evil, since the Nile had not come in my time for a space of seven years.[4] Grain was scant, fruits were dried up, and everything which they eat was short. Every man *robbed* his companion. They moved without going (*ahead*). The infant was wailing; the youth was *waiting*; the heart of the old men was in sorrow, their legs were bent, crouching on the ground, their arms were *folded.* The courtiers were in need. The temples were shut up; the sanctuaries held [*nothing but*] *air.* Every[*thing*] was found empty.[5]

I extended my heart back to the beginnings, and I asked him who was the *Chamberlain,* the Ibis, the Chief Lector Priest Ii-em-(ho)tep,[6] the son of Ptah, South-of-His-Wall: "What is the birthplace of the Nile? *Who is . . .* the god there? Who is the god?"

Then he answered (5) me: "I need the guidance of Him Who Presides over the House of the Fowling Net,[7] . . . *for the heart's confidence* of all men about what they should do. I shall enter into the House of Life and spread out the Souls of Re,[8] (to see) if some guidance be in them."

So he went, and he returned to me immediately, that he might *instruct* me on the inundation of the Nile, . . . and everything about which they had written. He uncovered for me the hidden spells thereof, to which the ancestors had taken (their) way, without their equal among kings since the limits *of time. He said* to me:

"There is a city in the midst of the waters [*from which*] the Nile *rises,* named Elephantine. It is the Beginning of the Beginning, the Beginning Nome, (*facing*) *toward* Wawat.[9] It is the *joining* of the land, the primeval hillock[10] *of earth, the throne* of Re, when he *reckons to cast* life beside everybody. 'Pleasant of Life' is the name of its dwelling. 'The Two Caverns' is the name of the water; they are the two breasts which pour

3 To Madir, the Governor at Elephantine.

4 Or: "in a pause of seven years."

5 "Found empty" may be used of the desolation of buildings. However, it is particularly common as a scribal notation to mark a lacuna in an older text. Its appearance here might be raised as an argument that our inscription derived from an earlier and damaged original.

6 Ii-em-hotep was the famed minister of Djoser, whose reputation for wisdom (cf. pp. 432, n.4; 467, n.4 below) later brought him deification. On his career, see K. Sethe, *Imhotep, der Asklepios der Aegypter* (*Untersuch.* II, Leipzig, 1902), 95-118.

7 Thoth of Hermopolis, the god of wisdom and of priestly lore.

8 For this passage see A. H. Gardiner in *JEA,* XXIV (1938), 166. The House of Life was the scriptorium in which the sacred and magic books were kept. "The Souls of Re," or emanations from the creator-god, were the books themselves.

9 As the southernmost of Egyptian administrative districts, Elephantine was the "Nome of the Beginning." Wawat was that part of Nubia immediately south of the First Cataract.

10 In a context which has many uncertainties, it is certain that Elephantine is likened to the mound on which creation took place; see p. 4, n.7.

forth all good things.[11] It is the couch of the Nile, in which he becomes young (again). . . . He fecundates (the land) by mounting as the male, the bull, to the female; he renews (his) virility, assuaging his desire. He rushes twenty-eight cubits (high at Elephantine); he hastens at Diospolis seven cubits (high).[12] Khnum is there as a god. . . ." . . .[13]

(18) . . . As I slept in life and satisfaction, I discovered the god standing over against me.[14] I propitiated him with praise; I prayed to him in his presence. He *revealed* himself to me, *his face* being fresh. His words were:

"I am Khnum, thy fashioner. . . .[15] I know the Nile. When he is introduced into the fields, his introduction gives life to every nostril, like the introduction (of life) to the fields . . . The Nile will pour forth for thee, without a year of cessation or laxness for any land. Plants will grow, bowing down under the *fruit*. Renenut[16] will be at the head of everything. . . . Dependents *will fulfill* the purposes in their hearts, (22) as well as the master. The starvation year will have gone, and (people's) *borrowing* from their granaries will have departed. Egypt will come into the fields, the banks will sparkle, . . . and contentment will be in their hearts more than that which was formerly."

Then I awoke *quickly*, my heart cutting off weariness. I made this decree beside my father Khnum:[17]

"An offering which the King gives to Khnum, the Lord of the Cataract Region, Who Presides over Nubia, in recompense for these things which thou wilt do for me:

"I offer to thee thy west in Manu and thy east (in) Bakhu,[18] from Elephantine as far as [Takompso], for twelve *iters*[19] on the east and west, whether arable land or desert or river in every part of these *iters* . . ."

(The remainder of the text continues Djoser's promise to Khnum, the essence of which is that the land presented to the god shall be tithed for his temple. It is finally provided that the decree shall be inscribed on a stela in the temple of Khnum.)

[11] In Egyptian mythology the Nile emerged from two underground caverns at Elephantine.

[12] *Sema-behdet*=Diospolis Inferior has been located by A. H. Gardiner at Tell el-Balamûn in the northern Delta: *JEA*, XXX (1944), 33-41. In context with Elephantine, it was the "Dan to Beersheba" of the Egyptians. It is not easy to interpret the measurements given here, since we do not know what zero datum was used. The Nile was 28 cubits high (about 14.5 m. or 48 ft.) at Elephantine, and 7 cubits (about 3.75 m. or 12 ft.) at Diospolis. Baedeker's *Aegypten und der Sudan* (8th ed., Leipzig, 1928), lxviii, gives the mean average difference between low and high Nile at Assuan as 7 m. (23 ft.) and at Cairo as 4.9 m. (16 ft.).

[13] Ii-em-hotep's report goes on to recite the divine powers of the god Khnum and of the other deities of Elephantine, as well as the mineral wealth of the region. Having received the report, the pharaoh performed services for the gods of Elephantine.

[14] Khnum appeared to the pharaoh in a dream.

[15] This translation omits Khnum's recital of his powers.

[16] The goddess of the harvest.

[17] That is, in the temple of Khnum.

[18] Manu was the western and Bakhu the eastern mountain range bordering the Nile.

[19] The stretch of 12 *iters* from Elephantine south to a place called Takompso constituted the *Dodekaschoinos* known from the Greek writers. Unfortunately, the location of Takompso and the length of the *iter* at the time in question are unknown. See Sethe, *op.cit.*, 59 ff.

Mortuary Texts: Life after Death

THE CONQUEST OF DEATH

These two extracts from the Pyramid Texts insist upon the immortality of the pharaoh. The device used is to identify him with the gods, whose death would not come into question, particularly with Osiris and his son Horus.

These two texts are carved inside the pyramids of Unis of the Fifth Dynasty and Pepi II of the Sixth Dynasty (25th and 24th centuries B.C.). Originally used for the pharaoh only, the texts were extended to queens by the end of the Sixth Dynasty and to worthy nonroyal persons by the Eleventh-Twelfth Dynasties (21st century B.C. and after). The pyramids of Unis and Pepi II are at Sakkarah. The material used in these two utterances is demonstrably much older than the Fifth Dynasty, as indicated by the archaic linguistic usages and—less certainly—by mythological references.

The texts are published in K. Sethe, *Die altägyptischen Pyramidentexte*, I (Leipzig, 1908), and *Uebersetzung und Kommentar zu den altägyptischen Pyramidentexten*, I, (Glückstadt und Hamburg, undated). Extract *a*, which is Pyramid Utterance 213, will be found as §134-35; extract *b*, from Utterance 219, as §167-93.

a

O King Unis, thou hast not at all departed dead, thou hast departed living! For thou sittest upon the throne of Osiris,[1] with thy scepter in thy hand, that thou mightest give command to the living, and with the *grip* of thy wand in thy hand, that thou mightest give command to those secret of place.[2] Thy arm is Atum, thy shoulders are Atum, thy belly is Atum, thy back is Atum, thy rear is Atum, thy legs are Atum, and thy face is Anubis.[3] The regions of Horus serve thee, and the regions of Seth serve thee.[4]

b

O Atum, the one here is that son of thine, Osiris, whom thou hast caused to survive and to live on.[5] He lives—(so also) this King Unis lives. He does not die—(so also) this King Unis does not die. He does not perish—(so also) this King Unis does not perish. He *is* not *judged*—(so also) this King Unis *is* not *judged*. (But) he *judges*—(so also) this King Unis *judges*. . . .[6]

What thou hast eaten is an eye. Thy belly is rounded out with it. Thy son Horus leaves it for thee, that thou

[1] Thus as Horus, the son of Osiris.

[2] The dead.

[3] The deceased is here the god of the dead, Anubis, who is depicted as jackal-headed on a human body. Thus here the parts of the body other than the head are equated with the god Atum, who is depicted in human form.

[4] Lower and Upper Egypt.

[5] The deceased is introduced to Atum as his (great-grand)son Osiris. Thus the deceased shares the immortality of Osiris.

[6] In successive stanzas, the deceased is then introduced as Osiris to Shu, Tefnut, Geb, Nut, Isis, Seth, Nephthys, Thoth, Horus, the Great Ennead, the Little Ennead, and Naunet(?). The language is almost the same in every case, except for such variants as relationship would require. For example, it would be absurd to state that Seth, who had murdered Osiris, had caused him to live on. In that case the address therefore runs: "O Seth, the one here is that brother of thine, Osiris, who has been caused to survive and to live on, that he might punish thee." Following the addresses to the several gods, the text proceeds to enunciate the immortality of Osiris in each of several cult-centers.

mayest live on it.[7] He lives—this King Unis lives. He does not die—this King Unis does not die. He does not perish—this King Unis does not perish. He *is* not *judged* —this King Unis *is* not *judged*. He *judges*—this King Unis *judges*.

Thy body is the body of this King Unis.[8] Thy flesh is the flesh of this King Unis. Thy bones are the bones of this King Unis. When thou departest, this King Unis departs. When this King Unis departs, thou departest.

THE FIELDS OF PARADISE

As the sun went to rest every night and was gloriously reborn every morning, so also a mortal left this world but was reborn for eternal happiness in the other world. The eastern horizon of heaven was thus an analogue for entry into paradise. The following text gives a few of the wonders of that home of the blessed.

The spell first occurs in the coffins of the Middle Kingdom. The hieroglyphic text is given by A. de Buck, *The Egyptian Coffin Texts*, II (*OIP* XLIX, Chicago, 1938), Spell 159, pp. 363 ff. It later became the 109th chapter of the Book of the Dead and is studied by K. Sethe *et al.* in *ZAeS*, LIX (1924), 1 ff. (cf. also the 107th and 149th chapters and the vignette to the 110th chapter).

Title

GOING IN AND OUT OF THE EASTERN DOORS OF HEAVEN AMONG THE FOLLOWERS OF RE. I know the Eastern Souls.[1]

The Place of Rebirth

I know that central door from which Re issues in the east.[2] Its south is the pool of *ḳha*-birds, in the place where Re sails with the breeze; its north is the waters of *ro*-fowl, in the place where Re sails with rowing.[3] I am the keeper of the halyard in the boat of the god; I am the oarsman who does not weary in the barque of Re.[4]

I know those two sycamores of turquoise(-green) between which Re comes forth, the two which came from the sowing of Shu at every eastern door at which Re rises.[5]

I know that Field of Reeds of Re.[6] The wall which is around it is of metal. The height of its barley is four

[7] These sentences show that this Utterance was used as an offering text to maintain the deceased. When a survivor made offering to the dead, he played the part of Horus offering his eye to his father Osiris.

[8] Again there is identification of the dead pharaoh with Osiris.

---

[1] For the claim of acquaintance with otherworldly forces, cf. pp. 10, n.2; 12a, n.1.

[2] The 17th chapter of the Book of the Dead (H. Grapow, *Religiöse Urḳunden* [*Urḳ.*, V], 28) mentions this door, with explanatory glosses: "I reach the land of the horizon-dwellers; I go forth from the august door. What is it? It is the Field of Reeds, which brings forth provisions for the gods who are about the shrine (of the sun-god). Further, as for that 'august door,' it is the door of the liftings of (the air-god) Shu. Another version: it is the door of the Underworld. Another version: it is the leaves of the door through which my father Atum proceeds, when he proceeds to the eastern horizon of heaven."

[3] The door has pleasant waters, where birds delight to be. On the Nile, movement south or upstream uses the prevailing north wind and a raised sail, movement north or downstream uses the current and the aid of oars. So also, in paradise the waters must be the same as in this world.

[4] Whether the movement is with the breeze or by rowing, the deceased has a useful function in the sun barque.

[5] As the air-god, Shu was responsible for lifting heaven from earth; cf. n.2 above. Here he planted trees as supports.

[6] The Elysian Fields of the Egyptians included a *seḳhet iaru* "Field of Reeds" and a *seḳhet hetep* "Field of Offerings." See n.10 below.

cubits; its beard is one cubit, and its stalk is three cubits.[7] Its emmer is seven cubits; its beard is two cubits, and its stalk is five cubits.[8] It is the horizon-dwellers, nine cubits in height,[9] who reap it, by the side of the Eastern Souls.[10]

Conclusion

I KNOW THE EASTERN SOULS. THEY ARE HAR-AKHTI, THE *KHURER*-CALF, AND THE MORNING STAR.[11]

THE GOOD FORTUNE OF THE DEAD

The Egyptians looked upon death as a continuation of this life and a fulfillment of the good things of this life. The following text sets forth the quietude which is the happy lot of the dead.

Carved on the wall of the tomb of Nefer-hotep at Thebes (Tomb No. 50) and dated to the reign of Hor-em-heb (about 1349-1319 B.C.). From the same tomb comes the Song of the Harper (p. 467 below). Published by A. H. Gardiner in *PSBA*, XXXV (1913), 165-70, and by M. Lichtheim, with translation and bibliography, in *JNES*, IV (1945), 197-98, 212. The setting and significance of the text are discussed by Gardiner, *The Attitude of the Ancient Egyptians to Death and the Dead* (Cambridge, 1935), 32.

The Singer with the Harp of the God's Father of Amon, Nefer-hotep, the triumphant, said:

All ye excellent nobles, the Ennead of the Mistress of Life,[1]
Hear ye how praises are made to the God's Father,
With homage paid to the excellent noble's efficacious soul,
Now that he is a god living forever,
Magnified in the West.
May they become a remembrance for the future,
For all who come to pass by.

I have heard those songs which are in the ancient tombs
And what they tell in magnifying (life) on earth
And in belittling the necropolis.
Why is it that such is done to the land of eternity,
The right and true, without terrors?
Quarreling is its abomination,
And there is no one who arrays himself against his fellow.
This land which has no opponent—

[7] Almost 7 feet tall, of which the ear was about 20 inches long.

[8] About 12 feet tall, of which the ear was about 41 inches long.

[9] Over 15 feet tall. We are not clear about the "horizon-dwellers." Some later texts change them from *aḳhtiu* to *aḳhu* "effective personalities," that is, the blessed dead.

[10] The vignette to the 110th chapter of the Book of the Dead shows the fields of paradise. For example, in the Papyrus of Ani (British Museum 10470; E. A. W. Budge, *The Booḳ of the Dead* [London 1898], Translation Volume, Pl. opp. p. 170), fields surrounded and cut by waterways are shown, with the deceased plowing, reaping, and threshing. Part of this area is labeled as the "Field of Reeds" and as the "place of the effective personalities, whose length is 7 cubits; the barley is of 3 cubits. It is the noble dead who reap it."

[11] Har-akhti, that is, Horus of the (Morning) Horizon, and the Morning Star are obviously in place in the east. We know little about the *ḳhurer*-calf, possibly a newborn suckling calf.

---

[1] The song is addressed to the honored dead and the gods of the necropolis.

All our kinsfolk rest in it since the first day of time.
They who are to be, for millions of millions,
Will all have come to it.
There exists none who may tarry in the land of Egypt;
There is not one who fails to reach yon place.

As for the duration of what is done on earth,
It is a kind of a dream;
(But) they say: "Welcome, safe and sound!"
To him who reaches the West.

THE PROTESTATION OF GUILTLESSNESS

Among the literary remains from ancient Egypt, a large proportion of the texts seeks to secure eternal happiness for the deceased individual. Under the Empire and later, such mortuary texts were normally on papyrus and have been gathered together by modern scholars under the title, the "Book of the Dead." A common part of this collection of miscellaneous texts envisages the deceased as testifying before a posthumous court and denying any guilt in various crimes and shortcomings. This so-called "negative confession" is one of our few sources for Egyptian social law. Its negative protestations must be studied together with the positive attitudes in the wisdom literature (pp. 412-425).

The following translation takes extracts from a portion of the 125th chapter of the Book of the Dead, as gathered by Ch. Maystre, *Les déclarations d'innocence* (*Livre des morts, chapitre 125*), (Cairo, 1937). Maystre's texts run from the Eighteenth through the Twenty-first Dynasty (1550-950 B.C.).[1]

Many other texts here translated were employed for mortuary purposes, e.g., pp. 3-4, 10-11, 11-12, etc. For a funerary ritual, see p. 325. For the judgment after death, see p. 415. For attitudes toward death, see pp. 412-414, 467. For a brief description of an Egyptian funeral, see pp. 20-21.

What is said on reaching the Broad-Hall of the Two Justices,[2] absolving *X*[3] of every sin which he has committed, and seeing the faces of the gods:

Hail to thee, O great god, lord of the Two Justices![4] I have come to thee, my lord, I have been brought that I might see thy beauty. I know thee; I know thy name and the names of the forty-two gods who are with thee in the Broad-Hall of the Two Justices,[5] who live on them who *preserve* evil and who drink their blood on that day of reckoning up character in the presence of Wennofer.[6] Behold, "*Sati-mertifi*, Lord of Justice," is thy name.[7] I have come to thee; I have brought thee justice; I have expelled deceit for thee.

(A1) I have not committed evil against men.

(A2) I have not mistreated cattle.

(A3) I have not committed sin in the place of truth.[8]

(A4) I have not known that which is not.[9]

(A5) I have not seen evil. . . .[10]

(A7) My name has not reached the Master of the Barque.[11]

(A8) I have not blasphemed a god.

(A9) I have not *done violence to* a poor man.

(A10) I have not done that which the gods abominate.

(A11) I have not defamed a slave to his superior.

(A12) I have not made (anyone) sick.

(A13) I have not made (anyone) weep.

(A14) I have not killed.

(A15) I have given no order to a killer.

(A16) I have not caused anyone suffering.

(A17) I have not cut down on the food-(income) in the temples.

(A18) I have not damaged the bread of the gods.

(A19) I have not taken the loaves of the blessed (dead).

(A20) I have not had sexual relations with a boy.

(A21) I have not defiled myself.

(A22) I have neither increased or diminished the grain-measure.

(A23) I have not disminished the *aroura*.[12]

(A24) I have not falsified a half-*aroura* of land.

(A25) I have not added to the weight of the balance.

(A26) I have not *weakened* the plummet of the scales.

(A27) I have not taken milk from the mouths of children.

(A28) I have not driven cattle away from their pasturage.

(A29) I have not snared the birds *of* the gods.

(A30) I have not caught fish in their marshes.[13]

(A31) I have not held up the water in its season.[14]

(A32) I have not built a dam against running water.

(A33) I have not quenched a fire at its (proper) time.

(A34) I have not neglected the (appointed) times and their meat-offerings.[15]

(A35) I have not driven away the cattle of the god's property.

(A36) I have not stopped a god on his procession.

I am pure!—four times.[16] My purity is the purity of that great *benu*-bird which is in Herakleopolis, because I am really that nose of the Lord of Breath, who makes all men to live, on that day of filling out the Eye (of Horus) in Heliopolis, in the second month of the second season, the last day, in the presence of the lord of this land.[17] I am the one who has seen the filling out of the

[1] The numbering of the A and B series of protestations is that of Maystre. The concluding statement, following the B series, is taken from the 18th dynasty Papyrus of Nu, as given in E. A. W. Budge, *The Book of the Dead* (London, 1898), Text Vol., 259 ff.

[2] The place of the next-world judgment. The meaning of the dual is obscure, although it is clearly a part of that balanced dualism which was so dear to the ancient Egyptian.

[3] The name and title of the deceased.

[4] Osiris, the judge of the dead.

[5] The knowledge of a name was an important force for control or influence. cf. pp. 12-14. Why the divine jurors were 42 in number we do not know.

[6] Wen-nofer is Osiris. The 42 jurors are also avengers of guilt.

[7] *Sati-mertifi* means "the Two Daughters, His Two Eyes," but its application to Osiris is inexplicable.

[8] The temple or the necropolis.

[9] I have not tried to learn that which is not meant for mortals.

[10] A6 is untranslatable, perhaps corrupt.

[11] The sun barque, but the application here is not clear.

[12] A measure of land area.

[13] If "their" refers to the gods of A29, the marshes were temple preserves. If "their" refers to the fish, the idea of preserves may still be present.

[14] Denying the inundation waters to others.

[15] The offerings at the regular feasts.

[16] The exclamation is to be repeated four times.

[17] What is mentioned is a moon feast, but much of the allusion here is obscure.

Eye in Heliopolis. Evil will never happen to me in this land or in this Broad-Hall of the Two Justices, because I know the names of these gods who are in it, the followers of the great god.[18]

(B1) O Wide-of-Stride, who comes forth from Heliopolis, I have not committed evil.

(B2) O Embracer-of-Fire, who comes forth from Babylon,[19] I have not stolen.

(B3) O Nosey, who comes forth from Hermopolis, I have not been covetous.

(B4) O Swallower-of-Shadows, who comes forth from the pit, I have not robbed.

(B5) O Dangerous-of-Face, who came forth from *Rostau*, I have not killed men.

(B6) O *Ruti*, who comes forth from heaven, I have not damaged the grain-measure.

(B7) O His-Eyes-are-of-Flint, who comes forth from the shrine, I have not caused *crookedness*.

(B8) O Flamer, who comes forth *backward*, I have not stolen the property of a god.

(B9) O Breaker-of-Bones, who comes forth from Herakleopolis, I have not told lies.

(B10) O *Commander-of-Fire*, who comes forth from Memphis, I have not taken away food.

(B11) O Dweller-in-the-Pit, who comes forth from the west, I have not been contentious.

(B12) O White-of-Teeth, who comes forth from the Faiyum, I have not trespassed.

(B13) O Eater-of-Blood, who comes forth from the execution-block, I have not slain the cattle of the god.

(B14) O Eater-of-Entrails, who comes forth from the Thirty,[20] I have not *practised usury*.

(B15) O Lord-of-Justice, who comes forth from *Ma'ati*, I have not stolen the *bread-ration*.

(B16) O Wanderer, who comes forth from Bubastis, I have not *gossiped*.

(B17) O *Aadi*, who comes forth from Heliopolis, my mouth has not gone (on unchecked).

(B18) O *Djudju*-serpent, who comes forth from Busiris, I have not argued with *some one summoned because of* his property.

(B19) O *Wamemti*-serpent, who comes forth from the place of judgment, I have not committed adultery.[21]

(B20) O *Maa-Intef*, who comes forth from the Temple of Min, I have not defiled myself.

(B21) O Superior-of-the-Nobles, who comes forth from *Imau*, I have not caused terror.

(B22) O Wrecker, who comes forth from *the Saite Nome*, I have not trespassed.

(B23) O Mischief-Maker, who comes forth from the sanctuary, I have not been (over)heated.

(B24) O Child, who comes forth from the Heliopolitan Nome, I have not been unresponsive to a matter of justice.

(B25) O *Ser-kheru*, who comes forth from *Wensi*, I have not been quarrelsome.

(B26) O Bastet, who comes forth from the sanctum, I have not winked.[22]

(B27) O His-Face-Behind-Him, who comes forth from *Tep-het-djat*, I have not *been perverted*; I have not had sexual relations with a boy.

(B28) O Hot-of-Leg, who comes forth from the twilight, I have not swallowed my heart.[23]

(B29) O Dark-One, who comes forth from the darkness, I have not been abusive.

(B30) O Bringer-of-His-Peace, who comes forth from Sais, I have not been (over)-energetic.

(B31) O Lord-of-Faces, who comes forth from the Heroonpolite Nome, my heart has not been hasty.

(B32) O Plan-Maker, who comes forth from *Utenet*, I have not transgressed my color; I have not washed the god.[24]

(B33) O Lord-of-Horns, who comes forth from Siut, my voice is not (too) much about matters.

(B34) O *Nefer-tem*, who comes forth from Memphis, I have not committed sins; I have not done evil.

(B35) O *Tem-sep*, who comes forth from Busiris, I have not been abusive against a king.

(B36) O Acting-with-His-Heart, who comes forth from *Tjebu*, I have not waded in water.[25]

(B37) O Flowing-One, who comes forth from Nun,[26] my voice has not been loud.

(B38) O Commander-of-the-People, who comes forth from *his shrine*, I have not been abusive against a god.

(B39) O *Neheb-nefert*, who comes forth from *the Saite Nome*, I have never made puffings-up.[27]

(B40) O *Neheb-kau*, who comes forth from the town, I have not made *discriminations for* myself.

(B41) O High-of-Head serpent, who comes forth from the cavern, my portion has not been (too) large, *not even* in my (own) property.

(B42) O *In-af* serpent, who comes forth from the cemetery, I have not blasphemed against my local god.

WORDS TO BE SPOKEN BY *X*:[28]

Hail to you, ye gods who are in this Broad-Hall of the Two Justices! I know you; I know your names. I shall not fall for dread of you. Ye have not reported guilt of mine up to this god in whose retinue ye are; no deed of mine has come *from* you. Ye have spoken truth about me in the presence of the All-Lord, because I acted justly in Egypt. I have not been abusive to a god. No deed of mine has come *from* a king who is in his day.

Hail to you who are in the Broad-Hall of the Two

[18] In the B part of this protestation, which follows, the deceased addresses each of the 42 divine jurors by name. Some of the names defy translation; some show power or frightfulness, but many apply to the judgment scene rather indifferently.

[19] Egyptian Babylon, near modern Cairo.

[20] A law court of Egyptian magistrates in this world.

[21] "I have not had sexual relations with the wife of (another) male."

[22] Winked at injustice?

[23] Have not been evasive, over-secret?

[24] Meaning of both parts obscure.

[25] An idiom?

[26] The abysmal waters.

[27] An idiom?

[28] *X* stands for the name and title of the deceased. One text has: "those words which follow (the hearing in) the Broad-Hall of the Two Justices." From here on the translation is based on one manuscript; see n.1 above.

Justices,[29] (5) who have no deceit in your bodies, who live on truth and who eat of truth in the presence of Horus, who is in his sun disc. May ye rescue me from Babi, who lives on the entrails *of elders* on that day of the great reckoning.[30] Behold me—I have come to you without sin, without guilt, without evil, without a witness (against me), without one against whom I have taken action. I live on truth, and I eat of truth. I have done that which men said and that with which gods are content. I have satisfied a god with that which he desires. I have given bread to the hungry, water to the thirsty, clothing to the naked, (10) and a ferry-boat to him who was marooned.[31] I have provided divine offerings for the gods and mortuary offerings for the dead.[32] (So) rescue me, you; protect me, you. Ye will not make report against me in the presence [of the great god.] I am one pure of mouth and pure of hands, one to whom "Welcome, welcome, in peace!" is said by those who see him, because I have heard those great words which the ass discussed with the cat in the house of *the hippopotamus*, when the witness was His-Face-Behind-Him and he gave out a cry.[33] I have seen the splitting of the *ished*-tree in *Rostau*.[34] I am one who has a concern for the gods, who knows the *nature* of their bodies. I have come here to testify to justice and to bring the scales[35] (15) to their (proper) position in the cemetery.

O thou who art high upon his standard, Lord of the *Atef*-Crown, whose name has been made "Lord of Breath,"[36] mayest thou rescue me from thy messengers who give forth uncleanliness and create *destruction*, who have no covering up of their faces,[37] because I have effected justice for the Lord of Justice, being pure—my front is pure, my rear is clean, my middle is in the flowing water of justice; there is no part of me free of justice. . . .[38]

(36) . . . "I will not announce thee," says the doorkeeper of the Broad-Hall of the Two Justices, "unless thou tellest my name." "Understander of Hearts, Searcher of Bodies is thy name." "Then to whom should I announce thee?" "To the god who is in his hour (of service)." "Thou shouldst tell it to the interpreter of the Two Lands." "Well, who is the interpreter of the Two Lands?" "It is Thoth."[39]

"Come," says Thoth, "why hast thou come?" "I have come here to be announced." "What is thy condition?" "I am pure of sin. I have protected myself from the strife of those who are in (40) their days. I am not among them." "Then to whom shall I announce thee? I shall announce thee to (him whose) ceiling is of fire, (whose) walls are living serpents, and whose pavement is water. Who is he?" "He is Osiris." (45) "Then go thou. Behold, thou art announced. Thy bread is the Restored Eye; thy beer is the Restored Eye. Thou hast invocation-offerings upon earth in the Restored Eye."[40] So spoke Osiris to *X*, the deceased.

Instructions for the Use of the Spell

To be done in conformance with what takes place in this Broad-Hall of the Two Justices. This spell is to be recited when one is clean and pure, clothed in (fresh) garments, shod with white sandals, painted with stibium, and anointed with myrrh, to whom cattle, fowl, incense, bread, beer, and vegetables have been offered. Then make thou this text in writing on a clean pavement with *ochre* smeared with (50) earth upon which pigs and (other) small cattle have not trodden. As for him on whose behalf this book is made, he shall be prosperous and his children shall be prosperous, without *greed*, because he shall be a trusted man of the king and his courtiers. Loaves, jars, bread, and joints of meat shall be given to him from the altar of the great god. He cannot be held back at any door of the West, (but) he shall be ushered in with the Kings of Upper and Lower Egypt, and he shall be in the retinue of Osiris.

Right and true a million times.

29 The 42 divine jurors and other gods attendant upon the court.

30 Babi is one name for the devourer of the condemned dead.

31 The protestations of benevolence in this sentence were common in the mortuary texts carved in Egyptian tombs.

32 "And goings-forth at the voice for the effective personalities." The "invocation-offerings" for the dead might be evoked by the right words.

33 The episode is unknown.

34 This episode, the splitting of a tree by a cat, occurs also in the 17th chapter of the Book of the Dead, but without great clarity.

35 In which the character of the deceased was weighed.

36 Osiris.

37 Have no compassion?

38 The translation omits three examinations undergone by the deceased before he enters the judgment hall. First he is questioned about mythological allusions by unknown examiners, who let him proceed to the door of the court because of his successful answers. Then the various parts of the door demand that he give their magical names before he passes through. Then the pavement of the hall will not let him tread upon it until he tells the magical names of his two treading feet. He passes these information tests successfully, and then is confronted by the doorkeeper.

39 On Thoth as the interpreter, or Master of Protocol, see K. Sethe in *Studies Presented to F. Ll. Griffith* (London, 1932), 433.

40 The restored eye of Horus, symbol of offerings.

Sumerian Myths and Epic Tales

TRANSLATOR: S. N. KRAMER

Enki and Ninhursag: a Paradise Myth

"Enki and Ninhursag" is one of the best preserved of the Sumerian myths uncovered to date. The story it tells is well nigh complete and at least on the surface most of the details of its rather complicated plot are reasonably intelligible. Unfortunately, the main purpose of the myth as a whole is by no means clear and the literary and mythological implications of its numerous and varied motifs are not readily analyzable.[1] Nevertheless it adds much that is significant for the Near Eastern mythological horizon, and perhaps even provides a number of interesting parallels to the motifs of the biblical paradise story as told in the second and third chapters of Genesis.[2] Briefly sketched, the contents of "Enki and Ninhursag" run as follows: The poem begins with a eulogy of Dilmun,[3] described as both a "land" and a "city," where the action of the story takes place. This Dilmun, according to our poem, is a place that is pure, clean, and bright (lines 1-13). It is a land in which there is probably neither sickness nor death (lines 14-30). It is a city which, by the command of the Sumerian water-god Enki, has become full of sweet water and of crop-bearing fields and farms and has thus become known as "the house of the *bank-quays* of the land" (lines 31-64).

Following a brief passage whose interpretation is far from clear (lines 65-72),[4] the main action of the myth begins. Enki impregnates the goddess Ninhursag, "the mother of the land," who, after nine days of pregnancy gives birth, without pain and effort, to the goddess Ninmu. Enki then proceeds to impregnate his daughter Ninmu, who in the same way as her mother Ninhursag, gives birth to the goddess named Ninkurra (lines 89-108). Enki then impregnates his granddaughter Ninkurra, and the latter gives birth to the goddess Uttu[5] (lines 109-127). Enki is now evidently prepared to impregnate his great-granddaughter Uttu when Ninhursag, the great-grandmother, intervenes and offers the latter some pertinent advice. Unfortunately the relevant passage (lines 128-152) is almost completely destroyed. But to judge from the passage that follows (lines 153-185) Uttu may have been instructed by Ninhursag not to cohabit with Enki until and unless he brings her a gift of cucumbers, *apples*, and grapes. Be that as it may, we next see Enki obtain the cucumbers, *apples*, and grapes from a gardener[6] who probably brought them to him in gratitude for his watering the dikes, ditches, and uncultivated places (lines 153-167). Enki brings them to Uttu as a gift, and the latter now joyfully receives his advances and cohabits with him (lines 165-185).

But of this union probably no new goddess is born. Instead, Ninhursag seems to utilize Enki's semen in a way which leads to the sprouting of eight different plants: the "tree"-plant, the "honey"-plant, the *roadweed*-plant, the *apasar*-plant,[7] the *thorn*-plant, the *caper*-plant, a plant whose name is illegible, and the cassia-plant (lines 186-195). And now Enki commits a sinful deed. As he looked about him in the marshland, he noticed the eight plants and probably determined to decide their fate. But first, it seems, he had to *know* their heart, that is, he probably had to taste what they were like. And so his messenger, the two-faced god Isimud, plucks each of the eight plants for Enki, and the latter eats them one by one (lines 196-217). Angered by this act, Ninhursag, the goddess who is so largely responsible for their first coming into existence, utters a curse against Enki, saying that until he dies she will not look upon him with the "eye of life." And, as good as her word, she immediately disappears.

Whereupon, Enki no doubt begins to pine away, and the Anunnaki, the "great" but nameless Sumerian gods, sit in the dust. At this point the fox[8] comes to the rescue; he asks Enlil, the leader of the Sumerian pantheon,[9] what would be his reward if he brought Ninhursag back to the gods. Enlil names his reward, and the fox, sure enough, succeeds in some way in having Ninhursag return to the gods in Dilmun (lines 221-249). Ninhursag then seats the dying Enki *by* her vulva,[10] and asks where he feels pain. Enki names an organ of the body which hurts him, and Ninhursag then informs him that she has caused a certain deity to be born for him,[11] the implication being that the birth of the deity will result in the healing of the sick member. All in all, Ninhursag repeats the question eight times.[12] Each time Enki names an organ of the body which pains him, and in each case Ninhursag announces the birth of a corresponding deity (lines 250-268).[13] Finally, probably at the request of Ninhursag, Enki decreed the fate of the newborn deities, the last of whom, Enshag by name, is destined to be "the lord of Dilmun."

The text of "Enki and Ninhursag" is based primarily on a fairly well-preserved six-column tablet excavated in Nippur and

[1] For a discussion of the aims and techniques of the Sumerian mythographers, cf. the writer's review of *The Intellectual Adventure of Ancient Man* in *JCS*, II, 39 ff.

[2] cf. *BASOR SS*, No. 1, 8-9.

[3] For a detailed discussion of Dilmun and its location, cf. the writer's Dilmun, the Land of the Living, *BASOR*, 96, 18-28; for a contrary opinion, cf. now P. B. Cornwall, *BASOR*, 103 (1946), 3-11.

[4] The suggestion in *SS*, No. 1, that the passage "may contain a description in anthropomorphic terms of the poet's notion of the formation of the marshlands in the neighborhood of the deltas bordering the Persian Gulf" (pp. 4-5) is highly dubious and might perhaps better not have been made in the first place.

[5] The mythological motifs involved in the birth of the goddesses Ninmu, Ninkurra and Uttu (note, too, that according to a variant of our text, a goddess by the name of Ninsig is to be added as a fourth in this chain of births) are obscure; Ninmu and Ninsig, to judge from their names ("the Lady who brings forth" and "the Lady who makes green"), seem to be deities whose activities originally concerned vegetation; the goddess Ninkurra, "Lady of the mountain-land" or perhaps "Lady of the nether world," is a deity whose activities seem to be restricted to stone working; the goddess Uttu seems to be a deity whose activities had to do with clothing (cf. now Jacobsen, *JNES*, V, 143).

[6] The presence of the gardener is not to be taken as an indication that our myth deals in any way with human beings; the gardener is no doubt to be considered as one of a host of minor deities in charge of a particular activity in the service of the gods.

[7] The reading of the name of this plant is uncertain.

[8] At least in Dilmun, therefore, which may perhaps be characterized as a divine paradise (cf. *SS* No. 1, 8, note 28), some animals were conceived as existing at the time when the action of our myth is supposed to take place.

[9] Note that Enlil, too, thus seems to be present in Dilmun.

[10] Actually the text seems to say "in her vulva."

[11] For the difficulties involved in the interpretation of the relevant lines, cf. *SS*, No. 1, 6, note 22.

[12] Note that the number of Enki's sick organs corresponds to the number of plants which he had eaten.

[13] The correspondence between the sick member and the healing deity rests on the superficial and punlike etymologizing of the ancient scribes; the Sumerian word for the sick organ contains at least one syllable in common with the name of the deity. Thus e.g. one of the organs that pained Enki was the "mouth," the Sumerian word for which is *ka*, and the deity created to alleviate this pain is called Nin*ka*si; similarly, the goddess born to alleviate the pain of the rib, the Sumerian word for which is *ti*, is named Nin*ti*, etc.

now in the University Museum; it was copied and published by Stephen Langdon under the title *Sumerian Epic of Paradise, the Flood, and the Fall of Man* in *PBS*, x, Pt. 1 (1915). Since then a fragment of unknown provenience has been published by Henri De Genouillac in *TRS*, 62, but the nature of its contents was first recognized by Edward Chiera (cf. *JAOS*, LIV, 417). Both tablets were actually inscribed some time in the first half of the second millennium B.C.; the date when the myth was first composed is unknown. A transliteration and translation of the poem were published by the writer in *BASOR SS* No. 1 (1945); here will be found references to earlier literature. A translation of the poem based on the transliteration in *SS* No. 1 has been published by M. Witzel in *Orientalia NS*, xv (1946), 239-285. A résumé of the contents of the myth and a translation of the first 25 lines were published by T. Jacobsen in *The Intellectual Adventure of Ancient Man*, pp. 157-160 (cf. the present writer's comment in *JCS*, II, 58, note 40).[14]

[15][The *place*] is [pure] . . . ,
. . . [the land] Dilmun is pure;
[The land Dilmun] is [pu]re . . . ,
. . . the [la]nd D[il]mun is pure;
The land Dilmun is pure, the land Dilmun is clean;
The land Dilmun is clean, the land Dilmun is most
bright.
Who had lain by himself in Dilmun—
The place, after Enki had lain with his wife,
That place is clean, that place is most bright;
(Who had lain) by himself (in Dilmun)—
The place, (after) Enki (had lain) by Ninsikilla,
That place is clean, (that place is bright).
In Dilmun the raven utters no cries,[16]
The *ittidu*-bird[17] utters not the cry of the *ittidu*-bird,
The lion kills not,
The wolf snatches not the lamb,
Unknown is the kid-devouring *wild dog*,
Unknown is the grain-devouring . . . ,
[*Unknown*][18] is the . . . widow,
The bird on high . . . s not its . . . ,
The dove *droops* not the head,
The sick-eyed says not "I am sick-eyed,"
The sick-headed (says) not "I am sick-headed,"
Its[19] old woman (says) not "I am an old woman,"
Its old man (says) not "I am an old man,"
Unbathed is the maid, no sparkling water is poured in
the city,
Who crosses the river utters no . . . ,
The wailing priest walks not round about him,
The singer utters no *wail*,
By the side of the city he (utters) no *lament*.
Ninsikilla says to her father[20] Enki:
"The city thou hast given, the city thou hast given,
thy . . . ,
Dilmun, the city thou hast given, the city (thou hast
given, thy . . .),
Has not . . . *of* the river;
Dilmun, the city thou hast given, the city (thou hast
given, thy . . .),
. . . ,
. . . *furrowed fields* (*and*) farms,[21]
. . . ,
. . . ."
[Father Enki answers Ninsikilla, his daughter]:
["Let Utu[22] *standing* in heaven],
[From the . . . , the *breast* of his . . .],
[From the . . . of Nanna],[23]
[From the 'mouth whence issues the water of the earth,'
bring thee sweet water from the earth];
Let him bring up the water into thy large . . . ,
Let him make thy city drink from it the waters of
abundance,
(Let him make) Dilmun (drink from it) the waters of
ab(undance),
Let thy well of bitter water become a well of sweet
water,
[Let thy *furrowed* fields (and) farms
bear thee grain],[24]
Let thy city become the *bank-quay*[25]
house of the land,[26]
Now Utu is a . . ."
Utu *standing* in heaven,
From the . . . , the *breast* of his . . . ,
From the . . . of Nanna,
From the "mouth whence issues the water of the earth,"
brought her sweet water from the earth;
He brings up the water into her large . . . ,
Makes her city drink from it the waters of abundance,
Makes Dilmun (drink from it) the waters
of ab(undance),
Her well of bitter water, verily it is become a well
of sweet water,
Her *furrowed* fields (and) farms *bore* her grain,
Her city, verily it is become the *bank-quay* house of the
land
Dilmun, (verily it is become) the *bank-(quay)* house
(of the land),
Now Utu is . . . ;[27] verily it was so.
Who is alone, *before* the wise Nintu, the mother of the
land,[28]

[14] Note also the review of *SS* No. 1 by Raymond Jestin in *Syria*, xxv (1946-1948), 150-155.

[15] The scribe of the tablet on which the text of the poem is based, often omitted words and complexes (or parts of words and complexes) that were obvious repetitions; such omissions are given in parentheses throughout this translation.

[16] Lines 13-25 seem to fit the assumption that Dilmun is a land in which there is neither sickness nor death; the implications of lines 26-30, however, are obscure even where the renderings are relatively certain.

[17] The *ittidu*-bird is probably a bird whose cry is a mark of death and desolation.

[18] Brackets erroneously omitted in *SS* No. 1.

[19] "Its" in this and the next line refers to Dilmun.

[20] The word "father" is here used as an honorific title and does not denote actual paternity.

[21] Note that this rendering differs slightly from that in *SS* No. 1.

[22] Utu (not to be confused with the goddess Uttu) is the sun-god.

[23] Nanna is the moon-god.

[24] This line must have been accidentally omitted by the scribe, cf. line 61; note too, the slightly varying rendering of these two lines from that in *SS* No. 1.

[25] Note this new rendering, and cf. Witzel, *Orientalia*, xv, 268.

[26] The Sumerian word here rendered "land" usually refers to Sumer; but since "thy city" refers to Dilmun, the implications of the line are not too clear.

[27] The first half of this line corresponds to line 51.

[28] Perhaps the rendering of this line and the next should read: "Who is alone, the wise, *before* Nintu, the mother of the land; Enki, the wise, before Nintu, the mother of the land," cf. *SS* No. 1, 24; for the word "land" cf. note 26.

Enki (*before*) the wise Nintu, (the mother of the land),
Causes his phallus to water the dikes,[29]
Causes his phallus to submerge the reeds,
Verily *causes his phallus to*[30] . . . ,
Thereupon he said, "*Let* no one walk in the marshland,"
Thereupon Enki said: ("*Let* no one walk in the marshland),"
He swore by the life of Anu.[31]
His . . . *of* the marshland, . . . *of* the marshland,
Enki . . . d *his* semen of Damgalnunna,[32]
Poured the semen in the womb of Ninhursag.
She took the semen into the womb, the semen of Enki.
One day being her one month,
Two days being her two months,
Three days being her three months,
Four days being her four months,
Five days (being her five months),
Six days (being her six months),
Seven days (being her seven months),
Eight [days] (being her eight months),
Nine [days] being her nine months, the months of "womanhood,"
L[ike . . . fat], like . . . fat, like good princely fat,
[Nintu], the mother of the land, like [. . . fat], (like . . . fat, like good princely fat),
Gave birth to [Ninmu].
Ninmu . . . d *at* the bank of the river,[33]
Enki in the marshland *looks about, looks about,*
He says to his messenger Isimud:
"Shall I not kiss the young one, the fair?
(Shall I not kiss) Ninmu, the fair?"
His messenger Isimud answers him:
"Kiss the young one, the fair,[34]
(Kiss) Ninmu, the fair,
For my king I shall *blow up a mighty wind*, I shall *blow up a mighty wind.*"
First he set his foot in the boat,[35]
Then he set it on *dry land,*
He embraced her, he kissed her,
Enki poured the semen into the womb,
She took the semen into the womb, the semen of Enki,
One day being her one month,
Two days being her two months,
Nine days being her nine months, the months of "womanhood,"[36]
[Like . . .] fat, like [. . . fat], like good princely fat,
[Ninmu], (like) . . . [fat], (like . . . fat, like good princely fat),
Gave birth to Nink[urra].
Ninkurra . . . d *at* the bank of the river,
Enki in the marshland [*looks about, looks about*],
He [says] to his messenger Isimud:
"Shall I not [kiss] the young one, the fair?
(Shall I not kiss) Ninkurra, the fair?"
His messenger Isimud answers him:
"Kiss the young one, the fair,
(Kiss) Ninkurra, the fair.
For my king I shall *blow up a mighty wind*, I shall *blow up a mighty wind.*"
First he set his foot in the boat,
Then he set it on *dry land,*
He embraced her, he kissed her,
Enki poured the semen into the womb,
She took the semen into the womb, the semen of Enki,
One day being her one month,
Nine days being her nine months, the months [of] "womanhood,"[37]
Like . . . fat, like . . . fat, like good, princely fat,
Ninkurra, (like) . . . fat, (like . . . fat, like good, princely fat),
Gave birth to Uttu, the *fair* lady.
Nintu says [to] Uttu, [the *fair* lady]:
"Instruction I offer thee, [take] my instruction,
A word I speak to thee, [take] my word.
Someone in the marshland *look*[*s*] *about,* [*looks about*],
Enki in the marshland [*looks about, looks about*],
The eye . . .
. . . (approximately 10 lines destroyed)
. . . Uttu, the fair lady . . . ,
. . . ,
. . . *in his* . . . ,
. . . *heart* . . .
Bring [the cucumbers in *their* . . .],
Bring [*the apples*] in their [. . .],
Bring the grapes in their . . . ,
In the house may he take hold of my leash,[38]
May Enki there take hold of my leash."
A second time while he[39] was filling with water,
He filled the dikes with water,
He filled the ditches with water,
He filled the uncultivated places with water.
The gardener *in the dust* in his joy . . . ,
He embrac[es] him.
"Who art thou who . . . [my] garden?"
Enki [answers] the gardener:
" . . . ,
[*Bring me the cucumbers in their* . . .],
[*Bring me the apples in their* . . .],
[*Bring me the grapes in their*. . . .]"
[He] *brought* him the cucumbers in *their* . . . ,
He *brought* him *the apples* in their . . . ,

29 "Dikes" instead of "ditches," as in *SS* No. 1.

30 Should have been italicized as doubtful in *SS* No. 1.

31 Anu is the god of heaven, who early in Sumerian history was the leading deity of the pantheon.

32 The implications of the phrase "the semen of Damgalnunna" are obscure; Damgalnunna is well known as the wife of Enki, and it is hardly likely that she is identical with the goddess Ninhursag (also known as Nintu throughout our poem) mentioned in the following line, cf. too, n.53.

33 Note the new rendering which differs considerably from that in *SS* No. 1; so also line 109.

34 The rendering is based on the assumption of a scribal error; cf. lines 115-116.

35 Note the new renderings of lines 98-99 and 118-119.

36 Note that the scribe does not repeat days three to eight.

37 Note that the scribe does not repeat days two to eight.

38 "To take hold of the leash" probably connotes "to follow the lead of someone" "to do exactly as had been planned by someone."

39 "He" probably refers to Enki.

He *brought* him the grapes in their . . . , he heaped them on his lap.
Enki, his face turned green, he gripped the staff,
To Uttu Enki directed his step.
"Who . . . st *in her house*, open."[40]
"Thou, who art thou?"
"I, the gardener, would give thee cucumbers, *apples*, and grapes as a 'so be it.' "[41]
Uttu with joyful heart opened the door of the house.
Enki to Uttu, the *fair lady*,
Gives the cucumbers in their . . . ,
Gives *the apples* in their . . . ,
Gives the grapes in their. . . .
Uttu, the fair lady . . . s the . . . for *him*, . . . s the . . . for *him*.[42]
Enki took his joy of Uttu,
He embraced her, lay in her lap,
He . . . s the thighs,[43] he touches the . . . ,
He embraced her, lay in her lap,
With the young one he cohabited, he kissed her.
Enki poured the semen into the womb,
She took the semen into the womb, the semen of Enki.
Uttu, the fair lady . . . ,
Ninhursag . . . d the *semen from the thighs*,
[The "tree"-plant sprouted],
[The "honey"-plant spro]uted,
[The *roadweed*-plant spro]uted,
[The . . .-plant s]prouted,
[The *thorn* s]prouted,
[The *caper*-plant] sp(routed),
[The . . .-plant] sp(routed),
[The cassia-plant s]prouted.
Enki in the marshland *looks about, looks about*,
He says to his messenger Isimud:
"Of the plants, their fate . . . ,
What, pray, is this? What, pray, is this?"
His messenger Isimud answers him:
"My [king], the 'tree'-plant," he says to him;
He[44] cuts it down for him, he eats it.
"My king, the 'honey'-plant," he says to him;[45]
He plucks it for him, he eats it.
"My king, the *r*[*oadwee*]*d*-plant, he (says to him),
He cuts it down for him, he eats it).
"My king, the . . .-plant," he (says to him);
[He plucks it for him, he (eats it)].
"[My king, the t]horn-plant," he (says to him);
[He cuts it down for him], he (eats it).
"[My king, the ca]per-[plant]," he (says to him),
[He plucks it for him, he (eats it)].
["My king, the . . .-plant," he (says to him)];
[He cuts it down for him], he (eats it).
"My king, the cassia-plant," he says to him;

[40] In *SS* No. 1, there is one "open" too many.
[41] For a leading god like Enki to give something as a "so be it," may be another way of saying "to present as a permanent gift."
[42] Note the slightly variant rendering from that of *SS* No. 1.
[43] "Thighs" instead of "buttocks" as in *SS* No. 1; cf., too, line 187.
[44] The first "he" refers to Isimud, the second "he" refers to Enki.
[45] Note that the scribe omits the text corresponding to line 199 before lines 203, 205, 207, etc.

[He plucks it for him], he eats it.
Of the plants, [Enki] decreed their fate, *knew* their "heart."
(Thereupon[46]) Ninhursag cursed Enki's name:
"Until he is dead I shall not look upon him with the 'eye of life.' "[47]
The Anunnaki sat in the dust,
(When)[48] up speaks the fox to Enlil:
"If I bring Ninhursag before thee, what shall be my reward?"
Enlil answers the fox:
"If thou wilt bring Ninhursag before me,
In my city[49] I will *plant* trees *(and) fields* for thee, verily thy name will be uttered."
The fox, *as one* . . . d *his skin*,
As one, loosened his . . . ,
As one, painted *his face*.
(four lines destroyed)
"[*To Nippur*] *I shall go*, Enlil . . . ,[50]
[*T*]*o* [*Ur*] *I shall go*, Nanna . . . ,
To [*Larsa*] *I shall go, Utu* . . . ,
To [*Erech*] *I shall go*, Inanna . . . ,
. . . *is, my name* . . . *bring*."
Enlil . . .
Ninhursag. . . .
(four lines destroyed)
. . . *stood by him*.
Ninhursag . . . d . . . ,
The Anunnaki seized her garments,
Made . . . ,[51]
Decreed the fate,
Interpreted the . . . ,
Ninhursag seated Enki *by*[52] her vulva:
"My brother,[53] what hurts thee?"
"My . . . hurts me."
"Abu I have caused to be born for thee."[54]
"My brother, what hurts thee?"
"My *jaw* hurts me."
"Nintulla I have caused to be born for thee."
"My brother, what hurts thee?" "My tooth hurts me."
"Ninsutu I have caused to be born for thee."
"My brother, what hurts thee?" "My mouth hurts me."
"Ninkasi I have [caused] to be [born] for thee."
"My brother what hurts thee?" "My . . [. hurts me]."

[46] "Thereupon" should have been placed in parentheses in *SS* No. 1.
[47] "The eye of life" had its opposite in the "eye of death," cf. e.g. line 164 of "Inanna's Descent to the Nether World" on p. 55.
[48] So, rather than as in *SS* No. 1.
[49] That is Nippur, the city where Enlil had his great temple, the Ekur.
[50] For the restoration of the place names in lines 233-236, cf. Witzel's excellent suggestion in *Orientalia*, NS, xv, 282. In *SS* No. 1, note that Uttu in line 235 is an error for *Utu*.
[51] In *SS* No. 1, two dots are superflous; so too, in line 249.
[52] Actually the text seems to say "in her vulva."
[53] Note that if the words "my brother" are to be taken literally, Enki and Ninhursag were conceived as brother and sister, at least by the mythographers of this period; at present it is not clear how this concept was justified.
[54] For the nature of the correspondence between the sick members and the healing deities listed in this passage, cf. n.13. As for the deities listed throughout this passage, they are relatively minor and comparatively little is known of their place in the Sumerian pantheon; among the better known are the god Abu; Ninkasi, the goddess of strong drink; Ninazu, a netherworld deity (cf. *SM*, 46, for the story of his birth); for the god Ningishzida, cf. E. Douglas Van Buren's study in *Iraq*, 1, 60-89.

"Nazi I have caused to be [born] for thee."
"My brother, what hurts thee?" "[My] arm [hurts me]."
"Azimua I have [caused] to be [born] for thee."
"My brother, what hurts thee?" "[My] rib [hurts me]."
"Ninti I have caused to be [born] for thee."
"My brother, what hurts thee?" "My . . . [hurts me]."
"Enshag I have caused to be [born] for thee.
For the little ones which I have caused to be born. . . ."[55]
"Let Abu be the king of the plants,
Let Nintulla be the lord of Magan,[56]
Let Ninsutu marry Ninazu,
Let Ninkasi be she who *sates the desires*,
Let Nazi marry *Nindara*,
Let Azi[mua] marry [Nin]gishzida,
Let N[inti] be the [qu]een *of the months*,
Let [Ensha]g be the lord of Dilmun."
[O Father Enki], praise!

Dumuzi and Enkimdu: the Dispute between the Shepherd-God and the Farmer-God

This poem is one of a group of Sumerian compositions whose plot is based on what may not inaptly be described as the "Cain-Abel" motif; their contents consist in large part of disputes between two gods, two demigods, or two kings,[1] each of whom attempts to convince the other of his superiority by extolling his own virtues and achievements and belittling those of his opponent. To be sure, in all our extant compositions, the dispute ends in a reconciliation, or at least in a peaceful settlement, rather than in a murder; indeed in the case of the present poem, one of the characters, the shepherd-god, is an unusually meek and peaceful person who takes the wind out of his opponent's sails by refusing to quarrel in the first place.[2] But the psychological ingredient is the same throughout, an aggressive attitude on the part of one of the characters resulting, at least in some cases, from a feeling of inferiority and frustration. In the case of the present poem, it is Dumuzi, the shepherd-god, who, having been rejected by the goddess Inanna in favor of the farmer-god,[3] is impelled to enumerate his superior qualities in elaborate detail, and to pick a quarrel with his peace-loving rival.

The characters of our poem are four in number: the goddess Inanna; her brother, the sun-god Utu; the shepherd-god Dumuzi; and the farmer-god Enkimdu. Its contents may be summarized as follows: Following a brief introduction, whose contents are largely fragmentary (lines 1-9), we find Utu addressing his sister and urging her to become the wife of the shepherd Dumuzi (lines 10-19). Inanna's answer (lines 20-34?)[4] consists of a flat refusal; she is determined instead to marry the farmer Enkimdu. Following several fragmentary lines of uncertain meaning (lines 35?-39), the text continues with a long address of the shepherd, directed probably to Inanna, in which he details his superior qualities (lines 40-64). We then find the shepherd rejoicing on the riverbank, probably because his argument had convinced Inanna and induced her to change her mind.[5] There he meets Enkimdu and starts a quarrel with him (lines 65-73). But the latter refuses to quarrel and agrees to allow Dumuzi's flocks to pasture anywhere in his territory (lines 74-79). The latter, thus appeased, invited the farmer to his wedding as one of his friends (lines 80-83). Whereupon, Enkimdu offers to bring him and Inanna several selected farm products as a wedding gift (lines 84-87). The poet then ends the composition with the conventional literary notations.

The text of the poem is reconstructed from three tablets and fragments excavated in Nippur; they date from the first half of the second millennium B.C. A transliteration and translation of the poem prepared recently by the writer will be found in *JCS*, II (1948), pp. 60-68. A preliminary sketch of the plot of the poem under the title Inanna Prefers the Farmer, together with translations of several excerpts from the poem was published by the writer in *SM*, (1944), 101-103. An interpretation of the contents of the poem under the title, The Wooing of Inanna: Relative Merits of Shepherd and Farmer, was published by Thorkild Jacobsen in *The Intellectual Adventure of Ancient Man* (1946), 166-168.

Who is a maid, the stable . . .
The maid Inanna, the sheepfold . . .
Kneeling in the furrows . . .
Inanna . . .
A garment . . .
. . .
. . . *I* am not . . .
From . . .
. . . wife of the shepherd . . .
Her brother, the hero, the warrior, Utu
Says [to] the pure Inanna:
"O my sister, let the shepherd marry thee,
O maid Inanna, why art thou unwilling?
His fat is good, his milk is good,
The shepherd, everything his hand touches is bright,
O Inanna, let the shepherd Dumuzi marry thee,
O thou who . . . , why art thou unwilling?
His good fat he will eat with thee,
O *protector of* the king, why art thou unwilling?"
"[*Me*] the shepherd shall not marry,
In his new [*garment*] he shall not *drape* me,
When I . . . he shall not . . . me,
Me, the maid, let the farmer marry,

[55] The translation assumes that this line contains the words of Ninhursag; it is not altogether impossible, however, that it is Enki who is speaking; in this case the line should be rendered "For the little ones which thou hast caused to be born. . . ." Similarly, the translation assumes that lines 270-277 contain the words of Enki; there is a bare possibility, however, that it is Ninhursag who is speaking.

[56] The land Magan is usually identified either with Arabia or with Egypt.

[1] cf. for the present the poems "Emesh and Enten" (*SM*, 49-51), "Cattle and Grain" (*ibid.*, 53-54), "Enmerkar and Ensukushsiranna" (*PAPS*, xc, [1946], 122-123). The motif was extended to include disputes between animals and inanimate objects; cf. the four wisdom compositions mentioned on p. 15 of *SM*; cf. also Jacobsen in *The Intellectual Adventure of Ancient Man*, 165-166.

[2] Note, on the other hand that, in the Cain-Abel story as told in the book of Genesis, it is the farmer, Cain, who seems to be the more aggressive throughout.

[3] In the Cain-Abel story, it is the farmer who feels rejected by his god.

[4] The reader will do well to note that there is no introductory statement to indicate who addresses whom in any of the speeches in our poem except in case of the first, that is, in the case of Utu's address to Inanna; in all other instances it is only from the context that we can gather who the speaker is. Helpful to the translator, however, is the Sumerian dialect in which the speech is reproduced; when it is in the Emesal dialect, the speaker must be Inanna.

[5] It must be stressed, however, that this is only an inference from the context, it is not expressly stated anywhere in the text.

The farmer who makes *plants* grow abundantly,
The farmer who makes grain grow abundantly,
. . . (Approximately 8 lines are destroyed.)
Me . . .
This *matter . . .*
To the shepherd . . .
The king of [dike, ditch, and plow] . . .
The shepherd Dumuzi . . .
. . . to speak . . .
"The f[arme]r (more) than I, the farmer (more) than I, the farmer what has he more (than I)?
Enkimdu, the man of dike, ditch, and plow,
(More) than I, the farmer, what has he more (than I)?
Should he give me his black garment,
I would give him, the farmer, my black ewe for it,
Should he give me his white garment,
I would give him, the farmer, my white ewe for it,
Should he pour me his prime date wine,
I would pour him, the farmer, my yellow milk for it
Should he pour me his good date wine,
I would pour him, the farmer my *kisim*-milk for it,
Should he pour me his . . . date wine,[6]
I would pour him, the farmer, my . . . milk for it,
Should he pour me his diluted date wine,
I would pour him, the farmer, my *plant*-milk for it,
Should he give me his good *portions*,
I would give him, the farmer, my *itirda*-milk for them,
Should he give me his good bread,
I would give him, the farmer, my *honey*-cheese for it,
Should he give me his small beans,
I would give him, the farmer, my small cheeses for them;
After *I* shall have eaten, shall have drunk,
I would *leave* for him the extra fat,
I would *leave* for him the extra milk;
(More) than I, the farmer, what has he more (than I)?"
He rejoiced, he rejoiced, . . . *on* the riverbank rejoiced,
On the riverbank, the shepherd on the riverbank [*rejoiced*],
The shepherd, moreover, [*led*] the sheep *on* the riverbank.
To the shepherd *walking to and fro on* the riverbank,
To him who is a shepherd, the farmer [*approached*],
The farmer Enkimdu [*approached*].
Dumuzi, the farmer, the king of dike and ditch . . . ,
In his plain, the shepherd in his [plain starts] a quarrel with him,
The [sh]epherd Dumuzi in his plain starts a quarrel with him.
"I against thee, O shepherd, against thee, O shepherd, I against thee
Why shall I strive?
Let thy sheep eat the grass of the riverbank,
In my *meadowland* let thy sheep walk about,
In the bright fields of Erech let them eat grain,
Let thy *kids* and *lambs* drink the water of my *Unun* canal."

[6] So, rather than as in *JCS*, II, 66.

"As for me, who am a shepherd, at my marriage,
O farmer, mayest thou be counted as my friend,
O farmer Enkimdu, as my friend, O farmer, as my friend,
Mayest thou be counted as my friend."
"I would bring thee wheat, I would bring thee beans,
I would bring thee . . . ,
O thou who art a maid, whatever is . . . to thee,
O maid Inanna, . . . I would bring thee."
In the dispute which took place between the shepherd and the farmer,[7]
O maid Inanna, thy praise is good.
It is a *balbale*.[8]

The Deluge

This Sumerian myth concerning the flood, with its Sumerian counterpart of the antediluvian Noah, offers the closest and most striking parallel to biblical material as yet uncovered in Sumerian literature. Moreover, its introductory passages are of considerable significance for Mesopotamian cosmogony; they include a number of important statements concerning the creation of man, the origin of kingship, and the existence of at least five antediluvian cities. Unfortunately, only one tablet inscribed with the myth has been uncovered to date, and of that tablet only the lower third is preserved. As a result, much of the context of the story is obscure, and but a few of the passages can be rendered with any degree of certainty. Briefly sketched, the contents run as follows: Following a break of about 37 lines, we find a deity[1] addressing other deities and probably stating that he will save mankind from destruction.[2] As a result, the deity continues, man will build the cities and temples of the gods. Following the address are three lines which are difficult to relate to the context; they seem to describe the actions performed by the deity to make his words effective. These lines are in turn followed by four lines concerned with the creation of man, animals, and, perhaps, plants. Here another break of about 37 lines follows, after which we learn that kingship was lowered from heaven, and that five cities were founded. A break of about 37 lines now follows; these must have dealt largely with the decision of the gods to bring the flood and destroy mankind. When the text becomes intelligible again we find some of the gods dissatisfied and unhappy over the cruel decision. We are then introduced to Ziusudra, the counterpart of the biblical Noah, who is described as a pious, a god-fearing king,[3] constantly on the lookout for divine revelations in dreams or incantations. Ziusudra seems to station himself by a wall, where he hears the voice of a deity[4] informing him of the decision taken by the assembly of the gods to send a flood and "to destroy the seed of mankind." The text

[7] To judge from the other compositions of this literary genre, one might have expected here a line reading approximately "The shepherd having proved the victor over the farmer."

[8] *Balbale* is the technical name for a category of Sumerian compositions which, to judge from the extant material, are hymnal in character; the actual meaning of the complex is still uncertain.

[1] There is some possibility that it is more than one deity who is speaking; the relevant Sumerian verbal forms in this passage seem to be inconsistent in regard to the use of the singular and plural. The name of the speaker (or speakers) is destroyed; probably it is either Enki or Anu and Enlil (perhaps better Anu Enlil; cf. n.7).

[2] The nature of this destruction is not known; it is rather unlikely that it refers to the deluge.

[3] The text does not give the name of the state over which he ruled, but we know from the Sumerian king list that he is supposed to have ruled over Sumer from his capital city Shuruppak; cf. *AS* 11, p. 26, n.34.

[4] Probably Enki; the name of the deity is not given in the text.

must have continued with detailed instructions to Ziusudra to build a giant boat and thus save himself from destruction.[5] But, all this is missing since there is another break of about 40 lines at this point. When the text becomes intelligible once again, we find that the flood in all its violence had already come upon the "land,"[6] and raged there for seven days and nights. But then the sun-god Utu came forth again, bringing his precious light everywhere, and Ziusudra prostrates himself before him and offers sacrifices. Here again there follows a break of about 39 lines. The last extant lines of our text describe the deification of Ziusudra. After he had prostrated himself before Anu and Enlil,[7] he was given "life like a god" and breath eternal, and translated to Dilmun,[8] "the place where the sun rises." The remainder of the poem, about 39 lines of text, is destroyed.[9]

The "deluge" tablet, or rather the lower third of it which is extant, was excavated in Nippur, and is now in the University Museum. It was published by Arno Poebel in *PBS*, v (1914), No. 1; a transliteration and translation of the text, together with a detailed commentary, were published by the same author in *PBS*, iv, Pt. 1, pp. 9-70. Poebel's translation is still standard, and except for slight modifications, underlies the present translation.[10]

(approximately first 37 lines destroyed)

"My mankind, *in* its destruction I will . . . ,[11]
To Nintu[12] I will *return the . . . of* my creatures,
I[13] will *return* the people *to*[14] their *settlements*,
Of the cities, verily they[15] will build their *places of (divine) ordinances*,[16] I[17] will make peaceful their shade,[18]
Of *our*[19] houses, verily they will lay their bricks in pure places,
The places of our decisions verily they will found in pure places."
He[20] directed[21] the . . . *of the temenos*,
Perfected the rites (and) the exalted (divine) ordinances,
On the earth he . . . d, placed the . . . there.[22]
After Anu, Enlil, Enki, and Ninhursag
Had fashioned the black-headed (people),[23]
Vegetation luxuriated from the earth,[24]
Animals, four-legged (creatures) of the plain, were brought artfully into existence.

(approximately 37 lines destroyed)

After the . . .[25] of kingship had been lowered from heaven,
After the exalted [*tiara*[26]] (and) the throne of kingship had been lowered from heaven,
He[27] [pe]rfected the [rites (and) the ex]alted [(divine) ordinances] . . . ,[28]
Founded the [*five*] *ci*[*ties*] in . . . p[ure places],
Cal[led] their names, [appor]tioned[29] them *as* [*cu*]*lt-centers*.[30]
The *first*[31] of these cities, Eridu, he gave to Nudimmud,[32] the leader,
The second, Badtibira, he gave to . . . ,[33]
The third, Larak, he gave to Endurbilhursag,[34]
The fourth, Sippar, he gave to the hero Utu,[35]
The fifth, Shuruppak, he gave to Sud.[36]
When he had called the names of these cities, apportioned them *as cult-centers*,
He *brought* . . . ,[37]
Established the *cleaning* of the small rivers *as* . . .

(approximately 37 lines destroyed)

[5] Whom else and what else he took with him in the boat are not found in the extant text, but note that, to judge from line 211, he had certainly taken along a number of animals.

[6] The Sumerian word here rendered as "land" usually seems to refer to Sumer.

[7] Perhaps a rendering "Anu Enlil" for "Anu and Enlil" is preferable; that is, the Enlil to whom the powers of Anu were delegated when the former took Anu's place as the leading deity of the Sumerian pantheon; cf. for the problem involved, Poebel, *PBS*, iv, Pt. 2, pp. 36 ff.

[8] For the location of Dilmun, cf. now p. 37 of this work.

[9] That is, if we assume that the last column was fully inscribed. Note, too, that there is the possibility that this tablet contained only part of the myth and that the latter may have been continued on another tablet or even other tablets, though on the whole this does not seem too likely. As for the so-called colophon to this tablet (cf. *PBS*, iv, Pt. 2, p. 63), cf. n.57.

[10] cf. also King, *Legends of Babylon and Egypt in Relation to Hebrew Tradition* (1918); Jacobsen, *AS* 11, pp. 58-59; Heidel, *The Gilgamesh Epic and Old Testament Parallels* (1946); Kramer, *SM*, 97-98. The numbering of the lines in the present translation is based on the assumption that each column of the tablet originally contained approximately 50 lines of text.

[11] Our interpretation of the text assumes that the speaking deity (or deities) plans to save mankind from destruction, but this is of course by no means certain.

[12] Nintu is the Sumerian mother goddess known also under the names Ninhursag and Ninmah; cf. n.32 on p. 39 of this work. She is not to be confused with the goddess Inanna, the Semitic Ishtar, a goddess noted primarily for love and war; cf. Poebel, *PBS*, iv, Pt. 2, pp. 24 ff.

[13] The verbal form in this line seems to be plural in form; if so, the rendering should be "we" rather than "I."

[14] Actually the Sumerian seems to say "from" rather than "to"; indeed the meaning of the entire line is highly doubtful.

[15] That is "the people" mentioned in the preceding line.

[16] The implications of this phrase, even if the translation should prove correct, are obscure; note particularly that the Sumerian word rendered by "(divine) ordinances" is the same as that rendered "our" in the following two lines.

[17] Perhaps "we" instead of "I"; the verbal form in this case seems to be incorrect, since it corresponds neither to the singular nor the plural form of the verb.

[18] Perhaps "I will be soothed by their shade."

[19] Perhaps "of the houses of the (divine) ordinances," cf. n.16.

[20] That is probably the same deity or deities whose address has just come to an end; cf. n.1.

[21] The Sumerian verbal form in this and the next line contains an infix which should be rendered "in (or upon) it (or him, them)," but at present it is difficult to see what this infix relates to.

[22] Note that the translation of this line was accidentally omitted in *PBS*, iv, Pt. 2, p. 17.

[23] The word "black-headed" usually refers to the inhabitants of Sumer and Babylon; in the present context, however, it seems to refer to mankind as a whole. For Sumerian concepts concerning the creation of man, cf. *SM*, 68 ff., and Jacobsen, *JNES*, v (1946), pp. 134 ff.

[24] "From the earth" seems to be repeated in the Sumerian text.

[25] Jacobsen, in *AS* 11, p. 58, restores *men* at the beginning of the line; there is, however, room for more than one sign in the break.

[26] In favor of this restoration, cf. *PBS*, v, No. 25, rev. v, line 4.

[27] Identity of deity or deities uncertain; perhaps it is Anu Enlil, cf. n.1.

[28] The translation in *PBS*, iv, Pt. 2, p. 18, seems to take care of only part of the break in this and the following line.

[29] Our translation does not treat the verbal forms in this line as relatives in spite of their form.

[30] cf. now Jacobsen, *AS* 11, p. 59, n.111.

[31] The word rendered tentatively as "first" in this line is represented by a sign whose reading cannot as yet be identified.

[32] Nudimmud is another name for the water-god Enki.

[33] To judge from the surrounding lines one would expect here the name of the tutelary deity of Badtibira, that is Latarak (cf. p. 57 of this work). However, the relevant Sumerian complex is not preceded by the "god" determinative, and seems on the surface to mean "the tabooed garment."

[34] Nothing is known of this deity; for the reading of the first part of the name as Hendur- rather than Pa-, cf. K. Tallquist, *Akkadische Götterepitheta* (1938), p. 435; Poebel, *ZA*, xxxix, 143 ff.

[35] That is, the sun-god, well known as the tutelary deity of both Sippar and Larsa.

[36] The tutelary goddess of Shuruppak identified by the later Babylonian theologians with the goddess Ninlil, the wife of Enlil.

[37] The rest of the line is unintelligible, although practically all the Sumerian signs are legible; it may deal with rain and water supply.

The flood . . .[38]
. . .
Thu[s w]as treated[39] . . .
Then did Nin[tu *weep*] like a . . . ,
The pure Inanna [set up] a lament for *its*[40] people,
Enki took coun[sel] with himself,
Anu, Enlil, Enki, (and) Ninhursag . . . ,
The gods of heaven and earth [uttered] the name of[41] Anu (and) Enlil.[42]
Then did Ziusudra, the king, the *pašišu*[43] [of] . . . ,
Build giant . . . ;
Humbly obedient, reverent*ly* [he] . . . ,
Attending daily, constantly [he] . . . ,
Bringing forth all kinds of dreams,[44] [he] . . . ,
Uttering the name of heaven (and) earth,[45] [he] . . .
. . . the gods a *wall* . . . ,[46]
Ziusudra, standing at *its* side, list[ened].
"Stand *by the wall* at my left side . . . ,[47]
By the wall I will say a word to thee, [take my word],[48]
[Give] ear to my instruction:
By our . . . a flood [*will sweep*] over the cult-centers;
To destroy the seed of mankind . . . ,
Is the decision, the word of the assembly [of the gods].
By the word commanded by Anu (and) Enlil[49] . . . ,
Its kingship, its rule [*will be put to an end*]."
(approximately 40 lines destroyed)
All the windstorms, exceedingly powerful, attacked as one,
At the same time, the flood sweeps *over the cult-centers*.[50]
After, for seven days (and) seven nights,
The flood had *swept over*[51] the land,[52]
(And) the huge boat had been tossed about by the windstorms on the great waters,[53]
Utu came forth, who sheds light on heaven (and) earth.
Ziusudra opened a *window of*[54] the huge boat,
The hero Utu *brought his rays into* the giant boat.[55]
Ziusudra, the king,
Prostrated himself before Utu,
The king kills an ox, *slaughters* a sheep.
(approximately 39 lines destroyed)
"Ye will utter 'breath of heaven,' 'breath of earth,' verily it will *stretch* itself by *your*. . . ."[56]
Anu (and) Enlil *uttered* "breath of heaven," "breath of earth," *by their* . . . , it stretched itself.
Vegetation, coming up out of the earth, rises up.
Ziusudra, the king,
Prostrated himself before Anu (and) Enlil.
Anu (and) Enlil cherished Ziusudra,[57]
Life like (that of) a god they give him,
Breath eternal like (that of) a god they *bring down* for him.
Then, Ziusudra the king,
The *preserver of the name*[58] *of vegetation (and)* of the seed of mankind,
In the land[59] *of crossing*,[60] the land of Dilmun, the place where the sun rises, they[61] caused to dwell.
(Remainder of the tablet,
about 39 lines of text, destroyed.)

[38] The punctuation for this and the following line is uncertain.

[39] The beginning of the line is to be restored to read *ḫur-gim bi-in-ag*.

[40] That is "the earth's" or "the land's."

[41] That is "conjured by Anu (and) Enlil."

[42] Or perhaps better Anu Enlil; cf. n.1.

[43] A priestly title.

[44] For the rendering instead of "dreams which had not been (before)" (cf. *PBS*, IV, Pt. 2, p. 18), see Poebel, *Grundzüge der sumerischen Grammatik* (Rostock, 1923), §264.

[45] That is "to conjure by."

[46] It is difficult to relate this sentence to the context.

[47] The name of the speaking deity is not given in the text, but he is, no doubt, Enki; cf. *PBS*, IV, Pt. 2, p. 52.

[48] For the restoration and translation of this and the following line, cf. *JCS*, I (1947), 33, notes 208 and 209, and the references there cited.

[49] For Anu (and) Enlil, here, and in the remainder of the myth, cf. the comment in n.7.

[50] cf. now Jacobsen, *AS* 11, p. 58.

[51] The Sumerian verb used for "swept" is the same as that in line 202, but instead of "over," the Sumerian has here "in."

[52] For "land" cf. n.6.

[53] "By the windstorms" was erroneously omitted in *SM*, p. 98.

[54] In *SM*, p. 98, the word "of," too, should have been rendered as doubtful.

[55] The entire line was erroneously omitted in *SM*, p. 98.

[56] Lines 251-253, although fully preserved, are at present extremely difficult to render, and the present translation is to be considered as highly doubtful. For not only is the relation of the passage to the context quite obscure, but it contains a number of grammatical difficulties which cannot be explained unless scribal errors are postulated. Thus, to list only some of the contextual problems, the identity of the individual whose speech probably ends with line 251, is uncertain (note that our translation assumes that he is addressing Anu (and Enlil); the antecedent of "it" in lines 251 and 252 (perhaps "he" or "she") is unknown; the Sumerian word rendered by the English word "stretch" in these two lines may have a different meaning here; the relation of the contents of line 253 to the preceding two lines is quite uncertain. As for the grammatical problems, note that the verbal form in line 251 might have been expected to read "utter ye" instead of "ye will utter"; the Sumerian words and complexes rendered as "your" in line 251, "uttered" and "by their" in line 252, are grammatically unjustified unless scribal errors are assumed; line 253, whose rendering is quite literal, seems clumsy and partially redundant.

[57] This line is actually written not below the preceding line but on the left edge; it was therefore assumed to be a colophon in *PBS*, IV, Pt. 2, p. 63 (cf. also Heidel, *loc. cit.*, p. 105). In all likelihood, however, it is a line that was accidentally omitted by the scribe in its proper place, and was therefore inserted on the left edge, where its correct position on the reverse of the tablet was indicated by means of a short horizontal line. The line is poorly preserved; the restoration assumed by our translation is by no means certain.

[58] If the rendering is correct, "name" might perhaps connote here "existence."

[59] The Sumerian word twice rendered by "land" in this line may also be translated as "mountain" or "mountain-land."

[60] Perhaps the crossing of the sun immediately upon his rising in the east; the Sumerian word used may also mean "of rule."

[61] That is, probably Anu and Enlil.

Gilgamesh and Agga

The Sumerian poem, "Gilgamesh and Agga," is one of the shortest of all Sumerian epic tales; it consists of no more than 115 lines of text. In spite of its brevity, however, it is of unusual significance from several points of view. In the first place, its plot deals with humans only; unlike the rest of the Sumerian epic tales, it introduces no mythological motifs involving any of the Sumerian deities. Secondly it is of considerable historical importance; it provides a number of hitherto unknown facts concerning the early struggles of the Sumerian city states. Finally, it is of very special significance for the history of political thought and practice. For as Thorkild Jacobsen was the first to point out,[1] it records what are, by all odds, the oldest two political assemblies

[1] See last paragraph of this introduction.

as yet known to man. To be sure, the tablets on which the poem has been found inscribed date back no earlier than the first half of the second millennium B.C.; however, the events recorded in them go back to the days of Gilgamesh and Agga, that is probably to the first quarter of the third millennium B.C [2]

The contents of the poem may be summarized as follows:[3] Agga, the king of Kish has sent envoys to Gilgamesh in Erech (lines 1-2); the purpose of the mission is not stated, but the context makes it obvious that they brought an ultimatum demanding of the Erechites to submit to Kish or take the consequences. Gilgamesh seeks the advice of the assembly of elders and urges them, for reasons that are far from clear, to fight rather than submit (lines 3-8). But the elders are contrary-minded; they would rather submit to Kish than fight it out (lines 9-14). Gilgamesh, displeased with this answer, now turns to the assembly of "men," that is, of arms-bearing males, and repeats his plea for war with Kish rather than submission to its rule (lines 15-23). In a long statement ending with a eulogy of Gilgamesh and highly encouraging words of victory, the assembly of "men" declares for war and independence (lines 24-39). Gilgamesh is now well pleased; in a speech to Enkidu, in which he seems to urge him to take to arms, he shows himself highly confident of victory over Agga (lines 40-47). In a very short time, however, Agga besieges Erech, and in spite of their brave words, the Erechites are dumbfounded (lines 48-50). Gilgamesh then addresses the "heroes" of Erech and asks for a volunteer to go before Agga (lines 51-54). A hero by the name of Birhurturri readily volunteers; he is confident that he can confound Agga's judgment (lines 55-58). No sooner does Birhurturri pass through the city gates, however, than he is seized, beaten, and brought before Agga. He begins to speak to Agga, but before he has finished, another hero from Erech, one Zabar . . . ga by name, ascends the wall (lines 59-67). There now follows a series of passages which are of utmost importance for the understanding of the plot of the tale, but which, for reasons outlined in notes 19, 20, and 22 are difficult and obscure. Certain it is, however, that in some way Agga has been induced to take a more friendly attitude and probably to lift the siege (lines 68-99). We then come to a passage whose meaning is quite certain; it consists of an address by Gilgamesh to Agga thanking him for all his kindness (lines 100-106). The poem concludes with a paean of praise to Gilgamesh (lines 107-end).

The text of "Gilgamesh and Agga" is reconstructed from six tablets and fragments; five of these were excavated in Nippur, while the sixth is of unknown provenience. All six pieces date from the first half of the second millennium B.C.; the date of the actual composition of the poem, however, is still unknown. A transliteration and translation of the poem based on the four of the six texts then known was published by M. Witzel, *Orientalia* NS, v (1936), 331-346. An excellent translation of most of the first forty-one lines of the poem was published by Jacobsen, *JNES*, II (1943), 165-166. A brief résumé of the contents of the poem was published by the writer in *JAOS*, LXIV (1944), 17-18. The writer's scientific edition of the poem (with commentary by Jacobsen) appeared in *AJA*, LIII, 1 ff.

[The en]voys of Agga, the son of Enmebaraggesi
Proceeded [*from Kish*] to Gilgamesh *in* Erech.
[The lord] Gilgamesh before the elders of his city
Put the [matter], seeks out (their) word:
"*To complete the* [*wells*], *to complete all the wells of the land,*[4]
To complete the [*wells*] *(and) the small bowls of the land,*
To dig the wells, to complete the fastening ropes,
Let us not submit to the house of Kish, let us smite it with weapons."
The convened assembly of the elders of his city
Answer Gilgamesh:
"*To complete the wells, to complete all the wells of the land,*[5]
To complete the wells (and) the small bowls of the land,
To dig the wells, to complete the fastening ropes,
Let us submit to the house of Kish, let us not smite it with weapons."
Gilgamesh, the lord of Kullab,[6]
Who performs heroic deeds for Inanna,[7]
Took not the word of the elders of his city to heart.
A second time Gilgamesh, the lord of Kullab,
Before the men of his city put the matter, seeks out (their) word:
To complete all the wells, to complete all the wells of the land,[8]
To complete the wells (and) the small bowls of the land,
To dig the wells, to complete the fastening ropes,
Do not submit to the house of Kish, let us smite it with weapons."
The convened assembly of the men of his city answer Gilgamesh:
"*O ye* who stand, *O ye* who sit,[9]

[2] cf. the writer's New Light on the Early History of the Ancient Near East, *AJA*, LII (1948), 156-64.

[3] It is well to note at this point that our poem provides an excellent example of one of the major difficulties confronting the translator of the Sumerian unilingual material. Here is a composition whose text is in practically perfect condition; there is hardly a single word broken or missing. Moreover, the reading of almost all the signs is certain; so, too, the meaning of most of the individual words. In spite of these favorable conditions, the translation of several crucial passages remains uncertain and obscure; cf. particularly lines 5-7, a passage repeated in lines 11-13 and lines 20-22; lines 75-80 and the corresponding passage in lines 94-99. The major difficulty with these passages consists of their laconic style; the aphoristic, riddle-like character of their contents, obscures, at least for the present, their real meaning. As for the historical background behind our poem, the reader should bear in mind that the Sumerian historians divided the history of their land into two major periods, the period before the flood and the one after the flood. The first dynasty immediately after the flood, according to these ancient historians, was that of the city of Kish; its last king was the Agga of our poem. The Dynasty of Kish was followed by the Dynasty of Eanna, or Erech (Erech is used more or less as a synonym of Eanna); the Gilgamesh of our poem is the fifth ruler of this dynasty. However, since Gilgamesh was preceded by four rulers of the Dynasty of Erech, who between them reigned over a considerable span of time, it is obvious that the dynasties of Kish and Erech must have overlapped to a large extent.

[4] Lines 5-7, and the identical lines 11-13 and 20-22, contain a proverb-like or riddlelike passage whose meaning in the context is altogether obscure; the renderings given are those usually attributed to the individual words, but they may prove unjustified. Similarly, the grammatical relationships between the various complexes are by no means certain. To judge from the contents of line 8, one might be led to conclude that the passage contained in lines 5-7 gives Gilgamesh's reasons for his plea to fight rather than submit to Kish. It will be noted, however, that in the passage immediately following, the very same words are used by the assembly of elders to justify their decision to submit to Kish rather than go to war. In short we may have here an early example of what is now generally described as "double-talk."

[5] For lines 11-13, cf. comment to lines 5-7.

[6] Kullab is a district in or close to Erech; the two are frequently mentioned together.

[7] Next to the heaven-god Anu, the goddess Inanna, more commonly known by her Semitic name Ishtar, was the most important deity of Erech.

[8] For lines 20-22, cf. comment to lines 5-7. In line 23, note that while the second verb is the expected first person plural, the first verb is the second person plural; it is difficult to see the reason for the change.

[9] Lines 24-27, if the rendering is correct, seem to describe the aristocrats ruling Erech; just what the relationship between these individuals and the two assemblies may have been, however, remains uncertain.

O ye who are raised with the sons of the king,
O ye who *press* the donkey's thigh,
Whoever *holds* its[10] life,
Do not submit to the house of Kish, let us smite it with weapons.
Erech, the *handiwork* of the gods,
Eanna,[11] the house ascending from heaven—
It is the great gods who have fashioned its parts—
Its great wall touching the clouds,
Its lofty dwelling place established by Anu,
Thou hast cared for, thou who art king (and) hero.
O *thou* . . .-headed, *thou* prince beloved of Anu,
How hast *thou* feared his[12] coming!
Its[13] army is small, it is scattered *behind it*,
Its men *do* not *hold high (their) face*."
Then—Gilgamesh, the lord of Kullab—
At the word of the men of his city his heart rejoiced, his spirit brightened;
He says to his servant Enkidu:
"Therefore let the *šukara*[14]-implement *be put aside for the violence* of battle,
Let the weapons of battle return to your side,
Let them *produce* fear (and) terror.
As for him,[15] when he comes, verily my great fear will fall upon him,
Verily his judgment will be confounded, verily his counsel will be dissipated."
The days were not five, the days were not ten,[16]
Agga, the son of Enmebaraggesi *besieged*[17] Erech;
Erech—its judgment was confounded.
Gilgamesh, the lord of Kullab,
Says to its heroes:
"My heroes *frown*;
Who has heart, let him stand up, to Agga I would *have him* go."
Birhurturri, his head . . . man,
Utters praises to his king:
"I would go to Agga,
Verily his judgment will be confounded, verily his counsel will be dissipated."
Birhurturri went out through the city gate.
As Birhurturri went out through the city gate,
They[18] seized him at the entrance of the city gate,
Birhurturri—they crush his *flesh*;
He was brought before Agga,
He speaks to Agga.
He had not finished his word (when) Zabar . . . ga ascends toward the wall;
He *peered over* the wall,
He saw Agga.
Birhurturri says to him:[19]
"O servant of the *stout man*, thy king
The *stout man*—is he not also my king?
Verily the *stout man* is my king,
Verily it is his . . . forehead,
Verily it is his . . . face,
Verily it is his beard of lapis lazuli,
Verily it is his gracious finger."
The multitude did not cast itself down, the multitude did not rise,[20]
The multitude did not cover itself with dust,
(*The people*) of all the foreign lands were not *overwhelmed*
On the mouths of (the people) of the lands, dust was not heaped,
The prow of the *magurru*-boat was not cut down,
Agga, the king of Kish, *restrained* not his *soldierly* heart.
They keep on striking him, they keep on beating him,[21]
Birhurturri—they crush his flesh.
After Zabar . . . ga, Gilgamesh ascends toward the wall,
Terror fell upon the old and young of Kullab,
The men of Erech held their battle weapons at their sides,
The door of the city gate—they stationed themselves at its *approaches*,
Enkidu went out toward the city gate.
Gilgamesh *peered over* the wall,
He saw Agga:
"O servant of the *stout man*, thy king[22]

10 "Its" presumably refers to Erech.

11 Eanna was the main temple of Erech; literally it is "the House of Anu."

12 "His" presumably refers to Agga.

13 "Its" presumably refers to Kish.

14 The *šukara* is probably an agricultural implement.

15 "Him" presumably refers to Agga.

16 A Sumerian idiomatic expression for a very brief passage of time.

17 The Sumerian verb for "besieged," is a third person plural; perhaps therefore the poet intended to include Agga's army as well.

18 "They" presumably refers to Agga's men.

19 Lines 68-75 presumably contain the words uttered by Birhurturri in the hope of soothing Agga and inducing him to call off his men and lift the siege; their meaning is however uncertain and obscure. The major difficulty results from the ambiguity of the "him" of line 68. If we assume that it refers to Agga, then Birhurturri seems to say to him that an individual described as a "*stout man*" is not only Agga's king but also his, that is, Birhurturri's. Presumably this "*stout man*" would be Gilgamesh, since the latter is not only Birhurturri's overlord, but also, as lines 102-103 seem to indicate, that of Agga as well. But just how was this statement expected to pacify Agga? Indeed, if Agga recognized Gilgamesh as his king, why did he proceed against Erech in the first place? Moreover, what is the purpose of Zabar . . . ga's presence on the wall? Perhaps, therefore, we must assume that the "him" of line 68 refers to Zabar . . . ga, and that the "*stout man*" refers to Agga, not to Gilgamesh; that is, Birhurturri while standing before Agga cries out to Zabar . . . ga who is looking down on the scene from the wall, that Agga is the acknowledged king of both.

20 The highly doubtful rendering of lines 76-81 assumes that Birhurturri's words had failed to satisfy Agga and his men, and that as a result the siege continued. The "multitude" of lines 76-77, the "people of all the foreign lands" of line 78, the "people of all the lands" of line 79, if the translations are correct, all refer to Agga's motley host besieging Erech; the acts attributed to them in these lines are descriptive of their complete indifference to Birhurturri's words. Line 80 may indicate that the siege was conducted by sea as well as by land; just what the cutting down of the prow of the *magurru*-boat signified, however, is not clear.

21 According to lines 82-90, Gilgamesh, seeing that Birhurturri's words had no effect on Agga and his men, in spite of Zabar . . . ga's presence on the wall, himself ascends the wall. At this act, the young and old of Erech are terrified, presumably because of the danger threatening Gilgamesh; the men of Erech now hold their weapons in readiness while Enkidu goes out to the city gate, perhaps to take charge of the Erechites in the expected battle.

22 Lines 91-92 probably represent a much abbreviated form of the passage contained in lines 69-75; note, too, that the crucial line corresponding to line 68, that is "Birhurturri says to him," is omitted. As in the case of the former and fuller passage, the interpretation of lines 91-92 hinges on the ambiguous "him" whom Birhurturri is addressing. If this "him" refers to Agga, then the "*stout man*" of lines 91-92 is Gilgamesh; if, on the other hand, it refers to Gilgamesh, then the "*stout man*" is Agga; cf. the comment to lines 69-75. In any case, this time Birhurturri's words seem to have

The *stout man* is my king."
As he spoke,
The multitude cast itself down, the multitude rose,
The multitude covered itself with dust,
(*The people*) of all the foreign lands were *overwhelmed,*
On the mouths of (the people) of the lands dust was heaped,
The prow of the *magurru*-boat was cut down,
Agga, the king of Kish, *restrained* his *soldierly* heart.
Gilgamesh, the lord of Kullab
Says to Agga:[23]
"O Agga, my overseer, O Agga, my steward,
O Agga, my army leader,
O Agga, the fleeing bird thou hast filled with grain,
O Agga, thou hast given me breath, thou hast given me life,
O Agga, thou bringest the fleeing man *to rest.*"
Erech, the *handiwork* of the gods,[24]
The great wall touching the sky,
The lofty dwelling place established by Anu,
Thou hast cared for, thou who art king
(and) hero.
O *thou* . . .-headed, *thou* prince beloved of Anu,
Agga has *set thee free for Kish,*
Before Utu he has returned to thee the power of former days;
O Gilgamesh, lord of Kullab,
Thy praise is good.

Gilgamesh and the Land of the Living

The poem "Gilgamesh and the Land of the Living" is one of the Sumerian epic tales probably utilized by the Semitic authors in their redaction of the Babylonian Epic of Gilgamesh.[1] Unfortunately, to date only 175 lines of the poem have been recovered;[2] even so, it is recognizable as a literary creation which must have had a profound emotional and aesthetic appeal to its highly credulous ancient audience. Its motivating theme, man's anxiety about death and its sublimation in the notion of an immortal name, has a universal significance that lends it high poetic value. Its plot structure reveals a careful and imaginative selection of just those details which are essential to its predominantly poignant mood and heroic temper. Stylistically, too, the poet obtains the appropriate rhythmic effect by the skillful use of an uncommonly varied assortment of repetition and parallelism patterns. All in all, there is little doubt that the poem before us is one of the finest Sumerian literary works as yet uncovered.

The contents of the poem may be briefly summarized as follows: The "lord" Gilgamesh, realizing that, like all mortals, he too must die sooner or later, is determined at least to raise up a name for himself before he meets his destined end. He therefore sets his heart on journeying to the far distant Land of the Living[3] with the probable intention of felling its cedars and bringing them to Erech. He informs his loyal servant and constant companion, Enkidu, of his proposed undertaking, and the latter advises him first to acquaint the sun-god Utu with this plan, for it is Utu who has charge of this cedar land (lines 1-12). Acting upon his advice, Gilgamesh brings offerings to Utu and pleads for his support of the contemplated journey to the Land of the Living (lines 13-18). Utu at first seems rather skeptical about Gilgamesh's qualifications. But Gilgamesh only repeats his plea in more persuasive language (lines 19-33). Utu takes pity on him and decides to help him, probably by immobilizing in some way the seven vicious demons personifying the destructive weather phenomena that might menace Gilgamesh in the course of his journey across the mountains situated between Erech and the Land of the Living (lines 34-45). Overjoyed, Gilgamesh gathers fifty volunteers from Erech, unattached men who have neither "house" nor "mother" and who are ready to follow him in whatever he does (lines 46-53). After having weapons of bronze and wood prepared for himself and his companions, they cross the seven mountains with the help of Utu (lines 54-61). Just what happens immediately after the crossing of the last of the seven mountains is not clear, since the relevant passage (lines 62-70) is poorly preserved. When the text becomes intelligible again we find that Gilgamesh had fallen into a heavy sleep from which he is awakened only after considerable time and effort (lines 71-83). Thoroughly aroused by this unexpected delay, he swears by his mother Ninsun and by his father Lugalbanda that he will enter the Land of the Living and brook no interference from either man or god (lines 84-97). Enkidu pleads with him to turn back, for the guardian of the cedars is the fearful monster Huwawa, whose destructive attack none may withstand (lines 95-105). But Gilgamesh will have none of this caution. Convinced that with Enkidu's help no harm can befall either of them, he bids him put away fear and go forward with him (lines 106-119). Spying from his cedar house, however, is the monster Huwawa who seems to make vain, but frantic, efforts to drive off Gilgamesh and his adventurous band (lines 120-126). Following a break of some lines we learn that, after cutting down seven trees, Gilgamesh had probably come to Huwawa's inner chamber (lines 127-141). Strangely enough, at the very first, and seem-

the desired effect. For according to lines 94-99, which are an exact repetition of lines 76-81 except that the verbs are all positive instead of negative in form, the multitudinous host from many lands which was besieging Erech was now prostrate and overwhelmed, and presumably no longer threatened Erech.

[23] In lines 100-106 Gilgamesh thanks Agga for some extraordinary kindness, presumably for the lifting of the siege; unless there has been a shift of scene unmentioned in the text, Gilgamesh is addressing Agga from the wall of Erech. Note, too, that according to lines 103-105, unless we are prepared to read in implications contrary to the obvious meaning of the words, Gilgamesh addresses Agga as his, that is Agga's, superior and overlord in spite of the fact that Agga seems to be the more powerful of the two; cf. comment to lines 68-75. In line 104, "the fleeing bird," and in line 106, "the fleeing man" refer no doubt to Gilgamesh.

[24] Lines 107-end are assumed to contain the poet's concluding eulogy of Gilgamesh. With lines 107-111, cf. lines 30-36, which are almost identical. The implications of lines 112-113 are not clear. On the surface they seem to say that Agga has restored Gilgamesh to his former greatness, which again tends to indicate that at one time Gilgamesh was the ruler of the entire land, including Kish; cf. comment to lines 100-106 and lines 68-75. As for the phrase "before Utu" in line 113, it may refer to the sun-god Utu as the god of justice; it is worth noting, however, that two predecessors of Gilgamesh in the first Erech dynasty are described in the Sumerian texts as "the son of Utu." The last two lines of our poem contain the conventional phrases concluding a myth or epic tale.

[1] For a detailed discussion of the Sumerian sources of the Babylonian epic of Gilgamesh, cf. *JAOS*, LXIV (1944), 8-23; note that our poem is there entitled "Gilgamesh and Huwawa."

[2] There is some possibility that the fragmentary extract of a Sumerian poem tentatively entitled "The Death of Gilgamesh," might belong to our poem; cf. *BASOR*, No. 94 (1944), 2-12, and particularly n.4. Note that the line numbering in *JCS*, I, 3-46, is off by one, following line 70.

[3] For the possibility that Dilmun was the Land of the Living, cf. *BASOR*, No. 96 (1944), 18-28. Note, however, that to judge from the contents of lines 145-149, particularly when compared with the text quoted in *JCS*, I (1947), 45, note 252 (it reads: Huwawa answers Gilgamesh: "My mother who gave birth to me is the 'land' (so, instead of 'highland') Hurrum, My father who begot me is the mountain Hurrum, Utu has made me dwell all alone with him in the 'land.' "), it is perhaps the highland Hurrum which is to be taken as the Land of the Living.

ingly very light, attack on the part of Gilgamesh, Huwawa is overcome with fright; he thereupon utters a prayer to the sun-god Utu and adjures Gilgamesh not to kill him (lines 142-151). Gilgamesh would like to act the generous victor, and in riddle-like phrases suggests to Enkidu that Huwawa be set free. But Enkidu, fearful of the consequences, advises against such unwise action (lines 152-161). Following Huwawa's indignant criticism of Enkidu's ungenerous attitude, our two heroes proceed to cut off his neck (lines 162-166). They then seem to bring Huwawa's corpse before Enlil and Ninlil, but what follows is quite uncertain, for after several fragmentary lines our available material comes to an end.

The text of "Gilgamesh and the Land of the Living" is reconstructed from fourteen tablets and fragments; eleven were excavated in Nippur, one in Kish, while the provenience of two is unknown. All the available tablets and fragments date from the first half of the second millennium B.C. A scientific edition of the poem, including copies of unpublished material in the University Museum, transliteration, translation, and commentary, was published by the writer in *JCS*, I (1947), 3-46; here, too, will be found a copy of a tablet in the Yale Babylonian Collection, copied by Ferris J. Stephens, and a copy of a tablet in the Oriental Museum of the University of Illinois, copied by Albrecht Goetze.

The lord, toward the Land of the Living set his mind,
The lord, Gilgamesh, toward the Land of the Living set his mind,
He says to his servant Enkidu:
"O Enkidu, not *(yet) have brick and stamp* brought forth *the fated end*,
I would enter the 'land,' I would set up my name,
In its places where the names have been raised up, I would raise up my name,
In its places where the names have not been raised up, I would raise up the names of the gods."
His servant Enkidu answers him:
"O my master, if thou wouldst enter the 'land,' inform Utu,
Inform Utu, the hero Utu—
The 'land,' it is Utu's charge,
The land *of the cut-down* cedar,[4] it is the hero Utu's charge—inform Utu."
Gilgamesh laid his hands on an all-white kid,
A brown kid, an offering, he pressed to his breast,
In his hand he placed the silver staff of his . . . ,
He says to Utu of heaven:
"O Utu, I would enter the 'land,' be thou my ally,
I would enter the land *of the cut-down* cedar, be thou my ally."
Utu of heaven answers him:
". . . verily thou art, but what art thou to the 'land?' "
"O Utu, a word I would speak to thee, to my word thy ear,[5]
I would have it reach thee, give ear to it.
In my city man dies, oppressed is the heart,
Man perishes, heavy is the heart,
I *peered over* the wall,
Saw the dead bodies . . . *floating on* the river;
As for me, I too will be served thus; verily 'tis so.
Man, the tallest, cannot stretch to heaven,
Man the widest, cannot *cover* the earth.
Not *(yet) have brick and stamp* brought forth *the fated end*,
I would enter the 'land,' I would set up my name,
In its places where the names have been raised up, I would raise up my name,
In its places where the names have not been raised up, I would raise up the names of the gods."
Utu accepted his tears as an offering,
Like a man of mercy, he showed him mercy,
The seven heroes, the sons of one mother,
The first, a . . . that . . . ,
The second a viper that . . . ,
The third, a dragon that . . . ,
The fourth, a *scorching fire* that . . . ,
The fifth, a *raging* snake that *turns the heart*, that . . . ,
The sixth, a destructive deluge that *floods* the land,
The seventh, the speeding . . . [lightning] which cannot be [*turned back*],
These seven . . . ,
He brings into the . . . of the mountains.
Who felled the cedar, acted joyfully,
The lord Gilgamesh acted joyfully,
In his city, as one man, *he* . . . ,
As two companions, *he* . . . :
"Who has a house, to his house! Who has a mother, to his mother!
Let single males who *would do as I* (do), fifty, *stand* at my side."
Who had a house, to his house; who had a mother, to his mother,
Single males who *would do as he* (did), fifty, *stood* at his side.
To the house of the smiths he directed his step,
The . . . , the . . .-axe, his "Might of Heroism" he caused to be cast there.
To the . . . garden of the plain he [directed] his step,
The . . .-tree, the *willow*, the *apple tree*, the *box* tree, the . . .-[tree] he [*felled*] there.
The "sons" of his city who accompanied him [*placed them*] in their hands.
The first, a . . . that . . . ,
Hav[*ing been brought*] into the . . . of the mountains,
The first [mo]untain they cross, *he comes not upon his* . . .
Upon their crossing the seventh mountain,[6]
. . . he did not wander about,
[The lord Gil]gamesh *fells* the cedar.
. . . *to* Gilgamesh,
. . . Gilgamesh . . . brought,
. . . *stretched out*,
. . . like . . . seized,

[4] So, instead of as in *JCS*. Note, too, that the present translation varies from that in *JCS* in lines 14, 22, 25, 26, 28, 42, 83, 86, 94, 100, 106, 121, 136, 139, 145, 174; most of the variations are very slight.

[5] Note the omission of a line approximating: "Gilgamesh answers him."

[6] Lines 62-72 are so fragmentary that is impossible to make any connected sense out of them; the punctuation, too, is of course altogether uncertain.

. . . set up for him,
[The "sons" of his city] who accompanied him,
. . .
. . . *it is* a dream, . . . it is a sleep,
. . . silence . . .
He touches him, he rises not,
He speaks to him, he [an]swers not.
"Who art lying, who art lying,
O Gilgamesh, lord, son of Kullab, how long wilt thou lie?
The 'land' has become dark, the shadows have spread over it,
Dusk has [*brought forth*] its light,
Utu has gone with lifted head to the bosom of his mother Ningal,
O Gilgamesh, how long [wilt thou] lie?
Let not the 'sons' of thy city [who] have accompanied thee,
Stand *waiting* for thee at the foot of the mountain,
Let not thy mother who gave birth to thee be *driven off* to the 'square' of thy city."
He gave heed,
With his "word of heroism" he [covered himself] like a garment,
His garment of thirty shekels which he *carried in his hand* he . . . d on his breast,
Like a bull he stood on the "great earth,"
He put (*his*) mouth to the ground, (*his*) *teeth shook*.
"By the life of Ninsun, my mother who gave birth to me, of pure Lugalbanda, my father,
May I become as one who sits to be wondered at on the knee of Ninsun, my mother who gave birth to me."
A second time moreover he says to *him*:
"By the life of Ninsun, my mother who gave birth to me, of pure Lugalbanda, my father,
Until I will have *fought* that 'man,' if he be a man, [until] I will have *fought* him, if he be a god,
My step directed to the 'land,' I shall not direct to the city."
The *faithful* servant *pleaded*, . . . d life,
He answers his master:
"O my master, thou who hast not seen that 'man,' art not terror-stricken,
I, who have seen that 'man,' am terror-stricken.
The hero, his *teeth* are the *teeth* of a dragon,
His face is the face of a lion,
His . . . is the onrushing floodwater,
From his forehead which devours trees and reeds none escapes.
O my master, journey thou to the 'land,' I will journey to the *city*,
I will *tell* thy mother of thy *glory, let her shout*,
I will *tell* her of thy *ensuing* death, [*let her*] shed bitter tears."
"*For me another* will not die, the *loaded* boat will not sink,
The three-ply cloth will not be cut,
The . . . will not be overwhelmed,
House (*and*) hut, fire will not destroy.
Do thou *help* me (and) I will *help* thee, *what can happen to us*?
After it had sunk, after it had sunk,[7]
After the Magan-boat had sunk,
After the boat, 'the might of Magilum,' had sunk,
In the . . . , the boat of the living creatures, *are seated those who come out of the womb*;
Come, let us go forward, we will cast eyes upon him,
If we go forward,
(And) there be fear, there be fear, turn it back,
There be terror, there be terror, turn it back,
In thy . . . , come, let us go forward."
Who is . . . , *is not at peace*,
Huwawa, moreover, . . . d his cedar house,
He fastened his eye upon him, the eye of death,
He *nodded* his head to him, shook his head at him,
He *spoke* to him . . . ,
Who are . . . *men* he . . . like . . .
Gilgamesh . . . ,
(break of approximately 7 lines)
"By the life [of Ninsun,] my mother who gave birth to me, [of pure Lugalbanda, my father],
In the 'land' verily *I* have known thy dwelling . . . ,
My little weak . . . verily I have brought into the 'land' for thee as . . . ,
. . . in thy . . . I would enter."
He himself uprooted *the first for him*,
The "sons" of his city who accompanied him
Cut down its crown, bundle it,
Lay it at the foot of the mountain.
After *he himself had finished off* for him the seventh, he approached *his chamber*,
He . . . d the "snake of the wine-quay" *in his wall*,
Like one pressing a kiss he slapped his cheek.
Huwawa, (*his*) *teeth shook*,[8]
He *warded off* Gilgamesh:
"To Utu I would say a word:
'O Utu, a mother who gave birth to me I know not, a father who reared me I know not,
In the "land" thou didst give birth to me, thou dost rear me.' "
He adjured Gilgamesh by the life of heaven, life of earth, life of the nether world,
Took him by the hand, *brought him to* . . .
Then did the heart of Gilgamesh take pity on the . . . ,
He says to his servant Enkidu:
"O Enkidu, let the caught bird go (back) to its place,
Let the caught man return to the bosom of his mother."
Enkidu answers Gilgamesh:
"The tallest who has not judgment,
Namtar[9] will devour, Namtar who knows *no distinctions*.

[7] The implications of lines 111-114 are obscure; it is not even certain that Gilgamesh is the speaker as assumed in the translation.

[8] Note the important new renderings in lines 145-151; they are based largely on a still unpublished fragment copied by me in Istanbul's Museum of the Ancient Orient.

[9] The evil demon "Fate."

If the caught bird goes (back) to its place,
If the caught man returns to the bosom of his mother,
Thou wilt not return to the city of the mother who gave birth to thee."
Huwawa says to Enkidu:
"Against me, O Enkidu, thou hast spoken evil to him,
O hired man who . . . the food, *who* stands next to the . . . *of* the rival, thou hast spoken evil words to him."
When he had thus spoken,
They cut off his neck,[10]
They placed upon him . . . ,
They brought him before Enlil and Ninlil.
Enlil brought forth his palace servant
from the sea,
And Ninlil brought forth . . .
When Enlil and Ninlil . . . :
"Why thus . . . ?
. . . *let him* come forth, *let him seize*,
. . ."[11]

The Death of Gilgamesh

The "Death of Gilgamesh" consists of a text which is but a small part of a poem of unknown length.[1] Fragmentary as the text is, its contents are of rather unusual significance for the light they shed on the Sumerian ideas concerning death and the nether world. The text is divided into two sections, A and B, between which there is a break of unknown size.[2] The contents of A may be briefly sketched as follows: Following a passage whose meaning is altogether obscure, Gilgamesh is informed that he must cherish no hope for immortality; that Enlil, the father of all the gods, has not destined him for eternal life. He is not to take it to heart, however, for Enlil has granted him kingship, prominence, and heroism in battle. There follows the death of Gilgamesh, described in a passage of typical Sumerian poetic form, consisting of at least ten lines ending with the refrain "lies, rises not," the first part of eight of the lines containing epithets descriptive of Gilgamesh. The section ends with a description of the ensuing mourning.

Section B consists of the last forty-two lines of the poem.[3] It begins with a list of Gilgamesh's family and retinue—wives, children, musicians, chief valet, attendants—and continues with the presentation by Gilgamesh of their gifts and offerings to the numerous deities of the nether world. That is, according to at least one plausible interpretation of the available material, Gilgamesh has died and descended to the nether world to become its king.[4] Moreover, we must reckon with the possibility that a large palace retinue was buried with Gilgamesh—if so, we have here the first mention of human sacrifices of the type uncovered by Woolley in the tombs of Ur—and that Gilgamesh performs the placation rites essential to their comfortable sojourn in the nether world. The remainder of the poem is poorly preserved; it probably ends with a special tribute to the glory and memory of Gilgamesh.

The text of the "Death of Gilgamesh" is reconstructed from three tablets excavated in Nippur, dating from the first half of the second millennium B.C. A translation and transliteration of the available material, together with a copy of one of the tablets, have been published by the writer in *BASOR*, No. 94 (1944), 2-12.[5]

[10] Note this important new rendering.

[11] A variant and considerably expanded version of our poem is found on a fragmentary tablet from Nippur dating from the same period as the other Nippur tablets and fragments; its contents will be found transliterated and analyzed in the *JCS* study in notes 205, 206, 217, 222, 226, 241, 245, 250, 252.

[1] There is some possibility that the text of our poem is a continuation of the epic tale "Gilgamesh and Huwawa"; cf. pp. 47-50 of the present volume.

[2] It is by no means certain, however, that the two sections are part of the same poem.

[3] That this section contains the last lines of whatever poem it is a part of, is certain from its last line which is typical of the end of Sumerian compositions.

[4] That Gilgamesh was conceived by the Sumerian theologians and myth makers as king of the nether world is known especially from a text discussed in *BASOR*, No. 94, 6, n.11.

Section A

. . . the road taken . . . ,[6]
. . . who brings up from its . . . ,
. . . *with* the killing from its . . . ,
. . . daily unto distant days.
After . . . had been placed,
. . . which had been granted,
. . . destruction old and ancient,
. . . the weapon which he *brought* up,
. . . which he directed,
. . . the *flood* which *destroyed* the land,
(lines 11-24 destroyed)
. . . the son of Utu[7]
In the nether world, the place of darkness, verily will give him light.
Mankind, as much as has been named,
Who beside him will *build* its *form* unto distant days?
The mighty heroes, the *seers*, like the new moon verily have . . .[8]
Who *beside him* has directed the power and the might before them?
In the month of Ab, *the . . . of the shades*,
Without him verily there is no light before them.
Enlil, the great mountain, the father of the gods—
O lord Gilgamesh, the *meaning* of the dream (is)—
Has destined thy fate, O Gilgamesh, for kingship, for eternal life he has not destined it.
(But) . . . of life, be not sad of heart,
Be not aggrieved, be not depressed.
Who of man committed a wrong . . . ,
The forbidden, thy bond cut loose . . .
The light (and) darkness of mankind
he has granted thee,[9]
Supremacy over mankind he has granted thee,
Unmatched . . . he has granted thee,
Battle *from which none may retreat* he has granted thee,
Onslaughts unrivalled he has granted thee,

[5] The present translation differs somewhat from that in *BASOR*; the more significant variations are pointed out in the notes.

[6] Because of the fragmentary condition of lines 1-10, the attempted renderings are to be taken as pointers only; the punctuation, too, is of course altogether uncertain.

[7] Lines 25-49 form part of an address by some deity or individual whose name was no doubt stated in the lines now destroyed. In lines 25-32, the crucial difficulty involves the subject of the verbal forms; from the extant text it seems impossible to offer an intelligent conjecture.

[8] Note the new rendering which omits the translation of the last two complexes of this line; their rendering in *BASOR* with "verily *made (sic!) the thresholds* with them" is based on a literal interpretation of the text which may be unjustified. Note, too, the new rendering of line 31.

[9] If the rendering is correct, which is not too likely, the line might be taken to indicate the extent of Gilgamesh's power and influence.

Attacks from which none may escape, he has granted thee.
Do not . . . thy faithful . . . palace servant,
Before Utu thou shalt . . . ,
A garment[10] . . . ,
The leader . . .
(break of approximately 10 lines)
Who [*destroyed*] evil [lies,[11] rises not],
Who [*established justice in the land* lies, rises not],
Who . . . li[es, rises not],
Who is *firm of muscle*, li[es, rises not],
The lord of Kullab li[es, rises not],
Who is *wise of features*, lies, [rises not],
Who . . . lies, [rises] not,
With him who ascends the mountain[12] he lies, he [rises] not,
On the bed of Fate he lies, he rises not,
[*On*] the multicolored . . . *couch* he lies, he rises not.
The standing are not silent, the sitting[13] are not silent, they set up a lament,
Who eat food are not silent, who drink water are not silent, they set up a lament.
Namtar[14] . . . is not silent,
Like . . . fish he has *stretched out*,
Like a gazelle held fast by the *gišburru*,[15] he . . . the couch.
Namtar who has no hands, who has no feet, [*who drinks*] *no water*, [*who eats no food*],[16]
(2 lines destroyed)[17]
. . . . made heavy.
. . . Gilgamesh,
After its . . . had been *interpreted*,
. . . which he *interpreted* to them,
. . . they answer:
". . . [*w*]*hy* dost thou cry?
. . . why *has it been* made?
. . . that *which* Nintu has not fashioned,
. . . he brought forth.
. . . there is not.
. . . strength, firm muscle . . . ,
. . . *escaped* not the hand.
. . . he looked not upon . . . ,
. . . from the . . . he seizes.
. . . ,
. . . upon which he looked,
. . . verily he decreed the fate.
Of . . . called by name . . ."

Section B

His beloved wife, [his] be[loved] son,
The . . .-wife, [his] be[loved] concubine,
His musician, [his beloved] *entertainer*,
[His] beloved chief valet, [his beloved] . . . ,
[His] be[loved] household,[18] the palace *attendants*,
His beloved *caretaker*,[19]
The *purified* palace . . . the heart of Erech—whoever lay with him in *that place*,[20]
Gilgamesh, the son of Ninsun,
Weighed out their offerings to Ereshkigal,[21]
Weighed out their gifts to Namtar,
Weighed out (*their*) *presents* to Dimpikug,
Weighed out their bread-offerings to Neti,
Weighed out their bread-offerings to Ningishzida and Dumuzi.
To Enki and Ninki, to Enmul and Ninmul,[22]
To Endukugga and Nindukugga,
To *Enindashurimma* and *Nindashurimma*,
To Enmu . . . la and Enmesharra,
The parents of Enlil,
Shulpae, the lord of the table,[23]
Sumugan, Ninhursag,
The Anunnaki of the Dukug
The Igigi of the Dukug,
The dead . . . , the dead . . . *sangu*,[24]
The *maḫḫu, entu* . . . ,
The *pašišu*, clad in linen . . . ,
Offerings[25] . . .
. . . ,
The lord [*Gilgamesh*] weighed out their bread[26]-offerings.

[10] Note that this line was omitted in the translation in *BASOR*.

[11] A more literal rendering may perhaps be "lay down" instead of "lies."

[12] Note the new rendering for this line; "who ascends the mountain" may perhaps be a euphemism for "who dies." "The bed of Fate" in the next line refers, of course, to death.

[13] "The standing" and "the sitting" may perhaps refer to those citizens who participate in the city assembly; cf. now Kramer, *AJA*, LIII, 14.

[14] Namtar, "Fate," is the nether-world demon responsible for death.

[15] For the *gišburru*, cf. lines 195 and 220 of the "Lamentation over the Destruction of Ur."

[16] Note the new rendering of the line.

[17] Because of the fragmentary condition of lines 76-96, the attempted renderings and punctuation are to be taken as pointers only; note the new rendering of line 82, the restoration of the Sumerian word for "why" is reasonably certain. In line 84, the goddess Nintu, also known under the names Ninhursag, Ninmah, etc., is particularly noted for her activities in the creation of man; cf. e.g. *SM*, 68-75.

[18] Note the new rendering; it is due to the suggestion of Frederick Geers, of the Oriental Institute of the University of Chicago, that the second Sumerian sign in the line is SI rather than KUG.

[19] The new rendering assumes that the contents of this line parallel those of the preceding lines; a more literal rendering might perhaps read "*one who puts* (his) hand on everything."

[20] Note the new rendering; the real meaning of the line and its relationship to what precedes and follows, remain obscure.

[21] The gods listed in lines 9-13 are all underworld deities: Ereshkigal is the well-known queen of the nether world; Namtar is the demon of death; Dimpikug's duties are unknown; *Neti* is the chief gatekeeper of the nether world; Ningishzida and Dumuzi are two well-known chthonic deities.

[22] The deities listed in lines 14-17 are described in line 18 as "the parents" of the leading Sumerian deity Enlil; they are all known as such from other texts, and were no doubt conceived by the theologians and mythographers as dwelling in the nether world.

[23] Note the new renderings in lines 19-28; particularly the word "to" at the beginning of lines 19-26 is by no means assured; nor is the assumption that the deities and priests listed in them are to be thought of as inhabiting the nether world. In the present fragmentary state of the text, and particularly of the crucial lines 26-27, it is difficult to get at the real meaning of the passage contained in lines 14-28. As for the deities mentioned, Shulpae, "the lord of the table," is the husband of Ninhursag, one of the four creating deities of Sumer (see note 17); Sumugan is known as the god in charge of the "plain," and the animal and plant life which fills it; the Anunnaki and the Igigi are groups of deities whose individual members are unnamed (the Anunnaki in particular are frequently mentioned as participating in the divine assemblies); the Dukug is the chamber in heaven where Igigi and particularly the Anunnaki are said to live; it seems to be described in one text as "the place of the creation of the gods."

[24] The *sangu*, *maḫḫu*, and *pašišu* are priests; the *entu* is a priestess.

[25] "*Offerings*" instead of "to the seer" in *BASOR*.

[26] The word "bread" was erroneously omitted in *BASOR*.

. . . *lies*,
Gilgamesh, the son of Ninsun,
At the place of libations . . . poured out date wine,
. . . *caused to be inhaled* for him.
. . . ,[27]
The people of *Erech*,
. . . *have no possessions*,
. . . d their . . . in dust.
In those days, . . . the lord[28] Gilgamesh,
For . . . who neglected not Enlil—
Gilgamesh, the son of Ninsun,
Of . . . *their* rival king has not been
born to *Nintu*;
Who has no [*rival*], *who is without* [*equ*]*al*,
O Gilga[mesh, lord of] Kullab, good is thy [pr]aise.

Inanna's Descent to the Nether World

The Sumerian myth "Inanna's Descent to the Nether World" is highly significant for the light on the Sumero-Babylonian religious tenets, particularly those concerning death and the nether world. Moreover, as the predecessor and prototype of the Semitic myth "Ishtar's Descent to the Nether World," it provides us with an ancient and highly instructive example of literary borrowing and transformation. Briefly sketched, its contents run as follows: For some unknown reason,[1] Inanna, queen of heaven, has set her heart upon visiting the nether world. She therefore collects all the appropriate divine ordinances, adorns herself with her queenly robes and jewels, and is ready to enter the "land of no return." Queen of the nether world is her older sister, and—at least so it seems—bitter enemy, Ereshkigal. Fearing lest her sister put her to death in the nether world, Inanna instructs her messenger Ninshubur, who is always at her beck and call, that if after three days she shall have failed to return,[2] he is to set up a hue and cry for her in heaven, in the assembly hall of the gods. He is then to go to Nippur, the city of Enlil, and plead with the latter to save Inanna and not let her be put to death in the nether world. If Enlil refuses he is to go to Ur, the city of the moon-god Nanna, and repeat his plea. If Nanna, too, refuses, he is to go to Eridu, the city of Enki, the god of wisdom, and the latter, who "knows the food of life," who "knows the water of life," will surely come to her rescue.

Inanna then descends to the nether world and approaches Ereshkigal's temple of lapis lazuli. At the gate she is met by the chief gatekeeper, who demands to know who she is and why she has come. Inanna concocts a false excuse for her visit, and the gatekeeper, upon instructions from his mistress, leads her through the seven gates of the nether world. As she passes through each of the gates her garments and jewels are removed piece by piece in spite of her protests. Finally, after entering the last gate, she is brought stark naked and on bended knees before Ereshkigal and the Anunnaki,[3] the seven dreaded judges of the nether world. These fasten upon her their "eye" of death and she is turned into a corpse which is then hung from a stake.[4] So pass three days and three nights. On the fourth day Ninshubur, seeing that his mistress has not returned, proceeds to make the rounds of the gods in accordance with his instructions. As Inanna had predicted, both Enlil and Nanna refuse all help. Enki, however, devises a plan to restore her to life. He fashions the *kurgarru* and the *kalaturru*, two sexless creatures, and entrusts to them the "food of life" and the "water of life," with instructions to proceed to the nether world and sprinkle this "food" and "water" (probably) sixty times upon Inanna's impaled corpse.[5] This they do, and Inanna revives. As she leaves the nether world, however, she is accompanied by the dead and by the bogeys and harpies who have their home there. Surrounded by this ghostly, ghastly crowd she wanders from city to city in Sumer.[6]

The text of "Inanna's Descent to the Nether World," is reconstructed from thirteen tablets and fragments, all of which were excavated in Nippur and are now either in the Museum of the Ancient Orient in Istanbul or in the University Museum in Philadelphia. All were actually inscribed in the first half of the second millennium B.C. but the date of the first composition

[27] Because of its fragmentary state, the meaning of the passage contained in lines 33-40 is altogether obscure; the renderings and the punctuation are quite uncertain throughout these lines. Note, too, the new renderings of lines 38 and 40.

[28] The word "lord" was erroneously omitted in *BASOR*.

[1] Hitherto it has been almost universally assumed that Inanna's descent to the nether world was for the purpose of saving Dumuzi (i.e. Tammuz), who supposedly was being held there against his will. As can be seen from note 6 (below), however, these assumptions were quite erroneous; the reason for Inanna's descent to the land of no return still remains unknown.

[2] This time limit is not stated explicitly in Inanna's instructions, but cf. lines 169 ff.

[3] The Anunnaki, to judge from the available Sumerian material, are the unnamed "great gods" of the Sumerian pantheon who participated in the assemblies called by the leading deities before making final decisions; they were conceived as begotten by the heaven-god Anu on the "mountain of heaven and earth" (cf. *SM*, 72-3). Presumably, therefore, they were sky-gods, and just how the Sumerian mythographers got seven of them to the nether world to act as judges in it (cf. line 63 of our myth) is as yet unknown.

[4] This seems to be the literal meaning of the Sumerian; presumably, the stake projected from a wall and pierced the dead body which thus "hung from it."

[5] Enki gave the two creatures quite a number of additional instructions, which would, no doubt, prove highly revealing for Sumerian mythological concepts and religious tenets concerning death and the nether world; but unfortunately the relevant lines (224-242 and lines 246-265) are largely destroyed.

[6] To this summary, which is based on the text of the myth as reconstructed in *PAPS*, LXXXV (cf. the paragraph following our summary) there can now be made a most important addition based on an as-yet-unpublished tablet in the Yale Babylonian Collection, which I had the opportunity of studying some time ago through the courtesy of Ferris J. Stephens, curator of the Yale Babylonian Collection, and Albrecht Goetze, his colleague. This tablet contains 91 lines of text; it begins with line 264 of the text as reconstructed in *PAPS* and duplicates the latter until line 323; from there on the text of the Yale tablet fills in part of the 40-line gap mentioned on p. 302 of *PAPS*, LXXXV. With the help of this new material, the events which took place upon Inanna's departure from the nether world are seen to be as follows: As soon as Inanna leaves the nether world with her ghostly and demoniac companions, she is met by her messenger Ninshubur, who throws himself at her feet, sits in the dirt, and dresses in mourning. The demons accompanying Inanna seem to threaten to carry him off to the nether world, but Inanna tells them who he is and how he had served her faithfully, and—this is not quite certain—that consequently they should do him no harm. They then proceed to Umma and its temple Sigkurshagga; here Shara, the tutelary deity of Umma, threw himself at her feet, sat in the dirt and dressed in mourning. The demons accompanying Inanna seem to threaten to carry him off to the nether world, but Inanna (if the interpretation is correct) dissuades them. They then proceed to Badtibira and its temple Emushkalamma; here Latarak, the tutelary deity of Badtibira, threw himself at her feet, sat in the dirt, and dressed in mourning. Once again the demons seem to threaten to carry off the god, and once again Inanna seems to dissuade them. They then proceed to a city whose name is uncertain; it may perhaps be Inanna's own city Erech, since its temple complex seems to be named Kullab, a district in, or adjacent to, Erech. And here comes what is, no doubt, the most surprising and revealing part of the text. In Kullab(?), the god Dumuzi, unlike the gods Ninshubur, Shara of Umma, and Latarak of Badtibira, does not throw himself at Inanna's feet; nor does he show any signs of mourning. Instead, he seats himself on a "high seat" totally unmindful of Inanna and her companions. Whereupon Inanna hands Dumuzi over into the hands of the demons, no doubt to carry him off to the nether world. Dumuzi bursts into tears and raises his hands in prayer to the sun-god Utu to save him from the demons. At this point our text breaks off, so that the end of the myth is still unknown.

of the myth is unknown. A first edition of the text of the myth, based on the eight tablets and fragments then available, was published by the writer in *RA*, xxxiv (1937), 93-134. Following the publication of several additional pieces belonging to the myth,[7] the writer published a new edition of the text based on all the thirteen pieces in *PAPS*, lxxxv (1942), 293-323, Pls. i-x. A study and translation of the text based on the writer's first edition, that in *RA*, xxxiv, were published by A. Falkenstein in *AfO*, xiv (1942), 113-138. A study and translation of the text based on the writer's first edition and on the additional material published by the writer in *RA*, xxxvi, together with an analysis of the Falkenstein article in *AfO*, xiv, were published by Maurus Witzel in *Orientalia* NS, xiv (1945), 24-69.[8]

From the ["great above"][9] she set her mind toward the "great below,"
The *goddess*, from the "great above," she set her mind towards the "great below,"
Inanna, from the "great above," she set her mind towards the "great below."
My lady abandoned heaven, abandoned earth, to the nether world she descended,
Inanna abandoned heaven, abandoned earth, to the nether world she descended,
Abandoned lordship, abandoned ladyship, to the nether world she descended.
In Erech she abandoned Eanna,[10] to the nether world she descended,
In Badtibira she abandoned Emushkalamma, to the nether world she descended,
In Zabalam she abandoned Giguna, to the nether world she descended,
In Adab she abandoned Esharra, to the nether world she descended,
In Nippur she abandoned Baratushgarra, to the nether world she descended,
In Kish she abandoned Hursagkalamma, to the nether world she descended,
In Agade she abandoned Eulmash, to the nether world she descended.
She *arrayed herself* in the seven ordinances,[11]
She gathered the ordinances, placed them in her hand,
All the ordinances she set up at (her) waiting foot,
The *šugurra*, the crown of the plain, she put upon her head,
The *wig* of her forehead she took,
The measuring rod (and) line of lapis lazuli she gripped in her hand,
Small lapis lazuli stones she tied about her neck,
Sparkling ... stones she *fastened* to her breast,
A gold ring she *put about* her hand,
A breastplate *which* ..., she *tightened* about her breast,
With the *pala*-garment, the garment of ladyship, she covered her body,
Kohl *which* ..., she daubed on her eyes.
Inanna walked towards the nether world.
Her messenger Ninshubur walked at her [*side*],
The pure Inanna says to Ninshubur:
"O (thou who art) my constant support,[12]
My messenger of favorable words,
My carrier of true[13] words,
I am now descending to the nether world.
When I shall have come to the nether world,
Fill heaven *with complaints for me*,
In the assembly shrine cry out for me,
In the house of the gods *rush about* for me,[14]
Scratch thy eyes for me, *scratch* thy mouth for me,[15]
Scratch thy large ... which ... s not with man,[16]
Like a pauper in a single garment dress for me,
To the Ekur, the house of Enlil, all alone direct thy step.[17]
Upon thy entering the Ekur, the house of Enlil,
Weep before Enlil:
'O Father Enlil, let not thy daughter be *put to death* in the nether world,
Let not thy good metal be covered with the dust of the nether world,[18]

[7] cf. *RA*, xxxvi (1939), 68-80; *BASOR*, 79 (1940), 18-27.

[8] cf. also B. A. van Proosdij in *JEOL*, vi (1939), 138-147. B. Landsberger has sent me some valuable comment on the *PAPS* edition, some of which will be quoted in the notes.

[9] The "great above" is the space above the sky; the "great below" is the space below the surface of the earth.

[10] This and the following lines mention seven important cities of Sumer together with Inanna's temple in each; the order is not significant since it varies considerably in one of the duplicates.

[11] For "ordinances" which attempts to render the Sumerian word *me*, cf. p. 43 of this work. It is to be noted that judging from our text, these "ordinances" seem to be concrete and tangible objects; note, too, that in the myth "Inanna and Enki: The Transfer of the Arts of Civilization from Eridu to Erech" (*SM*, 64-68), they were transported on a boat. The rendering of lines 14-25 varies to some extent from that in *PAPS*, lxxxv. In line 14, the new rendering is based on Landsberger's (cf. note 8) note that *zag—SÌR* is equated with *ḳiṣṣuru* in *CT*, xvi, 25, 49 (Falkenstein's interpretation of the compound in *AfO*, xiv, 115 and *ZA*, xlvii, 168 f., is therefore incorrect). For "gathered" instead of "sought out" in line 14, cf. Falkenstein, *AfO*, xiv, 115; for "*wig*" instead of "*radiance*," in line 18 cf. *ibid.*, 117-118. For the new rendering of line 19, cf. Witzel's excellent comment in *Orientalia* NS, xiv, 32-33; Landsberger, moreover, refers to the Burney Relief discussed by Frankfort in *AfO*, xii, 129 ff. which actually shows the rod and line in the hands of a female deity. While, therefore, the translations "measuring rod" and "line" are reasonably certain, there is some difficulty with the words "of lapis lazuli" since "the line" should, of course, be made of rope, not of stone; Landsberger therefore suggests the possibility that "lapis lazuli" is here used for the color "blue." In line 21, "twin" may be preferable to "sparkling"; the Sumerian word is ambiguous. For "*put about*" instead of "gripped in," (line 22) cf. Falkenstein, *loc. cit.*, 116; for the new rendering of line 24, cf. *ibid.*, 116-117; "kohl" (line 25) was suggested by Landsberger, but cf. already Falkenstein, *loc. cit.*, 11.

[12] One of the duplicates has an interesting variant for lines 29-31, which reads as follows: "Come, my faithful messenger of Eanna, Instruction I offer thee, take my instruction, A word I speak to thee, give ear to it."

[13] "True" rather than "supporting" as in *PAPS*, lxxx, cf. Falkenstein, *loc. cit.*, 130.

[14] The translation assumes that "the house of the gods" (line 36) and the "assembly shrine" of the preceding line refer to places in heaven where the gods met in assembly. Perhaps, however, the two lines refer to Ninshubur's making the rounds of the gods in Nippur, Ur, and Eridu; if so, "shrine" and "house" (lines 35, 36) should read "shrines" and "houses," and "rush about" might perhaps read "make the rounds."

[15] The rendering "scratch" is suggested by Landsberger. cf. perhaps, the similar practices in connection with the dead, which are prohibited in the Old Testament.

[16] For the rendering "with man," cf. Falkenstein, *loc. cit.*, 119.

[17] "All alone" was accidentally omitted in *PAPS*, lxxxv.

[18] For "be covered" instead of "be ground up," in *PAPS*, lxxxv, cf. Falkenstein, *loc. cit.*, 120. It is difficult to see what "thy good metal," "thy good lapis lazuli," "thy *boxwod*," are intended to refer to; on the surface it might seem that they refer to the jewels and ornaments carried by Inanna, but if so, what does "thy *boxwood*" refer to? Falkenstein (*loc. cit.*, 121) suggests that these phrases are figurative descriptions of Inanna's body; such usage, however, is as yet without parallel in Sumerian literature.

Let not thy good lapis lazuli be broken up[19] into the stone of the stoneworker,
Let not thy *boxwod* be cut up into the wood of the woodworker,
Let not the maid Inanna be *put to death* in the nether world.'
If Enlil stands not by thee in this matter, go to Ur.
In Ur, upon thy entering the house of . . . of the land,[20]
The Ekishnugal[21] the house of Nanna,
Weep before Nanna:
'O Father Nanna, let not thy daughter be *put to death* in the nether world,
Let not thy good metal be covered with the dust of the nether world,
Let not thy good lapis lazuli be broken up into the stone of the stoneworker,
Let not thy *boxwood* be cut up into the wood of the woodworker,
Let not the maid Inanna be *put to death* in the nether world.'
If Nanna stands not by thee in this matter, go to Eridu.
In Eridu, upon thy entering the house of Enki,
Weep before Enki:
'O Father Enki, let not thy daughter be *put to death* in the nether world,
Let not thy good metal be covered with the dust of the nether world,
Let not thy good lapis lazuli be broken up into the stone of the stoneworker,
Let not thy *boxwood* be cut up into the wood of the woodworker,
Let not the maid Inanna be *put to death* in the nether world.'
Father Enki, the lord of *wisdom*,[22]
Who knows the food of life, who knows the water of life,
He will surely bring me to life."[23]
Inanna walked towards the nether world,
To her messenger Ninshubur she says:
"Go, Ninshubur,
The word which I have commanded thee do not neglect."[24]
When Inanna arrived at the lapis lazuli palace of the nether world,[25]
At the door of the nether world she *acted* evilly,[26]
In the palace of the nether world she spoke evilly:
"Open the house, gatekeeper, open the house,
Open the house, Neti,[27] open the house, all alone I would enter."
Neti, the chief gatekeeper of the nether world,
Answers the pure Inanna:
"Who, pray, art thou?"
"I am Inanna of the place where the sun rises."[28]
"If thou art Inanna of the place where the sun rises,
Why pray hast thou come to the land of no return?
On the road whose traveler returns not, how hath thy heart led thee?"[29]
The pure Inanna answers him:
"My elder sister Ereshkigal,
Because her husband, the lord Gugalanna, had been killed,[30]
To witness his funeral rites,
. . . ; verily 'tis so."[31]
Neti, the chief gatekeeper of the nether world,
Answers the pure Inanna:
"*Stay*, Inanna, to my queen let me speak,
To my queen Ereshkigal let me speak, . . . let me speak."
Neti, the chief gatekeeper of the nether world,
Enters the house of his queen Ereshkigal (and) says to her:
"O my queen, a maid,
Like a god . . . ,
The door . . . ,
. . . ,
In Eanna . . . ,
She has *arrayed* herself in the seven ordinances,[32]
She has gathered the ordinances, has placed them in her hand,
All the ordinances she has set up at (her) waiting foot,
The *šugurra*, the crown of the plain, she has put upon her head,
The *wig* of her forehead she has taken,
The measuring rod (and) line of lapis lazuli she has gripped in her hand,
Small lapis lazuli stones she has tied about her neck,
Sparkling . . . stones she has *fastened* to her breast,
A gold ring she has *put about* her hand,
A breastplate *which* . . . , she has *tightened* about her breast,
Kohl *which* . . . , she has daubed on her eyes,
With the *pala*-garment, the garment of ladyship, she has covered her body."
Then Ereshkigal . . . ,
[Answers] Neti, her chief gatekeeper:
"Come, Neti, chief gatekeeper of the [nether world],
The word which I (shall) have commanded thee, do [not] ne[glect].[33]

[19] "Be broken up" (line 45) and "be cut up" (line 46) are reasonably certain renderings and should not have been italicized as doubtful in *PAPS*, LXXXV.

[20] The word "land" renders the Sumerian word *ḳalam* and usually refers to Sumer.

[21] For "Ekishnugal" instead of "Ekishshirgal," cf. p. 455 of this work.

[22] Should have been rendered as doubtful in *PAPS*, LXXXV.

[23] The rendering of this crucial line is still uncertain and should have been so indicated in *PAPS*, LXXXV.

[24] For the rendering "do not neglect," cf. Falkenstein, *loc. cit.*, 122-123, and 129.

[25] This line may perhaps be better rendered "When Inanna arrived at the palace, the lapis lazuli mountain," cf. Falkenstein, *loc. cit.*, 131.

[26] More literally, "set up that which is evil."

[27] Pronunciation of the first syllable of the name is still uncertain.

[28] Note the rendering which varies somewhat from that in *PAPS*, LXXXV, and cf. Falkenstein, *loc. cit.*, 131.

[29] Note that the word order differs from that in *PAPS*, LXXXV.

[30] The mythological implications of the statement made in this line are unknown.

[31] Note the new rendering of this line, and cf. *JCS*, I, 35, note 214.

[32] For lines 100-111, cf. lines 14-25, but note the inverted order of the last two lines of the passage.

[33] The new rendering is based on a collation of text A (cf. *PAPS*, LXXXV,

Of the seven gates of the nether world, [open their locks],
Of the gate [Ganzir, the *face* of the nether world,[34] *define its rules*].
Upon her entering,
Bowed low[35] . . . ."
Neti, the chief gatekeeper of the nether world,
Heeded[36] the word of his queen.
Of the seven gates of the nether world, [he opened] their locks,
Of the gate Ganzir, the *face* of the nether world, [*he defined*] *its rules*.
To the pure Inanna he says:
"Come, Inanna, enter."
Upon her entering,[37]
The *šugurra*, the crown of the plain of her head was removed.[38]
"What, pray, is this?"[39]
"*Be silent*,[40] Inanna, the ordinances of the nether world are perfect,[41]
O Inanna do not [question] the rites of the nether world."
Upon her entering the second gate,
The measuring rod (and) line of lapis lazuli was removed.
"What, pray, is this?"
"*Be silent*, Inanna, the ordinances of the nether world are perfect,
O Inanna, *do not* [*question*] the rites of the nether world."
Upon her entering the third gate,
The small lapis lazuli stones of her neck were removed.
"What, pray, is this?"
"*Be silent*, Inanna, the ordinances of the nether world are perfect,
O Inanna, do not [question] the rites of the nether world."
Upon her entering the fourth gate,
The *sparkling* . . . stones of her breast were removed.
"What, pray, is this?"
"*Be silent*, Inanna, the ordinances of the nether world are perfect,
O Inanna, *do not* [*question*] the rites of the nether world."
Upon her entering the fifth gate,
The gold ring of her hand was removed.
"What, pray, is this?"
"*Be silent*, Inanna, the ordinances of the nether world are perfect,
O Inanna, *do not* [*question*] the rites of the nether world."
Upon her entering the sixth gate,
The breastplate *which* . . . of her breast was removed.
"What, pray, is this?"
"*Be silent*, Inanna, the ordinances of the nether world are perfect,
O Inanna, *do not* [*question*] the rites of the nether world."
Upon her entering the seventh gate,
The *pala*-garment, the garment of ladyship of her body, was removed.
"What, pray, is this?"
"Be silent, Inanna, the ordinances of the nether world are perfect,
O Inanna, *do not* [*question*] the rites of the nether world."
Bowed low. . . .
The pure Ereshkigal seated herself upon her throne,
The Anunnaki, the seven judges, pronounced judgment before her,
They fastened (their) eyes upon her, the eyes of death,
At their word, the word which tortures the spirit,
. . . ,
The sick "woman" was turned into *a corpse*,
The *corpse* was hung from a *stake*.
After three days and three nights had passed,
Her messenger Ninshubur,[42]
Her messenger of favorable words,
Her carrier of true words,
Fills the heaven *with complaints for her*,
Cried out for her in the assembly shrine,
Rushed about for her in the house of the gods,
Scratched his eyes for her, *scratched* his mouth for her,
Scratched his large . . . *which* . . . s not with man,
Like a pauper in a single garment dressed for her,
To the Ekur, the house of Enlil, all alone[43] he directed his step.
Upon his entering the Ekur, the house of Enlil,
Before Enlil he weeps,
"O, Father Enlil, let not thy daughter be *put to death* in the nether world,[44]
Let not thy good metal be covered with the dust of the nether world,
Let not thy good lapis lazuli be broken up into the stone of the stoneworker,

303) which seems to make the following reading probable *inim-a-ra-dug$_4$-ga-mu gú-zu l*[*a-ba-ši-šub-bi-en*]. In G, on the other hand, the only other text available at this point, the line may read [*inim-a-ra-dug$_4$*]*-ga giz*[*zal ḫé*]*-im-*[*ši-ag*], "[To the com]manded [word giv]e e[ar]."

34 The implications of this phrase are not clear.

35 Should have been italicized as doubtful in *PAPS*, LXXXV.

36 For this new rendering, cf. Falkenstein, *loc. cit.*, 125.

37 A variant text reads: "Upon her entering the first gate."

38 According to the passage contained in lines 126-160, Inanna wore seven bits of apparel, which were removed piece by piece as she passed through each of the seven gates of the nether world. On the other hand, the passage describing Inanna's dress preparatory to her descent (lines 17-25), consists of nine lines, each of which seems to describe a specific unit of apparel or ornament; omitted in the later passage are the *wig* and the kohl. Interesting, too, is a variant text in which the measuring rod and line were removed even before she entered the first gate.

39 This phrase should not have been italicized on p. 308 of *PAPS*, LXXXV.

40 This translation which makes excellent sense is suggested by Falkenstein, *loc. cit.*, 126; it is nevertheless italicized as doubtful in our translation, since, as Witzel points out (*loc. cit.*, 44-45), the form would be expected to read *si-ga* rather than *si-a* as it appears in our text.

41 A more literal rendering of the verb would read "have been perfected."

42 cf. lines 30-39.

43 "All alone" was accidentally omitted in *PAPS*, LXXXV.

44 cf. lines 43 ff.

Let not thy *boxwood*[45] be cut up into the wood of the woodworker,
Let not the maid Inanna be *put to death* in the nether world."
Father Enlil answers Ninshubur:
"My daughter *has asḳed for* the 'great above,' *has asḳed for* the 'great below,'[46]
Inanna *has asḳed for* the 'great above,' *has asḳed for* the 'great below,'
The ordinances of the nether world, the . . . ordinances, the ordinances—she has *reached their* place,[47]
Who is it *that to their* place . . . ?"
Father Enlil stood not by him in this matter, he [went] to Ur.
In Ur, upon his entering the house of . . . of the land,
The Ekishnugal, the house of Nanna,
Before Nanna he weeps:
"O Father Nanna, let not thy daughter be *put to death* in the nether world,
Let not thy good metal be covered with the dust of the nether world,
Let not thy good lapis lazuli be broken up into the stone of the stoneworker,
Let not thy *boxwood* be cut up into the wood of the woodworker,
Let not the maid Inanna be *put to death* in the nether world."
Father Nanna answers Ninshubur:
"My daughter *has asḳed for* the 'great above,' *has asḳed for* the 'great below,'
Inanna *has asḳed for* the 'great above,' *has asḳed for* the 'great below,'
The ordinances of the nether world, the . . . ordinances the . . . ordinances—she has *reached their* place,
Who is it *that to their* place . . . ?"
Father Nanna stood not by him in this matter, he went to Eridu.
In Eridu upon his entering the house of Enki,
Before Enki he weeps:
"O Father Enki, let not thy daughter be *put to death* in the nether world,
Let not thy good metal be covered with the dust of the nether world,
Let not thy good lapis lazuli be broken up into the stone of the stoneworker,
Let not thy *boxwood* be cut up into the wood of the woodworker,
Let not the maid Inanna be *put to death* in the nether world."
Father Enki answers Ninshubur:
"What has happened to my daughter![49] I am troubled,
What has happened to Inanna! I am troubled,
What has happened to the queen of all the lands! I am troubled,
What has happened to the hierodule of heaven! I am troubled."
From his fingernail[50] he brought forth dirt (and) fashioned the *ḳurgarru*,
From his *red-painted* fingernail[51] he brought forth dirt (and) fashioned the *ḳalaturru*.
To the *ḳurgarru* he gave the food of life,
To the *ḳalaturru* he gave the water of life,
Father Enki says to the *ḳalaturru* and *ḳurgarru*:
"... (nineteen lines badly damaged)[52]
Upon the corpse hung from a staḳe direct the pulḫu (and) the melammu,[53]
Sixty times the food of life, *sixty times* the water of life, sprinkle upon it,
Surely Inanna will arise."
(break of approximately twenty lines)
[Upon the corpse hung] from a stake . . .
The pure Ereshkigal answers the *ḳa*[*laturru* and *ḳurgarru*]:
"*The corpse . . .*"
Upon the corpse[54] they . . . ,
Upon the corpse hung from a staḳe they directed the pulḫu (and) the melammu,
Sixty times the food of life, *sixty times* the water of life, they sprinkled upon it,
Inanna arose.
Inanna ascends from the nether world,
The Anunnaki *fled*,[55]
Who *now of the* dwellers of the nether world *will descend peacefully to* the nether world![56]
When Inanna ascends from the nether world,
Verily the dead *hasten ahead of her*.
Inanna ascends from the nether world,
The small demons like the spear shafts,[57]
The large demons like . . . s,[58]
Walked at her side.

[45] "Boxwood" should have been italicized as doubtful wherever it appears in *PAPS*, LXXXV.

[46] Note the new renderings of lines 189-190; it is due primarily to Landsberger's suggestion that *al—dug₄* is identical *al—di*, Akk. *erēšu*, "to desire," etc.; the lines may also be rendered "My daughter has desired it (death?) in the 'great above,' has desired it in the 'great below,' " etc.

[47] Note the attempted new rendering of this difficult but crucial line.

[48] Note the slightly modified rendering from that in *PAPS*, LXXXV.

[49] For this variant rendering, cf. Witzel's excellent comment (*loc. cit.*, 47); cf. now especially *JCS*, I, 10, line 27.

[50] Witzel as well as Landsberger read the Sumerian sign for this word correctly.

[51] This probably correct rendering was suggested by Landsberger who read the Sumerian complex *dubbin-su₄-še-gín(!)-na*.

[52] These lines contained a number of instructions to the *ḳalaturru* and *ḳurgarru* (cf. note 5); many of the broken lines end in a second person plural imperative.

[53] Note the variant rendering of the end of the line; for some possible interpretations of the *pulḫu* and *melammu*, cf. Oppenheim's study of the words in *JAOS*, LXIII, 31-34.

[54] Note the new rendering.

[55] "Fled" should have been rendered as doubtful in *PAPS*, LXXXV.

[56] The rendering of this line is quite uncertain and its implications are obscure; as it stands now, it seems to say that the incoming dead may raise difficulties, now that the Anunnaki, the judges in the nether world (cf. note 3), are no longer there to judge them. For the suggestion that this line contains a rhetorical question, cf. Falkenstein, *loc. cit.*, 127.

[57] The new rendering of the line follows Falkenstein's excellent comment, *loc. cit.*, 127-128. The "demons" throughout the text refer to a type known as *galla*-demons.

[58] Landsberger notes that the *gi-dub-ba-an* probably has nothing to do with tablet styluses, and the present evidence seems to bear him out.

Who *by his face* was no [messenger], held a staff in her hand,[59]
Who *by his body* was no [carrier], carried a weapon on the loin.
They who accompanied her,[60]
They who accompanied Inanna,
(Were beings who) know not food, who know not water,
Who eat not sprinkled flour,
Who drink not libated [water],[61]
Who take away the wife from the loins of man,
Who take away the child from the . . .
of the nursemaid.[62]
Inanna ascends from the nether world.
Upon Inanna's ascending from the nether world,
[Her messenger] Ninshubur threw himself[63] at her feet,
Sat in the dust, dressed in *sackcloth*.[64]
The demons say to the pure Inanna:
"O Inanna, *wait before* thy city, let us *carry him off*."[65]
The pure Inanna answers the demons:
"My messenger of favorable words,[66]
My carrier of true words,
(Who) fails not my directions,
Neglected not my commanded word,
Fills the heaven *with complaints for me*,
Cried out for me in the assembly shrine,
Rushed about for me in the house of the gods,
Scratched his eyes for me, *scratched* his mouth for me,
Scratched his large . . . which . . . s not with man,
Like a pauper in a single garment dressed for me,
To the Ekur, the house of Enlil,[67]
In Ur, to the house of Nanna,
In Eridu, to the house of Enki,
He brought me to life."[68]
"Let us accompany her, in Umma to the Sigkurshagga let us accompany her."[69]
In Umma, from the Sigkurshagga,
Shara threw himself[70] at her feet,
Sat in the dust, dressed in *sackcloth*,
The demons say to the pure Inanna:
"O Inanna, *wait before* thy city, let us *carry him off*."
The pure Inanna answers the demons:
(three lines broken and unintelligible)[71]
"Let us accompany her, in Badtibira to the Emushkalamma let us accompany her."
In Badtibira, from the Emushkalamma
Latarak threw himself at her feet,
Sat in the dust, dressed in *sackcloth*.
The demons say to the pure Inanna:
"O Inanna, *wait before* thy city, let us *carry him off*."
The pure Inanna answers the demons:
(rest of the myth still unknown)[72]

[59] Note the new renderings of this line and the next; the restorations "messenger" and "carrier" are from the Yale tablet described in note 6.

[60] Note the slightly variant rendering of this and the following line from that in *PAPS*, LXXXV; cf. Falkenstein, *loc. cit.*, 135.

[61] "Water" instead of "wine" follows the excellent comment by Falkenstein, *loc. cit.*, 128; the restoration is fully confirmed by the tablet in the Yale Babylonian Collection discussed in note 6.

[62] Note the variant rendering of the end of the line from that in *PAPS*, LXXXV.

[63] "Herself" in *PAPS*, LXXXV, is an accidental error.

[64] "Sackcloth" or some mourning garb for "dirt," cf. Falkenstein, *loc. cit.*, 135.

[65] Note the new rendering of the line, and cf. note 6 for the interpretation of this part of the myth.

[66] cf. lines 30 ff. and lines 170 ff. The passage recites Ninshubur's faithful services to Inanna; cf. note 6.

[67] This line is probably a kind of abbreviation for lines 179-191; the next line is an abbreviation for lines 192-205; the next line for lines 206-213.

[68] Following this line one might have expected a line in which Inanna asks the demons not to harm Ninshubur; the tablet in the Yale Babylonian Collection does have an added line here, but unfortunately its meaning is obscure.

[69] This line seems to contain words of exhortation uttered by the demons to each other.

[70] "Herself" in *PAPS*, LXXXV, is an accidental error.

[71] The first two lines might be expected to contain words of praise for Inanna; the third probably contained a statement not to harm him (cf. note 68).

[72] cf. however note 6.

The Duties and Powers of the Gods: Inscription on the Statue of King Kurigalzu

Aqar Quf, the tell covering the ancient city Dur-Kurigalzu, is situated approximately twenty miles west of Baghdad. Excavations at the site in recent years have laid bare several temples, the most important of which is the Eugal, that is probably "the house of the great lord," dedicated to the god Enlil. In the debris covering this temple, or in its immediate neighborhood, were found four inscribed fragments[1] of a larger-than-life statue of the Kassite King Kurigalzu.[2] The inscription, written throughout in the Sumerian language and not in the Semitic Akkadian that was actually current in those days, is of great importance for the light it sheds on the religious tenets of the Babylonians of the second millennium B.C. For, fragmentary and obscure as the extant text is,[3] it is clear that much of the original inscription was devoted to a description of the duties and powers of the more important deities of the Sumerian pantheon. A scientific edition of the text of the four fragments, including copies of the originals, and a transliteration and translation of the more intelligible portions, was published by Selim Levy, Taha Baqir, and the present writer in *Sumer*, IV (1948), 1-29+ix plates.[4]

Fragment A[5]

This fragment begins with a passage running from col. i to perhaps col. v, which seems to concern the Igigi, the gods

[1] One tiny fragment not included here contains only two legible signs.

[2] Probably Kurigalzu I; cf. Poebel, *AS*, No. 14, 5 ff. and note 20; he lived sometime in the fifteenth century B.C.

[3] Unfortunately there is but little that can be gleaned with certainty from the contents of these fragments. In the first place they contain but a small portion of the entire text of the statue. Moreover, none of the pieces joins; there is a break of unknown length between each two of them, and so there is very little connected text to provide us with a controlling context. In addition we find, of course, the expected number of roots and complexes whose meaning is either uncertain or altogether unknown. And, to crown all these difficulties which the cuneiformist has learned more or less to expect as routine, our Kurigalzu inscription presents an unusual feature which is particularly confusing. As was first pointed out by C. J. Gadd, the columns are divided into cases usually containing two or three signs written without any regard to the expected word division, so that it is often difficult to tell where one word or complex ends and another begins.

[4] cf. C. J. Gadd's comment in *Iraq*, Supplement, 1944, p. 15, and Arno Poebel's illuminating study, The City of Esa, in *AS*, No. 14, 1-22.

[5] The order of the four fragments is far from assured; cf. *Sumer*, IV, 2-3, for a discussion of the problems involved.

Badna, and the Anunnaki;[6] it is so fragmentary, however, that its sense escapes us. Beginning with, perhaps, the middle of col. v and ending with col. vii, we find a description of the duties assigned to the moon-god Nanna which ends in a passage stating that the Igigi directed the cult-rites for Nanna from the Eugal of heaven, and that Kurigalzu reestablished "the ancient days." The remainder of the fragment continues with a description of the duties and powers assigned, perhaps by the gods Enlil and Ninlil, to a deity whose name is not found in the extant text. The translation of the more intelligible portions of this fragment reads as follows:

(i) (practically completely destroyed)

(ii) . . . they . . . d. The light of the Igigi (*and*) *the gods Badna*[7] was covered up by its (their?) . . . The Igi[gi]. . . .

(iii) He (she?) does not. . . . Becau[se] their king had *punished* the Anunnaki, (because) he had put them out of the . . . of all the lands, out of heaven. . . .

(iv) To lift (bear?) the . . . , to give all the minute directions, they . . . d in its (their?) midst. . . .

(v)[8] Its (their?) pure . . . they did not bring close; the . . . they did not give. That Nanna might make bright the night, that during the day he might . . . in the . . . , that he might make known the signs in (of?) the night. . . .

(vi) (practically entirely unintelligible[9])

(vii) [From the Eugal of heaven, the place of the wide-knowing Anu, the Igigi . . . who are kings who *pronounce the word*], who are [pure gods]; from the place of Enlil and Ninlil, the Igigi . . . who are kings *who pronounce the word*, who are gods of true decrees, directed the *cult-rites* for Nanna from him who knows the heart. [I, Kurigalzu, who caused the Eugal to appear .] . . [. set up there the old days unto future days].[10]

(viii) . . . ; of the pure places of the fisherman of the gods, *he* returned their . . . To return to Nammu,[11] they charge the mission of . . . To *raise up* . . . ; *to multiply* riches and treasure. . . .

(ix) After he had fashioned there . . . , as the exalted head-goat of his chosen heir, Enlil and Ninlil. . . .

Fragment B

This fragment consists of two parts, a and b, whose relative positions in the inscription are quite uncertain. Bb is here given first since it seems to treat of matters involving the moon, and its text may therefore have preceded or followed that of fragment A.

(Bb i) *For* the . . . *of* his *trust* they made known its (their?) task(s) (and) its (their?) power(s). For *kingship*. . . .

(Bb ii) That he whose rays cover the black-headed people *at* the horizon and zenith might bring in the small watchers, that he might plan one month . . . of thirty days. . . .

(Bb iii) *Ashgirbabbar*[12] *whose* "horn" *is covered up by* Urash, *who overpowers* Urash, who makes bright the land, the wide . . . *of* the black-headed people. . . .

(Ba i) (largely destroyed)

(Ba ii) To . . . ; to fashion the image of mankind.[13] . . .

Fragment C

Fragment C begins with the assignment of duties and powers to the goddess Ninisinna,[14] and ends with a passage stating that the Igigi directed the cult-rites for her from the Eugal of heaven, and that Kurigalzu reestablished "the ancient days"; in other words, a passage which, except for the name of the deity, is identical with that which closes the portion of the text of A, dealing with the god Nanna. The fragment then continues with the duties and powers assigned to the god Nergal, the husband of Ninisinna and king of the nether world; it, too, probably ends with the "cult-rites" passage that marks the close of the Nanna and Ninisinna passages. The fragment then seems to continue with the "portions" and "lots" assigned to the goddess Inanna.

(i) (practically entirely destroyed)

(ii) (Only the phrases "[Enlil and Nin]lil," "*wifehood*," and the temple name "Eugal" can be made out.)

(iii) Enlil and Ninlil as fate . . . ; to make . . . very wisely from its (their?) good *garment* . . . *whatever is brought forth*, Enlil and Ninlil. . . .

(iv) [From the Eugal of heaven, the place of the wide-knowing Anu, the Igigi . . . who are kings who *pronounce the word*, who are pure gods; from the place of Enlil and Ninlil, the Igigi . . . who are kings who *pronounce the word*], who are gods of true decrees, [di]rected the *cult-rites* for Ninisinna from him who knows the heart. I, Kurigalzu, who caused the Eugal to appear . . . set up there the old days unto future days. For Nergal, Enlil [and] Nin[lil . . . d] the tail end and the "mouth" of the nether world, the place *whither* the Anunnaki drew nigh. . . .

(v) Of that which *overwhelms* . . . , to . . . its net; to *weaken* its *strength* . . . ; to bring in the . . . who have neither a *covering roof*, nor a headdress, nor a . . . ; as *for* those *without* head or hand, the snatching demons who did not submit *to* the Eugal . . . , their great. . . .

(vi) . . . *of* the earth, they presented to him[15] all sleeping mankind. . . . From the Eugal of heaven, the place of the wide-knowing Anu, the Igigi . . . who are kings who *pronounce the word*, who are pure gods; from the place of Enlil and Ninlil, the Igigi . . . [. . . who are kings who *pronounce the word*, who are gods of true

6 The rendering "the gods Badna" is quite uncertain; according to a suggestion from Falkenstein, it may represent a phrase descriptive of the preceding Igigi.

7 cf. preceding note.

8 cf. for this column also Poebel, *AS*, No. 14, 19.

9 It begins with a phrase which seems to read "*held* (so! not "hold" as in *Sumer*, IV, 6) in their *arms*." This is followed by the end of the sentence which seems to read: "A *naditu*-priestess (in *Sumer*, IV, 6 *munus-diš* is an error for SAL.ME) a hierodule who marks the . . . of the fields in accordance with the judgment of (the sun-god) Utu (*and*) the *lord* filled with wailing prepared . . . (*as*) a betrothal." The remaining cases contain the words "sickness," "lament," and "*outcry*."

10 cf. also Poebel, *AS*, No. 14, 19-20.

11 Nammu, the mother of the Sumerian water-god and god of wisdom, Enki, is probably the goddess of the primeval sea and was said to have given "birth to heaven and earth," cf. *SM*, 39 and 68 ff.

12 Ashgirbabbar (the reading of the name is uncertain) is the name of the god of the new moon. Urash is the wife of the heaven-god Anu.

13 To judge from this phrase, the deity involved might be Ninhursag, cf. p. 37 of this volume.

14 Ninisinna, as her name indicates, is the queen of Isin, a city dominant in Babylonia in the first quarter of the second millennium B.C. Nergal is the husband of Ninisinna.

15 "Him" refers to Nergal, the king of the nether world.

decrees, directed the *cult-rites* for Nergal from him who knows the heart. I, Kurigalzu, who caused the Eugal to appear . . . set up there the old days unto future days . . .].

(vii) The great Igigi who *parade in* the sky, whose brilliance, like fire, . . . s the *evening* and the black night, did not at all enlarge the . . . As *for* Belitili[16] who crosses the sky, in the earth . . . , from the district(s) of the sky. . . .

(viii) As *for her*[17] who, like . . . had been *put out* from the *district(s)* of the sky, they[18] gave her as (her) portion the built Eshaga, the Eshaga,[19] where all good things are stored; they filled her hands with the good word which soothes the flesh and the spirit *for* wife and husband. . . . *On* those who heed her, a firm eye. . . .

(ix)[20] . . . they gave to Inanna . . . as a share; they built for Belitili the . . . , the large grove, her abode of lordship; [they] adorned for her. . . .

16 Belitili seems to be used in this inscription as another name of Inanna; note that in *Sumer*, IV, 12 ff., the name was erroneously read as Ninzalli (note 66 on p. 26 of *Sumer*, IV, is to be omitted altogether); cf. Poebel, *AS*, No. 14, 18 ff.

17 "Her" refers to the goddess Inanna.

18 Note that the rendering "they" here, and in col. ix is probably not to be questioned as it is in *Sumer*, IV, 13; cf. Poebel, *AS*, No. 14, p. 18 and note 49 for the reading of the sign *KU* following *mu-na-an-sì* as mu_4, while it is not unlikely that the sign *GANAM* had the reading $uš_4$, so that we have here a plural form of the verb.

19 Eshaga, literally rendered, probably means "the house of the heart."

20 For the rendering of this passage, cf. also Poebel, *AS*, No. 14, 18-19.

(x) (This seems to deal with parts of a temple; its relation to what precedes is obscure. It reads:) . . . ; its outside which is . . . ; its *shrines* which are bright; its *rooms* which are pure; its . . . which are. . . .

(xi) (almost entirely destroyed)

Fragment D

This fragment, too, seems to deal with the tasks and duties assigned to the goddess Inanna. Col. i is practically entirely destroyed. In col. ii only the phrase "that *mankind* might do *its* work" is intelligible. Col. iii is almost altogether unintelligible in spite of the fact that the signs are well preserved; the major difficulty lies with the extreme uncertainty of the word division. The remainder of the fragment reads:

(iv) To *devour* the . . . ; to . . . *as* . . . ; to *raise high* the position of those who turn evil to good, *they gave* to Inanna . . . *among* her portions. . . .

(v) [From the Eugal of heaven, the place of the wide-knowing Anu, the Igigi . . . who are kings who *pronounce the word*], who are [pure gods; from] the place of E[nlil and Ninlil], the Igigi . . . who are kings who *pronounce the word*, who are gods of true decrees, [directed the *cult-rites* for Inanna from him who knows the heart. I, Kurigalzu, who caused the Eugal to appear . . . set up there the old days unto future days . . .].

(vi) For . . . they directed there the. . . .

Akkadian Myths and Epics

TRANSLATOR: E. A. SPEISER

The material here offered is intended to be representative rather than exhaustive. It is not always possible to draw a sharp line between Akkadian compositions devoted to myths and related material, and those that concern other types of religious literature, not to mention special categories of historical nature. Furthermore, considerations of space and time have tended to exclude sundry literary remains whose bearing on the purpose of this work is not immediately apparent. It is hoped, however, that nothing of genuine relevance has been omitted.

As regards the order of the individual subjects, it was deemed advisable to present in succession the two major survivals of this group of texts, namely, *The Creation Epic* and *The Epic of Gilgamesh*. The alternative procedure would have been to group some of the minor subjects with the one epic, and some with the other. The present arrangement has a sound biblical precedent in the order of the books of the Prophets.

In translating material which has come down to us in poetic form, there arises the inevitable conflict between adherence to the force and flavor of the original idiom—as that idiom is understood—and adherence to the given poetic form. In the present instance, preference was given to the demands of meaning, whenever necessary. Elsewhere slight exceptions have been made in an effort to reflect the measures of the Akkadian verse—normally a unit of two distinct halves with two beats in each half. Where the text presents an overlong line as a result of a mechanical combination of two verses, the added verse has been indented in the translation so as not to alter the line count of the text. In lines grown unwieldy for other reasons—such as theological addition in the original, or the helplessness of the translator when confronted with the economy or the elusiveness of the Akkadian idiom—indentation has likewise proved to be a convenient device.

The strong temptation to indicate logical transitions in the context by means of paragraphing has been resisted on the ground that such divisions might be regarded as arbitrary. Where, however, the text suggests paragraphing by means of horizontal lines (as in *The Epic of Gilgamesh*), the translation has followed suit by resorting to added spacing.

Virtually all of the material included under this heading has had the benefit of painstaking study over a period of many years. The principal editions of the texts and the latest discussions and translations are listed in the respective introductions to the individual subjects. Each revision is indebted to some extent to its various predecessors. My own debt to my colleagues, past and present, is too great to be acknowledged in detail. I have tried, however, to note explicitly such appropriated improvements and observations as may not as yet have become the common property of Assyriological scholarship. In fairness to others, it was necessary also to call attention to the occasional departures for which I alone must bear the responsibility. The existing gaps in the texts, at any rate, and the lacunae in our understanding of what is extant, are still much too formidable for anything like a definitive translation.

The Creation Epic

The struggle between cosmic order and chaos was to the ancient Mesopotamians a fateful drama that was renewed at the turn of each new year. The epic which deals with these events was therefore the most significant expression of the religious literature of Mesopotamia. The work, consisting of seven tablets, was known in Akkadian as *Enūma eliš* "When on high," after its opening words. It was recited with due solemnity on the fourth day of the New Year's festival.

Portions of this work were first made available in modern times by George Smith, in *The Chaldean Account of Genesis* (1876). The flow of material has continued intermittently ever since. We owe these texts to three main sources: (a) The British excavations at Nineveh; the relevant texts have been published in *CT*, XIII (1901) and in L. W. King's *The Seven Tablets of Creation* (2 Vols., 1902). (b) The German excavations at Ashur; texts in E. Ebeling's *Keilschrifttexte aus Assur religiösen Inhalts* (1915 ff.). (c) The British-American excavations at Kish; texts in S. Langdon's *Oxford Editions of Cuneiform Texts* (1923 ff.; Vol. VI). Scattered fragments have appeared in the periodical publications. A convenient compilation of the texts has been given by A. Deimel in his *Enuma Eliš* (2nd ed., 1936). This book contains a useful textual apparatus, but it does not altogether eliminate the need for comparison with the basic publications. In recent years, large gaps in Tablet VII have been filled by E. Ebeling in *MAOG*, XII (1939), part 4, and these additions have been supplemented and elucidated by W. von Soden in *ZA*, XLVII (1942), 1-26. The only part that still is largely unknown is Tablet V.

The various studies and translations of this epic are too numerous for a complete survey. The more recent ones include: S. Langdon, *The Babylonian Epic of Creation* (1923); E. Ebeling, *AOT*, 108 ff.; R. Labat, *Le poème babylonien de la création* (1935); and A. Heidel, *The Babylonian Genesis* (1942). For the sake of ready reference, I have retained the line count employed by Labat. Heidel's careful translation could scarcely be overestimated in its usefulness. Except for the portions of Tablet VII, which have appeared since, it constituted the fullest rendering possible at the time of its publication. Attention should also be called to W. von Soden's grammatical study, Der hymnisch-epische Dialekt des Akkadischen, *ZA*, XL-XLI (1932 f.), and to A. L. Oppenheim's notes on Mesopotamian Mythology I, *Orientalia*, XVI (1947), 207-38.

There is as yet no general agreement as regards the date of composition. None of the extant texts antedates the first millennium B.C. On the internal evidence, however, of the context and the linguistic criteria, the majority of the scholars would assign the epic to the Old Babylonian period, i.e. the early part of the second millennium B.C. There does not appear to be any convincing reason against this earlier dating.

The poem is cast in metric form. One seventh-century copy of Tablet IV, for instance, still shows plainly the division of lines into halves, thus bringing out the two beats of each half. Theological, political, and exegetical considerations have led to various changes and additions, but these are readily recognized for the most part thanks to the underlying metric framework.[1] Unfortunately, a translation cannot make use of this type of evidence, however obvious it may be. In general, the successive revisions have marred the poetic effect of the whole. Nevertheless, enough passages have come down intact to bear witness to a genuine literary inspiration in many instances.

Tablet I

When on high the heaven had not been named,

[1] A metric rendering of Tablet I into Dutch has been published by F. M. Th. Böhl in *JEOL*, IX (1944), 145 ff.

Firm ground below had not been called by name,
Naught but primordial Apsu, their begetter,
(And) Mummu[2]-Tiamat, she who bore them all,
Their[3] waters commingling as a single body;
No reed hut[4] had been matted, no marsh land had appeared,
When no gods whatever had been brought into being,
Uncalled by name, their destinies undetermined—
Then it was that the gods were formed within them.[5]
Lahmu and Lahamu were brought forth, by name they were called.
For aeons they grew in age and stature.
Anshar and Kishar were formed, surpassing the others.
They prolonged the days, added on the years.[6]
Anu was their son, of his fathers the rival;
Yea, Anshar's first-born, Anu, was his equal.
Anu begot in his image Nudimmud.[7]
This Nudimmud was of his fathers the master;[8]
Of broad wisdom, understanding, mighty in strength,
Mightier by far than his grandfather, Anshar.
He had no rival among the gods, his brothers.[9]
The divine brothers banded together,
They disturbed Tiamat *as they surged back and forth*,[10]
Yea, they troubled the mood[11] of Tiamat
By their *hilarity*[12] in the Abode of Heaven.
Apsu could not lessen their clamor
And Tiamat was speechless at their [*ways*].
Their doings were loathsome unto [. . .].
Unsavory were their ways; they were *overbearing*.[13]
Then Apsu, the begetter of the great gods,
Cried out, addressing Mummu, his vizier:
"O Mummu, my vizier, who rejoicest my spirit,[14]
Come hither and let us go to Tiamat!"
They went and sat down before Tiamat,
Exchanging counsel about the gods, their first-born.
Apsu, opening his mouth,
Said unto *resplendent*[15] Tiamat:
"Their ways are verily loathsome unto me.
By day I find no relief,[16] nor repose by night.
I will destroy, I will wreck their ways,
That quiet may be restored. Let us have rest!"
As soon as Tiamat heard this,
She was wroth and called out to her husband.
She cried out aggrieved, as she raged all alone,
Injecting woe into her mood:
"What? Should we destroy that which we have built?
Their ways indeed are most troublesome, but let us attend[17] kindly!"
Then answered Mummu, giving counsel to Apsu;
[*Ill-wishing*] and ungracious was Mummu's advice:
"Do destroy, my father, the mutinous ways.
Then shalt thou have relief by day and rest by night!"
When Apsu heard this, his face grew radiant
Because of the evil he planned against the gods, his sons.
As for Mummu, by the neck he embraced him
As (that one) sat down on his knees to kiss him.[18]
(Now) whatever they had plotted between them,
Was repeated unto the gods, their first-born.
When the gods heard (this),[19] they were astir,
(Then) lapsed into silence and remained speechless.
Surpassing in wisdom, accomplished, resourceful,
Ea, the all-wise, saw through their[20] scheme.
A master design against it he devised and set up,
Made artful his spell against it, surpassing and holy.
He recited it and made it subsist in the deep,[21]
As he poured sleep upon him. Sound asleep he lay.[22]
When Apsu he had made prone, drenched with sleep,
Mummu, the adviser,[23] was *impotent to move*.[24]
He loosened his band, tore off his tiara,
Removed his halo[25] (and) put it on himself.[26]
Having fettered Apsu, he slew him.
Mummu he bound and left behind lock.
Having thus upon Apsu established his dwelling,
He laid hold on Mummu, holding him by the nose-rope.
After he had vanquished and trodden down his foes,
Ea, his triumph over his enemies secured,
In his sacred chamber in profound peace he rested.
He named it "Apsu," for shrines he assigned (it).
In that same place his cult hut[27] he founded.

[2] Not to be confused with the vizier Mummu, for grammatical reasons. Perhaps an epithet in the sense of "mother," as has long been suspected. On the various meanings of the term see now A. Heidel in *JNES*, VII (1948), 98-105.

[3] i.e. the fresh waters of Apsū and the marine waters of Tiamat "the sea."

[4] In this epic *gipāru* indicates both the primitive building material—as in this passage; cf. E. Douglas Van Buren, *Orientalia*, XIII (1944), 32—and a cult hut (Tablet I, 77). Both meanings can be reconciled on the basis of W. Andrae's researches into the origin of Mesopotamian shrine architecture; cf. his *Das Gotteshaus und die Urformen des Bauens im alten Orient* (1930). Note, however, that the initial *gi* of this word is not to be confused with Sumerian *gi* "reed."

[5] The waters of Apsū and Tiamat.

[6] i.e. a long time elapsed.

[7] One of the names of Ea, the earth- and water-god.

[8] Reading *ša-liṭ*, with one Ashur text, for *a-lid* "begetter."

[9] Var. "fathers."

[10] Reading *na-muš-šu-nu*, with a number of interpreters. Others read the ambiguous second sign as *-ṣir-*, thus obtaining the sense "assaulted their keeper"; cf. Heidel, *BG*, 9.

[11] Lit. "belly."

[12] cf. W. v. Soden, *ZA*, XLIV (1938), 38.

[13] For the approximate sense cf. A. L. Oppenheim, *Orientalia*, XVI (1947), 210, n. 2.

[14] Lit. "liver."

[15] This translation ignores a minor grammatical difficulty; the alternative "(spoke) with raised voice" (cf. Tablet III, 125) would have to contend with etymological objections.

[16] Not merely "rest," because of the "elative" force of the prefix *š*-, a function as yet ignored in Akkadian grammars.

[17] For this value of *šadādu* cf. Gilg. XII, 32 and the semantic range of the terms listed in Deimel, *ŠL*, 371, 73.

[18] The Akkadian appears ambiguous as to subject and object. It would seem, however, that as Mummu came down to his knees, Apsū embraced him by the neck.

[19] Var. "The gods were in tears."

[20] That of Apsū and Mummu.

[21] Lit. "caused it to be in the waters," viz. those of Apsū.

[22] cf. F. W. Geers, *JNES*, IV (1945), 66.

[23] Reading *tam-la-ku* with Heidel, *BG*, 10, n. 22.

[24] cf. also the suggestion of B. Landsberger, *ZA*, XLI (1933), 222.

[25] Following the interpretation of A. L. Oppenheim, *JAOS*, LXIII (1943), 31 ff.

[26] The rich crop of variant readings which the Akkadian versions furnish for this passage, and the consequent variety of interpretations, appear to be due to the use of an archaic pronominal form (*šu'a*); cf. W. v. Soden, *ZA*, XL (1932), 182.

[27] See above, note 4.

Ea and Damkina,[28] his wife, dwelled (there) in splendor.
In the chamber of fates, the abode of destinies,
A god was engendered, most potent and wisest of gods.
In the heart of Apsu[29] was Marduk[30] created,
In the heart of holy Apsu was Marduk created.
He who begot him was Ea, his father;
She who conceived him was Damkina, his mother.
The breast of goddesses he did suck.[31]
The nurse that nursed him filled him with awesomeness.
Alluring was his figure, sparkling the lift of his eyes.
Lordly was his gait, commanding from of old.
When Ea saw him, the father who begot him,
He exulted and glowed, his heart filled with gladness.
He rendered him perfect[32] and endowed him with a double godhead.[33]
Greatly exalted was he above them, exceeding throughout.
Perfect were his members beyond comprehension,
Unsuited for understanding, difficult to perceive.
Four were his eyes, four were his ears;
When he moved his lips, fire blazed forth.
Large were all four[34] hearing organs,
And the eyes, in like number, scanned all things.
He was the loftiest of the gods, surpassing was his stature;
His members were enormous, he was exceeding tall.
"My little son, my little son![35]
My son, the Sun! Sun of the heavens!"
Clothed with the halo of ten gods, he was strong to the utmost,
As their [awe]some flashes were heaped upon him.
[. . .] the four winds Anu begot
To restrain the griffin, leader of the host.
[. . .] . . . to disturb Tiamat.
Disturbed was Tiamat, astir day and night.
[*The gods*], in malice, *contribute to the storm*.[36]
Their insides having plotted evil,
To Tiamat these brothers[37] said:
"When they slew Apsu, thy consort,
Thou didst not aid him but remainedst still.
Although he fashioned the awesome Saw,[38]
Thy insides are diluted and so we can have no rest.
Let Apsu, thy consort, be in thy mind[39]
And Mummu, who has been vanquished! Thou art left alone!
[. . .] thou pacest about hurriedly,
[. . . without ce]ase. Thou dost not love us!
[. . .] clouded are our eyes,
[. . .] without cease. Let us have rest!
[. . . *to batt*]*le*. Do thou avenge them!
[. . .] and render (them) as the wind!"
[When] Tiamat [heard] (these) words, she was pleased:[40]
"[. . .] you have given. Let us make *monsters*,
[. . .] and the gods in the mid[st . . .].
[. . . let us do] battle and against the gods [. . .]!"
They thronged and marched at the side of Tiamat.
Enraged, they plot without cease night and day,
They are set for combat, growling, raging,
They form a council to prepare for the fight.
Mother Hubur,[41] she who fashions all things,
Added matchless weapons, bore monster-serpents,
Sharp of tooth, unsparing of *fang*.
[With venom] for blood she has filled their bodies.
Roaring dragons she has clothed with terror,
Has crowned them with haloes, making them like gods,
So that he who beholds them shall perish abjectly,
(And) that, with their bodies reared up, none might turn [them back].[42]
She set up the Viper, the Dragon, and the *Sphinx*,
The Great-Lion, the Mad-Dog, and the Scorpion-Man,
Mighty lion-demons, the Dragon-Fly, the Centaur—
Bearing weapons that spare not, fearless in battle.
Firm were her decrees, past withstanding were they.
Withal eleven of this kind she brought [forth].
From among the gods, her first-born, who formed [her Assembly],
She elevated Kingu, made him chief among them.
The leading of the ranks, command of the Assembly,
The raising of weapons for the encounter, advancing to combat,
In battle the command-in-chief—
These[43] to his hand she entrusted as she seated him in the Council:
"I have cast for thee the spell, exalting thee in the Assembly of the gods.
To counsel all the gods I have given thee full power.[44]
Verily, thou art supreme, my only consort art thou!

28 The Assyrian versions substitute here and elsewhere Laḫmu and Laḫāmu for the Babylonian Ea and Damkina; similarly, Anshar-Ashur replaces Marduk.

29 "The Deep."

30 Var. "Ashur" here and in the next line.

31 Var. "she caused him to suck."

32 The technical term *šuteṣbū* refers primarily to the final inspection of their work by craftsmen before it is pronounced ready for use. cf. also Th. Bauer, *Das Inschriftenwerk Assurbanipals* (Leipzig, 1933), II, 84.

33 cf. Oppenheim, *Orientalia*, XVI (1947), 215.

34 The word play of the Akkadian *irbū erbā* cannot readily be reflected.

35 Here we have again a learned word play which is continued in the next line. The Akkadian *ma-ri-ya-u-tu* (for the meaning see J. Lewy, *Orientalia*, XV, 1946, p. 380, n.6) alludes to the Sumerian values (A) MAR.UTU, which constitute the so-called ideogram for Marduk. In turn, "(my) son (of the) Sun" is *mār(i) Utu(k)*, again a word play on Marduk. cf. H. Zimmern, *ZA*, XXXV (1923), 239, and P. Jensen, *ZA*, XXVI (1924), 77-79.

36 Obscure. Another possible rendering is "carry to the wind."

37 Var. "To Tiamat they mentioned trouble."

38 The weapon of the sun-god.

39 Lit. "heart."

40 Reading *i-ṭib* with F. Delitzsch, *AfO*, VI (1930-31), 222.

41 For this term, which in its application to a goddess represents in effect a female counterpart of Ea, cf. I. J. Gelb, *Hurrians and Subarians* (1944), 92 ff. and E. A. Speiser, *JAOS*, LXVIII (1948), 12.

42 Lit. "turn back their breasts." Another possibility is "they will not turn back." For lines 132-139, which recur several times later on, cf. Th. Jacobsen, in *The Intellectual Adventure of Ancient Man* (1946), 175-6. The entire epic is reviewed, and various passages are translated, *ibid.* 172 ff.

43 Rendering in this fashion the particle *-ma*.

44 The literal translation of this idiomatic phrase is "Into thy hand(s) I have charged (filled)."

Thy utterance shall prevail over all the Anunnaki!"
She gave him the Tablets of Fate, fastened on his breast:
"As for thee, thy command shall be unchangeable,
[Thy word] shall endure!"
As soon as Kingu was elevated, possessed of [the rank of Anu],
For the gods, his[45] sons, [they[46] decreed] the fate:
"Your word shall make the fire subside,
Shall humble the 'Power-Weapon,' so potent in (its) *sweep*!"[47]

Tablet II

When Tiamat had thus lent import to her handiwork,
She prepared for battle against the gods, her offspring.
To avenge Apsu, Tiamat wrought evil.
That she was girding for battle, was divulged to Ea.
As soon as Ea heard of this matter,
He lapsed into dark silence and sat right still.
Then, on further thought, his anger subsided,
To Anshar, his (fore)father he betook himself.
When he came before his grandfather, Anshar,
All that Tiamat had plotted to him
he repeated:
"My father, Tiamat, she who bore us, detests us.
She has set up the Assembly[48] and is furious with rage.
All the gods have rallied to her;
Even those whom you brought forth march at her side.
They throng and march at the side of Tiamat,
Enraged, they plot without cease night and day.
They are set for combat, growling, raging,
They have formed a council to prepare for the fight.
Mother Hubur, she who fashions all things,
Has added matchless weapons, has born
monster-serpents,
Sharp of tooth, unsparing of *fang*.
With venom for blood she has filled their bodies.
Roaring dragons she has clothed with terror,
Has crowned them with haloes, making them like gods,
So that he who beholds them shall perish abjectly,
(And) that, with their bodies reared up, none might turn them back.
She has set up the Viper, the Dragon, and the *Sphinx*,
The Great-Lion, the Mad-Dog, and the Scorpion-Man,
Mighty lion-demons, the Dragon-Fly, the Centaur—
Bearing weapons that spare not,
fearless in battle.
Firm are her decrees, past withstanding are they.
Withal eleven of this kind she has brought forth.
From among the gods, her first-born, who formed her Assembly,
She has elevated Kingu, has made him chief among them.
The leading of the ranks, command of the Assembly,
The raising of weapons for the encounter, advancing to combat,
In battle the command-in-chief—
These[49] to his hands [she entrusted] as she seated him in the Council:
'[I have cast the spell] for thee, exalting thee in the Assembly of the gods.
[To counsel all the] gods [I have given thee] full power.[44]
[Verily, thou art supreme, my only consort] art thou!
[Thy utterance shall prevail over all the Anun]naki!'
[She has given him the Tablets of Fate, fastened on his breast]:
'[As for thee, thy command shall be unchangeable],
They word shall endure!'
[As soon as Kingu was elevated], possessed of the rank of Anu,
[For the gods, her[50] sons, they decreed the fate:
'[Your word] shall make the fire subside,
Shall humble the "Power-Weapon," [so potent in (its) *sweep*!]' "
[When Anshar heard that Tiamat] was sorely troubled,
[He smote his loins[51] and] bit his lips.
[Gloomy was his heart], restless his mood.
[He *covered*] his [*mouth*] to stifle his outcry:[52]
"[. . .] battle.
[The weapon thou hast made], up, bear thou!
[*Lo*, Mummu and] Apsu thou didst slay.
[Now, slay thou Kin]gu, who marches before her.
[. . .] wisdom."
[Answered the counselor of] the gods, Nudimmud.

(The reply of Ea-Nudimmud is lost in the break. Apparently, Ea had no remedy, for Anshar next turns to Anu:)

[To Anu,] his son, [a word] he addressed:
"[. . .] this, the most puissant of heroes,
Whose strength [is outstanding], past resisting his onslaught.
[Go] and stand thou up to Tiamat,
That her mood [be calmed], that her heart expand.
[If] she will not hearken to thy word,
Then tell her our [word], that she might be calmed."
When [he heard] the command of his father, Anshar,
[He made straight] for her way, following
the road to her.
[But when Anu was near (enough)] to see the plan of Tiamat,
[He was not able to face her and] he turned back.
[He came abjectly to his father], Anshar.
[*As though he were* Tiamat[53] thus he] addressed him:

45 Var. "her."

46 Tiamat and Kingu.

47 The word play of the original *gašru : magšaru* is difficult to reproduce. For this passage see A. L. Oppenheim, *Orientalia*, XVI (1947), 219. I retain, however, *ḳit-mu-ru* in place of Oppenheim's *šit-mu-ru*.

48 For the all-important place of the *puḫrum* or "assembly" in Mesopotamian society, celestial as well as human, cf. Th. Jacobsen, Primitive Democracy in Mesopotamia, *JNES*, II (1943), 159 ff., and my remarks on Some Sources of Intellectual and Social Progress in the Ancient Near East, *Studies in the History of Culture* (1942), 51 ff. When used in its technical sense, the word has been capitalized in this translation.

49 cf. note 47.

50 Tablet I, 159 has "his."

51 As a sign of distress.

52 cf. Oppenheim, *loc. cit.*, 220, n.1. Note also the intransitive forms of this verb in the *Legend of Zu* (below), A 23, B 52.

53 The suffix *-ḳi* in the next line makes it apparent that the statement addressed to Anshar is an exact quotation of Anu's previous speech to Tiamat. The context bears out this interpretation.

"My hand [suffi]ces not for me to subdue thee."
Speechless was Anshar as he started at the ground,
Frowning and shaking his head at Ea.
All the Anunnaki gathered at that place;
Their lips closed tight, [they sat] in silence.
"No god" (thought they) "can go [to *battle* and],
Facing Tiamat, escape [with his life]."
Lord Anshar, father of the gods, [rose up] in grandeur,
And having pondered in his heart, he [said to the Anunnaki]:
"He whose [strength] is potent shall be [our] avenger,
He who is *keen* in battle, Marduk, the hero!"
Ea called [Marduk] to his place of seclusion.
[Giv]ing counsel, he told him what was in his heart:[54]
"O Marduk, consider my advice. Hearken to thy father,
For thou art my son who comforts his[55] heart.
When facing Anshar, approach as though in combat;
Stand up as thou speakest; seeing thee, he will grow restful."
The lord rejoiced at the word of his father;
He approached and stood up facing Anshar.
When Anshar saw him, his heart filled with joy.
He kissed his lips, his (own) gloom dispelled.
"[Anshar], be not muted; open wide thy lips.
I will go and attain thy heart's desire.
[Anshar], be not muted; open wide thy lips.
I will go and attain thy heart's desire!
What male is it who has pressed his fight against thee?
[*It is but*] Tiamat, a woman, that opposes thee with weapons!
[O my father-]creator, be glad and rejoice;
The neck of Tiamat thou shalt soon tread upon!
[O my father-]creator, be glad and rejoice;
[The neck] of Tiamat thou shalt soon tread upon!"
"My son, (thou) who knowest all wisdom,
Calm [Tiamat] with thy holy spell.
On the storm-ch[ariot] proceed with all speed.
From her [*presence*] they shall not drive (thee)! Turn (*them*) back!"
The lord [*rejoiced*] at the word of his father.
His heart exulting, he said to his father:
"Creator of the gods, destiny of the great gods,
If I indeed, as your avenger,
Am to vanquish Tiamat and save your lives,
Set up the Assembly, proclaim supreme my destiny!
When jointly in Ubshukinna[56] you have sat down rejoicing,
Let my word, instead of you, determine the fates.
Unalterable shall be what I may bring into being;
Neither recalled nor changed shall be the command of my lips."

Tablet III

Anshar opened his mouth and
To Gaga, his vizier, a word he addressed:
"O Gaga, my vizier, who gladdens my spirit,
To Lahmu and Lahamu I will dispatch thee.
Thou knowest discernment, art adept at fine talk;
The gods, thy fathers, produce thou before me!
Let all the gods proceed hither,
Let them hold converse, sit down to a banquet,
Let them eat festive bread, partake of wine;
For Marduk,[57] their avenger, let them fix the decrees.
Be on thy way, Gaga, take the stand before them,
And that which I shall tell thee repeat thou unto them:
'Anshar, your son, has sent me hither,
Charging me to give voice to [the dictates] of his heart,
[Saying]: "Tiamat, she who bore us, detests us.
She has set up the [Assembly] and is furious with rage.
All the gods have rallied to her;
Even those whom you brought forth march at her side.
They throng and march at the side of Tiamat.
Enraged, they plot without cease night and day.
They are set for combat, growling, raging,
They have formed a council to prepare for the fight.
Mother Hubur, she who fashions all things,
Has added matchless weapons, has born monster-serpents,
Sharp of tooth, unsparing of *fang*.
With venom for blood she has filled their bodies.
Roaring dragons she has clothed with terror,
Has crowned them with haloes, making them like gods,
So that he who beholds them shall perish abjectly,
(And) that, with their bodies reared up, none might turn them back.
She has set up the Viper, the Dragon, and the *Sphinx*,
The Great-Lion, the Mad-Dog, and the Scorpion-Man,
Mighty lion-demons, the Dragon-Fly, the Centaur—
Bearing weapons that spare not, fearless in battle.
Firm are her decrees, past withstanding are they.
Withal eleven of this kind she has brought forth.
From among the gods, her first-born, who formed [her Assembly],
She has elevated Kingu, has made [him] chief among them.
The leading of the ranks, [command of the Assembly],
The raising of weapons for the encounter, ad[vancing to combat],
In battle the comm[and]-in-chief—
These to his hands [she entrusted] as she se[ated him in the Council]:
'[I have] cast the spell for thee, [exalting thee] in the Assembly of the gods.
To counsel all the gods [I have given thee full power].
[Verily], thou art supreme, my [only consort art thou]!
Thy utterance shall prevail over all the [Anunnaki]!'
She has given him the Tablets of Fate, [fastened on his] breast:

[54] Reading: [*im*]-*li-ka-ma ak lib-bi-šu i-ta-mi-šu.*
[55] i.e. his father's.
[56] The Assembly Hall.
[57] Var. Ashur.

'As for thee, thy command shall be unchangeable,
Thy word shall endure!'
As soon as Kingu was elevated, possessed of the rank of Anu,
For the gods, her sons, they decreed the fate:
'Your word shall make the fire subside,
Shall humble the "Power-Weapon," so potent in (its) sweep!'
I sent forth Anu; he could not face her.
Nudimmud was afraid and turned back.
Forth came Marduk, the wisest of gods, your son,
His heart having prompted him to set out to face Tiamat.
He opened his mouth, saying unto me:
'If I indeed, as your avenger,
Am to vanquish Tiamat and save your lives,
Set up the Assembly, proclaim supreme my destiny!
When jointly in Ubshukinna you have sat down rejoicing,
Let my word, instead of you, determine the fates.
Unalterable shall be what I may bring into being;
Neither recalled nor changed shall be the command of my lips!'
Now hasten hither and promptly fix for him your decrees,
That he may go forth to face your mighty foe!" ' "
Gaga departed, proceeding on his way.
Before Lahmu and Lahamu, the gods, his fathers,
He made obeisance, kissing the ground at their feet.
He bowed low as he took his place to address them:
"It was Anshar, your son, who has sent me hither,
Charging me to give voice to the dictates of his heart,
Saying: 'Tiamat, she who bore us, detests us.
She has set up the Assembly and is furious with rage.
All the gods have rallied to her,
Even those whom you brought forth march at her side.
They throng and march at the side of Tiamat.
Enraged, they plot without cease night and day.
They are set for combat, growling, raging,
They have formed a council to prepare for the fight.
Mother Hubur, she who fashions all things,
Has added matchless weapons, has born monster-serpents,
Sharp of tooth, unsparing of *fang*.
With venom for blood she has filled their bodies,
Roaring dragons she has clothed with terror,
Has crowned them with haloes, making them like gods,
So that he who beholds them shall perish abjectly,
(And) that, with their bodies reared up, none might turn them back.
She has set up vipers,[58] dragons, and *sphinxes*,
Great-lions, mad-dogs, and scorpion-men,
Mighty lion-demons, dragon-flies, and centaurs—
Bearing weapons that spare not, fearless in battle.
Firm are decrees, past withstanding are they.
Withal eleven of this kind she has brought forth.
From among the gods, her first-born, who formed her Assembly,
She has elevated Kingu, has made him chief among them.
The leading of the ranks, command of the Assembly,
The raising of weapons for the encounter, advancing to combat,
In battle the command-in-chief—
These to his hands she has entrusted as she seated him in the Council:
'I have cast the spell for thee, exalting thee in the Assembly of the gods.
To counsel all the gods I have given thee full power.
Verily, thou art supreme, my only consort art thou!
Thy utterance shall prevail over all the Anunnaki!'
She has given him the Tablets of Fate, [fastened on his breast]:
'As for thee, thy command shall be un[changeable,
Thy word shall endure]!'
As soon as Kingu was elevated, [possessed of the rank of Anu],
For the gods, her sons, [they decreed the fate]:
'Your word shall make the fire subside,
[Shall humble the "Power-]Weapon," so potent in (its) *sweep*!'
I sent forth Anu; he could not [face her].
Nudimmud was afraid [and turned back].
Forth came Marduk, the wisest [of gods, your son],
[His heart having prompted him to set out] to face Tiamat.
He opened his mouth, [saying unto me]:
'If I indeed, [as your avenger],
Am to vanquish Tiamat [and save your lives],
Set up the Assembly, [proclaim supreme my destiny]!
When in Ubshukinna [jointly you sit down rejoicing],
Let my word, instead of [you, determine the fates].
Unalterable shall be what [I] may bring into being;
Neither recalled nor changed shall be the command [of my lips]!'
Now hasten hither and promptly [fix for him] your decrees,
That he may go forth to face your mighty foe!"
When Lahmu and Lahamu heard this, they cried out aloud,
All the Igigi[59] wailed in distress:
"How strange[60] that they should have made [this] decision!
We cannot fathom the doings of Tiamat!"
They made ready[61] to leave on their journey,
All the great gods who decree the fates.
They entered before Anshar, filling [Ubshukinna].
They kissed one another in the Assembly.

[58] In view of the plurals in this passage (one text, however, retains the singulars), the names of the monsters are this time given in lower case.

[59] The heavenly deities.

[60] Lit. "What has turned strange?"

[61] cf. Oppenheim, *Orientalia*, XVI (1947), 223.

They held converse as they [sat down] to the banquet.
They ate festive bread, partook of [the wine],
They wetted their drinking-tubes[62] with sweet intoxicant.
As they drank the strong drink, [their] bodies swelled.
They became very languid as their spirits rose.
For Marduk, their avenger, they fixed the decrees.

Tablet IV

They erected for him a princely throne.
Facing his fathers, he sat down, presiding.[63]
"Thou art the most honored of the great gods,
Thy decree is unrivaled, thy command is Anu.[64]
Thou, Marduk, art the most honored of the great gods,
Thy decree is unrivaled, thy word is Anu.
From this day unchangeable shall be thy pronouncement.
To raise or bring low—these shall be (in) thy hand.
Thy utterance shall come true, thy command shall not be doubted.
No one among the gods shall transgress thy bounds!
Adornment being wanted for the seats of the gods,
Let the place of their shrines ever be in thy place.
O Marduk, thou art indeed our avenger.
We have granted thee kingship over the universe entire.
When in Assembly thou sittest, thy word shall be supreme.
Thy weapons shall not fail; they shall smash thy foes!
O lord, spare the life of him who trusts thee,
But pour out the life of the god who seized evil."
Having placed in their midst a piece of cloth,
They addressed themselves to Marduk, their first-born:
"Lord, truly thy decree is first among gods.
Say but to wreck or create; it shall be.
Open thy mouth: the cloth will vanish!
Speak again, and the cloth shall be whole!"
At the word of his mouth the cloth vanished.
He spoke again, and the cloth was restored.
When the gods, his fathers, saw the fruit of his word,[65]
Joyfully they did homage: "Marduk is king!"
They conferred on him scepter, throne, and palū;
They gave him matchless weapons that ward off the foes:
"Go and cut off the life of Tiamat.
May the winds bear her blood to places undisclosed."
Bel's destiny thus fixed, the gods, his fathers,
Caused him to go the way of success and attainment.
He constructed a bow, marked it as his weapon,
Attached thereto the arrow, fixed its bow-cord.
He raised the mace, made his right hand grasp it;
Bow and quiver he hung at his side.
In front of him he set the lightning,
With a blazing flame he filled his body.
He then made a net to enfold Tiamat therein.
The four winds he stationed that nothing of her might escape,
The South Wind, the North Wind, the East Wind, the West Wind.
Close to his side he held the net, the gift of his father, Anu.
He brought forth Imhullu "the Evil Wind," the Whirlwind, the Hurricane,
The Fourfold Wind, the Sevenfold Wind, the Cyclone, the Matchless Wind;
Then he sent forth the winds he had brought forth, the seven of them.
To stir up the inside of Tiamat they rose up behind him.
Then the lord raised up the flood-storm, his mighty weapon.
He mounted the storm-chariot irresistible [and] terrifying.
He harnessed (and) yoked to it a team-of-four,
The Killer, the Relentless, the Trampler, the Swift.
Sharp were their teeth, bearing poison.
They were versed in ravage, in destruction skilled.
[.] . . they smote, they were fearsome in battle.
To the left or [the right] *they will not open* [.] . .[66]
For a cloak he was wrapped in [an armor] of terror;[67]
With his fearsome halo his head was turbaned.
The lord went forth and followed his course,
Towards the raging Tiamat he set his face.
In his lips he held [*a* . . .] of red paste;[68]
A plant to put out poison was grasped in his hand.
Then they milled about him, the gods milled about him,
The gods, his fathers, milled about him, the gods milled about him.
The lord approached to scan the inside of Tiamat,
(And) of Kingu, her consort, the scheme to perceive.
As he looks on, his course becomes upset,
His will is distracted and his doings are confused.
And when the gods, his helpers, who marched at his side,
Saw the valiant hero, blurred became their vision.
Tiamat emitted [a cry],[69] without turning her neck,
Framing[70] savage[71] defiance in her lips:[72]
"Too [imp]ortant art thou [for][73] the lord of the gods to rise up against thee!

[62] The term *rāṭum* "tube, pipe" refers here obviously to the drinking-tubes which are pictured commonly in representations of banquets.

[63] Lit. "for advising."

[64] i.e. it has the authority of the sky-god Anu.

[65] Lit. "outcome of his mouth."

[66] The text reads: [*l*] *a-a i-pat-tu* [.]*-en-d*[*i*]?, probably some idiom analogous to *purīdā petū* "to open the legs." Perhaps "swerve," but the syntax would be far from flawless.

[67] The assonance of the original, viz. *naḫlapti* [*apluḫti*] *pulḫāti ḫalipma* cannot be reproduced.

[68] Red being the magic color for warding off evil influence.

[69] cf. E. Weidner, *AfO*, III (1926), 123 for the reading [*rigm*]*a*, although [*tāš*]*a* "her incantation" is not impossible. For lines 64-83 see the fragment published by Weidner, *ibid*., 122-24.

[70] For a close semantic parallel cf. *Judg*. 12:6.

[71] To give *lullū* the same sense as in Tablet VI, 6-7, and Gilg. I, iv 7.

[72] Tiamat's taunt, as recorded in the next two lines, is not transparently clear.

[73] Reading [*ḳa*]*b-ta-t*[*a a?-n*]*a ša*, cf. *CT*, XIII, 17; the third sign does not appear to be adequately reproduced in Deimel, *Enuma Eliš*, 17, and the fifth sign cannot be read *šu* (for [*n*]*a*) as is done by Labat, *PBC*, 128.

Is it in their place that they have gathered, (or) in thy place?"
Thereupon the lord, having [raised] the flood-storm, his mighty weapon,
[To] enraged [Tiamat] he sent word as follows:
"[*Mightily*] art thou risen,[74] art haughtily exalted;
[Thou hast] charged thine own heart to stir up conflict,
[So that] sons reject their own fathers,
[And thou], who hast born them, dost hate . . [.]!
Thou hast aggrandized Kingu to be (thy) consort;
[A rule], not rightfully his,[75] thou hast substituted for the rule of Anu.
Against Anshar, king of the gods, thou seekest evil;
[Against] the gods, my fathers, thou hast confirmed thy wickedness.
[Though] drawn up be thy forces, girded on thy weapons,
Stand thou up, that I and thou meet in single combat!"
When Tiamat heard this,
She was like one possessed; she took leave of her senses.
In fury Tiamat cried out aloud.
To the roots her legs shook both together.[76]
She recites a charm, keeps casting her spell,
While the gods of battle sharpen their weapons.
Then joined issue Tiamat and Marduk, wisest of gods.
They *swayed*[77] in single combat, locked in battle.
The lord spread out his net to enfold her,
The Evil Wind, which followed behind, he let loose in her face.
When Tiamat opened her mouth to consume him,
He drove in the Evil Wind that she close not her lips.
As the fierce winds charged her belly,
Her body was distended[78] and her mouth was wide open.
He released the arrow, it tore her belly,
It cut through her insides, splitting the heart.
Having thus subdued her, he extinguished her life.
He cast down her carcass to stand upon it.
After he had slain Tiamat, the leader,
Her band was shattered, her troupe broken up;
And the gods, her helpers who marched at her side,
Trembling with terror, turned their backs about,
In order to save and preserve their lives.
Tightly encircled, they could not escape.
He made them captives and he smashed their weapons.
Thrown into the net, they found themselves ensnared;
Placed in cells, they were filled with wailing;
Bearing his wrath, they were held imprisoned.

[74] For lines 77-83 important additions are supplied by the Weidner fragment, for which cf. n.69.

[75] Weidner's fragment has *-ya* "mine"; this is an obvious slip. It has commonly been corrected to *-ḳi* "thine." Since, however, it is Kingu who is said to have received the authority of Anu (Tablet I, 158; II, 45; III, 49, 107), the required suffix is *-šu* "his."

[76] For *malmališ* cf. J. Lewy, *Orientalia*, XI (1942), 336, n.1; H. G. Güterbock, *AfO*, XIII (1939), 48.

[77] Reading *id-lu-bu*, with Heidel, *BG*, 30, n.84, but translating the verb in the sense established by B. Landsberger, in *ZA*, XLI (1933), 221 f.

[78] cf. Heidel, *BG*, 30, n.85.

And the eleven creatures which she had charged with awe,
The band of demons that marched . [. .] before her,
He cast into fetters, their hands [. . .].
For all their resistance, he trampled (them) underfoot.
And Kingu, who had been made chief among them,
He bound and accounted him to Uggae.[79]
He took from him the Tablets of Fate, not rightfully his,
Sealed (them) with a seal[80] and fastened (them) on his breast.
When he had vanquished and subdued his adversaries,
Had wholly established Anshar's triumph over the foe,
Had . . . the vainglorious foe,
Nudimmud's desire had achieved, valiant Marduk
Strengthened his hold on the vanquished gods,
And turned back to Tiamat whom he had bound.
The lord trod on the legs of Tiamat,
With his unsparing mace he crushed her skull.
When the arteries of her blood he had severed,
The North Wind bore (it) to places undisclosed.
On seeing this, his fathers were joyful and jubilant,
They brought gifts of homage, they to him.
Then the lord paused to view her dead body,
That he might divide the monster and do artful works.
He split her like a shellfish into two parts:
Half of her he set up and ceiled it as sky,
Pulled down the bar and posted guards.
He bade them to allow not her waters to escape.
He crossed the heavens and surveyed (its) regions.
He squared Apsu's quarter,[81] the abode of Nudimmud,
As the lord measured the dimensions of Apsu.
The Great Abode, its likeness, he fixed as Esharra,
The Great Abode, Esharra, which he made as the firmament.
Anu, Enlil, and Ea he made occupy their places.

Tablet V

He constructed stations for the great gods,
Fixing their astral likenesses as constellations.
He determined the year by designating the zones:
He set up three constellations for each of the twelve months.
After defining the days of the year [by means] of (heavenly) figures,
He founded the station of Nebiru[82] to determine their (heavenly) bands,
That none might transgress or fall short.
Alongside it he set up the stations of Enlil and Ea.
Having opened up the gates on both sides,
He strengthened the locks to the left and the right.

[79] God of death.

[80] This was an essential act of attestation in Mesopotamian society.

[81] For this rendering cf. A. Schott, *ZA*, XLII (1934), 137.

[82] i.e. the planet Jupiter. This station was taken to lie between the band (*riḳsu*; cf. I. 6) of the north, which belonged to Enlil, and the band of the south, which belonged to Ea.

In her[83] belly he established the zenith.
The Moon he caused to shine, the night (to him) entrusting.
He appointed him a creature of the night to signify the days:
"Monthly, without cease, form designs with a crown.
At the month's very start, rising over the land,
Thou shalt have luminous horns to signify six days.
On the seventh day be thou a [half]-crown.
At full moon[84] stand in opposition[85] in mid-month.
When the sun [overtakes] thee at the base of heaven,
Diminish [thy crown] and retrogress in light.
[At the time of disappearance] approach thou the course of the sun,
And [on the twenty-ninth] thou shalt again stand in opposition to the sun."

(The remainder of this tablet is broken away or too fragmentary for translation.)

Tablet VI

When Marduk hears the words of the gods,
His heart prompts (him) to fashion artful works.
Opening his mouth, he addresses Ea
To impart the plan he had conceived in his heart:
"Blood I will mass and cause bones to be.
I will establish a savage,[86] 'man' shall be his name.
Verily, savage-man I will create.
He shall be charged with the service of the gods
That they might be at ease!
The ways of the gods I will artfully alter.
Though alike revered, into two (groups) they shall be divided."
Ea answered him, speaking a word to him,
To relate to him a scheme for the relief of the gods:
"Let but one of their brothers be handed over;
He alone shall perish that mankind may be fashioned.[87]
Let the great gods be here in Assembly,
Let the guilty be handed over that they may endure."
Marduk summoned the great gods to Assembly;
Presiding[88] graciously, he issued instructions.
To his utterance the gods pay heed.[89]
The king addresses a word to the Anunnaki:
"If your former statement was true,
Do (now) the truth on oath by me declare![90]
Who was it that contrived the uprising,
And made Tiamat rebel, and joined battle?
Let him be handed over who contrived the uprising.
His guilt I will make him bear that you may dwell in peace!"
The Igigi, the great gods, replied to him,
To Lugaldimmerankia,[91] counselor of the gods, their lord:[92]
"It was Kingu who contrived the uprising,
And made Tiamat rebel, and joined battle."
They bound him, holding him before Ea.
They imposed on him his guilt and severed his blood (vessels).
Out of his blood they fashioned mankind.
He[93] imposed the service and let free the gods.
After Ea, the wise, had created mankind,
Had imposed upon it the service of the gods—
That work was beyond comprehension;
As artfully planned by Marduk, did Nudimmud create it—
Marduk, the king of the gods divided
All the Anunnaki above and below.[94]
He assigned (them) to Anu to guard his instructions.
Three hundred in the heavens he stationed as a guard.
In like manner the ways of the earth he defined.
In heaven and on earth six hundred (thus) he settled.
After he had ordered all the instructions,
To the Anunnaki of heaven and earth had allotted their portions,
The Anunnaki opened their mouths
And said to Marduk, their lord:
"Now,[95] O lord, thou who hast caused our deliverance,
What shall be our homage to thee?
Let us build a shrine whose name shall be called
'Lo, a chamber for our nightly rest'; let us repose in it!
Let us build a shrine, a recess for his abode![96]
On the day that we arrive[97] we shall repose in it."
When Marduk heard this,
Brightly glowed his features, like the day:
"Like that of *lofty* Babylon, whose building you have requested,
Let its brickwork be fashioned. You shall name it[98] 'The Sanctuary.'"
The Anunnaki applied the implement;
For one whole year they molded bricks.
When the second year arrived,

[83] Tiamat's.

[84] Akkadian *šapattu*, the prototype of the "Sabbath" in so far as the injunctions against all types of activity are concerned.

[85] i.e. with regard to the sun. This verb was a technical term in Babylonian astronomy.

[86] For this value of the term, probably a derivative of the ethnic name *Lullu*, cf. B. Landsberger, *Kleinasiatische Forschungen*, I (1929), 321-334 and *MAOG*, IV (1928), 320, n. 2; also E. A. Speiser, *Mesopotamian Origins* (1930), 95, n. 35. That the Lullu were linked by Akkadian sources with the remote and dim past may be gathered from the evidence which I listed in *JAOS*, LXVIII (1948), 8, as well as from the fact that the flood ship (Gilg., XI, 140) lands on Mount Nisir, in Lullu country.

[87] Out of his blood.

[88] Lit. "ordering."

[89] Reading *u-paq-qu-uš*! (var. *-šu*!), with W. von Soden, *ZA*, XLVII (1942), 3. Von Soden's notes on the remainder of Tablet VI and on Tablet VII, together with his translation of the hitherto unknown or obscure parts of Tablet VII—based on new fragments and on corrected readings of the text published by E. Ebeling in *MAOG*, XII (1939), part 4—(see *loc. cit.*, 1-26) have proved very illuminating, as may be seen from the numerous references below.

[90] cf. Oppenheim, *Orientalia*, XVI (1947), 234.

[91] "The king of the gods of heaven and earth."

[92] For lines 28-50 see the fragment published by E. Weidner in *AfO*, XI (1936) 72-74. This material was not available to Labat; von Soden's additions (cf. note 89) came too late to be utilized by Heidel.

[93] Ea.

[94] Here and elsewhere in this epic the Anunnaki are understood to be the celestial gods (normally Igigi) as well as those of the lower regions.

[95] Not "O Nannar," as translated by some. For this rebus writing signifying *inanna* "now" cf. *AfO*, XI (1936), 73.

[96] Reading *a-šar!-šu*, with v. Soden, *loc. cit.*, 4.

[97] For the New Year's festival.

[98] For this and the preceding line cf. v. Soden, *loc. cit.*

They raised high the head[99] of Esagila equaling Apsu.[100]
Having built a stage-tower *as high as* Apsu,
They set up *in it* an abode for Marduk, Enlil, (and) Ea.
In their presence he *adorned* (it) in grandeur.[101]
To the base of Esharra[102] its horns look down.
After they had achieved the building of Esagila,
The Anunnaki *themselves* erected their shrines.
[. . .] all of them gathered,
[. . .] they had built as his dwelling.
The gods, his fathers, at his banquet[103] he seated:
"This is Babylon, the place that is your home![104]
Make merry in its precincts, occupy its broad [places]."[105]
The great gods took their seats,
They set up festive drink, sat down to a banquet.
After they had made merry within it,
In Esagila, the *splendid*, had performed their rites,[106]
The norms had been fixed (and) *all* [their] portents,
All the gods apportioned the stations of heaven and earth.[107]
The fifty great gods took their seats.
The seven gods of destiny set up the three hundred [in heaven].[108]
Enlil raised the bo[w, his wea]pon,[109] and laid (it) before them.
The gods, his fathers, saw the net he had made.
When they beheld the bow, how skillful its shape,
His fathers praised the work he had wrought.
Raising (it), Anu spoke up in the Assembly of the gods,
As he kissed the bow: "This [. . .]."
He named the names of the bow as follows:
"Longwood is the first, the second is [. . .];
Its third name is Bow-Star, in heaven [. . .]."
He fixed its place [. . .].
After he had [decreed] the destinies of [. . .],
He set up a throne [. . .];
Another in [. . .].

(Lines 95-105 are too fragmentary for translation. Labat's assumed line 98 is to be deleted, following von Soden, *ZA*, XL (1932), 169. For convenience, however, Labat's numbering of the subsequent lines has been retained.)

"Verily, most exalted is the son [. . .].
His sovereignty is surpassing [. . .].
May he shepherd the black-headed ones[110] [. . .].
To the end of days, without forgetting, they shall proclaim [. . .].
May he establish for his fathers the great food-offerings;
Their support they shall furnish, shall tend their sanctuaries.
May he cause incense to be smelled, . . [.] their spells,
A likeness on earth of what he has wrought in heaven.
May he order the black-headed to *re*[*vere him*],
May the subjects ever bear in mind their god,
And may they at his word pay heed[111] to the goddess.
May food-offerings be borne (*for*) their gods and goddesses.
Without forgetting let them support their gods!
Their lands let them improve, build their shrines,
Let the black-headed wait on their gods.
As for us, by however many names we call him, he is our god!
Let us then proclaim his fifty names:[112]
"He whose ways are glorious, whose deeds are likewise,
(1) Marduk, as Anu, his father,[113] called him from his birth;[114]
Who provides grazing and drinking places, enriches their stalls,
Who with the flood-storm, his weapon, vanquished the detractors,
(And) who the gods, his fathers, rescued from distress.
Truly, the Son of the Sun,[115] most radiant of gods is he.
In his brilliant light may they walk forever!
On the people he brought forth, endowed with *li*[*fe*],
The service of the gods he imposed that these may have ease.
Creation, destruction, deliverance, grace—
Shall be by his command.[116] They shall look up to him!
(2) Marukka verily is the god, creator of all,
Who gladdens the heart of the Anunnaki, appeases their [*spirits*].
(3) Marutukku verily is the refuge of the land, *pro*-[*tection of its people*].
Unto him shall the people give praise.
(4) Barashakushu[117] stood up and took hold of its[118] reins;
Wide is his heart, warm his sympathy.
(5) Lugaldimmerankia is his name which we proclaimed in our Assembly.
His commands we have exalted above the gods, his fathers.
Verily, he is lord of all the gods of heaven and earth,
The king at whose discipline the gods above and below are in terror.[119]

99 A play on the sense of Sumerian "Esagila."

100 Meaning apparently that the height of Esagila corresponded to the depth of Apsû's waters.

101 cf. v. Soden, *loc. cit.*

102 *ibid.*

103 *ibid.*

104 Var. "which you love," a virtual homonym of "your home" in Akkadian.

105 v. Soden, *loc. cit.*, 6.

106 *ibid.*

107 *ibid.*

108 *ibid.*

109 *ibid.*

110 A common Akkadian metaphor for "the human race." In the preceding line the term *enūtu* has been taken to reflect the primary sense of Sumerian e n "lord" rather than "high priest."

111 Reading *i-piq-qu*, with v. Soden, *loc. cit.*, 6.

112 A penetrating discussion of these names has been furnished by F. M. Th. Böhl in *AfO*, XI (1936), 191-218. The text etymologizes the names in a manner made familiar by the Bible; the etymologies, which accompany virtually every name on the long list are meant to be cabalistic and symbolic rather than strictly linguistic, although some of them happen to be linguistically sound. The name count has in each case been indicated in parentheses.

113 Here and elsewhere "father" is used for "grandfather" or "ancestor."

114 Lit. "emergence."

115 cf. Tablet I, 101-02.

116 Reading *bal-ši-ma* in this line and *a-bal-tu* in the line above, with v. Soden, *loc. cit.*, 7. For *nannû* "command" see *ZA*, XLIV (1938), 42.

117 Var. Shudunshakushe.

118 i.e. those of the land.

119 For the remainder of this tablet cf. the new fragment published by E. Ebeling in *MAOG*, XII (1939), part 4 and the remarks of W. v. Soden in *ZA*, XLVII (1942), 7-8.

(6) NARI-LUGALDIMMERANKIA is the name of him
Whom we have called the monitor[120] of the gods;
Who in heaven and on earth founds for us retreats[121] in trouble,
And who allots stations to the Igigi and Anunnaki.
At his name the gods shall tremble and quake in retreat.
(7) ASARULUDU is that name of his
Which Anu, his father, proclaimed for him.
He is truly the light of the gods, the mighty leader,
Who, as the protecting deities[122] of gods and land,
In fierce single combat saved our retreats in distress.
Asaruludu, secondly, they have named (8) NAMTILLAKU,
The god who maintains life,[123]
Who restored the lost gods, as though his own creation;
The lord who revives the dead gods by his pure incantation,
Who destroys the wayward foes. Let us praise his prowess![124]
Asaruludu, whose name was thirdly called (9) NAMRU,
The shining god who illumines our ways."
Three each of his names[125] have Anshar, Lahmu, and Lahamu proclaimed;
Unto the gods, their sons, they did utter them:
"We have proclaimed three each of his names.
Like us, do you utter his names!"
Joyfully the gods did heed their command,
As in Ubshukinna their exchanged counsels:
"Of the heroic son, our avenger,
Of our supporter we will exalt the name!"
They sat down in their Assembly to fashion[126] destinies,
All of them uttering his names in the sanctuary.

Tablet VII

(10) ASARU, bestower of cultivation, who established *seed-land*;
Creator of grain and herbs, who causes [vegetation to sprout].[127]
(11) ASARUALIM, who is honored in the place of counsel, [who excels in counsel];
To whom the gods hope,[128] when pos[sessed of fear].
(12) ASARUALIMNUNNA, the gracious, light of [the father, his begetter],
Who directs the decrees of Anu, Enlil, [and Ea].
He is their provider who assigns [their *portions*],
Who mul[tiplies] their spears[129] in abundance.
(13) TUTU [is he], who effects their restoration.
Let him purify their shrines that they [may have ease].
Let him devise the spell that the gods may be [at rest].
Should they rise in anger, let him turn [them back].
Verily, he is supreme in the Assembly of the gods;
No one among the gods is his eq[ual].
Tutu is (14) ZIUKKINNA, life of the host of [the gods],
Who established[130] for the gods the holy heavens;
Who keeps a hold on their ways, determines [their *courses*];
He shall not be forgotten by the beclouded.[131] Let them [remember][132] his deeds!
Tutu they thirdly called (15) ZIKU, who establishes holiness,
The god of the benign breath, the lord who hearkens and acceeds;
Who produces riches and treasures, establishes abundance;[133]
Who has turned all our wants to plenty;
Whose benign breath we smelled in sore distress.
Let them speak, let them exalt, let them sing his praises!
Tutu, fourthly, let the people magnify as (16) AGAKU,
The lord of the holy charm, who revives the dead;
Who had mercy on the vanquished gods,
Who removed the yoke imposed on the gods, his enemies,
(And) who, to redeem them, created mankind;
The merciful, in whose power it lies to grant life.
May his words endure, not to be forgotten,
In the mouth of the black-headed, whom his hands have created.
Tutu, fifthly, is (17) TUKU, whose holy spell their mouths shall murmur;
Who with his holy charm has uprooted all the evil ones.
(18) SHAZU, who knows the heart of the gods,
Who examines the inside;
From whom the evildoer cannot escape;
Who sets up the Assembly of the gods, gladdens their hearts;
Who subdues the insubmissive; their wide-spread [pro]tection;
Who directs justice, roots [out] crooked talk,
Who wrong and right in his place keeps apart.
Shazu may they, secondly, exalt as (19) ZISI,
Who silences the insurgent;
Who banishes consternation from the body of the gods, his fathers.[134]
Shazu is, thirdly, (20) SUHRIM, who with the weapon roots out all enemies,
Who frustrates their plans, scatters (them) to the winds;
Who blots out all the wicked ones who *tremble* before him.

[120] This verse confirms the equation of *ašir* with Sumerian nari made by S. N. Kramer, *BASOR*, 79 (1940), 25, n. 25. The meaning "monitor" for this form and "admonition, instruction" for *aširtu* would seem to fit all known instances.

[121] Lit. "seats."

[122] The *šēdu* and *lamassu*.

[123] v. Soden, *loc. cit.*, 7.

[124] *ibid.*

[125] *ibid.* The reading III-ÁM on a new fragment brings the numbers into agreement with the actual enumeration and eliminates the discrepancies entailed in previous mistaken readings.

[126] Var. "proclaim."

[127] The restoration at the end of the lines are based on the ancient commentaries to *Enūma eliš*; cf. King, *STC*, I, 158 ff. and II, li ff.

[128] Lit. "wait."

[129] v. Soden, *loc. cit.*

[130] Akk. *uḳinnu*, a word play on the -UKKINNA of the name.

[131] Another metaphor for "mankind."

[132] Supplying [*li-ḳil-la*], with v. Soden, *loc. cit.*, 8-9.

[133] For lines 21-45 cf. A. Falkenstein, *Literarische Keilschrifttexte aus Uruḳ* (1931), No. 38, obv.

[134] Lines 43-130, most of them hitherto wanting or scarcely intelligible, have been translated by v. Soden in *ZA*, XLVII (1942), 10-17.

Let the gods exult, let them . . [.]!
Shazu is, fourthly, (21) SUHGURIM, who insures[135] a hearing,
Creator of the gods, his fathers,
Who roots out the enemies, destroys their progeny;
Who frustrates their doings, leaving nothing of them.
May his name be uttered and spoken
in the land!
Shazu, fifthly, they shall praise as (22) ZAHRIM, *the lord of the living*,
Who destroys all adversaries, who recompenses good and evil;
Who all the fugitive gods brought home to their shrines.
May this his name endure!
To Shazu, moreover, they shall, sixthly render all honor as (23) ZAHGURIM,
Who all the foes destroyed as though in battle.
(24) ENBILULU, the lord who makes them flourish, is he;
The mighty one who named them, who instituted roast-offerings;
Who ever regulates for the land the grazing and watering places;
Who opened the wells, apportioning waters
of *abundance*.
Enbilulu, secondly, they shall glorify as (25) EPADUN,
The lord who sprinkles the *field*,
Irrigator[136] of heaven and earth, who establishes seed-rows,
Who plow land and *grazing land*,
Dam and ditch regulates, who delimits the furrow;
Enbilulu, thirdly, they shall praise as (26) ENBILULU-GUGAL,
The irrigator of the plantations of the gods;
Lord of abundance, opulence, *and* of ample crops,
Who provides wealth, enriches all dwellings,
Who furnishes millet, causes barley to appear.
Enbilulu is (27) HEGAL, who heaps up abundance for the people's consumption;[137]
Who causes rich rains over the wide earth, provides vegetation.
(28) SIR.SIR,[137a] who heaped up a mountain over *her*,
Tiamat,
Who the corpse of Tiamat carried off with *his* weapon;
Who directs the land—their faithful shepherd;
Whose . . . means cultivation, whose spear means furrows;
Who the wide-spreading Tiamat vaulted in his wrath,
Crossing (her) like a bridge at the place of single combat.
Sirsir, secondly, they named (29) MALAH—and so forth—[138]
Tiamat is his vessel and he the rider.
(30) GIL, who stores up grain heaps—massive mounds—
Who brings forth barley and millet, furnishes the seed of the land.
(31) GILMA, who makes lasting the lofty abode
of the gods,
Creator of permanence,
The hoop that holds the . . . together, who presents good things.
(32) AGILMA, the exalted one, who tears off the crown [. . .],
Who creates the clouds above the waters, makes enduring [the *heavens*].
(33) ZULUM, who designates the fields [. . .],
Who grants portions and food-offerings, tends [the . . .].
(34) MUMMU, creator of heaven and earth, who directs [. . .].
The god who sanctifies heaven and earth is, secondly, (35) ZULUMMAR,
Whom no other among the gods can match in strength.
(35) GISHNUMUNAB, creator of all people, who made the (world) regions,
Destroyer of the gods of Tiamat; who made men
out of their substance.
(36) LUGALABDUBUR, the king who frustrated the work of Tiamat,
Rooted out her weapons;
Whose foundation is firm in front and in the rear.
(37) PAGALGUENNA, the foremost of all the lords, whose strength is outstanding;
Who is pre-eminent among the gods, his brothers, master of them all.
(38) LUGALDURMAH, the king, band of the gods, lord of the Durmah,[139]
Who is pre-eminent in the abode of the gods, most exalted of the gods.
(39) ARANUNNA, counselor of Ea, creator of the gods, his fathers,
Whose princely ways no god whatever can equal.
(40) DUMUDUKU, whose pure dwelling is renewed in Duku;[140]
Dumuduku, without whom Lugalkuduga
makes no decision.
(41) LUGALANNA, the king whose strength is outstanding among the gods,
The lord, strength of Anu, who became supreme *at the call*[141] of Anshar.
(42) LUGALUGGA, who carried off all of them amidst the struggle,[142]
Who all wisdom encompasses, broad in perception.

135 Lit. "sets up."

136 This meaning of *gugallu* fails to come through in v. Soden's rendering as "Walter." Attention may be called to my translation in *AASOR*, XVI (1936), 95. The term starts out with the value of "inspector of canals" and is thence transferred to the weather-gods (Adad; cf. Ennuge in Gilg., XI, 6). Eventually it comes to be applied to gods of vegetation and fertility, but in most contexts, including the present, the original connection is still apparent. cf. Th. Jacobsen, *JNES*, v (1946), 130.

137 v. Soden, *loc. cit.*, 20-21.

137a I owe this reading to a personal communication from Prof. Landsberger. A significant parallel passage (King, *STC*, II, lxiii, 16,) reads dSIR.SIR *šá pi-ti-iq šadî*i for the *šá-pi-iḳ š*. of our passage, hence perhaps "who is a mountain structure (with the Sea above it)."

138 For this odd phrase in the present context see v. Soden, *loc. cit.*, 21.

139 "Lofty Abode." The phrase "Lord of the Durmaḫ" merely reflects the full name.

140 "Pure Dwelling," a sacred chamber in the Temple at Babylon.

141 v. Soden, *loc. cit.*, 22.

142 cf. A. Goetze, *Analecta Orientalia*, XII (1935), 184 ff.

(43) IRKINGU, who carried off Kingu in the *thick*[143] of the battle,
Who conveys guidance for all, establishes rulership.
(44) KINMA, who directs all the gods, the giver of counsel,
At whose name the gods quake in fear, as at the storm.
(45) ESIZKUR shall sit aloft in the house of prayer;
May the gods bring their presents before him,
That (from him) they may receive their assignments;
None can without him create artful works.
Four black-headed ones are in his measurements;[144]
Aside from him no god *knows* the answer as to their days.
(46) GIBIL, who maintains the *sharp point* of the weapon,
Who wrought artful works in the battle with Tiamat;
Who has broad wisdom, is accomplished in insight,
Whose mind[145] is so vast that the gods, all of them, cannot fathom (it).
(47) ADDU be his name, the whole sky may he *occupy*.
May his beneficent roar be *heavy* over the earth;
May he, as Mummu,[146] diminish the clouds;[147]
Below, for the people may he furnish sustenance.
(48) ASHARU, who, as is his name, guided[148] the gods of destiny;
[. .] . of all the gods is verily in his charge.
(49) NEBIRU shall hold the crossings of heaven and earth;
Those who failed of crossing above and below,
Ever of him shall inquire.
Nebiru is the star[149] which in the skies is brilliant.
Verily, he governs their turnings,[150] to him indeed they look,
Saying: "He who the midst of the Sea restlessly crosses,
Let 'Crossing' be his name who controls[151] its midst.
May they uphold the course of the stars of heaven;
May he shepherd all the gods like sheep.
May he vanquish Tiamat; may her life be strait and short![152]
Into the future of mankind, when days have grown old,
May she recede[153] without cease and stay away forever.[154]

Because he created the spaces and fashioned the firm ground,
Father Enlil called his name (50) LORD OF THE LANDS."[155]
When all the names which the Igigi proclaimed,
Ea had heard, his spirit rejoiced,
Thus: "He whose names his fathers have glorified,
He is indeed even as I; his name shall be Ea.
All my combined rites he shall administer;
All my instructions he shall carry out!"
With the title "Fifty" the great gods
Proclaimed him whose names are fifty and made his way supreme.

Epilogue

Let them be kept (in mind) and let the leader explain them.[156]
Let the wise and the knowing discuss (them) together.
Let the father recite (them) and impart to his son.
Let the ears of shepherd and herdsman be opened.
Let him rejoice in Marduk, the Enlil of the gods,
That his land may be fertile and that he may prosper.
Firm in his order, his command unalterable,
The utterance of his mouth no god shall change.
When he looks he does not turn away his neck;
When he is angry, no god can withstand his wrath.
Vast is his mind, broad his sympathy;
Sinner and transgressor will be con[founded] before him.
The teaching which the leader has voiced in his presence,
[. . .]

(The few remaining lines are too fragmentary for translation.)

[143] Modifying slightly v. Soden's suggestion, *loc. cit.*, 23.
[144] This would seem to be the literal translation of the obscure verse; cf. v. Soden, *loc. cit.*, 23.
[145] Lit. "heart."
[146] For Mummu in the sense of "thunder" see A. Heidel, *JNES*, VII (1948), 104; the accompanying verb, however, has been given its normal meaning, cf. Tablet V, 20.
[147] Obviously two verses, combined into one on some of the tablets. The present line count follows Labat's and, with him, the count by tens as found in some of the texts.
[148] We have here apparently another ancient allusion to a connection between Akk. *ašāru* and Sumerian n a r i; cf. Tablet VI, 144.
[149] Jupiter.
[150] cf. F. M. Th. Böhl, *AfO*, XI (1936), 212.
[151] Lit. "holds."
[152] cf. v. Soden, *loc. cit.*, 25.
[153] i.e. Tiamat "the Sea." The variant form of the verb is *li-is-se-e-ma*.
[154] The reading *li-ri-iq* for *li-bi-il* (cf. v. Soden's variant *li-riq*!, *loc. cit.*, 25) makes the verse intelligible.

The Epic of Gilgamesh

The theme of this epic is essentially a secular one. The poem deals with such earthy things as man and nature, love and adventure, friendship and combat—all masterfully blended into a background for the stark reality of death. The climactic struggle of the protagonist to change his eventual fate, by learning the secret of immortality from the hero of the Great Flood of long ago, ends in failure; but with the failure comes a sense of quiet resignation. For the first time in the history of the world a profound experience on such a heroic scale has found expression in a noble style. The scope and sweep of the epic, and its sheer poetic power, give it a timeless appeal. In antiquity, the influence of the poem spread to various tongues and cultures. Today it captivates student and poet alike.

The Akkadian title of the poem, which was taken as usual from the opening words, is *Ša nagba imuru*, "He who saw everything." The prevailing meter has the normal four beats to a line. The work is divided into twelve tablets. The longest of these contains over three hundred lines. It happens to be the so-called Flood Tablet (XI), virtually in a perfect state of preservation. The rest has survived in portions, some of considerable size and others in relatively small fragments. All but a few of the Ak-

[155] Akk. *Bēl mātāti*. This is the fiftieth and last name of Marduk, not counting the honorific identification of Ea as given in line 140.
[156] For the concluding lines cf. A. L. Oppenheim, *Orientalia*, XVI (1947), 237.

kadian texts come from the library of Ashurbanipal at Nineveh. Unlike the Creation Epic, however, the Gilgamesh Epic is known also from versions which antedate the first millennium B.C. From the middle of the second millennium have come down fragments of an Akkadian recension current in the Hittite Empire, and the same Boğazköy archives have yielded also important fragments of a Hittite translation, as well as a fragment of a Hurrian rendering of the epic. From the first half of the second millennium we possess representative portions of the Old Babylonian version of the epic, which pertain to Tablets I-III, and X. That this version was itself a copy of an earlier text is suggested by the internal evidence of the material. The original date of composition of the Akkadian work has to be placed at the turn of the second millennium, if not slightly earlier.

The connection between the Epic of Gilgamesh as we know it in its Akkadian form, and its various Sumerian analogues, has been clarified in recent years thanks to the work of C. J. Gadd on the Epic of Gilgamesh, Tablet XII, *RA*, xxxi (1933), 126 ff., and especially by the studies of S. N. Kramer; see his summary in The Epic of Gilgamesh and its Sumerian Sources, *JAOS*, lxiv (1944), 7 ff. It has been demonstrated that Tablet XII is not of a piece with the other eleven tablets of the poem, but is instead a literal translation from the Sumerian. The epic proper, on the other hand, while utilizing certain motifs which are featured in Sumerian poems, does so largely in the course of developing a central theme that has no Sumerian prototype. In other words, the first eleven tablets of the Akkadian poem of Gilgamesh constitute an instance of creative borrowing which, substantially, amounts to an independent creation.[1]

The text of the Assyrian version is now available in the model edition published, with transliteration and notes, by R. Campbell Thompson under the title of *The Epic of Gilgamish* (1930). Thompson's arrangement and line count have been adopted in this translation, except for the passages that have been allocated otherwise, as will be noted in each given instance. The sources of the texts not given by Thompson will be cited in detail in the course of the translation.

Of the literature on the subject only a small selection can be listed. One cannot fail, however, to cite the work of Peter Jensen, antiquated though it may be in some respects, for no scholar has done more than he to bring the epic to the attention of the modern world. The translation, transliteration, and notes in his *Assyrisch-babylonische Mythen und Epen* (*Keilinschriftliche Bibliothek*, vi, 1900) remain useful to this day; and his monumental *Das Gilgamesch-Epos in der Weltliteratur* (Vol. i, 1906; Vol. ii, 1926) testifies to his enduring preoccupation with this subject. Important progress was made by A. Ungnad and H. Gressmann, *Das Gilgamesch-Epos* (1919), and Ungnad returned to the subject on two subsequent occasions: *Die Religion der Babylonier und Assyrer* (1921), and *Gilgamesch-Epos und Odyssee* (*Kulturfragen*, 4/5, 1923). E. Ebeling contributed a translation to *AOT* (2nd ed., 1926). The standard German translation is now that of A. Schott, *Das Gilgamesch-Epos* (1934). In English we have R. Campbell Thompson's translation into hexameters, entitled *The Epic of Gilgamish* (1928). To W. E. Leonard we owe a rendering into free rhythms, entitled *Gilgamesh* (1934), based on a German translation by H. Ranke. The book of G. Contenau, *L'épopée de Gilgamesh* is more valuable perhaps for its general orientation than for the particular contribution of the translation. An informed translation accompanied by brief notes has been published by F. M. Böhl under the Dutch title *Het Gilgamesj-Epos* (1941). The latest and most dependable translation in English, with brief notes and an extensive discussion of the biblical parallels is that of A. Heidel, *The Gilgamesh Epic and Old Testament Parallels* (1946). I have profited considerably from Heidel's treatment, as I have also from that of Schott (see above). The same holds true of Schott's notes, published in *ZA*, xlii (1934), 92 ff., and of the notes by A. L. Oppenheim, Mesopotamian Mythology II, *Orientalia*, xvii (1948), 17 ff.

[1] cf. S. N. Kramer, *loc. cit.*, 23, n.116. To the material listed in that article add now *id.*, *JCS*, i (1947), 3-46.

Tablet I

(i)

He who saw everything [to the end]s of the land,
[Who all thing]s experienced, [conside]red all![2]
[. . .] together [. . .],
[. . .] of wisdom, who all things . [. .].
The [hi]dden he saw, [laid bare] the undisclosed.
He brought report of before the Flood,
Achieved a long journey, weary and [w]orn.
All his toil he engraved on a stone stela.
Of ramparted[3] Uruk the wall he built,
Of holy Eanna,[4] the pure sanctuary.
Behold its outer wall, whose cornice[5] is like copper,
Peer at the inner wall, which none can equal!
Draw near to Eanna, the dwelling of Ishtar,
Which no future king, no man, can equal.
Go up and walk[6] on the walls of Uruk,
Inspect the base terrace, examine the brickwork:
Is not its brickwork of burnt brick?
Did not the Seven [Sages][7] lay its foundations?

(Remainder of the column broken away. A Hittite fragment [cf. J. Friedrich, *ZA*, xxxix (1929), 2-5] corresponds in part with the damaged initial portion of our column ii, and hence appears to contain some of the material from the end of the first column. We gather from this fragment that several gods had a hand in fashioning Gilgamesh, whom they endowed with superhuman dimensions. At length, Gilgamesh arrives in Uruk.)

(ii)

Two-thirds of him is god, [one-third of him is human].
The form of his body [. . .]
(mutilated or missing) (3-7)
[. . .] like a wild ox lofty [. . .]; (8)
The onslaught of his weapons verily has no equal.
By the *drum*[8] are aroused [his] companions.
The nobles of Uruk *are gloo*[*my*] in [their chamb]ers:
"Gilgamesh[9] leaves not the son to [his] father;
[Day] and [night] is unbridled his arro[gance].
[Yet] th[is is Gil]gamesh, [the shepherd of Uruk].
He *should be* [our] shepherd: [strong, stately, (and) wise]!
[Gilgamesh] leaves not [the maid to her mother],

[2] For the restoration of the first two lines cf. *GETh*, 111, and Böhl, *HGE*, 111.

[3] For this translation of *Uruk-supūri* cf. Leonard, *Gilgamesh*, 3.

[4] The temple of Anu and Ishtar in Uruk.

[5] Oppenheim, *Orientalia*, xvii (1948), 19, n.2.

[6] Text: *im-ta-lak* "take counsel," but the parallel passage, XI, 303, reads *i-tal-lak* "walk about."

[7] For the seven sages, who brought civilization to seven of the oldest cities in the land, see H. Zimmern, *ZA*, xxxv (1923), 151 ff.

[8] For *pukku* cf. the introduction to Tablet XII and note 233. Here perhaps the reference is to the abuse for personal purposes of an instrument intended for civic or religious use.

[9] For the various writings of the name cf. *GETh*, 8 f.; Th. Jacobsen, *The Sumerian King List* (1939), 89 f., n.128; and S. N. Kramer, *JAOS*, lxiv (1944), 11, n.15, and A. Goetze, *JCS*, i (1937), 254.

The warrior's daughter, [the noble's spouse]!"
The [gods hearkened] to their plaint,
The gods of heaven, Uruk's lord(s) [. . .]:
"Did not [*Aruru*][10] bring forth this strong
wild ox?
[The onslaught of his weapons] verily has no equal.
By the *drum* are aroused his [companions].
Gilgamesh leaves not the son to his father;
Day and night [is unbridled his arrogance].
Yet he is the shepherd of [ramparted] Uruk;
He *should be* their shepherd and [. . .],
Strong, stately, (and) wise [. . .]!
Gilgamesh leaves not the maid to [her mother],
The warrior's daughter, the noble's spouse!"
When [Anu] had heard out their plaint,
The great Aruru they called:
"Thou, Aruru, didst create [Gilgamesh];
Create now his double;[11]
His stormy heart[12] let him match.
Let them contend, that Uruk may have peace!"
When Aruru heard this,
A double of Anu she conceived within her.
Aruru washed her hands,
Pinched off clay and cast it on the steppe.[13]
[On the step]pe she created valiant Enkidu,
Offspring of . . . , liegeman[14] of Ninurta.
[Sha]ggy[15] with hair is his whole body,
He is endowed with head hair like a woman.
The locks of his hair sprout like Nisaba.[16]
He knows neither people nor land;
Garbed is he like Sumuqan.[17]
With the gazelles he feeds on grass,
With the wild beasts he jostles[18] at the
watering-place,
With the teeming creatures his heart delights in water.
(Now) a hunter, a trapping-man,[19]
Faced him at the watering-place.
[One] day, a second, and a third
He faced him at the watering-place.
When the hunter saw him, his face became motionless.

[10] A goddess.
[11] Lit. "evocation, image."
[12] Lit. "the storm of his heart."
[13] Where Enkidu was to be born. Other possible translations are "drew a design upon it," or "spat upon it."
[14] The second of the four Akkadian terms used to describe Enkidu remains uncertain as to meaning; even the pronunciation of the ambiguous first sign is still undecided. As regards *ḳi-ṣir*, there are too many possible meanings. Furthermore, the one adopted for this passage should also apply to I, iii, 4, 31; VI, 3, 23; II, i, 7: the war-god Ninurta, and the sky-god Anu, Enkidu, and something that fell down from heaven. The common assumption that the author may have used in these passages the same term in more than one sense is unsatisfactory.
The root meaning of *ḳaṣāru* is to "bind, attach." The noun is commonly used in the legal sense of "rental," i.e. an obligation to pay a given amount for the use of property for a stated period. "Tie-up with (or within)" will yield also "host, soldier (servant)," which are other attested meanings of the noun. I have adopted, therefore, in these passages the translation "liegeman," which hearks back to the etymology of the term and reflects a degree of association with another body such as is required in our contexts.
[15] Reading [*šu*]-*'u-ur* with Schott, *ZA*, XLII (1934), 96.
[16] Goddess of grain.
[17] God of cattle.
[18] Root *dapāru* "push, press."
[19] The epic employs a number of compound phrases, particularly with *amēlu* "man" as the second element.

He and his beasts went into his house,
[Sore a]fraid, still, without a sound,
(While) his heart [was disturbed], overclouded his face.
For woe had [entered] his belly;
His face was like that [of a wayfarer]
from[20] afar.

(iii)

The hunter opened [his mouth] to speak,
Saying to [his father]:
"My father, there is [a] fellow who [has come from the
hills],
He is the might[iest in the land]; strength he has.
[Like a liegeman] of Anu, so mighty his strength!
[Ever] he ranges over the hills,
[Ever] with the beasts [he feeds on grass].
[Ever sets he] his feet at the watering-place.
[I am so frightened that] I dare not approach him!
[He filled in] the pits that I had dug,
[He tore up] my *traps* which I had [set],
The beasts and creatures of the steppe
[He has made slip through my hands].[21]
[He does not allow] me to engage in fieldcraft!"[22]

[His father opened his mouth to speak],
Saying to the hunter:
"[My son], in Uruk [there lives] Gilgamesh.
[No one is there more mighty] than he.
[Like a liegeman of Anu, so mi]ghty is his strength!
[Go, then, toward Uruk set] thy face,
[Speak to him of] the power of the man.
[Let him give thee a harlot-lass[23]]. Take (her) [with
thee];
[Let her prevail against him] by dint of
[greater] might.
[When he waters the beasts at] the watering-place,
[She shall pull off] her cloth[ing, laying bare] her ripeness.
[As soon as he sees] her, he will draw near to her.
Reject him[24] will his beasts [that grew up on] his
steppe!"
[Giving heed to] the advice of his father,
The hunter went forth [to Gilgamesh].
He took the road, in Uruk he set [his foot]:
"[. . .] Gilga[mesh . . .],
There is a fellow [who has come from the hills],
He is the might[iest in the land; strength
he has].
Like a liegeman of Anu, so mighty [his strength]!

[20] The verb *alāḳu* means both "come" and "go." The state here described suggests the end, not the beginning, of a journey.
[21] Or perhaps "he has made me forfeit," the causative form of a phrase which, with the verb in the simple stem, has a well-established legal connotation.
[22] cf. Thompson, *EG*, 11.
[23] The two terms seem to be employed here often as a compound of the type used with *amēlu*; cf. above, note 19. For *ḫarimtu* the meaning "(temple-)prostitute" is amply established. The root *šamāḫ/ḳu*, in the sense of "be happy," occurs as a verbal noun in VIII, iii, 5. The noun means here "pleasure-girl."
[24] Lit. "regard as stranger, deny."

[Ever] he ranges over the hills,
Ever with the beasts [he feeds on grass],
Ever [sets] he his feet at the watering-place.
I am so frightened that I dare not approach [him]!
He filled in the pits that [I] had dug,
He tore up my *traps* [which I had set],
The beasts and creatures [of the steppe]
He has made slip through my hands.
He does not allow me to engage in fieldcraft!"
Gilgamesh says to him, [to] the hunter:
"Go, my hunter, take with thee a harlot-lass.
When he waters the beasts at the watering-place,
She shall pull off her clothing, laying bare her ripeness.
As soon as he sees her, he will draw near to her.
Reject him will his beasts that grew up on his steppe!"
Forth went the hunter, taking with him a harlot-lass.
They took the road, going straight on (their) way.
On the third day at the appointed spot they arrived.
The hunter and the harlot sat down in their places.
One day, a second day, they sat by the watering-place.
The wild beasts came to the watering-place to drink.

(iv)

The creeping creatures came, their heart delighting in water.
But as for him, Enkidu, born in the hills—
With the gazelles he feeds on grass,
With the wild beasts he drinks at the watering-place,
With the creeping creatures his heart delights in water—
The lass beheld him, the savage-man,[25]
The barbarous fellow from the depths of the steppe:
"There he is, O lass! Free thy breasts,
Bare thy bosom that he may possess thy ripeness!
Be not bashful! Welcome his ardor![26]
As soon as he sees thee, he will draw near to thee.
Lay aside[26a] thy cloth that he may rest upon thee.
Treat him, the savage, to a woman's task!
Reject him will his wild beasts that grew up on his steppe,
As his love is drawn unto thee."[27]
The lass freed her breasts, bared her bosom,
And he possessed her ripeness.
She was not bashful as she welcomed his ardor.
She laid aside her cloth and he rested upon her.
She treated him, the savage, to a woman's task,
As his love was drawn unto her.
For six days and seven nights Enkidu comes forth,
Mating with the lass.
After he had had (his) fill of her charms,
He set his face toward his wild beasts.
On seeing him, Enkidu, the gazelles ran off,
The wild beasts of the steppe drew away from his body.
Startled was Enkidu, as his body became taut,
His knees were motionless—for his wild beasts had gone.
Enkidu had to slacken his pace—it was not as before;
But he now had [wi]sdom, [br]oader understanding.[28]
Returning, he sits at the feet of the harlot.
He looks up at the face of the harlot,
His ears attentive, as the harlot speaks;
[The harlot] says to him, to Enkidu:
"Thou art [wi]se,[29] Enkidu, art become like a god!
Why with the wild creatures dost thou roam over the steppe?
Come, let me lead thee [to] ramparted Uruk,
To the holy temple, abode of Anu and Ishtar,
Where lives Gilgamesh, accomplished in strength,
And like a wild ox lords it over the folk."
As she speaks to him, her words find favor,
His heart enlightened,[30] he yearns for[31] a friend.
Enkidu says to her, to the harlot:
"Up, lass, escort thou me,[32]
To the pure sacred temple, abode of Anu and Ishtar,
Where lives Gilgamesh, accomplished in strength,
And like a wild ox lords it over the folk.
I will challenge him [and will bo]ldly address him,

(v)

[I will] shout in Uruk: 'I am he who is mighty!
[I am the] one who can alter destinies,
[(He) who] was born on the steppe is mighty; strength he has.'
[Up then, let us go, that he may see] thy face.
[I will show thee Gilgamesh; where] he is I know well.
Come then, O Enkidu, to ramparted [Uruk],
Where people are re[splend]ent in festal attire,
(Where) each day is made a holiday,
Where [. . .] lads . . . ,
And la[ss]es [. .] . of figure.
Their ripeness [. . .] full of perfume.
They drive the great ones from their couches!
To thee, O Enkidu, who rejoicest in living,
I will show Gilgamesh, the joyful man!
Look thou at him, regard his face;
He is radiant with manhood, vigor he has.
With ripeness gorgeous is the whole of his body,
Mightier strength has he than thou,
Never resting by day or by night.
O Enkidu, renounce thy presumption!
Gilgamesh—of him Shamash is fond;
Anu, Enlil, and Ea have broadened his wisdom.
Before thou comest down from the hills,
Gilgamesh will see thee in (his) dreams in Uruk:
For[33] Gilgamesh arose to reveal his dreams,
Saying to his mother:

[25] cf. *Creation Epic*, VI, 6, and n.86, *ibid*.
[26] Lit. "breathing," cf. B. Landsberger, *ZA*, XLII (1934), 100, n.2.
[26a] For the technical use of *muṣṣûm* "lay aside," *mutaṣṣûm* "take off" cf. *Descent of Ishtar* (below) 42 ff.
[27] cf. Th. Jacobsen, *Acta Orientalia*, VIII (1929), 67, n.2, and Schott, *ZA*, XLII, 101. The general connotation of the verb is clear, but its precise shading remains to be determined. It is plain, however, that the form is intransitive.
[28] Reading *i-ši ṭé-[ma ú-r]a-pa-aš ḫa-si-sa*, with Schott, *loc. cit.* The general parallel to Gen. 3:7 is highly suggestive.
[29] Reading [*en-*]*qa-ta*.
[30] Or "one who knows his heart," an object phrase.
[31] Lit. "seeks."
[32] Lit. "call."
[33] The particle *-ma* appears to introduce here a shift in the scene. It is not entirely clear whether the girl continues speaking, as is here assumed.

'My mother, I saw a dream this night:
There appeared the stars in the heavens.
Like a liegeman[34] of Anu it[35] descends upon me.
I sought to lift it; it was too stout for me.
I sought to drive it off,[36] but I could not
remove it.
Uruk-land was standing about [it],
[The land was gathered round it],
The populace jost[led towards it],
[The nobles] thronged about it.
[. . .] my companions were kissing its feet.
[I] was drawn to it[37] as though to a woman.
And I placed it at [thy] feet,
For thou didst make it vie with me.'
[The wise mother of Gilgamesh, who] is versed in all
knowledge,[38]
Says to her lord;
[Wise Ninsun], who is versed in all
knowledge,
Says to Gilgamesh:
'Thy [*rival*],—the star of heaven,
Which descended upon thee like a [liegeman of Anu];
[Thou didst seek to lift it], it was too stout for thee;
[Thou wouldst drive it off], but couldst not remove it;
[Thou didst place] it at my feet,
[For it was I who made] it vie with thee;
Thou wert drawn to it as though to a woman—

(vi)

[This means a stout com]rade who rescues a friend.
[He is the mightiest in the land]; strength he has.
[Like to a liegeman of Anu], so mighty is his strength.
[That thou wert] drawn to him [as though to a woman],
[Means that he will never] forsake [th]ee.
[This is the mean]ing of thy dream.'
[Again Gilgamesh says] to his mother:
'[My mother, I] saw another dream:
[In ramparted Uruk] lay an axe;
There was a gathering round it.
[Uruk-land] was standing about it,
[The land was gathered] round it,
[The populace jostled] towards it.
[I] placed it at thy feet.
As though to a woman I was drawn to it,
[For thou didst] make it vie with me.'
[The] wise one, who is versed in all knowledge,
Says to her son:
[Ninsun, the wi]se, who is versed in all knowledge,
Says to Gilgamesh:
'[The axe] which thou sawest is a man.
[That thou] wert drawn to it as though to a woman,
[For it was I] who made it vie with thee—
[This means] a stout comrade who rescues a friend.
[He is the mightiest in the land]; strength he has.
[Like to a liegeman of] Anu, so mighty is his strength.'

[34] cf. above, n.14.
[35] One of the stars?
[36] Reading *ul-tab-lak-ki-is-su* (from *blkt*), with Ungnad and Landsberger, cf. *ZA*, XLII (1934), 102 and n.2.
[37] cf. above, n.27.
[38] cf. Heidel, *EG*, 24.

[Gilgamesh opened his mouth], saying to his mother:
'[May it] fall to me as a great [lo]t[39]
[That a mighty comrade] I should acquire,
[. . .] I.' "
[Thus did Gilgamesh reveal] his dreams,
[And thus did the lass] speak to Gilgamesh,
[As they sat], the two (of them).

Tablet II

OLD BABYLONIAN VERSION

In the Assyrian Version, Tablet II has come down in only a few disjointed and mutilated fragments. The text here followed (in agreement with Böhl and Heidel) is that of the Old Babylonian Version as found on the "Pennsylvania Tablet." It was published by S. Langdon in *UM*, x, 3 (1917), and was revised in transliteration by M. Jastrow and A. T. Clay; cf. their *An Old Babylonian Version of the Gilgamesh Epic* (1920; abbr. *YOS*, IV, 3), 62-68. cf. also *GETh*, 20-24. The beginning of this tablet goes back to Tablet I, v, 25 of the Assyrian Version. The resulting repetition of some of the incidents should not prove to be unduly disturbing in an epic, particularly since the two accounts are by no means identical. It will be noted that many of the lines on the present tablet contain only two beats, an arrangement which affects the line count but does not alter the meter.

(ii)

Gilgamesh arose to reveal the dream,
Saying to his mother:
"My mother, in the time of night
I felt joyful and I walked about
In the midst of the nobles.
The stars appeared in the heavens.
A liegeman of Anu descended towards me.
I sought to lift it; it was too heavy for me!
I sought to move it; move it I could not!
Uruk-land was gathered about it,
While the nobles kissed its feet.
As I set my forehead,[40]
They gave me support.
I raised it and brought it to thee."
The mother of Gilgamesh, who knows all,
Says to Gilgamesh:
"Forsooth,[41] Gilgamesh, one like thee
Was born on the steppe,
And the hills have reared him.
When thou seest him, [*as (over) a woman*]
thou wilt rejoice.
The nobles will kiss his feet;
Thou wilt embrace him and [. .] . him;
Thou wilt lead him to me."
He lay down and saw another
[Dream]: he says to his mother:
[My mother], I saw another
[. . .] in *the confusion*.[42] In the street
[Of] broad-marted Uruk

[39] Reading [*ina is*]-*qí*, with Schott, *ZA*, XLII, 104.
[40] To press the carrying strap against it; for this method, which is witnessed on the Ur Standard and is still practiced in modern Iraq, cf. Th. Jacobsen, *Acta Orientalia* (1929), 67, n.3.
[41] For *mi-in-di* cf. *JCS*, I (1947), 322, n.6.
[42] If *ina e-ši-e* may be read and so interpreted.

There lay an axe, and
They were gathered round it.
That axe, strange was its shape.
As soon as I saw it, I rejoiced.
I loved it, and as though to a woman,
I was drawn[43] to it.
I took it and placed it
At my side."
The mother of Gilgamesh, who knows all,
[Says to Gilgamesh]:

(small break)

(ii)

"Because I made it vie with thee."
While Gilgamesh reveals his dream,
Enkidu sits before the harlot.
[. . .] *the two of them.*[44]
[Enki]du forgot where he was born.
For six days and seven nights was Enkidu come forth
Mating with the l[ass].
Then the harlot opened her mouth,
Saying to Enkidu:
"As I look at thee, Enkidu, thou art become like a god;
Wherefore with the wild creatures
Dost thou range over the steppe?
Up, I will lead thee
To broad-marted Uruk,[45]
To the holy temple, the abode of Anu,
Enkidu, arise, I will lead thee
To Eanna, the abode of Anu,
Where lives [Gilgamesh, accomplished] in deeds,
And thou, li[ke . . .],
Wilt love [him like] thyself.
Up, arise from the ground,
The shepherd's bed!"
He hearkened to her words, approved[46] her speech;
The woman's counsel
Fell upon his heart.
She pulled off (her) clothing;
With one (piece) she clothed him,
With the other garment
She clothed herself.
Holding on to his hand,
She leads him like a mother[47]
To the board[48] of shepherds,
The place of the sheepfold.
Round him the shepherds gathered.

(several lines missing)

(iii)

The milk of wild creatures
He was wont to suck.
Food they placed before him;
He was uneasy, he gaped
And he stared.
Nothing does Enkidu know
Of eating food;
To drink strong drink
He has not been taught.
The harlot opened her mouth,
Saying to Enkidu:
"Eat the food, Enkidu,
As is life's due;
Drink the strong drink, as is the custom of the land."
Enkidu ate the food,
Until he was sated;
Of strong drink he drank
Seven goblets.
Carefree became his mood (and) cheerful,
His heart exulted
And his face glowed.
He rubbed [the *shaggy growth*],[49]
The hair of his body,
Anointed himself with oil,
Became like a man.
He put on clothing,
He is like a groom!
He took his weapon
To chase the lions,
That shepherds might rest at night.
He caught wolves,
He captured lions,
The chief cattlemen could lie down;
Enkidu is their watchman,
The mighty man,
The unique hero!
To [. . .] he says:

(several lines missing)

(iv)

(some eight lines missing)

He made merry.
When he lifted his eyes,
He beheld a man.
He says to the harlot:
"Lass, fetch the man!
Why has he come hither?
His name let me hear."[50]
The harlot called the man,
Going up to him and saying to him:[51]
"Sir, whither hastenest thou?
What is this thy toilsome course?"
The man opened his mouth,
Saying to En[kidu]:
"Into the meeting-house he has [*intruded*],
Which is set aside[52] for the people,

43 See above, n.27.
44 Reading *ki!-la!-al-lu-un*, cf. Schott, *ZA*, XLII, 104.
45 cf. Thompson, *EG*, 16 (line 15). The designation *Uruk-rībitim* "Uruk-of-the-broad-place(s)" in the Old Babylonian Version alternates with *Uruk-supūri* "Uruk-of-the-enclosure" in the Assyrian Version.
46 Lit. "accepted."
47 Reading *ummim* with Schott, *loc. cit.*
48 For *gupru* "table" cf. P. Jensen, *OLZ*, 1921, 261.
49 Reading [*ma-li*]-*i*, with Schott, *ZA*, XLII, 105.
50 Reading *lu-uš-me*! with Böhl, *HGE*, 123.
51 Reading with Schott, *OLZ*, 1933, 520: *i-ku!-uš-šu-ma i-ta-wa!-šu.*
52 Lit. "decreed." For the nature of the offense see Th. Jacobsen, *Acta Orientalia*, VIII (1929), 70 ff.

. . . for *wedlock*.[53]
On the city he has heaped *defilement*,
Imposing strange things on the *hapless* city.
For the king of broad-marted Uruk
The *drum*[54] of the people is free for
nuptial choice.
For Gilgamesh, king of broad-marted Uruk,
The *drum* of the people is free
For nuptial choice,
That with lawful[55] wives he might mate!
He is the first,
The *husband*[56] comes after.
By the counsel of the gods it has (so) been ordained.
With the cutting of his umbilical cord
It was decreed for him!"
At the words of the man
His face grew pale.[57]

(some three lines missing)

(v)

(some six lines missing)

[Enkidu] walks [in front]
And the lass behind him.
When he entered broad-marted Uruk,
The populace gathered about him.
As he stopped in the street
Of broad-marted Uruk,
The people were gathered,
Saying about him:
"He is like Gilgamesh *to a hair*![58]
Though shorter in stature,
He is stronger of bone.
[. . .] . . .
[He is the strongest in the land]; strength he has.
The milk of wild creatures
He was wont to suck.
In Uruk (there will be) a constant (*clatter of*) *arms*."
The nobles rejoiced:
"A hero has appeared
For the man of proper mien!
For Gilgamesh, the godlike,
His equal has come forth."
For Ishhara[59] the bed
Is laid out.
Gilgamesh. [. .],
At night . . [.],
As he approaches,
[Enkidu] stands in the street
To bar the way

[53] If the sign before *-lu-tim* is to be read *kal-*. The literal meaning would be "brideship."

[54] Very obscure. But if *pukku* is to be given here the same meaning as in I, ii, 10 and XII, 1 ff., then one must seek here a reference to some such instrument whose sound could summon the listeners to a given task or occasion.

[55] Lit. "decreed," i.e. to their husbands.

[56] Reading *mu-tum*! with Schott, *OLZ*, 1933, 521.

[57] Reading *i-ri-qu*. For the end of column iii and the whole of column iv cf. G. Dossin, *La pâleur d'Enkidu* (1931).

[58] Reading *pi-ri!-tam*, with E. Ebeling, *AfO*, VIII (1932/33), 228.

[59] A form of Ishtar, as goddess of love.

To Gilgamesh
[. . .] in his might.

(some three lines missing)

(vi)

(some five lines missing)

Gilgamesh [. . .]
On the steppe [. . .]
Sprouts [. . .].
He rose up and [. . .]
Before him.
They met in the Market-of-the-Land.
Enkidu barred the gate
With his foot,
Not allowing Gilgamesh to enter.
They grappled each other,
Butting like bulls.
They shattered the doorpost,
As the wall shook.
Gilgamesh and Enkidu
Grappled each other,
Butting like bulls;
They shattered the doorpost,
As the wall shook.
As Gilgamesh bent the knee—
His foot on the ground—[60]
His fury abated
And he turned away.
When he had turned away,
Enkidu to him
Speaks up, to Gilgamesh:
"As one alone thy mother
Bore thee,
The wild cow of the steer-folds,
Ninsunna!
Raised up above men is thy head.
Kingship over the people
Enlil has granted thee!"

Tablet III

OLD BABYLONIAN VERSION

In the Assyrian Version, this tablet is extant only in fragments, which will be translated below, under B. The older text is that of the "Yale Tablet" (*YOS*, IV, 3, Pls. 1-7), which continues the account of the "Pennsylvania Tablet."

(i)

(Mutilated or missing. Gilgamesh has decided on an expedition against monstrous Ḫuwawa [Assyrian Ḫumbaba], who resides in the Cedar Forest. Enkidu tries to dissuade him, but is unsuccessful, as may be gathered from the following verses.)

"[Why] dost thou desire (13)
To do [this thing]?"
. . .

[60] For the form of wrestling to which this episode refers cf. C. H. Gordon, *JNES*, VII (1948), 264, and Oppenheim, *Orientalia*, XVII (1948), 30.

They kissed each other[61] (19)
And formed a friendship.

(remainder missing or mutilated)

(ii)

(some twenty-five lines missing or mutilated)

The eyes [of Enkidu filled] with t[ears].
[Ill was] his heart,
[As bitterly] he sighed.
[Yea, En]kidu's eyes filled with tears.
[Ill was] his heart, (30)
[As bitterly] he sighed.
[Gilgamesh], bearing with him,[62]
[Says] to Enkidu:
"[My friend, why] do thine eyes
[Fill with tear]s?
[Is ill] thy [heart],
[As bitterly thou sigh]est?"
En[kidu opened his mouth],
Saying to Gilgamesh:
"*A cry,*[63] my friend, (40)
Chokes my throat;[64]
My arms are limp,
And my strength has turned to weakness."
Gilgamesh opened his mouth,
Saying to Enkidu:

(iii)

(some four lines missing)

"[In the forest resides] fierce Huwawa. (5)
[Let us, me and thee, s]lay [him],
[That all evil from the land we may ban]ish![65]
(too fragmentary for translation) (8-11)
Enkidu opened his mouth,
Saying to Gilgamesh:
"I found it out, my friend, in the hills,
As I was roaming with the wild beasts.
For ten thousand leagues[66] *extends* the forest.
[Who is there] that would go down into it?
[Huwa]wa—his roaring is the flood-storm,
His mouth is fire,
His breath is death! (20)
Why dost thou desire
To do this thing?
An unequal struggle
Is *tangling with* Huwawa."
Gilgamesh opened his mouth,
Saying to Enkidu:
"[*The cedar*]—its mountain I would scale!"
(mostly destroyed) (28-35)
Enkidu opened his mouth,

[61] Reading *it-ta-aš-qú-ú-ma.*

[62] For this idiom cf. Schott, *ZA*, XLII (1934), 107.

[63] The noun *ta-ab-bi-a-tum* is generally derived from *tappû* and taken to refer, in the sense of "female companions," to "Enkidu's sorrow at the loss of his Love"; cf. Thompson, *EG*, 20. The context, however, would seem to favor Schott's derivation as based on *nubbû* "to wail," *loc. cit.*, 107.

[64] Lit. "has bound my neck veins."

[65] Restored (with Schott, *loc. cit.*, 108) from Assyrian Version, III, ii, 17-18.

[66] Lit. "double-hours," a measure of distance as well as of time.

Saying to [Gilgamesh]:
"How can we go down
To the Cedar Forest?
Its keeper, Gilgamesh, is a warrior.
He is mighty, never res[ting]. (40)
Huwawa [. . .]
Adad [. . .]
He [. . .]

(iv)

To safeguard [the Cedar Forest],
As a terror *to* [mortals[67] has Enlil appointed him]."

(Here fits in the fragment of the Assyrian Version, II, v, published in *GETh*, Pl. x, top. Line 4 of this text is restored from an unpublished fragment in the Oriental Institute, cited by Heidel, *GE*, 36, n.64.)

"To safeguard the Cedar Forest,
As a terror to mortals has Enlil appointed him.
Humbaba—his roaring is the storm-flood,
    His mouth is fire, his breath is death!
At sixty leagues he can hear the wild cows of the forest;
    Who is there that would go down to the Forest?
To safeguard the cedars,
    As a terror to mortals has Enlil appointed him;
Weakness lays hold on him who goes down to the forest."

(the Old Babylonian Version continues)

Gilgamesh opened his mouth, (3)
Saying to [Enkidu]:
"Who, my friend *is superior to de*[*ath*]?
Only the gods [live] forever under the sun.
As for mankind, numbered are their days;
Whatever they achieve is but the wind!
Even here thou art afraid of death.
What of thy heroic might? (10)
Let me go then before thee,
Let thy mouth call to me, 'Advance, fear not!'
Should I fall, I shall have made me a name:
'Gilgamesh'—they will say—against fierce Huwawa
Has fallen!' (Long) after
My offspring has been born in my house,"

(obscure; 18-21 mutilated)

"[Thus calling] to me, thou hast grieved my heart.
[My hand] I will poise
And [will fe]ll the cedars.
A [name] that endures I will make for me!
[. . .], my friend, the smith I will *commission*,
[Weapons] they shall cast in our presence."
[. . .] the smith they *commissioned*,
The artisans sat down to discuss (it).
Mighty adzes they cast; (30)
Axes of three talents[68] each they cast.
Mighty swords they cast—
The blades, two talents each,
The *knobs* on their *sheaths*, two talents each,

[67] Lit. "men."

[68] A talent contained sixty minas (pounds).

[. . .] of the swords, thirty minas gold each.
Gilgamesh and Enkidu were each laden with ten talents.
[In the] gate of Uruk, whose bolts are seven,
[. . .] the populace gathered.
[. . .] in the street of broad-marted Uruk.
[. . .] Gilgamesh
[. . .] of broad-marted [Uruk].
[. . .] sat down before him,
[Sp]eaking [. . .]:
"[. . .] of broad-marted [Uruk]."

(one line missing)

(v)

"Him of whom they speak, I, Gilgamesh, will see,
Him with whose name the lands are ever filled.
I will conquer him in the Cedar Forest!
How strong is the offspring of Uruk
I will cause the lands to hear!
My hand I will poise and will fell the cedars,
A name that endures I will make for me!"
The elders of broad-marted Uruk
Said to Gilgamesh in reply:
"Thou art yet young, Gilgamesh, thy heart
has carried thee away.
That which thou wouldst achieve thou knowest not.
We have heard that Huwawa is wondrous in appearance;
Who is there to face his weapons?
For ten thousand leagues *extends* the forest;
Who is there that would go down into it?
Huwawa—his roaring is the storm-flood,
His mouth is fire, his breath is death!
Why dost thou wish to do this thing?
An unequal struggle is *tangling with* Huwawa."
When Gilgamesh heard this speech
of his counsellors,
He looked round, smiling, towards [his] friend:
"Now, my friend, thus [. . .]."

(Rest of the speech destroyed. When the text again becomes intelligible, the elders are addressing Gilgamesh:) (23-31)

"May thy god [protect] thee.
[May he lead thee] on the road back in safety.
To the landing-place at Uruk [may he bring thee
back]!"
Gilgamesh kneels down [before Shamash],
The words which he speaks [. . .]:
"I go, O Shamash, my hands [raised up in prayer].
May it henceforth be well with my soul.
Bring me back to the landing-place at [Uruk];
Establish [over me] (thy) protection!"
Gilgamesh called [his] friend
[And inspected] his omen.

(This appears to have been unfavorable, for the text continues after a small break:)

(vi)

Tears run down [the face] of Gilgamesh:
"[. . .] a road I have never traveled,
[. . .] . . . I know not.
[. . .] I should fare well.
[. . .] with joyful heart.
[. . .] . . .
[. . .] . . . thrones."
[*They brought him*] his gear,
[. . .] mighty [*sw*]*ords*,
[Bow] and quiver
They placed [in] his hands.
[He] took the axes,
[. . .] his quiver,
[The bow] of Anshan.[69]
His sw[ord he placed] in his girdle.
[. . .] they could start on their journey,
[*The populace*] presses close [to Gilgamesh]:
"[. . .] mayest thou return to Uruk!"
[The elder]s pay him homage,
As they counsel Gilgamesh [about]
the journey:
"Trust [not], Gilgamesh, in thine own strength!
Let thine [eyes] be clear;[70] guard thyself!
Let Enkidu go before thee;
He knows[71] the [way], has traveled the road.
[Within] the forest, all the passes
Of Huwawa let him penetrate![72]
[He who goes] in front protects the companion;
Let his [ey]es be clear; [let him guard himself].
May Shamash [grant] thee thy desire;
What thy mouth has spoken may he show
thine eyes!
May he open for thee the barred path,
The road unclose for thy treading,
The mountain unclose for thy foot!
May the night bring thee things of delight,
And may Lugalbanda stand by thee
In regard to thy wish.
Childlike, mayest thou attain thy wish!
In the stream of Huwawa, for which thou art headed,
Wash thou thy feet!
At rest time at night dig thou a well;
Ever pure shall be the water in thy waterskin!
Cool water offer thou[73] to Shamash.
And be thou ever mindful of Lugalbanda!"
[Enkidu] opened his mouth, saying to Gilgamesh:
"[*Since*] *contend thou wilt*, be on (thy) way.
Let thy heart be [un]afraid. Follow me!
[. . .] I know his dwelling place,
[And also the road] which Huwawa travels."

(Mutilated or missing. Gilgamesh had bid adieu.) (49-56)

[69] A district in Elam.

[70] cf. Landsberger, *ZA*, XLII (1934), 110, n.2. The sense of [*i-na*]-*ka lu šu-wu-ra-ma* would be close to our "look sharp!" cf. Assyrian Version, III, i, 3.

[71] Lit. "has seen."

[72] Lit. "make him slip through," Akk. *ḫul-lip-šu*, cf. Schott, *ZA*, XLII (1934), 111.

[73] Reading *ta-na-qí*.

[When the elders heard] this speech of his,
They sent [off] the hero upon his way:
"Go, Gilgamesh, may [. . .],
May thy god [be at thy side]."

(four lines mutilated)

ASSYRIAN VERSION

The beginning of this section links up with column vi 19 of the preceding so that there is only a slight overlap.

(i)

[The elders opened their mouths, saying to Gilgamesh]:
"Trust not, Gilgamesh, in all thine own strength.
Let thine [eyes] be sated;[74] make trust[worthy] thy stroke.
He who goes in front saves the companion;
He who knows the path protects his friend.
Let Enkidu go in front of thee.
He knows the way to the Cedar Forest,
He has seen battle, is versed in combat.
Enkidu shall protect the friend, safeguard the companion.
Over the pitfalls he shall carry his body!
We, the Assembly, entrust the King to thee.
Bring thou back safe the King unto us!"
Gilgamesh opened his mouth to speak,
Saying to Enkidu:
"Up, my friend, let us go to Egalmah,[75]
To the presence of Ninsun, the great Queen.
Ninsun, the wise, who is versed in all knowledge,
Will lend reasoned steps to our feet."
Grasping each other, hand in hand,
Gilgamesh and Enkidu go to Egalmah,
To the presence of Ninsun, the great Queen.
Gilgamesh came forward as he entered [*the palace*]:
"O Ninsun, *I make bold*[76] [. . .]
A far journey, to the pl[ace of Humbaba].
An uncertain battle[77] [I am about to face],
An uncertain [road I am about to travel].
[Until the day that I go and return],
[Until I reach the Cedar Forest],
[And banish from the land all evil, hateful to Shamash],
[Pray thou to Shamash on my behalf]!"

(The above restorations are based on column ii 12 ff. The remainder of the break cannot be restored.)

(ii)

[Ninsun] entered [her chamber],
[. . .] . . .
[She put on a garment] as beseems her bo[dy],
[She put on an ornament] as beseems her breast,
[. . .] and donned her tiara.
[. . .] the ground . . .
She cl[imbed the stairs], mounted to the parapet,
Ascended the [*roof*], to Shamash offered incense.
The smoke-offering set up, to Shamash she raised her hands:
"Why, having given me Gilgamesh for a son,
With a restless heart didst thou endow him?
And now thou didst affect him to go
On a far journey, to the place of Humbaba,
To face an uncertain battle,
To travel an uncertain road!
Until the day that he goes and returns,
Until he reaches the Cedar Forest,
Until he has slain the fierce Humbaba,
And has banished from the land all evil thou dost hate—
In day time, when thou . . . ,
May Aya, thy bride, fearlessly[78] remind thee,
And may she [commend] him to the watchmen of the night!"

(long break)

(iv)

She put out the incense, *pro*[*nouncing the spell*].
She then called Enkidu to impart (this) message:
"Mighty Enkidu, thou not my womb's issue,
I herewith *pronounce* thee
With the *devotees* of Gilgamesh,
The priestesses, the votaries, and the cult women!"[79]
. . . she placed round the neck of Enkidu.

(The remainder of this column, the whole of column v, and the first seven lines of column vi are missing or too mutilated for translation.)

(vi)

"Let [Enkidu] pr[otect the friend, safeguard the companion].
Over the pitfalls [let him carry his body]!
We, the Assembly, [entrust the King to thee];
Bring thou back sa[fe the King unto us]."
Enkidu opened his mouth [to speak],
Saying [to Gilgamesh]:
"My friend tu[rn . . .],
A way not [. . .]."

(remainder of the tablet destroyed)

Tablet IV

For this tablet, and for several of the following, the sequence of the extant texts is at times uncertain since the context must be pieced together from scattered Assyrian fragments and from such additions as have come to light elsewhere, particularly at Boğazköy (in Hittite as well as in Akkadian). The arrangement here followed has been adopted from A. Schott, cf. *ZA*, XLII (1934), 113 ff. No existing fragments can be assigned with certainty to any of the first columns of the Assyrian Version. A small portion of the missing record of the journey to the Cedar Forest is preserved on a fragment from Uruk, published by A.

[74] In accordance with Landsberger's reading (cf. n.70, above) and a personal suggestion by Goetze, the first word should be [*i*]-*na-ka*. I read the last word of this line *tuk-k*[*il*].

[75] "The Great Palace."

[76] Reading *ag-da-šir*, with Landsberger, *ZA*, XLII (1934), 111, n.3. For the meaning, cf. the intensive form *ugdaššaru* "who lords it," I, iv, 46.

[77] Lit. "a battle I know not."

[78] Reading, with two of the copies (cf. *ZA*, XLII, 112 n.1) *ši-i! a-a i-dur-ka* "may she not fear thee."

[79] cf. Oppenheim, *Orientalia*, XVII (1948), 33 f.

Falkenstein, *Literarische Keilschrifttexte aus Uruk* (1931), No. 39.

[At twenty] leagues they broke off a morsel;
[At thir]ty (further) leagues they prepared for the night.
[Fifty leagu]es they walked all day.
[The distance of a mon]th and fifteen days they *traversed* in three days.
[Before Shamash] they dug [a well].

(v)

(The beginning is missing.[80] The two friends have arrived at the gate of the forest, which is guarded by Ḫumbaba's watchman. Gilgamesh appears to need encouragement from Enkidu.)

"[Bethink thee of what] thou didst say in Uruk!
[Arise] and stand up [that thou mayest
slay him].
[. . . Gil]gamesh, the offshoot of Uruk."
[When Gilgamesh] heard the words of [his] mouth,
He was inspired with confidence:[81]
"[Hur]ry, step up to him, that he may not *de*[*part*],[82]
[Go] down to the woods and [*disappear*]!
He is wont to cloak himself with seven cloaks;
[One] he has donned; six are still off [. . .]."
Like a raging wild ox he [. . .],
. . . he departed . . . [. . .].
The watchman of the forest calls out [. . .].
Humbaba, like [. . .].

(vi)

(beginning missing)

[Enkidu] opened his [mouth] to speak, (23)
[Saying to Gilgamesh]:
"[Let us not go] down [into the heart of the forest]!
[In open]ing [the gate my hand] became limp."

[Gil]gamesh opened his mouth to speak,
Saying [to Enkidu]:
"[. . .], my friend, like weaklings [. . .].
[. . . we] have traveled, all of them [. . .].
[. . .] before us [. . .].
My [friend], who art versed in combat,
ac[complished] in battle,
Touch but my [garment], and thou wilt not fear [death].
(unintelligible) (32-33)
That the limpness may depart from thy arm,
And the weakness pass [from thy hand].
[Do but] stand by, my friend, that we may go down together [. . .].
Let thy heart [*lux*]*uriate*[83] in combat;
Forget death and do not [. . .].
A man, resolute (yet) discreet, [. . .],
When he goes in front, he guards himself
And safeguards the companion.
[Even though] they fa[ll],[84] they establish a name."
[At the] green [mountain] the two arrived.
Their words were [silen]ced;[85] they themselves stood still.

Tablet V

(i)

They stood still and gazed at the forest,
They looked at the height of the cedars,
They looked at the entrance to the forest.
Where Humbaba was wont to walk was a path;
Straight were the tracks and good was the going.
They beheld the cedar mountain, abode of the gods,
Throne-seat of Irnini.[86]
From the face of the mountain
The cedars[87] raise aloft their luxuriance.
Good is their shadow, full of delight.
There is cover in their brushwood, cover in their [. . .].

(The remainder of the column is missing or mutilated, and the same applies to column ii and most of column iii. An Akkadian fragment from Boğazköy—published by E. F. Weidner, *KUB*, IV [1922], 12, and Pl. 48—helps to fill in some of the gaps while duplicating other parts.)

They grasped each other to go for their
nightly rest.
Sleep overcame [them]—the surge of the night.
At midnight, sleep [departed] from him.[88]
A dream he tells to Enkidu, [his] friend:
"If thou didst not arouse me, why [am I awake]?
Enkidu, my friend, I must have seen a dream!
Didst thou arouse me? Why [. . .]?

Aside from my first dream, a second [dream] I saw:
In my dream, my friend, a mountain [toppled].
It laid me low, taking hold of my feet [. . .].
The glare was overpowering! A man [appeared].
The fairest in the land was he; his grace [. . .].
From under the mountain he pulled me out,
Gave me water to drink; my heart qui[eted].
On the ground he set [my] feet."

Enkidu said to this god [. . .],
To Gilgamesh: "My friend, let us go [. . .]."

(remainder fragmentary)

(iii)

"[The other] dream which I saw: (32)
[In] mountain gorges[89] [. . .]
[A mountain] toppled [. . .]
Like small reed flies we [. . .]."

[80] *GETh*, Pl. 15, numbers the lines 39 and ff., but his transliteration (*ibid.*, p. 34) gives the line count as 1 ff.
[81] cf. *GETh*, Pl. 15, n.13.
[82] Adopting Schott's reading *ir-*[*te-iq?*], *ZA*, XLII (1934), 116.
[83] Schott suggests [*liḫ*]*-nu-ub* (?), *ibid.*, 117.
[84] Reading [*i-na mi-i*]*t-qú-ti-šu-nu*, *ibid.*
[85] Reading [*sa-ak*]*-ta*, *ibid.*
[86] A form of Ishtar.
[87] Text has singular, probably in a collective sense.
[88] Gilgamesh.
[89] Reading [*sa*]*-pan-ni*, with Schott, *loc. cit.*, 118.

[He] who was born on the st[eppe . . .],
Enkidu, said to his friend, [explaining] the dr[eam]:
"My friend, favorable is [thy] dream,
The dream is most precious [. . .].
The mountain, my friend, which thou sawest,
[is Humbaba].
[We] shall seize Humbaba, sh[all kill him],
[And shall cast] his corpse on the plain.
On the morrow [. . .]."
At twenty leagues they br[oke off a morsel];
At thirty (further) leagues they prepared [for the night].
Before Shamash they dug a well [. . .].
Gilgamesh went up to [the mountain],
His fine-meal he offered up [. . .]:
"Mountain, bring me a dream [. . .],
Furnish for him [. . .]!"

(iv)

[The mountain] brought a dr[eam for Enkidu],
It furnished for him [. . .].
A cold shower passed over [. . .];
It made him lie down [. . .],
[. . .] and like mountain barley [. . .].
[Gil]gamesh plants his chin on his knees.
Sleep, which is shed on mankind, overcame him.
In the middle watch he ended his sleep.
He started up, saying to his friend:
"My friend, didst thou not call me? Why did I waken?
Didst thou not touch me? Why am I startled?
Did some god go by? Why is my flesh aquiver?
My friend, I saw a third dream,
And the dream that I saw was wholly awesome!
The heavens shrieked, the earth boomed,
[Day]light had failed, darkness had come.
Lightning flashed, a flame shot up,
[*The clouds*] swelled, it rained death!
Then the glow[90] [vanished], the fire went out,
[And all that] had fallen was turned to ashes.
Let us go down! Outside[91] we can take counsel."
[When] Enkidu [heard][92] the dream he had brought him,
He said to Gilgamesh.

(Enkidu's reply is lost. The subsequent break in the Assyrian version is made up in part by the Hittite recension; cf. J. Friedrich, *ZA*, XXXIX [1929], 8 ff.)

[Gilgamesh] seized [the axe in (his) hand]
[. . . and] felled [the cedar].
[*But when Huwawa*] heard the *noise*,
[He] became angry: "Who has [come],
[*Has slighted the trees, which*] had been grown in my mountains,
And has felled the cedar?"

[Then] down from heaven spoke to them
Heavenly Shamash: "Draw near,
Fear you not, and [. . .]
March, as long [as . . .]
Into (his) house he does not [enter . . .]."

(Remainder of fragment mutilated. A further fragment implies that things had not gone well with the two friends, for)

His tears [came down in] streams. (6)
And Gilgamesh [said] to heavenly Shamash:

(two lines fragmentary and obscure)

"But I have [come] to heavenly Shamash
And have taken the road assigned [. . .]."
Heavenly Shamash hearkened to the prayer of Gilgamesh;
And against Huwawa mighty winds
Rise up: the great wind, the north wind, [. . .],
The storm wind, the chill wind, the tem[pestuous] wind,
The hot wind; eight winds rose up against him and
Beat against the eyes [of Huwawa].
And he is unable to move forward,
Nor is he able to move back.
Then Huwawa let up.

Thereupon Huwawa replied to Gilgamesh:
"Let me go, Gilgamesh; thou [wilt be] my [master],
And I shall be thy servant. And of [the trees]
Which I have grown, I shall [. . .]
Strong . . . [. . .]
Cut down and houses [. . .]."
But Enkidu [said] to [Gilgamesh]:
"To the word which Huwawa [has spoken]
H[ark] not [. . .]
Let not Huwawa [. . .]."

(The sequel seems to be found in the mutilated Assyrian fragment, *GETh*, Pl. 19, which ends [line 43] with these words:)

[. . .] the head of Humba[ba *they* cut down . . .].

Tablet VI

He[93] washed his grimy hair, polished his *weapons*,
The braid of his hair he shook out against his back.
He cast off his soiled (things), put on his clean things,
Wrapped a fringed cloak about and fastened a sash.
When Gilgamesh had put on his tiara,
Glorious Ishtar raised an eye at the beauty of Gilgamesh:
"Come, Gilgamesh, be thou (my) lover!
Do but grant me of thy fruit.
Thou shalt be my husband and I will be thy wife.
I will harness for thee a chariot of lapis
and gold,
Whose wheels are gold and whose horns are *electrum*.[94]

90 For *ni-bu-tu*, cf. *ibid.*, 120.
91 This idiomatic sense appears to be more suitable here than "steppe."
92 Supplying [*iš-me-m*]*a*, with Schott, *loc. cit.*, 120.
93 Gilgamesh.
94 This seems to be a plausible identification, especially in view of the occurrence of ornaments made of electrum in various Mesopotamian sites.

Thou shalt have storm-demons to hitch on for mighty mules.
Under the fragrance of cedars thou shalt enter our house.
When our house thou enterest,
Threshold (and) dais shall kiss thy feet!
Humbled before thee shall be kings, lords, and princes!
The *yield* of hills and plain they shall bring thee as tribute.
Thy goats shall cast triplets, thy sheep twins,
Thy he-ass in lading shall surpass thy mule.
Thy chariot horses shall be famed for racing,
[Thine ox] under yoke shall not have a rival!"

[Gilgamesh] opened his mouth to speak,
[Saying] to glorious Ishtar:
["What am I to give] thee, that I may take thee in marriage?
[Should I give oil] for the body, and clothing?
[Should I give] bread and victuals?
[. . .] food fit for divinity,
[. . .] drink fit for royalty.

(mutilated)

[. . . if I] take thee in marriage?
[Thou art but a brazier which goes out[95]] in the cold;
A back door [which does not] keep out blast and windstorm;
A palace which crushes the valiant [. . .];
A *turban*[96] whose cover [. . .];
Pitch which [soils] its bearers;
A waterskin which [soaks through] its bearer;
Limestone which [*springs*] the stone rampart;
Jasper [which . . .] enemy land;
A shoe which [pinches the foot[97]] of its owner!
Which lover didst thou love forever?
Which of thy shepherds[98] pleased[99] [thee for all time]?
Come, and I will *na*[*me* for thee] thy lovers:

Of . . . [. . .] . . .
For Tammuz, the lover of thy youth,
Thou hast ordained wailing year after year.
Having loved the dappled shepherd-bird,
Thou smotest him, breaking his wing.
In the grooves he sits,[100] crying 'My wing!'[101]
Then thou lovedst a lion, perfect in strength;
Seven pits and seven thou didst dig for him.
Then a stallion thou lovedst, famed in battle;
The whip, the spur, and the lash thou ordainedst for him.
Thou decreedst for him to gallop seven leagues,
Thou decreedst for him the muddied to drink;[102]
For his mother, Silili, thou ordainedst wailing!
Then thou lovedst the keeper of the herd,
Who ash-cakes ever did heap up for thee,
Daily slaughtered kids for thee;
Yet thou smotest him, turning him into a wolf,
So that his own herd boys drive him off,
And his dogs bite his thighs.[103]
Then thou lovedst Ishullanu, thy father's gardener,
Who baskets of dates ever did bring to thee,
And daily did brighten thy table.
Thine eyes raised at him, thou didst go to him:
'O my Ishullanu, let us taste of thy vigor!
Put forth thy "hand" and touch our "modesty!" '[104]
Ishullanu said to thee:
'What dost thou want with me?
Has my mother not baked, have I not eaten,
That I should taste the food of offense[105] and curses?
Does reed-work afford cover against the cold?'[106]
As thou heardst this his talk,
Thou smotest him and turn[edst] him into a spider.
Thou placedst him in the midst of . . [.] ;
He cannot go up . . . nor can he come down . . .[107]
If thou shouldst love me, thou wouldst [treat me] like them."

When Ishtar heard this,
Ishtar was enraged and [mounted] to heaven.
Forth went Ishtar before Anu, her father,
To Antum, her mother, she went and [said]:
"My father, Gilgamesh has heaped insults upon me!
Gilgamesh has recounted my offenses,
My offenses and my curses."
Anu opened his mouth to speak,
Saying to glorious Ishtar:
"But surely, thou didst invite . [. .],
And so Gilgamesh has recounted thy offenses,
Thy offenses and thy cu[rses]."

Ishtar opened her mouth to speak,
Saying to [Anu, her father]:
"My father, make me the Bull of Heaven [that he smite Gilgamesh],
[And] fill Gil[gamesh . . .]!
If thou [dost not make] me [the Bull of Heaven],
I will smash [the doors of the nether world],[108]
I will [. . .],
I will [raise up the dead eating (and) alive],
So that the dead shall outnumber the living!"

Anu [opened his mouth to speak],

95 This, rather than the generally supplied "oven," accords with the cultural background of the passage. Read [*at-ti-ma ḳi-nu-nu bi-lu-u*].

96 cf. Böhl, *HGE*, 134. "Elephant" would surely not be appropriate.

97 Reading *mu-na-*[*ši-ḳat šēp*] *be-li-ša*. For an omen based on the death of Bur-Sin, "who died of the bite of a shoe," see Goetze, *JCS*, I (1947), 261.

98 cf. Oppenheim, *BASOR*, 104 (1947), 12-13.

99 Reading *i-ṭib-u*.

100 Var. "stands."

101 Akk. *ḳappi*, plainly a word play on the cry of the bird; cf. Thompson, *EG*, 33, n.3.

102 Lit. "to make turbid (and) drink."

103 cf. E. Ebeling, *Tod und Leben* (1931), 103, n. c.

104 cf. W. F. Albright, *RA*, XVI (1919), 183.

105 Comparison with Heb. *pšʿ* "to sin" (with E. Ebeling, *AfO*, VIII [1932/33], 229) seems appropriate, especially since the biblical term is used primarily of moral offenses.

106 This appears to be a proverbial expression.

107 For suggestions about the meaning of the terms which have been left untranslated, cf. Oppenheim, *Orientalia*, XVII (1948), 37, n.4.

108 For lines 96-100 cf. *Descent of Ishtar*, obv. 17-20.

Saying [to glorious Ishtar]:
"[If I do what] thou askedst [of me],
[There will be] seven years of (barren) husks.
Hast thou gathered [grain for the people]?
Has thou grown grass [for the beasts]?"

[Ishtar opened her mouth] to speak,
[Saying to A]nu, her father:
"[Grain for the people] I have stored,
[Grass for the beasts] I have provided.
[If there should be seven] years of husks,
[I have ga]thered [grain for the people],
[I have grown] grass [for the beasts]."

(Lines 114-28 are too fragmentary for translation. It is plain, however, that Anu did Ishtar's bidding, for the Bull comes down and kills hundreds of men with his first two snorts.)

With [his] third snort [. . .] upon Enkidu.
Enkidu *parried*[109] his onslaught.
Up leaped Enkidu, seizing the Bull of Heaven by the horns.
The Bull of Heaven hurled [his] foam in [his] face,
Brushed[110] him with the thick of his tail.

Enkidu opened his mouth to speak,
Saying [to Gilgamesh]:
"My friend, we have gloried [. . .]."

(Lines 137-51 mutilated, but the course of the battle is made plain by the following:)

Between neck and horns [he thrust]
his sword.
When they had slain the Bull, they tore out his heart,
Placing it before Shamash.
They drew back and did homage before Shamash.
The two brothers sat down.

Then Ishtar mounted the wall of ramparted Uruk,
Sprang on the battlements, uttering a curse:
"Woe unto Gilgamesh because he insulted me[111]
By slaying the Bull of Heaven!"
When Enkidu heard this speech of Ishtar,
He *tore loose* the right thigh of the Bull of Heaven
And tossed it in her face:
"Could I but get thee, like unto him
I would do unto thee.
His entrails I would hang at thy side!"
(Thereupon) Ishtar assembled the votaries,
The (pleasure-)lasses and the (temple-)harlots.
Over the right thigh of the Bull of Heaven she set up a wail.
But Gilgamesh called the craftsmen, the armorers,
All (of them).

The artisans admire the thickness of his[112] horns:
Each is cast from thirty minas of lapis;
The coating[113] on each is two fingers (thick);
Six measures[114] of oil, the capacity of the two,
He offered as ointment to his god, Lugalbanda.
He brought (them) and hung them in his princely bed-chamber.[115]

In the Euphrates they washed their hands,
They embraced each other as they went on,
Riding through the market-street of Uruk.
The people of Uruk are gathered to gaze [upon them].
Gilgamesh to the *lyre maids*[116] [of Uruk]
Says (these) words:
"Who is most splendid among the heroes?
Who is most glorious among men?"
"Gilgamesh is most splendid among the heroes,
[Gilgamesh is most glori]ous among men."

(mutilated) (186-188)

Gilgamesh in his palace holds a celebration.
Down lie the heroes on their beds of night.
Also Enkidu lies down, a dream beholding.
Up rose Enkidu to relate his dream,
Saying to his friend:
"My friend, why are the great gods in council?"[117]

Tablet VII

The first two columns of this tablet are missing in the Assyrian Version. Enkidu's dream, however, is the subject of *KUB*, VIII, 48, and this Hittite text has been dealt with by J. Friedrich in *ZA*, XXXIX (1929), 16-19.

"[. . .] . . . Then daylight came."
[And] Enkidu answered Gilgamesh:
"[*He*]*ar* the dream which I had this night:
Anu, Enlil, Ea, and heavenly Shamash
[Were in council].
And Anu said to Ea:
'Because the Bull of Heaven they have slain, and Huwawa
They have slain, therefore'—said Anu—'the one of them
Who stripped the mountains of the cedar
[Must die!]'
But Enlil said: 'Enkidu must die;
Gilgamesh, however, shall not die!'

Then heavenly Shamash answered valiant Enlil:
'Was it not at my[118] command

[109] This translation is required by the context; but neither a derivation from *m(w)adū* nor from *maṭū* is satisfactory as the text stands, unless the first sign, *im-* is an error for *um-*; the meaning of *um!-ta-[a]ṭ-ṭi* would be "diminished."

[110] Reading *[il]-pu-us-su*, with Oppenheim, *loc. cit.*, 38.

[111] For *ṭuppulu* in this sense cf. B. Meissner, *MAOG*, XI (1937), 46-47. Comparison with Arab. *ṭfl* "little" may be suggested in further support.

[112] The Bull's.

[113] For this meaning of *taḫ(a)bātu* cf. Oppenheim, *loc. cit.*, 40, n.2. The singular is common in the Nuzi texts.

[114] The *gur*-measure was the equivalent of about 250 quarts.

[115] For this meaning of *ina urši ḫammūti* cf. Landsberger, *MAOG*, IV (1928/29), 299, n.2.

[116] The context calls clearly for musicians or singers, not servant girls; hence neither *ṭuppulu* (cf. n.111) nor *tabālu* can underlie the present term. However, Heb. *nēbel* "psaltery" suggests an excellent semantic and morphological background.

[117] Catch-line of the following tablet.

[118] Text "thy." See, however, Schott, *GE*, 45, n.1.

That they slew the Bull of Heaven and Huwawa?
Should now innocent
Enkidu die?' But Enlil turned
In anger to heavenly Shamash: 'Because, *much like*
One of their[119] comrades, thou didst daily go down to them.' "
Enkidu lay down (ill) before Gilgamesh.
And as his[120] tears were streaming down, (he said):
"O my brother, my dear brother! Me they would
Clear at the expense of my brother!"
Furthermore:
"Must I by the spirit (of the dead)
Sit down, at the spirit's door,
Never again [to behold] my dear brother with (mine) eyes?"

(The remainder is lost. In a deathbed review of his life, Enkidu seems to bemoan the events that had led up to this sorry state, cursing the successive steps in his fated life. One of his curses, preserved in an Assyrian fragment,[121] is directed against the gate that lamed his hand.)

Enkidu [. . .] lifted up [his eyes],
Speaking with the door as though [it were human]:
"Thou door of the woods, uncom[prehending],
Not endowed with understanding!
At twenty leagues away I found choice
thy wood,
(Long) before I beheld the lofty cedar.
There is no counterpart of thy wood [*in the land*].
Six dozen cubits is thy height, two dozen thy breadth [. . .].
Thy pole, thy pole-ferrule, and thy pole-knob[122] [. . .].
A *master-craftsman* in Nippur built thee [. . .].
Had I known, O door, that this [*would come to pass*]
And that this [thy] beauty [. . .],
I would have lifted the axe, would have [. . .],
I would have *set* a reed frame *upon* [*thee*]!"[123]

(A long gap follows. When the text sets in again, Enkidu—continuing his bitter survey—invokes the curse of Shamash upon the hunter.)

(iii)

"[. . .] destroy his wealth,[124] diminish his power!
May his [way be *repugnant*] before thee.
May [*the beasts he would trap*] escape from before him.
[Let not] the hunter at[tain] the fullness of his heart!"
[Then his heart] prompted (him) to curse [the harlo]t-lass:
"Come, lass, I will decree (thy) [fa]te,
[A fa]te that shall not end for all eternity!
[I will] curse thee with a great curse,
[*An oath*], whose curses shall soon overtake thee.
[. . .] surfeit of thy charms.
(mutilated)
[. . .] shall cast into thy house.
[. . .] the road shall be thy dwelling place,
[The shadow of the wall] shall be
thy station,
[. . .] thy feet,
[The besotted and the thirsty shall smite] thy cheek![125]
(mutilated)
Because me [thou hast . . .]
And because [. . .] upon me."
When Shamash heard [these words] of his mouth,
Forthwith he called down to him [from] heaven:
"Why, O Enkidu, cursest thou the harlot-lass,
Who made thee eat food fit for divinity,
And gave thee to drink wine fit for royalty,
Who clothed thee with noble garments,
And made thee have fair Gilgamesh for a comrade?
And has (not) now Gilgamesh, thy bosom
friend,[126]
Made thee lie on a noble couch?
He has made thee lie on a couch of honor,
Has placed thee on the seat of ease, the seat at the left,
That [the prin]ces of the earth may kiss thy feet!
He will make Uruk's people weep over thee (and) lament,
Will fill [joyful] people with woe over thee.
And, when thou art gone,[127]
He will his body with uncut hair invest,
Will don a lion skin and roam over the steppe."

[When] Enkidu [heard] the words of valiant Shamash,
[. . .] his vexed heart grew quiet.

(Short break. Relenting, Enkidu changes his curse into a blessing. He addresses himself once again to the girl:)

(iv)

"May [. . .] return to thy pl[ace . . .].
[Kings, prin]ces, and nobles shall love [thee].
[None shall on account of thee] smite his thigh.[128]
[Over thee shall the old man] shake his beard.
[. . .] shall unloose his girdle.
[. . .] *carnelian*, lapis, and gold.
[May he be paid] back who defiled thee,
[*May his home be emptied*], his heaped-up storehouse.[129]
[To the presence of] the gods [the priest] shall leave thee enter,

[119] Text "his."
[120] Referring to Gilgamesh; cf. Friedrich, *loc. cit.*, 51.
[121] The episode of the gate (K 3588, *GETh*, Pls. 14-15) was assigned by Thompson to the beginning of Tablet IV. See, however, Schott, *ZA*, XLII (1934), 113 ff.
[122] For the meaning of the terms employed in this line cf. my note in *JCS*, II (1948/49), 225 ff.
[123] Perhaps *u-šar-ḳi-b[a]* "made ride upon." One can scarcely "construct" (*u-šar-ḳi-i[s]*) a reed frame out of a door.
[124] Reading *ni-mil-šu*.
[125] With the last three lines cf. *Descent of Ishtar*, rev. 24-28.
[126] Taking *ib-ri ta-li-me-ḳa* as the type of compound that is not uncommon in this epic; see above, notes 19, 23. For *talīmu* "intimate, germane" see P. Koschaker, *ZA*, XLI (1933), 64 ff. Lines 40-41 have been interpreted in an interrogative sense, in view of the lengthened penult vowels at the beginning of the clauses. "Has now . . .?" would seem to have the force of our "Has not now . . .?"
[127] Lit. "after him," an idiomatic use of *arḳi*.
[128] In derision or embarrassment, cf. Oppenheim, *Orientalia*, XVII (1948), 42, n.2.
[129] Oppenheim, *ibid.* The missing verb might be a form of *gullubu*.

[On thy account] shall be forsaken the wife,
(though) a mother of seven."
[. . . Enki]du, whose mood is bitter,
[. . .] lies down all alone.
That night [he pours out] his feelings to his friend:
"[My friend], I saw a dream this night:
The heavens [moaned], the earth responded;[130]
[. . .] I stood [alo]ne.
[. . .] his face was darkened.
Like unto [. . .] was his face.
[. . . like] the talons of an eagle were his claws.
[. . .] he *overpowered* me.
[. . .] he leaps.
[. . .] he submerged me.
(mutilated or missing) (23-30)
[. . .] . . . he transformed me,
So that my arms were [. . .] like those of a bird.
Looking at me, he leads me to the House of Darkness,
The abode of Irkalla,
To the house which none leave who have entered it,
On the road from which there is no way back,
To the house wherein the dwellers are bereft of light,
Where dust is their fare and clay their food.
They are clothed like birds, with wings for garments,
And see no light, residing in darkness.[131]
In the House of Dust, which I entered,
I looked at [rulers], their crowns put away;
I [saw princes], those (born to) the crown,
Who had ruled the land from the days of yore.
[These *doubl*]*es*[132] of Anu and Enlil were serving meat roasts;
They were serving bake[meats] and pouring
Cool water from the waterskins.
In the House of Dust, which I entered,
Reside High Priest and acolyte,
Reside incantatory and ecstatic,
Reside the laver-anointers of the great gods,
Resides Etana,[133] resides Sumuqan.[134]
Ereshkigal [lives there], Queen of the nether world,
[And Belit-]Seri, recorder of the nether world, kneels before her.
[She holds a tablet] and reads out to her.
[Lifting] up her head, she beheld me:
[Saying: 'Who] has brought this one hither?' "

(The remainder of the tablet in the Assyrian Version is missing. The following fragment [*GETh*, 34; Pls. 15-16] may be relevant, as argued by Schott, *ZA*, XLII [1934], 113 ff.)

"Remember all my travels [with him]! (4)
My friend saw a dream whose [*portents*] were un[favorable]:
The day on which he saw the dream was ended.
Stricken is Enkidu, one day, [a second day].
Enkidu's [suffering],[135] on his bed, [increases].
A third day, a fourth,
Enkidu's [suffering], on his bed, increases.
A fifth day, a sixth, and a seventh;
An eighth, a ninth, [and a tenth day],
Enkidu's suffering, on his bed, [increases].
[Stricken] is Enkidu on his bed [*of pain*]!
At length he called Gilgamesh [and said to him]:
'My friend, [. . .] has cursed me!
[Not] like one [fallen] in battle [shall I die],
For I feared the battle [. . .].
My friend, he who [is slain] in battle [is blessed].
But as for me, [. . .].' "

Tablet VIII

[With the] first [glow of dawn],[136]
Gilgamesh [opened his mouth], saying to [his friend]:
"O En[kidu . . . like] a gazelle,
And [. . .] thee.
[. . .] reared thee,
And [. . .] pastures.

Moun[tains we scaled and *reached*] the Cedar Forest,
[. . .] night and day."

(The remainder of the column mutilated or lost. With the next column we find Gilgamesh addressing the elders of Uruk at the deathbed of Enkidu:)

(ii)

"Hear me, O elders [and give ear] unto me!
It is for Enkidu, my [friend], that I weep,
Moaning bitterly like a wailing woman.
The axe at my side, the [bow] in my hand,
The dirk in my belt, [the shield] in front of me,
My festal robe, my [*greatest*] joy—
An evil [*demon*] rose up and [*robbed*] me!
[O my younger[137] friend], thou chasedst
The wild ass[138] of the hills, the panther of the steppe!
Enkidu, my younger friend, thou who chasedst
The wild ass of the hills, the panther of the steppe!
We who [have conquered] all things, scaled
[the mountains],
Who seized the Bull [and slew him],
Brought affliction[139] on Hubaba,[140] who [dwelled in the Cedar Forest]!
What, now, is this sleep that has laid hold [on thee]?
Thou art benighted and canst not hear [me]!"
But he lifts not up [his eyes];

130 A portent of death. For this association cf. the elegiac passage in the text published by E. Ebeling, *Tod und Leben* (1931), 58, rev. The verb to be supplied is therefore [*ú-nam-bu-ú*].
131 Lines 33-39 are paralleled in *Descent of Ishtar*, obv. 4-10.
132 If [*di-n*]*a-an* may be read.
133 Legendary king of Kish who was carried to heaven by an eagle.
134 God of cattle.
135 cf. below, line 11.
136 Lit. "As soon as something of the day glowed."
137 For *quṭānu* cf. P. Jensen, *Keilinschriftliche Bibliotheḳ*, VI (1900) 464-65.
138 On *aḳḳannu* see B. Meissner, *MAOG*, XI (1937), 11 f.
139 The verb *lapātu* offers a close semantic parallel to Heb. *pgʿ* "touch, afflict."
140 Variant of Ḫumbaba, the Ḫuwawa of the Old Babylonian and Boğazköy texts.

When he touches his heart, it does not beat.
Then he veiled (his) friend like a bride [. . .].
Like a lion he raises up [his voice],
Like a lioness deprived of [her] whelps.
He paces back and forth before [*the couch*],
Pulling out (his hair) and strewing [it forth],
Tearing off and flinging down his finery [. . .].[141]

With the first glow [of dawn], Gil[gamesh . . .].

(long break)

(iii)

"On a couch [of honor I made thee lie],[142]
I placed thee [on the seat of ease, the seat at the left],
That the princes of the earth [might kiss thy feet]!
Over thee I will make [Uruk's] people weep (and) [lament],
Joyful people [I will fill with woe over thee].
And, when thou art gone,
[I shall invest my body with uncut hair],
And, clad in a [lion] skin, [I shall roam over the steppe]!"

With the first glow of dawn, [Gilgamesh]
Loosened his band [. . .].

(The remainder of the tablet is missing or too fragmentary for translation, with the exception of the following lines:)

(v)

With the first glow of dawn, Gilgamesh
fashioned [. . .],
Brought out a large table of Elammaqu wood,
Filled with honey a bowl of *carnelian*,
Filled with curds a bowl of lapis,
[. . .] he decorated and exposed to the sun.

Tablet IX

(i)

For Enkidu, his friend, Gilgamesh
Weeps bitterly, as he ranges over the steppe:
"When I die, shall I not be like Enkidu?
Woe has entered my belly.
Fearing death, I roam over the steppe.
To Utnapishtim,[143] Ubar-Tutu's[144] son,
I have taken the road to proceed in all haste.
When arriving by night at mountain passes,
I saw lions and grew afraid.
I lifted my head to Sin[145] to pray.
To [. . .] of the gods went out my orisons.
[. . .] preserve thou me!"

[As at night] he lay, he awoke from a dream.
[There were . . .], rejoicing in life.
He raised his axe in his hand,
He drew [the dirk] from his belt.
Like an ar[row] he descended among them.
He smote [them] and hacked away at them.

(The remainder of the column is broken away. When he next appears, Gilgamesh had arrived before a mountain.)

(ii)

The name of the mountain is Mashu.
When [he arrived] at the mountain range[146] of Mashu,
Which daily keeps watch over sun[rise and sunset]—
Whose peaks[147] [reach to] the vault of heaven
(And) whose breasts reach to the nether world below—
Scorpion-men guard its gate,
Whose terror is awesome and whose glance was death.
Their shimmering[148] halo sweeps the mountains
That at sunrise and sunset keep watch over the sun.
When Gilgamesh beheld them, with fear
And terror was darkened his face.
He took hold[149] of his senses and bowed before them.
A scorpion-man calls to his wife:
"He who has come to us—his body is the flesh of the gods!"
His wife answers the scorpion-man:
"Two-thirds of him is god, one-third of him is human."
[The scorpi]on-man calls to the fellow,
Addressing (these) words [to the offspring] of the gods:
"[Why hast thou come on this] far journey?
[Why hast thou arrived] before me,
[Traversing seas][150] whose crossings are difficult?
[The purpose of thy com]ing I would learn."

(remainder of the column broken away)

(iii)

(Lines 1-2 destroyed. Gilgamesh replies:)
"On account of Utnapishtim, my father, [have I come],
Who joined the Assembly [of the gods, in search of life].
About death and life [I wish to ask him]."
The scorpion-man opened his mouth [to speak],
Saying to [Gilgamesh]:
"Never was there, Gilgamesh, [a mortal who could achieve that].[151]
The mountain's trail no one [has traveled].
For twelve leagues [extends] its inside.
Dense is the darkness and [light there is] none.
To the rising of the sun [. . .];
To the setting of the sun [. . .]."

(remainder mutilated or broken)

141 For a sensitive translation of this passage cf. Th. Jacobsen, *The Intellectual Adventure of Ancient Man* (1946), 207-08.
142 cf. VII, iii, 41 ff.
143 For Utnapishtim (Old Babylonian Utanapishtim), Mesopotamian hero of the Flood—Sumerian Z i u s u d r a and Greek Xisouthros—cf. Th. Jacobsen, *The Sumerian King List* (1939), 76-77, n.34.
144 On this name see Jacobsen, *op. cit.*, 75-76, n.32.
145 The moon-god.
146 For this passage cf. H. and J. Lewy, *HUCA*, XVII (1943), 13 f.
147 Since the name means "twins" in Akkadian, it is treated in the text either as singular or plural.
148 cf. Oppenheim, *Orientalia*, XVII (1948), 46, n.3.
149 Reading *iṣ-bat*.
150 For the restoration cf. Heidel, *GE*, 66, n.141.
151 *ibid.*

(iv)

(top missing)

"Whether in sorrow [or pain],
In cold or [heat],
Sighing [or weeping—I will go].
Now [open the gate of the mountain]!"
The scorpion-man [opened his mouth to speak];
To Gilgamesh he [says]:
"Go, Gilga[mesh . . .].
The mountains of Mashu [. . .].
The mountains (and) ranges [. . .].
In safety may [. . .].
The gate of the mountain [is open to thee]!"
When Gilga[mesh heard this],
To the word [of the scorpion-man he gave heed].
Along the road of the sun [he went].[152]
When one league [he had attained],
Dense is the dark[ness and light there is none];
He can [see nothing ahead or behind].[153]
When two leagues [he had attained]

(v)

(top broken)

When four leagues [he had attained],
Dense is the dark[ness and light there is none];
He can [see nothing ahead or behind].
When five leagues [he had attained],
Dense is the dark[ness and light there is none];
He can [see nothing ahead or behind].
[When six league]s he [had attained],
Dense is the darkness and [light there
is none];
He can [see nothing ahead or behind].
When seven leagues he had attained,
Dense is the darkness and [light there is] none;
He can [see nothing] ahead or behind.
Eight leagues he has tr[aveled] and he cries out.
Dense is the dark[ness and] light there is none;
He can [see] nothing ahead or behind.
Nine leagues [he has traveled and he *feels*] the north
wind
[. . . fan]ning his face.[154]
[Dense is the darkness and] light
there is [none];
[He can see nothing a]head or behind.
[When ten leagues] he [had attained],
[. . .] is near;
[. . .] of the league.

[152] Apparently from east to west; cf. X (Old Babylonian Version), iv, 11. In favor of this direction may be citied the fact that the ale-wife Siduri, whom Gilgamesh encounters in the course of his present journey, is a Hurrian term for "young woman" used to describe Ḫebat, a form of Ishtar in the Hurrian texts; cf. e.g. *KUB*, xxvii, 38, iv, 8; 42; obv. 23. Note also the Hurrian fragment of the epic, *KUB*, viii, 61, which writes this name with š (line 4), thus confirming Jensen's old suggestion that Siduri and Šiduri should be equated.

[153] Lit. "It permits him not [to see the fr]ont of it or his back"; restored from col. v, 34 and 41.

[154] For the entire passage cf. Oppenheim, *loc. cit.*, 47.

[When eleven leagues he had attained], the dawn
breaks.[155]
[And when he attained twelve leagues], it had grown
bright.
On seeing the grove of *stones*, he heads for [. . .].[156]
The carnelian bears its fruit;
It is hung with vines good to look at.
The lapis bears *foliage*;
It, too, bears fruit lush to behold.

(vi)

(This entire column is mutilated or lost. What little remains suggests a further account of the marvels to be seen in this garden of jewels.)

Tablet X

This tablet, which traces further the successive stages in Gilgamesh's quest of immortality, happens to be represented by as many as four separate versions. Two of these, however, the Hittite (cf. *ZA*, xxxix [1929], 20 ff.) and the Hurrian (cf. *ZA*, xxxv [1924], 133 ff.), are extant only in fragments that are too slight for connected translation. Substantial portions are available, on the other hand, in the Old Babylonian and Assyrian recensions. The Old Babylonian material was published by B. Meissner, *MVAG*, vii (1902).

OLD BABYLONIAN VERSION

(i)

(top broken away)

"[. . .] . . .
With their skins [he clothes himself],[157] as he eats flesh.
[.] . . , O Gilgamesh, which has not happened
As long as my wind drives the waters."
Shamash was distraught, as he betook himself to him;
He says to Gilgamesh:
"Gilgamesh, whither rovest thou?
The life thou pursuest thou shalt not find."
Gilgamesh says to him, to valiant Shamash:
"After marching (and) roving over the steppe,
Must I lay my head in the heart of the earth
That I may sleep through all the years?
Let mine eyes behold the sun
That I may have my fill of the light!
Darkness withdraws when there is enough light.
May he who has died a death behold the radiance of the
sun!"

(ii)

(Beginning lost. Gilgamesh is addressing Siduri, the ale-wife:)

"He who with me underwent all hard[ships]—
Enkidu, whom I loved dearly,
Who with me underwent all hardships—
Has now gone to the fate of mankind!
Day and night I have wept over him.
I would not give him up for burial—

[155] *ibid.*

[156] *ibid.*

[157] Supplying [*il-ta-ba-aš*].

In case[158] my friend should rise at my plaint—
Seven days and seven nights,
Until[159] a worm fell out of his nose.
Since his passing I have not found life,
I have roamed like a hunter in the midst of the steppe.
O ale-wife, now that I have seen thy face,
Let me not see the death which I ever dread."
The ale-wife said to him, to Gilgamesh:

(iii)

"Gilgamesh, whither rovest thou?
The life thou pursuest thou shalt not find.
When the gods created mankind,
Death for mankind they set aside,
Life in their own hands retaining.
Thou, Gilgamesh, let full be thy belly,
Make thou merry[160] by day and by night.
Of each day make thou a feast of rejoicing,
Day and night dance thou and play!
Let thy garments be sparkling fresh,
Thy head be washed; bathe thou in water.
Pay heed to the little one that holds on to thy hand,
Let thy spouse delight in thy bosom!
For this is the task of [mankind]!"

(remainder of the column broken away)

(iv)

In his wrath he shatters them.[161]
When he returned, he goes up to him.[162]
Sursunabu[163] his eyes behold.
Sursunabu says to him, to Gilgamesh:
"Tell me, thou, what is thy name?
I am Sursunabu, (he) of Utanapishtim[164] the Faraway."
Gilgamesh said to him, to Sursunabu:
"As for me, Gilgamesh is my name,
Who have come from Uruk-Eanna,[165]
Who have traversed[166] the mountains,
A distant journey, as the sun *rises*.[167]
O Sursunabu, now that I have seen thy face,
Show me Utanapishtim the Faraway."
Sursunabu [says] to him, to Gilgamesh.

(remainder broken away)

THE ASSYRIAN VERSION

Although the two versions overlap in several instances, it has seemed best to present each separately. For the beginning of this account cf. the Hittite fragments, *ZA*, XXXIX (1929) 22, lines 9 ff.

(i)

The ale-wife Siduri, who dwells by the deep sea
And sits [. . .].
For her they made a jug,
They made for her [a mashing bowl of gold].[168]
With a veil she is covered and [. . .].
Gilgamesh comes up to her and [. . .].
He is clad in skins [. . .],
The flesh of the gods is in [his body].
There is woe in [his belly],
His face is [like] that of a wayfarer from afar.
The ale-wife gazes afar off;
Speaking in her own heart [she says] (these) words,
As she [takes counsel] with herself:
"Surely, this one is a kill[er]![169]
Whither is he heading [. . .]?"
As the ale-wife saw him, she locked [the door],
She barred her gate, securing [the bolt].
But he, Gilgamesh, on hearing [the sounds],
Held up his point(ed staff) and pla[ced . . .].

Gilgamesh [says] to her, [to the ale-wife]:
"Ale-wife, what sawest thou [that thou hast
locked thy door],
Hast barred thy gate, [hast secured the bolt]?
I will smash [thy] door, shat[ter thy gate]!"

(The remainder of the column is badly mutilated. Much can be restored, however, from the repetitious sections of the succeeding columns and from a fragment [Sp. 299], published in *GETh*, Pl. 42. cf. also A. Schott, *ZA*, XLII [1934], 132 f., whose restorations and numbering of the lines have here been adopted; cf. also Heidel, *GE*, 72-3.)

[Gilgamesh says to her, to the ale-wife]:
"[I slew the watchman of the forest],
[Brought affliction on Humbaba who dwelled in the]
Ce[dar Forest],
[Sle]w the lions [in the mountain passes]."
[The ale-wife said to him], to Gilgamesh:
"[If thou art Gilgamesh], who didst slay
the watchman,
[Bring affliction on Hum]baba who dwelled in the
Cedar Forest,
Slay the lions in the mountain [passes],
[Seize and] slay the Bull that came down from heaven,
[Why then are] thy cheeks [wasted], is sunken thy face,
[Is so sad thy heart], are worn thy features?
[(Why) should there be woe] in *thy* belly,
Thy face be like [that of a wayfarer from afar],
[With] cold and heat be seared thy countenance,

158 For this approximate meaning of the particle *-man*, cf. *ZA*, LX (1932), 200, n.4.

159 Reading *a-di*!

160 Interpreting *ḫi-ta-at-tu* as the imperative form *ḫitaddu*, with Landsberger, *ZA*, XLII (1934), 134, n.1.

161 Apparently the mysterious "Stone Things," cf. Assyrian Version, x, ii, 29.

162 To the boatman.

163 The Urshanabi of the Assyrian Version. For a suggested value *zur* as a reading of the first syllable in the Assyrian form of the name cf. A. Poebel, *JAOS*, LVII (1937), 54, n.22.

164 Assyrian Utnapishtim. Perhaps "I have found life," (in a somewhat anomalous grammatical construction), in contrast to the warning *balāṭam lā tuttā* (i, 8; iii, 2) "life thou shalt not find," with which Gilgamesh is confronted.

165 This time the entire phrase seems to be treated as a grammatical compound, which would explain the Akkadian genitive as referring to the whole; unless, of course, an error is to be assumed.

166 Reading *ša ás-ḫu-ra-am*, with W. von Soden, *ZA*, XLII (1934), 135, n.1.

167 See above, n.152.

168 Restored with J. Friedrich and H. Zimmern, *ZA*, XXXIX (1929), 53.

169 Reading *mu-na-'-[i-ru]*.

[As in quest of a wind-puff[170]] thou roamest over the steppe?"
[Gilgamesh says to her, to the ale-wife]:
"[O ale-wife, why should my cheeks not be so wasted],
[So sunken my face],
[So sad my heart, so worn my features]?
[(Why) should there not be woe in my belly],
[My face not be like that of a wayfarer from afar],
[Not be so seared my countenance with cold and heat],
[And in quest of a wind-puff should I not roam over the steppe]?[171]
[My younger friend],
[Who chased the wild ass of the hills, the panther of the steppe],
[Enkidu, my younger friend],
[Who chased the wild ass of the hills, the panther of the steppe],
[We who conquered all things, scaled the mountains],

(ii)

[Who seized the Bull of Heaven and slew him],
[Brought affliction on Humbaba who dwelled in the Cedar Forest]—
[My friend, whom I loved so dearly],
[Who underwent with me all hardships],
[Him has overtaken the fate of mankind]!
[Six days and seven nights I wept over him],
[Until the worm fell out of his nose].
[Fearing death, I roam over the steppe];
The matter of my friend [rests (heavy) upon me].
[On faraway paths] I roam [over the steppe];
The matter of Enkidu, [my friend, rests (heavy) upon me].
[How can I be silen]t? How can I be still?
[My friend, whom I loved, has turn]ed to clay!
[Must I, too, like] him, lay me down,
[Not to rise] again for ever and ever?"

[Gilgamesh] also says to her, to the ale-wife:
"[Now], ale-wife, which is the way to Utnapishtim?
[What are] its markers? Give me, O give me, its markers!
If it be possible, the sea I will cross;
If it be not possible, over the steppe I will range!"

The ale-wife said to him, to Gilgamesh:
"Never, O Gilgamesh, has there been a crossing,
And none who came since the beginning of days could cross the sea.
Only valiant Shamash crosses the sea;
Other than Shamash, who can cross (it)?
Toilsome is the place of crossing,
Very toilsome the way thereto,
And deep are the Waters of Death that bar its approaches!
Where then, O Gilgamesh, wouldst thou cross the sea?
On reaching the Waters of Death, what wouldst thou do?
Gilgamesh, there is Urshanabi,[172] boatman to Utnapishtim.
With him are the Stone Things.[173] In the woods he picks *'urnu'-snaḳes.*[174]
[Hi]m let thy face behold.
[If it be] suitable, cross thou with him;
If it be not suitable, draw thou back."
[When Gilgamesh] heard this,
[He raised the a]xe in [his hand],
[Drew the dirk from his belt], slipped into (the forest),
And went down to them.[175]
[Like *an arrow*] he descended among them.

(remainder too fragmentary for translation)

(iii)

Urshanabi said to him, to Gilgamesh:
"Why are thy cheeks wasted, is sunken [thy face],
Is so sad thy heart, [are worn thy features]?
(Why) should there be woe in [thy belly],
[Thy face be like that] of a wayfarer from afar,
With cold and heat be seared [thy countenance],
[As in quest of a wind-puff] thou roamest over the steppe"
[Gilgamesh] said [to him], to [Urshanabi]:
"[Urshanabi, why should my] cheeks [not be so wasted],
[So sunken my face],
[So sad] my [heart], so worn my features?
[(Why) should there not be] woe in [my belly],
[My face not be like that of a wayfarer from afar],
Not be so seared [my countenance with cold and heat],
[And in quest of a wind-puff should I not roam over the steppe]?
[My younger friend],
[Who chased the wild ass of the hills, the panther of the steppe],
[Enkidu, my younger friend],
[Who chased the wild ass of the hills, the panther of the steppe],
[We who conquered all things, scaled the mountains],
[Who seized the Bull of Heaven and slew him],
[Brought affliction on Humbaba who dwelled in the Cedar Forest]—
My friend, [whom I loved so dearly],
[Who underwent with me all hardships],

170 For *šiḳit šāri* Oppenheim, *Orientalia*, XVII (1948), 49, proposes 'mirage.' We obtain, however, much the same sense by translating "wind-puff," lit. "deposit, creation of the wind." cf. the *ziqiqu-amēlūtu* "wind-puff people," E. Ebeling, *Tod und Leben* (1931), 30 and 33, 35; and, below, XII, 82.

171 For this passage see the rendering of Leonard, *Gilgamesh*, 47 f.

172 Sursunabu in Old Babylonian.

173 The *šūt abnē* "those of stone" are apparently stone figures of unusual properties, to judge from the relevant Hittite fragment, *ZA*, XXXIX (1929), 26, line 3, and pp. 59-60. cf. also the Sumerian NIG.NA$_4$ "thing(s) of stone," to which Goetze has called attention in *JCS*, I (1947), 261, n.51.

174 In referring to this passage, Landsberger, *Fauna* (1934), 63, points out that the *urnu*-snake has long been supposed to be a favorite with sailors. At all events, whatever the meaning of the term may be in the present connection, its properties seem to be on a par with those of the Stone Things.

175 The Stone Things.

Enk[idu, my friend, whom I loved so dearly,
Who underwent with me all hardships]
[Him] has overtaken [the fate of mankind]!
Six days [and seven nights I wept over him],
Until [the worm fell out of his nose].
Fea[ring death, I roam over the steppe],
The mat[ter of my friend rests (heavy) upon me].
On [faraway] paths [I roam over the steppe],
[On] distant roa[ds] I [roam over the steppe];
[The matter of my friend rests (heavy) upon me].
How can I be sile[nt? How can I be still]?
My friend, whom I loved, has turn[ed to clay]!
Must I too, like him, lay me [down],
[Not to rise again forever and ever]?"

Gilgamesh further says to him, to [Urshanabi]:
"Now, Urshanabi, which is [the road to Utnapishtim]?
What are its markers? Give me, O give [me, its markers]!
If it be possible, the sea I will cross;
If it be not possible, [over the steppe I will range]."

Urshanabi said to him, to [Gilgamesh]:
"Thy hands, Gilgamesh, have hindered [the crossing]!
Thou hast broken the Stone Things, hast picked [the *'urnu'-snakes*].
The Stone Things are broken, the *'urnu'* is not [*in the woods*].
Gilgamesh, raise the axe in [thy hand],[176]
Go down to the woods and [cut down twice-sixty] poles
Of sixty cubits each.
Apply the bitumen and attach *ferrules*;[177]
Then bring (them) [to me]!"
When Gilgamesh [heard] this,
He raised the axe in his hand,
Drew [the dirk from his belt],
Went down to the woods and cut [twice-sixty poles]
Of sixty cubits each.
He applied the bitumen and attached the *ferrules*;
And he brought [(them) to him].
Gilgamesh and Urshanabi boarded [the boat].
They launched the boat on the waves and they [sailed away].
A run of a month and fifteen days they left behind by the third day.
Urshanabi arrived thus at the Waters
[of Death].

(iv)

Urshanabi [said] to him, [to Gilgamesh]:
"Press on, Gilgamesh, [take a pole],
(But) let thy hand not touch the Waters of Death. [..]!
A second, a third, and a fourth pole take thou, Gilgamesh,
A fifth, a sixth, and a seventh pole take thou, Gilgamesh,
An eighth, a ninth, and a tenth pole take thou, Gilgamesh,
An eleventh, a twelfth pole take thou, Gilgamesh!"
At twice-sixty Gilgamesh had used up the poles.[178]
Then he ungirded his loins. [..].
Gilgamesh pulled off [his] cl[oth ...].
With his hand he holds it aloft as a *sail*.
Utnapishtim peers into the distance.
Speaking to his heart, [he says] (these) words,
As [he takes counsel] with himself:
"Why have [the Stone Things] of the boat been broken,
And rides [in her] one who is not her master?
He who has come hither is not a man of mine;
And [...].
I peer, but I [cannot ...],
I peer, but [I cannot ...],
I peer, but [...]."

(The remainder of this column and the beginning of the next are lost. Gilgamesh meets Utnapishtim and, to judge from the available fragments, is greeted with questions that are exact duplicates of those previously put to him by Siduri and Urshanabi. The same holds true of the first part of his reply. The concluding part follows:)

(v)

Gilgamesh also said to him, to Utnapishtim:
"That now I might come and behold Utnapishtim,
Whom they call the Faraway,
I ranged and wandered over all the lands,
I traversed difficult mountains,
I crossed all the seas!
My face was not sated with sweet sleep,
I fretted myself with wakefulness;
I filled my joints with aches.
I had not reached the ale-wife's house,
When my clothing was used up.
[I sl]ew bear,[179] hyena, lion, panther,
Tiger, stag, (and) ibex—
The wild beasts and creeping things of the steppe.
Their [flesh] I ate and their skins I *wr*[*apped about me*]."

(The remainder of this column is too mutilated for translation. The beginning of the last column is broken away, except for the conclusion of the sage observations of Utnapishtim:)

(vi)

"Do we build houses for ever?
Do we seal (contracts) for ever?
Do brothers divide shares for ever?
Does hatred persist for ever in [the land]?
Does the river for ever raise up (and) bring on floods?
The dragon-fly [leaves] (its) shell[180]
That its face might (but) glance at the face of the sun?

176 For the remainder of the column cf. the Hittite recension, *ZA*, XXXIX (1929), 24-25.

177 cf. Thompson, *EG*, 48, n.1.

178 Each pole was good only for a single thrust, since not a drop of the water must touch the hand; cf. *GETh*, 85.

179 Reading [*a-du*]-*ka a-sa*.

180 For *qilippu* cf. Oppenheim, *Orientalia*, XVII (1948), 50, n.3, although his precise interpretation has not been followed here.

Since the days of yore there has been no [permanence];
The *resting* and the dead, how alike [they are]!
Do they not compose[181] a picture of death,
The commoner and the noble,
Once they are near to [their fate]?
The Anunnaki, the great gods, foregather;
Mammetum, maker of fate, with them the fate decrees:
Death and life they determine.
(But) of death, its days are not revealed."

Tablet XI

Gilgamesh said to him, to Utnapishtim the Faraway:
"As I look upon thee, Utnapishtim,
Thy features are not strange; even as I art thou.
Thou art not strange at all; even as I art thou.
My heart had regarded thee as resolved[182] to do battle,
[Yet] thou liest indolent upon thy back!
[Tell me,] how joinedst thou the Assembly of the gods,
In thy quest of life?"

Utnapishtim said to him, to Gilgamesh:
"I will reveal to thee, Gilgamesh, a hidden matter
And a secret of the gods will I tell thee:
Shurippak—a city which thou knowest,
[(And) which on Euphrates' [banks] is set—
That city was ancient, (as were) the gods within it,
When their heart led the great gods to produce the flood.
[*There*] *were* Anu, their father,
Valiant Enlil, their counselor,
Ninurta, their herald,
Ennuge, their irrigator.[183]
Ninigiku-Ea was also present with them;
Their words he repeats to the reed-hut:[184]
'Reed-hut, reed-hut! Wall, wall!
Reed-hut, hearken! Wall, reflect!
Man of Shuruppak,[185] son of Ubar-Tutu,
Tear down (this) house, build a ship!
Give up possessions, seek thou life.
Despise property and keep the soul alive!
Aboard the ship take thou the seed of all living things.
The ship that thou shalt build,
Her[186] dimensions shall be to measure.
Equal shall be her width and her length.
Like the Apsu thou shalt ceil her."[187]
I understood, and I said to Ea, my lord:
'[Behold], my lord, what thou hast thus ordered,
I shall be honored to carry out.
[But what] shall I answer the city, the people and elders?'[188]

Ea opened his mouth to speak,
Saying to me, his servant:
'Thou shalt then thus speak unto them:
"I have learned that Enlil is hostile to me,
So that I cannot reside in your city,
Nor set my f[oo]t in Enlil's territory.
To the Deep I will therefore go down,
To dwell with my lord Ea.
[But upon] you he will shower down abundance,
[The *choicest*] birds, the *rarest*[189] fishes.
[*The land shall have its fill*] of harvest riches.
[He who at dusk orders] the husk-greens,
Will shower down upon you a rain of wheat." '[190]

With the first glow of dawn,
The land was gathered [about me].
(too fragmentary for translation)
The little ones [carr]ied bitumen,
While the grown ones brought [all else] that was needful.
On the fifth day I laid her framework.
One (whole) acre[191] was her floor space,[192]
Ten dozen cubits the height of each of her walls,
Ten dozen cubits each edge of the square deck.[193]
I laid out the shape of her sides and joined her together.[194]
I provided her with six decks,
Dividing her (thus) into seven parts.
Her floor plan I divided into nine parts.
I hammered water-plugs into her.[195]
I saw to the punting-poles and laid in supplies.[196]
Six 'sar' (measures)[197] of bitumen I poured into the furnace,
Three sar of asphalt [I also] poured inside.
Three sar of oil the basket-bearers transferred,
Aside from the one sar of oil which the *calking*[198] consumed,
And the two sar of oil [which] the boatman stowed away.
Bullocks I slaughtered for the [people],
And I killed sheep every day.
Must, red wine, oil, and white wine[199]
[I gave the] workmen [to drink], as though river water,
That they might feast as on New Year's Day.
I op[ened . . .] ointment, applying (it) to my hand.

181 Lit. "draw, design."

182 For the sense of *tagmir libbi* cf. F. Thureau-Dangin, *Huitième campagne de Sargon* (1912), line 52, and p. 11, n.7. And for the factitive force of the intensive conjugation cf. Heidel, *EG*, 80, n.164.

183 More specifically, "inspector of canals," cf. *Creation Epic*, VII, 62.

184 Presumably, the dwelling place of Utnapishtim. Ea addresses him through the barrier of the wall.

185 Line 11 has the uncommon form Shurippak instead.

186 The Akkadian for "ship" is feminine, although without the grammatical feminine ending.

187 For the description of the subterranean waters of the Apsū cf. *Creation Epic*, IV, 62.

188 cf. my remarks in *Studies in the History of Culture* (1942), 60.

189 I take these genitive forms to denote the superlative, in accordance with Semitic usage. The literal sense would be "[A choice of] birds, a hiding of fishes."

190 Restored from lines 87, 90. As has long been recognized, these lines feature word plays in that both *kukku* and *kibāti* may designate either food or misfortune; cf. C. Frank, *ZA*, XXXVI (1935), 218. Wily Ea plays on this ambiguity: To the populace, the statement would be a promise of prosperity; to Utnapishtim it would signalize the impending deluge.

191 cf. Heidel, *EG*, 82, n.170.

192 Schott and Landsberger, *ZA*, XLII (1934), 137.

193 The ship was thus an exact cube, cf. Heidel, *EG*, 82, n.173.

194 cf. Oppenheim, *Orientalia*, XVII (1948), 52.

195 For O. Neugebauer's explanation of the plugs cf. *ZA*, XLII, 138.

196 Lit. "the needful."

197 Var. "three *šar*." The *šar* was the number 3,600. If the measure understood with it was the *sūtu* (seah), each *šar* designated about 8,000 gallons; cf. Heidel, *EG*, 83, n.178.

198 For *niqqu* cf. A. Salonen, *Die Wasserfahrzeuge in Babylonien* (1939), 149, n.2.

199 See A. Poebel, *ZA*, XXXIX (1929), 149.

[On the sev]enth [day] the ship was completed.
[*The launching*] was very difficult,
So that they had to shift the floor planks[200] above and below,
[*Until*] two-thirds of [*the structure*][201] [*had g*]*one* [*into the water*].

[Whatever I had] I laded upon her:
Whatever I had of silver I laded upon her;
Whatever I [had] of gold I laded upon her;
Whatever I had of all the living beings I [laded] upon her.
All my family and kin I made go aboard the ship.
The beasts of the field, the wild creatures of the field,
All the craftsmen I made go aboard.
Shamash had set for me a stated time:
'When he who orders unease at night,[202]
Will shower down a rain of blight,
Board thou the ship and batten up the gate!'
That stated time had arrived:
'He who orders unease at night, showers down a rain of blight.'
I watched the appearance of the weather.
The weather was awesome to behold.
I boarded the ship and battened up the gate.
To batten up[203] the (whole) ship, to Puzur-Amurri, the boatman,
I handed over the structure together with its contents.

With the first glow of dawn,
A black cloud rose up from the horizon.
Inside it Adad thunders,
While Shullat and Hanish[204] go in front,
Moving as heralds over hill and plain.
Erragal[205] tears out the posts;[206]
Forth comes Ninurta and causes the dikes to follow.
The Anunnaki lift up the torches,
Setting the land ablaze with their glare.
Consternation[207] over Adad reaches to the heavens,
Turning to blackness all that had been light.
[The wide] land was shattered like [a pot]!
For one day the south-storm [blew],
Gathering speed as it blew, [submerging the mountains],
Overtaking the [people] like a battle.
No one can see his fellow,
Nor can the people be recognized from heaven.
The gods were frightened by the deluge,
And, shrinking back, they ascended to the heaven of Anu.[208]
The gods cowered like dogs
Crouched against the outer wall.
Ishtar cried out like a woman in travail,
The sweet-voiced mistress of the [gods] moans aloud:
'The olden days are alas turned to clay,
Because I bespoke evil in the Assembly of the gods.
How could I bespeak evil in the Assembly of the gods,
Ordering battle for the destruction of my people,
When it is I myself who give birth to my people!
Like the spawn of the fishes they fill the sea!'
The Anunnaki gods weep with her,
The gods, all humbled, sit and weep,
Their lips *drawn tight*,[209] [. . .] one and all.
Six days and [six] nights
Blows the flood wind, as the south-storm sweeps the land.
When the seventh day arrived,
The flood(-carrying) south-storm subsided in the battle,
Which it had fought like an army.
The sea grew quiet, the tempest was still, the flood ceased.
I looked at the weather: stillness had set in,
And all of mankind had returned to clay.
The landscape was as level as a flat roof.
I opened a hatch, and light fell upon my face.
Bowing low, I sat and wept,
Tears running down on my face.
I looked about for coast lines in the expanse of the sea:
In each of fourteen[210] (regions)
There emerged a region(-mountain).[211]
On Mount Nisir[212] the ship came to a halt.
Mount Nisir held the ship fast,
Allowing no motion.
One day, a second day, Mount Nisir held the ship fast,
Allowing no motion.
A third day, a fourth day, Mount Nisir held the ship fast,
Allowing no motion.
A fifth, and a sixth (day), Mount Nisir held the ship fast,
Allowing no motion.

When the seventh day arrived,
I sent forth and set free a dove.
The dove went forth, but came back;
There was[212a] no resting-place for it and she turned round.
Then I sent forth and set free a swallow.

200 Read *ge-er-má-dù*, with Salonen, *op. cit.*, 93. I take the sense to be, however, that the weight had to be shifted around (*uštabbalu*) on the upper and lower decks (*eliš u šapliš*) to make the launching possible.

201 Because of the masculine suffix (*šinīpat-su*), the antecedent cannot be the feminine *eleppu* "ship." Perhaps *ekallu*, as in line 95.

202 The true bearing of the word plays mentioned in lines 46-47. In order to reflect the rhyme of the Akkadian, which the two halves of this line contain—perhaps to bring out the proverbial content—I have translated here *līlāti* as "night," instead of "evening, dusk."

203 Lit. "to calk," cf. Salonen, *op. cit.*, 152. This expression seems to mean here "to put the finishing touches to."

204 For this reading of the names of the two heralds cf. *CT*, XXXV, 7, lines 19-20.

205 i.e. Nergal, god of the nether world.

206 Of the world dam.

207 The term *šuḫarratu*, with the elative element *š*-, does not mean "rage," but "stark stillness, bewilderment, consternation." cf. line 131, below.

208 The highest of several heavens in the Mesopotamian conception of the cosmos.

209 Var. "covered."

210 Var. "twelve."

211 cf. Oppenheim, *Orientalia*, XVII (1948), 54; for *nagû* see H. and J. Lewy, *HUCA*, XVII (1943), 11-15.

212 For the identification of Mount Niṣir with modern Pir Omar Gudrun, cf. my report in *AASOR*, VIII (1926/27), 17-18.

The swallow went forth, but came back;
There was[212a] no resting-place for it and she turned round.
Then I sent forth and set free a raven.
The raven went forth and, seeing that the waters had diminished,
He eats, circles, caws, and turns not round.
Then I let out (all) to the four winds
And offered a sacrifice.
I poured out a libation on the top of the mountain.
Seven and seven cult-vessels I set up,
Upon their plate-stands I heaped cane, cedarwood, and myrtle.
The gods smelled the savor,
The gods smelled the sweet savor,
The gods crowded like flies about the sacrificer.
As soon as the great goddess[213] arrived,
She lifted up the great jewels which Anu had fashioned to her liking:
'Ye gods here, as surely as this lapis
Upon my neck I shall not forget,
I shall be mindful of these days, forgetting (them) never.
Let the gods come to the offering;
(But) let not Enlil come to the offering,
For he, unreasoning, brought on the deluge
And my people consigned to destruction.'
As soon as Enlil arrived,
And saw the ship, Enlil was wroth,
He was filled with wrath against the Igigi gods:[214]
'Has some living soul escaped?
No man was to survive the destruction!'
Ninurta opened his mouth to speak,
Saying to valiant Enlil:
'Who, other than Ea, can devise plans?[215]
It is Ea alone who knows every matter.'
Ea opened his mouth to speak,
Saying to valiant Enlil:
'Thou wisest of gods, thou hero,
How couldst thou, unreasoning, bring on the deluge?
On the sinner impose his sin,
On the transgressor impose his transgression!
(Yet) be lenient, lest he be cut off,
Be patient,[216] lest he be dis[lodged]!
Instead of thy bringing on the deluge,
Would that a lion had risen up to diminish mankind!
Instead of thy bringing on the deluge,
Would that a wolf had risen up to diminish mankind!
Instead of thy bringing on the deluge,
Would that a famine had risen up to l[ay low] mankind!
Instead of thy bringing on the deluge,

212a Perhaps better "appeared," from **(w)apū*, in view of the repeated writing with *p*.
213 Ishtar.
214 The heavenly gods.
215 An allusion to one of the common epithets of Ea.
216 For *šadādu* in the sense of "heed," and the like, see XII, 32.

Would that pestilence[217] had risen up to smi[te down] mankind!
It was not I who disclosed the secret of the great gods.
I let Atrahasis[218] see a dream,
And he perceived the secret of the gods.
Now then take counsel in regard to him!'
Thereupon Enlil went aboard the ship.
Holding me by the hand, he took me aboard.
He took my wife aboard and made (her) kneel by my side.
Standing between us, he touched our foreheads to bless us:
'Hitherto Utnapishtim has been but human.
Henceforth Utnapishtim and his wife shall be like unto us gods.
Utnapishtim shall reside far away, at the mouth of the rivers!'
Thus they took me and made me reside far away,
At the mouth of the rivers.
But now, who will for thy sake call the gods to Assembly
That the life which thou seekest thou mayest find?
Up, lie not down to sleep
For six days and seven nights."
As he sits there on his haunches,
Sleep fans him like a mist.
Utnapishtim says to her, to his spouse:
"Behold this hero who seeks life!
Sleep fans him like a mist."
His spouse says to him, to Utnapishtim the Faraway:
"Touch him that the man may awake,
That he may return safe on the way whence he came,
That through the gate by which he left he may return to his land."
Utnapishtim says to her, to his spouse:
"Since to deceive is human, he will seek
to deceive thee.[219]
Up, bake for him wafers, put (them) at his head,
And mark on the wall the days he sleeps."
She baked for him wafers, put (them) at his head,
And marked on the wall the days he slept.
His first wafer is dried out,
The second is *leathery*,[220] the third is soggy;
The crust[221] of the fourth has turned white;
The fifth has a moldy cast,
The sixth (still) is fresh-colored;[222]
And just as he touched the seventh, the man awoke.

Gilgamesh says to him, to Utnapishtim the Faraway:

217 Lit. "Erra," the god of pestilence.
218 "Exceeding Wise," an epithet of Utnapishtim.
219 By asserting that he had not slept at all. Lit. "Mankind being wicked, he will seek to deceive thee." For *raggu: ruggū* cf. B. Landsberger, *ana ittišu* (1937), 233.
220 Connecting *muššuḳat*, very doubtfully, with *mašḳu* "skin, leather."
221 For the Heb. cognate *ḳawwān*, cf. Jer. 7:18.
222 For *bašlu* in reference to color cf. my remarks in *JAOS*, LXVIII (1948), 13. The entire episode, as has long been recognized (cf. especially, Landsberger, *ZA*, XLII, 141, n.1), depicts the progressive deterioration of the bread wafers (not loaves) day by day. The technical problem is how this was indicated. The key would seem to be the specialized use of the term *bašlu*, not in the sense of "ripe, cooked," but in the independently attested meaning of "light-colored." The first three stages would thus be light-colored, moldy gray, and white.

"Scarcely[223] had sleep surged over me,
When straightway thou dost touch and rouse me!"
Utnapishtim [says to him], to Gilgamesh:
"[Go], Gilgamesh, count thy wafers,
[That the days thou hast slept] may become known to thee:
Thy [first] wafer is dried out,
[The second is *leathe*]*ry*, the third is soggy;
The crust of the fourth has turned white;
The fifth has a moldy cast,
The sixth (still) is fresh-colored.
[As for the seventh], at this instant thou hast awakened."
Gilgamesh says to him, to Utnapishtim the Faraway:
"[What then] shall I do, Utnapishtim,
Whither shall I go,
[Now] that the Bereaver has laid hold on my [members]?
In my bedchamber lurks death,
And wherever I se[t my foot], there is death!"

Utnapishtim [says to him], to Urshanabi, the boatman:
"Urshanabi, may the landing-pl[ace not rejoice in thee],
May the place of crossing despise thee!
To him who wanders on its shore, deny thou its shore!
The man thou hast led (hither), whose body is covered with grime,
The grace of whose members skins have distorted,
Take him, Urshanabi, and bring him to the washing-place.
Let him wash off his grime in water
clean as snow,
Let him cast off his skins, let the sea carry (them) away,
That the fairness of his body may be seen.
Let him renew the band round his head,
Let him put on a cloak to clothe his nakedness,
That he may arrive in his city,
That he may achieve his journey.
Let not (his) cloak have a moldy cast,
Let it be wholly new."
Urshanabi took him and brought him to the washing-place.
He washed off his grime in water clean as snow.
He cast off his skins, the sea carried (them) away,
That the fairness of his body might be seen.
He renewed [the band] round his head,
He put on a cloak to clothe his nakedness,
That he might ar[rive in his city],
That he might achieve his journey.
[The cloak had not a moldy cast, but] was [wholly] new.
Gilgamesh and Urshanabi boarded the boat,
[They launch]ed the boat on the waves (and) they sailed away.

His spouse says to him, to Utnapishtim the Faraway:
"Gilgamesh has come hither, toiling and straining.
What wilt thou give (him) that he may return
to his land?"
At that he, Gilgamesh, raised up (his) pole,
To bring the boat nigh to the shore.
Utnapishtim [says] to him, [to] Gilgamesh:
"Gilgamesh, thou hast come hither, toiling and straining.
What shall I give thee that thou mayest return to thy land?
I will disclose, O Gilgamesh, a hidden thing,
And [... about a plant I will] tell thee:
This plant, like the buckthorn is [its ...].
Its thorns will pr[ick thy hands] just as does the *rose*.
If thy hands obtain the plant, [thou wilt
attain life]."
No sooner had Gilgamesh heard this,
Than he opened the *wa*[*ter-pipe*],[224]
He tied heavy stones [to his feet].
They pulled him down into the deep [and he saw the plant].
He took the plant, though it pr[icked his hands].
He cut the heavy stones [from his feet].
The [s]ea[225] cast him up upon its shore.

Gilgamesh says to him, to Urshanabi, the boatman:
"Urshanabi, this plant is a plant *apart*,[226]
Whereby a man may regain his *life's breath*.
I will take it to ramparted Uruk,
Will cause [...] to eat the plant ... !
Its name shall be 'Man Becomes Young in Old Age.'
I myself shall eat (it)
And thus return to the state of my youth."
After twenty leagues they broke off a morsel,
After thirty (further) leagues they prepared for the night.
Gilgamesh saw a well whose water was cool.
He went down into it to bathe in the water.
A serpent snuffed the fragrance of the plant;
It came up [from the water] and carried off the plant.
Going back it shed [its] slough.[227]

Thereupon Gilgamesh sits down and weeps,
His tears running down over his face.
[He took the hand][228] of Urshanabi, the boatman:
"[For] whom,[229] Urshanabi, have my hands toiled?
For whom is being spent the blood of my heart?
I have not obtained a boon for myself.
For the earth-lion[230] have I effected a boon!
And now the tide[231] will bear (it) twenty leagues away!
When I opened the *water-pipe*[232] and spilled the gear,

223 Reading *an-ni-miš*, for which see W. von Soden, *ZA*, XLI (1933), 129, n.3.

224 See below, line 298.

225 Reading [*t*]*am-tum*, with W. F. Albright, *RA*, XVI (1919), 176.

226 Reading *ni-siḫ-ti*.

227 cf. Albright, *loc. cit.*, 189 f.

228 cf. Böhl, *HGE*, 161.

229 For *man-ni-ya* cf. v. Soden, *ZA*, XL (1932), 199.

230 An allusion to the serpent?

231 See Albright, *loc. cit.*, 175 f.

232 The opening of the *rāṭu* (normally "pipe, tube," apparently took place in connection with Gilgamesh's dive (cf. also l. 271). But the details remain obscure. Note, however, the *Eridu Creation Story*, II, where

I found that which has been placed as a sign for me:
I shall withdraw,
And leave the boat on the shore!"
After twenty leagues they broke off a morsel,
After thirty (further) leagues they prepared for the night.
When they arrived in ramparted Uruk,
Gilgamesh says to him, to Urshanabi, the boatman:
"Go up, Urshanabi, walk on the ramparts of Uruk.
Inspect the base terrace, examine its brickwork,
If its brickwork is not of burnt brick,
And if the Seven Wise Ones laid not its foundation!
One 'sar' is city, one sar orchards,
One sar margin land; (further) the *precinct* of the Temple of Ishtar.
Three sar and the *precinct* comprise Uruk."

Tablet XII

Contents and circumstantial evidence mark this tablet as an inorganic appendage to the epic proper. The basic theme is concluded with the hero's failure to attain his quest. Moreover, the last lines of Tablet XI are the same as the final lines of the introduction to the entire work (I, i, 16-19). Lastly, Gadd (*RA*, xxxi [1933], 126 ff.) and Kramer *JAOS*, lxiv (1944), 7 ff. have demonstrated that Tablet XII is a direct translation from the Sumerian; the remaining tablets—as pointed out by Kramer—give every indication of creative borrowing and independent formulation. The Akkadian version of the present tablet is a translation of the second part of a Sumerian legend. The first part—disregarded by the Akkadian translator—is fortunately extant and has been published by Kramer in his monograph *Gilgamesh and the Ḫuluppu-Tree* (1938). Since the beginning is essential as an introduction to Tablet XII, it may be summarized briefly, as follows:

Shortly after the creation of the universe, a tree growing on the bank of the Euphrates was uprooted by the south wind. Inanna (Ishtar) took the floating trunk and planted it in her garden in Uruk. She intended to use it, in due time, as timber for her bed and chair. When several hostile beings interfered with Inanna's plan, Gilgamesh came to her rescue. In gratitude, Inanna made from the base of the tree a *pukku*, probably a magic Drum, and from the crown a *mikkū*, apparently a Drumstick of similar magic potency, and gave them both to Gilgamesh. One day both these precious objects fell into the nether world. Gilgamesh sought to retrieve them but could not. Lamenting his loss, he cried "O my *pukku*, O my *mikkū*." It is at this point that the Akkadian translation, known to us as Tablet XII, sets in, a fact witnessed by the catch-line at the end of Tablet XI.

To Kramer (*loc. cit.*, 22-23 and n.113) and to Gadd we owe the further recognition that the small fragment containing the beginning of the first eight lines in Thompson's edition (*GETh*, Pl. 55) is not part of the main portion of the tablet, but a duplicate (as shown, among other things, by the fact that no proper join has been made). What Thompson mistook for the beginning of the tablet is in reality line 4, corresponding to line 48 in Gadd's Sumerian text. Line 1 is, of course, given by the catch-line. In the translation given below, restorations based on the Sumerian text will be indicated by square brackets. I had the opportunity to talk over the whole problem with Dr. Kramer and I have adopted from him several new observations which will be pointed out in the footnotes.

the same term is used, perhaps to a pipe connecting with a source of sweet waters which would nourish the miraculous plant.

"That time when I verily ha[d][233] the *Drum* in the carpenter's house,
[(When] the carpenter's wife was verily like my mother who bore me],
[(When) the carpenter's daughter was verily like my younger sister]!
Lo, [who will bring up] the *Dr*[*um* from the nether world]?
[Who will bring up] the *Drumstick* [from the nether world]?"
[Enkidu[234] says to him, to Gilgamesh, his lord]:
"My lord, why [criest thou (and) why is so ill thy heart]?
Lo, [I will bring up] the *Dr*[*um* from the nether world],
[I will bring up] the *Drumst*[*ick* from the nether world]."
Gi[lgamesh says to him, to Enkidu,
his servant]:
"If [thou wilt go down] to [the nether world],
[I will speak a word to thee, take my word];[235]
My admonition(s)[236] [heed thou well]:
Clean raiment [thou shalt not put on]!
As a sojourner[237] they would ma[rk thee].[238]
With sweet oil from the cruse thou shalt not anoint thee!
At its fragrance they would gather about thee.
A throw stick into the nether world thou shalt not hurl!
Those struck with the throw stick would surround thee.
A staff into thy hands thou shalt not take!
The spirits would tremble[239] on thy account.
Sandals to thy feet thou shalt not fasten,
A sound against the nether world thou shalt not make,
Thy wife whom thou lovest thou shalt not kiss,
Thy wife whom thou hatest thou shalt not strike,
Thy son whom thou lovest thou shalt not kiss,
Thy son whom thou hatest thou shalt not strike!
The wailing of the nether world would seize thee!"—
"She who rests, she who rests,
The mother of Ninazu,[240] she who rests;
Her holy shoulders are not covered
with raiment,
Her cruse-shaped breasts are not wrapped with cloth."[241]
[To his lord's admonitions Enkidu gave no] heed.[242]

233 Kramer (*JAOS*, lxiv [1944], 22, n.113) restores the end of the catch-line as *e-š*[*ú-u*], on the basis of the Sumerian passage. The current restoration *e-z*[*ib*] makes excellent sense. If correct, it might represent a somewhat free rendering. For the translation of *pukku* and *mi/ekkū* cf. Landsberger, *ZDMG*, lxxxviii (1934), 210, and S. Smith, *RA*, xxxi (1934), 153 ff.

234 This line is found only in the corresponding Sumerian passage.

235 This line occurs only in the Sumerian text, Gadd, *loc. cit.*, line 55, restored by Kramer, *BASOR*, 79 (1940), 25, n.25. By incorporating the verse, we obtain the same count as is given in *GETh*.

236 For *aširtu*(*tu*), Sum. n a . r i, cf. Kramer, *ibid.*, and *Creation Epic*, VI, 144, note 120.

237 For *ubāru* cf. *AASOR*, xvi (1935/36), 124, note, and J. J. Stamm, *Die akkadische Namengebung* (1939), 264.

238 Reading *ú-a-a*[*d-du-ka*], with Kramer, *loc. cit.*, 21, n.105.

239 For the verb cf. *Creation Epic*, VII, 45.

240 Husband of Ereshkigal, queen of the nether world.

241 These three lines are repeated in 47-49. They appear to constitute a refrain, but the precise import is now lost.

242 For *šadādu*, when corresponding to Sumerian b u . i, cf. the associated terms *maḫāru, nekelmû, redû*, which taken together point to the semantic range "observe, follow, give heed"; cf. Deimel, *ŠL*, 371, 73.

[He] put [on clean raiment]:
[They mar]ked him as a soj[ourner].
With [sweet] oil from the cruse [he anoin]ted himself:
At the frag[rance of it they gath]ered about him.
[He hurled] the throw stick in[to the nether world]:
[Those struck] with the throw stick surrounded him.[243]
A staff [he took into his] hand:
The spirits trembled [on his account].
Sandals to [his feet he fastened],
A sound [against the nether world he ma]de,
[He kissed his beloved] wife,
[He struck his] hated wife,
[He kissed his be]lov[ed son],
He str[uck his] hated [son]:
The wailing of the nether world seized him.
"She who rests, she who rests,
The mother of Ninazu, she who rests;
Her holy shoulders are not covered with raiment,
Her cruse-shaped breasts are not wrapped with cloth."
She allow[ed] not Enkidu to ascend from the nether world.
Nam[tar did not seize] him, Fever[244] did not seize him;
The nether world seized him.
[Nergal's] unsparing waylayer did not seize him;
The nether world [seized] him.
On the [battle]field of men he did not fall;
The nether world [seized him]!
The[n] my l[ord], the son of Ninsun,[245]
Weeping over Enkidu, his servant,
Went all alone to [Ekur], the temple of Enlil:
"Father [Enlil], lo, my *Drum* fell[246] into the nether world,
My *Drumstick* [fell into the nether world];
Namtar did not seize him,[247] Fever did not seize him;
The nether world seized him.
Nergal's unsparing waylayer did not seize him;
The nether world seized him.
On the battlefield of men he did not fall;
The nether world seized him!"
Father Enlil did not intercede for him in the matter;[248]
[To Ur][249] he went:
"Father Sin, lo, my *Drum* fell into the nether world,
My *Drumstick* fell into the nether world.
Enkidu, whom [I sent] to bring them up, the nether world seized.
Namtar did not seize him, Fever did not [seize] him;
The nether world seized him.
Nergal's unsparing waylayer did not seize him;
The nether world seized him.
On [the battlefield of men he did not] fall;
The nether world seized him!"
[Father Sin did not intercede for him in the matter];
[To Eridu[250] he went]:
"[Father Ea, lo, my *Drum* fell into the nether world],
[My *Drumstick* fell into the nether world].
[Enkidu, whom I sent to bring them up, the nether world seized].
Na[mtar did not seize him, Fever did not seize him];
[The nether world seized him].
Nergal's unsparing waylayer [did not seize him];
[The nether world seized him].
On the battlefield of men [he did not fall];
[The nether world seized him]!"
Father Ea [did intercede for him in the matter].[251]
[He said] to [Nergal],[252] the valiant hero:
"O valiant hero, Ne[rgal . . .],
[Open] forthwith a hole[253] [in the earth,]
That the spirit of [Enkidu may issue forth from the nether world],
That to his brother [he might tell the ways of the nether world]."
Nergal, the valiant hero, [hearkened to Ea],
Forthwith he opened a hole in the earth.
The spirit of Enkidu, like a wind-puff,
Issued forth from the nether world.
They embraced and kissed each other.[254]
They exchanged counsel, sighing at each other:[255]
"Tell me, my friend, tell me, my friend,
Tell me the order of the nether world which thou hast seen."
"I shall not tell thee, I shall not tell thee!
(But) if I tell thee the order of the nether world which I have seen,
Sit thou down (and) weep!"
"[. . .] I will sit down and weep."

243 In the Akkadian copies of the text, the latter halves of lines 37 and 39 have been transposed. The correct sequence is indicated by lines 18-21, above.

244 cf. *ZA*, XLI (1933), 219; Sumerian A s i g , personified, see Kramer, *loc. cit.*, 21-22 and n.106.

245 i.e. Gilgamesh.

246 Lit. "the *pukku* fell for me."

247 Lines 59-68 can now be almost completely restored with the aid of the fragment published by E. F. Weidner, *AfO*, x (1935/36), 363 ff.

248 Dr. Kramer has called to my attention the fact that the Sumerian (which is to be pieced together from texts already published and others which he expects to utilize for a connected publication of the whole tale) has here i n i m . b i n u . m u (. e) . dè . gub "in this matter he did not stand by him." The corresponding Akkadian phrase *amat ul ipul-šu* (preserved on the Weidner fragment) has hitherto been rendered "answered him not a word." In view of the evidence of the Sumerian, however, I now suggest that *apālu* should be taken in its common legal sense "to satisfy," the whole yielding thus "gave him no satisfaction in the matter"; or better still, in the sense of *idā apālu* "to intercede for," cf. J. J. Stamm, *Die akkadische Namengebung* (1939), 171, the entire clause meaning "did not intercede for him in the matter." It is noteworthy, also, that the noun is *amat*, not *amatam*, i.e. in a predicative and not in an objective sense: "in what the matter was."

249 The Sumerian omits this stage. But the analogy of the two other relevant instances, and the space available on the Weidner fragment leave little doubt that *Ur* is to be supplied.

250 cf. Kramer, *JAOS*, XL (1940), 246, No. 35.

251 This important change in the usual restoration of the text is demanded by Kramer's material which yields the reading i n i m . b i b a . dè . gub ; cf. *ibid.*

252 The Sumerian clearly reads U t u , but the Assyrian text has evidently *Nergal* in line 82; cf. Kramer, *ibid.*

253 For *takkabu* "hole" cf. Jensen, *Keilschriftliche Bibliothek* VI, 528 f. A hole in the lid of the gigantic sarcophagus of Ashurnasirpal II (cf. W. Andrae, *Das wiedererstandene Assur* [1938], 139) may have been intended for just such a purpose of allowing the spirit of the dead to issue forth.

254 Reading *ul-ta-ša-qú*, with E. Ebeling, *AfO*, VIII (1932/33), 232.

255 In view of the corresponding Sumerian *k ú š* (Kramer), Thompson's reading *uš-ta-an-na-ḫ[u]* (*GETh*, 69) proves right as against Ebeling's suggested *uš-ta-an-na-a*! (*loc. cit.*) "conversed," which Heidel has adopted (*GE*, 100).

"[*My body* . . .], which thou didst touch as thy heart rejoiced,
Vermin devour [as though] an old garment.
[*My body* . . .], which thou didst touch as thy heart rejoiced,
[. . .] is filled with dust."
He cried "[Woe!]" and threw himself [in the dust],[256]
[Gilgamesh] cried "[Woe!]" and threw himself [in the dust].
"[. . . has thou seen]?" "I have seen."

(Lines 100-101 mutilated. 102-117, and 119-144 in Thompson's edition lost except for two signs. Probably before line 118 belongs the reverse of the Weidner fragment, *AfO*, x, 363, which supplies the concluding parts of twelve lines [numbered 2′-13′ in the following translation]. Although Heidel's restorations from the Sumerian [Heidel, *GE*, 100-01] are probable, it seemed advisable at this time to render only what is available in Akkadian.)

"[. . .]?" "I have seen:
[. . .] weeps over (it)."
"[. . .]?" "I have seen:
[. . .] eats bread."
"[. . .]?" "I have seen:
[. . .] drinks water."
"[. . . hast thou se]en?" "I have seen:
[. . .] his heart rejoices."
"[. . .] hast thou seen?" "I have seen:
[Like that of a] good [scribe] is his arm bared.[257]
[. . .] he enters the palace."
"[. . .] hast thou seen?" "I have seen:
Like a beautiful standard [. . .]."

(twenty-six lines destroyed)

"Him who [*fell down*] from the mast hast thou seen?"
"[I have seen]:
Forthwith [. . .], as the pegs are pulled out."
"Him [who died] a sud[den] death[258] hast thou seen?"
"[I have seen]:
He lies upon the night couch and drinks pure water."
"Him who was killed in battle hast thou seen?"
"I have seen:
His father and his mother raise up his head,
And his wife [weeps] over him."
"Him whose corpse was cast out upon the steppe hast thou seen?"
"I have seen:
His spirit finds no rest in the nether world."
"Him whose spirit has no one to tend (it) hast thou seen?"
"I have seen:
Lees of the pot, crumbs of bread, offals of the street he eats."

[256] For this and the following line cf. Heidel, *GE*, 100.
[257] cf. Heidel, *ibid.*, n.244.
[258] Reading *ša-mu-ti sur-*[*ri i-mu-tu*], with Ebeling, *loc. cit.*

Creation of Man by the Mother Goddess

The basic theme of this myth is the creation of man out of clay mixed with the flesh and blood of a slain god. Unfortunately, the Old Babylonian text which deals with this subject (A) is incomplete and in a singularly poor state of preservation. Furthermore, the account came to be used as part of an incantation to facilitate childbirth, with the result that the myth itself seems to have been restated only in its bare outlines. It is too important, however, to be ignored, in spite of its lacunae and its uncertainties.

The ritual part of this Old Babylonian text agrees closely with the concluding portion of the Assyrian Version of the Atrahasis Epic—a fact which was first recognized by E. Ebeling.[1] Accordingly, the Assyrian analogue in question has been detached from the Atrahasis Epic—with which it has only an incidental connection—and has been appended in this place as Version B.

Texts: (A) T. G. Pinches, *CT*, vi (1898), Pl. 5; republished with minor changes by S. Langdon, *UM*, x, 1 (1915), Pls. iii-iv. (B) L. W. King, *CT*, xv (1902), Pl. 49, col. iv, and K. D. Macmillan, *Beiträge zur Assyriologie*, v (1906), 688. Principal edition and translation: E. Ebeling, *Tod und Leben* (1931), No. 37, pp. 172-77. Other translations: (A, obverse only) Langdon, *op. cit.*, 25-26, and Heidel, *BG*, 54-56. (B) P. Jensen, *KB*, vi, 1, 286-87, and Heidel, *GE*, 115-16. The line count here followed is that of Ebeling, *loc. cit.*[2]

OLD BABYLONIAN TEXT

(obverse)
(preceding column and top of the present column destroyed)

"That which is slight shall grow to abundance;
The *burden*[3] of creation man shall bear!"
The goddess they called, [. . .], [the *mot*]*her*,[4]
The most helpful of the gods, the wise Mami:
"Thou art the mother-womb,
The one who creates mankind.
Create, then, Lullu[5] and let him bear the yoke!
The yoke he shall bear, . . . [. . .];
The *burden* of creation man shall bear!"
. [.] . opened her mouth,
Saying to the great gods:
"With me is the *doing* of all that is suitable;[6]
With his . . . let Lullu appear!
He who shall be [. . .] of all [. . .],
Let him *be formed* out of clay, be *animated* with blood!"
Enki opened his mouth,
Saying to the great gods:
"On the . . . and [. . .] of the month
The purification of the land . . . !

[1] *Tod und Leben* (1931), 172.
[2] It starts, however, with the first intelligible line and not with the first line of which there is any trace. Although Ebeling's additions and interpretations are offered with great reserve, they are not uniformly satisfactory.
[3] This translation of *šu-q/ḳat* is a pure guess; it is based mainly on the context of line 9, which is preceded by the mention of "yoke."
[4] cf. Ebeling, *MAOG*, xii 1 (1937), 33.
[5] i.e. "the savage, the first man," cf. *The Creation Epic*, VI, 6, p. 68, n. 86. Lullu corresponds in effect to Adam.
[6] The reading *it-ti-ya-ma la na-tu-ú* "with me it is impossible" is not admissible in this context; it would be strange indeed in reference to a mother goddess. I suggest *it-ti-ya ma-la na-tu-ú*.

Let them slay one god,
And let the gods be purified in the *judgment.*
With his flesh and his blood
Let Ninhursag[7] mix clay.
God and man
Shall [...] therein, ... in the clay!
Unto eternity [...] we shall hear."

(remainder of obverse too fragmentary for translation)

(reverse)

[...] her breast,
[...] the beard,
[...] the cheek of the man.
[...] and the raising
[...] of both eyes, the wife and her husband.
[Fourteen mother]-wombs were assembled
[Before] Nintu.[8]
[At the ti]me of the new moon
[To the House] of Fates they called the *votaries.*
[*Enkidu* ...] came and
[*Kneel*]*ed down,*[9] opening the womb.
[...] ... and happy was his countenance.
[... bent] the knees [...],
[...] made an opening,
She brought forth her issue,[10]
Praying.
Fashion[11] a clay brick into a core,
Make ... stone in the midst of [...];
Let the vexed rejoice in the house of the one in travail!
As the Bearing One[12] gives birth,
May the mo[ther of the ch]ild bring forth by herself!

(remainder too fragmentary for translation)

ASSYRIAN VERSION

(beginning mutilated)

[... they kis]sed her feet,
[Saying: "The creatress of mankind] we call thee;
[The mistr]ess of all the gods be thy name!"
[They went] to the House of Fate,
[Nin]igiku-Ea (and) the wise Mama.
[Fourteen mother]-wombs were assembled
To tread upon the [c]lay before her.[13]
[...] Ea says, as he recites the incantation.
Sitting before her, Ea causes her to recite the incantation.
[Mama reci]ted the incantation; when she completed[14] [her] incantation,
[...] she drew upon her clay.
[Fourteen pie]ces she pinched off; seven pieces she placed on the right,
[Seven pie]ces she placed on the left; between them she placed a brick.

[7] One of the names of the mother goddess.
[8] Another name of the mother goddess.
[9] For the supplementations in this column cf. Ebeling, *Tod und Leben,* 174-75.
[10] cf. *ibid.,* 174c.
[11] There follow instructions to the attendant at the delivery.
[12] Apparently a reference to the mother goddess.
[13] cf. Ebeling, *op. cit.,* 176f.
[14] Var. "had recited."

[*E*]*a* was kneeling on the *matting*; he opened its[15] navel;
[... he c]alled the wise wives.
(Of the) [seven] and seven mother-wombs, seven brought forth males,
[Seven] brought forth females.
The Mother-Womb, the creatress of destiny,
In pairs[16] she completed them,
In pairs she completed before her.
The forms of the people Mami forms.
In the house of the bearing woman in travail,
Seven days shall the brick lie.
... from the house of Mah, the wise Mami.
The vexed shall rejoice in the house of the one in travail.
As the Bearing One gives birth,
May the mother of the child bring forth by [her]self.

(remainder destroyed)

A Cosmological Incantation: The Worm and the Toothache

Among the incantations which contain cosmological material, one of the best-known attributes toothache to a worm that had obtained the permission of the gods to dwell among the teeth and gums. The present text, which is designated ideographically as an "Incantation against Toothache," dates from Neo-Babylonian times and was published by R. Campbell Thompson in *CT,* XVII (1903), Pl. 50. But the colophon indicates that the copy had been made from an ancient text. And indeed, the Mari documents of the Old Babylonian period include a tablet with the Akkadian label *ši-pa-at tu-ul-tim* "Toothache Incantation." The text itself, however,[1] is in Hurrian. But although it cites various deities of the Hurrian pantheon—and is thus clearly religious in nature—the context does not correspond to the Neo-Babylonian legend, to judge from the intelligible portions.

Selected translations: B. Meissner, *MVAG,* IX/3 (1904), 42-45; E. Ebeling, *AOT,* 133 f.; F. Thureau-Dangin, *RA,* XXXVI (1939), 3-4; and A. Heidel, *BG,* 60-61.

After Anu [had created heaven],
Heaven had created [the earth],
The earth had created the rivers,
The rivers had created the canals,
The canals had created the marsh,
(And) the marsh had created the worm—
The worm went, weeping, before Shamash,
His tears flowing before Ea:
"What wilt thou give for my food?
What wilt thou give me for my sucking?"
"I shall give thee the ripe fig,
(And) the apricot."
"Of what use are they to me, the ripe fig
And the apricot?
Lift me up and among the teeth
And the gums cause me to dwell!
The blood of the tooth I will suck,

[15] Of the brick figure?
[16] cf. v. Soden, *ZA,* XLI (1933), 113, n.5 (on p. 114).

[1] cf. F. Thureau-Dangin, *RA,* XXXVI (1939), 1 ff.

And of the gum I will gnaw
Its *roots*!"
Fix the pin and seize its foot.[2]
Because thou hast said this, O worm,
May Ea smite thee with the might
Of his hand!

(There follow details about the treatment, the injunction to recite this incantation three times, the remark that the text had been copied from an ancient tablet, and the name of the scribe.)

[2] This is the instruction to the dentist, as pointed out by A. David, Operation dentaire en Babylonie, *RA*, xxv (1928), 95 ff.

Adapa

The story of Adapa* shares with the Epic of Gilgamesh the *motif* of man's squandered opportunity for gaining immortality. It is extant in four fragmentary accounts. The oldest and longest of these (B) comes from the El-Amarna archives (fourteenth century B.C.), whereas the other three (A, C, and D) derive from the library of Ashurbanipal. The order of presentation is contextual, except that C is roughly parallel to parts of B.

Sources: (A) A. T. Clay, *YOS*, v, 3 (1922), Pls. iv, vi; (B) O. Schroeder, *VS*, xii (1915), No. 194; (C) R. Campbell Thompson, *The Epic of Gilgamish* (1930), Pl. 31 (K.8743); (D) S. A. Strong, *PSBA*, xvi (1894), 274 f. Selected translations: P. Jensen, *KB*, vi, 1 (1900), 92-101; J. A. Knudtzon, *Die El-Amarna-Tafeln* (1915), 965-69; S. Langdon, *UM*, x, 1 (1915), 42-43 and 46-48; A. T. Clay, *op. cit.*, 40-41; E. Ebeling, *AOT*, 143-46; and A. Heidel, *BG* (1942), 126-31.

A

[Wis]dom . . . [. . .].
His command was indeed . . . [. . .] like the command of [Ea].
Wide understanding he had perfected for him to disclose[1] the designs of the land.
To him he had given wisdom; eternal life he had not given him.
In those days, in those years, the sage from Eridu,
Ea, created him as the *model*[1a] of men.
The sage—his command no one can set aside—
The capable, the most wise[2] among the Anunnaki is he;
The blameless, the clean of hands, the ointment priest, the observer of rites.
With the bakers he can do the baking,
With the bakers of Eridu he can do the baking;
Bread and water for Eridu daily he provides,
With his clean hand(s) he arranges the (offering) table,
Without him the table cannot be cleared.
He steers the ship, he does the fishing and *stalking* for Eridu.
In those days Adapa, the one of Eridu,
While [. . .] Ea . . . upon the couch,
Daily did attend to the sanctuary of Eridu.
At the holy quay, the Quay of the New Moon, he boarded the sailboat;
Then a wind blew thither and his boat drifted;
[With the o]ar he steers his boat[3]
[. . .] upon the wide sea.

(remainder destroyed)

* According to E. Ebeling, *Tod und Leben*, 27a, an unpublished syllabary equates *a-da-ap* with "man" (hence "Adam"?).

[1] Reading *ḳul!-lu-mu*.

[1a] In the sense of "something to be followed." cf. *lā āḫiz riddi* "unprincipled."

[2] Akk. *atraḫāsisa*, applied here as an epithet and not as a proper name.

B[4]

. . . [. . .]
The south wind b[lew and submerged him],
[Causing him to go down] to the home [of the fish]:
"South wind, [. .] . me thy *venom* . . . [. . .].
I will break thy wi[ng]!" Just as he had said (this) with his mouth,
The wing of the sou[th wi]nd was broken. For seven days
The [south win]d blew not upon the land. Anu
Calls [to] Ilabrat, his vizier:
"Why has the south wind not blown over the land these seven days?"
His vizier, Ilabrat, answered him: "My lord,
Adapa, the son of Ea, the wing of the south wind
Has broken." When Anu heard this speech,
He cried, "Mercy!" Rising from his throne: "[Let] them fetch him hither!"
At that, Ea, he who knows what pertains to heaven, took hold of him,
[Adapa], caused him to wear (his) [hai]r unkempt, a mourning garb
[He made him put on], and gave him (this) [ad]vice:
"[Adapa], thou art going [before Anu], the king;
[The road to heaven thou wilt take. When to] heaven
[Thou hast] go[ne up and] hast [approached the gate of Anu],
[Tammuz and Gizzida] at the gate of Anu
Will be standing. When they see thee, they will [as]k thee: 'Man,
For whom dost thou look thus? Adapa, for whom
Art thou clad with mourning garb?'
'From our land two gods have disappeared,
Hence I am thus.' 'Who are the two gods who from the land
Have disappeared?' 'Tammuz and Gizzida.' They will glance at each other
And will smile.[5] A good word they
Will speak to Anu, (and) Anu's benign face
They will cause to be shown thee. As thou standest before Anu,
When they offer thee bread of death,

[3] For lines 19-21 cf. A. Salonen, *Die Wasserfahrzeuge in Babylonien* (1939), 20. If should be added that Adapa's purpose was plainly to catch fish for Ea's temple, hence that god's primary interest in Adapa. For the importance of fishing to the temple economy cf. the so-called Weidner Chronicle, which employs this *motif* as a reason for the rise and fall of dynasties (and, incidentally, mentions Adapa). See especially H. G. Güterbock *ZA*, xlii (1934), 51 ff.

[4] This text lacks the normal metric form. For the sake of uniformity, however, each line has been treated in the translation as a verse of poetry.

[5] cf. B. Landsberger, *ZA*, xl (1932), 297-98.

Thou shalt not eat (it). When they offer thee water of death,
Thou shalt not drink (it). When they offer thee a garment,
Put (it) on. When they offer thee oil, anoint thyself (therewith).
(This) advice that I have given thee, neglect not; the words
That I have spoken to thee, hold fast!" The messenger
Of Anu arrived there: "Adapa, him who the south wind's
Wing has broken, bring him before me!"

He made him take the road to heaven, and to heaven he went up.
When he had ascended to heaven and approached the gate of Anu,
Tammuz and Gizzida were standing at the gate of Anu.
When they saw Adapa, they cried, "Mercy!
Man, for whom dost thou look thus? Adapa,
For whom art thou clad with mourning garb?"
"Two gods have disappeared from the land, therefore with mourning garb
I am clad." "Who are the two gods who from the land have disappeared?"
"Tammuz and Gizzida." They glanced at each other
And smiled.[6] As Adapa before Anu, the king,
Drew near and Anu saw him, he called:
"Come now, Adapa, wherefore the south wind's wing
Didst thou break?" Adapa replied to Anu: "My lord,
For the household of my master, in the midst of the sea
I was catching fish. The sea was like a mirror.
But the south wind came blowing and submerged me,
Causing me to go down to the home of the fish. In the wrath of my heart
I cursed the [south wind]." Speaking up at [his] side, Tammuz
[And] Gizzida to Anu [a g]ood word
Addressed. His heart quieted as he was *won over*:[7]
"Why did Ea to a *worthless* human of the heaven
And of the earth the plan[8] disclose,
Rendering him *distinguished* and making a name for him?
As for us, what shall we do about him? Bread of life
Fetch for him and he shall eat (it)." When the bread of life
They brought him, he did not eat; when the water of life
They brought him, he did not drink. When a garment
They brought him, he put (it) on; when oil
They brought him, he anointed himself (therewith).
As Anu looked at him, he laughed at him:
"Come now, Adapa! Why didst thou neither eat nor drink?' "
Thou shalt not have (eternal) life! Ah, *per*[*ver*]*se*[9] mankind!"
"Ea, my master,
Commanded me: 'Thou shalt not eat, thou shalt not drink' "
"Take him away and return him to his earth."

(remainder destroyed)

C

When [Anu] heard th[is],
[. . . in the wr]ath of his heart
[. . .] he dispatches a messenger,
[. . . , who] knows the heart of the great gods,
That he [. . .] . . .
To reach [. . . of Ea], the king.
[. . .] he discussed the matter.[10]
[. . .] to Ea, the king.
[. . .] . . .
[. . .], the wise, who knows the heart of the great gods
[. . .] heaven . . .
[. . .] unkempt hair he caused him to wear,
[. . .] . . . and clad him with a mourning garb,
[He gave him advice], saying to him (these) [wor]ds:
["Adapa,] thou art going [before Anu], the king;
[Neglect not my advice], the words hold fast!
[When thou hast gone up to heaven and] hast approached the gate of Anu,
[Tammuz and Gizzida] will be standing [at the gate of Anu]."

(remainder missing)

D

[. . .] he [. . .]
[Oil] he commanded for him, and he an[ointed himself],
[A ga]rment he commanded for him, and he was clothed.
Anu laughed aloud[11] at the doing of Ea, [saying]:
"Of the gods of heaven and earth, as many as there be,
Who [ever] gave such a command?
Who will make his own command exceed the command of Anu?"
As Adapa from the horizon of heaven to the zenith of heaven
Cast a glance, he saw its awesomeness.
[Th]en Anu imposed on Adapa [. . .];
For [the city] of Ea[12] he decreed release,
His [pri]esthood to glorify in the future he [*decreed*] as destiny.
[. . .] . . . as for Adapa, the human offspring,

[6] Apparently pleased because Adapa mourned their loss.
[7] Lit. "was seized," perhaps in the sense of "captivated."
[8] Lit. "heart."

[9] The attributive element which here accompanies *ni-ši* "mankind" is preserved as *d/ṭa-a-?-ti*; in the third position there is room at most for a short sign. Do we have here *ṭa-a-*[*a-*]*ti* (pl.), in the sense of "corrupt," etc.? The other possibilities that come to mind e.g., relating the form to *ṭi'u* "dizziness" or *di'u* "depression, niche," are even more dubious.
[10] For *šutābulu amāti* cf. Th. Bauer, *ZA*, XLII (1934), 168, n.1.
[11] For *šāqiš*, lit. "highly," cf. *issū elītum* "they cried out aloud," *Creation Epic*, III, 125.
[12] Eridu. The release in question signifies freeing from feudal obligations; cf. F. M. Th. Böhl, *MAOG*, XI/3 (1937), 18.

[Who . . .], lord-like, broke the south wind's wing,
Went up to heaven—and so forth—
[And] what ill he has brought upon mankind,
[And] the disease that he brought upon the bodies of men,
These Ninkarrak[13] will allay.
[Let] malady be lifted,[14] let disease turn aside.
[Upon] this [. . .] let horror fall,
Let him [*in*] sweet sleep not lie down,
[. . .] . . . joy of human heart(s).

(remainder broken off)

Nergal and Ereshkigal

This Mesopotamian myth is so far known only from two fragments of a school text dating from the fourteenth century B.C. and unearthed at Tell El-Amarna, in Egypt. In antiquity the myth was evidently used to train the Egyptian foreign-language student in acquiring a knowledge of Akkadian, at that time the common cultural medium of the whole region. This secondary use, however, did not enhance the reliability of the text. Furthermore, the tablet has suffered badly since then, one fragment (A) now belonging to the British Museum (published by C. Bezold and E. A. Wallis Budge, *The Tell El-Amarna Tablets in the British Museum*, 1892, No. 82), and the other (B) to the Berlin Museum (published by O. Schroeder in *VAB*, XII [1915], No. 195). The basic study is that of J. A. Knudtzon, *Die El-Amarna Tafeln* (1915), 969 ff.; Knudtzon's line count has here been retained. For later translations cf. Ebeling, *AOT*, 210 ff. and Heidel, *GE*, 129 ff.

(obverse)

Fragment A

When the gods were preparing a banquet,
To their sister, Ereshkigal,
They sent a messenger:
"Whereas we can go down to thee,
Thou canst not come up to us.
Send up, therefore, that they take thy food-portion."
Hence [Eresh]kigal sent Namtar, her vizier.
N[amt]ar went up to lofty heaven.
He enter[ed the place where the gods were *con*]*versing*.[1]
They [. . . and greeted] Namtar,
The messenger of their great [sister].

(Several lines mutilated or missing. It is clear, however, from what follows that Nergal, alone among the gods, failed to show the proper respect to the envoy of Ereshkigal. When this has been reported to her, she sends Namtar back.)

Fragment B

Saying: "The god [who] did not rise [before] my messenger,
Bring *him* to me that I may kill him."
Namtar went forth to speak to the gods.
The gods hailed him to speak to him [. . .]:
"Look and, as for the god who rose not before thee,
Take him to the presence of thy mistress."
When Namtar counted them, a god in the rear *was missing*:
"The god is not here who did not rise before me."
[Off w]ent Namtar [to make] his [r]eport.
"[. . . I counted] them,
[A g]od in the rear [was missing].
[The god who had not risen before me] was not there."

(Several lines mutilated or missing. In line 41 Ea is introduced into the story. Nergal appears to be in trouble, for the text goes on:)

"Take (him) to Ereshkigal!" Weeping, [he goes]
Before Ea, his father: "*If she catches* [*me*],
She will not let me live!"[2] "Be not afr[aid]!
I will give thee seven and seven [. . .]
To go with thee: [. . . ,[3] Mutabriqu],
Sharabdu, [Rabisu, Tirid, Idibtu],
Be[nnu, Sidanu, Miqit, Beluri[3a]],
Ummu [(and) Libu. They shall go]
With thee." [When Nergal arrives at the g]ate of
Ereshkigal, he calls out: "Gate[keeper, open] thy gate,
Loosen the latchstring[4] that I may enter!
To the presence of thy mistress,
Ereshkigal, I have been sent." Forth went the gatekeeper
And said to Namtar: "A certain god is standing at the entrance of the gate.
Come and inspect him that he may enter." Out went Namtar.
When he saw him, rejoicing[5] [. . .] he said
To his [mis]tress: "My lady, [it is the god w]ho months
Ago [dis]appeared, not having risen [before] me!"
"Bring (him) in! [When he c]omes in, I will kill [him]!"
Out went Namtar [and said]: "Enter, my lord,
Into the house of thy sister. [. . .] be thy departure."
[Answered] Nergal: "May thy heart rejoice in me."

(several lines destroyed)

(reverse)

Fragment A

[. . .] at the third, Mutabriqu at the fourth,
[Shar]abdu at the fifth, Rabisu at the sixth, Tirid
At the seventh, Idibtu at the eighth, Bennu
At the ninth, Sidanu at the tenth, Miqit
At the eleventh, Beluri at the twelfth,
Ummu at the thirteenth, (and) Libu at the fourteenth
Gate he stationed as *deterrents*. In the court he cut down

[13] Goddess of healing.
[14] Lit. "rise, move."

[1] Or, possibly "[sit]ting."

[2] Highly uncertain. The translation follows Heidel's reading *i-ba!-ra-an-ni* (*GE*, 130, n.96) in line 44, but assumes *ú-lu-ba-la-ṭa-an-ni* to be a case of crasis for *ul ubal(l)aṭanni*.
[3] The names of the first three demons are missing. Most of the extant names represent demons of disease.
[3a] Reading here and in line 72 *ᵈBi-e-el-ú!-ti*, not *ᵈBi-e-el-u*[b]*-ri*; see A. Ungnad, *AfO*, XIV (1944), 268.
[4] cf. Heidel, *GE*, 131, n.100.
[5] *Ibid.*, n.101.

Namtar. To his troop he gave (this) order: "The gates
Shall remain open, (or) presently I will let go at you!"
Inside the house he took hold of Ereshkigal,
By her hair he brought her down from the throne
To the ground, to cut off her head.
"Kill me not, my brother! Let me speak a word to thee!"
When Nergal heard her, his hands relaxed. She weeps, humbled:[6]
"Be thou my husband and I will be thy wife. I will let thee hold
Dominion over the wide nether world. I will place the tablet
Of wisdom in thy hand. That shalt be master,
I will be mistress!" When Nergal heard this her speech,
He took hold of her and kissed her, wiping away her tears:
"Whatever thou hast wished of me since months past,
So be it now!"

[6] Deriving the form from *duḫḫusu*, with v. Soden, *Orientalia*, XVIII (1949), 403.

Atrahasis

The name Atrahasis (Old Babylonian Atramhasis), i.e. "Exceeding Wise," is associated with more than one hero of the epic literature of Mesopotamia. The Epic of Gilgamesh (XI, 196) applies it to Utnapishtim, the hero of the Flood. The poems of Etana and Adapa make use of the same epithet. More specifically, however, the name is associated with a large epic cycle dealing with man's sins and his consequent punishment through plagues and the deluge. This cycle, which thus provides a parallel to the biblical motivation for the Flood, bore originally the name *Enūma ilu awēlum* "When God Man . . ." Today it is commonly known as the Atrahasis Epic.

Fragments of this epic have come down to us in separate Old Babylonian and Assyrian recensions—as is also true of Gilgamesh. The Assyrian Version (Fragments C, D) dates from the time of Ashurbanipal. The Old Babylonian Version (Fragments A, B) is approximately a thousand years older, going back to the reign of Ammizaduga, at which time it was copied from a still earlier text. Unfortunately, the extant material is but a small fraction of the original total. For according to the colophon on B, the Old Babylonian Version consisted of three tablets aggregating 1,245 lines, or about twenty times as many as are now available. The gaps in the Assyrian recension are only relatively less serious. The underlying relationship of all four pieces is assured by the joint evidence of phraseology, subject matter, and principal characters. Fragments of B and C, moreover, establish a direct connection with Gilgamesh, Tablet XI.

For the sake of convenience, a further fragment of an Old Babylonian flood text has been included in the present group. It has been marked as Fragment X and given a place immediately after Fragment B. For the present it cannot be determined whether this fragment ever did form an integral part of the earliest version of the epic; it might well have done so. On the other hand, column iv of Fragment D has been omitted from this context and placed instead at the end of Creation of Man by the Mother Goddess (pp. 99f.), where it clearly belongs. The eventual displacement is due to the fact that the present epic came to be used in Assyrian times (if not earlier) as an incantation for childbirth, for which column iv was apparently regarded as the proper accompaniment.

The source material is as follows: (A) A. T. Clay, *YOS*, v, 3 (1922), Pls. I-II and *Babylonian Records in the Morgan Library*, IV (1923), 1. (B) A. Boissier, *RA*, XXVIII (1931), 92-95. (X) H. V. Hilprecht, *BE*, D, v (1910), 1. (C) F. Delitzsch, *Assyrische Lesestücke* (1885), 101. (D) L. W. King, *CT*, XV (1902), 49. Recent translations: Clay, *op. cit.*, 58 ff.; Ebeling, *AOT*, 200 ff.; A. Boissier, *op. cit.*; Heidel, *GE*, 105 ff.

A

(i)

[. . .]
The land became wide, the peop[le became nu]merous,
The land *bellowed*[1] like wild oxen.
The god[1a] was disturbed by their uproar.[2]
[*Enlil*] heard their clamor
(And) said to the great gods:
"Oppressive has become the clamor of mankind.
By their uproar they prevent sleep.[3]
[Let] the fig [be c]ut off for the people,
[In] their [belli]es[4] let the greens be too few.
[Above] let Adad make scarce his [rain],
[Below[5] let not] flow
[The flood, let it not rise from the] source.
[Let] the wind come,
Laying bare the . . .
Let the clouds *hold back*[6]
[That rain from heaven] pour not forth.
[Let] the land [with]draw its yield,
[Let it turn] the breast of Nisaba."[7]

(ii)

(beginning destroyed)

"In the morning let him cause . . . to pour [down],
Let it extend through the night [. . .],
Let him cause to rain [. . .]
Let it come upon the field like a thief, let . . .
Which Adad had created in the city [. . .]."
So saying, they called [. . .],
Raising up a clamor [. . .],
They feared not [. . .].

(over three hundred lines destroyed)

(vii)

Enki [opened] his mouth,
Saying to *En*[*lil*]:
"Why hast thou sworn [. . .]?
I will stretch out my hand to the [. . .]

[1] cf. v. Soden, *ZA*, XLIII (1936), 261.

[1a] i.e. Enlil, the head of the pantheon.

[2] For this noun cf. v. Soden, *ZA*, XL (1932), 168, n.2.

[3] cf. Sidney Smith, *RA*, XXII (1925), 67-68. cf. also D iii, 3, 8, 41 and A Vision of the Nether World, rev. 21 (p. 110). It is worth noting that various phrases from this epic recur in the omens, e.g., the failure of the water to rise from its source, or the resort of mankind to cannibalism; for such passages cf. *Orientalia*, v (1936), 212.

[4] For the restorations in this and the following lines cf. Fragment D, iii, 42 ff., 52 ff.

[5] For the copyist's notation *ḫi-pí iš-*[*šu*] "new break," see Heidel, *GE*, 108, n.19.

[6] cf. A. T. Clay, *YOS*, v, 3 (1922), 60.

[7] Nisaba was the goddess of grain. To "turn the breast" is "to repel." The whole phrase, which is repeated several times in the present epic, refers to the cessation of growth.

The flood which thou commandest [. . .].
Who is he? I [. . .],
For I am he who gives birth [to my people]."[8]

(remainder of this and beginning of next column mutilated)

(viii)

Atramhasis opened his mouth, (438)
Saying to his lord:

(There follows the colophon which states that this is Tablet II of the series *Enūma ilu awēlum,* that it consists of 439 lines, and that it was written by Ellit-Aya, the "junior" scribe, in the eleventh year of Ammizaduga.)

B

[Atramhasis] opened his mouth,
[Saying] to his lord:
"[. . . make known unto me its content
[. . .] that I may *seek* its . . ."
[Ea] opened his mouth,
[Say]ing to his servant:
"Thou sayest 'let me *seek* . . .'
The task which I am about to tell thee
Guard thou well:[9]
'Wall, hearken to me, (10)
Reed-hut, guard well all my words![10]
Destroy the house, build a ship,
Despise goods,
Keep the soul alive!
The ship that thou shalt build.' "

(Remainder destroyed except for the significant colophon: " . . . Total 1,245 [lines] of three tablets. By the hand of Ellit-Aya, the junior scribe. . . . ")

X

(For the inclusion of this fragment cf. the introductory remarks. Largely destroyed.)

"[. . .] I will loosen. (2)
[. . .] he will seize all the people together,
[. . .], before the flood appears.
[. . .], as many as there are,
I will cause overthrow, affliction, . . .
[. . .] build a large ship.
[. . .] of good . . . shall be its structure.
That [ship] shall be an ark,[11] and its name
Shall be 'Preserver of Life.'
[. . .] ceil (it) with a mighty cover.
[Into the ship which] thou shalt make, (10)
[Thou shalt take] the beasts of the field,
The fowl of the heavens."

(remainder broken away)

[8] cf. Gilgamesh, XI, 122.
[9] For the following lines cf. the virtually identical passage in Gilgamesh, XI, 21 ff.
[10] Reading *zi-iḳ-ri-ya* with W. F. Geers, cf. Heidel, *GE,* 109, no. 25.
[11] cf. A. Salonen, *Die Wasserfahrzeuge in Babylonien* (1939), 51, under *eleppu qurqurru.*

C

"[. . .] like the vault of [. . .], (2)
[. . .] stout above and b[elow],
[. . .] calk [. . .].
[. . .] at the stated time of which I will inform t[hee],
Enter [the ship] and close the door of the ship.
Aboard her [bring] thy grain, thy possessions, thy goods,
Thy [wife], thy family, thy relations, and thy craftsmen.
Beasts of the field, creatures of the field, as many as eat herbs,
I will send to thee and they shall guard thy door." (10)
Atra[hasis] opened his mouth to speak,
[Say]ing to Ea, [his] lord:
"I have never built a ship [. . .].
Draw a design [of it on the gr]ound
That, seeing the [des]ign, I may [build] the ship.
[. . .] draw on the ground [. . .],
[. . .] what thou hast commanded [. . .]."

(remainder destroyed)

D

(i)

[When the th]ird year [arrived], (26)
The people *became hostile* in their [. . .].
When the fourth year [arrived],
Their places became cramped,
Their wide [. . .] became too narrow.
Downcast[12] the people wandered in the streets. (30)
When the fifth year arrived,
The daughter seeks entry to the mother,
(But) the mother opens not [her] door to the daughter.
The daughter watches the balances of the mother,
[The mother] watches the balances of the daughter.[13]
When the sixth year arrived,
They prepared [the daughter] for a meal,
The child they prepared for food.
Filled were [. . .].
One house de[voured] the other.
Like *ghosts of the dead* their faces [were veiled].
The people [lived] with bated [breath].
They received a message [. . .]. (40)
They entered and [. . .].

(remainder mutilated)

(ii)

(beginning missing)

Above [Adad made scarce his rain], (29)
Below [was dammed up the flood], (30)
[So that it rose not from the source].
The land withdrew its yield,
[It turned the breast of] Nisaba.
[During the nights the fields turned white].
[The broad plain] brought forth sa[lt crystals],[14]
[So that no plant cam]e forth, [no] grain [sprouted].

[12] See Heidel, *GE,* 111, n.28.
[13] That is, nobody trusted anyone.
[14] cf. Sidney Smith, *RA,* XXII (1925), 63-64.

[Fever was placed upon the people].
[The womb was bound so that it could not issue off-spring].
[. . .]
[When the second year arrived],
[. . .] the stores.
[When the third year] arrived,
[The people] *became hostile* [in their . . .].
[When the fourth year arrived],
Their [places] became cramped,
[Their wide . . .] became too narrow.
[Downcast the people wandered] in the streets.
[When the fifth year arrived],
The daughter seeks [entry] to the mother,
[(But) the mother op]ens [not] her door [to the daughter].
[The daughter] watches [the balances of the mother],
The mother watches [the balances of the daughter].
[When the sixth year arrived],
[They prepared] the daughter for a meal,
[The child] they prepared [for food].
[Filled were . . .].
One [house] devoured the other.
[Like *ghosts of the dead* their faces] were veiled.
[The people] lived [with bated] breath.
[Endowed with wis]dom, the man Atrahasis—
His mind alert [to Ea, his lord]—
[Converses] with his god.
[His lord, E]a, converses with him.[15]
[. . .] the gate of his god.
Opposite the river he places his bed.
[. . .] his *rain* . . .[16]

(iii)

(beginning destroyed)

[Because of] their clamor he is disturb[ed],
[Because of] their uproar [sleep] cannot seize him.
[En]lil set up [his] Assembly,
[Say]ing to the gods, his sons:
"Oppressive has become the clamor of mankind.
[Because of their] clamor I am disturbed,
[Because of th]eir [up]roar sleep cannot seize me.
[. . .] let there be chills.
The pestilence shall [prompt]ly put an end
to their clamor!
[Like] a storm it shall blow upon them
Aches, dizziness, chills, (and) fever."
[. . .] there developed chills.
The pestilence [prompt]ly put an end to their clamor.
[Like] a storm it blew upon them
Aches, dizziness, chills, (and) fever.
[Endowed with w]isdom, the man Atrahasis—
His mind alert [to] Ea, his [lord]—
Converses with his god.
His [lord], Ea, converses with him.
Atrahasis opened his mouth, saying
To Ea, his lord:
"O lord, mankind cries out.
Your [*an*]*ger* consumes the land.
[E]a, O lord, mankind cries out.
[The *anger*] of the gods consumes the land.
[. . .] ye have created us.
[Let there c]ease the aches, the dizziness, the chills, the fever!"
[Ea opened his mouth to s]peak,
Addressing Atrahasis:
"[. . .] let there appear in the land.
[. . .] pray to your goddess."

(mutilated)[17]

[Enlil] set up his Assembly,
Speaking to the gods, his sons:
"[. . .] do not arrange for them.
[The people] have not diminished;
They are more numerous than before.
[Because of] their clamor I am disturbed,
[Because of] their uproar sleep cannot seize me.
[Let] the fig tree be [cut] off for the people.
[In] their bellies let the greens be too few.
[Ab]ove let Adad make scarce his rain,
Below let the flood be dammed up,
Let it not rise from the source.
[Let] the land withdraw its yield,
[Let] it turn the breast of Nisaba.
During the nights let the fields turn white,
Let the broad plain bring forth salt crystals,
Let her[18] bosom revolt,
That no plant come forth, no grain sprout.
Let fever be placed upon the people,
Let [the womb] be bound that it issue not offspring!"
They c[u]t off the fig tree for the people,
In their bellies the greens became too few.
Above Adad made scarce his rain,
Below was dammed up the flood,
So that it rose not from its source.
The land withdrew its yield,
It turned the breast of Nisaba.
During the nights the fields turned white,
(As) the broad plain brought forth salt crystals.
Her bosom revolted,
So that no plant came forth, no grain sprouted.
Upon the people was placed fever,
The womb was bound and issued not offspring.

(For column iv, which has been treated with another myth, see the introductory remarks.)

Descent of Ishtar to the Nether World

This myth has as its central theme the detention of the goddess of fertility—Sumerian Inanna, Akkadian Ishtar—in the realm

[15] At this point the tablet contains the scribal notation *la-šú* "there is not," indicating a blank space in the original. The context, however, is not interrupted. cf. Heidel, *GE*, 113, n.37.

[16] Atrahasis evidently sought to obtain rain for his fellow men by means of some magic practices. Evidently he succeeded, but mankind presently reverted to its earlier ways.

[17] To judge from the sequel, the plagues were halted once again, but only temporarily.

[18] That of Nisaba.

of the dead and her eventual return to the land of the living. The cuneiform material is extant in Sumerian and Akkadian formulations. The Sumerian version is obviously primary. But although the Semitic version has various points of contact with the older source, it is by no means a mere translation from the Sumerian, for which cf. Kramer, pp. 52-57.

The Semitic version has come down to us in two recensions. The older of these (A) comes from Ashur. (For a fragment of a still older recension—which comes from Ashur and dates from the end of the second millennium B.C.—cf. the eleven initial lines published by Ebeling in *Orientalia*, XVIII [1949], 32, 37. To judge from this small piece, this older version represented an independent formulation.) Its text has been published in *KAR*, No. 1 (Pls. 1-4), and p. 321. The other recension (N) comes from the library of Ashurbanipal at Nineveh. Its text is found in *CT*, 15, Pls. 45-48. The translations include those by Jensen, *KB*, VI, 80 ff. (N only); S. Geller, in *OLZ*, XX (1917), cols. 41 ff. (the first translation of recension A); Ebeling, in *AOT*, 206 ff.; and Heidel, *GE*, 121 ff. The present translation is a composite one in that it makes use, in common with all the renderings subsequent to the publication of A, of both the Nineveh and the Ashur version. Where the difference between the two is more than stylistic, the recension here followed will be explicitly indicated.

(obverse)

To the Land of no Return, the realm of [*Ereshkigal*],
Ishtar, the daughter of Sin, [set] her mind.[1]
Yea, the daughter of Sin set [her] mind
To the dark house, the abode of Irkal[la],[2]
To the house which none leave who have entered it,
To the road from which there is no way back,
To the house wherein the dwellers are bereft of li[ght],
Where dust is their fare and clay their food,
(Where) they see no light, residing in darkness,
(Where) they are clothed like birds, with wings for garments,[3]
(And where) over door and bolt is spread dust.[4]
When Ishtar reached the gate of the Land of no Return,
She said (these) words to the gatekeeper:
"O gatekeeper, open thy gate,
Open thy gate that I may enter!
If thou openest not the gate so that I cannot enter,
I will smash the door, I will shatter the bolt,
I will smash the doorpost, I will move the doors,
I will raise up the dead, eating the living,
So that the dead will outnumber the living."[5]
The gatekeeper opened his mouth to speak,
Saying to exalted Ishtar:
"Stop, my lady, do not throw it[6] down!
I will go to announce thy name to Queen E[reshk]igal."
The gatekeeper entered, saying [to] Eresh[kigal]:
"Behold,[7] thy sister Ishtar is waiting at [the gate],
She who upholds[8] the great festivals,
Who stirs up the deep before Ea, the k[ing]."[9]
When Ereshkigal heard this,
Her face turned pale[10] like a cut-down tamarisk,
While her lips turned dark like a bruised *kunīnu*-reed.[11]
"What drove her heart to me? What impelled her spirit hither?
Lo, should I drink water with the Anunnaki?
Should I eat clay for bread, drink muddied water for beer?
Should I bemoan the men who left their wives behind?
Should I bemoan the maidens who were wrenched from the laps of their lovers?
(Or) should I bemoan the tender little one who was sent off before his time?[12]
Go, gatekeeper, open the gate for her,
Treat her in accordance with the ancient rules."
Forth went the gatekeeper (to) open the door for her:
"Enter, my lady, that Cutha[13] may rejoice over thee,
That the palace of the Land of no Return may be glad at thy presence."
When the first door he had made her enter,
He stripped[14] and took away the great crown on her head.
"Why, O gatekeeper, didst thou take the great crown on my head?"
"Enter, my lady, thus are the rules of the Mistress of the Nether World."
When the second gate he had made her enter,
He stripped and took away the pendants on her ears.
"Why, O gatekeeper, didst thou take the pendants on my ears?"
"Enter, my lady, thus are the rules of the Mistress of the Nether World."
When the third gate he had made her enter,
He stripped and took away the chains round her neck.
"Why, O gatekeeper, didst thou take the chains round my neck?"
"Enter, my lady, thus are the rules of the Mistress of the Nether World."
When the fourth gate he had made her enter,
He stripped and took away the ornaments on her breast.
"Why, O gatekeeper, didst thou take the ornaments on my breast?"
"Enter, my lady, thus are the rules of the Mistress of the Nether World."
When the fifth gate he had made her enter,
He stripped and took away the girdle of birth-stones on her hips.

[1] Lit. "ear."
[2] Ereshkigal, Queen of the Nether World.
[3] cf. Gilgamesh, VII, iv, 33-39.
[4] A adds: "[. . .] stillness is poured out."
[5] A reads: "So that the living will outnumber the dead."
[6] The door.
[7] This meaning of *annītu* in N is indicated by A's *annū*.
[8] A reads *mul-ḳi-il-tu*.
[9] This half of the verse in A only.
[10] From A.
[11] Word play *šabaṭ* "bruised": *šapat-š[a]* "her lips."
[12] i.e. Ereshkigal would have cause for weeping if all these occupants of the nether world should be liberated by Ishtar. cf. Heidel, *GE*, 123, n.70.
[13] A name of the nether world, the Akkadian city-name *Kutū*.
[14] The form *muṣṣū* "spread out" (clothing), as in Gilgamesh, I, iv, 12, 18, is paralleled by *šaḫāṭu* "strip," *ibid.* iii, 43. It may well correspond to our *mutaṣū*, cf. already, Jensen, *KB*, VI, 396. cf. also the analogous construction *esip tabal*.

"Why, O gatekeeper, didst thou take the girdle of birthstones on my hips?"
"Enter, my lady, thus are the rules of the Mistress of the Nether World."
When the sixth gate he had made her enter,
He stripped and took away the clasps round her hands and feet.
"Why, O gatekeeper, didst thou take the clasps round my hands and feet?"
"Enter, my lady, thus are the rules of the Mistress of the Nether World."
When the seventh gate he had made her enter,
He stripped and took away the clasps round her body.
"Why, O gatekeeper, didst thou take the breechcloth on my body?"
"Enter, my lady, thus are the rules of the Mistress of the Nether World."
As soon as Ishtar had descended to the Land of no Return,
Ereshkigal saw her and was enraged at her presence.
Ishtar, unreasoning, flew at her.
Ereshkigal opened her mouth to speak,
Saying (these) words to Namtar, her vizier:
"Go, Namtar, lock [her] up [in] my [palace]!
Release against her, [against] Ishtar, the sixty mis[eries]:
Misery of the eyes [against] her [eyes],
Misery of the sides ag[ainst] her [sides],
Misery of the feet ag[ainst] her [feet],
Misery of the head ag[ainst her head]—
Against every part of her, against [her whole body]!"
After Lady Ishtar [had descended to the Land of no Return],
The bull springs not upon the cow, [the ass impregnates not the jenny],
In the street [the man impregnates not] the maiden.
The man lay [in his (own) chamber, the maiden lay on her side],
[. . . l]ay [. . .].

(reverse)

The countenance of Papsukkal, the vizier of the great gods,
Was fallen, his face was [clouded].
He was clad in mourning, long hair he wore.
Forth went Papsukkal[15] before Sin his father, weeping,
[His] tears flowing before Ea, the king:
"Ishtar has gone down to the nether world, she has not come up.
Since Ishtar has gone down to the Land of no Return,
The bull springs not upon the cow, the ass impregnates not[16] the jenny,
In the street the man impregnates not the maiden.
The man lay down in his (own) chamber,
The maiden lay down on her side."
Ea[17] in his wise heart conceived an image,

[15] N reads "Shamash."

[16] Causative form of *arū* "to conceive," cf. Landsberger, *ZA*, XLI (1933), 228.

[17] A adds "the king."

And created Asushunamir,[18] a eunuch:
"Up, Asushunamir, set thy face to the gate of the Land of no Return;
The seven gates of the Land of no Return shall be opened for thee.
Ereshkigal shall see thee and rejoice at thy presence.
When her heart has calmed, her mood is happy,
Let her utter the oath[19] of the great gods.
(Then) lift up thy head, paying mind to the life-water bag:[20]
"Pray, Lady, let them give me the life-water bag
That water therefrom I may drink."[21]
As soon as Ereshkigal heard this,
She smote her thigh,[22] bit her finger:
"Thou didst request of me a thing that should not be requested.
Come, Asushunamir, I will curse thee with a mighty curse![23]
The food of the city's plows[24] shall be thy food,
The *sewers* of the city shall be thy drink.
The shadow of the wall shall be thy station,
The threshold shall be thy habitation,
The besotted and the thirsty shall smite thy cheek!"[25]
Ereshkigal opened her mouth to speak,
Saying (these) words to Namtar, her vizier:
"Up, Namtar, knock at Egalgina,[26]
Adorn the thresholds with *coral*-stone,
Bring forth the Anunnaki and seat (them) on thrones of gold,
Sprinkle Ishtar with the water of life and take her from my presence!"
Forth went Namtar, knocked at Egalgina,
Adorned the thresholds with *coral*-stone,
Brought forth the Anunnaki, seated (them) on thrones of gold,
Sprinkled Ishtar with the water of life and took her from her presence.[27]
When through the first gate he had made her go out,
He returned to her the breechcloth for her body.
When through the second gate he had made her go out,
He returned to her the clasps for her hands and feet.
When through the third gate he had made her go out,
He returned to her the birthstone girdle for her hips.

[18] A reads *Aṣnamer* throughout.

[19] A reads explicitly *ne-eš̌* "oath."

[20] Akk. *ḫalziq(q)u*.

[21] The scheme evidently succeeds as Ereshkigal, distracted by the beauty of *Aṣūšunamir* "His Appearance is Brilliant," does not recover until it is too late.

[22] A gesture of annoyance, or derision.

[23] A reads instead:
"I will decree for thee a fate not to be forgotten,
A fate will I decree for thee,
Not to be forgotten throughout eternity."

[24] A has *e-pi-it*, for which cf. v. Soden, *Orientalia*, XVI (1947), 171. The meaning of "food of the plows" can scarcely be other than "dirt."

[25] For lines 24-28 cf. Gilgamesh VII, iii, 19-22.

[26] "Palace of Justice."

[27] There appears to be at this point a lacuna in N. A adds:
"[. . .], up, O Namtar, [ta]ke [Ishtar] away.
[But i]f she does not give thee her ransom price, [br]ing her back."
Namtar [t]ook her away and [. . .].

When through the fourth gate he had made her go out,
He returned to her the ornaments for her breasts.
When through the fifth gate he had made her go out,
He returned to her the chains for her neck.
When through the sixth gate he had made her go out,
He returned to her the pendants for her ears.
When through the seventh gate he had made her go out,
He returned to her the great crown for her head.
"If she does not give thee her ransom price, bring her back.[28]
As for Tammuz, the lover of her youth,
Wash him with pure water, anoint him with sweet oil;
Clothe him with a red garment, let him *play* on a flute of lapis.
Let courtesans *turn* [*his*][29] mood."
[When] Belili[30] had [. . .] her jewelry,
[And her] lap was filled with "eye-stones,"[31]
On hearing the sound of her brother, Belili struck the jewelry on [. . .]
So that the "eye-stones" filled [her] *chamber.*
"My only brother, bring no harm to me!
On the day when Tammuz *welcomes* me,
When with him the lapis flute (and) the carnelian ring welcome me,
When with him the wailing men and the wailing women welcome me,
May the dead rise and smell the incense."

A Vision of the Nether World

Among the thirty-seven texts which E. Ebeling collected in his *Tod und Leben* (1931) there are several that bear on the subject of myths and epics. For the most part, however, the pertinent material is introduced indirectly, in connection with specific ritual processes.[1] Only Nos. 1 and 37—the first and last in the book—are directly relevant to the present section and hence have been utilized.[2]

Such understanding of No. 1 as we now enjoy is due primarily to W. v. Soden, who in *ZA*, XLIII (1936) produced a thoroughly revised transliteration, accompanied by photographs, translation, introduction, and brief commentary (pp. 1-31). Ebeling came back with a new transliteration in *MAOG*, X, 2 (1937), 5 ff., which adds a few further improvements. A translation of the reverse of the text (v. Soden's lines 41-75) is given also by Heidel, *GE*, 132-136.

[28] This continuation of Ereshkigal's instructions appears to be out of place here, as regards the N version. A speaks of the ransom before Ishtar is led away (see the preceding note). The mention of Tammuz is likewise startling in this context. There is no indication in the Sumerian version—contrary to earlier assumptions—that Tammuz had gone down to the nether world. The concluding part of the myth, therefore, will remain obscure in its allusions so long as additional material is not available.

[29] This seems required by the context. It is by no means certain, however, that the final [. . .]-*i-šu* of A goes with [*ḳabittu*].

[30] Apparently, Ishtar; cf. Heidel, *GE*, 128, n.88.

[31] Interpreted as "beads" by R. Campbell Thompson, *A Dictionary of Assyrian Chemistry and Geology* (1936), xl.

[1] The same is true also of the large text (*KAR*, 1, 1915, No. 143) which deals with the passion and eventual triumph of Bēl-Marduk; cf. the study by H. Zimmern, *Berichte der sächsischen Akademie der Wissenschaften, phil.-hist. Klasse*, LXX (1918), v, 1-52; see also S. Langdon, *Babylonian Epic of Creation*, 33-59, and the discussion by S. A. Pallis, *The Babylonian Akītu Festival* (1926), pp. 221-34.

[2] For No. 37 cf. Creation of Man by the Mother Goddess, pp. 99-100.

The text is inscribed on a large tablet from Ashur, dating from the middle of the seventh century B.C. It is in the form of a prose poem whose lines average over fifty signs each. The background of the story is political, but its mundane allusions are enigmatic and are further obscured by the mutilated character of the obverse. What does emerge is that an Assyrian prince, who is called Kummâ[3]—evidently a pseudonym—is so presumptuous as to desire a view of the nether world. His desire is at last granted and the realm of Nergal and Ereshkigal is revealed to him in a dream, as recorded on the reverse of the tablet. In the following translation each line of the original is presented as a brief paragraph. The line count follows the count of the reverse; line 1 corresponds to v. Soden's 41, and so on.

(reverse)

[Kum]ma lay down and beheld a night vision in his dream: "[. . .] *I held* and I saw his awe-inspiring splendor [. . .].

[Na]mtar, the vizier of the nether world, who creates the decrees, I beheld; a man stood before him; the hair of his head he held in his left, while in his right [he held] a sword [. . .].

[Na]mtartu, (his) *concubine*, was provided with the head of a *ḳurību*,[4] (her) hands (and) feet were human. The death-god was provided with the head of a serpent-dragon, his hands were human, his feet were [. . .].

The evil [. . .] (had) the head (and) hands of men; his headgear was a crown; the feet were (those of) a . . .-bird; with his left foot he trod on a *crocodile*. Alluhappu[5] (had) the head (of) a lion, four human hands (and) feet.

'The Upholder of Evil'[6] (had) the head of a bird; his wings were open as he flew to and fro, (his) hands (and) feet were human. 'Remove Hastily,'[7] the boatman of the nether world, (had) the head (of the) Zu-bird; his four hands (and) feet [. . .].

[. . .] (had) the head (of) an ox, four human hands (and) feet. The evil Utukku (had) the head (of) a lion, hands (and) feet (of) the Zu-bird. Shulak was a normal lion stand[ing] on his hind legs.

[Ma]mitu (had) the head (of) a goat, human hands (and) feet. Nedu, the gatekeeper of the nether world, (had) the head (of) a lion, human hands, feet (of) a bird. 'All that is Evil'[8] (had) two heads; one head was (that of) a lion, the other head [. . .].

[. . .]ra (had) three feet; the two in front were (those of) a bird, the hind one was (that of) an ox; he was possessed of an awesome brilliance. Two gods—I know not their names—one (had) the head, hands (and) feet (of) the Zu-bird; in his left [. . .];

The other was provided with a human head; the headgear was a tiara; in his right he carried a Mace; in his left [. . .]. *In all*, fifteen gods were present. When I saw them, I prayed [*to them*].

[3] The full form of the name is given in obverse, 27 as [I] *Ku-um-ma-a*. This is normalized by v. Soden as "Kummâ," and by Heidel as "Kummaya." Either view would seem tenable.

[4] A demon pictured as a sphinx.

[5] The term itself (a loan word from the Sumerian) means a "hunting net."

[6] Akk. *Muḳīl-rēš-lemutti.*

[7] Akk. *Ḫumuṭ-tabal.* V. Soden (*OLZ*, 1934, 414) calls attention to the analogous "Speed spoil, Haste prey" in Isaiah 8:3.

[8] Akk. *Mimma-lemnu.*

A man (also), his body was black as pitch; his face was like that of Zu; he was clad in a red cloak; in his left he carried a bow, in his right he[ld] a sword; *with* the left fo[ot] he *trod* on a *serp*[*ent*].

When I moved mine eyes, valiant Nergal was seated on a royal throne; his headgear was the crown of royalty; in his two hands he held two wrathful *Maces*;[9] two heads [. . .].

[. . .] they were cast down; *from* [. . .] of his *arms* lightning was flashing; the Anunnaki, the great gods, stood bowed to the right (and) to the left [. . .].

The nether world[10] was filled with terror; before the prince lay utter *st*[*ill*]*ness*.[11] [. . .] took me by the locks of my forehead and dre[w me] into his presence.

When [I] saw him, my legs trembled as his wrathful brilliance overwhelmed me; I kissed the feet of his [great] godhead as I bowed down; when I stood up, he looked at me, shaking his [head].

With a fierce [c]ry he shrieked at me wrathfully like a fu[rio]us storm; the scepter, which befits his divinity, one which is full of terror, like a viper,

He drew [tow]ards me in order to kill [me]; Ishum, his counselor, the intercessor who spares life, who loves truth, and so forth, spoke up: 'Put not the fellow to death, thou *do*[*ugh*]*ty* ruler of the nether world!

Let the subjects of all the land ever hear [. . .] of thy fame!' The heart of the all-powerful, the almighty, who vanquishes the evil ones, he soothed like clear water of the well.

Nergal *delivered* this his statement: 'Why didst thou *slight* my beloved wife, the Queen of the Nether World?[12]

[A]t her exalted command, which is not to be altered, Bib*lu*,[13] the slaughterer of the nether world, shall entrust thee to Lugalsula, the gatekeeper, that he may lead [thee] out through the Ishtar-Aya gate.

[For]get and forsake me not, and I will not impose the death sentence; (yet) at the command of Shamash, shall distress, oppression, and disorders

[. . .] shall together blow thee down;[14] because of their *fierce* uproar sleep shall not engulf thee.[15]

This [*spirit of the dead*], whom [thou] hast seen in the nether world, is that of the exalted shepherd to whom my father, [. . .], the king of the gods, granted all that was in his heart;

[It is that of him] who all the lands from east to west fattened like . . . as he ruled over all;

[Of him to whom] Ashur, in view of his priesthood, [. . .] the celebration of the holy New-Year's-Festival-in-the-Plain, in the Garden of Plenty,[16] the image of Lebanon, [. . .] forever

[*Decr*]*eed*, and whose body Yabru, Humba, (and) Naprushu[17] protected, whose seed, whose army (and) camp they rescued, so that in battle no *charioteer* came near him.

[And h]e, thy begetter, the *e*[*min*]*ent*, the one experienced in matters, of wide understanding, broad and wise in spirit, who ponders[18] the designs of the earth mass,

(Who), *nevertheless*, sealed his mind to his[19] speech, who partook of the forbidden and trampled on the consecrated—you (two) will the fearsome brilliance of his majesty overwhelm speedily *everywhere*.[20]

May this word be laid[21] on your hearts like unto a thorn! Go (back) to the upper regions, until I bethink me of thee!' As he spoke to me,

I awoke." And like a man who has shed blood, who wanders alone in the marshes, (and) whom a catchpole has overcome,[22] while his heart pounded,

Or like a young boar just matured, who has mounted on his mate—his insides constantly expanding —he ejected dirt[23] to the front and back of him.

He emitted a lamentation,[24] saying, "Woe, my heart!" Flying into the street like an arrow, he scooped up the dust of the road (and) market place into his mouth, as he uttered a fearsome *cry*, "Woe! Ah me!

Why hast thou decreed this for me?" (Thus) calling, he poignantly praised, before the subjects of Ashur the valor of Nergal (and) Ereshkigal, who had helpfully stood by this prince.

And as for that scribe who had previously accepted bribe(s) as he occupied the post of his father, owing to the clever understanding which Ea had imparted to him

He heeded[25] in his heart the *w*[*ord*]*s* of praise, speaking thus inside him: "In order that the oaths for evil draw not close to me nor press upon me,

I will carry out the deeds [that *Nergal*] has commanded!" He went forth and repeated it to the palace, saying: "This shall be my expiation."

[9] Reading *me-i-ṭi*!

[10] Akk. *arallū* (a Sumerian loan word), in stylistic contrast to *erṣetum*, lit. "earth," which was used in the preceding lines.

[11] cf. v. Soden, *ZA*, XLIII (1936), 29.

[12] By being so presumptuous as to enter her realm.

[13] Reading highly uncertain. On the photograph (*ZA*, XLIII, Pl. III) the sign is damaged and ambiguous. Ebeling reads *Bi-ib-bu*.

[14] Reading *lid-dib-ba-ni-ḳa-ma* (root *edēbu*), with v. Soden, *ZA*, XLII, 30.

[15] cf. Atraḫasis, A, 8; D, iii, 2, 8, 41; for the verbal root cf. Gilgamesh, V (Boghazköy fragment, *KUB*, IV, No. 12, 6): *šittu rāḫit muši*.

[16] A reference, obviously, to the celebration in the Country Temple at Ashur, for which cf. W. Andrae, *Das wiedererstandene Assur* (1938), 37-39, 214-15.

[17] For these three Elamite deities cf. v. Soden, *loc. cit.*, 30.

[18] For this as a possible nuance of *ḫâṭu* cf. the material collected by A. L. Oppenheim, in *Orientalia*, XIV (1945), 235-38.

[19] Referring to some unnamed deity.

[20] The Sumerian equivalent of this phrase, which Ebeling cites (*Tod und Leben*, 9, d) and v. Soden repeats (*loc. cit.*, 31), is in itself obscure in some respects. The Akk. may perhaps mean "as far as the wind (can penetrate)," hence "everywhere."

[21] Less probable, for syntactic reasons, would be the derivation of the verbal form from *naṭū* "scourge," cf. (*The Assyrian Laws*) *KAV*, I VI, 44.

[22] For *bēl birḳi* cf. the reference cited by v. Soden, *loc. cit.*, 31, but add, also, *KAR*, 174, rev., 3, line 25. Of special importance in this connection is a passage from the Erra Myth, *KAR*, 169, rev., 2, line 15, where *eṭel(?) bir-ḳi i-la-'-a* is followed by *a-ḳu-u bēl e-mu-qí i-ḳat-tam* "the weak shall overcome the mighty." Here *ḳatāmu* is parallel to *le'ū* "prevail," and *bēl emūqi* to an apparent synonym of *bēl birḳi*. Accordingly, the form *iḳtummūšūma* in our verse cannot be derived, with v. Soden, from *ḳamū*, but must be connected with *ḳatāmu*.

[23] Lit. "clay."

[24] For the reading *si!-pit-tu* cf. Ebeling, *MAOG*, X, 2, p. 20.

[25] For this force of *šadādu* cf. Gilgamesh, XII, 32, and note 242, *ibid*.

The Myth of Zu

This myth deals, in its Akkadian formulation, with the theft of the Tablets of Destinies and the arrogation of the supreme authority of the gods by the bird-god, Zu, who is eventually vanquished by one of the benign deities. It is probable that Zu belongs to the realm of the nether world.[1] The extant Sumerian material does not connect him with the episode that constitutes the core of the Akkadian myth. The Semitic versions are fragmentary, so that an adequate comparative study is as yet impossible. Until 1938 there was available only a portion of the Ashurbanipal recension (B). In that year, however, Father V. Scheil published two incomplete tablets of a Susa recension, which is approximately a thousand years older. This new material (A) helps to fill the gaps in the Assyrian Version in a number of passages and carries the story appreciably further. Unfortunately, the last sections are badly mutilated. Moreover, Father Scheil could not have meant his accompanying transliteration and translation to be more than a preliminary draft—which he never had the opportunity to revise. At any rate, the transliteration does not always agree with the autographed copy of the text, and there is not a single explanatory note in his publication. The translation given below follows the copy.

The myth is of outstanding importance in that it throws light on a primary aspect of the idea of sovereignty in Mesopotamia; supreme authority in heaven (*Enlilūtu* "Enlilship, Sovereignty") was linked to the possession of the Tablets of Fate (cf. *Epic of Creation*, I, 106)—and could be usurped by one who seized these symbols by fair means or foul. The concept of such symbols (Sumerian m e, Akkadian *parṣū* "norms") came to be reflected among the Hittites (*parā ḫandandātar*) and it underlies also the O. T. Urim and Thummim. It bears, moreover, on the profound difference between the concept of kingship in Egypt and the remainder of the Near East.

Literature: (A) Text, *RA*, xxxv (1938), 20-23; transliteration and translation, *ibid.*, 14-19, 22-25. (B) Text, *CT*, xv (1902), 39-40; translation, P. Jensen, *KB*, vi, 1 (1900), 47-55, Ebeling, *AOT*, 141-43, and Heidel, *BG*, 122-25.

SUSA VERSION

(Tablet 1 missing)

Tablet 2

He[2] took away the Enlilship; suspended are the norms.[3]
Father Enlil, their counselor, was speechless;
(All) brightness poured out, silence prevailed.
All the Igigi, in their totality, *were put out*;
The sanctuary took off its brightness.
The gods of the land gathered from all quarters at the news.
Anu opened his mouth,
Saying to the gods, his sons:
"Which god will slay Zu,
So that his name will remain the greatest of all?"
They called the Irrigator,[4] the son of Anu;
He who gives the orders said to him:
"[*In* thy *migh*]*ty* onslaught cut down Zu with thy weapons!
[Thy name shall be the greatest] of the great gods,
[Among the gods, thy brothers], thou shalt ha[ve] no equal.
[Glorified before] the gods, pot[ent] shall be thy name!"
[To Anu, his father, Adad add]re[ssed (these) words]:
"[My father], [to the trackless mountain] w[ho] will hasten?
[Who is like Z]u among thy sons?
[. . .] took away from the god [his Enlilship],
[. . .] *what is there that will bring him to justice?*[5]
His [comm]and [*has become*] like that of the god of Duranki.
[He who opposes] him will become like clay,
[*At*] his [. . .] the gods *waste away*."[6]
[Anu] commanded not to go on (this) journey.
[*The Igi*]*gi* [called][7] the first-born of Anunitum;[8]
[H]e who gives the orders addressed him;
[*Sh*]*ara* they called, the first-born of Ishtar;
[H]e who gives the orders addressed him;[9]
As the gods calmed, [. . .]ing counsel.
The Igigi gathered, [. . .] troubled;
He who possesses wisdom, who dwells in the Deep,[10]
[. . .] went up to him,
The matter that was in the heart [of] his father he told him:
"[. . .] the scheme [. . .] of Zu, I shall make known to the Assembly!"
The gods heard [this] his speech,
[They *were st*]*ir*[*red* and kissed] his feet.
The glory [of *Nanshe*[11] . . .] Marduk proclaimed in the Assembly:
"[. . .] the potent one, the res[plen]dent, thy beloved,
[The w]ide of breast, who conducts the Seven to combat;
[. . .] the potent one, the res[plen]dent, thy beloved,
[The] wide of breast, who conducts the Seven to combat."

(reverse)[12]

[Anu] heard this his speech,
Most glorious Nanshe indicated assent.

[1] cf. T. Fish, The Zu Bird, *Bulletin of the John Rylands Library*, xxxi (1948), 162-71.

[2] Zu.

[3] This section corresponds to lines 21 ff. of the Assyrian Version. The unambiguous nominative *parṣū* confirms B. Landsberger's interpretation of the phrase (*AfO*, ii, 1924, 66) in the Assyrian version as against the otherwise universal "the issuing of decrees."

[4] Epithet of Adad, the storm-god.

[5] One of the several idioms combining *rēšu* and *našū* (cf. A. L. Oppenheim, *JAOS*, lxi (1941), 252 ff. Before *it-ta-ši ri-ši-š*[*u*] I would read [*mi*]*-iš!-su*; cf. Gilgamesh, Old Babylonian (Yale Tablet) III, iv, 10 and cf. *ZA*, xl (1932), 200.

[6] The verb *saḫāḫu* (cf. also line 57, below) is paralleled by *šaḫāḫu* in the Assyrian Version. For the range of meaning cf. Th. Bauer, *Das Inschriftenwerk Assurbanipals* (1933), 33, n.1 (after Landsberger).

[7] The verb [*ís-su-ú*] is obviously to be supplied at the end of the line. Instead of the suggested [^{d}*I-gi*]*-gi*, some epithet of Shara (perhaps *māliku*, i.e. [AD.GI].GI) is entirely probable; the meaning would then be "*Malik* they called."

[8] A form of Ishtar.

[9] Here our text ceases to correspond to the Assyrian Version.

[10] Ea.

[11] The identity and relevance of some of the gods who are either mentioned or alluded to in this text are quite uncertain, owing mainly to the fragmentary and mutilated nature of the tablet. If Nanshe (cf. line 41) has been copied and read correctly, is this goddess another name for Ishtar, and is this also true of Mammi (line 48)? And what is Marduk's part? Does he merely sing the praises of the goddess, or does he actually take over the task of subduing Zu? Lastly, did Ninurta figure in this version, as he does in some Assyrian accounts? cf. E. Ebeling, *Tod und Leben*, nos. 7-8.

[12] Scheil numbers the reverse separately.

The gods of the land rejoiced at her word,
They were *stirred* and kissed his(!) feet.
She called out in the Assembly [. . .] the gods
Leading her son, the beloved of her heart, she said to him:
"Before Anu and Dagan, the exalted ones,
[. . .] *all* their regulations[12a] they will proclaim in the Assembly.
[. . .] . . . I gave birth to all of them,
[. . .] of the gods, I, Mammi!
[. . .] for my brother and for Anu ascertain the kingship of heaven;
[. . .] I will make known!
[. . .] thy father form thou,
[. . .] make it be well!
[. . .] bring forth light.
[. . .] wage thou thy combat!
[. . .] that they may *exclaim, 'My Mountain!'*[13]
[. . .] seize thou Zu,
[. . .] lay waste his dwelling.

(58-63 mutilated or missing)

May the curse of thy voice [. . .] overtake him,
May he carry [off] darkness, may his sight change (and) fail!
Let him not escape thee in the encounter,
Let his vigor sink!
Thou great one, never resting, unique,
Send forth before thee the mist
That he recognize not thy features.
(But) let no breeze blow above,
Let the bright day turn for him to dusk!
Cut down his life, shackle Zu,
Let the scorching wind carry (him) to places unknown,
Towards Ekur, towards his father,
Let the scorching wind carry him to places unknown!"
The valiant one heard the speech of his mother,
As she bade him valor in battle [. . .]—
Of her who hitches up seven [. . .],
[. . . *of seven w*]*inds* (and) seven tempests—
[. . .] who hitches up seven . . .
[. . . he waged] his combat.
[. . .] the gods *exclaimed "My Mountain!"*
[. . .] before the Ekur of Zu the god appeared.
[. . .] *he* entered before him;
[. . .] . . . like the *day*, his brilliance illumined the mountains.

Tablet 3

[. . .] *he* entered before him;
[. . . like the *d*]*ay*, his brilliance illumined the mountains.
[. . .] like . . . may they be goodly!
[. . .] of his heart he called out to . . . [. . .]:
"[. . .] the totality of all their regulations [. . .].
[. . .] . . . thou didst come, thy . . . [. . .]."
[With] his mouth valiant [*Mar*]*duk*[14] replied to Zu:
[. . . of Duran]ki, who foundedst Duranki, who decreest the destinies,
[. . .] it is I who have come, one who will crush thee.
[. . .] raise up the shield!
[. . .] the thief of the Mountain howled, [. . .] roared.
[. . .] washed with blood.
[. . .] the combat thundered.
[. . .] Mammi, the trust of the gods, *Z*[*u*] . . .
[. . .] to him . . .[15] drew near to Zu:
"[. . .] thou didst come here [. . .]"

(19-25-rev. 6, too fragmentary for translation)

"[. . .] may his life fail!
[. . .] let the norms return to Ekur, to the father who begot thee!
[Let b]uilt shrines [appear],
[In the f]our [quarters] establish thy places!"
[. . .] the commission of his father,
As he bade him [valor in bat]tle; he returned to . . .
[. . .] of combat the four winds he raised against him.
[. . .] the ground shook as . . . [. . .],
[. . .] the heavens . . .
As for Zu, at the onrush of the storm [his] vigor [sank].

ASSYRIAN VERSION

(Column i is almost entirely destroyed except for a few line finals, which furnish, among other forms, the names of Mammi—who figures prominently in A—and Enlil.)

(ii)

And all the decrees of the gods he directed.[15a]
. . . he dispatched Zu,
[. . .] . . . Enlil entrusted to him,
The [. . .]ing of pure water before him.
The exercise of his Enlilship his eyes view.
The crown of his sovereignty, the robe of his godhead,
His divine tablets of destinies Zu views constantly.
As he views constantly the father of the gods, the god of Duranki,[16]
The removal[17] of Enlilship he conceives in his heart.
As Zu views constantly the father of the gods, the god of Duranki,
The removal of Enlilship he conceives in his heart.
"I will take the divine tablets of destinies, I,
And the decrees of all the gods I will rule!

12a Here *parṣu* has its alternative meaning "rite, regulation," cf. *AfO*, II, 67.

13 Written ideographically ḫ u r . s a g . m u here and in line 79, which—if correct—can only be an exclamation, inasmuch as in line 79 the pronoun would otherwise be out of place. Is this an allusion to the nether world (cf. K. Tallquist, *Studia Orientalia*, V [1934], 4, pp. 23-25)?

14 So Scheil. The copy shows only faint traces of a possible UTU at the end. If read correctly, the name would give us the ultimate conqueror of Zu; cf., however, the following note.

15 Copy shows [. . .] *šum ma* GIŠ *iṭ-ḫi-a-am*. Scheil translates "when Gilgamesh approached." The appearance of Gilgamesh comes as a surprise, even though the father of Gilgamesh, Lugalbanda, is associated with Zu in a Sumero-Akkadian myth. For the present, at any rate, it seems preferable to regard *-šum-ma-*GIŠ(*níš?*) as the termination of an adverbial form.

15a Reading *ú-ma-*[*'-ir*], which alone fits the extant traces and parallels most closely the verbs used normally with *tērēti* and *parṣū*.

16 Here and in A (2, 21; 3, 8) the Temple Tower at Nippur rather than the city of Dēr.

17 Reading *uk-kuš*.

I will make firm my throne and be the master of the norms,
I will direct the totality of all the Igigi."
His heart having thus plotted aggression,
At the entrance of the sanctuary, which he had been viewing,
He awaits the start of day.
As Enlil was washing with pure water,
Having stepped down from the throne and deposited his crown,
He[18] seized the tablets of destinies in his hands,[19]
Taking away the Enlilship; suspended were [the norms].
When Zu had flown away and *was remote*[20] in his mountain,[21]
Father Enlil, their counselor, was speechless.[22]
Stillness spread abroad,[23] si[lence] prevailed.
The sanctuary took off[24] its brightness.
The deities tu[rn]ed in from all sides[25] at the ne[ws].
Anu op[ened] his mouth to speak,
Saying to the gods, his sons:
"[Wh]o[26] will slay Zu,
And make his name the greatest [in] the settlements?"

They called the [Irriga]tor, the son of Anu;
[He who gives the or]ders[27] addressed him.
They called the [Irriga]tor, the son of Anu;
[He who gives the or]ders addressed him:
"[Thou pot]ent one, all-conquering Adad—immovable thy onslaught—
[Cut thou down[28]] Zu with thy weapons!
[Thy name shall be the g]reatest in the Assembly of the gods,
[Among the god]s, thy brothers, thou shalt have no equal!
[Let] built shrines [appear],
[In the] four [quarters] establish thy places,
[Thy places] shall have entry into Ekur!
[Glorified] before the gods and potent shall be thy name!"
[Adad] replied to the command,
Saying (these) words [to Anu], his father:
"[My father, to the] trackless [mountain] who will hasten?
[Who is li]ke Zu among the gods, thy sons?
[The tablets of destinies] he has seized in his hands,
[The Enlilship] he has taken away; suspended are the norms.
[Zu] has flown away and *is remote* in his mountain.
His [utteran]ce has become like that of the god of Duranki.
[He who opposes] him will become [like clay],
[*At*] his [. . . the gods *waste away*]."
[Anu commanded Adad not to go on (this) journey].[29]

(iii)

(The first twenty-three lines of this column [54-76 in consecutive line count] are almost totally destroyed, except for portions of the last five lines. These correspond to lines 49-53 above. Apparently another deity had been called in, but declined to go against Zu. It should be noted that in the Susa Version the first-born of Ishtar is the second god to be called [the third in the Assyrian Version]. Moreover, he appears to have accepted the challenge, unlike his counterpart in the present instance.)

[They] called [Shara], the first-born[30] of Ishtar.
[He who gives the or]ders addressed him:
"[Thou pot]ent one, all-conquering Shara—immovable thy onslaught—
[Cut thou down] Zu with thy weapons!
[Thy name] shall be the greatest in the Assembly of the gods,
[Am]ong the gods, thy brothers, thou shalt have no equal!
[Let] built shrines appear,
In the four quarters establish thy places,
Thy places shall have entry into Ekur!
Glorified before the gods and potent shall be thy name!"
Shara replied to the command,
Saying (these) words to Anu, his father:
"My father, to the trackless mountain who will hasten?
Who is like Zu among the gods, thy sons?
The tablets of destinies he has seized in his hands,
The Enlilship he has taken away, the issuing of ordinan[ces].
Zu has flown away and is *re*[*mo*]*te* in his mountain.
[His] utter[ance] has [be]come [like that of the god of Duranki].
[He who opposes him will become like clay],
[*At* his . . . the gods *waste away*]."
[Anu commanded Shara not to go on (this) journey].

(The remainder of the tablet is too fragmentary for translation. Another incomplete tablet [*CT*, xv, Pls. 41-42] belongs to the Lugalbanda cycle—represented primarily in Sumerian—which tells us that Lugalbanda set out to conquer Zu by first plying him with intoxicants. In a hymn of Ashurbanipal it is Marduk who is celebrated as "the one who crushed the skull of Zu." And we have seen that the Susa Version records the downfall of Zu, but the identity of his conqueror remains in doubt.)

[18] Zu.
[19] Here begins the parallel account of the Susa Version.
[20] Reading *ik-kuš*; cf. n.17.
[21] The parallel text in A, 20 has *it-ta-ši re-ši-š*[*u*]. The sense appears to be here "to be distant in one's mountain, be secure." For "the mountain" as a place of ultimate security cf. *Etana*, A-2, line 2.
[22] Reading *š*[*u-ḫa-ru*]*-ur*, with A, 2.
[23] The same form *ittatbak* is used here of "stillness" and in A, 3 of "brightness." Both meanings ("disappear" and "spread") are attested, deriving from an underlying "be poured out." For a close parallel to the present text cf. the passage in the Old Babylonian Legend, *CT*, xv, Pl. iv, 5.
[24] The form *iš-ta-ḫa-aṭ* in A, 5 gives us the correct reading of the present form as *iš-ta-ḫaṭ*.
[25] A, 5 has *iptanaḫḫuru* "gathered time and again, from all sides."
[26] Perhaps [*a-a*]*-ú* ⟨*ilu*⟩ "which god?" in view of *i-lu ma-an-nu-um* in A, 9.
[27] cf. A, 11, which now gives us the correct supplementation.
[28] Supplying [*šu-up-ri-iq*] from A, 11.
[29] The last three lines have been supplemented from 74-77.
[30] Reading *bu-kùr* (not *bu-nu*), in view of *bu-kur* in A, 27.

Etana

The legendary dynasty of Kish which followed the Flood lists among its rulers "Etana, a shepherd, the one who to heaven ascended."[1] Cylinder seals of the Old Akkadian period depict a shepherd rising heavenwards on the wings of an eagle.[2] And a figure by the name of Etana—a mortal in all respects, except that his name may be written with the determinative for "god," a usage applied also to kings of the Old Akkadian and some of the succeeding dynasties—is the subject of an elaborate legend. The subject matter is thus clearly one of great antiquity. Its popularity, moreover, is attested by the fact that the legend has come down to us in fragments of three recensions: The Old Babylonian (A); the Middle Assyrian (B); and the Neo-Assyrian—from the library of Ashurbanipal (C). With the aid of these three versions, of which the latest is by far the best-preserved, the outlines of the story may be reconstructed as follows:

Etana had been designated to bring to mankind the security that kingship affords. But his life was blighted so long as he remained childless. The one known remedy appeared to be the plant of birth, which Etana must bring down in person from heaven. The difficult problem of the flight to heaven was eventually solved by Etana's enlisting the aid of an eagle. The eagle had betrayed his friend, the serpent, and was languishing in a pit as a result of his perfidy. Etana rescues the bird and, as a reward, is carried by the eagle on a spectacular and fitful flight. The text fails us at the critical juncture. But the fact that the king list records the name of Etana's son and heir, and the further fact that myths depicted on seals do not normally commemorate disaster,[3] permit the conclusion that the ending was a happy one after all.

The various texts which represent the Old Babylonian and the Neo-Assyrian recensions (A and C) have been republished by S. Langdon in *Babyloniaca*, XII (1931), Pls. I-XIV, and have been discussed by him, *ibid.*, pp. 1-53. Our text references will be limited in the main to Langdon's copies, which furnish also an adequate guide to the respective sources. But Langdon's attempt to piece together a consecutive story from documents separated by more than a millennium has not been followed in this translation. Instead, the material has been grouped according to periods. Thirteen years after Langdon's publication, E. Ebeling was able to add to the Etana material by publishing fragments of a Middle Assyrian version, *AfO*, XIV (1944), Pls. IX-X, and pp. 298-303, together with new Neo-Assyrian fragments, *ibid.*, Pls. XI-XII, and pp. 303-07. Older translations include those of P. Jensen, *KB*, VI, 1 (1900), 100-15, and 581-88; and of E. Ebeling, *AOT*, 235-40.[4] Detailed references will be given with each of the headings in the translation which follows.

OLD BABYLONIAN VERSION

A-1[5]

(i)

The great Anunnaki, who decree the fate,
Sat down, taking counsel about the land.
They who created the regions, who set up the establishments,
The Igigi, who were hostile to mankind,
A stated time for mankind decreed.
The beclouded[6] people, in all, had not set up a king.
At that time, no tiara had been tied on, nor crown,
And no scepter had been inlaid with lapis;
The quarters had not been built altogether.
The Seven[7] had barred the gates against the *settlers*.[8] (10)
Scepter, crown, tiara, and (shepherd's) crook
Lay deposited before Anu in heaven,
There being no counseling for its[9] people.
(Then) kingship descended from heaven.

(The remaining lines of this column, and nearly all of the following four columns, are missing. When the text becomes connected again, the eagle had appeared in the account:)

(v)

"O Shamash, ta[ke] my hand [. . .], (13)
Me [. . .]."
Shamash op[ened] his mouth, [saying to the eagle]:
"Thou hast dealt wickedly [. . .].
The detested of the g[ods and the forbidden thou didst eat]."

(vi)

By his [h]and he seized him . . . [. . .].
In the eighth month he caused (him) to pass by his pit.
The eagle, having received the food like a howling lion,
Gained strength.
The eagle opened his [mou]th, saying to Etana:
"My friend, verily we are joined in friendship, I and thou!
Say but to me what thou wishest of me, and I will grant it to thee."
Etana opened his mouth, saying to the eagle:
". . [. . .] . a hidden thing."

(tablet ends)

A-2[10]

(obverse)

"May the path be lost for him that he find not the way!
May the mountain withhold from him its passage.
May the darting weapon head straight for him!"[11]
They swore (this) oath to each other.
All were conceived, all were born.
In the shade of the *styrax*-tree[12] begets the serpent;
On its crown begets the eagle.

[1] cf. Th. Jacobsen, *The Sumerian King List* (1939), 80-81.
[2] H. Frankfort, *Cylinder Seals* (1939), 138-39, and Pl. XXIV-*h*.
[3] *ibid.*, 138.
[4] cf. also, P. Dhorme, *Choix de textes religieux assyro-babyloniens* (1907), 162-81.
[5] *Babyloniaca*, XII (1931), Pl. XII and p. 10 ff.; *KB*, VI, V (1900), 582 ff.

[6] A metaphor for "mankind."
[7] Not "the seven gates were locked" (Langdon, *Babyloniaca*, XII, 11), but "the divine Seven (barred the gates)," cf., below, C-1, line 17, where these deities are equated with the Igigi.
[8] Reading *da-ad!-nim*; cf. *da-ad-me* in the parallel passage, C-1, 18; the word means "settlements" and, by extension, "settlers," cf. B. Meissner, *Beiträge zum assyrischen Wörterbuch*, I (1931), 35-37. For the interchange *m/n* cf. *šašm/nu* "dual combat," W. v. Soden, *ZA*, XLI (1933), 169, and 166 n.1.
[9] Evidently, the earth's. The term *mitluku* "counseling, consultation" refers here to the function of the *māliku*, a cognate of the Hebrew word for "king." It is a significant commentary on the nature of kingship in Mesopotamian civilization.
[10] *Babyloniaca*, XII, Pls. XIII-XIV and pp. 14 ff.
[11] This is the concluding part of the oath taken by the eagle and the serpent; cf. the Middle Assyrian Version (B), 4-7, and the Neo-Assyrian passage, C-2, lines 11-16.
[12] For this identification cf. R. Campbell Thompson, *A Dictionary of Assyrian Chemistry and Geology* (1936), xxvi.

When the serpent has caught a wild ox (or) a wild sheep,[13]
The eagle feeds, his young feed.
When the serpent has caught a leopard (or) a *tiger*,[14]
The eagle feeds, his young feed.
After his young had grown in age [and size],
[*Their*] wings had *ac*[*quired* . . .],
The eagle [plotted evil] in his heart:
"My young [have grown in age and size];
They will go forth to seek [. . .],
They will seek the plant(s) [. . .],
Then I will devour the young of the serpent [. . .]!
I will go up and in [heaven]
I will dwell [. . .]!
Who is there that [. . .]?"
The [little] fledgling, [exceeding wise],[15]
To the ea[gle, his father (these) words addressed]:
"My father, [. . .]."

(remainder of obverse destroyed)

(reverse)

(beginning mutilated)

The serpent cast down [his burden] before [his young].[16]
He glanced round: [his young] were not there!
With his claws he [*scrapes*] the ground;[17]
[*The dust of the nest covers*] the sky.
[The serpent . . .] weeps,
His te[ars][18] flowing [before Shamash]:
"I put my trust in thee, valiant Shamash;
To the eagle I extended goodwill.
I revered and honored thine oath,
I upheld not evil against my friend.
Yet he, his nest is whole, but [my] nest is shattered,
The nest of the serpent has become the object of laments;
His fledglings are whole, my young are not there!
He came down and devoured my offspring.
Thou knowest, O Shamash, that he pursues evil.
Thy net is the wi[de] field,
Thy snare [is the far-away sky].
May the eagle not [escape] from thy net,
The doer of ev[il and abo]mination,
Who upholds e[vil] against his friend!"

MIDDLE ASSYRIAN VERSION[19]

(i)

(beginning mutilated)

"May the da[rt]ing [weapon] head straight for him,
May Shamash single him out[20] from among the killers,
May Shamash hand over the wicked one to the executioner!
May he place the wicked demon upon his land!"[21]

On the crown of the tree the eagle begets,
At the base of the *styrax*-tree begets the serpent.
In the shade of that *styrax*-tree
The eagle and the serpent formed a friendship,
Taking the oath to remain companions.
The desire of their hearts
They expounded to each other.

The serpent goes forth to hunt;
When *wild sheep* and *wild goats*[22]
The serpent has caught,
The eagle feeds, withdraws,[23]
His young feed.
When the serpent has caught mountain goats, gazelles of the steppe,
The [ea]gle feeds, withdraws, his young feed.
When the serpent has caught [the leopard] of the steppe, the creatures of the earth,
[The eagle] feeds, withdraws, his young feed.
[After the young] of the eagle
[Had grow]n in age and size,
Had acquired [*stature*],
[The eagle the young of] his [friend]
[To devour set] his [mind].

(Remainder of the column destroyed. Column ii too fragmentary for translation. The context corresponds to our C-3, 39 ff.)

NEO-ASSYRIAN VERSION

C-1[24]

(beginning mutilated)

The great Anunnaki [who decree the fate],
[Sat] exchanging their counsels [about the land].
They who created the four[25] regions [. . .],
All the Igigi were hostile [. . .].
The [. . .] had not set up a king.
In those days, [no tiara had been tied on, nor crown],
And [no] scepter had been [inlaid] with lapis.
The regions had not been created altogether.
The divine Seven against the people barred [the gates],
Against the settlers they barred [. . .].
The Igigi had turned away from the city.
Ishtar a shepherd [for the people . . .],
And a king she seeks [for the city].
Enlil inspects the quarters of heaven [. . .],
As he continues searching [. . .].
In the land a king [. . .],
Kingship [. . .].
Then [his heart] prompted Enlil [. . .].
The gods [. . .].

13 cf. B. Landsberger, *Fauna* (1934), 10, 144.
14 *ibid.*, 84.
15 cf. the new fragment, *AfO*, XIV (1944), Pl. XII (K 5299) and pp. 304 f.
16 *ibid.*, 305, line 9.
17 Reading *qa-qa!-ra*[*-am*], cf. *qaq-qa-ra, AfO*, XIV, *loc. cit.*, 11.
18 Reading *di!-*[*ma-a-*]*šu*, cf. *ibid.*, 13 and n.52.
19 E. Ebeling, *AfO*, XIV, Pl. IX and pp. 299-303.
20 Lit. "lift up his head," in the sense of "call to account"; cf. The Myth of Zu, p. 111, n.5.
21 Oath sworn by the eagle and the serpent, cf. above, A-2, 1-3, and below C-2, 11-16.
22 cf. Ebeling, *loc. cit.*, 300 f., n.15.
23 See Langdon, *Babyloniaca*, XII, 15, n.5.
24 *Babyloniaca*, XII, Pl. VII and pp. 7 ff.; cf. A-1, above.
25 Reading *4-im* in place of Langdon's *šá im-*.

C-2[26]

(beginning mutilated)

"Come, let us arise [. . .],
We have sworn by the *nether world* [. . .]!"
The oath that they sw[ore] before valiant Shamash:
"[He who transgresses] the boundary of Shamash,
May Shamash [hand him over] for evil to the executioner!
He who [transgresses] the boundary of Shamash,
May [the mountain] remove from him [its] pas[sage]!
May the darting weapon [head straight] for him,
May the snare, the curse of Shamash, overthrow him and catch him!"
When they had sworn the oath by the *nether world* [. . .],
They arose and went up to the mountain.
Each day they watch [. . .].
When the eagle has caught a wild ox or a wild ass,
The serpent feeds, withdraws, his young feed.
When the serpent has caught mountain goats (or) gazelles,
The eagle feeds, withdraws, his young feed.
When the eagle has caught *wild sheep* (or) *wild goats*,
The serpent feeds, withdraws, [his] young feed.
When the serpent has caught [leopards (or) *ground t*]*igers*,
[The eagle feeds, withdra]ws, [his] young feed.
The eagle received the food; his young grew in age and size.
When his young had grown in age and size,
The eagle's heart plotted evil.
And as his heart plotted evil,
He set his mind upon devouring the young of his friend.
The eagle opened his mouth, saying to his young:
"I will eat the young of the serpent; the serpent [. . .].
I will ascend to heaven that I may d[well there],
And I will descend to the crown of the tree to eat the fruit."
The little fledgling, exceeding wise,
(These) words to his father [addres]sed:[27]
"Eat not, my father! The net of Shamash may cat[ch thee],
The snare, the curse of Shamash, may overthrow thee and catch thee!
He who transgresses the boundary of Shamash,
[Him] Shamash [will hand over] for evil to the executioner!"
But he heard them not, he hearkened not [to the words of his son].
He descended and devoured the young [of the serpent].
[. . .], in the middle of the day the [serpent came],[28]

[26] *Babyloniaca*, XII, Pls. I-II, and pp. 12 ff.; E. Ebeling, *AOT*, 235 f., Fragment A.

[27] For this episode cf. the Middle Assyrian fragment, *AfO*, XIV, Pl. IX, ii, and pp. 301 ff.; also the Neo-Assyrian fragment, *ibid*., Pl. XII, and pp. 304 ff.

[28] The concluding part of this fragment is pieced together from *Babyloniaca*, XII, Pl. II, 43 ff. and *AfO*, XIV, Pl. XII (K 5299), obv. 8 ff.

Carrying his load (of flesh); at the entrance to the nest
H[e cast it down for his young].
As the serpent [glanced round], his nest was not there;
When he bent low, [he saw] (it) not.
With his claws he [scrapes] the ground;
The dust [of the ne]st [covers] the sky!

C-3[29]

The serpent [*li*]*es down* and weeps,
[His tears flowing] before Shamash:[30]
"I put my trust in thee, [valiant Shamash],
To the eagle [I extended goodwill].
Now my nest [. . .],
My nest is destroyed [. . .],
Shattered are my young [. . .].
He came down and devoured [my offspring].
[Thou knowest], O Shamash, the evil which he did to me.
Verily, O Shamash, thy net is the [wide] earth,
Thy snare is the [far-away] sky.
May [the eagle] not escape from thy net,
That evildoer, Zu,[31] who upholds [evil against his friend]!"
[When Shamash heard] the plea of the serpent,
Shamash opened his mouth, [saying] to [the serpent]:
"Go on (thy) way, cross [the mountain]!
I will bind[32] for thee a wild ox.
Open his inside, [rend his belly],
Pitch (thy) dwelling [in his belly]!
[Every kind] of bird of heaven [will descend to devour the flesh];
The eagle [will descend] with them [to devour the flesh],[33]
[Since] he knows not [his ill fortune].
Looking for the succulent flesh, he will proceed *cautiously*,[34]
Crawling to the recesses of the interior.
When he enters the interior, seize thou him by his wings;
Tear off his wings, his pinions, and his [talons];
Pluck him and cast him into a pit [. . .].
Let him die the death of hunger and thirst!"
At the command of valiant Shamash,
The serpent went and crossed the mountain.
When the serpent reached the wild ox,
He opened his inside, rent his belly.
He pitched (his) dwelling in his belly.
Every kind of bird of heaven descended to devour the flesh.

[29] *Babyloniaca*, XII, Pls. IV-V and II-III (Marsh Reverse); pp. 22 ff.; *KB*, VI, I, 104-08 (Jensen I*b*); *AOT*, 236-38 (Ebeling B).

[30] cf. *AfO*, XIV, 305, line 13.

[31] cf. pp. 111-13.

[32] In the sense of "charm, cast a spell upon."

[33] This is the beginning of K 2527 rev. (*Babyloniaca*, XII, Pl. IV), which Langdon provides with a separate line count, as he does also the sequel, viz., the reverse of the Jastrow Fragment, Pls. II-III. Our line count is consecutive, paralleling that of Jensen's fragment I*b*, except only that Jensen's numbers are ahead by one; he had assumed a gap of one line after 21, which assumption proved subsequently to be erroneous.

[34] Reading *sa-ṭa-a-ti* and adducing Aramaic-Hebrew *sūṭ*, or *sūd*, with W. F. Albright, *RA*, XVI (1919), 187. At any rate, the form cannot be read *id!-da-a-ti* with Ebeling, *AfO*, XIV, 305, n.57.

If the eagle but knew his ill fortune,[35]
He would not eat the flesh with the (other) birds!
The eagle opened his mouth saying to his young:
"Come ye, let us go down and devour the flesh of this wild ox!"
The little fledgling, exceeding wise,
To the eagle, his father,[36] (these) words addressed:
"Go [not] down, my father! Perchance
Inside this wild ox crouches the serpent?"
The eagle [*consulting not*] with [*his heart*],[37]
[Said] (these) [wor]ds:
"[I will g]o down [and eat the flesh of the wild ox]!
How could [the serpent] devour me?"[38]
He heard them not, he heeded not the words of his son,
He came down and lighted upon the wild ox.
The eagle inspected the flesh,
He examined its front and its hind parts.
Again he inspected the flesh, examining its front and its hind parts.
Proceeding *cautiously*, he *crawled* to the recesses of the interior.
When he entered the interior, the serpent seized him by his wings:
". . . !"[39]
The eagle opened his mouth, saying to the serpent:
"Have mercy upon me, and I will bestow upon thee
A marriage gift, like unto a bridegroom!"
The serpent opened his mouth, saying to the eagle:
"If I release thee, how shall I satisfy Shamash on high?
Thy punishment would be turned against me,
The punishment that I am imposing upon thee!"
He tore off his wings, his pinions, and his talons,
[He pl]ucked him and ca[st him] into a pi[t],
[Saying]: "He shall d[ie] a death of hunger [and thirst]!"
[. . .] the eagle daily beseeches Shamash:
"Am I to perish in the pit?
Who knows how thy *punishment* was imposed upon me?
Save the life of me, the eagle,
And I will sound thy name unto eternity!"
Shamash opened his mouth, saying to the eagle:
"Thou art evil and hast grieved me gravely!
The detested of the gods (and) the forbidden thou didst eat.
Though thou *diest*, I should not come near thee!
(But) lo, a man that I will send to thee,
He will take thy hand!"
Etana daily beseeches Shamash:
"Thou hast consumed, O Shamash, my fattest sheep,
The earth drinking up the blood of my lambs.

[35] Here begins the parallel text, Marsh Reverse, *Babyloniaca*, XII, Pls. II-III.

[36] These words are supplied from *AfO*, XIV, Pl. IX, ii, 4.

[37] Ebeling, *ibid.*, 305, line 3, would read *it-ti* [*lib-bi-šu ul im-lik-ma*], which yields excellent sense; it should be noted, however, that the copy (Langdon's Pl. II, 7) does not altogether favor these additions.

[38] This reading by Ebeling (*ibid.*, line 4), accords well with the traces on the Marsh Fragment (*Babyloniaca*, XII, Pl. II, line 8) and the new Ebeling text.

[39] Apparently some sort of exclamation, now unintelligible.

I honored the gods and revered the spirits;
The oracle priestesses have done the needful to my offerings,
The lambs, by their slaughter, have done the needful to the gods.
O lord, may it issue from thy mouth;
Grant thou me the plant of birth!
Show me the plant of birth,
Remove my burden and produce for me a name!"[40]
Shamash opened his mouth, saying to Etana:
"Go on (thy) way, cross the mountain.
On seeing a pit, examine its inside!
Inside it lies an eagle;
He will show thee the plant [of birth]!"
At the command of valiant Shamash,
Etana went on (his) wa[y, crossed the mountain].
When he saw the pit, he examined its inside;
Inside [it lay an eagle].
It was there that [Shamash] had caused him to await [him].

C-4[41]

The eagle opened his mouth,
[Saying] (these) words to Shamash, his lord:
[. . .].
"The young of a bird [. . .],
[*Le*]*ad him hither* [. . .].
[Wh]atever he says [. . .],
[Wh]atever I say [. . .]."
At the command of valiant Shamash [. . .],
The young of a bird [. . .].
The eagle opened his mouth, saying [to] Etana:
"Why thou didst come [tell me thou]!"
Etana opened his mouth, saying [to] the eagle:
"My friend, give me the plant of birth,
Show thou to me the plant of birth!
[Remove my burden and] produce for me a name!"

(At approximately this point comes in the Neo-Assyrian fragment, *AfO*, XIV, Pl. XI, and pp. 306-07. The text is badly damaged and Ebeling's suggested additions have been offered by him with all due reserve. The line count is that of Ebeling.)

(obverse)

[. . .] the eagle looked at [him],
Saying [. . .] to Etana:
"Thou art, indeed, Etana, the king of animals!
Thou art Etana [. . .] . . . !
Lift [me] up from the midst [of this pit],
Give me [. . .] . . . ,
[And *I will give* thee] a human *offspring*!
[Unto] eternity I will sing thy praises."
Etana [says] (these) words t[o the e]agle:
"I will save thy life [. . .],
[Fro]m the pit I will [lift thee],
[Unto d]istant times we [. . .]!"

(remainder broken away)

[40] Meaning "son."

[41] *Babyloniaca*, XII, Pl. VIII, pp. 39 ff.; *KB*, VI, I, 108-11 (Jensen II); *AOT*, 238 (Ebeling C).

(reverse)

"Upon me [. . .]
From sunrise until [. . .].
When he comes out of [. . .]
. . . [. . .]
I will give thee [the plant] of birth!"

When Etana [heard] this,
He filled the front of the pit with [. . .],
Next he put down two [. . .],
He put (them) down before him [. . .].
The eagle [*was unable*] *to rise* from the pit;
He [. . .].
[. . .] and [. . .]
Again [*he was unable*] *to rise* from the pit;
He flaps [his] w[ings . . .]ly.
[. . .] and [. . .];
[*For the third time* from the p]it [*he was unable*] to rise.
[He] flaps [his] w[ings . . .]ly.

(remainder destroyed)

C-5[42]

The eagle [opened] his mouth, [saying to Etana]:
"[. . .] . . .
At the entrance of the gate of Anu, Enlil, [and Ea],
We did obeisance.
At the entrance of the gate of Sin, Shamash, Adad, and [Ishtar]
I opened the . . . [. . .].
I *look round* as I go down [. . .].
She[43] was sitting in the midst of brilliance [. . .],
[. . .] she was laden [. . .].[44]
A throne was placed and [. . .].
At the foot of the throne lions [. . .].
As I got up, the lions [. . .].
Then I awoke, trembling [. . .]."
The eagle [says] to him, to Etana:
"My friend, brighten [. . .].
Up, I will bear thee to the heaven [of Anu]!
Upon my breast place thou [thy breast],
Upon the feathers of my wings place thou [thy hands],
Upon my sides place thou [thine arms]!"[45]
Upon his breast he placed [his breast],
Upon the feathers of his wings he placed [his] hands,
Upon his sides he placed [his] arms.
Excessively great was the burden of him!
When he had borne [him] aloft one league,
The eagle says to [him], to Etana:
"See, my friend, how the land appears!
Peer at the sea at the sides of E[kur]!"[46]
"The land has indeed *become* a hill;[47]
The sea has turned into the water [*of a stream*]!"
When he had borne [him] aloft a second league,
The eagle says to [him], to Etana:
"See, my friend, how the land appears!"
"The land has become [. . .]!"
When he had borne him aloft a third league,
The eagle [says] to him, to Etana:
"See, my friend, how the land appe[ars]!"
"The land has turned into a gardener's ditch!"
After they had ascended to the heaven of A[nu],
Had come to the gate of Anu, Enlil, and Ea,
The eagle (and) E[tana to]gether did o[beisance].
[. . .] the eagle (and) Etana.

(long gap)

C-6[48]

"The burden [. . .].
Leave [. . .]
[. . .]."
The eagle thus [speaks to him]:
". . . [. . .]
I will bear thee [. . .].
. . . [. . .] . . .
The eagle [. . .] a bird [. . .]
There is not [. . .]
Up, my friend, [. . .],
With Ishtar, the mistress [. . .],
Alongside Ishtar, the mistress [. . .].
Upon my sides [place thou thine arms],
Upon the feathers of my wings [place thou thy hands]!"
Upon his sides he placed [his arms],
Upon the feathers of his wings [he placed his hands].
[When he had borne him aloft] one league:
"My friend, take a glance at how the land [appears]!"
"Of the land . . . [. . .],
And the wide sea is just like an enclosure."
[When he had borne him aloft] a second league:
"My friend, cast a glance at how the land appears!"
"The land has turned into a furrow [. . .],
And the wide sea is just like a bread basket."
[When he had borne him aloft] a third league:
"My friend, cast a glance at how the land appears."
"As I glanced round, the land [*had disappeared*],
And upon the wide sea [mine eyes] could not feast!
My friend, I will not ascend to heaven!
Halt in (thy) tracks that [. . .]!"
One league he plunged down;
The eagle went down, and he abreast of him [. . .].
A second league he plunged down;
The eagle went down, and he abreast [of him . . .].
A third league he plunged down;
The eagle went down, and he abreast [of him . . .].
[To within three cubits][49] of the ground [of *Anu*],
The eagle had fallen, and he abre[ast of him . . .].
[. . .] the eagle . . . [50]; of Etana [. . .].

[42] *Babyloniaca*, XII, Pls. IX-X, pp. 43 ff.; *KB*, VI, I, 110-12 (Jensen III*a*); *AOT*, 239 (Ebeling E).

[43] Apparently, Ishtar.

[44] For the root-meaning of *rṣn* cf. v. Soden, *ZA*, XLI (1933), 166, n.5.

[45] Note the word plays *kappu* "wing," and "hand" (from different roots), and *idu* "arm" and "side."

[46] "Mountain House," in the sense of "World Mountain."

[47] If the reading li-*mid*-da is right, we have here a possible extension of the idiomatic, but still obscure, phrase *šadā(-šu) emēdu*, which is usually applied in a derogatory sense; cf. E. F. Weidner, *AfO*, XIII (1939-41), 233 f.

[48] *Babyloniaca*, XII, Pls. IX, XI, pp. 48 ff.; *KB*, VI, I 113-15 (Jensen III*b*); *AOT* 240 (Ebeling F).

[49] cf. v. Soden, *ZA*, XLV (1939), 77 f.

[50] At this decisive juncture the text unfortunately breaks off. The one verb that is preserved, *i-tar-rak*, is ambiguous in this context; v. Soden,

The Legend of Sargon

The legend concerning the birth of Sargon of Agade is available in two incomplete Neo-Assyrian copies (A and B) and in a Neo-Babylonian fragment (C). All three were published in *CT*, XIII (1901): A—Pl. 42; B and C—Pl. 43. Text B alone contains incomplete lines of a second column; it is uncertain whether this column bore any relation to the Sargon legend. A composite text of the actual legend, with variant readings, transliteration, and translation was published by L. W. King in his *Chronicles Concerning Early Babylonian Kings*, II (1907), 87-96. Latest (partial) translation and discussion: H. G. Güterbock, *ZA*, XLII (1934), 62-64.[1]

Sargon, the mighty king, king of Agade, am I.
My mother was a *changeling*,[2] my father I knew not.
The brother(s) of my father *loved* the hills.
My city is Azupiranu, which is situated on the banks of the Euphrates.
My *changeling* mother conceived me, in secret she bore me.
She set me in a basket of rushes, with bitumen she sealed my lid.[3]

loc. cit., has even suggested *i-ḫaš-šal* "he grinds" as a possible reading. In view, however, of the points made in the Introduction, it is improbable that the adventure ended in death.

Langdon would fill part of the break with the small fragment K 8563 rev. (*Babyloniaca*, XII, Pl. IX, and p. 52). It is too slight and inconclusive for a connected translation. But mention is made in it of Etana's wife, his kingship, and his ghost. Do we have here a speech addressed to Etana's son, Baliḫ, whom the king list places immediately after Etana (Th. Jacobsen, *The Sumerian King List*, 1939, 80-81)? At all events, the prevailing view that Etana's flight resulted in misfortune would seem to stand in need of confirmation.

1 For some parallel accounts cf. P. Jensen's article, Aussetzungsgeschichten, *Reallexikon der Assyriologie*, I (1928), 322-24.

2 The meaning of Akk. *enītum* remains doubtful. The obvious etymology is from *enū* "to change"; but—if the derivation is correct—there is no indication as to whether the term refers to a change in the social, religious, or national status. cf. Güterbock, *ZA*, XLII, 62, n.2.

3 Lit. "door."

She cast me into the river which rose not (over) me.[4]
The river bore me up and carried me to Akki, the drawer of water.
Akki, the drawer of water lifted me out as he dipped his e[w]er.[5]
Akki, the drawer of water, [took me] as his son (and) reared me.
Akki, the drawer of water, appointed me as his gardener.
While I was a gardener, Ishtar granted me (her) love,
And for four and [. . .] years I exercised kingship.
The black-headed [people] I ruled, I gov[erned];
Mighty [moun]tains with chip-axes of bronze I conquered,
The upper ranges I scaled,
The lower ranges I [trav]ersed,
The sea [*lan*]*ds* three times I circled.
Dilmun my [hand] cap[tured],
[To] the great Der I [went up], I [. . .],
[. . .] I altered and [. . .].
Whatever king may come up after me,
[. . .],
Let him r[ule, let him govern] the black-headed [peo]ple;
[Let him conquer] mighty [mountains] with chip-axe[s of bronze],
[Let] him scale the upper ranges,
[Let him traverse the lower ranges],
Let him circle the sea [*lan*]*ds* three times!
[Dilmun let his hand capture],
Let him go up [to] the great Der and [. . .]!
[. . .] from my city, Aga[de . . .]
[. . .] . . . [. . .].

(Remainder broken away. The remains of column ii, as extant in Text B, are too fragmentary for translation.)

4 cf. Güterbock, *loc. cit.*, 63.

5 Reading *i-na ṭí-ib d*[*a*]-*li*-[*šu*], with Landsberger, *ZA*, XLII, 63, n.2.

Hittite Myths, Epics, and Legends

TRANSLATOR: ALBRECHT GOETZE[1]

The Moon that Fell from Heaven

Text: *KUB*, XXVIII, 5 and its duplicate 4; the text is bilingual, in Hattic and Hittite. Literature: J. Friedrich, *AfO*, XI (1936/37) 76 f.; H. Th. Bossert, *Asia* (Istanbul, 1947), 164 ff.

(10) The Moon-god[2] (Hattic: *Kašku*) fell down from heaven. He fell upon the *kilammar*. But no one saw him. The Storm-god[2] (Hattic: *Taru*) sent rain after him, he sent rainstorms after him so that fear seized him (and) fright seized him.

(15) Hapantalliyas (Hattic: *Ḫapantalli*) went and took his place at his side so as to bespeak him. Kamrusepas (Hattic: *Kataḫziwuri*) saw what had fallen from heaven speaking as follows: "The Moon-god (Hattic: *Kašku*) has fallen from heaven. He fell upon the *kilammar*.

(20) "The Storm-god (Hattic: *Taru*) saw him and he sent rain after him, he sent rainstorms after him, he sent the winds after him so that fear seized him (and) fright seized him."

Hapantalliyas (Hattic: *Ḫapantalli*) went and took his place at his side (25) so as to bespeak him: "What art thou going to do? . . ."

Kingship in Heaven

Text: *KUB*, XXXIII, 120. Literature: E. Forrer, *Eine Geschichte des Götterkönigtums aus dem Hatti-Reiche (Annuaire de l'institut de philologie et d'histoire orientales*, IV [1936], 687-713); H. G. Güterbock, *Kumarbi Efsanesi* (Ankara, 1945), 11-16; the same, *Kumarbi, Mythen vom churritischen Kronos* (Zürich-New York, 1946), 6-12; the same, *AJA*, LII (1948), 123-125.

(i) [Let there listen the gods who are in heaven] and those who are in the dark earth! Let there listen the mighty [. . .] . . . gods, Naras, [Napsaras, Mink]is (and) Ammunkis! Let there listen Ammezadus [and the gods of the olden days, the god]s' fathers (and) mothers!

(5) Let there listen [Anus, Ant]us (and) Isharas, the fathers (and) mothers! Let there listen Ellilas, [Ninlilas and] also those who are mighty (and) firmly established gods! . . .—Once in the olden days Alalus was king in heaven. (As long as) Alalus was seated on the throne, the mighty Anus, first among the gods, (10) was standing before him. He would sink at his feet and set the drinking cup in his hand.

Nine in number were the years that Alalus was king in heaven. In the ninth year Anus gave battle to Alalus and he vanquished Alalus. He fled before him and *went* down to the dark earth. (15) Down he went to the dark earth, but Anus took his seat upon the throne. (As long as) Anus was seated upon the throne, the mighty Kumarbis would give him his food. He would sink at his feet and set the drinking cup in his hand.

Nine in number were the years that Anus was king in heaven. In the ninth year Anus gave battle to Kumarbis and *like* Alalus Kumarbis gave battle (20) to Anus. (When) he could no longer withstand Kumarbis' eyes, (he) Anus, he struggled forth from the hands of Kumarbis. He fled, (he) Anus; (like) a bird he moved in the sky. After him rushed Kumarbis, seized (him) Anus, by his feet and dragged him down from the sky.

(25) He (Kumarbis) bit his "knees"[1] and his manhood *went down* into his inside. When it lodged there, (and) when Kumarbis had swallowed Anus' manhood, he rejoiced and laughed. Anus turned back to him, to Kumarbis he began to speak: "Thou rejoicest over thine inside, because thou hast swallowed my manhood.

(30) "Rejoice not over thine inside! In thine inside I have planted a heavy burden. Firstly I have impregnated thee with the noble *Storm-god*. Secondly I have impregnated thee with the river Aranzahas,[2] not to be endured. Thirdly I have impregnated thee with the noble Tasmisus.[3] *Three* dreadful gods have I planted in thy belly as *seed*. Thou shalt go (35) and end by striking the rocks of thine own mountain with thy head!"

When Anus had finished speaking, he w[ent] up to heaven and hid himself. Out of his mouth spat [Kumarbis], the wise king. Out of his mouth he spat . . . [. . .] (40) mixed with. . . . That which Kumarbis spat out, [fell on] Mount Kanzuras; [. . .] an awesome god therein.

Filled with fury Kumarbis went to Nipp[ur,[4] . . .]. At the *lordly* . . . [. . .] he settled down. Kumarbis did not [. . .] (while) he counts [the months[5]]. The seventh month ca[me . . .].

(lower third of column i missing)

(Columns ii and iii are in the worst possible state of preservation. This makes it very difficult to follow the course of events. What is offered here, is far from certain. For the most part I have to limit myself to a paraphrase

[1] The nature of this publication has made it necessary to be liberal with restorations and to adopt sometimes rather free translations. Some scholars may feel that on occasion I have gone beyond the justifiable in this respect. It gives me great pleasure to express here my thanks to Mr. R. A. Crossland, M.A., who has greatly assisted me in putting my translations in adequate English. For a general discussion of Hittite texts see Introduction, pp. xvii-xviii.

[2] These translations are a makeshift. The real names of the gods are not known to us since they are always written with the respective ideograms.

[1] This is a euphemism for "male parts."

[2] The Hurrian name of the Tigris.

[3] Later (see below, The Song of Ullikummis) Tasmisus is the attendant of the Storm-god.

[4] The Mesopotamian city which was the center of the Sumero-Akkadian cult of Ellil.

[5] i.e. the months of pregnancy.

of such sections as seem intelligible. The main theme of column ii is the birth of the Storm-god.)

(Anus addresses the Storm-god who is still unborn inside Kumarbis and advises him of the various parts of Kumarbis' body through which he may come forth [ii 1-3].

(The Storm-god answers from within Kumarbis: "Long life to thee! *exalted* lord of wisdom! . . . The earth will give me its strength, the sky will give me its valor, Anus will give me his manliness, Kumarbis will give me his wisdom, Naras will give me his . . . , *Napsaras* will give me his. . . . " The giving of the bull Seris,[6] a wagon or chariot and of other objects is also mentioned. It seems as though the Storm-god speaks of his future greatness and promises Anus to revenge him [ii 4-22].

(Anus repeats his advice as to the places from which the Storm-god may come forth, among them Kumarbis' mouth and the "good place" [ii 23-28].

(The Storm-god replies: ". . . If I come forth from his . . . , it will *derange* (my) mind. If I come forth from his . . . , it will defile me at that spot, . . . it will defile me at the ear. . . . If I come forth from the 'good place,' a woman will . . . me." In the following the Storm-god, it seems, is forewarned of what will happen, if he should come forth by rending asunder Kumarbis' *tarnassas* [ii 29-38].

("As he walked along and took his place before Ayas,[7] Kumarbis became [*dizzy*] and collapsed. . . . Kumarbis began to speak to Ayas: 'Give me my son, I want to devour [my son]!' " Indeed it seems that Kumarbis received something to eat. However it hurts his mouth and he begins to moan [ii 39-54].

(On Kumarbis' complaint Ayas advises him to call in certain experts: "Let them go (and) summon the 'poor'! Let the 'poor' work magic on the heroes, the lords (and) the bulls for thee! Let the 'poor' bring sacrifices of meal for thee!" This then is done [ii 55-70].

("They began to work magic [on him] with [. . .], they kept bringing sacrifices of meal to him, they kept [. . .]. From the *tarnassas* [he wanted to come forth, but] they made Kumarbis' [*tarnassas*] secure. [Thus from the 'good pl]ace' came forth the valiant Storm-god" [ii 71-75].

(The birth of the Storm-god is completed and reported to Anus [ii 76-87].

(gap)

(Anus plots to destroy Kumarbis with the help of the Storm-god [iii 2-18].

(The Storm-god prepares for battle [iii 19-29].

(The outcome of the battle is not narrated on the preserved part of the tablet. Apparently the two other children that developed from Anus' "manhood" that Kumarbis' had spat out upon the earth also played a role therein [their birth being narrated in col. iv]. At any event, we have to assume that the Storm-god defeated Kumarbis and took over the kingship in heaven.)

[6] One of the two bulls sacred to the Storm-god.

[7] This is the Hittite-Hurrian pronunciation of the Sumerian name Ea.

The Song of Ullikummis

The texts are mentioned under the respective sections. Literature: H. G. Güterbock, *Kumarbi Efsanesi* (Ankara, 1945); the same, *Kumarbi, Mythen vom churritischen Kronos* (Zürich-New York, 1946); the same, *AJA*, LII (1948), 125-130. Güterbock offers a full reconstruction of the preserved parts of the composition. Furthermore, A. Goetze, *JAOS*, 69 (1949), 178-183; H. Otten, *Forschungen und Fortschritte*, 25 (1949), 145-147 (with information which could not be used here).

(1-a) *KUB*, XXXIII, 96 i *and duplicate* 98 i

[Of the god who . . .], who wise thoughts thinks out . . . in his mind, the father of all gods, of Kumarbis let me sing!

Kumarbis thinks out wise thoughts in his mind. He nurses the thought of (creating) misfortune (and) an evil being. He plots evil against the Storm-god. He nurses the thought of (raising up) a rival for the Storm-god.

Kumarbis thinks out wise thoughts in his mind and strings them together like beads.

When Kumarbis had thought out the wise thoughts in his mind, he instantly rose from his seat. He took his staff in his hand, put swift shoes on his feet. He set forth from Urkis,[1] his city, and betook himself to the . . . [. . .].

(1-b) *KUB*, XVII, 7 + XXXIII, 93 ii

(Imbaluris, Kumarbis' messenger, is being instructed:) ["Go to the Sea and tell her: '. . .] Kumarbis must remain father of the gods!' " [When Imbaluris] saw (that) Kumarbis [had finished (?)], he walked on to the Sea.

[Imbaluris] began [to] re[peat] the words to the Sea: "The words which my lord has [told me to say, I want to pass on] to the Sea. I have [them] committed [to memory: '. . . ; Ku]marbis must remain father of the gods!' "

[When the Sea] heard [Imbal]uris' words, [the Sea] began to reply to [Imbaluris:] "[Listen, O Imbaluris! and to the wo]rds which [I am speaking] to thee, [give] ear! [Go (and)] speak firm [words to Kumarbis: 'Why hast thou come in anger], Kumarbis? [Turn in favor] back to my house! Fear [has seized the hou]se. . . .' "

(1-c) *KUB*, XXXIII, 98 ii 1-30 *and duplicate* *KUB*, XXXIII, 102 ii 1-37

Imbaluris began to answer the Sea: "Kumarbis shall *forever* remain the father of the gods." The Sea answers Imbaluris: "Listen to these my words, and go to impress them upon Kumarbis!

"Go and speak to Kumarbis: 'Why hast thou come in anger toward (my) house? Fear has seized the house, and fright the house-slaves. For thee cedarwood is al-

[1] A city in Hurrian territory probably east of the Tigris.

ready split, food is already prepared. The musicians hold their instruments in readiness for thee day and night. So arise and come to my house!'" He arose, (he) Kumarbis, and Imbaluris walked before him. Kumarbis [came forth from his] house; he journeyed, (he) Kumarbis, and betook himself to the house of the Sea.

The Sea said: "For Kumarbis let them set up a seat to sit upon! Let them set up a table before him! Let them bring him food! Let them bring him beer to drink! The cooks brought dishes, the cupbearers brought ... wine for him to drink. They drank once, they drank twice, they drank three times, they drank four times, they drank five times, they drank six times, they drank seven times. And Kumarbis began to speak to his vizier Mukisanus: "Mukisanus, my vizier! Give ear to the word I speak to thee! Take (thy) staff in (thy) hand, put (thy) shoes [on thy feet]! [From ... set forth] and [betake thyself] to the Waters! [These wor]ds [speak] in the presence of the Waters: '[...].'"

(1-d) *KUB*, XVII, 7 + XXXIII, 93 iii[2]

... Stone [...] stone. [They] attended her[3] when she gave birth. [They cleared(?)] away the rocks [... and then] Kumarbis' son [made his] *appea[rance]*.

The [...] women brought him into the world, and the Good-women[4] and the Mother-goddesses [also attended]. [They] set him [upon his father's] knees [and Kumar]bis began to fondle his son [and] let him dance up and down. He proceeded to give [the child] a propitious name!

Kumarbis began to say to his soul: "What name [shall I give] him? The child which the Good-women and the Mother-goddesses presented me, [for the reason that he] shot forth from (her) body (as) a shaft, let him go and [his] name be Ullikummis! Let him ascend to heaven in [...]! Let him vanquish Kummiya, the beautiful city! Let him attack the Storm-god and tear [him] to pieces like a mortal! Let him tread him under foot [like] a ... ! Let him crush Tasmisus like a reed in the *brake*! Let him shoot down all the gods from the [sky] like birds and let him break them to pieces [like] empty pots!"

When Kumarbis [had finished] speak[ing] (these) words, [he began] to say to his soul: "To [...] will I give him, this child. He who [takes] him shall carry him and [... him]. He shall [bring] him to the [dark] earth...."

(Six lines are almost completely destroyed; they seem to have contained the scheme of having him grow into a giant as it is later executed.)

[Kumarbis] began to speak [these wor]ds [to Imbaluris: "Imbaluris! To the words] I speak [to thee] give [ear! Take (thy) staff] in (thy) hand and [put] swift shoes on thy [feet! *Set forth* and] go to the Irsirra deities! [When thou reachest them], tell the Irsirra deities [these] words: '[Come ye here!] Kumarbis, the father of the gods, [is ca]lling you. [... The err]and on which he is calling you, [ye are not to know.] Come ye instantly!'

"[The Irsirra deities] shall take [him], (him) my son, and they [shall bring] him [down to the dark] earth...."

(1-e) *KUB*, XXXIII, 98 iii *and duplicate* 102 iii (*immediate continuation*)

[When] Imbaluris [heard these words, he took] (his) staff in (his) hand, put [(his) shoes on (his) feet] and journeyed. Imbaluris betook himself [to the ... Irsir]ra deities.

[Imbaluris] began to [speak these wo]rds to the Irsirra deities: "Come ye here! Kumarbis, the father of the gods, [is calling] you. But the errand on which [he is calling] you, [ye are not to know]! Hasten and come!" When [the Irs]irra deities heard the words, [they hastened] (and) hurried. [They set forth and journe]yed and they covered the distance without stopping a single time. They betook themselves to Kumarbis and Kumarbis began [to speak] to the Irsirra deities:

"[Ta]ke ye [this child] and carry him with you! Bring him to the dark earth! [Ha]sten (and) hurry! Place him—a shaft—upon Ubelluris'[5] right shoulder! In one day he shall increase a cubit, in one month he shall increase one acre. The stone which is added to his stature shall present an amazing spectacle...."

(1-f and 1-g) *KUB*, XXXIII, 93 + 95 + 96 iv *and duplicate* 92 iii (*immediate continuation*)

When the Irsirra deities heard [the] words, they took [the child] from Kumarbis' knees. The Irsirra deities lifted the child and pressed it to their breasts like a cloth. They lifted him and placed him upon Ellil's knees. The ... lifted his eyes and b[eheld] the child as it stood in his divine presence. His body was made of diorite.

Ellil began to speak [(these) words]: "Who is that? Did the Good-women (and) the Mother-goddesses rear [him]? No one among the great gods will see mightier battles. No one's vileness [*equals*] Kumarbis'. Just as Kumarbis raised the Storm-god, he has [now raised] this awesome diorite man as his rival."

When Ellil [had finished] his words, [the Irsirra deities took the child] and placed it—a shaft—upon Ubelluris' right shoulder.

The diorite grows, the strong [*waters*] make him grow. In one day he increases one cubit, in one month he increases one acre. The stone which is added to his stature presents an amazing spectacle.

When the 15th day came, the stone had grown high. He [was standing] in the sea with his knees (as) a shaft. It stood out above the water, the stone, and in height it (was) like [a pillar]. The sea reached up to its belt like a (loin)cloth. Like a tower the stone is raised

[2] The correct arrangement of the two fragments is due to E. Laroche, *RHA*, VIII, 22 f.

[3] The deplorable state of preservation prevents us from knowing who is meant. Perhaps it is the earth.

[4] Here adopted as translation of the Hittite name of the Gulses (or GULses) goddesses.

[5] A kind of giant carrying the world on his shoulders, like Atlas.

up and reaches up to the temples and the *kuntarra* house[6] in heaven.

The Sun-god *looked* down from the sky and *caught sight* of Ullikummis. Ullikummis too *saw* the Sun-god. The Sun-god [said]: "What *vigorous* god [is standing there] in the sea? His body is not like (that of) the [other] gods."

The Sun-god of Heaven [descended(?)] and went out into the sea. [. . .]. The Sun-god laid his hand to his forehead [. . .]. In wrath he shook his fists.[6a]

[Whe]n [the Sun-god of] Heaven had seen [Ullikummis], the Sun-god [entered] the *horizon* for a second time again, set forth [from . . .] and [betook himself] to the Storm-god. [When he] saw the Sun-god coming, Tasmisus[7] [began to speak these words]: "Is this not the Sun-god of Heaven coming? The errand on which he is coming, that errand must be [momentous]. . . . It (must be) a grave vexation, [it] (must be) a grave [menace]. It fore[bodes] upheaval in heaven."

The Storm-god began to speak to Tasmisus: "Let them set up [a seat for him on which to sit down]! Let them set a table from which to eat!"

No sooner had they spoken thus, than the Sun-god [reached] them. They set up a seat for him on which to sit down, but he [sat] not. They set a table (with food), but he served himself not. They gave [him drink], but he took not a drop.[8]

The god, the Storm-god, began to speak to the Sun-god: "Who is the bad chamberlain who set up a chair for thee and thou sittest not? Who is the bad table man who set a table (with food) and thou eatest not? Who is the bad cupbearer who gave [thee wine] and thou drinkest not? [. . .]."

(There must have followed the Storm-god's report on what he had seen.)

(II-a) *KUB*, XXXIII, 113

[. . . The Storm-god and] Ishtar hastened [and hurried]. They took each other by the hand [. . .]. From the house of god they [set] forth and journeyed [to. . . . The storm-god] lost his courage [when] he saw [the monster]. Ishtar says: "Where [are] the two brothers[9] [*lingering*]? Shall I *p[erhaps]* go (and) seek them?" But Ishtar stood up before the Storm-god, her brother, and sent [a message] to the two [brothers]. They took each other by the hand [and journeyed]. They went up Mount Hazzi[10] [and looked out]. The sight appalled the King of Kummiya [and he said]: "The sight of the awesome diorite man is appalling." He looked at the awesome diorite man and in wrath he shook his fists.

The Storm-god sat down on the ground, while tears streamed [from his eyes] as in water courses. With tears streaming from his eyes the Storm-god speaks the word: "Who can bear to look upon so vexatious a sight? Who will dare go and battle [against the monster]? Who can bear seeing his terrifying [. . .] . . . s?" Ishtar replies t[o the Storm-god, her brother]: "My brother! Is there *really* not a single . . . [. . .] to whom *sufficient* courage [has been] gi[ven?] Dost thou *really* not know the son whom [. . .] . . . [has] begotten? [. . .]."

(II-b) *KUB*, XXXIII, 106 i

When the gods heard the word, [they . . .]. They made ready their wagons and handed [. . . to . . .]. Astabis[11] jumped [upon his wagon like a . . .] and [drove] the wagon to [. . .]. He gathered the chariots together [. . .] and thundered the while, he Astabis. Amid thunder Astabis let [a . . .] down into the sea. [With] the [. . .] they drew [*up the water*].[12] Astabis [. . .] and the seventy gods held [the . . .]. Yet he could not [. . .]. As[tabis . . .] and the seventy gods [*tumbled*] down into the sea. The diorite man [*stayed unchanged*], his body [even grew taller]. He made the heaven tremble and made [the earth shak]e. He [pushed upward] the sky like an empty garment. The diorite man increased in height [. . .]. Before [. . . his height was] 1,900 leagues as he stood [upon the dark ear]th. Like a tower he was lifted up, (he) the diorite man, so that he reached up to the *kuntarra* house. [Altogeth]er his height was 9,000 leagues, that diorite man, and his girth 9,000 leagues. He stood [over] the gate of Kummiya like [a . . .]. He, the diorite man, made Hebat[13] leave her temple. Hence Hebat could no longer hear the message of the gods, nor could she see with her eyes the Storm-god and Suwaliyattas.[14]

Hebat began to speak this word to Takitis:[15] "I cannot hear the mighty word of the Storm-god. Nor can I hear the message of Suwaliyattas and of all the gods. Should that being whom they call Ullikummis, the diorite man, have vanquished my [husband] the mighty [Storm-god]?"

Hebat began to speak this word to Takitis: "O Takitis, listen! Take thy staff in thy hand, put swift shoes on thy feet! Go and [call] the gods into a[ssembly!] The diorite man may have killed [my husband the no]ble king. [Bring] n[ews back] to me!"

[When Takitis heard Hebat's words], he hastened (and) hu[rried. . . .] was stretched. [. . .] he goes, but there is no road. [He could not get through], so he [returned] to Hebat.

[Takitis be]gan [to speak to Hebat]: . . . [. . .].

(Considerable gap, in which apparently the defeat of the Storm-god was related.)

(II-c) *KUB*, XXXIII, 106 ii

[Whe]n Tasmisus heard the Storm-god's words, he rose instantly, [took] his staff in his hand, put swift

6 Apparently the dwelling of the gods.

6a Literally "his arms became lowered (to the side)."

7 The Storm-god's personal attendant.

8 Differently Friedrich, *JCS*, I, 288.

9 It is not clear who is meant. Perhaps the Storm-god's bulls?

10 Mount Casius near ancient Ugarit on the Mediterranean coast.

11 The Hurrian Warrior-god who was identified with Zamama or Ninurta.

12 This seems to be an attempt at preventing the monster's growth by depriving it of the water in which it is standing.

13 The Storm-god's wife.

14 A warrior-god, probably brother of the Storm-god.

15 Hebat's messenger.

shoes on his feet and went forth to the high watchtower. Facing Hebat he took [his stand] (saying): "In a lowly place [my lord will have to stay] until he has fulfilled the years ordained for him." When Hebat saw Tasmisus, she barely missed falling from the roof. She would have fallen down, but her girls caught her and stopped her (falling). When Tasmisus had ended speaking his word, he descended from the watchtower and went to the Storm-god. Tasmisus began to speak to the Storm-god: "Where shall we sit down?—on Mount Kandurna? [While] we sit on Mount Kandurna, someone else will be seated on Mount Lalapaduwa. [If] we move anywhere else, there will be no king in heaven."

Tasmisus began to speak to the Storm-god: "My lord! Hearken to my words! To the words I am telling thee give ear! Come! Le us go before Ea to Apsu,[16] let us ask for the old tablets with the words [*of fate*]! [When] we arrive at the door of Ea's house, [we shall bow] to Ea's doors [five times, and] we shall bow to Ea's . . . five times. [But when] we arrive [before E]a (himself), we shall bow down to Ea (himself) fifteen times. [By then] Ea's [heart] will perhaps have been *softened* and Ea [will] perhaps [*listen*] and do us a favor. He will hand over to us the old [. . . tablets]."

[When the Storm-god] heard [Tasmisus'] words, he hastened (and) hurried. Instantly he rose from his seat. [The Storm-god] and [Tasmisus] took each other by the hand, covered the distance without stopping a single time and [arrived] in Apsu. [When the Storm-god] came [to the entrance of] Ea's house, [he bowed at] the front [door five times], [and at] their [. . .] . . . he bowed five times. [But before Ea (himself) he] bowed [fiftee]n times.

(II-d) *KUB*, XXXIII, 100 *and duplicate* 103 ii

(Assembly of the gods; the Storm-god complains:)

"[If ye allowed] the di[orite man to annihilate mankind, ye] would [bring] sacrif[ices to an end. . . .] mountains [. . . No] one will [celebrate the gods' festivals] any[more. . . .] sees [. . . . Our knees will shake, and our heads will whirl] like a potter's wheel."

[Ea], the king of wisdom, spoke among the gods; to the gods he began to speak: "Why will ye destroy [mankind]? Do they not give sacrifices to the gods and *lavish* cedarwood on them? [If] ye destroy mankind, no one will [care] for the gods any more, no one will sacrifice to them loaves and libations any more. It will come to pass that the Storm-god, the valiant king of Kummiya, will have to take to the plow himself. It will come to pass that Ishtar and Hebat will have to work at the grinding stones."

[Ea], the king of wisdom, began to speak to Kumarbis: "Why dost thou, Kumarbis, seek evil for mankind? Does not man take . . . and promptly sacrifice to thee, Kumarbis? Does he not promptly and joyfully sacrifice to thee, Kumarbis, the father of the gods, in thy temple? Do they not sacrifice to Ishtar [and to Astabis(?)], man's enemy? Do they not sacrifice to me, Ea, the king [of wisdom]? [Wilt thou] act against the council of all [the gods?]" [. . .] and tears [. . .].

(II-e) *KUB*, XXXIII, 106 iii

[Ea . . .], further[more . . .]. They[17] [took each other] by the hand [and . . .] until [they . . .]. From the assembly [he went to Ellil]. [As he] began to lament, [Ellil began to speak to Ea:] "Long life to thee, Ea! [He] who worships [the gods, brings sacrifices to the gods, lavishes the fine and] soothing [cedarwood] on the gods—why hast thou [come to persecute] him?"

Ea [began to speak] to Ellil: ["Listen, Ellil!] To the word [which I am telling thee give ear! Kumarbis has created] a rival to the Storm-god. [. . .] he has thrived and in hei[ght he is like a *pillar*], like [a tower] he is raised up [. . .]. [A rival] to thee [. . .] the olden [. . . . Doest thou know that *vig*]*orous* [god]?"

[. . . , but E]llil [did not know him].

[. . . ,] Ea [began to speak to Ellil: "What] can I [say to thee?] He who [. . . , will block off heaven and the gods'] holy houses."

When Ea [had ended his] wo[rds, he set forth and betook himself] to Ubelluris.[18] [. . .]. Ubelluris [lifted] (his) eyes [and beheld him]. Ubelluris [began to speak] to Ea: "Long life to thee, Ea! [What makes thee come] up [here?" Ea wished] life to Ubelluris [. . .] and [. . .] Ubelluris [was standing on] the dark earth, he upon whom [. . .] . . . was built.

Ea began to speak [these words] to Ubelluris: "Knowest thou not, O Ubelluris? Did no one bring thee the news? Doest thou not know him, that *vigorous* god whom Kumarbis has fashioned to oppose the gods? or the *frightful* death which Kumarbis is plotting for the Storm-god? He is fashioning for him a rival who has thriven in the sea as a diorite stone. Doest thou not know him? Like a tower he is lifted up and has blocked off heaven, the holy houses of the gods, and Hebat. (Is it) because thou art far away from the dark earth, Ubelluris, (that) thou doest not know of that *vigorous* god?"

Ubelluris began to speak to Ea: "When they built heaven and earth upon me I did not know anything. When they came and severed the heaven from the earth with a cleaver, I did not know that either. Now my right shoulder is a little sore. But I do not know who that god is."

When Ea heard these words, he turned Ubelluris' shoulder as the diorite man stood upon Ubelluris' right shoulder like a shaft.

Ea began to speak to the olden gods the words: "Listen ye, olden gods, ye who know the olden words! Open ye the ancient storehouses of the fathers and forefathers! Let them bring the olden seals of the fathers and let them seal them up again with them afterward! Let them bring [for]th the olden copper *knife* with

[16] Apsu, the watery deep where Ea is living, has become here a city.

[17] Ea and who? Perhaps the Storm-god.

[18] The giant who carries the world on his shoulder and now also Ullikummis.

which they severed heaven from earth. Let them *cut* through the feet of Ullikummis, the diorite man, whom Kumarbis has fashioned as a rival to oppose the gods!"

(II-f) *KUB*, XXXIII, 103 iii

(The gods are frightened and lament:)

[. . .] *affliction* [. . .]. The Storm-god and Ishtar . . . [. . .] us. The [. . .] . . . do not come out of the water as yet. [. . .] . . . we do not see as yet. Our knees are shaking and our heads are whirling like a potter's wheel. Like a kid sick with diarrhea our [*bowels move*. . .].

(II-g) *KUB*, XXXIII, 106 iv

Tasmisus [. . .] was on his knees. [. . .] he began to speak [: ". . .] In his body [(is) . . .]." His fists are thrust up, upon his head the hair [stands on end]. . . .

Ea began to speak to Tasmisus: "Move on! Thou wast assigned to my son[19] as [a . . .]. My soul is sad. I have seen with mine own eyes the dead [people] on the [dark] earth; they (are) str[ewn *about as*] dust while [. . .] stand (around)."

[Ea] began to speak [to the gods]: "Firstly, I have crippled, [and secondly I have . . .] the diorite man. Go ye and battle him again! [. . . .] Let him no longer stand like a shaft!" Tasmisus [*took courage*] and began to [re]joice. He clapped his hands three times and up [to the gods he shouted and] they heard (him). He clapped again, and the Storm-god, the valiant king of Kummiya, [hea]rd (him). They came to the place of assembly. All the gods began to bellow like cattle against Ullikummis, the diorite man.

The Storm-god jumped upon his chariot like a . . . . With thunder he went down to the sea and engaged him in battle, the Storm-god the diorite man.

The diorite man began to speak to [the Storm-]god: "What shall I say to thee, O Storm-god? Keep fighting!" Of his mind [. . .] while he stands (there)in.

"What shall I say to thee, O Storm-god! [Keep fighting!] Before [. . .] string together (thy) wise thoughts like pearls! [Up to heaven] I shall go to assume the kingship. Kummiya [I shall *destroy*] and the *kuntarra* house I shall take over. The gods I shall [drive out from] hea[ven]."

(The closing lines are almost completely destroyed. They must have told how Ullikummis, despite his boasting, was defeated by the Storm-god.)

The Myth of Illuyankas

Texts: *KBo*, III, 7 and its duplicates *KUB*, XII, 66, *KUB*, XVII, 5 and 6. Literature: H. Zimmern in Lehmann-Haas, *Textbuch zur Religionsgeschichte* (1922), 339 f.; A. H. Sayce, *JRAS*, 1922, 177-90; H. Zimmern, *Streitberg-Festgabe* (1924), 430-41; A. Götze, *Kulturgeschichte Kleinasiens* (1933), 131 f.

[19] i.e. the Storm-god.

OLDER VERSION

(i) These are the words of Kellas, the "anointed"[1] of the Storm-god of Nerik. What follows is the cult legend of the *Purulli* Festival[2] of the Storm-god of Heaven, (the version which) they no longer tell:

(5) May the land flourish (and) prosper! May the land be (well) protected! If it flourishes (and) prospers, they will celebrate the *Purulli* Festival.

When the Storm-god and the Dragon Illuyankas (10) *came to grips* in Kiskilussa, the Dragon Illuyankas vanquished the Storm-god.

The Storm-god besought all the gods: "Come ye to my aid! Let Inaras prepare a celebration!"

(15) He made everything ready on a grand scale: amphorae of wine, amphorae of *marnuwan*, (and) amphorae of *walhi*.[3] The amphorae he had filled to the brim.

Inaras went to Zigaratta (and) encountered Hupasiyas, a mortal.

Thus spoke Inaras "See, Hupasiyas! Such and such[4] I want to do. I would have thee aid me!"

Thus spoke Hupasiyas to Inaras: (25) "So be it! Let me sleep with thee, and I will come (and) fulfill thy wishes!" And he slept with her.

Inaras took Hupasiyas to the place and hid him. Inaras (ii 5[5]) put on her finery and lured the Dragon Illuyankas up from his lair: "See! I am holding a celebration. Come thou to eat and to drink!"

The Dragon Illuyankas came up with [his children] (10) and they ate (and) drank. They drank every amphora dry and quenched their thirst.

Thereupon they are no longer able to descend to their lair. Hupasiyas came (15) and trussed the Dragon Illuyankas with a rope.

[6]The Storm-god came and killed the Dragon Illuyankas and the gods were with him.

Inaras built herself a house on a cliff (15) in the land of Tarukka. She made Hupasiya live in that house. Inaras instructs him: "When I go to the country, thou shalt not look out of the window! If thou lookest out, thou mayest see thy wife and thy children."

When twenty days had passed, that man opened the window and [he saw] his wife and his children.

(25) When Inaras came home from the country, he began to moan: "Let me go home!"

(ii[7]) Thus spoke Ina[ras to Hupasiyas]: "Thou shalt [not] open the [window again]!" She [killed him] in the quarrel and the Storm-god sowed *sahlū*[8] [over the ruins of the house]. That man [came to a] griev[ous end].

(15) Inaras [returned] to Kiskil[ussa. But] her house . . . she placed . . . [in] the hand of the king. From the time on that we celebrated the first *Purulli* Festival, the hand of [the king has been supreme] in the . . . of Inaras.

[1] A priest.
[2] Probably the New Year's festival.
[3] Alcoholic beverages.
[4] Lit.: this and this.
[5] From here on *KUB*, XVII, 5 offers the best text.
[6] From here on *KUB*, XVII, 6 is followed.
[7] Second column of *KBo*, III, 7.
[8] A weed commonly found on ruins.

(There follow two more sections before a break. The word "rain" seems to play an important part in them.)

LATER VERSION

(iii[9]) [This is the way in] which [. . .] told it [later]: The Dragon Illuyankas vanquished the Storm-god and took (his) heart and (his) eyes away from him. The Storm-god [sought to revenge himself] upon him.

He took the daughter of the poor man for his wife and he begat a son. When he grew up, he took the daughter of the Dragon Illuyankas in marriage.

The Storm-god instructs his son: "When thou goest to the house of thy wife, ask them for (my) heart and (mine) eyes!"

When he went there, he asked them for (the) heart and they gave that to him. Later he asked for (the) eyes, and they gave him those too. He brought them to the Storm-god, his father. Thus the Storm-god got back his heart and his eyes.

When his frame had been restored to its old state, he left to the Sea for battle. When he had engaged the Dragon Illuyankas in battle, he came close to vanquishing him. But the son of the Storm-god, who was with Illuyankas, shouted up to heaven to his father:

"Count me as with (him)! Spare me not!" So the Storm-god killed the Dragon Illuyankas and his son too. In this way the Storm-god got even with the Dragon Illuyankas.

(After a considerable break a quite enigmatic text follows in col. iv. It seems to tell us about a procedure by which the rank and the order of the gods were established. The most significant verb in the text is *pu-u-ul(-)tiyanzi*; it may contain an etymology of the name of the *Purulli* Festival. Unfortunately its meaning is not clear; the context suggests "compete" or "race" as a possibility.)

All the gods arrive and they *compete*. Of all the gods Zashapunas of Kastama was the greatest. Because Zalanuisas is his wife, and Tazzuwasis his concubine, they made these three live in Tanipiyas.

(An estate is endowed for them there.)

Thus it is found on the tablet. I have told the holy saga as it is found there.

The Telepinus Myth

Texts: The main text is *KUB*, XVII, 10. Numerous additional fragments of a similar character have been edited and classified by H. Otten in *KUB*, XXXIII. The same author has dealt with the whole material in great detail in his book *Die Überlieferungen des Telipinu-Mythus* (*MVAG*, XLVI/1 [1942]). He assigns the surviving material to four different versions. A similar tale is also associated with the Storm-god. Literature: Besides the book just quoted, the translation of the main text by A. Götze in *Kulturgeschichte Kleinasiens* (1933) 134 ff.—although in need of revision—is still of interest; Otten's book does not deal with the main text.

[9] Third column of *KBo*, III, 7.

a. The God's Anger, His Disappearance and Its Consequences

(The upper third of the tablet, about 20 lines, is broken off. It probably told the reasons for the god's anger.)

(i) Telepinus [flew into a rage and shouted:] "There must be no inter[ference!" In his agitation] he tried to put [his right shoe] on his left foot and his left [shoe on his right foot]. . . . [. . .].

Mist seized the windows, *vapor* seized the house. In the fireplace the logs were stifled, at the altars the gods were stifled, in the fold the sheep were stifled, in the stable the cattle were stifled. The sheep neglected its lamb, the cow neglected its calf.

Telepinus walked away and took grain, (fertile) breeze, . . . , . . . and satiation to the country, the meadow, the *steppes*. Telepinus went and lost himself in the *steppe*; *fatigue* overcame him. So grain (and) spelt thrive no longer. So cattle, sheep and man no longer breed. And even those with young cannot bring them forth.

The *vegetation* dried up; the trees dried up and would bring forth no fresh shoots. The pastures dried up, the springs dried up. In the land famine arose so that man and gods perished from hunger. The great Sun-god arranged for a feast and invited the thousand gods. They ate, but they did not satisfy their hunger; they drank, but they did not quench their thirst.

b. The Search for the Vanished God

The Storm-god became anxious about Telepinus, his son: "Telepinus, my son, (he said) is not here. He has flown into a rage and taken (with him) every good thing." The great gods and the lesser gods began to search for Telepinus. The Sun-god sent out the swift Eagle (saying): "Go! Search every high mountain!"

"Search the deep valleys! Search the watery depth!" The Eagle went, but he could not find him. Back to the Sun-god he brought his message: "I could not find him, him, Telepinus, the noble god." The Storm-god said to Hannahannas[1]: "What shall we do? We shall die of hunger." Hannahannas said to the Storm-god: "Do something, O Storm-god! Go! Search for Telepinus thyself!"

The Storm-god began to search for Telepinus. In his city he [knock]s at the gate, but he is not there and opens not. He broke open his bolt and his lock, [but he has no luck], the Storm-god. So he gave up and sat down to rest. Hannahannas sent [out the Bee]: "Go! Search thou for Telepinus!"[2]

[The Storm-god s]aid [to Hannahannas]: "The great gods (and) the lesser gods have searched for him, but [did not find] him. Shall then this [Bee] go out [and

[1] The name is ideographically written NIN.TU or MAḪ; she is the mother of the gods.

[2] For the text of this and the next section see Otten, *loc. cit.*, p. 9.

find him]? Its wings are small, it is small itself. Shall they admit that it is greater then they?"

[3]Hannahannas said to the Storm-god: "Enough! It will go (and) find him." Hannahannas sent out the little Bee: "Go! Search thou for Telepinus! When thou findest him, sting him on his hands (and) his feet! Bring him to his feet! Take wax and wipe his eyes and his feet, purify him and bring him before me!"

The Bee went away and searched . . . the streaming rivers, and searched the murmuring springs. The honey within it gave out, [the wax within it] gave out. Then [it found] him in a meadow in the grove at Lihzina. It stung him on his hands and his feet. It brought him to his feet, it took wax and wiped his eyes (and) his feet, [it purified him] and [. . .].

[Telepinus . . .] declares: "For my part I had flown into a rage [and walked away. How dare] ye a[rouse me] from my sleep? How dare ye force me to talk when enraged?" He grew [still more infu]riated. [He stopped] the murmuring springs, he diverted the flowing rivers and made them flow over their banks. He [*blocked off*] the clay pits, he shattered [the windo]ws, he shattered the houses.

He had men perish, he had sheep and cattle perish. [It came to] pass that the gods [*despaire*]*d* (asking): "Wh[y has Te]lepinus become [so infur]iated? [Wh]at shall we do? [What] shall we do?"

[The great Sun-god(??) decl]ares: "[Fetch ye] man! Let him [t]ake the spring Hattara on mount Ammuna [as . . .]! Let him (man) make him move! With the eagle's wing let him make him move![4] Let man make him move! With the eagle's wing [let man make him move]!"

(A gap follows in which Kamrusepas, the goddess of magic and healing, is commissioned to pacify Telepinus and to bring him back.)

c. The Ritual

ENTREATY

(The beginning[5] is mutilated.)

(ii) "O Telepinus! [Here lies] sweet and soothing [cedar essence. Just as it is . . .], [even so let] the stifled [be set right] again!

"Here [I have] *upthrusting sap* [with which to purify thee]. (10) Let it [invigorate] thy heart and thy soul, O Telepinus! Toward the king [turn] in favor!

"Here lies *chaff*. [Let his heart (and) soul] be *segregated* [like it]! Here lies an ear [of grain]. Let it attract his heart [(and) his soul]!

"(15) Here lies sesame. [Let his heart (and) his soul] be *comforted* by it. Here [lie] figs. Just as [figs] are sweet, even so let Te[lepinus' heart (and) soul] become sweet!

"Just as the olive [holds] oil within it, [as the grape] (20) holds wine within it, so hold thou, Telepinus, in (thy) heart (and thy) soul good feelings [toward the king]!

"Here lies *ointment*. Let it anoint Telepin[us' heart (and) soul]! Just as malt (and) malt-loaves are harmoniously fused, even so let thy soul be in harmony with the affairs of mankind! [Just as spelt] (25) is clean, even so let Telepinus' soul become clean! J[ust as] honey is sweet, as cream is smooth, even so let Telepinus' soul become sweet and even so let him become smooth!

"See, O Telepinus! I have now sprinkled thy ways with fine oil. So walk thou, Telepinus, over these ways that are sprinkled with fine oil! (30) Let *šaḫiš* wood and *ḫappuriašaš* wood be at hand! Let us set thee right, O Telepinus, into whatever state of mind is the right one!"

Telepinus came in his fury. Lightning flashed, it thundered while the dark earth was in turmoil. (35) Kamrusepas saw him. The eagle's wing made him move out there. It took off him (iii) the rage, it took off him the anger, it took off him [the ire], it took off him the fury.

KAMRUSEPAS' RITUAL OF PURIFICATION

Kamrusepas tells the gods: "Come ye, O gods! See! Hapantallis is shepherding the Sun-god's sheep. (5) Select ye twelve rams! I want to fix long days for Telepinus. I have taken death, one thousand eyes.[6] I have strewn about the selected sheep of Kamrusepas.

"Over Telepinus I have swung them this way and that. (10) From Telepinus' body I have taken the evil, I have taken the malice. I have taken the rage, I have taken the anger, I have taken the ire, I have taken the fury.

"When Telepinus was angry, his heart (and) his soul were stifled (like) firebrands. (15) Just as they burned these brands, even so let Telepinus' rage, anger, malice (and) fury burn themselves out! Just as [malt] is barren, (as) people do not bring it to the field to use it for seed, (as) people do not make it into bread (or) put it in the storehouse, even so let Telepinus' rage, [anger], (20) malice (and) fury become barren!

"When Telepinus was angry, [his heart (and) his soul] were a burning fire. Just as this fire [is quenched], even so let (his) rage, anger (and) fury [be quenched] too!

"O Telepinus, give up thy rage, [give up] thine anger, (25) give up thy fury! Just as (water in) a pipe flows not upward, even so let Telepinus' [rage, anger (and)] fury not [come] back!

"The gods [were gathered] in assembly under the *ḫarikešnaš* tree. For the *ḫarikešnaš* tree I have fixed long [years]. (30) All gods are now present, (including) the [. . .] *tustayas*, the Good-women (and) the Mother-

[3] The text of the end of the mythological part of the text is regained by combining *KUB*, XXXIII, 5 (and fragment Chantre), i.e. Otten's B, with *KUB*, XXXIII, 9 and 10, i.e. Otten's C. The reconstruction may not be correct as to its exact wording; it will, however, cover the course of events adequately.

[4] A certain ritual.

[5] The rendered text is mainly that of *KUB*, XVII, 10 ii 6 ff.; at the beginning parallel texts are used for restoration.

[6] The meaning of this phrase is unclear.

goddesses, the Grain-god, Miyatanzipas, Telepinus, the Patron-god, Hapantaliyas (and) the Patron of the field. For these gods I have fixed long years; I have purified him, [O Telepinus]!

(35) "[. . .] I have taken the evil [from] Telepinus' body, I have taken away his [rage], [I have taken away] his an[ger], I have taken away his [ire], [I have taken away] his fury, I have taken away his malice, [I have taken away his] ev[il]."

(small gap)

MAN'S RITUAL

(The beginning is lost, but Telepinus is addressed:)[7] ". . . (When) thou [departedst] from the *ḫariḳešnaš* tree on a summer day, the crop got *smutted.* (When) the ox departed [with thee], (iv)[8] thou *wastedst* its *shape.* (When) the sheep departed with thee, thou *wastedst* its form. O Telepinus, stop rage, anger, malice (and) fury!

"(When) the Storm-god comes in his wrath, the Storm-god's priest (5) stops him. (When) a pot of food boils over, the (stirring) *spoon* stops it. Even so let the word of me, the mortal, stop Telepinus' rage, anger, and fury!

"Let Telepinus' rage, anger, malice, (and) fury depart! Let the house let them go, let the interior . . . let them go, (10) let the window let them go! In the . . . let the interior courtyard let them go, let the gate let them go, let the gateway let them go, let the road of the king let them go! Let it not go to the thriving field, garden (or) grove! Let it go the way of the Sun-god of the nether world!

"The doorkeeper has opened the seven doors, has unlocked the seven bolts. (15) Down in the dark earth there stand bronze cauldrons, their lids are of *abaru*-metal, their *handles* of iron. Whatever goes in there comes not out again; it perishes therein. Let them also receive Telepinus' rage, anger, malice (and) fury! Let them not come back!"

d. The God's Home-Coming

(20) Telepinus came home to his house and cared (again) for his land. The *mist* let go of the windows, the *vapor* let go of the house. The altars were set right for the gods, the hearth let go of the log. He let the sheep go to the fold, he let the cattle go to the pen. The mother tended her child, the ewe tended her lamb, (25) the cow tended her calf. Also Telepinus tended the king and the queen and provided them with enduring life and vigor.

Telepinus cared for the king. A pole was erected before Telepinus and from this pole the fleece of a sheep was suspended. It signifies fat of the sheep, it signifies grains of corn (and) (30) wine, it signifies cattle (and) sheep, it signifies long years and progeny.

It signifies the lamb's favorable message.[9] It signifies . . . . . . It signifies *fruitful* breeze. It signifies . . . satiation. . . .[10]

(end of the text lost)

[7] Text for the first few lines is taken from *KUB*, XXXIII, 54 13-15.

[8] Here the fourth column of *KUB*, XVII, 10 begins.

[9] i.e. favorable omens when the intestines of the sacrificial lamb are inspected.

[10] Compare *KUB*, XXXIII, 12 iv 15 ff. and 24 iv 19 ff.

Ugaritic Myths, Epics, and Legends

TRANSLATOR: H. L. GINSBERG

Ugaritic poetry falls into distinct metrical units, but these were not indicated outwardly by the scribes. In the following translation, every colon is printed on a separate line. Isolated cola are not common. As a rule there are two, and sometimes there are three, to a stich. In the translation, the second and third cola in each stich are indented. The numbers in the left margin are those of the lines in the Ugaritic tablet, which, as has been explained, do not coincide with the cola.

Poems about Baal and Anath

Both large and small fragments of tablets containing poetic mythological texts in which the leading role is played by the rain- and fertility-god Baal and the next in importance by the warrior-goddess Anath came to light in the French excavations of Ras Shamra-Ugarit in the years 1930, 1931, and 1933, and at least one small fragment (which may be a duplicate of one of the others) in 1929. Because so many letters, words, lines, columns, and probably some whole tablets are missing, not all of the tablets can be declared, with certainty, to be parts of the great epic of Baal and arranged in their proper order within it. However, in the following translations, even small fragments whose pertinence to the larger epic is probable have, for the most part, been included (if only, in a few desperate cases, in the form of sketchy summaries) and assigned tentative positions within it. Tablets whose pertinence to the larger poem is doubtful have been added at the end by way of an appendix.

In view of all these uncertainties, the tablets will not be designated as B'L A, B'L B, etc., but by the original sigla of the first editor, Ch. Virolleaud. They are all studied together by C. H. Gordon, *Ugaritic Literature*, Rome (1949), pp. 9-55 (56?). Other literature will be given separately for each tablet.

a. VI AB

Editions: Ch. Virolleaud, *La déesse 'Anat* (Paris, 1938), pp. 91-102 and the last photograph; C. H. Gordon, *Ugaritic Handbook*, II, pp. 189-190, 'nt, pls. ix-x (transliteration only). Studies: A. Herdner, *Syria*, XXIII (1942-43), 283-285. Owing to the very poor state of preservation, connected translation is possible only for groups of lines which, because they are stereotyped, can be completed with the help of parallels; while just the crucial passages are very doubtful. It seems, however, that El, the head of the pantheon, (1) instructs the craftsman-god Kothar wa-Khasis to build a palace on his (El's) grounds, the name of the latter being Khurshan-zur-kas (col. iii), (2) announces that his (eldest? favorite?) son is to be known as El's Beloved Yamm (= Sea) and as Master (cf. iv 15, 20 with II AB ii 34-35, and iv 17 with III AB B 17, 33-34), and (3) perhaps authorizes Yamm to banish Baal from his throne (iii 22-25).

b. III AB C

Editions: Ch. Virolleaud, *Syria*, XXIV (1944-45), 1-12; C. H. Gordon, *Ugaritic Handbook*, II, Text 129. This fragment comprises 24 very mutilated lines from the right-hand column on one of the sides of a tablet with two very broad columns on each side. Such a tablet is the one of whose col. i, III AB B is the lower part, and of whose col. iv, III AB A is the upper part; Virolleaud therefore surmises that III AB C is part of (the lower half of) col. iii of the same tablet. For its content, however, a position between III AB B and III AB A seems strange; so, perhaps, it belongs to a tablet which preceded, and in outward disposition resembled, the tablet of which III AB B-A is a remnant.

In it, El instructs Kothar to build a palace for Yamm. Ashtar complains of not being accorded the like favor.

[... There] he is off on his way (3)
    To El of the Sources [of the Floods,
    In the midst of the headwaters of the Two Oceans.
He penetrates] E[l]'s *field* and *enters*
    The [pa]vilion of King [Father Shunem.[1]
At El's feet he bows] and falls down,
    Prostrates himself, doing [him] *homage.*
(... "... O) Kothar wa-Kha[sis!
Quic]*kly* bu(ild the h)ouse of Yamm,
    [Ere]ct the palace of Judge Nahar.
...
    ...
Build the house of Prince Yamm,
    [Ere]ct the pala[ce *of Judge*] Nahar,
    In the midst of [....
Quickly] his [hou]se shalt thou build, (10)
    Quickly erec[t his palace].
..."
  (All that can be made out is that Ashtar is displeased.)
Quoth the Gods' Torch Shapsh,[2]
    Raising her voice and [crying:
"Heark]en, I pray thee!
Thy father Bull El *favors*
    Prince Yamm ... [...] ...
[Sh]ould thy father Bull [E]l hear thee,
    He will pull out [the *pillars* of thy dwelling!
Yea, overt]urn [the throne of thy] kingship!
    Yea, break the sce[pter] of thy dominion!"
Quoth [Ashtar] of the [...] ...:
    "*Oh*, my father Bull El!
I have no house [like] the gods,
    [Nor] court like [*the holy on*]*es.* (20)
..."

(the rest obscure)

c. III AB B-A

Editions: (1) Of III AB B: *Ugaritic Handbook*, II, Text 137. (2) Of III AB A: Ch. Virolleaud, *Syria*, XVI (1935), 29-45, with Pl. XI; H. L. Ginsberg, *JPOS*, XV (1935), 327-331; *Kitbe Ugarit*, 73-76; H. Bauer, *AKTRSch.*, Ca. Studies: W. F. Albright, *JPOS*, XVI (1936), 17-20; T. H. Gaster, *Iraq*, 4 (1937), 21-23; J. Obermann, *JAOS*, LXVII (1947), 195-208. See the paragraph preceding the translation of III AB C.

[1] One of El's epithets; vocalization uncertain. Some render "Father of Years."

[2] The sun-goddess.

(1) III AB B

... [... Quoth] Puissant Baal: (3)
"[May'st thou be driven from the throne of thy kingship,
From the seat of thy do]minion!
... [...]
Ayamur[3] upon thy head, [O Yamm;
Upon thy back Yagrush,[4]][5] Judge Nahar.
May [Horon] break, [O Yamm,
May Horon break] thy head,
Ashtoreth [Name of Baal thy pate.
...] down may'st thou fall in ... [...] (10)
... [...]."
[Me]ssengers Yamm doth send.

(Two lines defective and unintelligible.)

"Depart ye, lad[s, don't tarry.
There now, be off] on your way
Towards the Assembled Body[6]
In the m[idst of the Mount of Lala.
At the feet of El] fall not down,
Prostrate you not to the Assembled [Body.
Proudly standing] say ye your speech.
And say unto Bull [my] father [El,
Declare unto the Assembled] Body:
'Message of Yamm your lord,
Of your master Ju[dge Nahar].
Surrender the god *with a following,*
Him whom the multitudes worship:
Give Baal [to me to lord over],
Dagon's son whose spoil I'll possess.' "—
The lads depart, they delay not.
[There, they are off] on their way (20)
To the midst of the Mount of Lala,
Towards the Assembled Body.
Now, the gods were sitting to *e*[*at*],
The holy ones for to dine,
Baal attending upon El.
As soon as the gods espy them,
Espy the messengers of Yamm,
The envoys of Judge Nahar,
The gods do drop their heads
Down upon their knees
And on the thrones of their princeship.
Them doth Baal rebuke:
"Why, O gods, have ye dropt
Your head[s] down upon your knees
And on your thrones of princeship?
I see the gods are cowed
With terror of the messengers of Yamm,
Of the envoys of Judge Naha[r].
Lift up, O gods, your heads
From upon your knees,
From upon the thrones of your princeship,
And I'll answer[7] the messengers of Yamm,
The envoys of Judge Nahar."
The gods lift up their heads
From upon their knees,
From upon [their] thrones of prin[ceship].
Then come the messengers of Yamm, (30)
The envoys of Judge Nahar.
At El's feet they do [not] fall down,
Prostrate them not to the Assembled Body.
Prou[*dly*] *standing*, [they] say their speech.
Fire, burning fire, *doth flash*;
A whetted sword [are their *e*]*yes*.
They say to Bull his father El:
"Message of Yamm your lord,
Of your master Judge Nahar.
Surrender the god *with* a following,
etc." (see 18-19)
[Quoth] Bull, his father, El: (36)
"Thy slave is Baal, O Yamm,
Thy slave is Baal [for eve]r,
Dagon's Son is thy captive;
He shall be brought as thy tribute.
For the gods bring [thy gift],
The holy ones are thy tributaries."—
Now, Prince Baa[l] *was wroth*.
[Sei]zing [*a cudgel*] in his hand,
A *bludgeon* in his right hand,
He *r*[*eached*] to strike the lads.
[His right hand Ashtore]th[8] seizes, (40)
Ashtoreth seizes his left hand.
"How [canst thou strike the messengers of Yamm,
The en]voys of Judge Nahar?
A messenger ... [...
...] a messenger [bears];
Upon his shoulders the words of his lord,
And ... [...]."
But Prince Baal was wroth.
The *cudgel* in ha[nd he ...
He *con*]*fronts* the messengers of Yamm,
The [en]voys of Judge Naha[r.
...] ... "I say unto Yamm your lord,
[Your] ma[ster Judge Nahar]:
..."

(lines 46-47 too defective for understanding)

(2) III AB A

(defective and obscure) (1-4)

"... [ho]uses.
To the earth shall fall the strong,
To the dust the mighty."—
Scarce had the word lef[t] her mouth,
Her speech left her lips,
As she uttered her ... voice
Under the throne of Prince Yamm,
Quoth Kothar wa-Khasis:
"I tell thee, O Prince Baal,
I declare, O Rider of the Clouds.

[3] Name of a bludgeon, meaning something like "Driver"; see episode (2).
[4] Name of a bludgeon, meaning "Chaser"; see episode (2).
[5] Evidently Kothar has already promised Baal the two cudgels which he wields so effectively in episode (2).
[6] The assembly of the gods.
[7] Or, perhaps, humble.
[8] *Ana*]*th* or *Ashera*]*h* are also possible restorations.

Now thine enemy, O Baal,
Now thine enemy wilt thou smite,
Now wilt thou cut off thine adversary.
Thou'lt take thine eternal kingdom,
Thine everlasting dominion."
Kothar brings down two clubs
And gives them names.
"Thou, thy name is Yagrush ('Chaser').
Yagrush, chase Yamm!
Chase Yamm from his throne,
[Na]har from his seat of dominion.
Do thou swoop in the hand of Baal,
Like an eagle between his fingers;
Strike the back of Prince Yamm,
Between the arms[9] of [J]udge Nahar."
The club swoops in the hand of Baal,
Like an eagle between his [fi]ngers;
It strikes the back of Prince Yamm,
Between the arms of Judge Nahar.
Yamm is firm, he is not bowed;
His joints bend not,
Nor breaks his frame.—
Kothar brings down two clubs
And gives them names.
"Thou, thy name is Ayamur ('Driver'?).
Ayamur, drive Yamm!
Drive Yamm from his throne,
Nahar from his seat of dominion.
Do thou swoop in the hand of Baal,
Like an eagle between his fingers;
Strike the pate of Prince Yamm,
Between the eyes[10] of Judge Nahar.
Yamm shall collapse
And fall to the ground."
The club swoops in the hand of Baal,
[Like] an eagle between his fingers;
It strikes the pate of Prince [Yamm],
Between the eyes of Judge Nahar.
Yamm collapses,
He falls to the ground;
His joints bend,
His frame breaks.
Baal would rend, would smash Yamm,
Would annihilate Judge Nahar.
By name Ashtoreth rebukes [him].
"For shame, O Puissant [Baal];
For shame, O Rider of the Clouds!
For our captive is Prin[ce Yamm],
Our captive is Judge Nahar."
As [the word] left [her mouth],
Puissant Baal was ashamed . . .

(The rest is too defective for any meaning to be extracted, except that Yamm seems to say twice "I am dying, Baal will reign." But apparently Yamm does not die, but is only confined to his proper sphere, the seas. Hence there is still talk of him, e.g. at the end of col. ii of the next piece.)

[9] i.e. on the back; cf. II Kings 9:24; Zech. 13:6.
[10] i.e. on the front of the head; cf. Exod. 13:9, 16; Deut. 6:8; 11:18; Dan. 8:5.

d. Fragment b

This is the current designation of a piece—representing the top of the middle column of the obverse or reverse of a tablet with three columns on each side—of which a copy was published by Ch. Virolleaud, *Syria*, XIII (1932), 158; and transliterated by H. Bauer, *AKTRSch.*, p. 57, and C. H. Gordon, *Ugaritic Handbook*, II, p. 144a, middle. Here Baal apparently sends his messengers to Anath to tell her to join him in a démarche before Asherah with a view to procuring a palace.

". . . Homage to Lady Asherah of [the Sea],
Obeisance to the Progenitress of the Gods,
(So) [she] will give a house to Baal like the [g]ods',
And a court like [A]sherah's sons'."—
Loudly to his lads Baal cries:
"Look ye, Gapn and Ugar sons of Ghulumat,[11]
'Amamis twain, *sons* of Zulumat (*Ẓlmt*)[11]
The stately, win[g]-spreading, . . . ;
Winged ones twain, flock of clouds,
'Neath [. . .];
Birdlike ones twain, *fl*[*ock* of . . . snow].
. . ."

(obscure beginnings of 5 more lines)

e. II AB

Editions: Ch. Virolleaud, *Syria*, XIII (1932), 113-163; H. L. Ginsberg, *Tarbiz*, V (1933), 85-96; J. A. Montgomery, Z. S. Harris, *The Ras Shamra Mythological Texts* (1935), 58-74; H. L. Ginsberg, *Kitbe Ugarit*, pp. 18-46; H. Bauer, *AKTRSch.*, 48-56; C. H. Gordon, *Ugaritic Handbook*, II, Text 51. Studies: J. A. Montgomery, *JAOS*, LIII (1933), 115-123; W. F. Albright, *JPOS*, XIV (1934), 115-132; U. Cassuto, *Orientalia* NS, VII (1938), 265-90; *JBL*, LXI (1942), 51-56; T. H. Gaster, *BASOR*, 101 (Feb., 1946), 21-30; *JQR*, XXXVII (1946-7), 55-56. At the beginning, Baal's messengers explain to Anath why a démarche before Asherah is indicated.

(some 20 lines missing, 3 obliterated)

. . .
But alas!
He cri]es unto Bull El [his father,
To E]l the King [his begetter;
He cries] unto Ashe[rah and her children],
To [E]lath [and the band of] her [kindred:
Look, no house has Baal like the gods,
Nor court like the children of Ashe]*r*[ah].
The abode of El is the shelter of his son.
The abode of Lady Asherah of the Sea
Is the abode of the perfect brides:
'Tis the dwelling of Padriya daughter of Ar,
The shelter of Talliya(*ṭly*) the daughter of Rabb,
(And) the abode of Arsiya (*arṣy*) the daughter of Ya'abdar.[12]

[11] Means "darkness." Ghulumat is also known as the name of a goddess from RSh 1929, 1:19; 3:25.
[12] The three names mean "Flashie (or, Lightningette) daughter of Light, Dewie daughter of Distillation, Earthie daughter of . . ." They are Baal's wives or daughters, and Baal is the god of rain and dew and "the Prince, Lord of the Earth."

And here's something more I would tell thee:
Just try doing homage to Lady Asherah of the Sea,
Obeisance to the Progenitress of the Gods.
Hayyin[13] would go up to the bellows,
In Khasis' hands would be the tongs,
To melt silver,
To beat out gold.
He'd melt silver by the thousands (of shekels),
Gold he'd melt by the myriads.
He'd melt . . . and . . . :
A gorgeous dais weighing twice ten thousand (shekels),
A gorgeous dais cast in silver,
Coated with a film of gold;
A gorgeous throne resting above
A gorgeous footstool o'erspread with a mat;
A gorgeous couch having a . . . ,
He pours it over with gold;
A gorgeous table which is filled
With all manner of game[14] from the foundations of the earth;
Gorgeous bowls shaped like small beasts like those of Amurru,
Stelae shaped like the wild beasts of Yam'an,
Wherein are wild oxen by the myriads.[15]

(The first lines of the following scene perhaps show Asherah, "Lady Asherah of the Sea," presenting an offering of fish to El.)

(ii)

(Some 16 lines entirely missing, then 4 defective and obscure.)

Its[16] *skin*, the covering of its flesh.
She[17] *flings* its vestment into the sea,
Both its *skins* into the deeps.
She puts fire on the brazier,
A pot upon the coals,
(And) *propitiates* Bull El Benign,
Does obeisance to the Creator of Creatures.—
Lifting up her eyes she beholds.
The advance of Baal Asherah doth espy,
The advance of the Maiden Anath,
The onrush of Yabamat [Liimmim].
Thereat her feet [do stumble];
Her loins [do crack be]hind her,
Her [face breaks out in s]weat [above her].
Bent are the [joints of her loins],
Weakened those of [her] back.[18]
She lifts up her voice and cries:
"*Why* is Puissant [Ba]al come?
And why the Ma[id]en Anath?
Have my children slain [each other],
O[r the b]and of my kinsmen [destroyed one another]?"
[The *work*] of silver Asherah doth espy,
The *work* of silver and of gold.
Lady A[sherah] of the Sea rejoices;
Loudly unto her lad [she] doth [cry]:
"Look thou, Deft One, yea [give heed],
O fisherman of Lady Asher[ah of the Sea].
Take a net in thy hand,
A large [*seine*] *on thy two hands.*
[*Cast it*] into El's Beloved [Yamm][19]
Into the Sea of El *Be*[*nign*,
Into the De]ep of El . . . [. . .].
. . ."

(Only the beginnings of 37-47 preserved, and no connected sense recoverable.)

(iii)

(about 12 lines missing, 9 lines defective)

C[*ome*]*s* Puissant Baal,
Advances the Rider of the Clouds.
Lo, he takes his stand and *cries defiance*,
He stands erect and spits
In the midst of the *as*[*sem*]*bly* of the divine beings:
"*Ab*[*omination*] has been placed upon my table,
Filth in the cup I drink.
For two [kinds of] banquets Baal hates,
Three the Rider of the Clouds:
A banquet of shamefulness,
A banquet {banquet}[20] of baseness,
And a banquet of handmaids' *lewdness*.
Yet herein is flagrant shamefulness,
And herein is handmaids' *lewdness*."—
After this goes Puissant Baal,
Also goes the Maiden Anath.
As they do homage to Lady Asherah of the Sea,
Obeisance to the Progenitress of the Gods,
Quoth Lady Asherah of the Sea:
"Why do ye homage to Lady Asherah of the Sea,
Obeisance to the Progenitress of the Gods?
Have ye done homage to Bull El Benign,
Or obeisance to the Creator of Creatures?"
Quoth the Maiden Anath:
"We do homage to [*th*]*ee*, Lady Asherah of the Sea,
[Obei]sance to the Progenitress of the Gods.
. . ."

(Rest of column badly damaged. It is clear that Asherah makes a feast for her visitors, and it may be inferred that they urge her to intercede for Baal with El, as she does in the next column.)

(iv-v)

(Some 10 lines missing; lines 1-2a too fragmentary to be restored.)

[Loudly unto her lad] Ashe[rah doth cry:

13 "Deft," another name of the craftsman-god.

14 If the translation is correct: rhytons, or vessels having the shape of animals.

15 Uncertain rendering.

16 Of some beast or fish.

17 Apparently, Lady Asherah of the Sea.

18 Because she fears the unexpected visitors bring bad news (cf. Ezek. 21:11-12). This is the standard reaction of a female character to an unexpected visit.

19 Yamm (=Sea) is apparently still El's Beloved, despite what he went through above, in episode III AB A.

20 Dittography.

"Look thou, Qadesh wa-Amrur,
Fisherman of Lady] Asherah of the Sea!
[Saddle a donkey],
Harness a jackass.
[Attach trappings of] silver,
[A housing] of gol[d],
Put on the trappings of [thy] she-asses."
Qad[esh] wa-Amrur obeys.
He saddles a donkey,
Harnesses a jackass.
He attaches trappings of silver,
A *housing* of gold,
Puts on the trappings of his she-asses.
Qadesh wa-Amrur embraces
And places Asherah on the donkey's back,
On the beautiful back of the jackass.
Qadesh proceeds to lead,
Amrur is like a star in front;
The Maiden Anath follows,
While Baal leaves for Zaphon's summit.—
There, she[21] is off on her way
Towards El of the Sources of the Two Floods
In the midst of the headwaters of the Two Oceans.
She penetrates El's field and enters
The pavilion of King Father Shunem.
At El's feet she bows and falls down,
Prostrates her and does him reverence.
As soon as El espies her,
He *parts his jaws* and laughs.
His feet upon the footstool he puts
And doth twiddle his fingers.
He lifts up his voice and [cri]es:
"Why is come Lady Asher[ah of the S]ea?
Why hither the Progenitress of the G[ods]?
Art thou become hungry and *fa*[*int*],
Or art become thirsty and *pa*[*rched*]?
Eat, pray, yea drink.
Ea[t] thou from the tables bread;
Drink from the flagons wine,
From the golden gob⟨lets⟩ blood of vines.
See, El the King's love stays thee,
Bull's affection sustains thee."
Quoth Lady Asherah of the Sea:
"Thy decree, O El, is wise:
Wisdom with ever-life thy portion.
Thy decree is: our king's Puissant Baal,
Our sovereign second to none;
All of us must bear his gi[ft],
All of us [must b]ear his purse.[22]
[But alas!]
He cries unto Bull El his father,
To [El] the King his begetter;
He cries unto *Asherah* and her children,
Elath and the band of her kin[dred]:
Look, no house has Baal like the gods,
Nor court like the children of Asherah.

[21] Asherah.
[22] Must be tributary to him. But the translation is uncertain.

The abode of El is the shelter of his son.
The abode of Lady Asherah of the Sea
Is the abode of the perfect brides:
The abode of Padriya daughter of Ar,
The shelter of Talliya daughter of Rabb,
(And) the abode of Arsiya daughter of Ya'abdar."
Quoth the Kindly One El Ben[ign]:
"Am I a slave, an attendant of Asherah?
Am I a slave, to handle . . . ?
Or is Asherah a handmaid, to make bricks?

(v)

Let a house be built for Baal like the gods',
And a court like the children of Asherah's!"
Quoth Lady Asherah of the Sea:
"Art great indeed, O El, and wise,
Thy beard's gray hair instructs thee,
. . . , [. . .] to thy breast.
Now, too, the *seasons* of his rains will Baal *observe*,
The *seasons* of . . . with *snow*;
And ⟨he will⟩ peal his thunder in the clouds,
Flashing his lightnings to the earth.
The house of cedar—*let him burn it*;
Yea, the house of brick—*remove it*.
Be it told to Puissant Baal:
Summon *weeds* into thy house,
Herbs into the midst of thy palace.[23]
The mountains shall bring thee much silver,
The hills a treasure of gold;
They'll bring thee *god's grandeur aplenty*.
So build thou a silver and gold house,
A house of most pure lapis lazuli."
The Maiden Anath rejoices,
Stamps with her foot so the earth *quakes*.
There, she is off on her way
Unto Baal upon Zaphon's summit,
O'er a thousand fields, ten thousand acres.
Laughing, the Maiden Anath
Lifts up her voice and cries:
"Receive, Baal, the glad tidings I bring thee.
They will build thee a house like thy brethren's
And a court like unto thy kindred's.
Summon *weeds* into thy house,
Herbs into the midst of thy palace.
The mountains shall bring thee much silver,
The hills a treasure of gold;
They'll bring thee *god's grandeur aplenty*.
So build thou a silver and gold house,
A house of most pure lapis lazuli."
Puissant Baal rejoiced.
He summoned *weeds* into his house,
Herbs into the midst of his palace.
The mountains did bring him much silver,
The hills a treasure of gold;
They brought *him god's grandeur aplenty*.
Then he ⟨se⟩nt unto Kothar wa-Khasis.

[23] This seems—if the sense is correctly guessed—to imply that Baal had some sort of habitation before, but that it was not one worthy of a "ranking" god, such as Baal had become by vanquishing Yamm.

(Direction to the reciter):
Now turn to the account of the sending of the lads.[24]

After this comes Kothar wa-Khasis.
Before him an ox is set,
A fatted one at his disposal.
A throne is placed and he's seated
To the right of Puissant Baal.
So ate [the gods] and drank.
Then answered *Puiss*[*ant Baal,*
Responded the Ri]*d*[*er of the Clouds*]:
"Quickly, a house, *O K*[*othar*],
Quickly raise up a pal[ace].
Quickly the house shalt thou build,
Quickly shalt raise up the pa[lace]
In the midst of the fastness of Zaphon.
A thousand fields the house shall cover,
A myriad of acres the palace."
Quoth Kothar wa-Khasis:
"Hearken, O Puissant Baal:
Give heed, O rider of the Clouds.
A window I'll make in the House,
A casement within the palace."
But Puissant Baal replied:
"Make not a window in [the house],
[A casement] within the pal[ace]."

(2 or 3 lines missing?)

(vi)

Quoth Ko[thar wa-Khas]is:
"Thou'lt heed [my words], O Baal."
Again spake Ko[thar wa]-Khasis:
"Hark, pray, Pu[is]sant Baal!
A wi[nd]ow I'll make in the house,
A casement withi[n the pa]lace."
But Puissa[nt] Baal replied:
"Make not a w[ind]ow in the house,
A casement with[in the pa]lace.
Let not [Padriya] daughter of Ar [*be seen*]
Or T[alliya] daughter of Rabb *be espied*
By [. . .] El's Beloved Yamm!"
[. . .] *cried defiance*
And spat [. . .].
Quoth Kothar [wa-Khasis]:
"Thou'lt heed my words, O Baal."
[*As for Baal*] his house is built,
[*As for Hadd*][25] his palace is raised.
They [. . .] from Lebanon and its trees,
From [Siri]on its precious cedars.
. . . [. . . Le]banon and its trees,
Si[r]ion its precious cedars.
Fire is set to the house,
Flame to the palace.

[24] No doubt refers to an earlier passage, lost to us, in which Baal dispatched Gapn and Ugar to Kothar. The reciter is directed simply to repeat that passage verbatim here.

[25] Another name of Baal.

Lo, a [d]ay and a second,
Fire feeds on the house,
Flame upon the palace:
A third, a fourth day,
[Fi]re feeds on the house,
Flam[e] upon the palace.
A fifth, a s[ix]th day,
Fire feeds [on] the house, flame u[pon]
the palace.
There, on the seventh d[ay],
The fire *dies down* in the house,
The f[la]me in the palace.
The silver turns into blocks,
The gold is turned into bricks.
Puissant Baal exults:
"My h⟨ouse⟩ have I builded of silver;
My palace, indeed, of gold."
For (his) house preparations [Baa]l makes,
[Prepa]rations makes Hadd for his palace.
He slaughters both neat [and] small cattle,
Fells bulls [*together with*] fatlings;
Rams (and) one-year-ol[d] calves;
Lambs . . . k[i]ds.
He summons his brethren to his house,
His ki[nd]red within his palace:
Summons Asherah's seventy children.
He sates the he-lamb gods with *w*[*ine*],
He sates the ewe-lamb goddesses [. . . ?]
He sates the bull-gods with *w*[*ine*],
He sates the cow-goddesses [. . . ?]
He sates the throne-gods with *wi*[*ne*],
He sates the chair-goddesses [. . . ?]
He sates the gods with jars of wine,
He sates the goddesses with pitchers.
So eat the gods and drink.
They sate them with fatness abundant,
With tender [fat]ling by bounteous knife;[26]
While drinking the [wine] from flag[ons,
From gold cups the blood of vines].

(some 9-10 lines missing)

(vii)

(The first 8 lines are very defective. El's Beloved Yamm—see above vi 12—figures in lines 3-4. Since Baal's misgivings about a window are thereupon dispelled—15 ff.—perhaps Yamm is here given his quietus.)

Sixty-six towns he took,
Seventy-seven hamlets;
Eighty (took) Baal of [Zaphon's] s[ummit],
Ninety Baal of the *sum*[*mit.*
Baal] *dwells in his house,*
Baal in the midst of the house.
Quoth Puissant Baal:
"I will make (one), Kothar, this day;
Kothar, this very hour.

[26] Literally: They were sated with sucking of breast; by milch knife, with fatling's teat. (cf. Isa. 60:16; 66:11.)

A casement shall be opened in the house,
A window within the palace.
Yea, *I'll open rifts in* the clouds
At *thy word*, O Kothar wa-Khasis!"
Kothar wa-Khasis laughs,
He lifts up his voice and cries:
"Said I not to thee, Puissant Baal,
'Thou'lt heed my words, O Baal'?"—
He opens a casement in the house,
A window within the pa[lace].
Baal op[ens] *rifts in* [the cloud]s.
Ba[al gives] forth his holy voice,
Baal discharges the *ut*[*terance of his li*]*ps*.
His h[oly] voice [convulses] the earth, . . . the mountains quake,
A-tremble are . . .
East and west, earth's high places reel.
Baal's enemies take to the woods,
Hadd's enemies to the sides of the mountain.
Quoth Puissant Baal:
"Baal's enemies, why do you quake?
Why do you quake . . . ?"
Baal's eye seeks out for his hand
When the yew-club swings in his right hand.
So Baal dwells in his house.
"Nor king nor commoner
The earth my dominion shall . . .
Tribute I'll send not to Divine Mot,[27]
Not dispatch to El's Darling Ghazir.
Mot calls out in his soul,
The Beloved thinks in his heart,
'I alone will have sway o'er the gods
So that gods and men may feed,
Who satisfies the multitudes of the earth.' "
Aloud unto [his l]ads Baal doth cry:
"Look ye, [Gapn and] Ugar so⟨ns⟩ of Ghulumat,
['*Amami*]s twain, sons of Zulumat
[The stately, wing]-spreading, . . . ;
Winged ones twain, flock of clouds,
['Neath . . . ;
Birdlike ones twain, *flock* of . . . snow].

(some 5 lines missing)

(viii)

There now, be off on your way
Unto the Mount of Targhuzizza,
Unto the Mount of Tharumegi,
Unto the Ridge of the Loam of the Earth.
Lift the mount on your hands,
The elevation upon your palms,
And descend to the depth of the earth,
Be of those who descend into earth.
There now, be off on your way
Into his city *Pit*,
Low the throne that he sits on,
Filth the land of his inheritance.

[27] God of the rainless season and, apparently, of the nether world.

Yet beware, divine messengers.
Approach not Divine Mot,
Lest he make you like a lamb in his mouth,
Ye be crushed like a kid in his *gullet*.
Even the Gods' Torch Shapsh,
Who wings over heaven's expanse,
Is in Mot El's Beloved's hand![28]
From a thousand fields, ten thousand acres,[29]
To Mot's feet bow and fall down,
Prostrate you and show him honor.
And say unto Divine Mot,
Declare unto El's Darling Ghazir:
Message of Puissant Baal,
Work of the Mighty Wa[rrior]:
'My house I have builded [of silver,
My palace, indeed, of gold.]
. . .' "

(Ten lines of which only the ends are preserved, and approximately another 15 lines missing altogether.)
(Broken colophon in margin:)

[Written by Elimelech(?) Do]nated by Niqmadd,
King of Ugarit.

f. V AB

Only about one-half of this tablet is preserved, essentially the half containing the bottom of the obverse (cols. i-iii) and the top of the reverse (cols. iv-vi). Since the top of the first column on the reverse is always continuous with the bottom of the last column on the obverse, there are not six but only five pieces of continuous text. However, the first editor found it convenient to divide one of these into two episodes, making a total of six episodes designated as V AB A-F.

The position assigned to V AB in this translation of the Baal epic was determined by E 25-26; from which its appears that El's favorite-and-bully is now Mot, whereas he is still Yamm in II AB (our e) vi 12. But final judgment must be reserved.

Editions: Ch. Virolleaud, *La déesse 'Anat* (*Mission de Ras Shamra*, iv), 1938 (Part A, already *Syria*, xvii [1936], 335-345; Part B, *Syria*, xviii [1937], 85-102; Part C, *ibid.*, 256-270); *Ugaritic Handbook*, ii, pp. 187-9.

Studies: U. Cassuto, *Bulletin of the Jewish Palestine Exploration Society*, x, 2-3 (1943), 47-54; xii (1945-6), 40-42; T. H. Gaster, *Iraq*, vi (1939), 131-143; H. L. Ginsberg, *BASOR*, 84 (Dec. 1941), 12-14; W. F. Albright, *BASOR*, 83 (Oct. 1941), 39-42; 84 (Dec. 1941), 14-17; C. H. Gordon, *The Loves and Wars of Baal and Anat* (1943), pp. 21-27; A. Goetze, *BASOR*, 93 (Feb. 1944), 17-20; J. Obermann, *Ugaritic Mythology* (1948), *passim* (see Index); J. Aistleitner, *ZAW*, 57 (1939), 193-211; A. Herdner, *RÉS-Babyloniaca*, i (1942-45), 33-49.

A

. . . . . .
[. . .] . . .
Serves Puis[sant] Baal,
Ministers to the Prince, Lord of Earth.
He rises, . . . , and gives him to eat.
He cuts the fat meat before him,
With bounteous knife fatling's tenderness.

[28] After Yamm, this is the next favorite-and-bully of El that Baal has to vanquish. That is logical: first the earth—Baal's domain—must be made safe from the encroachments of the sea, then from the blight of sterility.

[29] From a safe distance.

He stands, *serves liquor*, and gives him drink.
He places a cup in his hand,
A flagon *in the grasp of* his hand;
A vessel large and conspicuous,
A jar to dumbfound a mortal;
A cup of woman *ne'er* seen,
Only Asherah[1] beholds such a flagon.
He takes a thousand pots of wine,
Mixes ten thousand in his mixture.
He rises, plays, and sings,
The musician plays the cymbals;
The sweet-voiced youth doth sing
Of Baal in the *Fastness* of Zaphon.—
Baal *regards* his lasses,[2]
Looks at Padriya daughter of Ar,
Also at Talliya [daughter of Ra]bb.
. . . . . . [. . .].
. . . [. . .] . . .

B

[. . .] . . .
Henna of seven maids,
Smell of coriander and *ambergris.*
She[3] *locked the gates* of Anath's house
And met the picked fighters in . . .
Now Anath[4] doth battle in the plain,
Fighting between the two towns;
Smiting the *Westland's* peoples,
Smashing the folk of the Sunrise.
Under her, *hea[ds]* like *sheaves;*
Over her, *hands* like locusts,
Like a grassho[pper]-mass heroes' hands.
She binds the *heads* to her back,
Fastens the hands in her girdle.
She p[lunges] knee-deep in knights' blood,
Hip-deep in the gore of heroes.
With darts she drives . . . ,
With the . . . of her bow . . .
Now Anath goes to her house,
The goddess proceeds to her palace.
Not sated with battling in the plain,
With her fighting between the two towns,
She *pictures* the chairs as heroes,
Pretending a table is warriors,
And that the footstools are troops.
Much battle she does and beholds,
Her fighting contemplates Anath:
Her liver *swells* with laughter,
Her heart fills up with joy,
Anath's liver *exults;*
For she plunges knee-deep in knights' blood,
Hip-deep in the gore of heroes.
Then, sated with battling in the house,
Fighting between the two tables,
. . . [. . .]s the knights' blood,
Pours the fatness of [de]w in a bowl.
Ma[id]en Anath washes her hands,
Yabamat Liimmim her fingers;
[She w]ashes her hands of knights' blood,
Her [fi]ngers of gore of heroes.
[. . .] . . . to chairs,
Table also to table;
Footstools *turn back* into footstools.
[She] draws some water and bathes;
Sky-[d]ew, fatness of earth,[5]
Spray of the Rider of Clouds;
Dew that the heavens do shed,
[Spray] that is shed by the stars.
She rubs herself in with *ambergris*
[*From a sperm-whale*] *whose home's* in the sea.
[. . .] . . .

C

"...[6]
. . .
For the friendship of Puissant Baal,
Affection of Padriya daughter of Ar,
Love of Talliya daughter of Rabb,
Friendship of Arsiya daughter of Ya'abdar
So then, O lads, *enter* ye;
At Anath's feet bow and fall down,
Prostrate you, do her honor.
And say unto Maiden Anath,
Declare unto Yamamat[7] Liimmim:
'Message of Puissant Baal,
Word of the Powerful Hero:
Take war [*away*] from the earth,
Banish (all) *strife* from the soil;
Pour peace into earth's very bowels,
Much amity into earth's bosom.
Hasten! Hurry! Rush!
To me thy feet shall trot,
To me shall sprint thy legs.
For
I've a word I fain would tell thee,
A speech I would utter to thee:
Speech of tree and whisper of stone,
Converse of heaven with earth,
E'en of the deeps with the stars;
Yea, *a thunderbolt* unknown to heaven,
A word not known to men,
Nor sensed by the masses on earth.
Come, pray, and I will reveal it
In the midst of my mount Godly Zaphon:
In the sanctuary, mount of my portion,
In the pleasance, the hill I possess.' "

D

No sooner espies she the gods,[8]
Than Anath's feet do stumble.

1 Or perhaps "a goddess"; cf. the appellative use of Ishtar in Akkadian.
2 Really his wives.
3 Anath herself?
4 Her character as a war-goddess is nowhere in oriental literature illustrated as graphically as in the following. But what is the carnage all about?
5 cf. Gen. 27:28, 39.
6 The speech, whose beginning is missing, is one by Baal to his messengers Gapn and Ugar.
7 Unique variant of the commoner *Yabamat.*
8 Gapn and Ugar, Baal's messengers.

Behind, her loins do break;
Above, her face doth sweat:
Bent are the joints of her loins,
Weakened those of her back.[9]
She lifts up her voice and cries:
"Why come Gapn and Ugar?
What enemy's ris[en] 'gainst Baal,
What foe 'gainst the Rider of Clouds?
Crushed I not El's Belov'd Yamm?
Destroyed I not El's Flood Rabbim?
Did I not, pray, muzzle the Dragon?
I did crush the crooked serpent,[10]
Shalyat [*šlyṭ*] the seven-headed.
I did crush El's Belov'd Ar[. . . ?],
Cut off El's *Bullock* 'Atak.
I did crush *the Godly Bitch Hashat,*
Destroy the house of El-Dhubub,
Who fought thee (and) seized the gold;
Who drave Baal from the Heights of Zaphon,
Sans frontlet,[11] *his ear piercèd through*;[12]
Chas'd him from his throne of kingship,
From the dais, the seat of his dominion.
What enemy's risen 'gainst Baal,
What foe 'gainst the Rider of Clouds?"—
[A]nswer the lads twain make:
"No enemy's risen 'gainst Baal,
No foe 'gainst the Rider of Clouds!
Message of Puissant Baal,
Word of the Powerful Hero:
Take war *away* from the earth,
Banish (all) strife from the soil, etc. etc."

(see above, lines 10 ff.)

[An]swers the Maiden [An]ath,
Replies [Yabamat] Liimmim:
"I'll *take* war *away* [from the earth,
Banish] (all) *strife* from the soil,
Pour [peace] into earth's very bowels,
Mu[ch amity into] earth's bos[om].
Let Baal [. . .] . . . ,
Let him . . . [. . .] . . .
I'll *take* war *away* from the earth, etc.
Yet another word will I say:
Go, go, attendants divine.
Ye *are slow* and I *am swift.*
From (my) Mount to the godhead afar,[13]
Enibaba[14] to the distant divinity,
Is two mathpads[15] under earth's furrows,
Three underneath *the hollows.*"—
There, she is off on her way
To Baal of the Summit of Zaphon.
From a thousand fields, ten thousand acres,

[9] The standard reaction of a female character to an unexpected visit: it must mean bad news!
[10] His proper name is Lotan=Leviathan (Isa. 27:1); see g, beginning.
[11] If *ṣṣ*=Heb. *ṣîṣ*, Exod. 28:36.
[12] cf. Exod. 21:6.
[13] i.e. Baal, the sender of the messengers.
[14] Name of Anath's abode. Could it be Hurrian, meaning "god's mountain"?
[15] Measure of time or length?

His sister's approach Baal sees,
The advance of his own father's-daughter.
He dismisses (his) wives from her presence.
He places an ox before her,
A fatted one in front of her.
She draws some water and bathes
Sky-dew, fatness of earth;
Dew that the heavens do [sh]ed,
Spray that is shed by the stars.
She rubs herself in with *ambergris*
From a sperm-whale
. . . [. . .].

E

[". . .[16]
No house hath Baal like the gods',
Nor court like Asherah's] children's. Etc. etc."[17]
Quoth [the Maiden Anath]:
"He'll heed me, will Bull E[l my father],
He'll heed me for his own good!
[For I'll] fell him like a lamb to the ground,
[Make] his gray hair [flow with] blood,
The gray hair of his beard [with gore];
Unless he give
A house unto Baal like the gods',
[And a cour]t like Asherah's children's."—
[She stamps] her foot [and the ea]rth [trembles].
[There, she is off on her] way
[Towards El of the S]ources of the Flo[ods,
In the m]idst of [the Headwaters of the Two De]eps.
She penetrates *El's Field and enters*
[The pavi]lion of K[i]ng Father [Shunem].

(couplet too damaged for sense)

Her voice Bull [El] her father [. . .] hea[rs].
[He replies] in the seven ch[am]bers,
[In]side the eight enclosures:

(lines 20-24 almost completely abraded)

". . .
Even the God's Torch Shapsh,
[*Who wings*] *the expanse of* heav[en],
Is in El's Belovèd Mot's hand."—
Quoth the Maiden Anath:
"[. . .] O El,
. . .
Rejoice not [. . .],
. . . [. . .]
[. . .] . . .
My long hand will [*smash*] thy skull.
I'll make thy gray hair flow [with blood],
The gray hair of thy beard with gore."—
El replies in the seven chambers,
Inside the eight enclosures:
"[I w]eened, daughter mine, thou wa[st gentle],
And contumely 'mong goddesses was not.

[16] In this speech Baal is explaining to Anath why he summoned her.
[17] See e, beginning.

What wouldst thou, O Maiden Anath?"—
And the Maiden Ana[th] re[pl]ied:
"Thy decree, O El, is wise:
  Wisdom with ever-life thy portion.
Thy decree: 'Our king's Puissant Baal,
  Our ruler, second to none. Etc.,' Etc."

(see above, e, iv-v 41 ff.)

F

"...
[O'er] thousand ['fields' in the] sea,
  Ten thousand [acres] in the floods.
[Tra]verse Gabal, traverse Qa'al,
  Traverse Ihat-nop-shamem.
Proceed, O Fisherman of Asherah,
  Go, O Qadesh wa-Amrur.[18]
There now, be off on thy way
  To the midst of Hikpat-El, all of it,[19]
To Kaphtor the throne that he sits on,
  Hikpat the land of his portion
From a thousand fields, ten thousand acres,[20]
  At Kotha[r]'s feet bow and fall down,
  Prostrate thee and do him honor.
And say unto Kothar wa-Khasis,
  Repeat unto Hayyin of the Handicrafts:
'Message of Pui[ssant Baal,
  Word of the Powerful Hero:
...]'"

g. I* AB

Two fragments, discovered in 1930 and 1931 respectively, were found to fit together, but about an equal amount of text is still missing from the tablet to which they belong. Though the top of col. i happens to be preserved, it does not exhibit the copyist's signature "Pertaining to 'Baal'" which ought to have occupied line 1 according to rule. However, thanks to the circumstance that the bottom of col. vi is also preserved, it is obvious that the direct continuation of this tablet is I AB, which has the expected superscription.

Editions: Ch. Virolleaud, *Syria*, xv (1934), 305-336; H. L. Ginsberg, *Orientalia* NS, v (1936), 161-196; *Kitbe Ugarit*, 47-56; *The Ras Shamra Mythological Texts*, 78-84; *AKTRSch.*, 35-41; *Ugaritic Handbook*, II, No. 67.

Studies: U. Cassuto, *Dissertationes in Honorem Dr. Eduardi Mahler* (Budapest, 1937), 53-57; *Tarbiz*, XII (1941), 169-180.

Col. i lines 1-8 represent the conclusion of a message which Mot has been instructing Gapn and Ugar, the messengers of Baal, to deliver to the latter. In order to be in Mot's presence, they must previously have been sent to him by Baal. Since we read of just such a mission in the incomplete last column of II AB (our e), it is possible that if that column were complete its text would be found to precede ours directly, in other words, to end with the first half of Mot's message; but other considerations suggest that V AB (our f) may have intervened. In any case the first half of Mot's original speech can for the most part easily be restored, since the entire speech is repeated by Gapn and Ugar in full—though slightly damaged—in the first column of our tablet. But it is so obscure that we shall skip most of it.

(i)

"...
If[1] thou smite Lotan, the serpent slant,
  Destroy the serpent tortuous,
  Shalyat (*šlyṭ*) of the seven heads,[2]
..."

(two couplets very obscure)

From the *tomb* of the Godly Mot,
  From the pit of El's Belov'd Ghazir,
  The gods twain[3] depart, tarry not.
There, they are off on their way
  To Baal of the Summit of Zaphon.
Then Gapn and Ugar declare:
"Message of Godly Mot,
  Word of the God-Belov'd Ghazir:

(even the gist of 14-27 still eludes savants)

If thou smite Lotan, the serpent slant,
  Destroy the serpent tortuous,
  Shalyat of the seven heads,
..."

(Traces of the two obscure couplets mentioned above. Some 30 lines missing.)

(ii)

(12 lines missing at the top)

One lip to earth and one to heaven,[4]
  [He stretches his to]ngue to the stars.
Baal enters his mouth,
  Descends into him like an olive-cake,[5]
  Like the yield of the earth and trees' fruit.
Sore afraid is Puissant Baal,
  Filled with dread is the Rider of Clouds:
"Begone![6] Say unto Godly Mot,
  Repeat unto El's Belov'd Ghazir:
'Message of Puissant Baal,
  Word of the Powerful Hero:
Be gracious, O Godly Mot;
  Thy slave I, thy bondman for ever.'"—
The gods depart, tarry not.
There, they are off on their way
  Unto Godly Mot,
Into his city Hamriya,
  Down to the throne that ⌈he⌉ sits on
  His ⌈filthy⌉ land of inher'tance.
They lift up their voice and cry:
"Message of Puissant Son Baal,
  Word of the Powerful Hero:
Be gracious, O Godly Mot;
  Thy slave I, thy bondman for ever."—

18 Attendant of Asherah, but on this occasion, it seems, he for some reason acts as messenger for Baal (see end).

19 *Ḥkpt il klh*, home of Kothar.

20 It is curious that this precaution (cf. e, viii 25 ff.) should be necessary with Kothar, who is otherwise an obliging deity and a friend of Baal.

1 Perhaps: even if. It depends on what the following lines mean.

2 cf. Ps. 74:14 for the last phrase; for the rest Isa. 27:1.

3 Gapn and Ugar. See the introductory paragraph.

4 Also occurs elsewhere in describing some ravenous creature opening its mouth.

5 Apparently a flat loaf of bread with olives, a common meal in ancient and modern times.

6 Said by Baal to Gapn and Ugar. A quotation without an introduction, not unexampled.

The Godly Mot rejoices
    [And lifting] his [vo]ice he cries:
"How *humbled is* [. . .]."

(Several ends of lines, then about 20-25 lines missing. Cols. iii-iv too damaged for connected sense.)

(v)

(About 25 lines missing at the top. Then 1-5 defective.)

". . .[7]
But thou, take thy cloud, thy wind,
    Thy . . . , thy rains;
With thee thy seven lads,
    Thine eight *boars*.
With thee Padriya, daughter of Ar;
    With thee Tatalliya (*Ṭṭly*),[8] daughter of Rabb.
There now, be off on thy way
    Unto the Mount of Kankaniya.
Lift the mount upon thy hands,
    The elevation upon thy palms,
And descend to the depth of the earth,
    Be of those who descend into earth,
    And . . ."—
Puissant Baal complies.
He desires a cow-calf in Dubr,
    A heifer in Shihlmemat-field (*šd šḫlmmt*);
Lies with her times seventy-seven,
    [. . .] . . . times eighty-eight.
    She [conc]eives and gives birth to Math.

(fragments of 3 more lines; another 11 missing)

(vi)

(about 30 lines missing at the top)

[They[9] penetrate El's Field and enter
    The pavilion of King El Father] Shunem.
[And lifting their voice they cr]y:
"We went [. . .],
    . . .
We [ca]me to the pleasance of Dubr-land,
    To the beauty of Shihlmemat-field.
We came upon Baal
    Fallen on the ground:
Puissant Baal is dead,
    The Prince, Lord of Earth, is perished."
Straightway Kindly El Benign
    Descends from the throne,
    Sits on the footstool;
From the footstool,
    And sits on the ground;
Pours dust of mourning on his head,
    Earth of mortification on his pate;
    And puts on *sacḳcloth and loincloth.*
He *cuts a gash* with a stone,
    Incisions with . . .
He *gashes* his cheeks and his chin,
    He *harrows* the *roll* of his *arm.*
He plows his chest like a garden,
    Harrows his back like a plain.
He lifts up his voice and cries:
"Baal's dead!—What becomes of the people?
    Dagon's Son!—What of the masses?
    After Baal I'll descend into earth."
Anath also goes and wanders
    Every mount to the heart of the earth,
    Every hill to the earth's very bo[we]ls.
She comes to the pleasance of Dubr-[land],
    To the beauty of Shihlmemat-field.
She [comes] upon Baal
    Fal[len] on the ground:
    She puts on *(sacḳcloth) and loincloth.*

[7] Addressed (by Mot?) to Baal.

[8] A variant of *Ṭly*. For some reason *ṭṭl* also occurs as a variant of the appellative *ṭl* ("dew").

[9] Probably Gapn and Ugar.

h. I AB

A tablet with three columns of writing on each side. It consists of two fragments: a larger one exhumed in 1930 and a smaller one brought to light in 1933. The latter constitutes the top of col. i and the bottom of col. vi and fits exactly onto the former.

Editions: Virolleaud, *Syria*, XII (1931), 193-224; *Syria*, XV (1934), 226-243; Montgomery-Harris, *The Ras Shamra Mythological Texts*, 49-57; Ginsberg, *Kitbe Ugarit*, 57-70; *AKTRSch.*, 42-48; *Ugaritic Handbooḳ*, II, Texts 49 (pp. 137-9) and 62 (pp. 146-7).

Studies: Albright, *BASOR*, 46 (Apr. 1932), 15-19; *JPOS*, XII (1932), 185-203; Montgomery, *JAOS*, LIII (1933), 97-123.

(Pertaining to "Baal.")
She *cuts a gash* with a stone,
    Incisions with . . . etc.

(See g, col. vi.)

Then weeps she her fill of weeping;
    Deep she drinks tears, like wine.
Loudly she calls
    Unto the Gods' Torch Shapsh.
"Lift Puissant Baal, I pray,
    Onto me."
Hearkening, Gods' Torch Shapsh
    Picks up Puissant Baal,
    Sets him on Anath's shoulder.
Up to Zaphon's *Fastness* she brings him,
    Bewails him and buries him too,
    Lays him in the hollows of the earth-ghosts.
She slaughters seventy buffaloes
    As tribute to Puissant Baal;
She slaughters seventy neat
    [As tr]ibute to Puissant Baal;
[She slaugh]ters seventy small cattle
    [As tribu]te to Puissant Baal;
[She slaugh]ters seventy deer
    [As tribute to] Puissant Baal;
[She slaughters] seventy mountain-goats
    [As tribute to Pu]issant Baal;
[She slaughters seventy ro]ebucks
    [As tribu]te to Puissant Baal.
[. . .] . . . A[nath],
    [. . .] Yabama[t] Liimmim.—

[The]re, she is off on her way
To [E]l of the Sources of the Floods,
In the midst of [the Hea]dwaters of the Two Deeps.
She penetrates El's Field and enters
The pavilion of King Father Shunem.
At El's feet she bows and falls down,
Prostrates her and does him honor.
She lifts up her voice and cries:
"Now let Asherah rejoice and her sons,
Elath and the band of her kinsmen;
For dead is Puissant Baal,
Perished the Prince, Lord of Earth."[1]
Loudly El doth cry
To Lady Asherah of the Sea:
"Hark, Lady A[sherah of the S]ea,
Give one of thy s[ons] I'll make king."
Quoth Lady Asherah of the Sea:
"Why, let's make Yadi' Yalhan (*yd' ylḥn*) king."
Answered Kindly One El Benign:
"Too weakly. He can't race with Baal,
Throw jav'lin with Dagon's Son *Glory-Crown*!"
Replied Lady Asherah of the Sea:
"Well, let's make it Ashtar the Tyrant;
Let Ashtar the Tyrant be king."—
Straightway Ashtar the Tyrant
Goes up to the *Fastness* of Zaphon
(And) sits on Baal Puissant's throne.
(But) his feet reach not down to the footstool,
Nor his head reaches up to the top.
So Ashtar the Tyrant declares:
"I'll not reign in Zaphon's *Fastness*!"
Down goes Ashtar the Tyrant,
Down from the throne of Baal Puissant,
And reigns in El's Earth, all of it.
[. . .] . . .
[. . .] . . .

(ii)

(some 30 lines missing on top)

[. . .]. A day, days go by,
[And Anath the Lass] draws nigh him.
Like the heart of a c[ow] for her calf,
Like the heart of a ew[e] for her lamb,
So's the heart of Ana[th] for Baal.
She grabs Mot by the fold of his garment,
Seizes [him] by the hem of his robe.
She lifts up her voice and [cries]:
"Now, Mot! Deliver my brother."
Responds the Godly Mot:
"What wouldst thou, O Maiden Anath?
I indeed have gone and have wander'd
Every mount to the heart of the earth,
Every hill to the earth's very bowels.
Lifebreath was wanting 'mong men,
Lifebreath among earth's masses.
I came to the pleasance of Dubr-land,
The beauty of Shihlmemat-field.
I did *masticate* Puissant Baal.
I made him like a lamb in my mouth;
Like a kid in my gullet he's crushed.
Even the Gods' Torch Shapsh,
Who wings over heaven's expanse,
Is in Mot the Godly's hand."
A day, even days pass by,
From days unto months.
Then Anath the Lass draws nigh him.
Like the heart of a cow for her calf,
Like the heart of a ewe for her lamb,
So's the heart of Anath for Baal.
She seizes the Godly Mot—
With sword she doth cleave him.
With fan she doth winnow him—
With fire she doth burn him.[2]
With hand-mill she grinds him—
In the field she doth sow him.
Birds eat his *remnants*,
Consuming his *portions*,
Flitting from remnant to remnant.[3]

(iii-iv)

(some 40 lines missing on top of col. iii)

". . .[4]
[That Puissant Baal had died],
That the Prince [Lord of Earth] had perished.
And behold, alive is [Puissant Baal]!
And behold, existent the Prince, Lo[rd of Earth]!
In a dream, O Kindly El Benign,
In a vision, Creator of Creatures,
The heavens fat did rain,
The wadies flow with honey.
So I knew
That alive was Puissant Baal!
Existent the Prince, Lord of Earth!
In a dream, Kindly El Benign,
In a vision, Creator of Creatures,
The heavens fat did rain,
The wadies flow with honey!"—
The Kindly One El Benign's glad.
His feet on the footstool he sets,
And parts his *jaws* and laughs.
He lifts up his voice and cries:
"Now will I sit and rest
And my soul be at ease in my breast.
For alive is Puissant Baal,
Existent the Prince, Lord of Earth!" (edge)
Loudly El doth cry
Unto the Maiden Anath.
"Hearken, O Maiden Anath!
Say to the Gods' Torch Shapsh:

[1] Now a son of Asherah can rule the earth. In col. v Asherah's sons are Baal's enemies. His epithet "Dagon's Son" may echo a stage of tradition in which he was not a son of El, either.

[2] That is to say, the parts of him corresponding to chaff and straw in cereals.

[3] But somehow Mot comes to life entire in col. vi, and Baal even earlier.

[4] Who the speaker is is not known.

(iv)

'Parch'd is the furrow of Soil, O Shapsh;
    Parched is El's Soil's furrow:
    Baal neglects the furrow of his tillage.
Where is Puissant Baal?
    Where is the Prince, Lord of Earth?' "—
The Maiden Anath departs.
There, she is off on her way
    Unto the Gods' Torch Shapsh.
She lifts up her voice and cries:
"Message of Bull El thy father,
    Word of the Kindly, thy begetter:
Parch'd is the furrow of Soil, O [Shapsh];
    Parched is El's Soil's furrow:
    Baal ne[glects] the furrow of his tillage.
Where is Puissant Baal?
    Where is the Prince, Lord of Earth?"—
Answer'd the Gods' Torch Sha[psh]:
". . . in the . . . [of thy brother],
    In the . . . of thy sibling,
    And I'll look for Puissant Baal."—
Quoth the Maiden Anath:
". . . . . . , O Shapsh;
. . .
May . . .[. . .] guard thee,
    . . . [. . .]."(?)
. . . [. . .]
    . . . [. . .].
        (some 35 lines missing)

(v)

Baal seizes the sons of Asherah.
    Rabbim[5] he strikes in the back.
Dokyamm he strikes with a bludgeon,
    . . . he fells to the earth.
Baal [mounts] his throne of kingship,
    [Dagon's Son] his seat of dominion.
[From] days to months, from months to years.
    Lo, after seven years,
The Godly Mot [. . .]
    Unto Puissant Baal.
He lifts up his voice and says:
"Upon thee . . . may I see,[5a]
    Downfall upon thee may I see.
Winnowing ⟨with fan
    Upon thee may I see.
Cleaving⟩ with sword
    Upon thee may I see.
Burning with fire
    Upon thee [may I see.
Gri]nding with hand-mill
    Up[on thee] may I s[ee
    Siftin]*g* with *sieve*
    Upon thee [may I] see.
[. . .] . [. . .] in the soil
    Upon thee may I see.
Sowing on the sea
    [. . .] . . [. . .]."
(Lines 20-28 defective and obscure. Some further 35 lines missing.)

(vi)

Returning to Baal of Zaphon's *Fastness*,
    He lifts *up* his voice and cries:
"My brothers hast thou given, Baal, my . . . [s?];
    My mother's sons, my . . ."
They . . . like *camels*:
    Mot's firm, Baal's firm.
They gore like buffaloes:
    Mot's firm. Baal's firm.
They bite like snakes:
    Mot's firm. Baal's firm.
They *kick* like *chargers*:
    Mot falls. Baal falls.
Above Shapsh cries to Mot:
"Hearken, now, Godly Mot!
    Why striv'st thou with Puissant Baal? Why?
Should Bull El thy father hear thee,
    He'll pull out thy dwelling's *pillars*.
Overturn thy throne of kingship,
    Break thy staff of dominion!"
Sore afraid was Godly Mot,
    Filled with dread El's Belovèd Ghazir.
Mot . . .
    . . [. . . .]
Baal seats him [on] his kingdom's [throne],
    Upon his dominion's [seat].
        (36-42 missing, defective, or unintelligible)
" . . .[6]
Thou'lt[7] eat the bread of honor,
    Thou'lt[7] drink the wine of favor.
Shapsh *shall govern* the *gathered ones*,[8]
    Shapsh *shall govern* the divine ones.
. . . gods . . . mortals,
    . . . Kothar thy fellow,
    Even Khasis thine intimate."
On the sea of *monster* and dragon,
    Proceedeth Kothar wa-Khasis,
    Kothar wa-Khasis doth journey.[8a]

(colophon)

Written by Elimelech the Shabnite.
Dictated by Attani-puruleni, Chief of Priests, Chief of (Temple)-herdsmen.
Donated by Niqmadd, King of Ugarit, Master of Yargub, Lord of Tharumeni.

APPENDIX. IV AB+RŠ 319 (and BH)

There exist a large (IV AB) and a very small piece (RŠ 319) of a tablet with three columns of writing on only one side. That they both belong to the same tablet is not certain but very

5 According to f (between lines 30 and 40), Anath has already destroyed Rabbim once.
5a Or, "Because of thee . . . have I seen." So also in the following.

6 Apparently Baal is handing out rewards to his allies.
7 Or, "she'll."
8 The *rephaim*, or shades?
8a Perhaps the quotation should rather be closed here.

probable. That only one side of the tablet is written on is probably due to the fact that it contained the whole of the composition in question, which was quite short. It has no colophon. It is distinct from the Baal epic which we have been following in the preceding pieces. RŠ 319, which is apparently the missing top right-hand corner of IV AB, contains a graphic account of sexual intercourse between Baal and Anath; and IV AB itself is suggestive of something more than platonic relations between the two. This is entirely at variance with the epic, as everyone will realize who has read the former without reading into it.

[A similar complete short episode about Baal, likewise covering only one side of a tablet is BH, which, however, is so defective that a translation here would be of little use.]

Editions: Virolleaud, *Syria*, XVII (1936), 150-173; XXIV, fasc. 1-2 (1944-45), 14-17; *Ugaritic Handbook*, II, Nos. 76 (pp. 152 f.) and 132 (pp. 166 f.); Ginsberg, *Orientalia* NS, VII (1938), 1-11 (main portion only).

(col. i too fragmentary for use)

(ii)

(some 20 lines missing on top?)

"... Baal in his house,
The God Hadd in the midst of his palace?"[1]
The lads of Baal make answer:
"Baal *is not* in his house,
[The God] Hadd in the midst of his palace.
His bow he has ta'en in his hand,
Also his *darts* in his right hand.
There he is off on his way
To Shimak Canebrake,[2] the [buf]falo-*filled*."—
The Maiden Ana[th] lifts her wing,
Lifts her wing and speeds in flight,
To Shimak Canebrake,[2] the [buf]falo-*filled*.—
Puissant Baal lifts up his eyes,
Lifts up his eyes and beholds,
Beholds the Maiden Anath,
Fairest *among* Baal's sisters.
Before her he rises, he stands,
At her feet he kneels and falls down.
And he lifts up his voice and cries:
"Hail, sister, and ... !
The horns of thy ..., O Maiden Anath,
The horns of thy ... Baal will anoint,
Baal will *anoint* them in flight.
We'll thrust my foes into the earth,
To the ground them that rise 'gainst thy brother!"—
The Maiden Anath lifts up her eyes,
Lifts up her eyes and beholds,
Beholds a cow and proceeds a-walking,
Proceeds a-walking and proceeds *a-dancing*,
In the pleasant spots, in the lovely places.

(RŠ 319)

(8 or 9 badly damaged lines at the bottom)

He seizes and holds [her] womb;
[She] seizes and holds [his] stones.
Baal ... *to an ox*.
[Th Mai]den Anath
[...] to conceive and bear.

[1] The inquirer is evidently Anath.

[2] Semachonitis, the modern Lake Ḥûleh in Galilee?

(another 14 lines very fragmentary)

(IV AB iii)

[Calve]s the cows dr[op]:
An ox for Maiden Anath
And a heifer for Yahamat Liimmim.
Quoth Puissant [Baal]:
"... that our progenitor is eternal,
To all generations our begetter."
Baal scoops [his hands] full,
⌜The God⌝ Hadd [his] fin[gers] full.
... the mouth of Maiden An[ath],
E'en the mouth of [his] fairest sister.
Baal goes up in the mou[ntain],
Dagon's Son in the s[ky].
Baal sits upon [his th]rone,
Dagon's Son upon [his se]at.

(In lines 16-29, which are poorly preserved, there is again talk of a buffalo being born to Baal, it being still not absolutely clear that his bovine mother was Anath herself.)

And so she goes up to Arar,
Up to Arar and Zaphon.
In the pleasance, the Mount of Possession,
She cries aloud to Baal:
"Receive, Baal, godly tidings,
Yea receive, O Son of Dagon:
A wild-ox is [born] to Baal,
A buffalo to Rider of Clouds."
Puissant Baal rejoices.

The Legend of King Keret

In the campaigns of 1930 and 1931 the French excavators of ancient Ugarit recovered fragments belonging to three clay tablets of an epic about a king designated by a name whose consonants are *k̠-r-t* and whose vowels are unknown; it is conventionally transcribed *Keret*.

There are six columns of writing (three on each side) on each tablet. According to the order in which they were published, they are designated as I K, II K, and III K, but according to their organic sequence as KRT A (=I K), KRT B (=III K), KRT C (=II K). KRT A was probably preceded, and KRT C was certainly followed, by one or more lost tablets. There may also be one or more missing between B and C.

Our text was copied in the reign of a certain king of Ugarit by the name of Niqmadd (see the colophon at the end of KRT C), who is known to have reigned in the second quarter of the fourteenth century B.C. That it contains a certain core of history is probable.

First publication: Of KRT A (with copies and photographs of the original), Ch. Virolleaud, *La légende de Keret, roi des Sidoniens* (*Mission de Ras Shamra II*), 1936. Of KRT B (with copies of the original), Ch. Virolleaud, Le mariage du roi Keret (III K), *Syria*, XXIII/3-4 (1942-43, actual date of publication 1945), 137-172. Of KRT C (with copies of the original), Ch. Virolleaud, Le roi Keret et son fils (II K), *Syria*, XXII (1941), 105-136, 197-217; *Syria*, XXIII/1-2 (1942-43), 1-20. Other editions: H. L. Ginsberg, *The Legend of King Keret* (*BASOR SS*, 2-3), 1946 (includes bibliography). C. H. Gordon, *Ugaritic Handbook* (*Analecta Orientalia*, XXV), 1947, II, pp. 162-166, 184-187; Texts 125-128, Krt (transliterations only). Other bibliography (not included in Ginsberg's edition): R. de Langhe, *Miscellanea historica Alberti de Meyer* (1946), 92-108; R. de Vaux, *RB*, LV (1948), 146-147; T. H. Gaster, *JQR*, XXXVII (1946-47), 285-293; C. H. Gordon, *BASOR*, 105 (February, 1947), 11-12; A. Herdner, *Syria*, XXV (1946-48), 162-165; J. Obermann, *JBL*, LXV (1946), 241-248; F. Rosenthal, *Orientalia* NS, XVI (1947), 399-402; D. W. Thomas, *Journal of Jewish Studies*, I (1948), 63-64; C. H. Gordon, *Ugaritic Literature*, pp. 66-83.

KRT A

(i)

([Pertaining to "Ke]ret.")[1]
. . .
. . . The house of [a k]ing *is destroyed*,
Who had seven [bre]thren,
Eight mother's sons.
Keret in offspring *is ruined*,
Keret *is undermined* of establishment.
His lawful wife he did find,
His legitimate spouse.
He married the woman, and she "departed."[2]
Flesh of kinship had he:
One-third died *in health*,
One-fourth of sickness;
One-fifth pestilence gathered unto itself,
One-sixth *calamity*;
One-seventh thereof fell by the sword.[3]—
He sees his offspring, doth Keret;
He sees his offspring ruined,
Wholly *undermined* his seat,
And in its entirety a posterity perishing,
And in its totality a succession.
(So) he enters his cubicle (and) weeps,
An inner chamber and cries.
His tears do drop
Like shekels to the ground.
His bed *is soaked* by his weeping,[4]
And he falls asleep as he cries.
Sleep prevails over him, and he lies;
Slumber, and he reclines.
And in his dream El descends,
In his vision the Father of Man.[5]
And he approaches asking Keret:
"What ails Keret that he weeps,
The Beloved, Lad of El,[6] that he cries?
Is it a kingship like Bull his father's he desires,
Or authority like the Father of Man's?"

(At the bottom of col. i, lines 44-53 are abraded. They doubtless contained an offer by El of "silver and gold . . . and perpetual slaves" etc. [cf. lines 53 ff., 126 ff., 37 ff., 250 ff., 269 ff., 282 ff.] and the beginning of Keret's reply, as follows: "What need have I of silver and yellow-glittering—)

(ii)

[gold];
Friendship by convenant [and vassa]lage for ever;
One-third of the chariot-[steeds]
In the stable of a handmaid's son?[7]
[*Grant*] I may beget [*chil*]*dren*;
[Grant that] I multiply [kins]men."—
And Bull, his father El, [replied]:
"*E*[*nough*] *for thee* of weeping, Keret;
Of crying, Beloved, Lad of El.
Do thou wash and rouge thee.
Wash from hand to elbow,
From [thy] fing[ers] up to the shoulder.
Enter [the shade of a pavilion].
Take a lam[b in thy hand],
A lamb of sac[rifice in thy] right hand;
A kid *in th*[*e grasp of* thy han]d,
All thy most tempting food.
Take a *turtle*[*dove*],
Bird of sacrifice.
[In a bo]wl of silver pour wine,
Honey in a bowl of [g]old.
{Go up to the top of a [to]wer.}[8]
And go up to the top of a [to]wer;
Bestride the top of the wal[l];
Lift up thy hands to heaven,
Sacrifice to Bull, thy father El;
Honor Baal with thy sacrifice,
Dagon's Son[9] with thine oblation.
Then descend, Keret, from the housetops.
Prepare thou corn from the granaries,
Wheat from the storehouses.
Let bread be baked for a fifth,
Food for a sixth month.
Muster the people and let it come forth,
The host of the troops of the people.
Yea, let come forth the assembled multitude,
Thy troops, a mighty force:
Three hundred myriads;
Serfs without number,
Peasants beyond counting.
They march in thousands *serried*,
And in myriads *massed.*
After two, two march;
After three, all of them.
The solitary man closes his house,
The widow *locks herself in*;[10]
The sick man is carried in bed,
The blind man *gropes his way.*
E'en the new-wed groom[11] goes forth.

[1] The first line in each tablet of a series indicates (where preserved) the series to which it belongs.
[2] A euphemism for "died."
[3] The poet either did not know or did not care if his fractions added up to more than unity.
[4] cf. Ps. 6:7.
[5] The word for "man" is identical with the proper name "Adam," and "Father (i.e. Creator) of the *First* Man" may be the meaning intended. El is also frequently called "Creator of Creatures."
[6] This epithet, like "Servant of El" (below, ll. 153, 155, 299), has the connotations of "favorite" and "intimate." cf. Num. 12:6-9; Deut. 34:5-10; Isa 41:8; etc.
[7] i.e. of a (slave or) vassal; cf. Ps. 86:16; 116:16; Wisd. 9:5.
[8] A dittography of the next line; cf. ll. 165 ff.
[9] = Baal.
[10] This sense is strongly indicated by the parallelism, though hard to confirm etymologically.
[11] Who was sometimes exempted, Deut. 24:5 (cf. 20:7).

He *drives*[12] to another his wife,
To a stranger his well-beloved.
(They are)
Like the locusts that dwell on the steppe,

(iii)

Like grasshoppers on the borders of the desert.[13]—
March a day and a second;
A third, a fourth day;
A fifth, a sixth day—
Lo! at the sun[14] on the seventh:
Thou arrivest at Udum the Great,
Even at Udum the Grand.
—Now do thou *attack* the villages,
Harass the towns.
Sweep from the fields the wood-cutting ⌜wives⌝,
From the threshing floors the straw-picking ones;
Sweep from the spring the women that draw,
From the fountain those that fill.[15]
Tarry a day and a second;
A third, a fourth day;
A fifth, a sixth day.
Thine arrows shoot *not* into the city,
(*Nor*) thy hand-stones *flung headlong*.
And behold, at the sun on the seventh,
King Pabel will sleep
Till the noise of the neighing of his stallion,
Till the sound of the braying of his he-ass,
Until the lowing of the plow ox,
(Until) the howling of the watchdog.
Then will he send two messengers unto thee,
Unto Keret, *to the camp*:
'Message of King Pabel:—
Take silver and yellow-glittering gold;
Friendship by covenant and vassalage for ever;
One-third of the chariot-steeds
In the stable of a handmaid's son.
Take it, Keret,
In peace, in peace.
And flee, O king, from my house;
Withdraw, O Keret, from my court.
Vex not Udum the Great,
Even Udum the Grand.
Udum is a gift of El,
Even a present of the Father of Man.'
Then send thou the two messengers back to him:—
'What need have I of silver and yellow-glittering gold;
Friendship by covenant and vassalage
for ever;
One-third of the chariot-steeds
In the stables of a handmaid's son?
Nay, what's not in my house shalt thou give!
Give me Lady Hurriya (*ḥry*),
The fair, thy first-begotten;
Whose fairness is like Anath's fairness,
[Whose] beau[ty] like Ashtoreth's beauty;
Whose eyeballs are the pureness of lapis,
Whose pup[ils] the gleam of *jet*;
. . . *Let me bask in the brightness of* her eyes;
Whom in my dream El bestowed,
In my vision the Father of Man.
And let her bear offspring to Keret,
And a lad to the Servant of El.' "—
Keret awoke, and (lo, it was) a dream;
The Servant of El, and (lo, it was) a fantasy.—
Then washèd he and roug'd him:
He washed from hand to elbow,
From his fingers up to the shoulder.
He entered the shade of a pavilion, (edge)
Took a lamb of sacrifice in his hand,
A kid *in the grasp of* his hand,
All his most tempting food.
He took a *turtledove*,
Bird of sacrif[ice].

(iv)

In a bowl of silver he poured wine,
Honey in a bowl of gold.
He went up to the top of a tower,
Bestrode the top of the wall;
Lifted up his [han]ds to heaven,
Sacrificed to Bull, his father El;
Honored Baal with his sacrifice,
Dagon's Son with his [ob]lation.
Keret descended [from the housetop]s.
He prepared corn from the granaries,
Wheat from the storehouses.
Bread [was ba]ked for a fifth,
[Food] for a sixth mon[th].
He mu[st]ered the people and [it came forth,
The host] of the troops of the peop[le.
And forth came the assembled] *multitude*,
His troops, [a mighty force]:
Thr[ee] hundred myriads.
They march in thousands *serried*,
And in myriads massed.
After two, two march;
After three, all of them.
The solitary man closes his house,
The widow *locks herself in*;
The sick man is carried in his bed,
The blind man *gropes his way*.
Forth comes,[16] too, the new-wed groom.
He *drives* to another his wife,
And to a stranger his well-beloved.
(They are) like the locusts that dwell on the steppe,
Like grasshoppers on the border of the desert.—
They march a day and a second;
Then, at the su[n] on the third,

[12] Or "leaves"?
[13] A stock simile for a vast multitude, Jud. 6:5; 7:12; Jer. 46:23; 51:27; Nah. 3:16, 17.
[14] Probably "sunrise."
[15] Evidently these, the most menial, tasks—cf. Deut. 29:10b; Josh. 9:20, 23, 27—devolved upon women in this society.
[16] The text has *wybl*, but this is probably miswritten for *wyṣu*; cf. above, line 100.

They co[me] to the shrine of Asherah of Tyre,[17]
Even that of Elath of Sidon.[17]
There [Ke]ret the Noble vo[ws]:
"As Asherah of Tyre exists,
As Elath of Sidon!
If Hurriya to my house I take,
Bring the lass into my court,
Her double I'll give in silver,
And her treble in gold."[18]
He marches a day and a second;
A third, a fourth day.
Then at the sun on the fourth,[19]
He arrives at Udum the Great,
Even Udum the [Gr]and.
He did attack the villages,
Harassed the towns.
He *swept* from the fields the wood-cutting ⟨wives⟩,
And from the threshing floors the straw-picking ones;

(v)

He *swept* from the spring the women that drew,
And from the fountain those that filled.
He tarr[ied] a day and a second,
A thi[rd, a fou]rth day;
A fifth, a sixth day.
And behold, at the sun on the seventh,
King Pabel slept
Till the noise of the neighing of his stallion,
Till the sound of the braying of his he-ass,
Until the lowing of the plow ox,
[(Until) the how]ling of the [wa]tchdog.
[*Straightw*]*ay* [King Pabe]l
[Lou]dly unto [his] wife doth [cry]:
"Hearken, I pray thee, [O . . .] *my wife*,
[. . .]
(lines 231-5 too fragmentary for rendering)
[*To Keret*] I will *surely* send [. . .]." (236)
Loudly [unto . . . he do]th cry:
["O . . . , *m*]*ount* ye an ass
(lines 240-5 destroyed except for a few letters)
. . . [There now, be off on your wa]y (246)
Towards [Keret the Noble].
And s[ay unto Keret the Noble]:
'Message of (King Pabel):—
Take [silver and yellow-glittering gold]; (250-261)
[*Friendship by covena*]*nt*, vass[alage for ever; Etc.] etc.'"
(see above, lines 125-136)

(vi)

(Lines 262-264, wanting, related how the two messengers did what Pabel had commanded in lines 239-245.)
[There, they are off on their way (265)
Towar]ds [Keret the Noble.
They] r[aise their voices and cry]:
"Mess[age of King Pabel:
Take silver and yellow-glittering gold; etc. etc." (269-280)
(see above, lines 125-136)
And [Ker]et the Nob[le replied: (281-299)
"Wh]at [need ha]ve I of silver and yellow-gl[ittering gold]; etc., etc."
(Till "and a lad to the Servant of El" [see lines 136-153] minus the clause "*let me bask in the brightness of her eyes.*")
The messengers twain depart,
They tarry not.
There, they are off on their way
Towards King Pabel.
They raise their voices and cry:
"Message of Keret the Nob[le],
Word of the [Be]loved, [Lad of]

KRT B

(i)

(All but the bottom, or some 35 lines, missing. They repeated Keret's message more or less verbatim. Then they related that Pabel said, in effect, "Return and say unto Keret:—All right, you may have her. But we shall miss her sorely. Everybody loves her because she is the embodiment of virtue.
The starved *she takes by the hand*,
The parched *she takes by the hand*.
They will follow her lamenting
Unto Keret, *to the camp*.
(As) the cow moans for her calf,
The *young of the flock* for their mothers,
Even so will Udum (*or*, the Udumians) wail."
Finally they told how:
The messengers twain depart,
They tarry not.
Behold, they do set (their) faces
Towards Keret the Noble.
They lift up their voices and cry: "Message of King Pabel:—All right you may have her. Etc.)

[The starved *she takes*] *by the hand*. (1)
The parched she takes by the hand.
They will follow her [*la*]*menting*
Unto Keret, *to the camp*.
(As) the cow moans for her calf,
The *young of the flock* for their mothers,
Even so will Udum[20] wail."—
And Keret the Noble replied:

(ii)

(At the top of the column, 10 or more lines are missing altogether, and lines 1-10 of the remainder are very defective. The missing lines may have related how Keret fulfilled the vow of KRT A 199 ff. and how he

[17] Perhaps better "the Tyrians," "the Sidonians." In either case, the shrine will have been situated not too far from Tyre and Sidon.
[18] Or, "two parts (i.e. thirds) of her . . . and the third. . . ."
[19] Apparently a mistake for "fifth."
[20] Perhaps better "the Udumians" (cf. n.17).

made new ones, referred to below, iii 23 ff. The defective lines tell that some of the leading gods are about to visit Keret and that Keret makes some obscure preparations.)

[The]n came the companies of the gods. (11)
And Puissant Baal spake up:
"[Now] come, O Kindly One [El Be]nign!
Wilt thou not bless [Keret] the Noble,
Not beatify the Beloved, Lad of El?"—
A cup [El] takes [in] (his) hand,
A flagon in (his) [right hand].
Indeed he blesses [*his servant*].
El blesses Keret,
[Beatifi]es the Beloved, Lad of El: (20)
"The wo[man thou ta]k'st, O Keret,
The woman thou tak'st into thy house,
The maid thou bring'st into thy court,
Shall bear seven sons unto thee;
Yea, eight she'll produce for thee.
She shall bear Yassib (*yṣb*) the Lad,[21]
Who shall draw the milk of A[she]rah,
Suck the breasts of the maiden Anath,
The two wet nurs[es *of the gods*].[21a]

(iii)

(About 10 lines missing entirely: they enumerated the sons Hurriya would bear after Yassib. The first line is almost entirely obliterated.)

[. . . Be greatly exalted], Keret, (2)
[In the midst of the *community*] of the land,
[In the number] of *the population of the realm.*
Also, she shall conceive and bear [dau]ghters to thee:
She shall bear the maiden T[. . .] t;
She shall bear the maid[en . . .];
She shall bear the mai[den . . .];
She shall bear the mai[den . . .]; (10)
She shall bear the mai[den(s?)[22] . . .];
She shall bear the mai[den(s?)[22] . . .]
Be greatly exalted, [Keret],
In the midst of the *community* of the land,
In the number of *the population of the realm.*
To the youngest of them will I give the birthright."—
The gods bless (and) proceed.
The gods proceed to their tents,
The family of El to their habitations.
And she conceives and bears son⟨s⟩ to him, (20)
And conceives and bears daughters to him.
Lo! in seven years,
The sons of Keret are even *as was stipulated in the vows*;
The daughters, also, of Hurriya are even so.
And Asherah remembers his vows,
Even Elath his de[dications],
And lifts up her voice and [cries]:
"Look, now. Doth Ker[et], then, [break],
Or [the king] alter vo[ws]?
So shall I break [. . .]."

(The missing fragment of tablet, which constituted the bottom of col. iii and the top of col. iv, contained a total of some 12-14 lines.)

(iv)

[His] fe[et upon the foostool he sets].[23]
Loudly unto (his wife he doth cry):
"Hearken, [O Lady Hurriya]!
Prep[are] the fattest of thy stall-fed ones;
Open a jar of wine.
Summon my seven[ty] peers,
My eighty barons:
The peers of Khubur the Great,
Khubur [the G]r[and]."
(10-13 broken and unintelligible)
Lady [Hu]rriya obeys. (14)
She prepares the fattest of her [stall-fed ones];
She opens a jar of wine.
Into her presence she causes his peers to come,
Into her presence his barons she causes to come:
The peers of Khubur the Great,
Khubur the Grand. (20)
Into the house of [Ke]ret they come,
Into the dwelling . . .
And into the *pavilion . . . they advance.*
Hand to the bowl she stretches forth,
Knife to the flesh she doth apply.
[And] Lady Hurriya [dec]lared:
"[To ea]t, to drink have I summoned you:
Your lord Keret [hath a sacrifice]."

(About 10 lines missing at the bottom of col. iv, and 5 or 6 at the top of col. v.)

(v)

[She prepares the fat]test of [her] sta[ll-fed ones;
She opens a ja]r of wi[ne].[24]
(3 lines too damaged for translation)
[Into] the dwelling . . . (6)
[. . . And into the *pavilion* . . . they advance.]
Hand to the bowl [she stretches] forth;
[Knife] to the flesh she doth apply.
[And] Lady Hurriya [declared]:
"[To ea]t, to drink have I summoned you. (10)
[. . .] . . . [. . .]."—
For Keret they do weep,
[Even as] spake the peers.
They weep [as one weeps] for the dead.
[. . .] and in (their) heart they . . .
(lines 16-17 unintelligible)
"At the setting of the sun Keret will come,
As the sun goes down our lord;" (20)

(Lines 21-29 too broken for coherent sense; then 10 lines missing.)

[21] i.e. the son who ministers personally to his father (cf. AQHT A i 26 ff., 43 ff., etc.); Mal. 3:17; also above, n.6.

[21a] Does the child thereby become a demi-god by adoption, or acquire godlike qualities?

[22] One of the girls was called Thitmanet, KRT C i-ii 29, 39, which may mean "the eighth"; so perhaps these two lines named two girls each.

[23] Always a sign of good spirits. But the restoration is uncertain.

[24] This time, perhaps, for the peeresses.

(vi)

Hearken . . .
That they might eat and drink.
And Lady Hurriya declared:
"To e[a]t, to dri[nk] have I summoned you:
Your sire[25] [Keret hath a sacrifice]."
Into Keret's presence they enter.
Like the speech of the peer[s] *is their speech.*
In a vision [. . .] . . . Keret.

(Some 40 lines missing. If KRT C is the *direct* continuation of KRT B, these 40 lines certainly indicated that Keret was ill, and that the opening lines of KRT C were what his son Elhau (*ilḫu*) was advised—perhaps by his own heart (cf. KRT C vi 25 ff.)—to say to his father. Also, the passing of the years which presumably elapsed between the 7th year of Keret's marriage (above, iii 20-25) and the apparent maturity of Elhau and Thitmanet as well as Yassib is more likely to have been indicated in this lacuna than in any of the preceding ones.)

KRT C

(i-ii)

([Pertaining to] "Keret.") "Like [a do]g thine aspect is changed,
Like a cur thy joyous countenance.
Wilt thou die, then, father, like the mortals,
Or thy joy change to mourning,
To a woman's dirge, O father, *my song*?
For thee, father, weeps the mount of Baal,
Zaphon, the sacred circuit.
The mighty circuit laments,
The circuit broad of span:
'Is, then, [Ke]ret a son of El,
An offspring of the Kindly One, and a holy being?' "—
Into the presence of his father he goes,
Weeping bitter tears,
Giving forth his voice in weeping:
"In thy life, our father, we rejoiced,
Exulted in thy not dying.
(But) like a dog thine aspect is changed,
Like a cur thy joyous countenance.
Wilt thou die then, father, like the mortals,
Or thy joy change to mourning,
To a woman's dirge, O father, my song?
How can it be said, 'A son of El is Keret,
An offspring of the Kindly One, and a holy being'?
Shall, then, a god die,
An offspring of the Kindly One not live?"
And Keret the Noble answers:
"My son, weep not for me,
Do thou not wail for me.
Waste not thine eye with flowing,
The brain in thy head with tears.
Call thy sister Thitmanet,
A maid *whose passion is strong.*
Let her weep and wail for me.
(sense of lines 31-37 obscure)
And say unto thy sister Thitmanet:
'*Our* Keret is making a sacrifice,
The king is preparing a banquet.
Take thy *drum* in thy hand,
Thy [*tam*]*bo*[*urine*] in thy right hand.
Go, *take thy stand by the songstresses of thy sire.*
Present [*thy petitions*] with thy *music*,
And *he will consent to* all.' "
Straightway the youth Elhau
His [l]ance in his hand doth take,
His [s]pear in his right hand,
And setteth out on a run.
[Ev]en as he arrives, it grows dark:
His sister kindles a lamp.
His lance *upon the threshold* he stands:
Its sheen lights up the gateway.
As soon as she sees her brother,
Her [loins] to the ground do break;[26]
[*Upon*] her brother['s *neck*] she weeps:
"Is, [then,] the king s[ick],
[*Or*] thy sire Keret [ill]?"
[And] the youth Elhau [replied]:
"The king is [not] sick,
Thy sire Keret [is not ill.
Keret] is making a [sac]rifice;
[The king is] preparing a banquet."

(ii)

(Of lines 63-78 only the beginnings are preserved, but it seems that Thitmanet asks a further question and Elhau's answer does not satisfy her; so that she tries to loosen his tongue with liquor,[27] and then)
She approaches [her] brother[28] [and asks]:
"Why dost thou *deceive me*, [my brother]?
How many moons hath he been s[ick],
How many hath Ker[et] been ill?"
And the youth [Elhau] replies:
"Three moons hath he been [sick],
Four hath Ke[ret] been ill."
(lines 86-96 defective and obscure)
She weeps bitt[er tears];
She gives forth her voice in weeping:
"In thy life, our [fa]ther, we rejoiced,
Exulted in thy not dying.
(But) like a dog thine aspect is changed,
Like a cur thy joyous countenance.
Wilt thou die, then, father, like the mortals,
Or thy joy change to weeping,
To a woman's dirge, O father, my song?
Shall, then, a god die,

[25] This time she uses a word which means both "master" and "father," so probably the third banquet is for her own children. The point of all these banquets remains obscure owing to the great gaps in the text.

[26] Because she guesses that he brings bad news; cf. Ezek. 21:11-12. Divine ladies who receive unexpected callers react in the same way; see pp. 132 and 137.

[27] A standard womanly wile; cf. AQHT C 214 ff.

[28] Or, "[his] sis[ter] approaches."

An offspring of the Kindly One not live?
For thee, father, weeps the mount of Baal,
Za[pho]n, the sacred circuit.
The mighty [circu]it laments,
The circuit broad of s[pan]:
'Is, then, Keret a son [of El],
An offspring of the Kindly One [and a holy being]?' "—
And so she comes in [to *her father's presence*],
She enters the *ch*[*amber* of Keret].
(Of lines 114-120 only the beginnings preserved; 2-3 more lines entirely abraded.)

(iii)

(about 30 lines missing at the top)
They pour *fat*[29] [. . .] *earth* and sky;
Turn to *the* . . . *of* the earth,
To the . . . of the *plowland*.
Unto the earth Baal rains,
And unto the field rains 'Aliyy.[30]
Sweet to the earth is Baa[l's] r[ai]n,
And to the field the rain of 'Aliyy.
'Tis sweet to the wheat in the *plowland*,
In the tilth to the emmer.
. . .
The plowmen raise their heads,
Upward the *growers* of corn.[31]
Spent is the bread corn [from] their *jars*,
Spent the wine from their skin-bottles,
Spent the oil from [their] *jugs*.
Keret's house[32] . . .
(about 14 lines missing)

(iv)

(about 18 lines missing at the top)
(abraded)
El hath heard thy . . .
(Thou) hast insight like El,
Art wise as Bull the Kindly One.
Call the carpenter-god Ilish,
Ili[sh] and his wives the carpenter-goddesses,
. . .
He calls the carpenter-god Ilish—
Ilish, carpenter of the house of Baal—
And his wives the carpenter-goddesses.
And the Kindly One, El Benign, spake:
"Hearken, O carpenter-god Il[ish]—
Ilish, carpenter of the house of Baal—
And thy wives the carpenter-goddesses.
Go up upon the top of *the structure*,
Upon *the platform* . . .
(Three lines defective and unintelligible, 25 more missing.)

(v)

(Of the first 7 lines, too little preserved for determining the sense.)
A second time [. . .],
A third time [. . . .
Then spake] the Kindly One, [El Benign:
"Who] among the gods can [remove the sickness],
Driving out the m[alady?"
None among the gods] answers him.
[A fourth time *El*] doth speak:
"Who among [the gods can remove] the illness,
Dr[iving out the malady]?"
None among the gods a[nswers him].
A fifth time he doth speak:
"[Who among the gods] can remove the illness,
Dr[iving out the malady]?"
None among the gods an[swers him].
A sixth, seventh time he speaks:
"[Who] among the gods can remove the illness,
Driving out the malady?"
None among the gods answers him.
Then spake the Kindly One, El Benign:
"Sit ye, my sons, upon your seat[s],
Upon yo[ur] thrones of princeship.
I will work magic
And will surely compass
The removal of illness,
Driving out the malady."
—With *clay* [*his hand*] he fills,
With goodly *clay* [*his fingers*].
He. . . .
(Lines 30-53 very defective, after that, about 8 lines missing entirely. The gist of it all can be seen to have been that El instructed a female being called Sha'taqat—to judge by the Aruru-Enkidu analogy [see p. 74], the one he had moulded out of the clay—to visit and cure Keret. The very end of these instructions constitutes the first sentence in col. vi.)

(vi)

". . .
[D]eath, do thou be broken;
Sha'taqat, do thou prevail."—
And so Sha'taqat departs;
Into Keret's house she goes.
Bḳt she penetrates and enters,
Nṣrt she enters to its innermost recess.
Towns she flies *over a hundred*,
Villages she flies *over a multitude*.
The *invalid* she . . . ,
The suffering one upon his[33] head,
And proceeds to wash him clean of sweat.

[29] If the reading is correct, the fat, or oil, is either literal, in which case we have a description of an act of sympathetic magic meant to induce precipitation; or figurative, in which case actual rain (cf. p. 136) is described.

[30] Evidently identical with Baal. Baal is the god of rain; cf. p. 153.

[31] All this certainly sounds more like the end of a drought (or dry season) than the beginning or middle of one, yet Keret is still ill. It is therefore anything but obvious that the drought is considered to be a consequence of the king's illness.

[32] Or, "daughter."

[33] Or, "her."

His desire for bread she opens,
His appetite for food.
Death, on the one hand, is broken;
Sha'taqat, on the other, has prevailed.—
Then Keret the Noble commands,
Raising his voice and crying:
"Hearken, O Lady Hurriya.
Prepare a lamb that I may eat,
A *yeanling* that I may dine."
Lady Hurriya hearkens.
She prepares a lamb and he eats,
A *yeanling* and he dines.
Behold a day and a second,
Keret returns to his former estate;
He sits upon the throne of kingship;
Upon the dais, the seat of authority.
Now, Yassib sits in the palace,
And his inward parts do instruct him:
"Go unto thy father, Yassib;
Go unto thy fa[ther] and speak,
Repeat unto Ke[ret the Noble]:
'List and incline [thine ear].
(one couplet unintelligible)
Thou hast let thy hand fall into mischief.[34]
Thou judgest not the cause of the widow,
Nor adjudicat'st the case of the wretched.
Having become a brother of the sickbed,
A companion of the bed of the suffering,
Descend from the kingship—I'll reign;
From thine authority—I'll sit enthroned.' "—
Yassib the Lad[35] departs,
Enters his father's presence,
And lifts up his voice and cries:
"Hearken, I pray thee, Keret the Noble!
List and incline thine ear.
(here again the unintelligible couplet)
Thou hast let thy hand fall into mischief.
Thou judgest not the cause of the widow,
Nor adjudicat'st the case of the wretched;
Driv'st not out them that prey on the poor;
Feed'st not the fatherless before thee,
The widow behind thy back,[36]
Having become a brother of the sickbed,
A companion of the bed of suffering,
Descend from the kingship—I'll reign;
From thine authority—I'll sit enthroned."—
And [K]eret the Noble makes answer:
"May Horon[37] break, O my son,
May Horon break thy head,
Ashtoreth name of Baal thy pate.
May'st thou fall into. . . ."
(last line unintelligible)
(colophon)
(Lengthwise of the left margin of col. vi is inscribed the following colophon:)

[34] Or possibly, "raised thy hand in mischief."
[35] cf. n.20.
[36] "Before thee . . . behind thy back" is probably a merism.
[37] God of the nether world.

Written by Elimelech; donated by ⟨Niqmadd, king of Ugarit⟩.[38]

The Tale of Aqhat

The rich epigraphic harvests of the French excavations of 1930 and 1931 at the site of ancient Ugarit included large portions of three tablets, and a possible fragment of a fourth, belonging to an epic about a youth whose name is spelled *a-q-h-t* and conventionally vocalized *Aqhat.* The text was at first called the Epic of Daniel, or Danel, for Aqhat's father; but on the one tablet of which the first line, containing the title of the composition to which the tablet belongs, is preserved, it reads "Pertaining to 'Aqhat,' " and closer study reveals that the text really tells about Daniel only what concerns Aqhat.

According to the order in which they were originally published, which is the descending order of magnitude, the three tablets are referred to as I D, II D, and III D (D = Daniel), or I Aqh(a)t, II Aqh(a)t, and III Aqh(a)t; but in accordance with their organic sequence they will be designated herein as AQHT A (= II D), AQHT B (= III D), and AQHT C (= I D). AQHT A originally counted 3 columns on each side, but the part containing col. iii on the obverse and col. iv on the reverse is missing entirely; AQHT B apparently contains parts of the first and last columns of a four-column tablet; while AQHT C is an almost complete tablet of four columns.

Part of the colophon of AQHT A is preserved, and enables us to date its copying in the same period as that of "The Legend of King Keret," namely about the second quarter of the fourteenth century B.C. (see below, n.26). The story borders on the mythical, and seems to have less of a historical core than that of Keret. There is a considerable probability that Aqhat's father, Daniel, is the ancient saint and sage of that name to whom the prophet Ezekiel refers in Ezek. 14:14, 20; 28:3.

First edition: Ch. Virolleaud, *La légende phénicienne de Danel* (*Mission de Ras-Shamra I*), 1936 (with copies and photographs of the original). Subsequent edition: C. H. Gordon, *Ugaritic Handbook* (*Analecta Orientalia,* xxv), 1947, II, pp. 179-184 (transliteration only). Special studies: S. Spiegel, Noah, Daniel, and Job, in *Louis Ginzberg Jubilee Volume,* 1945, English Section pp. 305-355 (copious bibliography of earlier Aqhat literature on pp. 310-11, n.1). J. Obermann, *How Daniel was Blessed with a Son* (*Publications of the American Oriental Society, Offprint Series* No. 20), 1946 (= *JAOS, Supplement* No. 6 [1946]). Y. Sukenik, The Composite Bow of the Canaanite Goddess Anath, *BASOR,* No. 107, pp. 11-15; A. Herdner, La légende cananéenne d'Aqhat d'après les travaux recents, *Syria,* 26 (1949), 1-16; C. H. Gordon, *Ugaritic Literature,* pp. 84-103.

AQHT A

(i)

(about 10 lines missing at top)
[. . . Straightway Daniel[1] the Raph]a[2]-man,
Forthwith [Ghazir[3] the Harnamiyy[4]-man],
Gives oblation to the gods to eat,

[38] cf. the colophons on pp. 135, 141.

[1] The name means "God judges." Judging the cause of the widow and the fatherless is Daniel's special concern; see v 4-8 etc. His wife's name, Danatiya (v 16, 22), is from the same root.

[2] This Rapha is perhaps identical with the aboriginal giant race of Canaan; II Sam. 21:16, 18, 20, 22; cf. Gen. 14:5; Deut. 2:11, 20; 3:11, 13 etc.

[3] As a common noun, *ġzr* means "boy."

[4] Perhaps connected with *Hrnm*, a Syrian locality named in an early Egyptian source; see p. 477 (Harnaim).

Gives oblation to drink to the holy ones.
A couch of sackcloth he mounts and lies,
A couch of [loincloth] and ⸢passes the night⸣.
Behold a day and a second,
Oblation to the gods gives Daniel,
Oblation to the gods to eat,
Oblation to drink to the holy ones.
A third, a fourth day,
Oblation to the gods gives Daniel,
Oblation to the gods to eat,
Oblation to drink to the holy ones.
A fifth, a sixth, a seventh day,
Oblation to the gods gives Daniel,
Oblation to the gods to eat,
Oblation to drink to the holy ones.
A *sackcloth couch* doth Daniel,
A *sackcloth couch* mount and lie,
A couch of loincloth and pass the night.
But lo, on the seventh day,
Baal approaches with his plea:[5]
"Unhappy is Daniel the Rapha-man,
A-sighing is Ghazir the Harnamiyy-man;
Who hath no son like his brethren,
Nor scion hath like his kindred.
Surely there's a son for him ⸢like⸣ his brethren's,
And a scion like unto his kindred's!
He gives oblation to the gods to eat,
Oblation to drink to the holy ones.
Wilt thou not bless him, O Bull El, my father,
Beatify him, O Creator of Creatures?
So shall there be a son in his house,[6]
A scion in the midst of his palace:
Who sets up the stelae of his ancestral spirits,
In the holy place the protectors of his clan;
Who frees his spirit from the earth,
From the dust guards his footsteps;
Who smothers the life-force of his detractor,
Drives off who attacks his abode;[7]
Who takes him by the hand when he's drunk,
Carries him when he's sated with wine;[8]
Consumes his funerary offering in Baal's house,
(Even) his *portion in* El's house;
Who plasters his roof when it leaks,
Washes his clothes when they're soiled."—
[*By the hand*] El takes his servant,
Blessing Daniel the Rapha-man,
Beatifying Ghazir the Harnamiyy-man:
"With life-breath shall be quickened Daniel the Rapha-man,
With spirit Ghazir the Harnamiyy-man.
[*With life-breath*] he is *invigorated*.[9]
Let him mount his bed [. . .].
In the kissing of his wife [she'll conceive],
In her embracing become pregnant.

[5] Compare Baal's role in KRT B ii 12 ff., p. 146.
[6] Literally "his son in a house."
[7] The translation of the preceding relative clauses is doubtful.
[8] cf. Isa. 51:17 ff. (note verse 18).
[9] This does not imply that Daniel's vigor was previously below average; cf. below, C 198-201.

[By conception] (and) pregnancy she'll bear
[A man-child to Daniel the Ra]pha-[man].
So shall there be a son [in his house,[10]
A scion] in the midst of his palace:
[Who sets up the stelae of his ances]tral spirits,
In the holy place [the protectors of his clan];
Who frees [his spirit from the e]arth,
[From the dust gu]ards his footsteps;
[Who smothers the life-force of his detractor],
Drives off who attacks [his abode;
Etc.]"

(After line 48 some 10 lines are missing, but the first 4 of these were obviously identical with lines 31-34 above. After that it was related that somebody was instructed to tell the good news to Daniel.)

(ii)

(Another 10 lines, approximately, missing here. The messenger obeyed instructions and addressed Daniel as follows: ". . . A son shall be borne thee like thy brethren's,
A scion like unto thy kindred's:
Who sets up the stelae of thine ancestral spirits,
In the holy place)
the pro[tectors of thy clan;
Who frees thy spirit from the earth], (1)
From the dust etc., etc." (2-8c)
(see above, i 25 ff.)
Daniel's face lights up, (8d)
While above his forehead shines.
He *parts his jaws* and laughs,
Places his foot on the footstool,
And lifts up his voice and cries:
Now will I sit and rest
And my soul be at ease in my breast.
For a son's born to me like my brethren's
A scion like unto my kindred's
Etc., etc.
Daniel goes to his house,
To his palace Daniel betakes him.
Into his house come skillful ones,[11]
Daughters of joyful noise, *swallows*.
Straightway Daniel the Rapha-man,
Forthwith Ghazir the Harnamiyy-man,
Prepares an ox for the skillful ones,
Gives food to the [ski]llful ones and gives drink
To the daughters of joy[ful noise], the *swallows*.
Behold a day and a second,
He give[s f]ood to the skillful ones and dr[in]k
To the daughters of joyful noise, the *swallows*;
A third, a fo[urth] day,
He gives food to the skillful ones and drink
To the daughters of joyful noise, the *swallows*;
A fifth, a sixth day,
He gives food to the skill[ful] ones and d[rink
To the d]aughters of joyful noise, the *swallows*.
Lo, on the seventh day,

[10] cf. n.6.
[11] "Artistes."

Away from his house go the skillful ones,
The daughters of joyful noise, the *swallows*.—
[. . .] the fairness of the bed [*of conception*],
The beauty of the bed of *childbirth*.
Daniel sits [and cou]nts her months.
A month follows a month;
A third, a fou[rth (a fifth?) month.
But in the fifth (sixth?)] month,
He goes [*to the shrine of* . . .].
(ten lines of col. ii and all of cols. iii-iv missing)

(v)

(Some 13 lines missing at the top. The preserved portion begins in the middle of a speech of the craftsman-god addressed to Daniel:)

(abraded except for traces)

". . .
I myself will bring the bow,
Even I will convey the *darts*."
And behold, on the seventh day—
Straightway Daniel the Rapha-man,
Forthwith Ghazir the Harnam[iyy]-man,
Is upright, sitting before the gate,
Beneath *a mighty tree* on the threshing floor,
Judging the cause of the widow,
Adjudicating the case of the fatherless.
Lifting up his eyes, he beholds:
From a thousand fields, ten thousand acres,[12]
The march of Kothar[13] he espies,
He espies the onrush of Khasis,[14]
See, he bringeth a bow;
Lo, he conveyeth *darts*.
Straightway Daniel the Rapha-man,
Forthwith Daniel the Harnamiyy-man,
Loudly unto his wife doth call:
"Hearken, Lady Danatiya,[15]
Prepare a lamb from the flock
For the desire of Ko[th]ar wa-Khasis,[16]
For the appetite of Hayyin[17] of the Handicrafts.
Give food, give drink to the godhead;
Serve, honor him,
The Lord of Hikpat-El,[18] all of it.
Lady Danatiya obeys,
She prepares a lamb from the flock
For the desire of Kothar wa-Khasis,
For the appetite of Hayyin of the Handicrafts.
Afterwards, Kothar wa-Khasis comes.
The bow he delivers into Daniel's hand;
The *darts* he places upon his knees.
Straightway Lady Danatiya
Gives food, gives drink to the godhead;
She serves, honors him,
The Lord of Hikpat-El, all of it.

[12] i.e. in the distance.
[13] "Skillful," the commonest name of the craftsman-god.
[14] "Clever," another of his names.
[15] See n.1.
[16] "Skillful and Clever"; see nn.13 and 14.
[17] "Deft," still another of his monickers.
[18] *ḥkpt il*, the name of the craftsman-god's "estate."

Kothar departs for[19] his tent,
Hayyin departs for[19] his tabernacle.
Straightway Daniel the Rapha-man,
Forthwith Ghazir the Harnamiyy-man,
The bow doth [. . .] . . . , upon Aqhat he doth . . . [. . .]:
"*The choicest* of thy game, O my son,
The choicest of thy game . . . [. . .],
The game of thy . . . [. . .]."[20]
(some 12 lines missing)

(vi)

(Some 19 lines missing. Then come 15 broken lines which tell about a feast and about the warrior-goddess Anath coveting Aqhat's bow: Aqhat will have been entertaining her tête-à-tête.)

[She lifts up her voice and] cries:
"Hearken, I pray thee, [Aqhat the Youth!
A]sk for silver, and I'll give it thee;
[For gold, and I'll be]stow't on thee;
But give thou thy bow [to me;
Let] Yabamat-Liimmim[21] *take* thy *darts*."
But Aqhat the Youth answers:
"*I vow yew trees* of Lebanon,
I vow sinews from wild oxen;
I vow horns from mountain goats,
Tendons from the hocks of a bull;
I vow from a *cane-forest* reeds:
Give (these) to Kothar wa-Khasis.
He'll make a bow for thee,
Darts for Yabamat-Liimmim."[22]
Then quoth the Maiden Anath:
"Ask for life, O Aqhat the Youth.
Ask for life and I'll give it thee,
For deathlessness, and I'll bestow't on thee.
I'll make thee count years with Baal,
With the sons of El shalt thou count months.[23]
And Baal when he gives life gives a feast,
Gives a feast to the life-given and bids him drink;
Sings and chants over him,
Sweetly serenad[es] him:
So give I life to Aqhat the Youth."
But Aqhat the Youth answers:
"Fib not to me, O Maiden;
For to a Youth thy fibbing is *loathsome*.
Further life—how can mortal attain it?
How can mortal attain life enduring?
Glaze will be poured [on] my head,
Plaster upon my pate;[24]
And I'll die as everyone dies,
I too shall assuredly die.
Moreover, this will I say:

[19] Or "from," if Daniel's tent is meant rather than Kothar's.
[20] Perhaps Daniel here impresses upon his son the duty of offering some of his game to the gods.
[21] An alternative designation of the Maiden Anath; meaning doubtful.
[22] Yew-wood, horn, sinew, and tendon go into the making of a composite bow; reed into that of arrows.
[23] i.e. shalt be immortal like them.
[24] My hair will turn white.

My bow is [*a weapon for*] warriors.
　Shall now females [*with it*] to the chase?"
—[Loud]ly Anath doth laugh,
　While forging [a plot] in her heart:
"Give heed *to* me, Aqhat the Youth,
　Give heed to me for thine own good.
[. . .] I'll meet thee in the path of arrogance,
　[Encounter thee] in the path of presumption,
Hurl thee down at [my feet *and trample*] thee,
　My darling great big he-man!"—
[She *stamps* with her fe]et and *traverses* the earth.
There, [she is off on her w]ay
　Towards El of the Source of the Floods
　[In the midst of the headwaters] of the Two Oceans.
She penetrates El's field [and enters
　The pavili]on of King Father Shunem.[25]
[At El's feet she] bows and falls down,
　Prostr[ates herself, doing him rever]ence.
She denounces Aqhat the Youth,
　[Damns the child of Dani]el the Rapha-man.
Quoth [the Maiden Anath,
　Lifting up] her [voice] and crying:

(In 54-55 only the word "Aqhat" can be made out. A further 10 lines or so are missing. In them Anath may well have told a cock-and-bull story about the unaccommodating youth. In any case, El declared he could, or would, do nothing against Aqhat.)

(colophon on edge of tablet)

[Dictated by Attani]-puruleni.[26]

AQHT B

(The preserved fragment of this four-column tablet bears the top of col. i on the obverse and the bottom of col. iv on the reverse, the surface of the obverse being largely abraded.)

(i)

[. . . But the Maiden Anath] [replied]:
"[. . .], O El!
　[. . . rejoice not.
Re]joice not [. . . ,
　Exult] not [. . . .
With] the *might* [of my] *lon*[*g hand*,
　I'll verily smash] thy [pa]te,
Make [thy gray hair] flow [with blood,
　The gray hair of] thy [beard] with gore.
And [call] Aqhat and let him save thee,
　The son [of Daniel] and let him deliver thee,
　From the hand of the Maiden [Anath]!"—
Answered the Kindly One El Be[nign]:
"I ween'd, daughter mine, thou wast *gentle*,
　And goddesses fr[ee from] *contumely*.
On, then, *perverse* daughter;
　[Thou'lt ta]ke whatsoever thou wilt.
Thou'lt compass [whatever thou] list:
　Who hinders thee will be crushed."—
[The Maid]en Anath [rejoices].
There, she is off [on her way
　Towards A]qhat the Youth,
　O'er thousand fi[elds, ten thousand a]cres.
Now laughs the Maiden [Anath,
　And lifts up] her voice and cries:
"Oh, hearken bu[t, Aqhat the Youth],
　Thou'rt my brother, and I [*thy sister*]. . . ."

(Lines 25-35 too damaged to yield anything but the probable general sense that Anath offers to show Aqhat a particularly good place to hunt in, namely, the environs of the home-town of Yatpan [*ytpn*], on whom see further on. Probably in the additional 20 lines of this column and in the whole of cols. ii-iii, which are missing altogether, the twain betook them thither; Aqhat had good luck, and Anath left him for a while.)

(iv)

(some 20 lines missing, 4 lines fragmentary)

The Maiden Anath [depar]ts.
[There, she is off on her way]
　Towards Yatpan [*the Drunken*] *Soldier*.
[She lifts up her voice] and cries:

(The sense of her imperfectly preserved utterance has not yet been determined, except that it shows that Yatpan dwelt in "the city of Abelim, Abelim the city of Prince Yarikh [= Moon].")

Quoth Yatpan [*the Drunken Soldier*]:
　"Hearken, O Maiden Anath.
Wouldst thou slay him[27] fo[r his bow],
　Slay him for his *darts*,
　Him ma[ke live again]?
The darling Youth has set meat and [*drink*].
　He is left in the fields and . . . [. . .]."
Quoth the Maiden Anath:
　"Give heed, Yatp,[28] and [I'll tell] thee.
I'll make thee like a vulture in my girdle,
　Like a swift flier in my pouch.
[As] Aqhat [sits] to eat,
　The son of Daniel to [dine],
[Over him] vultures will soar,
　[A flock of sw]ift fliers will *coast*.
'Mong the vultures will I be soaring;
　Above Aqhat will I pose thee.
Strike him twice on the crown,
　Thrice above the ear;
Pour out his blood like *sap*,
　Like *juice*[29] to his knees.
Let his breath escape like wind,
　His soul like vapor,
　Like smoke from his nostrils {from nostrils}.[30]
⌜His vigor⌝ I will revive."

[25] One of El's names; vocalization uncertain.

[26] Known from the colophon at the end of the Baal epic to have been chief of priests in the reign of Niqmadd, king of Ugarit, second quarter of the 14th century B.C.

[27] Aqhat.

[28] Hypocoristicon of, or mistake for, Yaṭpan.

[29] *Šḥṭ*, perhaps connected with Heb. *šḥṭ* "to press out (liquid)."

[30] Apparently dittography.

—She takes Yatpan *the Drunken Soldier*,
Makes him like a vulture in her girdle,
Like a swift flier in her pouch.
As Aqhat sits to e[at],
The son of Daniel to dine,
Over him vulture[s] soar,
A flock of swift flier[s] coasts.
[Among] the vultures soars Anath;
Above [Aqhat] she poses him.
He smites him twice [on the crown],
Thrice above the ear;
Pou[rs out] his blood [like] *sap*,
Like *ju*[*ice* to his knees.
His] breath escapes like wind,
His soul [like vapor],
Like smoke [from his nostrils].
Anath, [seeing] his vigor extinguished—
[The vigor of] Aqhat—doth weep.
"*Woe*! [Would] I could heal [thy corse]!
'Twas but for [thy bow I slew thee,
'Twas but for] thy *darts*.
But thou, would thou didst l[ive.
...] and perished ... [...]."

AQHT C

(i)

(In the first 13 lines, defective in various degrees, it is only clear that Anath figures there. She is apparently speaking; it is not known to whom.)

"...
I smote him *but* for his bow,
I smote him for his *darts*.
So his bow has been given to me.
But *through his death* ...,
The [*fr*]*uits* of summer *are withered*,
The ear [in] its husk."—
Straightway Daniel the Rapha-man,
Forthwith Ghaz*ir* [the Harna]miyy-[man],
*Is up*right, [sitting before the g]at[e,
Un]der [a mighty tree on the threshing floor,
Judging] the cause [of the widow,
Adjudicating] the case [of the fatherless.
...]

(lines 25-28 almost entirely missing)

[Lift]ing her eyes she[31] beholds:
[...] on the threshing floors *dries up*;
[...] *droops*;
Blasted are the buds [...].
O'er her father's house vultures are soaring
A flock of swift fliers is coasting.
Paghat weeps in her heart,
Cries in her inward parts.
She rends the garment of Daniel the Rapha-man,
The vest⟨ment⟩ of Ghazir the Harnamiyy-man.[32]

[31] Daniel's daughter Paghat.

[32] Because she realizes the blight upon the land must be due to the murder of some innocent person. She has the gift of divination; see further on.

Straightway Daniel the Rapha-man,
... s a cloud in the heat of the *season*;
... s a cloud raining upon the figs,
Dew distilling upon the grapes.[33]
"Seven years shall Baal fail,
Eight the Rider of the Clouds.
No dew,
No rain;
No welling-up of the deep,[34]
No sweetness of Baal's voice.[35]
For rent
Is the garment of Daniel the Rapha-man,
The vestment of Ghazir [the Harnamiyy-man]."—
Loudly to h[is] daughter he doth cry:

(ii)

"Hearken, Paghat who observes the wat[er],
Who studies the dew from the drip,
Who knows the course of the stars.[36]
Saddle a donkey, harness a jackass.
Attach my trappings of silver,
My golden housing."—
She obeys, Paghat who observes the water,
Who studies the ⌜dew [from the drip]⌝,
Who knows the course of the stars. ⌜ ... ⌝
See, she saddles a donkey;
See, she harnesses a ja⌜ck⌝ass.
See, she lifts up her father,
Places him on the donkey's back,
On the comely back of the jackass.—
Yadinel[37] turns to the *vegetable-patch*;
He sees a *stalk* in the *vegetable-patch*;
Seeing a *stalk* in the *seedbeds*,
H[e embraces] the *stalk* and kisses it:
"Ah, if it may be, *stalk*,
Let the *stalk* grow in the *vegetable-patch*;
Let it grow in the *beds* of the *plants*.
May the hand of Aqhat the Youth gather thee,
Deposit thee in the granary."—
Yadin⌜e⌝⟨l⟩ turns to the *grainfields*;
In the *grainfi*[*el*]*ds* he sees a corn-ear;
Seeing an ear in the unwatered land,
He em[braces] the ear and kisses it:
"Ah, if it may be, co[rn-ear],
Let the corn-ear grow in the unwatered land;
Let it grow in the [*beds*] of the *plants*.
May the hand of Aqhat the You[th] gather thee,
Deposit thee in the granary."—
Scarce hath the word left his mouth,
His speech left his lips,
When he lifts up his eyes and they behold:[38]

(Lines 77-89 rather mutilated and obscure. The gist

[33] In Syria rain sometimes falls in September.

[34] Through springs; cf. Gen. 7:11b. What Daniel here either predicts or wishes, David wishes for Gilboa, the scene of Saul and Jonathan's death in battle; see II Sam. 1:21, where "nor welling up of the deep" (*wšrʿ thwmwt*) is to be read for "nor fields of offering."

[35] Baal is the god of rain and thunder.

[36] Apparently forms of weather-wisdom bordering on divination.

[37] Apparently variant of "Daniel."

[38] Or "as she (Paghat) lifts up her eyes, she beholds."

of them is that somebody finds out what has happened to Aqhat; either because Paghat sees two supernatural beings act it out in dumb show, or because two attendants of Daniel hear the tale from the dying boy.)

[. . .] they come.
They lift up [their] voice, [and cry]:
"Hearken, O Daniel the [Rapha]-man!
Aqhat the Youth is dead.
The Maiden Anath [has caused
His breath to escape] like [wind],
His soul like vapor."
[Daniel's legs] tremble.
Abo[ve, his face sweats;
Behind, he is broken] in the loins.
[The joints of his loins are bent],
Weakened [those of his back.[39]
He lifts up his voice] and cri[es:
"*Cursed be*] the slayer [of my son].
(lines 100-104 missing)
Lift[ing up his eyes he beholds:
. . . vultures . . . .

(iii)

He lifts up his voice] and cries:
"The vultures' wings may Baal bre⟨ak⟩,
May Ba[a]l br[eak the pinions of them].
Let them fall down at my feet.
I'll spl[it their bellies and] gaze.
An there be fat,
An the[re be] bone,
I'll w⌜ee⌝p and inter it,
Lay't in the hollows of the ear⌜th⌝-ghosts."
Scarce hath the word left his mouth,
[His] speech left his lips,
The vultures' wings Baal doth break,
Baal doth break the pinions of them.
They do fall down at his feet,
He splits their bellies a[nd gazes]:
No fat is there,
No bone.
He lifts up his voice and cr*ies*:
"The vultures' wings may Baa*l* mend,
May ⟨Baal⟩ mend the pinions of them.
Vultures, flutter and fly."—
Lifting his eyes, he s[ees];
Beholds Hargab, the *vul*tures' father.
He lifts up his voice and cries:
"The *wi*ngs of Har[ga]b may Baal bre⟨ak⟩,
May Baal b[re]ak the pinions of [him].
And let him fall down at my feet.
I'll split [his] b[elly] and gaze.
An there be fat,
An there be [bone],
I'll weep and inter it,
Lay't in the *ho*[llo]*ws* of [the earth-ghosts]."
[Scarce hath the word left his mouth],
His speech [left] his [li]ps,
Hargab's wings Baal doth [br]eak,
Baal doth break the pinions of him.
He doth fall down at his feet.
So he splits his belly and gazes:
No fat is there,
No bone.
He lifts up [his] voice *and* cries:
"The wings of Hargab may Baal [mend,
May Ba]al mend the pinions of him.
Hargab, may'st flutter and fly."—
Lifting his eyes he sees,
Beholds Samal (*ṣml*), the vultures' mother.
He lifts up his voice and cries:
"The wings of Samal may Baal break,
May Baal break the [pi]nions of her.
Let her fall down at my feet.
I'll split her belly and gaze.
An there be fat,
An there be bone,
I'll weep and inter it,
Lay't in the hollows of the earth-ghosts."
Scarce hath the word [left] his mouth,
His speech left his lips,
Samal's wings [Ba]a[l doth break],
Baal doth break the pinions of her.
She doth fa[ll down at] his feet.
So he splits her belly and gazes.
There is fat,
There is bone.
Taking them for Aqhat he ⟨we⟩eps,
Weeps and inters him.
He inters him in . . . , in . . . ,
Then lifts up his voice and cries:
"The wings of the vultures may Baal break,
May Baal break the pinions of them,
An they fly over the grave of my son,
Rousing him from his sleep."—
Qiru-mayim[40] the king doth *curse*:
"Woe to thee, O Qiru-mayim,
O[n] which rests the blood-guilt of Aqhat the Youth!
. . . the dwellers of the house of El;
Now, *tomorrow*, and for evermore,
From now unto all generations!"
Again he waves the staff of his hand,
And comes to Marurat-taghullal-banir.[41]
He lifts up his voice and cries:
"Woe to thee, Marurat-taghullal-banir,
On which rests the blood-guilt of Aqhat the Youth!
Thy root grow not in the earth;
In uprooter's hand droop thy head—
Now, *tomorrow*, and for evermore,
From now unto all generations!"
Again he waves the staff of his hand,

[39] He is overcome with dismay. cf. p. 147, n.26.

[40] Perhaps "Water-Sources." In any case a locality near the scene of the murder.

[41] Perhaps "Blessed One Harnessed with a Yoke." See preceding note.

(iv)

And comes to the city of Abelim,
Abelim the city of Prince Yarikh.[42]
He lifts up his voice and cries:
"Woe to thee, city of Abelim,
On which rests the blood-guilt of Aqhat the Youth!
May Baal make thee blind
From now for evermore,
From now unto all generations!"
Again he waves the staff of his hand.
Daniel goes to his house,
To his palace Daniel betakes him.
Into his palace come weeping-women,
Wailing-women into his court *Pẓġm ġr*.[43]
He weeps for Aqhat the Youth,
Cries for the child, does Daniel the Rapha-man.
From days to months, from months to years,
Until seven years,
He weeps for Aqhat the Youth,
Cr[ie]s for the child, does Daniel the [Rapha]-man.
But after seven years,
[Daniel] the Rapha-[man] speaks up,
Ghazir [the Harnamiyy-m]an makes answer.
[He] lifts up his voice and cries:
"De[part], weeping-women, from my pala[ce];
Wailing-women, from my court *Pẓġm ġr*."—
He ta[kes] a sacrifice for the gods,
Offers up a *clan-offering* to heaven,
The *clan-offering* of Harnamiyy to the stars.
(three and one-half lines mutilated)
Quoth Paghat who observes the *flowing* water:
"Father has sacrificed to the gods,
Has offered up a *clan-offering* to heaven,
The *clan-offering* of Harnamiyy to the stars.
Do thou bless me, so I'll go blessed;
Beatify me, so I'll go beatified.
I'll slay the slayer of my brother,
[Destroy] the [de]stroyer of my [si]bling."—
[Dani]e[l] the Ra[p]ha-man makes answer:
"With life-breath shall be quickened [Paghat],
She who observes the water,
Who studies the dew from the drip,
Who knows the courses of the stars.
With life-breath she is *invigorated*.
She'll slay the slayer [of her brother],
Destroy the destroyer of [her] sibling."
. . . in the sea she bat[hes],
And stains herself red with murex,
. . .
She emerges, dons a youth's raiment,
Puts a *ḳ[nife]* in her sheath,
A sword she puts in her scabbard,
And o'er all dons woman's garb.
At the rising of Gods' Torch Shapsh,[44]
Paghat . . .
At the set[ting] of Gods' Torch Shapsh,
Paghat arriv[es] at the tents.
Word [is b]rought to Yat[pan]:
"*Our hired woman* has entered thy fields,
[. . .] has entered the *t⟨e⟩nts*."
And Yatpan *the Drunḳen Soldier* makes answer:
"Take her and let her give me wine to drink.
[Let her place] the cup in my hand,
The goblet in my right hand."
Paghat [t]akes and gives him drink:
Pl[aces the cup] in his hand,
The goblet in his right hand.
Then spake Yat[pa]n *the Drunḳen* [*Sold*]*ier*:
(one and one-half lines partly defective and obscure)
"The hand that slew [Aqha]t the Youth
Can slay thousands of foes."
(Two and one-half lines obscure, except that Paghat's "heart is like a serpent's," i.e. filled with fury.)
A second time she gives the mixture to him to drink,
Gives the [mi]xt[ure] to drink
(Direction to the reciter, along the edge to the left of 172-186:)
Here one proceeds to tell about the daughter.

(The story, continuing on one or more missing tablets, no doubt went on to relate that [a] Paghat killed Yatpan while he lay unconscious in the arms of Bacchus, and [b] between El's pity and Anath's remorse some modus was found for restoring Aqhat to his father, perhaps only for half—the fertile half—of the year. The familiar Adonis-Tammuz theme.)

[42] The actual home of the murderer; see B i end and B iv.

[43] It has been suggested that this is the proper name of Daniel's court.

[44] The sun-goddess.

II. Legal Texts

Collections of Laws from Mesopotamia and Asia Minor

Lipit-Ishtar Lawcode

(Translator: S. N. Kramer)

Like the Hammurabi Code, that of Lipit-Ishtar consists of three main sections: a Prologue; the legal text proper consisting of a large number of laws introduced by a Sumerian complex which is roughly the equivalent of the English word "if"; an Epilogue. The Prologue begins with a statement by King Lipit-Ishtar, the fifth ruler of the Dynasty of Isin, that after the leading Sumero-Babylonian deities Anu and Enlil had given the goddess Ninisinna[1] a favorable reign in her city Isin, and after they had called him, Lipit-Ishtar, "to the princeship of the land" in order "to bring well-being to the Sumerians and the Akkadians," he established justice in Sumer and Akkad. He then cites some of his achievements in regard to the welfare of his subjects: he freed "the sons and daughters of Sumer and Akkad" from slaveship which had been imposed upon them; he re-established equitable family practices. The end of the Prologue unfortunately is destroyed; so, too, is the beginning of the legal text proper.

As for the legal body of the Lipit-Ishtar Code, the available text permits the restoration, wholly or in part, of some thirty-eight laws; practically all belong to the second half of the code, the first half being almost entirely destroyed. The subject matter treated in these laws is as follows: hiring of boats (laws 4 and 5); real estate, particularly orchards (laws 7-11); slaves and perhaps servants (laws 12-17); defaulting of taxes (law 18 and probably 19); inheritance and marriage (laws 20-33); rented oxen (34-37). Immediately following the last of the thirty-eight laws extant wholly or in part, follows the Epilogue; because of the numerous breaks in the text, the latter is only partially intelligible. It begins with a reiteration by Lipit-Ishtar that he established justice in the land, and that he brought well-being to its people. He then states that he had set up "this stela," that is the stela on which the original code was inscribed,[2] and proceeds to bless those who will not damage it in any way, and to curse those who will.

The text of the code is reconstructed from seven clay tablets and fragments. Four of these are "excerpt tablets," that is, they are one- or two-column tablets which did not contain the entire code, but only small parts of it excerpted for scribal purposes. The remaining three pieces are all parts of a large, probably twenty-column tablet, which in its original state had contained the entire lawcode, including Prologue and Epilogue. Six of the seven tablets and fragments were excavated at Nippur and are now in the University Museum; one, of unknown provenience, is in the Louvre. All seven pieces date from the Early Post-Sumerian period, that is, they were actually inscribed sometime in the first half of the second millennium B.C. As for the first compilation of the code, it must have taken place sometime during the eleven-year reign of Lipit-Ishtar, who ruled probably during the first half of the nineteenth century B.C.; it thus antedates the Hammurabi Code by more than a century and a half. A scientific edition of the available text of the code, including copies of the unpublished material in the University Museum, was published by Francis R. Steele in *AJA*, LII (1948), pp. 425-450; there, too, the relevant earlier studies are cited;[3] the present translation follows the Steele publication throughout.

[1] Ninisinna, "Queen of Isin," is the tutelary deity of Isin, just as Marduk was that of Babylon.

[2] The contents of our "code" tablet may be presumed to be identical with those of the original stela on which a scene similar to that on the Hammurabi stela may have been sculptured.

Prologue[4]

[When] the great [Anu, the father of the go]ds, (and) [En]lil, [the king of all the lan]ds, [the lord who determines ordinan]ces, had . . . d to [Nini]sinna, [the daughter of A]nu the . . . *for* her . . . (*and*) the rejoicing . . . for her bright [forehead]; when they had giv[en h]er the kingship of Sumer (and) Akkad (and) a favorable reign in her (city) Isin, the . . . established by Anu; when Anu (and) Enlil had called Lipit-Ishtar—Lipit-Ishtar, the wise shepherd whose name had been pronounced by Nunamnir[5]—to the princeship of the land in order to establish justice in the land, to banish complaints, to turn back enmity and rebellion by the force of arms, (and) to bring well-being to the Sumerians and Akkadians, then I, Lipit-Ishtar, the humble shepherd of Nippur, the stalwart farmer of Ur, who abandons not Eridu, the suitable lord of Erech, [king] of I[sin], [kin]g of Sum[er and Akkad], who am f[it] for the heart of Inanna, [estab]lished [jus]tice in [Su]mer and Akkad in accordance with the word of Enlil. Verily, in those [days] I *procured* . . . the [fre]edom of the [so]ns and daughters of [Nippur], the [so]ns and daughters of Ur, the sons and daughters of [I]sin, the [so]ns and daughters of [Sum]er (and) Akkad *upon whom* . . . slaveship . . . *had been imposed*. Verily, in accordance with . . . , I made the father *support* his children (and) I made the children [*support* their] father; I made the father *sta*[*nd by* hi]s children (and) I made the children *stand by* their father; in the father's house (and) [in the brother's] house I. . . . Verily, I, Lipit-Ishtar, the son of Enlil,[6] *brought* seventy into the father's house (and) the brother's house; *into* the bachelor's house I *brought* . . . *for ten months* . . . 10 . . . the wife of a man, . . . the child of a man. . . .[7]

The Laws

1: . . . which had been set up. . . .[8]

[3] cf. also Steele's preliminary announcement in *AJA*, LI (1947), 158-164.

[4] For a brief comparative survey of the contents of the Lipit-Ishtar and Hammurabi codes, cf. Steele, *AJA*, LII (1948), pp. 446-450.

[5] Nunamnir is another name for the god Enlil; Lipit-Ishtar is frequently called "son of Enlil" in the relevant hymnal literature.

[6] cf. preceding note.

[7] A break of more than two columns of text follows; at some point in this break the prologue ended and the laws began.

[8] Remainder of the column destroyed.

2: . . . the property of the father's house from its. . . .[9]

3: . . . the son of the state official, the son of the palace official, the son of the supervisor. . . .[10]

4: . . . a boat . . . a boat he shall. . . .

5: I[f] a man hired a boat (and) *set it on a . . . journey for him. . . .*[11]

6: . . . the gift . . . he shall. . . .

7: If he gave his orchard to a gardener to raise . . . (and) the gardener . . . to the owner of the garden. . . .[12]

8: If a man gave bare ground to (another) man to set out an orchard (and the latter) did not complete setting out that bare ground as an orchard, he shall give to the man who set out the orchard the bare ground which he neglected, as part of his share.

9: If a man entered the orchard of (another) man (and) was seized there for stealing, he shall pay ten shekels of silver.

10: If a man cut down a tree in the garden of (another) man, he shall pay one-half mina of silver.

11: If adjacent to the house of a man the bare ground of (another) man has been neglected and the owner of the house has said to the owner of the bare ground, "Because your ground has been neglected someone may break into my house; strengthen your house,"[13] (and) this agreement has been confirmed by him, the owner of the bare ground shall restore to the owner of the house any of his property that is lost.

12: If a slave-girl or slave of a man has fled into the heart of the city (and) *it has been confirmed* that he (or she) dwelt in the house of (another) man for one month, he shall give slave for slave.

13: If he has no slave, he shall pay fifteen shekels of silver.

14: If a man's slave has *compensated* his slaveship to his master (and) *it is confirmed (that he has compensated)* his master twofold, that slave shall be freed.

15: If a *miqtum*[14] is a grant of the king, he shall not be taken away.

16: If a *miqtum* went to a man *of his own free will*, that man shall not *hold* him; he (the *miqtum*) may go where he desires.

17: If a man *without authorization bound* (another) man *to a matter* to which he (the latter) had no knowledge, that man is not *affirmed*; he (the first man) shall bear the penalty in regard *to the matter to which he has bound him.*[15]

18: If the master of an estate or the mistress of an estate has defaulted on the tax of the estate (and) a stranger has borne it, for three years he (the owner) may not be evicted. (Afterwards) the man who bore the tax of the estate shall possess that estate and the (former) owner of the estate shall not raise any claim.

19: If the master of an estate. . . .[16]

20: If a man from the heir(s) seized. . . .[17]

21: . . . the house of the father . . . he [married], the gift of the house of *her* father which was presented to *her* as *her* heir he shall take.

22: If the father (is) living, his daughter whether she be an *entu*,[18] a *naṭītu*,[18] or a hierodule, shall dwell *in* his house like an heir.

23: If the daughter *in* the house of (her) living father. . . .[19]

24: [I]f the secon[d wife] whom [he had] married bore him [chil]dren, the dowry which she brought from her father's house belongs to her children, (but) the children of (his) *first* wife and the children of (his) second wife shall divide equally the property of their father.

25: If a man married a wife (and) she bore him children and those children are living, and a slave also bore children for her master (but) the father granted freedom to the slave and her children, the children of the slave shall not divide the estate with the children of their (former) master.

26: [I]f his *first* [wife di]ed (and) [af]ter her (death) he takes his [slave] as a wife, the [children] of [his *first*] wife [are his he]irs; the children which [the slave] bore for her master shall be like . . . , his house they shall. . . .

27: If a man's wife has not borne him children (but) a harlot (from) the public square has borne him children, he shall provide grain, oil, and clothing for that harlot; the children which the harlot has borne him shall be his heirs, and as long as his wife lives the harlot shall not live in the house with his wife.

28: If a man has turned his face away from his *first* wife . . . (but) she has not gone out of the [house], his wife which he married *as his favorite* is a second wife; he shall continue to support his *first* wife.

29: If a son-in-law has entered the house of his (prospective) father-in-law (and) he made his betrothal (but) afterwards they made him go out (of the house) and gave his wife to his companion, they shall present to him the betrothal-gifts which he brought (and) that wife may not marry his companion.

30: If a young married man married a harlot (from) the public square (and) the judges have *ordered* him not to *visit* her, (but) afterwards he *divorced* his wife, money. . . .

31: . . . he has given him, after their father's death the heirs shall divide the estate of their father (but) the inheritance of the estate they shall not divide; they shall not "cook their father's word in water."[20]

[9] Remainder of the column destroyed.

[10] The remainder of this column and two additional columns are destroyed.

[11] Remainder of column and beginning of following column destroyed.

[12] Almost the entire remainder of the column destroyed.

[13] That is, presumably, the broken-down house in the neglected grounds.

[14] The meaning of the term *miqtum* (it is a Semitic, not a Sumerian, word) is unknown.

[15] The rendering of this law is doubtful in many parts and its meaning is quite uncertain.

[16] About ten lines destroyed.

[17] About 34 lines destroyed.

[18] Class of priestesses.

[19] About 22 lines destroyed.

[20] "Cook someone's word in water" seems to be an idiomatic expression for "disobey."

32: If a father while living has [set aside] a betrothal-gift for his eldest son[21] (and) [in] the presence of the father who was still alive he (the son) [married] a wife, after the father('s death) the heir. . . .[22]

33: If it has been *confirmed* that the . . . had not divided the estate, he shall pay ten shekels of silver.

34: If a man rented an ox (and) injured the flesh at the nose ring, he shall pay one third of (its) price.

35: If a man rented an ox (and) damaged its eye, he shall pay one half of (its) price.

36: If a man rented an ox (and) broke its horn, he shall pay one fourth of (its) price.

37: If a man rented an ox (and) damaged its tail, he shall pay one fourth of (its) price.

38: . . . [he shall] pay.

Epilogue

Verily in accordance with the tr[ue word] of Utu, I caused [Su]mer and Akkad to hold to true justice. Verily in accordance with the pronouncement of Enlil, I, Lipit-Ishtar, the son of Enlil,[23] *abolished* enmity and rebellion; made weeping, lamentations, outcries . . . taboo; caused righteousness and truth to exist; brought well-being to the Sumerians and the Akkadians. . . .[24]

Verily when I had established the wealth of Sumer and Akkad, I erected this stela. May he who will not commit any evil deed *with regard to it*, who will not damage my handiwork, who will [not] erase its inscription, who will not write his own name upon it—be presented with life and breath of long days; may he rise high in the Ekur;[25] may Enlil's bright forehead *look down upon him.* (On the other hand) he who will commit some evil deed *with regard to it*, who will damage my handiwork, who will enter the storeroom (and) *change* its pedestal, who will erase its inscription, who will write his own [name] upon it (or) who, because of this [curse], will [substi]tute someone else for himself—[that man, whe]ther he be a . . . , [whether he] be a . . .[26] may *he* take away from him . . . (and) bring to *him* . . . in his . . . whoever, may Ashnan and Sumugan,[27] the lords[28] of abundance, take away from him[29] . . . his . . . may he *abolish*. . . . May Utu, the judge of heaven and earth . . . take away . . . his . . . its foundation . . . as . . . may he be counted; let not the foundation of his land be firm; its king, whoever he may be, may Ninurta,[30] the mighty hero, the son of Enlil. . . .[31]

21 "Eldest son" is expressed here by the words "son, big brother."

22 About 17 lines destroyed.

23 cf. n.5.

24 About 19 lines missing.

25 Enlil's main temple in Nippur.

26 About 7 lines destroyed.

27 Ashnan is the goddess of grain and Sumugan is the god of the "plain."

28 In more exact language "the lords" should read "the lady and the lord."

29 About 22 lines destroyed.

30 Ninurta, the son of Enlil, is the god of the South Wind; for some of the heroic feats ascribed to him, cf. *SM*, 79-82.

31 Probably only a few lines missing.

The Laws of Eshnunna

(Translator: Albrecht Goetze)

Texts: Iraq Museum 51059 and 52614 excavated at Tell Abu Harmal[1] near Baghdad by the Iraq Directorate of Antiquities in Pre-Hammurabi layers.

Literature: Taha Baqir, *Sumer*, IV (1948) 52 f.; A. Goetze, *ibid.*, 54, 63-102, Plates I-IV; Taha Baqir, *ibid.* 153-173; A. Pohl, *Orientalia* NS, 18 (1949), 124-128; Plates X-XX (republication of Goetze's transliteration and of Goetze's copies); M. David, *Een nieuw-ontdekte Babylonische wet uit de tijd vóór Hammurabi* (1949); M. San Nicolò, *Orientalia* NS, 18 (1949), 258-262; A. Goetze, *JAOS*, 69 (1949), 115-120; J. Klima, *Archiv Orientální*, 16 (1949), 326-333; J. Miles and O. Gurney, *Archiv Orientální*, 17/2 (1949), 174-188; W. von Soden, *Archiv Orientální*, 17/2 (1949), 359-373.

Preamble: [. . . in the month of . . .] on the 21st day, [. . .] Bilalama[2] [. . .] kingship of Eshnunna [. . . st]atue into the house of his father [. . .] . . . Supur-Shamash [. . .] . . . Tigris river, in that individual year when he brought the mighty weapon there.

1: 1 kor of barley is (priced) at 1 shekel of silver; 3 *qa* of "best oil" are (priced) at 1 shekel of silver; 1 seah (and) 2 *qa* of sesame oil are (priced) at 1 shekel of silver; 1 seah (and) 5 *qa* of lard are (priced) at 1 shekel of silver; 4 seah of "river oil" are (priced) at 1 shekel of silver; 6 minas of wool are (priced) at 1 shekel of silver; 2 kor of . . .[3] are (priced) at 1 shekel of silver; 1 kor . . . is (priced) at 1 shekel of silver; 3 minas of copper are (priced) at 1 shekel of silver; 2 minas of refined copper are (priced) at 1 shekel of silver.

2: 1 *qa* of sesame oil *ša nisḫātim*—its (value in) barley is 3 seah; 1 *qa* of lard *ša nisḫātim*—its (value in) barley is 2 seah and 5 *qa*; 1 *qa* of "river oil" *ša nisḫātim*—its (value in) barley is 8 *qa*.

3: The hire for a wagon together with its oxen and its driver is 1 *massiktum* (and) 4 seah of barley. If it is (paid in) silver, the hire is one third of a shekel. He shall drive it the whole day.

4: The hire for a boat is 2 *qa* per kor (of capacity), and 4(?) *qa* is the hire for the boatman. He shall drive it the whole day.

5: If the boatman is negligent and causes the sinking of the boat, he shall pay in full for everything the sinking of which he caused.

6: If a man . . .[4] takes possession of a boat (which is) not his, he shall pay 10 shekels of silver.

7: The wages of a harvester are 2 seah of barley; if they are (paid in) silver, his wages are 12 grain.

8: The wages of winnowers are 1 seah of barley.

1 Abu Ḫarmal formed part of the kingdom of Eshnunna—the Diyala region east of Baghdad—which flourished between the downfall of the Third Dynasty of Ur (about 2000 B.C.) and the creation of Hammurabi's empire. Eshnunna was one of the numerous Amurrite-controlled states of the period. The city of Eshnunna itself is located at Tell Asmar which was excavated by the Oriental Institute of the University of Chicago.

2 One of the earliest kings of Eshnunna shortly after the downfall of Ibbi-Sin of Ur.

3 The sign encountered here looks like the ideogram for "salt."

4 Possibly "without that an emergency exists" or the like.

9: Should a man pay 1 shekel of silver to a hired man for harvesting—if he (the hired man) does not place himself at his disposal and does not complete for him the harvest work everywhere, he [shall p]ay 10 shekels of silver. He shall receive 1 seah (and) 5 *qa* (of barley) as wages and leave; he shall moreover return his rations of [barley], oil (and) cloth.[4a]

10: The hire for a donkey is 1 seah of barley, and the wages for its driver are 1 seah of barley. He shall drive it the whole day.

11: The wages of a hired man are 1 shekel of silver; his provender is 1 grain of silver. He shall work for one month.

12: A man who is caught in the field of a *muškēnum*[5] in the *crop* during daytime, shall pay 10 shekels of silver. He who is caught in the *crop* [at ni]ght, shall die, he shall not get away alive.

13: A man who is caught in the house of a *muškēnum*, in the house, during daytime, shall pay 10 shekels of silver. He who is caught in the house at night, shall die, he shall not get away alive.

14: The fee of a . . .[6]—should he bring 5 shekels of silver the fee is 1 shekel of silver; should he bring 10 shekels of silver the fee is 2 shekels of silver.

15: The *tamkarrum*[7] and the *sabītum*[8] shall not receive silver, barley, wool (or) sesame oil from a slave or a slave-girl *as an investment.*

16: To a coparcener or a slave a mortgage cannot be furnished.

17: Should the son of a man bring bride-money to the house of (his) father-in-law—, if one of the two deceases, the money shall revert to its owner.

18: If he takes her (the girl) and she enters his house, but *afterward* the young woman should decease, he (the husband) shall get refunded not (merely) that which he brought (to his father-in-law), he shall (also) receive its accrued interest; he shall add one sixth (of a shekel) and 6 grain per shekel, 1 *massiktum* (and) 4 seah per kor as interest.

19: The man who gives (a loan) in terms of his retake shall make (the debtor) pay on the threshing floor.

20: If a man gives a loan . . . expressing the value of the silver in barley, he shall at harvest time receive the barley and its interest, 1 *massiktum* (and) 4(?) seah per kor.

21: If a man gives silver (as a loan) *at face value*, he shall receive the silver and its interest, one sixth (of a shekel) and [6 grain] per shekel.

22: If a man has no claim against a(nother) man, but (nevertheless) distrains on the (other) man's slave-girl, the owner of the slave-girl shall [decla]re under oath: "Thou hast no claim against me" and he shall pay (him) silver in full compensation for the slave-girl.

23: If a man has no claim against a(nother) man, but (nevertheless) distrains on the (other) man's slave-girl, detains the distrainee in his house and causes (her) death, he shall give two slave-girls to the owner of the slave-girl as a replacement.

24: If he has no claim against him, but (nevertheless) distrains on the wife of a *muškēnum* (or) the child of a *muškēnum* and causes (their) death, it is a capital offence. The distrainer who distrained shall die.

25: If a man calls at the house of (his) father-in-law, and his father-in-law *accepts* him *in servitude*, but (nevertheless) gives his daughter to [another man], the father of the girl shall refund the bride-money which he received twofold.

26: If a man gives bride-money for a(nother) man's daughter, but another man seizes her forcibly without asking the permission of her father and her mother and deprives her of her virginity, it is a capital offence and he shall die.

27: If a man takes a(nother) man's daughter without asking the permission of her father and her mother and concludes no formal marriage contract with her father and her mother, even though she may live in his house for a year, she is not a housewife.

28: *On the other hand*, if he concludes a formal contract with her father and her mother and cohabits with her, she is a housewife. When she is caught with a(nother) man, she shall die, she shall not get away alive.[9]

29: If a man has been made prisoner during a raid or an invasion or (if) he has been carried off forcibly and [stayed in] a foreign [count]ry for a [long] time, (and if) another man has taken his wife and she has born him a son—when he returns, he shall [get] his wife back.

30: If a man hates his town and his lord and becomes a fugitive, (and if) another man takes his wife—when he returns, he shall have no right to claim his wife.

31: If a man deprives another man's slave-girl of her virginity, he shall pay two-thirds of a mina of silver; the slave-girl remains the property of her owner.

32: If a man gives his son (away) for having (him) nursed and brought up, but does not give (the nurse) rations of barley, oil (and) wool for three years, he shall pay (her) 10 minas (of silver) for bringing up his son and they shall return his son.

33: If a slave-girl by subterfuge gives her child to a(nother) man's daughter, (if) its lord sees it when it has become older, he may seize it and they shall return it (to him).

34: If a slave-girl of the palace gives her son or her daughter to a *muškēnum* for bringing (him/her) up, the palace may take back the son or the daughter whom she gave.

35: Also the adoptant of the child of a slave-girl of the palace shall recompense the palace with its equivalent.

[4a] The last two sentences are rather uncertain.

[5] The *muškēnum* is a member of a social class which at Eshnunna seems to be closely connected with the palace or the temple.

[6] The undeciphered word must denote some kind of "money-lender" or "merchant."

[7] The official "finance officer" who has a state monopoly on certain commercial transactions.

[8] The woman to whom trade in liquor is entrusted.

[9] The last sentence is contained only in IM 51059.

36: If a man gives property of his as a deposit to . . . and if the property he gives disappears without that the house was burglarized, the *sippu*[10] broken down (or) the window forced, he (the depositary) will replace his (the depositor's) property.

37: If the man's (the depositary's) house either collapses or is burglarized and together with the (property of the) deposit(or) which he gave him loss on the part of the owner of the house is incurred, the owner of the house shall swear him an oath in the gate of Tishpak[11] (saying): "Together with your property my property was lost; I have done nothing *improper* or fraudulent." If he swears him (such an oath), he shall have no claim against him.

38: If one of several brothers wants to sell his share (in a property common to them) and his brother wants to buy it, he shall pay. . . .[12]

39: If a man is hard up and sells his house, the owner of the house shall (be entitled to) redeem (it) whenever the purchaser (re)sells it.

40: If a man buys a slave, a slave-girl, an ox or any other valuable good but cannot (legally) establish the seller, he is a thief.

41: If an *ubārum*, a *napṭarum* or a *mudūm*[13] wants to sell his beer, the *sabītum*[14] shall sell the beer for him at the current price.

42: If a man bites the nose of a(nother) man and severs it, he shall pay 1 mina of silver. (For) an eye (he shall pay) 1 mina of silver; (for) a tooth ½ mina; (for) an ear ½ mina; (for) a slap in the face 10 shekels of silver.

43: If a man severs a(nother) man's finger, he shall pay two-thirds of a mina of silver.

44: If a man throws a(nother) man to the floor in an *altercation* and breaks his *hand*, he shall pay ½ mina of silver.

45: If he breaks his foot, he shall pay ½ mina of silver.

46: If a man assaults a(nother) man and breaks his . . . , he shall pay two-thirds of a mina of silver.

47: If a man *hits* a(nother) man *accidentally*, he shall pay 10 shekels of silver.

48: And in *addition*, (in cases involving penalties) from two-thirds of a mina to 1 mina, they shall formally try the man. A capital offence comes before the king.

49: If a man is caught with a stolen slave (or) a stolen slave-girl, he shall surrender slave by slave (and) slave-girl by slave-girl.

50: If the governor, the river commissioner (or) an(other) official whoever it may be seizes a lost slave, a lost slave-girl, a lost ox, a lost donkey belonging to the palace or a *muškēnum*[15] and does not surrender it to Eshnunna but keeps it in his house, even though he may let pass only seven days, the palace shall prosecute him for theft.

51: A slave or a slave-girl of Eshnunna which is marked with a *kannum*, a *maškanum* or an *abbuttum*[16] shall not leave the gate of Eshnunna without its owner's permission.

52: A slave or a slave-girl which has entered the gate of Eshnunna in the custody of a (foreign) envoy shall be marked with a *kannum*, a *maškanum* or an *abbuttum* but remains in the custody of its master.

53: If an ox gores an(other) ox and causes (its) death, both ox owners shall divide (among themselves) the price of the live ox and also the equivalent of the dead ox.

54: If an ox is known to gore habitually and the authorities have brought the fact to the knowledge of its owner, but he does not have his ox *dehorned*, it gores a man and causes (his) death, then the owner of the ox shall pay two-thirds of a mina of silver.

55: If it gores a slave and causes (his) death, he shall pay 15 shekels of silver.

56: If a dog is mad and the authorities have brought the fact to the knowledge of its owner, (if nevertheless) he does not keep it in, it bites a man and causes (his) death, then the owner of the dog shall pay two-thirds of a mina of silver.

57: If it bites a slave and causes (its) death, he shall pay 15 shekels of silver.

58: If a wall is threatening to fall and the authorities have brought the fact to the knowledge of its owner, (if nevertheless) he does not strengthen his wall, the wall collapses and causes a free man's death, then it is a capital offence; jurisdiction of the king.

59: If a man divorces his wife after having made her bear children and takes [ano]ther wife, he shall be driven from his house and from whatever he owns and may go after (the woman) whom *he loves*.

(60 and 61 badly mutilated and therefore incomprehensible)

[10] A part of the house at or near the door.

[11] The main god of Eshnunna.

[12] This expression, not yet fully understood, seems to imply a preferential treatment.

[13] Social classes who seem to be entitled to a ration of beer.

[14] See n.8.

[15] See n.5.

[16] Markings that can easily be removed.

The Code of Hammurabi

(Translator: Theophile J. Meek)

Hammurabi (also spelled Hammurapi) was the sixth of eleven kings in the Old Babylonian (Amorite) Dynasty. He ruled for 43 years, from 1728 to 1686 according to the most recent calculations.[1] The date-formula for his second year, "The year he enacted the law of the land," indicates that he promulgated his famous lawcode at the very beginning of his reign, but the copy which we have could not have been written so early because the Prologue refers to events much later than this. Our copy was written on a diorite stela, topped by a bas-relief showing Hammurabi in the act of receiving the commission to write the lawbook from the god of justice, the sun-god Shamash. The stela

[1] For the most recent discussion, fully documented, see R. P. R. de Vaux, *RB*, LIII (1946), 328 ff.; also P. van der Meer, *The Ancient Chronology of Western Asia and Egypt* (1947). F. Cornelius, *Klio*, XXXV (1942), 1 ff.; B. L. van der Waerden, *JEOL*, X (1946), 414 ff.

was carried off to the old Elamite capital, Susa (the Shushan of Esther and Daniel), by some Elamite raider (apparently Shutruk-Nahhunte, about 1207-1171 B.C.) as a trophy of war. It was discovered there by French archaeologists in the winter of 1901-1902 and was carried off by them to the Louvre in Paris as a trophy of archaeology. All the laws from col. xvi 77 to the end of the obverse (from the end of §65 to the beginning of §100) were chiseled off by the Elamites, but these have been preserved in large part on other copies of the Code. The Prologue and Epilogue are written in semi-poetic style, marked by parallelism but not by regular metrical structure.

The original stela was published by V. Scheil, *Mémoires de la délégation en Perse*, IV (1902), 11 ff. The best edition of the Code in all its known copies is A. Deimel, *Codex Ḫammurabi: transscriptio et translatio Latina* (1930). The English edition by R. F. Harper, *The Code of Hammurabi* (1904), includes only the stela and its translation is naturally antiquated and was little improved in the revision by D. D. Luckenbill and Edward Chiera in J. M. P. Smith, *The Origin and History of Hebrew Law* (1931). Both are far inferior to the German translation by Wilhelm Eilers, *AO*, XXXI (1931), Heft 3/4. The latest French translation, by Pierre Chruveillier, *Commentaire du code d'Hammourabi* (1938), is shockingly antiquated for such a recent work. The present translation, like that of other legal texts in this volume, is much influenced by two articles: A. Goetze, The t-Form of the Old Babylonian Verb, *JAOS*, LVI (1936), 297-334, and T. J. Meek, The Asyndeton Clause in the Code of Hammurabi, *JNES*, V (1946), 64-72.

THE PROLOGUE

(i)

When lofty Anum,[2] king of the Anunnaki,[3]
(and) Enlil,[4] lord of heaven and earth,
the determiner of the destinies of the land,
determined for Marduk,[5] the first-born of Enki,[6]
the Enlil functions over all mankind,
made him great among the Igigi,[3]
called Babylon by its exalted name,
made it supreme in the world,
established for him in its midst an enduring kingship,
whose foundations are as firm as heaven and earth—
at that time Anum and Enlil named me
to promote the welfare of the people,[7]
me, Hammurabi, the devout, god-fearing prince,
to cause justice to prevail in the land,
to destroy the wicked and the evil,
that the strong might not oppress the weak,
to rise like the sun over the black-headed (people),[8]
and to light up the land.
Hammurabi, the shepherd, called by Enlil, am I;
the one who makes affluence and plenty abound;
who provides in abundance all sorts of things for Nippur-Duranki;[9]
the devout patron of Ekur;
the efficient king, who restored Eridu[6] to its place;

(ii)

who purified the cult of Eabzu;
the one who strides through the four quarters of the world;
who makes the name of Babylon great;
who rejoices the heart of Marduk, his lord;
the one who throughout his lifetime stands responsible for Esagila;
the descendant of royalty, whom Sin[10] begat;
the one who made Ur prosper;
the pious, suppliant one, who brought abundance to Egishshirgal;
the wise king, obedient to mighty Shamash;[11]
the one who relaid the foundations of Sippar;
who decked with green the *chapels* of Aya;
the designer of the temple of Ebabbar, which is like a heavenly dwelling;
the warrior, the protector of Larsa;[12]
the one who rebuilt Ebabbar for Shamash, his helper;
the lord, who revived Uruk;[13]
who supplied water in abundance to its people;
who raised aloft the head of Eanna;
who made riches abound for Anum and Inanna;
the shelter of the land, who collected the scattered people of Isin;[14]
who makes the temple of Egalmah abound with affluence;
the monarch of kings, full brother of Zababa;[15]
the refounder of the settlement of Kish,
who has surrounded Emete-ursag with splendor;
the one who has made secure the great shrines of Inanna;

[2] The sky-god, the leader of the pantheon, worshiped especially in the temple of Eanna in Uruk along with the goddess Inanna.

[3] In this inscription the Anunnaki are the lesser gods attendant upon Anum and the Igigi are the lesser gods attendant on Enlil.

[4] The storm-god, the chief executive of the pantheon, worshiped especially in the temple of Ekur in Nippur in central Babylonia, modern Nuffar.

[5] The son of Enki and consort of Sarpanit; the god of Babylon and in Hammurabi's time the god of the Babylonian Empire with the functions of Enlil delegated to him; worshiped especially in the temple of Esagila in Babylon.

[6] Lord of the earth and the mass of life-giving waters within it, issuing in streams and fountains; the father of Marduk; worshiped especially in the temple of Eabzu in Eridu, in southern Babylonia, modern Abu Shahrein.

[7] Lit., "to make good the flesh of the people."

[8] The late-Sumerian expression for men in general.

[9] Duranki "bond of heaven and earth," was a time-honored Sumerian name of Nippur, the cult-center of Enlil, whose temple was Ekur.

[10] The moon-god, the son of Enlil, father of Shamash, and consort of Ningal; worshiped especially in the temple of Egishshirgal in Ur in southern Babylonia, modern Muqayyar.

[11] The sun-god and the god of justice, the consort of Aya, worshiped especially in the temple of Ebabbar in Sippar in northern Babylonia, modern Abu Habba.

[12] Another cult-center of Shamash, situated in southern Babylonia, modern Senkereh, with a temple also called Ebabbar. The city was captured by Hammurabi in the 30th year of his reign and its powerful dynasty brought to an end with the dethronement of its king, Rim-Sin. This event is set down as the formula for Hammurabi's 31st year, but the formula for the year always comes from an event in the preceding year; hence our year-numbers will be one less than those generally given.

[13] An ancient and important city in southern Babylonia, the biblical Erech (Gen. 10:10), modern Warka, conquered by Hammurabi in the 6th year of his reign. It was the cult-center of Anum and Inanna, with its temple Eanna.

[14] A city south of Nippur in southern Babylonia, conquered by Rim-Sin of Larsa in his 29th year, and then by Hammurabi in the 6th year of his reign. It was the cult-center of Ninkarrak, with its temple Egalmah.

[15] A form of Ninurta, worshiped especially in the temple of Emete-ursag in Kish, northeast of Babylon, modern Tell el-Oheimir.

the patron of the temple of Hursag-kalama;[16]
the *terror* of the enemy;

(iii)

the one whom Irra,[17] his comrade, caused to attain his desire;
who made Kutha preeminent;
who expanded every kind of facility for Meslam;
the fiery wild-bull who gores the foe;
the beloved of Tutu;[18] the one who brings joy to Borsippa;
the devout one, never a hindrance to Ezida;
god among kings, acquainted with wisdom;
the one who extended the cultivated land belonging to Dilbat;[19]
who stores up grain for mighty Urash;
the lord, adorned with scepter and crown;
the one whom the sage, Mama,[20] brought to perfection;
who laid out the plans for Kesh;
who makes sumptuous the splendid banquets for Nintu;
the solicitous, the perfect one,
who fixes the pastures and watering places for Lagash and Girsu,[21]
who provides bountiful sacrifices for Eninnu;
the one who seizes the foe; the favorite of Telitum;[22]
who fulfils the oracles of Hallab;[23]
the one who makes the heart of Ishtar[24] glad;
the illustrious prince, whose prayers[25] Adad[26] recognizes;
who pacifies the heart of Adad, the warrior, in Bet-karkar;
who has reestablished the appointments in Eudgalgal;
the king, who granted life to Adab;[27]
the director of the temple of Emah;
the chief of kings, a fighter without peer;

(iv)

the one who granted life to Mashkan-shabrim;[28]
who supplies drink in abundance to Meslam;
the wise one, the administrator;
the one who plumbed the depths of wisdom;
the rescuer of the people of Malka[29] from trouble;
the founder of dwelling places for them in abundance for the sake of Enki and Damgalnuna;
the enlarger of his kingdom;
the one who prescribed splendid sacrifices for all time;
the first of kings;
the subduer of the settlements along the Euphrates through the strength of Dagan,[30] his creator;
the one who spared the people of Mera and Tutul;[31]
the devout prince, who brightens up the face of Inanna;
the provider of splendid banquets for Ninazu;[32]
the savior of his people from distress,
who establishes in security their portion in the midst of Babylon;
the shepherd of the people, whose deeds are pleasing to Ishtar;
who installed Ishtar in Eulmash in the midst of Akkad[33] square;
who makes law prevail; who guides the people aright;
who returned to Ashur[34] its kindly protecting genius;
who overpowered the *agitators*;
the king, who made the name of Inanna glorious in Nineveh[35] in Emishmish;
the devout one, who prays fervently to the great gods;
the descendant of Sumu-la-el;[36]
the powerful son and heir[37] of Sin-muballit,

(v)

the ancient seed of royalty, the powerful king, the sun of Babylon,
who causes light to go forth over the lands of Sumer and Akkad;[38]
the king who has made the four quarters of the world subservient;
the favorite of Inanna am I.
When Marduk commissioned me to guide the people aright,
to direct the land,
I established law and justice in the language of the land,
thereby promoting the welfare of the people.
At that time (I decreed):

[16] The temple of Inanna in Kish, where she was the consort of Zababa.

[17] The god of pestilence and war, often identified with Nergal. His temple, Meslam, was in Kutha in northern Babylonia, modern Tell Ibrahim.

[18] Strictly a title of Marduk, but here applied to his son Nabum, the god of writing. His cult-center was Borsippa, near Babylon, with its temple Ezida.

[19] A city not far from Borsippa, the cult-center of the god Urash.

[20] A goddess worshiped in Kesh, near Lagash, in central Babylonia; also known as Nintu.

[21] Lagash, modern Telloh, and Girsu were twin cities in central Babylonia. Ningirsu was the city god and his temple was Eninnu.

[22] A title of Inanna.

[23] A city in Babylonia as yet unidentified; a cult-center of Ishtar.

[24] The Semitic name of Inanna.

[25] Lit., "the lifting up of whose hands."

[26] The weather-god, whose temple was Eudgalgal in Bet-karkar, a city as yet unidentified.

[27] A city on the Euphrates in central Babylonia, modern Bismaya. Its deity was Mah and her temple was Emah.

[28] A city not far from Adab, modern Dshidr.

[29] A city apparently on the middle Euphrates, conquered by Hammurabi in the 9th year of his reign and punished for a revolt in his 34th year. It was the seat of Enki and his consort Damgalnuna, also known as Damkina, the mother of Marduk.

[30] The Dagon of the Bible; a west Semitic grain-god, early imported into Mesopotamia and worshiped chiefly along the middle Euphrates.

[31] Two cities on the middle Euphrates. Mera may possibly be Mari, modern Tell Hariri, conquered by Hammurabi in his 32nd year.

[32] The god of medicine, worshiped particularly at Eshnunna in his temple Esikil.

[33] An ancient city of northern Babylonia, founded by Sargon the Great as his capital; a seat of Ishtar, with her temple Eulmash.

[34] The name of Assyria, of its ancient capital, modern Qal'at Shergat, on the upper Tigris, and of its national god. It is manifestly the city that is intended here.

[35] The later capital of Assyria on the upper Tigris, modern Kouyunjik, an important seat of Inanna, with her temple Emishmish.

[36] The second king of the Old Babylonian Dynasty.

[37] "Son and heir," a single word in Babylonian.

[38] Sumer was the ancient name of southern Babylonia and Akkad of northern Babylonia, the two together constituting a common name of the country as a whole.

The Laws

1: If a seignior[39] accused a(nother) seignior and brought a charge of murder against him, but has not proved it, his accuser shall be put to death.[40]

2: If a seignior brought a charge of sorcery against a(nother) seignior, but has not proved it, the one against whom the charge of sorcery was brought, upon going to the river,[41] shall throw himself into the river, and if the river has then overpowered him, his accuser shall take over his estate; if the river has shown that seignior to be innocent and he has accordingly come forth safe, the one who brought the charge of sorcery against him shall be put to death, while the one who threw himself into the river shall take over the estate of his accuser.

3: If a seignior came forward with false testimony in a case, and has not proved the word which he spoke, if that case was a case involving life, that seignior shall be put to death.

4: If he came forward with (false) testimony concerning grain or money, he shall bear the penalty of that case.

5: If a judge gave a judgment, rendered a decision, deposited a sealed document, but later has altered his judgment, they shall prove that that judge altered the judgment which he gave and he shall pay twelvefold the claim which holds in that case; furthermore, they shall expel him in the assembly from his seat of judgment and he shall never again sit[42] with the judges in a case.

6: If a seignior stole the property of church or state,[43] that seignior shall be put to death; also the one who received the stolen goods from his hand shall be put to death.

7: If a seignior has purchased or he received for safekeeping either silver or gold or a male slave or a female slave or an ox or a sheep or an ass or any sort of thing from the hand of a seignior's son or a seignior's slave without witnesses and contracts, since that seignior is a thief, he shall be put to death.

8: If a seignior stole either an ox or a sheep or an ass or a pig or a boat, if it belonged to the church (or) if it belonged to the state, he shall make thirtyfold restitution; if it belonged to a private citizen,[44] he shall make good tenfold. If the thief does not have sufficient to make restitution, he shall be put to death.[45]

9: When a seignior, (some of) whose property was lost, has found his lost property in the possession of a(nother) seignior, if the seignior in whose possession the lost (property) was found has declared, "A seller sold (it) to me; I made the purchase in the presence of witnesses," and the owner of the lost (property) in turn has declared, "I will produce witnesses attesting to my lost (property)"; the purchaser having then produced the seller who made the sale to him and the witnesses in whose presence he made the purchase, and the owner of the lost (property) having also produced the witnesses attesting to his lost (property), the judges shall consider their evidence, and the witnesses in whose presence the purchase was made, along with the witnesses attesting to the lost (property), shall declare what they know in the presence of god, and since the seller was the thief, he shall be put to death, while the owner of the lost (property) shall take his lost (property), with the purchaser obtaining from the estate of the seller the money that he paid out.[46]

10: If the (professed) purchaser has not produced the seller who made the sale to him and the witnesses in whose presence he made the purchase, but the owner of the lost property has produced witnesses attesting to his lost property, since the (professed) purchaser was the thief, he shall be put to death, while the owner of the lost property shall take his lost property.

11: If the (professed) owner of the lost property has not produced witnesses attesting to his lost property, since he was a cheat and started a false report, he shall be put to death.

12: If the seller has gone to (his) fate, the purchaser shall take from the estate of the seller fivefold the claim for that case.

13: If the witnesses of that seignior were not at hand, the judge shall set a time-limit of six months for him, and if he did not produce his witnesses within six months, since that seignior was a cheat, he shall bear the penalty of that case.

14: If a seignior has stolen the young son of a(nother) seignior, he shall be put to death.[47]

15: If a seignior has helped either a male slave of the state or a female slave of the state or a male slave of a

[39] The word *awēlum*, used here, is literally "man," but in the legal literature it seems to be used in at least three senses: (1) sometimes to indicate a man of the higher class, a noble; (2) sometimes a free man of any class, high or low; and (3) occasionally a man of any class, from king to slave (see, e.g. CH, reverse xxvi, 39-44). For the last I use the inclusive word "man," but for the first two, since it is seldom clear which of the two is intended in a given context, I follow the ambiguity of the original and use the rather general term "seignior," which I employ as the term is employed in Italian and Spanish, to indicate any free man of standing, and not in the strict feudal sense, although the ancient Near East did have something approximating the feudal system, and that is another reason for using "seignior."

[40] With this law and the three following cf. Deut. 5:20; 19:16 ff.; Exod. 23:1-3.

[41] The word for "river" throughout this section has the determinative of deity, indicating that the river (the Euphrates) as judge in the case was regarded as god.

[42] Lit., "he shall not return and sit."

[43] Lit., "the property of god or palace."

[44] The word is *muškēnum*, which in the Code ordinarily indicates a man of the middle class, a commoner, but here and in §§15, 16, 175, and 176 it manifestly refers to a private citizen as distinct from the church and state.

[45] The laws on theft in the Code (§§6-13, 22, 23, 25, 259, 260, 265) do not agree among themselves, indicating that we have laws of different dates in the Code. According to the earliest laws (§§7, 9, 10, 22, 25) theft was to be punished by death; later (§6) the death penalty was confined to the theft of church or state property; later still severalfold restitution (§§8, 265) or a fine (§§259, 260) came to be substituted for the death penalty; see T. J. Meek, *Hebrew Origins* (1936), pp. 61 f. For the Hebrew laws on theft see Exod. 20:15 (=Deut. 5:19); 22:1-4; Lev. 19:11, 13.

[46] Lit., "he weighed out." In the time of Hammurabi coinage had of course not yet been invented and the money (usually silver, as here) was weighed out in bars.

[47] cf. Exod. 21:16; Deut. 24:7.

private citizen or a female slave of a private citizen to escape through the city-gate, he shall be put to death.

16: If a seignior has harbored in his house either a fugitive male or female slave belonging to the state or to a private citizen and has not brought him forth at the summons of the police, that householder shall be put to death.

17: If a seignior caught a fugitive male or female slave in the open and has taken him to his owner, the owner of the slave shall pay him two shekels[48] of silver.

18: If that slave will not name his owner, he shall take him to the palace in order that his record may be investigated, and they shall return him to his owner.

19: If he has kept that slave in his house (and) later the slave has been found in his possession, that seignior shall be put to death.

20: If the slave has escaped from the hand of his captor, that seignior shall (so) affirm by god to the owner of the slave and he shall then go free.

21: If a seignior made a breach in a house, they shall put him to death in front of that breach and wall him in.[49]

22: If a seignior committed robbery and has been caught, that seignior shall be put to death.

23: If the robber has not been caught, the robbed seignior shall set forth the particulars regarding his lost property in the presence of god, and the city and governor, in whose territory and district the robbery was committed, shall make good to him his lost property.

24: If it was a life (that was lost), the city and governor shall pay one mina[50] of silver to his people.[51]

25: If fire broke out in a seignior's house and a seignior, who went to extinguish (it), cast his eye on the goods of the owner of the house and has appropriated the goods of the owner of the house, that seignior shall be thrown into that fire.

26: If either a private soldier or a commissary,[52] whose despatch on a campaign of the king was ordered, did not go or he hired a substitute[53] and has sent (him) in his place, that soldier or commissary shall be put to death, while the one who was hired by him shall take over his estate.

27: In the case of either a private soldier or a commissary who was carried off while in the armed service of the king, if after his (disappearance) they gave his field and orchard to another and he has looked after his feudal obligations—if he has returned and reached his city, they shall restore his field and orchard to him and he shall himself look after his feudal obligations.

28: In the case of either a private soldier or a commissary, who was carried off while in the armed service of the king, if his son is able to look after the feudal obligations, the field and orchard shall be given to him and he shall look after the feudal obligations of his father.

29: If his son is so young that he is not able to look after the feudal obligations of his father, one-third of the field and orchard shall be given to his mother in order that his mother may rear him.

30: If either a private soldier or a commissary gave up his field, orchard and house on account of the feudal obligations and has then absented himself, (and) after his (departure) another took over his field, orchard and house and has looked after the feudal obligations for three years—if he has returned and demands his field, orchard and house, they shall not be given to him; the one who has taken over and looked after his feudal obligations shall himself become the feudatory.

31: If he has absented himself for only one year and has returned, his field, orchard and house shall be given back to him and he shall look after his feudal obligations himself.

32: If a merchant has ransomed either a private soldier or a commissary, who was carried off in a campaign of the king, and has enabled him to reach his city, if there is sufficient to ransom (him) in his house, he himself shall ransom himself; if there is not sufficient to ransom him in his house, he shall be ransomed from the estate of his city-god; if there is not sufficient to ransom him in the estate of his city-god, the state shall ransom him, since his own field, orchard and house may not be ceded for his ransom.

33: If either a sergeant or a captain[54] has obtained a soldier by conscription or he accepted and has sent a hired substitute for a campaign of the king, that sergeant or captain shall be put to death.

34: If either a sergeant or a captain has appropriated the household goods of a soldier, has wronged a soldier, has let a soldier for hire, has abandoned a soldier to a superior in a lawsuit, has appropriated the grant which the king gave to a soldier, that sergeant or captain shall be put to death.

35: If a seignior has bought from the hand of a soldier the cattle or sheep which the king gave to the soldier, he shall forfeit his money.[55]

36: In no case is the field, orchard, or house belonging to a soldier, a commissary, or a feudatory[56] salable.[57]

37: If a seignior has purchased the field, orchard, or house belonging to a soldier, a commissary, or a feudatory, his contract-tablet shall be broken and he shall also forfeit his money, with the field, orchard, or house reverting to its owner.

38: In no case may a soldier, a commissary, or a feudatory deed any of his field, orchard, or house belonging

48 A weight of about 8 gr.

49 cf. Exod. 22:2, 3a.

50 A weight of about 500 gr., divided into 60 shekels.

51 With §§23 and 24 cf. Deut. 21:1 ff.

52 The exact meaning of the two military terms used here, *rēdūm* and *bā'irum*, is uncertain. The former means literally "follower" and is regularly used for the ordinary foot-soldier; the latter means literally "fisher, hunter," hence "commissary" here.

53 Lit., "hireling."

54 The exact meaning of these two military terms, *dēkūm* and *luputtūm*, is not known; they refer to officers of some sort.

55 Lit., "he shall go up from his silver," with the separative use of the *t*-form of the verb.

56 Lit., "bearer of dues."

57 Lit., "does not sell for silver"; the active *inaddin* would seem to be a scribal error for the passive *innaddin*, "to be sold."

to his fief to his wife or daughter, and in no case may he assign (them) for an obligation of his.

39: He may deed to his wife or daughter any of the field, orchard, or house which he purchases and accordingly owns,[58] and he may assign (them) for an obligation of his.

40: A hierodule,[59] a merchant, and a feudatory extraordinary may sell his field, orchard and house, with the purchaser assuming the feudal obligations of the field, orchard and house which he purchases.

41: If a seignior acquired by barter the field, orchard, or house belonging to a soldier, a commissary, or a feudatory, and also made an additional payment, the soldier, commissary, or feudatory shall repossess his field, orchard, or house, and he shall also keep the additional payment that was made to him.

42: If a seignior rented a field for cultivation, but has not produced grain in the field, they shall prove that he did no work on the field and he shall give grain to the owner of the field on the basis of those adjoining it.

43: If he did not cultivate the field, but has neglected (it), he shall give grain to the owner of the field on the basis of those adjoining it; furthermore, the field which he neglected he shall break up with mattocks, harrow and return to the owner of the field.

44: If a seignior rented a fallow field for three years for development, but became so lazy that he has not developed the field, in the fourth year he shall break up the field with mattocks, plow and harrow (it), and he shall return (it) to the owner of the field; furthermore, he shall measure out ten *kur*[60] of grain per eighteen *iku.*[61]

45: If a seignior let his field to a tenant[62] and has already received the rent of his field, (and) later Adad has inundated the field or a flood has ravaged (it), the loss shall be the tenant's.

46: If he has not received the rent of the field, whether he let the field for one-half or one-third (the crop), the tenant and the owner of the field shall divide proportionately the grain which is produced in the field.

47: If the tenant has asked (another) to cultivate the field because he did not get back his investment in the previous year, the owner of the field shall not object; his (new) tenant[63] shall cultivate[64] his field and at harvest-time he shall take grain in accordance with his contracts.

48: If a debt is outstanding against a seignior and Adad has inundated his field or a flood has ravaged (it) or through lack of water grain has not been produced in the field, he shall not make any return of grain to his creditor[65] in that year; he shall cancel[66] his contract-tablet and he shall pay no interest for that year.

49: When a seignior borrowed money from a merchant and pledged to the merchant a field prepared for grain or sesame, if he said to him, "Cultivate the field, then harvest (and) take the grain or sesame that is produced," if the tenant has produced grain or sesame in the field, the owner of the field at harvest-time shall himself take the grain or sesame that was produced in the field and he shall give to the merchant grain for his money, which he borrowed from the merchant, together with its interest, and also for the cost of cultivation.

50: If he pledged a field planted with ⟨grain⟩ or a field planted with sesame, the owner of the field shall himself take the grain or sesame that was produced in the field and he shall pay back the money with its interest to the merchant.

51: If he does not have the money to pay back, ⟨grain or⟩ sesame at their market value in accordance with the ratio fixed by the king[67] he shall give to the merchant for his money, which he borrowed from the merchant, together with its interest.

52: If the tenant has not produced grain or sesame in the field, he may not change his contract.

53: If a seignior was too lazy to make [the dike of] his field strong and did not make his dike strong and a break has opened up in his dike and he has accordingly let the water ravage the farmland, the seignior in whose dike the break was opened shall make good the grain that he let get destroyed.

54: If he is not able to make good the grain, they shall sell him and his goods, and the farmers whose grain the water carried off shall divide (the proceeds).

55: If a seignior, upon opening his canal for irrigation, became so lazy that he has let the water ravage a field adjoining his, he shall measure out grain on the basis of those adjoining his.

56: If a seignior opened up the water and then has let the water carry off the work done on a field adjoining his, he shall measure out ten *kur* of grain per eighteen *iku.*

57: If a shepherd has not come to an agreement with the owner of a field to pasture sheep on the grass, but has pastured sheep on the field without the consent of the owner of the field, when the owner of the field harvests his field, the shepherd who pastured the sheep on the field without the consent of the owner of the field shall give in addition twenty *kur* of grain per eighteen *iku* to the owner of the field.

58: If after the sheep have gone up from the meadow, when the whole flock[68] has been shut up within the city-

[58] i.e. in fee simple and not as a fief.

[59] The exact meaning of the term used here, *nadītum*, is unknown, but it indicates some kind of religious functionary.

[60] A measure equal to a little more than 7 bushels, divided into 300 *qu*.

[61] A land measure equal to about ⅞ of an acre.

[62] Lit., "gave his field for rent to a cultivator."

[63] The word has the emphatic *ma*-ending to indicate that the reference is not to the first tenant but the second, the sub-tenant.

[64] The original here, *i-ni-ri-iš-ma*, is clearly a scribal error for *i-ir-ri-iš-ma* and not the IV 1 form, which would of course be *in-ne-ri-iš-ma*.

[65] Reading *be-el ḫu-bu-ul-li-šu*, lit., "the owner of his debt."

[66] Lit., "he shall wash off."

[67] In ancient Mesopotamia the ratio between silver (the money of the time) and various commodities was fixed by the state, showing that price control is not such a modern institution after all.

[68] Lit., "the flock of the totality." The word *kannū* is plural construct here and manifestly means "flock."

gate,[69] the shepherd drove the sheep into a field and has then pastured the sheep on the field, the shepherd shall look after the field on which he pastured and at harvest-time he shall measure out sixty *kur* of grain per eighteen *iku* to the owner of the field.

59: If a seignior cut down a tree in a(nother) seignior's orchard without the consent of the owner of the orchard, he shall pay one-half mina of silver.

60: If, when a seignior gave a field to a gardener to set out an orchard, the gardener set out the orchard, he shall develop the orchard for four years; in the fifth year the owner of the orchard and the gardener shall divide equally, with the owner of the orchard receiving his preferential share.[70]

61: If the gardener did not set out the whole field,[71] but left a portion bare, they shall assign the bare portion to him as his share.

62: If he did not set out the field that was given to him as an orchard, if it was a cultivated field, the gardener shall pay[72] to the owner of the field rent for the field for the years that it was neglected on the basis of those adjoining it; also he shall do the (necessary) work on the field and return (it) to the owner of the field.

63: If it was fallow land, he shall do the (necessary) work on the field and return (it) to the owner of the field; also he shall measure out ten *kur* of grain per eighteen *iku* for each year.

64: If a seignior gave his orchard to a gardener to pollinate,[73] the gardener shall give to the owner of the orchard two-thirds of the produce of the orchard as rent of the orchard as long as the orchard is held, with himself taking one-third.

65: If the gardener did not pollinate the orchard and so has let the yield decline, the gardener [shall measure out] rent for the orchard on the basis of those adjoining it.

66: When a seignior borrowed money from a merchant and his merchant foreclosed on him and he has nothing to pay (it) back, if he gave his orchard after pollination to the merchant and said to him, "Take for your money as many dates as there are produced in the orchard," that merchant shall not be allowed; the owner of the orchard shall himself take the dates that were produced in the orchard and repay the merchant for the money and its interest in accordance with the wording of his tablet and the owner of the orchard shall in turn take the remaining dates that were produced in the orchard.

67: If a seignior built a house, his neighbor. . . .

68: f.: (not preserved)

70: . . . he shall give to him.

71: If he is giving grain, money, or goods for a fief estate belonging to an estate adjoining his, which he wishes to purchase, he shall forfeit whatever he paid, while the estate shall revert to its [owner]. If that estate does not carry feudal obligations, he may purchase (it), since he may give grain, money, or goods for such an estate.

72-77: (Only a few words preserved, having to do with house building.)

78: [If a seignior let a house to a(nother) seignior and] the seignior (who was) the tenant paid his rental money in full for the year to the owner of [the house] and the owner of the house has then said to the [tenant] while his term[74] was (still) incomplete, "Move out," the owner of the house [shall forfeit] the money which the tenant paid to him [because] he made the tenant [move out] of his house while his term was (still) incomplete.

79-87: (not preserved)

88: If a merchant [lent] grain[75] at interest, he shall receive sixty *qu* of grain per *kur* as interest.[76] If he lent money at interest, he shall receive one-sixth (shekel) six *še* (i.e. one-fifth shekel) per shekel of silver as interest.[77]

89: If a seignior, who [incurred] a debt, does not have the money to pay (it) back, but has the grain, [the merchant] shall take grain for his money [with its interest] in accordance with the ratio fixed by the king.

90: If the merchant increased the interest beyond [sixty *qu*] per *kur* [of grain] (or) one-sixth (shekel) six *še* [per shekel of money] and has collected (it), he shall forfeit whatever he lent.

91: If a merchant [lent] grain at interest and has collected money [for the full interest] on the grain, the grain along with the money may not [*be charged to the account*].

92: (not preserved)

93: [If the merchant] . . . or he has not had the full amount of grain [which he received] deducted and did not write a new contract, or he has added the interest to the principal, that merchant shall pay back double the full amount of grain that he received.

94: If a merchant lent grain or money at interest and when he lent (it) at interest he paid out the money by the small weight and the grain by the small measure, but when he got (it) back he got the money by the [large] weight (and) the grain by the large measure, [that merchant shall forfeit] whatever he lent.

95: If a [merchant lent grain or money] at interest and gave . . . , he shall forfeit whatever he lent.

96: If a seignior borrowed grain or money from a merchant and does not have the grain or money to pay (it) back, but has (other) goods, he shall give to his merchant whatever there is in his possession, (affirming)

69 The reference to the city-gate evidently reflects the Near Eastern custom in both ancient and modern times of bringing the sheep into the shelter of the town or village at night.

70 A circumstantial clause, grammatically co-ordinate but logically subordinate, reading literally "the owner of the orchard shall choose and take his share." With this law cf. Lev. 19:23-25.

71 Lit., "did not complete the field in setting (it) out."

72 Lit., "measure out," indicating that the rent was to be paid in grain.

73 The orchard was a date orchard (see §66) and hence had to be artificially fertilized.

74 Lit., "his days."

75 Through a scribal error the original has "silver."

76 Since there were 300 *qu* in a *kur*, the interest rate was 20%.

77 Since there were 180 *še* in a shekel, the interest rate was again 20%.

before witnesses that he will bring (it), while the merchant shall accept (it) without making any objections.

97: . . . , he shall be put to death.

98: If a seignior gave money to a(nother) seignior for a partnership, they shall divide equally in the presence of god the profit or loss which was incurred.

99: If a merchant lent money at interest to a trader[78] for the purpose of trading [and making purchases] and sent him out on the road, the trader shall . . . on the road [the money which was entrusted] to him.

100: If he has realized a profit where he went, he shall write down the interest on the full amount of money that he borrowed and they shall count up the days against him and he shall repay his merchant.

101: If he has not realized a profit where he went, the trader shall repay to the merchant double[79] the money that he borrowed.

102: If a merchant has lent money to a trader as a favor[80] and he has experienced a loss where he went, he shall pay back the principal of the money to the merchant.

103: If, when he went on the road, an enemy has made him give up whatever he was carrying, the trader shall (so) affirm by god and then he shall go free.

104: If a merchant lent grain, wool, oil, or any goods at all to a trader to retail, the trader shall write down the value and pay (it) back to the merchant, with the trader obtaining a sealed receipt for the money which he pays to the merchant.

105: If the trader has been careless and so has not obtained a sealed receipt for the money which he paid to the merchant, the money with no sealed receipt may not be credited to the account.

106: If a trader borrowed money from a merchant and has then disputed (the fact) with his merchant, that merchant in the presence of god and witnesses shall prove that the trader borrowed the money and the trader shall pay to the merchant threefold the full amount of money that he borrowed.

107: When a merchant entrusted (something) to a trader and the trader has returned to his merchant whatever the merchant gave him, if the merchant has then disputed with him whatever the trader gave him, that trader shall prove it against the merchant in the presence of god and witnesses and the merchant shall pay to the trader sixfold whatever he received because he had a dispute with his trader.

108: If a woman wine seller, instead of receiving grain for the price of a drink, has received money by the large weight and so has made the value of the drink less than the value of the grain, they shall prove it against that wine seller[81] and throw her into the water.

109: If outlaws have congregated in the establishment of a woman wine seller and she has not arrested those outlaws and did not take them to the palace, that wine seller shall be put to death.

110: If a hierodule, a nun,[82] who is not living in a convent, has opened (the door of) a wineshop or has entered a wineshop for a drink, they shall burn that woman.

111: If a woman wine seller gave one (flask) of *pīḫum*-drink[83] on credit,[84] she shall receive fifty *qu*[85] of grain at harvest-time.

112: When a seignior was engaged in a (trading) journey and gave silver, gold, (precious) stones, or (other) goods in his possession[86] to a(nother) seignior and consigned (them) to him for transport, if that seignior did not deliver whatever was to be transported where it was to be transported, but has appropriated (it), the owner of the goods to be transported shall prove the charge against[87] that seignior in the matter of whatever was to be transported, but which he did not deliver, and that seignior shall pay to the owner of the goods to be transported fivefold whatever was given to him.

113: If a seignior held (a debt of) grain or money against a(nother) seignior and he has then taken grain from the granary or threshing floor without the consent of the owner of the grain, they shall prove that that seignior took grain from the granary or threshing floor without the consent of the owner of the grain and he shall return the full amount of grain that he took and he shall also forfeit everything else that he lent.

114: If a seignior did not hold (a debt of) grain or money against a(nother) seignior, but has distrained (someone as) his pledge, he shall pay one-third mina of silver for each distraint.

115: If a seignior held (a debt of) grain or money against a(nother) seignior and distrained (someone as) his pledge and the pledge has then died a natural death[88] in the house of his distrainer, that case is not subject to claim.

116: If the pledge has died from beating or abuse in the house of his distrainer, the owner of the pledge shall prove it against his merchant, and if it was the seignior's son, they shall put his son to death; if it was the seignior's slave, he shall pay one-third mina of silver and also forfeit everything else that he lent.

117: If an obligation came due against a seignior[89] and he sold (the services of) his wife, his son, or his daughter, or he has been bound over[90] to service, they shall work (in) the house of their purchaser or obligee for

[78] i.e. a traveling salesman peddling his wares wherever he could find a buyer.

[79] Lit., "shall double and give to the merchant."

[80] i.e. without interest.

[81] A variant, *UM* v, No. 93, col. iv, lines 37-8, reads, "they shall bind that wine seller."

[82] This word may be in apposition to the preceding or the particle "or" may be understood before it. The exact meaning of the word, *entum*, is not known, but the ideogram means literally "lady of a god," hence my translation "nun."

[83] The exact meaning of *pīḫum* is not known.

[84] The original has *di-ip-tim*, but this is a scribal error for *qí-ip-tim*.

[85] A measure equal to a little more than ¾ of a quart, dry measure.

[86] Lit., "goods of his hand."

[87] The verb is impersonal plural, a scribal error for the singular.

[88] Lit., "in accordance with his fate."

[89] Lit., "If with respect to a seignior (*emphatic accusative of specification*) an obligation has seized him."

[90] The verb used here, *ittandin*, is IV 2 preterit with passive force, and not I 2 present, as regularly interpreted. For a discussion of this section and the following two see T. J. Meek, *JNES*, VII (1948), 180-3.

three years, with their freedom reestablished in the fourth year.[91]

118: When a male slave or a female slave has been bound over to service, if the merchant foreclosed,[92] he may sell (him), with no possibility of his being reclaimed.

119: If an obligation came due against a seignior and he has accordingly sold (the services of) his female slave who bore him children, the owner of the female slave may repay the money which the merchant paid out and thus redeem his female slave.

120: If a seignior deposited his grain in a(nother) seignior's house for storage and a loss has then occurred at the granary or the owner of the house opened the storage-room and took grain or he has denied completely[93] (the receipt of) the grain which was stored in his house, the owner of the grain shall set forth the particulars regarding his grain in the presence of god and the owner of the house shall give to the owner of the grain double the grain that he took.[94]

121: If a seignior stored grain in a(nother) seignior's house, he shall pay five *qu* of grain per *kur* of grain[95] as the storage-charge per year.

122: If a seignior wishes to give silver, gold, or any sort of thing to a(nother) seignior for safekeeping, he shall show to witnesses the full amount that he wishes to give, arrange the contracts, and then commit (it) to safekeeping.

123: If he gave (it) for safekeeping without witnesses and contracts and they have denied (its receipt) to him at the place where he made the deposit, that case is not subject to claim.

124: If a seignior gave silver, gold, or any sort of thing for safekeeping to a(nother) seignior in the presence of witnesses and he has denied (the fact) to him, they shall prove it against that seignior and he shall pay double whatever he denied.

125: If a seignior deposited property of his for safekeeping and at the place where he made the deposit his property has disappeared along with the property of the owner of the house, either through breaking in or through scaling (the wall), the owner of the house, who was so careless that he let whatever was given to him for safekeeping get lost, shall make (it) good and make restitution to the owner of the goods, while the owner of the house shall make a thorough search for his lost property and take (it) from its thief.

126: If the seignior's property was not lost, but he has declared, "My property is lost," thus deceiving his city council,[96] his city council shall set forth the facts regarding him in the presence of god, that his property was not lost, and he shall give to his city council double whatever he laid claim to.

127: If a seignior pointed the finger at a nun or the wife of a(nother) seignior, but has proved nothing, they shall drag that seignior into the presence of the judges and also cut off half his (hair).

128: If a seignior acquired a wife, but did not draw up the contracts for her, that woman is no wife.

129: If the wife of a seignior has been caught while lying with another man, they shall bind them and throw them into the water. If the husband[97] of the woman wishes to spare his wife, then the king in turn may spare his subject.[98]

130: If a seignior bound the (betrothed) wife of a(nother) seignior, who had had no intercourse with[99] a male and was still living in her father's house, and he has lain in her bosom and they have caught him, that seignior shall be put to death, while that woman shall go free.[100]

131: If a seignior's wife was accused by her husband,[101] but she was not caught while lying with another man, she shall make affirmation by god and return to her house.

132: If the finger was pointed at the wife of a seignior because of another man, but she has not been caught while lying with the other man, she shall throw herself into the river[102] for the sake of her husband.[103]

133: If a seignior was taken captive, but there was sufficient to live on in his house, his wife [shall not leave her house, but she shall take care of her person by not] entering [the house of another].[104]

133*a*: If that woman did not take care of her person, but has entered the house of another, they shall prove it against that woman and throw her into the water.[105]

134: If the seignior was taken captive and there was not sufficient to live on in his house, his wife may enter the house of another, with that woman incurring no blame at all.

135: If, when a seignior was taken captive and there was not sufficient to live on in his house, his wife has then entered the house of another before his (return) and has borne children, (and) later her husband has returned and has reached his city, that woman shall return to her first husband, while the children shall go with their father.

136: If, when a seignior deserted his city and then ran away, his wife has entered the house of another after his (departure), if that seignior has returned and wishes to take back his wife, the wife of the fugitive shall not return to her husband because he scorned his city and ran away.

91 cf. Exod. 21:2-11; Deut. 15:12-18.

92 Lit., "he caused (the time-limit) to expire."

93 Lit., "denied unto completeness."

94 cf. Exod. 22:7-9.

95 i.e. 1 2/3% since there were 300 *qu* in a *kur*.

96 This would seem to be the best translation of *bābtum*, a feminine formation from *bābum* "gate." Its use here is identical with that of *ša'ar* "gate," in Ruth 3:11; 4:10.

97 Lit., "owner, master."

98 Lit., "his slave." With this law cf. Deut. 22:22.

99 Lit., "had not known."

100 cf. Deut. 22:23-27.

101 Lit., "If with respect to a seignior's wife (*casus pendens*) her husband accused her."

102 i.e. submit to the water ordeal, with the river as divine judge; cf. §2 above and note 41.

103 cf. Num. 5:11-31.

104 i.e. in order to live there as another man's wife.

105 i.e. to be drowned.

137: If a seignior has made up his mind[106] to divorce a lay priestess,[107] who bore him children, or a hierodule who provided him with children, they shall return her dowry to that woman and also give her half of the field, orchard and goods in order that she may rear her children; after she has brought up her children, from whatever was given to her children they shall give her a portion corresponding to (that of) an individual heir in order that the man who chooses her[108] may marry her.

138: If a seignior wishes to divorce his wife who did not bear him children, he shall give her money to the full amount of her marriage-price and he shall also make good to her the dowry which she brought from her father's house and then he may divorce her.

139: If there was no marriage-price, he shall give her one mina of silver as the divorce-settlement.

140: If he is a peasant,[109] he shall give her one-third mina of silver.

141: If a seignior's wife, who was living in the house of the seignior, has made up her mind to leave in order that she may engage in business, thus neglecting her house (and) humiliating her husband, they shall prove it against her; and if her husband has then decided on her divorce, he may divorce her, with nothing to be given her as her divorce-settlement upon her departure.[110] If her husband has not decided on her divorce, her husband may marry another woman, with the former woman[111] living in the house of her husband like a maidservant.

142: If a woman so hated her husband that she has declared, "You may not have me," her record shall be investigated at her city council, and if she was careful and was not at fault, even though her husband has been going out and disparaging her greatly, that woman, without incurring any blame at all, may take her dowry and go off to her father's house.

143: If she was not careful, but was a gadabout, thus neglecting her house (and) humiliating her husband, they shall throw that woman into the water.

144: When a seignior married a hierodule and that hierodule gave a female slave to her husband and she has then produced children, if that seignior has made up his mind to marry a lay priestess, they may not allow that seignior, since he may not marry the lay priestess.

145: If a seignior married a hierodule and she did not provide him with children and he has made up his mind to marry a lay priestess, that seignior may marry the lay priestess, thus bringing her into his house, (but) with that lay priestess ranking in no way with the hierodule.

146: When a seignior married a hierodule and she gave a female slave to her husband and she has then borne children, if later that female slave has claimed equality with her mistress because she bore children, her mistress may not sell her; she may mark her with the slave-mark and count her among the slaves.

147: If she did not bear children, her mistress may sell her.

148: When a seignior married a woman and a fever[112] has then seized her, if he has made up his mind to marry another, he may marry (her), without divorcing his wife whom the fever seized; she shall live in the house which he built and he shall continue to support her as long as she lives.

149: If that woman has refused to live in her husband's house, he shall make good her dowry to her which she brought from her father's house and then she may leave.

150: If a seignior, upon presenting a field, orchard, house, or goods to his wife, left a sealed document with her, her children may not enter a claim against her after (the death of) her husband, since the mother may give her inheritance to that son of hers whom she likes, (but) she may not give (it) to an outsider.

151: If a woman, who was living in a seignior's house, having made a contract with her husband that a creditor[113] of her husband may not distrain her, has then had (him) deliver a written statement;[114] if there was a debt against that seignior before he married that woman, his creditors may not distrain his wife; also, if there was a debt against that woman before she entered the seignior's house, her creditors may not distrain her husband.

152: If a debt has developed against them after that woman entered the seignior's house, both of them shall be answerable to the merchant.[115]

153: If a seignior's wife has brought about the death of her husband because of another man, they shall impale that woman on stakes.

154: If a seignior has had intercourse with his daughter, they shall make that seignior leave the city.

155: If a seignior chose a bride for his son and his son had intercourse with her, but later he himself has lain in her bosom and they have caught him, they shall bind that seignior and throw him[116] into the water.

156: If a seignior chose a bride for his son and his son did not have intercourse with her, but he himself has lain in her bosom, he shall pay to her one-half mina of silver and he shall also make good to her whatever she brought from her father's house in order that the man who chooses her may marry her.

157: If a seignior has lain in the bosom of his mother after (the death of) his father, they shall burn both of them.

158: If a seignior after (the death of) his father has

106 Lit. "has set his face."

107 The exact meaning of the word used here, ŠU.GE$_4$-*tum*, is unknown, but it indicates some kind of priestess.

108 Lit., "her man of heart," *mutu libbiša*, where the suffix *-ša* is objective and not subjective, as hitherto understood. It was scarcely possible that a woman in ancient Babylonia was ever allowed to choose her husband!

109 The word is *muškēnum*; see note 44 above.

110 Lit., "her journey," a noun in the adverbial accusative of manner.

111 Lit., "that woman."

112 The exact meaning of the word used here, *la'bum*, is not known.

113 Lit., "the owner of a debt," here to be construed as singular, but elsewhere in this paragraph as plural because of the plural verbs to which they belong.

114 Lit. "a tablet."

115 i.e. the money-lender who made the loan.

116 Through a scribal error the original has "her."

been caught in the bosom of his foster mother[117] who was the bearer of children, that seignior shall be cut off from the parental home.[118]

159: If a seignior, who had the betrothal-gift brought to the house of his (prospective) father-in-law (and) paid the marriage-price, has then fallen in love with[119] another woman and has said to his (prospective) father-in-law, "I will not marry your daughter," the father of the daughter shall keep whatever was brought to him.

160: If a seignior had the betrothal-gift brought to the house of the (prospective) father-in-law (and) paid the marriage-price, and the father of the daughter has then said, "I will not give my daughter to you," he shall pay back double the full amount that was brought to him.

161: If a seignior had the betrothal-gift brought to the house of his (prospective) father-in-law (and) paid the marriage-price, and then a friend of his has so maligned him that his (prospective) father-in-law has said to the (prospective) husband,[120] "You may not marry my daughter," he shall pay back double the full amount that was brought to him, but his friend may not marry his (intended) wife.

162: If, when a seignior acquired a wife, she bore him children and that woman has then gone to (her) fate, her father may not lay claim to her dowry, since her dowry belongs to her children.

163: If a seignior acquired a wife and that woman has gone to (her) fate without providing him with children, if his father-in-law has then returned to him the marriage-price which that seignior brought to the house of his father-in-law, her husband may not lay claim to the dowry of that woman, since her dowry belongs to her father's house.

164: If his father-in-law has not returned the marriage-price to him, he shall deduct the full amount of her marriage-price from her dowry and return (the rest of) her dowry to her father's house.

165: If a seignior, upon presenting a field, orchard, or house to his first-born, who is the favorite in his eye, wrote a sealed document for him, when the brothers divide after the father has gone to (his) fate, he shall keep the present which the father gave him, but otherwise they shall share equally in the goods of the paternal estate.

166: If a seignior, upon acquiring wives for the sons that he got, did not acquire a wife for his youngest son, when the brothers divide after the father has gone to (his) fate, to their youngest brother who did not acquire a wife, to him in addition to his share they shall assign money (enough)for the marriage-price from the goods of the paternal estate and thus enable him to acquire a wife.

167: If, when a seignior acquired a wife and she bore him children, that woman has gone to (her) fate (and) after her (death) he has then married another woman and she has borne children, when later the father has gone to (his) fate, the children shall not divide according to mothers; they shall take the dowries of their (respective) mothers and then divide equally the goods of the paternal estate.

168: If a seignior, having made up his mind to disinherit his son, has said to the judges, "I wish to disinherit my son," the judges shall investigate his record, and if the son did not incur wrong grave (enough) to cut (him) off from sonship, the father may not cut his son off from sonship.

169: If he has incurred wrong against his father grave (enough) to cut (him) off from sonship, they shall condone his first (offense); if he has incurred grave wrong a second time, the father may cut off his son from sonship.

170: When a seignior's first wife bore him children and his female slave also bore him children, if the father during his lifetime has ever said "My children!" to the children whom the slave bore him, thus having counted them with the children of the first wife, after the father has gone to (his) fate, the children of the first wife and the children of the slave shall share equally in the goods of the paternal estate, with the first-born, the son of the first wife, receiving a preferential share.

171: However, if the father during his lifetime has never said "My children!" to the children whom the slave bore him, after the father has gone to (his) fate, the children of the slave may not share in the goods of the paternal estate along with the children of the first wife; freedom for the slave and her children shall be effected,[121] with the children of the first wife having no claim at all against the children of the slave for service; the first wife shall take her dowry and the marriage-gift which her husband, upon giving (it) to her, wrote down on a tablet for her, and living in the home of her husband, she shall have the usufruct (of it) as long as she lives, without ever selling (it), since her heritage belongs to her children.

172: If her husband did not give her a marriage-gift, they shall make good her dowry to her and she shall obtain from the goods of her husband's estate a portion corresponding to (that of) an individual heir; if her children keep plaguing her in order to make her leave the house, the judges shall investigate her record and place the blame on the children, so that woman need never leave her husband's house; if that woman has made up her mind to leave, she shall leave to her children the marriage-gift which her husband gave her (but) take the dowry from[122] her father's house in order that the man who chooses her may marry her.

173: If that woman has borne children to her later husband in the place that she entered, after that woman

[117] The text has *ra-bi-ti-šu*, but this must be a scribal error for *mu-ra-bi-ti-šu*.

[118] Lit. "the house of the father." With the laws in §§154-158 cf. Lev. 18:6-18; 20:10-21; Deut. 27:20, 22 f.

[119] Lit. "has then stared at, has made eyes at."

[120] Lit. "owner of a wife."

[121] The active form of the verb used here, *iš-ta-ak-ka-an*, must be a scribal error for the passive, *iš-ša-ak-ka-an*.

[122] Lit. "belonging to."

has died, the earlier with the later children shall divide the dowry.

174: If she has not borne children to her later husband, only the children of her first husband shall receive her dowry.

175: If either a palace slave or a private citizen's slave married the daughter of a seignior and she has borne children, the owner of the slave may not lay claim to the children of the seignior's daughter for service.

176: Furthermore, if a palace slave or a private citizen's slave married the daughter of a seignior and when he married her she entered the house of the palace slave or the private citizen's slave with the dowry from[122] her father's house and after they were joined together they set up a household and so acquired goods, but later either the palace slave or the private citizen's slave has gone to (his) fate, the seignior's daughter shall take her dowry, but they shall divide into two parts whatever her husband and she acquired after they were joined together and the owner of the slave shall take one-half, with the seignior's daughter taking one-half for her children.

176*a*: If the seignior's daughter has no dowry, they shall divide into two parts whatever her husband and she acquired after they were joined together and the owner of the slave shall take one-half, with the seignior's daughter taking one-half for her children.

177: If a widow, whose children are minors, has made up her mind to enter the house of another, she may not enter without the consent of the judges; when she wishes to enter the house of another, the judges shall investigate the condition of her former husband's estate and they shall entrust her former husband's estate to her later husband and that woman and they shall have them deposit a tablet (to the effect that) they will look after the estate and also rear the young (children), without ever selling the household goods, since the purchaser who purchases the household goods of a widow's children shall forfeit his money, with the goods reverting to their owner.

178: In the case of a nun, a hierodule, or a votary,[123] whose father, upon presenting a dowry to her, wrote a tablet for her, if he did not write for her on the tablet which he wrote for her (permission) to give her heritage to whom she pleased and did not grant her full discretion,[124] after the father has gone to (his) fate, her brothers shall take her field and orchard and they shall give her food, oil and clothing proportionate to the value of her share and thus make her comfortable;[125] if her brothers have not given her food, oil and clothing proportionate to the value of her share and so have not made her comfortable, she may give her field and orchard to any tenant that she pleases and her tenant shall support her, since she shall have the usufruct of the field, orchard or whatever her father gave her as long as she lives, without selling (it or) willing (it) to another, since her patrimony belongs to her brothers.

179: In the case of a nun, a hierodule, or a votary, whose father, upon presenting a dowry to her, wrote a sealed document for her, if he wrote for her on the tablet which he wrote for her (permission) to give her heritage to whomever she pleased and has granted her full discretion, after her father has gone to (his) fate, she may give her heritage to whomever she pleases, with her brothers having no claim against her.

180: If a father did not present a dowry to his daughter, a hierodule in a convent or a votary, after the father has gone to (his) fate, she shall receive as her share in the goods of the paternal estate a portion like (that of) an individual heir, but she shall have only the usufruct of (it) as long as she lives, since her heritage belongs to her brothers.

181: If a father dedicated[126] (his daughter) to deity as a hierodule, a sacred prostitute, or a devotee[127] and did not present a dowry to her, after the father has gone to (his) fate, she shall receive as her share in the goods of the paternal estate her one-third patrimony, but she shall have only the usufruct of (it) as long as she lives, since her heritage belongs to her brothers.

182: If a father, since he did not present a dowry to his daughter, a hierodule of Marduk of Babylon, did not write a sealed document for her, after the father has gone to (his) fate, she shall share along with her brothers in the goods of the paternal estate to the extent of her one-third patrimony, but she shall not assume any feudal obligations, since a hierodule of Marduk may give her heritage to whomever she pleases.

183: If a father, upon presenting a dowry to his daughter, a lay priestess, when he gave her to a husband, wrote a sealed document for her, after the father has gone to (his) fate, she may not share in the goods of the paternal estate.

184: If a seignior did not present a dowry to his daughter, a lay priestess, since he did not give her to a husband, after the father has gone to (his) fate, her brothers shall present her with a dowry proportionate to the value of the father's estate and they shall give her to a husband.

185: If a seignior adopted[128] a boy in his own name and has reared him, that foster child may never be reclaimed.

186: If a seignior, upon adopting a boy, seeks out his father and mother when he had taken him, that foster child may return to his father's house.

187: The (adopted) son of a chamberlain, a palace servant, or the (adopted) son of a votary, may never be reclaimed.

188: If a member of the artisan class[129] took a son as a

[123] The exact meaning of the word used here, ZI.IK.RU.UM, is not known, but it manifestly indicates some kind of priestess.

[124] Lit. "cause her to attain her full heart."

[125] Lit. "make her heart good."

[126] Lit. "lifted up."

[127] The exact meaning of the word used here, *kulmašītum*, is not known, but it manifestly indicates some kind of priestess.

[128] Lit. "took into sonship."

[129] Lit. "the son of an artisan," where "son" is used in the technical sense of "belonging to the class of, species of," so common in the Semitic languages.

foster child and has taught him his handicraft, he may never be reclaimed.

189: If he has not taught him his handicraft, that foster child may return to his father's house.

190: If a seignior has not counted among his sons the boy that he adopted and reared, that foster child may return to his father's house.

191: If a seignior, who adopted a boy and reared him, set up a family of his own, has later acquired children and so has made up (his) mind to cut off the foster child, that son shall not go off empty-handed; his foster father shall give him from his goods his one-third patrimony and then he shall go off, since he may not give him any of the field, orchard, or house.

192: If the (adopted) son of a chamberlain or the (adopted) son of a votary has said to his foster father or his foster mother, "You are not my father," "You are not my mother," they shall cut out his tongue.

193: If the (adopted) son of a chamberlain or the (adopted) son of a votary found out his parentage[130] and came to hate his foster father and his foster mother and so has gone off to his paternal home, they shall pluck out his eye.

194: When a seignior gave his son to a nurse and that son has died in the care[131] of the nurse, if the nurse has then made a contract for another son without the knowledge of his father and mother, they shall prove it against her and they shall cut off her breast because she made a contract for another son without the knowledge of his father and mother.

195: If a son has struck his father, they shall cut off his hand.[132]

196: If a seignior has destroyed the eye of a member of the aristocracy,[133] they shall destroy his eye.[134]

197: If he has broken a(nother) seignior's bone, they shall break his bone.[134]

198: If he has destroyed the eye of a commoner or broken the bone of a commoner, he shall pay one mina of silver.

199: If he has destroyed the eye of a seignior's slave or broken the bone of a seignior's slave, he shall pay one-half his value.

200: If a seignior has knocked out a tooth of a seignior of his own rank, they shall knock out his tooth.[134]

201: If he has knocked out a commoner's tooth, he shall pay one-third mina of silver.

202: If a seignior has struck the cheek of a seignior who is superior to him, he shall be beaten sixty (times) with an oxtail whip in the assembly.

203: If a member of the aristocracy has struck the cheek of a(nother) member of the aristocracy who is of the same rank as[135] himself, he shall pay one mina of silver.

204: If a commoner has struck the cheek of a(nother) commoner, he shall pay ten shekels of silver.

205: If a seignior's slave has struck the cheek of a member of the aristocracy, they shall cut off his ear.

206: If a seignior has struck a(nother) seignior in a brawl and has inflicted an injury on him, that seignior shall swear, "I did not strike him deliberately";[136] and he shall also pay for the physician.

207: If he has died because of his blow, he shall swear (as before), and if it was a member of the aristocracy, he shall pay one-half mina of silver.

208: If it was a member of the commonalty, he shall pay one-third mina of silver.

209: If a seignior struck a(nother) seignior's daughter and has caused her to have a miscarriage,[137] he shall pay ten shekels of silver for her fetus.

210: If that woman has died, they shall put his daughter to death.

211: If by a blow he has caused a commoner's daughter to have a miscarriage, he shall pay five shekels of silver.

212: If that woman has died, he shall pay one-half mina of silver.

213: If he struck a seignior's female slave and has caused her to a have a miscarriage, he shall pay two shekels of silver.

214: If that female slave has died, he shall pay one-third mina of silver.

215: If a physician performed a major operation on a seignior with a bronze lancet and has saved the seignior's life, or he opened up the eye-socket of a seignior with a bronze lancet and has saved the seignior's eye, he shall receive ten shekels of silver.

216: If it was a member of the commonalty, he shall receive five shekels.

217: If it was a seignior's slave, the owner of the slave shall give two shekels of silver to the physician.

218: If a physician performed a major operation on a seignior with a bronze lancet and has caused the seignior's death, or he opened up the eye-socket of a seignior and has destroyed the seignior's eye, they shall cut off his hand.

219: If a physican performed a major operation on a commoner's slave with a bronze lancet and has caused (his) death, he shall make good slave for slave.

220: If he opened up his eye-socket with a bronze lancet and has destroyed[138] his eye, he shall pay one-half his value in silver.

221: If a physician has set a seignior's broken bone, or has healed a sprained tendon, the patient[139] shall give five shekels of silver to the physician.

130 Lit. "found out his father's house."

131 Lit. "in the hand."

132 cf. Exod. 21:15. For the whole collection of laws dealing with personal injuries, §§195-214, cf. the similiar collection in Exod. 21:12-27.

133 Lit. "the son of a man," with "son" used in the technical sense already explained in note 129 above and "man" clearly in the sense of "noble, aristocrat"; or it is possible that "son" here is to be taken in its regular sense to indicate a person younger than the assailant.

134 cf. Exod. 21:23-25; Lev. 24:19 f.; Deut. 19:21.

135 Lit. "who is like."

136 Lit. "while I was aware of (it)."

137 Lit. "caused her to drop that of her womb (her fetus)." With this and the following five laws cf. Exod. 21:22-25.

138 The text has *úḫ-tap-da*, but this must be a scribal error for *úḫ-tap-pí-id*.

139 Lit. "owner of the injury."

222: If it was a member of the commonalty, he shall give three shekels of silver.

223: If it was a seignior's slave, the owner of the slave shall give two shekels of silver to the physician.

224: If a veterinary surgeon[140] performed a major operation on either an ox or an ass and has saved (its) life, the owner of the ox or ass shall give to the surgeon one-sixth (shekel) of silver as his fee.

225: If he performed a major operation on an ox or an ass and has caused (its) death, he shall give to the owner of the ox or ass one-fourth its value.

226: If a brander cut off the slave-mark of a slave not his own without the consent of the owner of the slave, they shall cut off the hand of that brander.

227: If a seignior deceived a brander so that he has cut off the slave-mark of a slave not his own, they shall put that seignior to death and immure him at his gate; the brander shall swear, "I did not cut (it) off knowingly," and then he shall go free.

228: If a builder constructed a house for a seignior and finished (it) for him, he shall give him two shekels of silver per *sar*[141] of house as his remuneration.

229: If a builder constructed a house for a seignior, but did not make his work strong, with the result that the house which he built collapsed and so has caused the death of the owner of the house, that builder shall be put to death.

230: If it has caused the death of a son of the owner of the house, they shall put the son of that builder to death.

231: If it has caused the death of a slave of the owner of the house, he shall give slave for slave to the owner of the house.

232: If it has destroyed goods, he shall make good whatever it destroyed; also, because he did not make the house strong which he built and it collapsed, he shall reconstruct the house which collapsed at his own expense.[142]

233: If a builder constructed a house for a seignior and has not made his work secure so that a wall has become unsafe, that builder shall strengthen that wall at his own expense.[143]

234: If a boatman calked a boat of sixty *kur* for a seignior, he shall give him two shekels of silver as his remuneration.

235: If a boatman calked a boat for a seignior and did not do his work well with the result that that boat has sprung a leak in that very year, since it has developed a defect, the boatman shall dismantle that boat and strengthen (it) at his own expense[142] and give the strengthened boat back to the owner of the boat.

236: If a seignior let his boat for hire to a boatman and the boatman was so careless that he has sunk or wrecked the boat, the boatman shall make good the boat to the owner of the boat.

237: When a seignior hired a boatman and a boat and loaded it with grain, wool, oil, dates, or any kind of freight, if that boatman was so careless that he has sunk the boat and lost what was in it as well, the boatman shall make good the boat which he sank and whatever he lost that was in it.

238: If a boatman sank the boat of a seignior and has then refloated it, he shall give one-half its value in silver.

239: If a seignior hired a boatman, he shall give him six *kur* of grain per year.

240: If a rowboat rammed a sailboat and has sunk (it), the owner of the boat whose boat was sunk shall in the presence of god set forth the particulars regarding whatever was lost in his boat and the one in charge of the rowboat[144] which sank the sailboat shall make good to him his boat and his lost property.

241: If a seignior has distrained an ox as a pledge, he shall pay one-third mina of silver.[145]

242, 243: If a seignior hired (it) for one year, he shall give to its owner four *kur* of grain as the hire of an ox in tandem, three *kur* of grain as the hire of a young lead-ox.

244: If a seignior hired an ox or an ass and a lion has killed it in the open, (the loss) shall be its owner's.

245: If a seignior hired an ox and has caused its death through carelessness or through beating, he shall make good ox for ox to the owner of the ox.

246: If a seignior hired an ox and has broken its foot or has cut its neck tendon, he shall make good ox for ox to the owner of the ox.

247: If a seignior hired an ox and has destroyed its eye, he shall give one-half its value in silver to the owner of the ox.

248: If a seignior hired an ox and has broken its horn, cut off its tail, or injured the flesh of its back, he shall give one-quarter its value in silver.

249: If a seignior hired an ox and god struck it and it has died, the seignior who hired the ox shall (so) affirm by god and then he shall go free.

250: If an ox, when it was walking along the street, gored a seignior to death,[146] that case is not subject to claim.

251: If a seignior's ox was a gorer and his city council made it known to him that it was a gorer, but he did not pad its horns (or) tie up his ox, and that ox gored to death a member of the aristocracy, he shall give one-half mina of silver.[147]

252: If it was a seignior's slave, he shall give one-third mina of silver.

253: If a seignior hired a(nother) seignior to oversee his field, and lending him *feed-grain*, entrusting him with oxen, contracted with him to cultivate the field, if that seignior stole the seed or fodder and it has been found in his possession, they shall cut off his hand.

254: If he appropriated the *feed-grain* and thus has

140 Lit. "physician of an ox or an ass."

141 A measure equal to about 42 1/5 square yards.

142 Lit. "out of his own goods."

143 Lit. "out of his own money."

144 Lit. "he of the rowboat."

145 cf. §114 above.

146 Lit. "and has caused his death."

147 With §§250-2 cf. Exod. 21:28-36.

starved the oxen, he shall make good twofold the grain which he received.[148]

255: If he has let the seignior's oxen out on hire or he stole the seed-grain and so has raised nothing in the field, they shall prove it against that seignior and at harvest-time he shall measure out sixty *ḳur* of grain per eighteen *iḳu*.

256: If he was not able to meet his obligation, they shall drag him through that field with the oxen.

257: If a seignior hired a *cultivator*, he shall give him eight *ḳur* of grain per year.

258: If a seignior hired a cattle-herder, he shall pay him six *ḳur* of grain per year.

259: If a seignior stole a plow from a field, he shall give five shekels of silver to the owner of the plow.

260: If he has stolen a *seeder* or a harrow, he shall give three shekels of silver.

261: If a seignior hired a shepherd to pasture cattle or sheep, he shall give him eight *ḳur* of grain per year.

262: If a seignior . . . and ox or a sheep to. . . .

263: If he has lost [the ox] or sheep which was committed to him, he shall make good ox for [ox], sheep for [sheep] to their owner.

264: If [a shepherd], to whom cattle or sheep were given to pasture, being in receipt of his wages in full, to his satisfaction, has then let the cattle decrease, has let the sheep decrease, thus lessening the birth rate, he shall give increase and profit in accordance with the terms of his contract.

265: If a shepherd, to whom cattle or sheep were given to pasture, became unfaithful and hence has altered the cattlemark or has sold (them), they shall prove it against him and he shall make good in cattle and sheep to their owner tenfold what he stole.

266: If a visitation of god has occurred in a sheepfold or a lion has made a kill, the shepherd shall prove himself innocent in the presence of god, but the owner of the sheepfold shall receive from him the animal stricken in the fold.[149]

267: If the shepherd was careless and has let lameness develop in the fold, the shepherd shall make good in cattle and sheep the loss through the lameness which he let develop in the fold and give (them) to their owner.[149]

268: If a seignior hired an ox to thresh, twenty *qu* of grain shall be its hire.

269: If he hired an ass to thresh, ten *qu* of grain shall be its hire.

270: If he hired a goat to thresh, one *qu* of grain shall be its hire.

271: If a seignior hired oxen, a wagon and a driver for it, he shall give 180 *qu* of grain per day.

272: If a seignior hired simply a wagon by itself, he shall give forty *qu* of grain per day.

273: If a seignior hired a laborer, he shall give six *še* of silver per day from the beginning of the year till the fifth month; from the sixth month till the end of the year he shall give five *še* of silver per day.

274: If a seignior wishes to hire an artisan, he shall pay per day as the wage of a . . . five [*še*] of silver; as the wage of a *brickmaker* five *še* of silver; [as the wage of] a *linen-weaver* . . . [*še*] of silver; [as the wage] of a *seal-cutter* . . . [*še*] of silver; [as the wage of] a *jeweller* . . . [*še* of] silver; [as the wage of] a *smith* . . . [*še* of] silver; [as the wage of] a carpenter four *še* of silver; as the wage of a leatherworker . . . *še* of silver; as the wage of a basketmaker . . . *še* of silver; [as the wage of] a builder . . . *še* of silver.

275: [If] a seignior hired a *long-boat*, its hire shall be three *še* of silver per day.

276: If a seignior hired a rowboat, he shall give two and one-half *še* of silver per day as its hire.

277: If a seignior hired a boat of sixty *ḳur*, he shall give one-sixth (shekel) of silver per day as its hire.

278: If a seignior purchased a male (or) female slave and when his month was not yet complete, epilepsy attacked him, he shall return (him) to his seller and the purchaser shall get back the money which he paid out.

279: If a seignior purchased a male (or) female slave and he has then received a claim (against him), his seller shall be responsible for the claim.

280: If a seignior has purchased in a foreign land the male (or) female slave of a(nother) seignior and when he has arrived home[150] the owner of the male or female slave has identified either his male or his female slave, if that male and female slave are natives of the land, their freedom shall be effected without any money (payment).

281: If they are natives of another land, the purchaser shall state in the presence of god what money he paid out and the owner of the male or female slave shall give to the merchant the money he paid out and thus redeem[151] his male or female slave.

282: If a male slave has said to his master, "You are not my master," his master shall prove him to be his slave and cut off his ear.

THE EPILOGUE

(reverse xxiv)

The laws of justice, which Hammurabi, the efficient king, set up,
and by which he caused the land to secure firm guidance and good government.

I, Hammurabi, the perfect king,
was not careless (or) neglectful of the black-headed (people),
whom Enlil had presented to me,
(and) whose shepherding Marduk had committed to me;
I sought out peaceful regions for them;
I overcame grievous difficulties;

[148] Reading *ta-[a]š-na* for *ta-a-na* and *im-ḫu-ru* for *im-ri-ru*.
[149] cf. Exod. 22:9 ff.

[150] Lit. "in the midst of the land."
[151] Reading *i-pa-ṭar* for *i-pa-aḳ*.

I caused light to rise on them.
With the mighty weapon which Zababa and Inanna entrusted to me,
with the insight that Enki allotted to me,
with the ability that Marduk gave me,
I rooted out the enemy above and below;
I made an end of war;
I promoted the welfare of the land;
I made the peoples rest in friendly habitations;
I did not let them have anyone to terrorize them.
The great gods called me,
so I became the beneficent shepherd whose scepter is righteous;
my benign shadow is spread over my city.
In my bosom I carried the peoples of the land of Sumer and Akkad;
they prospered under my protection;
I have governed them in peace;
I have sheltered them in my strength.
In order that the strong might not oppress the weak,
that justice might be dealt the orphan (and) the widow,
in Babylon, the city whose head Anum and Enlil raised aloft,
in Esagila, the temple whose foundations stand firm like heaven and earth,
I wrote my precious words on my stela,
and in the presence of my statue as the king of justice
I set (it) up in order to administer the law of the land,
to prescribe the ordinances of the land,
to give justice to the oppressed.

I am the king who is preeminent among kings;
my words are choice; my ability has no equal.
By the order of Shamash, the great judge of heaven and earth,
may my justice prevail in the land;
by the word of Marduk, my lord,
may my statutes have no one to scorn them;

(reverse xxv)

in Esagila, which I love, may my name be spoken in reverence forever!

Let any oppressed man who has a cause
come into the presence of my statue as the king of justice,
and then read my inscribed stela,
and give heed to my precious words,
and may my stela make the case clear to him;
may he understand his cause;
may he set his mind at ease!
"Hammurabi, the lord,
who is like a real father to the people,
bestirred himself for the word of Marduk, his lord,
and secured the triumph of Marduk above and below,
thus making glad the heart of Marduk, his lord,
and he also ensured prosperity for the people forever,
and led the land aright"—
let him proclaim this,
and let him pray with his whole heart for me
in the presence of Marduk, my lord, and Sarpanit,[152] my lady!
May the guardian spirit, the protecting genius,
the gods who enter Esagila, (and) Lebettum[153] of Esagila,
prosper the wishes (made) daily
in the presence of Marduk, my lord, (and) Sarpanit, my lady!

In the days to come, for all time,
let the king who appears in the land observe
the words of justice which I wrote on my stela;
let him not alter the law of the land which I enacted,
the ordinances of the land which I prescribed;
let him not scorn my statutes!
If that man has intelligence
and is able to guide his land aright,
let him heed the words which I wrote on my stela,
and may this stela show him the road (and) the way,
the law of the land which I enacted,
the ordinances of the land which I prescribed;
and let him guide aright his black-headed (people)!
Let him enact the law for them;
let him prescribe the ordinances for them!
Let him root out the wicked and the evil from his land;
let him promote the welfare of his people!

I, Hammurabi, am the king of justice,
to whom Shamash committed law.
My words are choice; my deeds have no equal;
it is only to the fool that they are empty;

(reverse xxvi)

to the wise they stand forth as an object of wonder.
If that man heeded my words which I wrote on my stela,
and did not scorn my law,
did not distort my words,
did not alter my statutes,
may Shamash make that man reign
as long as, the king of justice;
may he shepherd his people in justice!

If that man did not heed my words which I wrote on my stela,
and disregarded my curses,
and did not fear the curses of the gods,
but has abolished the law which I enacted,
has distorted my words,
has altered my statutes,

152 The consort of Marduk.
153 The god of brickmaking.

effaced my name inscribed (thereon),
and has written his own name,
(or) he has commissioned another (to do so) because of these curses—
as for that man, whether king or lord,
or governor or person of any rank,[154]
may mighty Anum, the father of the gods, who proclaimed my reign,
deprive him of the glory of sovereignty,
may he break his scepter, may he curse his fate!

May Enlil, the lord, the determiner of destinies,
whose orders cannot be altered,
who enlarged my kingdom,
kindle revolts against him in his abode which cannot be suppressed,
misfortune leading to his ruin!
May he determine as the fate for him a reign of woe,
days few in number, years of famine,
darkness without light, sudden death!
May he order by his forceful word the destruction of his city,
the dispersion of his people, the transfer of his kingdom,
the disappearance of his name and memory from the land!

May Ninlil,[155] the mighty mother,
whose orders carry weight in Ekur,
the lady who prospers my wishes,
vitiate his word at the place of judgment and decision in the presence of Enlil!
May she have Enlil, the king, decree[156] the ruin of his land,
the destruction of his people, the pouring-out of his life like water!

May Enki, the mighty prince whose decrees take precedence,
the wisest of the gods who knows every sort of thing,

(reverse xxvii)

who prolongs the days of my life,
deprive him of knowledge and understanding,
and constantly lead him astray!
May he dam up his rivers at the source;
may he not let there be grain, the life of the people, in his land!

May Shamash, the mighty judge of heaven and earth,
who guides aright living creatures,
the lord, my support, overthrow his kingdom;
may he not accord (him) his rights!
May he confuse his ways;
may he cause the foundations of his nation to crumble;
may he prepare for him in his vision an evil omen
predicting[157] the uprooting of the foundations of his kingdom,
and also the ruin of his land!
May the blighting word of Shamash come upon him quickly;
above, may he cut him off from among the living;
below, in the underworld, may he cause his shade to thirst for water!

May Sin, the lord of heaven, my divine creator,
whose chastening stands conspicuous among the gods,
deprive him of the crown (and) throne of sovereignty!
May he lay upon him heavy guilt as his great punishment,
which will not depart from his life,
and may he bring the days, months (and) years of his reign
to an end in woe and lamentation!
May he multiply for him the burdens of sovereignty;
may he determine as the fate for him
a life that is constantly wrestling with death!

May Adad, the lord of abundance,
the irrigator of heaven and earth, my helper,
deprive him of the rains from heaven
(and) the floodwaters from the springs!
May he bring his land to destruction through want and hunger;
may he thunder furiously over his city,
and turn his land into the desolation of a flood!

May Zababa, the mighty warrior,
the first-born son of Ekur,[158] who marches at my right hand,
shatter his weapons on the field of battle!
May he turn day into night for him,
and let his enemy trample upon him!

May Inanna, the lady of battle and conflict, who bares my weapons,
my gracious protecting genius, the admirer of my reign,
curse his rule with her great fury in her wrathful heart!
May she turn his good into evil;

(reverse xxviii)

may she shatter his weapons on the field of battle and conflict;
may she create confusion (and) revolt for him!
May she strike down his warriors,
(and) water the earth with their blood!
May she throw up a heap of his warriors' bodies on the plain;
may she show his warriors no mercy!
As for himself, may she deliver him into the hands of his enemies,

154 Lit. "person who is called a name."
155 The consort of Enlil.
156 Lit. "may she put in the mouth of Enlil, the king."
157 Lit. "of."
158 i.e. "of Enlil," since Ekur was Enlil's temple in Nippur.

and may they carry him away in bonds to a land hostile
to him!

May Nergal,[159] the strong one among the gods,
the fighter without peer, who achieves victory for me,
burn his people in his great power,
like the raging fire of swamp-reeds!
May he cut him off with his powerful weapons,
and break his body in pieces like an earthen image!

May Nintu, the exalted mistress of the lands,
the mother who bore me, deny him an heir;
may she not let him receive a name
or beget a male descendant in the midst of his people!

May Ninkarrak,[160] the daughter of Anum, my
advocate in Ekur,
inflict upon him in his body a grievous malady,
an evil disease, a serious injury which never heals,
whose nature no physician knows,
which he cannot allay with bandages,
which like a deadly bite cannot be rooted out,
and may he continue to lament (the loss of) his vigor
until his life comes to an end!

May the mighty gods of heaven and earth,
the Annunaki in their totality,
the guardian spirit of the temple, (and) Lebettum of
Ebabbar,
curse him, his descendants, his land, his warriors,
his people, and his nation, with a foul curse!

May Enlil, by his word which cannot be altered,
curse him with these[161] curses,
and may they come upon him quickly!

The Middle Assyrian Laws

(Translator: Theophile J. Meek)

The Middle Assyrian Laws are preserved to us, not on a stela as in the case of Hammurabi's laws, but on clay tablets, some of which are unfortunately badly broken, and the lacunae have not as yet been filled. The tablets were unearthed by German archaeologists in the course of their extensive excavation of ancient Ashur, modern Qal'at Shergat, from 1903 to the spring of 1914. The tablets themselves date from the time of Tiglath-pileser I in the 12th century B.C., but the laws on them may go back to the 15th century.

The texts were published by Otto Schroeder, *KAV*, supplemented later by five fragments published and translated by Ernst F. Weidner in *AfO*, XII (1937), 50 ff. The most elaborate treatment of the former texts is G. R. Driver and John C. Miles, *The Assyrian Laws, Edited with Translation and Commentary* (1935), where the extensive literature is cited in full. Driver's translation is one of the best and is far superior to that by D. D. Luckenbill and F. W. Geers in J. M. P. Smith, *The Origin and History of Hebrew Law* (1931). In the present translation Tablets C and G of the Driver-Miles edition are joined and Tablets D, H, and J are omitted altogether since it is now recognized that they do not belong here. The restoration of parts of Tablets C + G, M, and F follows closely that of M. David in *Symbolae ad iura orientis antiqui pertinentes Paulo Koschaker dedicatae* (1939), pp. 121 ff. Tablet K and the first part of Tablet L are hortatory in character and hence probably constituted the introduction to the laws, like the hortatory introduction to the laws in Deuteronomy.

The Laws

TABLET A[1]

1: If a woman, [whether] the wife of a seignior or the daughter of a seignior, has entered the temple of a god, has stolen something belonging to the sanctuary [from] the temple of the god, (and) it has been found [in her possession], when they have prosecuted [her] or convicted [her], [they shall take] the indictment and make inquiry of the god; as he orders [the woman to be treated], they shall treat her.

2: If a woman, whether the wife of a seignior or the daughter of a seignior, has uttered blasphemy or indulged in loose talk, that woman shall bear the penalty due her; they shall not touch her husband, her sons, (or) her daughters.

3: If, when a seignior was either sick or dead, his wife has stolen something from his house (and) has given (it) either to a seignior or to a lady or to anyone else, they shall put the seignior's wife to death along with the receivers as well. Also, if the wife of a seignior, whose husband is alive, has stolen (something) from her husband's house (and) has given (it) either to a seignior or to a lady or to anyone else, the seignior shall prosecute his wife and inflict the (proper) punishment; also the receiver who received (it) from the hand of the seignior's wife shall give up the stolen (property) and they shall inflict on the receiver the same punishment that the seignior inflicted on his wife.

4: If either a male slave or a female slave has received something (stolen) from the hand of a seignior's wife, they shall cut off the nose (and) ears of the male or female slave, thus compensating for the stolen (property), while the seignior shall cut off his wife's ears. However, if he lets his wife go free, without cutting off her ears, they shall not cut off those of the male or female slave and so they shall not compensate for the stolen (property).

5: If a seignior's wife has stolen something from another seignior's house, exceeding the value of five minas of lead, the owner of the stolen (property) shall swear, "I never let her take (it); there was a theft from my house," if her husband (so) desires, he may give up the stolen (property) and ransom her (but) cut off her ears. If her husband does not wish to ransom her, the owner of the stolen (property) shall take her and cut off her nose.

[159] The god of the underworld, whose cult-center was Kutha in northern Babylonia.

[160] A form of Gula, a goddess of healing, worshiped particularly at Isin.

[161] Reading *á-ni-a-tim*.

[1] Schroeder, *KAV*, No. 1, pp. 1-14.

6: If a seignior's wife has made a deposit abroad, the receiver shall be liable for the stolen (property).[2]

7: If a woman has laid hands on a seignior, when they have prosecuted her, she shall pay thirty minas of lead (and) they shall flog her twenty (times) with staves.

8: If a woman has crushed a seignior's testicle in a brawl, they shall cut off one finger of hers, and if the other testicle has become affected along with it by catching the infection even though a physician has bound (it) up, or she has crushed the other testicle in the brawl, they shall tear out both her [eyes].[3]

9: [If] a seignior laid hands on the wife of a(nother) seignior, thereby treating her like a young child, when they have prosecuted him (and) convicted him, they shall cut off [one] finger of his. If he has kissed her, they shall draw his lower lip along the edge of the *blade* of an ax (and) cut (it) off.

10: [If] either a seignior or a lady entered a(nother) seignior's [house] and killed [either a man] or a woman, [they shall give] the murderers [to the next-of-kin[4]], and if he chooses he may put them to death, or [if he chooses] he may spare (them but) take [their property]. [However, if] the murderers have nothing at home [to give], either a son or [a daughter] . . . in the house . . . belonging to. . . .

11: (not preserved)

12: If, as a seignior's wife passed along the street, a(nother) seignior has seized her, saying to her, "Let me lie with you," since she would not consent (and) kept defending herself, but he has taken her by force (and) lain with her, whether they found him on the seignior's wife or witnesses have charged him that he lay with the woman, they shall put the seignior to death, with no blame attaching to the woman.[5]

13: When a seignior's wife has left her own house and has visited a(nother) seignior where he is living, if he has lain with her, knowing that she was a seignior's wife, they shall put the seignior to death and the woman as well.

14: If a seignior has lain with the wife of a(nother) seignior either in a temple-brothel or in the street, knowing that she was a seignior's wife, they shall treat the adulterer as the seignior orders his wife to be treated. If he has lain with her without knowing that she was a seignior's wife, the adulterer is guiltless; the seignior shall prosecute his wife, treating her as he thinks fit.[6]

15: If a seignior has caught a(nother) seignior with his wife, when they have prosecuted him (and) convicted him, they shall put both of them to death, with no liability attaching to him. If, upon catching (him), he has brought him either into the presence of the king or into the presence of the judges, when they have prosecuted him (and) convicted him, if the woman's husband puts his wife to death, he shall also put the seignior to death, but if he cuts off his wife's nose, he shall turn the seignior into a eunuch and they shall mutilate his whole face. However, if he let his wife go free, they shall let the seignior go free.

16: If a seignior [has lain with a(nother) seignior's] wife at her invitation,[7] no blame attaches to the seignior; the (married) seignior shall inflict such punishment on his wife as he thinks fit. If he has lain with her by force, when they have prosecuted him (and) convicted him, his punishment shall be like that of the seignior's wife.

17: If a seignior has said to a(nother) seignior, "People have lain repeatedly with your wife," since there were no witnesses, they shall make an agreement (and) go to the river (for the water ordeal).

18: If a seignior said to his neighbor either in private or in a brawl, "People have lain repeatedly with your wife; I will prosecute (her) myself," since he is not able to prosecute (her and) did not prosecute (her), they shall flog that seignior forty (times) with staves (and) he shall do the work of the king for one full month;[8] they shall castrate him and he shall also pay one talent[9] of lead.

19: If a seignior started a rumor against his neighbor in private, saying, "People have lain repeatedly with him," or he said to him in a brawl in the presence of (other) people, "People have lain repeatedly with you; I will prosecute you," since he is not able to prosecute (him) (and) did not prosecute (him), they shall flog that seignior fifty (times) with staves (and) he shall do the work of the king for one full month; they shall castrate him and he shall also pay one talent of lead.

20: If a seignior lay with his neighbor, when they have prosecuted him (and) convicted him, they shall lie with him (and) turn him into a eunuch.[10]

21: If a seignior struck a(nother) seignior's daughter and has caused her to have a miscarriage, when they have prosecuted him (and) convicted him, he shall pay two talents thirty minas of lead; they shall flog him fifty (times) with staves (and) he shall do the work of the king for one full month.[11]

22: If in the case of a seignior's wife one not her father, nor her brother, nor her son, but another person, has caused her to take to the road, but he did not know that she was a seignior's wife, he shall (so) swear and he shall also pay two talents of lead to the woman's husband. If [he knew that she was a seignior's wife], he shall pay the damages [and swear], "I never lay with her." However, if the [seignior's] wife [has declared], "He did lie with me," when the man has paid the damages to the seignior, he shall go [to the] river, although he had no (such) agreement; if he has turned back from the river, they shall treat him as the woman's husband treated his wife.

[2] cf. Tablet C + G, §9.

[3] cf. Deut. 25:11 f.

[4] Restoring *a-na bêl nap-ša-a-te*, lit. "to the master of the life."

[5] With §§12-17, 55, 56 cf. Deut. 22:23-29.

[6] Lit. "in accordance with his heart."

[7] Restoring [*ki-i*] *pi-i-ša*, lit., "in accordance with her mouth."

[8] Lit. "one month of days."

[9] A talent contained 60 minas.

[10] cf. Lev. 18:22; 20:13.

[11] Other laws on the same topic are §§50-52 below, with all of which cf. Exod. 21:22-25; cf. also CH §§209-14.

23: If a seignior's wife, having taken a(nother) seignior's wife into her house, has given her to a man to lie with and the man knew that she was a seignior's wife, they shall treat him like one who had lain with a married woman and they shall treat the procuress as the woman's husband treats his adulterous wife. However, if the woman's husband does nothing to his adulterous wife, they shall do nothing to the adulterer or the procuress; they shall let them go free. However, if the seignior's wife did not know (the situation), but the woman who brought her into her house brought the man to her by *trickery* and he has lain with her, if when she left the house she has declared that she was ravished, they shall let the woman go free, since she is guiltless; they shall put the adulterer and procuress to death. However, if the woman has not (so) declared, the seignior shall inflict on his wife such punishment as he sees fit (and) they shall put the adulterer and the procuress to death.

24: If a seignior's wife, having deserted her husband,[12] has entered the house of an Assyrian,[13] whether it was in the same city or in some neighboring city, where he set her up in a house, (and) she stayed with the mistress of the house (and) spent the night (there) three (or) four times, without the master of the house knowing that the seignior's wife was staying in his house, (and) later that woman has been caught, the master of the house whose wife deserted him shall cut off (the ears of) his wife but take her back; they shall cut off the ears of the seignior's wife with whom his wife stayed; if he wishes, her husband may pay three talents thirty minas of lead as the (redemption) price for her, or if he wishes, they may take his wife away.[14] However, if the master of the house knew that the seignior's wife was staying in his house with his wife, he shall pay the (extra) third.[15] However, if he has denied (it) by declaring, "I did not know (it)," they shall go to the river (for the water ordeal). However, if the seignior in whose house the (other) seignior's wife was staying has turned back from the river, he shall pay the (extra) third; if the seignior whose wife deserted him has turned back from the river, he is quit since he fulfilled the total (requirement) for the river (ordeal). However, if the seignior whose wife deserted him does not cut off (the ears of) his wife (and) takes her back, there is no punishment at all.[16]

25: If a woman is living in her father's house and her husband is dead, since the brothers of her husband have as yet made no division (of the estate) and she has no son, the brothers of her husband, having made no division, shall take whatever ornaments her husband bestowed on her (and) are not lost; they shall have whatever remains submitted to the gods (and then) make claim (and) take (it); they shall not be forced to take the river (ordeal) or the oath.

[12] Lit. "betaken herself away from the face of her husband."

[13] An Assyrian was an ordinary citizen, manifestly lower in rank than a seignior.

[14] i.e. divorce her.

[15] i.e. he shall pay 1⅓ times the marriage-price.

[16] With §§22-24 cf. Lev. 20:10-21.

26: If a woman is living in her father's house and her husband is dead, if her husband has sons, they shall take whatever ornaments her husband bestowed on her; if her husband has no sons, she shall take (them) herself.

27: If a woman is living in her father's house (and) her husband has been coming in frequently, any marriage-gift, which her husband gave her, he may take back as his own, (but) he may not touch what belongs to her father's house.

28: When a widow has entered a seignior's house (as wife) and she has her infant son with her, if he has grown up in her (second) husband's house but no deed of adoption for him was written, he shall not receive a portion from the estate of his foster father (and) he shall not be liable for debts; he shall receive a portion according to his title from the estate of his real father.[17]

29: If a woman has entered her husband's house, her dowry and whatever she brought from her father's house or what her father-in-law gave her on her entry are vested in her sons, with her father-in-law's sons having no claim to (them); however, if her husband cut her off, he may give what he chooses to his sons.

30: If a father has conveyed (or) brought the betrothal-gift to the house of his son's (prospective) father-in-law, with the woman not yet married to his son and another son of his, whose wife is living in her father's house, died, he shall give his dead son's wife in marriage to his other son to whose father-in-law's house he brought (the gift); if the girl's master, who has received the gift, is not willing to give up his daughter, if he wishes, the father who brought the gift may take his (prospective) daughter-in-law (and) marry (her) to his son; however, if he wishes, he may take back in full[18] as much as he brought: lead, silver, gold, (and) what is edible, (but) with no claim to what is edible.

31: If a seignior brought the betrothal-gift to his (prospective) father-in-law's house and his (prospective) wife died, with his (prospective) father-in-law having (other) daughters, if the father-in-law wishes, he may marry a(nother) daughter of his father-in-law in place of his dead wife; or, if he wishes, he may take back the money which he gave, (but) they shall not give back to him either grain or sheep or anything edible; he shall receive only the money.

32: If a woman is still living in her father's house and her marriage-gift has been given (to her), whether she is taken or is not taken to her father-in-law's house, she shall be liable for the debts, misdemeanors, and crimes of her husband.

33: [If], while a woman is still living in her father's house, her husband died and she has sons, [she shall live where she chooses in] a house of theirs. [If] she has no [son, her father-in-law shall marry her to the son] of his choice . . . or if he wishes, he may give her in marriage to her father-in-law. If her husband and her father-in-law are both dead and she has no son, she becomes a widow; she may go where she wishes.[19]

[17] Lit. "his begetter."

[18] Lit. "the principal."

[19] With §§30, 31, 33 cf. Deut. 25:5-10.

34: If a seignior has married a widow, without sealing (it) with a contract, (and) she has lived in his house for two years, she becomes a wife; she need not leave.

35: If a widow has entered a seignior's house (as wife), anything at all that she brings becomes wholly her husband's; however, if the seignior has come in with the woman, anything at all that he brings becomes wholly the woman's.

36: If a woman is still living in her father's house or her husband made her live apart and her husband has gone off to the fields, without leaving her either oil or wool or clothing or food or anything at all (and) without having even an ear of grain brought to her from the field, that woman shall remain true to her husband for five years (and) not go to live with a(nother) husband. If she has sons (and) they hire themselves out and earn their living, the woman shall wait for her husband (and) not go to live with a(nother) husband. If she has no sons, she shall wait for her husband for five years; on the advent of the sixth year she may go to live with the man that chooses her; her husband upon coming back may not claim her; she is free for her later husband. If upon coming back he can prove that he was delayed beyond the period of five years (and) did not keep himself away of his own accord, since either an adversary[20] seized him and he had to flee or he was seized as a miscreant and so has been delayed, he shall give a woman equivalent to his wife and take back his wife. However, if the king has sent him to another country (and) he has been delayed beyond the period of five years, his wife shall wait for him (and) not go to live with a(nother) husband. However, if she has gone to live with a(nother) husband before the five years and has also borne children, her husband upon coming back shall get her back and her children as well because she did not respect the marriage-contract but got married.

37: If a seignior wishes to divorce his wife, if it is his will, he may give her something; if it is not his will, he need not give her anything; she shall go out empty.

38: If a woman is still living in her father's house and her husband has divorced her, he may take back the ornaments which he himself bestowed on her; he may not claim the marriage-price which he brought since it is vested in the woman.

39: If a seignior has given one not his daughter to a husband, if, her father being previously in debt (and) she made to live as a pledge, the earlier creditor has come forward, he shall be reimbursed for the value of the woman by the one who gave the woman (in marriage); if he has nothing to give, the seignior shall take the one who gave (her in marriage); but, if she was treated with cruelty, she is quit of the one who (so) treated her. However, if the seignior who became the husband of the woman, whether they have induced him to write a tablet or they have received a guarantee from him, makes restitution for the value of the woman, then the one who gave (her in marriage) [is quit].

40: Neither wives of seigniors nor [widows] nor [Assyrian women], who go out on the street [may have] their heads [uncovered]. The daughters of a seignior ... whether it is a shawl or a robe or [a *mantle*], must veil themselves; [they must not have] their heads [uncovered]. Whether . . . or . . . or . . . they must [not veil themselves, but] when they go out on the street alone, they must veil themselves. A concubine[21] who goes out on the street with her mistress must veil herself. A sacred prostitute whom a man married must veil herself on the street, but one whom a man did not marry must have her head uncovered on the street; she must not veil herself. A harlot must not veil herself; her head must be uncovered; he who has seen a harlot veiled must arrest her,[22] produce witnesses, (and) bring her to the palace tribunal;[23] they shall not take her jewelry away, (but) the one who arrested her may take her clothing; they shall flog her fifty (times) with staves (and) pour pitch on her head. However, if a seignior has seen a harlot veiled and has let (her) go without bringing her to the palace tribunal, they shall flog that seignior fifty (times) with staves; his prosecutor shall take his clothing; they shall pierce his ears, thread (them) with a cord, (and) tie (it) at his back, (and) he shall do the work of the king for one full month. Female slaves must not veil themselves and he who has seen a female slave veiled must arrest her (and) bring her to the palace tribunal; they shall cut off her ears (and) the one who arrested her shall take her clothes. If a seignior has seen a female slave veiled and has let her go without arresting her (and) bringing her to the palace tribunal, when they have prosecuted him (and) convicted him, they shall flog him fifty (times) with staves; they shall pierce his ears, thread (them) with a cord, (and) tie (it) at his back; his prosecutor shall take his clothes (and) he shall do the work of the king for one full month.[24]

41: If a seignior wishes to veil his concubine, he shall have five (or) six of his neighbors present (and) veil her in their presence (and) say, "She is my wife," (and so) she becomes his wife. A concubine who was not veiled in the presence of the men, whose husband did not say, "She is my wife," is not a wife; she is still a concubine. If a seignior died (and) his veiled wife has no sons, the sons by concubines become (legitimate) sons; they shall receive a share (of the estate).

42: If a seignior poured oil on the head of a(nother) seignior's daughter on a holiday or brought betrothal-

[20] Reading *qa-a-tu*, lit. "hand," for *qa-a-li*.

[21] Lit. "captive woman," the fate of whom was to become a concubine or secondary wife.

[22] Reading *i-⟨ṣa⟩-ba-as-si* for *i-ba-as-si*.

[23] Lit. "to the mouth of the palace."

[24] In this section we have a mixture of casuistic and apodictic law, just as we have in Hebrew legislation; see also Tablet A, §§57-9; Tablet B, §6; Code of Hammurabi, §§36, 38-40; and the Neo-Babylonian Laws. Hence those scholars are clearly wrong who say that apodictic law was unique and original with the Hebrews.

presents on a festival, they shall not make any return (of the gifts).

43: If the seignior either poured oil on (her) head or brought betrothal-presents (and) the son to whom he assigned the wife either died or fled, he may give (her) to whichever he wishes of his remaining sons from the oldest son to the youngest son who is at least ten years old. If the father died and the son to whom he assigned the wife also died, but the dead son has a son who is at least ten years old, he shall marry (her), but if the grandsons are younger than ten years, the girl's father, if he wishes, may give his daughter (to one of them); or if he wishes, he may make an equitable return (of the gifts). If there is no son, he shall return in full as much as he received, precious stones and whatever is not edible, but he need not return what is edible.

44: If there is an Assyrian man or if there is an Assyrian woman who is living in a seignior's house as a pledge for as much as his value (or) he was taken for the total value, when he deserves it, he (the seignior) may pull out (his hair); he may mutilate his ears by piercing (them).

45: When a woman has been given (in marriage) and the enemy has captured her husband, if she has no father-in-law and no son, she shall remain true to her husband for two years. During those two years, if she has not sufficient to live on, she shall come forward and (so) declare; she shall become a ward of the palace; her . . . shall support her (and) she shall do his work. [If she is the wife] of a peasant, . . . [shall support her (and) she shall do his work]. However, [if her husband held] a field and [a house as a fief in his city], she shall come forward [and say to the judges], ["I have nothing] to live on"; the judges shall inquire of the mayor (and) elders of the city (and) since he held a field in that city as a fief, they shall acquire the field and house for two years for her support (and) give (them) to her; she shall live (there) and they shall draw up her lease;[25] she shall complete two years (and then) she may go to live with the husband that chooses her, (and) they shall write a tablet for her as a widow. If in later days her missing husband has returned home,[26] he may take back his wife who was married to an outsider; he may not claim the sons whom she bore to her later husband, but her later husband shall take (them). The field and house which were leased to an outsider at the total value as her support, if he did not re-enter the armed service of the king, he shall pay for and take over (on the same terms) as they were leased. However, if he has not returned (but) died in another land, the king shall allocate his field and house where he wishes to allocate (them).

46: If a woman whose husband died does not wish to leave her house on her husband's death, if her husband assigned her nothing in writing, she shall live in a house of her sons where she chooses; her husband's sons shall support her; they shall make a contract with her for her food and drink as for a bride whom they love. If she is a later (wife and) has no sons, she shall live with one (of her husband's sons, and) they shall support her in common; if she has sons (and) the sons of the earlier (wife) are not willing to support her, she shall live in a house of her own sons where she chooses; it is her own sons who shall support her and she shall do their work. However, if there was actually one among her husband's sons who married her, it is the one who married her [that shall support her]; her own sons need not support her.

47: If either a man or a woman made up magical preparations and they were found in their possession, when they have prosecuted them (and) convicted them, they shall put the maker of the magical preparations to death.[27] The man who saw the making of the magical preparations (or) heard (of it) from the mouth of an eyewitness who declared to him, "I myself have seen (it)," shall come forward as an earwitness (and) so declare to the king; if the eyewitness has denied to the king what he said, he shall declare in the presence of the Bull-god, the son of Shamash, "He did indeed say (it)," (and then) he is quit. As for the eyewitness who made a statement and then denied (it), the king shall interrogate him as he is able (and) investigate his past; when the exorcist is brought, he shall make the man speak and he himself shall say, "He (the king) will not absolve you from the oath which you were made to swear to the king and his son; it is in accordance with the wording of the tablet which you were made to swear to the king and his son that you are sworn."

48: If a seignior, whose debtor's daughter is living in his house as (pledge for) a debt, asks her father, he may give her to a husband, (but) if her father is not willing, he may not give (her). If her father is dead, he shall ask one of her brothers and the latter shall speak to her (other) brothers; if a brother says, "I will redeem my sister within one full month," if he does not redeem her within one full month, the creditor, if he wishes, may declare her quit (of all claim and) give her to a husband. [However, if he wishes, he may] sell her [in accordance with] the terms [of his contract] . . . her . . . them . . . them . . . him.

49: . . . as a brother . . . . However, if the harlot died, because her brothers (so) declare, her . . . shall divide a share as a brother with the brothers of their *mother*.

50: [If a seignior] struck a(nother) seignior's [wife] and caused her to have [a miscarriage], they shall treat [the wife of the seignior], who caused the (other) seignior's wife to [have a miscarriage], as he treated her; he shall compensate for her fetus with a life. However, if that woman died, they shall put the seignior to death; he shall compensate for her fetus with a life. But, when that woman's husband has no son, if someone struck her so that she had a miscarriage, they shall put the striker to death; even if her fetus is a girl, he shall compensate with a life.

[25] Lit. "her tablet."

[26] Lit. "to the land."

[27] cf. Exod. 22:18; Lev. 20:27.

51: If a seignior struck a(nother) seignior's wife who does not rear her children and caused her to have a miscarriage, this punishment (shall hold): he shall pay two talents of lead.

52: If a seignior struck a harlot and caused her to have a miscarriage, they shall inflict blow for blow upon him; he shall compensate with a life.

53: If a woman has had a miscarriage by her own act, when they have prosecuted her (and) convicted her, they shall impale her on stakes without burying her. If she died in having the miscarriage, they shall impale her on stakes without burying her. If someone hid that woman when she had the miscarriage [without] informing [the king]....

54: (only a few signs preserved)

55: In the case of a seignior's daughter, a virgin who was living in her father's house, whose [father] had not been asked (for her in marriage), whose hymen had not been opened since she was not married, and no one had a claim against her father's house, if a seignior took the virgin by force and ravished her, either in the midst of the city or in the open country or at night in the street or in a granary or at a city festival, the father of the virgin shall take the wife of the virgin's ravisher and give her to be ravished; he shall not return her to her husband (but) take her; the father may give his daughter who was ravished to her ravisher in marriage. If he has no wife, the ravisher shall give the (extra) third in silver to her father as the value of a virgin (and) her ravisher shall marry her (and) not cast her off. If the father does not (so) wish, he shall receive the (extra) third for the virgin in silver (and) give his daughter to whom he wishes.[28]

56: If the virgin has given herself to the seignior, the seignior shall (so) swear and they shall not touch his wife; the seducer shall give the (extra) third in silver as the value of a virgin (and) the father shall treat his daughter as he wishes.

57: Whether it is flogging or ... [of] a seignior's wife [that] is prescribed [on] the tablet, [let it be done in the presence of the judges].

58. In all penalties, [whether tearing out (the eyes) or] cutting off (the ears) of [a seignior's wife], let the official be informed [and let him come] (and do) as [it is prescribed on the tablet].

59: Apart from the penalties for [a seignior's wife] which [are prescribed] on the tablet, [when she deserves it], a seignior may pull out (the hair of) his wife, mutilate (or) twist her ears, with no liability attaching to him.

The month of Sha-sarate, the 2nd day, the eponymy of Sagiu.[29]

TABLET B[30]

1: [If brothers divide the estate of their father ... the orchards and wells on] the land, [the oldest son] shall choose (and) take two portions [as his share[31]] and then his brothers one after the other shall choose (and) take (theirs). The youngest son shall divide up any *cultivated* land along with all the (produce of their) labors; the oldest son shall choose (and) take one portion and then cast lots with his brothers for his second portion.

2: If one among brothers who have not divided (the inheritance) took a life, they shall give him up to the next-of-kin; if he chooses, the next-of-kin may put him to death, or if he chooses, he may spare (him) [and] take his share.

3: If one among brothers who have not divided (the inheritance) uttered treason or ran away, the king (shall deal) with his share as he thinks fit.

4: [If], when brothers are in (joint occupation of) an undivided field, one brother among them ... sowed seed ... cultivated the field (but) another [brother] has come forward (and) [taken the grain] of his brother's tillage [for] the second time, when they have prosecuted him (and) convicted him, [the brother who] cultivated [the field] shall take [his share] as soon as the former comes forward.

5: [If, when brothers are in (joint occupation of) an un]divided [field], [one brother among] them dug up [the field with spades] ... and ... has come forward....

6: ... he shall acquire by purchase.[32] Before he acquires the field [and] house by purchase, he shall have the herald make proclamation within the city of Ashur (if the property is there) three times during one full month (or) he shall have (him) make proclamation three times within the city of the field and house that he is about to acquire, saying, "I am about to acquire by [purchase] the field and house of so-and-so, the son of so-and-so, in the precincts of this city; let those who have a right or a claim to them produce their deeds, lay (them) before the registrars, set forth their claim, show a clear title, and take (the property). Those who have produced their deeds for me during this one full month, while there is still time without forgetting it, (and) have placed (them) before the registrars—(such) person is secured to the extent of his field (and) shall take (it)." When the herald has made proclamation within the city of Ashur, one of the ministers (who stands) before the king, the city-clerk, the herald, and the king's registrars shall convene—in the case of another city where he is about to acquire a field and house, the mayor (and) three elders of the city shall convene—they shall have the herald make proclamation; they shall write their tablets (and) deliver (them), saying, "During this one full month the herald has made proclamation three times. He who has not produced his deed during this one full month (and) laid (it) before the registrars lost title to[33] the field and house; they are free to him who had the herald make proclamation." Three

[28] cf. Deut. 22:23-27.

[29] For this date in the reign of Tiglath-pileser I of Assyria see E. F. Weidner, *AfO* XII (1937), 48 f.

[30] Schroeder, *KAV*, No. 2, pp. 14-18, with §§1 and 17 restored in part by the duplicate, Weidner, *op. cit.*, Tafel v, No. 2.

[31] cf. Deut. 21:17.

[32] Lit. "for silver."

[33] Lit. "his hand went up from."

tablets containing the herald's proclamation belonging to the judges they shall write; one [tablet] the registrars....

7: [If a seignior destroyed the house of his neighbor,] ... as much as [the owner of the house] claims ... for ... and the value of the house ... which he destroyed ... twofold on the value of the house ... he shall give to the owner of the house ... ; for the one talent of lead they shall flog him five (times) [with staves] (and) he shall do the work of the king for one [full] month.

8: If a seignior has encroached on the more important bounded property[34] of his neighbor, when they have prosecuted him (and) convicted him, he shall give up one-third as much field as he encroached on; they shall cut off one finger of his; they shall flog him one hundred (times) with staves (and) he shall do the work of the king for one full month.

9: If a seignior infringed upon the less important bounded property from allotment,[35] when they have prosecuted him (and) convicted him, he shall pay one talent of lead (and) give up one-third as much field as he encroached on; they shall flog him fifty (times) with staves (and) he shall do the work of the king for one full month.

10: If a seignior dug a well (or) constructed a dike in a field not his, he lost title to his well (or) his dike; they shall flog him thirty (times) with [staves] (and) [he shall do] the work of the king for twenty days. The encroachment on the ground ... in the ... the dike ... he shall swear, ... "I did ... I did not ... the well; I did not ... the dike"; the owner of the field ... in ... the well ... and....

11: ... and ... a creditor ... to do ... or ... the creditor ... the tablets ... (the produce of) the labors ... to do ... the field ... to the creditor ... he shall give.

12: If a seignior set out an orchard, [dug] a well, (or) grew trees in [his neighbor's] field, with the owner of the field looking on (and) not [objecting], the orchard is free to the one who set it out, (but) he shall give field for field to the owner of the orchard-ground.

13: If a seignior either set out an orchard or dug a well or grew vegetables or trees on ground not his, when they have prosecuted him (and) convicted him, as soon as the owner of the field comes forward, he shall take the orchard together with (the produce of) his labors.

14: If a seignior occupied a piece of ground not his and made bricks, when they have prosecuted him (and) convicted him, he shall give up one-third as much ground (and) they shall appropriate his bricks; they shall flog him fifty (times) with staves (and) he shall do the work of the king [for one full month].

15: [If a seignior] ... on ground not his (and) made bricks, they shall appropriate [his bricks]; they shall flog him [fifty times with staves] (and) he shall do [the work of the king for one full month].

16: (not preserved)

17: [If] there is [water on the land] in the wells [which can] be brought[36] [on to] the irrigated land in order to prepare (it), the owners of the fields shall assist one another; each shall do the work to the extent of his field (and) irrigate his field. However, if there is no cooperation among them, the cooperative one among them shall apply to the judges (and) procure the judges' written order,[37] and then he may do the work, take that water for himself (and) irrigate his field, with no one else irrigating (from it).

18: If there is rain water[38] which can be brought on to the irrigated land in order to prepare (it), the owners of the fields shall assist one another; each shall do the work to the extent of his field (and) irrigate his field. However, if there is no cooperation among them and the cooperative one among them receives the judges' written order against the uncooperative ones, the mayor and five elders [of the city shall convene] ... they shall flog him [fifty (times) with staves] (and) he shall do [the work of the king for one full month].

19: [If a seignior] planted (and) [cultivated] his neighbor's [field] or occupied it, [if the owner of the field swears] by the king, "He planted it and cultivated (it)," as soon as he has objected, the cultivator of the field shall be deprived of his claim at the time of reaping [and] pour out [the grain] into a conveyance (and) return the grain measure by measure [to the owner of the field; in accordance with] the yield of the city's field ... he shall give [to the owner] of the field.

20: [If] a seignior ... in a field not his, surrounded (it) with a boundary-wall, set up a boundary-stone (and) declared, "The field was a gift," when they have prosecuted him (and) convicted him,....

TABLET C + G[39]

1: ... their master ... and if the taker ... which I *redeemed* ... [he shall compensate for the male slave at the rate of] ... talents of lead (and) for the female slave at the rate of four talents of lead.... However, if the receiver declares, ... he shall (so) swear in the presence of god and he shall take as much as....

2: [If a seignior sold] to another seignior [either a man of the aristocracy] or a woman of the aristocracy[40] who was living [in his house] as (security for) money or as [a pledge, or] he sold [anyone else] who was living in his house, [when they have prosecuted him], he shall forfeit[41] his money; he shall give [his equivalent in accordance with his value to] the owner of the

[34] This was property that came as the preferred share to the oldest son; cf. Tablet B, §1.

[35] This was property that came as the secondary share, selected by lot; cf. Tablet B, §1.

[36] Lit. "can come."

[37] Lit. "tablet."

[38] Lit. "water of Adad (the god of rain)."

[39] Schroeder, *KAV*, No. 6, pp. 20 f., plus No. 143, p. 89. The two tablets are combined by Weidner, *op. cit.*, Tafel III, No. 1.

[40] Lit. "the son of a seignior or the daughter of a seignior," where "son" and "daughter" are used in a technical sense, meaning one who belongs to the class of seigniors.

[41] Lit. "his hand shall go up from."

property; they shall flog him . . . (times) [with staves] (and) he shall do the work of the king for twenty days.

3: [If a seignior] sold into another country [either a man of the aristocracy] or a woman of the aristocracy who [was living in his house] as (security for) money or as a pledge, [when they have prosecuted him] (and) convicted him, he shall forfeit his money; he shall give [his equivalent in accordance with his value to] the owner of the property; they shall flog him . . . (times) [with staves] (and) he shall do the work of the king for forty days. [If the man that he sold] died in the other country, he shall [compensate with a life]. An Assyrian man or an Assyrian woman [who] was taken [at the total value] may be sold into another country.

4: [If a seignior] sold [either an ox or] an ass or a horse or any beast not [his own which] was stabled in his house [as a pledge], he shall give [a beast like it in value], (but) he need not return the money. If [he did not give] a beast, he shall forfeit [his money]; the owner of the property whose [beast] was stabled [in the seignior's house] shall seize his beast, while the receiver [of] the beast [shall be reimbursed] for his money by the seller.

5: [If a seignior], upon stealing either an ox or an ass or a horse [or any other beast] from the pasture, [sold it] to a(nother) seignior at the proper price and the purchaser [paid the proper] price without knowing [that it was stolen], should it be found [in his possession], the seller shall compensate [in full] for the thing stolen, as much as it turned out to be.

6: [When a seignior found either a] . . . or a beast or anything else [that was lost] and witnesses [saw it, if the seignior sold it and] the owner of that property recognized [his property] in the possession of [the purchaser] (and) seized (it), but the seignior [declared, "I] purchased it," the owner of the property shall [not] take his property [from his hand; he shall give it back and] get (it) from the hand of the seller and. . . . [Furthermore, the seignior] who bought the property and from whose hand [the owner of the property did take his property shall be reimbursed] by the seignior who sold (it) to him. [If] the seller declares, "I did not [know] that his property was lost," [the witnesses who] saw (it) shall prosecute [him]; . . . .

6*a*: . . . he shall take and . . . which for money . . . two goats to the owner of the silver . . . has come forward and whatever . . . he shall not take from him. . . .

7: [If there was a] . . . or anyone who was living [in the house of] an Assyrian as a pledge [or as (security for) money] and the time expired . . . if he . . . the money for as much as his value, he shall take . . . ; if he did not . . . his money value . . . he shall acquire and take . . . he shall make known; the principal of the money . . . there is not. . . .

8: [If a seignior stole a] . . . or a beast or anything else, when they have prosecuted him (and) convicted him, he shall pay . . . [minas] of lead; they shall flog him fifty (times) with staves (and) he shall do [the work of the king for . . . days]. The judges of the *land* [shall give] this judgment. [If the stolen] (property) has reached (the value of) . . . [minas of lead] and [he has sold] the stolen (property), as much as he stole, [for the full price], small or great, the king shall inflict on him such [punishment] as he thinks fit.

9: [If, when a seignior] entrusted everything of every sort [either to his wife] or to a slave, [*something from the house*] was placed in deposit elsewhere [and the receiver], in whose house the deposit was made, did not report [*the deposit* to the seignior], who entrusted his house, [and the property] was found [in] his possession, [the owner of the property shall take his property], while that seignior shall be liable for the stolen (property).

10: [If a seignior] has overvalued [a trust] from his neighbor (and) has put (it) in writing, when they have prosecuted him (and) convicted him, since he is a thief, (he shall bear) the punishment which the king, [as he thinks fit], inflicts on him.

11: [If a seignior] has overvalued . . . (and) has put (it) in writing [so as to] make the creditors lose [their money], when they have prosecuted him (and) convicted him, [*because*] he wrote down [*too large an amount*], they shall flog him . . . (times) with staves . . . the hand of the creditors . . . the clerk and. . . .

TABLET E[42]

1: . . . [when they have prosecuted him] (and) convicted him . . . which he paid back . . . they shall flog him; from . . . thirty minas of lead . . . and the rest of the fifteen minas . . . the sons of the king (and) the judges . . . which he paid back in accordance with what . . . which outside to the son . . . the king. . . .

2: [If] . . . he struck . . . to the head . . . which . . . one mina . . . him. . . .

3: [If] . . . everything, as much as . . . let him receive. However, if from . . . he seized and the work . . . he will not turn . . . his hire he shall not . . . the employer. . . .

4: [If] . . . the doer . . . they shall deposit . . . of the former creditor . . . of the creditor . . . and. . . .

TABLET F[43]

1: . . . to . . . the sheep which. . . . However, if [the seignior . . . and carried off] a sheep from the herd of his neighbor and changed [its ownership mark] and substituted his own ownership mark, [they shall flog] the seignior who carried off the sheep one hundred (times) with [staves] (and) they shall pull out (his hair); [he shall do] the work [of the king] for one full month and he shall also be liable for the theft of the sheep.

2: The herdsman of a herd of horses must not sell [a beast] either for money [or for] . . . without asking its owner; he must not . . . out of his hands; the herdsman of the herd and the receiver [of the beast] . . . the

[42] Schroeder, *KAV*, No. 4, p. 19.
[43] Schroeder, *KAV*, No. 5, p. 19.

beast which he sold . . . [*since he is a thief*], they shall mutilate his face; they shall. . . .

TABLET K[44]

1: . . . and he himself. . . .

2: . . . of the king you must not [take . . . ba]il in money from . . . you must not take; bail . . . you must not take; bail. . . .

3: . . . silver let him produce, any falling off before . . . let him pass over, let him . . . these . . . of silver and his quota. . . .

TABLET L[45]

1: . . . from him . . . you must not take.

2: . . . to the burgher . . . which was established. . . .

3: [If] . . . bribed a citizen of his land and . . . , when they have prosecuted him (and) convicted him, . . . he shall complete it and. . . .

4: [If] . . . of the judge his debtor to his house . . . the debtor need not repay the . . . of the judge; if . . . which his plaintiff. . . .

5: . . . which he keeps . . . the bribe . . . to. . . .

TABLET M[46]

1: . . . on his own initiative . . . , "Sell (it) to me," . . . it sank . . . whether it sank or was altered . . . they must make good the boat with its cargo . . . or they shall compensate that person who has laid claim to the boat . . . ; the boatman who . . . did not swear by the king shall not be reinstated.[47]

2: [If] . . . a boat whether it was drifting downstream[48] or crossing from one bank to the other, with the current . . . *carelessly* rammed a loaded boat and has sunk (it) [or] . . . rammed an empty boat and [has sunk it], as much cargo as was lost. . . .

3: [If a seignior], while [he was making] a journey, gave clothing to a clothier to wash [and when he returned the clothier] declared, "It is lost," [he shall make good] in full to the owner of the clothing whatever clothing was lost. However, if he sold (it) and it has been heard of [*in the city*, when they have prosecuted him] and convicted him, [or] it was found [in the possession of the purchaser], the seignior's . . . [shall make] . . .-fold [restitution] for the stolen (property).

TABLET N[49]

1: If a seignior [said] to a(nother) seignior . . . in a brawl, "You uttered blasphemy . . . and you have profaned the temple of god," . . . they shall flog him forty (times) with staves. . . .

2: If a seignior [said] to a(nother) seignior . . . in a brawl, "[You uttered] blasphemy . . . and you have profaned the temple of god," . . . , since he is not [able to prosecute (him and) did not prosecute (him), they shall flog] that seignior [forty (times) with staves (and) he shall do the work of the king] for one [full] month.[50]

TABLET O[51]

1: [If] . . . prescribed . . . for his sons, they shall do. . . .

2: . . . his mind was changed . . . his house he does not determine . . . which they did. . . .

3: . . . on the days . . . the houses which . . . the male slaves . . . and the orchards . . . after this . . . the tablets which . . . and the witnesses as many as. . . .

4: If brothers [divide] the estate of [their] father . . . the orchards and the wells [on the land, the oldest son shall choose (and) take two] portions [and then his brothers one] after the other shall choose (and) [take (theirs). The youngest son shall divide up any] *cultivated* land [along with all] the (produce of their) labors; [the oldest son shall choose (and) take one portion and then cast lots with his brothers for his second portion].[52]

5: If the owner . . . their (*fem.*) water . . . they shall make claim and give. . . .

6: If there is water on the land in [the wells which can be brought on to the irrigated land in order to prepare (it)], the owners [of the fields shall assist one another]; each shall do the work [to the extent of his field] (and) irrigate his field. [However, if] there is no cooperation [among them, the cooperative one among them] shall apply to [the judges] (and) procure the [judges'] written order, [and then he may do the work, take] that water for [himself (and) irrigate his field, with no one else irrigating (from it)].[53]

7: . . . his freedom . . . he cut off, he shall pay one mina of silver . . . he shall pay . . . minas of silver . . . he shall pay four *qu* . . . *by proper reckoning* . . . they shall take.

The Hittite Laws

(Translator: Albrecht Goetze)

The laws which have come down to us represent two tablets of a series called "If anyone." A label which is accidentally preserved (*ABoT*, 52) proves that there was a third tablet of which no text has become known as yet. The texts known up to 1922 were utilized in the following work, which is still the standard translation: F. Hrozný, *Code hittite provenant de l'Asie Mineure* (1922). Additional fragments have been published as *KUB*, XIII, 11-16; *KUB*, XXVI, 56; *KUB*, XXIX, 13-38.

Other translations of the Laws were presented by the following authors: H. Zimmern and J. Friedrich, *Hethitische Gesetze* (= *AO*, XXIII/2 [1922]) with "Nachträge" (1923); compare also J. Friedrich, *Aus dem hethitischen Schrifttum* 1 (= *AO*, XXIV/3 [1925]), 27 ff. G. A. Barton in *Archaeology and the Bible* (1927), 369-88. E. Ebeling, *AOT*, 423-31. G. Furlani, *Leggi dell' Asia anteriore antica* (1929), 61-88. A. Walther in J. M. P. Smith, *The Origin and History of Hebrew Law*

44 Weidner, *op. cit.*, Tafel V, No. 1.
45 Weidner, *op. cit.*, Tafel III, No. 2.
46 Weidner, *op. cit.*, Tafel VI, No. 1.
47 Lit. "shall not return."
48 Lit. "from above."
49 Weidner, *op. cit.*, Tafel VI, No. 2.
50 §§1 and 2 are similar to Tablet A, §§18 and 19, and have been restored in part from them.
51 Weidner, *op. cit.*, Tafel V, No. 2.
52 Restored in part from the duplicate, Tablet B, §1.
53 Restored in part from the duplicate, Tablet B, §17.

(1931), 246-79. A new treatment of the Hittite Laws by J. Friedrich is freely quoted by German Hittitologists, but has not been published so far. Excerpts from the first of the two tablets are also contained in Sturtevant-Bechtel, *A Hittite Chrestomathy* (1935), 202-223.

TABLET I

1: If anyone kills a man or a woman in a quarrel, he has to make amends for him/her. He shall give four persons, man or woman, and pledge his estate as security.

2: If anyone kills a male or a female slave in a quarrel, he has to make amends for him/her. He shall give two persons, man or woman, and pledge his estate as security.

3: If anyone strikes a free man or woman and he/she dies, (only) his hand doing wrong, he has to make amends for him/her. He shall give two persons and pledge his estate as security.

4: If anyone strikes a male or a female slave and he/she dies, (only) his hand doing wrong, he has to make amends for him/her. He shall give one person and pledge his estate as security.

Later version of 3 and 4: [If anyone stri]kes [a woman] and she dies, (only) his hand doing wrong, [he shall give x minas of silver]; but if the woman is a slave, he shall give 2 minas of silver.

5: If anyone kills a Hittite merchant, he shall give 100 minas of silver and pledge his estate as security. If (it happens) in the country of Luwiya or in the country of Pala, he shall give 100 minas of silver and replace his goods; if (it happens) in the Hatti land, he has (also) to make amends for the merchant himself.

Later version of 5: If anyone kills a Hittite merchant for (his) goods, he shall give [x minas of silver] and shall make threefold compensation for (his) goods. [If] he had no goods with him, and anyone kills him in a quarrel, he shall give 6 minas of silver. But if (only) the hand is doing wrong, he shall give 2 minas of silver.

6: If a person, man or woman, dies in *another* town, he on whose property he/she dies shall set aside 100 *gipeššar*[1] of his property and he[2] shall receive it.

Later version of 6: If a man dies on the field (or) fallow of another man, in case he is a free man, he shall give field (and) fallow, house (and) 1 mina (and) 20 shekels of silver. But if there is no other man's field (and) fallow, a distance of three leagues in one direction and (a distance) of three leagues in the other direction (shall be taken) and whatever village is found to fall within it, he[2] shall take those. If there is no village (within the area), he[2] forfeits (his claims).

7: If anyone blinds a free man or knocks out his teeth, he shall give 20 shekels of silver and pledge his estate as security.

8: If anyone blinds a male or female slave or knocks out his/her teeth, he shall give 10 shekels of silver and pledge his estate as security.

[1] A measure, probably a cubit.
[2] i.e. the heir.

Later version of 7 and 8: If anyone blinds a free man in a quarrel, he shall give 1 mina of silver. If (only) his hand does wrong, he shall give 20 shekels of silver.—If anyone blinds a slave in a quarrel, he shall give 30(?) shekels of silver. If (only) his hand is doing wrong, he shall give 10 shekels of silver.—If anyone knocks out the teeth of a free man, in case he knocks out 2 teeth or 3 teeth, he shall give 12 shekels of silver. If it is a slave, he shall give 6 shekels of silver.

9: If anyone bewitches a man's head, they would formerly give 6 shekels of silver; he who was bewitched would receive 3 shekels of silver, and they would receive 3 shekels of silver for the palace. Now the king has abolished the (share) of the palace and only he who was bewitched receives 3 shekels of silver.

Later version of 9: If anyone bewitches a man's head, the bewitched shall receive 3 shekels of silver.

10: If anyone bewitches a man so that he falls ill, he shall *take care* of him. He shall give a man in his stead who can look after his house until he recovers. When he recovers, he shall give him 6 shekels of silver, and he shall also pay the physician's fee.

Later version of 10: If anyone casts spells on a free man's head, he shall take care of him. He shall give a man in his stead who can look after his house until he recovers. When he recovers, he shall give him 10 shekels of silver, and he shall also pay the physician's fee. If it is a slave, he shall pay 2 shekels of silver.

11: If anyone breaks a free man's hand or foot, he shall give him 20 shekels of silver and pledge his estate as security.

12: If anyone breaks the hand or foot of a male or a female slave, he shall give 10 shekels of silver and pledge his estate as security.

Later version of 11 and 12: If anyone breaks a free man's hand or foot, in case he is permanently crippled, he shall give him 20 shekels of silver. But in case he is not permanently crippled, he shall give him 10 shekels of silver.—If anyone breaks a slave's hand or foot, in case he is permanently crippled, he shall give him 10 shekels of silver. But in case he is not permanently crippled, he shall give him 5 shekels of silver.

13: If anyone bites off a free man's nose, he shall give 1 mina of silver and pledge his estate as security.

Later version of 13: If anyone bites off a free man's nose, he shall give 30 shekels(!) of silver and pledge his estate as security.

14. If anyone bites off the nose of a male or female slave, he shall give 30(?) shekels of silver and pledge his estate as security.

Later version of 14: If anyone bites bites off a slave's nose, he shall give 15 shekels(!) of silver.

15: If anyone mutilates a free man's ear, he shall give 15 shekels of silver and pledge his estate as security.

Later version of 15: If anyone mutilates a free man's ear, he shall give 12 shekels of silver.

16: If anyone mutilates the ear of a male or female slave, he shall give 6 shekels of silver.

Later version of 16: If anyone mutilates a slave's ear, he shall give 6 shekels of silver.

17: If anyone causes a free woman to miscarry—if (it is) the 10th month, he shall give 10 shekels of silver, if (it is) the 5th month, he shall give 5 shekels of silver and pledge his estate as security.

Later version of 17: If anyone causes a free woman to miscarry, he shall give 20 shekels of silver.

18: If anyone causes a slave-woman to miscarry, if (it is) the 10th month, he shall give 5 shekels of silver.

Later version of 18: If anyone causes a slave-girl to miscarry, he shall give 10 shekels of silver.

19 (A): If any Luwian steals a person—man or woman—from Hattusa and carries him to the country of Arzawa, but his master traces him out, he shall forfeit his estate. (B): If in Hattusa any Hittite steals a Luwian and carries him to the country of Luwiya, they would formerly give 12 persons, now he shall give 6 persons and place his estate as security.

20: If any Hittite steals a Hittite slave from the country of Luwiya and carries him to the Hatti land, but his master traces him out, he shall give him 12 shekels of silver and pledge his estate as security.

21: If anyone steals the slave of a Luwian from the country of Luwiya and carries him to the Hatti land, but his master traces him out, he shall give just the slave; there will be no compensation.

22: If a slave runs away and anyone brings him back—if he seizes him in the vicinity, he shall give him shoes; if on this side of the river, he shall give him 2 shekels of silver; if on the other side of the river, he shall give him 3 shekels of silver.

23: If a slave runs away and goes to the country of Luwiya, he shall give to him who brings him back 6 shekels of silver. If a slave runs away and goes to an enemy country, whoever brings him nevertheless back, shall receive him (the slave) himself.

24: If a male or female slave runs away, the man at whose hearth his master finds him/her, shall give a man's wages for 1 year, (namely) x shekels of silver, but a woman's wages for 1 year, (namely) x[3] shekels of silver.

25: If a man fouls a storage vessel or a cistern, they would formerly give 6 shekels of silver; he who fouled would give 3 shekels of silver and for the palace they would take at random 3 shekels of silver. The king has now abandoned the (share) of the palace, and only the one who fouled gives 3 shekels of silver and pledges his estate as security.

26: (preserved only in traces)

26 (A):[4] If a woman send away a man, she shall give him . . . and. . . . The man shall get his children.

26 (B): If a man divorces a woman, and she . . . , he may sell her; whoever [buys her] shall give 12 shekels of silver.

27: If a man takes a wife and carries her [to his house], he takes her dowry with her. If the woman dies, they turn her property into (property) of the man, and the man also receives her dowry. But if she dies in the house of her father, and there are children, the man will not receive her dowry.

28: If a girl is promised to a man, but another (man) elopes with her,[5] as soon as he elopes, he shall compensate the first man for whatever he [has given]; her parents will not make any compensation. But if the parents give her to another man, the parents will make compensation. If the parents refuse (to make compensation), they shall withhold her from him.[6]

29: If a girl is betrothed to a man and he has given the bride-price for her, but the parents subsequently abrogate it (i.e. the contract) and withhold her from the man, they (i.e. the parents) shall make double compensation.

30: If the man has not yet taken the girl and refuses her, he loses the bride-price which he has brought.

31: If a free man and a slave-girl (are) *lovers* and they cohabit, he takes her for his wife, they found a family and have children, but subsequently, either (as) they quarrel or (as) they reach a friendly agreement, they break up the family, the man receives the children, but the woman receives one child.

32: If a slave takes a free woman, the provision of the law is the same for them.

33: If a slave takes a slave-girl, the provision of the law is the same for them.

34: If a slave brings the bride-price for a woman and takes her for his wife, no one shall change her social status.

35: If an overseer or a shepherd elopes with a free woman and does not bring the bride-price for her, she becomes a slave for three years.

36: If a slave brings the bride-price to the son of a free man and takes him as husband (*of his daughter*), no one shall change his social status.

37: If anyone elopes with a woman and an avenger goes after them, if two men or three men die, there be no compensation (the reason being): "Thou hast become a wolf."[7]

38: If men are implicated in a lawsuit and an avenger comes for them, (if) then the defendants get enraged and (one of them) strikes the avenger so that he dies, there will be no compensation.

39: If the inhabitant of a town has possession of another (inhabitant)'s fields, he shall also perform (the respective) service to the liege lord. If he allows fields to lie idle, another man may take the fields, but he[8] must not sell them.

40: If a craftsman disappears (and) a socman is assigned (in his stead), (if) the socman says: "This is my craftsman's fee, but this (other one) is my socage," he shall secure for himself a sealed deed concerning the fields; then he has (legal) possession of the craftsman's

[3] Probably 40.

[4] This and the following section are taken from *KUB*, XXVI, 56.

[5] Lit.: "makes her run."

[6] i.e. the authorities shall withhold the girl from the second man.

[7] The implications of this formula are not known.

[8] i.e. the other man.

fee and shall also perform the socage. If he refuses the craftsman's service, they will declare the fields of the craftsman vacant and the people of the town shall work them. If the king gives deportees, they shall give him the fields and he shall become a (landed) craftsman.

41: If a socman disappears (and) a craftsman is assigned (in his stead), (if) the craftsman says: "This is my craftsman's fee, but this (other one) is my socage," he shall secure for himself a sealed deed concerning the fields; then he has (legal) possession of the craftsman's fee and shall also perform the socage. If he refuses the socage, they take the fields of the socman for the palace, and the socage expires.

42: If anyone hires a man and he goes to war and dies, if the hire has been given, there will be no compensation. If his hire has not been given, he shall give one person and as hire he will give 12 shekels of silver, and as the hire of a woman he will give 6 shekels of silver.

43: If a man customarily fords a river with his ox, another (man) pushes him aside, seizes the tail of the ox and crosses the river, but the river carries the owner of the ox away, they[9] shall receive that very man.

44: If anyone pushes a man into a fire so that he dies, he will give his son. If anyone has performed a rite of purification on a man and disposes of the remnants of the offerings, if he disposes of them in anyone's field or house, it is sorcery and (a case for the) court of the king.

Later version of 44: [. . .] he shall purify him again. If anything in the house goes wrong, he shall purify him again. For whatever perishes in it, he shall make compensation once.

45: If anyone finds implements, he shall return them to their owner; he shall reward him. If he does not give them (back), he becomes a thief.

Later version of 45: If anyone finds implements or an ox, a sheep, a horse (or) an ass, he shall drive it back to its owner and he shall reward him. If he does not find the owner, but secures witnesses for himself, and (if) afterward its owner finds it out, he shall replace for him whatever was destroyed of the respective (property). But if he does not secure witnesses for himself, and afterward its owner finds it out, he shall be considered a thief and shall make threefold compensation.

46: If in a village anyone holds fields under socage as inheritance—if the fields have all been given to him, he shall render the services; if the fields have been given to him only to a small part, he shall not render the services, they shall render them from his father's house. If he *usurps* fields of the estate-leaver or the people of the village give a field (to him), he shall render the services.

Later version of 46: (The first part is almost identical with the earlier version. The second part is as follows:) If the field (and) fallow of the testator are vacant *or* the people of the village give him field (and) fallow, he shall render the services.

47: If anyone holds fields as a gift from the king, he shall not render the services. The king will take a loaf from (his) table and give it to him.—If anyone buys all the fields of a craftsman, he shall render the services. If he buys a great (part of) the fields, he shall not render the services. If he usurps the fields or the people of the village give them (to him), he shall render the services.

Later version of 47:[10] If anyone holds field (and) fallow as a gift from the king and if the king exempts him, he shall not render the services.—If anyone buys all the field (and) fallow of a craftsman and the owner of the field (and) fallow perishes, he shall perform the socage which the king imposes upon him. But if the owner of field (and) fallow is alive or the house of the owner of field (and) fallow is continued either in this country or in another country, he shall not perform the socage.—[11]If anyone holds field (and) fallow as a gift from the king, he shall render the services connected with the fields. If he *is exempted* by order of the palace, he shall not render the services. If anyone buys all the fields of a craftsman, they shall ask the king, and he shall render those services which the king orders. If there remain fields in the hands of the man from whom he buys, he shall not render the services. If field (and) fallow are vacant or the people of the village give it to him, he shall render the services.

48: A *ḫipparas* man renders the services, but no one shall transact business with a *ḫipparas* man. No one shall buy his son, his field (or) his vineyard. Whoever transacts business with a *ḫipparas* man, shall forfeit the purchasing-price. Whatever the *ḫipparas* man sold, he shall receive back.

Later version of 48: (It is virtually identical with the older version.)

49: If a *ḫipparas* man steals, there will be no compensation. If he is considered a felon, the community to which he belongs will make compensation. If one would indict them for theft, all of them were criminals or would have to be considered as thieves. Whether this (man) seize one (of them), or that (man) another, they would . . . a penalty.

50: The *people* who live in Nerik, in Arinna (and) in Ziplanta, (and) the priests in every town—their houses (shall be) exempt. But their associates shall render the services. The house of a man who stays in Arinna for 11 months, and he at whose gate an *eyan*[12] is erected, (shall be) free.

51: Formerly the house of a man who had become a weaver in Arinna (was) exempt, also his associates and his relations (were) exempt. Now (only) his own house (is) exempt, but his associates and his relations perform socage and render the services. In Zippalantiya it is just the same.

52: The slave of the seal-house, the slave of a royal prince (and) the master of a . . . who hold a field among craftsmen, render the services.

[9] i.e. the authorities of the respective village or town.

[10] The following precedes §46 of the later version.

[11] The following has its place after §46 of the later version.

[12] Otherwise translated by "pole."

53: If a craftsman and his associate live together, but decide when quarreling to divide their household, if there are on their land ten heads (of slaves), the craftsman receives 7 and his associate receives 3. The cattle (and) sheep on their land they shall divide in the same ratio. If anyone holds a royal gift with (special) deed, —in case they divide an old estate, the craftsman receives 2 parts of the gift and his associate receives one part.

54: Previously the Manda people, the Sala people, the people of the cities Tamalki, Hatra, Zalpa, Tashiniya, Hemuwa, the archers, the carpenters, the grooms and their *karuḫḫala* men did not render any services and did not perform socage.

55: When the Hittites, socmen, came (to) petition the father of the king and announce: "No one pays any wage and they refuse us (with the words): 'You are (only) socmen,'" the father of the king [rose] in the assembly and declared under his seal: "Go ye! Ye shall be just as your comrades!"

56: No one of the metal workers shall be freed from participating in a royal campaign in a fortress, (and) from cutting a vineyard. The gardeners shall render the full services.

57: If anyone steals a bull—if it is a weanling, it is not a bull; if it is a yearling, it is not a bull; if it is a two-year-old, that is a bull—they would formerly give 30 (head of) cattle. Now he shall give 15 (head of) cattle, (specifically) 5 two-year-olds, 5 yearlings (and) 5 weanlings and he shall pledge his estate as security.

58: If anyone steals a stallion—if it is a weanling, it is not a stallion; if it is a yearling, it is not a stallion; if it is a two-year-old, that is a stallion—they would formerly give 30 horses. Now they shall give 15 horses, (specifically) 5 two-year-old horses, 5 yearlings (and) 5 weanlings and he shall pledge his estate as security.

59: If anyone steals a ram, they used to give formerly 30 sheep. Now he shall give 15 sheep, (specifically) 5 ewes, 5 rams (and) 5 lambs.

60: If anyone finds a bull and removes the brand, (if) its owner traces it out, he shall give 7 (head of) cattle; he shall give (specifically) 2 two-year-olds, 3 yearlings (and) 2 weanlings and he shall pledge his estate as security.

61: If anyone finds a stallion and removes the brand, (if) its owner traces it out, he shall give 7 horses; he shall give (specifically) 2 two-year-olds, 3 yearlings (and) 2 weanlings and he shall pledge his estate as security.

62: If anyone finds a ram and removes the brand, (if) its owner traces it out, he shall give 7 sheep; he shall give (specifically) 2 ewes, 3 rams, (and) 2 lambs and he shall pledge his estate as security.

63: If anyone steals a plow-ox, they would formerly give 15 (head of) cattle. Now he shall give 10 (head of) cattle; he shall give (specifically) 3 two-year-olds, 3 yearlings (and) 4 weanlings and he shall pledge his estate as security.

64: If anyone steals a draft horse, its treatment is the same.

65: If anyone steals a *tamed* buck or a trained wild-goat or *tamed* mountain sheep, the compensation is as for a buck; and the compensation for it is the same.

66: If a plow-ox or a draft horse or a (milk-giving) cow or a brood ass-mare strays off to the corral, or if a *tamed* buck or a ewe or a ram strays off to the fold (and) its owner finds it, he shall receive the respective (animal); there shall be no question of a thief.

67: If anyone steals a cow, they would formerly give 12 (head of) cattle; now he shall give 6 (head of) cattle; he shall give (specifically) 2 two-year-olds, 2 yearlings (and) 2 weanlings and he shall pledge his estate as security.

68: If anyone steals a brood mare, its treatment is the same.

69: If anyone steals a ewe or a ram, they used to give formerly 12 sheep. Now he shall give 6 sheep; he shall give (specifically) 2 ewes, 2 rams (and) 2 lambs and he shall pledge his estate as security.

70: If anyone steals a horse, or a mule or an ass and its owner traces it out, he shall receive the respective (animal). In addition he (the thief) shall give it a second time and he shall pledge his estate as security.

71: If anyone finds an ox, a horse (or) a mule, he shall drive it to the king's court. If he finds it in the country, the elders may assign it to him and he may harness it. When its owner finds it, he shall receive the respective animal; there shall be no question of a thief. If the elders do not assign it (to him), he becomes a thief.

72: If an ox dies in anyone's field, the owner of the field shall give 2 oxen and pledge his estate as security.

73: If anyone disposes of a living ox (found on his property), he is as if he had committed theft.

74: If anyone breaks the horn or the foot of an ox, he shall receive that (animal) and give one in good condition to the owner of the ox. If the owner of the ox says: "I want to have my own ox," he shall receive his ox and he (i.e. the offender) shall give him 2 shekels of silver.

75: If anyone yokes an ox, a horse, a mule (or) an ass and it dies, or a wolf devours it or it gets lost, he shall give (the value of) the respective animal. But if he contends: "It died by the hand of god," he shall take an oath.

76: If anyone pawns an ox, a horse, a mule (or) an ass and it dies at his place, he has to make amends for it and he shall pay its hire.

77 (A): If anyone hits a bearing cow and causes it to miscarry, he shall give 2 shekels of silver. If anyone hits a bearing mare and causes it to miscarry, he shall give 2 shekels of silver.

77 (B): If anyone blinds the eye of an ox or a horse, he shall give 6 shekels of silver and pledge his estate as security.

78: If anyone hires an ox, applies to him the lash or the whip and its owner finds him out, he shall give 1 grain (of silver?) per streak.

79: If oxen go upon a field and the owner of the field finds them, he may yoke them for one day till the stars come out, and shall (then) drive them back to their owner.

80: If anyone throws a sheep to the wolves, its owner shall receive the meat and he himself shall keep the hide.

81: If anyone steals a fattened pig, they would formerly give 1 mina of silver. Now he shall give 12 shekels of silver and pledge his estate as security.

82: If anyone steals an *ordinary* pig, he shall give 6 shekels of silver and pledge his estate as security.

83: If anyone steals a bearing pig, he shall give 6 shekels of silver. They shall also count the little pigs, and he shall give a *pārisu* of grain[13] for each 2 little pigs.

84: If anyone strikes a bearing pig so that it dies, its treatment is the same.

85: If anyone *mistreats* a little pig and steals (it), he shall give 1 grain (of silver?) per streak.

86: If a pig goes to a threshing floor, or a field (or) a garden, and the owner of the threshing floor, the field (or) the garden strikes it so that it dies, he shall return it to its owner. If he does not return it, he becomes a thief.

87: If anyone strikes the dog of a herdsman so that it dies, he shall give 20 shekels of silver and pledge his estate as security.

88: If anyone strikes the dog of a dog fancier so that it dies, he shall give 12 shekels of silver and pledge his estate as security.

89: If anyone strikes an *ordinary* dog so that it dies, he shall give 1 shekel of silver.

90: If a dog devours pig's lard and the owner of the lard finds him out, he may kill it and recover the lard from its stomach. There will be no compensation.

91: If anyone steals bees from a *swarm*, they would formerly give 1 mina of silver. Now he shall give 5 shekels of silver and pledge his estate as security.

92: If anyone steals two beehives or three beehives, formerly (it meant exposure to) bee-sting; now he shall give 6 shekels of silver. If anyone steals a beehive while no bees are therein, he shall give 3 shekels of silver.

93: If they seize a free man while breaking in before he has entered the house, he shall give 12 shekels of silver. If they seize a slave while breaking in before he has entered the house, he shall give 24 shekels of silver.

94: If a free man steals in a house, he shall give (back) the respective goods; they would formerly give for the theft 1 mina of silver, now he shall give 12 shekels of silver. If he has stolen much, they shall impose a heavy fine upon him; if he has stolen little, they shall impose a small fine upon him and he shall pledge his estate as security.

95: If a slave steals in a house, he shall give (back) the respective goods. For the theft he shall give 6 shekels of silver. They shall also cut off the slave's nose and ears and give him back to his master. If he has stolen much, they shall impose a heavy fine upon him; if he has stolen little, they shall impose a small fine upon him. If his master says: "I will make compensation in his stead," he may do so; but if he refuses, he will lose the slave.

96: If a free man steals in a granary and obtains grain in the granary, he shall fill the granary with grain and give 12 shekels of silver and he shall pledge his estate as security.

97: If a slave steals in a granary and obtains grain in the granary, he shall fill the granary with grain and give 6 shekels of silver and he shall pledge his estate as security.

98: If a free man sets a house on fire, he shall rebuild the house. Whatever was lost in the house, whether it is man, cattle or sheep, he shall replace as a matter of course.

99: If a slave sets a house on fire, his master shall make compensation in his stead. They shall cut off the slave's nose (and) ears and shall give him back to his master. But if he does not make compensation, he will lose that (slave).

100: If anyone sets a shed on fire, he shall feed his cattle and make amends in the next spring, he shall (also) give back the shed. If there was no straw therein, he shall just rebuild the shed.

[13] A measure of capacity.

TABLET II

101: If anyone steals vine or fruit branch, or . . . s, or onions, they would formerly give for 1 vine x shekels of silver, for 1 fruit branch 1 shekel of silver, for 1 . . . x shekel of silver, for 1 *bunch* of onions 1 shekel of silver, and they would strike him with the spear in the palace. Formerly they proceeded like this. Now he shall give, if a free man, 6 shekels of silver, and if a slave, 3 shekels of silver.

102: If anyone steals timber from a pond—if (it is) 1 talent of wood, (he shall give) 3 shekels of silver; if (it is) 2 talents of wood, he shall give 6 shekels of silver; if (it is) 3 talents of wood, (it is a case for) the court of the king.

103: If anyone steals freshly planted things—if (it is) 1 *gipeššar*[14] of planting, he shall replant it and give one shekel of silver; if (it is) 2 *gipeššar* of planting, he shall replant it and give 2 shekels of silver.

104: If anyone cuts down *pomegranate* trees or *medlar* trees, he shall give x shekels of silver and pledge his estate as security.

105: If anyone sets a . . . on fire and (the fire) spreads to a fruit bearing orchard—if vines, fruit trees, *pomegranate* trees (or) *medlar* trees get burnt up, he shall give 6 shekels of silver for each tree; the planting he shall replant and he shall pledge his estate as security. If he is a slave, he shall give 3 shekels of silver.

106: If anyone makes fire on his field and sets another man's bearing field on fire, he who set the fire shall take the burnt-over field for himself and give a good field to the owner of the (burnt-over) field and (that man) shall reap it.

[14] See n.1.

107: If a man turns (his) sheep into a vineyard under cultivation and they ruin it—if (it is) fruit bearing, he shall give 10 shekels of silver for each acre, but if (it is) bare, he shall give 3 shekels of silver.

108: If anyone steals tendrils from a *fenced-in* vineyard —if (there are) 100 trees, he shall give 6 shekels of silver and pledge his estate as security. But if they (are) not fenced-in and he steals tendrils, he shall pay 3 shekels of silver.

109: If anyone disposes of fruit from an irrigated (orchard)—if (there are) 100 trees, he shall give 6 shekels of silver.

110: If anyone steals plaster from a bin—however much he steals, he shall give the same amount a second time over.

111: If anyone . . . s plaster (mud) in [a . . .], it is sorcery (and a case for) the court of the king.

112: If they give [to a . . .] the field of a craftsman (which produces) grain, for 3 years he shall not perform socage, he will begin to perform socage from the fourth year on, and shall rank with the craftsmen.

113: If anyone cuts down . . . vine, that (man) shall receive the cut-down vine and give a good one to the owner of the vine and he will vindemiate. [Until] that man's vine [recovers, he keeps the offender's vine. Afterward] he takes [his own back].

(some sections mutilated or missing)

119: If anyone steals a bird from a pond or a trained . . . , they would formerly give x shekels of silver. Now he shall give 12 shekels of silver and pledge his estate as security.

120: If anyone steals . . . birds . . . ,—if (they are) ten birds, he shall give 1 shekel of silver.

121: If anyone, a free man, steals a plow and its owner finds it out, he shall put him upon the . . . and. . . . Formerly they proceeded in this way. Now he shall give 6 shekels of silver and pledge his estate as security. If he is a slave, he will give 3 shekels of silver.

122: If anyone steals a cart with all its accessories, they would formerly give 1 shekel of silver. . . . Now he gives x shekel of silver and pledges his estate as security.

123: If [anyone steals a . . . , it was formerly considered] a capital crime. [Now . . .], he shall give three shekels of silver and pledge his estate as security.

124: If anyone steals a *šišiyama*, he shall give 3 shekels of silver and pledge his estate as security. If anyone loads a cart, leaves it in the fields and (if) anyone steals it, he shall give 3 shekels of silver and pledge his estate as security.

125: If anyone steals a water *trough*, he shall give x shekels of silver. If anyone steals a *lash* or a *whip*, he shall give 1 shekel of silver.

126: If anyone steals a *zaḫrai*(-emblem) in the gate of the palace, he shall give 6 shekels of silver. If anyone steals a bronze spear in the gate of the palace, he shall die. If anyone steals a copper *nail*, he will give one-half *pārisu* of grain. If anyone steals *curtains* (to the amount) of 1 (bolt of) cloth, he shall give 1 bolt of wool cloth.

127: If anyone steals a door in a quarrel, he shall replace everything that may get lost in the house. He will also give 1 mina of silver and pledge his estate as security.

128: If anyone steals bricks—however much he steals, he shall give the same amount a second time over. If anyone steals stones out of a foundation, for two (such) stones he shall give 10 stones. If anyone steals a stone . . .-[. . .] or a stone *ḫarmiyalli*, he shall give 2 shekels of silver.

129: If anybody steals the *reins*, the (leather) *annanu* . . . , the (leather) *gazzimuel* (or) the bronze *ḳatral* of a horse (or) a mule, they would formerly give 1 mina of silver. Now he shall give 12 shekels of silver and pledge his estate as security.

130: If anybody steals the [. . .] . . . of an ox or a horse, he shall give x shekels of silver and pledge his estate as security.

131: If anyone steals a (leather) *ḫapput* . . . , he shall give 6 shekels of silver and pledge his estate as security.

132: If anyone, a free man, steals [a . . .], he shall give 6 shekels of silver and pledge his estate as security. If he is a slave, he shall give 3 shekels of silver.

133: If anyone, a free man, steals [a . . .], he shall give x shekels of silver. If he is a slave, he shall give x shekels of silver.

(several sections missing)

142: [If a free man] drives [a chariot, leaves it in . . . , and (if) anybody steals] the wheels thereof—he shall give one-half *pārisu*[15] of grain for one wheel. If he (is) a slave, he shall give [. . .] of grain for one wheel.

143: If a free man steals a (copper) *ḳnife* [, a . . .], (or) a (copper) *šanḳuvalli*, he shall give 6 shekels of silver and pledge his estate as security. If he (is) a slave, he shall give 3 shekels of silver.

144: If a barber [cuts . . .] with a (copper) knife and ruins them, he shall give the respective [. . .]. If anyone cuts fine cloth with a . . . he shall give 10 shekels of silver. If anyone cuts [. . . with . . .] he shall give 5 shekels of silver.

145: If anyone builds a stable, [the . . .] shall give [him] 6 shekels of silver. If he leaves out [. . .], he shall forfeit his wages.

146: If anyone buys a house or a village or a garden or a pasture and the other man goes and beats him up and demands a purchasing price over and above the (first) price, he is a felon and he shall give 1 mina of silver. [The purchaser] will pay the first price.

147: If anyone buys an unskilled man, and another (man) beats him up, he is a felon and he shall give 5 shekels of silver.

148: If anyone buys a horse, a mule (or) an ass, and another (man) beats him up, he is a felon and he shall give x shekels of silver.

[15] See n.13.

149: If anyone has sold a trained man and (afterward) says: "He has died," but his owner traces him out, he shall receive him. In addition he shall give him 2 persons and pledge his estate as security.

150: If a man hires himself out for wages, his wages for 1 month shall be x shekels of silver. If (it is) a woman, her wages for one month shall be x shekels of silver.

151: If anyone hires a plow-ox, its hire for 1 month shall be 1 shekel of silver. If anyone hires a [. . .], its hire for 1 month shall be one-half shekel of silver.

152: If anyone hires a horse, a mule (or) an ass, he shall give (as its hire) for 1 month 1 shekel of silver.

(There is no gap between 152 and 157.)

157: If a bronze *ateš* weighs 3(?) mina, its rent for 1 month is 1 shekel of silver. If an *ateš* weighs 1 mina of silver, its rent for 1 month is one-half shekel of silver. If a bronze *tapulli* weighs 1 mina, its rent for 1 month is one-half shekel of silver.

158: If a man hires himself out for the harvest (on the understanding) that he will bind the sheaves, (that) the bound (sheaves) will get on the wagon, (that) he will bring it into the barn and (that) they will clear the threshing floor, his wages for three months shall be 30 *pārisu*[16] of grain. If a woman hires herself out for the harvest, her wages for 2 months shall be 12 *pārisu* of grain.

159: If anyone yokes a team of oxen for 1 day, its hire shall be one-half *pārisu* of grain.

160: If a smith makes a box weighing one-half mina, his wages are *one and a half pārisu* of grain. If he makes an *ateš* of two mina weight, his wages are 1 *pārisu* of spelt.

161: If he makes an *ateš* of one mina weight, his wages are 1 *pārisu* of grain.[17]

162: If anyone diverts a watering ditch, he shall give 1 shekel of silver. . . .

163: If anyone's animals are branded and (anyone else) removes the brand and drives them away, (if) *he puts them in (as his share) in a company*, does not tell his partner and the partner unknowingly drives his (the other man's) animals away and they perish, there shall be compensation.

164: If anyone goes (to a place) to get a pawn, starts a quarrel and *spoils* either the sacrificial loaf or the wine destined for libations, (165[18]), he shall give 1 sheep, 10 loaves (and) 1 jug of strong beer and shall make his house holy again. Until a year has elapsed, he shall keep away from his house.

166: If anyone sows seed upon seed, his neck shall be put upon the plow. They shall harness two yokes of oxen and direct the face of one (of them) this way, and the face of the other one that way; the man shall die, and the oxen shall die too. He who sowed the field first, shall take it for himself. Formerly they proceeded thus.

[16] See n.13.
[17] A variant offers "spelt" instead of "grain."
[18] The dividing line found here in our text should be disregarded.

167: Now a sheep is substituted for the man, and two sheep are substituted for the oxen. He shall give 30 loaves of bread (and) 3 jugs of strong beer and shall purify them. He who sowed the field first, shall reap it.

168: If anyone violates the boundary of a field and takes 1 *furrow* off (the neighbor's field), the owner of the field shall cut 1 *gipeššar*[19] of field (from the other's field) and take it for himself. He who violated the boundary, shall give 1 sheep, 10 loaves (and) 1 jug of strong beer and purify the field again.

169: If anyone buys a field and then violates the boundary, he shall take a sacrificial loaf, break it for the Sun-god and say: "Thou hast planted my balance in the ground."[20] Thus he shall say; (whether it is) the Sun-god (or) the Storm-god, does not make any difference.

170: If a free man kills a snake while pronouncing another man's name, he will give 1 mina of silver. If he (the offender) is a slave, he shall die.

171: If a mother draws her garment away from a son of hers, she is repudiating her sons. If her son enters (her house) again, and (if) she takes the door and *moves* it, takes his *iškiššana* (and) his *ḫuppulli* and moves it, then she accepts them again. She makes her son her son again.

172: If a man saves a free man's life in a year of famine, he shall give (a person) like himself. If he is a slave, he shall give 10 shekels of silver.

173: If anyone rejects the judgment of the king, his house shall be made a *shambles*. If anyone rejects the judgment of a dignitary, they shall cut off his head. If a slave rises against his master, he shall go into the *pit*.[21]

174: If men fight one another and one of them is killed, he (who killed) shall give one person.

175: If a shepherd or an overseer takes a free woman in marriage, she shall be a slave either for two years or for four years. . . .

176 (A): If anyone keeps a bull outside the pen, it is (a case for) the court of the king. They shall put (it) up for sale.—It breeds in the third year; the plow-ox, the wether (and) the he-goat breed in the third year.

176 (B): If anyone buys a craftsman, either a potter, a smith, a carpenter, a leatherworker, a fuller, a weaver or he buys a maker of *ḳapalli* garments, he shall give 10 shekels of silver.

177: If anyone buys a trained bird-fancier, he shall give 25 shekels of silver. If he buys a man or a woman who are not fully trained (therein), he shall give 20 shekels of silver.

178: The price of a plow-ox is 12 shekels of silver. The price of a bull is 10 shekels of silver. The price of a full-grown cow is 7 shekels of silver. The price of a one-year-old plow-ox (or) cow is 5 shekels of silver. The price of a weaned calf is 4 shekels of silver. If the cow is with calf, the price is 8 shekels of silver. The price of a calf is 3 shekels of silver. The prices for a stallion

[19] See n.1.
[20] The implications of this formula are obscure.
[21] A kind of punishment.

(and) a brood mare, of an ass (and) a brood ass-mare is analogous.

179: If it is a sheep, its price is 1 shekel of silver. The price for 3 goats is 2 shekels of silver. The price for 2 lambs is 1 shekel of silver. The price for 2 kids is one-half shekel of silver.

180: If it is a draft-horse, its price is 20 shekels of silver. The price for 1 mule is 1 mina of silver. The price for a horse in the pasture is 15 shekels of silver. The price for a one-year-old colt is 10 shekels of silver. The price of a one-year-old filly is 15 shekels of silver.

181: The price of a weaned colt and of a weaned filly is 4 shekels of silver. The price of 4 minas of copper is 1 shekel of silver. The price of 1 *tub* of fine oil is 2 shekels of silver, of 1 *tub* of lard 1 shekel of silver, of 1 *tub* of butter 1 shekel of silver, of 1 *tub* of honey 1 shekel of silver, of 2 cheeses 1 shekel of silver, of 3 (pieces) of yeast 1 shekel of silver.

182: The price of a *ḫappušanza* garment is 12 shekels of silver. The price of a fine garment is 30 shekels of silver. The price for a blue woolen garment is 20 shekels of silver. The price of an *adupli* garment is 10 shekels of silver. The price of an *iškalleššar* garment is 3 shekels of silver. The price of an . . . is 4 shekels of silver. The price of 1 fine shirt is 3 shekels of silver. [The price] of 1 (ordinary) sh[irt is x shekels of silver]. The price of 1 (bolt of) cloth of 7 mina weight is x [shekels of silver]. The price of 1 great (bolt of) linen is 5 shekels of silver.

183: The price of 3 *pārisu* of spelt is 1 shekel of silver. [The price] of 4 *pār*[*isu* of . . . is x shekels of silver]. The price of 1 *pārisu* of wine is one-half shekel of silver, of a *pārisu* [of . . . x shekels of silver]. The price of 1 acre of . . . field is 3 [shekels of silver]. The price of 1 acre of . . . field is 3 [shekels of silver]. The price of 1 acre of "partition" field is 2 shekels of silver. If the field is farther out, he [shall give] 1 shekel of silver.

184: This is the tariff. As it is (valid) in a village, [it is also valid *in the capital*].

185 (A): The price of 1 acre of vineyard is 1 mina of silver. The price of the hide of a full-grown ox is 1 shekel of silver. The price of 5 hides of weanlings is 1 shekel of silver, of 10 *calf*-hides is 1 mina of silver, of a shaggy sheepskin is 1 shekel of silver, of 10 plucked sheepskins is 1 shekel of silver, of 4 goatskins is 1 shekel of silver, of 15 sheared goatskins is 1 shekel of silver, of 20 lambskins is 1 shekel of silver, of 20 kidskins is 1 shekel of silver.

185 (B): Whoever buys the meat of 2 full-grown cattle shall give 1 sheep.

186: Whoever buys the meat of 2 one-year-old cattle shall give 1 sheep. Whoever buys the meat of 5 weanlings shall give 1 sheep. Whoever buys the meat of 10 calves shall give 1 sheep. Whoever buys the meat of 10 sheep shall give a sheep, the meat of 20 lambs shall give 1 sheep, the meat of 20 goats shall give 1 sheep.

187: If a man does evil with a head of cattle, it is a capital crime and he shall be killed. They bring him to the king's court. Whether the king orders him killed, or whether the king spares his life, he must not appeal to the king.

188: If a man does evil with a sheep, it is a capital crime and he shall be killed. They bring him to the king's court. Whether the king orders him killed, or whether the king spares his life, he must not appeal to the king.

189: If a man violates his own mother, it is a capital crime. If a man violates his daughter, it is a capital crime. If a man violates his son, it is a capital crime.

190: . . . If a man violates his stepmother, there shall be no punishment. (But) if his father is living, it is a capital crime.

191: If a free man cohabits with (several) free women, sisters and their mother, with this one in one country and that one in another country, there shall be no punishment. But if (it happens) in one and the same place knowing (of their relationship), it is a capital crime.

192: If a man's wife dies (and) he marries his wife's sister, there shall be no punishment.

193: If a man has a wife and then the man dies, his brother shall take his wife, then his father shall take her. If in turn also his father dies, one of his brother's sons shall take the wife whom he had. There shall be no punishment.

194: If a free man cohabits with (several) slave-girls, sisters and their mother, there shall be no punishment. If blood-relations sleep with (the same) free woman, there shall be no punishment. If father and son sleep with (the same) slave-girl or harlot, there shall be no punishment.

195: If however a man sleeps with the wife of his brother while his brother is living, it is a capital crime. If a man has a free woman (in marriage) and then lies also with her daughter, it is a capital crime. If a man has the daughter in marriage and then lies also with her mother or her sister, it is a capital crime.

196: If his slave (or) his slave-girl commit a capital crime, they move them away and have them settled the one in this town, the other in that town; a sheep will be proffered in this one's stead and a sheep in that one's stead.

197: If a man seizes a woman in the mountains, it is the man's crime and he will be killed. But if he seizes her in (her) house, it is the woman's crime and the woman shall be killed. If the husband finds them, he may kill them, there shall be no punishment for him.

198: If he brings them to the gate of the palace and declares: "My wife shall not be killed" and thereby spares his wife's life, he shall also spare the life of the adulterer and shall mark his head. If he says, "Let them die both of them!" they may ask for mercy. The king may order them killed, the king may spare their lives.

199: If anyone does evil with a pig, he shall die. They will bring them to the gate of the palace and the king may order them killed, the king may spare their lives;

but he must not appeal to the king. If an ox leaps at a man, the ox shall die, but the man shall not die. A sheep may be proffered in the man's stead and they shall kill that. If a pig leaps at a man, there shall be no punishment.

200 (A): If a man does evil with a horse or a mule, there shall be no punishment. He must not appeal to the king nor shall he become a case for the priest.—If anyone sleeps with a foreign (woman) and (also) with her mother or [her] si[ster], there will be no punishment.

200 (B): If anyone gives his son to be trained either as a carpenter, or as a smith, [or as a potter,] or as a leather-worker, or as a fuller, he shall give (as a fee) for the training 6 shekels of silver. If he has made him an expert, he shall give him one person.

The Neo-Babylonian Laws

(Translator: Theophile J. Meek)

These laws are found on a tablet in the British Museum, published and translated by F. E. Peiser, *SPAW*, 1889, pp. 823-8 and Tafel VII. They have been translated by B. Meissner, *ibid.*, 1918, pp. 280-97, and the better preserved portions of the tablet have been most recently translated by E. Ebeling in *AOT*, pp. 422-3. The tablet originally contained some sixteen paragraphs, of which only nine are well preserved. Peiser suggests a date in the time of Ashurbanipal, but what he regards as the remnants of a date is unquestionably a part of the legislation in §1. However, the script, orthography, and wording, all clearly indicate a date in the Neo-Babylonian Period.

1: (only a few words preserved)

2: . . . when they bring about his conviction, he shall give [rent in] one amount for the field [to] the owner of the field on the basis of those adjoining [and for the field which he did not] look after he shall give grain [on the basis of] those adjoining.

3: [The seignior, who *opened*] his well for irrigation purposes, but did not make [his *dike*] strong and hence caused a flood and inundated [a field] adjoining his, shall give [grain to the owner of the field on the basis of] those adjoining.

4: (only a few signs preserved)

5: In the case of a seignior, who sealed a tablet and deed for the owner of a field [or house] with the name of another and did not conclude an agreement in accordance with the terms thereon and also did not obtain a duplicate of the tablet—the seignior with whose name the tablet and deed were inscribed shall take that field or house.

6: In the case of a seignior, who sold a female slave when there was a claim outstanding against (her) and she was taken away—the seller shall give money to the purchaser in accordance with the terms of the deed in its full amount; if she bore children, he shall give her one-half shekel of silver for each.

7: The woman, who was guilty of using or of cutting (wood) from the field of a seignior or who cut off (wood) from [a boat] or from an oven or from any sort of thing, shall give to the owner of the field three times the amount of wood that she cut from there; if she cut off (wood) from a boat (or) cut off (wood) from an oven or from any sort of thing, she shall give three times the reduction that she caused in the field. When in the month. . . . Its (i.e. the paragraph's) law is not completed and so is not written.[1]

8: (not preserved)

9: In the case of a seignior, who gave his daughter (in marriage) to a(nother) seignior's son and the father set down a certain amount on the document and gave (it) to his son and the seignior set the dowry[2] for his daughter and they wrote a contract with one another—they may not contest their contract; the father may not make a deduction from anything that he wrote down for his son on the contract and indicated to his (son's) father-in-law. If, when fate carried off the father's wife, he has acquired another wife and she has borne him children, the children of the later (wife) shall take one-third of the remainder of his property.

10: The seignior, who promised a dowry to his daughter or wrote a deed for her, but whose property later dwindled, shall give his daughter a dowry commensurate with his property that is left; the father-in-law and son-in-law may not join together to contest (it).

11: In the case of a seignior, who gave his daughter a dowry and she had no son or daughter when fate carried her off—her dowry shall revert to her father's house . . . toward the son . . . she may give her dowry to her husband or to anyone that she chooses.

12: In the case of a wife, whose dowry her husband took, who had no son (or) daughter and whose husband fate carried off—a dowry shall be given her from her husband's property as large as the dowry should be. If her husband has presented her with a marriage-gift,[2] she shall take her husband's marriage-gift along with her dowry and then she is quit. If she has no dowry, the judges shall appraise her husband's property (and) something commensurate with her husband's property shall be given her.

13: When a seignior acquired a wife and she bore him children, when fate later carried off that seignior and that woman has made up her mind to enter the house of another—she may take the dowry which she brought from her father's house and whatever her husband presented her with and the husband that chooses her may marry [her]. As long as she lives, she shall have the usufruct thereof along with. . . . If she has borne children to her (later) husband, after her (death) the children of the [later (husband)] and the children of the earlier (husband) [shall share] equally her dowry [and her marriage-gift]. . . .

14: (not preserved)

1 This is a notation by the scribe, indicating that the tablet from which he was copying had this paragraph only partly preserved.

2 In these laws *nudunnû* is "dowry" and *šereqtu* is "marriage-gift," which represents an interchange of meanings between the two words from the earlier laws.

15: In the case of a seignior, who acquired a wife and she bore him children and, when fate carried off his wife, he acquired another wife and she bore him children—after the father has gone to (his) fate, the sons of the earlier (wife) shall take two-thirds of the property of the paternal estate and the sons of the later (wife) one-third; their sisters who are living in the paternal home and....

16: (Not preserved. At the end of the colophon the one word "Babylon" is preserved.)

Egyptian and Hittite Treaties

Egyptian Treaty

(Translator: John A. Wilson)

TREATY BETWEEN THE HITTITES AND EGYPT

The reign of Ramses II began in hostility against the Hittite state. However, by this pharaoh's twenty-first year (about 1280 B.C.), both powers were ready to conclude a treaty, so that they might turn their attention to other problems, such as the encroachments of the "Sea Peoples." The offensive and defensive alliance set forth in the following document mentions no effective frontier between the two empires. Perhaps there was no one firm line, but Egyptian hegemony was recognized in Palestine and southern Phoenicia, Hittite hegemony in Syria and northern Phoenicia.

Since Akkadian was the diplomatic language of the day, the Egyptian text was a translation, edited to give greater prominence to the role of Egypt in granting peace. The Hittite version (pp. 201-203) was probably much closer to the text formally agreed upon, and the two versions should be read together.

The Egyptian version was carved upon the walls of the Temple of Amon at Karnak and of the Ramesseum. The most satisfactory copy is by W. M. Müller in *MVAG*, VII (1902), No. 5. The standard study, with a comparison of the cuneiform and hieroglyphic texts, was made by S. Langdon and A. H. Gardiner, in *JEA*, VI (1920), 179-205. There is also a translation of the Egyptian in Breasted, *AR*, III, §§367-391.

Year 21, 1st month of the second season, day 21,[1] under the majesty of the King of Upper and Lower Egypt: User-maat-Re; Son of Re: Ramses Meri-Amon, given life forever, beloved of Amon-Re; Har-akhti; Ptah, South-of-His-Wall, Lord of Life of the Two Lands; Mut, the Lady of Ishru; and Khonsu Nefer-hotep; appearing on the Horus-Throne of the Living, like his father Har-akhti forever and ever.

On this day, while his majesty was in the town of Per-Ramses Meri-Amon,[2] doing the pleasure of his father Amon-Re; Har-akhti; Atum, Lord of the Two Lands, the Heliopolitan; Amon of Ramses Meri-Amon;[2] Ptah of Ramses Meri-Amon;[2] and [Seth], the Great of Strength, the Son of Nut, according as they give him an eternity of jubilees and an infinity of years of peace, while all lands and all foreign countries are prostrate under his soles forever—there came the Royal Envoy and Deputy . . . Royal Envoy . . . [User-maat-Re] Setep-en-[Re] . . . [Tar]-Teshub, and the Messenger of Hatti, . . .-silis, carrying [the *tablet of silver which*] the Great Prince of Hatti, Hattusilis [caused] to be brought to Pharaoh—life, prosperity, health!—in order to beg [peace from *the majesty of* User-maat-Re] Setep-en-Re, the Son of Re: Ramses Meri-Amon, [given] life forever and ever, like his father Re every day.

[1] Around 1280 B.C., this date would fall toward the end of November.
[2] The capital city of Ramses in the Delta.

Copy of the tablet of silver which the Great Prince of Hatti, Hattusilis, caused to be brought to Pharaoh—life, prosperity, health!—by the hand of his envoy (5) Tar-Teshub, and his envoy Ra-mose,[3] in order to beg peace from the majesty of [User-maat-Re], Son of Re: Ramses Meri-Amon, the bull of rulers, who has made his frontier where he wished in very land.

Preamble

The regulations[4] which the Great Prince of Hatti, Hattusilis, the powerful, the son of Mursilis, the Great Prince of Hatti, the powerful, the son of the son of Suppi[luliumas, the Great Prince of Hatti, the] powerful, made upon a tablet of silver for User-maat-Re, the great ruler of Egypt, the powerful, the son of Men-maat-Re, the great ruler of Egypt, the powerful, the son of Men-pehti-Re,[5] the great ruler of Egypt, the powerful; the good regulations of peace and of brotherhood, giving peace . . . forever.

Former Relations

Now from the beginning of the limits of eternity, as for the situation of the great ruler of Egypt with the Great Prince of Hatti, the god did not permit hostility to occur between them, through a regulation.[6] But in the time of Muwatallis, the Great Prince of Hatti, my brother,[7] he fought with [Ramses Meri-Amon], the great ruler of Egypt. But hereafter, from this day, behold Hattusilis, the Great Prince of Hatti, [is *under*] a regulation for making permanent the situation which the Re and Seth[8] made for the land of Egypt with the land of Hatti, in order not to permit hostility to occur between them forever.

The Present Treaty

Behold, Hattusilis, the Great Prince of Hatti, has set himself in a regulation with User-maat-Re Setep-en-Re, the great ruler of Egypt, beginning from this day, to cause that good peace and brotherhood occur between us forever, (10) while he is in brotherhood with me and he is at peace with me, and I am in brotherhood with him and I am at peace with him forever.

Now since Muwatallis, the Great Prince of Hatti, my brother, went in pursuit of his fate,[9] and Hattusilis sat as Great Prince of Hatti upon the throne of his father,

[3] Tar-Teshub bears a Hittite name, Ra-mose an Egyptian name. However, in the broken context above, two Hittite names apppear. See E. Edel in *JNES*, VII (1948), 17-18.
[4] The "prescribed form," used throughout this inscription for the treaty.
[5] Ramses II, the son of Seti I, the son of Ramses I.
[6] Reference to a previous treaty (in the reign of Hor-em-heb?).
[7] Whose best-known encounter with Ramses II was at the Battle of Kadesh, 16 years earlier; cf. pp. 255-256 below.
[8] Cuneiform version: "the Sun-god and the Storm-god." See n.15 below.
[9] This is an example of the non-Egyptian language resulting from a translation of the cuneiform.

behold, I have come to be with Ramses Meri-Amon, the great ruler of Egypt, for *we are* [*together in*] *our* peace and our brotherhood. It is better than the peace or the brotherhood which was formerly in the land.

Behold, I, as the Great Prince of Hatti, am with [Ramses Meri-Amon], in good peace and in good brotherhood. The children of the children [of] the Great Prince of Hatti *are* in brotherhood and peace with the children of the children of [Ra]mses Meri-[Amon], the great ruler of Egypt, for they are in our situation of brotherhood and our situation [of peace. *The land of Egypt*], with the land of Hatti, [*shall be*] at peace and in brotherhood like unto us forever. Hostilities shall not occur between them forever.

Mutual Renunciation of Invasion

The Great Prince of Hatti shall not trespass against the land of Egypt forever, to take anything from it. And User-maat-Re Setep-en-Re, the great ruler of Egypt, shall not trespass against the land [of Hatti, to take] from it forever.

Reaffirmation of Former Treaties

As to the traditional regulation[10] which had been here in the time of Suppiluliumas, the Great Prince of Hatti, as well as the traditional regulation which had been in the time of Muwatallis,[11] the Great Prince of Hatti, my father, I seize hold of it. Behold, Ramses Meri-Amon, the great ruler of Egypt, seizes hold of (15) [*the regulation which he makes*] together with us, beginning from this day. We seize hold of it, and we act in this traditional situation.

A Defensive Alliance—for Egypt

If another enemy come against the lands of User-maat-Re, the great ruler of Egypt, and he send to the Great Prince of Hatti, saying: "Come with me as reinforcement against him," the Great Prince of Hatti shall [come to him and] the Great Prince of Hatti shall slay his enemy. However, if it is not the desire of the Great Prince of Hatti to go (himself), he shall send his infantry and his chariotry, and he shall slay his enemy. Or, if Ramses Meri-Amon, [the great ruler of Egypt], is enraged against servants belonging to him, and they commit another offence against him, and he go to slay them, the Great Prince of Hatti shall act with him [to *slay*] everyone [against whom] they shall be enraged.

A Defensive Alliance—for Hatti

But [if] another enemy [come] against the Great Prince [of Hatti, User]-maat-[Re] Setep-en-Re, [the great ruler of Egypt, shall] come to him as reinforcement to slay his enemy. If it is (not)[12] the desire of Ramses Meri-Amon, the great ruler of Egypt, to come, he shall . . . Hatti, [and he shall send his infantry and his] chariotry, besides returning answer to the land of Hatti. Now if the servants of the Great Prince of Hatti trespass against him, and Ramses Meri-Amon. . . .

The Contingency of Death?

. . . the [land] of Hatti and the land [of Egypt] (20) . . . the life. *Should it be that* I shall go [in] pursuit of my fate, *then* Ramses Meri-[Amon], the great ruler of Egypt, living forever, *shall go and come* [*to*] the [land of] Hatti, . . . to cause . . . , to make him lord for them, to make User-maat-Re Setep-en-[Re], the great ruler of Egypt, silent with his mouth forever.[13] Now after he . . . the land of Hatti, and he *returns* . . . the Great Prince of Hatti, as well as the. . . .

Extradition of Refugees to Egypt

[If a great man flee from the land of Egypt and come to] the Great Prince of Hatti, or a town belonging to the lands of Ramses Meri-Amon, the great ruler of Egypt, and they come to the Great Prince of Hatti, the Great Prince of Hatti shall not receive them. The Great Prince of Hatti shall cause them to be brought to User-maat-Re Setep-en-Re, the great ruler of Egypt, their lord, [because] of it. Or if a man or two men—no matter who[14]—flee, and they come to the land of Hatti to be servants of someone else, they shall not be left in the land of Hatti; they shall be brought to Ramses Meri-Amon, the great ruler of Egypt.

Extradition of Refugees to Hatti

Or if a great man flee from the land of Hatti and [come to User]-maat-[Re] Setep-en-Re, the [great] ruler of Egypt, or a town or a district or a . . . belonging to the land of Hatti, and they come to Ramses Meri-Amon, the great ruler of Egypt, (then) User-maat-Re Setep-en-Re, the great ruler of Egypt, shall not receive them. Ramses Meri-Amon, the great ruler of Egypt, shall cause them to be brought to the Prince [*of Hatti*]. They shall not be left. Similarly, if a man or two men—(25) [no] matter who[14]—flee, and they come to the land of Egypt to be servants of other people, User-maat-Re Setep-en-Re, the great ruler of Egypt, shall not leave them. He shall cause them to be brought to the Great Prince of Hatti.

The Divine Witnesses to the Treaty

As for these words of the regulation [*which*] the Great Prince of Hatti [*made*] with Ramses [Meri-Amon], the great ruler [of Egypt], in writing upon this tablet of silver—as for these words, a thousand gods of the male gods and of the female gods of them of the land of Hatti, together with a thousand gods of the male gods and of the female gods of them of the land of

[10] The former treaty.

[11] Muwatallis was the brother of Hattusilis; Mursilis the father of Hattusilis. There seem to have been two former treaties—or one which was valid in two reigns.

[12] It is clear from the context and from the parallel above that the negative has dropped out.

[13] The meaning of this section is uncertain, but it seems to provide that Ramses II shall take helpful action in the succession to the Hittite throne, if Hattusilis dies. If so, the reciprocal section about Egypt does not appear. cf. the Hittite version.

[14] "They are unknown." The clause provides for the same treatment of individuals and of subject princes or subject states.

Egypt, are with me as witnesses [*hearing*] these words:[15] the Re, the lord of the sky; the Re of the town of Arinna; Seth, the lord of the sky; Seth of Hatti; Seth of the town of Arinna; Seth of the town of Zippalanda; Seth of the town of Pe(tt)iyarik; Seth of the town of Hissas(ha)pa; Seth of the town of Sarissa; Seth of the town of Aleppo; Seth of the town of Lihzina; Seth of the town . . . ; . . . ; Seth of the town of *Sahpin; Antaret*[16] of the land of Hatti; the god of Zithari(as); the god of *Karzis*; the god of Hapantaliyas; the goddess of the town of Karahna; the goddess of . . . . . .[17] . . . ; the Queen of the Sky; the gods, the lords of oaths; this goddess, the Lady of the Ground; the Lady of the Oath, Ishara; the Lady (30) (*of the*) mountains and the rivers of the land of Hatti; the gods of the land of Kizuwadna; Amon; the Re; Seth; the male gods; the female gods; the mountains; and the rivers of the land of Egypt; the sky; the earth; the great sea; the winds; and the clouds.

Curses and Blessings for this Treaty

As for these words which are on this tablet of silver of the land of Hatti and of the land of Egypt—as for him who shall not keep them, a thousand gods of the land of Hatti, together with a thousand gods of the land of Egypt, shall destroy his house, his land, and his servants. But, as for him who shall keep these words which are on this tablet of silver, whether they are Hatti or whether they are Egyptians, and they are not *neglectful of* them, a thousand gods of the land of Hatti, together with a thousand gods of the land of Egypt, shall cause that he be well, shall cause that he live, together with his houses and his (land) and his servants.

Extradition of Egyptians from Hatti

If a man flee from the land of Egypt—or two or three—and they come to the Great Prince of Hatti, the Great Prince of Hatti shall lay hold of them, and he shall cause that they be brought back to User-maat-Re Setep-en-Re, the great ruler of Egypt. But, as for the man who shall be brought to Ramses Meri-Amon, the great ruler of Egypt, do not cause that his crime be raised against him; do not cause that his house or his wives or his children be destroyed; [do not cause that] he be [slain]; do not cause that injury be done to his eyes, to his ears, to his mouth, or to his legs; do not let any [crime be raised] against him.

[15] Langdon and Gardiner, *op. cit.*, 194-97, show a number of the cuneiform originals of these Hittite deities. The present translation has profited by the suggestions of A. Goetze. For example, "the Re, the lord of the sky" from an original "the Sun-god, lord of heaven"; "the Re of the town of Arinna" from an original "the Sun-goddess of Arinna"; "Seth, lord of the sky" from an original "the Storm-god, lord of heaven"; etc.

[16] Goetze believes that the formerly proposed emendation of this name to "Astarte" is impossible and that the original here had "the (patron god) of the Hatti land," with the ideogram ^{d}KAL, Hittite reading unknown but designating the patron god, hidden behind the curious Egyptian *'ntrt* (fem.).

[17] Goetze rules out the previously proposed "the goddess of Tyre," and suggests that we have here an Egyptian attempt to render a Hittite original, "the goddess of the field." He believes that the previous "the goddess of the town of Karahna" stems from an original "the (patron god) of Karahna," ^{d}KAL again. The present translation omits a broken context following this note.

Extradition of Hittites from Egypt

Similarly, if men flee from the land of Hatti—whether he be one or two or three—and they come to User-maat-Re Setep-en-Re, (35) the great ruler of Egypt, let Ramses Meri-Amon, the [great] ruler [of Egypt], lay hold [of them and cause] that they be brought to the Great Prince of Hatti, and the Great Prince of Hatti shall not raise their crime against them, and they shall not destroy his house or his wives or his children, and they shall not slay him, and they shall not do injury to his ears, to his eyes, to his mouth, or to his legs, and they shall not raise any crime against him.

Description of the Tablet

What is in the middle of the tablet of silver. On its front side: figures consisting of an image of Seth embracing an image of the Great Prince [of Hatti], surrounded by a border with the words: "the seal of Seth, the ruler of the sky; the seal of the regulation which Hattusilis made, the Great Prince of Hatti, the powerful, the son of Mursilis, the Great Prince of Hatti, the powerful." What is within that which surrounds the figures: the seal [of *Seth*. What is on] its other side: figures consisting of a female image of [the] goddess of Hatti embracing a female image of the Princess of Hatti, surrounded by a border with the words: "the seal of the Re of the town of Arinna, the lord of the land; the seal of Putu-hepa, the Princess of the land of Hatti, the daughter of the land of Kizuwadna, the [*priestess*] *of* [*the town of*] Arinna, the Lady of the Land, the servant of the goddess." What is within the surrounding (frame) of the figures: the seal of the Re of Arinna, the lord of every land.

Hittite Treaties

(Translator: Albrecht Goetze)

Treaties, rare in other parts of the ancient Near East, are relatively frequent among the Hittite texts. Most of the surviving examples of this type have been translated previously. The most important publications are the following two: E. F. Weidner, *Politische Dokumente aus Kleinasien* (*Boghazköi Studien*, VIII and IX, 1923). J. Friedrich, *Staatsverträge des Ḫatti-Reiches in hethitischer Sprache* (*MVAG*, XXXI/1, 1926 and XXXIV/1, 1930). From the legal point of view the treaties have been dealt with in the following book: V. Korošec, *Hethitische Staatsverträge. Ein Beitrag zu ihrer juristischen Wertung* (*Leipziger Rechtswissenschaftliche Studien*, LX, 1931).

TREATY BETWEEN HATTUSILIS AND RAMSES II

Texts: *KBo*, I, 7 + *KUB*, III, 121 and its duplicates *KBo*, I, 25, *KUB*, III, 11 + Fragm. Likhachev (*Zapiski Vostočnago Otdieleniya Russkago Arkheologičeskago Obsčestva*, XXV [1918], p. 78) and *KUB*, III, 120. Literature: B. Meissner, *ZDMG*, LXXII (1918), 46-57; A. H. Gardiner and S. Langdon, *JEA*, VI (1920), 179-205; H. Zimmern in Lehmann-Haas, *Textbuch zur Religionsgeschichte* (2nd ed., 1922), 332; E. F. Weidner, *Politische*

Dokumente aus Kleinasien (*Boghazköi Studien*, IX, 1923), 112-123. For the Egyptian version see J. A. Wilson, above pp. 199-201.

Title

Treaty of Rea-mashesha mai Amana,[1] the great king, the king of the land of Egypt, the valiant, with Hattusilis, the great king of the Hatti land for establishing [good] peace [and] good brotherhood [worthy of] great [king]ship forever.

Preamble

These are the words of Rea-mashesha mai Amana, the great king of the land of Egypt, the valiant of all lands, the son (5) of Min-mua-rea,[2] the great king, the king of the land of Egypt, the valiant, the grandson of Min-pakhta-rea,[3] the great king, the king of the land of Egypt, the valiant, (spoken) to Hattusilis, the great king, the king of the Hatti land, the valiant, the son of Mursilis, the great king, the king of the Hatti land, the valiant, the grandson of Suppiluliumas, the great king, the king of the Hatti land, the valiant.

Relations up to the Conclusion of the Treaty

Now I have established good brotherhood (and) good peace between us forever. In order to establish good peace (and) good brotherhood in [the relationship] of the land of Egypt with the Hatti land forever (I speak) thus: Behold, as for the relationship between the land of Egypt (10) and the Hatti land, since eternity the god does not permit the making of hostility between them because of a treaty (valid) forever. Behold, Rea-mashesha mai Amana, the great king, the king of the land of Egypt, in order to bring about the relationship that the Sun-god[4] and the Storm-god[5] have effected for the land of Egypt with the Hatti land finds himself in a relationship valid since eternity which [does not permi]t the making of hostility between [them] until all and everlasting time.

The Present Treaty

Rea-mashesha mai Amana, the great king, the king of the land of Egypt, has entered into a treaty (written) upon a silver tablet (15) with Hattusilis, the great king, the king of the Hatti land, [his] brother, [from] this [da]y on to establish good peace (and) good brotherhood be[tween us] forever. He is a brother [to me] and I am a brother to him and at peace with him forever. And as for us, our brotherhood and our peace is being brought about and it will be better than the brotherhood and the peace which existed formerly for the land of Egypt with the Hatti land.

[1] This is Egyptian in cuneiform characters meaning "Ramses beloved of Amon."

[2] This is the "throne name" of Seti I in cuneiform transliteration.

[3] This is the "throne name" of Ramses I in cuneiform transliteration.

[4] Rea (Re), the chief god of the Egyptians.

[5] The chief god of the Hittites. His name cannot be put in the text because it is always written ideographically and his real name therefore unknown.

Future Relations of the Two Countries

Behold, Rea-mashesha mai Amana, the king of the land of Egypt, is in good peace (and) in good brotherhood with [Hattusilis], the great king, the king of the Hatti land.

Behold the sons of Rea-mashesha mai Amana, the king of the land of Egypt, (20) are in peace with (and) brothers of the sons of Hattusilis, the great king, the king of the Hatti land, forever. They are in the same relationship of brotherhood and peace as we.

And as for (the relationship of) the land of Egypt with the Hatti land, they are at peace and brothers like us forever.

Mutual Renunciation of Aggression

Rea-mashesha mai Amana, the great king, the king of the land of Egypt, shall not tresspass into the Hatti land to take anything therefrom in the future. And Hattusilis, the great king, the king of the Hatti land, shall not tresspass into the land of Egypt to take anything therefrom in the future.

Behold, the holy ordinance (valid) forever which the Sun-god and the Storm-god had brought about (25) for the land of Egypt with the Hatti land (calls for) peace and brotherhood so as not to make hostility between them. Behold, Rea-mashesha mai Amana, the great king, the king of the land of Egypt, has seized hold of it in order to bring about well-being from this day on. Behold, the land of Egypt (in its relation) with the Hatti land—they are at peace and brothers forever.

Defensive Alliance

If an enemy from abroad comes against the Hatti land, and Hattusilis, the great king, the king of the Hatti land, sends to me saying: "Come to me to help me against him," Rea-mashesha mai Amana, the great king, the king of the land of Egypt, (30) shall send his foot soldiers (and) his charioteers and they shall slay [his enemy and] take revenge upon him for the sake of the Hatti land.

And if Hattusilis, the great king, the king of the Hatti land, is angry with servants belonging to him (and if) they have failed against him and sends to Rea-mashesha mai Amana, the great king, the king of the land of Egypt, on their account—lo! Rea-mashesha mai Amana shall send his foot soldiers (and) his charioteers and they shall destroy all those with whom he is angry.

If an enemy from abroad comes against the land of Egypt and Rea-mashesha mai Amana, the king of the land of Egypt, your brother, sends to Hattusilis, (35) the king of the Hatti land, his brother, saying: "Come here to help me against him"—lo! Hattusilis, the king of the Hatti land, shall send his foot soldiers (and) his charioteers and shall slay my enemies.

And if Rea-mashesha ma[i Amana, the king of] the land of Egypt, is angry with servants belonging to him (and if) they have committed sin again[st him and I send] to Hattusilis, the king of the Hatti land, my brother, on his account—lo! Hattusilis, [the king of the Hatti land,] my brother, shall send his foot soldiers (and) his charioteers and they shall destroy all those with whom he is angry.

Succession to the Throne

(40) Behold, the son of Hattusilis, the king of the Hatti land, shall be made king of the Hatti land in place of Hattusilis, his father, after the many years of Hattusilis, the king of the Hatti land. If the noblemen of the Hatti land commit sin against him—lo! [Rea-mashesha mai Amana, the king of Egypt, shall send foot soldiers] (and) charioteers to take revenge upon them [for the sake of the Hatti land. And after they have re-established order] in the country of the king of the Hatti land, [they shall return[6]] to the country [of Egypt].

(Corresponding provision concerning Egypt lost in a gap.)

Extradition of Fugitives

(reverse 7) [If a nobleman flees from the Hatti land and i]f one (such) man comes [to Rea-mashesha mai Amana, the great king, the king of the land of Egypt,] in order to enter his services—[be it a . . . belonging to Ha]ttusilis, the king of the Hatti land, (10) [be it a . . .] or a single town—[Rea-mashesha mai Amana, the great king, the king of the Hatti land, shall seize them and] shall have them brought back to the king of the Hatti land.

(several badly broken lines)

(18) [If a nobleman] flees [from Rea-mashesha mai Amana, the king of the land of Egypt, and if one (such) man] comes to the [Hatti] land, [Ha]ttusilis, (20) [the great king, the king of the Hatti land, shall seize him and] shall have him brought back to R[ea-mashesha mai] Amana, the great king, the king of Egypt, his brother.

If one man flees from the [Hatti land or] two men, [or three men and come to] Rea-mashesha mai [Amana, the great king, the king of the land of Egyp]t, [Rea-mashesha] mai Amana, the great king, [the king of the land of Egypt, shall seize them and have them brought back t]o Hattusilis, his brother. [Rea-mashesha mai Amana and Hattusilis are verily] brothers; hence [let them not *exact punishment for*] their sins, [let them not] tear out [their eyes; (25) let them not *take revenge upon*] their people [. . . together with] their [wives and wi]th their children.

If [one man flees from Egypt] or two men or three men [and come to Hattusilis, the great king, the king of the Hatti land, Hattusilis, the great king], the king of the Hatti land, his brother, shall seize them and have them brought [back to Rea-mashesha mai Amana, the great king, the king of] the land of Egypt. [Hattusilis, the king of the Hatti land], and Rea-mashesha, the great king, the k[ing of the land of Egypt, are verily brothers; hence let them not *exact punishment for* their sins,] (30) [. . .] let them not tear out their eyes; [let them not *take revenge upon* their people . . . together with] their wives (and) with their children.

(After some fragmentary lines the text breaks off altogether. With the end of the treaty the list of the gods who were invoked as witnesses is missing.)

TREATY BETWEEN MURSILIS AND DUPPI-TESSUB OF AMURRU

Texts: Akkadian version: *KUB*, III, 14. Hittite version: *KBo*, V, 9; *KUB*, III, 119; *KUB*, XIV, 5; *KUB*, XIX, 48; *KUB*, XXI, 49. Literature: J. Friedrich, *Staatsverträge des Ḫatti-Reiches in hethitischer Sprache* (*MVAG*, XXXI/1, 1926), 1-48. E. F. Weidner, *Politische Dokumente aus Kleinasien* (*Boghazköi Studien*, VIII, 1923), 76-79.

Preamble

1. These are the words of the Sun[1] Mursilis, the great king, the king of the Hatti land, the valiant, the favorite of the Storm-god, the son of Suppiluliumas, the great king, the king of the Hatti land, the valiant.

Historical Introduction

2. Aziras[2] was the grandfather of you, Duppi-Tessub. He rebelled against my father, but submitted again to my father. When the kings of Nuhassi land[3] and the kings of Kinza[4] rebelled against my father, Aziras did not rebel. As he was bound by treaty, he remained bound by treaty. As my father fought against his enemies, in the same manner fought Aziras. Aziras remained loyal toward my father [as his overlord] and did not incite my father's anger. My father was loyal toward Aziras and his country; he did not undertake any unjust action against him or incite his or his country's anger in any way. 300 (shekels of) refined and first-class gold, the tribute which my father had imposed upon your father, he brought year for year; he never refused it.

3. When my father became god[5] and I seated myself on the throne of my father, Aziras behaved toward me just as he had behaved toward my father. It happened that the Nuhassi kings and the king of Kinza rebelled a second time against me. But Aziras, your grandfather, and DU-Tessub,[6] your father, [did not take their side]; they remained loyal to me as their lord. [When he grew too old] and could no longer go to war and fight, DU-Tessub fought against the enemy with the foot soldiers and the charioteers of the Amurru land just as he had fought with foot soldiers and charioteers against the enemy. And the Sun destroyed them.

(gap in which the reign of DU-Tessub was dealt with)

6*. (DU-Tessub recommends his son as his successor:) "[. . . When I die, accept my son] Duppi-Tessub as your vassal."

7*. When your father died, in accordance with your

[6] This restoration is suggested by the Egyptian parallel.

[1] Sun is the title with which the Hittite king is addressed.

[2] The king of Amurru who is well known from the Amarna letters.

[3] The region between Halba (Aleppo) and the Orontes River.

[4] Qadesh on the Orontes, today Tell Nebi Mendo.

[5] i.e. died.

[6] The first part of the name is an ideogram, the Hurrian pronunciation of which is not known; in this case even the meaning of the ideogram is obscure.

father's word I did not drop you. Since your father had mentioned to me your name *with great praise*, I sought after you. To be sure, you were sick and ailing, but although you were ailing, I, the Sun, put you in the place of your father and took your brothers (and) sisters and the Amurru land in oath for you.

Future Relations of the Two Countries

8*. When I, the Sun, sought after you in accordance with your father's word and put you in your father's place, I took you in oath for the king of the Hatti land, the Hatti land, and for my sons and grandsons. So honor the oath (of loyalty) to the king and the king's *kin*! And I, the king, will be loyal toward you, Duppi-Tessub. When you take a wife, and when you beget an heir, he shall be king in the Amurru land likewise. And just as I shall be loyal toward you, even so shall I be loyal toward your son. But you, Duppi-Tessub, remain loyal toward the king of the Hatti land, the Hatti land, my sons (and) my grandsons forever! The tribute which was imposed upon your grandfather and your father—they presented 300 shekels of good, refined first-class gold weighed with standard weights—you shall present them likewise. Do not turn your eyes to anyone else! Your fathers presented tribute to Egypt; you [shall not do that!]

(gap)

Military Clauses

9**.[7] [With my friend you shall be friend, and with my enemy you shall be enemy. If the king of the Hatti land is either in the Hurri land,[8] or in the land of Egypt, or in the country of Astata,[9] or in the country of Alse[10]—any country contiguous to the territory of your country that is friendly with the king of the Hatti land—(or in) any country contiguous to the territory of your country that is friendly with the king of the Hatti land—(as) the country of Mukis,[11] the country of Halba[12] (and) the country of Kinza[13]—but turns around and becomes inimical toward the king of the Hatti land while the king of the Hatti land is on a marauding campaign—if then you, Duppi-Tessub, do not remain loyal together with your foot soldiers and your charioteers and if you do not fight wholeheartedly; or if I should send out a prince (or) a high officer with foot soldiers and charioteers to re-enforce you, Duppi-Tessub, (for the purpose of) going out to maraud in an]other c[ountry—if then you, Duppi-Tessub, do not fight wholehea]rtedly (that) enemy with [your army and your charioteers] and speak as follows: "I am under an oath of loyalty, but [how am I to know] whether they will beat the enemy, or the enemy will beat them?"; or if you even send a man to that enemy and inform him as follows: "An army and charioteers of the Hatti land are on their way; be on your guard!"—(if you do such things) you act in disregard of your oath.

10**. As I, the Sun, am loyal toward you, do you extend military help to the Sun and the Hatti land. If an evil rumor originates in the Hatti land that someone is to rise in revolt against the Sun and you hear it, leave with your foot soldiers and your charioteers and go immediately to the aid of the king of the Hatti land! But if you are not able to leave yourself, dispatch either your son or your brother together with your foot soldiers (and) your charioteers to the aid of the king of the Hatti land! If you do not dispatch your son (or) your brother with your foot soldiers (and) your charioteers to the aid of the king of the Hatti land, you act in disregard of the gods of the oath.

11**. If anyone should press you hard, Duppi-Tessub, or (if) anyone should revolt against you, (if) you then write to the king of the Hatti land, and the king of the Hatti land dispatches foot soldiers and charioteers to your aid—⟨if you treat them in an unfair manner[14]⟩, you act in disregard of the gods of the oath.

12**. If they take Hittites—foot soldiers and charioteers—through Duppi-Tessub's territory and Duppi-Tessub provides them while passing through (his) towns with food and drink—(if that army) engages in any misconduct—pilfering in his country or his towns or in an attempt at deposing Duppi-Tessub from his kingship—it acts in disregard of the oath.

Dealings with Foreigners etc.

13**. If anyone of the deportees from the Nuhassi land or of the deportees from the country of Kinza whom my father removed and myself removed escapes and comes to you, (if) you do not seize him and turn him back to the king of the Hatti land, and even tell him as follows: "Go! Where you are going to, I do not want to know," you act in disregard of your oath.

14**. If anyone utters words unfriendly toward the king of the Hatti land before you, Duppi-Tessub, you shall not withhold his name from the king. Or if the Sun (iii) gives you an order in secrecy (saying): "Do this or that!" (if) that order cannot be executed, petition about it on the spot (stating): "This order I cannot execute and will not execute" and the king will *reconsider* it then and there. But if you do not execute an order which can (well) be executed and deceive the king, or (if) you do not keep to yourself the word which the king told you in secrecy, you act in disregard of the oath.

15**. If a country or a fugitive takes to the road and while betaking themselves to the Hatti land pass through your territory, put them on the right way, show them the way to the Hatti land and speak friendly words

[7] The bracketed first part of the section is here restored from the treaty between Mursilis and Tette of Nuhassi (*KBo*, I, 4 etc. in Akkadian, translated by Weidner, *loc. cit.*, 58 ff.). It is possible that not all the geographical names were the same here.

[8] Upper Mesopotamia between the Euphrates and Assyria.

[9] The region at the bend of the Euphrates south of Jerablus.

[10] The region on the upper Tigris.

[11] Its capital is Alalha, the ancient name of Atchana (Tell Açana) east of Antakya.

[12] Aleppo.

[13] Qadesh on the Orontes, today Tell Nebi Mendo.

[14] Inadvertently omitted by the scribe.

to them! Do not send them to anyone else! If you do not put them on the right way, (if) you do not guide them on the right way to the Hatti land, but direct them into the mountains or speak unfriendly words before them, you act in disregard of the oath.

16**. Or if the king of the Hatti land is getting the better of a country and puts them to flight, and they come to your country, if then you desire to take anything from them, ask the king of the Hatti land for it! You shall not take it on your own! If you lay hand on it by yourself or conceal it, (you act in disregard of the oath).

17**. Furthermore, if a fugitive comes to your country, seize him! . . .

(gap)

Invocation of the Gods[15]

18**. [The Sun-god of Heaven, the Sun-goddess of Arinna, the Storm-god of Heaven, the Hattian Storm-god, Seris (and) Hurris,[16] Mount Nanni (and) Mount Hazzi,[17] the Storm-god of [. . .], the Storm-god of Halab, the Storm-god of Zippalanda, the Storm-god of Nerik, the Storm-god of Lihzina, the Storm-god of Hissashapa, the Storm-god of Sabina, the Storm-god of Tahaya, the Storm-god of Bettiyarik, the Storm-god of Samuha, the Storm-god of Hurma, the Storm-god of Saressa, the Storm-god of . . . , the Storm-god of Uda, the Storm-god of Kizzuwatna, the Storm-god of Ishupitta, the Storm-god of Nuhassi;

the Patron-god, the Hattian Patron-god, Zithariyas, Hapantalliyas, the Patron-god of Karahna, the Patron-god of the shield, Ea, Allatum, Telepinus of Durmitta, Telepinus of Tawiniya, Telepinus of Hanhana, Ishtar the Mighty, Askasepas;

Sin, lord of the oath, Ishara, queen of the oath, Hebat, queen of heaven, Ishtar, Ishtar of the battlefield, Ishtar of Nineveh, Ishtar of Hattarina, Ninatta (and)] Kulitta, the Hattian Warrior-god, the Warrior-god of Ellaya, the Warrior-god of Arziya, Yarris, Zampanas;

Hantidassus of Hurma, Abaras of Samuhas, Katahhas of Ankuwa, the Queen of Katapa, Ammammas of Tahurpa, Hallaras of Dunna, Huwassanas of Hupisna, Tapisuwa of Ishupitta, the "Lady" of Landa, Kunniyawannis of Landa, NIN.PISAN.PISAN of Kinza, Mount Lablana,[18] Mount Sariyana,[19] Mount Pisaisa, the Lulahhi gods (and) the Hapiri[20] gods, Ereskigal, the gods and goddesses of the Hatti land, the gods and goddesses of Amurru land, all the olden gods, Naras, Napsaras, Minki, Tuhusi, Ammunki, Ammizadu, Allalu, Anu, Antu, Apantu, Ellil, Ninlil, the mountains, the rivers, the springs, the great Sea, heaven and earth, the winds (and) the clouds—let these be witnesses to this treaty and to the oath.

Curses and Blessings

20**. The words of the treaty and the oath that are inscribed on this tablet—should Duppi-Tessub not honor these words of the treaty and the oath, may these gods of the oath destroy Duppi-Tessub together with his person, his wife, his son, his grandson, his house, his land and together with everything that he owns.

21**. But if Duppi-Tessub honors these words of the treaty and the oath that are inscribed on this tablet, may these gods of the oath protect him together with his person, his wife, his son, his grandson, his house (and) his country.

[15] The bracketed part is again taken from the treaty with Tette of Nuhassi, see n.7.
[16] The two bulls of the Storm-god.
[17] Mons Casius near Ugarit.
[18] The Lebanon.
[19] The Hermon.
[20] Much discussed in connection with the question as to whether the Hapirū (widely quoted as Habirū), who are ubiquitous in cuneiform texts of the times, are to be equated with the Hebrews.

GOD LIST, BLESSINGS AND CURSES OF THE TREATY BETWEEN SUPPILULIUMAS AND MATTIWAZA

Text: *KBo*, I, I (and duplicates) reverse 35 ff. (in Akkadian). Literature: E. F. Weidner, *Politische Dokumente aus Kleinasien* (= *Boghazköi Studien*, VIII) 27 ff.

A duplicate of this tablet has been deposited before the Sun-goddess of Arinna, because the Sun-goddess of Arinna regulates kingship and queenship.

In the Mitanni land (a duplicate) has been deposited before Tessub, the lord of the *kurinnu*[1] of Kahat. At regular *intervals* shall they read it in the presence of the king of the Mitanni land and in the presence of the sons of the Hurri country. Whoever will remove this tablet from before Tessub, the lord of the *kurinnu* of Kahat, and put it in a hidden place, if he breaks it or causes anyone else to change the wording of the tablet—at the conclusion of this treaty we have called the gods to be assembled and the gods of the contracting parties to be present, to listen and to serve as witnesses: The Sun-goddess of Arinna who regulates kingship and queenship in the Hatti land, the Sun-god, the lord of heaven, the Storm-god, the lord of the Hatti land, Seris (and) Hurris,[2] the mountains Nanni (and) Hazzi,[3] the Storm-god, the lord of the KI.LAM, the Storm-god, the lord of the encampment, the Storm-god, the lord of aid, the Storm-god of Bettiyarik, the Storm-god of Nerik, the Storm-god, the lord of the mounds, the Storm-god of Halab, the Storm-god of Lihzina, the Storm-god of Samuha, the Storm-god of Hurma, the Storm-god of Saressa, the Storm-god of Sapinuwa, the Storm-god of Hissashapa, the Storm-god of Tahaya, the Storm-god of . . . , the Storm-god of Kizzuwatna, the Storm-god of Uda, the Hattian Patron-god of Karahna, Zithariyas, Karzis, Hapantalliyas, the Patron-god of the field, the Patron-god of the shield, Leliwanis, Ea and Damkina, Telepinus of Tawiniya, Telepinus of Durmitta, Telepinus of Hanhana, the warlike Ishtar, Askasipa, Halkis, the

[1] A kind of sanctuary or shrine.
[2] The two bulls sacred to the Storm-god.
[3] Mons Casius on the Mediterranean shore near Ugarit.

Moon-god lord of the oath, Ishara queen of the oath, Hebat queen of heaven, Hebat of Halba, Hebat of Uda, Hebat of Kizzuwatna, the Warrior-god, the Hattian Warrior-god, the Warrior-god of Ellaya, the Warrior-god of Arziya, Yarris, Zappanas, Hasammelis, Hantidassus of Hurma, Abaras of Samuha, Katahhas of Ankuwa, Katahhas of Katapa, Mammas of Tahurpa, Hallaras of Dunna, Huwassanas of Hupisna, the "Lady" of Landa, Kunniyawannis of Landa, the Lulahhi gods (and) the Hapiri gods,[4] all the gods and goddesses of the Hatti land, the gods and goddesses of the country of Kizzuwatna, Ereskigal, Nara, Namsara, Minku, Amminku, Tussi, Ammizadu, Alalu, Anu, Antu, Ellil, Ninlil, Bēlat-Ekalli, the mountains, the rivers, the Tigris (and) the Euphrates, heaven and earth, the winds (and) the clouds;

Tessub, the lord of heaven and earth,[5] Kusuh[6] and Simigi,[7] the Harranian Moon-god of heaven and earth, Tessub lord of the *ḳurinnu* of Kahat, the . . . of Gurta, Tessub lord of Uhusuman, Ea-sharru lord of wisdom, Anu and Antu, Ellil and Ninlil, the twin gods Mitra and Uruwana,[8] Indar,[9] the Nassatiyana gods,[10] ELLAT, Samaminuhi, Tessub lord of Wassukkanni, Tessub lord of the *ḳamari*[11] of Irrite, Partahi of Suta, Nabarbi, Suruhi, Ashur star, Sala, Bēlat-Ekalli, Damkina, Ishara, the mountains and the rivers, the gods of heaven and the gods of the earth;—

at the conclusion of the words of this treaty let them be present, let them listen and let them serve as witnesses. If you, Mattiwaza, the prince, and (you) the sons of the Hurri country do not fulfill the words of this treaty, may the gods, the lords of the oath, blot you out, (you) Mattiwaza and (you) the Hurri men together with your country, your wives and all that you have. May they draw you like malt from its hull. Just as one does not obtain a plant from *bubuwaḫi*, even so may you Mattiwaza with a second wife that you may take,[12] and (you) the Hurri men with your wives, your sons and your country have no seed. These gods of the contracting parties may bring misery and poverty over you. May they overturn your throne, (yours), of Mattiwaza. May the oaths sworn in the presence of these gods break you like reeds, you, Mattiwaza, together with your country. May they exterminate from the earth your name and your seed (born) from a second wife that you may take. Much as you may seek *uninterrupted* peace for your country, from the midst of the Hurrians may that be banned. May the earth be coldness so that you fall down slipping. May the soil of your country be a hardened quagmire so that you break in, but never get across. May you, Mattiwaza, and (you), the Hurrians, be hateful to the thousand gods, may they pursue you.

If (on the other hand) you, Mattiwaza, the prince, and (you), the Hurrians, fulfill this treaty and (this) oath, may these gods protect you, Mattiwaza, together with your wife, the daughter of the Hatti land, her children and her children's children, and also (you), the Hurrians, together with your wives, your children, and your children's children and together with your country. May the Mitanni country return to the place which it occupied before,[13] may it thrive and expand. May you, Mattiwaza, your sons and your sons' sons (descended) from the daughter of the Great King of the Hatti land, and (you), the Hurrians, exercise kingship forever. May the throne of your father persist, may the Mitanni country persist.

[4] Much discussed in connection with the question as to whether the Hapirū, ubiquitous in cuneiform texts of the times, are to be equated with the Hebrews.

[5] The Hurrian form of the Storm-god.

[6] The Hurrian Moon-god.

[7] The Hurrian Sun-god.

[8] Mitra and Varuna, the Indian gods, appear here among the Hurrian pantheon.

[9] Indra, also an Indian god.

[10] The Nasatyas of the Indians.

[11] A kind of sanctuary or shrine.

[12] Mattiwaza's main wife was a daughter of Suppiluliumas, his overlord.

[13] Lit.: to its place.

Hittite Instructions

TRANSLATOR: ALBRECHT GOETZE

Instructions for Palace Personnel to Insure the King's Purity

Text: *KUB*, XIII, 3. Literature: J. Friedrich, *MAOG*, IV (1928), 46-58.

(Less than half of the tablet—parts of the columns ii and iii—yields an intelligible text.)

(ii) [If] anyone does something [in an uncl]ean way (or if) anyone arouses the king's displeasure, (but) you say as follows: "[The king] is not seeing us," (be aware of the fact that) the king's gods will certainly observe you. They will treat you as a goat and pursue you over the mountains, they will treat you as a *sheep* and pursue you over the rocks.

When some day the king's anger is aroused and I (the king) summon you, all the kitchen personnel, and hand you over to the River (for an ordeal)—whoever will be proven innocent, will remain the king's servant. But whoever will be proven guilty, I, the king, would not wish (to retain) him. Together with his wife and his children I shall put him to death.

Further: You, all the kitchen personnel—the cupbearer, the table-man, the cook, the baker, the *tawal* man, the *walḫi* man, the *cellarius*, the *pašandalaš*, the dairy man, the *ķipliyalaš*, the *šurralaš*, the *tappalaš*, the keeper of the loaves, the *zuppalaš*—you will have to swear an oath of loyalty to the king every month. Fill a bitumen cup with water and pour it out toward the Sun-god and speak as follows: "Whoever does something in an unclean way and offers to the king polluted water, (iii) pour you, O gods, that man's soul out like water!"

Further: You who are the shoemakers who make the king's shoes, take always oxhides from the (royal) kitchen! Do not take any other! He who takes any other and it becomes known afterward, they will put him to death together with his offspring.

Further: You who are leatherworkers of the house of the *taršipaliyaš*, of the house of the *appaš* or the foreman of ten among the *taršipalaš* and you who produce the chariot on which the king is to stand, take always oxhides (and) goatskins from the (royal) kitchen! Do not take any other!

If you take any other and tell the king about it, it is no crime for you. I, the king, will send that abroad or give it to my servants.

But if you conceal it and it becomes known afterward, they will put you to death together with your wives (and) your children.

Further: You who are water carriers, be very careful with water! Strain the water with a strainer! At some time I, the king, found a hair in the water pitcher in Sanahuitta. The king became angry and I expressed my anger to the water carriers (saying): "This is *scandalous*." Then Arnilis (said): "Zuliyas was careless." The king said: "Let Zuliyas go to the . . .![1] If he proves innocent, let him clean himself! If he is found guilty, he shall be killed!"

Zuliyas went to the . . . and was found guilty. They placed Zuliyas [. . .] in Sures[. . .], the king [. . .] him and he died.

Instructions for Temple Officials

Texts: *KUB*, XIII, 4 and its duplicates *KUB*, XIII, 5 + *KUB*, XXXI, 95, *KUB*, XIII, 6 + 19 and furthermore *KUB*, XIII, 17, 18; *KUB*, XXVI, 31; *KUB*, XXXI, 92, 93 and 94, several of which may be remnants of the same tablet or belong to one of the duplicates. Literature: E. H. Sturtevant, *JAOS*, LIV (1934), 363-406, also separately as *Publications of the American Oriental Society, Offprint Series*, No. 4 (1934). Text, transliteration and translation are also found in Sturtevant-Bechtel, *A Hittite Chrestomathy* (1935), 127-174.

(The beginning of column i has not been recovered as yet.)

2. Furthermore, let those who prepare the daily loaves be clean. (15) Let them be bathed (and) *groomed*, let their *(body) hair* and nails be removed. Let them be clothed in clean dresses. [While unclean], let them not prepare (the loaves); let those who are [agreeable] to the gods' soul and person prepare them. The bakers' house in which they prepare them—let that be swept (and) scrubbed. (20) Furthermore, let a pig or a dog not stay at the door of the place where the loaves are broken. Are the minds of men and of the gods generally different? No! With regard to the matter with which we are dealing? No! Their minds are exactly alike. When a servant is to stand before his master, he is bathed and clothed in clean (garments); he either gives him his food, or he gives him his beverage. (25) And because he, his master, eats (and) drinks, he is relaxed in spirit and feels one with him. But if he (the servant) is ever remiss, (if) he is inattentive, his mind is alien to him. And if a slave causes his master's anger, they will either kill him or they will injure him at his nose, his eyes (or) (30) his ears; or [they will seize] him, his wife, his children, his brother, his sister, his in-laws, his kin whether it be a male slave or a slave-girl. They may (either) *impose the extreme penalty*, (or) they

[1] A kind of ordeal.

may do to him nothing at all. If ever he is to die, he will not die alone; his kin will accompany him.

3. If then, on the other hand, anyone arouses the anger of a god, does the god take revenge on him alone? Does he not take revenge on his wife, his children, his descendants, his kin, his slaves, and slave-girls, his cattle (and) sheep together with his crop and will utterly destroy him? Be very reverent indeed to the word of a god!

4. Further: The festival of the month, the festival of the year, the festival of the stag, the festival of autumn, the festival of spring, the festival of thunder, the festival of *ḫiyaraš*, the festival of *pudaḫaš*, the festival of *išuwaš*, the festival of [. . .]*dulaššaš*, the festival of the rhyton, the festivals of the holy priest, the festivals of the Old Men, the festivals of the mothers-of-god, the festival of *daḫiyaš*, the festivals of the *upati* men, the festivals of *pulaš*, the festivals of *ḫaḫratar*, or whatever festival else (will be celebrated) in Hattusa—if you do not celebrate them with all the cattle, sheep, loaves, beer (and) wine set (before the gods), and if you, the god's priests, make a deal with those who give all that, you can be sure that the gods will notice what is amiss.

5. Or if you ever take (sacrifices that have been) set (before the gods) and do not carry them right to the gods themselves, (if) you withhold (it) from them, keep (it) in your houses, and your wives, children (or) servants consume it, (if) you give it to a relative or some citizen befriended with you who happens to visit (you), if you give it to him and take it away from the god and do not carry it right to him, (or if) you give it (to him) in several portions—you will be held responsible for that matter of dividing. Do not divide it. He who divides it, shall be killed; there shall be no recourse for him.

6. Every bit of the loaves, the beer (and) the wine keep in the temple. Let no one appropriate for himself a sacrificial loaf of the god (or) a thin loaf. Let no one pour out beer (or) wine from the cup. Devote every bit to the god. Furthermore, in the presence of the god speak for yourselves (these) words: "Whoever has taken from thy divine loaves (or) from the libation bowl, may the god, my lord, [punish] him; may he hold this man's house responsible for it!" (ii) If you [*wish*] to eat and to drink [. . .] on that day, eat and drink. If you cannot finish it, keep on eating (and) drinking [for] three days. But your wives, your children (and) your servants must in no circumstances [. . . cross] the threshold of the gods. But a member of the community who may come to see someone is allowed to enter the house of the god and he may also cross the threshold of the king.[1] So let that man (whom he is visiting) conduct him up (to the temple) and let him eat (and) drink. But if it is [a foreigner], if it is not a Hittite man, and he ap[proach]es the gods, he shall be killed. And he who conducts him (into the temple), it makes him liable of the death penalty too.

7. If an ox (or) a sheep is driven up to the god as food, and you appropriate for yourselves either a fattened ox or a fattened sheep and substitute a lean one which you have slaughtered, and (if) you either consume that or put it into your pen, or put it under the yoke, or (if) you put the sheep into your fold or kill it for yourselves, and (if) you see fit [to *give it away*] or to turn it over to another man, or (if) you accept a price for it and thus [take it away from] the god and withhold it from (his) mouth, (if) you take it for yourselves or give it to another man and speak as follows: "Since he is a god, he will not say anything, and will not do anything to us"—just think how the man reacts who sees his *most valued possession* snatched away from before his eyes! The will of the gods is strong. It does not make haste to seize, but when it seizes, it does not let go (again). Now be very reverent of the will of the gods.

8. Further: Whatever silver, gold, garments or bronze implements of the gods you hold, you are (merely) (their) caretakers. You have no right to the silver, gold, garments (and) bronze implements of the gods, and none whatsoever to the things that are in the gods' houses. They belong to the god alone. Be very careful and let no temple official have silver (or) gold. Let him not carry it on his own body, and let him not make it into an ornament for his wife (or) his children. But if they give him silver, gold, garments (and) bronze implements as a gift from the palace, let them be specified: "So-and-so, the king has given it to him." How much its weight is, let also be set down. Furthermore let it be set down thus: "At such-and-such a festival have they given it to him." Let also the witnesses be set down at the end: "When they gave it to him, so-and-so and so-and-so were present." Furthermore let him not leave it in his house; let him offer it for sale. But when he sells it, let him not sell it in a secret place; let the Hittite lords be present and look on. Let that which (anyone) buys be listed on a tablet and let them seal it. And when the king comes up to Hattusa, let him take it (the tablet) up to the palace and let them seal it. If he puts them up for sale on his own, he is liable to the death penalty. He who does not put up for sale silver, gold, garments (or) implements of bronze in the same way (as here described), also he who receives it and hides it and does not bring it to the king's court, both of them are liable to the death penalty, they shall both be killed. They are [*disagreeable*] to the gods. There shall in no circumstances be recourse for them.

9. Further: You who are temple officials, if you do not celebrate the festivals at the time proper for the festivals and (if) you celebrate the festival of spring in the autumn, or (if)—when in the course of time a festival is about to be celebrated—he who is to perform it comes to you, the priests, the "anointed," the mothers-

[1] The beginning of the second column is preserved only on *KUB*, XIII, 5.

of-god, *and* to the temple officials and embraces your knees (saying): "The harvest is before me, or arranging for (my) marriage, or a journey, or some other business. Do me a favor and let me finish that business first. But when that business of mine is finished, I shall perform the festival as prescribed"—do not yield to a man's whim, let him not *take precedence* (of the gods). You must not make a deal of the gods' pleasure. Should with you a man *take precedence* (of the gods) and should you make a deal for yourselves, the gods will seek to take revenge on you in the future. They will hold a grudge against you, yourselves, your wives, your children (and) your servants. So act only according to the pleasure of the gods! And you will eat bread, drink water and establish a family. But do not act according to the pleasure of a man. Do not sell the death penalty, but do not buy the death penalty either.

10. Further: You who are temple officials, be very careful with respect to the precinct. At nightfall go promptly down (to the town); eat (and) drink, and if the desire for a woman [overcom]es anyone, let him sleep with a woman. (iii) But as long as [. . .] let him [. . .] and let e[very one] promptly come up to spend the night in the temple. Whoever is a temple official, all high priests, minor priests, "anointed" or whoever else is allowed to cross the threshold of the gods, let (them) not fail to spend the night in the temple one by one. Furthermore, there shall be watchmen employed by night who shall patrol all night through. Outside in the precinct keepers shall watch, inside the temples shall the temple officials patrol all night through and they shall not sleep. Night by night one of the high priests shall be in charge of the patrols. Furthermore, someone of those who are priests shall be in charge of the gate of the temple and guard the temple. In his own house no one (of these) shall spend the night with his wife. Whomsoever they will find down in his house, it will be a capital offense for him. Guard the temple very carefully and do not sleep. (Responsibility for) the precinct shall be divided among yourselves. He who commits an offense with respect to the precinct shall be killed; he shall not be pardoned.

11. If anyone has some (official) duty to perform in Hattusa, and (either) a priest (or) an "anointed" is to admit people who are accompanied by guards, he will admit those too. If a guard is assigned to anyone, he may also enter the precinct. He must not speak thus: "I am guarding the house of my god, but I shall not go in there."—If there is some talk of enmity, (namely) that someone will undertake to defile Hattusa and (the guards) at the outer wall do not recognize him, but the temple officials recognize him inside, the guard shall definitely go after him. (In) such (situation the) guard must not fail to spend the night with his god. If he fails however, in case they do not kill him, they shall humiliate him. Naked—there shall be no garment on his body—he shall bring three times water from the Labarnas' cistern to the house of his god. Such shall be his humiliation.

12. Further: O priests, "anointed," mothers-of-god (and) temple officials! Some *troublemaker* may rise in the temple or another sacred building. If he rises in the temple and causes a quarrel and thereby interferes with a festival, they shall interfere with him. Let him celebrate that festival with the usual expenditure of sheep, bread (and) beer, neither must he omit the thin loaf. Whoever fails (to provide) it and does not celebrate a fully set festival, it shall be a great offense for him and he shall make up for the festival. So be very careful with a quarrel.

13. Further: Be very careful with the matter of fire. If there is a festival in the temple, guard the fire carefully. When night falls, quench well with water whatever fire remains on the hearth. But if there is any flame in isolated spots and (also) dry wood, (if) he who is to quench it becomes criminally negligent in the temple—even if only the temple is destroyed, but Hattusa and the king's property is not destroyed—he who commits the crime will perish together with his descendants. Of those who are in the temple not one is to be spared; together with their descendants they shall perish. So for your own good be very careful in the matter of fire.

14. Further: All of you who are kitchen servants of the gods, cupbearers, table-men, cooks, bakers (or) vintners, be very careful with respect to the gods' mood. Spend much reverent care upon the gods' sacrificial loaves (and) libation bowls. The place where the bread is broken shall be swept (and) scrubbed; (the regulations concerning) the threshold shall be enforced for pigs and dogs. As to yourselves, you shall be bathed and dressed in clean garments. Furthermore, your (*body*) *hair* and your nails shall be removed. Let the mood of the gods not befall you. If a pig (or) a dog somehow approaches the implements of wood or bitumen which you have, and the kitchen servant does not discard it, but gives the god to eat from an unclean (vessel), to such a man the gods will give dung (and) urine to eat (and) to drink. Whoever is going to sleep with a woman, he shall go to that woman in the same condition in which he performs a rite for the gods and gives the god his portion to eat and to drink. Furthermore, [at . . .], as soon as the sun is up, he shall at once take a bath; and in the morning, at the time when the gods eat, he shall promptly be present. But, if he omits (to do so), it will be a sin for him. Whoever sleeps with a woman, if his superior (or) his chief constrains (him), he shall say so. If he himself does not dare tell him, he shall tell his fellow servant and shall bathe anyway. But if he knowingly postpones it and without having bathed approaches the gods' sacrificial loaves (and) libation bowl in an unclean condition, or (if) his fellow servant knows about him—namely that he placed himself first—but nevertheless conceals it, (if) afterward it becomes known, they are liable to the capital penalty; both of them shall be killed.

15. (iv) [Further: You who are the plowmen of the gods, . . .]. The young animals which you, the plowmen, are supposed to have ready, have them promptly ready at the correct time. (5) Before a man has eaten from them, carry them promptly to the presence of the gods; let the gods not wait for them. If you delay them, you commit a sin. They will consult the oracles about you, and just as the gods, my lords, direct, so they will do to you. (10) They will fine you an ox and ten sheep and will pacify the mind of the gods.

16. Further: If you plant grain, and if the priest does not send you a man to plant the seed, you shall manage by yourselves. Should you plant much, (15) but tell the priest (that) it (was) little, or should the gods' field be thriving, but the field of the plowmen be barren and you call the gods' field yours, but your field that of the god, or should you when you store the grain declare one half, but conceal the other half (20) and should you proceed to divide it afterward among yourselves and should it(!) afterward become known—you may get away with appropriating it from a man, but you cannot appropriate it from a god—, you will commit a sin. They will take all the grain away from you and put it in the magazines of the gods.

17. (25) Further: You who hold the plow-oxen of [the gods], if you sell a plow-ox, or kill it and consume it, (if) you appropriate it for yourselves (while it belongs) to the god (saying): "It died from emaciation, or it broke (its legs), or it ran away, or the bull gored it" (30) and consume it yourselves, and it afterwards becomes known, you will replace that ox. If however it does not become known, you will go before the god.[2] If you are acquitted, (it is due to) your patron god; if you are convicted, it is considered a capital sin for you.

18. Further: You who are the gods' cowherds (and) the gods' shepherds, (35) if there is a rite for any god at the time of bearing young and you are supposed to have ready for him either a calf, a lamb, a kid or *choice animals*, do not delay them! Have them ready at the right time; do not let the gods wait for them. Before a man eats of the young animals, (40) bring it promptly to the gods. Or if there is a "festival of the cup" for any god, (even) while they repair the cup, do not allow it to lapse; celebrate it for him. If you do not bring the young animals promptly to the gods, but eat first of them yourselves (45) or send them to your superiors, but it afterward becomes known, it is considered a capital sin for you. If it does not become known—at whatever time you will bring them, you will bring them with these words: "If we have given this young animal to ourselves first, (50) or have given it to our superiors, or to our wives, our children or to anyone else, we have offended the gods' feelings." Then you will drink dry the rhyton of the god of life.[3] If you are found innocent, (it is due to) your patron god; but if you are found guilty, you will perish together with (55) your wives (and) your children.

19. Further: If you ever make a selection (of animals) and drive them up to the gods, your lords, the cowherd and the shepherd shall go with that selection. In the same condition in which they are selected from the pen (and) the fold, (60) shall they bring them to the gods. On the road they must not exchange them. But if any cowherd or shepherd does wrong on the road, exchanges either a fattened ox or a fattened sheep, or makes a deal or kills it and (65) they eat it up, and put in its place an emaciated (animal), and it becomes known, it is considered a capital sin for them; they have taken the gods' *most valued possession*. But if it does not become known, whenever they arrive they shall take the rhyton of the god of life from the cult stand, (70) and while doing so they shall declare as follows: "If we have for ourselves withheld from the mouth of the gods their *most valued possession*, and have given it to ourselves, or (if) we have sold it for ourselves, or if we have exchanged it, made a deal (75) and substituted in its place an emaciated (animal), then do thou, O god, pursue us together with our wives (and) our children on account of thy most valued possession!"

[2] i.e. you will be subject to an ordeal.

[3] A kind of ordeal.

From the Instructions for the Commander of the Border Guards

Text: *KUB*, xiii, 2 ii 26-iii 35 and its duplicates *KUB*, xxxi, 90 ii 7 ff. and *KUB*, xxxi, 86 iv 1 ff. (+) 88 iii 1 ff. Literature: V. Korošec, *Zbornik znanstvenih razprav juridične fakultete*, viii (1942), 139-170 (with a summary in Italian).

In the town through which the commander of the border guards passes on his tour of inspection he shall attend to the necessary provisions for town-elders, priests, "anointed" (and) mothers-of-god. He shall speak to them as follows: "The sanctuary which exists in this town, whether it is of the Storm-god or of other gods, (30) is now collapsed and in disrepair. It is not provided with priests, mothers-of-god (and) 'anointed.' So provide it again with such (functionaries)! They shall restore it. As it was built previously, (35) so shall they rebuild it."

Furthermore, due reverence shall be shown to the gods, but to the Storm-god special reverence shall be shown. If some temple *has a leaking roof*, the commander of the border guards and the town commandant shall put it right, or (if) any rhyton of the Storm-god (40) or any implement of any other god is in disrepair, the priests, the "anointed" (and) the mothers-of-god shall restore it.

Furthermore, the commander of the border guards shall make an inventory of the god's utensils and send it before the Sun.[1] Furthermore, they shall worship the

[1] i.e. the Hittite king.

gods on the right dates. If a certain date is set for some god, they shall worship him on that date. If some god has no priest, mother-of-god (or) "anointed," they shall promptly appoint one.

(iii) [If] no provisions have been made [for sacrifices to the gods'] stone pillars, provide for them now! They shall arrange for them, and furthermore they shall present whatever sacrifices have long been customary.

The rites which are established for the springs that are in the town, they shall go to them and celebrate their rites. And those springs for which rites have not been established, they shall go to them all the same. In no circumstances shall they omit them. They shall regularly give sacrifices to the mountains (and) to the rivers for which such are established.

Furthermore, the commander of the border guards, the town commandant and the elders shall judge and decide legal cases in accordance with the law. As it has been from olden days—in a town in which they have been accustomed to imposing the death penalty, they shall continue to do so. But in a town where they have been accustomed to imposing exile, they shall continue that (custom). Furthermore, the citizens shall bathe afterward and there shall be a public announcement. No one shall let (the exiled) return. He who lets him return, shall be *put in prison*.

And when they worship the gods, let no one start a disturbance in the presence of the gods, let no one start a disturbance in the house of festival. Furthermore let reverence be paid to the priests, the lay brothers, the "anointed" (and) the mothers-of-god. Reverence toward the gods shall be the duty of the priests, the "anointed" and the mothers-of-god. If anyone brings suit by means of a sealed brief, the commander of the border guards shall judge it according to the law and set them right. If he rejects (the case), he shall send it before the Sun.[1]

He must not decide it in favor of his superior, he must not decide it in favor of his brother, his wife or his friend; no one shall be shown any favor. He must not make a just case unjust; he must not make an unjust case just. Whatever is right, that shall he do.

Whenever you arrive at a town, call all the people of the town together. For him who has a complaint, judge it and set him right. If a man's slave or a man's slave-girl has a complaint against a woman *of the upper class*, judge it for them and set them right. Should Kassiya people, Himmuwa people, Tagaramma people and Isuwa people[2] be there, attend to them in every way.

[2] These are privileged classes of people. cf. §54 of the Hittite Laws.

Documents from the Practice of Law

Egyptian Documents

(Translator: John A. Wilson)

A ROYAL DECREE OF TEMPLE PRIVILEGE

No codes of laws have been found for ancient Egypt. This means either that such collections of laws were written on papyrus and leather and so have not survived or that pharaonic Egypt did not codify law, but rather operated on the basis of topical justice originating in the word of the god-king. We do possess royal decrees, framed to meet particular situations.[1] Most common are the charters of immunity, granting a temple exemption from civil obligation. The following decree of the Fifth Dynasty pharaoh Nefer-iri-ka-Re (26th century B.C.) freed the personnel of the Temple of Osiris at Abydos from forced labor for the state.

The stela was found at Abydos and is now in the Boston Museum of Fine Arts (03.1896). The text was published by W. M. F. Petrie, *Abydos II* (London, 1903), Pls. XIV, XVIII, and by K. Sethe, *Urkunden des alten Reichs* (*Urk.*, I, Leipzig, 1933), 170-72. It was studied by Sethe in *GGA* (1912), 733 ff., and by A. Moret in *JA* (1917), 429 ff.

Other royal decrees or references thereto will be found at pp. 31-32; 252, n.9; 327; 329.

The Horus: User-khau.[2]
Royal decree (to) the Chief Prophet Hem-ur.

I

I do not permit that any man have the right to[3]—take away any prophets who are in the District in which thou art, for the corvée, as well as any (other) work of the District, except to do service for the god himself in the temple in which he is and to conserve the temples in which they are. They are exempt in the length of eternity by the decree of the King of Upper and Lower Egypt: Nefer-iri-ka-Re. There is no title to them in any (other) service.

II

(I do not permit that any man have the right to)—carry *(off) the necessary [equipment]* for any work to any *(other)* God's Field[4] on which there is priestly service by any prophets. (They are exempt in the length of eternity by the decree of the King of Upper and Lower Egypt: Nefer-iri-ka-Re. There is no title to them in any service.)

III

(I do not permit that any man have the right to)—take away any serfs who are on (any God's Field on which there is priestly service by any prophets), for the corvée, as well as any (other) work of the District. (They are exempt in the length of eternity by the decree of the King of Upper and Lower Egypt: Nefer-iri-ka-Re. There is no title to them in any service.)

IV

As for any man of the District who shall take away—any prophets who are *on* the God's Field on which they do priestly service in this District, for the corvée, as well as any (other) work of the District, thou shalt *consign* him to the temple workhouse, he [*him*]*self* being put on [*any*] *corvée*, or (to) the place of plowing . . .

V

(As for any man of the District who shall take away)—any serfs who are on the God's Field, (for the corvée, as well as any work of the District, thou shalt *consign* him to the temple workhouse, he [*him*]*self* being put on [*any*] *corvée*, or the place of plowing . . .)

VI

Any official or royal intimate or agricultural officer who shall act contrary to these things which I have decreed shall [*be removed*] and turned over to the law court, while the house, fields, people, and everything in his possession shall *be forfeited*, he being put on any corvée.

The Royal Person was present at the sealing. Second month of the third season, day 11 (+*x*).[5]

THE VIZIER OF EGYPT

By dogma the pharaoh of Egypt was the state, but in actual practice he had to delegate authority to others. The most important civil official was the vizier, who was directly responsible to the pharaoh and to whom most of the other officials were responsible. We possess a fair amount of material with regard to the vizier under the Egyptian Empire. The following texts relate to Rekh-mi-Re, the Vizier of Upper Egypt under the reign of Thut-mose III (about 1490-1436 B.C.).

The texts are from the tomb of Rekh-mi-Re, No. 100 at Thebes. They have been published by N. de G. Davies, *The Tomb of Rekh-mi-Re at Thebes* (*Publications of the Metropolitan Museum of Art*, XI, New York, 1943), two volumes, including translations. The texts were earlier presented in K.

[1] The decrees of the Old Kingdom were published together by R. Weill, *Les décrets royaux de l'ancien empire Égyptien* (Paris, 1912); see also W. C. Hayes in *JEA*, XXXII (1946), 3-23. The decree of Hor-em-heb, following the Amarna Revolution, was studied by K. Pflüger in *JNES*, V (1946), 260-76. A decree of Seti I was studied by W. F. Edgerton in *JNES*, VI (1947), 219-30.

[2] The Horus name of Nefer-iri-ka-Re.

[3] The physical arrangement of the inscription permitted certain elements—here given in the long parenthetical sections—to be used in repetition. The present introductory words serve also as the introductory words for sections II and III below.

[4] This is understood to mean a temple estate, including property within and without the temple precincts.

[5] The original decree was on a scroll, and pharaoh gave his sanctioning presence to the sealing of this document. Around 2530 B.C., the date would fall in February or March.

Sethe, *Urkunden der 18. Dynastie* (*Urk.*, IV, Leipzig, 1909), 1071-1117, and translated by Breasted, *AR*, II, §§663-711.

A. FROM THE AUTOBIOGRAPHY OF REKH-MI-RE

In a lengthy statement about his worldly position and success, the vizier tells about his appointment to that office. Davies, *op.cit.*, 79-83, Pls. XI-XII.

I was a noble, the second of the king and the *fourth* of him who judged the Pair.[1] ... It was the first occasion of my being summoned. All my brothers were in the outer *office*. I went (5) forth ... clad in fine linen. ... I reached the doorway of the palace gate. The courtiers bent their backs, and I found the masters of ceremonies clearing the way [before me]. ... My abilities were not as they had been: my yesterday's nature had altered itself, since I had come forth in the accoutrements [*of the vizier, having been promoted*] to be Prophet of Maat.[2] ...

I was [summoned] again into the presence of the good god (Thut-mose III). ... His majesty opened his mouth and spoke his words veritably (10) in my presence: "Now behold, I *see a face which* I send to my heart,[3] [*for my majesty knows*] that decisions are many, without limit to them, and the judging of cases never falls off. Would that thou mightest act in conformance with what I may say! Then Maat will rest in her place." He charged me very much: "Gather thyself together; *be strong in action*; do not flag. ..."

[*I acted*] in conformance with that which he had ordained. He gave me a tribunal under my authority, and there was none therein who could oppose me. ... I raised justice[4] to the height of heaven; I made its beauty circulate to the width of earth, so that it rested in their nostrils (20) like the north wind, when it has driven bitterness away from the body.[5] ... When I judged (37) the petitioner, I was not partial. I did not turn my brow for the sake of reward. I was not angry [at *him who came*] as [a petitioner], nor did I *rebuff* him, (but) I tolerated him in his moment of outburst. I rescued the timid from the violent. ...

B. THE INSTALLATION OF THE VIZIER

Another long text gives the charge which Thut-mose III laid upon his newly appointed vizier. Davies, *op.cit.*, 84-88, Pls. XIV-XV, with Pls. CXVI-CXVIII adding the same text from the tombs of two other viziers of the Eighteenth Dynasty.

The regulations laid upon the Vizier Re[kh-mi-Re], when the tribunal was ushered into audience hall of Pharaoh—life, prosperity, health!—and it was caused that the newly appointed Vizier [Rekh-mi-Re] be brought in.

(1) Then his majesty said to him: "Look thou to this office of vizier. Be vigilant over [everything that] is done in it. Behold, it is the support of the entire land. Behold, as to the vizierate, behold, it is not sweet at all, behold, it is as bitter as *gall*. ... Behold, it does not mean giving attention (only) to himself and to his officials and councillors, nor (yet) making [dependents] out of everybody. ... (5) Therefore, see to it for thyself that all [things] are done according to that which conforms to law and that all things are done in conformance to the precedent[6] thereof *in* [*setting every man in*] his just deserts. Behold, as for the official who is in public view, the (very) winds and waters report all that he does; so, behold, his deeds cannot be unknown. ... Behold, it is the official's place of refuge to act in conformance with the regulations. ... [The] (12) abomination of the god is partiality. This is the instruction, and thus shalt thou act: 'Thou shalt look upon him whom thou knowest like him whom thou knowest not, upon him who has access to thee like him who is far away.' ... (17). .. Behold, thou shouldst *attach to* thy carrying out of this office thy carrying out of justice. Behold, what is desired is that the carrying out of justice be the produce of the vizier.[7] ..."

C. THE JUDICIAL SITTING OF THE VIZIER

In a long and detailed text, Rekh-mi-Re tells of the several functions of his office. This translation deals only with the rules for the judicial hearings of the vizier in his hall of justice. Davies, *op.cit.*, 88-94; Pls. XXVI-XXVIII, with Pls. CXIX-CXXII giving parallels from the tombs of two other viziers of the Eighteenth Dynasty, and Pls. XXIV-XXV a scene showing the hall of justice, with the vizier enthroned, his supporting magistrates and clerks, court bailiffs, and humbly bowing appellants to the court.

(1) The regulations for the sitting of the Mayor and Vizier of the Southern City and of the Residence in the Hall of the Vizier.

As for everything which this official, the Vizier, shall do while holding hearings in the Hall of the Vizier—he shall sit upon a *judgment*-chair, with a matting on the floor, a *matting over* him, a cushion under his back and a cushion under his feet, a [*cape*] upon him, a sceptre at his hand, and the forty leather *straps*[8] spread out in front of him, the Chiefs of Southern Tens[9] on two sides in front of him, the Overseer of the Cabinet on his right hand, the Supervisor of Clients on his left hand,

[1] He was the immediate assistant of the king, just as if he were a partner of the god Thoth in judging Horus and Seth—thus making a fourth to these three gods.

[2] The goddess Maat was "Truth" or "Justice." In his capacity as the highest magistrate, Rekh-mi-Re was the priest of Maat.

[3] Translation uncertain, assumed to mean: I see someone with whom I have sympathy because of his arduous duties. Davies: "My eyes send me to my heart"—grammatically impeccable, but unintelligible.

[4] The same word *maat* as that of n.2 above, but not here determined with the picture of a goddess.

[5] The north wind was Egypt's refreshing wind.

[6] The word means "normal." Davies: "due regularity."

[7] The execution of justice is the "outcome" or "output" of the vizier.

[8] *Shesmu*, a critical word in the understanding of Egyptian law. The scene of hearing shows forty oblong or tubular things lying on mats in front of the vizier. The present word has a skin determinative. These have been assumed to be the scrolls of the law, written on leather, our only indication of codified law at this time. Unfortunately, Davies (pp. 31-32) shows evidence that they were used for maintaining authority or for punishment, citing a passage in which a man was "beaten with fifty *shesem*." He concludes that the forty which were spread out were symbols of authority.

[9] A body of magistrates.

and the Scribe of the Vizier beside him, one *confronting* another, with every man opposite him.[10]

Let one be heard after his fellow, not permitting the last to be heard before an earlier. If one who is earlier should say: "There is no one *hearing* near me," then he is to be taken in charge by the messengers of the Vizier.[11] . . .

RESULTS OF A TRIAL FOR CONSPIRACY

The Twentieth Dynasty has provided us with a mass of legal material, particularly on the proceedings occasioned by the plundering of Theban tombs.[1] We shall present here extracts from a document of different nature, dealing with a harem conspiracy and the plot to supplant Ramses III upon his throne by one of his sons.[2] It is uncertain whether the conspiracy was successful to the point of taking the life of Ramses III. In that case, the court of inquiry and punishment will have been constituted by Ramses IV in the name of his dead father. Alternatively, Ramses III survived the plot and himself constituted the court.

The manuscript is the Judicial Papyrus of Turin, dated to the end of the reign of Ramses III (about 1164 B.C.). The hieratic text was facsimiled by T. Devéria in *Bibliothèque égyptologique* (ed. by G. Maspero), v (Paris, 1897), Pls. v-vi, 97-251. It was translated by Breasted, *AR*, iv, §§416-53. Its most recent study was by A. de Buck in *JEA*, xxiii (1937), 152-64. The lost beginning of the manuscript probably gave the setting of the conspiracy.

Two other texts have a juridical setting: the story of the Eloquent Peasant (pp. 407-410) and the story of the contendings of Horus and Seth (pp. 14-17), although the latter is a burlesque on court procedure. For advice on conduct in court, see the Instruction of Amen-em-Opet (p. 424). For a prayer that the poor man may be protected against avarice in court, see p. 380.

. . . they are (ii 1) the abomination of the land. I laid the charge upon:[3] the Overseer of the Treasury Montu-em-tawi; the Overseer of the Treasury Paif-ru; the Standard-Bearer Kar; the Butler Pai-Bes; the Butler Qedendenen; the Butler Baal-mahar; the Butler Pa-ir-sun; the Butler Thut-rekh-nefer; the Royal Herald Pen-Renenut; the Scribe May; the Scribe of the Archives Pa-Re-em-heb; and the Standard-Bearer of the Garrison Hori, (5) saying: "As for the matters which the people—I do not know who[4]—have said, go and examine them." And they went and examined them, and they caused to die by their own hands those whom they caused to die—[I] do not know [who—and they] inflicted punishment [upon the] others—[I] do not know [who] also. But [I] charged [them *strictly*], saying: "Be careful, guard against having punishment inflicted (upon) a [person] *irregularly* [*by an official*] *who is not over him.*" So I said to them repeatedly. (iii 1) As for all that they have done, it is they who have done it. Let all that they have done come upon their (own) heads, whereas I am privileged and immune unto eternity, since I am among the righteous kings who are in the presence of Amon-Re, King of the Gods, and in the presence of Osiris, Ruler of Eternity.[5]

I

(iv 1) PERSONS brought in because of the great crimes which they had committed, and turned over to the Place of Examination, in the presence of the great officials of the Place of Examination, in order to be examined by: the Overseer of the Treasury Montu-em-tawi; the Overseer of the Treasury Paif-ru; the Standard-Bearer Kar; the Butler Pai-Bes; the Scribe of the Archives May; and the Standard-Bearer Hori.[6] They examined them. They found them guilty. They caused their sentences to overtake them. Their crimes seized them.[7]

The great enemy Pai-bak-kamen,[8] who had been Chief of the Chamber. HE WAS BROUGHT IN because he had been in collusion with Tiye and the women of the harem. He had made common cause with them. He had begun to take their words outside to their mothers and their brothers who were there, saying: "Gather people and stir up enemies to make rebellion against their lord!" He was placed in the presence of the great officials of the Place of Examination. They examined his crimes.

[10] The scene of the judgment hall shows two balanced groups of twenty men each on the two sides of the hall.

[11] The scene shows bailiffs bringing in the appellants, by the wrist or by the scruff of the neck. Our text is uncertain. The translation assumes that one whose position is far enough advanced has been neglected in the hearing; when he protests, he is hauled forward by a bailiff to an immediate hearing. Davies, on the contrary, assumes that the individual seeks unfair advantage and is then to be arrested: "Should one who is further forward say, 'No one near me is to be heard (before me),' he is to be arrested by the apparitors of the vizier."

The text continues with a long statement of the several duties of the vizier, including several passages on his judicial function.

[1] See T. E. Peet, *The Great Tomb-Robberies of the Twentieth Egyptian Dynasty* (Oxford, 1930), J. Capart *et al.* in *JEA* xxii (1936), 169-93.

[2] One conspiracy within the royal palace is indicated in the Instruction of King Amen-em-het I (pp. 418-419 below). Another, of the 6th dynasty, is in the text of Breasted, *AR*, i, §310:—"When a case was examined in secret in the royal harem against the King's Wife and Great of Wand, his majesty had me go down to hear it alone." There, as in our present text, the name of the accused is suppressed, and only her title is given.

[3] The court of inquiry consists of palace officials, apparently all persons in positions of intimate trust to the pharaoh. One among them, Baal-mahar, bears a Semitic name. This court divides into three groups. The two treasury overseers, the two standard-bearers, the Butler Pai-Bes, and the Scribe May are "the great officials of the Place of Examination," who try almost all of those under section I of the translation. A second group of four or five butlers, who try the last man of section I, are particularly concerned with the major criminals of section III. The Herald Pen-Renenut and the Scribe Pa-Re-em-heb are given in no other lists of judges, and may have been other officers of the court. Note that three of the "great officials" turn up as criminals in sections IV and V.

[4] As de Buck suggests, the insistence of the pharaoh that he does not know who were the criminals against his throne and who was punished for conspiracy probably means that he accepts no personal responsibility for the fate of individuals. See the next note.

[5] The pharaoh states explicitly that responsibility falls upon the heads of the judges and that he is "sheltered and protected" forever from any responsibility. In connection with the final clauses, one may argue that the pharaoh was already dead and was refusing to take into the presence of the gods any responsibility for taking the lives of others.

[6] Although these are the "great officials" (cf. n.3 above), the criminals whom they try and sentence are not of such calibre that they are permitted to take their own lives, contrasting with those in sections II and III.

[7] The sentences which were imposed are not stated.

[8] "This Blind Slave." It has frequently been pointed out that some of these criminals have fictitious names. To be sure, the name Pa-tjau-emdi-Amon, "The Breath (of Life) is With Amon," is a perfectly good Egyptian name. However, Mesed-su-Re, "Re Hates Him," Pen-Huy-bin, "He of the Wicked Huy," Bin-em-Waset, "The Wicked One in Thebes," and probably Pa-Re-kamenef, "The Re Will Blind (Him)," are all names of opprobrium, given either to degrade the criminals or to conceal their true and formerly honored names. See n.18 below.

They found that he had committed them. His crimes laid hold upon him. The officials who examined him caused his sentence to overtake him.

The great enemy Mesed-su-Re, who had been butler. He was brought in because he had been in collusion with Pai-bak-kamen, who had been Chief of the Chamber, and with the women, to gather enemies and to make rebellion against their lord. He was placed in the presence of the great officials of the Place of Examination. They examined his crimes. They found him guilty. They caused his sentence to overtake him. . . .[9]

(6) The great enemy Pa-tjau-emdi-Amon, who had been Agent of the Harem in the Retinue. He was brought in because he had heard the words which the men had plotted with the women of the harem, without reporting them. He was placed in the presence of the great officials of the Place of Examination. They examined his crimes. They found him guilty. They caused his sentence to overtake him. . . .[10]

(v 1) The wives of the men of the gate of the harem, who had joined the men who plotted the matters, who were placed in the presence of the officials of the Place of Examination. They found them guilty. They caused their sentences to overtake them. Six women.

The great enemy Pa-iry, son of Rem, who had been Overseer of the Treasury. He was brought in because he had been in collusion with the great enemy Pen-Huy-bin.[11] He had made common cause with him to stir up enemies and to make rebellion against their lord. He was placed in the presence of the officials of the Place of Examination. They found him guilty. They caused his sentence to overtake him.

The great enemy Bin-em-Waset, who had been Troop Commander of Ethiopia.[12] He was brought in because his sister, who was in the harem in the retinue, had written to him, saying: "Gather people, make enemies, and come back to make rebellion against your lord!" He was placed in the presence of Qedendenen, Baal-mahar, Pa-ir-sun, and Thut-rekh-nefer. They examined him. They found him guilty. They caused his sentence to overtake him.

II

Persons brought in because of their crimes, because they had been in collusion with Pai-bak-kamen, Pai-is, and Pen-ta-Uret.[13] They were placed in the presence of the officials of the Place of Examination, in order to examine them. They found them guilty. They left them in their (own) hands in the Place of Examination. They took their own lives; no penalty was carried out against them.[14]

(5) The great enemy Pai-is, who had been Commander of the Army; the great enemy Messui, who had been Scribe of the House of Life;[15] the great enemy Pa-Re-kamenef, who had been Chief (Lector Priest);[16] the great enemy Ii-roi, who had been Overseer of the Priests of Sekhmet; the great enemy Neb-djefa, who had been butler; and the great enemy Shad-mesdjer, who had been Scribe of the House of Life. Total: six.

III

Persons brought, because of their crimes, in to the Place of Examination, in the presence of Qedendenen, Baal-mahar, Pa-ir-sun, Thut-rekh-nefer, and Mer-usi-Amon. They examined them concerning their crimes. They found them guilty. They left them where they were. They took their own lives.[17]

Pen-ta-Urt, he who had been called by that other name.[18] He was brought in because he had been in collusion with Tiye, his mother, when she had plotted matters with the women of the harem about making rebellion against his lord. He was placed in the presence of the butlers in order to examine him. They found him guilty. They left him where he was. He took his own life.

The great enemy Henuten-Amon, who had been butler. He was brought in because of the crimes of the women of the harem, among whom he had been, which he had heard, without making report of them. He was placed in the presence of the butlers in order to examine him. They found him guilty. They left him where he was. He took his own life. . . .[19]

IV

(vi 1) Persons upon whom sentence was carried out by cutting off their noses and their ears, because they had abandoned the good instructions given to them.[20] The women had gone. They had reached them at the

[9] The translation omits the cases of two more officials of the royal harem, treated in the same terms as Pai-bak-kamen and Mesed-su-Re.

[10] The translation omits the cases of nine more officials of the harem or of the palace, also guilty of withholding knowledge of the conspiracy and treated in the same terms as Pa-tjau-emdi-Amon. One is named Pa-Luka, "The Lycian," and one is a Libyan.

[11] In another document Pen-Huy-bin was guilty of securing a magic scroll to be used for witchcraft against Ramses III (Breasted, *op. cit.*, IV, §455). It is not here stated whether Pa-iry's guilt was collusion in this witchcraft.

[12] This soldier had apparently been on duty in Ethiopia, and his sister had tried to get him to stir up a revolt in the provinces.

[13] It seems that these three names correspond to the three groups of criminals in sections I, II, and III.

[14] Either the particular crimes of which these persons were guilty called for suicide, or the criminals were of such a nature that they were permitted to take their own lives. cf. n.17.

[15] The archives in which were kept the sacred and magical writings. The present group includes two clerks from those archives; a priest of Sekhmet, which means priest, physician, and magician; and a lector priest, versed in the magical writings. The present group was apparently guilty of using magical texts for the conspiracy.

[16] It has been pointed out that this title gave rise to the word used (e.g. Gen. 41:8) for the Egyptian magicians; cf. de Buck, *op. cit.*, 163.

[17] Here, if Pen-ta-Urt was truly the pretender to the throne, the reason for permitting suicide is obvious. The prince was of too high a birth to incur a capital punishment.

[18] Apparently the prince who was the pretender of the conspiracy, being advanced by his mother, Tiye. Breasted assumes that the trial gives him an assumed name, to protect his own name. De Buck suggests that the conspirators had given him another name for his claim to kingship, that is, a full royal titulary.

[19] The translation omits two other officials, recorded in the same terms as Henuten-Amon.

[20] Two of the following four had been judges in the court of examination, two were of the military or police, perhaps attached to that court. The instructions which they had "abandoned" were those of the pharaoh in constituting the court.

place where they were. They had caroused[21] with them and with Pai-is. Their crime seized them.

The great enemy Pai-Bes, who had been butler. This sentence was carried out on him: he was left, and he took his own life.

The great enemy May, who had been Scribe of the Archives.

The great enemy Tai-nakhtet, who had been Lieutenant of the Garrison.

(5) The great enemy Nanai, who had been Chief of Bailiffs.

V

PERSON who had been in common with them. He was rebuked severely with wicked words.[22] He was left, and no penalty was carried out against him.

The great enemy Hori, who had been Standard-Bearer of the Garrison.

FROM THE RECORD OF A LAWSUIT

The following text has lost its beginning and its end, but it gives an adequate impression of legal proceedings under the Egyptian Empire. A merchant Raia offered the woman Iri-nofret a female slave from Palestine or Syria. Iri-nofret bought the slave for a price calculated in silver, but paid in goods, some of which she already had, but some of which she had to buy from other persons. Some time later, a soldier named Nekhy laid the legal charge that some of the payment for the slave had consisted of goods properly belonging to a woman named Bake-Mut. The court is examining this charge.

The papyrus was discovered by the Metropolitan Museum of Art at Thebes and is now Cairo Museum 65739. It dates to the Nineteenth Dynasty (13th century B.C.). It was published by A. H. Gardiner in *JEA*, XXI (1935), 140-46, Pls. XIII-XVI.

. . .[1] SAID BY the woman[2] Iri-nofret: "[*As for me, I am the wife of* the District Overseer Si-Mut], and I came to live in his house, and I worked and [*wove*] and took care of my (own) clothes. In the year 15, seven years after I had entered the house of the District Overseer Si-[Mut], the merchant Raia approached me with the Syrian slave Gemni-her-imentet,[3] while she was (still) a girl, [and he] (5) said to me: 'Buy this girl and give me the price for her'—so he spoke to me. And I took the girl and gave him [the price] for her. Now look, I shall tell the price which I gave for her:

1 *shroud* of Upper Egyptian linen, making 5 *ḳidet* of silver;[4]

1 sheet of Upper Egyptian linen, making 3⅓ *ḳidet* of silver; . . .[5]

bought from the woman Kafy, 1 bronze jar, making 18 *deben*, making 1 2/3 *ḳidet* of silver;[6] . . . (10) . . .

bought from the Chief Steward of the House of Amon, Tutu: 1 bronze jug, making 20 *deben*, making 2 *ḳidet* of silver; 10 shirts of fine Upper Egyptian linen, making 4 *ḳidet* of silver—

TOTAL of everything, 4 *deben*, 1 *ḳidet* of silver.[7]

And I gave them to the merchant Raia, and there was nothing in them belonging to the woman Bake-Mut. And he gave me this girl, and I called her by the name Gemni-her-imentet."

(15) SAID BY the tribunal of judges to the woman Iri-nofret: "Take the oath of the Lord—life, prosperity, health!—with the words: 'Should witnesses be brought up against me that any property belonged to the woman Bake-Mut within the silver which I gave for this servant and I concealed it, I shall be (liable) to one hundred blows, while I am deprived of her.' "

OATH of the Lord—life, prosperity, health!—spoken by the woman Iri-nofret: "As Amon endures and as the Ruler—life, prosperity, health!—endures, should witnesses be brought up against me that any property belonged to the woman Bake-Mut within the silver which I gave for this servant and I concealed it, I shall be (liable) to one hundred blows, while I am deprived of her!"

SAID BY the tribunal of judges to the soldier Nekhy: (20) "Produce for us the witnesses of whom you said that they knew that this silver belonging to the woman Bake-Mut was given to buy the slave Gemni-her-imentet, as well as the witnesses about this tomb of which you said that it was the woman Bake-Mut who made it, but the woman Iri-nofret gave it to the merchant Nakht, and he gave her the slave Tener-Ptah in exchange for it."[8]

QUANTITY OF witnesses whom the soldier Nekhy named in the presence of the tribunal: the Chief of Police Min-i . . . ; the Mayor of the West Ra-mose; the Priest Huy Phinehas, the elder brother of the District Overseer Si-Mut; the woman Kafy, (25) the wife of the Chief of Police Pa-shed, who is dead; the woman Weret-nofret: and the woman Hut-ia, the elder sister of the

21 "They had made a beer-hall." For officers of the court of inquiry to carouse in a friendly way with the harem women whom they were trying was obviously a serious breach of judicial behavior.

22 "One fought with him with bad words strongly," i.e. he was let off with a reprimand. Apparently Hori—also one of the original judges—had been friendly with the preceding group, but had not acted with them in the carousing.

1 The lost beginning probably included a date (presumably in the reign of Ramses II), the composition of the court, and the accusation of the soldier Nekhy.

2 Here and below, the title "Living-Woman of the Town" is rendered simply "woman."

3 The *Kharu* ("Horite") slave was given this Egyptian name after she was purchased by Iri-nofret. We are not told her Asiatic name.

4 Each element of the payment was calculated in a weight of silver. Ten *ḳidet* made one Egyptian *deben*, equal to about 91 grams or 3 oz. Troy. Thus the present piece of cloth (of Iri-nofret's own weaving?) was worth about 45 grams of silver.

5 The translation omits three other payments of Iri-nofret's own linen, totalling 14 *ḳidet* of silver.

6 The translation omits four other purchases by Iri-nofret, of bronze vessels, beaten copper, and honey. One of these purchases was from the Priest Huy Phinehas, mentioned below as a witness against her. From the conversions of bronze or copper into silver, the ratio of silver to copper in the 19th dynasty was 100:1, calculated to the nearest convenient fraction.

7 The price of the Syrian slave girl was 4.1 *deben* of silver, about 375 grams or 1 Troy pound. J. Černý, in *Archiv Orientální*, VI (1933), 173 ff., showed that, at the end of the 19th and beginning of the 20th dynasty, 1 *ḳhar* of emmer wheat was worth 1 *deben* of copper. Using the ratio of 100:1 of the preceding note, this would make 2.25 bushels of emmer worth 1 *deben* of copper, and the 410 *deben* of copper value given for the slave girl would work out at more than 900 bushels of emmer. But there are several uncertainties in the calculation; see Gardiner, *op. cit.*, 146.

8 It is not clear how this transaction of the tomb and the purchase of a male slave figures in the accusation. It is apparently a second charge against Iri-nofret.

woman Bake-Mut—TOTAL: three men and three women; TOTAL: six.[9] And they stood in the presence of the tribunal, and they took the oath of the Lord—life, prosperity, health!—as well as the oath of the god, with the words: "We shall speak truthfully; we shall not speak falsely. Should we speak falsely, the servants shall be taken away from us."[10]

SAID BY the tribunal of judges to the Priest Huy: "Tell us the matter of the Syrian slave..."

9 From two of these—the Priest Huy Phinehas and the woman Kafy—Iri-nofret had purchased some of the goods which she used to make up the price of the slave. There is a heavy weight of testimony against her, in the Chief of Police and the Mayor of the West side of Thebes, not to mention her brother-in-law.

10 They were testifying under oath about the legal possession of a slave. If they perjured themselves, the penalty would take its similarity to the case: they would lose their own slaves.

Mesopotamian Legal Documents

(Translator: Theophile J. Meek)

Out of the thousands of tablets that have been published in this field it was difficult to make a selection. The following were chosen because (1) they represent different periods and different types, (2) most of them are short and hence permit the inclusion of a considerable variety, (3) they are quite well preserved, and (4) they are not too complex or involved so that their translation is fairly certain.

A. SUMERIAN

Notation re Laborers[1]

Uru-ki-erima, En-udana, Lugal-nanga-ra-na, Ki-bi-batila, Shesh-tur, Ur-Enki, Ur-Ninsig, Lugal-mu, Nesag, (and) Lugal-sha-la-tuk, the overseer, have gone ahead; as for Uda, A-lu-lila, (and) En-tu, Lugal-sha-la-tuk, the fisherman, brought about their dispatch. A total of 12 men, who are sea-fishermen (in the employ) of the goddess Baba,[2] have gone to the sea, with Lugal-sha-⟨la-tuk⟩ as their overseer.

The fifth year.[3]

B. OLD AKKADIAN

(1) Amortization[4]

94 copper utensils the recorder, Zuzu, received. 21 copper utensils in the case of Ishma-il, the son of Shu-Dada, (and) 5 copper utensils in the case of Name, are still outstanding as a balance against them.

(2) Receipt of Balance Due[5]

110 *qu* of barley, the balance of the barley for rations, Ire-Shamash received. The month of Zalul.

(3) Receipt of Barley to be Sold[6]

. . Akkadian *kur*[7] of barley Ate, the merchant, received from Zuzu to be sold in Lulubum.[8]

(4) Receipt of Barley for Rations[9]

A certain Buzi at 120 *qu*, 4 workmen at 60 *qu*, 2 female slaves at 30 *qu*, 2 sons at 30 *qu*, 2 sons at 20 *qu*, 2 daughters at 20 *qu*, (making) 1 *kur* 260 *qu* of barley for rations per month: a total of 7 *kur* 140 *qu* of barley for rations for 4 months, the son of Absham of the city of Kinakum received.

C. NEW SUMERIAN

(1) Divorce Settlement[10]

Final judgment: Lu-Utu, the son of Nig-Baba, divorced Geme-Enlil. Dugidu, an officer and official,[11] took oath that Geme-Enlil had taken her stand[12] (and) said, "By the king! Give me 10 shekels of silver (and) I will not enter claim against you," (and) that she made him forfeit 10 shekels of silver. Ur-.. (was) the deputy; Ur-Lama (was) the governor.

The year Harshi and Humurti were sacked.[13]

(2) Receipt of Votive-gift[14]

180 *gur* of barley, the votive-gift of Lu-Nanna, the governor of Zimudar, Ur-Gal-alim has received on behalf of the divine Shulgi-Nanna, on the bank of the canal Dur-ul.

The month of Shegurkud, the year the divine Shu-Sin became king.[15]

(3) Loan at Interest[16]

120 shekels of silver, with its interest at 5 shekels per 60 shekels, Adda-kala has borrowed from Ur-dul-azaga. In the month of Sig he shall return it. By the king he swore.

(The names of three persons as witnesses, each preceded by the witness-sign.)

The month of Shegurkud, the year the divine Ibbi-Sin, the king, sacked Simurru.[17]

(Sealed in three places with a seal inscribed, "Adda-kala, the son of Ur-Sin.")

D. OLD ASSYRIAN

(1) Local Court Decision[18]

The council of Kanish[19] gave judgment having to do

1 Published and translated by Thorkild Jacobsen, *Cuneiform Texts in the National Museum, Copenhagen* (1939), No. 2.

2 Some scholars still prefer the older reading *Bau* for this name. Baba was the consort of Ningirsu, the city-god of Lagash.

3 i.e. the fifth year of Urukagina, king of Lagash, about 2375 B.C.

4 Published by T. J. Meek, *Old Akkadian, Sumerian, and Cappadocian Texts from Nuzi* (1935), No. 59.

5 Published by T. J. Meek, *op. cit.*, No. 63.

6 Published by T. J. Meek, *op. cit.*, No. 99.

7 The *kur* of Akkad contained 300 *qu*.

8 A district corresponding roughly to the modern district of Sulaimania, east of Kirkuk.

9 Published by T. J. Meek, *op. cit.*, No. 190.

10 Published by Fr. Thureau-Dangin, *Recueil de tablettes chaldéennes* (1903), No. 289; most recently translated by C. J. Gadd, *A Sumerian Reading-Book* (1924), p. 173.

11 The exact meaning of the titles used here, *ùg-íl* and *engar*, is not known.

12 Lit. "had set her face."

13 This is the date formula for the last year of Shulgi, king of Ur, about 2038-1990 B.C.

14 Published and translated by L. Legrain, *RA*, xxx (1933), 117-25, No. 7.

15 The date formula for the first year of Shu-Sin, king of Ur, about 1981-1972 B.C.

16 Published by J. B. Nies, *Ur Dynasty Tablets* (1920), No. 30.

17 The date formula for the third year of Ibbi-Sin, king of Ur, about 1972-1947 B.C.

18 Not published; transliterated and translated by G. Eisser and J. Lewy, *MVAG*, xxxiii (1930), No. 276.

19 A city in central Asia Minor where there was an important trading colony of Assyrians.

with Ashur-ammarum, the son of Enum-Ashur: Zibe-zibe, the daughter of Ashur-beli, (was) his wife; he divorced her and Ashur-ammarum gave Zibe-zibe, his wife, 1 mina of silver as her divorce-settlement;[20] so his three sons shall revert to Ashur-ammarum; Zibe-zibe has no further claim against Ashur-ammarum or his three sons.

The month of Sin; the eponymy of Aweliya.[21]

(2) Supreme (Ashur) Court Decision[22]

(The names of nine persons, the last four being three sons and a daughter, Ahaha, of Pushu-ken, each preceded by "The seal of.")

As for the 40 minas of silver, with which Ikuppiya, the son of Ata'a, became indebted to Pushu-ken, in Kanish, and which money Ashur-muttabil and Belanum, the bailiff, got—for this money neither the (other) sons of Pushu-ken nor the daughter of Pushu-ken, the nun, may file claim against their brother, Ashur-muttabil. On his arrival the sons of Pushu-ken and the daughter of Pushu-ken, the nun, shall give to Ashur-muttabil in Kanish the tablet having to do with the debt of Ikuppiya, the son of Ata'a.[23]

In conformity with the judgment of the city (i.e. Ashur) the sons of Pushu-ken and the daughter of Pushu-ken are content in the matter of the money. Idi-abum, the son of Ashur-malik, represented Ahaha.

(3) Divorce[24]

(The seals of six persons, each preceded by "The seal of.")

Hashusharna, the son of Gudgariya, divorced his wife, Taliya. If Taliya tries to reclaim her (former) husband Hashusharna, she shall pay 2 minas of silver and they shall put her to death in the *open*. If Gudgariya[25] and Hashusharna try to reclaim Taliya, they shall pay 2 minas of silver and they shall put them to death in the *open*.

E. OLD BABYLONIAN

(1) Lawsuit[26]

(Legal) Document: For a house in Durum-eshshum belonging to Manutum, the daughter of Abdirah, Hamazirum, the daughter of Abihar, filed claim against Manutum, the daughter of Abdirah, whereupon the judges in the temple of Shamash put Manutum under oath to god. When Manutum swore by Aya, her lady, she (i.e. the plaintiff Hamazirum) renounced her claim. On no account[27] shall Hamazirum ever again file claim for the house, patrimony, possessions, or heritage of Manutum, whatever it may be; by Shamash and Aya, Marduk and Sumu-la-el[28] she swore.

The judgment of the temple of Shamash.

(The names of the two judges.)

(The names of two persons and the scribe, a woman, as witnesses, each preceded by the witness-sign.)

(2) Receipt of Sheep to Pasture[29]

183 ewes, 178 rams, 30 female lambs, 35 male lambs, 20 large lambs, (a total of) 446 sheep belonging to Belitiya, Ahushunu, the shepherd, received from Sin-ishmeni to pasture. Should a sheep be lost, he shall make it good.[30] By the king he swore.

(The names of seven persons as witnesses, each preceded by the witness-sign.)

The seal of Ahushunu.

The month of Nisan, the year the great wall was built.[31]

(Sealed in six places with the seal of Ahushunu, the son of Imgur-Sin.)

(3) Division of Estate[32]

Nur-Shamash, Ilima-ahi, Palatum, and Humurum have divided the property of their father. On no account will they file claim against one another. By Shamash, Aya, Marduk, and Hammurabi they swore.

(The names of four persons as witnesses, each preceded by the witness-sign.)

The year the Hammurabi-canal.[33]

(4) Rent of House[34]

The house of Ribatum, a hierodule of Shamash, Mashqum, the son of Rim-Adad, has rented for one year from Ribatum, a hierodule of Shamash. As the rent per year he shall pay 1½ shekels of silver, with ⅔ shekel of silver received as the initial payment on his rent.

(The names of two persons as witnesses, each preceded by the witness-sign.)

The month of Iyyar, the 10th day, the year a shining weapon-emblem.[35]

(5) Purchase of Slave[36]

One female slave, Ina-Eulmash-banat by name, from the city of Ursum, the slave of Damiq-Marduk, the son of Lipit-Ishtar, Usriya, the son of Waraza, bought from Damiq-Marduk, the son of Lipit-Ishtar, her owner. As her full price he weighed out ⅚ mina 1 shekel of silver and he also delivered ⅔ shekel of silver as additional payment. Three days are allowed for in-

[20] This happens to be the amount prescribed in the Code of Hammurabi, §139.

[21] This is the Assyrian method of dating, but since we do not have complete eponym lists for the Old Assyrian period we can only date the texts in the most general terms as belonging in or close to the early 20th century B.C.

[22] Published by G. Contenau, *Louvre IV: tablettes cappadociennes* (1920), No. 79; translated by G. Eisser and J. Lewy, *MVAG*, XXXIII (1930), No. 11.

[23] i.e. the original tablet is to be surrendered and destroyed because the debt is now paid.

[24] Published by Fr. Thureau-Dangin, *Lettres et contrats de l'époque de la première dynastie babylonienne* (1910), No. 242; discussed at length by J. Lewy, *ZA*, XXXVI (1925), 139-61.

[25] Written defectively as *Udgari*.

[26] Published in *CT*, VIII, 28*a*; translated most recently by M. Schorr, *Urkunden des altbabylonischen Zivil- und Prozessrechts* (1913), No. 257.

[27] Lit., "not from straw to gold."

[28] King of Babylon, about 1816-1780 B.C.

[29] Published and translated by T. J. Meek, *AJSL*, XXXIII (1917), 203-44, No. 3; most recently translated by P. Koschaker und A. Ungnad, *Hammurabi's Gesetz*, VI (1923), No. 1502.

[30] This is also the prescription in the Code of Hammurabi, §263.

[31] The date formula for the 10th year of Warad-Sin, king of Larsa, about 1771-1759 B.C.

[32] Published by B. Meissner, *Beiträge zur altbabylonischen Privatrecht* (1893), No. 106; translated most recently by M. Schorr, *op. cit.*, No. 184.

[33] An abbreviated formula for the 9th year of Hammurabi, king of Babylon, about 1728-1686 B.C.

[34] Published and translated by E. Chiera, *Old Babylonian Contracts* (1922), No. 220.

[35] An abbreviated formula for the 7th year of Samsu-iluna, king of Babylon, about 1685-1647 B.C.

[36] Published in *VS*, VII (1909), No. 50; translated by M. Schorr, *op. cit.*, No. 84.

vestigation (and) one month for epilepsy in order to clear her, in accordance with the ordinances of the king.[37]

(The names of five persons and the scribe as witnesses, each preceded by the witness-sign.)

The month of Kislim, the 15th day, the year Ammi-ditana, the king, brought in his statue (representing him as) offering prayer, scepter in hand.[38]

F. LATE SUMERIAN

(1) Hire of Laborer[39]

Shep-Sin hired Sin-ishmeanni from his foreman, Ahum; his hire per year (is to be) 6 shekels of silver, of which Ahum has received 4 shekels of silver.

(The names of three persons as witnesses, each preceded by the witness-sign.)

The month of Ab, the 30th day, the 30th year (after) Isin was conquered.[40]

(Sealed in two places.)

(2) Marriage Contract[41]

Ama-sukkal, the daughter of Ninurta-mansum, has been taken in marriage by Enlil-izzu, the high priest of Enlil, the son of Lugal-azida; Ama-sukkal has brought 19 shekels of silver to Enlil-izzu, her husband (as dowry).

If Enlil-izzu ever says to Ama-sukkal, his wife, "You are no longer my wife," he shall return the 19 shekels of silver and he shall also weigh out ½ mina as her divorce-settlement. On the other hand, if Ama-sukkal ever says to Enlil-izzu, her husband, "You are no longer my husband," she shall forfeit the 19 shekels of silver and she shall also weigh out ½ mina of silver. In mutual agreement they have sworn together by the king.

(The names of eight men, two women, the scribe, and the notary as witnesses, each preceded by the witness-sign.)

(Sealed with two seals, twice each.)

The month of Nisan, the 28th day, the year Samsu-iluna, the king, by the command of Enlil brought Kisurra and Sabum to obedience.[42]

G. MIDDLE BABYLONIAN

(1) Court Decision[43]

One ox from pasture Iqisha-Enlil, the son of Hashma-Harbe, received from the hand of Belanu, the son of Urash-amela-uballit, to draw (water), and he broke its leg, whereupon Belanu spoke thus to Iqisha-Enlil, "Bring me an ox that I may plow in the field so that you may not hinder me from plowing." Iqisha-Enlil spoke thus to Belanu, "I will give you an ox in the month of Ab." Since Iqisha-Enlil has not given the ox to Belanu in the month of Ab, Iqisha-Enlil shall make good to Belanu the crop of the field.

(The names of two persons as witnesses, each preceded by the witness-sign.)

(Three thumbnail impressions on the left edge.)

The month of Sivan, the first year of Nazi-Maruttash, the all-powerful king.[44]

(2) Release on Bail[45]

As for Mina-egu-ana-Shamash, the son of Salli-lumur, the governor—Awel-Marduk, his lord, shut him up in prison, but Arkat-Nergal, the son of Ardu-nubatti, went bail for him and got him released. So he (i.e. Arkat-Nergal) shall take 13 1/3 shekels of gold and give it to Marduk-risua, and then Mina-egu-ana-Shamash and his wife, . . . , shall take (it) and give (it) to Awel-Marduk.

The month of Tammuz, the 9th day, the 8th year of Shagarakti-Shuriash, the king.[46]

The thumbnail impression of Arkat-Nergal as his seal.

(Six thumbnail impressions on the left edge.)

H. NUZI AKKADIAN

(1) Sale-Adoption[47]

The tablet of adoption belonging to Kuzu, the son of Karmishe: he adopted Tehip-tilla, the son of Puhi-shenni. As his share[48] (of the estate) Kuzu gave Tehip-tilla 40 imers[49] of land in the district of Iphushshi. If the land should have a claimant, Kuzu shall clear (it) and give (it) back to Tehip-tilla. Tehip-tilla in turn gave 1 mina of silver to Kuzu as his honorarium. Whoever defaults shall pay 2 minas of silver (and) 2 minas of gold.

(The names of fourteen persons and the scribe as witnesses, each preceded by the witness-sign.)

(The names of two of the witnesses, one other person, and the scribe, each preceded by "The seal of.")

(2) Sale-Adoption[50]

The tablet of adoption belonging to Nashwi, the son of Ar-shenni: he adopted Wullu, the son of Puhi-shenni. As long as Nashwi is alive, Wullu shall provide food and clothing; when Nashwi dies, Wullu shall become the heir. If Nashwi has a son of his own, he shall divide (the estate) equally with Wullu, but the son of Nashwi shall take the gods of Nashwi. However, if Nashwi does

[37] i.e. in the Code of Hammurabi, particularly §§278 f.

[38] The date formula for the 7th year of Ammi-ditana, king of Babylon, about 1619-1582 B.C.

[39] Published in *VS*, XIII (1914), No. 92; translated by P. Koschaker und A. Ungnad, *op. cit.*, No. 1676.

[40] The date formula for the 59th year of Rim-Sin, king of Larsa, about 1759-1698 B.C.

[41] Published and translated by A. Poebel, *Babylonian Business and Legal Documents* (1909), No. 40; most recently translated by M. Schorr, *op. cit.*, No. 1.

[42] The date formula for the 13th year of Samsu-iluna, king of Babylon, about 1685-1647 B.C.

[43] Published and translated by Albert T. Clay, *Documents from the Temple Archives of Nippur Dated in the Reigns of Cassite Rulers* (1906), No. 41.

[44] One of the kings of the Cassite dynasty in Babylonia who ruled about 1300 B.C.

[45] Published and translated by Albert T. Clay, *op. cit.*, No. 135.

[46] One of the kings of the Cassite dynasty in Babylonia who ruled about 1240 B.C.

[47] Published by E. Chiera, *Joint Expedition with the Iraq Museum at Nuzi* (1927), No. 1; translated by E. Chiera and E. A. Speiser, *JAOS*, XLVII (1927), 37 f. Sale-adoption was a legal device used in Nuzi whereby a landowner could circumvent the law prohibiting the sale of land outside the family by going through the form of adopting the purchaser. The Nuzi tablets come from the middle of the 2nd millennium B.C.

[48] The word used here, *zittu*, means the double share of the first-born son.

[49] An imer was approximately 4½ acres.

[50] Published and translated by C. J. Gadd, *RA*, XXIII (1926), 49-161, No. 51.

not have a son of his own, then Wullu shall take the gods of Nashwi.[51] Furthermore, he gave his daughter Nuhuya in marriage to Wullu, and if Wullu takes another wife he shall forfeit the lands and buildings of Nashwi. Whoever defaults shall make compensation with 1 mina of silver and 1 mina of gold.

(The names of five persons and the scribe as witnesses, each preceded by the witness-sign.)

(The names of four of the witnesses and the scribe, each preceded by "The seal of.")

(3) Real Adoption[52]

The tablet of adoption belonging to [Zike], the son of Akkuya: he gave his son Shennima in adoption to Shuriha-ilu, and Shuriha-ilu, with reference to Shennima, (from) all the lands . . . (and) his earnings of every sort gave to Shennima one (portion) of his property. If Shuriha-ilu should have a son of his own, as the principal (son) he shall take a double share; Shennima shall then be next in order (and) take his proper share. As long as Shuriha-ilu is alive, Shennima shall revere him. When Shuriha-ilu [dies], Shennima shall become the heir. Furthermore, Kelim-ninu has been given in marriage to Shennima. If Kelim-ninu bears (children), Shennima shall not take another wife; but if Kelim-ninu does not bear, Kelim-ninu shall acquire a woman of the land of Lullu as wife for Shennima, and Kelim-ninu may not send the offspring away. Any sons that may be born to Shennima from the womb of Kelim-ninu, to (these) sons shall be given [all] the lands (and) buildings of every sort. [However], if she does not bear a son, [then] the daughter of Kelim-ninu from the lands (and) buildings shall take one (portion) of the property. Furthermore, Shuriha-ilu shall not adopt another son in addition to Shennima. Whoever among them defaults shall compensate with 1 mina of silver (and) 1 mina of gold.

Furthermore, Yalampa is given as a handmaid to Kelim-ninu and Shatim-ninu has been made co-parent. As long as she is alive, she (i.e. Yalampa) shall revere her and Shatim-ninu shall not annul the [*agreement*].

If Kelim-ninu bears (children) and Shennima takes another wife, she may *take* her dowry and leave.

(The names of nine persons and the scribe as witnesses, each preceded by the witness-sign.)

The remaining sons of Zike may not lay claim to the lands (and) buildings belonging to the (above) one (portion) of the property.

The tablet was written after the proclamation.

(Sealed by eight persons, seven of whom were already named as witnesses.)

(4) Lawsuit[53]

Tarmiya, the son of Huya, appeared with Shukriya and Kula-hupi, with (these) two brothers of his, the sons of Huya, in a lawsuit before the judges of Nuzi with reference to the female slave [Sululi-Ishtar], whereupon Tarmiya spoke thus before the judges, "My father, Huya, was sick and lay on a couch; then my father seized my hand and spoke thus to me, 'My other sons, being older, have acquired wives, but you have not acquired a wife; so I give you herewith Sululi-Ishtar as your wife.' " Then the judges demanded the witnesses of Tarmiya [and Tarmiya] had his witnesses appear [before the judges]: . . . , the son of Hurshaya, . . . , the son of Ikkiya, . . . , the son of Itrusha, (and) . . . , the son of Hamanna. [These] witnesses of [Tarmiya] were examined before the judges, whereupon the judges spoke to Shukriya and Kula-hupi, "Go and take the oath of the gods against the witnesses of Tarmiya." Shukriya and Kula-hupi shrank from the gods[54] so that Tarmiya prevailed in the lawsuit and the judges assigned the female slave, Sululi-Ishtar, to Tarmiya.

(The names of three persons, each preceded by "The seal of.")

The signature of Iliya.

(5) Hebrew Slave Document[55]

Mar-Idiglat, a Hebrew from the land of Assyria, on his own initiative has entered (the house of) Tehip-tilla, the son of Puhi-shenni, as a slave.

(The names of eleven persons and the scribe as witnesses, each preceded by the witness-sign.)

(The names of two of the witnesses and the scribe, each preceded by "The seal of.")

(6) Hebrew Slave Document[56]

Sin-balti, a Hebrew woman, on her own initiative has entered the house of Tehip-tilla as a slave. Now if Sin-balti defaults and goes into the house of another, Tehip-tilla shall pluck out the eyes of Sin-balti and sell her.

(The names of nine persons and the scribe as witnesses, each preceded by the witness-sign.)

(The names of two of the witnesses and the scribe, each preceded by "The seal of.")

I. MIDDLE ASSYRIAN

(1) Deed of Gift[57]

The (first-born's) share of the palace together with its grain, belonging to the estate of Mushtepish-ilu, the son of Mar-Idigla, Ashur-uballit, the sovereign, has given to Abi-ilu, the son of Adad-nerari.

The month of Kinate, the 6th day, the eponymy of Adad-nasir.[58]

(Sealed with a seal inscribed, "The seal of Ashur-uballit, the king of Assyria, the son of [Eriba]-Adad.")

[51] Possession of the household gods marked a person as the legitimate heir, which explains Laban's anxiety in Gen. 31:26 ff. to recover his household gods from Jacob. It is to be noted too that Laban binds Jacob in verse 50 to marry no other wives beside his daughters, just as Wullu is bound in our text.

[52] Published by E. Chiera, *HSS*, v (1929), No. 67; translated by E. A. Speiser, *AASOR*, x (1930), 31 ff.

[53] Transliterated by R. H. Pfeiffer, *AASOR*, xvi (1936), No. 56; translated by E. A. Speiser, *ibid.*

[54] i.e. they refused to take the oath in fear of its consequences and thus showed themselves in the wrong.

[55] Published by E. Chiera, *Joint Expedition with the Iraq Museum at Nuzi* (1934), No. 459.

[56] Published by E. Chiera, *op. cit.*, No. 452; translated by E. Chiera and E. A. Speiser, *JAOS*, xlvii (1927), 44 f.

[57] Published by Erich Ebeling, *KAJ*, No. 173; translated by E. Ebeling, *MAOG*, vii (1933), 88.

[58] The date formula for a year in the reign of Ashur-uballit I, king of Assyria, 1363-1328 B.C.

(2) Sale of House[59]

The seal of Ashur-apla-eresh.

As for the 5 talents 30 minas of lead due Zer-iqisha, the son of Yakiya, debited to Ashur-apla-eresh, the son of Nusku-aha-iddina, the son of Ea-iddina, the goldsmith, of the inner city (i.e. Ashur)—he is in receipt of this lead as the price of his house in the inner city.

(The names of two persons and the scribe as witnesses, each preceded by the witness-sign.)

The month of Sin, the 23rd day, the eponymy of Tukulti-Ninurta, the sovereign.[60]

(The names of two persons, each preceded by "The seal of.")

(Sealed in two places.)

(3) Loan[61]

The seal of Shamash-tukulti.

He borrowed 12 homers[62] of barley by the old measure belonging to Sin-apla-eresh, the son of Ashur-kashid, the son of Bel-qarrad, debited to Shamash-tukulti, the son of Shamash-sharru, the son of Bel-qarrad. He shall [measure] out the principal of the barley at the threshing floor. When the time-limit has expired, the barley shall bear interest. As countervalue for this barley Sin-apla-eresh shall seize as security (and) have the usufruct of the unencumbered property of Shamash-tukulti.

(The names of three persons as witnesses, each preceded by the witness-sign.)

The month of Allanatu, the 16th day, the eponymy of Mushibshi-Sibita.[63]

J. NEO-ASSYRIAN

(1) Loan at Interest[64]

Three minas of silver according to (the mina) of Carchemish, belonging to Apliya (are) at the disposition of Sukaya; they shall increase 6 shekels per month.

The month of Ab, the 2nd day, the eponymy of Bel-emuranni, the field-marshal.[65]

(The names of five persons as witnesses, each preceded by the witness-sign.)

(2) Sentence for Murder[66]

(The names of eleven persons, each preceded by "The seal of.")

Siri (is) the murderer who murdered Silim-ili. In their presence[67] he shall compensate for that murder with either his wife or his brother or his son, whichever is forthcoming.

[59] Published by E. Ebeling, *KAJ*, No. 144; translated by E. Ebeling, *MAOG*, VII (1933), 74 f.

[60] Tukulti-Ninurta became king of Assyria in 1243 B.C.

[61] Not published; transliterated and translated by E. A. Speiser in *Symbolae ad iura orientis antiqui pertinentes Paulo Koschaker dedicatae* (1939), pp. 145-7.

[62] A homer or donkey-load contained a little more than 2¾ bushels.

[63] The date formula for a year in the reign of Shalmaneser I, king of Assyria about 1260 B.C.

[64] Published by C. H. W. Johns, *Assyrian Deeds and Documents*, I (1898), No. 28; translated by J. Kohler und A. Ungnad, *Assyrische Rechtsurkunden* (1913), No. 248.

[65] The date is 685 B.C., in the reign of Sennacherib, king of Assyria, 704-681 B.C.

[66] Published by C. H. W. Johns, *op. cit.*, No. 618; translated by J. Kohler und A. Ungnad, *op. cit.*, No. 660.

[67] i.e. in the presence of the eleven witnesses just named.

(The names of six persons and the scribe as witnesses, each preceded by the witness-sign.)

The month of Ab, the 21st day, the eponymy of Labashi.[68]

K. NEO-BABYLONIAN

(1) Sale of Slave[69]

As for Dunanu and Nabu-kullimanni, whom Ilu-bani, the son of Nabu-le'i, the descendant of Ilu-bani, sold to Nabu-mukin-zeri, the son of Apla'a, the descendant of Ilu-bani, for 2 1/3 minas of silver at the price agreed on—should there ever be a plaintiff or a claimant thereof, Ilu-bani shall hand back and give up (the purchase-price) to Nabu-mukin-zeri.

Borsippa, the month of Tammuz, the 29th day, the 2nd [year] of Nebuchadnezzar,[70] [the king of] Babylon.

(2) Partnership[71]

One mina of silver Itti-Marduk-balatu, the son of Nabu-ahhe-iddina, the descendant of Egibi, and Shapik-zeri, the son of Nabu-shuma-iddina, the descendant of Nadin-she'im, have undertaken a business in partnership; whatever profit they make therein they shall share equally.

(The names of three persons and the scribe as witnesses, each preceded by the witness-sign.)

Babylon, the month of Marchesvan, the 3rd day, the 5th year of Nabonidus, the king of Babylon.[72]

(3) Receipt of Feudal Dues[73] *(Late Babylonian)*

The feudal dues of Guzanu, the son of Hammaqu, the descendant of the appraiser, from the month of Nisan, the 26th year, to the end of the month of Adar, the 27th year of Darius, Shamash-iddina, the son of Arad-Marduk, the descendant of Diki, received from the hand of Shishku, the son of Iddina, the descendant of Egibi, on behalf of Guzanu, the son of Hammaqu, the descendant of the appraiser. They have taken one (document) each.

Babylon, the month of Nisan, the 11th day, the 27th year of Darius,[74] the king of Babylon, the king of the lands.

(4) Tax Receipt[75] *(Late Babylonian)*

From 1½ minas of silver, the taxes on a field for the 33rd year of Artaxerxes, the king, belonging to Enlil-aha-iddina, the son of Gahla, which is at the disposition of Enlil-nadin-shumi, the son of Murashu—therefrom Enlil-aha-iddina received (and) obtained payment of 1 mina from the hand of Enlil-nadin-shumi.

[68] The date is 656 B.C., in the reign of Ashurbanipal, king of Assyria, 668-633 B.C.

[69] Published by G. Contenau, *Louvre XII, Contrats néo-babyloniens* (1927), No. 27; translated by E. W. Moore, *Neo-Babylonian Business and Administrative Documents* (1935), No. 27.

[70] i.e. Nebuchadnezzar II, 605-562 B.C.

[71] Published by J. N. Strassmaier, *Nbn.*, No. 199; translated by Morris Jastrow, Jr., *The Civilization of Babylonia and Assyria* (1915), p. 354.

[72] Nabonidus was the last king of Babylonia, 555-539 B.C.

[73] Published by G. Contenau, *op. cit.*, No. 198; translated by E. W. Moore, *op. cit.*, No. 198.

[74] i.e. Darius I, king of Persia, 521-486 B.C.

[75] Published by Albert T. Clay, *Business Documents of Marashû Sons of Nippur, Dated in the Reign of Artaxerxes I* (1898), No. 33; translated by J. Kohler und A. Ungnad, *Hundert ausgewählte Rechtsurkunden* (1911), No. 28.

(The names of seven persons and the scribe as witnesses, each preceded by the witness-sign.)

Nippur, the month of Tebet, the 9th day, the 33rd year of Artaxerxes,[76] the king of the lands.

The thumbnail impression of Enlil-aha-iddina, the son of Gahla.

(5) Receipt of Provisions[77] *(Late Babylonian)*

27 *qu* of barley as provisions, which Nabu-belshunu, the son of Bel-ahhe-iddina, the expiation priest, and Marduk-eriba, the son of Iddina-Bel, the brewer, have received.

The month of Sivan, the 4th day, the 6th year of Alexander,[78] the son of Alexander.

The signet-ring impression of Nabu-belshunu and the signet-ring impression of Marduk-eriba.

(Sealed in one place.)

(6) Rent of House[79] *(Late Babylonian)*

A *ḳurubbu*-house belonging to Nana-iddina, the son of Tanittum-[Anu], the descendant of Ah'utu, which (is) in the district of the great grove which (is) in Erech, which (is) alongside the *ḳurubbu*-house of Mushe-zibitum, the daughter of Ishtar-aha-iddina, and alongside the center of the field, (is) at the disposal of Anu-uballit, the son of Kidin-Anu, for 4 shekels of silver as the rent of the house per year. Half the money he shall pay at the beginning of the year (and) the rest of the money in the middle of the year. The bareness (of the walls) he shall rectify; the cracks of the walls he shall close up. The work, the bricks, the reeds, and the beams, as much as he uses therefor, he shall reckon as a credit. He shall furnish 3 baskets of dates per year. From the 10th day of the month of Tammuz, the 8th year of Seleucus, the king, that *ḳurubbu*-house (is) at the disposal of Anu-uballit, the son of Kidin-Anu, for rent at 4 shekels of silver per year.

(The names of five persons and the scribe as witnesses, each preceded by the witness-sign.)

The month of Tammuz, the 5th day, the 8th year of Seleucus, the king.[80]

(The names of the five witnesses, each preceded by "The signet-ring impression of.")

The thumbnail impression of Anu-uballit.

Aramaic Papyri from Elephantine

(Translator: H. L. Ginsberg)

MIBTAHIAH'S FIRST MARRIAGE

Deed of 459 B.C., relating to reversion of property. Text: Sayce-Cowley, C; Cowley, 9.

On the 21st of Chisleu, that is the 1st of Mesore[1], year 6 of King Artaxerxes, Mahseiah b. Yedoniah, a Jew of Elephantine, of the detachment of Haumadata, said to Jezaniah b. Uriah of the said detachment as follows: There is the site of 1 house belonging to me, west of the house belonging to you, which I have given to your wife, my daughter Mibtahiah (*Mbṭḥyh*), and in respect of which I have written her a deed. The measurements of the house in question are 8 cubits and a handbreadth (5) by 11, *by the measuring-rod*. Now do I, Mahseiah, say to you, Build and equip that site . . . and dwell thereon with your wife. But you may not sell that house or give it as a present to others; only your children by my daughter Mibtahiah shall have power over it after you two. If tomorrow or some other day you build upon this land, and then my daughter divorces you and leaves you, she shall have no power to take it or give it to others; only your children by (10) Mibtahiah shall have power over it, in return for the work which you shall have done. If, on the other hand, she recovers from you,[2] she [may] take half of the house, and [the] othe[r] half shall be at your disposal in return for the building which you will have done on that house. And again as to that half, your children by Mibtahiah shall have power over it after you. If tomorrow or another day I should institute suit or process against you and say I did not give you this land to build on and did not draw up this deed for you, I (15) shall give you a sum of 10 *ḳarshin* by royal weight, at the rate of 2 *R*[3] to the ten, and no suit or process shall lie. This deed was written by 'Atharshuri b. Nabuzeribni in the fortress of Syene at the dictation of Mahseiah. Witnesses hereto (signatures).

IN LIQUIDATION OF MIBTAHIAH'S SECOND MARRIAGE

See the Aramaic letter, "Settlement of Claim by Oath," p. 491.

CONTRACT OF MIBTAHIAH'S THIRD MARRIAGE

Text: Sayce-Cowley, G; Cowley, 15. Date: about 440 B.C.

On the 2[5]th of Tishri, that is the 6th day of the month Epiphi,[4] [year . . . of] Kin[g Artaxerx]es, said Ashor b. [Seho],[5] builder to the king, to Mah[seiah, A]ramean of Syene, of the detachment of Varizata, as follows: I have [co]me to your house that you might give me your daughter Mipht⟨ah⟩iah in marriage. She is my wife and I am her husband from this day for ever. I have given you as the bride-price (5) of your daughter

[76] i.e. Artaxerxes I, king of Persia, 464-424 B.C.

[77] Published by J. N. Strassmaier, *ZA*, III (1888), 129 ff., No. 12; translated by J. Kohler und A. Ungnad, *op. cit.*, No. 90.

[78] i.e. Alexander II, the son of Alexander the Great, who became king in 316 B.C.

[79] Published and translated by Albert T. Clay, *Legal Documents from Erech Dated in the Seleucid Era* (1913), No 1.

[80] The Seleucid era began in 311 B.C. according to the Babylonian calendar; so this would be the year 304 B.C., in the reign of Seleucus I.

[1] Egyptian month-name.

[2] This must mean, "In the event of your divorcing her, in which case she does not forfeit all rights as when she divorces you." Perhaps there is a lacuna in the text.

[3] Probably stands for *rub̲'īn* "quarters" (of a shekel). Does 2/4 × 10 (=1/5) indicate the proportion of alloy?

[4] See n.1.

[5] The name of Asḥor's father (*ṣḥ'*) is preserved in another document. Both it and his own are Egyptian, but he eventually adopted the Hebrew one of Nathan.

Miphtahiah (a sum of) 5 shekels, royal weight. It has been received by you and your heart is content therewith. (Lines 6-16, Ashor's [or Mahseiah's] gifts to Miphtahiah and—perhaps—hers to him.) (17) Should Ashor die tomorrow or an[othe]r day having no child, male or female, by his wife Mi[phtah]iah, Miphtahiah shall be entitled to the house, chattels and all worldly goods of Ashor. (20) Should Miphtahiah die tomorrow or ⟨another⟩ day having no child, male or female, by her husband Ashor, Ashor shall inherit her property and chattels. Should [Miph]tahiah, tomorrow [or] another [d]ay stand up in a congregation and say, I divorce my husband Ashor, the price of divorce shall be upon her head: she shall sit by the balance and weigh out to [As]hor a sum of 7 shekels 2 *R.*[6] But all that which I[7] have settled (25) upon her she shall take out, shred and thread, and go whither she will, without suit or process. Should Ashor tomorrow or another day stand up in a congregation and say, I divorce my [wif]e Miphtahiah, [he shall] forfeit her bride-price, and all that which I[7] have settled upon her she shall take out, shred and thread, on one day at one stroke, and shall go whither she will, without suit or process. And [whoever] arises against Miphtahiah (30) to drive her away from the house, possessions, and chattels of Ashor shall give her the sum of 20 *ḳarash*,[8] and the law of this deed shall [. . .] for her. And I shall have no right to say I have another wife besides Mipht⟨ah⟩iah or other children besides any Miphtahiah may bear to me. If I say I have chi[ldren] and wife other than Miphtahiah and her children, I shall give to Miphtahiah a su[m] of 20 *ḳarash*, royal weight. (35) Neither shall I have the right to [wre]st my property and chattels from Miph[tah]iah. If I take *them* away from her (erasure), I shall give to Miphtahiah [a sum of] 20 *ḳarash*, royal weight. [This deed] was written by Nathan b. *Ananiah* [at the dictation of Ashor]. Witnesses: (signatures).

[6] In the light of n.3, this sum is exactly 1½ times the bride-price Ashor paid for her (line 5).

[7] Or, "you" (Mahseiah, line 2). The spelling of the verb is ambiguous.

[8] A *ḳarash* is 10 heavy shekels or 20 light ones.

III. Historical Texts

Egyptian Historical Texts

TRANSLATOR: JOHN A. WILSON

Brief Texts of the Old Kingdom

Inscriptional evidence on the relations of Egypt and Asia under the Old Kingdom is slight. For the most part, we rely upon the uninscribed materials coming out of excavations in both areas for evidence on the strength of such contacts. The following are samples of texts playing on the problem of Egyptian interest in Asia.

a

The jar-sealing of a Second Dynasty king, who lived about 2850 or 2800 B.C., may be read as the record of military activity in Asia. Such sealings have been found at Abydos: W. M. F. Petrie, *The Royal Tombs of the Earliest Dynasties*, II (London, 1901), Pl. XXII; E. Naville *et al.*, *The Cemeteries of Abydos*, I (London, 1914), Pl. X.

The Seth: Per-ibsen, who carries off Asia.[1]

b

Three notations from the "Annals" of the Old Kingdom on the reign of Snefru of the Fourth Dynasty (about 2650 or 2600 B.C.) show trade relations between Egypt and Phoenicia and the use to which the timber brought from Asia was put. These items are extracted from the records of three successive years. The Palermo Stone, recto vi 2-4, was published by H. Schäfer, *Ein Bruchstück altägyptischer Annalen* (*APAW*, 1902), and the present extracts by K. Sethe, *Urkunden des alten Reichs* (*Urk.*, I, Leipzig, 1933), 236-37. Translated by Breasted, *AR*, I, §§146-48. On the interpretation of the text see K. Sethe, in *ZAeS*, XLV (1908), 7-14.

Bringing forty ships filled (with) cedar logs.

Shipbuilding (of) cedarwood, one "Praise-of-the-Two-Lands" ship, 100 cubits (long), and (of) *meru*-wood, two ships, 100 cubits (long).

Making the doors of the royal palace (of) cedarwood.[2]

c

We have somewhat more information about the Egyptians' activity in Sinai, because of their interest in the turquoise and copper mines there. However, under the Old Kingdom the records in the mining area normally give little more than a depiction of the pharaoh smiting a nomad, with the pharaoh's name accompanying the scene. Such are the records of Semerkhet of the First Dynasty (about 2950 or 2900 B.C.), and of Djoser and Za-nakht of the Third Dynasty (about 2750 or 2700 B.C.), as published in A. H. Gardiner and T. E. Peet, *The Inscriptions of Sinai*, I (London, 1917), Pls. I, IV, Nos. 1-4. The same publication (Pl. II, Nos. 5, 7)[3] shows also scenes of Snefru and Khufu of the Fourth Dynasty (2650 or 2600 B.C.) clubbing kneeling figures and accompanied by the following legends:

Snefru, the great god, . . . Subjugating foreign countries.

Khnum-Khufu, the great god. Smiting the nomads [of Asia].

[1] Per-ibsen identified himself as a king with the god Seth, rather than the god Horus. The word *Setjet*, here translated "Asia," cannot as yet be made more precise. It applied to regions east and northeast of Egypt.

[2] The word here translated "cedar" probably applied to that wood and other coniferous woods also. At any rate, it and *meru*-wood were conifers, brought by sea from Phoenicia or Cilicia. The ships were over 50 meters (over 170 feet) long.

[3] These two texts also presented in Sethe's *Urkunden des alten Reichs*, I, 7-8, and translated in Breasted, *AR*, I, §§168-69, 176.

Asiatic Campaigns Under Pepi I

For the most part, it is an argument from silence to assume that military contact between Egypt and Asia was slight under the Old Kingdom. Rare bits of evidence indicate that a certain amount of aggressive activity was normal on the part of Egypt. We need to interpret the significance of the "prisoners" in Egyptian ships returning from Asia in the time of Sahu-Re of the Fifth Dynasty (about 2550 B.C.).[1] There is a tomb scene of the late Fifth or early Sixth Dynasty (2500-2350 B.C.) showing the Egyptians making a successful attack on a fortress peopled with Asiatics.[2] Finally, there is the text which follows, which may apply to a particularly aggravated situation or which may represent a normal situation of fighting, not otherwise stated to us. A certain career official of the Sixth Dynasty, named Uni, left an inscription in his cenotaph at Abydos, giving us the chief stages of his career under various pharaohs. Under Pepi I (about 2375 or 2350 B.C.), Uni was particularly active as a military commander against the Asiatics.

Cairo Museum 1435 has most recently been published by L. Borchardt, *Denkmäler des Alten Reiches* (*Catalogue général . . . du Musée du Caire*, Berlin, 1937), I, 115 ff., Pls. 29-30, with antecedent bibliography. See also P. Tresson, *L'inscription d'Ouni* (*Bibliothèque d'Étude*, VIII, Cairo, 1919), and K. Sethe, *Urkunden des alten Reichs* (*Urk.*, I, 2nd ed., Leipzig, 1932), I, 98-110. Translated in Breasted, *AR*, I, §§306-15.

For the presence of Asiatics in the Egyptian Delta between the Old and Middle Kingdoms, see the Instruction for King Meri-ka-Re (pp. 414-418 below), the Prophecy of Nefer-rohu (pp. 444-446 below), and the Admonitions of Ipu-wer (pp. 441-444 below).

For conditions at the beginning of the Middle Kingdom, see the Instruction of King Amen-em-het (pp. 418-419 below) and the Story of Si-nuhe (pp. 18-22 above).

When his majesty imposed punishment upon the Asiatics Who-are-Upon-the-Sands,[3] his majesty made an

[1] Shown in L. Borchardt, *Das Grabdenkmal des Königs S'aḥu-re'* (*Deutsche Orient-Gesellschaft. Wissenschaftliche Veröffentlichung*, 26, Leipzig, 1913), II, Pls. 12-13, or one boat in J. H. Breasted, *Ancient Times* (Boston, 1914), 58.

[2] Line-drawings in W. M. F. Petrie, *Deshasheh* (London, 1898), Pl. IV, and in W. S. Smith, *A History of Egyptian Sculpture and Painting in the Old Kingdom* (London, 1946), 212; photograph in W. Wreszinski, *Atlas zur altägyptischen Kulturgeschichte*, II (Leipzig, 1935), Pl. 4. Discussed in *Cambridge Ancient History*, I (Cambridge, 1923), 226, 289-90. Although the names Nedia and Ain-. . . are given in an accompanying broken text, it is not certain that either of these names applies to the fortress, and neither of the names can be located.

[3] This should mean desert nomads, and probably did mean that in the first instance. It came to be a term of scorn for all Asiatics. As will appear later in this inscription, these "Sand-Dwellers" were agriculturalists who built buildings.

army of many ten-thousands,[4] in the entire Upper Egypt, the south being Elephantine and the north being Aphroditopolis, and in Lower Egypt: in both of the (*administrative*) sides of the *realm*, (15) in the (*frontier*) *fortress*, and in the midst of the (*frontier*) *fortresses*; among the Nubians of Irtjet, the Nubians of Madjoi, the Nubians of Yam, among the Nubians of Wawat, among the Nubians of *Kaau*, and from the land of the Temeh-Libyans.[5] His majesty sent me at the head of this army, while the counts, while the Seal-Bearers of the King of Lower Egypt, while the Sole Companions of the Palace, while the nomarchs and mayors of Upper and Lower Egypt, the companions and chief dragomans, the chief prophets of Upper and Lower Egypt, and the chief bureaucrats were (each) at the head of a troop of Upper or Lower Egypt, or of the villages and towns which they might rule, or of the Nubians of these foreign countries. I was the one who used to make the plan for them, although my office was (only that of) Chief Domain Supervisor of the Palace, because I was (*so*) *fitted for* the post that not one of them (so much as) laid a hand upon his fellow, (20) that not one of them appropriated (so much as) a *lump of dough* or a pair of sandals from a wayfarer, that not one of them carried off (so much as) a *loin*cloth from any town, that not one of them carried off any goat from anybody.

I led them to Northern Island, Doorway of Ii-hotep, and the District of Horus: Neb-maat,[6] while I was in this office. . . . *All* these troops *explored for me*; never had *there been (such) exploration* for any other servant.[7]

This army returned in safety,
After it had hacked up the land of the [Sand]-Dwellers.
This army returned in safety,
After it had crushed the land of the Sand-Dwellers.
This army returned in safety,
After it had thrown down its[8] enclosures.
This army returned in safety,
After it had cut down its[8] fig trees and its vines. (25)
This army returned in safety,
After it had cast fire into all its[8] *dwellings*.
This army returned in safety,
After it had killed troops in it by many ten-thousands.
This army returned in safety,
[After it had taken troops] in it, a great multitude as living captives.[9]

His majesty praised me for it more than anything.

His majesty sent me to lead [this] army five times, in order to repel the land of the Sand-Dwellers each time that they rebelled, with these troops. I acted with regard to that [for which his] majesty would show me favor [more than anything].

When it was said that *backsliders* because of something were among these foreigners in *Antelope-Nose*,[10] I crossed over (30) in transports with these troops. I made a landing at the rear of the heights of the mountain range on the north of the land of the Sand-Dwellers.[11] While a full half of this army was (still) on the road, I arrived, I caught them all, and every *backslider* among them was slain.[12]

4 The figure is flamboyant, not to be taken literally.

5 There were levies on all parts of Egypt, and soldiers were recruited or drafted from the lands to the south and west of Egypt.

6 These three places cannot be located. One may argue that "Northern Island" might apply to one of the watered parts of the Delta, that a "Doorway" might be a frontier post, and that the pharaoh Snefru ("Horus: Neb-maat") was a patron of the Sinai area. This would provide three successive stages of exit from Egypt, but it would be based on three guesses.

7 Or, "I opened the number of these troops; never had there been opened for any servant," in the sense of finding the number of soldiers?

8 The land's.

9 This hymn of a victoriously returning army shows that the "Sand-Dwellers" had orchards and vineyards, fortified enclosures, and troops in considerable number. Sinai probably would not fit the case. Uni's army must have moved into Palestine.

10 The word translated "backsliders" seems to come from a root meaning "slide, be slippery." In Egyptian propaganda these expeditions into other countries were always punitive against rebellion. The place "Antelope-Nose"(?) cannot be located. The beast in question is not a gazelle; it is either a bubalis or a fallow deer. The place may have been a mountain range coming down to the sea, so-named by Egyptian sailors because of a characteristic profile. If so, the Carmel Range may be argued from the context which follows immediately.

11 Uni had gone by land against the "Sand-Dwellers." For a more northerly expedition his army travelled by boat. Where would a range come to the water so clearly as the Carmel Range?

12 The translation understands that Uni landed, marched inland, and won a victory while the rear half of his army was still on the march.

Middle Kingdom Egyptian Contacts with Asia

The Egyptian Middle Kingdom saw a number of contacts with Asia, even though these do not loom large in inscriptional records. There was exceptionally vigorous activity in the area of the Sinai mines.[1] Objects bearing the names of Twelfth Dynasty pharaohs or of members of their families have been found at Byblos, Beirut, and Ugarit on the Phoenician coast, and at Qatna in north central Syria.[2] At the minimum, these may have been royal gifts from Egyptian pharaohs to friendly but independent princes in Asia. At the maximum, they may show some kind of Egyptian hegemony in the area. Of a number of monuments found in Asia and bearing the names of Egyptian officials, two examples will suffice.

At Megiddo in Palestine there was found the statuette base of Thut-hotep, son of Kay and Sit-Kheper-ka, a High Priest of Thoth at Hermopolis and Nomarch of the Hare Nome, in which Hermopolis lay. This was an official whose career, somewhere between 1900 and 1850 B.C., was well known from his tomb in Egypt.[3]

At Ugarit (Ras Shamra) on the Phoenician coast there was found the statue group of the

Mayor of the Pyramid City, Vizier, and Chief Justice, Sen-Usert-onekh, . . . [to] whom [was given] the Gold of Honor in the presence of the courtiers.[4]

(The award of the "Gold of Honor" was normally

1 cf. the inscription of Hor-ur-Re on pp. 229-30 below.

2 References by A. Rowe, *A Catalogue of Egyptian Scarabs . . . in the Palestine Archaeological Museum* (Cairo, 1935), xviii-xxii, and by J. A. Wilson in *AJSL*, LVIII (1941), 235.

3 Wilson, *op.cit.*, 225-36.

4 P. Montet, in *Syria*, XV (1934), 131-33 and Pl. XIV; XVII (1936), 202-03; J. H. Breasted, in *Syria*, XVI (1935), 318-20. C. F. A. Schaeffer, *Ugaritica*, I (Paris, 1939), Pl. V.

made for service outside of Egypt. The presence of the statues of such important officials in Palestine and Syria shows fairly intimate relations between Egypt and Asia. It is possible that they saw service as diplomatic agents or as resident Egyptian commissioners in areas of strong commercial and cultural interest.

(The ties between Egypt and Byblos [Gebal] on the Phoenician coast were particularly close. By the end of the Middle Kingdom princes of Byblos, bearing Asiatic names, used Egyptian hieroglyphic inscriptions showing that they boasted the Egyptian title *haty-a* "Count," which *in Egypt* was a title conferred by the pharaoh. Even though we cannot be sure that the same applied in Phoenicia, the evidence of cultural leadership is clear. Two of these Byblite princes were:)[5]

The Count of Byblos, Yep-shemu-ib, who repeats life, son of the Count, Ib-shemu, the triumphant.

The Count of Byblos, Inten, who repeats life, son of the Count Reyen, the triumphant.

(Our evidence on Asiatics in Egypt is disappointingly slight. A testamentary enactment, probably of the time of Amen-em-het III [end of the 19th century B.C.], indicates the presence of Asiatic slaves or serfs in Egypt:)[6]

I give to her the four Asiatics which my brother *X* gave to me.

(Further, Asiatics seem to have been in some demand as dancers at Egyptian festivals.[7]

(The most famous record of an Asiatic visit to Egypt at this time is a scene in the tomb of a noble of Middle Egypt, depicting the arrival of gaily garbed Bedouin, who came to trade stibium, the black eye cosmetic loved by the Egyptians.[8] The two Egyptians who introduce the visitors are:)

The Royal Documents Scribe Nefer-hotep.

The Overseer of Hunters Khety.

(The sheikh of the Asiatic group is labeled:)

The Ruler of a Foreign Country Ibsha.[9]

(The general label for the scene runs:)

The arrival, bringing stibium, which thirty-seven Asiatics brought to him.

(The occasion was significant enough for a rather formal record. The Egyptian scribe holds a docket with the following inscription:)

[5] Yep-shemu-ib's name appears on a scimitar: P. Montet, *Byblos et l'Égypte* (Paris, 1928-29), 174-77, Pls. XCIX-C, and on a cloisonné pendant: *ibid.*, 165-66, Pl. XCVII. W. F. Albright, *The Vocalization of the Egyptian Syllabic Orthography* (New Haven, 1934), 8, suggests the readings Yapâ-shemu-abi and Abî-shemu for the two names. The name of Inten (Yin-naten?) appears on objects published in *Kêmi*, I (1928), 90-93; in *JEA*, XIV (1928), 109; and in *Syria*, X (1929), 12-15. An associated king's name dates him to the period following the 12th dynasty (after 1775 B.C.).

[6] F. Ll. Griffith, *Hieratic Papyri from Kahun and Gurob* (London, 1898), Pl. XII:10-11; cf. Pls. XIII:15-17; XXX:35.

[7] *ibid.*, Pl. XXIV:4-6, 13-14.

[8] A frequently published scene in the tomb of Khnum-hotep III at Beni Hasan. P. E. Newberry, *Beni Hasan*, I (London, 1893), Pls. XXX-XXXI. N. M. Davies and A. H. Gardiner, *Ancient Egyptian Paintings* (Chicago, 1936), I, Pls. X-XI. Other references in B. Porter and R. L. Moss, *Topographical Bibliography of Ancient Egyptian Hieroglyphic Texts, Reliefs, and Paintings*, IV (Oxford, 1934), 145-46. Texts also in K. Sethe, *Historisch-biographische Urkunden des Mittleren Reiches* (*Urk.*, VII, Leipzig, 1935), I, 36-37.

[9] Albright, *op.cit.*, 8, renders Abî-shar. On the title, "ruler of a foreign country," see pp. 20, n.16; 247, n.56.

Year 6, under the majesty of the Horus: Leader of the Two Lands; the King of Upper and Lower Egypt: Kha-kheper-Re.[10] List of the Asiatics whom the son of the Count Khnum-hotep brought on account of stibium, Asiatics of *Shut*.[11] List thereof: thirty-seven.

[10] Sen-Usert II. The year would be about 1890 B.C.

[11] The reading of the name and the location of this Asiatic area are uncertain.

The Egyptian Mines in Sinai

Mines in the southern part of the Sinai peninsula provided Egypt with copper, which was an important material for the advancement of her culture, and with turquoise, which she prized for adornment. The Sinai mines were worked by Egypt from predynastic times down into the Twentieth Dynasty. The necessity for securing the ore provided a reason for external conquest and the beginnings of empire. One of the Egyptian records of mining activity is here given as an example.

The inscription of Hor-ur-Re at Serabit el-Khadim in Sinai may be dated from other inscriptions in the same place to the reign of Amen-em-het III of the Twelfth Dynasty (about 1840-1790 B.C.). Published by A. H. Gardiner and T. E. Peet, *The Inscriptions of Sinai*, I (London, 1917), Pl. XXVI, No. 90, and by K. Sethe, *Aegyptische Lesestücke* (2nd ed., Leipzig, 1928), 86. Studied by V. Loret in *Kêmi*, I (1928), 109-14, and by A. M. Blackman, in *BIFAO*, XXX (1930), 97-101. Translated by Breasted, *AR*, I, §§733-38.

The majesty of this god[1] despatched the Seal-Bearer of the God, the Overseer of the Cabinet, and Director of *Lances*, Hor-ur-Re, to this mining area. This land was reached in the 3rd month of the second season, although it was not at all the season for coming to this mining area.[2] This Seal-Bearer of the God says to the officials who may come to this mining area at this season:

Let not your faces flag because of it. Behold ye, Hat-Hor *turns it* (5) *to good*.[3] I have seen (it so) with regard to myself; I have experienced the like in myself. I came from Egypt with my face flagging. It was difficult, in my experience,[4] to find the (proper) skin for it, when the land was burning hot, the highland was in summer, and the mountains branded an (*already*) *blistered* skin. When day broke *for my leading to the camp*,[5] I kept on addressing the craftsmen about it: "How fortunate is he who is in this mining area!" But they said: "Turquoise is (10) always in the mountain, (but) it is the (proper) skin which has to be sought at this season. We used to hear the like, that ore is forthcoming at this season, but, really, it is the skin that is lacking for it in this difficult season of summer!"

All the time that I was leading (the men) to this mining area, the glory of the king was directing me.[6] Then I reached this land, and I began the work under

[1] The pharaoh.

[2] About 1830 B.C., this month would start close to the beginning of June, an almost unbearably hot season in Sinai.

[3] The Egyptian goddess Hat-Hor was a patroness of the Sinai mines.

[4] "In my face."

[5] Problematical. The final word has an enclosure determinative and may be a designation or the name for the mines.

[6] "Was giving in my heart."

good auspices. (15) My entire army returned complete; no loss had ever occurred in it. My face did not flag at the prospect of the work. I succeeded in grasping the best auspices. I left off in the 1st month of the 3rd season,[7] and brought away this noble stone. I had surpassed anyone (else) who had come *or anything demanded*. There was no: "Oh for a good skin!", (but) eyes were in *festivity*. It was better than at its normal season. Offer (20) offerings to the Lady of Heaven; *pray*, satisfy ye Hat-Hor. If you do it, it will profit you. Ye shall surpass because of it; prosperity will be among you. I made my expedition very successfully. There (need be) no loudness of voice about my work: what I accomplished *was the success of the expedition*....

[7] About 1830 B.C., this month would fall chiefly in August.

The Inscription of Khu-Sebek, Called Djaa

The pharaohs of the Middle Kingdom have left us no direct record of their activities in Asia. Therefore we prize any indirect records, such as the following reference to an Asiatic campaign by Sen-Usert III (about 1880-1840 B.C.).

A stela found at Abydos, now No. 3306 in the Manchester Museum, England. Published by J. Garstang, *El Arabah* (London, 1901), Pls. IV-V, by T. E. Peet, *The Stela of Sebek-khu* (Manchester, 1914), and by K. Sethe, *Aegyptische Lesestücke* (2nd ed., Leipzig, 1928), 82-83. Translated by Breasted, *AR*, I, §§676-87.

For the real and potential enemies of Egypt at the end of the Middle Kingdom or shortly thereafter, see the Execration of Asiatic Princes (pp. 328-329 below).

(6) The Hereditary Prince and Count, firm of sandal, confident of stride, treading the path of his benefactor, whose good repute the Lord of the Two Lands has granted, whose position his love has advanced, the Chief District Supervisor of the Town, Djaa. He says:

I made for myself this cenotaph,[1] beatified, with its place established at the stairway of the great god, the lord of life, who presides over Abydos,[2] in the district "Lord of Offerings" and in the district "Mistress of Life," that I might smell for myself the incense coming forth therefrom and might be provided with the god's vapor.

The Chief District Supervisor of the Town, [Khu-Sebek]. (11) He says: I was born in the [year] 27, under the majesty of the King of Upper and Lower Egypt: Nub-kau-Re, the triumphant.[3] When the majesty of the King of Upper and Lower Egypt: Kha-kau-Re, the triumphant,[4] appeared in the crowns of Upper and Lower Egypt upon the Horus-Throne of the Living, his majesty had me work as a fighter behind and beside his majesty, with seven men of the Residence.[5] Thereupon I showed keenness in his presence, and his majesty had me made an Attendant of the Ruler, and sixty persons were given to me. His majesty proceeded [south]ward, to overthrow (16) the nomads of Nubia. Then I smote a Nubian *in Kenkef* in the presence of my town.[6] Then I sailed north, following (the king) with six (men) of the Residence. Then he made (me) Deputy of Attendants, and a hundred persons were given to me as a reward.

(1) His majesty proceeded northward to overthrow the Asiatics. His majesty reached a foreign country of which the name was Sekmem.[7] His majesty *took the right direction* in proceeding to the Residence of life, prosperity, and health.[8] Then Sekmem fell, together with the wretched Retenu.[9]

While I was acting as rear guard, then I rallied together the individuals of the army to fight with the Asiatics. Then I smote an Asiatic. Then I had his weapons taken by two individuals of the army, without deviating from the fight, for my face was *forward* and I did not turn my back to the Asiatic.[10]

As Se(n)-Usert lives for me, I have spoken in truth! Then he gave me a *throw-stick* of fine gold for my hand, a *scabbard* and a dagger worked with fine gold, together with *accessories*.[11]

[1] Egyptians were normally buried in their home districts, but those who could afford it might have a cenotaph at the Osiris shrine in Abydos.

[2] Osiris.

[3] Amen-em-het II (about 1930-1895 B.C.). Thus under Sen-Usert III (about 1880-40), Khu-Sebek's age range would be a minimum of 15 and a maximum of 50. In the 9th year of Amen-em-het III (about 1830 B.C.), Khu-Sebek, probably over 70, led a frontier patrol at the Second Cataract, where he left an inscription recording the height of the Nile at Semneh (cf. Peet, *op.cit.*, 13, bottom of Pl. II; Breasted, *op.cit.*, I, §679).

[4] Sen-Usert III.

[5] Apparently he headed the personal bodyguard of the pharaoh.

[6] His home contingent witnessed the feat.

[7] Possibly Shechem, although the equivalence is not satisfactory.

[8] "His majesty gave the good beginning in." This expression is usually employed for the beginning of an enterprise. Here it seems that the pharaoh decided to leave the attack on Sekmem and return to Egypt. Then the Asiatic city fell after his departure. The only alternative is to assume that this sentence has been misplaced in the context. cf. n.10 below, and note the necessity of reading this stela with lines 6-17 preceding lines 1-5.

[9] Syria-Palestine in general. The implication is that Sekmem was a focal center of an Asiatic "rebellion" against Egypt.

[10] Unless these lines are misplaced, they imply that the Egyptian army was under pressure on its return from the victory over Sekmem.

[11] A. M. Blackman, in *JEA*, II (1915), 13-14, claims "an indirect reference to Sesostris III's Syrian campaign" in a tomb scene showing "cattle of Retenu" in Egypt. Unfortunately, Blackman's "the cattle of *Rtnw* during the counting(?)" might equally be translated "the cattle at every counting," thus removing the assumed Asiatic country name.

The Hyksos in Egypt

The greatest indignity suffered by the ancient Egyptians was the conquest and rule of their land by foreigners out of Asia, the so-called "Shepherd Kings," or Hyksos (ca. 1725-1575 B.C.). There is surprisingly little in Egyptian literature, in view of the real change which this foreign domination made in the national psychology: the change from a confident sense of domestic security to an aggressive sense of national peril. To be sure, it was not in character for an ancient people to enlarge on defeat and subjection at the hands of others. Only the victorious elimination of peril would enter the literature. Josephus has given us something of the tradition of a harsh foreign rule.[1]

[1] Josephus, *Contra Apionem*, I, 14, in H. St. J. Thackeray's translation for the Loeb Library, *Josephus*, I (New York, 1926), 190-201.

a

In an inscription written almost a century after the expulsion of the Hyksos from Egypt, the queen Hat-shepsut (about 1486-1469 B.C.) gives some of the national sense of indignation. This inscription was carved on the façade of a temple of hers at Speos Artemidos (Istabl Antar) in Middle Egypt. A new edition by A. H. Gardiner, based on a copy by N. de G. Davies, *JEA*, XXXII (1946), 43-56, Pl. VI, supplants previous presentations of the text by W. Golenischeff, in *Recueil de travaux . . .*, VI (1885), Pl. opp. p. 20, and by K. Sethe, *Urkunden der 18. Dynastie* (*Urk.*, IV, Leipzig, 1906), II, 383-91, and the translation by Breasted, *AR*, II, §§296-303. The extract below comes from lines 35-42 of this inscription.

Hear ye, all people and the folk as many as they may be, I have done these things through the counsel of my heart. I have not slept forgetfully, (but) I have restored that which had been ruined. I have raised up that which had gone to pieces *formerly*, since the Asiatics were in the midst of Avaris of the Northland,[2] and vagabonds[3] were in the midst of them, overthrowing that which had been made. They ruled without Re, and he[4] did not act by divine command down to (the reign of) my majesty. (Now) I am established upon the thrones of Re. I was foretold for the limits of the years as a born conqueror.[5] I am come as the uraeus-serpent of Horus, flaming against my enemies. I have made distant those whom the gods abominate, and earth has carried off their foot(prints). This is the precept of the father of [my] fathers, who comes at his (appointed) times, Re, and there shall not occur damage to what Amon has commanded. My (own) command endures like the mountains, (while) the sun disc shines forth and spreads rays over the formal titles of my majesty and my falcon is high above (my) name-standard for the duration of eternity.[6]

b

Another document on the Hyksos rule might perhaps be among folk tales treated above. It is a legend of later date, carrying the story of a contest between two rulers in Egypt. The Hyksos King Apophis in the Delta held suzerainty over the Egyptian King Seqnen-Re at Thebes. Apophis laid before Seqnen-Re one of those difficult problems which oriental literature loves, an insulting demand which threatened the dignity of the Egyptian ruler. We lack the end of the story, but the logic of the situation suggests that Seqnen-Re must have extricated himself from the indignity by returning to Apophis a proposition which counterchecked the problem set by the Hyksos king.

Papyrus Sallier I (British Museum 10185), recto i 1-iii 3; verso ii-iii, was written in the late Nineteenth Dynasty (end of the 13th century B.C.) in the colloquial language.[7] It is facsimiled in *Select Papyri in the Hieratic Character from the Collections of the British Museum*, I (London, 1841), Pls. I-III, and in *Facsimiles of Egyptian Hieratic Papyri in the British Museum. Second Series* (ed. by E. A. W. Budge, London, 1923), Pls. LIII-LV. A transcription into hieroglyphic is given in A. H. Gardiner, *Late-Egyptian Stories* (*Bibliotheca Aegyptiaca*, I, Brussels, 1932), 85-89. Translations by B. Gunn and A. H. Gardiner, in *JEA*, V (1918), 40-45, and by Erman, *LAE*, 165-67.

Now IT SO HAPPENED THAT the land of Egypt was in distress. There was no Lord—life, prosperity, health!—or king of the time. However, it happened that, as for King Seqnen-Re—life, prosperity, health!—he was Ruler—life, prosperity, health!—of the Southern City.[8] Distress was in the town *of the Asiatics*, for Prince Apophis—life, prosperity, health—was in Avaris, and the entire land was subject to him with their dues, the *north* as well, with all the good produce of *the Delta*. THEN King Apophis—life, prosperity, health!—made him Seth as lord, and he would not serve any god who was in the land [except] Seth.[9] And [he] built a temple of good and eternal work beside the *House* of [King Apo]phis—life, prosperity, health!—[and] he appeared [*every*] day to have sacrifices made . . . daily to Seth. And the officials [*of the King*]—life, prosperity, health!—carried wreaths, just exactly as is done (in) the temple of the Re-Har-akhti. Now then, as for (5) [King] A[pophis]—life, prosperity, health!—he wanted to [send] an irritating message (to) King Seqnen-Re—[life, prosperity, health!—the] Prince of the Southern City.

Now [AFTER] MANY DAYS FOLLOWING THIS, then King [Apophis—life, prosperity, health!]—had summoned. . . .

(Here the papyrus is badly broken. Apophis appears to be in consultation with his "scribes and wise men," and they seem to suggest the arrogant demand about the hippopotamus pool at Thebes. If Seqnen-Re should accede to this demand he would lose face, but he was in no position to ignore it. His only recourse would be to devise a logical but equally absurd riposte.)

["*So we shall see the power of the god who*] (ii 1) is with him as protector. He relies upon no god who is in the [entire land] except Amon-Re, King of the Gods."[10]

Now AFTER MANY DAYS FOLLOWING THIS, then King Apophis—life, prosperity, health!—sent to the Prince of the Southern City (with) the message which his scribes and wise men had told him. Now when the messenger of King Apophis—life, prosperity, health!—reached the Prince of the Southern City, THEN HE WAS taken into the presence of the Prince of the Southern City. THEN THEY said to the messenger of King Apophis—life, prosperity, health!: "Why were you sent to the Southern City? How did you come to (make) this trip?" THEN the messenger (5) said to him: "King Apophis—life, prosperity, health!—sends to you as follows: 'Have the hippopotamus pool which is in the *orient* of the City

[2] The Hyksos capital, Avaris, has been located, with some probability, at the same site as Tanis, San el-Hagar, in the northeast Delta. cf. pp. 232, 233, 252 below.

[3] "Wanderers, nomads, strangers."

[4] Re. Gardiner, *op.cit.*, 55, explains that the pharaoh "ascribed all his official acts to obedience to orders given him by the deity."

[5] "As a she-becomes-(she)-seizes," a compound expression.

[6] The gods have blessed Hat-shepsut's rule, confirming the names under which she ruled.

[7] For example, the 2nd person singular is translated "you," rather than "thou."

[8] Thebes.

[9] The Egyptian god Seth served also as their equivalent for various Asiatic gods. cf. pp. 201, 249, 252, 257.

[10] This is taken to be the end of the advice of Apophis' wise men. It pits their god Seth against the Theban god Amon-Re.

done [away] with! For they do not let sleep come to me by day or by night,' and the noise is (in) the ears of his *city*." THEN the Prince of the Southern City was dumfounded for a long time, for it happened that he did not know how to return [answer] to the messenger of King Apophis—life, prosperity, health!

THEN the Prince of the Southern City said to him: "Well, your lord—life, prosperity, health!—should hear *something about [this pool which is in] the orient* of the Southern City *here*." THEN [the messenger said: "The] matter about which he sent me [*must be carried out*]!" [Then the Prince of the Southern City had] the [messenger of King Apophis—life, prosperity, health!] —taken care of, [with] good [things]: meat, cakes, . . . [*Then the Prince of the Southern City said to him: "Tell*] *your* [*lord*]: As for everything which you say to him,[11] I will do it. Tell [him] so." . . . [Then the messenger of King] Apophis—life, prosperity, health!— started out to travel to the place where (iii 1) his lord —life, prosperity, health!—was.

THEN the Prince of the Southern City had his chief officials summoned, as well as every superior soldier that he had, and he repeated to them every message about which King Apophis—life, prosperity, health!—had sent to him. THEN they were one and all silent for a long time, (for) they did not know how to answer him, whether good or bad.

THEN King Apophis—life, prosperity, health!—sent to . . .[12]

The War Against the Hyksos

The expulsion of the Hyksos from Egypt was not accomplished in a single generation. The Egyptians had to find their strength in a series of campaigns. The account of one such revolt against the foreign rule is found in a characteristic setting: the record of a pharaoh's superior judgment and prowess. Ka-mose, who reigned just before the Eighteenth Dynasty (before 1570 B.C.), rebelled against a truce which divided Egypt between his Theban rule and the rule of the Hyksos at Avaris, rejected the cautious advice of his officials, and set out to win back a larger dominion. Although the end of the inscription is lost, it may be assumed that Ka-mose was recording some measure of success.

The Carnarvon Tablet I, found in western Thebes, is a schoolboy exercise almost contemporaneous with the events it relates. As will be indicated below, it may have been copied from Ka-mose's own stela. The tablet was published by Lord Carnarvon and H. Carter, *Five Years' Exploration at Thebes* (London, 1912), 36-37, Pls. XXVII-XXVIII, and by A. H. Gardiner, in *JEA*, III (1916), 95-110, Pls. XII-XIII. It was translated by B. Gunn and A. H. Gardiner, in *JEA*, V (1918), 45-47, and by Erman, *LAE*, 52-54.

That this schoolboy's tablet derived from a genuine historical inscription was demonstrated by the discovery of fragments of a stela found at Karnak, noted in *ASAE*, XXXV (1935), 111, and published by P. Lacau, in *ASAE*, XXXIX (1939), 245-71, Pls. XXXVII-XXXVIII. After one allows for the schoolboy's mistakes, the congruence of the two texts is marked.

11 *Sic*, but it seems probable that it should be read "me."

12 The story breaks off in the middle of a sentence.

Year 3 of Horus: Appearing upon His Throne; the Two Goddesses: Repeating Monuments; Horus of Gold: Making the Two Lands Content; the King of Upper and Lower Egypt . . . : [Wadj]-kheper-[Re; the Son of Re . . . : Ka]-mose, given life, beloved of Amon-Re, Lord of the Thrones of the Two Lands, like Re forever and ever.

The mighty king in Thebes, Ka-mose, given life forever, was the beneficent king. It was [Re] himself [who made him] king and who assigned him strength in truth.

His majesty spoke in his palace to the council of nobles who were in his retinue: "Let me understand what this strength of mine is for! (One) prince is in Avaris, another is in Ethiopia, and (here) I sit associated with an Asiatic and a Negro![1] Each man has his slice of this Egypt, dividing up the land with me. I cannot *pass by* him as far as Memphis, *the waters of* Egypt, (but), behold, he *has* Hermopolis.[2] No man can settle down, being despoiled by the imposts of the Asiatics. I will grapple with him, that I may cut open his belly! My wish is to save Egypt and to *smite* (5) the Asiatics!"

The great men of his council spoke: "Behold, *it is* Asiatic *water* as far as Cusae,[3] and they have *pulled out* their tongues that they might speak all together,[4] (whereas) we are at ease in our (part of) Egypt. Elephantine is strong, and *the middle (of the land)* is with us as far as Cusae. The *sleekest* of their fields are plowed for us, and our cattle are pastured in the Delta.[5] Emmer is sent for our pigs. Our cattle have not been taken away. . . . He holds the land of the Asiatics; we hold Egypt. Should someone come *and act [against us]*, then we shall act against him!"

Then they were hurtful to the heart of his majesty: "As for this plan of yours, . . . He who divides the land with me will not respect me. [*Shall I res*]*pect* these Asiatics who . . . *from him*? I [shall] sail north to *reach Lower Egypt*. [*If I fight with*] the Asiatics, success will come.[6] If *he thinks to be content with . . . with* weeping, the entire land . . . (10) . . . [rul]er in the midst of Thebes, Ka-mose, the protector of Egypt!"[7]

I went north because I was strong (enough) to attack the Asiatics through the command of Amon, the just of counsels. My valiant army was in front of me like a blast of fire. The troops of the Madjoi were on

1 Avaris was the Hyksos capital in the Delta. The word translated "Ethiopia" is the same as the biblical Cush. In contexts of earlier times, the word *Nehsi* was rendered "Nubian," but is here rendered "Negro." See the article by H. Junker, The First Appearance of the Negroes in History, in *JEA*, VII (1921), 121-32.

2 "He" was the Hyksos ruler, holding as far south as Hermopolis in Middle Egypt, about 150 miles south of Memphis.

3 Cusae lay about 25 miles south of Hermopolis.

4 Perhaps a colloquialism for: They have over-extended themselves, since the following clause contrasts the ease of the Egyptians. The Karnak stela adds the words "that they might speak," lacking in the tablet.

5 The word "pastured" is in this place on the stela, is misplaced on the tablet. Upper Egypt commonly had herds at pasture in the Delta, a practice permitted by the present truce. Emmer wheat, used largely for fodder, was grown chiefly in the Delta.

6 In this section of the text both tablet and stela are broken, making the sense uncertain.

7 Since this ends the argument, pharaoh's bolder counsel prevailed.

the upper part of our cabins, to seek out the Asiatics and to push back their positions.[8] East and west had *their* fat, and the army *foraged for* things everywhere. I sent out a strong troop of the Madjoi, while I was *on the day's patrol* . . . to hem in . . . Teti, the son of Pepi, within Nefrusi.[9] I would not let him escape, while I held back the Asiatics who had withstood Egypt. He made Nefrusi *the nest*[10] of the Asiatics. I spent the night in my boat, with my heart happy.

When day broke, I was on him as if it were a falcon. When the time of breakfast had come, I attacked him. I broke down his walls, I killed his people, and I made his wife come down (15) to the riverbank.[11] My soldiers were as lions are, with their spoil, having serfs, cattle, *milk*, fat, and honey, dividing up their property, their hearts *gay*. The region of *Ne[frusi]* was something fallen; it was not (*too*) *much* for us *before* its soul was hemmed in.

The [*region*] *of Per-shaq* was missing when I reached it.[12] Their horses were fled inside. The patrol . . .[13]

The Expulsion of the Hyksos

It is an irony of history that our best contemporaneous source on the expulsion of the Hyksos from Egypt comes from the biographical record of a relatively modest citizen of Upper Egypt, the captain of a Nile vessel. In relating his participation in the campaigns of Ah-mose I (about 1570-1545 B.C.) and of Thut-mose I (about 1525-1495), Ah-mose, son of the woman Eben, tells of the successive attacks on the Hyksos in Egypt and then of the follow-up campaigns into Asia.

The inscriptions in Ah-mose's tomb in el-Kab of Upper Egypt were copied in C. R. Lepsius, *Denkmäler aus Aegypten und Aethiopien* (Berlin, 1849-59), III, 12 b, c, d, and are also set forth in K. Sethe, *Urkunden der 18. Dynastie* (*Urk.*, IV, Leipzig, 1905), I, 1-11, accompanied by a translation (Leipzig, 1914). The text was studied by V. Loret, *L'inscription d'Ahmès fils d'Abana* (*Bibliothèque d'Étude*, III, Cairo, 1910). There are translations by Breasted, *AR*, II, §§1-13, 81-82, and by B. Gunn and A. H. Gardiner, in *JEA*, V (1918), 48-54.

The commander of a crew, Ah-mose, son of Eben, the triumphant, says:

I speak to you, all mankind, that I may let you know the favors which have come to me. I have been awarded gold seven times in the presence of the entire land, and male and female slaves in like manner, and I have been vested with very many fields.[1] The reputation of a valiant man is from what he has done, not being destroyed in this land forever.[2]

He speaks thus:

I had my upbringing in the town of el-Kab, my father being a soldier of the King of Upper and Lower Egypt: Seqnen-Re, the triumphant,[3] his name being Bebe, (5) the son of (the woman) Ro-onet. Then I served as soldier in his place in the ship, "The Wild Bull," in the time of the Lord of the Two Lands: Neb-pehti-Re, the triumphant,[4] when I was (still) a boy, before I had taken a wife, (but) while I was (still) sleeping in a *net hammock*.[5]

But after I had set up a household, then I was taken on the ship, "Northern," because I was valiant. Thus I used to accompany the Sovereign—life, prosperity, health!—on foot, following his excursions in his chariot.[6] When the town of Avaris was besieged,[7] then I showed valor on foot in the presence of his majesty. Thereupon I was appointed to the ship, "Appearing in Memphis." Then there was fighting on the water in *the canal Pa-Djedku* of Avaris. Thereupon I made a capture, (10) and I carried away a hand.[8] It was reported to the king's herald. Then the Gold of Valor was given to me. Thereupon there was fighting again in this place. Then I made a capture again there and brought away a hand. Then the Gold of Valor was given to me over again.

Then there was fighting in the Egypt which is south of this town.[9] Thereupon I carried off a man (as) living prisoner. I went down into the water—now he was taken captive on the side of the town[10]—and crossed over the water carrying him. Report was made to the king's herald. Thereupon I was awarded gold another time.

Then Avaris was despoiled. Then I carried off spoil from there: one man, three women, a total of four persons. Then his majesty gave them to me to be slaves.[11]

Then (15) Sharuhen was besieged for three years.[12] Then his majesty despoiled it. Thereupon I carried off spoil from there: two women and a hand. Then the

8 The Madjoi mercenaries from south of Egypt were mounted high in the ships to spy out the enemy.

9 Nefrusi was a short distance north of Hermopolis. Nothing is known about Teti, the son of Pepi, whose Egyptian name suggests that he was a local vassal of the Hyksos king. See the next note.

10 These words are given on the stela. Perhaps: He (Teti) made the town of Nefrusi a nest for the Asiatic power, in Middle Egypt.

11 In token of submission and as part of the loot.

12 The reading of the place name—if such it is—and its location are uncertain.

13 The scanty remains cannot be translated.

1 In his tomb, Ah-mose gives a list of 9 male and 10 female slaves which were his booty; see n.11 below. His grants of land from the king came to something like 70 acres.

2 As B. Gunn has pointed out (*JEA*, XII [1926], 283), this is a proverb which occurs three times in 18th dynasty inscriptions.

3 One of the pharaohs named Seqnen-Re in the 17th dynasty.

4 Ah-mose I.

5 Perhaps: "I was (still) sleeping with the phallic sheath attached"? So B. Grdseloff, in *ASAE*, XLIII (1943), 357.

6 Note the first use of the horse and chariot by the Egyptians. The Hyksos had introduced this war force into Egypt. cf. p. 233a above.

7 "When one sat down at the town of Avaris." We are abruptly confronted with a curt statement that the Egyptians attacked the Hyksos in the latter's capital in the eastern Delta. It is significant that the following sentence names a boat as "He Who Has (Ceremonial) Appearance in Memphis," suggesting that Memphis had already been recaptured by the Egyptians.

8 It was an Egyptian army custom to cut off the hand of a dead enemy as a proof of killing.

9 South of Avaris. This looks like a temporary retirement by the Egyptians.

10 Beside the town, but across a body of water from the Egyptian army.

11 In Ah-mose's "list of the male and female slaves of the spoil," most of the 19 names are good Egyptian. However, there appear a Pa-ʿAam, "The Asiatic," a Tʿamutj, which is a feminine name similar to Amos, and an Ishtar-ummi, "Ishtar is My Mother."

12 "Then one sat down at Sharuhen in three years." Sharuhen (Josh. 19:6) lay in the extreme southwestern corner of the land of Canaan, in the territory of the tribe of Simeon. Perhaps it was modern Tell el-Fârʿah. It seems that it was the first stronghold of the Hyksos on their departure from Egypt. "In three years" is a little strange and may mean in three successive campaigning seasons, rather than an unbroken siege.

Gold of Valor was given to me, *and* my spoil was given to me to be slaves.

Now after his majesty had killed the Asiatics, then he sailed southward to Khenti-hen-nefer, to destroy the Nubian nomads. . . .[13]

After this (Thut-mose I) went forth to Retenu,[14] to assuage his heart throughout the foreign countries. His majesty reached Naharin,[15] (37) and his majesty—life, prosperity, health!—found that enemy[16] while he was marshaling the battle array. Then his majesty made a great slaughter among them. There was no number to the living prisoners whom his majesty carried off by his victory. Now I was in the van of our army,[17] and his majesty saw how valiant I was. I carried off a chariot, its horse, and him who was in it as a living prisoner. They were presented to his majesty. Then I was awarded gold another time.[18] . . .

The Asiatic Campaigns of Thut-mose III

THE FIRST CAMPAIGN: THE BATTLE OF MEGIDDO

Thut-mose III (about 1490-1436 B.C.) was the conquering pharaoh who set the Egyptian Empire on a foundation firm for almost a century. For twenty years he led campaigns into Asia almost every year. Some of these campaigns involved serious fighting, others were parades of strength. We have detailed information on his first campaign (perhaps 1468 B.C.), which attacked the focus of Asiatic resistance in the Canaanite city of Megiddo. The campaigns of subsequent years may have been just as fully recorded, but that detail has been condensed in the texts deriving from those years.[1]

A. THE ARMANT STELA

A red granite stela, broken and reused in later constructions, was found at Armant in Upper Egypt and published in R. Mond and O. H. Myers, *The Temples of Armant. A Preliminary Survey* (London, 1940), Pls. XI, No. 5; LXXXVIII, No. 8; and CIII; Text Volume, 182-84, with a translation and commentary by M. S. Drower. Like the Barkal Stela, treated below, this stela does not deal with events in chronological order. Those elements which belong to other campaigns will be noted in relation to those campaigns. Here only the material of the first campaign is translated.

Live the Horus: Mighty Bull, Appearing in Thebes; the Two Goddesses: Enduring of Kingship, like Re in Heaven; the Horus of Gold: Majestic of Appearances, Mighty of Strength; the King of Upper and Lower Egypt, Lord of the Two Lands, Lord of Making Offerings: Men-kheper-Re; the Son of Re, of his Body: Thut-mose Heqa-Maat, beloved of Montu, Lord of Thebes, Residing in Hermonthis,[2] living forever.

Year 22, 2nd month of the second season, day 10.[3] Summary of the deeds of valor and victory which this good god performed, being every effective deed of heroism, beginning from the first generation; that which the Lord of the Gods, the Lord of Hermonthis, did for him: the magnification of his victories, to cause that his deeds of valor be related for millions of years to come, apart from the deeds of heroism which his majesty did at all times. If (they) were to be related all together by their names, they would be (too) numerous to put them into writing. . . .

His majesty made no delay in proceeding to the land of (10) Djahi,[4] to kill the treacherous ones who were in it and to give things to those who were loyal to him; *witness, indeed,* [*their*] *names, each* [*country*] *according to its time.* His majesty returned on each occasion, when his attack had been effected in valor and victory, so that he caused Egypt to be in its condition as (it was) when Re was in it as king. [*Year 22, 4th month of the second season, day . . . Proceeding*] from Memphis,[5] to slay the countries of the wretched Retenu, on the first occasion of victory. It was his majesty who opened its roads and forced its every way for his army, after *it had made* [*rebellion, gathered in Megid*]*do.* His majesty entered upon that road which becomes very narrow,[6] as the first of his entire army, while every country had gathered, standing prepared at its mouth. . . . The enemy quailed, fleeing headlong to their town, together with the prince who was in . . . (15) . . . to them, beseeching [*breath*], their goods upon their backs. His majesty returned in gladness of heart, with this entire land as vassal . . . [*Asia*]*tics,* coming at one time, bearing [their] tribute . . .

B. THE ANNALS IN KARNAK

The "Annals" of Thut-mose III's military campaigns are carved on the walls of the Temple of Karnak, in recognition of

[13] This translation omits the account of campaigns in Nubia under Ah-mose I, Amen-hotep I, and Thut-mose I, and resumes with the record of an Asiatic campaign under Thut-mose I, when Ah-mose must have been a relatively old man.

[14] Syria-Palestine in general.

[15] "The Two Rivers," the area of the Euphrates bend.

[16] "That fallen one," a frequent designation of a major enemy.

[17] It has been pointed out that only in the stretch of patriotic enthusiasm of the first century of the 18th dynasty did the Egyptians speak of "our army," instead of ascribing the troops to the pharaoh.

[18] Two more documents may be cited on Ah-mose I's campaigning in Asia. In the tomb of a certain Ah-mose called Pen-Nekhbet at el-Kab (Sethe, *op.cit.*, 35; Breasted, *op.cit.*, §20), a notation runs: "I followed the King of Upper and Lower Egypt: Neb-pehti-Re, the triumphant. I took booty for him in Djahi: 1 person and 1 hand." In a text of Ah-mose I's 22nd year in the quarries of Maâsara, south of Cairo (Sethe, *op.cit.*, 25; Breasted, *op.cit.*, §27), there is a record of the reopening of the quarries for stone to be used in certain temples. Part of the inscription runs: "The stone was dragged by the cattle which his [*victories*] thoughout the lands of the Fenkhu had carried off." The accompanying scene shows Asiatics driving the cattle. Djahi and Fenkhu apply to the Phoenician coast running down into Palestine and including the hinterland—further north than southern Palestine.

[1] On the detail for the first campaign, cf. n.39 below. On the abbreviation in the carved record of subsequent campaigns see the text of the seventh campaign (p. 239 below).

[2] Hermonthis is modern Armant.

[3] For the first twenty-two years of his reign, Thut-mose III had been overshadowed by the queen Hat-shepsut. Then he seized power with some show of violence and indulged his desire for military activity almost immediately. The present date is two and a half months earlier than Thut-mose's departure from the Egyptian frontier (n.9 below). Drower, *op.cit.*, 183, n. *b*, suggests that the present date may be the beginning of his sole reign.

[4] Centrally Phoenicia, but here Syria-Palestine.

[5] The formal departure from Memphis must have preceded the passing of the Egyptian frontier (n.9 below).

[6] The pass through the Carmel range leading to Megiddo; cf. n.20 below.

the fact that the god Amon-Re had given victory. The text appears in C. R. Lepsius, *Denkmäler aus Aegypten und Aethiopien* (Berlin, 1849-59), III, 31b-32, and in K. Sethe, *Urkunden der 18. Dynastie* (*Urk.*, IV), III, 647-77. Translations and commentary will be found in Breasted, *AR*, II, §§391-443; H. H. Nelson, *The Battle of Megiddo* (Chicago, 1913), with topographical study; and R. Faulkner, in *JEA*, XXVIII (1942), 2-15.

The Horus: Mighty Bull, Appearing in Thebes; . . . (Thut-mose III).[7]

His majesty commanded that [the victories which his father Amon had given to him] should be established [upon] a monument in the temple which his majesty had made for [his father Amon, in order to set down] (5) each individual campaign,[8] together with the booty which [his majesty] carried [off from it, *and the dues of*] every [*foreign country*] which his father Re had given to him.

Year 22, 4th month of the second season, day 25.[9] [*His majesty passed the fortress of*] Sile,[10] on the first campaign of victory [*which his majesty made to extend*] the frontiers of Egypt, in valor, [in victory, in power, and in justification]. Now this was a [long] time in years . . . (10) plunder, while every man *was* [*tributary*] before . . .[11] But it happened in later times[12] that the garrison which was there was in the town of Sharuhen,[13] while from Iursa to the outer ends of the earth[14] had become rebellious against his majesty.[15]

Year 23, 1st month of the third season, day 4, the day of the feast of the king's coronation—as far as the town of "That-Which-the-Ruler-Seized," [*of which the Syrian name is*] Gaza.[16]

[Year 23,] (15) 1st month of the third season, day 5—departure from this place, in valor, [in victory,] in power, and in justification, in order to overthrow that wretched enemy,[17] and to extend the frontiers of Egypt, according to the command of his father Amon-Re, the [*valiant*] and victorious, that he should capture.

Year 23, 1st month of the third season, day 16[18]—as far as the town of Yehem. [His majesty] ordered a conference with his victorious army, speaking as follows: "That [wretched] enemy (20) of Kadesh has come and has entered into Megiddo. He is [there] at this moment. He has gathered to him the princes of [every] foreign country [which had been] loyal to Egypt, as well as (those) as far as Naharin and *M*[*itanni*], them of Hurru, them of Kode, their horses, their armies, [and their people], *for* he says—so it is reported—'I shall wait [here] (25) in Megiddo [to fight against his majesty].' Will ye tell me [what is in your hearts]?"[19]

They said in the presence of his majesty: "What is it like to go [on] this [road] which becomes (so) narrow? It is [reported] that the foe is there, waiting on [the outside, while they are] becoming (more) numerous. Will not horse (have to) go after [horse, and the army] (30) and the people similarly? Will the vanguard of us be fighting while the [rear guard] is waiting here in Aruna, unable to fight?[20] *Now* two (other) roads are here. One of the roads—behold, it is [*to the east of*] us, so that *it* comes out at Taanach. The other—behold, it is to the (35) north side of Djefti, and we will come out to the north of Megiddo.[21] Let our victorious lord proceed on the one of [them] which is [satisfactory to] his heart, (but) do not make us go on that difficult road!"

Then messages [were brought in *about that wretched enemy, and discussion was continued*] of [that] problem on which they had previously spoken. That which was said in the majesty of the Court—life, prosperity, health![22]—"I [swear], (40) as Re loves me, as my father Amon favors me, as my [nostrils] are rejuvenated with life and satisfaction, my majesty shall proceed upon this Aruna road! Let him of you who wishes go upon these roads of which you speak, and let him of you who wishes come in the following of my majesty! '*Behold*,' they will say, these (45) enemies whom Re abominates, 'has

[7] The royal titulary, much as translated above for the Armant Stela.

[8] "An expedition by its name." cf. n.39 below.

[9] Tentatively, April 16, 1468 B.C., accepting, for this translation, the date for the battle of Megiddo (n.35 below), as given by L. Borchardt, *Die Mittel zur zeitlichen Festlegung von Punkten der ägyptischen Geschichte* (*Quellen und Forschungen zur ägyptischen Geschichte*, II, Cairo, 1935), 120. The precise date will depend upon an establishment of what the ancient Egyptians meant by a "new moon."

[10] Or Tjaru, the Egyptian frontier post, at or near modern Kantarah.

[11] Sethe (see his justification in *ZAeS*, XLVII [1910], 74-84) restores a context referring to the Hyksos rule in Egypt, as a forerunner of the present "revolt" in Palestine: "Now it was a [long] time in years [that they had ruled this land, which had been] plundered, while every man was [tributary] before [their princes, who were in Avaris]." This is too specific for a restoration. See n.15 below.

[12] "In the times of other (persons)."

[13] In southwestern Canaan; see p. 233b, n.12, above.

[14] From southern Palestine to northern Syria.

[15] Sethe's restoration (n.11 above) assumes three steps: (a) the Hyksos ruled Egypt from Avaris; (b) they were driven by Ah-mose I to Sharuhen in Palestine; (c) now, a century later, Asia is in revolt against Thut-mose III—that is, the enemies are these same Hyksos. B. Gunn and A. H. Gardiner, in *JEA*, V (1918), 54, n.2, reject Sethe's restoration as assuming too much. They translate the last sentence: "But it happened in other times that the garrison which was there (i.e. in Palestine) was in Sharūḥen, when from *Yrḏ* to the ends of the earth had fallen into rebellion against His Majesty." This would take the Hyksos out of the context and would assume that an Asiatic rebellion had pushed back an Egyptian garrison from a northern town (like Megiddo) to Sharuhen at the extreme south of Palestine.

[16] Instead of the above translation, one may render: "as far as a town of the holding of the Ruler, [of which the name was] Gaza . . ." On Borchardt's reckoning, the Egyptians reached Gaza on April 25, 1468, having traveled at the respectable rate of 150 miles in 9 or 10 days. As this date was the anniversary of Thut-mose III's coronation, the year number changed from 22 to 23.

[17] Not yet specified by name or title. The Prince of Kadesh—probably Kadesh on the Orontes—was the leader of the coalition against Egypt. See n.19 below.

[18] May 7, 1468 (Borchardt). After leaving the Egyptian-held city of Gaza, the army's rate was notably slower through territory which was actually or potentially rebellious. Perhaps 80 miles were covered in 11 or 12 days. Yehem (possibly Jahmai or similar) is tentatively located by Nelson at Yemma on the south side of the Carmel ridge.

[19] It is probable from the nature of this coalition and from Thut-mose's subsequent campaigns that this Kadesh was the city on the Orontes. The Barkal Stela (p. 238) gives the coalition as 330 princes, i.e. rulers of city states. Naharin and Mitanni (restoration not certain) were at the bend of the Euphrates. Hurru (or Kharu) was generally Syria-Palestine, and Kode the coast of north Syria and of Cilicia.

[20] Nelson's topographic reconstruction gives the situation confronting the Egyptians. If they went straight ahead on the narrow track debouching just south of Megiddo, they had to go in single file and would be particularly vulnerable. Aruna, perhaps modern Tell 'Ârā in the pass, was not "here" at Yehem, since it was a few miles further north. It was "here" on the southern side of the mountain range.

[21] Two safer mountain tracks were offered as alternatives, one debouching at Taanach, 4 or 5 miles southeast of Megiddo, and one debouching at an unknown point north(west) of Megiddo.

[22] That is, the voice from the throne. The Court moved with the pharaoh.

his majesty set out on another road because he has become afraid of us?'—so they will speak."

They said in the presence of his majesty: "May thy father Amon, Lord of the Thrones of the Two Lands, Presiding over Karnak, act [*according to thy desire*]! Behold, we are following thy majesty everywhere that [thy majesty] goes, for a servant will be after [his] lord."

[*Then* his majesty *laid a charge*] (50) upon the entire army: "[*Ye*] *shall* [*hold fast to the stride of your victorious lord on*] that road which becomes (so) na[rrow. Behold, his majesty has taken] an oath, saying: 'I will not let [my victorious army] go forth ahead of my majesty in [this place!' " *Now his majesty had laid it in his heart*] that he himself should go forth at the head of his army. [Every man] was made aware (55) of his order of march, horse following horse, while [his majesty] was at the head of his army.

Year 23, 1st month of the third season, day 19[23]—the awakening in [life] in the tent of life, prosperity, and health, at the town of Aruna.[24] Proceeding northward by my majesty, carrying my father Amon-Re, Lord of the Thrones of the Two Lands, [that he might open the ways] before me,[25] while Har-akhti established [*the heart of my victorious army*] (60) and my father Amon strengthened the arm [of my majesty]. . . .

Then [his] majesty issued forth[26] [at the head of] his [army], which was [prepared] in many ranks. [*He had not met*] a single [*enemy*. Their] southern wing[27] was in Taanach, [while their] nothern wing was on the south side [of *the Qina Valley*.[28] Then] (65) his majesty *rallied them saying*: ". . . ! They are fallen![29] While that [wretched] enemy . . . [*May*] ye [*give praise*] to (70) [*him; may ye extol the might of*] his majesty, because his arm is greater than (that of) [*any king. It has indeed protected the rear of*] his majesty's army in Aruna!"

Now while the rear of his majesty's victorious army was (still) at [the town] of Aruna, the vanguard had come out into the [Qi]na Valley, and they filled the mouth of this valley.

Then they said to his majesty—life, prosperity, health! —(75) "Behold, his majesty has come forth with his victorious army, and they have filled the valley. Let our victorious lord listen to us this time, and let our lord guard for us the rear of his army and his people. When the rear of the army comes forth for us into the open, then we shall fight against these foreigners, then we shall not trouble our hearts [about] the rear of (80) our army."

A halt was made by his majesty outside, [*seated*] there and guarding the rear of his victorious army. Now the [*leaders*] had just finished coming forth on this road when the shadow turned.[30] His majesty reached the south of Megiddo on the bank of the Qina brook, when the seventh hour was in (its) course in the day.[31]

Then a camp was pitched there for his majesty, and a charge was laid upon the entire army, [saying]: "Prepare ye! Make your weapons ready, since one[32] will engage in combat with that wretched enemy in the morning, because one is . . . !"

Resting in the enclosure of life, prosperity, and health.[33] Providing for the officials. *Issuing rations* to the retinue. Posting the sentries of the army. Saying to them: "Be steadfast, be steadfast! Be vigilant, be vigilant!" Awakening in life in the tent of life, prosperity, and health. They came to tell his majesty: "The desert is well,[34] and the garrisons of the south and north also!"

Year 23, 1st month of the third season, day 21, the day of the feast of the *true* new moon.[35] Appearance of the king at dawn. Now a charge was laid upon the entire army to *pass by* . . . (85) His majesty set forth in a chariot of fine gold, adorned with his accoutrements of combat, like Horus, the Mighty of Arm, a lord of action like Montu, the Theban, while his father Amon made strong his arms. The southern wing of his majesty's army was at a hill south of [the] Qina [*brook*], and the northern wing was to the northwest of Megiddo, while his majesty was in their center, Amon being the protection of his person (in) the melee and the strength of [*Seth pervading*] his members.

Thereupon his majesty prevailed over them at the head of his army. Then they saw his majesty prevailing over them, and they fled headlong [to] Megiddo with faces of fear. They abandoned their horses and their chariots of gold and silver, so that someone might draw them (up) into this town by *hoisting* on their garments. Now the people had shut this town against them, (but) they [let down] garments to *hoist* them up into this town. Now, if only his majesty's army had not given up their hearts to capturing the possessions of the enemy, they would [have captured] Megiddo at this time, while the wretched enemy of Kadesh and the wretched enemy of this town were being dragged (up) *hastily* to get them into their town, for the fear of his majesty entered

23 Three days after the arrival in Yehem. See n.18 above, n.35 below.

24 An impersonal expression for the beginning of the day with the king's awaking.

25 The standard of Amon led the way. See it thus leading the way in the time of Ramses III, in the Epigraphic Survey, *Medinet Habu, I. The Earlier Historical Records of Ramses III* (*OIP*, VIII, Chicago, 1930), Pl. 17.

26 From the pass on to the Megiddo plain.

27 "Horn." This was the Asiatic wing. Why they were drawn up opposite the mouth of the pass and yet had not held the pass against the thin Egyptian line is inexplicable.

28 The Qina is still represented by a brook flowing south of Megiddo.

29 The preceding verb means "summon," rather than "cry out." Therefore, we should have Thut-mose's rallying cry to his army behind him. When he said: "They are fallen!" he was anticipating the fall of the Asiatics, because they had failed to guard the pass.

30 It was noon, and the shadow clock should be turned around. The Egyptian van thus reached the Megiddo plain seven hours (see the next note) before the rear of the army emerged and Thut-mose could go into camp.

31 Presumably seven hours after the turning of the sun, although this is not certain.

32 Pharaoh.

33 These brief notations, without true sentence form, probably derive from the army's daybook. The royal enclosure was doubtless an elaborate pavilion such as that shown in scenes of Ramses II's campaigns, e.g. A. Erman and H. Ranke, *Aegypten* (Tübingen, 1923), 635.

34 Faulkner suggests that this is the equivalent of "The coast is clear."

35 Borchardt's date for the battle is May 12, 1468. However, this rests on his understanding of "the true(?) new moon." In addition, Faulkner points out that "day 20" seems to have dropped out since the departure from Aruna (n.23 above).

[their bodies], their arms were weak, [*for*] his serpent-diadem had overpowered them.

Then their horses and their chariots of gold and silver were captured as an easy [prey.[36] *Ranks*] of them were lying stretched out on their backs, like fish in the *bight of a net*, while his majesty's victorious army counted up their possessions. Now there was captured [that] wretched [enemy's] tent, which was worked [with *silver*], . . .

Then the entire army rejoiced and gave praise to Amon [because of the victory] which he had given to his son on [this day. They *lauded*] his majesty and extolled his victories. Then they presented the plunder which they had taken: hands,[37] living prisoners, horses, and chariots of gold and silver and of *painted work*. (90). . . .

[Then his majesty commanded] his army with the words: "Capture ye [effectively, my] victorious [army]! Behold, [*all foreign countries*] have been put [*in this town by* the command] of Re on this day, inasmuch as every prince of every [northern] country is shut up within it, for the capturing of Megiddo is the capturing of a thousand towns! Capture ye firmly, firmly! . . ."

[*Orders were issued to* the com]manders of the troops to *pro*[*vide for their divisions and to inform*] each [man] *of* his place. They measured [this] city, which was corralled with a moat and enclosed with fresh timbers of all their pleasant trees, while his majesty himself was in a fortress east of this town, [being] watchful . . . . . . [enclosed] with a girdle wall, . . . *by* its girdle wall. Its name was called "Men-kheper-Re-is-the-Corraller-of-the-Asiatics." People were appointed as sentries at the enclosure of his majesty, and they were told: "Be steadfast, be steadfast! Be vigilant, [be vigilant]!" . . . his majesty . . . . [Not one] of them [was permitted to go] outside from behind this wall, except to come out *at a knock* on the door of their fortress.[38]

Now everything which his majesty did to this town and to that wretched enemy and his wretched army is set down by the individual day, by the individual expedition, and by the individual [troop] commanders.[39] . . . They [are] set down on a roll of leather in the temple of Amon today.

Now the princes of this foreign country came on their bellies to kiss the ground to the glory of his majesty and to beg breath for their nostrils, because his arm was (so) great, because the prowess of Amon was (so) great [over (95) every] foreign [country][40] . . . [all] the princes whom the prowess of his majesty carried off, bearing their tribute of silver, gold, lapis lazuli, and turquoise, and carrying grain, wine, and large and small cattle for the army of his majesty, with one gang of them bearing tribute southward.[41] Then his majesty appointed princes anew for [*every town*]. . . .

[List of the booty which his majesty's army carried off from the town of] Megiddo: 340 living prisoners and 83 hands; 2,041 horses, 191 foals, 6 stallions, and . . . colts; 1 chariot worked with gold, with a *body* of gold, belonging to that enemy, [*1*] fine chariot worked with gold belonging to the Prince of [*Megiddo*] . . . , and 892 chariots of his wretched army—total: 924; 1 fine bronze coat of mail belonging to that enemy, [*1*] fine bronze coat of mail belonging to the Prince of Meg[iddo, and] 200 [*leather*] coats of mail belonging to his wretched army; 502 bows; and 7 poles of *meru*-wood, worked with silver, of the tent of that enemy.

Now the army [of his majesty] carried off [*cattle*] . . . : 387 . . . , 1,929 cows, 2,000 goats, and 20,500 sheep.

List of what was carried off afterward by the king from the household goods of that enemy, who [was in] Yanoam, Nuges, and Herenkeru,[42] together with the property of those towns which had made themselves subject to him . . . : . . . ; 38 [*maryanu*] belonging to them,[43] 84 children of that enemy and of the princes who were with him, 5 *maryanu* belonging to them, 1,796 male and female slaves, as well as their children, and 103 pardoned persons, who had come out from that enemy because of hunger—total: 2,503—apart from bowls of costly stone and gold, various vessels, (100) . . . , a large *akunu*-jar in Syrian work, jars, bowls, *plates*, various drinking vessels, large kettles, [$x +$] 17 knives —making 1,784 *deben*;[44] gold in discs, found in the process of being worked, as well as abundant silver in discs —966 *deben* and 1 *kidet*;[45] a silver statue *in the form of* . . . , [*a statue*] . . . , with head of gold; 3 walking sticks with human heads; 6 carrying-chairs of that enemy, of ivory, ebony, and *carob*-wood, worked with gold, and the 6 footstools belonging to them; 6 large tables of

36 "As a go-[and-take]."

37 Cut off from the fallen foe as tokens of battle accomplishment.

38 The besieged Asiatics were permitted only to appear if Egyptians called them out? Alternatively: "except to come out to surrender(?) at the door of their fortress." The siege lasted seven months (Barkal Stela, p. 238 below). Further information on the siege is given on a stela from the Ptah Temple at Karnak (Sethe, *op.cit.*, 767): "My majesty returned from the foreign country of Retenu on the first occasion of the victories which my father Amon gave to me, when he gave me all the countries of Djahi, gathered together and shut up in a single town. The fear of my majesty pervaded their hearts; they were fallen and powerless when I reached them. There was no lack of runaways among them. I corralled them in a single town. I built a girdle wall around it, to cut them off from the breath of life."

39 "On the day in its name, in the name of the journey, and in the names of the commanders of [troops]." In the Theban tomb biography of "the Army Scribe" Tjaneni, who served under Thut-mose III (Sethe, *op.cit.*, 1004), we read: "I was the one who set down the victories which he achieved over every foreign country, put into writing as it was done."

40 On the surrender, see also the Barkal Stela (p. 238).

41 Toward Egypt.

42 Elsewhere in the Temple of Karnak (Sethe, *op.cit.*, 744), Thut-mose III states that he presented to Amon "three towns in Upper Retenu—Nuges the name of one, Yanoam the name of another, and Herenkeru the name of another—taxed with annual dues for the divine offerings of my father Amon." "Upper Retenu" properly stands for the mountain territory of north Palestine and southern Syria, and Yanoam seems to have been in the Lake Huleh area. The three towns would then be somewhere in that area. See A. H. Gardiner, *Ancient Egyptian Onomastica* (London, 1947), I, 168* ff. We do not know what is meant by "that enemy" being in these towns. The dedicatory inscriptions translated under D below suggest that Thut-mose had time for a campaign in the Lebanon while Megiddo was under siege.

43 The *maryanu* were the warrior or officer class in Asia at this time. cf. p. 22, n.2. "Belonging to them" refers to listed individuals in the lost context above (474 are missing from the total), and probably includes the women of the Asiatic princes.

44 About 435 lb. Troy of metal value (probably reckoned in silver) in the listed pieces.

45 About 235 lb. Troy. Uncertain whether of silver only, or of the combined value of gold and silver.

ivory and *carob*-wood; 1 bed belonging to that enemy, of *carob*-wood, worked with gold and with every (kind of) costly stone, in the manner of a *kerker*,[46] completely worked in gold; a statue of that enemy which was there, of ebony worked with gold, its head of lapis [lazuli] . . . ; bronze vessels, and much clothing of that enemy.

Now the fields were made into arable plots and assigned to inspectors of the palace—life, prosperity, health!—in order to reap their harvest. List of the harvest which his majesty carried off from the Megiddo acres: 207,300 [$+x$] sacks of wheat,[47] apart from what was cut as forage by his majesty's army, . . .

C. THE BARKAL STELA

In his 47th year, Thut-mose III erected at Gebel Barkal near the Fourth Cataract a granite stela summarizing some of the achievements of his reign. It was published, with photograph, transcription, and translation, by G. A. and M. B. Reisner in *ZAeS*, LXIX (1933), 24-39, Pls. III-V. Only that part of the text which deals with the first campaign is translated below. Another extract will be found below under the eighth campaign.

I repeat further to you—hear, O people! (19) He[48] entrusted to me the foreign countries of Retenu on the first campaign, when they had come to engage with my majesty, being millions and hundred-thousands of men, the individuals of every foreign country, waiting in their chariots—330 princes, every one of them having his (own) army.

When they were in the Qina Valley *and away from it*, in *a tight spot*, good fortune befell me among them, when my majesty attacked them. Then they fled immediately or fell prostrate. When they entered into Megiddo, my majesty shut them up for a period up to seven months, before they came out into the open, pleading to my majesty and saying: "Give us thy breath, our lord! The countries of Retenu will never repeat rebellion another time!"

Then that enemy and the princes who were with him sent out to my majesty, with all their *children* carrying abundant tribute: gold and silver, all their horses which were with them, their great chariots of gold and silver, as well as those *which were painted*, all their coats of mail, their bows, their arrows, and all their weapons of warfare. It was these with which they had come *from afar* to fight against my majesty, and now they were bringing them as tribute to my majesty, while they were standing on their walls, giving praise to my majesty, seeking that the breath of life might be given to them.

(24) Then my majesty had administered to them an oath *of fealty*, with the words: "We will not repeat evil against Men-kheper-Re, who lives forever, our good lord, in our time of life, inasmuch as we have seen his power, and he has given us breath as he wishes! It was his father who did it—[Amon-Re, Lord of the Thrones of the Two Lands]—it was not the *hand* of man!"

Then my majesty had them given leave to (go to) their cities. They all went on donkey(back), so that I might take their horses. I took captive the townspeople thereof for Egypt, and their possessions likewise.

[46] An unknown object of wood.

[47] Something like 450,000 bushels.

[48] Amon-Re.

D. FROM A DEDICATORY INSCRIPTION

In the Temple of Karnak Thut-mose III recorded the offerings and feasts which he established for the god Amon-Re in return for his victories. An extract from the beginning of this text gives further information on the first campaign. Perhaps during the seven months' siege of Megiddo, the pharaoh had been able to send a detachment north and establish a fortress outpost somewhere in the Lebanon. The text appears in Lepsius, *op. cit.*, 30b, and in Sethe, *op.cit.*, 739-40. It is translated in Breasted, *op.cit.*, §§548-49.

. . . in the country of Retenu, in a fortress which my majesty built through his victories, a central point of the princes of Lebanon, of which the name shall be "Men-kheper-Re-is-the-Binder-of-the-Vagabonds."

Now when he landed at Thebes, his father Amon was [*in joy*]. . . . My majesty established for him a Feast of Victory anew, at the time when my majesty returned from the first victorious campaign, overthrowing the wretched Retenu and extending the frontiers of Egypt, in the year 23, as the first of the victories which he decreed to me.

SUBSEQUENT CAMPAIGNS

Thut-mose III conducted at least sixteen campaigns into Asia in a period of twenty years. Some campaigns involved difficult fighting, some were mere parades of strength to organize the new empire. The records of some campaigns consist simply of statements of "tribute" to Egypt—from Retenu, Djahi, and Cyprus; from Nubia, Ethiopia, and Punt; and from Naharin, Hatti, Assyria, and Babylonia. Obviously, some of this was truly tribute from conquered countries, but some of it consisted of gifts from distant and sovereign lands. This translation includes only those campaigns having greater interest.

For Thut-mose III's Hymn of Victory, see pp. 373-375 below. For a legend about the capture of Joppa under Thut-mose III, see pp. 22-23 above.

A. FIFTH CAMPAIGN

By his fifth campaign, in his 29th year, Thut-mose was moving as far north as the towns of Tunip and Ardata, somewhere in north Syria. From the "Annals" in Karnak: Sethe, *op.cit.*, 685-88; bibliography on 680. Translation in Breasted, *op.cit.*, §§454-62.

(3) Year 29.[1] Now [his] majesty [was in Dja]hi, destroying the countries which had been rebellious to him, on the fifth victorious campaign. Now his majesty captured the town of *Wartet*.[2] . . . List of the plunder which was taken from this town, from the garrison of that enemy of Tunip: 1 prince of this town; 329 *teher-*

[1] A date isolated in broken context on the Armant Stela (p. 234 above) gives: "Year 29, 4th month of the second season, day . . . ," which would correspond to the earliest month dates in the first campaign. The Egyptian campaigning season normally fell just after the Egyptian harvest, but just before the Asiatic harvest, for maximum advantage to Egypt.

[2] Unknown, but apparently a garrison town for Tunip, which seems to have been in the north Syrian plain.

warriors;[3] 100 *deben* of silver;[4] 100 *deben* of gold;[4] lapis lazuli, turquoise, and vessels of bronze and copper.

Now there was a seizing of two ships, . . . loaded with everything, with male and female slaves, copper, lead, *emery*, and every good thing, after his majesty proceeded southward to Egypt, to his father Amon-Re, with joy of heart.[5]

Now his majesty destroyed the town of Ardata, with its grain. All its pleasant trees were cut down. Now [his majesty] found [the] entire [land of] Djahi, with their orchards filled with their fruit. Their (7) wines were found lying in their vats, as water flows, and their grains on the threshing floors, *being ground*. They were more plentiful than the sands of the shore. The army overflowed with its possessions. . . . Now his majesty's army was as drunk and anointed with oil every day as if at feasts in Egypt.

B. SIXTH CAMPAIGN

In his 30th year, Thut-mose moved against the focal center of opposition to Egypt, Kadesh on the Orontes. The word "destroy," used with reference to this town, is not to be taken literally; Thut-mose may have done no more than destroy its food supplies. The record of the year is notable for the statement of the policy of holding the heirs of Syrian princes in Egypt. From the "Annals" in Karnak: Sethe, *op.cit.*, 689-90. Translation by Breasted, *op.cit.*, §§463-67.

Year 30. Now his majesty was in the country of Retenu on his majesty's sixth victorious campaign. Arrival at the town of Kadesh. Destroying it. Felling its trees. Cutting down its grain. Proceeding by passing Reyet[6] and reaching the town of Simyra.[7] Reaching the town of Ardata. Doing the same to it.

List of the tribute (10) brought to the glory of his majesty by the princes of Retenu in this year. Now the children of the princes and their brothers were brought to be *hostages*[8] in Egypt. Now, whoever of these princes died, his majesty was accustomed to make his son go to stand in his place.[9] List of the children of princes carried off in this year: 36 men; 181 male and female slaves; 188 horses: and 40 chariots, worked with gold and silver *or painted*.

C. SEVENTH CAMPAIGN

In his 31st year, Thut-mose captured the Phoenician town of Ullaza. He had now proceeded so far north that the control of the Sea was essential to the maintenance of empire. The record of this year tells of the Egyptian concern for holding the Phoenican harbors. References as above: Sethe, *op.cit.*, 690-96; Breasted, *op.cit.*, §§468-75.

Year 31, 1st month of the third season, day 3.[10] Summary of the plunder of his majesty in this year.

Plunder which was carried off from the town of Ullaza, which is on the shore of *Meren*:[11] 492 living captives, [*1*] *commander* belonging to the son of the enemy of Tunip, 1 superior of the . . . who was there—total: 494 men—26 horses, 13 chariots, (12) and their equipment of all (kinds of) weapons of warfare. Then his majesty captured this town within a short hour, all its goods being an easy prey.[12] . . .

Now every port town which his majesty reached was supplied with good bread and with various (kinds of) bread, with olive oil, incense, wine, honey, fr[uit], . . . They were more abundant than anything, beyond the experience of his majesty's army, without equivocation. (15) They are set down in the daybook of the palace—life, prosperity, health! That the list of them has not been put upon this monument is in order not to multiply words and in order to put *their content* in that place [*in which*] I made [*them*].[13] . . .

D. EIGHTH CAMPAIGN

In his 33rd year, Thut-mose achieved one of his most ambitious campaigns, crossing the bend of the Euphrates and fighting against "that enemy of the wretched Naharin." It is not certain whether this opponent was the King of Naharin or was a lesser prince. We have four sources for the events of this campaign. On the campaign in general, see the discussion by R. Faulkner, in *JEA*, XXXII (1946), 39-42.

D.-A THE ANNALS IN KARNAK

The references are as above: Sethe, *op.cit.*, 696-703; Breasted, *op.cit.*, §§476-87.

Year 33. Now his majesty was in the country of Retenu.

Reach[ing *the district of Qatna on the eighth victorious campaign. Crossing the Great Bend of Naharin by his majesty at the head of his army, to* the] east of this water.[14] He set up beside the stela of his father, (20) the King of Upper and Lower Egypt: Aa-kheper-ka-Re,[15] another (stela). Now his majesty went *north*,[16] plunder-

[3] A foreign word (perhaps Hittite) for chariot-warriors. cf. pp. 258, n.23; 263, n.12; and 469, n.10.

[4] About 25 lb. Troy.

[5] The loaded cargo-vessels were seized after the pharaoh had left for Egypt. Thus this does not state that he returned by water. See T. Säve-Söderbergh, *The Navy of the Eighteenth Egyptian Dynasty* (Uppsala, 1946), 34-35.

[6] Unknown.

[7] A town on the north Phoenician coast. Its location and that of Ardata are still to be established with precision.

[8] Or "captives"; less likely: "to be in strongholds."

[9] Elsewhere in Karnak (p. 242 below), Thut-mose III listed "the foreign countries of Upper Retenu, . . . whose children his majesty carried off as living prisoners to the town . . . in Karnak." The name given to this section of Karnak is unfortunately unreadable. cf. pp. 247, 248-49, 257.

[10] This would be the last day of Thut-mose III's 31st year. See n.16 on the first campaign above.

[11] Reading and location uncertain. Ullaza was a north Phoenician coast town. The Egyptians located a garrison here; cf. against n.28 below.

[12] "Being a go-and-take."

[13] On the army daybook, cf. against n.39 of the first campaign.

[14] Sethe's restoration, used above, depends upon several other contexts. In a broken Karnak inscription (Sethe, *op.cit.*, 188), there is reference to ". . . [the dis]trict of Qatna on the 8th victorious campaign." Qatna lay northeast of modern Homs. Part of the restoration depends upon the Hymn of Victory (p. 374 below): "Thou hast crossed the waters of the Great Bend of Naharin," and on an inscription on the obelisk now in Istanbul (Sethe, *op.cit.*, 587): "He who crossed the Great Bend of Naharin in valor and victory at the head of his army and made a great slaughter." The general sense of the restoration is probably correct. On Naharin, see A. H. Gardiner, *Ancient Egyptian Onomastica*, I, 171* ff.

[15] Thut-mose I (ca. 1525-1495 B.C.). Thut-mose III's 33rd year should be about 1458 B.C.

[16] In Egypt this word would mean both "go north" and "go downstream." Since the Euphrates flows south, the direction is uncertain in the present context. See A. H. Gardiner, *Ancient Egyptian Onomastica* (London, 1947), I, 160* ff.

ing towns and laying waste encampments of that enemy of the wretched Naharin. . . .

[Then] he [*pursued*] after them an *iter* of sailing.[17] Not one (of them) looked behind him, but was fleeing continually like a *herd* of desert beasts. [Now] there were galloping horses. . . .

His majesty reached the town (23) of Ni, going *south*,[18] when his majesty returned, after he had set up his stela in Naharin, (thus) extending the frontiers of Egypt. . . .[19]

D.-B THE ARMANT STELA

See the reference, Mond and Myers, as the first text translated under the first campaign, p. 234 above.

He finished off 120 elephants in the country of Ni, on his return from Naharin. He crossed the river Great Bend, and he crushed the towns of its two sides, consumed by fire forever. He set up a stela of victory on its [east] side. . . .

D.-C THE BARKAL STELA

For the reference, G. A. and M. B. Reisner, see under the first campaign, p. 238 above.

(6) . . . The many troops (of) Mitanni were overthrown in the completion of an hour, quite gone, as if they had never come into being. . . . His southern frontier is to the horns of the earth, to the southern limit *of this land*; (his) northern to the marshes of Asia, to the supporting pillars of heaven. They come to him with bowed head, seeking his breath of life. He is a king, valiant like Montu;[20] a taker, from whom no one can take, who crushes all rebellious countries.

There is none who can protect them in that land of Naharin, which its lord abandoned because of fear. I desolated his towns and his tribes and set fire to them. My majesty made them mounds, and their (re)settlement will never take place. I captured all their people, carried off as living prisoners, the (10) cattle thereof without limit, and their goods as well. I took away the *very sources of life*, (for) I cut down their grain and felled all their groves and all their pleasant trees. . . . I destroyed it; it became a . . . upon which there are no trees.

When my majesty crossed over to the marshes of Asia, I had many ships of cedar built on the mountains of God's Land near the Lady of Byblos.[21] They were placed on chariots,[22] with cattle drawing (them). They journeyed in [front of] my majesty, in order to cross that great river which lies between this foreign country and Naharin.[23] A king indeed to be boasted of in proportion to (the success of) his arms in the melee, he who crossed the Great Bend in pursuit of him who had attacked him, as the foremost of his army, seeking for that wretched enemy [*in*][24] the countries of Mitanni, when he was a fugitive before my majesty to another land, a distant place, because of fear.

Then my majesty set up on that mountain of Naharin my stela, which was dug out of the mountain on the west side (of) the Great Bend. . . .

When I proceeded (15) south to Egypt, after I had put the sword (to) Naharin, *great was* the terror in the mouth of the Sand-Dwellers.[25] Their doors were closed because of it; they would not come out into the open for fear of the Bull. . . .

Still another instance of the victory which Re decreed to me: he repeated for me a great (feat of) valor (at) the *water hole* of Ni, when he let me make droves of elephants and my majesty fought them in a herd of 120. Never was the like done since (the time of) the god by a king (*of*) them who took the White Crown. I have said this without boasting therein, and without equivocation therein. . . .

[26]Every year there is hewed [for me in Dja]hi genuine cedar of Lebanon, which is brought to the Court—life, prosperity, health! *Timber* comes to Egypt for me, *advancing* (31) . . . New [*wood*] of Negau[27] [*is brought*], the choicest of God's Land . . . , to reach the Residence City, without passing over the seasons thereof, each and every year. When my army which is the garrison in Ullaza[28] comes, [*they bring the tribute*], which is the cedar of the victories of my majesty, through the plans of my father [Amon-Re], who entrusted to me all foreign countries. I have not given (any) of it to the Asiatics, (for) it is a wood which he loves. . . .

D.-D THE BIOGRAPHY OF AMEN-EM-HEB

Amen-em-heb was an Egyptian soldier of moderate military rank, who has left us a lively account of his deeds of valor in following Thut-mose III. His autobiography is painted on the walls of his tomb (No. 85) in Thebes. Although he gives us no chronology, it has been argued that his narrative "almost certainly deals with the events of this one campaign in chronological order, the only exception being the second assault on Kadesh, which is the last battle in which Amenemhab fought" (A. H. Gardiner, on the authority of R. Faulkner, in *JEA*, XXXII [1946], 39). The text appears in W. M. Müller, *Egyptological Researches* (Washington, 1906), I, Pls. XXXIII-XXXIX, and in Sethe, *op.cit.*, 889-97; a translation in Breasted, *op.cit.*, §§574-92. See also A. H. Gardiner, *Ancient Egyptian Onomastica* (London, 1947), I, 153* ff.

17 Perhaps two kilometers.

18 Or "going upstream," which would be north on the Euphrates; cf. n.16 above. Ni (or Niya) may be located south of Carchemish on the Euphrates, and the Amen-em-heb inscription (p. 241) makes the crossing possible in the Carchemish district.

19 On the elephant hunt in Ni, see the three texts which follow. The only other element of interest in the "Annals" of this year is in the tribute of an Asiatic country of which the name is lost: "4 birds of this country—now they [give] birth every day." This, as Sethe has pointed out (Die älteste Erwähnung des Haushuhns in einem ägyptischen Texte [*Festschrift für F. K. Andreas*, Leipzig, 1916; 109]), is the earliest record of the domestic hen.

20 The Egyptian god of war.

21 "God's Land" was the east in general. The goddess of Byblos, whom the Egyptians equated with their Hat-Hor, stands here for the town.

22 *Sic*, both in word and determinative, although heavier carts must have been used.

23 i.e. the Euphrates. This feat of transporting boats from Phoenicia to the Euphrates gives some measure of the military genius of Thut-mose III.

24 Or "[*of*]"?

25 The Asiatic nomads of the deserts near Egypt.

26 The following paragraph does not refer to the eighth campaign, but is a general statement of the pharaoh's power.

27 Probably a Lebanese or Phoenician area; cf. *Syria*, IV (1923), 181-92.

28 cf. n.11 above.

I made captives in the country of (5) Negeb.[29] I took three men, Asiatics, as living prisoners.

When his majesty reached Naharin, I took three men captive there, so that I might put them before thy[30] majesty as living prisoners. Again I made captives within this campaign in the country, the Ridge of Wan, on the west of Aleppo. I took Asiatics as living prisoners: 13 men; 70 live asses; 13 bronze battle-axes; and . . . of bronze, worked with gold. Again I took booty within this campaign in the country of Carchemish. I took (10) . . . as living prisoners, and I crossed over the water of Naharin, while they were in my hand . . . ; I [placed] them before my lord. Then he rewarded me with a great reward; the list thereof: . . .

I saw the victory of the King of Upper and Lower Egypt: Men-kheper-Re, given life, in the country of Sendjer,[31] when he made [a great] slaughter [among] them. I made captives in the king's presence; I took a hand there, and he gave me the Gold of Favor; the list thereof: . . . , and two rings of silver.

Again I saw how valiant he was, while I was in his retinue, when [he] captured the [city of] (15) Kadesh, without my swerving from the place where he was. I took two men, *maryanu*,[32] as [living prisoners and set them] before the king, the Lord of the Two Lands: Thut-mose-Ruler-of-Thebes, living forever. He gave me gold because of my valor, in the presence of everybody . . . ; the list thereof: a lion, two necklaces, two flies, and four rings of finished gold.[33] . . .

(20) Again I saw his victory in the country of the wretched Takhshi,[34] in the town of Meriu. . . I took booty from it in the presence of the king; I took three men, Asiatics, as living prisoners. Then my lord gave to me the Gold of Favor; the list thereof: two necklaces, four rings, two flies, and one lion of gold; a female slave and a male slave.

Again [I saw] another successful deed which the Lord of the Two Lands accomplished in Ni. He hunted 120 elephants *at their mudhole*.[35] Then the biggest elephant which was among them began to fight before the face of his majesty. I was the one who cut off his hand[36] while he was (still) alive, (25) in the presence of his majesty, while I was standing in the water between two rocks. Then my lord rewarded me with gold: . . . , and five pieces of clothing.

Then, when the Prince of Kadesh sent out a mare, which [*was swift*] on her feet and which entered among the army,[37] I ran after her on foot, carrying my *dagger*, and I (ripped) open her belly. I cut off her tail and set it before the king. Praise was given to god for it. He gave joy, and it filled my belly, jubilation, and it imbued my body. (30) His majesty sent forth every valiant man of his army, to breach the new wall which Kadesh had made. I was the one who breached it, being the first of every valiant man, and no other did (it) before me. When I came out, I brought two men, *maryanu*, as living prisoners. Then my lord again rewarded me for it, with every good thing of heart's satisfaction.

Now really, I made these captures while I was a soldier of [User-het-A]mon.[38] . . .

E. NINTH CAMPAIGN

The success of Thut-mose's first eight campaigns seems to be reflected in the dull, statistical character of the records of the final campaigns. They consist chiefly of lists of "tribute" from dependent or friendly countries. The 9th campaign, in the 34th year, contains a slightly different statement about pharaoh's concern for the harbors of Phoenicia. The references are to the "Annals" in Karnak: Sethe, *op.cit.*, 707; Breasted, *op.cit.*, §492.

Now every port town of his majesty was supplied with every good thing which [his] majesty received [in the country of Dja]hi, with Keftiu, Byblos, and Sektu ships of cedar,[39] loaded with columns and beams, as well as (37) large timbers for the [major wood]working of his majesty. . . .

F. FINAL CAMPAIGN

In his 42nd year, Thut-mose conducted his 16th or 17th campaign, the last listed. Apparently he met somewhat more resistance than in other late campaigns. The references are to the "Annals" in Karnak; Sethe, *op.cit.*, 729-34, with antecedent bibliography on 724; Breasted, *op.cit.*, §§528-40.

. . . the Fenkhu.[40] Now his majesty was on the coast road, in order to destroy the town of Irqata,[41] together with those towns which (11) [were *in its district*]. . . .

Arrival at Tunip. Destruction of the town. Cutting down its grain and felling its trees. . . .

Coming (back) successfully. Arrival at the region of Kadesh. Capturing three towns therein.[42] . . .

[*Now his majesty captured the foreigners*] of the wretched Naharin, who were auxiliaries among them, together with their horses: 691 individuals; 29 hands; 48 horses, . . .

(20) . . . Now his majesty commanded that the victories which he had accomplished from the year 23 to the year 42 should be set down at the time when this monument was established in this chapel, in order that he might achieve "given-life-forever."

29 Apparently the same as the modern Negeb, south of Palestine.

30 *Sic*, but read "his."

31 Perhaps modern Sheidjar, northwest of Hama.

32 cf. n.43 on the first campaign.

33 Decorations of gold in various forms. Flies and lions' heads of gold have been found in Egyptian excavation.

34 Takhshi lay near Damascus. Meriu . . . is unknown.

35 Their "slime-place"? Less likely: "because of their ivory."

36 *Sic*, for "trunk." See P. E. Newberry, in *JEA*, xxx (1944), 75.

37 To stampede the stallions of the Egyptian chariotry.

38 The sacred barge of Amon at Thebes. The implication seems to be that Amen-em-heb was only an official of relatively low rank. The text goes on to record the death of Thut-mose III and Amen-em-heb's elevation to the rank of "Lieutenant of the Army" under Amen-hotep II.

39 Keftiu was Crete—or the eastern Mediterranean coast generally—and Byblos was the Phoenician town. A geographical name fitting Sektu cannot now be supplied (*pace* S. R. K. Glanville, in *ZAeS*, LXVIII [1932], 14-15, who suggests an equation with Ras esh-Shaqqah, south of the Phoenician town of Tripoli). The names of these vessels indicate the commercial carriers of the time.

40 Phoenicians.

41 Modern 'Arqah, northeast of Tripoli.

42 These words do not actually claim the capture of Kadesh itself, although that may have been one of the three towns.

Lists of Asiatic Countries Under the Egyptian Empire

The conqueror Thut-mose III initiated the custom of listing the Asiatic and African countries which he had conquered or over which he claimed dominion. In the Temple of Amon at Karnak three of his lists bear superscriptions. The texts are published in K. Sethe, *Urkunden der 18. Dynastie* (*Urk.*, IV, Leipzig, 1907), 780-81, with translations in Breasted, *AR*, II, §402.

(a) Roster of the countries of Upper Retenu which his majesty shut up in the town of the wretched Megiddo, whose children his majesty carried off as living prisoners to the town . . . in Karnak,[1] on his first victorious campaign, according to the command of his father Amon, who led him to the good ways.

(b) All the mysterious lands of the marshes of Asia which his majesty carried off as living prisoners, while he made a great slaughter among them, (lands) which had not been trodden by other kings except for his majesty. The reputation of a valiant man is from [what he has done], not being destroyed in this land [forever].[2]

(c) Roster of the countries of Upper Retenu which his majesty shut up in the town of the wretched Megiddo, whose children his majesty carried off as living prisoners to the town of Thebes, to fill the workhouse of his father Amon in Karnak, on his first victorious campaign, according to the command of his father Amon, who led him to the good ways.

Subsequent kings followed Thut-mose III in compiling such lists. The result is only a partial historical gain. Identifications are often difficult or impossible, and some of the later lists are suspect as having a strong fictional coloring. Selections from these lists are given below, with attempted identifications. It will be understood that the name is not always the biblical site; it may be a Kadesh, a Hamath, or a Geba. Those names which are checked with numbers derive from the longer lists and—with the exception of Ramses III—may more truly represent historical achievement than those names which occur in briefer lists of strong propagandistic force (here checked with x).

The names are taken from J. Simons, *Handbook for the Study of Egyptian Topographical Lists Relating to Western Asia* (Leyden, 1937), in which antecedent bibliography is given. The numbers used below are those of Simons' lists. Important for the identification of place names are M. Burchardt, *Die altkanaanäischen Fremdworte und Eigennamen im ägyptischen* (Leipzig, 1909), and W. F. Albright, *The Vocalization of the Egyptian Syllabic Orthography* (New Haven, 1934).

	Thut-mose III	Amen-hotep II	Thut-mose IV	Amen-hotep III	Hor-em-heb	Seti I	Ramses II	Ramses III	Sheshonk I
[3]Achshaph	40								
Acre	47					54	x		
Adummim	36								98
Aijalon									26
Alashiya	213(?)					x			
Aleppo	311	x		x				6	
Altaku					x	x	x	x	
Anaharath	52								
Apheq							30(?)	80	
Arrapkha				x			x(?)		
Aruna	27								32
Arzawa	175(?)				x	x	x	x	x
Ashtaroth	28								
Assyria	x			x	x	x	x		x
Beeroth	19								
Beth-Anath	111(?)					59	x		124
Beth-Dagon								72	
Beth-Horon									24
Beth-Olam									36
Beth-Shan	110					51	x		16
Beth-Tappuah									39
Byblos				x					
Carchemish	270			x				29	
Chinneroth	34								
Damascus	13			x					
Deper							x		
Dibon	98								
Dothan	9								
Edrei	91								
Emeq	107								65
Field of Abram									71-72
Geba	114						x		
Geba-Shumen	41								
Gezer	104								
Gibeon									23
Ham	118								x
Hamath	16					x	x		
Hand of the King									29
Hapharaim									18
Hatti				x	x	22	x	x	x
Hazor	32	x				64			
Ibleam	43								
Isy (Cyprus)						31	x	x	
Iteren	230								
Iursa	60								
Jacob-El	102						9	104	
Joppa	62								
Jordan									150
Joseph-El	78			x					
Kadesh	1	x	x	x	x	28		x	x
Karmaim	96							74	
Keftiu ("Crete")				x			x		
Khashabu	55								
Kiriath-Anab						63	x		
Kishion	37								
Kumidi						55			
Laish	31								

The approximate working dates for the pharaohs are: Thut-mose III, 1490-1436 B.C.; Amen-hotep II, 1447-1421; Thut-mose IV, 1421-1413; Amen-hotep III, 1413-1377; Hor-em-heb, 1349-1319; Seti I, 1318-1301; Ramses II, 1301-1234; Ramses III, 1195-1164; Sheshonk I, 945-924. Sheshonk I is the Shishak of the Bible.

[1] The name of the town of captives at Karnak is unfortunately broken and untranslatable.

[2] A proverb. See n.2 on p. 233.

[3] Many identifications may be open to more question than is indicated.

	Thut-mose III	Amen-hotep II	Thut-mose IV	Amen-hotep III	Hor-em-heb	Seti I	Ramses II	Ramses III	Sheshonk I
Levi-El								111	
Lullu	x				x	x	x		
Lydda	64								
Mahanaim									22
Makkedah	30								
Megiddo	2					x			27
Merom	12						x		
Migdol	71						32(?)	82	58
Mishal	39								
Mitanni	x			x(?)			x	28	
Moab							x		
Naharin			x	x	x	23	x	x	x
Negeb	57								84
Ni	132	x							
Nukhashshe (Neges)				x					
Ono	65								
Papkhi					x	29	x	x	
Pella (Pahel)	33			x	x	49	x		
Qatna		x		x	x	30		x	
Qedem[4]	x								
Rabbah	105								13
Raphia						65			x
Rebi	82								
Rehob	87								17
Retenu, Lower		x				25	x		
Retenu, Upper		x				24		x	
Rosh-Kadesh	48						1	108	
Shamash-Edom	51								
Shankhar (Shinar)			x	x	x	26	x		x
Sharon	21								
Shasu (Bedouin)			x	x	x	x	x		x
Shunem	38								15
Socho	67								38
Taanach	42								14
Takhshi			x	x		x	x		
Tjerekh (Zalkhi)	342								
Tunip	127	x	x	x	x	x		x	x
Tyre				x(?)		57	x(?)	121	
Ugarit				x	x				
Ullaza	166					56	x		
Unqi	148								
Uzu						58	x		
Yaa[4]	x								
Yanoam				x		52	28	78	
Yehem	68								35

A Trip to the Lebanon for Cedar

An official of Thut-mose III has left us an inscription—unfortunately badly damaged—on a commission which he undertook to secure cedar from the Lebanon. The inscription appears in the tomb of the Chief Treasurer Sen-nefer (No. 99 at Thebes). The text appears in K. Sethe, *Urkunden der 18. Dynastie* (*Urk.*, IV, Leipzig, 1906), III, 531-36, and was studied by Sethe, Eine ägyptische Expedition nach dem Libanon im 15. Jahrhundert v. Chr. (*SPAW*, 1906, 356-63).

. . . *above the clouds.* I entered the forest-[preserve]. . . . [I caused] that there be presented to her offerings of millions of things on behalf of [*the life, prosperity, and health of thy majesty*].[1] . . . (10) *in* Byblos, that I might give them to her lord for her [heart's] satisfaction. . . . gave . . . of the choicest thereof. I brought away (timbers of) 60 cubits in [their] length.[2] . . . They were sharper than the beard of grain,[3] the middle thereof *as thick* . . . I [*brought*] them [*down*] from the highland of God's Land. They reached as far as the forest-preserve.[4] . . . [*I sailed* on the] Great [Green] Sea with a favorable breeze, land[ing *in Egypt*] . . .

Pharaoh as a Sportsman

The following texts have place in the record of the Egyptian Empire because they present to us the invincible being who conquered and held foreign countries. As a god-king, he was placed beyond any mortals of his day. Yet he led his armies into battle and arrows were aimed at him. He had to present himself and he had to be presented by the dogma of the state as unsurpassed and unsurpassable in physical prowess. In addition to the accumulating legend of his triumphs in battle, a legend was fostered of his invincibility in competitive sport.

a

The first document deals with Thut-mose III (about 1490-1436 B.C.) and is extracted from his Armant Stela, for which the bibliography was given on p. 234 above.

(4) He shot at an ingot of copper, every shaft being split like a reed. Then his majesty put a sample there in the House of Amon, being a target of worked copper of three fingers in thickness,[1] with his arrow therein. When it had passed through it, he made three palms[2] come out at the back of it, in order to grant the request of those who followed: the success of his arms in valor and victory. I speak to the water of what he did,[3] without *lying* and without equivocation therein, in the face of his entire army, without a phrase of boasting therein. If he spent a moment of recreation by hunting in any foreign country, the number of that which he carried off is greater than the bag of the entire army. He killed seven lions by shooting in the completion of a moment. He carried off a herd of twelve wild cattle within an hour, when breakfast time had taken place,

4 On the historical value of the names Yaa and Qedem, A. H. Gardiner, *Notes on the Story of Sinuhe* (Paris, 1916), 155, points out that in this one list the two names "occur beside one another, obviously reminiscences of the story of Sinuhe and without further historical value." cf. p. 19 above.

1 In the lost context there must have been reference to the goddess of Byblos, whom the Egyptians equated with their Hat-Hor. The "presentations" to her are a polite statement of the payment for cedar. The term *khenti-she*, here translated "forest-preserve," was used in Egypt for royal domains.

2 Slightly over 100 feet long. The numeral is partly destroyed on the wall, but is considered by Sethe to be certainly 60.

3 Not literally sharp. This word is elsewhere used in various forms of approval, somewhat like the modern juvenile "keen, neat."

4 Perhaps: "When I [brought] them [down] upon the country of God's Land," i.e. the Orient in general, they were so many that "they reached as far" back as the edge of the forest in the mountains.

1 A little over 2 in. in thickness.

2 Nearly 9 in. of the arrow protruding from the back of the target.

3 So literally. Is it an idiom for: I speak the unadulterated truth?

the tails thereof for his back.[4] . . . He carried off a rhinoceros by shooting, in the southern country (9) of Nubia,[5] after he proceeded to Miu[6] to seek him who had been rebellious to him in that country. He set up his stela there, like that which he had made *at the ends [of the earth]*.[7] ...

b

The pharaoh who has left us the most numerous records of his physical prowess was Amen-hotep II (about 1447-1421 B.C.).[8] A stela recently discovered near the Sphinx at Gizeh gives the most telling record of his triumphs at sport. It was published by Selim Hassan in *ASAE*, XXXVII (1937), 129-34, Pls. I-II, and by A. Varille in *BIFAO*, XLI (1942), 31-38, Pl. I. It was translated by G. Steindorff and K. C. Seele, *When Egypt Ruled the East* (Chicago, 1942), 68-70. The conventional praise of the pharaoh in the first ten and a half lines is here omitted.

Now, further, his majesty appeared as king as a goodly youth.[9] When he had matured[10] and completed eighteen years *on his thighs* in valor, (12) he was one who knew every task of Montu:[11] there was no one like him on the field of battle. He was one who knew horses: there was not his like in this numerous army. There was not one therein who could draw his bow.[12] He could not be approached in running.

Strong of arms, one who did not weary when he took the oar, he rowed at the stern of his falcon-boat as the *stroke* for two hundred men.[13] When there was a pause, after they had attained half an *iter's* course,[14] they were weak, their bodies were limp, they could not draw a breath, whereas his majesty was (still) strong under his oar of twenty cubits in its length.[15] He left off and moored his falcon-boat (only after) he had attained three *iters* in rowing,[16] without letting down (15) in pulling. Faces were bright at the sight of him, when he did this.

He drew three hundred stiff bows in comparing the work of the craftsmen of them, in order to distinguish the ignorant from the wise. When he had just come from doing this which I have called to your attention, he entered into his northern garden and found that there had been set up for him four targets of Asiatic copper of one palm in their thickness,[17] with twenty cubits[18] between one post and its fellow. Then his majesty appeared in a chariot like Montu in his power. He grasped his bow and gripped four arrows at the same time. So he rode northward, shooting at them like Montu in his regalia. His arrows had come out on the back thereof while he was attacking another post. It was really a deed which had never been done nor heard of by report: shooting at a target of copper an arrow which came out of it and dropped to the ground—except for the king, rich in glory, whom [Amon] made strong, the King of Upper and Lower Egypt: Aa-khepru-Re, heroic like Montu.

Now when he was (still) a lad,[19] he loved his horses and rejoiced in them. It was a strengthening of the heart to work them, to learn their natures, to be skilled in *training* them, and to enter into their ways. When (it) was heard (20) in the palace by his father, the Horus: Mighty Bull, Appearing in Thebes,[20] the heart of his majesty was glad when he heard it, rejoicing at what was said about his eldest son, while he said in his heart: "He it is who will act as Lord for the entire land, without being attacked, while the heart *moves* in valor, rejoicing in strength, though he is (only) a goodly, beloved youth. He is not yet sagacious; he is not (yet) at the time of doing the work of Montu. He is (still) unconcerned with *carnal desire*,[21] (but) he loves strength. It is a god who puts (it) into his heart to act so that Egypt may be protected for him and so that the land defers to him."[22] Then his majesty said to those who were at his side: "Let there be given to him the very best horses in my majesty's stable which is in Memphis, and tell him: 'Take care of them, instil fear into them, make them gallop, and handle them if there be resistance to thee!' " Now after it had been entrusted to the King's Son to take care of horses of the king's stable, well then, he did that which had been entrusted to him. Rashap and Astarte[23] were rejoicing in him for doing all that his heart desired.

He trained horses without their equal: they would not grow tired when he took the reins, nor would they sweat (even) at a high gallop. He would harness *with the bit* in Memphis and stop at the rest-house of (25) Harmakhis,[24] (so that) he might spend a moment there, going around and around it and seeing the charm of this rest-house of Khufu and Khaf-Re, the triumphant. His heart desired to perpetuate their names, (but) he still put it into his heart—so he said—until that which

[4] The pharaoh wore a bull's tail in ceremonial appearance. There follows the account of the elephant hunt, translated on p. 240 above.

[5] Also depicted at the temple of Armant (Mond and Myers, *op.cit.*, Pls. IX, XCIII; translation by Drower, pp. 159-60) is a rhinoceros, which may be this same beast, although the dating of the scene is uncertain. The depiction of the animal is accompanied by its dimensions.

[6] A Sudanese place name which occurs elsewhere, but which cannot be located.

[7] That is, the stela at the Euphrates, p. 239 above. There follows the text about the Battle of Megiddo, p. 234 above.

[8] Drower, in Mond and Myers, *op.cit.*, 184, n. *e*, gives a bibliography of the texts on the pharaoh as a sportsman. They are also treated by B. Van der Walle, *Les rois sportifs de l'ancienne Égypte*, in *Chronique d'Égypte*, No. 26 (1938), 234-57. New material to be added to these is in the Memphis Stela of Amen-hotep II, p. 246 below.

[9] For an uncertain number of years he was coregent with his father, Thut-mose III.

[10] "When he had counted his body," in the sense of developing to maturity.

[11] The god of war.

[12] The same claim in his Amada inscription, p. 247 below. Breasted, *AR*, II, p. 310, n. *d*, calls attention to the legend in Herodotus (III, 21) that Cambyses could not draw the bow of the king of Ethiopia.

[13] The "falcon-boat" was the king's official barge. The word translated "stroke" may come from a root, "to destine, to determine."

[14] Probably about a kilometer, five-eighths of a mile.

[15] About 34 feet.

[16] Probably about 4 miles.

[17] A little less than 3 inches.

[18] About 34 feet.

[19] The word means "puppy," but in no derogatory sense.

[20] Thut-mose III.

[21] "Thirst of the body."

[22] The old warrior king apparently feels that his son's athletic preparation for kingship is god-given.

[23] Two Asiatic deities. See pp. 249-50 below.

[24] The Sphinx at Gizeh, dominated by the pyramids of Khufu (Cheops) and Khaf-Re (Chephren).

his father Re had decreed to him should have come to pass.[25]

After this, when his majesty was made to appear as king, the uraeus-serpent took her place upon his brow, the image of Re[26] was established at its post, and the land was as (in) its first state, at peace under their lord, Aa-khepru-Re. He ruled the Two Lands, and every foreign country was bound under his soles. Then his majesty remembered the place where he had enjoyed himself in the vicinity of the pyramids and of Harmakhis, and One[27] ordered that it be caused that a rest-house be made there, in which was set up a stela of limestone, the face of which was engraved with the Great Name of Aa-khepru-Re, beloved of Harmakhis, given life forever.

[25] He postponed his act of appreciation until he should become king.
[26] The king.
[27] A circumlocution for the king.

The Asiatic Campaigning of Amen-hotep II

Amen-hotep II (about 1447-1421 B.C.) gloried in his reputation for personal strength and prowess. His records therefore contrast with those of his predecessor and father, Thut-mose III, in emphasizing individual achievement. cf. the translations immediately preceding.

A. THE MEMPHIS AND KARNAK STELAE

There are two sources, in partial duplicate, for Amen-hotep's first and second campaigns into Asia. The more extensive text was recently discovered at Memphis, having been reused by a prince of the Twenty-second Dynasty as the ceiling of his burial chamber about 875 B.C. It was published by A. M. Badawi, *Die neue historische Stele Amenophis' II*, in *ASAE*, XLII (1943), 1-23, Pl. I. The more damaged source is a stela standing at the south of the Eighth Pylon at Karnak. It was translated, with notes on antecedent bibliography, by Breasted, *AR*, II, §§781-90. Both stelae were hacked up under the Amarna Revolution and restored in the Nineteenth Dynasty—badly restored, in the case of the Karnak stela. Both stelae were collated in 1946, the Memphis stela being mounted in the Cairo Museum under exhibition No. 6301. The line numbers below follow the Memphis stela.

Year 7, 1st month of the third season, day 25,[1] under the majesty of Horus: Mighty Bull, Sharp of Horns; the Two Goddesses: Rich in *Dread, Made to* Appear in Thebes; Horus of Gold: Carrying Off and Gaining Power over All Lands; King of Upper and Lower Egypt, Lord of the Two Lands: Aa-khepru-Re; the Son of Re, Lord of Diadems, Lord of the Strong Arm: Amen-hotep-the-God-Ruler-of-Heliopolis, given life forever; the good god, likeness of Re, son of Amon upon His throne, for He built him as strong and powerful in distinction to that which had been. His majesty has trod Naharin, *which* his bow has crushed, *being devastated*, carrying off *by victory and power*, like Montu[2] adorned with his equipment. His heart is at rest when he sees them, (for) he has cut off the heads of *the attackers*.

His majesty proceeded to Retenu on his first victorious campaign to extend his frontiers, made *from* the property *of them who are not* loyal to him, his face terrible like (that of) Bastet,[3] like Seth in his moment of raging. His majesty reached Shamash-Edom.[4] He hacked it up in a short moment, like a lion fierce of face, when he *treads* the foreign countries.[5] (His) majesty was in his chariot, *of which* the name was: "Amon, the valiant . . ."[6] List of the booty *of* his arm: living Asiatics: 35; cattle: 22.[7]

His majesty crossed the Orontes[8] (5) on *dangerous* waters, like Rashap.[9] Then he turned about to watch his rear, and he saw a few Asiatics coming *furtively*,[10] adorned with weapons of warfare,[11] to attack the king's army. His majesty *burst* after them like the flight of a divine falcon. The *confidence* of their hearts was slackened, and one after another *fell* upon his fellow, up to their commander.[12] Not a single one was with his majesty, except for himself with his valiant arm. His majesty killed them by shooting.[13] He returned thence, his heart glad like Montu the valiant, when he had triumphed.[14] List of what his majesty captured within this day: two princes and six *maryanu*,[15] *in addition to*

[1] Around 1440 B.C., this date will have fallen in the latter part of May. The translator finds it impossible to reconcile the dates in these several stelae. The Memphis stela places the first campaign in Amen-hotep II's 7th year, the second in his 9th year. The Amada stela below is dated in his 3rd year, to record a celebration in Egypt after the return from the first campaign! Further, it is understood that Amen-hotep was coregent with his father, Thut-mose III, for a minimum of 1 year and up to a possible 11 years. A possible reconciliation would be that the 7th year after the coregency began was the 3rd year of sole reign.

[2] God of war.

[3] The slaughtering cat-goddess.

[4] The Karnak variant, abusively restored (*ASAE*, IV [1903], 126-32): "the town of Shamash-Edom." This town occurs also in the geographical lists of Thut-mose III (p. 243 above), in an association which seems to place it in Palestine.

[5] Karnak variant: "His majesty achieved a happy feat there, (for) his majesty himself took booty. Now he was like a fierce lion, *smit[ing the] foreign countries [of Ret]en[u]*. . . ."

[6] E. Drioton (*ASAE*, XLIV [1945], 5-9) objects that grammatically this should not be the name of the chariot and proposes: "His majesty was in his chariot, victorious Amon who led the success, of which the name is 'Beautiful of Disc.'" This seems somewhat of a strain on the sense.

[7] Karnak variant: "List of the booty of his majesty himself on this day: 26 (perhaps 18) living Asiatics; 19 cattle."

[8] Karnak variant: "1st month of the third season, day 26. His majesty's crossing the ford of the *Yerset* on this day, (*when*) [*he*] caused to cross. . . ." The date is the day following the date given at the beginning of the Memphis stela. The writing *Yerset* for *Yernet*, "Orontes," is probably a product of ignorant restoration under the 19th dynasty.

[9] On the Asiatic god Rashap, see p. 250 below. The Karnak variant: ". . . *being dangerous*, like the strength of Montu, the Theban." Drioton, *op.cit.*, 9-12, argues for the *hithpa'el* of the Hebrew verb *mawag*, "move, shake": "his majesty crossed the Orontes on waters shaking with fury."

[10] Karnak variant: "his majesty turned about to see the ends of the earth. *(Th)en* his majesty saw a few Asiatics coming in chariots."

[11] For once, the Karnak variant is preferable, since it adorns the pharaoh: "Now his majesty was adorned with his weapons of warfare, and his majesty *became terrible in proportion to the hidden strength of* Seth in his hour."

[12] Karnak variant: "They quailed when (they) saw his majesty alone . . . *among* them. Then his majesty felled their commander himself with his battle-axe." Karnak variant follows this with a text garbled by the restoration under the 19th dynasty.

[13] Karnak variant: "Now he carried off this Asiatic *at the side [of his chariot, and also captured]* his team, his chariot, and all his weapons of warfare."

[14] Karnak variant: "His majesty returned in joy of heart (*like*) his father Amon, *who* had given to him the earth, when he had triumphed."

[15] The term *maryanu* (related to the Vedic *márya* "male, noble") was used for Asiatic warriors in this period. cf. p. 22, n.2. Karnak variant: "List of what his majesty captured on this day: . . . , the 2 horses, 1 chariot, a coat of mail, 2 bows, a quiver filled with *arrows*, . . . and an *inlaid axe*."

their chariots, their teams, and all their weapons of warfare.

His majesty, going *south*, reached Ni.[16] Its prince and all his people, male as well as female, were at peace with his majesty, (for) their faces *had received a bedazzlement.*[17] His majesty reached Ikat.[18] He surrounded everyone rebellious to him and killed them, like those who have never existed, put on (their) side, upside down. He returned thence in joy of heart, with this entire country in bondage to him.

Rest in the tent of his majesty[19] in the neighborhood of Tjerekh on the east of Sheshrem. The settlements of Mendjet[20] were plundered. His majesty reached Hetjra.[20] Its prince came out in peace to his majesty, (10) bringing his children and all his goods. Submission was made to his majesty by Unqi.[21] His majesty reached Kadesh. Its prince came out in peace to his majesty. They were made to take the oath *of fealty*, and all their children *as* (*well*). Thereupon his majesty shot at two targets of copper *in hammered work*, in their presence, on the south side of this town.[22] *Excursions* were made in Rebi[20] in the forest, and there were brought back gazelles, *maset*, hares, and *wild*[23] asses without their limit.

His majesty proceeded by chariot to Khashabu,[24] alone, without having a companion. He returned thence in a short moment, and he brought back 16 living *maryanu* on the two sides of his chariot, 20 hands at the foreheads of his horses, and 60 cattle being driven before him. Submission was made to his majesty by this town.

While his majesty was going south in the midst of the *Plain of Sharon*,[25] he met a messenger of the Prince of Naharin, carrying a letter *of clay* at his throat.[26] He took him as a living prisoner at the side of his chariot. His majesty went forth in chariot *by a track*[27] to Egypt, (15) with the *marya*[28] as a living prisoner in the chariot alone with him.

His majesty reached Memphis, his heart joyful, the Mighty Bull. List of this booty:[29] *maryanu*: 550; their wives: 240; Canaanites: 640; princes' children: 232; princes' children, female: 323; *favorites*[30] of the princes of every foreign country: 270 women, in addition to their paraphernalia for entertaining the heart, of silver and gold, *(at) their shoulders*; total: 2,214;[31] horses: 820; chariots: 730, *in addition to* all their weapons of warfare. Now the God's Wife, King's Wife, and King's [Daughter] beheld the victory of his majesty.[32]

Year 9, 3rd month of the first season, day 25.[33] His majesty proceeded to Retenu on his second victorious campaign, against the town of Apheq.[34] It came out in surrender to the great victory of Pharaoh—life, prosperity, health! His majesty went forth by chariot, adorned with weapons of warfare, against the town of Yehem.[35] Now his majesty captured the settlements of Mepesen, together with the settlements of Khettjen, two towns on the west of Socho.[36] Now the Ruler was raging like a divine falcon, his horses flying like a star of heaven. His majesty entered, and (20) its princes, its children, and its women were carried off as living prisoners, and all its retainers similarly, all its goods, without their limit, its cattle, its horses, and all the small cattle *(which) were before him.*

Thereupon his majesty *rested*. The majesty of this august god, Amon, Lord of the Thrones of the Two Lands, came before his majesty in a dream, to give valor to his son, Aa-khepru-Re. His father Amon-Re was the magical protection of his person, guarding the Ruler.

[16] Karnak variant: "2nd month of the third season, day 10. Advancing *on . . . [by going sou]th* toward Egypt. His majesty proceeded by chariot against the town of Ni." The date will have been two weeks after the fording of the Orontes. Ni was somewhere near the bend of the Euphrates; cf. p. 240, n.18 above. The Karnak text tends to confirm the meaning, "to go south," for *em khentit*, since movement toward Egypt would be south, but the same doubt arises as on p. 239, n.16 above.

[17] Karnak variant: "Now the Asiatics of this town, male as well as female, were upon their wall, praising his majesty and . . . the good god."

[18] Karnak variant: "Now his majesty heard that certain [of] the Asiatics who were in the town of Ikat were *conspiring* to accomplish the abandonment of his majesty's garrison . . . in this town, in order to turn upside down . . . who was loyal to his majesty. . . . Then everyone rebellious to him was surrounded in this town. . . . He [*killed*] them immediately, and he quieted [this] town, . . . *the whole country*." The two texts agree on the writing of the town Ikat, the location of which is unknown. By a simple emendation one could read *Ikarit*, Ugarit.

[19] Karnak variant: "2nd month of the third season, day 20. . . . in the encampment which was made. . . ." The date would be 10 days after that of n.16 above.

[20] Unknown.

[21] Territory between the Euphrates and the sea. Thus the Kadesh which follows was Kadesh on the Orontes.

[22] Emphasizing the pharaoh's skill at sport (pp. 243-45 above), in order to impress the locals.

[23] Here written *khem*, with determinative of motion, as if related to the word "ignorant," but probably related to the later *'aa shema* "roaming =wild ass." The *maset* animal is unknown.

[24] Egyptian *Kh-sh-b*, cuneiform *Khashabu*, temptingly identified by Badawi with Hasbeya, west of Mt. Hermon.

[25] The stela is broken at this point, but *pa 'am . . w sau-ri-na* is probably visible, to be completed to "the *'Emeq* of Sharon."

[26] Although the text shows *sh'atu in*, there can be little doubt that it is to be corrected to *sh'at sin* "a letter of clay." "At his throat" would mean "hanging around his neck," probably in a pouch.

[27] An unknown *em sibiny*, with a determinative which looks like two plants. The tentative translation assumes that it is Hebrew *shebîl* "path"—perhaps "two tracks," not a road, but two traces of chariot wheels across the wilderness—and that the determinative is borrowed from the root which appears in Assyrian *shubultu* "ear (of grain)."

[28] This seems to be the only occurrence of the singular *marya*, for what normally appears in a plural or collective, *maryanu*, n.15 above. Of course, the writing here may be defective.

[29] The Karnak variant has a date: ". . . [*of the third*] *season*, day 27," followed by a broken and uncertain context, which seems to apply to the temple of Ptah at Memphis: "His majesty came forth from the House . . . of the Beautiful of Face." Then, "[*His majesty*] proceeded [*to*] Memphis, bearing the booty which he had carried off from the country of Retenu. List of the booty: living *maryanu*: 550; the[ir wi]ves: 240; *kin . . . of fine* gold: 6,800 *deben*; copper: 500,000 *deben*; . . . *total: 2 heads*; horses: 210; and chariots: 300." Thus, the Memphite text's *kin'anu*, which can only be understood as *Kena'ani* "Canaanite," has been turned by the Karnak text into some object related to gold—perhaps **kena'ah* "baggage, pack," of Jer. 10:17. The gold would amount to about 1,700 lb. Troy, the copper to 125,000 lb. Troy.

[30] Or "(woman) singers," particularly in view of their entertainment paraphernalia. However, 270 women minstrels seems a very high number, and the translation assumes that these were simply harem women, who would also have entertainment paraphernalia.

[31] *Sic*, 2,214, although the total by addition comes to 2,255.

[32] Probably the queen Ti-'aa or the queen Hat-shepsut II. Karnak variant: "The entire land beheld the victory of his majesty."

[33] See n.1 above. About 1440 B.C., the present date would fall in the early part of November, an unusual season for an Egyptian campaign in Asia.

[34] Of several Apheqs, the one at Ras el-Ain in Palestine seems to fit the apparent itinerary best.

[35] On Yehem see p. 235, n.18 above.

[36] Of these three names, only Socho can be identified. Karnak variant: "His majesty . . . ed the tribe of Khettjen . . . Now the prince . . . [*abandoned*] the city for fear of his majesty. His princes (or officials?), his women, his children, and all his [*retain*]*ers* as well, were carried off. List of that which his majesty himself captured: . . . , his horses."

His majesty went forth by chariot at dawn, against the town of Iteren, as well as Migdol-*yen*.[37] Then his majesty—life, prosperity, health!—prevailed like the prevailing of Sekhmet, like Montu over Thebes. He carried off their princes: 34; *merui*:[38] 57; living Asiatics: 231; hands: 372; horses: 54; chariots: 54; *in addition to* all the weapons of warfare, every able-bodied man[39] of Retenu, their children, their wives, and all their property. After his majesty saw the very abundant plunder, they were made into living prisoners, and two ditches were made *around all of them. Behold*, they were filled with fire, and his majesty kept watch over it until daybreak, while his (25) battle-axe was in his right hand, alone, without a single one with him, while the army was far from him, *far from hearing* the cry of Pharaoh.[40] Now after daybreak of a second day, his majesty went forth by chariot at dawn, adorned with the equipment of Montu. The day of the Feast of the Royal Coronation of his majesty:[41] Anaharath was plundered. List of the booty of his majesty alone within this day: living *maryanu*: 17; children of princes: 6; living Asiatics: 68; hands: 123; teams: 7; chariots of silver and gold: 7; *in addition to* all their weapons of warfare; *bulls*: 443; cows: 370; and all (kinds of) cattle, without their limit. Then the army presented very abundant booty, without its limit.

His majesty reached *Huakti*.[42] The Prince of Geba-Shumen,[43] whose name was Qaqa,[44] was brought, his wife, his children, and all his retainers as well. Another prince was appointed in his place.[45]

His majesty reached the town of Memphis, his heart appeased over all countries, with all lands beneath his soles. List of the plunder which his majesty carried off: princes of Retenu: *127*;[46] *brothers* of princes: (30) 179; *Apiru*:[47] 3,600; living *Shasu*: 15,200; *Kharu*: 36,300; living *Neges*: 15,070; the *adherents* thereof: *30,652*; total: 89,600 men;[48] similarly their goods, without their limit; all small cattle belonging to them; all (kinds of) cattle, without their limit; chariots of silver and gold: 60; painted chariots of wood: 1,032; *in addition to* all their weapons of warfare, *being 13,050*;[49] through the strength of his august father, his beloved, who is thy[50] magical protection, *Amon*, who decreed to him valor.

Now when the Prince of Naharin, the Prince of Hatti, and the Prince of Shanhar[51] heard of the great victory which I had made, *each one vied with his fellow in making offering*, while they said in their hearts to the father of their fathers, in order to beg peace from his majesty, seeking that there be given to them the breath of life: "We are under thy sway, *for* thy palace, O Son of Re: Amen-hotep-the-God-Ruler-of-Heliopolis, ruler of rulers, raging lion *in* . . . this land forever!"[52]

37 Two unknown places. The translation ignores the final *-t*, which might make a Migdol-yeneth.

38 Corrupt. Hardly to be emended to *maryanu*. Possibly to be emended to read: "their serfs."

39 "Every strong of arm," i.e. every adult.

40 This episode was sheer bravura on the part of the pharaoh, of a spectacular nature in order to create a legend of his personal prowess.

41 Which was the 4th month of the first season, day 1 (cf. A. H. Gardiner in *JEA*, xxxi [1945], 27), or 6 days after the date against n.33 above.

42 Perhaps "the vicinity of 'Akti." In either case, unknown.

43 Here *Qeb'asemen*. Elsewhere *Keb'asemen*, which M. Burchardt, *Die altkanaanäischen Fremdworte und Eigennamen im Aegyptischen* (Leipzig, 1909), ii, 49-50, makes into a possible Geba-shemoneh, "Hill of Eight."

44 Badawi suggests a name like Gargur.

45 cf. the policy of Thut-mose III on Asiatic princes, p. 239 above.

46 Or 217 or 144.

47 The appearance of the *Apiru* (cf. pp. 22, 255, 261) in a list of Asiatic captives is unusual. They are listed as the third element in a list, preceded by princes and princes' brothers(?), followed by three terms having geographic connotation—*Shasu*, the Bedouin, especially to the south of Palestine; *Kharu* "Horites," the settled people of Palestine-Syria; and *Neges*, perhaps "Nukhashshe," the people of northern Syria—and terminated by an expression of attribution, here translated: "the adherents(?) thereof," with a miscarved *ẖr* sign, but perhaps to be read: "the families thereof," with the word *abet* "family." The *Apiru* are notably greater in number than the princes and princes' brothers; they are notably fewer in number than the three regional listees or the retainers (or families). It is quite clear that the Egyptians recognized the *Apiru* as a distinct entity from other peoples, clearly countable. See also A. H. Gardiner, *Ancient Egyptian Onomastica*, i, 184*.

B. THE AMADA AND ELEPHANTINE STELAE

A different treatment of Amen-hotep II's achievements emphasizes the nature of his triumphs in Egypt after his return from Asiatic campaigning. This is also on two monuments, both published in Ch. Kuentz, *Deux stèles d'Aménophis II* (*Bibliothèque d'Étude*, x, Cairo, 1925). The stela in the Temple of Amada in Nubia was published by H. Gauthier, *Le temple d'Amada* (*Les temples immergés de la Nubie*, xiii, Cairo, 1913-1926), 19 ff., Pl. x. The stela from Elephantine is now divided between Cairo (No. 34019: P. Lacau, *Stèles du nouvel empire* [*Catalogue général . . . du Musée du Caire*, Cairo, 1909], 38-40, Pl. xii) and Vienna (W. Wreszinski, *Aegyptische Inschriften aus dem K. K. Hofmuseum in Wien* [Leipzig, 1906], No. 141). Translation in Breasted, *AR*, ii, §§791-97. The line numbers below follow the Amada Stela.

Year 3, 3rd month of the third season, day 15,[53] under the majesty of . . . Amen-hotep-the-God-Ruler-of-Heliopolis[54] . . . He is a king very weighty of arm: there is none who can draw his bow[55] in his army, among the rulers of foreign countries,[56] or the princes of Retenu, because his strength is so much greater than (that of) any (other) king who has existed. Raging like a panther when he treads the field of battle; there is none who can fight in his vicinity. . . . Prevailing instantly over every foreign country, whether people or horses, (though) they have come in millions of men, (for) they knew not that Amon-Re (5) was loyal to him.[57] . . . (15) . . . Then his majesty caused that this stela be

48 The figures given total 101,128, instead of 89,600. Even though two of the figures give questionable readings, no clear alternatives will supply the total given on the stela.

49 The phrasing is peculiar, and a palimpsestic text makes the reading uncertain.

50 *Sic*, but read "his."

51 Shin'ar, or Babylonia. Gardiner, *Ancient Egyptian Onomastica*, i, 209* ff.

52 The end of the inscription has been badly garbled by the restoration of the 19th dynasty. Of course, the historicity of the frightened submissiveness of distant and independent rulers is out of the question, and represents a literary device for the climax of a swashbuckling account.

53 See n.1 above. Around 1440 B.C., the present date would have fallen in July.

54 The long titulary of the king and many of the epithets applied to him are omitted in this translation.

55 See the claims made for him in the text describing his athletic accomplishments, p. 244 above.

56 "Rulers of foreign countries" here seems to be distinct from the princes of Syria-Palestine, and it was the term from which the designation "Hyksos" arose; cf. pp. 20, n.16; 229, n.9 above.

57 "Was upon his water," which normally means: "was subject to him."

made and set up in this temple at the place of the Station of the Lord,[58] engraved with the Great Name of the Lord of the Two Lands, the Son of Re: Amen-hotep-the-God-Ruler-of-Heliopolis, in the house of his fathers, the gods, after his majesty had returned from Upper Retenu, when he had overthrown all his foes, extending the frontiers of Egypt on the first victorious campaign.[53]

His majesty returned in joy of heart to his father Amon, when he had slain with his own mace the seven princes who had been in the district of Takhshi,[59] who had been put upside down at the prow of his majesty's falcon-boat, of which the name is "Aa-khepru-Re, the Establisher of the Two Lands." Then six men of these enemies were hanged on the face of the wall of Thebes, and the hands as well.[60] Then the other foe was taken upstream to the land of Nubia and hanged to the wall of Napata,[61] to show his majesty's victories forever and ever in all lands and all countries of the Negro land; inasmuch as he had carried off the southerners and bowed down the northerners, the (very) ends of the (20) entire earth upon which Re shines, (so that) he might set his frontier where he wishes without being opposed, according to the decree of his father Re. . . .

A Syrian Captive Colony in Thebes

Little is known of the activities of Thut-mose IV (about 1421-1413 B.C.) in Asia. The energies of Thut-mose III and of Amen-hotep II may have left him little need for military prowess. Some of the Asiatic regions which he claimed to have conquered will be found in the lists on pp. 242-43 above. He continued his predecessors' practice of introducing foreign captives into the Egyptian temple estates, as is evidenced by a brief text on a stela found in his mortuary temple in western Thebes. The inscription was published by W. M. F. Petrie, *Six Temples at Thebes* (London, 1896), Pl. I, No. 7, and translated by Breasted, *AR*, II, §821.

For the "Dream Stela" of Thut-mose IV, see p. 449 below. For a hymn of victory of Amen-hotep III, see pp. 373-375 below.

The settlement of the Fortification of Men-khepru-Re[1] with the Syrians[2] [of] his majesty's capturing in the town of *Gez*[*er*].[3]

Scenes of Asiatic Commerce in Theban Tombs

The Egyptian Empire brought an abundance of Asiatic goods into Egypt. The formal Egyptian records called all of this "tribute," whether it was enforced dues, the product of commerce, or came as princely gifts. Scenes in the Theban tombs often show subservient Asiatics humbly offering their produce and begging mercy from the pharaoh.

a

The first instance is from the Theban tomb (No. 100) of Rekh-mi-Re, vizier under Thut-mose III (about 1490-1436 B.C.). In two registers Asiatics are depicted bringing their characteristic goods to the vizier. It is definitively published by N. de G. Davies, *The Tomb of Rekh-mi-Re at Thebes* (*Publications of the Metropolitan Museum of Art. Egyptian Expedition*, XI, New York, 1943), I, 27-30; II, Pls. XXI-XXIII. Details of the scenes are shown in color by Davies, *Paintings from the Tomb of Rekh-mi-Re at Thebes* (*Publications of the Metropolitan Museum of Art. Egyptian Expedition*, X, New York, 1935), Pls. IX-XII. The text is also in K. Sethe, *Urkunden der 18. Dynastie* (*Urk.*, IV, Leipzig, 1909), IV, 1101-03.

Coming in peace by the princes of Retenu and all northern countries of the ends of Asia, bowing down in humility, with their tribute upon their backs, seeking that there be given them the breath of life and desiring to be subject to his majesty, for they have seen his very great victories and the terror of him has mastered their hearts. Now it is the Hereditary Prince, Count, Father and Beloved of the God, great trusted man of the Lord of the Two Lands, Mayor and Vizier, Rekh-mi-Re, who receives the tribute of all foreign countries . . .

Presenting the children of the princes of the southern countries, along with the children of the princes of the northern countries, who were brought as the best of the booty of his majesty, the King of Upper and Lower Egypt: Men-kheper-Re, given life, from all foreign countries, to fill the workshop and to be serfs of the divine offerings of his father Amon, Lord of the Thrones of the Two Lands, according as there have been given to him all foreign countries together in his grasp, with their princes prostrated under his sandals. . . .

b

Men-kheper-Re-seneb was High Priest of Amon under Thut-mose III. The scenes and texts in his Theban tomb (No. 86) give us a suggestion of the importance of the riches of Asia to the temple of the imperial god Amon. See N. and N. de G. Davies, *The Tombs of Menkheperrasonb, Amenmose, and Another* (*Theban Tomb Series*, V, London, 1933), Pls. IV, VII. Texts in K. Sethe, *op.cit.*, 929-30. Details in color in N. M. Davies and A. H. Gardiner, *Ancient Egyptian Paintings* (Chicago, 1936), I, Pls. XXI-XXIV.

In the scenes, an individual labeled "the Prince of Keftiu"[1] prostrates himself, "the Prince of Hatti" kneels in adoration, "the Prince of Tunip"[2] presents his infant son, and "the Prince of Kadesh" offers an elaborate vessel. A procession of Asiatics voices their submission in a broken text, of which the final words are legible: "The fear of thee is in all lands. Thou hast annihilated the lands of Mitanni; thou hast laid waste their towns, and their princes are in caves." The general legend for this scene runs:

[58] The king's official post in a temple; cf. pp. 375, 446 below.

[59] In the Damascus area. The temple scenes often show the pharaoh clubbing captured enemies with his mace. Our text shows that this depiction had its reality, carried further by the public and derogatory exposure of the enemies, here at the prow of the royal barges and on city walls.

[60] The hands of the enemy were cut off as recordable trophies.

[61] Near the Fourth Cataract of the Nile.

[1] Thut-mose IV. The "Fortification of Men-khepru-Re" may be a name for the compound of his mortuary temple, including the temple storehouses, workshops, and quarters for the temple serfs.

[2] Egyptian *Kharu*, or Horites.

[3] *Qedj* . . . , probably to be completed *Qedjer*, Gezer; less likely, to *Qedjet*, Gaza, which was more often written *Gedjet* in Egyptian.

[1] Crete and the Aegean world, probably including the Aegeanized coastlands.

[2] A city-state of north Syria.

Giving praise to the Lord of the Two Lands, kissing the ground to the good god by the princes of every land, as they extol the victories of his majesty, with their tribute upon their backs, consisting of every [substance] of God's Land:[3] silver, gold, lapis lazuli, turquoise, and every august costly stone, seeking that there be given them the breath of life.

c

Two generations later, under Thut-mose IV (about 1421-1413 B.C.), the form of expression remains the same, as in the Theban tomb (No. 74) of Tjaneni, an officer of the Egyptian army. The texts were published by Sethe, *op.cit.*, 1007; full publication of the tomb by J. V. Scheil, *Le tombeau de Djanni* (*Mission archéologique française au Caire. Mémoires*, v, Paris, 1894), 591-603.

Presenting the tribute of Retenu and the produce of the northern countries: silver, gold, turquoise, and all costly stones of God's Land, by the princes of all foreign countries, when they come to make supplication to the good god and to beg breath for their nostrils, and by the real Scribe of the King, his beloved, the Commander of the Army, and Scribe of Recruits, Tjaneni.

d

The Amarna Revolution drastically altered the direction of empire, but the modes of expression remained much the same—as, for example, in the Memphite tomb of Hor-em-heb, pp. 250-251 below. Huy, the Viceroy of Nubia under Tut-ankh-Amon (about 1361-1352 B.C.), continues the earlier scenes and texts in his Theban tomb (No. 40). The publication is N. de G. Davies and A. H. Gardiner, *The Tomb of Huy* (*Theban Tomb Series*, iv, London, 1926), 28-30, Pls. xix-xx. Translated in Breasted, *AR*, ii, §§1027-33.

Presenting tribute to the Lord of the Two Lands, the produce of the wretched Retenu, by the King's Envoy to Every Foreign Country, the King's Son of Ethiopia, the Overseer of Southern Countries, Amen-hotep,[4] the triumphant.

Vessels of all the choicest and best of their countries: silver, gold, lapis lazuli, turquoise, and every august costly stone.

The princes of Upper Retenu, who knew not Egypt since the time of the god,[5] begging for peace before his majesty. They say: "[Give] us the breath which thou givest! *Then* we shall relate thy victories. There are none rebellious in thy vicinity, (but) every land is at peace!"

[3] The orient as the land of the rising sun. Here Syria-Palestine—as the shipping source of the goods, not the native source of those ores listed.

[4] Huy was an abbreviated form of the name Amen-hotep.

[5] Since the time of the creator, i.e. for a long time.

The Egyptians and the Gods of Asia

In earlier history the Egyptians had identified foreign gods with their own deities, so that the goddess of Byblos was a Hat-Hor to them and various Asiatic gods were Seth to them.[1] This process of extending their own into other countries continued under the Empire. Ramses III built a temple of Amon in Asia,[2] and Ptah had a sanctuary at Ashkelon.[3] There were also two cosmopolitan forces at work: a worship of Asiatic gods as such at their shrines in Asia and a domestication of Asiatic gods in Egypt.

The first of these processes began at least as early as the time of Thut-mose III (15th century B.C.). A stela found at Beisan in Palestine shows the Egyptian architect Amen-em-Opet and his son worshiping the local god Mekal. "Mekal, the god of Beth-Shan," is depicted as unmistakably Asiatic in features and dress, with a pointed beard and a conical headdress with horns and streamers. Amen-em-Opet addresses a perfectly normal Egyptian mortuary prayer to this god.[4]

Beisan also yielded a stela of the Ramses III level (12th century B.C.), on which an Egyptian is shown worshiping the goddess "Anath, Lady of Heaven, Mistress of All the Gods."[5]

Near Sheikh Sa'ad, east of the Sea of Galilee, a badly worn stela was found depicting Ramses II making offering to a deity with an elaborate headdress. The name of this deity, with some uncertainty, might be read as Adon-Zaphon, "Lord of the North."[6]

From about the same period (13th century B.C.) comes a stela found at Ugarit (Ras Shamra) on the north Phoenician coast. Here the "Royal Scribe and Chief Steward of *the Palace* Memi" addresses his mortuary prayer to "Baal-Zaphon, the great god," a being with the Asiatic conical cap with streamers.[7]

From the end of the Eighteenth Dynasty on (14th century B.C.), there is an abundance of evidence on Asiatic gods worshiped in Egypt. The most frequently mentioned deity was Baal.[8] As the god of the heavens, the mountain tops, and of thunder—the Semitic Baal-Shamaim—he was the counterpart of the Egyptian god Seth, and his name was used in figures of speech relating to the pharaoh in battle:

His battle cry is like (that of) Baal in the heavens.[9]

In this terrorizing capacity the texts equate him with the Egyptian war-gods Montu and Seth.[10] He was used in magical texts to frighten away evil forces:

Baal smites thee with the cedar tree which is in his hand.[11]

However, his role might be beneficent, as when a woman musician wrote from Memphis, appealing to various gods on behalf of her correspondent:

. . . to the Ennead which is in the House of Ptah, to

[1] For example, such was still the case in the Egyptian-Hittite treaty at the time of Ramses II (13th century); cf. pp. 200-201 above: Seth of Hatti, equated to Teshub, lord of the land of Hatti; Seth of the town of Aleppo, equated to Teshub of Aleppo, etc.; also Re, lord of the sky, equated to Shamash, lord of the sky. cf. p. 231, n.9.

[2] pp. 260-261.

[3] p. 263.

[4] A. Rowe, *The Topography and History of Beth-Shan* (Philadelphia, 1930), i, 14-15; Pl. 33.

[5] *ibid.*, 32-33; Pl. 50, No. 2.

[6] So W. F. Albright, in *AASOR*, vi (1926), 45-46, n.104. This so-called "Job Stone" was originally published by G. Schumacher in an article by A. Erman, in *ZDPV*, xv (1892), 205-11. Erman, in *ZAeS*, xxxi (1893), 100-01, tentatively read the name as Arcana-Zaphon.

[7] C. F.-A. Schaeffer, *Ugaritica*, i (Paris, 1939), 39-41.

[8] Most of the occurrences of the name of Baal in Egyptian texts were covered by H. Gressmann, in *Beihefte zur ZAW*, xxxiii (1918), 191 ff.

[9] The Epigraphic Survey, *Later Historical Records of Ramses III* (*Medinet Habu*, ii, *OIP*, ix, Chicago, 1932), Pls. 79:22; 87:2-3. Translated in W. F. Edgerton and J. A. Wilson, *Historical Records of Ramses III* (*SAOC*, 12, Chicago, 1936), 73, 94.

[10] In the Poem on Ramses II's Battle of Kadesh, a Luxor text makes the pharaoh say: "I was like Seth in his time (of might)," where the Abydos text has "Montu" and a papyrus text has "Baal" (J. A. Wilson, in *AJSL*, xliii [1927], 271). The same poem puts into the mouths of the enemy the words: "It is not a man who is in our midst, (but) Seth, the great in strength, or Baal in person," (*ibid.*, 272).

[11] Papyrus Leyden 345, recto, iv 12-v 2, quoted in Gressmann, *op.cit.*, 201.

Baalat, to Qedesh, to *Meni*, (to) Baali-Zaphon, to Sopdu, . . .[12]

Baal had his own priesthood in Egypt from the late Eighteenth Dynasty on.[13] Toward the end of the Empire, the presence in Egypt of such a personal name as Baal-khepeshef, "Baal-is-(Upon)-His-Sword,"[14] corresponding to good Egyptian names like Amon-her-khepeshef, Montu-her-khepeshef, and Seth-her-khepeshef, shows the domestication of this immigrant god from Asia.

Also popular in Egypt were the Semitic goddesses Anath and Astarte (Ishtar).[15] They served as war-goddesses, with a particular interest in horses and chariots. As early as Thut-mose IV (late 15th century), the pharaoh was described as "mighty in the chariot like Astarte."[16] In a poem in praise of the king's war chariot (13th century), a dual part of the chariot is likened to Anath and Astarte.[17] It was said of Ramses III (12th century):

Montu and Seth are with him in every fray; Anath and Astarte are a shield to him.[18]

By the Eighteenth Dynasty, Astarte had become a goddess of healing in Egypt, in the name of "Astar of Syria."[19] Anath, Astarte, and Qedesh each bore the Egyptian title, "Lady of Heaven," generally equivalent to the Hebrew *Meleketh Hash-shamaim*, "Queen of the Heavens." Like Baal, Astarte had her own priesthood in Egypt.[20] The egyptianization of Anath and Astarte is indicated by the compounding of their names into personal names of normal formation.[21]

Something has already been said about the goddess Qedesh, "the Holy," and about the god Rashap (or Resheph or Reshpu).[22] These two, together with the Egyptian god Min, are associated on a stela in Vienna, where the goddess Qedesh stands on the back of a lion.[23] So also, on a stela in the British Museum, a goddess Kenet stands on the back of a lion, flanked by Min and by "Rashap, the great god, lord of heaven, and ruler of the Ennead."[24] On a stela in Turin are associated "Qedesh, Lady of Heaven, Mistress of All the gods, the Eye of Re, without her peer," and "Rashap, the great god, lord of heaven, ruler of the Ennead, and lord of eternity."[25] A stela in Aberdeen shows the worship of "Rashap-Shulman."[26] Rashap, like Baal, was a war-god and thunder-god. It was said of Ramses III's army:

The chariot-warriors are as mighty as Rashaps.[27]

Finally, as a forceful and exotic deity, Rashap was used in magical texts, as in this formula against some ailment:

with the poisons of the Upper God and Neker, his wife; the poisons of Rashap and Item, his wife.[28]

Texts from the Tomb of General Hor-em-heb

History may reach a point where the repetition of old and successful formulae is more important than the recording of contemporary events. The historian often cannot be sure whether he is dealing with truthful records or with stereotyped claims of accomplishment. The following extracts constitute a case in point. Under the Amarna Revolution, Egypt lost the greater part of her Asiatic Empire. A commander of the Egyptian armies at that time was the Hor-em-heb who later became pharaoh (reigning about 1349-1319 B.C.). While still an official, he erected a tomb at Sakkarah, of which the remains are now scattered in three continents. The claims of foreign conquest and tribute may enlarge a limited reality or may be the protestations which covered failure.

The texts of (a) below are in the British Museum, the Cairo Museum, and the Louvre; of (b) in a private collection in Alexandria; of (c) in the Civic Museum in Bologna; of (d) in the Rijksmuseum at Leyden; and of (e) in the Vienna Museum. The bibliography for these pieces is in B. Porter and R. L. B. Moss, *Topographical Bibliography of Ancient Egyptian Hieroglyphic Texts, Reliefs, and Paintings, III. Memphis* (Oxford, 1931), 195-97. Translations in Breasted, *AR*, III, §§1-21.

a

The titles of Hor-em-heb in his tomb show his responsibilities toward Asiatic countries. He was the "Hereditary Prince, Fan-

12 Papyrus Sallier IV, verso, i 5-6; text in A. H. Gardiner, *Late-Egyptian Miscellanies* (*Bibliotheca Aegyptiaca*, VII, Brussels, 1937), 89. The Ennead of gods in Memphis and Sopdu are good Egyptian, although the latter, as a god of the east, integrates with the Asiatic deities here. Baalat is, of course, the female counterpart of Baal. Baali-Zaphon, "the Baals of the North," may not be a true plural, but a plural of majesty. cf. the Baal-Zaphon, which Exodus 14:2 uses as a place-name on the Asiatic frontier of Egypt. The goddess Qedesh will be discussed below. The reading "Meni" is quite uncertain and attempts to relate the name to a god "Fortune" in Isaiah 65:11. The Egyptian might equally be read "Ini."

13 C. R. Lepsius, *Denkmäler aus Aegypten und Aethiopien*, Text (ed. by E. Naville *et al*; Leipzig, 1897), I, 16, shows a Memphite individual of the time of Akh-en-Aton, who was "Prophet of Baal" and "Prophet of Astarte." By the Twenty-second Dynasty, a family had several generations in which there had been a "Prophet of the House of Baal in Memphis," *Aegyptische Inschriften aus den staatlichen Museen zu Berlin* (ed. by G. Roeder; Leipzig, 1924), II, 233, no. 8169.

14 A. H. Gardiner, *The Wilbour Papyrus* (Oxford, 1941), I, Pl. 31, lxvi:28. A team of Ramses III's horses bears the same name; the Epigraphic Survey, *Earlier Historical Records of Ramses III* (*Medinet Habu*, I, *OIP*, VIII; Chicago 1930), Pl. 23:59.

15 For the two as wives of Seth, see p. 15. For the legend of Astarte and the Sea, see pp. 17-18. For a cult-seat of Astarte in the city Ramses, see p. 470. Much of the material on Astarte is assembled by H. Ranke in *Studies Presented to F. Ll. Griffith* (London, 1932), 412-18.

16 H. Carter and P. E. Newberry, *The Tomb of Thoutmôsis IV* (*Catalogue général . . . du Musée du Caire*, Westminster, 1904), 27, Pl. x. As late as the Ptolemaic period, a goddess depicted in a war chariot was designated as "Astarte, Mistress of Horses, Lady of the Chariot"; E. Naville, *Textes rélatifs au mythe d'Horus* (Geneva, 1870), Pl. XIII. For Asti (Astarte) on horseback, with shield and spear, in the 19th dynasty, see C. R. Lepsius, *Denkmäler aus Aegypten und Aethiopien* (Berlin, 1849-59), III, 138, o; *JEA*, IV (1917), 251.

17 W. R. Dawson and T. E. Peet in *JEA*, XIX (1933), 167-74; translated in Erman, *LAE*, 280-81.

18 Edgerton and Wilson, *op.cit.*, 75. For Astarte with shield and spear, see W. M. F. Petrie, *Memphis*, I (London, 1909), Pl. XV, No. 37, of the 19th dynasty. For Anath similarly equipped, see British Museum stela 191 (Exhibition No. 646), in *A Guide to the Egyptian Collections of the British Museum* (London, 1909), opp. p. 248. Papyrus Chester Beatty VII, verso i 8-9 (*Hieratic Papyri in the British Museum. Third Series. Chester Beatty Gift*, ed. by A. H. Gardiner [London, 1935], I, 62-63) has a passage in a myth about Anath, in which her warlike nature is taken up in the words: "Anath, the goddess, the victorious, a woman acting (as) a man, clad as a male and girt as a female." For Anath in the name of Seti I's team, see p. 254. For the delight of Astarte and the god Rashap in horsemanship, see p. 244.

19 Ranke, *op.cit.*, gives a stela of worship to "Astar of Kharu" and a statuette with a prayer for health addressed to "Asti of Kharu, the Lady of Heaven, the Mistress of the Two Lands, and the Mistress of All the Gods," and to "Qedesh, the Lady of Heaven and Mistress of All the Gods."

20 See n.13 above; also E. von Bergmann in *Recueil de travaux . . .*, XII (1892), 10, and H. Brugsch, *Recueil de monuments égyptiens* (Leipzig, 1862), I, Pl. IV, 3, the last being a prophet of the Moon, of the 5th dynasty pharaoh Sahu-Re, and of Astarte, "the Lady of the Two Lands."

21 e.g. Anath-em-nekhu, "Anath is a Protection" (H. Ranke, *Die ägyptischen Personennamen*, I [Glückstadt, 1935], 69:15) and Astart-em-heb, "Astarte is in Festival" (*ibid.*, 71:7).

22 Notes 12, 18, and 19 above.

23 E. von Bergmann, in *Recueil de travaux . . .*, VII (1886), 190-91.

24 This is the British Museum stela showing Anath in war panoply, mentioned in n.18 above.

25 H. Brugsch, *Thesaurus inscriptionum Aegyptiacarum*, VI (Leipzig, 1891), 1434. A late 18th dynasty stela (*Hieroglyphic Texts from Egyptian Stelae, etc., in the British Museum*, VII, ed. by H. R. Hall [London, 1925], Pl. 41) has a hymn to Rashap.

26 F. Ll. Griffith, in *PSBA*, XXII (1900), 271-72, with Plate; W. F. Albright, in *AfO*, VII (1931-32), 167.

27 Edgerton and Wilson, *op.cit.*, 24. Here the plural may be a true plural or a plural of majesty.

28 A passage in a Leyden papyrus (I 343), discussed by A. H. Gardiner in *ZAeS*, XLIII (1906), 97. The "Upper God" is assumed to be the sun-god, and Neker may stand for the Babylonian Ningal. The wife of Rashap, as here given, is unknown, but might be a goddess Edom.

Bearer on the King's Right Hand, and Chief Commander of the Army"; the "attendant of the King in his footsteps in the foreign countries of the south and the north"; the "King's Messenger in front of his army to the foreign countries of the south and the north"; and the "Sole Companion, he who is by the feet of his lord on the battlefield on that day of killing Asiatics."[1]

b

Hor-em-heb was sent by an unnamed pharaoh to bring tribute from countries to the south of Egypt, for the occasion of the formal presentation of tribute of Africa and Asia.

... He was sent as King's Messenger as far as the sun disc shines, returning when he had triumphed, when his [conquest] was effected. No land could stand before him, (but) he [*cap*]*tured* it in the completion of a moment. His name is pronounced *in* [*awe* in] the country of . . . ,[2] and he does not [*leave*] *off* in going north. Now his majesty appeared upon the throne of the offering of tribute, which the [countries] of the south and the north offered, while the Hereditary Prince Hor-em-heb, the triumphant, was standing beside ...

c

The following lines probably come from the same scene of the presentation of foreign tribute.

... introducing the tribute into its place and what was selected from it to clothe . . . , . . . the army, filling the storehouse of the god, who was satisfied of heart, . . . which Syria gave to them. . . . he was serviceable to the king.

d

When Hor-em-heb introduced to the unnamed pharaoh Asiatics, the king was graciously pleased to reward the general with gold.

. . . The princes of all foreign countries come to beg life from him. It is the Hereditary Prince, Sole Companion, and Royal Scribe Hor-em-heb, the triumphant, who will say, when he answers [*the king*: "*The countries*] which knew not Egypt—they are under thy feet forever and ever, for Amon has decreed them to thee. They mustered [*every*] foreign country [*into a confederacy*] unknown since Re. Their battle cry in their hearts was as one. (But) thy name is flaming [against them, *and they become*] subject to thee. Thou art the Re [*who causes*] that they [*abandon*] their towns . . ."

e

One of Hor-em-heb's responsibilities was the relocation of foreign refugees or transplanted peoples.

. . . foreigners, and others have been put into their places.[3] . . . destroying them, as well as desolating their towns and casting fire . . . The Great of Strength[4] will send his mighty sword before . . . Their countries are starving, and they live like the beasts of the desert. . . saying:[5] "Certain of the foreigners who know not how they may live have come [begging the] . . . of Pharaoh —life, prosperity, health!—after the manner of their fathers' fathers since the first times,[6] . . . So Pharaoh—life, prosperity, health!—gives them into your hands to guard their boundaries."

[1] The only one of the Amarna pharaohs who has left us visible claim to foreign conquest was Tut-ankh-Amon, whose decorated box (N. M. Davies and A. H. Gardiner, *Ancient Egyptian Paintings* [Chicago, 1936], II, Pl. LXXVIII) shows a battle scene of the pharaoh decimating the Asiatic enemy, with the legend: "The good god, son of Amon, hero without his peer, possessor of a strong arm, crushing hundred-thousands and making them prostrate." One may hold some scepticism about the historicity of any such encounter.

[2] In view of the following clause and the probable balanced statement of south and north, this unreadable name was probably that of a country to the south of Egypt—perhaps Nepau, which appears in a long list of African regions conquered by Thut-mose III.

[3] A reference to the system of transplanting conquered peoples.

[4] The pharaoh.

[5] This seems to be a charge by Hor-em-heb to his subordinate officers.

[6] The perennial Bedouin desire to sojourn in the fertile Nile valley. cf. pp. 258-259, 446.

Tut-ankh-Amon's Restoration after the Amarna Revolution

The Amarna movement barely survived the reign of Akh-en-Aton. His son-in-law Tut-ankh-Amon was forced to make his peace with the older priesthoods and civil officials and return to Thebes. On a stela erected in the Temple of Amon at Karnak, he tells of his pious acts of restoration after the heresy. The stela was later usurped by Hor-em-heb (about 1349-1319 B.C.), who inserted his name in place of the name of Tut-ankh-Amon (about 1361-1352 B.C.), since the latter had been stained by relation to the heresy.

The stela was found by G. Legrain at Karnak, and is now 34183 in the Cairo Museum. It was published by Legrain in *Recueil de travaux . . .* , XXIX (1907), 162-73, and by P. Lacau, *Stèles du nouvel empire* (*Catalogue général . . . du Musée du Caire*; Cairo, 1909), 224 ff., Pl. LXX, with the fragment of a duplicate inscription, Cairo 34184, on p. 230 f. There is a translation and commentary by J. Bennett in *JEA*, XXV (1939), 8-15. The year date at the beginning of the inscription is unfortunately lost.

. . . The good ruler, performing benefactions for his father (Amon) and all the gods, for he has made what was ruined to endure as a monument for the ages (5) of eternity and he has expelled deceit throughout the Two Lands, and justice was set up [*so that*] *it might make* lying to be an abomination of the land, as (in) its first time.[1]

Now when his majesty appeared as king, the temples of the gods and goddesses from Elephantine [down] to the marshes of the Delta [had . . . and] gone to pieces. Their shrines had become desolate, had become *mounds* overgrown with [*weeds*]. Their sanctuaries were as if they had never been. Their halls were a footpath. The land was topsy-turvy,[2] and the gods turned their backs upon this land. If [*the army* was] sent to Djahi to extend the frontiers of Egypt, no success of theirs came at all. If one prayed to a god to seek counsel from him, he would never come [at all]. If one made supplication to a goddess similarly, she would never come at all.

[1] Although the entire context was inevitably framed with reference to the restoration after the Amarna heresy, these same expressions were used about the accession of any pharaoh, who had a responsibility to restore order (*ma'at* "truth, justice") as order had been given by the gods.

[2] A compound expression, *seni-meni* "was passed-by-and-sick."

Their hearts *were hurt* in their bodies, (so that) they did damage to that which had been made.

Now after days had passed by this,[3] [his majesty] appeared [upon] the throne of his father. He ruled the regions of Horus; the Black Land and the Red Land[4] were under his authority, and every land was bowing down to the glory of him.

Now when his majesty was in his palace which is in the House of Aa-kheper-ka-Re,[5] like Re in the heavens, then his majesty was conducting the affairs of this land and the daily needs of the Two Banks. So his majesty deliberated plans with his heart, searching for any beneficial deed, seeking out acts of service for his father Amon, and fashioning his august image of genuine fine gold. He surpassed what had been done previously. He fashioned his father Amon upon thirteen carrying-poles, his holy image being of fine gold, lapis lazuli, [turquoise], and every august costly stone, whereas the majesty of this august god had formerly been upon eleven carrying-poles. He fashioned Ptah, South-of-His-Wall, Lord of Life of the Two Lands, his august image being of fine gold, [upon] eleven [carrying-poles], his holy image being of fine gold, lapis lazuli, turquoise, and every august costly stone, whereas the majesty of this august god had formerly been on [$x+$]3 carrying-poles.[6]

Then his majesty made monuments for the gods, [fashioning] their cult-statues of genuine fine gold from the highlands, building their sanctuaries anew as monuments for the ages of eternity, established with possessions forever, setting for them divine offerings as a regular daily observance, and provisioning their food-offerings upon earth. He surpassed what had been previously, [he] went beyond what had [been done] since the time of the ancestors. He has inducted priests and prophets from the children of the nobles of their towns, (each) the son of a known man, whose (own) name is known. He has increased their [property] in gold, silver, bronze, and copper, without limit in [any respect].[7] He has filled their workhouses with male and female slaves, the product of his majesty's capturing [*in every foreign country*]. All the [property] of the temples has been doubled, tripled, and quadrupled in silver, [gold], lapis lazuli, turquoise, every (kind of) august costly stone, royal linen, white linen, fine linen, olive oil, gum, fat, . . . incense, *benzoin*, and myrrh, without limit to any good thing. His majesty—life, prosperity, health!—has built their barques upon the river of new cedar from the terraces, of the choicest (wood) of Negau,[8] worked with gold from the highlands. They make the river shine.

His majesty—life, prosperity, health!—has consecrated male and female slaves, women singers and dancers, who had been maidservants in the palace. Their work is charged against the palace and against the . . . of the Lord of the Two Lands. I cause that they be privileged and protected to (the benefit of) my fathers, all the gods, through a desire to satisfy them by doing what their *ka* wishes, so that they may protect Egypt.[9]

The hearts of the gods and goddesses who are in this land are in joy; the possessors of shrines are rejoicing; the regions are in jubilee and exultation throughout the [entire] land:—the good [*times*] have come! The Ennead of gods who are in the Great House,[10] (raise) their arms in praise; their hands are filled with jubilees [for] ever and ever; all life and satisfaction are with them for the nose of the Horus who repeats births,[11] the beloved son [of Amon], . . . , for He fashioned him in order that He (Himself) might be fashioned.[12] . . .

[3] This was a phrase from story telling, and is not to be taken literally. It is an example of the vulgarization of the formal language under the influence of the Amarna movement and of empire.

[4] Egypt itself was the land of the fertile black soil; the desert was the Red Land.

[5] Thut-mose I (about 1525-1495 B.C.). From another inscription, this estate seems to have been at Memphis, a religious center which has unusual prominence in a text located at Karnak.

[6] The portable statues of Amon and Ptah seem to have had an "august image" (*tit shepset*) and also a "holy image" (*tit djesret*), the distinction between which is not clear. These were carried by priests, the number of carrying-poles being a factor in the number of priests and thus in the honor paid to the god.

[7] In this sentence and the following, "their" refers to the gods.

[8] Negau lay in or near the Lebanon, the area of the "terraces" from which came the wood which we conventionally translate "cedar."

[9] The use of the first person singular in this sentence suggests that it was a quotation from a royal decree for the immunity of temples from taxes. The expenses of the slaves and musicians whom the pharaoh gave to the temples were charged against the royal estate and not against the temples.

[10] Since this is the home of the Ennead, it is probably the Temple of Heliopolis.

[11] Pictorially a god held the hieroglyph of life to the nose of the king; or he might hold strings of "year" or "jubilee" hieroglyphs for the king's long life.

[12] Amon made Tut-ankh-Amon the divine king in order that Amon might be advanced.

The Era of the City of Tanis

About the year 1330 B.C., when Hor-em-heb was pharaoh, a vizier of Egypt named Seti came to the city Tanis in the Delta to celebrate a four hundredth anniversary. This anniversary took the form of the worship of the Egyptian god Seth, who is represented in the scene carved on the stela as an Asiatic deity in a distinctively Asiatic dress. Somewhere close to four hundred years before 1330 B.C., the Hyksos had begun their rule in Egypt, and the Hyksos capital Avaris was probably the later Tanis and the later city Ramses, while the god of the Hyksos was equated by the Egyptians with Seth.[1] The celebration therefore commemorated the four hundredth year of the rule of Seth as a king, and apparently also the four hundredth year since the founding of Tanis.[2] It was, of course, out of the question that the Egyptians should mention the hated Hyksos in such a commemoration, but Seth held a high position under the Ninteenth Dynasty, with two pharaohs named Seti, "Seth's Man."

Later the father of this vizier Seti became the pharaoh Ramses I and founded a dynastic line. Seti himself became the pharaoh Seti I. When his son Ramses II enlarged the city Tanis to be his capital city Ramses,[3] he set up a stela to justify Tanis' claim to rule, on the ground that the god Seth had ruled there for four hundred years.

[1] cf. p. 231, n.9.

[2] Numbers (13:22), carries the tradition that Tanis (Zoan) and Hebron in Palestine were founded at approximately the same time.

[3] For the argument that Tanis, the Hyksos capital Avaris, and the city Ramses were one and the same, see A. H. Gardiner in *JEA*, XIX (1933), 122-28.

The "Stela of the Year 400" was found at Tanis. See the latest publication by P. Montet in *Kêmi*, IV (1933), 191-215. The significance of the stela was stated by K. Sethe in *ZAeS*, LXV (1930), 85-89. There is a translation in Breasted, *AR*, III, §§538-42. The scene above the inscription designates the Asiatic-garbed Seth as "Seth of Ramses," thus locating him in the residence city of that name.

(1) Live the Horus: Mighty Bull, Who Loves Truth, . . . (Ramses II).[4] (5) His majesty commanded the making of a great stela of granite bearing the great name of his fathers, in order to set up the name of the father of his fathers[5] (and of) the King Men-maat-Re, the Son of Re: Seti Mer-ne-Ptah,[6] enduring and abiding forever like Re every day:

"Year 400, 4th month of the third season, day 4,[7] of the King of Upper and Lower Egypt: Seth-the-Great-of-Strength; the Son of Re, his beloved: The-Ombite,[8] beloved of Re-Har-akhti, so that he exists forever and ever. Now there came the Hereditary Prince; Mayor of the City and Vizier; Fan-Bearer on the Right Hand of the King, Troop Commander;[9] Overseer of Foreign Countries; Overseer of the Fortress of Sile;[10] Chief of Police, Royal Scribe; Master of Horse; Conductor of the Feast of the Ram-the-Lord-of-Mendes; High Priest of Seth; Lector Priest of Uto, She-Who-Opens-the-Two-Lands; and Overseer of the Prophets of All the Gods, Seti, the triumphant,[11] the son of the Hereditary Prince; Mayor of the City and Vizier; (10) Troop Commander; Overseer of Foreign Countries; Overseer of the Fortress of Sile; Royal Scribe; and Master of Horse, Pa-Ramses, the triumphant,[12] and child of the Lady of the House and Singer of the Re, Tiu, the triumphant. He said: 'Hail to thee, O Seth, Son of Nut, the Great of Strength in the Barque of Millions,[13] felling the enemy at the prow of the barque of Re, great of battle cry . . . ! *Mayest* [*thou*] *give me* a good lifetime serving [thy] *ka*, while I remain in [*thy favor*] . . .' "[14]

[4] The long titulary of Ramses II is here omitted.
[5] The god Seth, conceived as the ancestor of the royal line.
[6] Seti I.
[7] Around the year 1330 B.C., this date would have fallen late in June.
[8] The god is supplied with a "great name," a pharaonic titulary, to enforce the claim of dynastic ancestry.
[9] This title is carved twice through dittography.
[10] Or Tjaru, the frontier fortress on the eastern Delta.
[11] By the time his son Ramses II set up this stela, Seti was dead.
[12] "The Ramses," the later Ramses I.
[13] Referring to Seth's activity in repelling the serpent demon which attacked the sun barque. See pp. 6-7.
[14] The remainder of the stela is broken away.

A Campaign of Seti I in Northern Palestine

Internally and externally the Amarna Revolution had dealt a serious blow to Egyptian empire. Domestic reorganization was the first need. Then, when Seti I (about 1318-1301 B.C.) became pharaoh, he returned to campaigning in Asia. This stela from Palestinian soil gives a brief statement of his energy in meeting an attempted coalition of Asiatic princes.

A basalt stela, found by the University of Pennsylvania in the mound of Beisan (Beth-Shan) and now in the Palestine Museum at Jerusalem. Published by A. Rowe in *Museum Journal. University of Pennsylvania*, XX (1929), 88-98, and in *The Topography and History of Beth-Shan* (Philadelphia, 1930), I, 24-29, Pl. 41.

Year 1, 3rd month of the third season, day 10.[1] Live the Horus: Mighty Bull, Appearing in Thebes, Making the Two Lands to Live; the Two Goddesses: Repeating Births, Mighty of Arm, Repelling the Nine Bows; the Horus of Gold: Repeating Appearances, Mighty of Bows in All Lands; the King of Upper and Lower Egypt, Lord of the Two Lands: Men-maat-Re [Ir]-en-Re; the Son of Re, Lord of Diadems: Seti Mer-ne-Ptah, beloved of Re-Har-akhti, the great god. The good god, potent with his arm, heroic and valiant like Montu, rich in captives, (5) knowing (how to) place his hand, alert wherever he is; speaking with his mouth, acting with his hands, valiant leader of his army, valiant warrior in the very heart of the fray, a Bastet[2] terrible in combat, penetrating into a mass of Asiatics and making them prostrate, crushing the princes of Retenu, reaching the (very) ends of (10) him who transgresses against *his* way. He causes to *retreat* the princes of Syria,[3] *all* the boastfulness *of whose* mouth was *(so) great*. Every foreign country of the ends of the earth, their princes say: "Where shall we go?" They spend the night *giving testimony* in his name, *saying: "Behold it, behold it!" in* their hearts. It is the strength of his father Amon that decreed to him valor and victory.

On this day[4] one came to speak to his majesty, as follows: (15) "The wretched foe who is in the town of Hamath[5] is gathering to himself many people, while he is seizing the town of Beth-Shan. *Then there will be* an alliance with them of Pahel. He does not permit the Prince of Rehob to go outside."[6]

Thereupon his majesty sent the first army of Amon, (named) "Mighty of Bows," to the town of Hamath, the first army of the (20) Re, (named) "Plentiful of Valor," to the town of Beth-Shan, and the first army of Seth, (named) "Strong of Bows," to the town of Yanoam.[7] When the space of a day had passed, they were overthrown to the glory of his majesty, the King

[1] Around 1318 B.C., this date fell late in May.
[2] Bastet, an Egyptian cat-goddess, merged with Sekhmet, the lioness goddess of war.
[3] *Kharu*, Syria-Palestine in general.
[4] The date at the beginning of the inscription.
[5] Not necessarily the Prince of Hamath, for which we should expect "the wretched foe *of* the town of Hamath." This may have been a prince from the north; note that Seti sends one army division north to Yanoam.
[6] Ancient Beth-Shan is modern Tell el-Ḥuṣn, just northwest of modern Beisan. Hamath is almost certainly Tell el-Ḥammeh, about 10 mi. south of Beisan. Pahel or Pella is Khirbet Faḥil, about 7 mi. southeast of Beisan and across the Jordan. Rehob is probably Tell eṣ-Ṣârem, about 3 mi. south of Beisan. These cities all seem to have lain within a small range. It would seem that Hamath and Pahel were acting against Beth-Shan and Rehob.
[7] "First army" has something of the sense of *corps d'élite*. As in Ramses II's campaign against Kadesh, each division of the Egyptian army marched under the aegis of a god, whose image led the way. cf. pp. 255-56. Seti I's dispositions were rapid and effective. One problem here is the reason for sending a unit against Yanoam, which was apparently considerably north of the center of disaffection. Yanoam may be modern Tell en-Nâʿameh, north of Lake Huleh and thus nearly 50 mi. north of Beisan. Perhaps the real opposition to Egypt lay to the north, in the territory dominated by the Hittites. Perhaps the leader of this coalition came from the north; cf. n.5 above. By throwing a road-block against reinforcements from the north, Seti I would be able to deal with a localized rebellion around Beth-Shan, without outside interference.

of Upper and Lower Egypt: Men-maat-Re; the Son of Re: Seti Mer-ne-Ptah, given life.

Campaigns of Seti I in Asia

On the north exterior wall of the great hypostyle hall at Karnak Seti I (about 1318-1301 B.C.) has left scenes of his military activity with at least four objectives: against the *Shasu*-Bedouin of Sinai and southern Palestine, against the mountain region of Palestine-Syria, against the Hittites in central and northern Syria, and against the Libyans. Extracts from this material will illustrate the problem which this pharaoh faced in attempting to reconstitute the Egyptian Empire.

Bibliography of the publications and translations of the texts will be found in Breasted, *AR*, III, §§80-156, and bibliography also in B. Porter and R. L. B. Moss, *Topographical Bibliography . . . II. Theban Temples* (Oxford, 1929), 19-23. A convenient transcription of the texts, but without improvement over the earlier copyists, will be found in C. E. Sander-Hansen, *Historische Inschriften der 19. Dynastie* (*Bibliotheca Aegyptiaca*, IV, Brussels, 1933), 3-12.

In the following (a) is Breasted, scene 8 = Porter and Moss, scene 57 bottom; (b) is Breasted, scenes 8, 2, and 1 = Porter and Moss, scenes 55-57 bottom; (c) is Breasted, scenes 3, 4, and 5 = Porter and Moss, scenes 54, and 55 top; (d) is Breasted, scenes 9-10 = Porter and Moss, 59 top and bottom; (e) is Breasted, scenes 16, 17, 19 = Porter and Moss, scenes 62 top, 62 bottom, and 64 bottom.

a

This scene gives Seti's return from a campaign, but the text states the reasons for his activity. The restlessness in Palestine was an aftermath of the disturbances in the Amarna period.

Year 1 of the Renaissance,[1] and of the King of Upper and Lower Egypt, Lord of the Two Lands: Men-maat-Re, given life. Then one came to say to his majesty: "The foe belonging to the Shasu are plotting rebellion. Their tribal chiefs are gathered in one place, waiting on the mountain ranges of Kharu.[2] They have taken to clamoring and quarreling, one of them killing his fellow. They have no regard for the laws of the palace." The heart of his majesty—life, prosperity, health!—was glad at it.

Now as for the good god, he exults at undertaking combat; he delights at an attack on him; his heart is satisfied at the sight of blood. He cuts off the heads of the perverse of heart. He loves an instant of trampling more than a day of jubilation. His majesty kills them all at one time, and leaves no heirs among them. He who is spared by his hand is a living prisoner, carried off to Egypt.

b

Three scenes show the pharaoh on the march and list the stations on the military road through Sinai, running close to the sea between the Egyptian frontier at Sile (near modern Kantarah) and Raphia in Palestine. This was the main avenue of intercourse between Egypt and Palestine. The route has been studied by A. H. Gardiner in *JEA*, VI (1920), 99-116, in relation to the similar listing in the satirical letter of p. 478 below.

[1] "Repeating Births." Seti I's reign inaugurated a new era; see *ZAeS*, LXVI (1931), 4.

[2] Probably, as in the Beisan stela of this same year (pp. 253-54 above), the mountains of northern Palestine.

An interesting touch of evidence on the international forces playing upon the imperial religion of the time is the fact that the pharaoh's team of horses has an alternative name: "The great team of his majesty (named) 'Amon Decrees to Him the Valor,' which is (also) called 'Anath is Content.' "[3]

c

Somewhere in Palestine Seti I attacked a fortified place, "the town of the Canaan," which we cannot locate. As the accompanying text indicates, this was on the same expedition as that of the scenes just mentioned.

Year 1 of the King of Upper and Lower Egypt: Men-maat-Re. The desolation which the mighty arm of Pharaoh—life, prosperity, health!—made among the foe belonging to the Shasu from the fortress of Sile to the Canaan. His majesty [pre]vailed over them like a fierce lion. They were made into corpses throughout their valleys, stretched out in their (own) blood, like that which has never been.

Another scene shows the pharaoh capturing a town surrounded by a forest, "the town of Yanoam." This may have been the same thrust as that mentioned in the Beisan stela.[4]

A third scene depicts the Asiatics cutting down trees for the pharaoh, at "the town of Qeder in the land of Henem," which cannot be located.[5] However, the local rulers are "the great princes of Lebanon," and the descriptive legend runs:

. . . Lebanon. Cutting down [cedar for] the great barque upon the river, "[Amon]-U[ser-h]et,"[6] as well as for the great flagpoles of Amon . . .

d

The texts of the scenes following Seti's triumphal return to Egypt link the campaign against the Shasu-Bedouin with the mountain area of Syria-Palestine, called "Upper Retenu."

The return [of] his majesty from Upper Retenu, having extended the frontiers of Egypt.

The plunder which his majesty carried off from these Shasu, whom his majesty himself captured in the year 1 of the Renaissance.

e

Other scenes show Seti I engaged with the Hittites in Syria. He is shown attacking a mountainous settlement, "the town of Kadesh." That this was Kadesh on the Orontes seems certain from the fact that the fragment of a monumental stela of this pharaoh was found on that site.[7] The legend for the scene at Karnak runs:

The going up which Pharaoh—life, prosperity, health!—made to desolate the land of Kadesh and the land of *Amurru*.[8]

Either on this expedition or on a subsequent campaign, the pharaoh came into military competition with the powerful state of Hatti. He is shown in battle, with the legend:

The wretched land of the Hittites, among whom his

[3] On this goddess see pp. 249-50 above.

[4] cf. pp. 253-54 above.

[5] Perhaps a Gedor or Geder in a land of Hinnom.

[6] cf. Wen-Amon's expedition to get cedar for this sacred barque of Amon, pp. 25-29.

[7] M. Pézard, in *Syria*, III (1922), 108-10; G. Loukianoff, in *Ancient Egypt*, 1924, 101-08.

[8] A. H. Gardiner, *Ancient Egyptian Onomastica* (London, 1947), I, 140* f., does not believe this to be Amurru.

majesty—life, prosperity, health!—made a great slaughter.

On his return to Egypt, the pharaoh enjoyed the usual triumph and made the customary gift acknowledgement to the imperial god Amon.

[Presentation of] tribute by the good god to his father Amon-Re, Lord of the [Thrones] of [the Two Lands, at] his return from the country of Hatti, having annihilated the rebellious countries and crushed the Asiatics in their places . . .

The great princes of the wretched Retenu, whom his majesty carried off by his victories from the country of Hatti, to fill the workhouse of his father Amon-Re, Lord of the Thrones of the Two Lands, according as he had given valor against the south and victory against the north . . .

Beth-Shan Stelae of Seti I and Ramses II

In addition to the Beth-Shan stela of Seti I translated on pp. 253-54 above, there are two further commemorative stelae found in the same excavation, one of Seti I and one of Ramses II.

a

A broken and pitted basalt stela of Seti I is most difficult to read. It was published by A. Rowe, *The Topography and History of Beth-Shan* (Philadelphia, 1930), I, 29-30, Pls. 42-44. The only passage which can be discerned with some slight assurance is in lines 9-11 of the stela's 20 lines.[1]

On this day,[2] lo, his [majesty]—life, prosperity, health! —. . . the Apiru[3] of the mountain of Yer . . . ,[4] together with Tir . . . ,[5] . . . *who had trodden upon*[6] . . .

b

The basalt stela of Ramses II, now in the University Museum in Philadelphia, is thoroughly conventional. It was published by Rowe, *op.cit.*, 33-36, Pl. 46, with a translation also in *Museum Journal. The University of Pennsylvania*, xx (1929), 94-98. Only the date in line 1 and the passage about the Asiatics coming to the city of Ramses in Egypt in lines 8-10 will be translated here.

Year 9, 4th month of the second season, day 1.[7] . . . *When day had broken*,[8] he made to retreat the Asiatics. . . . They all come bowing down to him, to his palace of life and satisfaction, Per-Ramses-Meri-Amon-the-Great-of-Victories.[9] . . .

[1] I had intended to collate the stela in Jerusalem in the spring of 1946. Unfortunately I found that another visiting egyptologist, coming at a time when the Director of the Museum was away on war work, had covered the stone with his own collation in thick white ink. It was therefore impossible to discern the original carving, and the translation has to rest upon the published photographs.

[2] On a date lost at the beginning of the stela.

[3] The Apiru are probably etymologically related to the Habiru. See p. 247, n.47.

[4] Hardly Jordan. Yer[ḥem] = Jeroham seems a possibility.

[5] Also unknown, and only a portion of the name. Could it be a Tell-. . . ?

[6] The photograph seems to show *tehmu her* "who had exerted (some sort of) force upon."

[7] Around 1290, this date fell in the month of February.

[8] If the translation is correct, this will refer to the date above and refer to specific military action. Otherwise, it would be preferable to take the following context as customary: "he makes to retreat."

[9] "The House of Ramses," the Residence City Ramses or Raamses in the Egyptian Delta. See A. H. Gardiner in *JEA*, v (1918), 127 ff.

The Asiatic Campaigning of Ramses II

By length of years and sheer self-assertiveness Ramses II (about 1301-1234 B.C.) left his name scrawled across Egyptian history out of all proportion to his personal achievement. In physical content his texts bulk large, but they lack historical relevance or clear applicability to the Old Testament.

A. THE FIRST TWO CAMPAIGNS

At the mouth of the Dog River (Nahr el-Kelb) between Beirut and Byblos, Ramses II left three nearly illegible stelae of triumph, one of which bears the date, "Year 4," and testifies to his consolidation of territory north to that point by that date.[1]

In the following year the pharaoh engaged upon the exploit of his life, the battle against the Hittite king Muwatallis at Kadesh on the Orontes. No other text occupies so much wall space in Egypt and Nubia. However, it is clear that Ramses did not win a victory, but succeeded only in extricating himself from a tight spot by his personal valor. The full statement of this campaign is of little immediate concern here, as the action took place north in Syria and the Hittite confederation was almost completely northern. We give here only those extracts which relate to his crossing Palestine and southern Syria on his way to Kadesh.

The texts have been best gathered in Ch. Kuentz, *La bataille de Qadesch* (*Mémoires pub. par les membres de l'Institut Français d'Archéologie Orientale*, LV, Cairo, 1928), to which the most recent addition is an extract in Papyrus Beatty III (*Hieratic Papyri in the British Museum. Third Series. Chester Beatty Gift*, ed. by A. H. Gardiner [London, 1935], I, 23-24; II, Pls. 9-10). The texts appear also in Selim Hassan, *Le poème dit de Pentauor et le rapport officiel sur la bataille de Qadesh* (Cairo, 1929). There are translations in Breasted, *AR*, III, §§298-351, and by J. A. Wilson in *AJSL*, XLIII (1927), 266-87. The poem is also translated by Erman, *LAE*, 260-70.

The poem on the battle deals briefly with the departure from Egypt, the organization of the Egyptian army, and the approach to Kadesh (Kuentz, *op.cit.*, 220-25, 230-33).

Now then, his majesty had prepared (8) his infantry, his chariotry, and the Sherden[2] of his majesty's capturing, whom he had carried off by the victories of his arm, equipped with all their weapons, to whom the orders of combat had been given. His majesty journeyed northward, his infantry and chariotry with him. He began to march on the good way in the year 5, 2nd month of the third season, day 9, (when) his majesty passed the fortress of Sile.[3] [He] was mighty like Montu[4] when he goes forth, (so that) every foreign country was trembling before him, their chiefs were presenting their tribute, and all the rebels were coming, bowing down through fear of the glory of his majesty. His infantry went on the narrow passes as if on the highways of Egypt. Now after days had passed after this, then his majesty was in Ramses Meri-Amon, the town which is

[1] C. R. Lepsius, *Denkmäler aus Aegypten und Aethiopien* (Berlin, 1849-59), III, 197; F. H. Weissbach, *Die Denkmäler und Inschriften an der Mündung des Nahr el-Kelb* (Berlin und Leipzig, 1922), 17-22.

[2] One of the Peoples of the Sea who served as Egyptian mercenaries. cf. pp. 260, 262, 476.

[3] Or Tjaru, the fortress at the Suez frontier. The date, around 1296 B.C., would fall around the middle of April.

[4] The Egyptian god of war.

in the Valley of the Cedar.[5] His majesty proceeded northward. After his majesty reached the mountain range of Kadesh, then his majesty went forward like his father Montu, Lord of Thebes, and he crossed (12) the ford of the Orontes, with the first division of Amon (named) "He Gives Victory to User-maat-Re Setep-en-Re."[6] His majesty reached the town of Kadesh. . . .[7]

Now the wretched foe belonging to Hatti, with the numerous foreign countries which were with him, was waiting hidden and ready on the northeast of the town of Kadesh, while his majesty was alone by himself (17) with his retinue. The division of Amon was on the march behind him; the division of Re was crossing the ford in a district south of the town of Shabtuna, at the dis-stance of one *iter* from the place where his majesty was;[8] the division of Ptah was on the south of the town of Arnaim; and the division of Seth was marching on the road. His majesty had formed the first ranks of battle of all the leaders of his army, while they were (still) on the shore in the land of Amurru. . . .[9]

The briefer account of the battle, called the Record, adds only a few details to the account of the march toward Kadesh (Kuentz, *op.cit.*, 328-30).

Year 5, 3rd month of the third season, day 9, under the majesty of (Ramses II).[10] When his majesty was in Djahi on his second victorious campaign, the goodly awakening in life, prosperity, and health was at the tent of his majesty on the mountain range south of Kadesh. After this, at the time of dawn, his majesty appeared like the rising of Re, and he took the adornments of his father Montu. The lord proceeded northward, and his majesty arrived at a vicinity south of the town of Shabtuna.[11] . . .

The only other detail from the Battle of Kadesh which need be noted here comes from a legend attached to a scene in which a military detachment of Egyptians is shown coming to the rescue of the hard-pressed pharaoh. It seems that this was a separate unit from the four army divisions named above and came by a separate route, arriving in the nick of time for the pharaoh. Kuentz, *op.cit.*, 366.

The arrival of the *Nearin*-troops of Pharaoh—life, prosperity, health!—from the land of Amurru.[12] . . .

[5] An Asiatic town named after Ramses, presumably in the Lebanon. For the "Valley of the Cedar," see also the Story of the Two Brothers, p. 25.

[6] For the naming of the units of the army after gods, each one of whom extended his special sanction to that unit, cf. the Beisan Stela of Seti I, p. 253.

[7] The omitted context lists the northern confederation which the Hittite king had gathered.

[8] Ramses encamped west of the city of Kadesh. An *iter* may have been about 2 kilometers at this time.

[9] "The shore in the land of Amurru" must have been the Phoenician coast. The omitted continuation of the text then details the battle, beginning with the charge of the concealed Hittite chariotry.

[10] Just one month after the date of n.3 above, Ramses had marched from the Egyptian frontier to the highland south of Kadesh.

[11] The omitted continuation tells how the Hittite king employed Bedouin agents to lull Ramses II into a false security.

[12] *Nearin* is a Semitic word for "boys" or "young men." cf. pp. 476, 478 below. However, these troops are shown as Egyptian. The statement that they arrived from "the land of Amurru" must mean that they came by a different route from the rest of the army. One might assume that they were sent up the Phoenician coast to secure communications by water, and then cut inland to join the rest of the army. See A. H. Gardiner, *Ancient Egyptian Onomastica*, I, 171*, 188* f.

B. LATER CAMPAIGNING

The campaigns of Ramses II's subsequent years cannot be arranged in historical sequence and ran from southern Palestine to northern Syria. This is true for the activities of his eighth year, as indicated by the legends attached to four of a number of Asiatic strongholds, shown on the back of the first pylon of the Ramesseum at Thebes. These were published by W. M. Müller, *Egyptological Researches* (Washington, 1906-), II, Pls. 100-03; W. Wreszinski, *Atlas zur altägyptischen Kulturgeschichte*, II (Leipzig, 1935-), 90-91. Translations in Breasted, *AR*, III, §§356-62.

The town which his majesty desolated in the year 8, Merom.[13]

The town which his majesty desolated in the year 8, Salem.[13]

The town which his majesty desolated on the mountain of Beth-Anath, Kerep.

The town which his majesty desolated in the land of Amurru, Deper.

Here Beth-Anath is probably in Palestine, but Deper (not Tabor!) is to be located in north Syria, in the general region of Tunip.

In one of these campaigns Ramses II took action against Ashkelon in southern Palestine. The scene showing the storming of this town is carved in the Temple of Karnak, was published by Wreszinski, *op.cit.*, 58, and was translated by Breasted, *AR*, III, §§353-55.

The wretched town which his majesty took when it was wicked, Ashkelon. It says: "Happy is he who acts in fidelity to thee, (but) woe (to) him who transgresses thy frontier! Leave over a heritage, so that we may relate thy strength to every ignorant foreign country!"

The Egyptians related all this disturbance to the machinations of the Hittites, even down into Palestine. A scene in Karnak (Müller, *op.cit.*, Pls. 37-38; Wreszinski, *op.cit.*, 55a) shows an attack upon the "town which his majesty desolated, Acre," and has a broken text in which one may read the words: "when the princes of Kadesh see him, the [*terror*] of him is in their hearts." The Hittite confederation of the Battle of Kadesh was still considered the main foe of Ramses II.

Of the same general attitude are the references to the excursions into the region of Tunip and Deper in north Syria, as shown in scenes in the Temple of Luxor and the Ramesseum (Müller, *op.cit.*, Pls. 44-45; Wreszinski, *op.cit.*, 77-80; 107-09; Breasted, *op.cit.*, §§364-66). There the claim of Ramses II that he fought "the fallen ones of Hatti" shows this larger restlessness, covering all of the empire which he claimed in Asia.

C. PEACE BETWEEN EGYPT AND HATTI

Ultimately, both the Egyptians and the Hittites found the war expensive of energies which had to be saved against the encroachments of the Peoples of the Sea. In the 21st year of Ramses II (perhaps 1280 B.C.), a treaty was concluded between Egypt and Hatti, providing for an offensive and defensive alliance; see pp. 199-201.

By Ramses II's 34th year (perhaps 1267 B.C.), the alliance between Egypt and Hatti was given visible expression through a royal marriage between the pharaoh and the eldest daughter of the Hittite king. This was not the first international marriage, as the pharaohs preceding the Amarna period had taken royal

[13] The pictured determinative of the name Merom is a man with arms raised high in the air, corresponding to the meaning of "height" for the word Merom. The pictured determinative of the name Salem shows a man with arms raised in greeting or salutation, corresponding to the meaning of "Peace!" for this word.

wives from the Mitannian princesses. Egyptian texts treated such a marriage as a surrender of the Hittites, on the theme that the princess was the chief element of "tribute" sent to Egypt, after Hatti had been defeated by the pharaoh. The "Marriage Stela" is a document which mingles bombast with genuine relief at a successful peace after years of fighting.

The stelae at Karnak, Elephantine, and Abu Simbel are presented, with translation, by Ch. Kuentz in *ASAE*, xxv (1925), 181-238. A recently discovered version at Amarah in the Sudan is still unpublished (*JEA*, xxiv [1938], 155). An abbreviated version of the text from Karnak, published by G. Lefebvre in *ASAE*, xxv (1925), 34-45, aids in giving the end of the text. The earlier treatment of the text is given in Breasted, *AR*, iii, §§415-24.

. . . Then the (21) great princes of every land heard of the mysterious qualities of his majesty. Then they were dismayed and afraid, and the terror of his majesty was in their hearts, while they lauded his glory and gave praise to his beautiful face, . . . [*making offer*]*ing* to him with their children, namely the great lords of Retenu and of strange countries—no matter which[14]—in order to appease the heart of the Bull and to beg peace from him. *Ramses II.[15] They *despoiled* themselves of their own goods, being charged with their annual dues, with their children at the head of their tribute, in praise and homage to his [*name*]. *Ramses II. So every foreign country was in humility under the feet of this good god, for he made his frontiers (*so that*) they were *held in* [*check*]—except for *that* land of Hatti. It did not do the same as these princes.

Words spoken by his majesty: "As my father Re favors me forever as Ruler of the Two Lands, as I rise like the sun disc and shine like Re, as the heaven is firm upon its supports, I will attain the (25) limits of the land of Hatti, and they shall be prostrate under (my)[16] feet forever! *Ramses II. I will make them turn back from fighting at the pass and stop the boasting in their land, for I know that my father Seth *has made* victory *to* flourish against every land, since he has made my arm mighty to the height of heaven and my strength to the width of earth! *Ramses II."

Then his majesty prepared his infantry and his chariotry, and they were *launched* in the land of Hatti. He despoiled them alone by himself[17] . . . entirely, so that he [made] himself a name forever in the midst of it. *Ramses II. They have memory of the victories of his arm. He makes the survivors of his hand curse, for his prowess among them is like a blazing torch. No prince(s) remain upon their thrones, *or their brothers* [*either*]. *Ramses II.

They fulfilled many years while they were destroyed and . . . from year to year through the prowess of the great living god, *Ramses II. Then the Great Prince of Hatti sent [to] his majesty, magnifying his prowess and extolling . . . , saying: ". . . We are charged with [*dues*], and we [carry] them to thy august palace. Behold, we (30) are under thy feet, O victorious king! May we act according to all that thou hast commanded! *Ramses II." So the Great Prince of Hatti sent and appeased his majesty year by year. *Ramses II. (But) he never listened to them.

Now after they saw their land in this *destroyed* state under the great prowess of the Lord of the Two Lands, *Ramses II, then the Great Prince of Hatti said to his *army* and his officials: "What is this? Our land is desolated; our lord Seth is angry with us, and the skies do not give water over against us.[18] . . . Let us despoil ourselves of all our goods, with my eldest daughter at the head of them, and let us carry gifts of fealty[19] to the good god, so that he may give us peace, that we may live! *Ramses II." Then he caused to be brought [his] eldest daughter, with noble tribute before her: gold, silver, many great ores, horses without limit to them, cattle, goats, and sheep by the ten-thousands, without limit to the products of their [land.] *Ramses II.

[Then one] came to make communication to his majesty, saying: "Behold, even the Great Prince of Hatti! His eldest daughter is being brought, carrying abundant tribute of everything. They cover the [*valleys with*] their [*numbers*], *the daughter* of the Prince of Hatti and the [*daughter of the*] Great Princess of Hatti *among* them. They have passed difficult mountains and wicked ravines. *Ramses II. They have reached the frontier of his majesty. Let (35) *our* [*army*] and the officials [*come*] to receive them. *Ramses II." Then his majesty received [*great*] joy, and the palace was in happiness, when he heard these mysterious matters, which were completely unknown in Egypt.[20] So he despatched the army and the officials hastily, in order to make the reception before them. *Ramses II.

Then his majesty took deliberate counsel with his heart, saying: "How will it be with those whom I have sent, going on a mission to Djahi,[21] in these days of rain and snow which come in winter?" Then he offered a great oblation to his father Seth, appealing to him *about* [*it*] with the words: "Heaven is in thy hands, and earth is under thy feet. What happens is what thou commandest. Mayest thou [*delay*] to make the rain, the cold wind, and the snow, until the marvels which thou hast assigned to me shall reach me.[22] *Ramses II."

Then his father Seth heard all that he had said. So the skies were peaceful, and days of summer fell *to* [*him*], while his army went, being gay, their bodies freestriding, their hearts in joy. *Ramses II. So the daughter of the Great Prince of Hatti marched to Egypt, while the infantry, chariotry, and officials of his majesty accompanied her, mingling with the infantry and char-

14 "They are not known," in the sense: they need not be specified.

15 This text uses the two formal names of Ramses II as a mark of punctuation, here abbreviated with an asterisk for the purposes of this translation.

16 The two texts give "thy" and "his."

17 The theme of solitary victory derives from Ramses' personal achievements at the Battle of Kadesh.

18 Seth—corresponding to the Hittite god Teshub—is here working against Hatti to the advantage of Egypt. cf. the claim, p. 471, that the pharaoh is able to withhold rain from Hatti.

19 A Semitic word like the Hebrew *berakah*.

20 The Egyptian account insists that the entire initiative was Hittite.

21 The area of Phoenicia and its hinterland, down into Palestine. Note that this is claimed above as "the frontier of his majesty."

22 Seth is here in a dual role: the god of the Hittites and the god of storm; cf. p. 17, n.27.

iotry of Hatti, for they were (40) *teher*-warriors[23] like the troops of *Ramses II and like his chariotry, all the people of the land of Hatti being mingled with those of Egypt. They ate and drank *together*, being of one heart like brothers, without shunning one another, for peace and brotherhood were between them, after the manner of the god himself, *Ramses II.

Then the great princes of every land, when they passed *by them*, were dismayed, turned back, shrinking, when they saw all the people of Hatti as they [joined] with the army of the king *Ramses II. So one of these princes said to his fellow: "What his majesty has said is true. . . . How great are these [things] which we have seen with our own faces! Every foreign country is with [him] as slaves, in one accord with [Egypt]! *Ramses II. That which had been the land of Hatti, behold, it has come to be like Egypt with him. *What is* the heaven? It (also) is under his seal, so that it acts according to all that he has wished! *Ramses II."

Now after [*many days they*] reached (the city) Ramses Meri-Amon, . . . and we celebrated the great marvels of valor and victory in the year 34, 3rd month of the second season.[24] *Ramses II. Then they ushered the daughter of the Great Prince of Hatti, *who had come* marching to Egypt, into the presence of his majesty,[25] with very great tribute following her, without limit. . . . Then [his] majesty saw that she was fair of face [*like*] a goddess. Now (it was) a great, mysterious, marvellous, and fortunate affair. It was unknown, unheard of from mouth to mouth, not mentioned in the writings of the ancestors . . . *Ramses II. So she was beautiful in the heart of his majesty, and he loved her more than anything, as a good fortune *for him* through [*the command of*] his father Ptah-tenen.[26] *Ramses II. [27]Then his majesty caused that her name be made to be: the King's Wife Maat-nefru-Re,[28] the daughter of the Great Prince of Hatti and the daughter of the Great Princess of Hatti. . . .

And so it was that, if a man or a woman proceeded on their mission to Djahi, they could reach the land of Hatti without fear around about their hearts, because of the greatness of the victories of his [maj]esty.

For the treaty of peace between Egypt and the Hittites in the reign of Ramses II, see pp. 199-201 above.

For the "Israel Stela," a hymn of victory of Mer-ne-Ptah, see pp. 376-378 below.

For a literary document giving a satirical account of conditions in Syria-Palestine from the standpoint of an Egyptian official, see pp. 475-479 below.

[23] In the account of the Battle of Kadesh, this term is applied to the Hittite chariot-warriors. See also p. 239, n.3.

[24] About 1267 B.C., this date would coincide generally with the month of January.

[25] The relief above the inscription in the temple of Abu Simbel shows the Hittite king and his daughter coming into the presence of Ramses II.

[26] In the "Blessing of Ptah" (Breasted, *AR*, III, §410), it is this god who delivers Hatti and its princess to Ramses II.

[27] From this point on, the longer texts are badly damaged, and the translation uses the abbreviated version: Lefebvre, *op.cit.*, 40-41, lines 16-18.

[28] In Egyptian: "She Who Sees the Beauty of Re"; cf. p. 29.

The Journal of a Frontier Official

On the verso of a papyrus devoted to texts for school use, there are records of an official of the eastern frontier post of the Egyptian Delta. They illustrate the traffic between Egypt and Asia at the time of the pharaoh Mer-ne-Ptah.

Papyrus Anastasi III (British Museum 10246), verso vi 1-v 9, probably from Memphis. Facsimiled in *Select Papyri in the Hieratic Character from the Collections of the British Museum*, II (London, 1842), back of Pls. LXXIX-LXXVIII, and in G. Möller, *Hieratische Lesestücke*, III (Leipzig, 1935), 26-27. Transcription into hieroglyphic in A. H. Gardiner, *Late-Egyptian Miscellanies* (*Bibliotheca Aegyptiaca*, VII, Brussels, 1937), 31-32. Translated by Breasted, *AR*, §§629-35, by A. Erman and H. Ranke, *Aegypten* (Tübingen, 1923), 645-46, and by W. Wolf in *ZAeS*, LXIX (1933), 39-45.

I

Year 3, 1ST MONTH OF THE 3RD SEASON, DAY 15.[1] The Guardsman[2] Baal-roy, son of Zippor, of Gaza, went up,[3] who had two different despatches for Syria:[4] the Commander of the Garrison Khay, one despatch; the Prince of Tyre *Baal-termeg*,[5] one despatch.

II

(4) Year 3, 1ST MONTH OF THE 3RD SEASON, DAY 17. The Chief of Bowmen of the Wells of Mer-ne-Ptah Hotep-hir-Maat—life, prosperity, health!—which is (on) the mountain range,[6] arrived for a (judicial) investigation in the fortress which is in Sile.[7]

III

(6) Year 3, 1ST MONTH OF THE 3RD SEASON, DAY 22. The Guardsman Thuti, son of Tjekrem, of Gaza, came, in company with Tjedet, son of Shemu-Baal, of ditto, and Seth-mose, son of Apar-dagal, of ditto, who had with him, for the place where One was,[8] (for) the Commander of the Garrison Khay, *gifts* and one despatch.[9]

(V 1) THERE WENT UP the Guardsman Nakht-Amon, son of Tjer, of the Castle of Mer-ne-Ptah Hotep-hir-Maat—life, prosperity, health![10]—which is near Sar-ram, who had with him two different despatches for Syria: the Commander of the Garrison Pen-Amon, one despatch; the Steward (of) this town Ramses-nakht, one despatch.

(4) THERE CAME the Overseer of the Stable of the town Mer-ne-Ptah Hotep-hir-Maat—life, prosperity,

[1] About 1230 B.C., the dates in these entries would fall in the month of March.

[2] "Follower," i.e. one of the retinue, perhaps of the bodyguard.

[3] The text uses "go up" for the journey out of Egypt to Asia and "arrive" or "come" for the arrival from Asia.

[4] Egyptian *Kharu* or Hurru.

[5] The name contains the elements indicated, but perhaps should be divided Baalat-remeg.

[6] Of Palestine? If one reads Josh. 15:9 and 18:15 "the Fountain of Mer-ne-Ptah," instead of "the Fountain of the waters (*mai*) of Nephtoah," and if the equation is correct, the location will have been near Jerusalem.

[7] Egyptian *Tjaru* or *Tjile*, the chief frontier post, located near modern Kantarah.

[8] "One" is a respectful circumlocution for pharaoh.

[9] In Section I above Khay is in Syria; here apparently at the Egyptian capital. If the same man is meant the translation is faulty.

[10] The location of this castle is unknown, *pace* A. H. Gardiner in *JEA*, VI (1920), 111.

health!—which is in the district of *the Arem*,[11] Pa-mer-khetem, son of Ani, who had with him two different despatches for the place where One was: the Commander of the Garrison Pa-Re-em-heb, one despatch; the Deputy Pa-Re-em-heb, one despatch.[12]

IV

(8) Year 3, 1ST MONTH OF THE 3RD SEASON, DAY 25. The Charioteer of the Great Stable of Ba-(en)-Re Meri-Amon—life, prosperity, health!—[of] the Court, In-wau, went up.

The Report of a Frontier Official

In a group of letters which served as models for schoolboys, one communication presents the form in which an official on the eastern frontier of Egypt might report the passage of Asiatic tribes into the better pasturage of the Delta.

Papyrus Anastasi VI (British Museum 10245), lines 51-61 (=iv 11-v 5), of the late Nineteenth Dynasty (end of the 13th century B.C.) and presumably from Memphis. Facsimiled in *Select Papyri in the Hieratic Character from the Collections of the British Museum*, III (London, 1844), Pls. CXXV-CXXVI. Transcription into hieroglyphic by A. H. Gardiner, *Late Egyptian Miscellanies* (*Bibliotheca Aegyptiaca*, VII, Brussels, 1937), 76-77. Translated by Breasted, *AR*, III, §§636-38.

(51) The Scribe Inena communicating to his lord, the Scribe of the Treasury Qa-g[abu], . . . :—In life, prosperity, health! This is a letter [to] let [my lord] know: An[other communication to] my lord, to wit:[1]

[I] have carried out every commission laid upon me, in good shape and strong as metal. I have not been lax.

Another communication to my [lord], to [wit: We] have finished letting the Bedouin[2] tribes of Edom pass the Fortress [of] Mer-ne-Ptah Hotep-hir-Maat—life, prosperity, health!—which is (in) Tjeku,[3] (56) to the pools[4] of Per-Atum[5] [of] Mer-[ne]-Ptah Hotep-hir-Maat, which are (in) Tjeku, to keep them alive and to keep their cattle alive, through the great *ka* of Pharaoh—life, prosperity, health!—the good sun of every land, in the year 8, 5 [intercalary] days, [the Birth of] Seth.[6] I have had them brought in a copy of the *report* to the [place where] my lord is, *as well as* the other names of days[7] when the Fortress of Mer-ne-Ptah Hotep-hir-Maat—life, prosperity, health!—which is (in) [Tj]ek[u], may be passed. . . .

[11] Or Parem? Perhaps to be revised to Amurru.

[12] In *JEA*, XXV (1939), 103, P. C. Smither draws an interesting analogy between this postal register and one of Ptolemaic times.

[1] The pupil, Inena, addresses his master, Qa-gabu; cf. p. 25 above.

[2] The Egyptian word is *Shasu*, which became Coptic *shôs* "shepherd."

[3] The location is the eastern end of the Wadi Tumilat, the "land of Goshen." The Fortress of Mer-ne-Ptah will have been a frontier fortress. Tjeku—or probably Teku—could only with difficulty be Succoth and seems to be a broad designation for the region.

[4] The Semitic word *birkeh* is used.

[5] Per-Atum, "the House of Atum," is probably biblical Pithom, located by A. H. Gardiner (*JEA*, XIX [1933], 127) at Tell er-Retabeh, about 22 miles west of modern Ismailiyeh.

[6] "The Birth of Seth" was the 3rd intercalary day at the end of the year. Around 1215 B.C. this would be after the middle of June.

[7] That is, the names of other days.

The Pursuit of Runaway Slaves

Among the model letters set for the instruction of schoolboys, there is one reporting the pursuit of two slaves escaping from Egypt into Asia.

Papyrus Anastasi V (British Museum 10244), xix 2-xx 6, of the end of the 13th century B.C. and probably from Memphis. Facsimiled in *Select Papyri in the Hieratic Character from the Collections of the British Museum*, III (London, 1844), Pls. CXIII-CXIV. Transcribed into hieroglyphic by A. H. Gardiner, *Late-Egyptian Miscellanies* (*Bibliotheca Aegyptiaca*, VII, Brussels, 1937), 66-67. Translated by Erman, *LAE*, 198-99, and an extract by A. H. Gardiner in *JEA*, VI (1920), 109-10.

The Chief of Bowmen of Tjeku,[1] Ka-Kem-wer, to the Chief of Bowmen Ani and the Chief of Bowmen Bak-en-Ptah:

In life, prosperity, health! In the favor of Amon-Re, King of the Gods, and of the *ka* of the King of Upper and Lower Egypt: User-kheperu-Re Setep-en-Re[2]—life, prosperity, health!—our good lord—life, prosperity, health! I say to (xix 5) the Re-Har-akhti: "Keep Pharaoh—life, prosperity, health!—our good lord—life, prosperity, health!—in health! Let him celebrate millions of jubilees, while we are in his favor daily!"

Another matter, to wit: I was sent forth from the broad-halls of the palace—life, prosperity, health!—in the 3rd month of the third season, day 9,[3] at the time of evening, following after these two slaves.[4] Now when I reached the enclosure-wall of Tjeku on the 3rd month of the third season, day 10, they told [me] they were saying to the south that they[5] had passed by on the 3rd month of the third season, day 10.[6] (xx 1) [Now] when [I] reached the fortress,[7] they told me that the *scout*[8] had come from the desert [saying that] they had passed the walled place north of the Migdol of Seti Mer-ne-Ptah—life, prosperity, health!—Beloved like Seth.[9]

When my letter reaches you, write to me about all that has happened to [them]. Who found their tracks? Which watch found their tracks? What people are after them? Write to me about all that has happened to them and how many people you send out after them.[10]

[May your health] be good!

[1] Or Teku. Probably not Succoth. Gardiner (*JEA*, VI [1920], 109) locates it at Tell el-Maskhuteh in the Wadi Tumilat. It seems more likely that it is not yet identifiable, and it may be generally equivalent to the Wadi Tumilat.

[2] Seti II (about 1222-1212 B.C.).

[3] About 1220 B.C., this date would fall in the month of May.

[4] For the Egyptian word *bak* as "slave," rather than "servant," cf. *JEA*, XXVI (1941), 26, n.1; 73-74.

[5] The slaves. The two preceding uses of "they" are impersonal.

[6] Thus on the same day, but, on rumor, further south.

[7] Perhaps the frontier fortress of Sile, near modern Kantarah.

[8] This word *masharui* is probably corrupt and has usually been emended to *marui* "groom." In the present context it might be emended to a noun based on the Hebrew word *shamar* "watch, guard."

[9] For the location of this Migdol at Tell el-Her in Sinai and about a dozen miles northeast of Sile, see Gardiner in *JEA*, VI (1920), 109-10.

[10] Since Ani and Bak-en-Ptah seem to be still in pursuit of the slaves, these officers may have been located in Asia.

A Syrian Interregnum

For an unknown number of years between the Nineteenth and Twentieth Dynasties Egypt was in a chaotic state and for a part of the time was under the rule of a Syrian. All that we know of this episode comes from the following text.

The Great Papyrus Harris comes from Thebes and dates to the end of the reign of Ramses III (about 1164 B.C.), forming a kind of last will and testament for him. The troubles which he here describes lay between the reign of the last king of the Nineteenth Dynasty (about 1205 B.C.) and the beginning of the reign of Ramses III's father, Set-nakht (about 1197 B.C.).

Papyrus Harris I (British Museum 10053), lxxv 1-9. Facsimile of the text edited by S. Birch in *Facsimile of an Egyptian Hieratic Papyrus of the Reign of Rameses III, now in the British Museum* (London, 1876). Transcribed into hieroglyphic by W. Erichsen, *Papyrus Harris I* (*Bibliotheca Aegyptiaca*, v, Brussels, 1933), 91-92. Translated by Breasted, *AR*, iv, §§397-99.

Said King User-maat-Re Meri-Amon[1]—life, prosperity, health!—the great god,[2] to the officials and leaders of the land, the infantry, the chariotry, the Sherden,[3] the many bowmen, and all the souls of Egypt:

Hear ye, that I may make you aware of my benefactions which I accomplished while I was king of the people. The land of Egypt had been cast aside, with every man being his (*own standard of*) *right.* They had no chief spokesman for many years previously up to other times. The land of Egypt was officials and mayors,[4] one slaying his fellow, both exalted and lowly. Other *times* came afterwards in the empty years,[5] and . . . ,[6] a Syrian (5) with them, made himself prince. He set the entire land as tributary before him. One joined his companion that their property might be plundered. They treated the gods like the people, and no offerings were presented in the temples.

But when the gods reversed themselves to show mercy and to set the land right as was its normal state, they established their son, who had come forth from their body, to be Ruler—life, prosperity, health!—of every land, upon their great throne: User-kha-Re Setep-en-Re Meri-Amon—life, prosperity, health!—the Son of Re: Set-nakht Merer-Re Meri-Amon—life, prosperity, health! He was Khepri-Seth when he was enraged. He brought to order the entire land, which had been rebellious. He slew the disaffected of heart who had been in Egypt. He cleansed the great throne of Egypt.

[1] Ramses III (about 1195-1164 B.C.).

[2] The epithet normally means that the king is already dead. For the thesis that Papyrus Harris was actually promulgated by Ramses IV in the name of his father Ramses III, see W. Struve, in *Aegyptus*, vii (1926), 3 ff.

[3] Egyptian captive or mercenary troops, coming from the Mediterranean area. cf. p. 255, n.2.

[4] That is, broken down under local rule only, without king or other central government.

[5] Either years void of orderly rule, or years of emptiness, i.e. of economic distress.

[6] This translation treats the text on the assumption that the actual name of the Syrian has dropped out, leaving only the determinatives which show a foreigner. Alternatively, instead of translating "made himself," one may treat these elements as a proper name and read: "and Irsu, a Syrian, was with them as prince." In either case, the rule of an otherwise unknown Syrian ("Horite") is certain.

From the Lists of Ramses III

The course of the Egyptian Empire was marked by a rapid increase in the wealth and power of the Egyptian temples. We have a kind of testamentary enactment of Ramses III (about 1195-1164 B.C.) of the Twentieth Dynasty stating the accumulated properties of the temples through his benefactions. One authority has estimated that at the close of this pharaoh's reign the temples owned about 20% of the population of Egypt as serfs and about 30% of the arable land.[1] Our interest in the long document will be confined to the indications of Egyptian contacts with Asia.

Papyrus Harris I (British Museum 10053), edited by S. Birch in *Facsimile of an Egyptian Hieratic Papyrus of the Reign of Rameses III, now in the British Museum* (London, 1876). Transcribed into hieroglyphic by W. Erichsen, *Papyrus Harris I* (*Bibliotheca Aegyptiaca*, v, Brussels, 1933). Translated by Breasted, *AR*, iv, §§151-412. The extracts given below, with the §§ of Breasted's translation are: (a) activity on the Mediterranean: Papyrus Harris vii 8—Breasted §211; xxix 1—§270; xlviii 6—§328; (b) temple in Asia: ix 1-3—§219; (c) towns of Amon's estate: xi 10-11—§226; lxviii 1-2—§384; (d) serfs of the temples: viii 9—§217; x 15—§225; xxx 2—§278; xxxi 8—§281; xlvii 10—§322; lia 9—§338; (e) temple cattle: xiib 8—§229; lxix 10—§387; (f) temple grain: xxxiva 10—§287; liiia 7—§344; lxxib 1—§391; (g) temple oil: xva 4-6—§233; lxiiic 11-12—§376; (h) temple cedar: xvb 12-13—§234; liiia 12—§345; lxva 14—§379; lxxia 11—§391; (i) summary of northern wars: lxxvi 6-11—§§403-04.

A. ACTIVITY ON THE MEDITERRANEAN

Section for Amon of Thebes

(vii 8) I made for thee *qerer*-ships, *menesh*-ships, and *bari*-ships,[2] with bowmen equipped with their weapons on the Great Green Sea. I gave to them troop commanders and ship's captains, outfitted with many crews, without limit to them, in order to transport the goods of the land of Djahi and of the countries of the ends of the earth to thy great treasuries in Thebes-the-Victorious.

Section for Re of Heliopolis

(xxix 1) I made for thee *qerer*-ships and *menesh*-ships, outfitted with men, in order to transport the goods of God's Land[3] to thy treasury and thy storehouse.

Section for Ptah of Memphis

(xlviii 6) I made for thee *qerer*-ships and *menesh*-ships in the midst of the Great Green Sea, outfitted with crews of *menesh*-ships in abundant number, in order to transport the goods of God's Land and the dues of the land of Djahi to thy great treasuries of thy city Memphis.

B. TEMPLE OF AMON IN ASIA

(ix 1) I built for thee a mysterious house in the land of Djahi,[4] like the horizon of heaven which is in the

[1] So H. D. Schaedel, *Die Listen des grossen Papyrus Harris* (*Leipziger ägyptologische Studien*, 6, Glückstadt, 1936), 67. However, the true meaning of the lists is still in debate, and the number of unknown factors is large. Breasted, *op.cit.*, §§166-67, estimated that the temples owned 2% of the people and 15% of the land.

[2] Three separate types of ships, perhaps all cargo vessels capable of sea travel.

[3] The east generally, the Arabian or east African coast as well as the Palestinian-Phoenician coast.

[4] Djahi here clearly includes "the Canaan" and is an area to which the people of Retenu (the Syrian-Palestinian highland) normally would come. One may point to a settlement of Ramses III at Beth-Shan in Palestine, but this may have been one of several such settlements; see A. Rowe, *The Topography and History of Beth-Shan* (Philadelphia, 1930), 38 ff.

sky, (named) "the House of Ramses-Ruler-of-Heliopolis —life, prosperity, health!—in the Canaan," as the vested property of thy name. I fashioned thy great cult image which rests in it, (named) "Amon of Ramses-Ruler-of-Heliopolis—life, prosperity, health!" The foreigners of Retenu come to it, bearing their tribute before it, according as it is divine.

C. TOWNS OF AMON'S ESTATE

Theban Section

(xi 10)	Towns of Egypt	56
	Towns of Syria and Ethiopia[5]	9
	TOTAL	65

Summarizing Section

(lxviiia 1)	Towns of Egypt	160
	Towns of Syria	9
	TOTAL	169

D. SERFS OF THE TEMPLES

Theban Section

(viii 9) I fashioned thy august cult image. . . . I filled its house with male and female slaves whom I had carried off from the lands of the Asiatics.

(x 15) Syrians and Negroes[6] of the captivity of his majesty—life, prosperity, health!—whom he gave to the House of Amon-Re, King of the Gods, the House of Mut, and the House of Khonsu: 2,607 cases.[7]

Heliopolitan Section

(xxx 2) I made for thee a *fresh* foundation from the many classes whose sons I carried off to thy house, (named) "Taking the Others."[8]

(xxxi 8) Warriors, sons of (foreign) princes, *maryanu, apiru,*[9] and people settled who are in this place: 2,093 persons.[7]

Memphite Section

(xlvii 10) I made for thee workshops for the Feasts of Epiphany in thy divine house. They were built upon a ground effected with labor. I filled them with slaves whom I had carried off in captivity, in order to serve thy divine offerings, full and pure, in order to provision the House of Ptah with food and supplies, and in order to double what was before thee, O South-of-His-Wall! Thy Ennead is content of heart and gay over them.

(lia o) Syrians and Negroes of the captivity of his majesty—life, prosperity, health!—whom he gave to the House of Ptah: 205 cases.[7]

E. TEMPLE CATTLE

Theban Section

(xiib 8) Oxen, *steers,* various *long-horns, short-horns, and*[10] cattle from the dues of the lands of Syria: 19.[11]

Summarizing Section

(lxix 10) Oxen, *steers,* various *long-horns, short-horns, and* cattle from the dues of the lands of Syria: 19.

F. TEMPLE GRAIN

Heliopolitan Section

(xxxiva 10) Syrian grain: 5 *heḳet.*[12]

Memphite Section

(liiia 7) Syrian grain: 40 *heḳet.*

Summarizing Section

(lxxib 1) Syrian grain: 45 *heḳet.*[13]

G. TEMPLE OIL

Theban Section

(xva 4) Oil of Egypt: 2,743 *men*-measures.[14]
Oil of Syria: 53 *meseḳh*-measures.[14]
Oil of Syria: 1,757 *men*-measures.

Small Temples Section

(lxiiic 11) Oil of Egypt: 513 *men*-measures.
Oil of Syria: 542 *men*-measures.

H. TEMPLE CEDAR

Theban Section

(xvb 12) *Slabs* of cedar: 6.[15]
A *mast* of cedar: 1.[15]

Memphite Section

(liiia 12) *Beams* of cedar: 8.[16]

[5] "Towns of *Kharu* and *Cush*." Note that the summarizing section below —perhaps only by inadvertence—gives only "towns of *Kharu*," and that all the foreign towns are credited to the god Amon.

[6] "*Kharu*" (Hurru, Horites) and "*Nehsi*," the two terms used at this time for the northern and southern neighbors.

[7] Amon, Mut, and Khonsu formed the Theban triad of gods. The 2,607 foreigners are part of a total of 86,486 persons added to the Theban estates under Ramses III. The 2,093 foreigners are part of a total of 12,364 persons added to the Heliopolitan estates. The 205 foreigners are part of a total of 3,079 persons added to the Memphite estates. In these lists of temple serfs, the word *tep* "head," is regularly used for the Egyptian serfs. In the case of the Theban and Memphite lists, the word *sep* "case," is used for the foreign serfs.

[8] It is not absolutely certain that these were foreigners. "Others" may mean "outsiders, foreigners," or it may mean "the common people, the rabble."

[9] The term *maryanu* was used for Asiatic warriors in this period. cf. p. 22, n.2. The term *'apiru* has been argued to mean "aliens," particularly applicable to foreign slave labor, perhaps the same word as *Ḫabiru*, and thus etymologically related to "Hebrew"—but not implying that these captives were Israelites. See p. 247, n.47 above.

[10] Four or five terms for cattle are used, and we do not know enough about the different kinds to translate with precision. Further, it is not clear whether we have four kinds followed by a fifth or whether we have four kinds followed by an apposition: "(which are the) cattle from the dues of the lands of Syria."

[11] Amon's Asiatic cattle numbered 19, out of a total of 866 presented annually to his temple. For the argument that this was annual delivery, see A. H. Gardiner in *JEA*, XXVII (1941), 72-73. The summarizing section, here translated immediately after the Theban section, shows that only Amon received these Asiatic cattle.

[12] *Sherit* (a plant, assumed to be a kind of barley) of *Kharu*. The annual amount would be less than 3 pecks.

[13] A little over 6 bushels, of which Memphis received 8/9 annually.

[14] The amounts in volume of the *men*-jar measure and of the *meseḳh*-jar measure are unknown.

[15] The word translated "slabs" might mean "beams" or similar. The word translated "mast" was a major timber in shipbuilding.

[16] The word translated "beams" is used in shipbuilding—apparently for the ribs or side-planks.

Small Temples Section

(lxva 14) Various logs of cedar: 336.

Summarizing Section

(lxxia 11) Various logs of cedar: 351.[17]

I. SUMMARY OF NORTHERN WARS

I extended all the frontiers of Egypt and overthrew those who had attacked them from their (lxxvi 7) lands. I slew the Denyen in their islands, while the Tjeker and the Philistines were made ashes. The Sherden and the Weshesh of the Sea were made nonexistent, captured all together and brought in captivity to Egypt like the sands of the shore.[18] I settled them in strongholds, bound in my name.[19] Their military classes were as numerous as hundred-thousands. I assigned portions for them all with clothing and provisions from the treasuries and granaries every year.[20]

I destroyed the people of Seir among the Bedouin tribes.[21] I razed their tents: their people, their property, and their cattle as well, without number, pinioned and carried away in captivity, as the tribute of Egypt. I gave them to the Ennead of the gods, as slaves for their houses.

The War Against the Peoples of the Sea

In the latter half of the second millennium B.C. there were extensive movements in the eastern Mediterranean area. Masses of homeless peoples moved slowly across the sea and its coastlands, displacing or merging with the older populations. These migrations ended the Minoan civilization in Crete, contributed to the historical populations of Greece and Italy, wiped out the Hittite Empire, thrust the Philistines into Canaan, and washed up on the shores of Egypt. In Ramses III's eighth year (about 1188 B.C.) the pharaoh met and checked their attempt to push into the rich lands of the Nile. The victory was only a check, because the Egyptian Empire in Asia ended shortly after. The following accounts of this war come from Ramses III's temple of Medinet Habu at Thebes.

The texts were published by the Epigraphic Expedition, *Medinet Habu*, I. *Earlier Historical Records of Ramses III* (*OIP*, VIII, Chicago, 1930). They are translated in W. F. Edgerton and J. A. Wilson, *Historical Records of Ramses III* (*SAOC*, 12, Chicago, 1936), and by Breasted, *AR*, IV, §§59-82. See also the extract from Papyrus Harris, p. 262a above. In the following (a) is Pl. 46 of the Epigraphic Expedition publication; (b) Pl. 28; (c) Pl. 31; and (d) Pls. 37-39.

For the harem conspiracy at the end of the reign of Ramses III, see pp. 214-216 above.

a

(1) Year 8 under the majesty of (Ramses III)....

(16) . . . The foreign countries made a *conspiracy* in their islands. All at once the lands were removed and scattered in the fray. No land could stand before their arms, from Hatti, Kode, Carchemish, Arzawa, and Alashiya on,[1] being cut off *at* [*one time*]. A camp [was set up] in one place in Amor.[2] They desolated its people, and its land was like that which has never come into being. They were coming forward toward Egypt, while the flame was prepared before them. Their confederation was the Philistines, Tjeker, Shekelesh, Denye(n), and Weshesh,[3] lands united. They laid their hands upon the lands as far as the circuit of the earth, their hearts confident and trusting: "Our plans will succeed!"

Now the heart of this god, the Lord of the Gods, was prepared and ready to ensnare them like birds.... I organized my frontier in Djahi,[4] prepared before them:—princes, commanders of garrisons, (20) and *maryanu*.[5] I have the river-mouths[6] prepared like a strong wall, with warships, galleys and coasters, *(fully) equipped*, for they were manned completely from bow to stern with valiant warriors carrying their weapons. The troops consisted of every picked man of Egypt. They were like lions roaring upon the mountain tops. The chariotry consisted of runners, of *picked men*, of every good and capable chariot-warrior. The horses were quivering in every part of their bodies, prepared to crush the foreign countries under their hoofs. I was the valiant Montu,[7] standing fast at their head, so that they might gaze upon the capturing of my hands....

Those who reached my frontier, their seed is not, their heart and their soul are finished forever and ever. Those who came forward together on the sea, the full

[17] The total of the three preceding sections.

[18] The reference is to Ramses III's war against the Sea Peoples in his 8th year; cf. pp. 262-263 below. For the Tjeker, cf. the Wen-Amon story (p. 26, n.5 above). The Denyen (Danaoi), the Sherden (Sardians?), and the Weshesh (Wasasa?) were also participants in this great restlessness on the eastern Mediterranean in the latter half of the 2nd millennium B.C.

[19] Foreign captives were branded with the name of pharaoh. cf. Breasted, *op.cit.*, §405; The Epigraphic Survey, *Earlier Historical Records of Ramses III* (*Medinet Habu*, I, *OIP*, VIII, Chicago, 1930), Pl. 42.

[20] Not: "I taxed them all with," etc. Foreign captives were not taxworthy, but did need food and clothing from the state stores.

[21] It is interesting that Ramses III's only statement here of a campaign against Semitic peoples deals with the nomads of the region to the south of the Dead Sea. His scenes depicting campaigns into Syria-Palestine on the walls of his temple of Medinet Habu may all be pious or propagandistic forgeries—The Epigraphic Survey, *Later Historical Records of Ramses III* (*Medinet Habu*, II, *OIP*, IX, Chicago, 1932), Pls. 87-99; cf. W. F. Edgerton and J. A. Wilson, *Historical Records of Ramses III* (*SAOC*, 12, Chicago, 1936), 94, n.3b. Ramses III did have a temple at Beth-Shan and did have relations with Megiddo (p. 263 below), but he may have been unable to campaign north of Palestine, and he may have held garrison posts in Palestine without fighting. The complete collapse of the Egyptian Empire in Asia seems to have come shortly after his reign.

[1] Hatti was the Hittite Empire, Kode the coast of Cilicia and northern Syria, Carchemish the city on the Euphrates, Arzawa somewhere in or near Cilicia, and Alashiya probably Cyprus.

[2] Perhaps in the north Syrian plain or in Coele-Syria.

[3] Except for the Philistines (Peleset), these names are rendered close to the Egyptian writings. For the Tjeker, cf. the Wen-Amon story (pp. 25-29 above). The Shekelesh might be the Siculi, the Denyen (cuneiform Danuna) might be the Danaoi. The Weshesh cannot easily be related to any later people. cf. G. Bonfante, Who were the Philistines?, in *AJA*, L (1946) 251-62.

[4] The Phoenician coast, running down into Palestine. From what little we know of Ramses III's sway, his defensive frontier was not north of Palestine. It is possible that the land battle against the Peoples of the Sea was in Asia, whereas the sea battle was on the coast of Egypt; cf. n.6 below.

[5] From its pictured determinative, the word "princes" meant Asiatics. The *maryanu* were Asiatic warriors; see p. 22, n.2.

[6] Normally used for the mouths of the branches of the Nile in the Delta. Hence probably the line of defense in Egypt. Just possibly, the word might have been extended to harborages on the Asiatic coast.

[7] The Egyptian god of war.

flame was in front of them *at* the river-mouths, while a stockade of lances surrounded them on the shore.[8] They were dragged in, enclosed, and prostrated on the beach, killed, and made into heaps from tail to head. Their ships and their goods were as if fallen into the water.

I have made the lands turn back from (even) mentioning Egypt; for when they pronounce my name in their land, then (25) they are burned up. Since I sat upon the throne of Har-akhti and the Great-of-Magic[9] was fixed upon my head like Re, I have not let foreign countries behold the frontier of Egypt, to boast thereof to the Nine Bows.[10] I have taken away their land, their frontiers being added to mine. Their princes and their tribespeople are mine with praise, for I am on the ways of the plans of the All-Lord, my august, divine father, the Lord of the Gods.

b

[11](51) . . . The northern countries quivered in their bodies, the Philistines, Tjekk[er, and . . .]. They cut off their (own) land and were coming, their soul finished. They were *teher*-warriors on land;[12] another (group) was on the sea. Those who came on [land were *overthrown and killed* . . .]. Amon-Re was after them, destroying them. Those who entered the river-mouths were like birds *ensnared* in the net. . . . Their leaders were carried off and slain. They were cast down and pinioned. . . .

c

This is a scene showing Ramses III and his troops on the march against the Peoples of the Sea. It moves forward into a scene (Pl. 32 of the publication), in which the pharaoh is engaged in a land battle with the invaders. The logic of this arrangement is that the land battle was in Djahi.

His majesty sets out for Djahi, like unto Montu, to crush every foreign country that violates his frontier. His troops are like bulls ready upon the field of battle; his horses are like falcons in the midst of small birds. . . .

d

This scene shows a naval battle, in which the Egyptian ships grapple with the vessels of the Sea Peoples, while the pharaoh and his land troops fight from the shore.

Now then, the northern countries which were in their islands were quivering in their bodies. They penetrated the channels of the river-mouths. Their nostrils have ceased (to function, so) their desire is to breathe the breath. His majesty has gone forth like a whirlwind against them, fighting on the battlefield like a runner. The dread of him and the terror of him have entered into their bodies. They are capsized and overwhelmed where they are. Their heart is taken away, their soul is flown away. Their weapons are scattered upon the sea. His arrow pierces whom of them he may have wished, and the fugitive is become one fallen into the water.[13] His majesty is like an enraged lion, attacking his assailant with his arms: plundering on his right hand and powerful on his left hand, like Seth destroying the serpent "Evil of Character."[14] It is Amon-Re who has overthrown for him the lands and has crushed for him every land under his feet.

[8] One body had to be met on land (in Djahi?), whereas another body had to be met on sea (in the Delta?). The scenes show the boats of the Peoples of the Sea and also a movement by land in oxcarts, with women, children, and goods.

[9] The uraeus-serpent, symbol of kingship.

[10] The traditional enemies of Egypt.

[11] From "the Inscription of the Year 5," but here recording events in the Year 8.

[12] On *teher* as foreign warriors, see p. 239, n.3.

[13] The scene shows the capsized boats, the drowning Peoples of the Sea, and Ramses III shooting with unerring arrows.

[14] The god Seth defended the barque of the sun-god from a dragon, see pp. 11-12.

The Megiddo Ivories

A large collection of "Phoenician ivories" was found by excavation in a palace at Megiddo in Palestine. The carved designs were cosmopolitanly derived from various culture areas of the ancient Near East. The excavator tentatively dates the manufacture of the pieces between 1350 and 1150 B.C. Among the ivories are five bearing Egyptian hieroglyphs. A model pen case of an Egyptian envoy to foreign countries bears the name of Ramses III (about 1195-1164 B.C.), setting the *terminus ad quem* for the collection. The ivories were published by G. Loud, *The Megiddo Ivories* (*OIP*, LII, Chicago, 1939), with a translation of the hieroglyphic inscriptions by J. A. Wilson on pp. 11-13. Photographs of the Egyptian pieces appear on Pls. 62-63.

Three plaques, which may have been used for inlay in furniture, bear the name of

the Singer of Ptah, South-of-His-Wall, Lord of the Life of the Two Lands, and Great Prince of Ashkelon, Kerker.

Kerker (or Kurkur or Kulkul) seems to have been a woman minstrel for the Egyptian god Ptah in Palestine, like the woman singer at the court of Byblos in the Wen-Amon story (pp. 28, n.39; 246, n.30, above). The first two of Ptah's titles apply to his cult-home at Memphis in Egypt, the third—"Great Prince of Ashkelon"—implies a cult-seat at that Palestinian city.

For the relations of Egypt and Asia about 1100 B.C., see the Journey of Wen-Amon to Phoenicia (pp. 25-29 above).

The Campaign of Sheshonk I

Sheshonk I (about 945-924 B.C.) is the Shishak of the Old Testament. It is disappointing to find that the Egyptian texts do not enlarge our understanding of his campaign in Palestine in a sense which constitutes a real addition to the biblical account. To be sure, he has left us a listing of the Palestinian and Syrian towns which he claimed to have conquered, and this list may be reconstructed into a kind of itinerary.[1] There is, however, no narrative account of the campaign by the pharaoh. The references in his inscriptions to "tribute of the land of Syria" or to his victories over the "Asiatics of distant foreign countries" are vague and generalized. How unhistorical his large claims were is clear from a statement to the pharaoh by the god Amon: "I have subjugated [for] thee the Asiatics of the armies of

[1] See pp. 242-243 above. For the reconstruction of a possible itinerary, see A. T. Olmstead, *History of Palestine and Syria* (New York, 1931), 354-56.

Mitanni."[2] Mitanni as a nation had ceased to exist at least four centuries earlier.

In addition to the list of towns, we do possess two documents attesting the name of Sheshonk on Asiatic soil. At Megiddo in Palestine was found a fragment of a monumental stela bearing the name of Sheshonk I and permitting the conclusion that the pharaoh had set up a triumphal monument there.[3] At Byblos in Phoenicia another fragment, this time the chair of a seated statue, bears his name, although this monument may well be a princely gift, rather than a symbol of conquest.[4]

Finally, the Walters Art Gallery in Baltimore has a basalt statuette of an Egyptian, the "Envoy of the Canaan and of Palestine, Pa-di-Eset, the son of Apy," which may date to the Twenty-second Dynasty. This piece does not involve conquest, but rather diplomatic relations.[5]

[2] J. Lammeyer, *Das Siegesdenkmal des Königs Scheschonk I. zu Karnak* (Neuss a. Rhein, 1907), 29. This text and the list noted above are treated by Breasted, *AR*, IV, §§709-22, where additional bibliography will be found.

[3] R. S. Lamon and G. M. Shipton, *Megiddo* I (*OIP*, XLII, Chicago, 1939), 60-61.

[4] R. Dussaud in *Syria*, V (1924), 145-47.

[5] G. Steindorff in *JEA*, XXV (1939), 30-33, Pl. VII. Steindorff points out that the father's name may be Canaanite in origin.

Babylonian and Assyrian Historical Texts

TRANSLATOR: A. LEO OPPENHEIM

Texts from the Beginnings to the First Dynasty of Babylon

For this section, two documents have been selected to illustrate the content and the stylistic features of early Mesopotamian historiography, while two groups of texts have been translated to represent the historical source material, which is rather rare in this period.

The texts of the first part are: (1) an excerpt of the Sumerian King List, and (2) the "Sargon Chronicle." The second part contains (1) two inscriptions from statues of Sargon of Agade, (2) an excerpt from an inscription of Naram-Sin, and (3) excerpts from three inscriptions of the well-known Gudea of Lagash.

HISTORIOGRAPHIC DOCUMENTS

I. THE SUMERIAN KING LIST

In his book *The Sumerian King List* (*AS*, No. 11), Thorkild Jacobsen offers not only a critical edition of the entire text material[1] and an excellent translation,[2] but also critical examination of all textual, stylistic, and historical problems involved. On the basis of a systematic study of the numerous variant readings, Jacobsen has shown that all extant "manuscripts" go back to one single original written at the time of Utu-hegal, king of Uruk, the liberator of Sumer from the yoke of the Guti domination. To demonstrate that his country had always been united under one king—though these kings were ruling successively in different capitals—the learned and patriotic author compiled this interesting document from two types of literary sources: from lists containing the names of the kings, the places and the lengths of their rules (established originally for practical chronological purposes), and from epical texts, legendary stories, local anecdotic traditions, etc., dealing with the biography and the marvelous deeds of some of these primeval kings. This literary material is referred to in very succinct sentences scattered throughout the monotonous enumeration of royal names, figures, and place names. To this opus has later been added a section dealing with the events before the Flood. This "preamble" has an entirely different literary background[3] and does not appear in all manuscripts.

The entire text material has been utilized by Thorkild Jacobsen (*The Sumerian King List*) to establish a "standard version" of this document on the basis of the most extensive "manuscript" published by S. Langdon from the Weld-Blundell Collection (= *Oxford Edition of Cuneiform Texts*, Vol. II [Oxford, 1923]), No. 1923, 444, pp. 13 ff. and Pls. I-IV.

The following translation contains lines i 1—iv 5 with the "ante-diluvian" preamble (cf. above) and the historical survey from the beginnings to the end of the First Dynasty of Ur. This section has been selected because it contains the names of the kings who ruled for an excessive length of time as well as nearly all the passages of mythological and literary interest.

[1] An additional text has been published since by V. Scheil, Liste susienne des dynasties de Sumer-Accad, in *Mémoires, inst. franç. d'archéol. orientale . . . du Caire*, LXII (1934), (=*Mélanges Maspero*, I), 393-400.

[2] My translation differs only slightly and in minor points from that of T. Jacobsen.

[3] cf., for a more detailed discussion, Jacobsen, *op.cit.*, pp. 63 f.

When kingship was lowered from heaven, kingship was (first) in Eridu. (In) Eridu, A-lulim[4] (became) king and ruled 28,800 years. Alalgar ruled 36,000 years. Two kings (thus) ruled it for 64,800 years.

I drop (the topic) Eridu (because) its kingship was brought to Bad-tibira. (In) Bad-tibira, En-men-lu-Anna ruled 43,200 years; En-men-gal-Anna ruled 28,800 years; the god Dumu-zi, a shepherd, ruled 36,000 years. Three kings (thus) ruled it for 108,000 years.

I drop (the topic) Bad-tibira (because) its kingship was brought to Larak. (In) Larak, En-sipa-zi-Anna ruled 28,800 years. One king (thus) ruled it for 28,800 years.

I drop (the topic) Larak (because) its kingship was brought to Sippar. (In) Sippar, En-men-dur-Anna became king and ruled 21,000 years. One king (thus) ruled it for 21,000 years.

I drop (the topic) Sippar (because) its kingship was brought to Shuruppak. (In) Shuruppak, Ubar-Tutu became king and ruled 18,600 years. One king (thus) ruled it for 18,600 years.

These are five cities, eight kings ruled them for 241,000 years. (Then) the Flood swept over (the earth).

After the Flood had swept over (the earth) (and) when kingship was lowered (again) from heaven, kingship was (first) in Kish. In Kish, Ga[. . .]ur became king and ruled 1,200 years—(original) destroyed! legible (only) to heavenly Nidaba (the goddess of writing)—ruled 960 years. [Pala-kinatim ruled 900 years; Nangish-lishma ruled . . . years];[5] Bah[i]na ruled . . . years; BU.AN. [. .] . [um] ruled [8]40 ye[ars]; Kalibum ruled 960 years; Qalumum ruled 840 years; Zuqaqip ruled 900 years; Atab ruled 600 years; [Mashda, son][6] of Atab ruled 840 years; Arwi'um, son of Mashda, ruled 720 years; Etana, a shepherd, he who ascended to heaven (and) who consolidated all countries, became king and ruled 1,560 (var.: 1,500) years; Balih, son of Etana, ruled 400 (var.: 410) years; En-me-nunna ruled 660 years; Melam-Kishi, son of En-me-nunna ruled 900 years; Bar-sal-nunna, son of En-me-nunna, ruled 1,200 years; Samug, son of Bar-sal-nunna, ruled 140 years; Tizkar, son of Samug, ruled 305 years; Ilku' ruled 900 years; Ilta-sadum ruled 1,200 years; En-men-barage-si, he who carried away as spoil the "weapon" of Elam, became king and ruled 900 years; Aka, son of En-men-barage-si, ruled 629 years. Twenty-three kings (thus) ruled it for 24,510 years, 3 months, and 3½ days.

[4] For a late (Neo-Assyrian) reference to this first king of Mesopotamia, cf. my note in *BASOR*, 97 (1944), 26-27.

[5] The passage in square brackets does not appear in the Weld-Blundell text.

[6] Emendation of T. Jacobsen; cf. Jacobsen, *op.cit.*, p. 24.

Kish was defeated in battle (lit.: was smitten with weapons), its kingship was removed to Eanna (sacred precinct of Uruk).

In Eanna, Mes-kiag-gasher, the son of the (sun) god Utu, became high priest as well as king, and ruled 324 years. Mes-kiag-gasher went (daily) into the (Western) Sea and came forth (again) toward the (Sunrise) Mountains; En-me-kar, son of Mes-kiag-gasher, he who built Uruk, became king and ruled 420 years; the god Lugal-banda, a shepherd, ruled 1,200 years; the god Dumu-zi, a ŠU.PEŠ-fisherman[7]—his (native) city was Ku'a(ra),—ruled 100 years; the divine Gilgamesh, his father was a *lillû*,[8] a high priest of Kullab, ruled 126 years; Ur-Nungal (var.: Ur-lugal), son of Gilgamesh, ruled 30 years; Utul-kalamma, son of Ur-nun-gal (var.: Ur-lugal), ruled 15 years; Laba[h . . .]ir ruled 9 years; En-nun-dara-Anna ruled 8 years; MES(?).ḪÉ, a smith, ruled 36 years; Melam-Anna ruled 6 years; Lugal-ki-tun(?) ruled 36 years. Twelve kings (thus) ruled it for 2,310 years.

Uruk was defeated in battle, its kingship was removed to Ur.

In Ur, Mes-Anne-pada became king, ruled 80[9] years; Mes-kiag-Nanna[10] became king, ruled 36 years; [Elulu ruled 25 years; Balulu ruled 36 years. Four kings (thus) ruled it for 177 years. Ur was defeated in battle].

2. THE "SARGON CHRONICLE"

While in the Sumerian King List the references to legendary, pseudo-historical, and historical traditions occur only sporadically and are subordinated to the chronological framework elaborated by the author, here they have overgrown the basically annalistic structure in a type of chronicle to be represented by two tablets of the same series.[1] This literary work centers its attention around the most interesting of the historical figures and reports their outstanding achievements in peace and war with special regard to the unique and the memorable. Important events in neighboring countries as well as foreign invasions are recorded from time to time. For a literary evaluation of this document, cf. H. G. Güterbock, *ZA*, XLII (NF VIII), 1 ff.

a

The tablet (British Museum 26,472), written in the Neo-Babylonian Period, has been published by L. W. King in his *Chronicles Concerning Early Babylonian Kings* (London, 1907), II, 113-119. Transliteration and translation: *op.cit.*, pp. 3-14. Latest complete translation: Ebeling in *AOT*, 335-336.

Sargon (*Šarru-kên*), king of Agade, rose (to power) in the era of Ishtar[2] and had neither rival nor opponent. He spread his terror-inspiring glamor over all the countries. He crossed the Sea in the East and he, himself, conquered the country of the West, in its full extent,

[7] For this profession, cf. Jacobsen, *op.cit.*, p. 88, n.125.

[8] For this difficult word, cf. Jacobsen, *op.cit.*, p. 90, n.131; also, my remarks in *Orientalia*, NS XVI (1947), 233, n.3.

[9] For this figure, cf. Jacobsen, *op.cit.*, p. 93, n.145. From historical inscriptions of his own, we know that the name of the son of this king was A-anne-pada. For unknown reasons, he is not mentioned in the present list.

[10] *Nanna* to be emendated to *nunna*; cf. Jacobsen, *op.cit.*, p. 94, n.146.

[1] This tablet belongs to the same literary work as the text translated p. 303. cf. B. Landsberger-Th. Bauer, *ZA*, XXXVII, (NF III), 61 ff.

[2] For the latest discussion of the enigmatic expression "era of Ishtar," cf. J. Lewy, *HUCA*, XIX (1946), 420, 480.

in the 11th year (of his rule). He established there a central government (lit.: he made its mouth be one). He erected his stelae in the West. Their booty (i.e. the booty of the countries in the Eastern and Western Seas) he ferried over on rafts. He made his court officials live (around his residence, thus covering an area) of five double-miles, and held sway over the totality of the countries, without exception.

He marched against the country of Kazalla[3] and turned Kazalla into ruin-hills and heaps (of rubble).[3a] He (even) destroyed (there every possible) perching place for a bird.

Afterwards, in his old age, all the countries revolted against him and they besieged him in Agade. (But) Sargon made an armed sortie and defeated them, knocked them over, and crushed their vast army.

Later on, Subartu[4] rose with its multitudes, but it bowed to his military might. Sargon made sedentary this nomadic society.[5] Their possessions he brought into Agade. He took away earth from the (*foundation*)-pits[6] of Babylon and he built upon it a(nother) Babylon beside the town of Agade. On account of the sacrilege he (thus) committed, the great lord Marduk became enraged and destroyed his people by hunger. From the East to the West he alienated[7] (them) from him and inflicted upon [him] (as punishment) that he could not rest (in his grave).[8]

Naram-Sin, son of Sargon, marched against the town of Apishal[9] and made a breach (in its wall to conquer it). He personally caught Rish-Adad, king of Apishal, and the *sukkal* of Apishal. He (also) marched against the country Magan and personally caught Mannu-dannu, king of Magan.[10]

Shulgi,[11] son of Ur-Nanshe, took very good care of the town of Eridu which is on the seashore (but) he had evil intentions and he removed the property of the

[3] The British Museum text K 2130, a collection of hepatoscopic omina referring to historical events and personalities (first published in Rawlinson, Vol. IV, Pl. 34, No. 1), gives the name of the king of Kazalla, to wit: Kashtubila.

[3a] For this translation of the well-known nouns *tillu u ḳarmu* cf. E. F. Weidner in *Mélanges syriens*, II, 924, n.5.

[4] My translation differs from the usual by emending the vertical wedge before ^{mat}*Su-bir*$_4$^{ki}. The use of the verbs *tebû* and *ḳamâsu* fits much better into the thus corrected phrase, and so does the word *gipšu*, which normally describes an unorganized army and therefore seems more likely to refer to the army of Subartu than to that of Sargon. The lines 15-16 (*abiḳta-šú-nu im-ḫaṣ ḳa-mar-šú-nu iš-ḳun um-man-šú-nu rapaštim*^{tim} *ú-šam-qí-it*) have been omitted as an erroneous repetition of lines 12-13.

[5] Conjectural translation, text in disorder.

[6] This passage (and its parallel in the so-called "Weidner-Chronicle," cf. H. G. Güterbock, *ZA*, XLII [NF VIII], 47 ff., rev. 17) has been lately elucidated by Güterbock, in *AfO*, XIII (1940-41), 50, who connected it with *is(s)û* "pit." The passage seems therefore to suggest that the contents (clean earth and sand) of the well-known deep pits under the emplacements of the images were considered endowed with the very essence of the "holiness" which pervaded the image, its temple, and its sacred city.

[7] The subject of all three verbs is necessarily Marduk.

[8] For this punishment, cf. lately E. F. Weidner, *AfO*, XIII (1940-41), 236, n.26.

[9] For this town, cf. I. J. Gelb, *AJSL*, LV (1938), 70 f.

[10] For a recent statement concerning the often discussed problem of the identification of Mannu-dannu (var.: Manium) with Menes, the first king of the list of Manetho, cf. E. Drioton and J. Vandier, *L'Egypt* (Paris, 1946), pp. 162 ff.; and of Magan with Egypt, cf. A. Ungnad, *AfO*, XIV (1941-44), 199 f.

[11] For the still uncertain reading of this name of the second king of the Third Dynasty of Ur, formerly often read Dungi, cf. T. Jacobsen, in *BASOR*, 102 (1947), 16 ff., where the transliteration ŠAḪ - g i is proposed.

temple Esagila and of Babylon sacrilegiously. Bel be[came angry] and his corpse (i.e. of Shulgi) he (illegible) him.

Irra-imitti,[12] the king, installed Bel-ibni, the gardener, on his throne as a "substitute king"[13] and he (Irra-imitti) (even) placed his own royal crown on his (i.e. Bel-ibni's) head. (During the ceremonial rule of Bel-ibni) Irra-imitti died in his palace while sip[ping][14] hot porridge, and Bel-ibni who was (still) sitting on the throne did not rise (any more), he (thus) was elevated to (real) kingship.

Catchline:[15] Ilishuma was king of Assyria in the time of Su(mu)abu (king of Babylon).[16]

b

Continuation of the preceding text on tablet British Museum 96,152, published by King, *op.cit.*, pp. 121-127; transliteration and translation: *op.cit.*, pp. 17 ff. and Ebeling, *AOT*, 337.

(obverse 8—reverse 17)

Hammurabi, king of Babylon, called up his army and marched against Rim-Sin, king of Ur. He personally conquered Ur and Larsa, he took their possessions to Babylon. The . . . of . . . he threw down, the [booty of . . .] he carried away.

[Samsuilu]na, king of Babylon, son of Ha[mmura]bi, the king, [did . . . , his army he cal]led up and . . . Rim-Sin . . . he marched. He personally conquered [Ur and Larsa]; [he caught] him alive in the palace. . . . He marched [against . . .] and laid siege . . . its inhabitants. . . .

(end of obverse and beginning of reverse destroyed)

[Ili]ma-ilum . . . water, he built . . . and made an attack against him . . . , their corpses [filled] the sea. For a second time, Samsuiluna rose to [attack] Ilima-ilum and [he inflicted] a defeat [upon his army].

Abishi (= Abieshuh), son of Samsuiluna, did . . . to defeat Ilima-ilum and he had the idea of damming up the Tigris;[17] he actually dammed up the Tigris, but he did not [catch] Ilima-ilum.

In the time of Samsuditana, the country of Hatti [marched] against Akkad.[18]

Ea-gamil, king of the Sea-Country, [marched] against Elam.

After him, Ulamburiash, brother of Kashtiliash, of the country of the Kassites, called up his army and conquered the Sea-Country. He held (thus) sway over the (entire) country.

Agum, son of Kashtiliash, called up his army and marched against the Sea-Country. He conquered the town Dur-Ea. He demolished the temple é.egara.urù.na[19] of Ea in Dur-Ea.

[12] The ninth king of the Dynasty of Isin.

[13] cf. for this incident and its background R. Labat, *Le caractère religieux de la royauté assyro-babylonienne* (Paris, 1939), pp. 103 f., and H. Frankfort, *Kingship and the Gods* (Chicago 1947), pp. 263 f.

[14] According to the very suggestive explanation of A. Ungnad in *Orientalia*, NS XII (1943), 194 ff., this rite was performed on account of an eclipse of the moon which portended evil for the king. For *sarâpu* "to sip," cf. H. G. Güterbock, *ZA*, XLII (NF VIII), 60, n.2.

[15] This "catchline" (colophon) indicates the first line of the next—here the third—tablet of the series.

[16] The founder of the First Dynasty of Babylon ("Hammurabi Dynasty").

[17] For the strategic use made in war of the changing levels of the Mesopotamian rivers, cf. also the damaged evidence contained in the report on the first campaign of Samsuiluna against Ilimailum of the Sea-Country. cf., furthermore, n.12, p. 270.

[18] These words are written, in smaller characters, over the line which separates the paragraphs.

[19] Not in Deimel, *ŠL*. For the sign agara, cf. R. T. Hallock, *The Chicago Syllabary and the Louvre Syllabary AO 7661* (*AS*, No. 7 [1940]), line 244, =*bît ku-mu-ri-e* "store house." The name é.agara.urù.na could therefore mean "temple . . . with an *urunakku*" (cf. Deimel, *ŠL*, 331/20, for this building [?]).

HISTORICAL DOCUMENTS

I. SARGON OF AGADE

The tablet is large, with 14 columns on either side, containing copies of inscriptions on votive objects and statues set up in the temple Ekur in Nippur. According to its paleographic features, the tablet was written soon after the rule of the Dynasty of Agade. The inscriptions are those of Lugalzaggisi, king of Uruk, and of Sargon, Rimush, Manishtusu, kings of Agade. Two fragments of this tablet have been successively published by A. Poebel in *Historical and Grammatical Texts* (Philadelphia, 1914, *UM*, v), Pl. xx, No. 34, and by L. Legrain, *The Museum Journal* (University of Pennsylvania), XIV (1923), 203 ff., Figs. 42-44. Transliterations and translations: Poebel (*UM*, IV), 173 ff., Legrain (*UM*, XIV), 12 ff.; G. A. Barton, *The Royal Inscriptions of Sumer and Akkad* (New Haven, 1929), pp. 101 ff. (Inscription AB.) Latest translation of v-vi 5-52, Ebeling, *AOT*, 338.

(i-ii 1—iii-iv 44)

Sargon, king of Agade, overseer of Ishtar, king of Kish,[1] anointed priest of Anu, king of the country, great ensi[2] of Enlil; he defeated Uruk and tore down its wall; in the battle with the inhabitants of Uruk he was victorious. Lugalzaggisi, king of Uruk, he captured in (this) battle, he brought him in a (dog) collar to the gate of Enlil. Sargon, king of Agade, was victorious in the battle with the inhabitants of Ur, the(ir) town he defeated and tore down its wall. He defeated (the town) E-Ninmar and tore down its wall and defeated (also) its (entire) territory from Lagash as far as the sea. His weapon (then) he washed in the sea. In the battle with the inhabitants of Umma he was victorious, the(ir) town he defeated and tore down its wall.

Enlil did not let anybody oppose Sargon, the king of the country. Enlil gave him (the region from) the Upper Sea (to) the Lower Sea. From the Lower Sea onwards, natives of Agade are holding the governorships. Mari and Elam are standing (in obedience) before Sargon, king of the country. Sargon, king of the country, restored Kish, he ordered them to take (again) possession of the(ir) city.

May Shamash destroy the potency[3] and make perish every offspring of whosoever damages this inscription.

Inscription on the pedestal of (a statue of) Sargon, king of the country.

[1] For this title and its political implications, cf. T. Jacobsen, *The Sumerian King List*, pp. 181 f.; also, J. Lewy in *HUCA*, XIX (1946), 476. Furthermore, p. 274-275, n.2.

[2] Formerly read *patesi*; the new reading has been proposed by A. Falkenstein in *ZA*, XLII (NF VIII), 152 ff., and has been generally accepted (cf. F. M. Th. Boehl, *MAOG*, XI [1937], p. 37, n.1, but contrast A. Deimel in *ŠL*, *Šumerisch-akkadisches Glossar* [Rome, 1934], p. 94a).

[3] This is the exact meaning of the idiom *išdâ nasâhu*.

(v-vi 5-52)

. . . Sargon, king of Kish, was victorious in 34 campaigns and dismantled (all) the cities, as far as the shore of the sea. At the wharf of Agade he made moor ships from Meluhha,[4] ships from Magan,[4] (and) ships from Dilmun.[5] Sargon, the king, prostrated (himself) in prayer before the god Dagan in Tutul[6] (and) he gave (him) the Upper Region (i.e.) Mari, Iarmuti (and) Ibla as far as the Cedar Forest and the Silver Mountain. Enlil did not let anybody oppose Sargon, the king. 5,400 soldiers ate daily in his palace (lit.: presence).

May Anu destroy the name and Enlil finish off the offspring, Inanna do . . . to whosoever destroys this inscription.

Inscription on a statue the pedestal of which is not inscribed.

2. NARAM-SIN IN THE CEDAR MOUNTAIN[1]

The text, published, transliterated, and translated by C. J. Gadd and L. Legrain in *UET*, as No. 275 (Vol. I, pp. 74 ff.; Vol. II, Pl. LVI) is taken from a collection of late copies (approximately, Dynasty of Isin or First Babylonian Dynasty) made on a clay tablet from inscriptions of the kings of the dynasty of Agade The copies are negligently made and offer therefore many difficulties.

(i 1—ii 28)

Although since the era of the *si-ḳ[i]-ti*[2] of man(kind) none of the kings has ever destroyed[3] (the towns) Arman and Ibla, *now*[4] the god Nergal did open up the path *for* the mighty[5] Naram-Sin, and gave him Arman and Ibla, and he presented him (also) with the Amanus, the Cedar Mountain and (with) the Upper Sea. And mighty Naram-Sin slew Arman and Ibla with the "weapon" of the god Dagan who aggrandizes his kingdom. And he . . .[6] all the peoples with which Dagan had presented him for the first time,[7] from the Euphrates frontier as far as Ulisum and . . .[8] the corvée-basket for his god Amal. And he *overpowered*[9] the Amanus, the Cedar Mountain.

[4] At this period, Magan and Meluhha are probably denominations of still unidentified countries on the eastern shores of Arabia. With the expanding geographical horizon, these names shift constantly towards the southeastern peripheral regions of the known *orbis terrarum*. cf. e.g., W. F. Albright, *JAOS*, XLII (1922), 317 ff.

[5] For this country, its geographical location, and its meaning within a certain type of Mesopotamian literature, cf. S. N. Kramer, *BASOR*, 96 (1944), 18-28 (cf., also P. B. Cornwall, *BASOR*, 103 [1946], 3-10).

[6] cf. for this town I. J. Gelb in *AJSL*, LV (1938), 74.

[1] In the context, the expression "Cedar Mountain" clearly refers to the Amanus, but there are indications that this basically "mytho-geographic" term denotes also a region east of Mesopotamia. cf. S. N. Kramer *BASOR*, 96 (1944), 20 ff.

[2] Though one expects here a reference to the creation of man or the like, the term *šiḳittu* is difficult to interpret in this sense.

[3] Text: *u-sa-al-bi-tu*.

[4] For *in šu(?)-e* in this very dubious meaning, reference has to be made to Landsberger's guess in *OLZ*, XXXIV (1931), 131.

[5] Translation uncertain; "mighty" is nominative.

[6] Text: *u-ra-is* which is usually interpreted (cf. von Soden, *ZA*, XLI [NF VII], 170) as "he crushed," but the context and the reference to the corvée-basket suggest a verb (expected: *warā'u*) referring to a transfer of the conquered population for forced labor.

[7] For this translation, cf. Jacobsen in *AJSL*, XLVI (1929), 70.

[8] The text seems to have *na-sì-ni/um* (to *našā'u* "to carry"?) not *na-ab-num*.

[9] Text: *i-iḳ/g-mu-ur*.

3. GUDEA, ENSI OF LAGASH

a

From the "Cylinder A" published by E. de Sarzec and L. Heuzey, *Découvertes en Chaldée* (Paris, 1884 ff.), Pls. 33-35. Latest translation: G. A. Barton, *The Royal Inscriptions of Sumer and Akkad* (New Haven, 1929), pp. 205 ff.

(xv 1—xvi 24)

. . . from Elam came the Elamite(s), from Susa the Susian(s). Magan and Meluhha collected timber from their mountains, and—in order to build the temple of Ningirsu—Gudea brought (these materials) together in his town Girsu.

After the god Ninzagga had given him a (pertinent) order, they brought copper for Gudea, the temple-builder as if it be NI. š e . m a ḫ ; after the god Ninsikila had given him a (pertinent) order, they brought great willow-logs, ebony-logs, together with a b b a -logs to the e n s i, the temple-builder. Gudea, the e n -priest of Ningirsu, made a path in(to) the Cedar Mountain which nobody had entered (before); he cut its cedars with great axes. With axes he fashioned (them) for the SÁR.ÚR, the "Right Arm of Lagash," the "Floodstorm-Weapon" of his king. (Like) giant snakes, cedar rafts were floating down the water (of the river) from the Cedar Mountain, pine rafts from the Pine Mountain, z a b a l u m -wood rafts from the z a b a l u m -wood Mountain, and with them were floating down(stream) large rafts with great logs of ù -wood, t u l u b u m -wood and of e r a l u m -wood, in the main quay of Kasurra. . . .

[In the quarries which nobody had entered (before), Gudea], the e n -priest of Ningirsu, ma[de] a path and (thus) the stones were delivered in large blocks. Boats (loaded) with ḫ a l u n a -stone, boats (loaded) with n a l u -stone, they brought to Gudea, e n -priest of Ningirsu, also bitumen (filled) in buckets, i g i . e n g u r -bitumen[1] and gypsum from the mountains of Madga as (if they be) boats bringing in barley from the fields. Many other precious materials were carried to the e n s i, the builder of the Ninnu-temple: from the copper mountains of Kimash—(after) the soil had been prospected (for copper ore)—its copper was mined in clusters;[2] gold was delivered from its mine (lit.: mountain) as dust for the e n s i who wanted to build a house for his king, for Gudea they mined silver from its mine (lit.: mountain), delivered red stone from Meluhha in great amounts. In the š i r -quarry, they mined š i r -stone (alabaster) for him.

b

From the "Statue B" published by E. de Sarzec and L. Heuzey, *Découvertes en Chaldée* (Paris, 1884 ff.), Pls. 16 ff., and p. vii. Latest translation: G. A. Barton, *op.cit.*, pp. 181 ff.

(v 21—40, v 53—vi 63)

When he (Gudea) was building the temple of Nin-

[1] Probably, "bitumen from a well."

[2] Text: u š u b . b a which could refer to copper ore found in globular druses, rather than describe the way in which the ore was transported from the mine. For u š u b "nest, basketlike boat," cf. Deimel, *ŠL*, 85/242.

girsu, Ningirsu, his beloved king, opened up for him (all) the (trade) routes from the Upper to the Lower Sea. In (lit.: from) the Amanus, the Cedar Mountain, he formed into rafts cedar logs 60 cubits long, cedar logs 50 cubits long (and) KU-wood logs 25 cubits long, and brought them (thus) out of the mountain. He fashioned (from this wood) for him (i.e. Ningirsu) the SÁR.ÚR, his Floodstorm-Weapon for the battle, and he made for him the SÁR.GAZ-mace with seven copper knobs (lit.: eyes). In the town Ursu[1] in the mountains of Ibla,[1] he formed into rafts the timber of the mountain region: z a b a l u m -logs, great Ù.KU-wood logs and t u l u b u m -logs. He made them into roof beams for (lit.: in) the Ninnu-temple. In (lit.: from) Umanum, in the mountains of Menua, he quarried great blocks of stone (and also) in Basalla, in the mountains of Martu (i.e. the Westland). He made stelae of them and set them up in the courtyard of the Ninnu-temple. From Tidanum[2] in the mountains of Martu (Westland) he brought alabaster in great blocks and fashioned it into u r . p a d . d a *-slabs* and *erected* them in the temple as barriers. In KÁ.GAL.AD, a mountain (region) in Kimash, he mined copper and fashioned it into the Mace-of-the-Relentless-Storm. He imported (lit.: brought out) e s i -wood from the mountains of Meluhha and built ⟨ . . . ⟩. He imported n i r -stone and made it into a mace with three lion-heads; from the Hahhum[3]-mountains, he imported gold in dust-form and mounted with it the mace with the three lion-heads. From the mountains of Meluhha he imported gold in dust-form and made (out of it) a container (for the mace). He (also) imported a b r i , he imported willow logs from Gubin in the Willow Mountains and fashioned (them) into the bird(-shaped part) of the SÁR.ÚR-mace. From Madga in the mountains of the Luruda river, he imported bitumen[4] and built (with it) the supporting wall (k i s a) of the Ninnu temple. He imported (also) ḫ a . u m -earth. From the mountains of Barsip he loaded n a l u a -stones on large boats and surrounded (with them) the foundation of the Ninnu temple.

c

"Macehead A," published by E. de Sarzec and L. Heuzey, *op.cit.*, Pl. 25 *bis*, No. 1. Latest translation: G. A. Barton, *op.cit.*, p. 261.

For his king Ningirsu, the powerful hero of Enlil, Gudea, the e n s i of Lagash, had quarried and imported (this) š i r . g a l -stone (marble) from the Uringiraz-mountains of the Upper Sea (Mediterranean Sea) and fashioned (it) into a macehead with three lion-heads, and dedicated it to him for (the preservation of) his life.

[1] cf. for these place names, I. J. Gelb, *AJSL*, LV (1938), 77 and 84.
[2] For the location of this country, cf. A. Poebel, *JNES*, I (1942), 257 f.
[3] cf. Gelb, *AJSL*, LV, 75 f.
[4] Text: e s i r . g ú . ḪI + KASKAL. For the last sign (not in Deimel, *ŠL*), cf. F. Thureau-Dangin, *Recherches sur l'origine de l'écriture cunéiforme* (Paris, 1898), No. 214.

Texts from Hammurabi to the Downfall of the Assyrian Empire

The six texts of the first part (Historiographic Documents) illustrate the development of official historiography in Mesopotamia; at the same time, they give the chronological framework (in terms of the sequence of dynasties) and most of the royal names from the First Babylonian Dynasty to the end of the Assyrian domination in Babylonia.

The first text (1) contains the full wording of the names of the forty-three years during which Hammurabi was king of Babylon. The present list is based upon the compilation of A. Ungnad in his article, Datenlisten, in the *Reallexikon der Assyriologie*, II, 187 ff., in which he collected the names and arranged them in the sequence indicated by the official lists of abbreviated year-names. Such a list, compiled for obvious practical purposes, is given in the next text (2) which covers the thirty-eight years of the rule of Samsuiluna, son of Hammurabi.

The so-called Babylonian King List B, translated here under (3), shows a further step of this development. It contains the names of all the kings of the First Dynasty of Babylon with the lengths of their reigns and—as a rule—their relation to their predecessors. The last line sums up the number of kings and indicates the name of the dynasty. The reverse of the same tablet lists the kings of another dynasty in exactly the same way. The unfortunately damaged tablet known as Babylonian King List A (4) lists first the kings of the Hammurabi Dynasty and continues the sequence of dynasties to the domination of Babylon by Assyrian kings, Kandalanu, the Babylonian successor of Shamashshumukin, being the last name before a break. From this "raw material" the historiographers of later periods compiled such lists as are exemplified in the famous Assyrian King List of Khorsabad, for which I refer—provisionally—to the articles of A. Poebel in the *JNES*, I, 247 ff., 460 ff.; and II, 56 ff. (cf., also, E. F. Weidner, *AfO*, XIV [1944], 362 ff.)

The Synchronistic Chronicle (5) deals with the period covered by the preceding text; its author, however, is not interested in dynasties and lengths of rule, but in relating chronologically, or synchronizing, the kings of Assyria (left column) with those of Babylonia (right column). The basic principle of arrangement is to mention within the same paragraph the names of the kings of one country who ascended the throne during the reign of the king of the other country. As an interesting innovation, the name of the vizier is mentioned in certain cases beside that of the ruling king.

The Excerpts from the Lists of Assyrian Eponyms (6) illustrate these Assyrian historiographic documents as a source of historic information.

HISTORIOGRAPHIC DOCUMENTS

1. LIST OF DATE FORMULAE OF THE REIGN OF HAMMURABI

This list has been compiled by A. Ungnad, in *Reallexikon der Assyriologie*, II, 178-182. For the official lists containing the abbreviated names of the years of the kings of the First Dynasty of Babylon, cf. the text material collected by Ungnad, *op.cit.*, pp. 164 ff.

1. Hammurabi (became) king.
2. He established justice[1] in the country.

[1] This refers to a royal act aiming at the restoration of the social equity whenever economic or other changes created a discrepancy between the social status established and protected by law (termed *kittu* "correct/normal [status]") and the needs, or claims, of certain groups of the population. Under such circumstances, it is the official duty of the king to "make (Akk.: *šakânu*, Sum.: g a r) *mîšaru* (Sum.: n í g . s i . s á)" i.e., to readjust the law to the necessities of an ever changing world. In practice, however, *mîšaram šakânum* refers probably always to a remission of (certain) debts or to a moratory. cf. also B. Landsberger, Die baby-

3. He constructed a throne for the main dais of the god Nanna (var. adds: in the temple é.k i š.š i r$_5$.g a l) in Babylon.

4. The wall of (the sacred precinct) Gagia was built.

5. He constructed the e n k a.a š.b a r.r a[2].

6. He constructed the ŠIR$_3$ of the goddess Laz.

7. Uruk and Isin were conquered.

8. The country Emutbal (var.: the land on the embankment of the Shumundar-canal[3]).

9. The canal (called) Hammurabi-hegal (was dug).

10. Army (var.: City) (and) inhabitants of Malgia were crushed.

11. He conquered Rapiqum and Shalibi (var.: Rapiqum and Ibiq-Adad).

12. He constructed a throne for the goddess Sarpanit.

13. A copper stand for a royal statue (and) the pertinent d u$_8$.m a ḫ.[4]

14. He constructed a throne for the goddess Inanna of Babylon.

15. The seven statues.

16. He constructed the throne of the god Nabium (Nebo).

17. He made the image of the goddess Inanna of Kibalbarru "as high as the sky."

18. He constructed the main dais for Enlil in Babylon.

19. The big wall of Igi-hursag.

20. The year following: "The wall of Igi-hursag." Also: The throne of Meri (i.e., Adad).

21. The wall of the town Bazu[5] was built.

22. The statue of Hammurabi (as) king (granting) justice.

23. The APIN[6] of the wall of Sippar.

24. He redug the *tilida*[7]-canal for (the benefit of the temple of) Enlil, and (also the bed of) the Euphrates.

25. The great wall of Sippar[8] was built (var.: for the gods Shamash and Shenirda).

26. The great daises of gold.

27. He constructed the main emblem of reddish gold which is carried in front of the army, for the great gods, his helpers.

28. The temple é.n a m.ḫ é ("House of Abundance") of Adad in Babylon was built.

29. He constructed the image of the goddess Shala.

30. The year following, "He constructed the image of Shala."

Also: The leader, beloved of Marduk, after having defeated the army which Elam—(counting[9]) from the frontier of Marhashi, also Subartu, Gutium, Eshnunna, and Malgi—had raised in masses, through the mighty power of the great gods, re-established/consolidated the foundations of (the empire of) Sumer and Akkad.

31. (Encouraged) by an oracle (given) by Anu and Enlil who are advancing in front of his army, (and) through the mighty power which the great gods had given to him, he was a match[10] for the country (var.: army) of Emutbal and its king Rim-Sin, and . . . and (thus) forced Sumer and Akkad to (obey) his orders.

32. The hero who proclaims the triumphs of Marduk, overthrew in battle with his powerful weapon the army of Eshnunna, Subartu (and) Gutium and was a match (also) for the country Mankizum and the country along the bank of the Tigris as far as (the frontier of) the country Subartu.

33. He redug the canal (called) "Hammurabi-(spells)-abundance-for-the-people, the Beloved-of-Anu-and-Enlil," (thus) he provided Nippur, Eridu, Ur, Larsa, Uruk (and) Isin with a permanent and plentiful water supply, and reorganized Sumer and Akkad from (its) confusion (lit.: scattering). Mari and Malgi he overthrew in battle and made Mari, and . . . and also several other cities of Subartu, by a friendly agreement, (listen) to his orders.

34. He built the temple é.t ù r.k a l a m.m a ("Fold of the Country") for Anu, Inanna and Nana.

35. Upon the command of Anu and Enlil he destroyed the wall(s) of Mari and Malgia.

36. He restored the temple é.m e.t e.u r.s a g ("The Pride of the Hero") and built the temple tower, the mighty abode of Zababa[11] (and) Inanna, whose top is sky-high and (thus) he greatly increased the glamor of Zababa as well as of Inanna in a pious manner.

37. Through the great power of Marduk he overthrew the army of (var.: Sutium), Turukku, Kakmu and of the country Subartu.

38. Upon the command of Anu and Enlil—and with the splendid wisdom with which Marduk has endowed him—he . . . Eshnunna which a flood had destroyed[12] . . .

39. With the mighty power which Anu (and) Enlil have given him, he defeated all his enemies as far as the country of Subartu.

lonischen Termini fuer Gesetz und Recht (*Studia et Documenta ad Iura Orientis antiqui pertinentia*, II, pp. 219 ff.) and B. A. Prossdij, *Šar mišârim*, titre des rois babyloniens comme legislateurs (*ibid.* vol. III, p. 29 ff.).

2 For this obscure term, cf. Deimel, *ŠL*, 15/35, and 556/310 and 311.

3 For the country Sumandar, cf. B. Landsberger, *OLZ*, XIX (1916), 33 f.

4 cf. A. Schott, *ZA*, XL (NF VI), 20 ff. for this term.

5 This town was, later on, the seat of a dynasty, cf. p. 272.

6 For this term which corresponds to Akk. *uššu* and refers to the ledge of a wall, cf. my Mesopotamian Mythology III, *Orientalia*, NS XIX, 138, n.3.

7 Meaning: "Flowing Vase Canal" (reading after B. Landsberger, *AfO*, XII [1938], 140). For the pertinent implications and the iconographic material, cf. E. (Douglas) van Buren, *The Flowing Vase and the God with Streams* (Berlin, 1933).

8 For the wall of Sippar, cf. H. G. Güterbock, *ZA*, XLII (NF VIII), 85. Also, below, n.13.

9 The translation of this year name follows T. Jacobsen, *Philological Notes on Eshnunna and Its Inscriptions* (*AS*, No. 9 [1934]), p. 7.

10 The text uses the verb s i . . . s á which, in legal texts, means "to correspond in value."

11 The reading Ilbaba (cf. R. Labat, in *Revue des études semitiques* 1942-45/1, pp. 1-8) has been questioned recently (cf. E. F. Weidner, *AfO*, XIII [1939-40], 318) in favor of the older reading Zababa.

12 The reference to the wisdom which inspired this warlike exploit seems to suggest an attack made by Hammurabi upon the stricken city. This would offer an interesting parallel to the incident reported by the Pharaoh Pi-ankhi at the conquest of Memphis.

40. He made the temple é.mes.lam ("Temple of the spreading mes-tree") as high as a mountain.

41. The goddess Tashmetum (who listens) to his supplication.

42. After the year "Tashmetum."

Also: He made the great wall at the embankment of the Tigris high as a mountain, called its name "Pier of Shamash," and built also the wall of Rapiqu at the embankment of the Euphrates.

43. (As to) Sippar, the primeval city of the sun-god Utu, he provided (it) with a wall made of piled-up earth.[13]

2. LIST OF YEAR NAMES: SAMSUILUNA, KING OF BABYLON

British Museum Bu 91-5-9,284, published in *CT*, VI, Pls. 9 f. (rev. iii 45—iv 35) and by L. W. King, *Letters and Inscriptions of Hammurabi, etc.* (London, 1898 f.), II, Nos. 101, 217 ff. Latest translation: A. Ungnad, *Reallexikon der Assyriologie*, II, Nos. 146-183, p. 165 f.

Year: Samsuiluna (became) king.
Year: He established freedom (from taxation)[1] for Sumer and Akkad.
Year: Canal *Samsuiluna-naqab-nuḫši* ("Samsuiluna is a source of prosperity [for the people]").
Year:[2] Canal *Samsuiluna*-ḫegal ("Samsuiluna is abundance").
Year: bizem[3]-throne.
Year: Statues of adorants.
Year: Emblem weapon.
Year: Copper stand for royal statue.
Year: Kassite army.
Year: Army of Idamaras. (10)
Year: Wall of Uruk.
Year: All the enemies.
Year: Kisurra as well as Sabu.
Year: The evil usurper-king.
Year: The wall of Isin was demolished.
Year: The sky-reaching wall.
Year: The several great walls.
Year: É.babbar (the temple of the sun-god) Utu in Sippar.
Year: The two golden thrones for the dais.
Year: The rebellious (lit.: not obedient) foreign countries. (20)
Year: The throne for the great dais.
Year: The temple tower, the mighty abode.
Year: (Through) the terrible power.
Year: The wall of Kish.
Year: (His) statue brandishing the weapon.
Year: (In) the mountains of Amurru.
Year: A shining votive object.
Year: Upon the command of Enlil.
Year following (the year): Upon the command of Enlil.
Year following (the year): Following (the year): Upon the command of Enlil. (30)
Year: His statue of nim-wood he [fashioned].
Year: He redug the canal Durul and Taban.[4]
Year: The town Kagaratum.
Year: The palace of rulership.
Year: (The countries) Amal (and) Arkum.
Year: The army of (the country of) Amurru.
Year: In the land Akkad.
Year: Ubanuil (name of the mace of Ninurta).
38 year-(names) of king Samsuiluna.
(Written) Aiaru 2nd (of)
the year: Ammi-zaduga (son of Samsuiluna, became) king.

[13] cf. W. F. Albright in *BASOR*, 88 (1942), 33, for this date formula; also, A. Poebel in *AfO*, IX (1933-4), 283 f.

[1] cf. for this institution, E. F. Weidner, *ZA*, XLIII (NF IX), 122.

[2] Break in the tablet; restored after BrM No. 16,324 published by King, *op.cit.*, No. 102, p. 231.

[3] The sign which appears here is explained in the syllabary Poebel, *UM*, V, 108:7 as *pi-s[a]-an-nu*, Sumerian reading: [bi].zé.em. It recurs in the list of names of gods *CT*, XXV, 27c (K 2117), line 8, with the gloss bi.zi.èm while the parallel passage (*CT*, XXIV, 48, K 4349B, line 17) has clearly pisan₃. These quotations have been indicated to me by Dr. F. W. Geers. The bizem-throne could etymologically be explained as a "*covered* throne," because bizem (which through the process of *Rückentlehnung* became *pisannu* "box" in Akkadian) seems to be a loan from a Semitic word (*psn/m* "to cover").

[4] For the names of these canals, cf. the inscription of Samsuiluna published by A. Poebel, *AfO*, IX (1933-4), 241 ff., col. ii 27.

3. THE BABYLONIAN KING LIST B

British Museum 80,11-12-3 (now No. 38122), published by H. Winckler, *Untersuchungen zur altorientalischen Geschichte* (1889), p. 145, and P. Rost, *MVAG*, II/2 (1897), 240. Latest translation: E. Ebeling in *AOT*, 332.

(obverse)

Sumuabi,[1] king, 15[2] years.
Sumulail,[1] 35 years.
Sabu, his son, same (i.e. king) 14 years.
Apil-Sin, his son, same, 18 years.
Sinmuballit, his son, same, 30 years.
Hammurabi,[1] his son, same, 55 years.
Samsuiluna,[1] his son, same, 35 years.
Ebishum,[1] his son, same, 25 years.
Ammiditana,[1] same, 25 years.
Ammisaduga,[1] same, 22(!) years.
Samsuditana(!),[1] same, 31 years.
Eleven kings, dynasty of Babylon.

(reverse)

Uruku(g): Ilimailum, king.
Ittiilinibi.
Damqiilishu.
Ishkibal.
Shushshi.
Gulkishar.
Peshgaldaramash, his son, same (i.e. king).
Adarakalama, his son, same.
Akurulanna.
Melamkurkurra.
Eagam[il].
Ten (*sic*) kings, dynasty of Uruku(g).

[1] For these names (meaning and language), cf. Th. Bauer, *Die Ostkanaanäer* (Leipzig, 1926), pp. 10, 13, 19, and 38.

[2] For the figures of this list, cf. A. Poebel, The Use of Mathematical Mean Values in Babylonian King List B (Study V, *Miscellaneous Studies=AS*, No. 14 [1947]).

4. THE BABYLONIAN KING LIST A

BrM No. 33332; published by T. G. Pinches, *PSBA*, VI (1884), pp. 193 f. (*CT*, XXXVI, Pls. 24-25); H. Winckler, *Untersuchungen zur altorientalischen Geschichte* (Leipzig, 1889), pp. 146-147; P. Rost, *Untersuchungen zur altorientalischen Geschichte* (*MVAG*, II/2, 1897), 241-242. Latest translation: Ebeling in *AOT*, 332-333.

(i)

(11 lines missing)

[. . .] (years), 11 kings, dyn[asty of Babylon]

60 (years) Ilima[1]
56 Ittili
36 Damqiili
15 Ishki
26 Shushshi, brother
55 Gulki . . .[2]
50 Peshgal
28 Aiadara
26 Ekurul
7 Melamma
9 Eaga

368 (*sic*) (years), 11 kings, dynasty of Uruku(g)

16 Gandash
12 Agum the First, his son
22 Kashtiliashi
8 Ushshi, his son
[. . .] Abirattash
[. . .] Tazzigurumash

(ii)

(more than 13 lines missing)

x + 22 (years) [. . .]
26 [. . .]
18 [. . .]
[. . .] Kadash [. . .]
6 Kudur-[Enlil], his [so]n
13 Shagarak[ti], his [so]n
8 Kashtil, his son
1 year 6 months Ellilnadinshumi
1 year 6 months Kadashman-Harbe
6 Adadnadinshumi
30 Adadshumnasir
15 Melishipak
13 Mardukaplaiddin, his son
1 year Zababa[shumiddin]
3 Ellilnadin[ahhe]

576 (years) 9 months, 36 king[s, dynasty of . . .].

17 (years) Marduk[shapikzeri]
6 . . .

(destroyed)

(iii)

(destroyed)

22 (years) [. . .]
1 year 6 months Marduka[hheriba]
12 Mardukzer [. . .]
8 Nabushum[libur]

132 (years) 6 months, 11 kings, dynasty of Isin.

18 (years) Simmashshi
5 months Eamukin
3 (years) Kashshunadinahhe

21 (years) 5 months, 3 kings, dynasty of the Sea Country.

17 (years) Eulmashshakinshumi
3 Ninurtakudurra
3 months Shi[riqti]-Shuqamu

20 (years) 3 months, 3 kings, dynasty of Bas[u].

6(?) (years) I [. . .]

38(?) (years) [. . .]
8 months 12 [days . . .]

(destroyed)

(iv)

(destroyed)

[. . .] Nabushumishkun [his] s[on]
[. . .] Nabun[asir]
2 (years) Nabunadinzeri, his son,
1 month 12 days Nabushumukin, his son,

22 (years or kings?), dynasty of E.

3 (years) Ukinzer, dynasty of Shashi
2 Pulu[3]
5 Ululaia,[4] dynasty of Bal-til[5]
12 Mardukaplaiddin, dynasty of the Sea Country,
5 Sargon
2 Sennacherib, dynasty of Habigal,
1 month Mardukzakirshumi, son of Ardu,
9 months Mardukaplaiddin, a native of Habi,
3 (years) Belibni, dynasty of E,
6 Ashurnadinshumi, dynasty of Habigal,
1 Nergalushezib
5 Ushezib-Marduk, dynasty of E,
8 Sennacherib
[. . .] Esarhaddon
[. . .] Shamashshum[6]
[. . .] Kandal[7]

(destroyed)

[1] The names of the kings of this dynasty appear here in abbreviated forms; cf. King List B for the full names.

[2] Follows one horizontal wedge (as between lines 5 and 6) of obscure meaning.

[3] =Tiglath-pileser III of Assyria (744-727).

[4] =Shalmaneser V of Assyria (726-722).

[5] The name of this town (BAL.BAD or BAL.TIL) was discussed recently by J. Lewy in *HUCA*, XIX (1946), 467 ff. (especially, n.305), who considered it as denoting the "innermost, and, hence, oldest part of the city of Assur."

[6] Short for Shamashshumukin, son of Esarhaddon and brother of Ashurbanipal.

[7] Short for Kandalanu (formerly identified with Ashurbanipal), a Babylonian successor of Shamashshumukin ruling in Babylon for 22 years. cf. W. H. Dubberstein, *JNES*, III (1944), 38 ff.

5. THE SYNCHRONISTIC CHRONICLE

Berlin, Assur 14616c; latest publication by E. F. Weidner, Die grosse Königsliste aus Assur, *AfO*, III (1926), 66-70 (copy: 70-71). Latest translation: Ebeling, *AOT*, 333-335.

(i)

(destroyed)

Ad[asi, same (i.e., king of Assyria)]	[Damiqilishu, same (i.e., king of Babylon)]

Belbani, same	I[shk]ib[al, same]
Lubaia, same	Shush[i, same]
Sharma-Adad, same	Gulkisha[r, same]
LIK.KUD-Shamash, same	[. . .]en[. . . , same]
Bazaia, same	Pesh[gal]daramash, same
Lulla, same	Aiadarakalamma, same
Shininua, same	Ekurulanna, same
Sharma-Adad, same	Mela[m]kurra, same
Erishu[1]	Eagamil, G[and]ush, same
Shamshi-Adad, same	[Ag]um, the former, his son, same
same same	Kashtil[a]shu, same
same same	Abirattash, same
same same	Kashtil[ashu, same]
same same	Tazzigurumash, same
same same	Harba[shipa]k, same
same same	Tiptakzi, same
same same	Agu[m], same
[Ishme]-Dagan, same	Burnab[uri]ash, same
[Shamshi]-Adad, same	. . .
. . . same	Kashtil[ashu, same]
[Puzur-Ashur], same	Ula[mb]uri[ash, same]
[Enli]lnasir, same	same
[Nu]rili, same	same
[Ishme-Dag]an, same	same

(ii)

(one line destroyed)

Tukulti-[Ninurta, king of Assyria]	[Kashtiliash . . .]
. . .	[NN his vizier]
Ashurnadinapli, same	[Enlilnadinshumi, same]
same same	Ka[dashmanharbe, same]
[A]shurnirari, same	Adad[shumiddin, same]
Enlilkudurrausur, same	same
[Ni]nurtaapilekur, same	Adad-shumiddin, same
same same	M[el]ish[i]pak, same
same same	[Marduk]aplaiddin, same
[Ashurdan], same	Zababa[shumiddin, same]
same same	[Enlil]nadin[ahhe, same]
Ninurtatukulti-Ashur, same	Marduk[shapikzeri, same]
Mutakkil-Nusku, same	[NN his vizier]
Ashurreshishi, same	Ninurta[nadinshumi, same]
same same	Nabukudurrausur, same
same same	Enlilnadinapli, same
Tukultiapil[e]sarra, same	[Marduk]nadinahhe, same
Ni[nurta]apilekur, same	Itti-Mardukbalati, same
	NN his vizier
Ashurbelkala, same	Marduk[shapikzermati, same]
Enlilrabi, same	Adad[aplaiddin, same]
Ashurbelkala, same	[Mardukahheriba, same]
same same	[Mardukzer- . . .]
same same	[Nabushumlibûr, same]

(iii)

Eriba Adad, king [of Assyr]ia	. . .
	[NN his vizier . . .]
Shamshi-Adad, same	Ea[mukinshumi, same]
Ashurnasirpal, same	Kashshu[nadinahhe, same]
Shulmanuasharidu, same	Ulmash[shakinshumi, same]
Ashurnirari, same	Ninurtaku[durrausur, same]
Ashurrabi, same	Shiriqti[Shuqamuna, same]
Ashurreshishi, same	Marbiti[aplausur, same]
Tukultiapilesharra, same	[Nabumukin]apli, same
same same	[Ninurtakudurr]ausur, same
same same	[Marbiti]ahiddin, same
	. . . his vizier
Ashurdan, same	Shamashmudammiq, king of Babylon
Adad-nirari	same
	Qalia [his vizier]
Tukulti-Ninurta, same	Nabushum[ukin, same]
Gabbiilanieresh	[his] vizier
Ashurnasirpal, same	Nabuaplaiddin
Gabbiilanieresh	[his] vizi[er]
Shulmanuasharidu, same	[Nabuzakirshumi, same]
[Me]luhhaia [his] vi[zier]	

(destroyed)

(iv)

Sennacherib ([*Sîn*]*aḫḫērîba*), king of Assyria	[and of Babylon]
Nabuaplaiddin [his] vizier	(anepigraph)
	[for two] years Sennacherib was king of Akkad; then the inhabitants of Akkad revolted and
	Ashurnadinshumi, the father [ceded] him the throne,[2]
Sennacherib	Nergalushezib, son of Gahul,
	Mushezib-Marduk, a native[3] of Bit-Dakkuri
	were the kings of [Ak]kad.
Sennacherib, king of Assyria	and of Babylon,
Belupahhir (and)	Kalbu, his viziers;

[1] First of the royal names of the present list to be mentioned (as No. 33) in the Assyrian King List of Khorsabad, cf. A. Poebel in *JNES*, I (1942), 282.

[2] cf. for this passage E. F. Weidner in *AfO*, III (1926), 75 f.

[3] cf. below p. 308, n.9 for a possible different interpretation of the phrase *mâr Bît Dakkûri*.

Esarhaddon, son of Sennacherib, king of Assyria and of Babylonia
Nabuzerlishir (and) Ishtarshumeresh, his viziers,
Ashurbanipal, same   Shamashshumukin, same
same   same   Kandalanu, same
Ishtarshumeresh, his vizier.
82 kings of Assyria from (the time of) Erishu, son of Ilushuma, to Ashurbanipal, son of Esarhaddon (correspond to)
98 kings of Akkad
from (the time of) Sumulail to Kandalanu.

6. EXCERPTS FROM THE LISTS OF ASSYRIAN EPONYMS

In contradistinction to the Babylonian custom (attested from the time of the kings of Agade to that of the Kassite rulers) of naming each year after an important event, the Assyrians used the names of certain high officials for the same purpose. The first (full) year of the reign of a king is always named after himself, the following years have originally been named after that official who won when lots were thrown to determine the eponym.[1] Later on, the position of the official within the hierarchy was decisive for the sequence, the highest official (*tartanu*) following the king immediately, while important palace officers (such as, e.g. the *nāgir ekalli* "overseer of the royal property," the chief cupbearer, etc.) and the governors of the foremost provinces took their turn in well-established order. After the exhaustion of all eligible candidates for the office of the *lîmu*, within the rule of one and the same king, the sequence of officials started anew, beginning with the king.

For the throwing of lots (done by means of a "die" called *pûru* thrown into a bowl), cf. E. F. Weidner, *AfO*, XIII (1941), 308 f.;[2] for the sequence of officials, cf. E. Forrer, *Die Provinzeinteilung des assyrischen Reiches* (Leipzig, 1921), after p. 6, with an instructive diagram.

For practical and chronological purposes, the Assyrian scribes made elaborate lists[3] of the names of the *lîmu* -officials which either contain only name and rank (termed by Delitzsch: C[anon][a]) or additional short notices referring to historical events (C^b).[4] These lists have been studied and edited repeatedly, the most recent studies being those of A. Ungnad in *Reallexikon der Assyriologie*, II, *sub* Eponym, 412-457, and E. F. Weidner, *AfO*, XIII (1941), 308-318.

The following excerpts utilize A. Ungnad's transliteration and restoration of C^b on pp. 428 ff., to the arrangement of which the numbering of lines refers.

(Reign of Adad-nirari II)
(obverse)

(15) [In the eponymat of Ashurbaltinishe, (governor) of Arra]pha:
(campaign) against the sea; a plague.

(Reign of Shalmaneser IV)

(43) [In the eponymat of] Pali[lerish, (governor) of Ras]appa:
(campaign) against Damascus (*Di-maš-qa*).

(Reign of Tiglath-pileser III)
(reverse)

(40) [In the eponymat of Beldan], (governor) of Kalha:
(campaign) against Palestine (*matPi-liš-ta*).

(41) [In the eponymat of Ashurdanninanni], (governor) of Mazzamua:
(campaign) against Damascus (*Di-maš-qa*).

(42) [In the eponymat of Nabubelusu]r, (governor) of Si'me:
(campaign) against Damascus (*Di-maš-qa*).

1 For literature on *pûru*, cf. J. Lewy, *Revue Hittite et Asianique*, v (1939), 117 ff. (especially p. 117, n.2); also, A. Ungnad, in *Reallexikon*, II, 412, n.2; E. F. Weidner, *AfO*, XIII (1941), 308.

2 Such a "die" has been preserved—as Weidner has ingeniously established—and is published in F. J. Stephens, *Votive and Historical Texts from Babylonia and Assyria* (*YOS*, Vol. IX), No. 73, and Pl. XLV.

3 The possibility that the rows of stelae found in Ashur are meant to serve as a sort of monumental "index" of *lîmu* -officials, has been discussed by A. Ungnad, *op.cit.*, p. 412. These officials would then have had two essentially royal prerogatives: to give their name to the year and to set up stelae.

4 Various other types of such lists (rarely attested, however) are mentioned by Ungnad, *op.cit.*, p. 414.

HISTORICAL DOCUMENTS

This part contains the records which ten kings of Assyria have left us—on stone slabs, clay foundation documents, inscribed stelae, etc.—of their campaigns for the conquest of Syria, Palestine, the island of Cyprus, Arabia, and, eventually, of Egypt.

1. SHAMSHI-ADAD I (ABOUT 1726-1694):[1] FIRST CONTACT WITH THE WEST

L. Messerschmidt, *KAH*, I, No. 2. Transliteration and translation: B. Meissner, in *Die Inschriften der altassyrischen Koenige*, (*Altorientalische Bibliothek*), I (Leipzig, 1926), 24 f.

(iv 4—17)

At that time, I received in my town Ashur the tribute[2] of the kings of Tukrish and of the kings of the Upper Country.[3] I erected a stela (inscribed) with my great name in the country Lab'an (*La-ab-a-an*[ki]) on the shore of the Great Sea.

2. TIGLATH-PILESER I (1114-1076): EXPEDITIONS TO SYRIA, THE LEBANON, AND THE MEDITERRANEAN SEA

a

Foundation document (clay) of the Anu-Adad temple in Ashur. Published by O. Schroeder, in *KAH*, II, No. 68. Translation: Luckenbill, *AR*, I, §§300-303.

(1—29)

Tiglath-pileser, the legitimate[1] king, king of the world,[2] king of Assyria, king of (all) the four rims (of

1 The dates given after the names of Assyrian kings are those of A. Poebel in *JNES*, II (1943), pp. 85-88.

2 For the various terms appearing in the historical texts with the approximate meaning "tribute" or the like—such as *biltu, mandattu, miḫirtu*, etc. —cf. W. J. Martin, Tribut und Tributleistungen bei den Assyrern, *Studia Orientalia*, VIII (1936), 20 ff. The hendiadys *biltu mandattu* is, in the present pages, translated by one English term (to wit, "tribute"), because it is not admissible to render literally the well-known stylistic feature of the Akkadian (cf. H. Ehelolf, Ein Wortfolgeprinzip im Assyrisch-Babylonischen, *LSS*, VI/3 [1916]) to use two nearly synonymous nouns to express one concept on the level of a solemn and dignified diction. Therefore I translate, e.g., *qablu (u) tâḫazu* simply with "battle," *bûšu (u) makkuru* with "possessions," *kittu (u) mîšaru* with "justice," etc.

3 cf. B. Maisler, *Untersuchungen zur alten Geschichte und Ethnographie Syriens und Palästinas* (Giessen, 1930), p. 10.

1 In the title l u g a l . k a l a . g a (Akk.: *šarru dannu*), the adjective k a l a (g) or *dannu* has a definite meaning which is difficult to render exactly. From such references as e.g. *našparu dannu* (cf. below p. 309, n.4), *sukkallu dannu* ("regular *sukkallu* -official"), etc., the meaning "legitimate, orderly, correct" results (cf. also Deimel, *ŠL*, 322/18 for the Sum. verb k a l a (g) "to deliver regularly"), while other references point towards *dannu* in the meaning "potent, full-grown, powerful." With regard to the ancient Near Eastern concept of kingship, it seems possible that the title is meant to express both aspects: the legitimacy of the ruler and his full personal vigor, both being equally essential prerequisites for the exercise of kingship.

2 For the history of this age-old royal title, cf. p. 267, n.1. The rendering

the earth), the courageous hero who lives (guided) by the trust-inspiring oracles given (to him) by Ashur and Ninurta, the great gods and his lords, (and who thus) overthrew (all) his enemies; son of Ashurreshishi, king of the world, king of Assyria, (grand)son of Mutakkil-Nusku, also king of the world, king of Assyria.

At the command of my lord Ashur I was a conqueror (lit.: my hand conquered) from beyond the Lower Zab River to the Upper Sea which (lies towards) the West. Three times I did march against the Nairi countries. The widespread Nairi countries I conquered from the country Tumme as far as Daiaeni, Himua, and even as far as Paiteri and Kirhi. I made bow to my feet 30 kings of the Nairi countries, I took hostages from them. I received as their tribute horses, broken to the yoke. I imposed upon them (regular) tribute and *tâmartu*-gifts.

I went to the Lebanon (*Lab-na-a-ni*). I cut (there) timber of cedars for the temple of Anu and Adad, the great gods, my lords, and carried (them to Ashur). I continued (my march) towards the country of Amurru. I conquered the entire country of Amurru. I received tribute from Byblos (*Gu-bal*), Sidon (*Ṣi-du-ni*), and Arvad (*Ar-ma-da*). I crossed over in ships (belonging) to Arvad, from Arvad which is on the seashore, to the town Samuri which (lies) in Amurru (a distance of) 3 double-miles overland. I killed a narwhal[3] which they call "sea horse," on high sea.

And (afterwards) on my return march (towards Ashur) I did [conquer] the entire [country of . . .] tribute. . . .

b

Two excerpts from a fragmented octagonal prism (perhaps the foundation document of the royal palace). Published by O. Schroeder, in *KAH*, II, No. 63. Translation: Luckenbill, *AR*, I, §§286 and 287.

(ii 10—16)

Upon the command of Anu and Adad, the great gods, my lords, I went to the Lebanon mountains (*šadê*^{e} *Lab-na-ni*), [. . . tim]ber. . . .

(iii 3—14 = *KAH*, II, 71 [tablet] 19—23

Twenty-eight times (I fought) the Ahlamu peoples and the Arameans, (once) I even crossed the Euphrates twice in one year. I defeated them from Tadmar (Palmyra) which (lies) in the country Amurru, Anat[1] which (lies) in the country Suhu as far as the town Rapiqu which (lies) in Kar-Duniash (i.e. Babylonia). I brought their possessions as spoils to my town Ashur.

c

Rock Inscription from Sebeneh-Su. Published first by Rawlinson, Vol. III, Pl. 4, No. 6, and again by F. Lehmann-Haupt, in *Materialien zur aelteren Geschichte Armeniens und Mesopotamiens* (*Abh. Kgl. Ges. d. Wiss. Göttingen* NF IX/3, 1907), No. 7 (cf. also King, *AKA*, p. 127, n.1). Translation: Luckenbill, *AR*, I, §271.

With the help of Ashur (and) Shamash, the great gods, my lords, I, Tukultiapilesarra, king of Assyria, son of Ashurreshishi, king of Assyria, son of Mutakkil-Nusku, likewise king of Assyria, am a conqueror (of the regions) from the Great Sea which is in the country Amurru as far as the Great Sea which is in the Nairi country. I have marched three times against the Nairi country.

"king of the world" does not do justice to the complex political and emotional implications involved.

[3] For *nâḫiru* "narwhal," cf. B. Landsberger and I. Krumbiegel, *Die Fauna des alten Mesopotamiens etc.* (Leipzig, 1934), p. 142.

[1] For the town Anat, cf. J. Lewy in *HUCA*, XIX, 431, n.18.

3. ASHURNASIRPAL II (883-859): EXPEDITION TO CARCHEMISH AND THE LEBANON

From the annals inscribed on the large pavement slabs of the temple of Ninurta in Calah, the new royal residence built by Ashurnasirpal II. Published by Rawlinson, Vol. I, Pls. 17-26; also, by King, *AKA*, p. 254 ff. (with transliteration and translation) and I. Y. Le Gac, *Les inscriptions de Aššur-naṣir-aplu III* (Paris, 1907), p. 3 ff. Translation: Luckenbill, *AR*, I, §§475-479.

(iii 64—90)

I departed from the country Bit-Adini and crossed the Euphrates at the peak of its flood by means of (rafts made buoyant with inflated) goatskin (bottle)s. I advanced towards Carchemish. (There) I received from him(self) the tribute of Sangara, the king of the Hittites (amounting to): 20 talents of silver, a *sa'aru* object of gold, a ring of gold, golden daggers, 100 talents of copper, 250 talents of iron, (furthermore) bull-images[1] of copper, copper basin-and-ewer sets[2] for washing, a copper brazier—(all) his own furniture,[3] the weights of which were not taken (separately),—(furthermore) beds of boxwood,[4] a š t i -chairs[5] of boxwood, tables of boxwood, (all) inlaid with ivory, also 200 young females (clad in) linen garments with multi-colored trimmings[6] made of dark and reddish purple-(dyed) wool, (also) alabaster, elephants' tusks (and even) a shining chariot (and) a golden *nimattu* -chair[7] with panels[8]—his (own) royal insignia. I took over the chariot (-corps), the cavalry (and) the infantry of Carchemish. The kings of all (surrounding) countries came to me, embraced my feet and I took hostages from them and they marched (with me) towards the Lebanon (*Lab-na-na*) forming my vanguard.

[1] This translation is based upon the variants a m "wild bull," and d i n g i r "(image of a) god," describing the very same object. cf. for these variants, L. W. King, *AKA*, I, 366, n.3.

[2] The words *ḫarîtu* and *narmaktu* refer to the two containers needed in the Orient for washing and taking a bath: a spouted vessel to pour the water and a recipient with wide opening to collect it. cf. the corresponding Egyptian word *ḥsmn*.

[3] Literally: "furniture of his palace"; the term *ekallu* denotes in Mesopotamia the personal property of the king.

[4] The reading *taskarinnu* (instead of **urkarinnu*) was indicated to me by Dr. B. Landsberger, who made reference to syllabic spellings in Old-Assyrian and texts from Nuzi as well as to Aram. *'eškra'* "boxwood."

[5] The Sumerian words a š t i or a š t e denote a special type of chair, often a royal throne.

[6] This refers to linen garments decorated with sewn-on narrow woven bands or tresses made of wool thread in various colors (termed *birmu*). This typically Syrian technique is often depicted on Egyptian murals and reliefs. The Assyrian kings mention these garments always in their reports on booty or tribute received from Upper Mesopotamia, Syria, and Palestine.

[7] A certain type of easy chair.

[8] For the technical terms *iḫzu* "frame, border, mounting" and *tamlû* "panel, filling," cf. e.g., F. Thureau-Dangin, *Arslan Tash* (Paris 1931), p. 139.

I departed from Carchemish, taking the road between the mountains Munzigani and the Hamurga, leaving the country Ahanu on my left. I advanced towards the town Hazazu which belongs to Lubarna from Hattina. (There) I received gold and linen garments.

I proceeded and crossed the river Apre[9] (where) I passed the night. From the banks of the Apre I departed and advanced towards the town Kunulua, the royal residence of Lubarna from Hattina. Afraid of the terrible weapons of my ferocious army, he embraced my feet to save his life. Twenty talents of silver (the equivalent[10] of) one talent of gold, 100 talents of tin, 100 talents of iron, 1,000 (heads of big) cattle, 10,000 sheep, 1,000 linen garments with multicolored trimmings, easy chairs of boxwood with insets (and) mountings, beds of boxwood, beds provided with insets, tables with ivory(inlay) (on) boxwood—(all) his own furniture, the weights of which were not taken (separately), also female singers (with) [num]erous *ḳan*[. . .], large *pagûtu* -instruments[11] (and) great EN-objects I received from him as his tribute, and himself I pardoned. I took over the chariot (-corps), the cavalry (and) the infantry of Hattina and seized hostages from him.

At that time I received (also) the tribute of Gusi from Iahani (consisting of): gold, silver, tin, [iron], large and small cattle, linen garments with multicolored trimmings. From Kunulua, the royal residence of Lubarna from Hattina, I departed; I crossed the river Orontes ([*Aran*]*tu*) and passed the night on the banks of the Orontes. From the banks of the Orontes I departed, taking the road between the mountains Iaraqi and Ia'turi, and crossed over the [. . .] mountain to pass ⟨the night⟩[12] on the banks of the Sangura river. From the banks of the Sangura river I departed, taking the road between the mountains Saratini and Duppani, and ⟨passed the night⟩[12] on the banks of the . . . [la]ke. I entered Aribua, the fortress of Lubarna from Hattina, and seized (it) as my own (town). I harvested the grain as well as the straw[13] of the Luhuti country and stored (them) therein. In his own palace I performed the *tašîltu* -festival[14] and (then) settled natives of Assyria in it (the town). While I stayed in Aribua, I conquered the (other) towns of Luhuti, defeating their (inhabitants) in many bloody battles. I destroyed (them), tore down (the walls) and burned (the towns) with fire; I caught the survivors and impaled (them) on stakes in front of their towns. At that time I seized the entire extent of the Lebanon mountain and reached the Great Sea of the Amurru country. I cleaned my weapons in the deep[15] sea and performed sheep-offerings to (all) the gods. The tribute of the seacoast—from the inhabitants of Tyre, Sidon, Byblos, Mahallata, Maiza, Kaiza, Amurru, and (of) Arvad which is (an island) in the sea, (consisting of): gold, silver, tin, copper, copper containers, linen garments with multicolored trimmings, large and small monkeys,[16] ebony, boxwood, ivory from walrus tusk[17]—(thus ivory) a product of the sea,—(this) their tribute I received and they embraced my feet.

I ascended the mountains of the Amanus (*Ḫa-ma-ni*)[18] and cut down (there) logs of cedars, stone-pines, cypresses (and) pines, and performed sheep-offerings to my gods. I (had) made a sculptured stela (commemorating) my heroic achievements and erected (it) there. The cedar beams from the Amanus mountain I *destined/sent*[19] for/to the temple Esarra for (the construction of) a *iasmaḳu* -sanctuary[20] as a building for festivals serving the temples of Sin and Shamash, the light(giving) gods.

9 This is the river Afrîn of today. cf., also, Forrer, *Provinzeinteilung*, p. 56.

10 This interpretation of the frequent phrase "*x* silver, *y* gold" yields additional material for the study of the history of the gold-silver ratio in Mesopotamia.

11 For this musical instrument, cf. C. Frank, *Studien zur babylonischen Religion* (Strassburg, 1911), I, 70, n.175.

12 Omission of the scribe.

13 Since the stalks were cut rather high, it was necessary to cut them again to make use of this product as feed for animals, etc.

14 This seems to have been a ceremonial banquet of inauguration.

15 The adjective *rabû*, when referring to water, means always "deep, navigable."

16 Monkeys (here: *pagû*) appear rarely in lists of tributes, cf. the Black Obelisk of Shalmaneser III (below, p. 281b, n.4) where *baziâte-* and **udumi* -monkeys are mentioned and depicted as coming from Muṣru. cf. also [*ba*]*zâti-*, *pagû-*, and *uqupu-* monkeys taken from Thebes (cf. n.4, p. 297). Note in this context W. C. McDermott, *The Ape in Antiquity* (Baltimore, 1938) and M. F. Ashley Montague, Knowledge of the Ape in Antiquity, in *Isis*, XXXII (1947), 87 ff. The spelling **udumi* has to be corrected and read *ú-qup-pu(!)* according to Landsberger, *Fauna* p. 88, n.1.

17 For this passage, cf. P. Haupt, Der assyrische Name des Potwals, in *AJSL*, XXIII (1906/7), 253 ff.

18 For this mountain chain, cf. Julius Lewy, *HUCA*, XVIII (1944), 454 ff.

19 Text unintelligible: *šá-ḳu*-DU-*ḳa*(?).

20 Is *iasmaḳḳu* to be connected with *simaḳḳu* (cf. for the latter, von Soden, *ZA*, XLI [NF VII], 17)?

4. SHALMANESER III (858-824): THE FIGHT AGAINST THE ARAMEAN COALITION[1]

(a) Texts of a General Nature

(a) From the "Thron-Inschrift": A. H. Layard, *Inscriptions in the Cuneiform Character* (London, 1851), p. 76 f.; translation: F. Delitzsch, in *BA*, VI/1, 151 f., Luckenbill, *AR*, I, §674.

(1—20)

(I am) Shalmaneser, the legitimate king, the king of the world, the king without rival, the "Great Dragon,"[2] the (only) power within the (four) rims (of the earth), overlord of all the princes, who has smashed all his enemies as if (they be) earthenware, the strong man, unsparing, who shows no mercy in battle,—the son of Ashurnasirpal, king of the world, king of Assyria, (grand)son of Tukulti-Ninurta, likewise king of the world, king of Assyria, a conqueror from the Upper Sea

1 For the historical background, cf. E. G. H. Kraeling, *Aram and Israel* (New York, 1918); A. Jirku, *Der Kampf um Syrien-Palästina im orientalischen Altertum* (*AO*, XXV/4 [Leipzig, 1926]); A. T. Olmstead, *History of Palestine and Syria* (New York, 1931); A. Alt, *Völker und Staaten Syriens im frühen Altertum*, *AO*, XXXIV/4 [Leipzig, 1936]. Finally, B. Landsberger, *Sam'al*, Vol. I (Ankara, 1948).

2 The designation of a ruler as u š u m . g a l "Giant Snake" (attested already in the Prologue of the Code of Hammurabi, then taken up by the Assyrian kings) is borrowed from the vocabulary of hymnical religious texts which reserve this title to the most important figures of the pantheon (cf. K. Tallquist, *Akkadische Götterepitheta* [*Studia Orientalia* VII, Helsinki, 1938], p. 34). The terror-inspiring aspect of kingship is the *tertium comparationis* of this simile which, to a certain extent, can be compared with the function and role of the Egyptian uraeus.

to the Lower Sea (to wit) the countries Hatti, Luhuti, Adri, Lebanon (*Lab-na-na*), Que, Tabali, Militene (*Me-li-di*); who has visited the sources of (both) the Tigris and the Euphrates.

I marched against Akkad (= Babylonia) to avenge Mardukshumiddin and inflicted a defeat upon [Mar-]dukbelusate, his younger brother. I entered Kutha, Babylon, and Borsippa, offered sacrifices to the gods of the sacred cities of Akkad. I went (further) downstream to Chaldea and received tribute from all kings of Chaldea.

(b) From the inscription on the bronze gates of Balawat. First publication, T. G. Pinches, in *TSBA*, VII (1880-2), 89 f.; translation: F. Delitzsch, in *BA*, VI/I (1908), 133 ff., and Luckenbill, *AR*, I, §§616 ff.

(i 6—ii 5)

At that time [Ashur, the great lord . . . gave me scepter, staff] . . . necessary (to rule) the people, (and) I was acting (only) upon the trust-inspiring oracles given by Ashur, the great lord, my lord, who loves me to be his high priest and . . . all the countries and mountain regions to their full extent. [I (am) Shalmaneser . . . conqueror from] the sea of the Nairi country and the sea of the Zamua country which is nearer (to Assyria) as far (text: and) the Great Sea of Amurru. I swept over Hatti, in its full extent (making it look) like ruin-hills (left) by the flood. . . . (thus) I spread the terror-inspiring glare of my rule over Hatti.

On my (continued) march to the sea, I made a stela (representing) myself as the supreme ruler and set it up beside that of the god Hirbe.[1] . . . I marched [to the Great] Sea, washed my weapons in the Great Sea; I offered sacrifices (there) to my gods. I received the tribute from all the kings of the seacoast. [I made a stela representing myself as king and warrior] and inscribed upon it [the deeds which] I had performed [in the region of the] sea[coast]; I set it up by the sea.

(b) Annalistic Reports

First Year according to the so-called "Monolith Inscriptions" (from Kurkh), published by Rawlinson, Vol. III, Pls. 7-8. Translation: Luckenbill, *AR*, I, §§599-600.

(i 29—ii 13)

In the month Aiaru, the 13th day, I departed from Nineveh; I crossed the Tigris, by-passed the countries Hasamu and Dihnunu and approached the town of La'la'te which (belongs to) Ahuni, man of Adini. The terror and the glamor of Ashur, my lord, overwhelmed [them] . . . and they dispersed.[1] I destroyed the town, tore down (its wall) and burnt (it) down. From La'la'ti I departed, I approached the town of Ki[.]qa, the royal residence] of Ahuni, man of Adini. Ahuni, man of Adini, [putting his trust] upon his numerous [army, ro]se for a decisive battle. . . . I fought with him upon a trust(-inspiring) oracle of Ashur and the (other) great gods, my lords, (and) inflicted a . . . defeat upon him. I shut him up in his town. From the town Ki[.]qa I departed, the town Bur-mar'ana which (belongs to) Ahuni, man of Adini, [I approached]. I stormed and conquered (it). I slew with the sword 300 of their warriors. Pillars of skulls I erec[ted in front of the town]. I received the tribute of Hapini from the town Til-abna, of Ga'uni from the town Sa[ll]ate, (and) of Giri-Adad (to wit): . . . silver, gold, large and small cattle, wine. From Bur-mar'ana I departed, I crossed the Euphrates on rafts (made buoyant by means) of (inflated) goatskins and received the tribute of Qatazi[l]i from Commagene (*Kummuḫi*)[2] (to wit): silver, gold, large and small cattle, wine. I approached the town of Pakaruhbuni (and) the towns of Ahuni, man of Adini, on the other side of the Euphrates. I defeated (his) country, turning his towns into ruins. I covered the wide plain with the corpses of his warriors: 1,300 of their battle-experienced soldiers I slew with the sword. From Pakaruhbuni I departed, I approached the towns of Mutalli from Gurgume. I received the tribute of Mutalli from Gurgume (to wit): silver, gold, large and small cattle, wine (and) his daughter with her big dowry. From Gurgume I departed and I approached Lutibu, the fortress town of Hani from Sam'al.[2a] Hani from Sam'al, Sapalulme from Hattina, Ahuni, man of Adini, Sangara from Carchemish put their trust on mutual assistance, prepared for battle and rose against me to resist. I fought with them (assisted) by the mighty power of Nergal, my leader, by the ferocious weapons which Ashur, my lord, has presented to me, (and) I inflicted a defeat upon them. I slew their warriors with the sword, descending upon them like Adad when he makes a rainstorm pour down. In the moat (of the town) I piled them up, I covered the wide plain with the corpses of their fighting men, I dyed the mountains with their blood like red wool. I took away from him many chariots (and) horses broken to the yoke. I erected pillars of skulls in front of his town, destroyed his (other) towns, tore down (their walls) and burnt (them) down.

At that time, I paid homage to the greatness of (all) the great gods (and) extolled for posterity the heroic achievements of Ashur and Shamash by fashioning a (sculptured) stela with myself as king (depicted on it). I wrote thereupon my heroic behavior, my deeds in combat[3] and erected it beside the source of the Saluara river which is at the foot of the mountains of the Amanus. From the mountain Amanus I departed, crossed the Orontes river (*A-ra-an-tu*) and approached Alimush, the fortress town of Sapalulme from Hattina. To save his life, Sapalulme from Hattina [called for] Ahuni, man of Adini, Sangara from Carchemish, Haianu from Sam'al, Kate from Que, Pihirim from Hilukka, Bur-Anate from Iasbuq, Ada[. . .] . . . Assyria. . . .

[1] cf. E. Unger, Das Bild des Gottes Ḫirbe auf dem Atalur, in *MAOG*, IV (1930), 212 ff.

[1] Technical term: *elû*.

[2] For this identification, cf. L. W. King, Kummuḫ = Commagene, in *Manchester Egypt. and Oriental Soc.*, II (1913), 47 ff.

[2a] Ha(i)ani of Sam'al is the father of Kilamua, whose inscription is translated in *AOT*, 442.

[3] To *tašnintu*, cf. now von Soden in *Orientalia*, NS XVI (1946), 70 f.

(ii)

[their/his army] I scattered, I stormed and conquered the town . . . I carried away as booty . . . , his horses, broken to the yoke. I slew with the sword. . . . During this battle I personally captured Bur-Anate from [Iasbuk]. I con[quered] the great cities (*maḫâzu*) of Hattina. . . . I overthrew the . . . of the Upper [Sea] of Amurru and of the Western Sea (so that they became) like ruin-hills (left by) the flood. I received tribute from the kings of the seashore. I marched straightaway,[4] unopposed . . . throughout the wide seashore. I fashioned a stela with an image of myself as overlord in order to make my name/fame lasting forever and e[rected it] near the sea. I ascended the mountains of the Amanus, I cut there cedar and pine timber. I went to the mountain region Atalur, where the statue of the god Hirbe is set up and erected (there) a(nother) statue (of mine) beside his statue. I de[parted] from the sea; I conquered the towns Taia, Hazazu, Nulia (and) Butamu which (belong) to the country Hattina. I killed 2,900 of [their] battle-experienced soldiers; 14,600 I brought away as prisoners of war. I received the tribute of Arame, man of Gusi, (to wit): silver, gold, large [and small] cattle, wine, a couch of *whitish* gold.[5]

First Year according to the Annals inscribed on clay tablets found in Ashur. Published by O. Schroeder, in *KAH*, II, Nos. 112-114. Translation: Luckenbill, *AR*, I, §633.

(*KAH*, II, 113:12—9)

[I]n the first year of my rule, I crossed the Euphrates at its flood and marched towards the Western Sea. I washed my weapons in the sea, offered [sacrifices to] the gods. I ascended the mountains of the Amanus and cut (there) timber of cedar and pine. I ascended the Lallar mountain, I erected (there) an image (representing) myself as king.[6] The towns of the Hattineans, [those of] Ahuni, man of Adini, those (belonging) to the peoples of Carchemish, (and) to the Mar-Gus[i . . .] [(in short) all the to]wns on the other embankment of the Euphrates, I destroyed, tore down (the walls) and burnt (them) down.

First Year according to the Black Obelisk from Calah. Published by Layard, *Inscriptions*, Pls. 87 f. Translation: Luckenbill, *AR*, I, §558.[6a]

(face B, 26—31)

In the first year of my rule, I crossed the Euphrates at its flood; I marched to the Western Sea; my weapons I cleaned (ritually) in the sea; sheep-offerings I performed for my gods. I ascended the mountain Amanus; cedar and pine timber I cut (there). I ascended the mountain Lallare (and) there I set up a stela with my image as king.

Sixth Year according to the Monolith-Inscription (cf. above). Translation: Luckenbill, *AR*, I, §610.

(ii 78—102)

In the year of (the eponym) Daian-Ashur, in the month Aiaru, the 14th day, I departed from Nineveh. I crossed the Tigris and approached the towns of Giammu on the river Balih. They became afraid of the terror emanating from my position as overlord, as well as of the splendor of my fierce weapons, and killed their master[7] Giammu with their own weapons. I entered the towns Sahlala and Til-sha-Turahi and brought my gods/images into his palaces. I performed the *tašîltu* -festival in his (own) palaces. I opened (his) treasury, inspected what he had hidden; I carried away as booty his possessions, bringing (them) to my town Ashur. From Sahlala I departed and approached Kar-Shalmaneser. I crossed the Euphrates another time at its flood on rafts (made buoyant by means) of (inflated) goatskins. In Ina-Ashur-utir-asbat, which the people of Hattina call Pitru, on the other side of the Euphrates, on the river Sagur, I received tribute from the kings of the other side of the Euphrates—that is, of Sanagara from Carchemish, Kundashpi from Commagene, of Arame, man of Gusi, of Lalli from Melitene (*Melid*), of Haiani, son of Gabari, of Kalparuda from Hattina, (and) of Kalparuda of Gurgum—(consisting of): silver, gold, tin, copper (or bronze), copper containers. I departed from the banks of the Euphrates and approached Aleppo (*Ḫal-man*). They (i.e., the inhabitants of A.) were afraid to fight and seized my feet (in submission). I received silver and gold as their tribute and offered sacrifices before the Adad of Aleppo. I departed from Aleppo and approached the two towns of Irhuleni from Hamath (*Amat*). I captured the towns Adennu, Barga (and) Argana his royal residence. I removed from them his booty (as well as) his personal (lit.: of his palaces) possessions. I set his palaces afire. I departed from Argana and approached Karkara. I destroyed, tore down and burned down Karkara, his (text: my) royal residence. He brought along to help him 1,200 chariots, 1,200 cavalrymen, 20,000 foot soldiers of Adad-'idri (i.e. Hadadezer) of Damascus (*Imērišu*),[8]

[4] Read: [*i*]*-še-riš*.

[5] Uncertain; text: *ḫurâṣu ḳa-sap*.

[6] For the divergent designations of this mountain, cf. M. Streck, Assyriologische Miszellen (No. 10, Atalur und Lallar) in *OLZ*, IX (1906), 344 f. cf. also E. F. Weidner *apud* E. Michel in *Die Welt des Orients*, I (1947), p. 14, n.10.

[6a] cf. also the lines 15—reverse of 8 of the basalt tablet published by L. Messerschmidt, *KAH*, I, 77 and transliterated and translated by E. Michel, Die Assur-Texte Salmanassars III, *Die Welt des Orients*, I (1947), p. 11 f.

[7] The use of the Sumerian term e n in this context is rather puzzling. It might indicate a peculiar social set-up which compelled the Assyrian scribes to use this rare word.

[8] The problem of the often changing (and apparently interchangeable) Akkadian denominations for Damascus (apart from *Di-ma(-a)š-qi/u*) is still unsolved; for previous discussions I refer to A. T. Clay in *YOS*, I (1915), 2, n.1; Streck, *Assurbanipal* (=*VAB*, VII), III, 780, where literature is amply quoted. These denominations are *Ša-imērišu*, *Ša-imērē*pl*-šu*, *Ša-i-me-ri-šu* (cf., e.g., C. Bezold, *Catalogue*, I, 21) and *Imērišu* with *imēru* spelled either phonetically or respectively as a n š e and d ù r. I would like to draw attention, on one hand, to the name of a town Ša-i-me-ri-e on the stela of Shilhak-Inshushinak (V. Scheil, *Délégation en Perse, Mémoires*, XI [1911], 42, No. 14), also attested in texts from Nuzi (cf. R. H. Pfeiffer and E. A. Lacheman, *Miscellaneous Texts from Nuzi, HSS*, XIII [1942], No. 433:6 [road leading from Nuzi to *Ša-imēri*]), and, on the other hand, to certain Neo-Assyrian and Neo-Babylonian nouns (of the formation *amêl ša xxx-šu*) denoting traders in commodities (salt, wine, pottery, fruit, etc.) or animals (for the latter, cf. C. H. W. Johns, *Assyrian Deeds and Documents* [London, 1898 f.]. 1076 II:2 *amelšá bu-li-šu*). cf. also the name of the town Ša-birêšu (Forrer, *Provinzeinteilung*, p. 107).

700 chariots, 700 cavalrymen, 10,000 foot soldiers of Irhuleni from Hamath, 2,000 chariots, 10,000 foot soldiers of Ahab, the Israelite (*A-ḫa-ab-bu* ^{mat}*Sir-'i-la-a-a*), 500 soldiers from Que, 1,000 soldiers from Musri,[9] 10 chariots, 10,000 soldiers from Irqanata, 200 soldiers of Matinu-ba'lu from Arvad, 200 soldiers from Usanata, 30 chariots, 1[0?],000 soldiers of Adunu-ba'lu from Shian, 1,000 camel-(rider)s of Gindibu', from Arabia, [. . .],000 soldiers of Ba'sa, son of Ruhubi, from Ammon—(all together) these were twelve kings. They rose against me [for a] decisive battle. I fought with them with (the support of) the mighty forces of Ashur, which Ashur, my lord, has given to me, and the strong weapons which Nergal, my leader, has presented to me, (and) I did inflict a defeat upon them between the towns Karkara and Gilzau. I slew 14,000 of their soldiers with the sword, descending upon them like Adad when he makes a rainstorm pour down. I spread their corpses (everywhere), filling the entire plain with their widely scattered (fleeing) soldiers. During the battle I made their blood flow down the *ḫur-pa-lu* of the district. The plain was too small to let (all) their (text: his) souls descend[10] (into the nether world), the vast field[11] gave out (when it came) to bury them. With their (text: sing.) corpses[12] I spanned the Orontes before there was a bridge. Even during the battle I took from them their chariots, their horses broken to the yoke.

Sixth Year according to the Bull-Inscription from the bull statues found in Calah. Published by A. H. Layard, *Inscriptions in the Cuneiform Character from Assyrian Monuments* (London, 1851), Pls. 12 f. (Bull A), and Pls. 46 f. (Bull B). For transliteration and translation, cf. A. Billerbeck and F. Delitzsch, Die Palasttore Salmanassars II von Balawat, in *BA*, VI (1908), 144 ff. English translation: Luckenbill, *AR*, I, §§646-647.

(67—74 of the Billerbeck-Delitzsch Edition)

In the sixth year of my rule, I departed from Nineveh and approached the river Balih. [The country] became afraid of my powerful army and [they killed] Giammu [their "master"]. I entered Til-Turahi and seized that town for myself. From the region along the river Balih I departed, the river Euphrates I crossed at its flood. I received tribute from the kings of the Hittite country (^{mat}*Ḫat-ti*). From the Hittite country I departed and approached the town Aleppo (*Ḫal-man*). I made sheep-[offering to the god Adad] of Aleppo. From Aleppo I departed and approached the city of Karkara. Hadadezer (^{d}*Adad-id-ri*) of Damascus (^{mat}*Imērišu*), Irhuleni of Hamath with 12 kings from the seacoast, trusting their combined power, set out (to march) against me for a decisive battle. I fought with them. I slew in battle 25,000 of their experienced soldiers and took away from them their chariots, their cavalry-horses and their battle equipment—they (themselves) dispersed to save their lives.

I embarked upon boats and made a journey into the high sea.

Sixth Year according to the Black Obelisk published first by A. H. Layard, *Inscriptions*, Pl. 87 f. Translation: Luckenbill, *AR*, I, §563.

In the sixth year of my rule, I approached the towns of the region along the Balih river. (Upon this) they (revolted and) killed Giammu, the master of their cities. I entered the town Til-Turahi. I crossed the Euphrates at its flood. I received tribute from [all] the kings of Hatti. At that time Hadadezer [of] Damascus, Irhulina from Hamath, as well as the kings of Hatti and (of) the seashore put their trust on their mutual strength and rose against me to fight a decisive battle. Upon the (oracle-) command of Ashur, the great lord, my lord, I fought with them (and) inflicted a defeat upon them. I took away from them their chariots, their cavalry-horses and their battle equipment, slaying 20,500 of their battle-experienced soldiers.

Tenth Year according to the text Schroeder, *KAH*, II, 110. Translation: Ernst Michel, Die Assur-Texte Salmanassars III in *Die Welt des Orients*, I (1947), pp. 67 ff.

(6—11)

In the tenth year of my rule, I crossed the Euphrates for the eighth time . . . [I departed] from the cities (belonging) to the people of Carchemish . . . together with one thousand (smaller) cities in its neighborhood. . . . At that time Hadadezer of Da[mascus] . . . put their trust on their mutual strength . . . I inflicted a defeat upon them. [I took] their chariots. . . .

Eleventh Year according to the Bull Inscription (cf. above). Translation: Luckenbill, *AR*, I, §653.

(90—96 of the Billerbeck-Delitzsch Edition)

In the eleventh year of my rule, I departed from Nineveh, I crossed for the ninth time the Euphrates at its flood. I conquered 97 towns of Sangar, I conquered 100 towns of Arame, I destroyed (them), tore (their walls down) and burnt (them) down. I seized the region of the mountain Amanus, crossed over the mountain Iaruqu and descended (then) against the towns of (the inhabitants) of Hamath. I conquered the town Ashtamaku together with 90 (smaller) towns, I made a massacre (among) them and their booty I carried away. At that time, Hadadezer of Damascus, Irhuleni of Hamath together with 12 kings from the seacoast trusting their combined strength set out (to march) against me for a decisive battle. I fought with them

[9] Here, the name *Muṣru* refers probably to a country in southern Asia Minor (cf. H. Winckler, Arabisches Muṣri in *MVAG*, XI [1906], 102-116, and E. F. Weidner [*apud* H. Bauer] in *AfO*, VIII [1932-3], 4, n.3, as well as recently in *AfO*, XIV (1941), 45, for three, or even more, countries bearing this name). The basic meaning of *Muṣru* is always "march" (from *maṣâru* "to mark, draw a line"), i.e. "border country."

[10] Text: *ana šúm-pùl* ZI^{meš}-*šú*⟨*nu*⟩ (line 110). This expression seems to indicate that the "souls" of the numerous dying soldiers were conceived as slipping down to the nether world through holes or cavities in the ground and that the massed corpses actually did cover the battlefield so completely as to make this descent difficult.

[11] The word *naprarû* (equated with *ṣêru* in a list of synonymous Akkadian words, (cf. von Soden, *ZA*, XLIII [NF IX], 234, l.25) is to be derived from the stem *prr'* which has the same meaning as *šprr* (cf. A. Heidel, *AS*, No. 13 [1940]), i.e. "to spread."

[12] Read a d (d a), i.e. l ú + u g$_6$. For the sign and its reading, cf. A. Goetze, *JAOS*, LXV (1945), 231.

and inflicted a defeat upon them. I slew in battle 10,000 of their experienced soldiers and took away from them their chariots, cavalry-horses and their equipment.

On my return march I conquered the town Apparazu, the fortress of Arame. At that time I received the tribute of Karparundi, from Hattina, (to wit): silver, gold, tin, wine, large cattle, sheep, garments, linen. I ascended the Amanus (and) cut (there) cedar logs.

Eleventh Year according to the Black Obelisk (cf. above). Translation: Luckenbill, *AR*, I, §568.

(face A [base], 87—89)

In the eleventh year of my rule, I crossed the Euphrates for the ninth time. I conquered countless towns. I descended towards the towns of Hatti (and) of the country of the inhabitants of Hamath; I conquered (there) 89 towns. Hadadezer of Damascus and 12 kings of Hatti stood together (trusting) in their combined strength. I inflicted a defeat upon them.

Fourteenth Year according to the Bull Inscription (Bull B) (cf. above). Translation: Luckenbill, *AR*, I, §§658-659.

(99—102)

In the fourteenth year of my rule, I called up the innumerable (inhabitants) of my vast country and crossed the Euphrates, at its flood, with my army of 120,000 (men). At the same time, Hadadezer of Damascus, Irhuleni from Hamath as well as 12 (other) kings from the shore of the Upper and Lower Sea, called up the(ir) innumerably large army and rose against me. I fought with them and defeated them. I did destroy[13] their chariots (and) their cavalry-horses, taking away from them their battle equipment. To save their lives they dispersed.

Fourteenth Year according to the Black Obelisk (cf. above). Translation: Luckenbill, *AR*, I, §571.

(face A [base], 91—93)

In the fourteenth year of my rule, I called up the country; I crossed the Euphrates. The twelve kings rose against me. I fought (and) defeated them.

Eighteenth Year according to the Black Obelisk (cf. above). Translation: Luckenbill, *AR*, I, §575.

(face B [base], 97—99)

In the eighteenth year of my rule, I crossed the Euphrates for the sixteenth time. Hazael (*Ḫa-za-'-il*) of Damascus rose for battle. I took away from him 1,121 chariots, 470 cavalry-horses as well as his camp.

Eighteenth Year according to the fragment of an annalistic text published in Rawlinson, Vol. III, Pl. 5, No. 6. Translation: Luckenbill, *AR*, I, §672.

In the eighteenth year of my rule I crossed the Euphrates for the sixteenth time. Hazael of Damascus (*Imērišu*) put his trust upon his numerous army and called up his troops in great number, making the mountain Senir (Sa-ni-ru), a mountain, facing the Lebanon, to his fortress. I fought with him and inflicted a defeat upon him, killing with the sword 16,000 of his experienced soldiers. I took away from him 1,121 chariots, 470 riding horses as well as his camp. He disappeared to save his life (but) I followed him and besieged him in Damascus (*Di-maš-qi*), his royal residence. (There) I cut down his gardens (outside of the city, and departed). I marched as far as the mountains of Hauran (*šadê*^{e} ^{mat}*Ḫa-ú-ra-ni*),[14] destroying, tearing down and burning innumerable towns, carrying booty away from them which was beyond counting. I (also) marched as far as the mountains of Ba'li-ra'si which is a promontory (lit.: at the side of the sea) and erected there a stela with my image as king. At that time I received the tribute of the inhabitants of Tyre, Sidon, and of Jehu, son of Omri (*Ia-ú-a mâr Ḫu-um-ri-i*).

Twenty-first Year according to the Black Obelisk (cf. above). Translation: Luckenbill, *AR*, I, §578.

(face B [base], 102—104)

In my twenty-first year, I crossed the Euphrates for the twenty-first time. I marched against the towns of Hazael of Damascus. Four of his larger urban settlements (*maḫâzu*) I conquered. I received tribute from the countries of the inhabitants of Tyre, Sidon, and Byblos.

(c) Various Inscriptions

(a) On a basalt statue; text published by L. Messerschmidt in *KAH*, I, No. 30. Translation: Luckenbill, *AR*, I, §681. cf. also Ernst Michel, Die Assur-Texte Salmanassars III (858-824), *Die Welt des Orients*, I (1947), pp. 57 f.

(14—ii 1)

I defeated Hadadezer of Damascus (*Imēr*[*i*]) together with twelve princes, his allies (lit.: helpers). I stretched upon the ground 20,900 of his strong warriors like *šu-bi*,[1] the remnants of his troops I pushed into the Orontes (*Arantu*) river and they dispersed to save their lives; Hadadezer (himself) perished. Hazael, a commoner (lit.: son of nobody), seized the throne, called up a numerous army and rose against me. I fought with him and defeated him, taking the *chariots*[2] of his camp. He disappeared to save his life. I marched as far as Damascus (*Di-ma-áš-qi*), his royal residence [and cut down his] gardens.

(b) Two inscriptions from C. F. Lehmann-Haupt, *Materalien zur älteren Geschichte Armeniens und Mesopotamiens* (*Abh. Kgl. Ges. d. Wiss. Goettingen* NF, IX/3 [1907]), No. 20 (Pl. III and pp. 31 ff.), and No. 22 (Pl. III and pp. 38 f.). Translation: Luckenbill, *AR*, I, §691.

(i 21—27)

Hadadezer, king of Damascus (*Ša-imērišu*), Irhulini from Hamath, together with 15(!) kings from the

13 For the verb used here, cf. E. Ebeling, *AfO*, IX (1933-4), 327, n.16 (*nṣi*), and J. Seidmann, *MAOG*, IX/3 (1935), 18, n.1 (*ṣi'*).

14 cf. for this region, J. Lewy, in *HUCA*, XVIII, 449, n.107.

1 For this comparison, cf. Michel, *Die Welt des Orients*, I (1947), p. 60, n.12. Furthermore, Nassouhi, *AfO*, III, 65 f. and K. Fr. Mueller, *MVAG*, XLI/3, p. 69, n.5.

2 For this reading cf. B. Meissner, *OLZ*, XV (1912), p. 146, n.1.

towns of the region along [the sea], rose [against me]. I fought with them for the fourth time and inflicted a defeat upon them. [I took away from them their chariots, their cavalry-horses and] their battle equipment, they dispersed to save their lives.

(ii 14—17)

Hadadezer, king of Damascus (*Ša-imērišu*), together with 12 kings of Hatti-land, rose against me. For the fourth time I fought with them and inflicted a defeat upon them. I took away from them their chariots, their cavalry-horses[3] and their battle equipment. To save their lives they dispersed.

(c) Inscription from a marble bead published by O. Schroeder, in *AfK*, II (1924), 70. Translation: Ebeling in *AOT*, 344.

Booty (*kišitti*[ti]) of the temple of Sheru from the town of Mallaha, the royal residence of Hazael of Damascus (*Imērišu*) which Shalmaneser, son of Ashurnasirpal, has brought into the walls of Libbiali.[4]

(d) Epigraphs

From the rich iconographic documentation left by Shalmaneser III, five representations fall into the orbit of this book. They are provided with epigraphs which are given below in translation.

(a) From the Bronze Gates of Balawat (cf. L. W. King, *Bronze Reliefs from the Gates of Shalmaneser* (London, 1915), also E. Unger, *Zum Bronzetor von Balawat* (Diss.), (Leipzig, 1912). For publications, cf. King, *op.cit.*, and for translation, Luckenbill, *AR*, I, §614.

(Band III—Phoenicia, Tyre, Sidon, Gaza)

I received the tribute (brought) on ships from the inhabitants of Tyre and Sidon.

(Band XIII—Syria)

I conquered Ashtamaku,[1] the royal residence of Irhuleni of Hatti, together with 86 (other towns).

(b) From the Black Obelisk. Epigraphs published in Layard, *Inscriptions*, Pl. 98. Translation: Luckenbill, *AR*, I, §§590, 591, 593.

II

The tribute of Jehu (*Ia-ú-a*), son of Omri (*Ḫu-um-ri*); I received from him silver, gold, a golden *saplu* -bowl, a golden vase with pointed bottom, golden tumblers, golden buckets, tin, a staff for a king, (and) wooden *puruḫtu*.[2]

III

The tribute of the country Musri; I received from him camels whose backs were doubled,[3] a river ox (*hippopotamus*), a *sakēa* -animal (*rhinoceros*), a *susu* -antelope, elephants, *bazîtu*- (and) *uqupu*- monkeys.[4]

V

The tribute of Karparunda from Hattina; I received from him silver, gold, tin, bronze, copper[5] *širiḫu* -pots, ivory, (and) ebony-wood.

5. ADAD-NIRARI III (810-783): EXPEDITION TO PALESTINE

(a) Stone Slab. From a broken stone slab found at Calah. Published by Rawlinson, Vol. I, Pl. 35, No. 1. Translation: Luckenbill, *AR*, I, §§739-740.

(1—21)

Property of Adad-nirari, great king, legitimate king, king of the world, king of Assyria—a king whom Ashur, the king of the Igigi (i.e. the dei superi) had chosen (already) when he was a youngster, entrusting him with the position of a prince without rival, (a king) whose shepherding they made as agreeable to the people of Assyria as (is the smell of) the Plant of Life, (a king) whose throne they established firmly; the holy high priest (and) tireless caretaker of the temple é.sár.ra, who keeps up the rites of the sanctuary, who acts (only) upon the trust-inspiring oracles (given) by Ashur, his lord; who has made submit to his feet the princes within the four rims of the earth; conquering from the Siluna mountain of the Rising Sun, the countries Saban, Ellipi, Harhar, Araziash, Mesu, the (country of the) Medians, Gizilbunda in its (full) extent, the countries Munna, Persia (*Parsua*), Allabria, Apdadana, Na'iri with all its regions, Andiu which lies far away in the *pitḫu* of the mountains[1] with all its regions, as far as the Great Sea of the Rising Sun (and) from the banks of the Euphrates, the country of the Hittites, Amurru-country in its full extent, Tyre, Sidon, Israel (*[mat]Ḫu-um-ri*), Edom, Palestine (*Pa-la-as-tu*), as far as the shore of the Great Sea of the Setting Sun, I made them submit all to my feet, imposing upon them tribute.

I marched against the country *Ša-imērišu*: I shut up Mari',[2] king of Damascus (*Imērišu*) in Damascus (*Di-ma-áš-qi*), his royal residence. The terror-inspiring glamor of Ashur, my (text: his) lord, overwhelmed him and he seized my feet, assuming the position of a slave (of mine). (Then) I received in his (own) palace in Damascus (*Di-ma-áš-qi*), his royal residence, 2,300

[3] The meaning "cavalry-horse" for *pit-ḫallu* is well attested; only rarely this word denotes the chariot-horse, such as, e.g. in Thureau-Dangin, *VIIIe Campagne* line 403 "one statue (representing king) Ursâ with his two *sisē[mes]* *pit-ḫal-lì-tu*, his (chariot)-driver, together with its socle, made of cast bronze."

[4] The name *Libbi-âli* denotes the central section of the town Ashur, cf. E. Unger in *Reallexikon der Assyriologie*, I, 173.

[1] For this town, cf. R. R. Boudou, Liste de noms géographiques (*Orientalia* No. 36-38, Rome, 1929 f.), p. 27.

[2] Text: *b/pu-ru₄-ḫa-ti*. Meaning unknown.

[3] This reference to the Bactrian camel—especially in connection with the *alap nâri* "river ox" and with monkeys—is rather disturbing. cf. in this connection, E. Forrer, *Provinzeinteilung*, p. 23, and Landsberger-Bauer, in *ZA*, XXXVII (NF III), p. 76. Landsberger, *Fauna*, p. 143.

[4] cf. above n.16, p. 276 and below n.4, p. 297.

[5] The word *siparru* (usually "bronze") has to be translated here with "copper," because it refers to a container. The learned scribes in Mesopotamia were always rather careless in the use of the terms urudu ("copper") and zabar ("bronze"), while those of the temple and fiscal administration differentiate very exactly.

[1] Text: *pit-ḫu šadû[u]*, cf. E. Ebeling, *MAOG*, VII/1-2 (1933), 64, n.h, for this expression.

[2] The Assyrians have taken Aram. *mari'* "my lord" to be the name of the king and not his title, cf. my article, Une glose hurrite dans les Annales de Teglath-Phalasar I, *RHA*, V (1939), 112, for this and similar cases of such misunderstandings.

talents of silver (corresponding to) 20 talents of gold, 5,000 talents of iron, garments of linen with multicolored trimmings, a bed (inlaid) with ivory, a *nimattu* -couch mounted and inlaid with ivory, (and) countless (other objects being) his possessions.

(b) Saba'a Stela. Report on a campaign against Palestine from the Saba'a Stela. Published by E. Unger, *Relief Stele Adadniraris III aus Saba'a und Semiramis* (*Publicationen der Kaiserlichen osmanischen Museen*, No. 12, Konstantinopel, 1916). Translation: Luckenbill, *AR*, I, §§734-735.

(11—20)

In the fifth year (of my official rule) I sat down solemnly on my royal throne and called up the country (for war). I ordered the numerous army of Assyria to march against Palestine (*Pa-la-áš-tu*). I crossed the Euphrates at its flood. As to the numerous hostile kings who had rebelled in the time of my father Shamshi-Adad (i.e., Shamshi-Adad V) and had wi[thheld] their regular (tributes), [the terror-inspiring glam]or overwhelmed them (and) upon the command of Ashur, Sin, Shamash, Adad (and) Ishtar, my trust(-inspiring) gods, they seized my feet (in submission). I received all the tributes [. . .] which they brought to Assyria. I (then) ordered [to march] against the country Damascus (*Ša-imērišu*). I invested Mari' in Damascus (*Dimaš-qi*) [and he surrendered]. One hundred talents of gold (corresponding to) one thousand talents of [silver], 60 talents of . . . [I received as his tribute].

6. TIGLATH-PILESER III (744-727): CAMPAIGNS AGAINST SYRIA AND PALESTINE[1]

(a) Building Inscription

From a building inscription on clay preserved in various copies, published by Rawlinson, in Vol. II, Pl. 67. Translation: Luckenbill, *AR*, I, §§800-801, 803.

(56—63)

I installed Idi-bi'li as a Warden of Marches[2] on the border of Musur. In all the countries which . . . [I received] the tribute of Kushtashpi of Commagene[3] (*Kummuḫu*), Urik of Qu'e, Sibitti-be'l of Byblos, . . . Enil of Hamath, Panammu of Sam'al, Tarhulara of Gumgum, Sulumal of Militene, . . . Uassurme of Tabal, Ushhitti of Tuna, Urballa of Tuhana, Tuhamme of Ishtunda, . . . [Ma]tan-be'l of Arvad, Sanipu of Bit-Ammon, Salamanu of Moab, . . . Mitinti of Ashkelon, Jehoahaz (*Ia-ú-ḫa-zi*) of Judah (*Ia-ú-da-a-a*), Kaushmalaku of Edom (*Ú-du-mu-a-a*), Muzr[i . . .], Hanno (*Ḫa-a-nu-ú-nu*) of Gaza (*Ḫa-za-at-a-a*) (consisting of) gold, silver, tin, iron, antimony,[4] linen garments with multicolored trimmings, garments of their native (industries) (being made of) dark purple wool . . . all kinds of costly objects be they products of the sea or of the continent, the (choice) products of their regions, the treasures of (their) kings, horses, mules (trained for) the yoke. . . .

[1] cf. for the historical background—apart from the books listed in n.1, p. 276—also: A. Alt, Das System der assyrischen Provinzen auf dem Boden des Reiches Israel, in *ZDPV*, LII (1929), 220 ff.; Neue assyrische Nachrichten über Palästina und Syria, in *ZDPV*, LXVII (1945), 178 ff.; K. Galling, Assyrische und persische Präfekten in Geser, in *Palästina Jahrbuch*, XXXI (1935), 75 ff.; A. Jepsen, Israel und Damaskus, in *AfO*, XIV (1941-44), 153 ff.; A. Jirku, Der angebliche assyrische Bezirk Gile'ad, in *ZDPV*, LI (1928), 249 ff.; and R. de Vaux, La chronologie de Hazael et de Benhadad III, rois de Damas, *RB* (1932), 512 ff.

[2] Text: *a-na* ^{amel}*atûtu*${}^{u-tu}$ *ina muḫḫi* ^{mat}*Mu-uṣ-ri*.

[3] For the local names mentioned in this text, cf. P. Naster, *L'Asie Mineure et l'Assyrie aux VIII*e *et VII*e *siècles av. J.-C. d'après les annales des rois assyriens* (Louvain, 1938), index *s.v.*; and B. Landsberger, *Sam'al*, I, pp. 8 ff.

(66)

I sent an officer of mine, the *rabšaq*,[5] to Tyre [and received] from Metenna of Tyre 150 talents of gold. . . .

(b) Annalistic Records

From the so-called "Annals" engraved upon slabs found in Calah. Published by P. Rost, *Die Keilschrifttexte Tiglat-Pilesers III nach den Papierabklatschen und Originalen des Britischen Museums* (Leipzig, 1893).

Third Year, Rost, *op.cit.*, Pls. XX-XXI, text, pp. 19-23. Translation: Luckenbill, *AR*, I, §770.

(103—133)

[In] the (subsequent) course of my campaign [I received] the tribute of the kin[gs . . . A]zriau from Iuda[1] (*Ia-ú-da-a-a*), like a [. . . Azr]iau from Iuda in . . . countless, (reaching) sky high . . . eyes, like from heaven . . . by means of an attack with foot soldiers. . . . He heard [about the approach of the] massed [armies of] Ashur and was afraid. . . . I tore down, destroyed and burnt [down . . . for Azri]au they had annexed, they (thus) had reinforced him . . . like vine/trunks . . . was very difficult . . . was barred and high . . . was situated and its exit . . . I made deep . . . I surrounded his garrisons [with earthwork], against. . . . I made them carry [the corvée-basket] and . . . his great . . . like a pot [I did crush . . .] (lacuna of three lines) . . . Azriau . . . a royal palace of my own [I built in his city . . .] tribute like that [for Assyrian citizens I imposed upon them . . .] the city Kul[lani . . .] his ally . . . the cities[2] Usnu, Siannu, Si[mirra], Ra[sh]puna which are on the se[acoa]st as well as the cities up to the mountain[3] Saue, the mountain which abuts on the Lebanon proper; the mountain Ba'li-Sapuna as far as the Amanus, the Boxwood-tree Mountain (in short) the entire Sau-country; the provinces of Kar-Adad, Hatarikka,[4] the province of Nuqudina, the mountain Hasu as well as the (smaller) cities in its vicinity, the town Ara (and) the cities on

[4] The term *abaru* (Sumerogram: A.BAR) denotes a rarely used metal, probably magnesite (cf. R. C. Thompson, *A Dictionary of Assyrian Chemistry and Geology* [Oxford, 1936], p. 116; and J. R. Partington, *Origin and Development of Applied Chemistry* [London, 1935], index *s.v.*). For unknown reasons, it has mostly been used for small objects and tools (spoon, axe, etc.) prescribed for ritual purposes. For a foundation inscription on *abaru*, cf. Luckenbill, *AR*, II, §§106 f.

[5] For this official, cf. e.g. W. Manitius, in *ZA*, XXIV (1910), 199 f., and B. Meissner, *Babylonien und Assyrien* (Heidelberg, 1920), I, p. 103.

[1] For this country, cf. J. Lewy, in *HUCA*, XVIII, 479 f. cf. furthermore, P. Naster, *L'Asie Mineure*, etc., p. 19, n.33.

[2] For identification of these place names, cf. E. Forrer, *Provinzeinteilung*, pp. 57 ff.

[3] cf. L. Koehler, Lexikologisch-Geographisches (No. 3, Der Berg als Grenze), in *ZDPV*, LXII (1939), 115 f.

[4] cf. J. Lewy, in *HUCA*, XVIII, 449, n.108.

both sides of them as well as the cities in their vicinity, the mountain Sarbua—the entire mountain,—the towns Ashhani (and) Iadabi, the mountain Iaraqu—the entire mountain,—the towns . . . Illitarbi, Zitanu as far as Atinni, . . . Bumami—(together) 19 districts belonging to Hamath and the cities in their vicinity which are (situated) at the coast of the Western Sea and which they had (unlawfully) taken away for Azriau, I restored to the territory of Assyria. An officer of mine I installed as governor over them. [I deported] 30,300 inhabitants from their cities and settled them in the province of the town Ku[. . .]; 1,223 inhabitants I settled in the province of the Ullaba country.

Year Unknown, Rost, *op.cit.*, Pl. xv, xvi, text, pp. 26-27. Translation: Luckenbill, *AR*, I, §772.

(150—157)

I received tribute from Kushtashpi of Commagene (*Kummuḫu*), Rezon (*Ra-ḫi-a-nu*)[4a] of Damascus (*Ša-imērišu*), Menahem of Samaria (*Me-ni-ḫi-im-me* [al]*Sa-me-ri-na-a-a*), Hiram (*Ḫi-ru-um-mu*) of Tyre, Sibitti-bi'li of Byblos, Urikki of Qu'e, Pisiris of Carchemish, I'nil of Hamath, Panammu of Sam'al, Tarḫulara of Gurgum, Sulumal of Militene, Dadilu of Kaska, Uassurme of Tabal, Ushhitti of Tuna, Urballa of Tuhana, Tuhamme of Ishtunda, Urimme of Hubishna (and) Zabibe, the queen of Arabia,[5] (to wit) gold, silver, tin, iron, elephant-hides, ivory, linen garments with multicolored trimmings, blue-dyed wool, purple-dyed[6] wool, ebony-wood, boxwood-wood, whatever was precious (enough for a) royal treasure; also lambs whose stretched hides were dyed purple, (and) wild birds whose spread-out wings were dyed blue,[7] (furthermore) horses, mules, large and small cattle, (male) camels, female camels with their foals.

After the 9th Year, Rost, *op.cit.*, Pls. xxii, xxiii, text pp. 35-41. Translation: Luckenbill, *AR*, I, §§777-779.

(205—240)

I laid siege to and conquered the town Hadara, the inherited property of Rezon of Damascus (*Ša-imērišu*), [the place where] he was born. I brought away as prisoners 800 (of its) inhabitants with their possessions, . . . their large (and) small cattle. 750 prisoners from Kurussa [. . . prisoners] from Irma, 550 prisoners from Metuna I brought (also) away. 592 towns . . . of the 16 districts of the country of Damascus (*Ša-imērišu*) I destroyed (making them look) like hills of (ruined cities over which) the flood (had swept).

[4a] The much-damaged stone tablet published by E. Nassouhi in *MAOG*, III/1-2, as No. VII contains the names *Ra-ḫi-a-nu* and *Su-lu-ma-al*. The reading *Ra-ḫi-a-nu* instead of *Ra-ṣun-nu* has been shown by B. Landsberger in *Sam'al* (*Veroeffentlichungen der Tuerkischen historischen Gesellschaft*, Series VII, No. 16 [Ankara, 1948]), p. 66, n.169.

[5] For the female rulers of Arab tribes (attested in cuneiform documents from Tiglath-pileser III to Ashurbanipal, and perhaps [cf. n.7, p. 312] Nabonidus), cf. N. Abbot, Pre-Islamic Arab Queens, in *AJSL*, LVIII (1941), 1-22.

[6] The terms used in this context are *takiltu* and *argamannu*; the first denoting a darker, the second a reddish shade of blue purple. cf. F. Thureau-Dangin, Un comptoir de laine pourpre à Ras Shamra, etc., in *Syria*, XV (1934), 141.

[7] This unique reference seems to mention stuffed and decorated animals.

Samsi, the queen of Arabia who had acted against the oath (sworn) by Shamash and had . . . town . . . to the town I'zasi . . . Arabia in the country of Sa[ba' . . .] in her camp . . . she became afraid [of my mighty army] and [sent] to [me camels, camel-mares], . . . [I p]ut [an official/regent over her] and made (also) [the Bir'aians] bow to my feet. The inhabitants of Mas'a, of Tema (and) the inhabitants of Saba', Haiappa, Badana, Hatti, the tribe of the Idiba'ileans . . . whose countries [(are) far away], towards West, [*heard*] the fame of my rule [. . . and brought]—without ex[ception (lit.: like one man)]—as their tribute: gold, silver, [male and female ca]mels and all kinds of spices to [me and kis]sed my feet. . . . I estab[lished] a palace as be[fitting for my position as their king in . . .] and appointed Idibi'lu as governor over [the country Musru]. In my former campaigns I had considered all the cities [which . . . as . . .] and I had carried away as booty and . . . the town Samaria only I did le[ave/except . . .] their king [. . . like a] fog/snow-storm . . . districts of the country Bit-[. . . prisoners] of the town [. . .]bara, 625 prisoners of the town . . . of the town Hinatuna, 650 prisoners of the town Qana[. . . of the town . . .]atbiti, 650 prisoners of the town Ir[. . . all these] people together with their possessions [I brought away . . .] the town Aruma, the town Marum [. . . (as to) Mitinti from] Ashkelon (who) had [violated] the oath sworn to me [and had revolted], (when) he learned about [the defeat inflicted upon] Rezon he [perished] in in[sanity]. [Rukibtu, son of Mitinti] sat (himself) on his throne. To . . . and he implored me 500 . . . I entered his town. Fifteen towns . . . Idibi'lu of Arabia. . . .

Year Unknown. From a fragmentary annalistic text published by Rawlinson, Vol. III, Pl. 10, No. 2,1-45; also, Rost, Pls. xxv-xxvi, text, pp. 79-83. Translation: Luckenbill, *AR*, I, §§815-819; cf. also E. Forrer, *Provinzeinteilung*, pp. 59 f.

(1—34)

. . . the town Hatarikka as far as the mountain Saua, [. . . the towns:] Byb[los], . . . Simirra, Arqa, Zimarra, . . . Uznu, [Siannu], Ri'-raba, Ri'-sisu, . . . the towns . . . of the Upper Sea, I brought under my rule. Six officers of mine I installed as governors over them. [. . . the town R]ashpuna which is (situated) at the coast of the Upper Sea, [the towns . . .]nite, Gal'za, Abilakka which are adjacent to Israel (*Bît Ḫu-um-ri-a*) [and the] wide (land of) [Naphta]li,[8] in its entire extent, I united with Assyria. Officers of mine I installed as governors upon them.

As to Hanno of Gaza (*Ḫa-a-nu-ú-nu* [al]*Ḫa-az-za-at-a-a*) who had fled before my army and run away to Egypt, [I conquered] the town of Gaza, . . . his personal property, his images . . . [and I placed (?)] (the images of) my [. . . gods] and my royal image in his own palace . . . and declared (them) to be (thenceforward) the gods of their country. I imposed upon th[em tribute]. [As for Menahem I ov]erwhelmed him [like a

[8] The text has only: [. . .]-*li*.

snowstorm] and he . . . fled like a bird, alone, [and bowed to my feet(?)]. I returned him to his place [and imposed tribute upon him, to wit:] gold, silver, linen garments with multicolored trimmings, . . . great . . . [I re]ceived from him. Israel (lit.: "Omri-Land" *Bît Ḫumria*) . . . all its inhabitants (and) their possessions I led to Assyria. They overthrew their king Pekah (*Pa-qa-ḫa*) and I placed Hoshea (*A-ú-si-'*) as king over them. I received from them 10 talents of gold, 1,000(?) talents of silver as their [tri]bute and brought them to Assyria.

As for Samsi, queen of Arabia, . . . I killed, 1,100 inhabitants, 30,000 camels, 20,000 (heads of) cattle [. . .] 5,000 (containers with all kinds of spices, 11 *tûlu*[9] -bowls, the property of her gods, . . . her (own) possessions, I took away from her and she herself [fled] to save her life to the town Bazu, a waterless region (lit.: a place of thirst) like a wild donkey-mare. . . . forced by hunger, the people which were in her camp [did]. . . . (Then) she became apprehensive [of the power of] my strong [army] and brought to me male and female camels, . . . her. . . . [I put a regent over her. I made the Bir'ai bow to my feet.] The inhabitants of Mas'ai, Tema, the Sabaeans, the inhabitants of Haiappa, Badana, Hattia, the Idiba'leans, . . . from the region of the West [whose far] away countries [nobody knows, heard] of the fame of my rule [and] . . . they bowed to the yoke of my rule. [They brought to me]—without exception—as their tribute male and female camels and all kinds of spices and kissed my feet. . . . I appointed Idibi'lu to the office of Warden of Marches on (the frontier of) Musur (*Mu-ṣu-ri*).

7. SARGON II (721-705): THE FALL OF SAMARIA

(a) Inscriptions of a General Nature

(1) "Pavé des Portes," No. IV, lines 31-44. Published by H. Winckler, *Die Keilschrifttexte Sargons* (Leipzig, 1889), I, 147 f., II, Pl. 38. Translation: Luckenbill, *AR*, II, §99.

(Property of Sargon, etc., king of Assyria, etc.) conqueror of Samaria (*Sa-mir-i-na*) and of the entire (country of) Israel (*Bît-Ḫu-um-ri-a*) who despoiled Ashdod (and) Shinuhti, who caught the Greeks who (live on islands) in the sea, like fish, who exterminated Kasku, all Tabali and Cilicia (*Ḫilakku*), who chased away Midas (*Mi-ta-a*) king of Musku, who defeated Musur (*Mu-ṣu-ri*) in Rapihu, who declared Hanno, king of Gaza, as booty, who subdued the seven kings of the country Ia', a district on Cyprus (*Ia-ad-na-na*), (who) dwell (on an island) in the sea, at (a distance of) a seven-day journey.

(2) From the so-called Cyprus Stela, published by A. Ungnad, in *VS*, I, 71; cf. also H. Winckler, *op.cit.*, I, 174 ff., II, Pls. 46-47. Translation: Luckenbill, *AR*, II, §§183, 186.

(51—65, right face)

I smash[ed] like a flood-storm the country of Hamath (*A-ma-at-tu*) in its entire [extent]. I br[ought its] ki[ng] Iaubi'di as well as his family, (and) [his] warriors in fett[ers], as the prisoner (contingent) of his country, to Assyria. From these (prisoners) I set [up a troop] of 300 chariots (and) 600 moun[ted men] equipped with leather shields and lan[ces], and ad[ded them] to my royal corps. I se[ttled] 6,300 Assyrians of reliable [disposition][1] in the country of Hamath and installed an officer of mine as go[vernor] over them, imposing upon th[em] (the payment) of tri[bute].

(28—42, left face)

[and the seven ki]ngs of Ia', a district on [Cy]prus ([*Ad*]*nana*) which [lies a]midst the Western Sea at a distance of 7 days, their location being (so) far off (that) none of my royal forefathers [had ever he]ard the names of their countries (mentioned) [since the] far-off days of the *ṣi-bit mat* [d]*Aššš*[*ur*][2] [lea]rned, far away in the midst of the sea, [the feats which I have achie]ved in Chaldea and in Hatti, and their hearts began to pound, [terror] fell upon them. They sent me, [to] Babylon, gold, silver, objects made of ebony and boxwood (which are the) treasures of their country, and kissed my feet.

(b) From Annalistic Reports

So-called Annals and their parallels taken from the Display Inscriptions. The Annals are quoted here according to A. G. Lie, *The Inscriptions of Sargon II, King of Assyria*, Part I. The Annals (Paris, 1929). Their text, taken from stone slabs and wall inscriptions in Khorsabad (Dûr-Sharrukîn) has been published (latest publication) by H. Winckler (cf. above).[1] The latest English translation of the Annals is that of Lie (cf. above); that of the Display Inscriptions: Luckenbill, *AR*, II, §§53 ff.

(1) *First Year*. According to A. G. Lie, *op.cit.* (H. Winckler, No. 63). Translation: Luckenbill, *AR*, II, §4.

(10—17)

At the begi[nning of my royal rule, I . . . the town of the Sama]rians [I besieged, conquered] (2 lines destroyed) [for the god . . . who le]t me achieve (this) my triumph. . . . I led away as prisoners [27,290 inhabitants of it (and) [equipped] from among [them (soldiers to man)] 50 chariots for my royal corps. . . . [The town I] re[built] better than (it was) before and [settled] therein people from countries which [I] myself [had con]quered. I placed an officer of mine as governor over them and imposed upon them tribute as (is customary) for Assyrian citizens.

According to the Display Inscriptions; text: H. Winckler, II, Pls. 30 f., I, 101. Translation: Luckenbill, *AR*, II, §55.

(23—26)

I besieged and conquered Samaria (*Sa-me-ri-na*), led

[9] In Rawlinson: *tu-du-ni*, according to Rost: *tu-la(?)-ni*. The latter seems to be the better reading, *tûlu* being a well-known word for a bowl shaped like the female breast.

[1] Text: *be-el* [*ṭêmi*]. This term refers here obviously to the political reliability of the Assyrian subjects settled in Hamath.

[2] This enigmatic phrase has been discussed recently by J. Lewy, in *HUCA*, XIX, 466, and taken as referring to the "landnama" of Assyria by the Assyrians.

[1] For the textual and historical problems involved, cf. A. T. Olmstead, The Text of Sargon's Annals, in *AJSL*, XLVIII (1931), 259 ff.

away as booty 27,290 inhabitants of it. I formed from among them a contingent of 50 chariots and made remaining (inhabitants) assume their (social) positions.[2] I installed over them an officer of mine and imposed upon them the tribute of the former king. Hanno, king of Gaza and also Sib'e,[3] the *turtan*[4] of Egypt (*Mu-ṣu-ri*), set out from Rapihu against me to deliver a decisive battle. I defeated them; Sib'e ran away, afraid when he (only) heard the noise of my (approaching) army, and has not been seen again. Hanno, I captured personally. I received the tribute from Pir'u of Musuru,[5] from Samsi, queen of Arabia (and) It'amar the Sabaean, gold in dust-form, horses (and) camels.

According to the Annals of the Room XIV, published by H. Winckler, *op.cit.*, II, Pls. 26 ff.; transliterated and translated by F. H. Weissbach, in *ZDMG*, LXXII, 176 ff., and Luckenbill, *AR*, II, §§79-80.

(11—15)

Iamani from Ashdod, afraid of my armed force (lit.: weapons), left his wife and children and fled to the frontier of M[usru] which belongs to Meluhha (i.e., Ethiopia) and hid (lit.: stayed) there like a thief. I installed an officer of mine as governor over his entire large country and its prosperous inhabitants, (thus) aggrandizing (again) the territory belonging to Ashur, the king of the gods. The terror(-inspiring) glamor of Ashur, my lord, overpowered (however) the king of Meluhha and he threw him (i.e. Iamani) in fetters on hands and feet, and sent him to me, to Assyria. I conquered and sacked the towns Shinuhtu (and) Samaria, and all Israel (lit.: "Omri-Land" *Bît Ḫu-um-ri-ia*). I caught, like a fish, the Greek (Ionians) who live (on islands) amidst the Western Sea.

(2) *Second Year*. According to A. G. Lie, *op.cit.*; H. Winckler, *Annals*, I, 23-31. Translation: Luckenbill, *AR*, II, §5.

(23—57)

In the second year of my rule, Ilubi'[di, from Hamath] . . . a large [army] he brought together at the town Qarqar and, [forgetting] the oaths [which they had sworn . . .] the [cities of Arpad, Simirra], Damascus (*Di-maš-*[*qa*[ki]]) and Samaria [revolted against me] (lacuna of uncertain length) he (i.e. Hanno of Gaza) made [an agreement with him (i.e. the Pharaoh)] and he (i.e. the Pharaoh) called up Sib'e his *turtan* to assist him (i.e. Hanno) and he (i.e. Sib'e) set out against me to deliver a decisive battle. I inflicted a defeat upon them (i.e. Hanno and Sib'e) upon an (oracle-)order[6] (given) by my lord Ashur, and Sib'e, like a s i p a (i.e. shepherd)[7] whose flock has been stolen, fled alone and disappeared. Hanno (however), I captured personally and brought him (with me) in fetters to my city Ashur. I destroyed Rapihu, tore down (its walls) and burned (it). I led away as prisoners 9,033 inhabitants with their numerous possessions.

According to the Display Inscriptions; text: H. Winckler, I, 103-105, II, Pl. 31. Translation: Luckenbill, *AR*, II, §55.

(33—37)

Ia'ubidi from Hamath, a commoner[8] without claim to the throne, a cursed Hittite, schemed to become king of Hamath, induced the cities Arvad, Simirra, Damascus (*Di-maš-qa*[ki]) and Samaria to desert me, made them collaborate and fitted out an army. I called up the masses of the soldiers of Ashur and besieged him and his warriors in Qarqar, his favorite city. I conquered (it) and burnt (it). Himself I flayed; the rebels I killed in their cities and established (again) peace and harmony. A contingent of 200 chariots and 600 men on horseback I formed from among the inhabitants of Hamath and added them to my royal corps.

(3) *Fifth Year*. According to A. G. Lie, *op.cit.*; (H. Winckler, *Annals*, I, 46-50). Translation: Luckenbill, *AR*, II, §8.

(72—76)

In the fifth year of my rule, Pisiri of Carchemish broke the oath sworn by the great gods and wrote messages to Midas (*Mi-ta-a*), king of Muski, (full) of hostile plans against Assyria. I lifted my hands (in prayer) to my lord Ashur (with the result that) I (quickly) made him, and also his family, surrender (lit.: come out) (of Carchemish), (all) in fetters and with the gold, silver and his personal possessions. And the rebellious inhabitants of Carchemish who (had sided) with him, I led away as prisoners and brought (them) to Assyria. I formed from among them a contingent of 50 chariots, 200 men on horseback (and) 3,000 foot soldiers and added (it) to my royal corps. In the city of Carchemish I (then) settled inhabitants of Assyria and imposed upon their (neck) the yoke of Ashur, my lord.[9]

(4) *Seventh Year*. According to A. G. Lie, *op.cit.*; (H. Winckler, *Annals*, I, 94-99). Translation: Luckenbill, *AR*, II, §§17-18.

[2] To this meaning of *enû*, cf. *tênû* discussed below, n.1, p. 289

[3] For this Egyptian name (mentioned also in II Kings 17:4) and the historical problems involved, cf. G. Steindorff, Die keilschriftliche Wiedergabe. aegyptischer Eigennamen (*BA*, I, 339 ff.); also, Kees, *GGA*, 1926, p. 426; H. Ranke, *Keilschriftliches Material zur altaegyptischen Vokalisierung*, p. 38; and Helene von Zeissl, Aethiopen und Assyrer in Aegypten, *Beiträge zur Geschichte der ägyptischen "Spätzeit"* (*Aegyptologische Forschungen*, Heft 14, 1944), p. 18 ff. Further, A. T. Olmstead, *History of Assyria* (New York, 1923), p. 204.

[4] The Assyrian word (attested since Shalmaneser III, but *tertennûtu* already in Boğazköi-Akkadian, *KBo*, I, 3:29 and Ebeling, *KAJ*, 245:17 *amel**tar-te-ni-šu-nu*) refers to a high military and administrative official, second in rank only to the king (cf. E. Unger's translation *Vizekönig* in *ZATW*, 1923, 204ff.). Etymology uncertain; beside *turtanu,* also *tartanu* is attested.

[5] To the thorny problem of the identification of both, name of king and name of country, cf. E. F. Weidner, *AfO*, XIV (1941), 45 f. Also Helene von Zeissl, *op.cit.*, pp. 21 ff.

[6] The text has *siqru* "order," cf. von Soden, *ZA*, XLI (NF VII), 168.

[7] This is meant to be a pun.

[8] For the meaning of the term *ḫubšu* denoting in Akkadian (as well as Ugaritic) texts a special social class, cf. G. R. Driver and J. C. Miles, *The Assyrian Laws* (Oxford, 1935), p. 485 (with references); further, W. F. Albright, *BASOR*, 63 (1934), 29 f.; I. Mendelsohn, *BASOR*, 83 (1941), 36 ff.; and R. Lacheman, *BASOR*, 86 (1942), 36 f.

[9] Usually, the yoke of the king is mentioned in connection with the status of newly subjugated peoples. The present reference to the "Yoke of Ashur" could therefore indicate a special status of the Assyrians forcibly settled in Carchemish.

(120—125)

Upon a trust(-inspiring oracle given by) my lord Ashur, I crushed the tribes of Tamud, Ibadidi, Marsimanu, and Haiapa, the Arabs who live, far away, in the desert (and) who know neither overseers nor official(s) and who had not (yet) brought their tribute to any king. I deported their survivors and settled (them) in Samaria.

From Pir'u, the king of Musru, Samsi, the queen of Arabia, It'amra, the Sabaean,—the(se) are the kings of the seashore and from the desert—I received as their presents, gold in the form of dust, precious stones, ivory, ebony-seeds,[10] all kinds of aromatic substances, horses (and) camels.

(5) *Eleventh Year.* According to A. G. Lie, *op.cit.*; (H. Winckler, *Annals*, I, 215-228). Translation: Luckenbill, *AR*, II, §30.

(249—262)

Azuri, king of Ashdod, had schemed not to deliver tribute (any more) and sent messages (full) of hostilities against Assyria to the kings (living) in his neighborhood. On account of the misdeed which he (thus) committed, I abolished his rule over the inhabitants of his country and made Ahimiti, his younger[11] brother, king over them. But the(se) Hittites, (always) planning treachery, hated his (i.e. Ahimiti's) reign and elevated to rule over them a Greek[12] who, without claim to the throne, knew, just as they (themselves), no respect for authority. [In a sudden rage] I marched quickly—(even) in my state-chariot[13] and (only) with my cavalry which never, even in friendly territory,[14] leaves my side—against Ashdod, his royal residence, and I besieged and conquered the cities Ashdod, Gath (*Gi-im-tu*) (and) Asdudimmu. I declared the gods residing therein, himself, as well as the inhabitants of his country, the gold, silver (and) his personal possessions as booty. I reorganized (the administration of) these cities[15] and placed an officer of mine as governor over them and declared them Assyrian citizens and they bore (as such) my yoke.[16]

According to the Display Inscription (H. Winckler, *op.cit.*, I, 115-116; II, 33-34). Translation: Luckenbill, *AR*, II, §62.

(90—112)

Azuri, king of Ashdod, had schemed not to deliver tribute any more and sent messages (full) of hostilities against Assyria, to the kings (living) in his neighborhood. On account of the(se) act(s) which he committed, I abolished his rule over the people of his country and made Ahimiti, his younger brother, king over them. But the(se) Hittites, always planning evil deeds, hated his reign and elevated to rule over them a Greek (*Ia-ma-ni*) who, without any claim to the throne, had no respect for authority—just as they themselves. In a sudden rage, I did not (wait to) assemble the full might of my army (or to) prepare the camp(ing equipment), but started out towards Ashdod (only) with those of my warriors who, even in friendly areas, never leave my side. But this Greek heard about the advance of my expedition, from afar, and he fled into the territory of Musru—which belongs (now) to Ethiopia—and his (hiding) place could not be detected. I besieged (and) conquered the cities Ashdod, Gath, Asdudimmu; I declared his images, his wife, his children, all the possessions and treasures of his palace as well as the inhabitants of his country as booty. I reorganized (the administration of) these cities (and) settled therein people from the [regions] of the East which I had conquered personally. I installed an officer of mine over them and declared them Assyrian citizens and they pulled (as such) the straps (of my yoke). The king of Ethiopia who [lives] in [a distant country], in an inapproachable region, the road [to which is . . .], whose fathers never—from remote days until now[17]—had sent messengers to inquire after the health of my royal forefathers, he did hear, even (that) far away, of the might of Ashur, Nebo (and) Marduk. The awe-inspiring glamor of my kingship blinded him and terror overcame him. He threw him (i.e. the Greek) in fetters, shackles and iron bands, and they brought him to Assyria, a long journey.

(c) From Broken Prisms

(1) The fragmentary prism Assur 16587 (=VA 8412), published by E. F. Weidner, in *AfO*, XIV (1941), 40 ff. (text: p. 43), reports in col. B, lines 5-11, on these events as follows:

. . . in the region of the town *Naḫal-m*[*uṣur* ([1]) . . .] I made [my army] march [the road] towards sunset . . . the sheik[2] of the town Laban . . . Shilkanni (or: Shilheni),[3] king of Musri, who . . . the terror-inspiring glamor of Ashur, my lord, overwhelmed him and he brought as *tâmartu* -present 12 fine (lit.: big) horses from Musri which have not their equals in this country.

[10] These seeds are part of the Mesopotamian pharmacopoeia.

[11] For *talimu* "younger brother," cf. in extenso P. Koschaker, Fratriarchat, Hausgemeinschaft und Mutterrecht in Keilschriftrechten, in *ZA*, XLI (NF VII), 64 ff. In *RA*, XVI (1919), p. 193, and *JAOS*, XLVIII (1928), p. 182, W. F. Albright suggested the translation "uterine brother."

[12] The pertinent texts interchange the expressions *Iamani* (i.e. Ionian) and *Iadna*; cf. D. D. Luckenbill, *ZA*, XXVIII (1913), 92 ff.

[13] According to this passage, the vehicle termed *narkabat šêpē* was not destined for speedy transportation nor for warlike purposes.

[14] This translation is suggested by the context (differently Landsberger, *ZA*, XXXVII [NF III], 86 f. for *salimu*).

[15] For the meaning of the administrative terminus technicus *ana eššûti ṣabâtu*, cf. B. Meissner, *Babylonien und Assyrien* (Heidelberg, 1920), I, p. 141.

[16] A very similar version of this report is contained in the fragment BrM 81-7-23,3 published by E. F. Weidner, in *AfO*, XIV (1941), 40, with transliteration and translation on p. 50.

[17] *Sic*, against J. Lewy, in *HUCA*, XIX, 461.

[1] Lit.: "town (of the) Brook-of-Egypt." The location of this "brook" is still uncertain; it has been identified with the isthmus between Egypt and Palestine (cf. E. F. Weidner, *AfO*, XIV [1941], 43 f.), with the Wadi el-'Arish (Weissbach, in *ZA*, XXXVIII [NF IV], 110), and with a wadi near the town of Raphia (H. Winckler, in *MVAG*, III/1 [1898], 10 f.). cf. also A. Alt in *ZDPV*, LXVII (1945), 130 ff.

[2] For this meaning of *amêlnasiku*, cf., e.g. B. Meissner, in *MAOG*, III/3 (1929), 31, and the frequent occurrences in the letters of the Harper Collection (cf. L. Waterman, *Royal Correspondence of the Assyrian Empire* [Ann Arbor, 1936], IV, p. 144, for references).

[3] W. von Bissing (*apud* Weidner, *AfO*, XIV [1941], 44 f.) discusses the possibility that this name renders that of an Egyptian king of the 22nd or 23rd dynasty, while G. Ryckmans (Ši-il-kan-ni, Ši-il-ḫe-ni=arabe (pre-islamique) Slḥn, in *AfO*, XIV [1941], 54 f.) attempts to link it to Old Arabic names.

(2) According to the broken Prism A published by H. Winckler, *op.cit.*, I, 186-189, II, 44. Translation: Luckenbill, *AR*, II, §§193-195. Fragment D:

[Aziru, king] of Ashdod (lacuna) on account of [this crime . . .] *from* . . . Ahimiti[4] . . . his younger brother over [them . . .] I made (him) ruler . . . tribute . . . like (those of) the [former] kings, I imposed upon him. [But these] accursed [Hittites] conceived [the idea] of not delivering the tribute and [started] a rebellion against their ruler; they expelled him . . . (*Ia-ma-ni*) a Greek, comm[oner without claim to the throne] to be king over them, they made sit down [on the very throne] of his (former) master and [they . . .] their city of (or: for) the at[tack] (lacuna of 3 lines) . . . its neighborhood, a moat [they prepared] of a depth of 20 + x cubits . . . it (even) reached the underground water, in order to. . . . Then [to] the rulers of Palestine (*Pi-liš-te*), Judah (*Ia-ú-di*), Ed[om], Moab (and) those who live (on islands) and bring tribute [and] *tâmartu* -gifts to my lord Ashur—[he spread] countless evil lies to alienate (them) from me, and (also) sent bribes to Pir'u, king of Musru—a potentate, incapable to save them—and asked him to be an ally. But I, Sargon, the rightful ruler, devoted to the pronouncements (uttered by) Nebo and Marduk, (carefully) observing the orders of Ashur, led my army over the Tigris and the Euphrates, at the peak of the(ir) flood, the spring flood, as (if it be) dry ground. This Greek, however, their king who had put his trust in his own power and (therefore) did not bow to my (divinely ordained) rulership, heard about the approach of my expedition (while I was still) far away, and the splendor of my lord Ashur overwhelmed him and . . . he fled. . . .

(3) Nimrud Inscription; published by H. Winckler, *op.cit.*, I, 169-170; Vol. II, Pl. 48. Translation: Luckenbill, *AR*, II, §137.

(8)

(Property of Sargon, etc.) the subduer of the country Judah (*Ia-ú-du*) which is far away, the uprooter of Hamath, the ruler of which—Iau'bidi—he captured personally.[1]

8. SENNACHERIB (704-681)

(a) The Siege of Jerusalem[1]

(1) From the Oriental Institute Prism of Sennacherib, which contains—as does the so-called Taylor Prism (cf. Rawlinson, Vol. I, Pls. 37-42)—the final edition of the Annals of Sennacherib. Publication: D. D. Luckenbill, *The Annals of Sennacherib* (*OIP*, II, Chicago, 1924). Translation: *ibid.*, and Luckenbill, *AR*, II, §§233 ff.

(ii 37—iii 49)

In my third campaign I marched against Hatti. Luli, king of Sidon, whom the terror-inspiring glamor of my lordship had overwhelmed, fled far overseas and perished.[2] The awe-inspiring splendor of the "Weapon" of Ashur, my lord, overwhelmed his strong cities (such as) Great Sidon, Little Sidon, Bit-Zitti, Zaribtu, Mahalliba, Ushu (i.e. the mainland settlement of Tyre), Akzib (and) Akko, (all) his fortress cities, walled (and well) provided with feed and water for his garrisons, and they bowed in submission to my feet. I installed Ethba'al (*Tuba'lu*) upon the throne to be their king and imposed upon him tribute (due) to me (as his) overlord (to be paid) annually without interruption.

As to all the kings of Amurru—Menahem (*Mi-in-ḫi-im-mu*) from Samsimuruna, Tuba'lu from Sidon, Abdili'ti from Arvad, Urumilki from Byblos, Mitinti from Ashdod, Buduili from Beth-Ammon, Kammusunadbi from Moab (and) Aiarammu from Edom, they brought sumptuous gifts (*igisû*) and—fourfold—their heavy *tâmartu* -presents to me and kissed my feet. Sidqia, however, king of Ashkelon, who did not bow to my yoke, I deported and sent to Assyria, his family-gods, himself, his wife, his children, his brothers, all the male descendants of his family. I set Sharruludari, son of Rukibtu, their former king, over the inhabitants of Ashkelon and imposed upon him the payment of tribute (and of) *ḳatrû* -presents (due) to me (as) overlord—and he (now) pulls the straps (of my yoke)!

In the continuation of my campaign I besieged Beth-Dagon, Joppa, Banai-Barqa, Azuru, cities belonging to Sidqia who did not bow to my feet quickly (enough); I conquered (them) and carried their spoils away. The officials, the patricians and the (common) people of Ekron[3]—who had thrown Padi, their king, into fetters (because he was) loyal to (his) solemn oath (sworn) by the god Ashur, and had handed him over to Hezekiah, the Jew (*Ha-za-qi-(i)a-ú* ^{amel}*Ia-ú-da-ai*)—(and) he (Hezekiah) held him in prison, unlawfully, as if he (Padi) be an enemy—had become afraid and had called (for help) upon the kings of Egypt (*Muṣ(u)ri*) (and) the bowmen, the chariot(-corps) and the cavalry of the king of Ethiopia (*Meluḫḫa*), an army beyond counting—and they (actually) had come to their assistance. In the plain of Eltekeh (*Al-ta-qu-ú*), their battle lines were drawn up against me and they sharpened their weapons. Upon a trust(-inspiring) oracle (given) by Ashur, my lord, I fought with them and inflicted a defeat upon them. In the mêlée of the battle, I personally captured alive the Egyptian charioteers with the(ir) princes and (also) the charioteers of the king of

[4] Instead of Aḫimiti, the parallel version has the name Aḫimilki.

[1] After his victory over Iau-bi'di at Qarqar, Sargon erected various stelae commemorating this event. One, found near Hama on the Orontes, is extant and has been published by F. Thureau-Dangin, La Stèle d'Acharne, in *RA*, XXX (1933), 53 ff. The text is badly preserved and of little interest.

[1] For the problems involved, cf. the following bibliography: A. Alt, *Palästina Jahrbuch*, XXV (1929), 80-88; G. Boutflower, *Journal of the Transactions, Victoria Institute*, LX, 214-220; P. R. Dougherty, *JBL*, XLIX (1930), 160-171; O. Eissfeldt, *Palästina Jahrbuch*, XXVII (1931), 58-65; S. I. Feigin, *Missitrei Heavar* (New York, 1943), pp. 88-117, 202-209 (in Hebrew); K. Fullerton, *AJSL*, XLII (1925), 1-25; L. L. Honor, *Sennacherib's Invasion of Palestine, A Critical Source Study* (New York, 1926); J. Lewy, *OLZ*, XXXI (1928), 150-163; Th. Reinach, *Revue des études grecques*, 172, 257-260; R. W. Rogers, *Wellhausen-Festschrift* (Giessen, 1914), p. 322; W. Rudolph, *Palästina Jahrbuch*, XXV (1929), 59-80; A. Ungnad, Die Zahl der von Sanherib deportierten Judäer, *ZAW*, LIX, 199-202.

[2] For the enigmatic idiom *šadâ(šu) emêdu*, cf. lately E. F. Weidner, *AfO*, XIII (1940), 233 f. with the proposed translation "to die an infamous death."

[3] Note the social stratification indicated in this passage.

Ethiopia. I besieged Eltekeh (and) Timnah (*Ta-am-na-a*), conquered (them) and carried their spoils away. I assaulted Ekron and killed the officials and patricians who had committed the crime and hung their bodies on poles surrounding the city. The (common) citizens who were guilty of minor crimes, I considered prisoners of war. The rest of them, those who were not accused of crimes and misbehavior, I released. I made Padi, their king, come from Jerusalem (*Ur-sa-li-im-mu*) and set him as their lord on the throne, imposing upon him the tribute (due) to me (as) overlord.

As to Hezekiah, the Jew, he did not submit to my yoke, I laid siege to 46 of his strong cities, walled forts and to the countless small villages in their vicinity, and conquered (them) by means of well-stamped (earth-)ramps, and battering-rams brought (thus) near (to the walls) (combined with) the attack by foot soldiers, (using) mines, breeches as well as sapper work. I drove out (of them) 200,150 people, young and old, male and female, horses, mules, donkeys, camels, big and small cattle beyond counting, and considered (them) booty. Himself I made a prisoner in Jerusalem, his royal residence, like a bird in a cage. I surrounded him with earthwork in order to molest those who were leaving his city's gate. His towns which I had plundered, I took away from his country and gave them (over) to Mitinti, king of Ashdod, Padi, king of Ekron, and Sillibel, king of Gaza. Thus I reduced his country, but I still increased the tribute and the *ḳatrû* -presents (due) to me (as his) overlord which I imposed (later) upon him beyond the former tribute, to be delivered annually. Hezekiah himself, whom the terror-inspiring splendor of my lordship had overwhelmed and whose irregular[4] and elite troops which he had brought into Jerusalem, his royal residence, in order to strengthen (it), had deserted him, did send me, later, to Nineveh, my lordly city, together with 30 talents of gold, 800 talents of silver, precious stones, antimony,[5] large cuts of red stone, couches (inlaid) with ivory, *nîmedu* -chairs (inlaid) with ivory, elephant-hides, ebony-wood, boxwood (and) all kinds of valuable treasures, his (own) daughters, concubines, male and female musicians. In order to deliver the tribute and to do obeisance as a slave he sent his (personal) messenger.

(2) From the Bull Inscription published by George Smith, *History of Sennacherib* (London, 1878), as Nos. 1, 2, and 3. Translation: cf. Luckenbill, *op.cit.*, pp. 76 f.

(17—21)

And Luli, king of Sidon, was afraid to fight me and fled to the country Cyprus (*Iadnana*) which is (an island) in the midst of the sea, and sought refuge (there). But even in this land, he met infamous death before the awe-inspiring splendor of the "Weapon" of my lord Ashur. I installed Ethba'al (*Tuba'lu*) upon his royal throne and imposed upon him the tribute (due to) me (as his) overlord. I laid waste the large district of Judah (*Ia-ú-di*) and made the overbearing and proud Hezekiah (*Ḫa-za-qi-a-a-a*), its king, bow in submission.

(3) From the Nebi Yunus Slab, published by Rawlinson, Vol. I, Pl. 43. Translation: Luckenbill, *op.cit.*, p. 86, and *AR*, II, §347.

(13—15)

I deprived Luli, king of Sidon, of his kingdom. I installed Ethba'al (*Tuba'lu*) upon his throne and I imposed upon him the tribute (due to) me (as his) overlord. I laid waste the large district of Judah and put the straps (*abšāni*) of my (yoke) upon Hezekiah, its king.

(4) Epigraph from a relief showing the conquest of Lachish. cf. A. Paterson, *Assyrian Sculptures: The Palace of Sinacherib* (The Hague, 1912-13), Pls. 74-76. Translation: Luckenbill, *op.cit.*, p. 156.

Sennacherib, king of the world, king of Assyria, sat upon a *nîmedu* -throne and passed in review the booty (taken) from Lachish (*La-ḳi-su*).

(b) The Death of Sennacherib[1]

To illustrate the still mysterious circumstances of the death of Sennacherib, a passage of the annals of Ashurbanipal (Rassam Cylinder, published by Rawlinson, v, Pls. 1-10) is translated here. Translation: Luckenbill, *op.cit.; AR*, II, §§795, 796.

(iv 65—82)

I tore out the tongues of those whose slanderous mouths had uttered blasphemies against my god Ashur and had plotted against me, his god-fearing prince; I defeated them (completely). The others, I smashed alive with the very same statues of protective deities with which they had smashed my own grandfather Sennacherib—now (finally) as a (belated) burial sacrifice for his soul. I fed their corpses, cut into small pieces, to dogs, pigs, *zîbu* -birds, vultures, the birds of the sky and (also) to the fish of the ocean. After I had performed this and (thus) made quiet (again) the hearts of the great gods, my lords, I removed the corpses of those whom the pestilence had felled, whose leftovers (after) the dogs and pigs had fed on them were obstructing the streets, filling the places (of Babylon), (and) of those who had lost their lives through the terrible famine.

[4] For *amelurbu*, cf. H. Winckler, in *OLZ*, IX (1906), 334, and, recently, Th. Bauer, *Assurbanipal*, II, 1.

[5] This refers probably to stibnite, a native sulphide of antimony (cf. J. R. Partington, *Origin and Development of Applied Chemistry* [London, 1935], p. 256; also R. C. Thompson, *A Dictionary of Assyrian Chemistry and Geology* [Oxford, 1936], p. 49), which might have been used as an eye paint (beside the cheaper and efficient substitute, burnt shells of almond and soot). Stibium is easily reduced and the metal is sporadically attested in Mesopotamia since the Neo-Sumerian period. For the provenience of the stibnite, cf. B. Meissner, *OLZ*, XVII (1915), 52 ff.

[1] For discussions dealing with the mysterious events connected with the death of Sennacherib and the accession of Esarhaddon, cf. H. Hirschberg, *Studien zur Geschichte Esarhaddons, Königs von Assyrien (681-669)* (Ohlau, 1932), and the pertinent book reviews of J. Schawe, in *AfO*, IX (1933-34), 55-60; Th. Bauer, in *ZA*, XLII (NF VIII), 170-184; as well as the remarks of A. Boissier, in *RA*, XXX (1933), 73 ff. cf. also, B. Meissner, Neue Nachrichten über die Ermordung Sanheribs, in *Preuss. Ak. d. Wiss. Sitz.-Ber. Phil. Hist. Kl.* (1932), pp. 250 ff.; and Wo befand sich Asarhaddon zur Zeit der Ermordung Sanheribs? in *Analecta Orientalia*, XII (1936), 232 ff.

9. Esarhaddon (680-669)

(a) The Fight for the Throne

From the so-called Prism B, after R. Campbell Thompson, *The Prisms of Esarhaddon and of Ashurbanipal* (London, 1931). Translation: R. Campbell Thompson, *ibid.*; and Th. Bauer, *ZA*, XLII (NF VIII), pp. 171 ff.

(i 1—ii 11)

Property of Esarhaddon, great king, legitimate king, king of the world, king of Assyria, regent of Babylon, king of Sumer and Akkad, king of the four rims (of the earth), the true shepherd, favorite of the great gods, whom Ashur, Shamash, Bel and Nebo, the Ishtar of Nineveh (and) the Ishtar of Arbela have pronounced king of Assyria (ever) since he was a youngster.

I was (indeed) the(ir) youngest (brother) among my elder brothers, (but) my own father, upon the command of Ashur, Sin, Shamash, Bel and Nebo, the Ishtar of Nineveh (and) the Ishtar of Arbela, has chosen me—in due form and in the presence (lit.: assembly) of all my brothers—saying: "This is the son to (be elevated to) the position of a successor of mine." (Then) he put this question before Shamash and Adad by means of an oracle and they answered him: "He (verily) is your replacement."[1] He (i.e. Sennacherib) heeded their important pronouncement and called together the people of Assyria, young and old, my brothers (and all) the male[2] descendants of (the family of) my father and made them take a solemn oath in the presence of (the images of) the gods of Assyria: Ashur, Sin, Shamash, Nebo (and) Marduk, (and) of (all) the (other) gods residing in heaven and in the nether world, in order to secure my succession.

In a propitious month, on a favorable day, I happily entered—upon their exalted (oracle-)command—the palace of the crown prince, this highly venerable place in which (those) live (who are) destined for the kingship. (When) the real meaning (of this act) dawned upon my brothers, they abandoned godliness, put their trust on bold actions, planning an evil plot. They originated against me slander, false accusation, (whatever is) disliked by the gods, and constantly were spreading evil, incorrect and hostile (rumors) behind my back. (Thus) they alienated from me—against the will of the gods—the heart of my father which was (formerly) friendly, (though) in the bottom of his heart there was (always) love (for me) and his intentions were (always) that I should become king. I became apprehensive and asked myself as follows: "Are their bold actions based upon trust in their own ideas[3] or could they have acted (that) evil against the will of the gods?" I implored Ashur, the king of the gods (and) the merciful Marduk, to (both of) whom baseness is an abomination, by means of prayers, lamentations and prostrations, and they (eventually) agreed to (give) the (oracle-)answer (that the brothers acted) according to the decision of the great gods, my lords. And they (the gods) made me stay in a hiding place in the face of (these) evil machinations, spreading their sweet protecting shadow over me and (thus) preserving me for the kingship.

Thereupon, my brothers went out of their senses, doing everything that is wicked in (the eyes of) the gods and mankind, and (continued) their evil machinations. They (even) drew weapons in the midst of Nineveh (which is) against (the will of) the gods, and butted each other—like kids—to take over the kingship. Ashur, Sin, Shamash, Bel, Nebo, the Ishtar of Nineveh (and) the Ishtar of Arbela looked with displeasure upon these doings of the usurpers which had come to pass against the will of the gods, and they did not help them. (On the contrary) they changed their strength into weakness and (thus) made them (eventually) bow beneath me. (Also) the people of Assyria which had sworn the oath of the great gods, by means of water and oil, to protect my claim to the kingship, did not come to their assistance. But I, Esarhaddon, who never turns around in a battle, trusting in the great gods, his lords, soon heard of these sorry happenings and I cried out "Woe!" rent my princely robe and began to lament loudly. I became as mad as a lion, my soul was aflame and I (called up the gods by) clapping my hands, with regard to my (intention of) assuming the kingship, my paternal legacy. I prayed to Ashur, Sin, Shamash, Bel, Nebo and Nergal, (to) the Ishtar of Nineveh, the Ishtar of Arbela, and they agreed to give an (oracle-)answer. By means of their correct (and) positive answer, they sent me the (following) trustworthy oracle (received by) extispicy: "Go (ahead), do not tarry! We will march with you, kill your enemies!" I did not even wait for the next day,[4] nor for my army, did not turn back (for a moment), did not muster the contingents of horses broken to the yoke or the battle equipment, I did not (even) pile up provisions for my expedition, I was not afraid of the snow and the cold of the month Shabatu (in which) the winter is (at its) hard(est)—but I spread my wings like the (swift-)flying storm(bird) to overwhelm my enemies. I followed that road to Nineveh which is difficult for traveling but short. In front of me, in the territory of Hanigalbat, all their (i.e. the brothers') best soldiers blocked the advance of my expeditionary corps, sharpening their weapons (for the battle). But the terror(-inspiring sight) of the great gods, my lords, overwhelmed them and they turned into madmen when they saw the attack of my strong battle array. Ishtar, the Lady of Battle, who likes me (to be) her high priest, stood at my side breaking their bows, scattering their orderly battle array. And then they spoke among themselves: "This is our king!" Upon her lofty command they went over in masses to me and rallied behind me. Like lambs they gamboled and (recognized) me as their lord by praying (to me). The people of

[1] The term *tênû* (from *enû* "to change, replace") corresponds exactly to Arabic *caliph*.

[2] The reading *zêru* fits better into the context than the variant *šumu*.

[3] Translation suggested by context.

[4] Idiomatic expression, lit.: "one day, two days, I did not wait."

Assyria which had sworn an oath by the life of the great gods on my behalf, came to meet me and kissed my feet. But they, the usurpers, who had started the rebellion, deserted their (most) trustworthy troops, when they heard the approach of my expeditionary corps and fled to an unknown country.

I reached the embankment of the Tigris and upon the (oracle-)command of Sin and Shamash, the (two) lords of the (celestial) embankment, I had all my troops jump over the Tigris as if it be a small ditch.

(ii)

In the month of Addar, a favorable month, on the 8th day, the day of the Nebo festival, I entered joyfully into Nineveh, the town in which I (exercise) my lordship and sat down happily upon the throne of my father. The Southwind, the breeze (directed by) Ea, blew (at this moment), this wind, the blowing of which portends well for exercising kingship, came just in time for me. (Other) favorable omina on the sky and on earth (which to interpret is) the work of the seer, messages of the gods and goddesses, happened continuously to me and made my heart confident. The culpable military which had schemed to secure the sovereignty of Assyria for my brothers, I considered guilty as a collective group and meted out a grievous punishment to them; I (even) exterminated their male descendants.

(b) Texts of a General Nature

(1) From the Steinplatteninschrift published by L. Messerschmidt, in *KAH*, I, No. 75. Translation: Luckenbill, *AR*, II, §710.

(2—11 obverse)

I cut down with the sword and conquered . . . I caught like a fish (and) cut off his head. I trod up[on Arzani at] the "Brook of Eg[ypt]."[1] I put Asuhili, its king, in fetters and took [him to Assyria]. I conquered the town of Bazu in a district which is far away. Upon Qa[. . .]a, king of . . . I imposed tribute due to me as (his) lord. I conquered the country of Shupria in its full extent and slew with (my own) weapon Inip-Teshup, its king who did not listen to my personal orders. I conquered Tyre which is (an island) amidst the sea. I took away all the towns and the possessions of Ba'lu its king, who had put his trust on Tirhakah (*Tarqû*), king of Nubia (*Kûsu*). I conquered Egypt (*Muṣur*), Paturi[si][2] and Nubia. Its king, Tirhakah, I wounded five times with arrowshots and ruled over his entire country; I car[ried much booty away]. All the kings from (the islands) amidst the sea—from the country Iadanana (Cyprus), as far as Tarsisi,[3] bowed to my feet and I received heavy tribute (from them).

[1] cf. above n.1, p. 286.

[2] cf. for this name M. J. Leibovitch, Pathros, in *Bulletin de l'Institut d'Egypt*, XVII (1934-35), 69 ff.

[3] Text: *Nu-si-si* (identified with Knossos by Luckenbill, in *ZA*, XXVIII, 95) to be emended into *Tar(!)-si-si* according to Ed. Meyer, *Geschichte des Altertums*, Vol. III (2d ed.), p. 79, n.3. cf. now, also Weidner *Mélanges syriens*, II, 932, n.3.

(2) The door socket published (with transliteration and translation) by E. Nassouhi, *Textes divers rélatifs à l'histoire de l'Assyrie* (*MAOG*, III/1-2, Leipzig, 1927) No. x, 19 f.

To Ashur, his lord, Esarhaddon, king of the world, king of [Assyria], governor of Babylon, king of Kar-Duni[ash], king of kings, k[ing] of E[gypt] (*M[u-ṣur]*), Patur[isi] and Nubia (*Kûsu*), [has dedicated this door/building] for his (own) life and the prosperity (*šulmu*) of his country.

(3) From a clay barrel found in Ashur and published by E. Nassouhi, *ibid.* as No. XII, 22 ff.

(7—8)

Conqueror of the town Sidon which is situated (on an island) in the midst of the sea . . . [who plundered the country Arsa] which is (situated) along the "Brook of Egypt" (*i-te-e na-ḫal* ^{mat}*Mu-[u]ṣ-ri*), who put its [king] Asu[hili] in fetters together with his councilors (*māliku*). . . .

(c) The Syro-Palestinian Campaign

(1) From the Prism A, published by Rawlinson, Vol. I, Pls. 45 f. Translation: Luckenbill, *AR*, II, §§527-528.

(i 9—54)

(I am Esarhaddon), the conqueror of Sidon, which lies (on an island) amidst the sea, (he) who has leveled all its urban buildings—I even tore up and cast into the sea its wall and its foundation, destroying (thus) completely the (very) place it (i.e. Sidon) was built (upon). I caught out of the open sea, like a fish, Abdimilkutte, its king, who had fled before my attack into the high sea, and I cut off his head. I carried away as booty his piled-up possessions in large amounts (to wit): gold, silver, precious stones, elephant-hides, ivory, ebony and boxwood, garments (made) with multicolored trimmings and linen, all his personal valuables. I drove to Assyria his teeming people which could not be counted, (also) large and small cattle and donkeys. I (then) called together and made all the kings of the country Hatti and of the seashore (do corvée-work for me) by making them erect the walls of another [residence] and I called its name Kar-Esarhaddon. I settled therein people from the mountain regions and the sea(shore) of the East, (those) who belonged to me as my share of the booty.[1] I set over them officers of mine as governors.

As for Sanduarri, king of Kundi and Sizu, an inveterate enemy, unwilling to recognize me as ruler (and) whom the gods (therefore) forsook,—(who) had put his trust upon the rugged mountains (of his country) and had made Abdimilkutte, king of Sidon, his ally (lit.: helper) by taking mutual oaths by the life of the great gods—they put their trust upon their own force while I trusted Ashur, my lord,—I caught him like a bird in his mountains and (likewise) cut off his

[1] Text: *ḫubut* ^{is}*qašti*; this legal term recurs in the so-called "Erstbericht" of Esarhaddon (cf. Th. Bauer in *ZA*, XL, p. 259, IV:11) and in the Neo-Babylonian text Strassmaier, *Camb.* 334:4.

head. (Then) I hung the heads of Sanduarri and of Abdimilkutte around the neck of their nobles/chief-officials to demonstrate to the population the power of Ashur, my lord, and paraded (thus) through the wide main street of Nineveh with singers (playing on) *sammû*-harps.

(2) From Prism B, published by R. Campbell Thompson, *op.cit.* Translation: *ibid.*, p. 16.

(ii 65—82)

Abdimilkutte, king of Sidon, without respect for my position as lord, without listening to my personal orders, threw off the yoke of the god Ashur, trusting the heaving sea (to protect him). As to Sidon, his fortress town, which lies in the midst of the sea, I leveled it as (if) an *abûbu* -storm (had passed over it), its walls and foundations I tore out and threw (them) into the sea destroying (thus) its emplacement completely. I caught Abdimilkutte, its king, who fled before my attack into the sea, upon an oracle-command of Ashur, my lord, like a fish on high sea and cut off his head. I carried off as booty: his wife, his children, the personnel of his palace, gold, silver, (other) valuables, precious stones, garments made of multicolored trimmings and linen, elephant-hides, ivory, ebony and boxwood, whatever precious objects there were in his palace, (and) in great quantities. I led to Assyria his teeming subjects, which could not be counted, (and) large and small cattle and donkeys in great quantities. (There), I called together all the kings of the country Hatti and from the seacoast and made them build a town (for me) on a new location, calling its name Kar-Esarhaddon.

(3) From the fragmentary text K 2671(!) rev., published by H. Winckler, in *ZA*, II (1887), Pl. 1, after p. 314. Translation: Luckenbill, *AR*, II, §547.

(reverse 2—10)

[Ba'lu, king of Ty]re, living [on an island amidst the sea] . . . threw off my yoke . . . [of As]hur and the splendor of my lordship [overwhelmed him] . . . [he] bowed down and implored me, as his lord. . . . heavy [tribu]te, his daughters with dowries [as well as] all the [tribu]tes which he had omitted (to send). He kissed my feet. I took away from him those of his towns (which are situated on) the mainland [and re]organized [the region] turning it over to Assyria.

(4) From the Prism B, published by R. Campbell Thompson, *op.cit.* Translation: *ibid.*, pp. 25 f.

(v 54—vi 1)

I called up the kings of the country Hatti and (of the region) on the other side of the river (Euphrates) (to wit): Ba'lu, king of Tyre, Manasseh (*Me-na-si-i*), king of Judah (*Ia-ú-di*), Qaushgabri, king of Edom, Musuri, king of Moab, Sil-Bel, king of Gaza, Metinti, king of Ashkelon, Ikausu, king of Ekron, Milkiashapa, king of Byblos, Matanba'al, king of Arvad, Abiba'al, king of Samsimuruna, Puduil, king of Beth-Ammon, Ahimilki, king of Ashdod—12 kings from the seacoast;

Ekishtura, king of Edi'il (Idalion),[1] Pilagura (Pythagoras), king of Kitrusi (Chytros), Kisu, king of Sillu'ua (Soli), Ituandar, king of Pappa (Paphos), Erisu, king of Silli, Damasu, king of Kuri (Curium), Atmesu, king of Tamesi, Damusi, king of Qarti-hadasti (Carthage), Unasagusu, king of Lidir (Ledra), Busueu, king of Nuria,—10 kings from Cyprus (*Iadnana*) amidst the sea,

together 22 kings of Hatti, the seashore and the islands; all these I sent out and made them transport under terrible difficulties, to Nineveh, the town (where I exercise) my rulership, as building material for my palace: big logs, long beams (and) thin boards from cedar and pine trees, products of the Sirara and Lebanon (*Lab-na-na*) mountains, which had grown for a long time into tall and strong timber, (also) from their quarries (lit.: place of creation) in the mountains, statues of protective deities (lit.: of Lamassû and Shêdu) made of a š n a n -stone, statues of (female) *abzaztu*,[2] thresholds, slabs of limestone, of a š n a n -stone, of large- and small-grained breccia, of *alallu*-stone, (and) of g i . r i n . ḫ i . l i . b a -stone.[3]

(d) The Campaign against the Arabs and Egypt

(1) From the Prism B, published by R. Campbell Thompson, *op.cit.* Translation: *ibid.*, p. 20.[1]

(iv 1—13)

(From) Adumatu,[2] the stronghold of the Arabs which Sennacherib, king of Assyria, my own father, had conquered and (from where) he has taken as booty its possessions, its images as well as Iskallatu, the queen of the Arabs, and brought (all these) to Assyria, Hazail, the king of the Arabs, came with heavy gifts to Nineveh, the town (where I exercise) my rulership, and kissed my feet. He implored me to return his images and I had mercy upon him; I repaired the damages of the images of Atarsamain, Dai, Nuhai, Ruldaiu, Abirillu (and of) Atarquruma,[3] the gods of the Arabs, and returned them to him after having written upon them an inscription (proclaiming) the (superior) might of Ashur, my lord, and my own name. I made Tarbua who had grown up in the palace of my father their queen and returned her to her (native) country together

[1] For these more or less tentative identifications, cf. Sir George Hill, *A History of Cyprus* (London, 1940), I, 107 ff.

[2] cf. N. Schneider, *AfO*, XIV (1941), 70 ff. (with references to previous discussions).

[3] For this stone, cf. B. Meissner, in *MAOG*, XI (1937), 21 (No. 17), for the stones called *alallu* and a š n a n cf. respectively pp. 159 and 163 of R. C. Thompson, *A Dictionary of Assyrian Chemistry and Geology* (Oxford, 1936).

[1] For Arabia at this period, cf. Trude Weiss Rosmarin, Aribi und Arabien in den Babylonisch-Assyrischen Quellen, in *JSOR*, XVI (1932), 1 ff., especially 14 ff. For Egypt at this period, I can only refer to Helene von Zeissl, *Aethiopen und Assyrer in Aegypten* (*Aegyptologische Forschungen*, No. 14 [Glueckstadt, 1944]).

[2] Identified with Djof by E. Forrer, *Provinzeinteilung*, p. 64. cf. also W. F. Albright, The Conquests of Nabonid in Arabia, *JRAS*, 1925, pp. 293 ff.

[3] For this enumeration of pre-Islamic Arab deities, cf. Weiss Rosmarin, *JSOR*, XVI (1932), 32.

with her gods. As an additional tribute, I imposed upon him (the payment of) 65 camels (and) 10 foals (more than) before. When fate carried Hazail away, I set Iata', his son, upon his throne and assessed upon him an additional tribute of 10 minas of gold (and) 1,000 *birûti* -stones, 50 camels, 100 *ḳunzu* -bags[4] with aromatic matter (more than) his father (paid).

Afterwards, Wahb (*Uabu*) induced all the Arabs to revolt against Iata', (because) he wanted to become king (himself), but I, Esarhaddon, king of Assyria, king of the four rims (of the earth), who loves justice and to whom crookedness is an abomination, sent my army to the assistance of Iata', and they subdued all the Arabs. They threw Wahb and the warriors of his entourage in fetters and brought them (to me). I put collars on them and bound them to the posts of my gate.

(2) From the British Museum Fragment K 8523, published by H. Winckler, in *ZA*, II (1887), 299 ff., and Tafel II (after p. 314); cf. also, H. Winckler *Altorientalische Forschungen* (Leipzig, 1897), I, 526. Translation: Luckenbill, *AR*, II, §§550-552.

(13 obverse—end)

[Ar]zani which is (situated) on the "Brook of Egypt" I reached . . . I destroyed

(reverse)

I brought [NN with he]avy [booty] to Assyria . . . , like a pig I tied him [to the gate of]. . . . [As to Hazail, king of Arabia], my [awe-inspiring splendor] overwhelmed him and he brought to me gold, silver, precious stones [and . . .] and kissed my feet. I imposed upon him 65 camels more than [the trib]ute (imposed by) my father. Afterwards, Hazail [died and Iata', his son,] sat down [upon] his throne and I (again) imposed upon him an (additional) tribute of 10 minas of gold, 1,000 *birûte* -stones, 50 ca[mels above the tribute paid by] his father. Wahb (however) induced all the Arabs to rebel against Iata' and. . . . [But, I, Esarhaddon] to whom [. . . and croo]kedness is an abomination [sent out] (a contingent) of bowmen (mounted on) horse(back) from my army [and pa]cified [the Arabs] making (them) submit (again) to him (i.e. Iata'). They brought Wahb together with the [*other leaders* to Assyria and they tied him] to the left side of the Metalworker's Gate in Nineveh and made (him) guard the bar. . . . Abdimilkutte, ki[ng of] Sidon [and Sanduarri], king of Kundi (and) Si[zu] (destroyed).

(3) Report on the tenth campaign in the annalistic text British Museum K 3082 + S 2027 + K 3086, published by R. W. Rogers, *Haverford College Studies*, No. 2 (1889), pp. 65 ff. Translation: H. Winckler, *Untersuchungen zur altorientalischen Geschichte* (Leipzig, 1889), pp. 97-98; Luckenbill, *AR*, II, §§554-559.

(6 obverse—18 reverse)

In my tenth campaign, I directed my march [against . . . I ordered . . .] towards the country . . . which is called in the language of the people of Nubia (*Kûsu*) and Egypt (*Muṣur*). . . . I called up the numerous army of Ashur which was stationed in. . . . In the month of Nisanu, the first month (of the year), I departed from my city Ashur. I crossed the Tigris and the Euphrates at (the time of) their flood; I advanced over the difficult territory (of my route) (as quick-footed) as a wild-ox. In the course of my campaign I threw up earthwork (for a siege) against Ba'lu, king of Tyre who had put his trust upon his friend Tirhakah (*Tarqû*), king of Nubia (*Kûsu*), and (therefore) had thrown off the yoke of Ashur, my lord, answering (my admonitions with) insolence. I withheld from them (i.e. the inhabitants of besieged Tyre) food and (fresh) water which sustain life. (Then) I removed my camp from Musru and marched directly towards Meluhha[1]—a distance of 30 double-hours from the town of Apku which is in the region of Samaria (*Sa-me-[ri-na]*) as far as the town Rapihu (in) the region adjacent to the "Brook of Egypt"—and there is no river (all the way)! By means of cords,[1a] chains (and) buckets I had to provide water for my army by drawing from wells.

(reverse)

When the oracle-command of Ashur, my lord, came to my mind (during this calamity) my soul [rejoiced] (and) I put [water bottles] . . . upon the camels which all the kings of Arabia had brought. . . . A distance of 20 double-hours in a journey of 15 days through . . . I advanced. A distance of 4 double-hours I marched over a territory covered with alum[2] and *mûṣu*[- stone].[3] A distance of 4 double-hours in a journey of 2 days (there were) two-headed serpents [whose attack] (spelled) death—but I trampled (upon them) and marched on. A distance of 4 double-hours in a journey of 2 days (there were) green [animals][4] whose wings were batting. A distance of 4 double-hours in a journey of 2 days . . . upper. . . . A distance of 15 double-hours in a journey of 8 days, I advanced [through] . . . (then) Marduk, the great lord, came to my assistance [he did . . . and thus] kept my troops alive. For 20 days and 7 [double miles] (a town/region) which is on the frontier of . . . Magan.[1] [In . . .] I spent the night. From the town of Mag[da]li I advanced to the town of . . . , a distance of 40 double-hours measured . . . this territory was like KA[. . .][5] -stone, [. . . sharp] like the point of a spear/arrow . . . blood and pus . . . the wicked

[4] For this term denoting some kind of leather bag, cf. Ebeling, in *MAOG*, XI/I (1937), 25, n.13. cf. also R. C. Thompson, Notes to my Prisms of Esarhaddon, *AAA*, XX (1933), pp. 126 f.

[1] This text uses the geographical terms Muṣru, Magan, Meluḫḫa, etc. rather loosely.

[1a] For the words used in this context (*iblu, ḫarḫarru*, and *ḳalḳaltu*), cf. Landsberger, in *ZA*, XLIII (NF IX), 75.

[2] Text: *^{aban}gab-e*. The alum of this region seems to have been exported to Egypt where it was denoted with a Semitic loan word: *ỉbnm*, i.e. "stones."

[3] A stone called *mûṣu* is well attested; cf. B. Meissner, *OLZ*, XVII (1914), 54, n.1; also E. F. Weidner, *AfO*, VIII (1932-3), 58. In the present context, the word is, however, incompletely preserved.

[4] cf. perhaps, B. Landsberger (and I. Krumbiegel), *Die Fauna des Alten Mesopotamiens nach der 14. Tafel der Serie* ḪAR.RA = *ḫubullû* (*Saechs. Ak. d. Wissensch. Phil.-Hist. Kl. Abh.* XLII/VI [1934]), No. 314 or 319.

[5] Probably referring to obsidian.

enemy together as far as . . . to the town of Ishhup[ri][6] (balance destroyed).

(4) From the fragment, British Museum 80-7-19,15. Transliteration and translation only by H. Winckler, *Untersuchungen zur altorientalischen Geschichte* (Leipzig, 1889), p. 98.

I scattered their well arranged battle force . . . his brother, his governors [. . . from] Ishhupri as far as Memphis (destroyed).

(5) From the Senjirli Stela published by A. Ungnad, in *VS*, I, No. 78 (cf. also, *ibid.*, p. x). Translation: Luckenbill, *AR*, II, §580.

(37—53 reverse)

From the town of Ishhupri as far as Memphis, his royal residence, a distance of 15 days (march), I fought daily, without interruption, very bloody battles against Tirhakah (*Tarqû*), king of Egypt and Ethiopia, the one accursed by all the great gods. Five times I hit him with the point of (my) arrows (inflicting) wounds (from which he should) not recover, and (then) I led siege to Memphis, his royal residence, and conquered it in half a day by means of mines, breaches and assault ladders; I destroyed (it), tore down (its walls) and burnt it down. His "queen,"[1] the women of his palace,[2] Ushanahuru, his "heir apparent,"[3] his other children, his possessions, horses, large and small cattle beyond counting, I carried away as booty to Assyria. All Ethiopians I deported from Egypt—leaving not even one to do homage (to me). Everywhere in Egypt, I appointed new (local) kings, governors, officers (*šaknu*), harbor overseers, officials and administrative personnel. I installed regular sacrificial dues for Ashur and the (other) great gods, my lords, for all times. I imposed upon them tribute due to me (as their) overlord, (to be paid) annually without ceasing. I had (also) made (this) stela (bearing) my name-inscription and had written thereupon the praise of the valor of my lord Ashur, my own mighty deeds—when I was marching (against the enemy) upon the trustworthy oracles of my lord Ashur—as well as my triumphal personal achievements, and I erected it, for all days to come, (so that) it was to be seen by the entire country of the enemy.

(6) From the Dog River Stela, published by F. H. Weissbach, *Die Denkmäler und Inschriften des Nahr-el-Kelb* (Berlin-Leipzig, 1922) (= *Wissenschaftliche Veröffentlichungen des Deutsch-Türkischen Denkmalschutzkommandos*, Heft 6), Pls. XI-XII (and pp. 27 ff.). Translation: Luckenbill, *AR*, II, §§584-585.

(7—end)

I entered Memphis (*Me-im-pi*), his royal residence, amidst (general) jubilation and rejoicing. . . . [u]pon the *šadalum* which was plated with gold, I sa[t down] in happiness. . . . weapons, [. . .]KUR*nanâti* of gold, silver, plate[s of]. . . . Afterwards . . . [I en]tered and his personal property (lit.: palace), the gods and goddesses of Tirhakah (*Tarqû*), king of Nubia (*Kûsu*), together with their possessions . . . I declared as booty. [His] "queen," the female servants of his court, Ushanahuru, the heir to his throne, [. . .]miri, his court official(s), . . . his possessions, [. . .]s inlaid with KUR-stone, ivory, wooden . . . , the plating of which is of gold, their faucets/openings of . . . (other) utensils of gold, silver, [. . .]-stone, . . . whatever was in the palace which had no [equal in Assyria] and/or was artfully/interestingly constructed. And I (also) opened the chests, the baskets and . . . [in which were stored the tribute] of his kingdom, I did . . . king . . . they had left them (behind) as well as 16 t[iaras] 30 headgears for "queens" [. . .]-stone [. . .] stone slabs . . . in large quantities. The treasuries (full) with gold, silver, ant[imony . . .], byssus-linen,[1] . . . the *batbat* of which is like . . . , copper, tin, *abaru* -metal, ivory, [. . .]s of the Suti-people . . . his sons-in-law, his family (*qinnu*), . . . princes . . . physicians, divination-experts, . . . goldsmiths, cabinetmakers, . . . the son of Binzuqi . . . which Tirhakah [has made] to their strongholds, . . . (balance destroyed).[2]

(7) In *Altorientalische Forschungen*, Vol. II, p. 21, H. Winckler published a fragment of a prism in the British Museum (Bu 91-2-9, 218). This text of two columns has never been translated and is included here because it very likely refers to the Egyptian campaign of Esarhaddon. The first column parallels the enumeration of craftsmen and specialists deported from Egypt contained in the text of the badly damaged Dog River Stela. The second column lists the officials installed by the Assyrian conqueror in a series of cities, all mentioned with their new Assyrian names, and the regular sacrificial offerings imposed upon them.

(col. A)

. . . precious stones beyond counting . . . which . . . the offspring of his father's family . . . third-men-on-chariots, charioteers . . . [dri]vers, bowmen, shieldbearers . . . [. . .]s BAR.NUN-men HAR.DI.[. . . men], veterinarians, [. . .]-scribes, . . . *kāṣiru*,[1] singers, *bread*-(bakers), ditto, . . . brewers and their . . .[2] ditto, . . . [. . .]-men, fishermen, [. . .]-men, ditto, . . . cartwrights, shipwrights, . . . their [. . .], ditto, . . . black[smiths]. . . .

(col. B)

. . . [over the town . . .]mukin-palu-kussu-abishu, . . . over the town Mahri-gare-sarri, Sa[. . .] over the

[6] Against Landsberger-Bauer (*ZA*, XXXVII [NF III], 76 f.), who locate the above described region in Persia, this local name links our fragment immediately to the next, which clearly records the campaign against Egypt.

[1] Text: š à . é . g a l *-šu*; for this unique denomination of the wife of a ruler of royal rank, cf., e.g. Martin, *Tribut*, p. 50, n.1, who discusses the Sumerogram SAL.É.GAL denoting the wife of the Assyrian king. Actual ruling queens (on the divine as well as on the human level) are termed *šarratu* (in the Hittite texts SAL.LUGAL).

[2] Text: SAL.ERIN.É.GAL.

[3] Text: *mār ridûti.*

[1] Text: *sad-din bu-ú-ṣi*, as in the Neo-Assyrian letter, Harper, *ABL*, 568:11, and in C. H. W. Johns, *Assyrian Deeds and Documents*, 1129:3. For *saddin*, cf. W. J. Martin, *Tribut und Tributleistungen bei den Assyriern* (=*Studia Orientalia* VIII/1, 1936), p. 47; for *bûṣu* ("byssus"), H. Zimmern, *Fremdwörter*, p. 37, Jastrow, *AJSL*, XV (1899), 79; both terms denote linen fabrics of a special quality.

[2] A small and very damaged fragment (British Museum K 3127 + 4435) reports in two broken lines on the booty taken from Memphis. cf. Th. Bauer, *Assurbanipal*, I, Pl. 36, ii, 66.

[1] This name of profession cannot be identified with certainty. Certain indications point to a connection with the manufacturing of textiles.

[2] Text: l ú . n í g . g a . m e š *-šú-nu*. Hapax legomenon.

town Ashur-matsu-urappish, Sik[. . .] over the town Ashur-nakamte-LAL, Pudime[. . .] over the town Limmir-ishak-Ashur, Dimu[. . .] over the town Kar-Banite, Sin[. . .] over the town Bit-Marduk, the town Sha-Ashur-taru, the town . . . Arad-Nana, my *murakkisu*-officer . . . Uarbis in the town . . . Kisir-Ishtar in the town Sha-emuq-Ashur . . . (as) regular sacrificial offerings for Ashur and the great gods: 9 talents 19 minas of gold 300 . . . 1,585 garments . . . *ebony* wood/trees, 199 leather . . . 1[. . .]40 horses . . . 30,418 rams . . . 19,323 donkeys . . . as the tribute (paid for) the rule of Assyria . . . Ashur. . . .

10. ASHURBANIPAL (668-633)

(a) Campaigns against Egypt, Syria, and Palestine[1]

(1) From the so-called Rassam Cylinder found 1878 in the ruins of Kuyunjik, latest publication by Rawlinson, Vol. v, Pls. 1-10. Transliteration and translation: M. Streck, *Assurbanipal und die letzten assyrischen Könige bis zum Untergang* (*VAB*, VII) (Leipzig, 1916), Vol. II, pp. 2 ff. English translation: Luckenbill, *AR*, II, §§770-783.

(i 53—ii 94)

In my first campaign I marched against Egypt (Magan) and Ethiopia (Meluhha). Tirhakah (*Tarqû*), king of Egypt (*Muṣur*) and Nubia (*Kûsu*), whom Esarhaddon, king of Assyria, my own father, had defeated and in whose country he (Esarhaddon) had ruled, this (same) Tirhakah forgot[2] the might of Ashur, Ishtar and the (other) great gods, my lords, and put his trust upon his own power. He turned against the kings (and) regents whom my own father had appointed in Egypt.[3] He entered and took residence in Memphis (*Me-im-pi*), the city which my own father had conquered and incorporated into Assyrian territory. An express messenger came to Nineveh to report to me. I became very angry on account of these happenings, my soul was aflame. I lifted my hands, prayed to Ashur and to the Assyrian Ishtar. (Then) I called up my mighty armed forces which Ashur and Ishtar have entrusted to me and took the shortest (lit.: straight) road to Egypt (*Muṣur*) and Nubia. During my march (to Egypt) 22 kings from the seashore, the islands and the mainland,

A list of these kings is contained in the text of Cylinder C, composed of various fragments by M. Streck, *op.cit.*, pp. 139 ff. Translation: Luckenbill, AR, II, §876.

(i 24—46)

Ba'al, king of Tyre, Manasseh (*Mi-in-si-e*), king of Judah (*Ia-ú-di*), Qaushgabri, king of Edom, Musuri, king of Moab, Sil-Bel, king of Gaza, Mitinti, king of Ashkelon, Ikausu,[4] king of Ekron, Milkiashapa, king of Byblos, Iakinlu, king of Arvad, Abiba'al, king of Samsimuruna, Amminadbi, king of Beth-Ammon, Ahumilki, king of Ashdod, Ekishtura, king of Edi'li, Pilagura, king of Pitrusi, Kisu, king of Silua, Ituandar, king of Pappa, Erisu, king of Sillu, Damasu, king of Kuri, Admesu, king of Tamesu, Damusu, king of Qarti-hadasti, Unasagusu, king of Lidir, Pususu, king of Nure, together 12 kings from the seashore, the islands and the mainland;

servants who belong to me, brought heavy gifts (*tâmartu*) to me and kissed my feet. I made these kings accompany my army over the land—as well as (over) the sea-route with their armed forces and their ships (respectively). Quickly I advanced as far as Kar-Baniti to bring speedy relief to the kings and regents in Egypt, servants who belong to me. Tirhakah, king of Egypt (*Muṣur*) and Nubia, heard in Memphis of the coming of my expedition and he called up his warriors for a decisive battle against me. Upon a trust(-inspiring) oracle (given) by Ashur, Bel, Nebo, the great gods, my lords, who (always) march at my side, I defeated the battle(-experienced) soldiers of his army in a great open battle. Tirhakah heard in Memphis of the defeat of his army (and) the (terror-inspiring) splendor of Ashur and Ishtar blinded (lit.: overwhelmed) him (thus) that he became like a madman. The glamor of my kingship with which the gods of heaven and nether world have endowed me, dazzled him and he left Memphis and fled, to save his life, into the town Ni' (Thebes).[5] This town (too) I seized and led my army into it to repose (there).

Necho (*Ni-ku-ú*), king of Memphis and Sais (*Sa-a-a*),[6] Sharruludari, king of Si'nu, Pishanhuru, king of Nathu, Pakruru, king of (Pi)shaptu, Bukkunanni'pi, king of Athribis (*Ḫa-at-ḫi-ri-bi*), Nahke, king of Hininshi, Putubishti, king of Tanis (*Ṣa-'-nu*), Unamunu, king of Nathu, Harsiaeshu, king of Sabnuti, Buaima, king of Pitinti, Shishak (*Su-si-in-qu*), king of Busiris (*Bu-ši-ru*), Tabnahti, king of Punubu, Bukkananni'pi king of Ahni, Iptihardeshu, king of Pihattihurunpi(ki), Nahtihuruansini, king of Pishabdi'a, Bukurninip, king of Pahnuti, Siha, king of Siut (*Si-ia-a-ú-tú*), Lamentu, king of Himuni (Hermopolis), Ishpimatu, king of Taini, Mantimanhe, king of Thebes; these kings, governors and regents whom my own father had appointed in Egypt and who had left their offices in the face of the uprising of Tirhakah and had scattered into the open country, I reinstalled in their offices and in their (former) seats of office. (Thus) I seized anew (control over) Egypt (*Muṣur*) and Nubia which (already) my own father had conquered; I made the garrisons stronger than before and the(ir) regulations (more) severe. With many prisoners and heavy booty I returned safely to Nineveh.

Afterwards, (however), all the kings whom I had appointed broke the oaths (sworn to) me, did not keep the agreements sworn by the great gods, forgot that I had treated them mildly and conceived an evil (plot). They talked about rebellion and came, among them-

1 For reliefs concerning the Egyptian campaign of Ashurbanipal, cf. the references collected by J. Schawe, in *AfO*, x (1935-36), 170.

2 Text: *im-ši-ma*; variant: *i-mi-iš*, "he thought little of. . . ."

3 Variant adds: "in order to murder, to rob and to seize Egypt for himself."

4 The reading: *I-ka-šám-su* is likewise possible.

5 For the name of Thebes, cf. recently W. Vycichl, in *ZAeS*, LXXVI (1940), 82 ff.

6 For this and the subsequent names of Egyptian towns and persons, cf. Steindorff, in *BA*, I, 330 f., II, 593 ff.; also, M. Streck, *Assurbanipal*, II, 10, n.2-3, and H. Ranke, *Keilschriftliches Material zur altaegyptischen Vokalizierung* (*Kgl. Preuss. Ak. d. Wiss., Abh.* 1910), pp. 26 ff.

selves to the unholy decision: "(Now when even) Tirhakah has been driven out of Egypt (*Muṣur*), how can we, ourselves, (hope to) stay?" And they sent their mounted messengers to Tirhakah, king of Nubia, to establish a sworn agreement: "Let there be peace between us and let us come to mutual understanding; we will divide the country between us, no foreigner shall be ruler among us!" They continued to scheme against the Assyrian army, the forces (upon which) my rule (was based), (and) which I had stationed (in Egypt) for their (own) support. (But) my officers heard about these matters, seized their mounted messengers with their messages and (thus) learned about their rebellious doings. They arrested these kings and put their hands and feet in iron cuffs and fetters. The (consequences of the broken) oaths (sworn) by Ashur, the king of the gods, befell them, I called to account those who had sinned against the oath (sworn by) the great gods (and those) whom I had treated (before) with clemency. And they (the officers)[7] put to the sword the inhabitants, young and old, of the towns of Sais, Pindidi,

(ii)

Tanis and of all the other towns which had associated with them to plot, they did not spare anybody among (them). They hung their corpses from stakes, flayed their skins and covered (with them) the wall of the town(s). Those kings who had repeatedly schemed, they brought alive to me to Nineveh. From all of them, I had only mercy upon Necho and granted him life. I made (a treaty) with him (protected by) oaths which greatly surpassed (those of the former treaty). I clad him in a garment with multicolored trimmings, placed a golden chain on him (as the) insigne of his kingship,[8] put golden rings on his hands; I wrote my name (phonetically)[9] upon an iron dagger (to be worn in) the girdle, the mounting of which was golden, and gave it to him. I presented him (furthermore) with chariots, horses and mules as means of transportation (befitting) his position as ruler. I sent with him (and) for his assistance, officers of mine as governors. I returned to him Sais as residence (the place) where my own father had appointed him king. Nabushezibanni, his son, I appointed for Athribis (thus) treating him with more friendliness and favor than my own father did. The terror of the (sacred) weapon of Ashur, my lord, overcame Tirhakah where he had taken refuge and he was never heard of again.[10] Afterwards URdamane,[11] son of Shabaku (var.: son of his sister), sat down on the throne of his kingdom. He made Thebes and Heliopolis (*Ú-nu*) his fortresses and assembled his (armed) might. He called up his battle(-experienced soldiers) to attack my troops, (and) the Assyrians stationed in Memphis. He surrounded these men and seized (all) their communications (lit.: exits). An express messenger came to Nineveh and told me about this.

In my second campaign I marched directly against Egypt (*Muṣur*) and Nubia. URdamane heard of the approach of my expedition (only when) I had (already) set foot on Egyptian territory. He left Memphis and fled into Thebes to save his life. The kings, governors, and regents whom I had installed in Egypt came to meet me and kissed my feet. I followed URdamane (and) went as far as Thebes, his fortress. He saw my mighty battle array approaching, left Thebes and fled to Kipkipi. Upon a trust(-inspiring) oracle of Ashur and Ishtar I, myself, conquered this town completely. From Thebes[12] I carried away booty, heavy and beyond counting: silver, gold, precious stones, his entire personal possessions, linen garments with multicolored trimmings, fine horses, (certain) inhabitants, male and female. I pulled two high obelisks, cast[13] of shining *zaḫalû* -bronze,[14] the weight of which was 2,500 talents, standing at the door of the temple, out of their bases and took (them) to Assyria. (Thus) I carried off from Thebes heavy booty, beyond counting. I made Egypt (*Muṣur*) and Nubia feel my weapons bitterly and celebrated my triumph. With full hands and safely, I returned to Nineveh, the city (where I exercise) my rule.

In my third campaign I marched against Ba'il, king of Tyre, who lives (on an island) amidst the sea, because he did not heed my royal order, did not listen to my personal (lit.: of my lips) commands. I surrounded him with redoubts, seized his communications (lit.: roads) on sea and land. I (thus) intercepted (lit.: strangled) and made scarce their food supply and forced them to submit to my yoke. He brought his own daughter and the daughters of his brothers before me to do menial services.[15] At the same time, he brought his son Iahimilki who had not (yet) crossed the sea to greet me as (my) slave. I received from him his

[7] Here, the Cylinder B (cf. Streck, *op.cit.*, pp. 94 ff., Col. II:14) and the parallel text published by R. C. Thompson, in *Iraq*, VII (1941), 103 f., No. 104 on Pl. 14, No. 25 on Pl. 15, which is styled in the first person, has the following lines: "The hearts of the inhabitants of Sais, Bindidi, Tanis who had revolted and collaborated with Tirhakah I hung on poles; I flayed (them) and [covered] with their skins the wall of the town(s)."

[8] Here, Ashurbanipal follows the Egyptian customs.

[9] Lit.: "the pronunciation of my name"; for this meaning of *nibîtu*, cf. my remarks in *WZKM*, XLIV (1937), 179.

[10] For the idiom *namuššišu alâku*, cf. Th. Bauer, *Assurbanipal*, II, 1.

[11] For this name, cf. W. Struve, *ZAeS*, LXII (1926), 63 ff. and also, Weidner, *AfO*, XIII (1940), 208.

[12] The text published by E. Nassouhi, *AfO*, II (1924), 97 ff., shows the following variant (Col. ii:7-10): "I conquered the town Thebes, the capital of Egypt (*Mu-ṣir*) and Nubia (*Ku-ši*); I carried away as booty fine horses, linen garments with multicolored trimmings, gold, silver, and countless people."

[13] The term *pitqu* ("cast") is used here incorrectly because the Egyptian obelisks had only metal coatings.

[14] *Zaḫalû* (cf. also, Weissbach, *WVDOG*, LIX, 78, n.9) denotes a bright gold-copper alloy used—like a kindred alloy called *esmaru*—for casting objects and, at least in one instance (cf. D. D. Luckenbill, *Annals of Sennacherib*, 109:21), to provide a copper statue with a coating.

[15] The Sumerian word a g r i g (Akk. *abarakku*) seems to refer originally to a servant (male or female) of higher standing within the retinue of a man of rank, perhaps a steward (Landsberger, *AfO*, x [1935-36], 150, n.48, and *apud* Stamm, *MVAG*, XLIV [1938], 270, n.1). In the Neo-Assyrian period, it denoted a court official of consequence, while—in the present context—the term *abarakkûtu* refers to the status of those daughters of vanquished foreign rulers who were admitted to the royal Assyrian household. While, on one hand, they might have been hostages, much like the sons and brothers of such unhappy kings, admitted to court service, their legal status was certainly different as is indicated by the fact that they are endowed with dowries.

daughter and the daughters of his brothers with their great dowries. I had mercy upon him and returned to him the son, the offspring of his loins. Iakinlu, king of Arvad, living (also) on an island who had not submitted to (any of) the kings of my family, did (now) submit to my yoke and brought his daughter with a great dowry to Nineveh to do menial services, and he kissed my feet.

(Lines 68-80 deal with kings of Asia Minor bringing tribute, etc.)

After Iakinlu, king of Arvad, had perished,[16] Aziba'l, Abiba'l, Aduniba'l, Sapatiba'l, Budiba'l, Ba'liashupu, Ba'lhanunu, Ba'lmaluku, Abimilki, Ahimilki, the sons of Iakinlu who live (on an island) amidst the sea, came from the sea to me with their heavy presents (*tâmartu*) and kissed my feet. I liked Aziba'l (lit.: I looked with pleasure upon Aziba'l) and made him king of Arvad. I clad Abiba'l, Aduniba'l, Sapatiba'l, Budiba'l, Ba'liashupu, Ba'lhanûnu, Ba'lmaluku, Abimilki (and) Ahimilki in multicolored garments, put golden rings on their hands and made them do service at my court.[17]

(2) From the Cylinder E (cf. A. C. Piepkorn, *Historical Prism Inscriptions of Ashurbanipal* [*AS*, No. 5] [Chicago, 1933], I, 10; also, M. Streck, *op.cit.*, pp. 155 f.). Translation: Luckenbill, *AR*, II, §892.

(i 4—19)

Magan and Meluhha, a distant [region] . . . (to which) Esarhaddon, king of Assyria, my own father, had advanced and through which he had marched defeating there Tirhakah, king of Nubia (*Kûsu*), scattering his army. He conquered Egypt (*Muṣur*) and Nubia and carried off (from) it booty (beyond) counting. He ruled over the entire country and incorporated it into the territory of Assyria. The former names of the cities he changed, giving them new denominations.[1] He installed his (own) servants as kings (and) governors in these towns. He imposed upon them [annual] tribute to (be paid to) him as overlord. . . . *ašlu*[2] distance . . . Memphis. . . .

(3) From the British Museum text K 3083 (largely a parallel to the preceding text); cf. M. Streck, *op.cit.*, pp. 217 f., and Th. Bauer, *Das Inschriftwerk Assurbanipals* (Leipzig, 1933), II, 27. Translation: Luckenbill, *AR*, II, §989.

(6—8)

Fifty-five of their statues of kings of Egypt . . . and wrote [upon them . . .] the triumph achieved by his own hands. After my own father (i.e. Esarhaddon) had died. . . .

(4) From the British Museum text K 228 joined to K 2675 (literary type: annals written on tablets); cf. M. Streck, *op.cit.*, pp. 158 ff. Translation: Luckenbill, *AR*, II, §§900-907.

(I—reverse 5)

The kings from East and West came and kissed my feet. (But) Tirhakah (*Tarqû*), against (the will of) the gods, planned[1] to seize Egypt (and) to. . . . He thought little of the might of Ashur, my lord, and put his trust in his own power; the harsh way in which my own father had treated him, did not come to his mind. He marched out and entered Memphis, taking this town for himself. He sent his army against the Assyrians who were in Egypt, servants belonging to me, whom Esarhaddon, my own father, had appointed there as kings, to kill, to make prisoners and booty. An express-messenger came to Nineveh to report to me. I became very angry on account of these happenings, my soul was aflame. I called the *turtan* -official, the governors, and also their assistants and gave immediately the order to my mighty (battle-) forces for quick assistance to the kings and governors, servants who belong to me, and made them start out on the march to Egypt. In mad haste they marched on as far as the town Kar-Baniti.

(Lines 15-19 parallel the above translated report.)

He (i.e. *Tarqû*) left Memphis, his royal residence, the place in which he had put his trust, to save his life, boarded a ship, leaving his camp and fleeing alone. He entered Thebes (*Ni'*). The warriors (of Assyria) seized all the warships that were with him. They sent me the good tiding through a messenger (who) also reported to me orally. (Then) I ordered to add to my former (battle-)forces (in Egypt) the *rabšaq* -officer, all the governors (and) kings of (the region) beyond the river (Euphrates), servants who belong to me, together with their forces and their ships, and (also) the kings of Egypt, servants who belong to me, together with their forces and their ships, to chase Tirhakah out of Egypt (*Muṣur*) and Nubia. They marched towards Thebes, the fortress-town of Tirhakah, king of Nubia, (covering) a distance of a month march (in) 10 days. Tirhakah, who had heard of the coming of my army, left Thebes, his fortress-town, crossed the Nile (*Ia-ru-'-ú*)[2] and pitched camp on the other side (of the river). Necho, Sharruludari (and) Pakruru, kings whom my own father had installed in Egypt, did not keep the agreements sworn by Ashur and the great gods, my lords, they broke their oaths, forgot the friendliness (with which) my own father (had treated them) and began to plot.

(Lines 36-41 parallel the above translated report.)

They plotted constantly against the Assyrian army massed (in Egypt), in order to save their own lives, they schemed[3] towards (their) complete annihilation. (But)

[16] In *AfO*, XIII (1940), 233, Weidner conjectures that these sons of the king of Arvad had murdered their father and—unable to settle the problem of succession—appealed to Ashurbanipal for a pertinent decision.

[17] For the meaning of this idiom, cf. my remarks in *JAOS*, LXI (1941), 258.

[1] This seems to refer to a renaming of the major cities with Assyrian denominations; cf., e.g. the name *Limmir-išak -dAššur*, etc.

[2] Text: *ašlu qaqqar*. One *ašlu* corresponds roughly to 60 yards, but it is quite possible that the *ašlu qaqqar* denotes a larger unit.

[1] Text: *uš-tam-ṣa-a*; for the verb *maṣû* III/2, cf. G. Meier, in *AfO*, XII (1937-39), 142, n.35 (with literature).

[2] For the Semitic word denoting the Nile, cf. W. Vycichl, *ZAeS*, LXXVI (1941), 79 ff.

[3] This meaning of *karâmu* seems to be suggested by the context.

my officers heard of these matters and met their cunning with cunning. They arrested their mounted messengers together with their messages and learned (thus) about their rebellious plot. They arrested Sharruludari (and) Necho.

(Lines 47-51 parallel the above translated report.)

And I, Ashurbanipal, [inclined towards] friendliness, had mercy upon Necho, my own servant, whom Esarhaddon, my own father, had made king in Kar-Belmatate (= Sais).

(Lines 54-63 parallel the above translated report.)

His son Nabushezibanni I made king in Athribis (*Ḫatḫariba*), the (new) name of which is Limmirishak-Ashur.

(Lines 66-68 parallel the above translated report.)

He (URdamane) assembled his (armed) might; he made his weapons ready and marched on to deliver a decisive battle against my army. (But) upon a trustworthy oracle of Ashur, Sin and the great gods, my lords, they (my troops) defeated him in a great open battle and scattered his (armed) might. URdamane fled alone and entered Thebes, his royal residence. They (i.e. my army) marched after him (covering) a distance of one month (in) 10 days on difficult roads as far as Thebes. They conquered this city completely, smashed (it as if by) a floodstorm. They moved out of his town

(reverse)

gold, silver—(found) in dust-form in his mountains,—precious stones, all his personal treasures, linen garments with multicolored trimmings, fine horses, male and female personnel, *bazû-*, *pagû-*, and *uqupu* -monkeys,[4] native in his (URdamane's) mountains, (everything) in great quantities, beyond counting, and declared it booty. They brought (the booty) safely to Nineveh, the town (where I exercise) my rule, and kissed my feet.

(5) British Museum fragment 82-5-22,10 published by Th. Bauer, *Das Inschriftwerk Assurbanipals* (Leipzig, 1933), Vol. I, Pl. 60, ii, 56.

(4—9)

. . . in Egypt they assembled [. . . Ne]cho, Sharruludari, Pakruru, the ki[ngs . . .] in order to go to the place (from) where my army was marching out [. . . Pishanhu]ru whom [my own father] Esarhaddon [had installed] in Nathu, [forgot] the harsh way in which [I had treated] Necho, Sharruludari and Pa[kruru . . .] and addressed the officers who marched at the front of my army . . . they said as follows: "At the time of the night. . . ."

(6) From the *Warka Cylinder of Assurbanipal* published (autograph, transliteration, and translation) by H. F. Lutz, *University of California, Publications in Semitic Philology*, IX/8 (Berkeley, 1931), 385 ff. For the parallel text, A. T. Clay, *Miscellaneous Texts in the Yale Babylonian Collection* (New Haven, 1915) (*YOS*, I), No. 42, cf. the translation by A. Ungnad, in *ZA*, XXXI, 33 ff. (also, B. Meissner, in *AfO*, VIII [1932-33], 51).

[4] cf. n.16, p. 276.

(7—10)

Ashurbanipal, the great king, the legitimate king, the king of the world, king of Assyria, king of (all) the four rims (of the earth), king of kings,[1] prince without rival, who rules from the Upper Sea to the Lower Sea and has made bow to his feet all the (other) rulers and who has laid the yoke (*nîru*) of his overlordship (upon them) from Tyre which is (an island) in the Upper Sea and (read: as far as) Dilmun which is (an island) in the Lower Sea—and they pulled the straps (*abšānu*) (of) his (yoke).

(7) From the inscription in the temple of Ishtar published (with autographs, transliteration, and translation) by R. C. Thompson, in *AAA*, XX (1933), 71 ff. Text: Pls. XC ff. Translation: *ibid.*, 90 ff.

(78—84)

They (i.e. the great gods) made bo[w] to my yo[ke] all the countries from the Upper Sea to the Lower Sea . . . and they pulled the straps (*abšānu*) (of) my (yoke). Upon their mighty command, quickly.[1] . . . I conquered Thebes (*Ni'*), the royal residence of Egypt (*Muṣur*) and Nubia (*Kûsu*), [brought] its heavy spoils to Assyria. I made bow to my yoke Ba'lu, king of Tyre, who did not heed my royal orders, by surrounding him with earthworks and by seizing his communications on sea and land. (Also) Iakinlu, king of Arvad, and Sandasharme, king of Cilicia (*Ḫilakku*) who (both) did not submit to my royal forefathers, did bow to [my yoke].

(8) From the very small British Museum fragment K 6049 (published in *CT*, XXXV, Pl. 18) we learn that "[URdaman]e, son of the sister of Tirhakah, king of [Egypt]" had taken refuge in Elam. Translation: Luckenbill, *AR*, II, §1117.

(b) Campaign against the Arabs[1]

(1) From the Rassam Cylinder (cf. above). Translation: Luckenbill, *AR*, II, §§817-831.

(vii 82—x 5)

In my ninth campaign, I called up my troops (and) marched directly against Uate', king of Arabia (*Aribu*) because he had broken the (agreements protected by) oaths (sworn to) me, did not remember that I had treated him with clemency; he had cast away the yoke of my rule which Ashur (himself) has placed upon him and the ropes (*abšānu*) (of which) he has been pulling (till now). He refused to come (and) to inquire about (the state of) my health and held back the presents (*tâmartu*) and his heavy tribute. He

[1] cf. for this title, F. Bilabel, *Geschichte Vorderasiens und Ägyptens, vom 16.-11. Jahrhundert v. Chr.* (Heidelberg, 1927), pp. 207 ff.; also, C. W. McEwan, *The Oriental Origin of Hellenistic Kingship* (*SAOC*, No. 13, 1934), pp. 32 ff.

[1] Text: *kullamari* (lit.: "early morning"); for parallels to this semantic development, cf. my remarks in *Orientalia*, NS XIX (1950), p. 129, n.*.

[1] To this subject, cf. T. Weiss-Rosmarin, *JSOR*, XVI (1932), 1 ff. For the pertinent iconographic material, cf. D. Opitz, *AfO*, VII (1931), 7 ff.; and B. Meissner, *Islamica*, II (1927), 291 f.

listened—exactly as Elam (did)—to the rebellious propaganda of Akkad and did not care for the oaths sworn to me. He did leave me, Ashurbanipal, the holy high priest, the (ever)praying servant (of the gods), created by the hands of Ashur, and lent (lit.: gave) his armed forces to Abiiate' (and) Aamu, son of Te'ri. He ordered (them) expressly to the assistance of my evil brother Shamashshumukin. He persuaded the inhabitants of Arabia (to join) him and then plundered repeatedly those peoples which Ashur, Ishtar and the (other) great gods had given to me to be their shepherd and had entrusted into my hands. Upon the oracle-command of Ashur, and Ishtar ⟨I called up⟩ my army and defeated him in bloody battles, inflicted countless routs on him (to wit) in the *girû*[2] of the towns of Azaril (and) Hirata(-)kasaia, in Edom, in the pass of Iabrudu, in Beth-Ammon, in the district of Haurina, in Moab, in Sa'arri, in Harge, in the district of Zobah.[3] In the(se) battles I smashed all the inhabitants of Arabia who had revolted with him, but he himself escaped before the powerful "weapons" of Ashur to a distant region. They set fire to the tents in which they live and burnt (them) down. Uate' had misgivings[4] and he fled, alone, to the country Nabate.

The Cylinder C (cf. M. Streck, *op.cit.*, pp. 139 ff.) adds here a more explicit version. Translation: Luckenbill, *AR*, II, §880.

(ix 34—49)

[Iau]ta' . . . [fled] to the country Nabaiati. [He went] to see Natnu (and) Natnu said as follows to Iauta': "(How) can I be saved (now) from Assyria (since) you have put me (by your visit) in your power!" Natnu was afraid, he was seized with anxiety and sent his messengers to inquire after my health and they kissed my feet. He implored me repeatedly—as his lord—to make a peace agreement (secured by) oaths (and) to become my servant. (Finally) I looked with friendliness upon him, turning to him a smiling face. I imposed upon him an annual tribute.

(viii)

As to (that other) Uate', the son of Hazail, the nephew of Uate', the son of Bir-Dadda who had made himself king of Arabia, Ashur, the king of the gods, the Great Mountain, made him change his mind and he came to meet me (in submission). To demonstrate that Ashur and the great gods, my lords (are worthy of) the (highest) praise, I imposed (the following) heavy punishment (var.: he accepted the (following) verdict): I put a pillory (on) his (neck) together with a bear (and) a dog and made him stand on guard (duty) at the gate in Nineveh, (called) *Nîrib-masnaqti-adnāti*.[5] Ammuladi, however, king of Qedar (*Qi-id-ri*) rose to fight the kings of the Westland whom Ashur, Ishtar and the (other) great gods, have given me as my property. Upon a trust(-inspiring) oracle (given by) Ashur, Sin, Shamash, Adad, Bel, Nebo, the Ishtar of Nineveh—the Queen of Kidmuri[5a]—the Ishtar of Arbela, Ninurta, Nergal (and) Nusku, I inflicted a defeat upon him. They seized him alive and also Adia, the wife of Uate', king of Arabia, and brought (them) to me.

Here, the text British Museum K 2802 (cf. for publication and translation, M. Streck, *op.cit.*, pp. 197 ff. and 203) adds a more detailed account. English translation: Luckenbill, *AR*, II, §1084.

(v 26—30)

(As to) Adia, queen of Arabia, I inflicted a bloody defeat upon her, burnt down her tents, seized her alive (and) removed her, with many (other) prisoners, to Assyria.

Upon the (oracle-)command of the great gods, my lords, I put a dog's collar on him and made him watch the bar (of the city's gate). Upon the (oracle-)command of Ashur, Ishtar and the great gods, my lords, I defeated in a bloody battle and routed the soldiers of Abiate' (and of) Aamu, son of Te'ri, who marched to the assistance of Shamashshumukin, my evil brother, (when they were about) to enter Babylon. The remainders who succeeded to enter Babylon ate (there) each other's flesh in their ravenous hunger, and (later) they made a sortie from Babylon to save their lives. My forces, (however,) stationed (there) against Shamashshumukin, inflicted a second defeat upon him (so that) he (i.e. Abiate') escaped alone and seized my feet to save his own life. I had mercy upon him, made him take oaths by the life of the great gods, appointing him, instead of Uate', son of Hazail,[6] as king of Arabia.

A more explicit version appears in the Cylinder B (cf. M. Streck, *op.cit.*, pp. 135 ff.). Translation: Luckenbill, *AR*, II, §870.

(viii 24—44)

Abiate', son of Te'ri, came to Nineveh and kissed my feet. I made a sworn agreement with him concerning his status as a servant of mine. I made him king instead of Iauta' (or) of somebody else. I imposed upon him as annual tribute gold, eye-shaped beads of UD.AŠ-stone, antimony, camels and stud-donkeys. With the help of Ashur, Sin, Shamash, Adad, Bel, Nebo, the Ishtar of Nineveh—the Queen of Kidmuri—the Ishtar of Arbela, Ninurta, Nergal (and) Nusku and by pronouncing my name which Ashur has made powerful, Kamashaltu, king of Moab, a servant belonging to me, inflicted a defeat in an open battle upon Ammuladi, king of Qedar who, like him (Abiate'), had revolted and had continuously made razzias against the kings of the Westland. Ammuladi (himself) captured those of his (i.e. Abiate's) people who [escaped] before . . . , put them in handcuffs and iron foot fetters and sent them to me to Nineveh.

But he came to an understanding with the country of the Nabaiateans, was not afraid of the (oaths sworn by the) life of the great gods and made constantly razzias into the territory of my country. Natnu, king of Nabaiati which lies at a great distance and to whom Uate' had fled, heard—through an intervention[7] of Ashur, Sin, Shamash, Adad, Bel, Nebo, the Ishtar of

[2] Obscure word.

[3] For the identification of Ṣupite, cf. E. Forrer, *Provinzeinteilung*, pp. 62 f. (Zobah).

[4] This seems to be the meaning of the idiom: *marušta maḫāru*.

[5] For the names of the gates of Nineveh, cf. R. C. Thompson (*Iraq*, VII [1940], 91 ff.).

[5a] The temple of this Ishtar-figure was in Calah (*Kalḫu*) and was very famous in Assyria.

[6] Cylinder B shows here the variant "in so-and-so."

[7] Text: *ina tukultiti*. The context suggests that Ashurbanipal assumed that direct divine interference was instrumental in the submission of this king.

Nineveh—the Queen of Kidmuri—the Ishtar of Arbela, Ninurta, Nergal (and) Nusku—about the might of Ashur which endows me with strength, and he—who had never sent a messenger to my royal forefathers to greet them as kings by inquiring after their health—inquired (now)—afraid of the (ever) victorious arms of Ashur—very assiduously[8] after my royal health. But Abiate', son of Te'ri, devoid of any good intentions, unmindful of oaths sworn (even) by the great gods, spoke of rebellion against me and came to an understanding with Natni, king of Nabaiati; they called up their forces for a dangerous attack against my territory.

Upon an (oracle-)command of Ashur, Sin, Shamash, Adad, Bel, Nebo, the Ishtar of Nineveh—the Queen of Kidmuri—the Ishtar of Arbela, Ninurta, Nergal (and) Nusku, I called up my army and took the direct road against Abiate'. They (i.e. my army) crossed safely Tigris and Euphrates at the time of their highest flood; they took (lit.: followed) a path (leading to) far-away regions. They ascended high mountain chains, winding[9] their way through woods full of shadow, proceeding safely upon a thorny road between high trees and *sidra*[10] -shrubs (full) of spines. A distance of 100 double-hours from Nineveh, the town beloved by Ishtar, the spouse of Ellil, they marched forward through the desert where parching thirst is at home, where there are not even birds in the sky and wherein neither wild donkeys (nor) gazelles pasture, following Uate', king of Arabia, and Abiate' who marched with the forces of the country of the Nabaiateans. I departed from the town Hadata in the month of Simanu—the month of Sin, first-born son of Ellil and leader (of his brothers)—on the 25th day—(the day of) the procession of the Lady-of-Babylon, the most important among the great gods. I pitched camp in Laribda, a city with a wall of undressed stones,[11] at the (last) water cisterns. My army drew water (there) for their drinking-supply and (then) marched forward to the regions of parching thirst, as far as Hurarina. I inflicted a defeat upon the Isamme', a confederation[12] of (the worshipers of) the god Atarsamain, and of the Nabaiateans between the towns of Iarki and Azalla in a far-away desert where there are no wild animals and (where) not even the birds build their nests. I took as booty from them countless prisoners, donkeys, camels and small cattle. After my army had marched unopposed through a distance of 8 double-hours, they returned safely and drank (again) water in Azalla to quench their thirst. (Then) they marched forward as far as the town Qurasiti, a distance of 6 double-miles (through) a territory of parching thirst. (There) I rounded up the confederation of (the worshipers of) the god Atarsamain

(ix)

and the Qedareans under Uate', son of Bir-Dadda and made them march (with me) on the road to Damascus (*Di-maš-qa*), (also) his gods, his mother, his sister, his wife, his family (distaff side) (and) all the other women[13] of Qedar, the donkeys, camels and small cattle as many as I caught with the help of Ashur and Ishtar, my lords.

In the month of Abu—the month of the Bow-Star, the mighty daughter of Sin—the third day—the day before (the festival) of Marduk, king of the gods—I departed from Damascus (*Di-maš-qa*); I marched forward as far as Hulhuliti, a distance of 6 double-hours, in a single night. I caught the confederation of Abiate', son of Te'ri, (with) the Qedareans at the steep mountain Hukkurina and inflicted a defeat upon him, carrying (some) booty away from him. During the battle, according to the (oracle-)command (given) by Ashur and Ishtar, my lords, I myself caught Abiate' (and) Aammu, son of Te'ri, alive and fettered them with iron fetters on hands and feet. I brought them to Assyria together with the booty (collected) in their country. Those fugitives who escaped my onslaught occupied in their terror the mountain Hukkuruna (which is) a steep mountain peak. I ordered soldiers to stand on guard in the towns of Manhabbi, Apparu, Tenuquri, Zaiuran, Marqana, Sadaten, Enzikarme, Ta'na, Irrana, anywhere where there were cisterns or water in the springs, thus refusing them (the access to the) water (supply) which (alone) could keep them alive. I (thus) made water to be very rare for their lips, (and many) perished of parching thirst. The others slit open camels, their (only) means of transportation, drinking blood and filthy water against their thirst. None of those who ascended the mountain or entered (this region) to hide there, did escape; none was enough fleet of foot to get out of my hands. I caught them all myself in their hiding-places; countless people—male and female—,donkeys, camels, large and small cattle, I led as booty to Assyria. They filled up completely and to its entire extent all my land(s) which Ashur has given me. I formed flocks and distributed camels as if they be sheep, dividing (them) up to all inhabitants of Assyria. Camels were bought within my country for less than one shekel[14] of silver on the market place. The *ṣutammu* -workers received camels and (even) slaves as a present, the brewer as bakhshish, the gardener as an *additional payment*![15] Irra, the Warrior (i.e. pestilence) struck down Uate', as well as his army, who had not kept the oaths sworn to me and had fled before the onslaught of

[8] Hendiadys: *sanâqu* + *ša'âlu*.

[9] For the word *ḫalâpu* with the meaning "to walk through a wooded area" (lit.: "to slip through"), cf. the semantic parallel in *ḫalâlu* attested in the Epic of Gilgamesh: cf. Thompson's edition (Tablet X), Pl. 39, II:34 (*iḫ-lu-ul-ma it-tar-da*).

[10] For this identification of *amurdinnu*, cf. W. F. Albright, *ZA*, XXXVII (NF III), 140 f.

[11] Text: *bît dûri ša* n a$_4$. l a g . The Sumerian word is to be read in this context l a g (and not: k i š i b "cylinder seal") with regard to l a g a (b), i.e. undressed stone block.

[12] The passages interchange *amel**a'-lu* and g i š . DA. cf. Deimel, *ŠL*, 335/27. The contemporaneous royal correspondence (cf., e.g. Harper, *ABL*, 1114:rev. 17(!) and 1286:rev. 2) uses the writing *aiālu*.

[13] This meaning of *nišê* is attested in Neo-Assyrian and Neo-Babylonian texts.

[14] Idiomatic expression; lit.: "for one shekel (and) one-half shekel."

[15] The words *nidnu* (lit.: gift), *ḫabû* (attested in Neo-Babyl. business documents, cf. A. Ungnad, Glossar to M. San Nicolò and A. Ungnad, *Neubabylonische Rechts- und Verwaltungsurkunden* [Leipzig, 1937], p. 59) and *qîšu* (lit.: gift) are practically synonymous in this context.

Ashur, my lord,—had run away from them. Famine broke out among them and they ate the flesh of their children against their hunger. Ashur, Sin, Shamash, Adad, Bel, Nebo, the Ishtar of Nineveh—the Queen of Kidmuri—the Ishtar of Arbela, Ninurta, Nergal (and) Nusku (thus) inflicted quickly upon them (all) the curses written (down) in their sworn agreements. Even when the camel foals, the donkey foals,[16] calves or lambs were suckling many times (lit.: 7 times) on the mother animals, they could not fill (lit.: satiate) their stomachs with milk.[16a] Whenever the inhabitants of Arabia asked each other: "On account of what have these calamities befallen Arabia?" (they answered themselves:) "Because we did not keep the solemn oaths (sworn by) Ashur, because we offended the friendliness of Ashurbanipal, the king, beloved by Ellil!"

And (verily) Ninlil, the lordly Wild-Cow, the most heroic among the goddesses who rivals in rank (only) with Anu and Enlil, was butting my enemies with her mighty horns; the Ishtar who dwells in Arbela, clad in (divine) fire (and) carrying the *melammû* -headwear, was raining flames upon Arabia; Irra, the Warrior, armed with *anuntu*,[17] was crushing (underfoot) my foes; Ninurta, the Arrow, the great hero, the son of Ellil, was cutting the throats of my enemies with his sharp point; Nusku, the obedient messenger (of the gods) proclaimer of my lordship, who accompanied me upon the command of Ashur, (and) the courageous Ninlil, the Lady of [Arbela],[18] who protected me as king, took the lead of my army and threw down my foes. (When) the troops of Uate' heard the approach of the(se) mighty "weapons" of Ashur and Ishtar, the great gods, my lords, which during the battle had come to my assistance, they revolted against him. He became frightened and left the house (*sanctuary*) into which he had fled, so that I caught him personally according to the trustworthy oracle of Ashur, Sin, Shamash, Adad, Bel, Nebo, the Ishtar of Nineveh—the Queen of Kidmuri—the Ishtar of Arbela, Ninurta, Nergal (and) Nusku—and brought him to Assyria. Upon an oracle-command of Ashur and Ninlil I pierced his cheeks with the sharp-edged spear, my personal weapon, by laying the very hands on him which I had received to conquer opposition against me; I put the ring to his jaw, placed a dog collar around his neck and made him guard the bar of the east gate of Nineveh which is called *Nîrib-masnaq-adnāte*. (Later) I had mercy upon him and granted him life in order to praise the glory of Ashur, Ishtar (and) the great gods, my lords.

[16] The denomination of the donkey foal as *suḫiru* is very rare and recurs, to my knowledge, only in the Middle-Assyrian text Ebeling, *KAJ*, No. 311:8-9 where male (n i t á) and female (*si-ni-il-te*) *imer**su-ḫi-ru* are mentioned.

[16a] This situation is mentioned in nearly the same words in the curses of the Aramaic treaty studied by H. Bauer, Ein aramäischer Staatsvertrag aus dem 8. Jahr. v. Chr. in *AfO*, VIII, p. 11 (to lines x + 2-5).

[17] The difficult word *anuntu* (identified in lists of synonymous words with *qablu* and *tâḫazu* "battle") is used here in exactly the same context as *tuquntu*, in L. W. King, *STC*, I, 222:12.

[18] Dr. F. W. Geers indicated to me the parallel text BrM 1904-10-9,81 (cf. L. W. King, *Supplement*, p. 20, No. 117) which permits the filling of this gap.

On my return march, I conquered the town Ushu the emplacement of which is on the seacoast.[19] I killed those inhabitants of Ushu who did not obey their governors by refusing to deliver the tribute which they had to pay annually. I took to task those among them who were not submissive. Their images and the (surviving) people I led as booty to Assyria. I killed (also) those inhabitants of Accho who were not submissive, hanging their corpses on poles which I placed around the city. The others I took to Assyria, formed a contingent (out of them) and added (it) to the large army which

(x)

Ashur has presented to me. During the battle I seized personally Aamu, son of Te'ri (who) had sided with Abiate', his brother; I (had) him flayed in Nineveh, the town (where I exercise) my rule.

(2) From the inscription in the temple of Ishtar, published by R. C. Thompson, in *AAA*, XX (1933), 71 ff. Text: Pls. XC ff. and pp. 79 ff. Translation: pp. 90 ff.

(113—114)

I caught alive Uate', king of Ishmael (*Su-mu-ìl*)[1] [who was in agreement] with him (i.e. Shamashshumukin); Ammuladi, king of Qedar (*Qi-da-ri*), had fallen into the hands of my army in a battle engagement and they (i.e. the army) brought him (to me) alive.

(118—121)

I harnessed Tammaritu, Pa'e, Ummana[ldasi, king(s)] of Elam, (and) Iaute', king of Ishmael (*Su-mu-ìl*) whom I had captured personally upon the oracle-command of Ashur, Ninlil and the Ish[tar dwelling in Arbela], like choice foals to my (triumphal) char,[2] my royal means of transportation, after [I went forth in procession] from the temples é . s a r . r a , é . m a š . m a š , é . [. . .] in order to make the sacrifices and to perform the rites—and they actually held the straps (*abšānu*) (to pull the char).

(123—129)

[Natnu, king of Nabai]ati, which is (a country) far away, who did not submit to my royal forefathers, did bow to my y[oke] and (therefore), upon the oracle-command of Ashur and Ninlil, the great gods, my lords, who (thus) encouraged me, I defeated Iaute' who had put his trust upon (the assistance of) the Nabaiati country and [had therefore held back his *tâmartu* -gifts];[3] I turned his cities into ruin-hills and heaps (of debris). I [led away] himself, his wife, his children . . . as the he[avy] spoils of his country. Nuhuru,[4] his son,

[19] *Ušû* is the name of the mainland settlement of Tyre.

[1] For this identification, cf. Thompson, *AAA*, XX (1933), 98, and—more in detail—J. Lewy, in *HUCA*, XIX, 432, n.143.

[2] For this vehicle, cf. Th. Bauer, *Assurbanipal*, II, 53, n.4.

[3] Restoration proposed by Thompson, *op.cit.*

[4] This name has been compared with that of the grandfather and brother of Abraham (cf. Thompson, *op.cit.*, p. 99), Nahor. For the city of the same name mentioned in Mari Texts, cf., e.g. Ch. Jean, *Revue des études semitiques—Babyloniaca* (1941), 126.

who had fled before the attack (^{is}*kakku*) of Ashur and Ishtar . . . [the glamor] of their godhead had blinded him, he [came] to me with gifts and [kissed my feet]. I had mercy upon him and sat him on the throne of his father.

(3) British Museum K 3087 (M. Streck, *op.cit.*, pp. 217 f.) and K 3405 (M. Streck, *op.cit.*, pp. 223 f.). Translation: Luckenbill, *AR*, II, §§940 and 943.

(1—17)

[Te'elhunu], the *kumirtu*[1] -priestess of the [goddess Dilbat who] had become angry with Hazail, king of Arabia . . . and had him delivered into the hands of Sennacherib, my own grandfather, by causing his defeat, and who had declared not to live (any more) with the people of Arabia, had emigrated to Assyria. To Esarhaddon, king of Assyria, my own father, a favorite of the great gods who had obtained [success] because of his worship of (all) the gods and goddesses—who had reinstalled [Hazail] upon the throne of his own father [upon a command given by] Ashur and Shamash, and had returned all conquered images to their sanctuaries—came Hazail, king of Arabia, to see him with heavy gifts (*tâmartu*) and kissed his feet, approaching him to return (the image of) his goddess Ishtar. He (i.e. Esarhaddon) had mercy upon him and conceded [to give him] Te'elhunu, her former *kumirtu* -priestess. With respect to (the priestess) Tabua (however) he made an oracle inquiry to Shamash as follows: . . . Then he returned her together with the image of his goddess. He (also) made a star[2] of reddish gold which was decorated with precious stones and . . . for a happy life of his, long lasting span (of life), prosperity of his offspring . . . , permanency of his kingdom, over[throw of all his enemies]. . . .

(c) Receipt of Tribute from Palestine

The BrM text K 1295 is a receipt of tribute brought from Palestine. The text was published by R. F. Harper, *ABL*, Vol. VI, No. 632, and has been translated repeatedly; cf. G. G. Boson, *Les métaux et les pierres dans les inscriptions assyro-babyloniennes* (München, 1914), p. 51; R. H. Pfeiffer, in *JBL*, XLVII (1928), 185 f., and *State Letters of Assyria* (New Haven, 1935), No. 96; L. Waterman, *Royal Correspondence of the Assyrian Empire* (Ann Arbor, 1930), I, 440 f. The text is dated to the period between Sargon II and Esarhaddon.

Two minas of gold from the inhabitants of Bit-Ammon (^{mat}*Bît-Am-man-na-a-a*); one mina of gold from the inhabitants of Moab (^{mat}*Mu-'-ba-a-a*); ten minas of silver from the inhabitants of Judah (^{mat}*Ia-ú-da-a-a*); [. . . mi]nas of silver from the inhabitants of [Edom] (^{mat}[*U-du-ma*]-*a-a*). . . .

(reverse)

. . . the inhabitants of Byblos, the district officers of the king, my lord, have brought.

[1] For the (West-Semitic) term for priest: *kumru*, cf. J. Lewy, in *ZA*, XXXVIII (NF IV), 243 ff., and E. Ebeling, *MAOG*, VII/1-2 (1933), 86, n.a.

[2] The "symbol" of Ishtar.

The Neo-Babylonian Empire and its Successors

The historiographic literature of this period is represented by excerpts from four chronicles translated in the first part of this section. They cover—sometimes overlapping—the period from the first year of Esarhaddon to the seizure of Babylon by Cyrus. For the literary form and the political tendencies of these documents, reference should be made to the remarks of Landsberger-Bauer, in *ZA*, XXXVII (NF III), 61-65.

The second part contains historical inscriptions of Nebuchadnezzar II and of Nabonidus which refer to conquests made in the West (Syria and Palestine), to the foreign policy of the Chaldean dynasty, and describe, in his own words, Nabonidus' rise to royal power. To illustrate the particular background of this ruler, the Eski-Harran inscription is given, a memorial for the mother of the usurper. The end of this dynasty is illustrated by the account given by Cyrus on his famous cylinder and by the poetic text known under the misleading title of Persian Verse-Account of Nabonidus. Finally, the novel mood of the Persian domination is shown in one of the trilingual inscriptions of Xerxes and—to document the persistency of the literary tradition—an inscription of the Seleucid king Antiochus I, Soter, has been translated.

HISTORIOGRAPHIC DOCUMENTS

1. TEXT FROM THE FIRST YEAR OF BELIBNI TO THE ACCESSION YEAR OF SHAMASHSHUMUKIN

From the Babylonian Chronicle (British Museum 84-211,356 and 92, 502, last publication in *CT*, XXXIV, Pls. 46 ff.), translated by F. Delitzsch, *Die babylonische Chronik* (*Abh. d. Phil. Hist. Klasse; Kgl. Saechs. Ak. d. W.* XXV/1 [1906], 8 ff.), and partly by Luckenbill, *The Annals of Sennacherib* (*OIP*, II), 158 ff.

(ii 23—iv 38)

First year of Belibni: Sennacherib destroyed (lit.: broke) the towns Hirimma and Hararatum.

Third year of Belibni: Sennacherib marched down to the country of Akkad and carried away the booty (made) in Akkad. They brought Belibni and his nobles in fetters to Assyria. Three years was Belibni king in Babylon. Sennacherib placed his son Ashurnadinshumi upon the throne in Babylon.

First year of Ashurnadinshumi: Hallushu, the brother of Ishtarhundu, king of Elam, seized him (i.e. Ishtarhundu) and closed up the door (of his palace) in front of him.[1] Eighteen years was Ishtarhundu king in Elam. Hallushu, his brother, sat himself on the throne, in Elam.

Sixth year of Ashurnadinshumi: Sennacherib marched down to Elam, he destroyed (lit.: broke) the towns Nagitum, Hilmi, Pillatum and Hupapanu, and carried their booty away. Afterwards, Hallushu, king of Elam, marched against the country of Akkad; towards the end of the (month) Tashritu, he entered Sippar and killed its inhabitants. (The image of) Shamash did (therefore) not leave the temple Ebarra (in the procession). Ashurnadinshumi was made a prisoner and brought to Elam. Six years was Ashurnadinshumi king in Babylon. The king of Elam placed Nergalushe-

[1] The meaning of this phrase (which recurs in the report on the first year of Nergalushezib) remains obscure.

zib on the throne, in Babylon. He *declared* (a state of) *h[ostilitie]s* (against) Assyria.

First year of Nergalushezib: In the month of Tammuz, the 16th day, Nergalushezib seized Nippur and (unintelligible).[2] In the month of Tashritu, the 1st day,

(iii)

the Assyrian army entered Uruk; they carried away as booty the gods of Uruk and its inhabitants. (Thus while) Nergalushezib went after the Elamites (to ask for help), they (i.e. the Assyrians) snatched the gods of Uruk and its inhabitants. In the month of Tashritu, the 7th day, he (Nergalushezib) made an attack against the Assyrian army, in the province of Nippur, but he was seized in open battle and brought to Assyria. One year and 6 months was Nergalushezib king in Babylon. In the month of Tashritu, the 26th day, his people made a rebellion against Hallushu, king of Elam, and they closed up the door (of the palace) in front of him and killed him. Six years was Hallushu king in Elam. Kudurru sat himself on the throne in Elam. Afterwards Sennacherib marched down to Elam and destroyed (lit.: broke) (the country) from the land of Rishi as far as Bit-Burnaki, and carried away the booty thereof. Mushezib-Marduk sat himself on the throne in Babylon.

First year of Mushezib-Marduk: In the month of Abu, the 8(?)th day, Kudurru, king of Elam, was seized in a rebellion and killed. Ten months was Kudurru king in Elam. Menanu sat himself on the throne in Elam. In an unknown year, Menanu called up the armies of Elam and Akkad and made an attack against Assyria in the town of Halule. He (also) made a raid against Assyria.

Fourth year of Mushezib-Marduk: In the month of Nisanu, the 15th day, Menanu, king of Elam, suffered a stroke, his mouth was paralyzed, he was unable to speak. In the month of Kislimu, the 1st day, the city (i.e. Babylon) was seized, Mushezib-Marduk was made a prisoner and brought to Assyria. Four years was Mushezib-Marduk king in Babylon. In the month of Addaru, the 7th day, Menanu, king of Elam, died (lit.: "fate"). Four years [was] Menanu king in E[lam]. Hummahaldashu sat himself on the throne in Elam.

For eight years there was no king in Babylon. In the month of Tammuz, the 3rd day, the gods of Uruk entered Uruk (again) from.... In the month of Tashritu, the 23rd day, Hummahaldashu, king of Elam, was stricken at noon and [die]d at sun-set (of the same day). Eight years was Hummahaldashu king in Elam. Hummahaldashu, the second, sat himself on the throne in Elam. In the month of Tebitu, the 20th day, his son killed Sennacherib, king of Assyria, during a rebellion. [Twenty-thr]ee years was Sennacherib king in Assyria. From the month of Tebitu, the 20th day, till the month of Addaru, the 2nd day, there was continuous rebellion in Assyria. In the month of Addaru, the 18th day, Esarhaddon, his son, sat himself on the throne in Assyria.

First year of Esarhaddon: Zer-DU-lishir of the Sea-Country fled before the officials of Assyria and en[tered] Elam after he had marched upstream against Ur and had laid siege to the town. . . . In Elam (however), the king of Elam arrested him and [put him] to the sword. In Nippur the g ú . e n . n a -official[3] . . . in an unknown month. In the month of Ululu, the god Satran and the (other) gods . . . of Der went to Dur-Sharruken (i.e. Khorsabad). . . . In the month of Addaru the foundations of . . . [were laid].

[*Second*] year: The major-domo (*rab bîti*) of . . .

(iv)

. . . (two lines destroyed) [NN and . . . -]ahheshullim, the g ú . e n . n a -officials were [arrested], led away to Assyria and executed in Assyria.

[Fourth year]: Sidon was taken and looted. The major-domo of Akkad ordered a *biḫirtum*.[4]

Fifth year: In the month of Tashritu, the 2nd day, the Assyrian army seized (the town of) Bassa (*ba-aṣ-ṣa iṣ-ṣab-tu*). In the month of Tashritu, the head of the king of Sidon was cut off and brought to Assyria; in the month of Addaru, the head of the king of Kindu and Sizu was cut off and brought to Assyria.

Sixth year: The king of Elam entered Sippar and made a massacre (there). (The image of) Shamash did (therefore) not leave the temple Ebabbar (in procession). Assyria (marched) against Militene (*Mi-li-du*)[5]. . . . Hummahaldashu, king of Elam, died in his palace without having been sick.[6] Five years was Hummahaldashu king in Elam. His brother Urtagu sat down on the throne in Elam. In an unknown month the g ú . e n . n a -official Shum-iddin and the "Dakkurean"[7] Kudurru went to Assyria.

Seventh year: In the month of Addaru, the 5th day, the army of Assyria was defeated in a bloody battle in Egypt. In the month of Addaru, the (image of the) Ishtar of Agade and the (other) gods of Agade came from Elam and entered Agade, the 10th day.

Eighth year of Esarhaddon: In the month of Tebitu, the day (on the original) is broken (off), the country Shuprisa was conquered and looted. In the month of Kislimu, its booty entered Uruk. In the month of Addaru, the 5th day, the wife of the king died.

Tenth year: In the month of Nisanu, the Assyrian army marched against Egypt. Broken (passage on the original)! Three bloody battles were fought in Egypt

[2] Text: SAR.SAR^{ir} NI.LAL. cf. also, below, n.10, p. 306.

[3] For this office, attested from the Sumerian to the Neo-Babylonian periods—and always in relation to the town of Nippur—cf. e.g. Forrer, in *Reallexikon der Assyriologie*, II, 456.

[4] Obscure term.

[5] Text: *Mi-li-du-me* LUḪ ḪA (or: 7); Landsberger-Bauer seem to assume a haplology (*Mi-li-du* ⟨DU⟩^{me}), but do not explain the remaining two signs.

[6] Variant adds "alive." Langdon (*JRAS*, 1925, 166) translates "although in good health." The wording seems to imply that the king had been poisoned.

[7] On the country Dakuru, cf. B. Meissner, *OLZ*, XXI (1918), 220 ff. and E. Unger in *Reallexikon*, II 38 f. *mâr Da-ku-ru* seem to indicate here an official position, comparable, perhaps, with that of the *(w)akil amurrî* in the Old Babylonian period. cf., also, below n.9, p. 308 for a similar expression.

the 3rd, 16th and 18th days. On the 22nd day, Memphis (*Me-im-bi*), [its royal re]sidence [was con]quered. Its king escaped (but) his son and [brother] were [cap]tured. It (i.e. Egypt) was looted, its inhabitants were made prisoners, its possessions carried away.

Eleventh year: The king (remained) in Assyria. He executed m[any of his] officials.

Twelfth year: The king of Assyria [went to Egypt]. He fell sick on the way and died (lit.: "fate") in the month of Arahshamnu, the 10th day. For 12 years was Esarhaddon king of Assyria. Both his sons, Shamash-shumukin in Babylonia, Ashurbanipal in Assyria, sat down upon the throne.

Accession-year of Shamashshumukin: In the month of Aiaru, Bel and the (other) gods of Akkad went forth from *Libbi-âli* (i.e. Ashur) and entered Babylon in the month of Aiaru, the 12th day. In the same year, the town Kirbitum was seized, its king was caught. In the month of Tebitu, the 20th day, Beletir, the (chief) justice of Babylon was seized and executed.

2. TEXT FROM THE FIRST YEAR OF ESARHADDON TO THE FIRST YEAR OF SHAMASHSHUMUKIN

The Esarhaddon Chronicle (British Museum 25,091) published by Sidney Smith, in *Babylonian Historical Texts*, Pls. I-III; transliteration and translation, pp. 12 ff. It belongs to the same "series" as the text translated on pp. 266-267.

[First year: . . .] the king of Elam . . . Esarhaddon. . . . In the month Ululu the Great God and the (other) gods of Der [went] . . . the gods Humbabaia[1] and Shimali[a]. . . . In the month Tashritu the (illegible)[2] was inaugurated. In the month. . . .

Second year: The major-domo [ordered a *biḫirtu*] in Akkad. In the same year the town Arza[ni]a was seized, its booty ca[rried away . . .], the [inhabitant]s made prisoners, king and crown[prince] put in [fet]ters. Battles were foug[ht] against the Bu[da]u and the Cymmerians, (and) in Kushehni.

Third year: [. . .]-ahheshullim, the g ú . e n . n a -official (and) Shamashibni, the "Dakkurean," were brought to Assyria and killed in Assyria.

Fourth year: The town of Sidon (*Ṣi-da-nu*) was seized, its booty carried away. In the (same) year the major-domo ordered a *biḫirtu* in Akkad.

Fifth year: In the month Du'uzu, the 2nd day, the troops of Assyria seized the town Bassa. In the month of [Tashritu] the head of the king of Sidon (*Ṣa-'-i-du-nu*) was cut off and brought to Assyria.

Sixth year: The troops of Assyria marched against Militene (*Mi-li-du*).[3] They laid siege against Mugallu. In the month of Ululu, the 5th day, the life of Humbahaldashu, king of [Ela]m, came to an end in his palace; he was not sick but in good health. Humbahaldashu ruled as king in Elam for six years. His brother Urtagu sat down on the throne in Elam. The g ú . e n . n a -official Nadinshumi (and) Kudurru, the "Dakkurean," were brought away (to Assyria).

Seventh year: In the month of Addaru, the 8th day, the army of Assyria [fought] against the town Shamele.[4] In the same year, the Ishtar-(image) of Agade and the (other) gods of Agade [came] from [Elam], in the month of Addaru, the 10th day, [they entered] the town Agade.

Eighth year: In the month of Addaru, the 6th day, the wife of the king di[ed].

(reverse)

In the month of Addaru, the 18th day, the troops of Assyria seized the country Shupr[isa], they carried away its booty.

Tenth year: In the month of Nisanu, the troops of Assyria [marched against Egypt]. In the month Du'uzu, the 3rd day, a battle [was fought] in Egypt.

Eleventh year: The king of Assyria [slew] many of his high officials.

Twelfth year: The king of Assyria went to Egypt. He fell sick on the journey and died in the month of Arahshamnu, the 10th day. Esarhaddon ruled as king in Assyria for 12 years.

(For) 8 years (under) Sennacherib, (for) 12 years (under) Esarhaddon (in summa for) 20 years (the image of) Bel stayed in Ashur and the New Year's Festival was (therefore) interrupted; Nebo did not come from Bo[rsi]ppa for the ["Proc]ession of Bel." In the month of Kislimu, Ashurbanipal, [his] s[on] sat down on the throne in Assyria.

Accession-year of Shamashshumukin: In the month of Aiaru, Bel and the (other) gods of [Akkad] went out from Ashur and, in the month of Aiaru, the 25th day, [they entered] Babylon. Nebo and the (other) gods of Bor[si]ppa c[ame] to Babylon. In the same year the town of Kirbitu was seized, its king cap[tured]. In the month of Tebitu, the 20th day, the (chief) justice of Babylon was sei[zed and executed].

First year of Shamashshumukin: [The army of Assyria marched] against [Egypt], Tirhakah (*Tarqû*) king of Eg[ypt] . . . , the country of Eg[ypt] . . . Necho [king of] Egypt. . . .

(balance broken)

3. TEXT FROM THE TENTH TO THE SEVENTEENTH YEAR OF NABOPOLASSAR: EVENTS LEADING TO THE FALL OF NINEVEH

C. J. Gadd, *The Newly Discovered Babylonian Chronicle*, No. 21,901, in the British Museum (London, 1923), with transliteration and translation. cf. also, J. Lewy, Forschungen zur alten Geschichte Vorderasiens, in *MVAG*, XXIX (1924), 69 ff., and E. Ebeling, *AOT*, 362 ff.

Tenth year: In the month Aiaru, Nabopolassar called up the army of Akkad and marched (upstream) on the

1 For the god Humbaba, cf. S. I. Feigin, in *Analecta Orientalia*, XII (1936), 94 ff.; for Shimalia, A. Deimel, *Pantheon Babylonicum* (Rome, 1914), No. 3209.

2 Landsberger-Bauer (*ZA*, XXXVII [NF III], 74) transliterate *ḳisalla-šu šu-ur-ru*, but the first sign is certainly not k i s a l and the first of the two *šu* signs is different from the second. S. Smith's interpretation of this enigmatic passage (cf. *Babylonian Historical Texts*, p. 16) is not acceptable.

3 cf. for the reading, Landsberger-Bauer, *ZA*, XXXVII (NF III), 77.

4 cf. for this town, Landsberger-Bauer, *op.cit.*, p. 85.

embankment of the Euphrates. The people of the countries Suhu and Hindanu did not fight against him, but deposited their tributes before him. In the month Abu, the Assyrian army took up battle position[1] in the town Qablinu and Nabopolassar marched upstream against them. In the month Abu, the 12th day, he made an attack against the soldiers of Assyria and they fell back before him. A great defeat was (thus) inflicted upon Assyria and they took many of them as prisoners. They (also) seized the Mannaeans who had come to their (i.e. the Assyrians') assistance and high officials of Assyria. The same day the town of Qablinu was captured. In the same month of Abu, the king of Akkad[2] sent his soldiers against the towns Mane, Sahiru and Balihu[3] and they took much booty from them and carried many of them as prisoners away. They (also) led their gods away. In the month Ululu, the king of Akkad and his army turned back and on his march he took the (inhabitants of the) town Hindanu and their gods to Babylon. In the month Tashritu, the army of Egypt and the army of Assyria advanced as far as Qablinu—in the pursuit of the king of Akkad—(but) did not overtake the king of Akkad (and) they turned back.[4] In the month Addaru, the army of Assyria and the army of Akkad were fighting against each other in the town Madanu which (belongs to the district of) Arrapha. The army of Assyria fell back before the army of Akkad and they inflicted a great defeat upon them. They threw them into the river Zab. They seized their ch[ariots][5] and horses (and) took much booty from them. Many of his [high officials] they made cross the Tigris with them and brought them to Babylon.

[Eleventh year: The king] of Akkad called up his army and marched (upstream) on the embankment of the Tigris and pitched (his camp) against the town of Ashur. In the month Simanu, the [. . .]th day, he made an attack against the town, but he did not seize it. The king of Assyria called up[6] his army and the king of Akkad disengaged himself from Ashur and retired as far as the town Takritain, in Assyria, on the banks of the Tigris. The king of Akkad garrisoned his army in the citadel of Takritain. The king of Assyria and his soldiers pitched (camp) against the army of the king of Akkad which was (thus) [sh]ut up in Takritain and attacked them for 10 days but did not seize the town. The army of the king of Akkad (although) shut up in the citadel (thus) inflicted a great defeat on Assyria. The king of Assyria and his army [gave up] and he returned to his country. In the month Arahshamnu, the Medians came down into the province of Arrapha and attacked the town of. . . .

Twelfth year: When, in the month Abu, the Medians

1 Following Landsberger-Bauer, *ZA*, xxxvii (NF iii), 85.

2 cf. J. Lewy, Forschungen zur alten Geschichte Vorderasiens (*MVAG*, xxix/2, 1925), 93, for this change of style. The "king of Akkad" is simply called "Nabopolassar" in the preceding lines of the text.

3 For this town, cf. E. Forrer, *Provinzeinteilung*, pp. 8, 24.

4 Following Landsberger-Bauer, *op.cit.*, p. 85.

5 This restoration is suggested by the size of the break and by the context.

6 Instead of the usual *id-ḳi-e-ma* (cf., e.g. lines 1, 16, 32, etc.), the text has here: *id-ḳam-ma*.

. . . against Nineveh . . . they rushed and seized the town of Tarbisu, a town belonging to the province of Nineveh, . . . they went downstream on the embankment of the Tigris and pitched (camp) against Ashur. They made an attack against the town and [took the town], [the wall of] the town was torn down, a terrible defeat/massacre they inflicted upon the entire population. They took booty (and) carried pri[soners away]. The king of Akkad and his army who went to the aid of the Medians did not come (in time) for the battle. The to[wn was already taken]. The king of Akkad and Cyaxares (*U-ma-ḳiš-tar*) met each other before[7] the town and established among themselves good relations and friendship. . . . [Cyax]ares and his army returned to his country, the king of Akkad and his army returned to his country.

[Thirteenth year: In the month Ai]aru the inhabitants of the country of Suhu revolted against the king of Akkad and resorted to hostilities. The king of Akkad called up his army and marched against Suhu. In the month Simanu, the 4th day, he made an attack against Rahilu, a town situated (on an island) amidst the Euphrates, and seized the town the very same day. (Then) he built a . . . ; stones from the banks of the Euphrates they piled up in front of it . . . ; against the city Anat he pitched (camp). [He constru]cted a turret[8] [at] the west side . . . , he brought the turret near to the wall, and made an attack against the city [(but) he did not(?) seize it]. [In the month] . . . the king of Assyria and his army came downstream and the king of Akkad and his army made a turnabout and [returned to his country].[9]

(reverse)

[Fourteenth year:] The king of Akkad cal[led up] his army and [Cyaxar]es,[10] the king of the Manda-hordes (*Umman-manda*)[10a] marched towards the king of Akkad, [in] . . . they met each other. The king of Akkad . . . and [Cyaxar]es . . . [the . . .]s he ferried across and they marched (upstream) on the embankment of the Tigris and . . . [pitched camp] against Nineveh. . . . From the month Simanu till the month Abu, three ba[ttles were fought, then] they made a great attack against the city. In the month Abu, [the . . . th day, the city was seized and a great defeat] he inflicted [upon the] entire [population]. On that day, Sinsharishkun, king of Assy[ria fled to] . . . , many prisoners of the city, beyond counting, they carried

7 Text: *ina muḫḫi* (against Landsberger-Bauer, *op.cit.*, pp. 85 f.).

8 The word *ṣapîtu* refers here to a (wooden) tower used for the siege of a walled town. As indicated by the etymology of *ṣapîtu* (*ṣapû* "to look out, watch"), the word seems to refer primarily to wooden structures erected outside of the cities to watch the approach to fields and orchards. cf. the Neo-Babylonian letter, Thompson, *CT*, xxii 53:10, referring to this watch-duty with *ṣa-pi-tum*, and the contemporaneous texts, Strassmaier, *Cyr.* 236:1,6, *VS*, iii 69:15, 86:12, vi 271:16 (correct Ungnad, Glossar to *NRV*, i, 143!), denoting the fee paid by the tenant of an orchard for this service equally with *ṣapîtu*.

9 Restored after Gadd, *op.cit.*, p. 34, n.3.

10 Text: [*U-ma-ḳi-iš*]*-tar(!)* according to Landsberger-Bauer, *ZA*, xxxvii (NF iii), 87.

10a For the expression *umman-manda*, cf. Landsberger-Bauer, *ZA*, xxxvii (NF iii), 82 f.

away. The city [they turned] into ruin-hills and hea[ps (of debris). The king] and the army of Assyria escaped (however) before the king (of Akkad) and [the army] of the king of Akkad. . . . In the month Ululu, the 20th day, Cyaxares and his army returned to his country. Afterwards, the king of A[kkad] . . . marched as far as Nisibis. Booty and *ga-lu-tu* of . . . and (of) the country Rusapu they brought to the king of Akkad, to Nineveh. [In the month] . . . Ashuruballit[11] . . . sat down in Harran upon the throne to become king of Assyria. Till the month . . . [the king of Akkad stayed] in Nineveh. . . . From the 20th day of the month [Tashritu] the king [of Akkad] . . . in the same month of Tashritu in the town. . . .

Fifteenth year: In the month Du'uzu . . . [the king of] Akkad [called up his army and] marched against Assyria. . . . [He marched around in Assyria] unopposed (lit.: like a ruler). The army of the country Hazzu, Han[. . .] and of the country *Šu*[. . .][12] he met/reached. [Their] bo[oty] they took and prisoners [they carried away] from there. In the month Arahshamnu, the king of Akkad o[rdered] the return of his army and [pitched camp] against the town Rugguliti . . . he made an attack against the town and seized the town in the month Arahshamnu, the 28th day, not one man [escaped] . . . [and he] returned [to] his [country].

Sixteenth year: In the month Aiaru, the king of Akkad called up his army and marched against Assyria. From the month [Aiaru] to the month Arahshamnu they marched around in Assyria unopposed. In the month Arahshamnu, the Manda-hordes (*Umman-manda*) . . . came to the aid of the king of Akkad and they merged their armies and marched against Harran, against [Ashuruball]it who had sat down on the throne in Assyria. Fear of the enemy befell Ashuruballit and the soldiers of the country Gul[[13] . . . who] had come [to his aid] and they le[ft] the town and . . . crossed [the river Euphrates]. The king of Akkad arrived at the town Harran and [made an attack and] seized the town. Many prisoners, beyond counting, he carried away from the town. In the month Addaru the king of Akkad . . . he dismissed/left, and he returned to his country and the Manda-hordes who had come to the aid of the king of Akkad we[nt and re]turned [to their country].

⟨Seventeenth year:⟩ In the month Du'uzu, Ashuruballit, king of Assyria, (and) a large [army of] E[gy]pt [who had come to his aid] crossed the river (Euphrates) and [marched on] to conquer Harran. [He laid siege to the town and] entered it, but the garrison which the king of Akkad had laid therein killed them[14] (the assault party) and (then) he pit[ched (camp)] against the town Harran. Till the month Ululu he made attack(s) against the town. Nothing, however, did he ac[h]ieve and they returned.[15] . . . The king of Akkad came to the aid of his troops and . . . an attack. [Then] he went up to the country [I]zalla[16] and . . . the towns of many regions . . . their . . . he burnt down. At the same time the army [of the Manda-hordes] . . . as far as the province of Urartu . . . in the country Ahs[a . . .] they made booty . . . the garrisons which the ki[ng of . . .] they [. . .]ed and to the town . . . they went up. [In the month] . . . the king of Akkad returned to his country.

Catchline: In the [eighteenth] ye[ar]: [In the month] . . . the king of Akkad called up his army and. . . .

[11] cf. Gadd, *op.cit.*, p. 35, n.2.

[12] Lewy (*MVAG*, XXIX/2, 1925, 85) reads *Šu*[*ppa*].

[13] Lewy (*op.cit.*) proposes to read *Mi*(?)-[*ṣir*], i.e. E[gypt].

[14] cf. Landsberger-Bauer, *ZA*, XXXVII (NF III), 88.

[15] cf. W. F. Albright, *JBL*, LI (1932), 87, n.33.

[16] cf. Gadd, *op.cit.*, p. 36, n.2.

4. TEXT FROM THE ACCESSION YEAR OF NABONIDUS TO THE FALL OF BABYLON

So-called Nabonidus-Chronicle, first published by T. G. Pinches, *TSBA*, VII (1882), 139 ff., then by Sidney Smith, in *Babylonian Historical Texts, Relating to the Downfall of Babylon* (London, 1924), Pls. XI-XIV, pp. 110 ff.

(i)

(First line destroyed, accession year) . . . his . . . he lifted. The king . . . their [. . .]*mati* they brought to Babylon. (one line destroyed).

[First year:] . . . they did (unintelligible)[1] and he did not lift [his . . .]. All their families. . . . The king called up his army and . . . against (the country) Hume.[2] (one line destroyed)

[Second year: In] the month Tebitu in the country of Hamath . . .

(one line not inscribed)

[Third year: In] the month of Abu, to the Amananus, the mountains of . . . fruit trees, all kinds of fruits . . . [he sent] from them to Babylon.[3]

[The king fell] sick but he recovered. In the month Kislimu, the king [called up] his army . . . and ^{d}*Nabû*-^{d}EN(?).DAN.ŠEŠ . . . of Amurru to. . . . [Against the town A]dummu they pitched (camp) . . . and the numerous troops . . . the town Shindini . . . he killed him (one line destroyed).

[Sixth year: . . . King Ishtumegu] called up his

(ii)

troops and marched against Cyrus, king of Anshan, in order to me[et him in battle]. The army of Ishtumegu revolted against him and in fetters[4] they de[livered him] to Cyrus. Cyrus ⟨marched⟩ against the country Agamtanu; the royal residence ⟨he seized⟩; silver, gold, (other) valuables . . . of the country Agamtanu he took as booty and brought (them) to Anshan. The valuables of. . .

[1] Text: *iš-ḫu-ḫu-ma*.

[2] The country Ḫumê (cancel in Bezold, *Glossar*, pp. 122b **ḫumû*, "Aufruehrer" against Zehnpfund-Langdon, *VAB*, IV, 303) is also attested in contemporaneous administrative documents, cf., e.g. Strassmaier, *Nbn.*, 571 1:35, 37, 40, Tremayne, *YOS*, VI 210:14, and Dougherty, *GCCI*, II, 53:2—in all cases as the homeland of iron. cf. also, E. F. Weidner, in *Mélanges Dussaud*, II, 935. The location of this country remains obscure.

[3] The British Museum text Sp. II, 407 published by J. N. Strassmaier, *Hebraica*, IX (1892), 4 f., transliterated and translated by E. F. Weidner, *JSOR*, VI (1922), 112 ff. seems to report more in detail on the events of the third year (mentioning the country Hatti and the town *Am-ma-na-nu*). The nature of this text remains, however, obscure.

[4] Text: *ina qātē*^{II} *ṣa-bit*.

Seventh year: The king (i.e. Nabonidus, stayed) in Tema;[5] the crown prince, his officials and his army (were) in Akkad. The king did not come to Babylon [for the ceremonies of the month of Nisanu]; the (image of the) god Nebo did not come to Babylon, the (image of the) god Bel did not go out (of Esagila in procession), the fest[ival of the New Year was omitted], (but) the offerings within (the temples) Esagila and Ezida were given according [to the complete (ritual)]; the *urigallu*[6] -priest made the libation and asperged the temple.

Eighth year: (blank of two lines)

Ninth year: Nabonidus, the king, (stayed) in Tema; the crown prince, the officials and the army (were) in Akkad. The king did not come to Babylon for the (ceremony of the) month of Nisanu; the god Nebo did not come to Babylon, the god Bel did not go out (of Esagila in procession), the festival of the New Year was omitted. (But) the offerings in Esagila and Ezida for the gods of ⟨Babylon⟩ and Borsippa were given according to the complete (ritual). In the month of Nisanu the 5th day, the mother of the king died in Dur-karashu[7] which is on the banks of the Euphrates, above Sippar. The crown prince and his army were in deep mourning for three days, a(n official) "weeping" was performed. In Akkad, a(n official) "weeping" on behalf of the mother of the king was performed in the month of Simanu. In the month of Nisanu, Cyrus, king of Persia, called up his army and crossed the Tigris below the town Arbela. In the month Aiaru [he marched] against the country Ly[dia] . . . killed its king, took his possessions, put (there) a garrison of his own. Afterwards, his garrison as well as the king *remained* there.

Tenth year: The king (stayed) in Tema; the crown prince, his officials and his army (were) in Akkad. The king did not come to Babylon for the (ceremonies of the) month Nisanu, Nebo did not come to Babylon, Bel did not go out (of Esagila in procession), the festival of the New Year was omitted, (but) the offerings in Esagila and Ezida for the gods of Babylon and Borsippa were given according to the complete (ritual). In the month Simanu, the 21st day, . . . of the country of the Elamites in Akkad . . . the governor in Uruk. . . .

Eleventh year: The king (stayed) in Tema; the crown prince, the officials and his army (were) in Akkad. The king did not come to Babylon for the (ceremonies of the) month Nisanu, Nebo did not come to Babylon, Bel did not go out (from Esagila in procession), the festival of the New Year was omitted, (but) the offerings for the gods of Babylon and Borsippa were given according to the complete (ritual).

(iii reverse)

. . . Tigris . . . [In the month of] Addaru the (image of the) Ishtar of Uruk . . . the . . . [the . . .]s of the Sea Country . . . [arm]y [made an] at[tack]. . . .

[Seventeenth year:] . . . Nebo [went] from Borsippa for the procession of [Bel . . .] [the king] entered the temple É.tùr.kalam.ma, in the t[emple] . . . (partly unintelligible).[8] [Be]l went out (in procession), they performed the festival of the New Year according to the complete (ritual). In the month of . . . [Lugal-Marada and the other gods] of the town Marad, Zababa and the (other) gods of Kish, the goddess Ninlil [and the other gods of] Hursagkalama entered Babylon. Till the end of the month Ululu (all) the gods of Akkad . . . those from above the IM[9] and (those from) below the IM, entered Babylon. The gods from Borsippa, Kutha, . . . and Sippar (however) did not enter. In the month of Tashritu, when Cyrus attacked the army of Akkad in Opis on the Tigris, the inhabitants of Akkad revolted, but he (*Nabonidus*) massacred the confused inhabitants.[10] The 15th day, Sippar was seized without battle. Nabonidus fled. The 16th day, Gobryas (*Ugbaru*), the governor of Gutium and the army of Cyrus entered Babylon without battle. Afterwards Nabonidus was arrested in Babylon when he returned (there). Till the end of the month, the shield(-carrying)[11] Gutians were staying within Esagila (but) nobody carried arms[12] in Esagila and its (pertinent) buildings, the correct time (for a ceremony) was not missed. In the month of Arahshamnu, the 3rd day, Cyrus entered Babylon, green twigs[13] were spread in front of him—the state of "Peace" (*šulmu*) was imposed upon the city. Cyrus sent greetings to all Babylon. Gobryas, his governor, installed (sub-)governors in Babylon. From the month of Kislimu to the month of Addaru, the gods of Akkad which Nabonidus had made come down to Babylon . . . returned to their sacred cities. In the month of Arahshamnu, on the night of the 11th day, Gobyras died. In the month of [Arahshamnu, the . . .th day, the wi]fe of the king died. From the 27th day of Arahshamnu till the 3rd day of Nisanu a(n official) "weeping" was performed in Akkad, all the people (went around) with their hair disheveled.[14] When, the 4th day, Cambyses, son of Cyrus, went to the temple é.NÍG.PA[15].kalam.ma.sum.ma, the É.PA priest

[5] Nabonidus' prolonged and apparently unmotivated stay in Tema has given rise to an extended literature which has been recently discussed by Julius Lewy, in *HUCA*, XIX, 434 ff. (add: R. P. Dougherty, *Mizraim*, I [1933], 140 ff.; the same, *JAOS*, XLII [1922], 305 ff.; the same, in *AJA*, XXXIV [1930], 296 ff.; cf. also, W. F. Albright, *JRAS*, 1925, 293 ff.).

[6] For the important role of the *urigallu* -priest at the New Year's Festival of Esagila, cf. F. Thureau-Dangin, *Rituels accadiens* (Paris, 1921), p. 129, n.1.

[7] Lit.: Walled Camp.

[8] I propose to read this difficult passage: [^{ma}]^{t} *Tam-tim nabalkatum* (written: BAL^{tum}) *nabalkutum* (written: $^{nab(!)}$BAL.KI^{tum}) šà x[. . .] and to translate it tentatively: "The Sea Country made a short invasion. . . ." This incident seems to have occurred during the New Year's Festival.

[9] It does not seem likely—as S. Smith, *op.cit.*, p. 121, assumes—that this unique characterization refers to a division between the gods "above and below the earth," which is not attested elsewhere.

[10] Text: BAL.KI SAR.SAR *nišē*^{mes} *idûk*. cf. for SAR.SAR above n.2.

[11] For ^{masak}*tukku*, cf. Meissner, *BAWb.*, I, 66.

[12] Text: *til-la . . . ul is-sa-kin*, literally: "trappings" (for armor and/or weapons were not put on." cf. the parallel expression sub n.4, p. 315.

[13] For *ḫaranu* denoting stalks, cf. the syllabary passage, von Soden, *ZA*, XLIII (NF IX), 237:81 ff. (=von Soden, *Akkadische Synonymenlisten*, No. 9b) and the passages from Neo-Babylonian business documents: Dougherty, *GCCI*, I, 188:3-4, ^{qan}*di-pa-ra-nu sá ḫa-ra-ni-e* "torches made of (reed)stalks," and *ibid.*, 11:10, *uṭṭatu šá ḫa-ra-ni-e* "barley *on the stalk*."

[14] For *qaqqadu patâru*, cf. below n.14, p. 314.

[15] The sign NÍG.PA which occurs here and in other Neo-Babylonian historical inscriptions (while the scepter inscription published by E. Ebeling,

of Nebo who . . . the bull . . . they came (and) made the "weaving" by means of the *handles*[16] and when [he le]d the image of Ne[bo . . . sp]ears and leather quivers, from. . . . Nebo returned to Esagila, sheep-offerings in front of Bel and the god *Mâ*[*r*]-*b*[*îti*].

(iv reverse)

(After lacuna, only the ends of 9 lines are preserved.)

HISTORICAL DOCUMENTS

I. NEBUCHADNEZZAR II (605-562)

(a) The Expedition to Syria

From the so-called Wadi-Brisa Inscription, published by F. H. Weissbach: *Die Inschriften Nebukadnezars II im Wadi Brissa und am Nahr el-Kelb* (Leipzig, 1906) (*WVDOG*, v). For the latest translation, cf. Zehnpfund-Langdon, in *VAB*, iv, 151 ff.

(ix 1—x 40)

(Two lines destroyed) [from] the Upper Sea [to] the Lower Sea (one line destroyed) . . . which Marduk, my lord, has entrusted to me, I have made . . . the city of Babylon to the foremost among all the countries and every human habitation; its name I have [made/elevated] to the (most worthy of) praise among the sacred cities. . . . The sanctuaries of my lords Nebo and Marduk (as a) wise (ruler) . . . always. . . .

At that time, the Lebanon (*La-ab-na-a-nu*), the [Cedar] Mountain, the luxurious forest of Marduk, the smell of which is sweet, the hi[gh] cedars of which, (its) pro[duct], another god [*has not desired*, which] no other king has *fe*[*lled*] . . . my *nâbû*[1] Marduk [had desired] as a fitting adornment for the palace of the *ruler* of heaven and earth, (this Lebanon) over which a foreign enemy was ruling and robbing (it of) its riches—its people were scattered, had fled to a far (away region). (Trusting) in the power of my lords Nebo and Marduk, I organized [my army] for a[n expedition] to the Lebanon. I made that country happy by eradicating its enemy everywhere (lit.: below and above). All its scattered inhabitants I led back to their settlements (lit.: collected and reinstalled). What no former king had done (I achieved): I cut through steep mountains, I split rocks, opened passages and (thus) I constructed a straight road for the (transport of the) cedars. I made the Arahtu flo[at][2] (down) and carry to Marduk, my king, mighty cedars, high and strong, of precious beauty and of excellent dark quality, the abundant yield of the Lebanon, as (if they be) reed stalks (carried by) the river. Within Babylon [*I stored*] mulberry wood. I made the inhabitants of the Lebanon live in safety together and let nobody disturb them. In order that nobody might do any harm [to them] I ere[cted there] a stela (showing) me (as) everlasting king (of this region) and built . . . I, myself, . . . established . . .

(x)

(four lines destroyed) . . . people . . . to . . . towards the entrance to the mountain. . . . Beside my statue as king . . . I wrote an inscription mentioning my name, . . . I erected for posterity. May future [kings] res[pect the *monuments*], remember the praise of the gods (inscribed thereupon). [He who] respects . . . my royal name, who does not abrogate my statutes (and) not change my decrees, [his throne] shall be secure, his [li]fe last long, his dynasty shall continue (lit.: renew itself)! Rain from the sky, [fl]ood [water] from (the interior of) the earth shall be given to him con[tinually] as a present! He himself shall rule peacefully and in abundance.

O Marduk, my lord, do remember my deeds favorably as good [deeds], may (these) my good deeds be always before your mind (so that) my walking in Esagila and Ezida—which I love—may last to old age. May I (remain) always your legitimate governor (*šakanakku*), may I pull your yoke till (I am) sated with progeny, may my name be remembered in future (days) in a good sense, may my offspring rule forever over the black-headed.

(b) The Court of Nebuchadnezzar

From a prism in Istanbul (No. 7834), found in Babylon, and published (photograph, transliteration, and translation) by E. Unger, in *Babylon, die heilige Stadt* (Berlin-Leipzig, 1931), pp. 282-294 (Pls. 52-56).

(iii 33—v 29)

I ordered the (following) court officials in exercise of (their) duties to take up position in my (official) suite:

As *mašennu* -officials[1] Nabuzeriddinam, the chief cook, Nabuzeribni, the chief armorer (Lord High Steward), [E]rib[. . .] in charge of the palace officials, Sinshar[ilani(?)], the major-domo, Atkal-ana-Mar-Esagila

(iv)

[the . . .] (two names broken), Inaqibit-Bel [the . . .], Bel-erish, the chief [. . .], Ardia, the *mašennu* of the "House-of-the-Palace-Women," Beluballit, the secretary of the "House-of-the-Palace-Women," Silla,

in *Analecta Orientalia*, xii [1936] (Eine Weihinschrift Assuretililanis für Marduk, lines 10 and 18 and Legrain, *UM*, xv, 80, ii:19, show GIŠ.NÍG.PA) has no reading listed in Deimel, *ŠL*. Dr. Geers has drawn my attention to other occurrences of this sign group such as, e.g. *TCL*, vi, 53:7-8 (bilingual text).

16 Text: *ina šu-lu-pu uš-bi-nim-ma* "they made the ritual 'weaving' motions (*ba'û* iii/ii cf. F. K. Mueller, *MVAG*, xli/3 [1937], 83, and *ZA*, xlv [NF x], 213) by means of the *šulupu*." This word is also mentioned in Thureau-Dangin, *Rituels accadiens*, p. 91 (text, p. 72), rev. 4 *šul-pu ḫurāṣi mê*^{mes} *qātē*^{II} "golden handles/lugs of the hand-basin"; the same words recur in the text Strassmaier, *Darius*, 373:9 *šul-pu(!) šá me-e qātē*^{II} while an earthen *šulpu* -container is mentioned in A. Falkenstein, *Literarische Keilschrifttexte aus Uruk* (Berlin, 1931), No. 51:rev. 5. Further references to this word I intend to discuss elsewhere.

1 Text: *na-a-bu-u-a*.

2 Read: *uš(!)-te-qi*[*l-pu-ma*].

1 cf. for this word (cf. also Strassmaier, *Dar.* 244:12) denoting a high court-official, B. Landsberger, *ZA*, xli (NF vii), 298, who, however, rejects the obvious connection with Hebr. *mišneh* which is now made even more likely by the occurrence of Ugaritic *ṯnn* (cf. T. H. Gaster, in *JAOS*, lxvi [1946], 56, n.8; R. Langhe, *Les Textes de Ras Shamra-Ugarit, etc.* [Paris, 1945], ii, 398 f.) and—in the syllabic writing—of ^{amel}*šanani* (cf. Virolleaud, *RA*, xxxviii [1941], 8 f.). These references have been indicated to me by Dr. T. H. Gaster. cf. finally the denomination *šinaḫila* given a high official in the texts from Boğazköy and discussed by A. Ungnad, in *ZAW*, 1923, 207 (for further literature, cf. E. A. Speiser, in *AASOR*, xvi [1936], 134).

the chief master-of-*ceremonies*,[2] Nabuahusur, the chief of the engineers,[3] Mushallim-Marduk, Nabu-ushibshi (and) Eribshu, the overseers (lit.: heads) of the slave-girls, Nabubelusur, overseer of the slave-girls, Nabuzeribni, the cupbearer, Nergalresua, the chief of the singers, Ardi-Nabu, the *sipiru* -official[4] of the crown prince, Eaidanni, the chief of the cattle,[5] Rimutu, the chief of the cattle, Nabumarsharriusur, the chief of the sailors, (and) Hanunu,[6] the chief of the royal merchants;

(and as) the officials of the country Akkad (i.e. Babylon):[7] Eadaian, the governor of the Sea(-Country), Nergalsharusur, the *Sîn-magir*,[8] Emuqahi(?), (the governor) of Tupliash, Belshumishkun (the governor) of Puqudu, Bibbea, the Dakkurean,[9] Nadinahi, the "official"[10] of Der, Marduksharusur (the governor) of Gambulu, Marduksharrani, the district officer of Sumandar, Belidarum, the Amuqean,[9] Rimutu, the regular governor of Zame, Beletirnapshate, the governor of Iaptiru, the "official"[10] of

(v)

. . . , Mushezib-Bel, the "official" of . . . ,

(and as) the "officials":[10] Shumkenum, the "official" of the town Dur-[Iakin], Bania, the "official" of the town Limetum, Mardukzeribni, the "official" of the town Matakallu, Shula, the "official" of the town Nimid-Laguda, Shuma, the "official" of the town Kullab, Nergalzeribin, the "official" of the town Udannum, Mardukerish, the "official" of the town Larsa, Nabukinapli, the "official" of the town Kissik, Belupahhir, the "official" of the town of Bakushu;

(and as) *qêpu* -officials of cities: Iba, the district officer of Dur-[. . .], Shalambili, the district officer of . . . , Ziria, the district officer of . . . , Zabina, the *qêpu* -official of . . . , Shuma, the *qêpu* -official of . . . , Adadahiddinam, the district officer of the town . . . , Nabuzerukin (officer) of the country A[. . .], Anumepush, the *qêpu* -official of . . . , Belshumishkun, the *qêpu* -official of the town N[i . . .];

(furthermore): the king of Tyre, the king of Gaza, the king of Sidon, the king of Arvad, the king of Ashdod, the king of Mir[. . .], the king of . . .[11]

[2] Text: ^{amel}*rab ri-e-di ḳi-ib-su*. Both words mean "custom," "mores," "correct behavior," "intelligence," or the like.

[3] For *qallapu* "sapper," cf. Meissner, *BAWb.*, I, 86, n.93, Thureau-Dangin, *VIII*[e] *Campagne*, p. 66, n.1.

[4] For *sipiru*, cf. my remarks in *BASOR*, No. 93 (1944), 15, n.6.

[5] Text: ^{amel}*rab bu-ú-lu(!)*.

[6] Note the "Phoenician" name of this official.

[7] This line and lines iii 35, iv 20, v 3, 13 are probably to be considered the headings of the following enumerations of officials (against Landsberger, in *ZA*, XLI [NF VII], 298).

[8] For the official called *Sîn-māgir*, cf. Streck, *Assurbanipal*, II, 62, n.1; E. Unger, *Theologische Literaturzeitung* (1925), col. 482. Also, Pohl, *Analecta Orientalia*, VIII (1933), 56:7, 12, 14, with the spelling ^{amel}*si-im-ma-gir*.

[9] *mâr* ^{m}*Da-ḳu-ru* is here a title; cf. above n.3, p. 273. In line 30 we have an exactly parallel denomination of an official, *mâr* ^{m}*A-mu-ḳa-nim*.

[10] The ideogram-group l ú É.BAR cannot mean here *šangu* (cf. Deimel, *ŠL*, 324/27b); the translation "official" is only provisional.

[11] The king of Judah is not mentioned here, but E. F. Weidner has published a group of texts which indicates that this king was receiving a pension from the royal Babylonian household. cf. below.

(c) Varia

(1) From administrative documents found in Babylon, some information concerning the fate of Jehoiachin, king of Judah, can be gathered. *Text and translation*: E. F. Weidner, Jojachin, König von Juda, in babylonischen Keilschrifttexten (*Mélanges syriens offerts à Monsieur René Dussaud*, II [Paris, 1939], 923-935), has published a small group of texts excavated by the German expedition in Babylon and dating from the 10th to the 35th year of Nebuchadnezzar II. The tablets list deliveries of oil for the subsistence of individuals who are either prisoners of war or otherwise dependent upon the royal household. They are identified by name, profession, and/or nationality. The two tablets, so far published, also mention, beside Judeans, inhabitants of Ashkelon, Tyre, Byblos, Arvad, and, further, Egyptians, Medeans, Persians, Lydians, and Greeks.

(text Babylon 28122, obverse 29-33)

. . . t[o?] *Ia-'-ú-ḳin*, king . . .
to the *qîpūtu*-house of . . .
. . . for Shalamiamu, the . . .
. . . for 126 men from Tyre . . .
. . . for Zabiria, the Ly[dian] . . .

(text Babylon 28178, obverse ii 38-40)

10 (*sila* of oil) to . . . [*Ia*]-*'-ḳin*, king of *Ia*[. . .]
2½ *sila* (oil) to [. . . so]ns of the king of Judah (*Ia-a-ḫu-du*)
4 *sila* to 8 men from Judah (^{amel}*Ia-a-ḫu-da-a-a*) . . .

(text Babylon 28186, reverse ii 13-18)

1½ *sila* (oil) for 3 carpenters from Arvad, ½ *sila* each
11½ *sila* for 8 ditto from Byblos, 1 sila each . . .
3½ *sila* for 7 ditto, Greeks, ½ sila each
½ *sila* to *Nabû-êṭir* the carpenter
10 (*sila*) to *Ia-ḳu-ú-ḳi-nu*, the son of the king of *Ia-ḳu-du* (i.e. Judah)
2½ *sila* for the 5 sons of the king of Judah (*Ia-ḳu-du*) through Qana'a [. . .]

(2) From a fragmentary historical text (BrM 78-10-15, 22, 37, and 38), published (last publication) by N. Strassmaier, *Nbḳ.* No. 329. cf. also, H. Winckler, *Altorientalische Forschungen* (Leipzig, 1897), pp. 511 ff. ("Pittakos?"). Translation: Zehnpfund-Langdon, in *VAB*, IV, 206 f.

(13—22)

. . . [in] the 37th year, Nebuchadnezzar, king of Bab[ylon] mar[ched against] Egypt (*Mi-ṣir*) to deliver a battle. [*Ama*]*sis* (text: [. . .]-*a(?)-su*), of Egypt, [called up his a]rm[y] . . . [. . .]*ḳu* from the town *Puṭu-Iaman* . . . distant regions which (are situated on islands) amidst the sea . . . many . . . which/who (are) in Egypt . . . [car]rying weapons, horses and [chariot]s . . . he called up to assist him and . . . did [. . .] in front of him . . . he put his trust . . . (only the first signs at the beginning and the end of the following 7 or 8 lines are legible).

2. NABONIDUS (555-539)

(a) Nabonidus' Rise to Power

The basalt stela in Istanbul, first published by V. Scheil, *Inscription de Nabonide* (1896), in *RT*, XVIII, 15 ff. cf. also, L. Messerschmidt, *Die Stele Nabuna'ids*, in *MVAG*, 1/1 (1896),

1 ff. and 73 ff. Translation: Zehnpfund-Langdon, in *VAB*, IV, 270 ff.

(i)

(two or three lines missing) [Against Akkad] he (i.e. Sennacherib) had evil intentions, he thought out crimes [agai]nst the country (Babylon), [he had] no mercy for the inhabitants of the co[untry]. With evil intentions against Babylon he let its sanctuaries fall in disrepair, disturbed[1] the(ir) foundation outlines and let the cultic rites fall into oblivion. He (even) led the princely Marduk away and brought (him) into Ashur. (But) he acted (thus against the country only) according to the wrath(ful will) of the gods. The princely Marduk did not appease his anger, for 21 years he established his seat in Ashur. (But eventually) the time became full, the (predetermined) moment arrived, and the wrath of the king of the gods, the lord of lords calmed down; he remembered (again) Esagila and Babylon, his princely residence. (Therefore) he made his own son murder the king of Subartu (Assyria), he who (once) upon the wrath(ful command) of Marduk (himself) had brought about the downfall of the country. (two or three lines missing)

(ii[2])

He (i.e. Marduk) provided him (i.e. the king of Babylon) with helpers, made him acquire a friend and caused the king of the Manda-hordes who has no rival, to bow to his orders in submission and to come to his assistance. (And) he (the king of the Manda-hordes) swept on like a flood storm, above and below, right and left, avenging Babylon in retaliation. The king of the Manda-hordes, without (religious) fear, demolished the sanctuaries of all the gods of Subartu (Assyria). He also demolished the towns within the territory of Akkad which had been hostile against the king of Akkad and had not come to his assistance (in his fight against Subartu). None of their cult(-centers) he omitted, laying waste their (sacred) towns worse than a flood storm. The king of Babylon, however, for whom this sacrilegious action of Marduk was horrible, did not raise his hand against the cult(-places) of any of the great gods, but let his hair unkempt,[3] slept on the floor (to express his pious desperation).

(iii)

[The king of Akkad then rebuilt the temple of] those gods and [resto]red the [cu]lt of those whose sacred cities Marduk had expressly permitted to be resettled, and whose deserted ruin-hills—the (former) sanctuaries of the gods—he (Marduk) had put into his (Neriglissar's) hands. (Also) the Ishtar (Inanna) of Uruk, the exalted princess who (formerly) dwelt in a gold(-clad) cella (and on a chariot) to which were harnessed seven lions, whose cult the inhabitants of Uruk had changed during the rule of the king Erba-Marduk removing her cella and unharnessing her team, (and who) therefore had left Eanna angrily and stayed (hence) in an un(seemly) place while they had placed in her chapel some image (^{d}*Lamassu*) which was not appropriate for Eanna, (this) Ishtar (^{d}XV) he (the king of Akkad) appeased and he (re)installed her in her cella putting to her (chariot) the seven lions which befit her godhead. The incorrect (image of) Ishtar (^{d}XV) he took out of Eanna and brought back to her shrine Eanna (the correct image of) Inanna (I n . n i n . n a). (As to) the Ishtar (*Iš-tar*), the lady of Elam, the princess who dwells in Susa (two lines missing)

(iv)

sitting/dwelling . . . which is in . . . whom nobody has seen for a long time, her throne he erected of alabaster shining like the sun (lit.: day) and of reddish gold. (As to) the goddess Anunitum residing in Sippar, whose residence in old times a (victorious) enemy had removed to Arrapha and whose sanctuary the Gutians had destroyed, and whose cult Neriglissar had renewed and whose (image) he had clad with an attire befitting her godhead, he made her stay (provisionally)—her own temple being in ruins—in a chapel in Sippar-Amnanu arranging (only) for her *nidbû* (subsistence) -offerings.

After (his) days had become full and he had started out on the journey of (human) destiny his son Labashi-Marduk, a minor (who) had not (yet) learned how to behave, sat down on the royal throne against the intentions of the gods and (three lines missing).

(v)

They carried me into the palace and all prostrated themselves to my feet, they kissed my feet greeting me again and again as king. (Thus) I was elevated to rule the country by the order of my lord Marduk and (therefore) I shall obtain whatever I desire—there shall be no rival of mine!

I am the real executor[4] of the wills of Nebuchadnezzar and Neriglissar, my royal predecessors! Their armies are entrusted to me, I shall not treat carelessly their orders and I am (anxious) to please them (i.e. to execute their plans).

Awel-Marduk, son of Nebuchadnezzar, and Labashi-Marduk, son of Neriglissar [called up] their [troo]ps and . . . their . . . they dispersed. Their orders (7-8 lines missing)

(vi)

them and prayed to them; with regard to the impending constellation[5] of the Great Star[6] and the moon, I became

[1] Lit.: "to blot out" (*suḫḫû*). This seems to have been done to make it impossible to retrace the outlines of the original foundation-walls and therefore to rebuild the sanctuary.

[2] For a translation of this column, cf. J. Lewy, in *MVAG*, XXIX/2 (1924), 80 ff.

[3] For the phrase *našû malâ*, cf. B. Meissner, *BAWb.*, I, 52 f.

[4] Text: *našparu dannu*. As to the very rare denomination of a ruler as *našparu*, cf., for another instance, T. Jacobsen, *apud* H. Frankfort, *Tell Asmar and Khafaje* (*OIP*, XIII [1932]), p. 45, and H. Frankfort, Seton Lloyd and T. Jacobsen, *The Gimilsin Temple and the Palace of the Ruler at Tell Asmar* (*OIP*, XLIII [1940]), p. 136.

[5] This constellation caused also another dream which is reported on a small tablet (Yale Babylonian Collection, published by A. T. Clay, in *YOS*, I [1915], No. 39, with translation on p. 55). "In the month of Tebitu, the 15th day, of the 7th year of (the rule of) Nabonidus, king of Babylon, Shumukin reported (text: present tense) as follows: 'In a dream I saw

apprehensive (but) (in a dream) a (!)[7] man came to my assistance, saying to me: "There are no evil portents (involved) in the impending constellation!" In the same dream, when my royal predecessor Nebuchadnezzar and one attendant (appeared to me) standing on a chariot, the attendant said to Nebuchadnezzar: "Do speak to Nabonidus, that he should report to you the dream he has seen!" Nebuchadnezzar listened to him and said to me: "Tell me what good (signs) you have seen!" (And) I answered him, saying: "In my dream I beheld with joy the Great Star, the moon and Marduk (i.e. the planet Jupiter) high up on the sky and it (the Great Star) called me by my name!"

(vii)

(2-3 lines missing) [*altars of* the planet] Venus, the planet Saturn, the Shining Star,[8] the star AB(?)+ḪAL,[9] the great stars dwelling in heaven, the great witnesses (*of my dream*) I set up for them and prayed to them for a life lasting through many days, permanence of (my) throne, endurance of (my) rule, and that my words might be received favorably before Marduk my lord. (Then) I lay down and beheld in a night(ly vision) the goddess Gula who restores the health of the dead(ly sick) and bestows long life. I prayed to her for lasting life for myself and that she might turn her face towards me. And she actually did turn and looked steadily upon me with her shining face (thus) indicating (her) mercy. I entered the temple é.NÍG.PA.kalam.ma.sum.mu into the presence of Nebo, he who extends (the length of) my rule; he placed into my hands the correct scepter, the lawful staff, which (alone) ensures the aggrandizement of the country. I beheld the throne of the goddess Tashmetum (who is) Gula (in the role of) bestower of life. She did present my cause favorably before Marduk, my lord, with regard to the lengthening of (my) life into future days and the overthrowing of all opposition.[10] And the wrath of Marduk, my lord, did (eventually) calm down and—full of awe—I dared to praise him; (then) with fervent prayers I approached his sanctuary and (eventually) addressed my prayers to him (directly), telling him my very thoughts as follows: "If I am in reality a king who pleases your heart—and I am not certain (yet), I (still) do not know (this)—one in whose (text: my) hands you, lord of lords, intend to entrust a kingship which is more (important) than that of the kings whom you have nominated in former times to exercise the rule[11]—do make my days last long; (if) I live through long years (lit.: if my years grow old), I shall care for the sanctuaries

(viii)

(of the gods)!" (one line missing) [a fabric befitting a] god [. . . embroidered] and made sparkling with precious stones and gold(-appliqués) was its front, I had made (lit.: fit) beautifully into garments befitting their godheads, for my lord Ea who increases my royal power, for Nebo, the administrator of all the upper and nether world, who lengthens the span of my life, for my lady Tashmetum who watches over my life. I furthermore made—what no former king had done—an *arattû* -throne of reddish gold for my lord Ea, according to the (customs/models of the) past, and placed it, as a seat for him, in his shrine é.kar.za.gin.na (Lapis-Lazuli Quay).

I am a king who always, daily (and) without interruption, is interested in the maintenance of the temples Esagila and Ezida. I had plated with shining silver the wooden door-leaves of (all) the rooms in the temple of the gods of the upper and the nether world (to wit) the mystery-room (lit.: room of seclusion) of Marduk and Sarpanit, and the door-leaves of the temple ki.durun.KA[12] which are on both sides of the temple é.maḫ, and (also) those of the gate of the goddess Beltia (Madonna) for the procession of Sarpanit, the beloved of Marduk, she who makes firm/steadfast the foundations of my royal throne. As to the main gate, the gate of the temple é.maḫ, the door-leaves of which consisted (each) of one leaf covered with (ordinary) wood, I rebuilt these door-leaves as *lulimu* -doors[13] made of cedarwood and mounted them with gold-bronze making them as shining as the sun, so that the coating could show that excellency which is befitting to these (door-leaves). On (unintelligible)[14] I put them on (their) hinges (lit.: places). I [had also made] the bronze snakes which are upon the supporting walls of the temple é.maḫ and the bronze wild-oxen.

(ix)

(one line missing) I am (also) a caretaker who brings large gifts to the great gods. In the month of Nisanu, the 10th day, when Marduk, the king of the gods, as well as (all) the (other) gods from the upper and the

the Great Star, Venus (i.e. Dilbat), Sirius, the moon and the sun and I shall (now) study this (constellation) with regard to a favorable interpretation for my lord Nabonidus, king of Babylon, as well as to a favorable interpretation for my lord Belshazzar, the crown-prince!' The 17th of the month Tebitu of the 7th year of (the reign of) Nabonidus, king of Babylon, Shumukin reported (text: present tense) as follows: 'I have observed the Great Star and I shall study (this) with regard to a favorable interpretation for my lord Nabonidus, king of Babylon, as well as to my lord Belshazzar, the crown-prince!' "

6 Oaths sworn by this star (mul.gal "Great Star") are sometimes mentioned in contemporaneous legal documents, such as Strassmaier, *Dar.*, 468:8; Clay, *UM*, II/1, 140:11, 13; and in the letter Harper, *ABL*, 454:7. cf. also, Thureau-Dangin, *Rituels accadiens*, p. 78 (text: p. 64):11.

7 Read: 1*en(!)*.

8 Text: mul.šu.pa (cf. Deimel, *ŠL*, 354/259, for proposed identifications). The Sumerian word is obviously a loan from Akk. *šûpû* "shining forth."

9 This sign is not mentioned in Deimel, *ŠL*.

10 Text: *šum-qut šàr-šàr-ú-tú*. For *šaršaru* "rebel, enemy," cf. K 2401 II:10 (S. A. Strong, *BA*, II [1894], 627 ff.) and the letter Harper, *ABL*, 1341:9.

11 This passage is very difficult; my translation is necessarily provisional, based upon the peculiar situation (Marduk as the natural protector of legitimacy versus Nabonidus as usurper troubled by his conscience). Exactly as in the Eski-Harran Memorial, longevity is considered here a gift with which the deity endows her favorites among men.

12 The name of this temple or chapel must not be confused with that of the temple of the goddess Nin-Eanna in Babylon: é.ki.durun.PA.AN which appears sometimes (cf., e.g., Strassmaier, *Nbk.*, 247:12) as é.ki.durun.KA.NI. The latter is also the name of a sanctuary in Kish, cf. J. A. Craig, *Hebraica*, III (1897), 220, text BrM, Sm 289, obv.(?) line 11.

13 The meaning of this term remains obscure.

14 Text: *ina* KI.UŠ dNammu. Meaning?

nether world were seated in the é.sizkur.sizkur, the chapel of the offerings, the *akītu* -chapel of the "Lord of Justice," I brought in for them 100 talents (and) 21 minas of silver (corresponding in value to) 5 talents and 17 minas of gold, in (addition) to the annual *gurrû* -offerings which (come) from tokens of homage,[15] from the excessive abundance of the (flat) lands, the rich yield of the mountain regions, the incoming taxes of all inhabited regions, (from) tokens of esteem (given) by kings, (from) the vast treasures which the prince Marduk has entrusted to me, (all) as perpetual (and) voluntary *gurrû* -offerings for Bel, Nebo and Nergal, the great gods who love my rule and watch over my life. To Nebo and Nergal, my divine helpers, I (also) dedicated as temple slaves 2,850 men of the prisoners from the country Hume to carry the (earth) baskets (because) Marduk, my lord, has given more (prisoners) into my hands than to (any of) my royal predecessors. After they had performed the festival of the *akītu* -chapel, and Bel and the son of Bel (i.e. Nebo) had taken up their (respective) comfortable seats, I brought to them (further) sumptuous gifts. In the great sacred cities, I prostrated myself before (the other) god(s) and goddess(es): I went to Uruk, Larsa and Ur and brought silver, gold (and) precious stones to Sin, Shamash and Ishtar. When I (then) proceeded, (unintelligible)[16] to the town of the god *Maḫ* . . . beer, abundant sacrifices . . .

(x)

(more than 10 lines missing) [as to the temples of the gods] whose storehouses [were empty] (and) where since . . . their (gods) had not dwelt, these (temples) Marduk, my lord, called to my attention and entrusted me (lit.: put into my hands) with the restoration of the divine cults. In a sacred pronouncement he ordered the appeasement of the angry gods and the resettlement of their seats to (be the pious duty of) my rule. As to the temple é.ḫul.ḫul in Harran which was in ruins for 54 years—through a devastation by the Manda-hordes the(se) sanctuaries were laid waste—the time (predestined) by the gods, the moment for the appeasement (to wit) 54 years, had come near, when Sin should have returned to his place. Now, Sin, the crown-bearer, did return to his place and remembered his lofty seat—and as to all the (lesser) gods who had moved out with him from his shrine—it was again Marduk, the king of (all) the gods who ordered (me) to gather them. As to the cylinder seal of the costliest jasper, a stone (befitting) a king, upon which Ashurbanipal, king of Assyria, had improved by drawing upon it a picture of Sin—that his own name be remembered—and upon which he had written a eulogy of Sin and hung it around the neck of (the image of) Sin, (this stone) whose exterior had been damaged in these days, during the destruction (wrought by) the enemy, [I restored/mounted and deposited] in Esagila, the temple

[15] Text: *šukînû*.

[16] Text difficult: *ina* MAŠ?AN.ḪAR KI *âlu* ᵈMAḪ *ina i-te-et-tu-qí-ia*.

which keeps the great gods alive,[17] in order not to (permit an) interruption of the oracles given by him (Sin) (by means of this seal?)[18]

(xi)

(This column contains a list of quotations from hepatoscopic texts concerning the results obtained during the examination of the liver of a sheep sacrificed for that purpose probably when this stela was set up.)

(b) The Family of Nabonidus

Memorial written either for the mother or the grandmother of Nabonidus, published by H. Pognon, in *Inscriptions sémitiques de la Syrie, de la Mésopotamie et de la région de Mossoul* (Paris, 1907), Pls. XII-XIII, and pp. 1 ff. For important corrections, cf. E. Dhorme, *RB*, 1908, 130 ff., and—superseding previous literature—J. Lewy, The Late Assyro-Babylonian Cult of the Moon and its Culmination at the time of Nabonidus (*HUCA*, XIX [1946], 405-489), as well as B. Landsberger, Die Basaltstele Nabonid's von Eski-Harran, in *Halil Edhem Hatira Kitabi* (Ankara, 1947); cf. also, S. Smith, *Isaiah, Chapter XL-LV* (Schweich Lectures of the British Academy, 1940), (London, 1944), pp. 22-28; and E. Dhorme, *RA*, XLI (1947), pp. 1-22.

(i)

(one line destroyed);[1] day and night through month(s) and year(s) I . . . for the moment;[2] holding the hem (of the garment) of Sin, the king of the gods, looking at him (every) night and (every) day; [in] supplication and prostration, I remained before them (i.e. the gods) saying: "May your return (i.e. Sin's) to your town take place so that (its) black-headed inhabitants can worship for all days to come your great godhead!" [Upon an id]ea prompted by my (personal) god and goddess [I did not (anymore) let touch] my body garments (made) of sag[3] -wool, silver[finery], new underwear nor perfumes, sweet(smelling) oil; I was clad [only in] . . . and I was performing the religious duties [in] . . . and in (ritual) silence. For the [. . .]s of my town . . . what my heart desired, all my finery . . . to them [I offered] solemnly.

[*During* the time from Ashurbanipal], the king of Assyria, [in] whose [rule] I was born—(to wit): [21 years][4] under Ashurbanipal, [4 years under Ashur]-etillu-ilani, his son, [21 years under Nabupola]ssar, 43 years under Nebuchadnezzar, [2 years under Ewil-

[17] This seems to be an allusion to the well-established Mesopotamian concept that it is the function of the temple to receive and to transmit the sacrifices to the deity which "lives" on them.

[18] The meaning of the text seems to suggest this translation and the proposed interpretation—although no Mesopotamian parallels can be adduced to support it.

[1] J. Lewy proposes to restore this line as "I [am] Shumuadanq[a], the go[verness]."

[2] Landsberger reads: *ad-din*(?); Lewy (*HUCA*, XIX, 414, n.50): *ap(!)-laḫ(!)*.

[3] The term síg.sag does not denote "fine, first-(class) wool" as one would be inclined to think, but wool of a specific color. This results clearly from the Middle-Babylonian text, Clay, *UM*, II/2, 44:1-3, where various amounts of ˢⁱᵍ*ri-iš* and ˢⁱᵍ*ta-kil-tum* are summed up as ˢⁱᵍ*ṣir-pu*, i.e. "colored wool," or from the text *UM*, II/2, 135, 1:6-9, mentioning garments described as *ta-bar-rum* "red," *ta-kil-tum* "dark blue," síg.sag and *piṣû* "white." The Neo-Babyl. references for síg.sag are Dougherty, *GCCI*, II, 361:2; Clay, *BIN*, I 9:22; Harper, *ABL*, 511:9, Strassmaier, *Nbk.*, 455:2.

[4] The figures given here and in the following lines are those of Landsberger.

Merodach], 4 years under Neriglissar, [in summa 95 yea]rs, [the god was away] till Sin, the king of the gods, [*remembered the temple*] . . . of his [great] godhead, his clouded face[5] [shone up], [and he listened] to my prayers, [forgot] the angry command [which he had given, and decided to return t]o the temple é.ḫul.ḫul, the temple, [the mansion,] his heart's delight. [With regard to his impending return to] the [temp]le, Sin, the king of [the gods, said (to me)]: "Nabonidus, the king of Babylon, the son [of thy

(ii)

womb] [shall] make [me] en[ter/sit down (again)] in(to) the temple é.ḫul.ḫul!" I care[fully obeyed the orders] which [Sin], the king of the gods, had pronounced (and therefore) I did see myself (how) Nabonidus, the king of Babylon (DIN.TIR^{ki}), the offspring of my womb, reinstalled completely the forgotten rites of Sin, Ningal, Nusku (and) Sadarnunna, (how) he rebuilt the temple é.ḫul.ḫul and completed its construction. He (also) restored completely the town of Harran (making it bigger) than (it was) before. He led (the images of) Sin, Ningal, Nusku (and) Sadarnunna from Babylon, his royal residence, to Harran and made them take their seats in the temple é.ḫul.ḫul, the sanctuary which pleases their hearts, under the jubilant rejoicing (of the population).

In his love for me who (always) worshiped his godhead, held (in prayers) the hem of his garment, Sin, the king of the gods, did what he never did before, gave (to me) what he had not given to anybody (else); (to wit) Sin, the king of the gods, chose me (lit.: lifted my head) and made my name famous in the world by adding many (lit.: long) days (and) years of (full) mental capacity (to the normal span of life) and (thus) kept me alive—from the time of Ashurbanipal, king of Assyria, to the 6th year of Nabonidus, king of Babylon, the son of my womb, (that is) for 104 happy years, according to[6] what Sin, the king of the gods, had promised me (lit.: put into my heart). (And indeed all the time) my eyesight was keen, my hearing excellent, my hands and feet in perfect condition, my diction well chosen, food and drink agreed with me, . . . I was in good spirits, . . .

(iii)

He[7] served them (the Assyrian kings) as an official, did always what was agreeable to t[hem] and made me a fine name before them (treating me) like the[ir] own daughter, (they) chose me (to become a *governess*). Afterwards they died; none of their children, none of their families and of their officials to whom—when they had been put into office—they had given rich gifts, performed actually as much as a fumigation-offering, whereas I brought monthly, without interruption—in my best garments—offerings to their souls, fat lambs, bread, fine beer, wine, oil, honey, and all kinds of garden fruits, and established as perpetual offerings abundant fumigations (yielding) sweet smells for them and placed . . . before them.

[5] Following the suggestion of Landsberger.

[6] Thus I propose to translate: *ina pu-ú-ti šá* ^{d}*Sîn . . . ina lìb-bi-ia iš-ku-nu-ma*, assuming an idiom *ina libbi* NN *šakânu* "to promise to NN" (for Landsberger's treatment of this phrase, cf. *op.cit.*, pp. 141 f.). For *ina pûti* with the meaning "according to."

[7] This most enigmatic phrase of the entire inscription has found very divergent interpretations; cf. Landsberger, *op.cit.*, pp. 142 ff., and Lewy, *HUCA*, XIX, 413 f. and especially p. 420 f. for female rulers among Arab groups.

(Postscript) In the [ninth] year of Nabonidus, king of Babylon, she died a natural death, and Nabonidus, king of Babylon, the offspring of her womb, the favorite of his mother, deposited her corpse (in the coffin) (clad in) fine (woolen) garments, shining linen, (with) golden A.LU(?), precious and costly stones [he decked her out]; he [sprinkled] her corpse with perfumed oil. They de[posited] (the coffin) [in a] secure tomb and, in front of it, he (then) slaughtered cattle and fat sheep, and he assembled into [his] presence the inhabitants of Babylon and Borsippa (broken).

(c) Nabonidus and the Clergy of Babylon

The "Verse Account of Nabonidus" is preserved on the damaged tablet British Museum 38,299 which was published by Sidney Smith, in *Babylonian Historical Texts*, Pls. v-x, transliteration and translation, pp. 83 ff. The understanding of the difficult and partly very damaged poem was greatly furthered by Landsberger-Bauer, *ZA*, XXXVII (1926-27), (NF III), 88 ff. The following translation is to a large extent based upon the interpretation given by Landsberger-Bauer. cf. also, S. Smith, in *Isaiah, Chapter XL-LV Literary Criticism and History* (The Schweich Lectures of the British Academy, 1940), London, 1944.

(i)

(one line destroyed)

[. . . law (and)] order are not promulgated by him,
[. . . *he made perish the common people* through w]ant, the nobles he killed in war,
[. . . for] the trader he blocked the road.

[. . . for the farmer] he made rare the *kuruppu*[1]
[. . .] there is no . . .[2] in the country
[. . . the harvester] does not sing the *alalu* -song (any more)[3]
[. . .] he does not fence in (any more) the arable territory.
[. . .] . . .

[1] This word still remains obscure. From Neo-Babylonian legal texts, one may gather the following evidence: 1) Speleers, *Recueil des inscriptions de l'Asie antérieure, etc.* (Bruxelles, 1925) 293:2,5,9 mentions a *bît ku-ru-up-pu rik(?)-ki-tim* which was rented; also Clay, *Babylonian Records in the Library of J. Pierpont Morgan*, II, 1:1 where this type of house is described as adjacent to other *bît kuruppu*'s; and 2) the formula *mašiḫu ša kuruppi* is quite frequent in texts of this period, note also O. Krückmann, *Texte und Materialien der Frau Professor Hilprecht Babylonian Collection*, II/III, 193:10 (context damaged) "silver (given) *a-na ku-ru-up-pu-šú*," and 3) R. Dougherty, *YOS*, VII, 78: 5 (cf. also M. San Nicolò in *Archiv orientální*, V [1933], 299 f. and 300, n.1) where it is reported that somebody was sitting on the *ku-ru-up-pu* of a goldsmith while witnessing a nocturnal burglarly. One is perhaps allowed to deduce from these passages that the word *kuruppu* denoted a type of wall used to build warehouses, then also such warehouses.

[2] Read perhaps [*iš*]-*pu-ku*.

[3] For the *alalu* -song, cf. my remarks in *BASOR*, 103 (1946), 11 ff.

[. . . he took away] their property, scattered their possessions,
[. . .] he ruined completely,
[. . .] their corpses[4] on a dark/obscure [pla]ce,
[. . .] became narrow/small.

[. . .] their faces became changed/hostile,
[. . .] they do not parade along the wide street,
[. . .] you do not see happiness (any more);
[. . . is] unpleasant, they decided.

[As to Nabonidus] (his) protective deity became hostile to him,
[And he, the former favorite of the g]ods (is now) seized by misfortunes:
[. . . against the will of the g]ods he performed an unholy action,
[. . .] he thought out something worthless:

[He had made the image of a deity] which nobody had (ever) seen in (this) country
[He introduced it into the temple] he placed (it) upon a pedestal;
[. . .] he called it by the name of Nanna,
[. . . it is adorned with a . . . of lapis]lazuli,[5] crowned with a tiara,

[. . .] its appearance is (that of) the eclipsed moon,[6]
[. . . the gest]ure[7] of its hand is like that of the god L u g a l . ŠU.DU,
[. . .] its head of hair [rea]ches to the pedestal,
[. . . in fr]ont of it are (placed) the Storm (*abûbu*) Dragon and the Wild Bull.

[When he worshiped it] its appearance became [like that of a . . . demon crowned with] a tiara
[. . .] his [. . . became . . .] his face turned hostile,
[. . .] his form became [. . .]
[. . .-]GAL was his name.

[. . .] at his [fe]et.

(ii)

(at least one line missing)

[His form] not (even) Ea-Mummu could have formed,
Not (even) the learned Adapa knows his name.

(Nabonidus said): "I shall build a temple for him, I shall construct his (holy) seat,
I shall form its (first) brick (for) him, I shall establish firmly its foundation,
I shall make a replica even to the temple Ekur,
I shall call its name é . ḫ u l . ḫ u l for all days to come!

"When I will have fully executed what I have planned,
I shall lead him by his hand and establish him on his seat.
(Yet) till I have achieved this, till I have obtained what is my desire,
I shall omit (all) festivals, I shall order (even) the New Year's Festival to cease!"

And he formed its (first) brick, did lay out the outlines,
He spread[8] out the foundation, made high its summit,
By means of (wall-decorations made of) gypsum and bitumen he made its facing brilliant,
As in the temple Esagila he made a ferocious wild-bull stand (on guard) in front of it.

After he had obtained what he desired, a work of utter deceit,
Had built (this) abomination, a work of unholiness —when the third year was about to begin—
He entrusted the "Camp" to his oldest (son), the first-born,
The troops everywhere in the country he ordered under his (command).

He let (everything) go,[9] entrusted the kingship to him
And, himself, he started out for a long journey,
The (military) forces of Akkad marching with him;
He turned towards Tema (deep) in the west.

He started out the expedition on a path (leading) to a distant (region). When he arrived there,
He killed in battle the prince of Tema,
Slaughtered the flocks of those who dwell in the city (as well as) in the countryside,
And he, himself, took his residence in [Te]ma, the forces of Akkad [were also stationed] there.

He made the town beautiful, built (there) [his palace]
Like the palace in Š u . a n . n a (Babylon), he (also) built [walls]

[4] Read: [*pa*]*g-ri-šú-nu.*
[5] Landsberger reads [*ziqnu*] *za-qin.*
[6] Obscure simile.
[7] Read: [*ta-ra*]*-aṣ qát-su* and cf. E. F. Weidner, *AfO*, XI (1936-7), 361, n.12.
[8] For *šeṭû* "to spread out," cf. Thureau-Dangin *VIIIe Camp.* p. 134, n.9, and R. C. Thompson, *RA*, XXVI (1929), 51, n.1.
[9] Idiomatic expression: *qātē paṭāru*; cf. also, F. R. Kraus, in *ZA*, XLII (NF IX), 109.

(For) the fortifications of the town and [. . .].
He surrounded the town with sentinels [. . .].

[The inhabitants] became troubled [. . .]
The brick form [and the brick basket he imposed upon them]
Through the (hard) work [they . . .]
(break of some lines)

(iii)

(two or more lines destroyed)
He killed the inhabitants [. . .]
Women and youngsters [. . .]
Their prosperity (lit.: possessions) he brought to an end [. . .]
(All) the barley which he fo[und] therein [. . .]

His tired/weary army [grumbled . . .]
. . . [. . .]
The *ḫazânu*-official of Cy[rus . . .]
[. . .].

(iv)

(This column contains now only ten lines, of which but few words at their beginnings are preserved, such as "after," "[the symbol] stylus," "the king is mad," "the Lord-of-the-Stylus," . . . . , "portents were o[bserved . . .], "How?")

(v)

(break)
The pra[is]e of the Lord of Lords [and the names of the countries]
Which he has not conquered he wrote upon [this stela . . .].

(While) Cyrus (is) the king of the world whose tri[umph(s) are true]
And [whose yoke] the kings of all the countries are pulli[ng,]
He (Nabonidus) has written upon his stone tablets: "[I have made . . . bow] to my feet
I personally have conquered his countries, his possessions I took to my residence."

(It was) he (who) stood up in the assembly to praise hi[mself]
(Saying): "I am wise, I know, I have seen (what is) hi[dden]
(Even) if I do not know how to write (with the stylus), yet I have seen se[cret things]
The god Ilte'ri[10] has made me see a vision, he ha[s shown to me] everything.
[I am] aw[are] of a wisdom which greatly surpasses (even that of)
(The series) u_4.sar.^{d}A.num.^{d}En.líl.lá which Adapa has composed!"

(Yet) he (continues to) mix up the rites, he confuses the (hepatoscopic) oracles [. . .].
To the most important ritual observances he makes (lit.: orders) an end;
As to the (sacred) representations in Esagila—representations which Ea-Mummu (himself) had fashioned—
He looks at the representations and utters blasphemies,

When he saw the u_4.sar-symbol of Esagila he makes a . . . gesture[11]
He assembled the (priestly) scholars, he expounded to them (as follows):
"Is not this the sign (of ownership indicating) for whom the temple was built?
If[12] it belong (really) to Bel, it would have been marked with the spade,
(Therefore) Sin (himself) has marked (already) his (own) temple with his u_4.sar-symbol!"

And Zeria, the *šatammu*-official who used to crouch[13] (as his secretary) in front of him,
Rimut, the bookkeeper, who used to have his (court-) position (quite) near to him,
Do confirm the royal dictum, stand by his words, they (even) bare their heads[14] to pronounce under oath:
"Now (only) we understand (this situation), after the king has explained (lit.: has spoken) (about it)!"

In the month of Nisanu, the 11th day, till the god [was present on] his seat,
(break)

(vi)

(break)
[. . . for] the inhabitants of Babylon he (i.e. Cyrus) declared the state of "peace,"
[. . .] . . . (the troops) he kept away from Ekur.

10 For this deity, cf. J. Lewy, *HUCA*, XIX, 426 ff.

11 Text: *i-s/šal-lal qātē*^{II}*-šu*.

12 Conditional phrase introduced by *lu*.

13 This is the typical posture of the scribe as is indicated by the passage in the Epic of Gilgamesh (cf. R. C. Thompson's edition, Pl. 30, line 51, transliteration p. 47) *dup-šar-ra-at irṣitim*^{tim} *ma-ḫar-ša ḳam-sa-at* "(lady)-scribe, crouching in front of her."

14 Here, *qaqqadu puṭṭuru* could also mean "to clap one's forehead (as a gesture of regret)" and indicate that the subservient court official wanted to express, in an exaggerated way, his regret at not having made himself this obvious observation and to stress, at the same time, the cleverness of the argumentation of the king.

[Big cattle he slaughtered with the a]xe,[15] he slaughtered many *aslu* -sheep[16]
[Incense he put] on the censer, the regular offerings for the Lord of Lords he ordered increased,
[He constantly prayed to] the gods, prostrated on his face,
[To be/do . . .] is dear to his heart.

[To build up/repair the town of Babylon] he conceived the idea
[And he himself took up hoe, spade and] earth basket and began to complete the wall of Babylon!
[The original plan of] Nebuchadnezzar they (the inhabitants) executed with a willing heart,
[. . .] . . . he built fortifications on the *Imgur-Enlil*-wall.

[The images of Babyl]on(ia), male and female, he returned to their cellas,
[The . . . who] had abandoned their [cha]pels he returned to their mansions,
[Their wrath] he appeased, their mind he put at rest,
[. . . those whose power was] at a low he brought back to life
[Because] their food is served (to them) [regular]ly.

[. . .] (these) deeds he effaced,
[. . . which] he has constructed, all the sanctuaries
[. . .] of his [royal ru]le . . . he has eradicated,
[. . .] of his [. . .] the wind carried away.

[. . .] his picture/symbol he effaced,
[. . . in all] the sanctuaries the inscriptions of his name are erased,
[. . . whatever he (Nabonidus) had cre]ated, he (Cyrus) let fire burn up
[. . . what he (Nabonidus) had cre]ated, he (Cyrus) fed to the flames!

[To the inhabitants of] Babylon a (joyful) heart is given now
[They are like prisoners when] the prisons are opened
[Liberty is restored to] those who were surrounded by oppression
[All rejoice] to look upon him as king!

(broken)

[15] Text: [*ú-pal*]*-liq* from *palāqu* "to slaughter with the *pilaqqu-* axe" attested, e.g., in Thureau-Dangin, *Rituels accadiens*, p. 14 (text p. 4) II:16; also, C. Mullo-Weir, in *JRAS* (1929), 554 (*KAR*, 360), line 14 (in parallelism to *ṭabaḫu*). For the pertinent tool, cf., e.g. ^{urudu}*naplaqtum*^{zabar} on the Obelisk of Man-ištusu (V. Scheil, *Délégation en Perse, Mém.*, Vol. II, face C VIII:12).

[16] For this animal, cf. L. F. Hartman-A. L. Oppenheim, The Domestic Animals of Ancient Mesopotamia (*JNES*, IV [1945]), 156, line 12.

3. CYRUS (557-529)

Inscription on a clay barrel, published in Rawlinson, v, 35. Transliteration and translation: F. H. Weissbach, in *Die Keilinschriften der Achämeniden* (*VAB*, III), 2 ff. Translations: Ebeling, in *AOT*, 368 ff., and R. W. Rogers, *Cuneiform Parallels to the Old Testament* (New York, 1926), pp. 380 ff.

(one line destroyed)

. . . [r]ims (of the world) . . . a weakling has been installed as the *enû*[1] of his country; [the correct images of the gods he removed from their thrones, imi]tations he ordered to place upon them. A replica of the temple Esagila he has[2] . . . for Ur and the other sacred cities inappropriate rituals . . . daily he did blabber [incorrect prayers]. He (furthermore) interrupted in a fiendish way the regular offerings, he did . . . he established within the sacred cities. The worship of Marduk, the king of the gods, he [chang]ed into abomination, daily he used to do evil against his (i.e. Marduk's) city. . . . He [tormented] its [inhabitant]s with corvée-work (lit.: a yoke) without relief, he ruined them all.

Upon their complaints the lord of the gods became terribly angry and [he departed from] their region, (also) the (other) gods living among them left their mansions, wroth that he had brought (them) into Babylon (Šu.an.na^{ki}). (But) Marduk [who does care for] . . . on account of (the fact that) the sanctuaries of all their settlements were in ruins and the inhabitants of Sumer and Akkad had become like (living) dead, turned back (his countenance) [his] an[ger] [abated] and he had mercy (upon them). He scanned and looked (through) all the countries, searching for a righteous ruler willing to lead him (i.e. Marduk) (in the annual procession).[3] (Then) he pronounced the name of Cyrus (*Ku-ra-aš*), king of Anshan, declared him (lit.: pronounced [his] name) to be(come) the ruler of all the world. He made the Guti country and all the Manda-hordes bow in submission to his (i.e. Cyrus') feet. And he (Cyrus) did always endeavour to treat according to justice the black-headed whom he (Marduk) has made him conquer. Marduk, the great lord, a protector of his people/worshipers, beheld with pleasure his (i.e. Cyrus') good deeds and his upright mind (lit.: heart) (and therefore) ordered him to march against his city Babylon (Ká.dingir.ra). He made him set out on the road to Babylon (DIN.TIR^{ki}) going at his side like a real friend. His widespread troops—their number, like that of the water of a river, could not be established—strolled along, their weapons packed away.[4] Without any battle, he made him enter his town Babylon (Šu.an.na), sparing Babylon (Ká.dingir.ra^{ki}) any calamity. He delivered into his (i.e. Cyrus') hands Nabonidus, the king who did not

[1] The old Sumerian title appears here in a context which seems to indicate that the primitive concept concerning the intimate connection between the physical vitality of the ruler and the prosperity of the country, was still valid in the political speculations of the Babylonian clergy.

[2] Text: *i-te-*[. . .] which could also mean "bes[ide . . .]."

[3] For this meaning of the idiomatic phrase: *qātē* NN *ṣabātu*, cf. my remarks in *JAOS*, LXII (1941), 270.

[4] Text: ^{is}*kakkē*^{pl}*-šú-nu ṣa-an-du-ma*.

worship him (i.e. Marduk). All the inhabitants of Babylon (DIN.TIR^{ki}) as well as of the entire country of Sumer and Akkad, princes and governors (included), bowed to him (Cyrus) and kissed his feet, jubilant that he (had received) the kingship, and with shining faces. Happily they greeted him as a master through whose help they had come (again) to life from death (and) had all been spared damage and disaster,[5] and they worshiped his (very) name.

I am Cyrus, king of the world, great king, legitimate king, king of Babylon, king of Sumer and Akkad, king of the four rims (of the earth), son of Cambyses (*Ka-am-bu-zi-ia*), great king, king of Anshan, grandson of Cyrus, great king, king of Anshan, descendant of Teispes (*Ši-iš-pi-iš*), great king, king of Anshan, of a family (which) always (exercised) kingship; whose rule Bel and Nebo love, whom they want as king to please their hearts.

When I entered Babylon (DIN.TIR^{ki}) as a friend and (when) I established the seat of the government in the palace of the ruler under jubilation and rejoicing, Marduk, the great lord, [induced] the magnanimous inhabitants of Babylon (DIN.TIR^{ki}) [to love me], and I was daily endeavouring to worship him. My numerous troops walked around in Babylon (DIN.TIR^{ki}) in peace, I did not allow anybody to terrorize (any place) of the [country of Sumer] and Akkad. I strove for peace in Babylon (K á . d i n g i r . r a^{ki}) and in all his (other) sacred cities. As to the inhabitants of Babylon (DIN.TIR^{ki}), [they saw their] hearts con[tent] (because) [I abolished] the corvée (lit.: yoke) which was against their (social) standing. I brought relief to their dilapidated housing, putting (thus) an end to their (main) complaints. Marduk, the great lord, was well pleased with my deeds and sent friendly blessings to myself, Cyrus, the king who worships him, to Cambyses, my son, the offspring of [my] loins, as well as to all my troops, and we all [praised] his great [godhead] joyously, standing before him in peace.

All the kings of the entire world from the Upper to the Lower Sea, those who are seated in throne rooms, (those who) live in other [types of buildings as well as] all the kings of the West land living in tents,[6] brought their heavy tributes and kissed my feet in Babylon (Š u . a n . n a). (As to the region) from . . . as far as Ashur and Susa, Agade, Eshnunna, the towns Zamban, Me-Turnu,[7] Der as well as the region of the Gutians, I returned to (these) sacred cities on the other side of the Tigris, the sanctuaries of which have been ruins for a long time, the images which (used) to live therein and established for them permanent sanctuaries. I (also) gathered all their (former) inhabitants and returned (to them) their habitations. Furthermore, I resettled upon the command of Marduk, the great lord, all the gods of Sumer and Akkad whom Nabonidus has brought into Babylon (Š u . a n . n a^{ki}) to the anger of the lord of the gods, unharmed, in their (former) chapels, the places which make them happy.

May all the gods whom I have resettled in their sacred cities ask daily Bel and Nebo for a long life for me and may they recommend me (to him); to Marduk, my lord, they may say this: "Cyrus, the king who worships you, and Cambyses, his son, . . ." . . . all of them I settled in a peaceful place . . . ducks and doves, . . . I endeavoured to fortify/repair their dwelling places. . . .

(six lines destroyed)

4. XERXES (485-465)

Akkadian version of a foundation tablet from Persepolis; SE corner of the *terrasse*. Text: E. Herzfeld, *Archaeologische Mitteilungen aus dem Iran*, VIII (1937), 56 ff.; transliteration and translation with extensive annotations by E. Herzfeld, *Altpersische Inschriften* (Berlin, 1938), No. 14, pp. 27 ff.[1]

Ahuramazda is the great god who gave (us) this earth, who gave (us) that sky, who gave (us) mankind, who gave to his worshipers[2] prosperity,[3] who made Xerxes, the king, (rule) the multitudes (as) only king, give alone orders to the other (kings).[4]

I am Xerxes, the great king, the only king (lit.: king of kings), the king of (all) countries (which speak) all kinds of languages, the king of this (entire) big and far(-reaching) earth,—the son of king Darius, the Achaemenian, a Persian, son of a Persian, an Aryan (*ar-ri-i*) of Aryan descent (lit.: seed).[5]

Thus speaks king Xerxes: These are the countries—in addition to Persia—over which I am king under the "shadow" of Ahuramazda, over which I hold sway, which are bringing their tribute to me—whatever is commanded them by me, that they do and they abide by my law(s)—: Media, Elam, Arachosia, Urartu (Pers. version: Armenia), Drangiana, Parthia, (H)aria, Bactria, Sogdia, Chorasmia, Babylonia, Assyria, Sattagydia, Sardis, Egypt (*Mi-ṣir*), the Ionians who live on the salty sea and (those) who live beyond (lit.: on the other shore of) the salty sea, Maka, Arabia, Gandara, India, Cappadocia, Da'an, the Amyrgian Cimmerians (Pers. and Elam. versions: Sakans), the Cimmerians (wearing) pointed caps, the Skudra, the Akupish, Libya,[6] Banneshu (Carians) (and) Kush.

[5] Text: *pa-ḳi-e*. Meaning unknown.

[6] This phrase refers either to the way of life of a nomadic or a primitive society in contradistinction to that of an urban. cf. A. Poebel, in *JNES*, I (1942), 252 f., and also the passage *Aḫ-la-me-i šu-ut ḳuš-ta-ri* "Ahlamû peoples (living) in tents" (Craig, *Ass. and Babyl. Religious Texts*, I, 81 f., text K 8608 + 2623 + 3016 + 3435, obv. line 4).

[7] *Me-tur-nu* (instead of the usual *Me-tur-nat*) appears also as *Me-e-tur-ni* (cf. Deimel, *ŠL*, 381/197). For this name of a river, the literature quoted by A. Falkenstein and L. Matous, *ZA*, XLII (NF VIII), 151, and A. Falkenstein, *ZA*, XLV (NF XI), 69 f.

[1] Dr. G. G. Cameron is to be thanked for his expert assistance in translating certain difficult passages of this text.

[2] The Persian and Elamite versions do not differentiate between the term which the Akkadian version renders respectively as "mankind" (*amēlūtu*) and "worshipers" (*nišē*).

[3] The Persian word is connected etymologically with Latin *quies* (cf. also, Herzfeld, *Altpersische Inschriften*, pp. 318 ff.), but refers there—as Dr. Cameron pointed out to me—to "earthly affairs."

[4] This renders the Akk. *ma'dūtu*, the Persian text means literally: one of many kings or *framatars*.

[5] The Akk. text—unable to render the foreign concept—uses here a transliteration of the Old Persian original: *ar-ri-i-si-tir* for *ar^{i}yačith^{r}a*.

[6] cf. for this translation (of Akk. ^{m}*Pu-ú-ṭu*), G. G. Cameron, in *JNES*, II (1943), 308 f.

Thus speaks king Xerxes: After I became king, there were (some) among these countries (names of which) are written above, which revolted (but) I crushed (lit.: killed) these countries, after Ahuramazda had given me his support, under the "shadow" of Ahuramazda, and I put them (again) into their (former political) status. Furthermore, there were among these countries (some) which performed (religious) service (lit.: festival) to the "Evil (God)s," (but) under the "shadow" of Ahuramazda I destroyed (lit.: eradicated) these temples of the "Evil (God)s" and proclaimed (as follows): "You must not perform (religious) service to the 'Evil (God)s' (any more)!" Wherever formerly (religious) service was performed to the "Evil (God)s," I, myself, performed a (religious) service to Ahuramazda and the *arta* (cosmic order)[7] reverently. Furthermore, there were other things which were done in a bad way, and these (too) I made in the correct way.

All these things which I did, I performed under the "shadow" of Ahuramazda and Ahuramazda gave me his support until I had accomplished everything.

Whosoever you are, in future (days) who thinks (as follows): "May I be prosperous in this life and blessed[8] after my death!"—do live according to this law which Ahuramazda has promulgated: "Perform (religious) service (only) for Ahuramazda and the *arta* (cosmic order) reverently." A man who lives according to this law which Ahuramazda has promulgated, and (who) performs (religious) service (only) to Ahuramazda and the *arta* (cosmic order) reverently, will be prosperous while he is alive and—(when) dead—he will become blessed.

Thus speaks king Xerxes: May Ahuramazda protect me, my family and these countries from all evil. This I do ask of Ahuramazda and this Ahuramazda may grant me!

5. ANTIOCHUS SOTER (280-262/1)

Published in Rawlinson, Vol. v, Pl. 66; latest translation: F. H. Weissbach, *Die Keilinschriften der Achämeniden* (*VAB*, III, Leipzig, 1911), pp. 132 ff.

I am Antiochus (*An-ti-'u-ku-us*), the great king, the legitimate king, the king of the world, king of Babylon (E^{ki}), king of all countries,[1] the caretaker of the temples Esagila and Ezida, the first(-born) son of king Seleucus (*Si-lu-uk-ku*), the Macedonian (^{amel}*Ma-ak-ka-du-na-a-a*), king of Babylon.

[7] For this translation of a religious terminus technicus which the Akk. version was again unable to render (the Akk. text has *ar-ta-šá-' bi-ra-za-am-man-ni-i* corresponding to the Old Persian *rtača brazmani*^{y}), Dr. Cameron referred me to R. Kent, *Language*, XXI (1945), 223 ff.

[8] Again, the Akk. text uses a transliteration of an Old Persian word: *ar-ta-wa* (for *ṛtava*) when faced with the problem of rendering a concept alien to the Mesopotamian religious thought.

[1] For this title which appears in Mesopotamia with the Persian domination, cf. R. D. Wilson, Titles of Persian Kings (in *Festschrift*, E. Sachau, Berlin 1905, pp. 179 ff.), pp. 183 f., No. 9-11.

When I conceived the idea of (re)constructing Esagila and Ezida, I formed with my august hands (when I was still) in the country Hatti[2] the (first) brick for Esagila and Ezida with the finest oil[3] and brought (it with me) for the laying of the foundation of Esagila and Ezida. And in the month of Addaru, the 20th day, the 43rd year (of the Seleucid era), I did lay the foundation of Ezida, the (only) true temple of Nebo which is in Borsippa.

O Nebo, lofty son, (most) wise among the gods, splendid (and) worthy of all praise, first-born son of Marduk, child of Arua, the queen who fashioned all creation, do look friendly (upon me) and may—upon your lofty command which is never revoked—the overthrow of the country of my enemy, the fulfillment of (all) my wishes against my foes, constant predominance, a kingdom (ruled) in justice (to all),[4] an *orderly* government,[5] years of happiness, enough progeny (lit.: to be sated with progeny) be your permanent gift to the (joint) kingship of Antiochus and his son, king Seleucus!

When you, prince Nebo, born in (lit.: son of) Esagila, first-born of Marduk, child of Arua the queen, enter —under jubilant rejoicings—Ezida, the (only) true temple, the temple (befitting) your position as Anu (i.e. highermost of the gods), the seat which gladdens your heart, may—upon your trustworthy command which cannot be made void—my days (on earth) be long, my years many, my throne firm, my rule lasting, under your lofty scepter which determines the borderline between the heaven and the nether world. May (only words of) favor be on your sacred lips (lit.: mouth) with regard to me, and may I personally conquer (all) the countries from sunrise to sunset, gather their tribute and bring it (home) for the perfection of Esagila and Ezida.

O Nebo, foremost son, when you enter Ezida, the (only) true temple, may there be on your lips (lit.: mouth) (words of) favor for Antiochus, the king of all countries, for Seleucus, the king, his son (and) for Stratonike (*As-ta-ar-ta-ni-ik-ku*), his consort, the queen!

[2] Antiochus was, at that time, in Syria; cf. W. W. Tarn, *The Cambridge Ancient History*, VII (Cambridge, 1933), 701 f.

[3] Oil was presumably used to keep the brick, prepared by the king himself as his first royal act, in a state of "freshness" till it was actually deposited in the ground. For the use of substitutes for clay when this common matter was to be touched by royal hands, I refer here to two misunderstood passages; Nabopolassar (text: *ZA*, IV [1889], 129 ff., col. III:2-3) reports: "I made my first-born son Nebuchadnezzar carry clay (which was in reality) a mixture of wine, oil, and resin-cuttings (*ṭi-it-tam be-el-la-at karāni šamni u ḫi-bi-iš-tim*)," and Ashurbanipal (cf. E. Nassouhi, *AfO*, II [1924], 98, I:17) refers to the same technique with the words "by means of a brick-mould made of ebony and m e s -wood from Magan and (from) cuttings of aromatic matters (*ḫi-biš-ti* š i m . ḫ i . a), I made the (first) brick for it."

[4] For this translation of *šarrūtu*$^{u-tu}$ *mi-šá-ri*, cf. my remarks above in n.1, p. 269b.

[5] Text: *pa-li-e bu-a-ri.*

Hittite Historical Texts

TRANSLATOR: ALBRECHT GOETZE

Suppiluliumas Destroys the Kingdom of Mitanni

Excerpt from the historical introduction to the treaty between Suppiluliumas and Mattiwaza of Mitanni. Texts: *KBo*, I, 1 obv. 17-47 and its duplicates *KBo*, I, 2 and *KUB*, III, 1 (in Akkadian). Literature: E. F. Weidner, *Politische Dokumente aus Kleinasien* (*Boghazköi-Studien* VIII, 1923), 6-15.

I, the Sun Suppiluliumas, the great king, the king of the Hatti land, the valiant, the favorite of the Storm-god, went to war. Because of king Tusratta's[1] presumptuousness I crossed the Euphrates and invaded the country of Isuwa.[2] The country of Isuwa I vanquished for the second time and made them again my subjects. The countries which in the time of my father (20) had crossed over into the country of Isuwa,[3] (namely) people from Gurtalissa, people from Arawanna, the country of Zazzisa, the country of Kalasma,[4] the country of Tim(mi)na, the mountain district of Haliwa, the mountain district of Karna, people from Turmitta, the country of Alha, the country of Hurma, the mountain district of Harana, half of the country of Tegarama,[5] people from Tepurziya, people from Hazga, people from Armatana—these peoples and these countries I vanquished, and reconquered them for the Hatti land. The countries which I captured I set free and they remained in their respective places; but all the people whom I set free, they returned to their people and the Hatti land took over their places.

(25) I, the Sun Suppiluliumas, the great king, the king of the Hatti land, the valiant, the favorite of the Storm-god, reached the country of Alse[6] and captured the provincial center Kutmar.[7] To Antar-atal of the country of Alse I presented it as a gift. I proceeded to the provincial center Suta[8] and ransacked it. I reached Wassukanni.[9] The inhabitants of the provincial center Suta together with their cattle, sheep (and) horses, together with their possessions and together with their deportees I brought to the Hatti land. Tusratta, the king, had departed, he did not come to meet me in battle.

(30) I turned around and (re)crossed the Euphrates. I vanquished the country of Halba[10] and the country of Mukishi.[11] Takuya, the king of Neya,[12] came before me to the country of Mukishi to sue for peace. But in Takuwa's absence, his brother Akit-Tessub persuaded the country of Neya and the city Neya to revolt. Akit-Tessub entered into a conspiracy with the *mariyannu*,[13] (namely) Hismiya, Asiri, Zulkiya, Utriya and Niruwa. Together with their charioteers and their foot soldiers they entered into a conspiracy with Akiya, the king of Arahti. They occupied Arahti and rebelled; this is what they said: "Let us battle with the great king, the king of the Hatti land!" (35) I, the great king, the king of the Hatti land, vanquished them at Arahti. I took prisoner Akiya, the king of Arahti, Akit-Tessub, Akuwa's brother, and their *mariyannu*, all of them with all that they owned and brought them to the Hatti land. I also brought Qatna[14] with its possessions and all that they owned to the Hatti land.

When I proceeded to the Nuhassi land,[15] I conquered all its countries. Sarrupsi[16] had met a violent death; I took prisoner his mother, his brothers and his sons and brought them to the Hatti land. Takib-sar, his servant, (40) I placed as king over Ukulzat. I proceeded to Apina[17] without expecting that I would have to fight with the country of Kinza.[18] However, Sutatarra together with Aitakama, his son, and together with his charioteers went out to fight with me. I defeated him and they retreated into Abzuya; I had Abzuya besieged. I took prisoner Sutatarra together with his son, his *mariyannu*, his brothers and with all that they owned and brought them to the Hatti land. I then proceeded to the country of Apina; Ariwanahi, the king of Apina, Wambadura, Akparu and Artaya, his great, went out to fight with me. (45) ⟨I took prisoner⟩ all of them with their countries and with all that they owned and brought them to the Hatti land. Because of king Tusratta's presumptuousness I raided all these countries in a single year and conquered them for the Hatti land. On this side I made Mount Niblani,[19] on the other side the Euphrates my frontier.

1 The ruler of the Mitanni kingdom in Upper Mesopotamia and contemporary of the pharaohs Amen-hotep III and IV, well-known from the Amarna letters.

2 Region in the bend of the Euphrates near Harput.

3 The mentioned countries seem to stretch from the region of Malatya toward the northwest.

4 The text gives here Tegarama; this is clearly a mistake—Tegarama follows presently—which the parallel passage obverse 12 allows us to correct.

5 Biblical Togarmah.

6 Region on the upper Tigris.

7 Assyrian Kullimeri east of the Batman Su and north of the upper Tigris.

8 In the hill country between upper Tigris and the Habur.

9 The Mitannian capital, probably opposite Tell Halaf (near modern Ras el-Ain) on the upper Habur.

10 Aleppo.

11 Today Atchana (Tell Açana) east of Antakya.

12 Near the northernmost point of the Orontes river.

13 The nobility of the Mitanni states.

14 Today Mishrife east of the middle Orontes.

15 Region south of Aleppo toward the Orontes.

16 He had been made king there by Suppiluliumas on an earlier campaign.

17 The region of Damascus. The name is the same as Apa; the final *-na* is the Hurrian article.

18 Qadesh on the Orontes.

19 The Lebanon.

Suppiluliumas and the Egyptian Queen

From Suppiluliumas' annals compiled by his son Mursilis. Texts: *KBo*, v, 6 (=2*BoTU*, 41) iii 1 ff. and its duplicate 639/f (*MDOG*, LXXV, 63 f.). Literature: H. Zimmern, *ZA*, NF 1 (1923), 37 ff.; A. Götze, *OLZ*, 1924, 581 ff.; J. Friedrich, *AO*, XXIV/3 (1925), 12 ff.; E. Cavaignac, *Les annales de Subbiluliuma* (1931), 20 ff.

(iii) While my father was down in the country of Karkamis,[1] he dispatched Lupakkis and Tessub-zalmas to the country of Amqa.[2] They proceeded to attack the country of Amqa and brought deportees, cattle (and) sheep home before my father. When the people of the land of Egypt heard about the attack on Amqa, they became frightened. Because, to make matters worse, their lord Bibhururiyas[3] had just died, the Egyptian queen who had become a *widow*, sent an envoy to my father and wrote him as follows: "My husband died and I have no son. People say that you have many sons. If you were to send me one of your sons, he might become my husband. I am loath to take a servant of mine and make him my husband." When my father heard that, he called the great into council (saying): "Since of old such a thing has never happened before me" He proceeded to dispatch Hattu-zitis, the chamberlain, (saying): "Go! Bring you reliable information back to me. They may try to deceive me: As to whether perhaps they have a prince bring reliable information back to me!"

During Hattu-zitis' absence in the land of Egypt my father vanquished the city of Karkamis....

The Egyptian envoy, the Honorable Hanis, came to him. Because my father had instructed Hattu-zitis while sending him to the land of Egypt as follows: "Perhaps they have a prince; they may try to deceive me and do not really want one of my sons to (take over) the kingship," the Egyptian queen answered my father in a letter as follows: "Why do you say: 'They may try to deceive me'? If I had a son, would I (iv) write to a foreign country in a manner which is humiliating to myself and to my country? You do not trust me and tell me even such a thing. He who was my husband died and I have no sons. Shall I perhaps take one of my servants and make him my husband? I have not written to any other country, I have written (only) to you. People say that you have many sons. Give me one of your sons and he is my husband and king in the land of Egypt." Because my father was generous, he complied with the lady's wishes and decided for (sending) the son.

(From the text translated below on p. 395, we know that the Hittite prince never reached Egypt but was murdered on his way.)

[1] Today Jerablus on the Euphrates.

[2] Between Lebanon and Antilibanus.

[3] A parallel text (*KUB*, XXXIV, 24 4) offers the variant Nibhururiyas. The much discussed question as to whether Amen-hotep IV (*Nfr. -ḫpr.w-rʿ*) or Tut-ankh-Amon (*Nb-ḫpr.w-rʿ*) is meant is thereby decided in favor of the latter.

Hattusilis on Muwatallis' War Against Egypt

Text: *KUB*, XXI, 17 i 14-21 and its duplicate *KUB*, XXXI, 27 2-8. Literature: A. Götze, *OLZ*, 1929, 837.

At the time that Muwatallis took the field against the king of the land of Egypt and the country of Amurru, and when he then had defeated the king of the land of Egypt and the country of Amurru,[1] he returned to the country Apa.[2] When Muwatallis, my brother, had (also) defeated Apa, he [returned to] the Hatti land, but [left] me in the country of Apa.

[1] On the coast of the Mediterranean between the sea and the upper Orontes. The defeat was accomplished in the famous battle of Qadesh when Muwatallis met Ramses II.

[2] The region of Damascus.

Palestinian Inscriptions

TRANSLATOR: W. F. ALBRIGHT

The Gezer Calendar

This little inscription was discovered at Gezer in 1908 by R. A. S. Macalister; it is on a school exercise tablet of soft limestone. For a number of years its date was uncertain, but recent discoveries establish its relative archaism and point to the second half of the tenth century or the very beginning of the ninth as its probable time. The writer would date it in or about the third quarter of the tenth century—about 925 B.C. in round numbers. The language is good biblical Hebrew, in a very early spelling; it is written in verse and seems to have been a kind of mnemonic ditty for children.

The official publication will be found in Macalister, *Gezer*, II, pp. 24-28, and III, Pl. CXXVII. For a nearly exhaustive bibliography up to 1934 see Diringer, *Le iscrizioni antico-ebraiche palestinesi* (Florence, 1934), pp. 1-20, supplemented by Albright, *BASOR*, 92, pp. 16-26. Additional items from 1936 to 1946 are the following: U. Cassuto, *Studi e materiali di storia delle religioni*, XII, pp. 107-25; S. Birnbaum and D. Diringer, *PEQ*, 1942/3, pp. 104-107; 1943, pp. 50-53; 1944, pp. 213-17; G. R. Driver, *PEQ*, 1945, pp. 5-9; E. Zolli, *Biblica*, 1946, pp. 129-131; H. Torczyner, *BJPES*, XIII, pp. 1-7.

His two months are (olive) harvest, (tricolon, 2:2:2)
His two months are planting (grain),
His two months are late planting;
His month is hoeing up of flax, (tricolon, 3:3:3)
His month is harvest of barley,
His month is harvest and *feasting*;
His two months are vine-tending, (bicolon, 2:2)
His month is summer fruit.

The Moabite Stone

This important inscription was discovered intact in 1868; it was subsequently broken by the Arabs and in 1873 it was taken to the Louvre. The best publication is found in Dussaud, *Les monuments palestiniens et judaïques (Musée du Louvre)*, 1912, pp. 4-22, with a magnificent photograph of the stela and a good bibliography. The work of Smend and Socin, *Die Inschrift des Königs Mesa von Moab* (1886), which was long standard, is not reliable, as was pointed out in detail by Renan and Clermont-Ganneau; see especially Lidzbarski, *Ephemeris*, I, pp. 1-10. The most recent competent translation is that of Gressmann, *AOT*, pp. 440-42. On the question of the authenticity of the text, which was strangely disputed for a long time (in spite of the fact that no forger of that time could possibly have divined the correct forms of letters in the ninth century B.C.), cf. Albright, *JQR*, XXXV, 1945, pp. 247-250.

For details of translation which depend on recent discoveries see especially Poebel, *Das appositionell bestimmte Pronomen* (Chicago, 1932), pp. 7-11; Albright, *BASOR*, 89, p. 16. n.55. There are a number of words which were formerly obscure but which have now been found in other Northwest-Semitic inscriptions.

The date of the Mesha Stone is roughly fixed by the reference to Mesha, king of Moab, in II Kings 3:4, after 849 B.C. However, since the contents of the stela point to a date toward the end of the king's reign, it seems probable that it should be placed between 840 and 820, perhaps about 830 B.C. in round numbers.

I (am) Mesha, son of Chemosh-[. . .], king of Moab, the Dibonite—my father (had) reigned over Moab thirty years, and I reigned after my father,—(who) made this high place for Chemosh in Qarhoh [. . .] because he saved me from all the kings and caused me to triumph over all my adversaries. As for Omri, (5) king of Israel, he humbled Moab many years (lit., days), for Chemosh was angry at his land. And his son followed him and he also said, "I will humble Moab." In my time he spoke (thus), but I have triumphed over him and over his house, while Israel hath perished for ever! (Now) Omri had occupied the land of Medeba, and (Israel) had dwelt there in his time and half the time of his son (Ahab), forty years; but Chemosh dwelt there in my time.

And I built Baal-meon, making a reservoir in it, and I built (10) Qaryaten. Now the men of Gad had always dwelt in the land of Ataroth, and the king of Israel had built Ataroth for them; but I fought against the town and took it and slew all the people of the town as satiation (intoxication) for Chemosh and Moab. And I brought back from there Arel (or Oriel), its chieftain, dragging him before Chemosh in Kerioth, and I settled there men of Sharon and men of Maharith. And Chemosh said to me, "Go, take Nebo from Israel!" (15) So I went by night and fought against it from the break of dawn until noon, taking it and slaying all, seven thousand men, boys, women, girls and maid-servants, for I had devoted them to destruction for (the god) Ashtar-Chemosh. And I took from there the [. . .] of Yahweh, dragging them before Chemosh. And the king of Israel had built Jahaz, and he dwelt there while he was fighting against me, but Chemosh drove him out before me. And (20) I took from Moab two hundred men, all first class (warriors), and set them against Jahaz and took it in order to attach it to (the district of) Dibon.

It was I (who) built Qarhoh, the wall of *the forests* and the wall of the citadel; I also built its gates and I built its towers and I built the king's house, and I made both of its reservoirs for water inside the town. And there was no cistern inside the town at Qarhoh, so I said to all the people, "Let each of you make (25) a cistern for himself in his house!" And I cut *beams* for Qarhoh with Israelite captives. I built Aroer, and I made the highway in the Arnon (valley); I built Beth-bamoth, for it had been destroyed; I built Bezer—

for it lay in ruins—with fifty men of Dibon, for all Dibon is (my) loyal dependency.

And I reigned [*in peace*] *over* the hundred towns which I had added to the land. And I built (30) [. . .] Medeba and Beth-diblathen and Beth-baal-meon, and I set there the [. . .] of the land. And as for Hauronen, there dwelt in it [. . . . And] Chemosh said to me, "Go down, fight against Hauronen. And I went down [and I fought against the town and I took it], and Chemosh dwelt there in my time. . . .

The Ostraca of Samaria

This name is applied to a homogeneous group of 63 dockets on Israelite potsherds which were found by G. A. Reisner in 1910, while excavating a floor-level from the first phase of the second period of palace construction at Samaria. Owing to a mistake in stratigraphy, which was subsequently corrected by J. W. Crowfoot and his associates, this level was first attributed to Ahab; it is now reasonably certain that it should be assigned to the reign of Jeroboam II (about 786-746 B.C.). The four regnal years mentioned on the Ostraca extend from the ninth to the seventeenth (about 778-770 B.C.). These documents, though jejune in themselves, are of great significance for the script, spelling, personal names, topography, religion, administrative system, and clan distribution of the period.

The documents were published first by G. A. Reisner in his rare book, *Israelite Ostraca from Samaria* (no date). A revised form of this study was then incorporated in the *Harvard Excavations at Samaria*, by Reisner, Fisher and Lyon (Cambridge, Mass., 1924), pp. 227-246. For a full bibliography up to 1933 see Diringer, *Le iscrizioni antico-ebraiche palestinesi* (Florence, 1934), pp. 21-68, especially pp. 66-68. Subsequent treatments deal mainly with the question of chronology or with the personal names; cf. especially J. W. Crowfoot, *The Buildings at Samaria* (London, 1942), pp. 5-9, 24-27; Albright, *BASOR*, 73, p. 21, n.38.

Samaria Ostracon, No. 1

In the tenth year. To Shamaryau (Shemariah) from Beer-yam, a jar of old wine. Pega (son of) Elisha, 2; Uzza (son of) . . . , 1; Eliba, 1; Baala (son of) Elisha, 1; Jedaiah, 1.

Samaria Ostracon, No. 2

In the tenth year. To Gaddiyau from Azzo. Abibaal, 2; Ahaz, 2; Sheba, 1; Merib-baal, 1.

Samaria Ostracon, No. 18

In the tenth year. From Hazeroth to Gaddiyau. A jar of fine oil.

Samaria Ostracon, No. 30

In the fifteenth year. From Shemida to Hillez (son of) Gaddiyau. Gera (son of) Hanniab.

Samaria Ostracon, No. 55

In the tenth year. (From the) vineyard of Yehau-eli. A jar of fine oil.

An Order for Barley from Samaria

In 1932 several ostraca were found at Samaria, and were published the following year by E. L. Sukenik. One of them is outstanding because of its length and relative completeness. The script belongs to the eighth century, probably to its third quarter; it is characterized by extraordinarily long shafts of such letters as *l*, *m*, *n*, like other Israelite documents of this general period. The text is difficult, and the rendering below is tentative.

For the official publication see Sukenik, *PEQ*, 1933, pp. 152-154; the text has subsequently been treated by Diringer, *Le iscrizioni antico-ebraiche palestinesi* (Florence, 1934), pp. 71-72, and Albright, *PEQ*, 1936, pp. 211-15.

Baruch *(son of) Shallum* [. . .]

O Baruch . . . pay attention and [give (?) to . . . (son of)] Yimnah (Imnah) barley (to the amount of) two (or three?) *measures*.

The Siloam Inscription

Accidentally discovered in 1880 in the rock wall of the lower entrance to the tunnel of Hezekiah south of the temple area in Jerusalem, the inscription is now in the Museum of the Ancient Orient at Istanbul. Its six lines occupy the lower half of a prepared surface, the upper part of which was found bare of inscription. It is, accordingly, almost certain that the first half of the original document is missing. Its contents and script point to the reign of Hezekiah (about 715-687 B.C.), a dating confirmed by II Kings 20:20 and especially II Chron. 32:30.

There is a very extensive bibliography, which is collected up to 1932 by Diringer, *Le iscrizioni antico-ebraiche palestinesi* (Florence, 1934), pp. 95-102. Among subsequently published items mention may be made of H. Torczyner, *BJPES*, 7, pp. 1-4, and Albright, *JBL*, 62, p. 370. The language is perfect classical Hebrew prose, but the spelling is not entirely consistent; translations can easily be judged by the quality of Hebrew which they presuppose.

[. . . when] (the tunnel) was driven through. And this was the way in which it was cut through:—While [. . .] (were) still [. . .] axe(s), each man toward his fellow, and while there were still three cubits to be cut through, [there was heard] the voice of a man calling to his fellow, for there was *an overlap* in the rock on the right [and on the left]. And when the tunnel was driven through, the quarrymen hewed (the rock), each man toward his fellow, axe against axe; and the water flowed from the spring toward the reservoir for 1,200 cubits, and the height of the rock above the head(s) of the quarrymen was 100 cubits.

The Lachish Ostraca

These ostraca were discovered in the ruins of the latest Israelite occupation at Tell ed-Duweir in southern Palestine, which unquestionably represents biblical Lachish. The first 18 were found by the late J. L. Starkey in 1935; three more (making 21 in all) were added during a supplementary campaign in 1938. Most of the ostraca were letters, while others were lists of names, etc., but only a third of the documents are preserved well enough to be reasonably intelligible throughout. Nearly all of the ostraca come from the latest occupation level of the Israelite gate-tower, and they are generally placed immediately before the beginning of the Chaldean siege of Lachish, perhaps in the autumn of 589 (or 588) B.C. Since they form the only known corpus of documents in classical Hebrew prose, they have unusual philological significance, quite aside from the light which they shed on the time of Jeremiah.

The texts were published by Harry Torczyner of the Hebrew University in *The Lachish Letters* (Lachish I), (London, 1938), and *Te'udot Lakhish* (Jerusalem, 1940). There is a large scattered bibliography, for which see Torczyner's second publication, pp. viii-x, and *BASOR*, 82, p. 18. Among the more useful items will be found Albright, *BASOR*, 61, pp. 10-16; 70, pp. 11-17; 73, pp. 16-21; 82, pp. 18-24; H. L. Ginsberg, *BASOR*, 71, pp. 24-26; 80, pp. 10-13; Roland de Vaux, *RB*, 1939, pp. 181-206; S. Birnbaum, *PEQ*, 1939, pp. 20-28, 91-110; Winton Thomas, *Journal of Theological Studies*, 40, pp. 1-15. Since the latest bibliography two contributions should be mentioned: H. G. May, *BASOR*, 97, pp. 22-26; Bernard Chapira, *Revue des études sémitiques*, 1942-45, pp. 105-173 (practically worthless, since it wholly lacks philological discipline).

Lachish Ostracon II

To my lord Yaosh: May Yahweh cause my lord to hear tidings of peace this very day, this very day! Who is thy servant (but) a dog that my lord hath remembered his servant? May Yahweh afflict those who re[port] an (evil) rumor about which thou art not informed!

Lachish Ostracon III

Thy servant Hoshaiah hath sent to inform my lord Yaosh: May Yahweh cause my lord to hear tidings of peace! And now thou hast sent a letter, but my lord did not enlighten thy servant concerning the letter which thou didst send to thy servant yesterday evening, though the heart of thy servant hath been sick since thou didst write to thy servant. And as for what my lord said, "Dost thou not understand?—call a scribe!", as Yahweh liveth no one hath ever undertaken to call a scribe for me; and as for any scribe who might have come to me, truly I did not call him nor would I give anything at all for him!

And it hath been reported to thy servant, saying, "The commander of the host, Coniah son of Elnathan, hath come down in order to go into Egypt; and unto Hodaviah son of Ahijah and his men hath he sent to obtain . . . from him."

And as for the letter of Tobiah, servant of the king, which came to Shallum son of Jaddua through the prophet, saying, "Beware!", thy servant hath sent it to my lord.

Lachish Ostracon IV

May Yahweh cause my lord to hear this very day tidings of good! And now according to everything that my lord hath written, so hath thy servant done; I have written on the door according to all that my lord hath written to me. And with respect to what my lord hath written about the matter of *Beth-haraphid*, there is no one there.

And as for Semachiah, Shemaiah hath taken him and hath brought him up to the city. And as for thy servant, I am not sending *anyone* thither [today(?), but I will send] tomorrow morning.

And let (my lord) know that we are watching for the signals of Lachish, according to all the indications which my lord hath given, for we cannot see Azekah.

Lachish Ostracon V

May Yahweh cause my lord to hear [tidings of peace] and good [this very day, this very day!] Who is thy servant (but) a dog that thou hast sent to thy servant the [letters . . . Now] thy servant hath returned the letters to my lord. May Yahweh cause thee to see [. . .]. How can thy servant benefit or injure the king?

Lachish Ostracon VI

To my lord Yaosh: May Yahweh cause my lord to see this season in good health! Who is thy servant (but) a dog that my lord hath sent the [let]ter of the king and the letters of the prince[s, say]ing, "Pray, read them!" And behold the words of the pr[inces] are not good, (but) to weaken our hands [and to sla]cken the hands of the *m[en] who are informed about them* [. . . And now] my lord, wilt thou not write to them, saying, "Why do ye thus [*even*] in Jerusalem? Behold unto the king and unto [*his house*] are ye doing this thing!" [And,] as Yahweh thy God liveth, truly since thy servant read the letters there hath been no [*peace*] for [thy ser]vant. . . .

Lachish Ostracon VIII

May Yahweh cause my lord to hear tidings of good this very day! [. . .]. *The Lord hath humbled me* before thee. *Nedabiah* hath fled to the mountains [. . .]. Truly I lie not—let my lord *send* thither!

Lachish Ostracon IX

May Yahweh cause my lord to hear [tidings] of peace! [. . .] let him send [. . .] *fifteen* [. . .]. Return word to thy servant through *Shelemiah* (telling us) what we shall do tomorrow!

Lachish Ostracon XIII

. . . they did not wish to do (any) work . . . and Semachiah. . . .

IV. Rituals, Incantations, and Descriptions of Festivals

Egyptian Rituals and Incantations

TRANSLATOR: JOHN A. WILSON

A Ritual for Offering Food

The ancient Egyptian texts contain an abundance of material on the ritual to be performed in making offerings. The most common setting is the mortuary offering to the dead, in which the material offered is called "the Eye of Horus." The deceased was thought of as Osiris, and the servitor thus became his pious son Horus, who offered up his eye fighting on behalf of his father. The brief extract which follows is accompanied by the directions to the servitor for his manual acts.

The passages come from the pyramids of Unis and Pepi I (Nefer-ka-Re) of the Fifth and Sixth Dynasties (25th-24th centuries B.C.). Published by K. Sethe, *Die altägyptischen Pyramidentexte* (Leipzig, 1908), I, §§61c-63c.

Words to be spoken: "O Osiris King Nefer-ka-Re, take to thyself the Eye of Horus. Lift thou it to thy face." A lifting of bread and beer.

Lifting before his face. Words to be spoken: "Lift thy face, O Osiris. Lift thy face, O this King Nefer-ka-Re, *whose state of glory has departed*.[1] Lift thy face, O this King Nefer-ka-Re, honored and keen, that thou mayest look at that which came forth from thee,[2] . . . Wash thyself, O King Nefer-ka-Re. Open thy mouth with the Eye of Horus.[3] Thou callest thy *ka*, like Osiris, that it may protect thee from all wrath of the dead.[4] O King Nefer-ka-Re, receive thou this thy bread, which is the Eye of Horus." Laid on the ground before him.

The Daily Ritual in the Temple

The temple ceremonial on behalf of gods or deified pharaohs was elaborate and detailed. Brief extracts are here given of the ritual whereby Amon-Re of Karnak was awakened each morning and prepared for his daily activities. One episode has to do with the preliminary burning of incense, the other two with the opening of the shrine within which the god rested.

The texts are from Berlin Papyrus 3055, facsimiled in *Hieratische Papyrus aus den königlichen Museen zu Berlin*, I (Leipzig, 1901), Pls. I-XXXVII. The manuscript comes from Thebes and dates to the Twenty-second Dynasty (10th-9th centuries B.C.). It was treated by O. von Lemm, *Das Ritualbuch des Amondienstes* (Leipzig, 1882), and by A. Moret, *Le rituel du culte divin journalier en Égypte* (Paris, 1902). For a similar ritual on behalf of the deified Amen-hotep I, see *Hieratic Papyri in the British Museum. Third Series. Chester Beatty Gift* (ed. by A. H. Gardiner, London, 1935), I, 78-106.

For a text which was used in the daily ritual of the temple, see p. 6 above.

(i 1) THE BEGINNING OF THE UTTERANCES OF the sacred rites which are carried out for the House of Amon-Re, King of the Gods, in the course of every day by the major priest who is in his day's (service).

THE UTTERANCE FOR striking the fire. WORDS TO BE SPOKEN: "Welcome, welcome in peace, O Eye of Horus,[1] who art glorious, unharmed, and youthful in peace! It shines forth like Re upon the horizon. The power of Seth has hidden itself before the Eye of Horus, who took it away and brought it back, (so that) it is put in its place (again) for Horus. Triumphant is Horus because of his Eye.[2] The Eye of Horus drives away enemies (5) [for] Amon-Re, Lord of the Thrones of the Two Lands, wherever they may be. An offering which the king gives: I am pure."[3] . . .

(iii 5) . . . THE UTTERANCE FOR breaking the clay.[4] WORDS TO BE SPOKEN: "The clay is broken; the cool waters are opened; the veins of Osiris are drawn.[5] I have certainly not come to drive the god from his throne; I have come to put the god upon his throne. (Thus) thou abidest upon thy great throne, O Amon-Re, Lord of the Thrones of the Two Lands.[6] I am one whom the gods inducted. An offering which the king gives: I am pure."

THE UTTERANCE FOR loosening the shrine.[7] WORDS TO BE SPOKEN: "The finger of Seth is drawn out of the Eye of Horus, (so that) it may become well.[8] The finger of Seth is loosed from the Eye of Horus, (so that) it may become well. The *leather covering* on the back of the god is laid off.[9] O Amon-Re, Lord of the Thrones of the Two Lands, (iv 1) receive thou thy two feathers and thy white crown as the Eye of Horus, the right

---

1 Grammar uncertain, but not: whose glory is lost to him; rather: whose state of other-world being has departed (to the other world).

2 Probably some confusion of Osiris and Horus here, as the Eye came from Horus. Alternatively, the bread which was offered came forth from Osiris as god of the grain.

3 An elaborate ceremonial of "Opening the Mouth" was performed upon a statue of the deceased, in order to enable him to eat, drink, and speak.

4 It is clear that the *ka* could function to protect the deceased from the malignity of other dead, but the significance of the phrase "like Osiris" is not clear.

1 The flame for the incense, like other offerings, was called the Eye of Horus.

2 "True is the voice of Horus because of his Eye," i.e. he triumphed in the legal contest against Seth.

3 Dogmatically the pharaoh was the priest of all the gods. Since it was impossible for him to fulfill this function, he delegated authority to priests, who were thus made pure for the designated activity. There follow this utterance the utterances for taking the censer, for laying the bowl of the censer upon its arm, for putting the incense upon the fire, and for proceeding to the shrine.

4 Breaking the clay sealing of the doors of the shrine.

5 The breaking of the clay is like the opening of an earthen dam in order to release irrigating waters. This, in turn, is likened to the opening of the veins of Osiris, god of the Nile waters.

6 The god, awakened from his night's sleep, must be assured that the priest has no hostile intention and is fit for his role.

7 A variant title in the daily ritual for the goddess Mut (Berlin Papyrus 3014, ii 10, in the same publication) gives: "THE UTTERANCE FOR THE DRAWING BACK OF THE BOLT" (of the shrine door).

8 The door-bolt of the shrine is likened to the finger of Seth with which he damaged the eye of Horus. When the finger was withdrawn, the eye might heal.

9 If the translation is correct, this must refer to a shroud which covered the image of the god by night.

(feather) as a right eye and the left as a left eye.[10] Thou hast thy beauty, O Amon-Re, Lord of the Thrones of the Two Lands: naked, thou art covered; clothed, thou art (further) clothed. Now I am verily a priest; it was the king who sent me to see the god."[11]

[10] Confusing to the modern. The god's headdress consisted of a crown flanked with two feathers. Each feather was an "eye" and the composite headdress the "Eye."

[11] cf. n.3 above. The sense may be: "To be sure, I am (only) a priest, (but) it was the king who sent me to see the god."

Circumcision in Egypt

References to circumcision are rare in ancient Egypt. In the following text the man wishes to record the fact that he came successfully through that rite. The inscription should be studied in conjunction with a scene of circumcision mentioned in the notes to the translation.

The stela probably comes from Naga ed-Der in Middle Egypt and is now at the University of Chicago, Oriental Institute 16956. It was published by D. Dunham, *Naga-ed-Der Stelae of the First Intermediate Period* (London, 1937), Pl. XXXII, No. 84, pp. 102-04. Dunham considers the stela to date from the early part of the First Intermediate Period (23rd century B.C.).

An offering which the king and Anubis, Who is Upon His Mountain, He Who is In Ut, the Lord of the Holy Land, give: an invocation-offering to the Count, Seal-Bearer of the King of Lower Egypt, Sole Companion, and Lector Priest, honored with the great god, the Lord of Heaven, Uha, who says:

"I was one beloved of his father, favored of his mother, whom his brothers and sisters loved. When I was circumcised,[1] together with one hundred and twenty men, there was none thereof who hit out, there was none thereof who was hit, there was none (5) thereof who scratched, there was none thereof who was scratched.[2] I was a commoner of repute, who lived on his (own) property, plowed with (his own) span of oxen, and sailed in his (own) ship, and not through that which I had found in the possession of my father, the honored Uha."[3]

[1] As Dunham points out, this word *sab* may be connected with the Coptic word for "circumcise," *sebbe* or *sebi.* Further, it is probably the same word as the *sebet* attached as a legend to the scene referred to in the following note.

[2] Dunham suggests that these phrases may have referred to the circumcision ceremony or may have been general, that Uha in his career abused no one and was abused by no one. We have taken it as meaning that it was remarkable that so large a group should have been circumcised without injury to the youths or without any youth reacting violently. In support of that possibility, there may be cited the Sixth Dynasty scene at Sakkarah, in the tomb of Ankh-ma-Hor (J. Capart, *Une rue de tombeaux à Saqqarah* [Brussels, 1897], II, Pl. LXVI; W. Wreszinski, *Atlas zur altägyptischen Kulturgeschichte,* III [Leipzig, 1936-], 25-26). This scene shows that the youth might fear the operation sufficiently so that he might have to be held firmly. The legend to the scene is "circumcision," the word being the one of n.1 above, and its determinative suggesting that a flint knife was used. The operator is, interestingly enough, a "mortuary priest," who says to the attendant who is holding the youth: "Hold on to him; do not let him faint." The attendant answers: "I shall act to thy pleasure!" In the neighboring scene the youth says to the operator "*Rub off what is* (*there*) thoroughly." The operator answers: "I shall make (it) heal." These passages indicate that the fear of pain was present. An interesting point in our inscription is the large number who were circumcised at one time. One might conclude that circumcision was effected periodically in a mass ceremony, rather than individually.

[3] An expression of the independent spirit of the end of the Old Kingdom and the beginning of the Middle Kingdom.

Charms Against Snakes

The fear of snakes and scorpions in the ground, of crocodiles in the water, and of lions in the desert was ever-present in ancient Egypt. For an example of a charm which might be used against snakes or scorpions, see pp. 12-14 above.[1] Since the dead were buried in the ground, they also needed protection against the beasts of the ground, so that the mortuary texts in tombs provided adequate magic against snakes.

The following charms come from the pyramids of pharaohs Unis, Teti, and Pepi I of the Fifth-Sixth Dynasties (25th-24th centuries B.C.) at Sakkarah. They are published in K. Sethe, *Die altägyptischen Pyramidentexte* (Leipzig, 1908), I, and translated in his *Uebersetzung und Kommentar zu den altägyptischen Pyramidentexten* (Glückstadt, n.d.), I-II. (a) is Sethe's *Spruch* 228 (§228), (b) is *Spruch* 229 (§229), and (c) is *Spruch* 293 (§§434-35).

a

Words to be spoken: "A face has fallen against a face; a face has seen a face.[2] The mottled knife, black and green, goes forth against it. It has swallowed for itself that which it tasted."[3]

b

Words to be spoken: "This is the fingernail of Atum, which was on the backbone of *Nehebu-ḳau* and which brought to an end the strife in Hermopolis.[4] Fall, roll up!"

c

Words to be spoken: "Back with thee, hidden snake! Hide thyself! Thou shalt not make King Unis see thee. Back with thee, hidden snake! Hide thyself! Thou shalt not come to the place where King Unis is, lest he tell that name of thine against thee: *Nemi,* the son of *Nemit.*[5] The *servant of the Ennead* fell into the Nile.[6] Turn about, turn about! O monster, lie down!"

Curses and Threats

a

In the Sakkarah pyramid of the pharaoh Unis (25th century B.C.), the earth-god Geb is cited as the authority to restrain mortals from abusing the name of the deceased king. The text is in K. Sethe, *Die altägyptischen Pyramidentexte* (Leipzig, 1908), I, §§137-38; translation in Sethe, *Ueberzetsung und*

[1] For amuletic tablets of late times, used against stings or bites, cf. the article by K. C. Seele, Horus on the Crocodiles, in *JNES,* VI (1947), 43-52.

[2] The lurking snake is seen, so that hostile action may be taken against it.

[3] We do not know the significance of the coloring of the knife which consumes the snake. Some mythological reference may be involved.

[4] That which clamps the snake to the ground is likened to the finger (or toe) nail of the god Atum in a myth—otherwise unknown to us—in which he pinned down the snake called *Nehebu-ḳau* and thus concluded some mythological quarrel in Hermopolis. The magical application of known myth to exorcism is obvious in these texts.

[5] The knowledge of a hidden name of power and the ability to release that name and thus weaken the power are themes also of the text in pp. 34-36 above. The hidden name of the snake may be: "Wanderer, the son of Wanderess"; its application is not known.

[6] Another mythological parallel of which the significance escapes us, although it is obvious that, as such a being fell into the Nile, the snake cannot escape. The rendering of the designation of the being is uncertain, perhaps: "the majesty of the shining one." At any rate, the texts determine the designation with the picture of a pelican, which—in myth—must have suffered such a fate.

Kommentar zu den altägyptischen Pyramidentexten (Glückstadt, n.d.), I, 4-5, 11-13.

Other curses will be found in the texts of pp. 25, 201, 377.

Everyone who shall speak evilly against the name of King Unis, when thou ascendest—Geb has decreed that he be a poor man in his town, (so that) he flees and is exhausted.

b

Even the gods were not immune to the threatening magic which might withhold from them their offerings and privileges.[1] The text, in the Sakkarah pyramid of Meri-Re Pepi I (25th-24th century B.C.), is in Sethe, *op. cit.*, II, §§1322-24; translation in H. Kees, *Totenglauben und Jenseitsvorstellungen der alten Aegypter* (Leipzig, 1926), 108.

Every god who will not build the staircase of this Meri-Re for him, when he goes up and when he ascends to heaven—he shall have no offering bread, he shall have no sunshade, he shall not wash himself in the basin, he shall not smell the joint of meat, he shall not taste the leg of meat, earth shall not be hacked up for him, offerings shall not be struck for him—when he goes up, when this Meri-Re ascends to heaven. It is not really this Pepi who says this against you, O gods; it is magic which says this against you, O gods.

c

The tomb was a man's "house of eternity," and violators of a tomb were threatened with an afterlife judgment or with the other-world vengeance of the deceased, who dwelt with the gods. The following text, from the Sakkarah tomb of the Sixth Dynasty magistrate Nenki (24th-23rd century B.C.), appears in K. Sethe, *Urkunden des Alten Reichs* (*Urk.*, I, Leipzig, 1933), 260, and in A. H. Gardiner and K. Sethe, *Egyptian Letters to the Dead* (London, 1928), 10, Pl. x, 1.

As for this tomb, which I have made in the necropolis of the West, I made it (in) a clean and central place. As for any noble, any official, or any man who shall rip out any stone or any brick from this tomb, I will be judged with him by the Great God,[2] I (will) seize his neck like a bird, and I will cause all the living who are upon earth to be afraid of the spirits who are in the West, *which is (still) far from them.*

d

The following text, from the Sakkarah tomb of the Sixth Dynasty vizier Ankh-ma-Hor, is published in Sethe, *op. cit.*, 201-02, and in Gardiner and Sethe, *op. cit.*, 10, Pl. x, 2.

[May it *go well* with you], my successors; may it prosper you, my predecessors! As for anything which ye may do against this my tomb (of) the necropolis, [the like shall be done] against your property. I was a successful and knowing lector priest. *No* magic was *ever* effectively secret from me.[3] [As for] all [people] who may enter into this tomb in their *impurity*,[4] when they have eaten *fish*,[5] the abomination of an effective spirit—(thus) they are not pure for me as they would be pure for an effective spirit who does what his lord praises—[I will seize] him like a bird, (so that) the fear of me is cast into him, so that the spirits and those who are upon earth may see and may be afraid of me, an effective spirit; [I will be] judged with him in that august council of the Great God. But as for every man who may enter [into this tomb] being pure and satisfied with it, I will be his partisan in the necropolis, in the council of the Great God.

e

In addition to afterlife vengeance, perils upon earth might be invoked against an evildoer. The following text is from the Gizeh tomb of the Sixth Dynasty official Meni and is now in the Glyptothek at Munich. Published by Sethe, *op. cit.*, 23, and by A. Scharff in *MDIK*, VIII (1939), 17-33, Pl. 12.

The Eldest of the House Meni says: The crocodile be against him in the water, the snake be against him on land—(against) him who may do a thing to this (tomb). I never did a thing to him. It is the god who will judge (him).

f

The divine king of Egypt might—in effect—excommunicate any violators of a royal decree. The following text is a promise on behalf of the property of a vizier of the First Intermediate Period (23rd century B.C.). It was found in the Temple of Koptos and is now Cairo Museum 41894. Published by R. Weill, *Les decrets royaux de l'ancien empire égyptien* (Paris, 1912), 59-67, Pls. IV, IX, and by Sethe, *op. cit.*, 304-06.

As to all people of this entire land who may do an injurious or evil thing to any statues, offering-stones, chapels, *woodwork*, or monuments of thine which are in any temple precincts or any temples, my majesty does not permit that their property or that of their fathers remain with them, that they join the spirits in the necropolis, or that they remain among the living [*upon earth*].

g

In royal decrees the pharaoh might set mundane legal penalties against acts which could be established by evidence. However, where the evidence might be obscure, he could invoke divine vengeance. The following text is from a decree of Seti I (about 1318-1301 B.C.) at Nauri near the Third Cataract in the Sudan, and is on behalf of a temple of Osiris at Abydos. It was published by F. Ll. Griffith in *JEA*, XIII (1927), 193-206, and translated by W. F. Edgerton in *JNES*, VI (1947), 219-30. This extract is from lines 109-19.

[As to any people] who are in the entire land, to whom shall *come* anybody of the House-of-Men-maat-Re-Heart's-Content-in-Abydos[6] to say: "[*A certain agent*] wronged [me], (for) he took my ox, . . . he took

[1] For this attitude to the gods cf. H. Grapow, Bedrohungen der Götter durch den Verstorbenen, in *ZAeS*, XLIX (1911), 48-54.

[2] The "Great God" in these Old Kingdom contexts was probably the sun-god Re, although Osiris may have been meant (cf. Gardiner and Sethe, *op. cit.*, 11-12).

[3] The lector priest was learned in magic.

[4] The word here and in similar contexts is written as if "purity," but it is obviously undesirable and, by the principle of invoking opposites for magic prophylaxis, probably means "impurity."

[5] Or "abominations." The two words are written identically.

[6] The name of the temple protected by this decree.

my goat"—or anything which may be taken from people, or (to say): "A certain agent took my man by (unlawful) seizure"—and they do not fly at his word to have his opponent brought quickly, in order to judge him—Osiris, the Foremost of the Westerners, the owner of the people and the owner of the property,[7] shall be after him, after his wife, and after his children, to wipe out his name, to destroy his soul, and to prevent his corpse from resting in the necropolis.

But as to any [*magistrate*] who is in any city, to [whom] shall come anybody of the House-of-Men-maat-Re-Heart's-Ease-in-Abydos in order to make complaint to him—and he shall be deaf to him, in order not to fly at his word to do his *business* quickly—the law shall be carried out against him by beating him with one hundred blows, *he being removed* from his office and made a peasant-farmer in [the House-of]-Men-maat-Re-Heart's-Ease-in-Abydos.

h

By a nice application of magic, divine vengeance might be apportioned to a triad of gods. This text, from a temple of Seti I at Wadi Abbad east of Redesiyeh on the Nile, was last published by C. E. Sander-Hansen, *Historische Inschriften der 19. Dynastie* (*Bibliotheca Aegyptiaca*, IV, Brussels, 1933), 29; was translated by Breasted, *AR*, III, §194, and by B. Gunn and A. H. Gardiner in *JEA*, IV (1917), 248.

As to anyone who shall be deaf to this decree, Osiris shall be after him, Isis after his wife, and Horus after his children,[8] and the great ones, the lords of the Holy Land, will make their reckoning with him.

Magical Protection for a Child

A brief extract will serve as an example of protective magic, in this case the mother protecting her sleeping child at night.

Berlin Papyrus 3027, perhaps from the 16th century B.C., was published by A. Erman, *Zaubersprüche für Mutter und Kind* (*APAW*, 1901). The following extract, recto i 9-ii 6, is also in K. Sethe, *Aegyptische Lesestücke* (2nd ed., Leipzig, 1928), 51-52. There is a translation in G. Roeder, *Urkunden zur Religion des alten Aegypten* (Jena, 1923), 116-19.

ANOTHER (CHARM). Mayest thou flow away, he who comes in the darkness and enters in furtively, with his nose behind him, and his face reversed, failing in that for which he came![1]

Mayest thou flow away, she who comes in the darkness and enters in furtively, with her nose behind her, and her face turned backwards, failing in that for which she came!

Hast thou come to kiss this child? I will not let thee kiss him! Hast thou come to silence (him)? I will not let thee set silence over him![2] Hast thou come to injure him? I will not let thee injure him! Hast thou come to take him away? I will not let thee take him away from me!

I have made his magical protection against thee out of *clover*—that is what *sets an obstacle*[3]—out of onions—what injures thee[4]—out of honey—sweet for men, (but) bitter for those who are yonder[5]—out of the *roe* of the *abdju*-fish, out of the jawbone of the *meret*-fish, and out of the backbone of the perch.

[7] Osiris, as the god of the temple, would act to preserve his property.

[8] Similarly in a 20th dynasty tomb at Aniba in Nubia (G. Steindorff, *Aniba* [Glückstadt, 1937], Pl. 101; Breasted, *op. cit.*, IV, §483): "As to anyone who shall speak against it, Amon-Re, King of the Gods, shall be after (him) to destroy him, Mut shall be after his wife, and Khonsu after his child, (so that) he shall hunger, he shall thirst, he shall become weak, and he shall suffer."

[1] Male or female ghosts—it is indicated below that they may be the dead—looking back as the dead look backward, and coveting a child, might slip in at night.

[2] This may be either soothing the child, just as the spirit desired to kiss the child and thus gain its affection, or imposing the silence of death.

[3] Some of the magic packet, which kept the spirits away, had known efficacy, here specifically stated.

[4] Here the magic efficacy arises out of a pun: *hedjw* "onions," and *hedjet* "what injures."

[5] The dead.

The Execration of Asiatic Princes

In the period of the Middle Kingdom the Egyptians resorted to a formal magical cursing of actual or potential enemies of the state. The Berlin Museum possesses numerous fragments of pottery bowls which were inscribed with names and designations of such foes and then smashed. In the Cairo and Brussels Museums inscribed figurines of bound captives carry the same kind of curse. It is clear that the effective magic was: as we smash this pottery, so we break the power of our enemies. The exorcised elements are the Nubians, the Asiatics, the Libyans, hostile Egyptians, and evil forces. The translation below, from the Berlin material, gives some of the Asiatics, the Egyptians, and the forces.

The Berlin fragments were purchased in Thebes; the Cairo and Brussels fragments came from Sakkarah. The period is the latter part of the Twelfth Dynasty or the Thirteenth Dynasty (19th-18th centuries B.C.).[1] The Berlin material was published by K. Sethe, *Die Aechtung feindlicher Fürsten, Völker und Dinge auf altägyptischen Tongefässscherben des mittleren Reiches* (*APAW*, 1926). The numbering below is that of Sethe. The figurines were published by G. Posener, *Princes et pays d'Asie et de Nubie. Textes hiératiques sur des figurines d'envoûtement du Moyen Empire* (Brussels, 1940), with added remarks on the Berlin bowls by B. van de Walle. The extensive literature of comment and identification is not listed here.

Asiatics

(e 1) The Ruler of Iy'aneq,[2] 'Aam, and all the *retainers*[3] who are with him; the Ruler of Iy'aneq, Abi-imamu, and all the *retainers* who are with him; the Ruler of Iy'aneq, 'Akam, and all the *retainers* who are with him;

[1] Posener, *op. cit.*, 31-35, believes that the figurines cannot be earlier than Sen-Usert III (about 1880-1840 B.C.), but may be later, and that the bowls may be slightly older. W. F. Edgerton, in *JAOS*, LX (1940), 492, n.44, states that the Berlin texts "cannot be earlier than Sesostris [=Sen-Usert] III and are more probably to be placed in the Second Intermediate Period." W. F. Albright, in *BASOR*, 88 (1942), 32, places the figurines in the mid-19th century B.C.

[2] Many of the geographic names are unknown, and identifications for most of the others must be tentative. The present name has been related to the *'Anaqim* "giants" who were in the land of Canaan at the time of the Conquest: e.g. Deut. 2:10.

[3] Taken as the Egyptian word for "trusted men." Perhaps the same word as the **hanik* of Gen. 14:14. Posener, on the other hand (26-28), proposes a different word, "smitten ones" or "captives."

(4) the Ruler of Shutu,[4] Ayyabum,[5] and all the *retainers* who are with him; the Ruler of Shutu, Kusher, and all the *retainers* who are with him; the Ruler of Shutu, Tjebanu,[6] and all the *retainers* who are with him; . . .

(23) the Ruler of Isqanu,[7] Khaykim, and all the *retainers* who are with him; . . .

(27) the Ruler of Aushamem,[8] Iyqa-'ammu, and all the *retainers* who are with him; the Ruler of Aushamem, Setj-'anu, and all the *retainers* who are with him; . . .[9]

(31) all the rulers of Iysipi[10] and all the *retainers* who are with them;

(f 1) all the Asiatics—of Byblos, of Iuatji,[11] of Iy'aneq, of Shutu, of Iymu'aru, of Qehermu, of Iahebu, of Iyamut,[12] of Inhia, of Aqhi, of 'Aaqtem,[13] of Iyamut, of Isinu, of Isqanu, of Demitiu, of Mutia, of Aushamem, of 'Akhmut, of Iahenu, and of Iysipi;

(g 1) their strong men, their swift runners, their allies, their associates, and the Mentu[14] in Asia;

(h 1) who may rebel, who may plot, who may fight, who may talk of fighting, or who may talk of rebelling —in this entire land.

Egyptians

(m 1) All men, all people, all folk, all males, all *eunuchs*, all women, and all officials,

(n 1) who may rebel, who may plot, who may fight, who may talk of fighting, or who may talk of rebelling, and every rebel who talks of rebelling—in this entire land.

(o 1) Ameni shall die, the tutor of Sit-Bastet, the *chancellor* of Sit-Hat-Hor, (daughter of) Nefru.[15]

Sen-Usert the younger, called Ketu, shall die, the tutor of Sit-Ipi, (daughter of) Sit-Hat-Hor, and tutor of Sit-Ipi, (daughter of) Sit-Ameni, the *chancellor* of Ii-menet, (daughter of) Sit-Hat-Hor. . . .

(8) Ameni, born to Hetep and son of Sen-Usert, shall die.

Baneful Forces

(p 1) Every evil word, every evil speech, every evil slander, every evil thought, every evil plot, every evil fight, every evil quarrel, every evil plan, every evil thing, all evil dreams, and all evil slumber.

[4] Possibly of Moab; cf. the "sons of Sheth" in Num. 24:17.

[5] The translation has given some of the personal names an Asiatic cast. The Egyptian shows Iy-bem.

[6] Zebulon?

[7] Ashkelon.

[8] Jerusalem.

[9] The figurines in Brussels and Cairo have a number of further identifiable names. (E6 of Posener's numbering) "the Ruler of Shechem, Abesh-Hadad"; (E8) "the Ruler of Pella, 'Aper-'Anu"; (E9) "the Ruler of Aphek, Yenki-Ilu"; (E11) "the Ruler of Achshaph, *Yapanu*"; (E15) "the Ruler of Hazor, Getji"; (E49) "the Ruler of Acre, Ta-'amu"; (E55) "the Ruler of Shemu'anu (Simeon?), Abu-reheni"; (E60) "the Ruler of Beth-Shemesh, *Yetep*-Ilu"; (E61) "the tribe of Irkata"; (E63) "the tribe of Byblos."

[10] Since this region is unknown, it is impossible to say why it employs a different formula, with "rulers" in the plural.

[11] Probably Uzu, "Old Tyre," opposite Tyre.

[12] Perhaps the cuneiform *Iarmuti* of north Syria.

[13] Perhaps *'Irqatum* of Phoenicia.

[14] The "Mentu in Setet" is an old designation for Egypt's immediate neighbors to the northeast.

[15] There are two significant factors about these specifically named Egyptians. First, the names are names characteristic of the 12th dynasty royal family. Second, several of them are functionaries of women who seem to be princesses or queens. One thinks of a harem conspiracy as the setting for such curses. cf. p. 419, n.11.

Religious Drama in Egypt

Much of Egyptian religious ceremonial was carried on in dramatic form. Priests and other initiated persons assumed roles and recited parts in a drama appropriate to a religious purpose. For the most part, such a use of the ceremonial texts is not stated; only occasionally is our evidence more explicit.[1] The following Twelfth Dynasty text records the satisfaction of an official at his opportunity to take part in a passion play of Osiris at Abydos.

The stela of Ii-kher-nofret was found at Abydos and is now 1204 in the Berlin Museum. It was published by H. Schäfer, *Die Mysterien des Osiris in Abydos unter König Sesostris III* (*Untersuch.*, IV, Leipzig, 1904), and the text appears in K. Sethe, *Aegyptische Lesestücke* (2nd ed., Leipzig, 1928), 70-71. Translated by Breasted, *AR*, I, §§661-70.

For a text to present religious drama in an Egyptian temple, see pp. 4-6 above.

For other texts used for magical purposes see pp. 6-7, 12-14, and 29-31 above. For further references to magic, see p. 215, n.11; p. 215, n.15-16; p. 442, n.18.

Live the Horus: Divine of Form; the Two Goddesses: Divine of Birth; the Horus of Gold: Who Comes into Being; the King of Upper and Lower Egypt: Khakau-Re; the Son of Re: Sen-Usert, given life like Re forever.[2] Royal decree to the Hereditary Prince and Count, Seal-Bearer of the King of Lower Egypt, Sole Companion, Overseer of the Two Houses of Gold, Overseer of the Two Houses of Silver, and Chief Treasurer, Ii-kher-nofret, the possessor of reverence:

"My majesty has commanded that thou be sent upstream to Abydos of the Thinite nome, to make monuments for my father Osiris, the Foremost of the Westerners, and to embellish his mysterious image with the fine gold which he caused my majesty to bring out of the land of Nubia in victory and in triumph. Now thou shalt do this in (5) the truest way to do a thing, . . . inasmuch as it is the case that thou hast had recourse to the teaching of my majesty—for thou didst really grow up as my majesty's ward, the sole pupil of my palace, and I made thee a *courtier* when thou wert a youth of twenty-six years. . . . Go thou, and return when thou hast acted according to all that my majesty has commanded."

(10) I acted according to all that his majesty commanded in accomplishing what my lord had commanded for his father Osiris, the Foremost of the Westerners, the Lord of Abydos, the great power residing in the Thinite nome.

I acted as the "Son-Whom-He-Loves"[3] for Osiris, the Foremost of the Westerners. I adorned his great barque of eternity and everlastingness. I made for him a port-

[1] For example, in the two documents studied by K. Sethe, *Dramatische Texte zu altägyptischen Mysterienspielen* (*Untersuch.*, x, Leipzig, 1928); cf. pp. 4-5 above.

[2] Sen-Usert III (about 1880-1840 B.C.).

[3] The pious son who performs funerary rites for his father—here the role of Horus for his father Osiris.

able shrine which would carry the beauty of the Foremost of the Westerners, of gold, silver, lapis lazuli, *carob*-wood, and *meru*-wood. The gods who attended him were fashioned, and their shrines were made anew. I laid [*a charge upon*] the hour-priests of the temple to do their duties, and they were made to know the regulations for every day and the feasts of the beginnings of the seasons. I conducted the work on the *neshmet*-barque,[4] and I fashioned the cabin. (15) I decked the breast of the Lord of Abydos with lapis lazuli and turquoise, fine gold, and all costly stones which are the ornaments of a god's body. I clothed the god with his regalia in my office of privy councilor and my duty of *ritualist*. I was pure of hand in decking the god, a *sem*-priest purified of fingers.

I celebrated the Procession of Up-wawet, when he went forth to champion his father.[5] I opposed those rebellious to the *neshmet*-barque, and I overthrew the enemies of Osiris. I celebrated the Great Procession, following the god in his footsteps. I caused the god's boat to sail, while Thoth guided the journey.[6] I outfitted with a cabin the barque (named) "Appearing in Truth, the Lord of Abydos." (20) His beautiful regalia was fixed, when he proceeded to the *domain* of Peqer.[7] I cleared the ways of the god to his tomb which is in Peqer. I championed Wen-nofer[8] on that day of the Great Fight, and I overthrew all his enemies on the *flats* of Nedit.[9] I caused him to proceed into the *weret*-barque,[10] and it carried his beauty. I made the eastern deserts glad; I [*caused* re]joicing in the western deserts, when they saw the beauty of the *neshmet*-barque, as it landed at Abydos and brought [Osiris, the Foremost of the Westerners, the Lord] of Abydos, to his palace. I accompanied the god into his house. When his purification had taken place and his place had been widened, I loosened the knot within the . . . , [*and he came to rest* among] his [*retinue*] and among his court.

4 Osiris' sacred barque at Abydos.

5 The god Up-wawet, the "Opener of the Ways," led off with the "First Procession" at the Osiris mysteries. cf. the text published by A. N. Dakin in *JEA*, XXIV (1938), 190-97: "Kissing the ground to the Foremost of the Westerners in the Great Procession, when the god is ferried across to Peqer, and seeing the beauty of Up-wawet in the First Procession."

6 A priestly actor playing the role of the god Thoth. Perhaps this was Ii-kher-nofret himself, as it is possible to translate: "a Thoth in guiding the journey."

7 The part of Abydos in which the Egyptians located the tomb of Osiris, probably the area in which the tombs of the kings of the first two dynasties lay.

8 Osiris.

9 In Egyptian mythology, Seth slew Osiris on the "shore of Nedit." Here it is the scene of a drama in which Osiris repulses attack.

10 Perhaps a separate boat from the *neshmet*. cf. J. A. Wilson in *JNES*, III (1944), 206-07.

Akkadian Rituals

TRANSLATOR: A. SACHS

Temple Program for the New Year's Festivals at Babylon

Copies, transcriptions, and translations: F. Thureau-Dangin, *Rituels accadiens* (Paris, 1921), 127-154; translation only: E. Ebeling, *AOT*, 295-303. Two duplicate texts are involved, one in Paris and the other in London, both tablets dating to the Seleucid period. The program described may go back to a much earlier time.

On the second day of the month Nisannu, two hours of the night (remaining?), the *urigallu*-priest shall arise and wash with river water. He shall enter into the presence of the god Bel, and he shall . . . a linen *gadalū* in front of Bel. He shall recite the following prayer.

O Bel, who has no equal when angry,
O Bel, excellent king, lord of the countries,
Who makes the great gods friendly,
O Bel, who fells the mighty with his glance,
Lord of the kings, light of mankind, who divides the portions—
O Bel, your dwelling is the city of Babylon, your tiara is the (neighboring) city of Borsippa,
Broad heaven is the "totality of your liver."
O Bel, with your eyes you see all things,
[With] your oracles you *verify* the oracles,
[With] your glance you hand down the law.
[With] your . . . you . . . the mighty;
When you look (at them), you grant them mercy;
You show them the light, (and) they speak of your valor.
Lord of the countries, light of the Igigi deities (who) bless—
Who (does not speak) of you, does not speak of your valor?
Who does not speak of your glory, does not glorify your sovereignty?
Lord of the countries, who dwells in the temple Eudul, who grasps the hand of the fallen,
Grant mercy to your city, Babylon!
Turn your face to the temple Esagil, your house!
Establish the "liberty" of the people of Babylon, your subordinates.

(Colophon:) Twenty-one lines (of writing): secrets of the temple Esagil. [Whoever rev]eres the god Bel shall show (them) to nobody except the *urigallu*-priest of the temple Ekua.

[After] he speaks the recitation, he shall [open the gate]. The *ēribbīti*-priests [shall arise] and perform their rites, in the traditional manner, [before] the deities Bel and Beltiya. [The *kalū*-priests and the] singers (shall do) likewise.

(eight lines missing or hopelessly broken)

. . . he shall place . . . ; a seal . . . in the tiara of the god Anu . . . of the second day, upon . . . he shall place . . . before them. Three times he shall speak. . . .

The evil enemies . . . who in their strength . . . this which in . . . of the exorcism . . . because the enemy and the bandit . . . the great lord, Marduk . . . has uttered a curse that cannot be altered . . . has decreed a fate that cannot be withdrawn . . . who . . . the god Bel, my lord; who . . . the lord of the countries, who . . . the city of Babylon. In the middle of the earth . . . who . . . the temple Eudul, the purification of . . . like heaven and earth . . . who extracts . . . the temples of . . . the forgetting of their rites . . . who overwhelms . . . the people dwelling in . . . the maidservants . . . of the city Babylon . . . who . . . the temple Eudul, he bound (all) of you . . . (all) of you dwell. . . .

(about 75 lines missing)

(157) On the [third] day of the month Nisannu, [at . . . o'clock, the *urigallu*-priest] shall arise [and] wash with [. . . . He shall speak the following] prayer to the god Bel.

(about 25 lines missing or hopeless)

. . . He shall open the doors. [All the *ēribbīti*-priests] shall enter and perform [their rites in the traditional manner. The *kalū*-priests and the singers shall do likewise.]

(two lines missing)

When it is three hours after sunrise, [he shall call] a metalworker and give him precious stones and gold [from] the treasury of the god Marduk to make two images for (the ceremonies of) the sixth day (of Nisannu). He shall call a woodworker and give him (some) cedar and tamarisk (pieces). He shall call a goldsmith and give him (some) gold. From the third day (of the month Nisannu) to the sixth day, (pieces of meat) from (the slaughtered sheep offered) before the god Bel (are to be distributed as follows:) the *tail* to the metalworker, the breast to the goldsmith, the thigh to the woodworker, the rib(s) to the weaver. These (pieces of meat) from (the slaughtered sheep offered) before the god Bel shall be delivered to the *urigallu*-priest for the artisans.

Those two images (which the artisans are to make) shall be 7 finger(-widths) high. One (shall be made) of cedar, one of tamarisk. *Four dušū*-stones shall be mounted in settings of gold weighing *four* shekels. [One image] shall hold in its left hand a snake (made) of cedar, raising its right [hand] to the god Nabu. The second (image) shall hold in its [left hand] a scorpion, raising its right hand [to the god] Nabu. They shall be clothed in red garments, [bou]nd in the middle [with] a palm [br]anch. Until the sixth day (of the month Nisannu), [they shall be placed] in the house of the god Madan. *Food* (from) the tray of the god Madan shall be presented to them. On the sixth day (of the month), when the god Nabu reaches the temple Ehursagtila, the slaughterer . . . shall strike off their heads. Then, a *fire* having been started in the presence of the god Nabu, they shall be thrown into it.

On the fourth day of the month Nisannu, three and one-third hours of the night (remaining?), the *urigallu*-priest shall arise and wash with river water. A linen *gadalū* he shall . . . in front of the god Bel and the goddess Beltiya. He shall recite the following prayer, while lifting his hand, to the god Bel.

Powerful master of the Igigi gods, exalted among the great gods,
Lord of the world, king of the gods, divine Marduk, who establishes the plan,
Important, elevated, exalted, superior,
Who holds kingship, grasps lordship,
Bright light, god Marduk, who dwells in the temple Eudul,
. . . who sweeps the enemy's land,
. . . (three lines missing) . . .
Who . . .s heaven, heaps up the earth,
Who measures the waters of the sea, cultivates the fields,
Who dwells in the temple Eudul; lord of Babylon, exalted Marduk,
Who decrees the fates of all the gods,
Who turns over the pure scepter to the king who reveres him—
I am the *urigallu*-priest of the temple Ekua, who *blesses* you.
To your city, Babylon, grant release!
To Esaggil, your temple, grant mercy!
At your exalted command, O lord of the great gods,
Let light be set before the people of Babylon.

He shall (then) withdraw from the presence of the god Bel and recite the following prayer to the goddess Beltiya.

Powerful, goddess, (most) exalted of the female divinities,
Sarpanitu, who shines brilliantly (among) the stars, who dwells in the temple Eudul,
. . . of the goddesses, whose garment is (bright) light,
Who . . .s heaven, heaps up the earth,
Sarpanitu, whose position is exalted,
Bright, Beltiya, sublime and elevated—
There is none like her among the female divinities—
Who brings complaints, who defends,
Who impoverishes the rich, who causes the poor to become wealthy,
Who fells the enemy who does not fear her divinity,
Who releases the prisoner, grasps the hand of the fallen—
Bless the slave who *blesses* you!
Decree the destiny for the king who reveres you!
Grant life to the people of Babylon, who are your subordinates,
Defend them in the presence of Marduk, king of the gods!
May (the people) speak your praise, magnify your lordship,
Speak of your heroism, exalt your name.
Grant mercy to the servant who blesses you,
Take his hand (when he is) in great difficulty and need!
Present him with life when he is sick and in pain,
(So that) he may constantly walk in happiness and joy,
Speaking of your heroism to all people.

He shall (then) go out to the Exalted Courtyard, turn to the north and bless the temple Esagil three times with the blessing: "Iku-star, Esagil, image of heaven and earth." He shall (then) open the doors. All the *ēribbīti*-priests shall enter and perform their rites in the traditional manner. The *kalū*-priests and the singers (shall do) likewise.

When this is done, [and after] the second meal of the late afternoon, the *urigallu*-priest of the temple Ekua shall recite (while lifting his hand?) to the god Bel the (composition entitled) *Enūma eliš*. While he recites *Enūma eliš* to the god Bel, the front of the tiara of the god Anu and the resting place of the god Enlil shall be covered.

On the fifth day of the month Nisannu, four hours of the night (remaining?), the *urigallu*-priest shall arise and wash with water from the Tigris and Euphrates. [He shall enter into the presence of the god Bel, and] he shall . . . a linen *gadalū* in front of the god Bel and the goddess Beltiya. He shall recite the following prayer [to Bel].

My Lord, is he not my lord?
My Lord, . . . , is not his name My Lord?
My Lord, . . . , My Lord, king of the countries,
My Lord, . . . , My Lord, . . . ,
Is it not My Lord who gives, My Lord who . . . ?
My Lord, . . . , My Lord, . . . ,
My Lord, . . . , My Lord, . . . ,
My Lord, . . . , My Lord, who dwells in the temple Eudul,
My Lord, . . . , My Lord, . . . ,
My Lord, . . . , My Lord, who gives,
My Lord, . . . , My Lord, who dwells in the chapel,
My Lord, . . . , My Lord, he is my lord.
God of heaven and earth, who decrees the fates—My Lord, be calm!

The star Musirkeshda, who carries the (royal) scepter and circle, My Lord—My Lord, be calm!
The Eridu star, the possessor of wisdom, My Lord—My Lord, be calm!
Asari, who grants the gift of cultivation, My Lord—My Lord, be calm!
Planet Jupiter, who carries the *sign* for all, My Lord—My Lord, be calm!
Planet Mercury, who causes it to rain, My Lord—My Lord, be calm!
Planet Saturn, star of justice and righteousness, My Lord—My Lord, be calm!
Planet Mars, fierce flame, My Lord—My Lord, be calm!
The star Sirius, who measures the waters of the sea, My Lord—My Lord, be calm!
The star Shupa, lord of the Enlil gods, My Lord—My Lord, be calm!
The star Nenegar, who was self-created, My Lord—My Lord, be calm!
The star Numushda, who causes the rains to *continue*, My Lord—My Lord, be calm!
The *Sting*-of-the-Scorpion star, who . . . the breast of the ocean, My Lord—My Lord, be calm!
Sun, light of the world, My Lord—My Lord, be calm!
Moon, who brings the darkness, My Lord—My Lord, be calm!
My Lord is my god, My Lord is my lord. Who, except for you, is lord?

To the goddess he shall recite the following prayer.

My *merciful* Lady—My Lady, be calm!
My Lady, who does not become angry, who is calm,
My Lady, who gives, My Lady, who is so very good,
My Lady, . . . , My Lady, who is so very good,
The *calm* lady, who does not become angry, My Lady, who confers *gifts*,
My Lady, (who receives) prayer, My Lady, who confers *gifts*,
Damkianna, mistress of heaven and earth, whose name is My Lady,
Planet Venus, who shines brilliantly (among) the stars, whose name is My Lady,
The star Ban, who fells the mighty, whose name is My Lady.
The star Uz, who views heaven, whose name is My Lady,
The star Hegala, the star of abundance, whose name is My Lady,
The star Baltesha, the star of *sensuousness*, whose name is My Lady,
The star Margidda, the bond of heaven, whose name is My Lady,
The star Eru, who creates sperm, whose name is My Lady,
The star Ninmah, who makes a gift of life, whose name is My Lady,
My Lady, her name is My Lady. Is not her name My Lady?

After the recitation has been recited, he shall open the doors. All the *ēribbīti*-priests shall (then) enter and perform their rites in the traditional manner. The *ḳalū*-priests and the singers (shall do) likewise.

When it is two hours after sunrise, after the trays of the god Bel and the goddess Beltiya have been set, he shall call a *mašmašu*-priest to purify the temple and sprinkle water, (taken from) a cistern of the Tigris and a cistern of the Euphrates, on the temple. He shall beat the kettle-drum inside the temple. He shall have a censer and a torch brought into the temple. [He(?)] shall *remain* in the courtyard; he shall not enter the sanctuary of the deities Bel and Beltiya. When the purification of the temple is completed, he shall enter the temple Ezida, into the sanctuary of the god Nabu, with censer, torch, and *egubbū*-vessel to purify the temple, and he shall sprinkle water (from) the Tigris and Euphrates cisterns on the sanctuary. He shall smear all the doors of the sanctuary with cedar *resin*. In the court of the sanctuary, he shall place a silver censer, upon which he shall mix aromatic ingredients and cypress. He shall call a slaughterer to decapitate a ram, the body of which the *mašmašu*-priest shall use in performing the *ḳuppuru*-ritual for the temple. He shall recite the incantations for exorcising the temple. He shall purify the whole sanctuary, including its environs, and shall remove the censer. The *mašmašu*-priest shall lift up the body of the aforementioned ram and proceed to the river. Facing west, he shall throw the body of the ram into the river. He shall (then) go out into the open country. The slaughterer shall do the same thing with the ram's head. The *mašmašu*-priest and the slaughterer shall go out into the open country. As long as the god Nabu is in Babylon, they shall not enter Babylon, but stay in the open country from the fifth to the twelfth day (of the month Nisannu). The *urigallu*-priest of the temple Ekua shall not view the purification of the temple. If he does view (it), he is no (longer) pure. After the purification of the temple, when it is three and one-third hours after sunrise, the *urigallu*-priest of the temple Ekua shall go out and call all the artisans. They shall bring forth the Golden Heaven from the treasury of the god Marduk and (use it to?) cover the temple Ezida, the sanctuary of the god Nabu, from (its) . . . to the foundation of the temple. The *urigallu*-priest and the artisans shall recite the following *loud* recital.

They purify the temple,
The god Marduk from Eridu, who dwells in the temple Eudul,
The god Kusug . . . ,
The deity Ningirim, who listens to prayers,

The god Marduk purifies the temple,
The god Kusug draws the plans,
The deity Ningirim casts the spell.
Go forth, evil that happens to be in this temple!
May the god Bel kill you, evil demon!
Wherever you are, be suppressed!

All the artisans shall (then) go out to the gate.

[. . . hours . . .] the day, the *urigallu*-priest [shall enter] into the presence of the god Bel, and shall . . . [in front of B]el. He shall [prepare] the golden tray, placing upon it *roasted* meat, [. . .], twelve of the usual *loaves*, a gold . . . filled with salt, a gold . . . filled with honey, . . . , four gold dishes. He shall place a gold censer . . . in front of the tray; aromatic ingredients and cypress. . . . He shall make a libation of wine. . . . . He shall recite the following.

[Marduk], exalted among the gods,
[Who dwells in the temple Esag]il, who creates the laws,
[Who . . .] to the great gods,
[. . .] I praise your heroism.
[May] your heart [be sympathetic] to whoever seizes your hands.
[In Esiz]kur, the temple of prayer,
[In . . .], your place, may he raise up his head.

After he recites the [recitation], he shall clear the tray. He shall summon all the artisans and shall turn the whole tray over to them to bring to the god Nabu. The artisans shall take it, and in . . . they shall go. When Nabu arrives [at . . .], they shall . . . it to Nabu. [When] they have set the tray before the god Nabu, they shall lift up the *loaves* (which are on?) the tray as soon as Nabu [leaves] the ship called Iddahedu, and then on the tray. . . . They shall bring water (for washing) the king's hands and then shall accompany him [to the temple Esag]il. The artisans shall go out to the gate. When he (that is, the king) reaches [the presence of the god Bel], the *urigallu*-priest shall leave (the sanctuary) and take away the scepter, the circle, and the sword [from the king]. He shall bring them [before the god Bel] and place them [on] a chair. He shall leave (the sanctuary) and strike the king's cheek. He shall place the . . . behind him. He shall accompany him (that is, the king) into the presence of the god Bel. . . . he shall drag (him by) the ears and make him bow down to the ground. . . . The king shall speak the following (only) once: "I did [not] sin, lord of the countries. I was not neglectful (of the requirements) of your godship. [I did not] destroy Babylon; I did not command its overthrow [I did not .] . . the temple Esagil, I did not forget its rites. [I did not] rain blows on the cheek of a subordinate. . . . I did [not] humiliate them. [I watched out] for Babylon; I did not smash its walls." . . . (About five lines are missing. The *urigallu*-priest is speaking when the text begins again.) ". . . Have no fear . . . which the god Bel. . . . The god Bel [will listen to] your prayer . . . he will magnify your lordship . . . he will exalt your kingship. . . . On the day of the *eššešu*-festival, do . . . in the festival of the Opening of the Gate, purify [your] hands . . . day and night. . . . [The god Bel], whose city is Babylon . . . , whose temple is Esagil . . . whose dependents are the people of Babylon. . . . The god Bel will bless you . . . forever. He will destroy your enemy, fell your adversary." After (the *urigallu*-priest) says (this), the king shall regain his *composure*. . . . The scepter, circle, and sword [shall be restored] to the king. He shall strike the king's cheek. If, when [he strikes] the king's cheek, the tears flow, (it means that) the god Bel is friendly; if no tears appear, the god Bel is angry: the enemy will rise up and bring about his downfall.

When (these things) have been done, at *sunset*, the *urigallu*-priest shall tie together forty reeds—each three cubits long, uncut, unbroken, straight—using a palm branch as the bond. A hole shall be dug in the Exalted Courtyard and he shall put (the bundle into it). He shall put (in it) honey, cream, first-quality oil. . . . He shall . . . a white bull [before the hole]. The king shall [set all this afire] with a burning reed. The king [and the *urigallu*-priest shall recite] the following recitation.

O Divine Bull, brilliant light which lig[hts up the darkness], . . . (The remainder of the prayer and the ritual is broken away.)

Ritual to be Followed by the *Kalū*-Priest when Covering the Temple Kettle-Drum

This ritual is known from four texts, designated below as A, B, C, and D; all four texts are transcribed and translated by F. Thureau-Dangin, *Rituels accadiens* (Paris, 1921), 10 ff. Text A, now in the Louvre, was copied in the Seleucid period in the city of Uruk; the latest copy is by F. Thureau-Dangin, *TCL*, VI, No. 44, the latest translation by E. Ebeling, *AOT*, 303 ff. Text B, now in Berlin, was excavated at Ashur, where it had been copied from older Babylonian texts in the seventh century B.C.; a copy of the text was published by E. Ebeling, *KAR*, I, No. 60. Text C consists of two duplicate texts, in Berlin and London, the former excavated at Ashur and the latter at Nineveh, both having been copied in the seventh century B.C. from older tablets which came from Babylonia; one was published by E. Ebeling, *KAR*, I, No. 50, the other by H. Zimmern, *Beiträge zur Kenntnis der bab. Rel.*, Ritualtafeln No. 56. Text D, from Nineveh, was published in Vol. IV of Rawlinson, No. 1 of Plate 23; it is a copy of an older text which came from Babylonia.

TEXT A

(i) When you [are confronted with the task of] covering (that is, replacing the head of) the kettle-drum (used in the temple, proceed as follows). An expert shall inspect—from head to tip of tail—a sound black bull whose horns and hooves are whole. If its body is black as pitch, it shall be taken for the ceremony. (5) If it is spotted by (as many as?) seven white tufts (which look like) stars, or if it has (ever?) been struck with a staff or touched by a goad, it shall not be taken for the ceremony.

When you have the bull led into the *mummu*-house, on an auspicious day you shall stand at its side, sweep the ground, sprinkle pure water, (and) . . . the *mummu*-house. You shall lay two bricks, (one) at the right, (the other) at the left of the doorway of the *mummu*-house. (10) You shall scatter *flour* for the god(s) of heaven, the god(s) of heaven and earth, and the great gods. You shall make a libation of prime beer. You shall (then) have the bull led into the *mummu*-house. You shall lay down a reed mat. You shall scatter sand beneath the reed mat, and you shall surround the reed mat with sand. You shall set the bull on the reed mat, tying his legs with a bond made of goat's hair. (15) Opposite the bull, you shall place beer (made of) . . . , in a bronze *drum*. You shall set up [two] *egubbû*-vessels for the deities Kusug and Ningirim. You shall set up [two] stands; on each you shall place seven loaves of barley bread, seven loaves of emmer bread, a paste of honey and cream, dates, and *šasqû*-flour. You shall set up (vessels containing?) [beer, wine,] and milk. You shall set up an *adagurru*-vessel. (Of lines 20-36 only the following ends of lines are preserved:) . . . cypress . . . you shall set up a drinking cup . . . one-third of a pound of white wool . . . seven and one-half (pounds?) of goat's hair you shall put down . . . beer (made of) . . . tamarisk . . . reed . . . thorn . . . you shall lay down an *egubbû*-vessel . . . cedar *sap*, honey, cream . . . you shall lay down; [you shall purify] with a censer and a torch . . . thigh, . . . , and *roasted* meat you shall offer; you shall make a libation of [prime beer, wine], and milk . . . you shall lay down . . . *egubbû*-vessel . . . you shall lay twelve bricks. (ii) On (the bricks) you shall lay twelve (pieces of) linen. On them you shall seat all twelve gods. You shall lift up the *egubbû*-vessel of the deity Ningirim and with its water you shall clean the equipment prepared for the ceremony. You shall sprinkle some (aromatic?) barley seed. You shall set up the kettle-drum. (5) You shall lay a brick for the deity Lumha. You shall set up a stand. You shall slaughter a sheep. You shall offer the thigh, . . . , and *roasted* meat. You shall make a libation of prime beer, wine, and milk. Before these (gods) you shall place water. You shall draw the curtains shut. On the bull you shall perform the rite of Washing the Mouth. You shall whisper through a reed tube into the bull's right ear the incantation entitled "*Gugal gumaḫ u ḳiuš ḳuga.*" (10) You shall whisper through a reed tube into the bull's left ear the incantation entitled "*Alpu ilittu Zī attāma.*" You shall besprinkle the bull with cedar *resin*. You shall purify the bull, using a brazier and a torch. You shall draw a ring of *zisurra*-flour around the bull. Standing at its head, you shall sing (the composition called) "*Nitugḳi niginna*" to the accompaniment of a bronze *ḫalḫallatu*. (15) After that, you shall recite (the composition entitled) "*Dimmer . . . anḳia mundimma.*" Then you shall cut open that bull and start a fire with cedar. You shall burn the bull's heart with cedar, cypress, and *maṣḫatu*-flour before the kettle-drum. You shall remove the tendon of its left shoulder and shall bury the body of that bull (wrapped) in a single red . . . cloth. (20) You shall throw some *gunnu*-oil on it (and) arrange it so that its face points to the west. You shall take the hide of that bull and dip it in fine flour made from clean barley, in water, prime beer, (and) wine. You shall then lay it in the pure fat of a bull and aromatic ingredients, (taken) from the hearts of plants, with four *qa*-measures of ground malt, four *qa*-measures of *bitqa*-flour, (and) one (*qa*-measure?) of. . . . (25) You shall press (it) with gall-nuts and alum from the land of the Hittites. (With it) you shall cover the bronze kettle-drum. On it you shall stretch a linen cord. Drumsticks (or pegs?) of *musuḳannu*-wood, . . .-wood, cedar, and *ušu*-wood, and all the rest of the *drum-sticḳs* (of?) *maštu*-wood *for* the bronze kettle-drum you shall *cover* with *varnish*. (30) With the tendon of (the bull's) left shoulder you shall . . . its *opening*. You shall loosen the (linen) cord, and lay it on a *napdû*. You shall bury the . . . . You shall make preparations for a sacrifice to the god Lumha. You shall sacrifice a sheep and shall offer the thigh, the . . . , and *roasted* meat. (35) You shall make a libation of prime beer, wine, and milk.

(iii) Anu, Enlil, and Ea, the great gods. The deities Lugalgirra and Meslamtaea. The deity Zisummu (or) Ninsig, who is in the city Nippur. (5) The deity Bigirhush (or) Shuzianna, of the *apsû*-ocean. The deity Sabarragimgimme (or) Ennugi, who cultivates the fields. The deity Urbadda (or) Kusug, the exalted lord. (10) The deity Urbadgumgum (or) Ninsar, the son of the temple Eshabba. The deity Gubbagarrae (or) Ninkasi, the son of the new city. The deity Abarralah (or) Nusku, *born* on the thirtieth day (of the month, when the moon is) invisible.

(15) On the fifteenth day, you shall cause the bronze kettle-drum to be brought forth to the presence of the god Shamash. You shall prepare five sacrifices for the deities Ea, Shamash, Marduk, Lumha, and the Divine Kettle-Drum. You shall sacrifice a sheep and offer the thigh, the . . . , and *roasted* meat. You shall make a libation of (20) prime beer, wi[ne, and milk]. You shall perform the purifications with brazier and torch and with water from the *egubbû*-vessel. You shall recite three times (the composition entitled) "*Enḳi Utu . . . zadede.*" You shall cause to be performed the rite of the Washing of the Mouth . . . on it (that is, the kettle-drum). You shall anoint it with *animal fat* and filtered oil. The *ḳalamaḫḫu*-priest (25) shall lay . . . upon the bronze kettle-drum. You shall (then) remove the (sacrificial) accoutrements (and) shall purify it (that is, the kettle-drum) with brazier and torch. You shall grasp the "hand" of the kettle-drum (and bring it?)

to the presence of the gods, setting it in (aromatic?) barley seed. You shall *perform* the lamentation (called?) "*Lugale dimmer ankia.*"

(Colophon:) This ritual, which you perform, (only) the properly *qualified* person (30) shall view. An outsider who has nothing to do with the ritual shall not view (it); if he does, may his remaining days be few! The informed person may show (this tablet) to the informed person. The uninformed shall not see (it)—it is among the forbidden things of Anu, Enlil, and Ea, the great gods. (iv) [Whoever . . .], may his [remaining days] be many!

(Equipment to be assembled:) . . . the bronze kettle-drum . . . cypress, one-half pound of *sweet-smelling* reed, (5) . . . of *roses*, ten shekels of aromatic *annabu*, . . . of *kasisiḫatu*, . . . of *kanaktu*, . . . of *suadi*, two *qa*-measures of filtered oil, . . . two *qa*-measures of wine, (10) . . . of *bitqa*-flour, four *qa*-measures of ground malt, . . . one-half *qa*-measure of cedar *sap*, . . . *varnish*, . . . the *wrappings* of the *drum-sticks*.

. . . white . . .-cloth, one red . . .-cloth, (15) . . . pounds of wool, seven pounds of . . . , . . . seven pounds of blue wool, . . . [goat's] hair, two *kur*-measures and four *pan*-measures of barley, one *pan*-measure of (aromatic?) barley seed, . . . emmer, salt, and cypress, one reed, . . . utensils (20) of iron . . . one-half pound of alum from the land of the Hittites, one pound of bright *varnish; drum-sticks*, three *of musukannu*-wood, three of . . .-wood, three of cedar, three of *ušu*-wood, three of tamarisk—all the rest of the *drum-sticks* of *maštu*-wood; (25) ten linen cords, each cord ten cubits long; one linen cord, one-hundred cubits long; ten cords of goat's hair, four cubits long; one cord, with which the bull was bound; one . . . ; one cover.

The equipment (to be made by) the potter are: four *egubbû*-vessels, four *kandurû*-vessels, (30) four *saḫḫaru*-vessels, twenty-four *ḫabû*-vessels, 120 *malittu*-vessels, 300 *bagurru*-vessels, sixty braziers, five *ṣabittu*, six *aggannu*, six *nisippu*, two *ṣindû*, two *namḫaru*. The equipment (to be made by) the woodworker: one *kummu*, four iron pegs, wood for the pegs (or drum-sticks?). The equipment for the wickerworker: twenty-four stands, twenty-four *baskets*, five *hand baskets*, three mats, three covers.

(Colophon:) Ritual of the *kalû*-priest. Tablet belonging to Anuahaiddin, the son of Rihatanu, the *kalamaḫḫu*-priest of the deities Anu and Antu, citizen of Uruk. It was copied from an old(er) tablet, checked, and rechecked.

TEXT B

(beginning and end of tablet broken)

. . . water before them . . . the *kalû*-priest in a bronze *drum*. . . . You shall lay down a reed mat, [strewing sand] beneath the mat and (5) surrounding the sides of the reed mat with sand. You shall set the bull upon the reed mat and besprinkle him with water from the *egubbû*-vessel; you shall wash the bull's mouth. You shall encircle the bull with a circle made of *zisurra*-flour and lay a brick in front of the bull. You shall sprinkle some cypress on the brazier and make a libation of prime beer. (10) You shall whisper through a reed tube into the bull's right ear the incantation entitled "*Gugal gumaḫ u kiuš kuga.*" You shall whisper through a reed tube into his left ear the incantation entitled "*Alpu ilittu Zī attāma.*" You shall place the bull before the god Lumha and . . . with cedar *sap*. (15) Then you shall *cut open* that bull and (burn) the bull's heart before the god Lumha with cypress, (cedar, and *maṣḫatu*-flour). You shall sprinkle (some cypress upon the brazier) and make a libation of beer. The *kalû*-priest shall remove his head, . . . he shall bow down and remain at the bull's head, reciting three times the composition entitled "*Mulu na.*" Furthermore, he shall recite the following words three times: "These acts—it is the totality of the gods who have performed (them); it is not (really) I who performed them." You shall then take away the water and open the curtains. (5) You shall take the above-mentioned hide and *dip* it in crushed flour made from clean barley, in water, beer and first-class wine. You shall press (it) with fat from a clean bullock, alum from the land of the Hittites, and gall-nuts. (With it) you shall cover the bronze kettle-drum. With the left tendon of the (bull's) shoulder you shall . . . its *opening*. (10) You shall wrap the *drum-sticks* with *fluffy* wool and *cover* it with *varnish*; you shall. . . . In an auspicious month, you shall find a favorable day, and then you shall perform all these acts. The *kalamaḫḫu*-priest shall not eat any of the flesh of the above-mentioned bull. . . .

TEXT C

(obverse)

Incantation: You are the Exalted Bull, created by the great gods.
You were created for the service of the great gods. . . .
In the heavens your image . . . for the rites of divinity. (5)
When the gods Anu, Enlil, Ea, and Ninmah [decreed] the destinies of the great gods,
Your skin (and) your muscles were destined for the secrets of the great gods. (10)
Remain for everlasting days in this secret!
(O great gods,) fix the destiny of this image with the gods, his brothers!
As for this god, may his temple be holy
and pure! (15)
May the evil tongue remain outside!

(reverse)

The ritual (is as follows). On a good day in the correct month, in the morning, before sunrise, you shall prepare three sacrificial stands for the gods Ea, Shamash, and Marduk. (On the stands,) you shall sprinkle some dates and *šasqû*-flour and shall set a mixture of honey and *cream*. (5) You shall slaughter three white sheep and offer the thighs, the . . . , and the *roasted* meat. You shall put down a brazier filled with cypress and sprinkle some *maṣḫatu*-flour (on it?). You shall pull the curtains shut. You shall scatter (about?) heaps of flour. You shall place the Exalted Bull in a place forbidden (to the outsider), and then you shall whisper three times into his right ear and his left one. You shall then cut (open?) the Exalted Bull and take his hide and tendon for this work (which you are about to perform).

Incantation: "*Karzaginna ḳar* . . ." . . .

TEXT D

(beginning of col. i broken)

The deity Gabbagararae (or) Ninkasi, the son of the new city. The deity Ebarralah (or) Nusku, *born* on the thirtieth day (of the month, when the moon) is invisible.

(These) seven gods, children of the god Enmesharra, are (represented by) the heaps of flour.

You shall lay the twelve bronze gods in the bronze kettle-drum and then you shall cover (that is, attach the head of) the bronze kettle-drum.

Great Bull, Exalted Bull, who treads upon clean pasture,
Who walks upon the fields, who holds abundance,
The cultivator of grain, who causes the countryside to be *fertile*,
My clean hands have made a sacrifice before you.

(The above is) the word of the *apsū*-ocean which you shall whisper through a reed tube into the right ear of the bull used to cover the bronze kettle-drum.

O Bull, you are the offspring of the deity Zu.
You have been chosen for the rites and ceremonies.
The deity Ningizzida is your friend for eternity.
The great . . . , guard the (heavenly) plans!
. . . fix the scheme of heaven and earth!
. . . be entrusted to the god Lumha!
. . . be . . . to the god Bel.

(The above is) [the word of the *apsū*-ocean which you shall whisper into] the left ear of the bull used to cover the bronze kettle-drum.

He who is lying down, the lord who is lying down, how long will he remain lying down?
The great Mountain, the father, Mullil, who is lying down, how long (will he remain lying down)?
The Shepherd who decrees the destinies, who is lying down, how long?

(ii) . . .

The god Mullil, who has given his city away—together (the foe) devoured it.
The person who had good clothing perished of cold,
He who owned vast fields perished of hunger.

The above composition is for the occasion when the twelve bronze gods are laid in the bronze kettle-drum.

Faithful Shepherd, faithful Shepherd,
God Enlil, faithful Shepherd,
Master of all countries, [faithful] Shepherd,
Lord of all the Igigi deities, faithful Shepherd,
Lord of the . . . , faithful Shepherd,
The lord who drew the outline of his land, who . . . his land,
The lord who drew the outline of his land, . . . ,
You gave the accumulated possessions [to the enemy],
[You gave] the stored treasure [to the enemy].
[The enemy dwelt] in a clean house,
The enemy dwelt in a clean place,
[The stranger lay] in a clean bedroom.

(iii)

(So) beautiful a city—[how could you turn it over to the enemy]?
May lord Ea, the king [of the *apsū*-ocean, calm you]!
May lord Marduk [pacify your liver]!
May the lordly father Adad [calm you]!
May the lordly hero Shamash [pacify your liver]!
May lord Ninurta [calm you]!
May exalted lord Shulpae [calm you]!
Point my hands in the straight direction, [point my hands in the straight direction]!
Point my hands in the straight direction, [point] my hands [in the straight direction]!
Make these words be right, [make] these words [be right]!
As for the kettle-drum, [make] its word be right.

(The above is) the incantation (to recite) [when performing] the rite of the Mouth Washing of the bronze kettle-drum.

Before the god Lumha and the bronze kettle-drum, you shall set up a stand and prepare it (for the ceremony). You shall sprinkle some *šasqū*-flour (on?) a paste of honey and *cream* and some dates. You shall [sacrifice] a sheep and [make an offering] of the thigh, the . . . , and *roasted* meat. . . .

(iv)

(The above—broken away in the text—is) the incantation (to recite) when placing water (on the stand) and when drawing the curtains shut. [Having placed the water (on the stand)], you shall draw the curtains shut.

Wash [your hands], wash your hands,
You are the god Enlil, wash [your hands],

You are Enlil, . . . ,
You are . . . , (10)
. . . , wash [your hands]!
. . . the earth . . . , (15)
May all [the gods] rejoice in you!
[O god Marduk], for your king speak (the words): "You are released." (20)
O god Adad, for your king speak (the words): "You are released."

(The above is) the incantation (to recite) when removing the water. Having removed the water, you shall open the curtains.

(25) (The next tablet of this series begins with the words:) When you have had the bull led into the *mummu*-house.

(Colophon:) Ritual for the *ḳalū*-priesthood, copied from an older tablet and checked.

Temple Ritual for the Sixteenth and Seventeenth Days of an Unknown Month at Uruk

Latest copy: F. Thureau-Dangin, *TCL*, VI, No. 41. Copy, transcription, and translation: F. Thureau-Dangin, *Rituels accadiens* (Paris, 1921), p. 68 f. and 118 ff. Translation: E. Ebeling, *AOT*, 317 ff. The beginning and end of this text are not preserved. The tablet belongs to an archive of tablets from Uruk written (if not composed) in the Seleucid period.

(obverse)

. . . upon . . . he shall pay his respects to the Scepter, just as. . . . The Scepter and the Shoe shall "arise," and then the gods and goddesses shall, exactly as before, proceed before him and behind him. They shall descend to the Exalted Court and shall turn toward the god Anu. The *mašmašu*-priest shall purify the Scepter; the Scepter shall enter and be seated. The deities Papsukkal, Nusku, (5) and Sha(?) shall be seated in the court of the god Anu. Furthermore, the Shoe, the divine Daughters of Anu, and the divine Daughters of Uruk shall return, and the Shoe shall enter the Enir, the house of the golden bed of the goddess Antu, and shall be placed upon a stool. The divine Daughters of Anu and the divine Daughters of Uruk shall be seated in the court of the goddess Antu. (The priest) shall mix wine and good oil, and shall make a libation at the gate of the sanctuary of Anu, Antu, and all the gods. (10) He shall smear (some of it) on the door-sockets of the gate of the sanctuary (and on) the doors and gates. He shall fill the golden censers, and then he shall sacrifice a bull and a ram to Anu, Antu, and all the gods. He shall serve the evening meal to Anu, Antu, and all the gods without interruption. He shall *spend* the night (there?). The door shall not be shut. He shall offer the meal to all the deities dwelling in the court.

In the first watch of the night, on the roof of the *topmost* stage of the temple-tower of the (15) Resh temple, when the star Great Anu of Heaven rises and the star Great Antu of Heaven rises in the constellation Wagon, (he shall recite the compositions beginning?) "*Ana tamšīl zīmu bunnē ḳakḳab šamāmi Anu šarru*" and "*Ittaṣā ṣalam banū.*" You shall prepare a golden tray for the deities Anu and Antu of heaven. You shall present water (for washing) hands to the deities Anu and Antu of heaven, and then you shall set the tray, serving bull meat, ram meat, and fowl. You shall also serve prime beer (20) together with "pressed" wine. You shall heap up all (types of) garden produce. You shall sprinkle some cedar *resin* and *maṣḫatu*-flour upon a golden censer, and then you shall make a libation of "pressed" wine from a golden libation vessel. Upon seven large golden trays, you shall present water (for washing) hands to the planets Jupiter, Venus, Mercury, Saturn, Mars, the moon, and the sun, *as soon as* they appear. Then you shall set the tray (25) and serve bull meat, ram meat, and fowl. You shall also serve prime beer together with "pressed" wine. You shall heap up all (types of) garden produce. You shall sprinkle cedar *resin* and *maṣḫatu*-flour upon seven golden censers, and then you shall make a libation of "pressed" wine from a golden libation vessel. The *maḫḫū*-priest, wearing a *sash*, shall use a *naphtha* fire to light a large torch, in which spices have been inserted, which has been sprinkled with oil, and upon which the rite of "Washing of the Mouth" has been performed. (30) He shall then face the tray, raise his hand to the deity Great Anu of Heaven, and recite (the composition beginning?) "*Kakḳab Anu etellu šamāmi.*" You shall (then) clear the large tray, and you shall present water (for washing) hands. The chief *ēribbīti*-priest shall take the "hand" of the torch among the *mašmašu*-priests, the *ḳalū*-priests, and the singers (on leaving) the temple-tower, and then, (by) the Holy Gate which is behind the sanctuary, he shall enter the Exalted Court, and, at the side of the Kizalagga, he shall turn toward the deity Anu. In his presence, (reverse) a *ḫarū*-pot shall be broken. He shall speak a recitation. The chief *ēribbīti*-priest shall then take the "hand" of the torch of the deities Papsukkal, Nusku, Sha(?), and Pisangunuqu, and they shall proceed to the sanctuary of the goddess Antu. He shall turn toward Antu. In her presence a *ḫarū*-pot shall be broken. The deities Papsukkal, (5) Nusku, Sha(?) and Pisangunuqu, with the torch, shall go forth toward the Ubshukkinakku. Near the Sanctuary of Destinies, a bull shall be sacrificed in their presence. The torch shall (be used to) start a fire in the Ubshukkinakku. The thigh of the bull, together with its skin, shall be removed and shall then be *seared* at the right and left of the fire. The deities Papsukkal, Nusku, Sha(?) and Pisangunuqu, with the torch, shall go forth from the Ubshukkinakku, by the High Gate, (10) into the street. Then, with Pisangunuqu at the head, Papsukkal,

Nusku, and Sha(?) shall proceed, circling the temple. They shall then return, Papsukkal by the High Gate, Nusku by the (ordinary?) gate, and Sha(?) by the *Main* Gate. The *ēribbīti*-priest shall use the torch to start a fire in their presence, and they shall be seated until daybreak. The priests of the temples of Uruk—and similarly the *ēribbīti*-priests of all the temples—(15) shall use the torch to start fires and shall carry (the fires) to their temples. Then they shall perform the ceremony of *šalām biti*. They shall light fires at the gates of their temples and shall recite (the compositions entitled) "*Anu uštapā ina napḫar mātāti*" and "*Ittaṣā ṣalam banū*." The torch and the deity Pisangunuqu shall return, entering the court of Anu, turning toward the goddess Antu. The *mašmašu*-priest shall use water from the *egubbū*-vessels, prime beer, milk, wine, and oil to extinguish the torch. (20) The deity Pisangunuqu shall again move on and shall be seated in the Ubshukkinakku until daybreak. The deities Adad, Sin, Shamash, and Beletile shall be seated in the court until daybreak. The people of the land shall light fires in their homes and shall offer banquets to all the gods. They shall speak the recitations mentioned above. The guards of the city shall light fires (25) in the streets and squares. The gates of the city of Uruk shall not be . . . until daybreak. The guards of the gates shall set up reed *poles* to the left and right of the gates. They shall light fires in the gates (and keep them going) until daybreak.

On the seventeenth day (of the month), forty minutes after sunrise, the gate shall be opened before the deities Anu and Antu, bringing an end to the(ir) overnight stay. The main meal of the morning shall be offered to Anu, Antu, and all the gods. (30) When the main (meal) is over, the second meal shall be offered. The (priest) shall fill the golden censers and then shall sacrifice a bull and a ram. The singers shall [sing] (the hymn entitled) "*Elum gud sunna*." (The priest) shall then fill the censers and shall sacrifice a bull and a ram. [He shall grasp?] the hands of the deities Adad, Sin, Shamash, Pisangunuqu, and Beletile *through* the linen curtain. . . .

Ritual for the Repair of a Temple

Two of the texts (A and B) come from Uruk and were written in the Seleucid period, the third (C) was excavated at Babylon and is probably only a century or two older. All of these texts are probably copies of older ones. The latest copies of A and B are by F. Thureau-Dangin, *TCL*, VI, Nos. 45 and 46; text C was published by F. H. Weissbach, *Babylonische Miscellen*, No. 12. For transcriptions and translations of all three texts, see F. Thureau-Dangin, *Rituels accadiens* (Paris, 1921), 34 ff.

TEXT A

(obverse)

When the wall of the temple of the god Anu falls into ruin—[for the purpose of demolishing and founding anew the temple in question], you shall prepare three sac[rificial stands for the god of the temple, the goddess of the temple, and the household god of the temple] in an auspicious month, on a favorable day, in the night. You shall sacrifice [the sheep] (and) offer the thigh, the . . . , and *roas*[*ted* meat. You shall make a libation of beer, wine, and milk.] You shall light a fire for the gods Ea and Marduk, (5) sacrifice [a sheep to Ea and Marduk], and make a libation of prime beer, wine, (and) milk. You shall sing the lamentation (entitled) "*Utudim eta*" and the lamentation (entitled) "*U'uaba muḫul*." In the morning, [on the roof of the temple in question, at a spot which is forbidden to the outsider], you shall sprinkle pure water (and) set up three sacrificial stands for the gods Ea, Shamash, and Marduk. You shall place [three pieces of linen] on the seats; and you shall put down some paste made of honey and *cream as well as* some [dates, *šasqū*-flour], and filtered oil. You shall put in place three *adagurru*-vessels (filled with) prime beer, wine, (and) milk. You shall put down [a brazier (containing) cypress]. (10) You shall scatter (about?) some (aromatic?) barley seed of *all* (kinds?). You shall sacrifice three sheep and offer the thigh, the . . . , and *roasted* meat; you shall make a libation of prime beer, wine, (and) milk. You shall have some water available. Then you shall draw the curtains shut. Facing the temple, you shall sing (the compositions entitled) "*Ezi gulgullude*," "*Nibišu*," and "*Er imšeše*." After this, accompanied on the *ḫalḫallatu*-instrument, you shall sing for the gods Ea, Shamash, and Marduk (the compositions entitled) "*Nitug niginna*," "*Utu lugalam*," and "*Ešabḫungata*." He(!) shall then stop (singing); you shall take up some water and shall open the curtains.

(15) (The above is) the ritual of the *kalū*-priest.

(An old omen reads:) if the earth trembles, (this means that) an enemy will arise and the dwelling(s) of the country will be unstable. (Another omen reads:) if the earth moves, (this means that) there will be *injustice* in the whole country, the country will go *mad*. On a favorable day, the king shall purify and cleanse himself and shall call out the admission of sin to the gods Anu, Enlil, and Ea. After that, you shall make preparations for two sacrifices to his god and his goddess. You shall sacrifice the sheep, and shall make a lamentation. You shall cause the king to *speak* the (special) poems of appeasement of these (deities).

(20) In the morning, you shall set up three sacrificial stands for the gods Anu, Enlil, and Ea. You shall sacrifice the sheep, offer the thigh, the . . . , and *roasted* meat, and then you shall make a libation of prime beer, wine, (and) milk. You shall make a lamentation. You shall cause the king to *speak* the poem of appeasement (called) "*Barra umun etamakil annam*" for the god Anu, "*Meeumunmu šišim*" for the gods Enlil (and) Ea, "*Mee ansar*" for the god Shamash. He (that is, the king) shall prostrate himself. He shall be shaved, (and) the hair of his body (25) you shall hide

away in a *laḫansaḫar*-vessel. And (then) you shall leave it (that is, the vessel) at the enemy's border. He (that is, the king) shall go straight back to his palace. You shall offer a major sacrifice to the god Anu. You shall make a lamentation. After that, you shall make lamentations and special poems of appeasement on the Royal Fringed Garment (reverse) in all the cities. If you do all this, no evil will approach the king.

(The above is) the ritual of the *ḳalū*-priest.

(An omen reads:) If a dog enters a temple, (this means that) the gods will show no mercy to the land. (Another omen reads:) If a beast of the desert, different and rare, enters the city and . . . , (this means) the overthrow of the city and the destruction of the people.

(5) On a favorable day, you shall set up three sacrificial stands for the god of the city, the goddess of the city, and the household god of the city. You shall sacrifice the sheep and offer the thigh, the . . . , and *roasted* meat. You shall make a libation of prime beer, wine, (and) milk. You shall light a fire. You shall make a lamentation. You shall recite the special poems of appeasement on the Royal Fringed Garment.

In the morning, in the desert or on the bank of a river, at a place which is not public, you shall sprinkle the earth with pure water. You shall set up three sacrificial stands for the gods Anu, Enlil, and Ea. You shall sacrifice the sheep and offer the thigh, the . . . , and *roasted* meat. (10) You shall make a libation of prime beer, wine, (and) milk. You shall light a fire. You shall make a lamentation. You shall recite the special poems of appeasement on the Royal Fringed Garment. After that, you shall set up two sacrificial stands for the god and goddess of the desert. You shall sacrifice the sheep and offer the thigh, the . . . , and *roasted* meat. You shall make a libation of prime beer, wine, (and) milk. You shall make a lamentation. The *mašmašu*-priest and the *ḳalū*-priest shall perform the *ḳuppuru*-ritual for the city in question.

If you do all this, no evil will approach the king.

(An omen reads:) If the image of the king of the country in question or the image of his father or the image of his grandfather falls over and breaks, or if its *shape warps*, (this means that) the days of the king of that country will be few in number.

(An omen reads:) If . . . in a temple, (this denotes) divine anger, the king's treasure will go forth outside (the city). (Another omen reads:) If an evil sign, a strange sign, is seen in the temple, (this means that) nobody will be able to enter that temple.

On an auspicious day, during the night, you shall set up three sacrificial stands for the god (or?) goddess in question, for the deity . . . , and for the god Shamash. You shall sacrifice the sheep and offer the thigh, the . . . , and *roasted* meat. You shall make a libation of prime beer, wine, and milk. You shall make a lamentation. You shall cause special poems of appeasement to be *spoḳen on behalf of* the king.

(20) In the morning, you shall sprinkle clean water on the roof of the temple in question and shall set up three sacrificial stands for the gods Ea, Shamash, and Marduk. You shall place three pieces of linen on the chairs. You shall sacrifice the sheep and offer the thigh, the . . . , and *roasted* meat. You shall make a libation of prime beer, wine, (and) milk. You shall light a fire and make a lamentation. You shall cause special poems of appeasement to be *spoḳen on behalf of* the king. You shall purify the temple in question. After that, the king shall call out the admission of sin and present a gift to the god in question.

(25) (Colophon:) Tablet belonging to Anubelshunu, son of Nidintuanu. (Written by) his own hand. (Dated at) Uruk, the month Adaru, the twenty-second day, Seleucus being king.

TEXT B

(obverse)

[When] the wall of the temple falls into ruin—for the purpose of demolishing and founding anew the temple in question, the *bārū*-priest shall *investigate* [*its plans*]. Then you shall set up three sacrificial stands [for] the god of the temple, the goddess of the temple, and the household god of the temple in an auspicious month, on a favorable day, at night. You shall sacrifice the sheep and offer the thigh, the . . . , and *roasted* meat. You shall make a libation of beer, wine, (and) milk. (5) You shall light a fire for the gods Ea and Marduk and shall sacrifice the sheep to Ea and Marduk. You shall make a libation of beer, wine, (and) milk. You shall sing the lamentation (called) "*Utudim eta*" and the lamentation (called) "*Ulili enzu marmar.*" In the morning, on the roof of the temple in question, at a spot [which is forbidden to the outsider], you shall sprinkle pure water. You shall set up three sacrificial stands for the gods Ea, Shamash, and Marduk. You shall sacrifice three sheep. You shall scatter (about) some (aromatic?) barley seed of *all* (kinds?). You shall have some water available. (10) You shall light a fire. Facing the temple, you shall sing (the compositions called) "*Ezi gulgullede,*" "*Nibišu,*" and "*Er imšeše.*" After that, accompanied on the *ḫalḫallatu*-instrument, you shall sing for the gods Ea, Shamash, and Marduk (the compositions entitled) "*Nitug niginna,*" "*Utu lugalam,*" and "*Ešabḫungata.*" He(!) shall then stop (singing); you shall take up some water and shall open the curtains. The director of the reconstruction of the temple in question shall put on clean clothes, place a *tin* bracelet on his hand, (15) take up an axe of basalt, shall *lift up* the first brick, and put (it) away in an inaccessible place. You shall set up a single sacrificial stand in front of the brick for the god of the foundations and shall sacrifice the sheep. (On it?) you shall scatter some (aromatic?) barley seed of *all* (sorts?) and shall make a libation of beer, [wine], and milk. He(!) shall prostrate (himself). While you are engaged in the job of demolishing and reconstructing, you shall . . . water. The *ḳalū*-priest shall strew some (aromatic?) *flour.* They shall make a libation of honey, *cream*, milk, beer, wine, and [good] oil on (the brick).

[(Standing) before the brick], the *ḳalū*-priest [shall recite] the (composition called) "*Enūma Anu ibnū šamē.*"

(The above is) the ritual of the *ḳalū*-priest.

. . . the demolition of the temple and *the accomplishment* of the rites. When the wall of the temple falls into ruin—for the purpose of demolishing and founding the temple anew, the *bārū*-priest shall *sacrifice* a lamb upon the Fringed Garment of the king, and then . . . he shall recite [the incantation] of the *bārū*-priesthood for the case of a temple wall's falling into ruin. . . . this lamb (and) shall inspect (the internal organs). If (the inspection) reveals good omens, this [work] of demolition and founding anew will be for the good of the king and his country. . . . while the demolishing and refounding (are going on), offerings and lamentations shall be made, (and) the *ḳalū*-priest shall not cease strewing (aromatic?) flour (about?) and making libations and recitations.

(reverse)

(The above is) a tablet (describing) what is required of the *ḳalū*-priest.

When the foundations of a temple collapse, you shall open up the foundations in an auspicious month, on a favorable day. When you are laying the foundations of the temple, you shall prepare during the night five sacrifices for the deities Sin, Marduk, Ninmah, Kulla, and Ninshubur. You shall sacrifice the sheep, strew some (aromatic?) barley seed of *all* (sorts?), start a fire, (and) make a libation of beer, wine, (and) milk. You shall sing the lamentation (called) "*Uddam ḳimuš*" and the lamentation (called) "*Umun barḳugga.*" After this, you shall set up three sacrificial stands for the god of the temple, the goddess of the temple, (and) the household god of the temple. You shall light a fire, make some water available, (and) draw the curtains shut. Facing the temple, you shall sing (the composition entitled) "*Ešabḫungata,*" accompanied on the *ḫalḫallatu*-instrument. After this, you shall prepare three sacrifices for the gods Anu, Enlil, and [Ea] in the morning. You shall sing the lamentations (called) "*Umunšermallašu anḳia*" and "*Nitug niginam.*" You shall sing (the composition entitled) "*Ud Ana Enlilla Enḳi anḳia mundimdimene.*" . . . You shall remove the sacrificial accoutrements and shall lay the foundation until the temple is completed. You shall not interrupt making sacrifices and lamentations. Once the foundation is laid, you shall purify that place with purification rituals.

(The above is) the ritual of the *ḳalū*-priest.

(The next tablet of this series begins with the words:) when the door-sockets are installed.

(Colophon:) Tablet belonging to Nidintuanu. (Written by) the hand of Anubelshunu, his son, the apprentice *ḳalū*-priest. (Dated at) Uruk, the month of Simannu, twenty-eighth day, the year eighty-one (of the Seleucid period, corresponding to 231 B.C.), Seleucus being the king.

TEXT C

When the wall of the temple falls into ruin—for the purpose of demolishing and founding anew the temple in question, the *bārū*-priest shall *investigate* its *plans.* Then, in an auspicious month, on a favorable day, during the night, they shall light a fire for the gods Ea and Marduk and make a sacrifice to Ea and Marduk. The *ḳalū*-priest shall make a lamentation, and the singer shall make *groaning* noises. In the morning you shall make preparations on the roof of the temple in question for three sacrifices to the gods Ea, Shamash, and Marduk. You shall strew (about) nine *loaves* of emmer bread, dates, (and) *šasqū*-flour. [You shall lay down] a mixture of honey, *cream,* and filtered oil. You shall set down three *adagurru*-vessels. [You shall make a libation] of prime beer, [wine, and milk]. You shall put down a brazier (filled with) cypress. [You shall strew (about?) (aromatic?) barley seed of *all* (sorts?)]. You shall slaughter two sheep. The *ḳalū*-priest, accompanied on the *ḫalḫallatu*-instrument, shall sing [for the gods Ea], Shamash, and Marduk [the (compositions entitled) "*Nitug niginna,*" "*Utu lugalam,*" (and) "*Ešabḫungata*"]. After this, he shall sing (the compositions called) "*Ezi* [*gulgullude*]," "*Nibišu,*" and "*Er imšeše.*" He shall (then) stop. [The director of the reconstruction] of the temple in question shall put on clean clothes, place a *tin* [bracelet] on his hand, take up a basalt axe, shall *lift up* [the first bri]ck, shall mourn [for the] house, shall say "Woe," and shall put that brick away in an inaccessible place. Then the *ḳalū*-priest shall strew some (aromatic?) flour [on] the brazier. He shall pour [honey], *cream,* milk, prime beer, wine, and good oil [on] it (that is, the brick). And then he shall recite in front of the brick (the composition called) "*Enūma Anu ibnū šamē.*"

(This composition now follows.)

When the god Anu created heaven,
(When) the god Nudimmud created the *apsū*-ocean, his dwelling,
The god Ea pinched off a piece of clay in the *apsū* ocean,
Created the (brick-god) Kulla for the restoration of [temples],
Created the reed marsh and the forest for the work of their construction,
Created the gods Ninildu, Ninsimug, and Arazu to be the completers of their construction work,
Created mountains and oceans for everything . . . ,
Created the deities Gushkinbanda, Ninagal, Ninzadim, and Ninkurra for their work,
(Created) the abundant products (of mountain and ocean) to be offerings . . . ,
Created the deities Ashnan, Lahar, Siris, Ningizzida, Ninsar, . . .
For making their revenues abundant . . . ,
Created the deities Umunmutamku and Umunmutamnag to be presenters of offerings,

Created the god Kusug, high-priest of the great gods, to be the one who completes their rites and ceremonies.
Created the king to be the provider . . . ,
Created men to be the makers . . . ,
. . . the gods Anu, Enlil, Ea, . . .
. . . (40)

Program of the Pageant of the Statue of the God Anu at Uruk

A copy of this text was published by Clay, *Babylonian Records in the Library of J. Pierpont Morgan*, IV, No. 7; for a transcription and translation, see F. Thureau-Dangin, *RA*, XX (1923), 107 ff. and A. Falkenstein, *Topographie von Uruk*, I (Leipzig, 1941), 45 ff.; for another translation, see E. Ebeling, *AOT*, 313 f.

(45) At the command of the deities Anu and Antu, may (everything which I do) go well![1]

(1) . . . after the (statue of the) god Anu has left the chapel (called) Enamenna and has reached the Exalted Gate, all the *mašmašu*-priests shall recite three times the incantation (entitled) "*Šarru ittaṣā.*" The *mašmašu*-priests shall (then) stop (reciting), and the *urigallu*-priest, the *mašmašu*-priests, the *ēribbīti*-priests, and the brewers—who are harnessed to the cross-beam (supporting the moving statue of Anu)—(5) shall bless Anu with the blessing (entitled) "*Anu rabū šamē u erṣetu likrubūka.*"[2]

After the blessing, the *mašmašu*-priests shall (again) recite four times the incantation (entitled) "*Šarru ittaṣā*" as far as the Street of the Gods. The *urigallu*-priest, the *mašmašu*-priests, the *ēribbītu*-priests, and the brewers—who are harnessed to the cross-beam—shall (again) bless Anu with the blessing (entitled) "*Anu rabū šamē u erṣetu likrubūka.*"[2]

After the blessing, the *mašmašu*-priests (10) shall recite four times the incantation (entitled) "*Lugale ankia lugaltaea*" when they are in the Street of the Gods. They shall (then) stop (reciting) the incantation, and the *urigallu*-priest, the *mašmašu*-priests, the *ēribbīti*-priests, and the people carrying the cross-beam shall bless Anu exactly as before.

After the blessing, the *mašmašu*-priests shall recite seven times both the incantation (entitled) "*Lugale ezen šinmundu*" and the incantation (entitled) "*Egubbakugata*" as far as the Holy Quay, the Dike of the Ship of Anu, the Path of the Gods. They shall (then) stop (reciting) the incantation, and the *urigallu*-priest, (15) the *mašmašu*-priests, the *ēribbīti*-priests, and the people carrying the cross-beam shall bless Anu.

As soon as Anu is on the Dike of the Ship of Anu, the *mašmašu*-priests (and) the *ēribbīti*-priests shall recite with hand-raising gestures the incantation (entitled) "*Magur munu*" to Anu. Thereafter, the *urigallu*-priest, the *mašmašu*-priests, the *ēribbīti*-priests, and the people carrying the cross-beam shall bless Anu exactly as before.

(20) From the Upper Dike of the Holy Quay to the Royal Gate, the *mašmašu*-priests shall recite seven times the incantation (entitled) "*Lugaltaea sila kuga badibata.*" They shall (then) stop (reciting) the incantation, and, in the Royal Gate, the *urigallu*-priest, the *mašmašu*-priests, the *ēribbīti*-priests, and the people carrying the cross-beam shall bless Anu exactly as before.

From the Royal Gate to the Akitu House (outside the city), the house of worship, the *mašmašu*-priests shall recite the incantations (25) (which they recited before) in the Street of the Gods. They shall (then) stop (reciting) the incantation, and the *urigallu*-priest, the *mašmašu*-priests, the *ēribbīti*-priests, and the brewers—who are harnessed to the cross-beam—shall bless Anu seven full times.

As soon as Anu has reached the Akitu House, the *mašmašu*-priests shall recite the incantation (entitled) "*Ekuga edingirene,*" the incantation (entitled) "*An lugalmu šadugazuše,*" the incantation (entitled) (30) "*Unu kinsigannake,*" the incantation (entitled) "*Šubtu ša ilāni.*"

(39) The following is the blessing with which the *urigallu*-priest, the *mašmašu*-priests, the *ēribbīti*-priests, (40) and the brewers—who are harnessed to the cross-beam—shall bless Anu seven times, on the way to the Akitu House from the Resh House:

Great Anu, may heaven and earth bless you! (32)
May the deities Enlil, Ea, and Beletile bless you joyfully!
May both the gods Sin and Shamash bless you when you appear!
May the deities Nergal and Sibi bless you with firm hearts! (35)
May the Igigi gods of heaven and the Anunnaki gods of earth bless you!
May the gods of the Deep and the gods of the Holy Shrine bless you!
May they bless you daily (every) day, month, and year!

(The next tablet of these instructions begins with the words:) Incantation (entitled) "*Šarru ittaṣā šarru ittaṣā.*"

(Colophon:) Copied from an old tablet, verified and collated. Copy of an old tablet which is the property of (the temple of) Anu and Antu. (This) tablet (belongs) to Anuahaushabshi, the son of Kidinanu, the descendant of Ekurzakir, the *mašmašu*-priest of Anu and Antu, the *urigallu*-priest of the Resh Temple, citizen of the city Uruk. (This tablet was written by) the hand of Anubalatsuiqbi, his son. He wrote (this tablet) for his own instruction, for the prolongation of his days, for the continuation of his life, (and) for the "establishment of his foundation(s)"; and then he deposited it in the city of Uruk, in the Resh Temple,

[1] This is an invocation that appears quite frequently at the beginning of literary and scientific texts of the Seleucid period at Uruk.
[2] This blessing is given in full in lines 32-38.

the house of his (that is, Anu's) divinity. Whoever reveres Anu shall not steal it! (Dated at) Uruk, in the month Du'uzu, the twenty-*fifth* day, the year sixty-one (of the Seleucid Era, corresponding to the year 251 B.C.), Antiochus (being) king of the lands (at that time).

Daily Sacrifices to the Gods of the City of Uruk

For a complete edition of this text, see F. Thureau-Dangin, *Rituels accadiens* (Paris, 1921), 62 ff. and 74 ff.; the copy was later republished by F. Thureau-Dangin, *TCL*, VI, No. 38; for another translation, see E. Ebeling, *AOT*, 305 ff.

(obverse)

Every day in the year, for the main meal of the morning, you shall prepare—in addition to the *sappu*-vessels of the *maqqānē*—eighteen gold *sappu*-vessels on the tray of the god Anu. Of these (eighteen vessels), you shall prepare before the god Anu seven *sappu*-vessels on the right—three for barley-beer and four for mixed beer—and seven *sappu*-vessels on the left—three for barley-beer, one for mixed beer, one for *nāšu*-beer, one for *zarbabu*-beer, and one alabaster *sappu*-vessel for milk—and four gold *sappu*-vessels for "pressed" wine. Similar (preparations shall be made) for the second (meal) of the morning as well as for the main and second (meals) of the evening. No milk shall be served at the main and second (meals) of the evening. Among the gold *sappu*-vessels for the tray, there are five gold *sappu*-vessels which are *bound* with (strings of?) *inexpensive* stone(s).

He shall grasp the five gold *sappu*-vessels, each with a capacity of one *qa*-measure, and [shall perform] the *maqqānē* of the sanctuary [of the god Anu]. (These five vessels should contain different liquids:) one for barley-beer, one for mixed beer, one for *nāšu*-beer, one for "pressed" wine, [and one for milk]. He shall grasp a *sappu*-vessel with a capacity of five *akālu*-measures (=one-half *qa*), containing wine of the land Azallu. Four [gold] *tigidū*-vessels of the sanctuary of the god Anu, of which one gold *tigidū*-vessel . . . , one gold *tigidū*-vessel is *painted* with blossoms, one gold *tigidū*-vessel has rope wrapped around its neck, (and) one [gold] *tigidū*-vessel is. . . . (This makes a) total of four gold *tigidū*-vessels on a *kandurū*-vessel . . . of the deities Anu and Antu. . . .

You shall prepare fourteen gold *sappu*-vessels upon the tray of the goddess Antu. (These are to contain) prime beer, exactly [as in the case of the tray of Anu]. Twelve gold *sappu*-vessels (are to be set) before the goddess Ishtar, ten gold *sappu*-vessels before [the goddess Nana]. (These vessels do) not include the gold *sappu*-vessels (used) throughout the year for the (other) deities dwelling in [the city of Uruk].

(Furthermore, these vessels do) not include the gold *sappu*-vessels (which are filled) with the food prepared for the god's trip or the two *tigidū*-vessels. . . .

Every day in the year, a *būru*-vessel containing three *gur*-measures and three *pan*-measures of barley [and emmer]—(in other words, expressed sexagesimally), 1,48 *sāt*-measures, or, (expressed decimally), one hundred and eight *sāt*-measures—the *basic* quantity for the regular offerings, according to the *sāt*-measure of "ten pounds" . . . which the millers in the kitchen shall turn over to the chefs every day for the four meals of the deities [Anu], Antu, Ishtar, Nana, and the (other) deities dwelling in the city of Uruk.

Of these (108 *sāt*-measures, there shall be) eighty-one *sāt*-measures of barley flour and twenty-seven *sāt*-measures of emmer flour which the chef shall use in baking two hundred and forty-three *ṣibtu*-loaves. Of these (loaves), the chef shall supply for the four (daily) meals thirty *ṣibtu*-loaves to be placed on the tray before the god Anu. (To itemize these more specifically,) the chef shall supply eight *ṣibtu*-loaves for the main meal of the morning and (eight for) the second meal of the morning; the chef shall supply seven *ṣibtu*-loaves for the main meal of the evening and (seven) for the second meal of the evening. (Furthermore,) the chef shall supply thirty *ṣibtu*-loaves (to be set) before the goddess Antu, thirty *ṣibtu*-loaves (to be set) before the goddess Ishtar, thirty *ṣibtu*-loaves (to be set) before the goddess Nana, twelve *ṣibtu*-loaves (to be set) before the seat of the god Anu and the household god of the sanctuary of the goddess Antu, four *ṣibtu*-loaves (to be set) before the two tiaras of the god Anu, sixteen loaves (to be set) before the temple-tower and the household god of the temple-tower, (and) sixteen loaves (to be set) before the other (gods) of the sanctuary of the deities Anu and Antu—totalling one hundred and sixty-eight *ṣibtu*-loaves for the four (daily) meals. (These loaves are) in addition to the seventy-five *ṣibtu*-loaves which shall be offered to the (other) deities dwelling in the city of Uruk, in their temples at the four (daily) meals. (These loaves are also) in addition to the loave(s) of(?) the *rabbū* and the date cakes (to be prepared) for the god's trip, for the *guqqānū*-sacrifice, for the *eššešu*-festivals, for (the ceremonies of) the Opening of the Gate, for the (ceremony) of the Clothing, for the *egubbū*-vessel (ceremonies?), for the overnight (ceremonies), for the brazier (ceremonies?), for the ritual of the (divine) marriage, for the "blessers," for the sacrifices of the king, ... And one thousand and two hundred . . . oil, which is placed beneath the (ordinary) dates and the dates of the land of Tilmun, and filtered oil shall be offered upon the *kalakku* of Anu, Antu, and the (other) deities of the city of Uruk. And *maṣhatu*-flour in storage baskets which the miller shall supply every day of the year to the *ēribbīti*-priest. The miller, while grinding flour on the millstone, shall recite (the composition entitled?) ". . . *mulapin ina ṣēri epinni zēri iṣmidu*." And the chef, while (working at) the kneading trough with the lumps (of dough) and while *withdrawing* the hot (loaves?), shall recite (the composition beginning with the words?) "*Nisaba ḫengal duššū mākalū ellu.*"

Every day of the year, for the four (daily) meals, 1,48 *sāt*-measures—(that is, expressed decimally,) one hundred and eight *sāt*-measures—of ordinary dates, dates from the land of Tilmun, figs, and *raisins*, in addition to the . . . and the . . . , shall be offered to the deities Anu, Antu, Ishtar, Nana, and the (other) deities dwelling in the city of Uruk.

(reverse)

(Below are enumerated) the bulls and rams for the regular offerings (to be made) every day of the year to the deities Anu, Antu, Ishtar, Nana, and the (other) gods dwelling in the Resh Temple, the Irigal Temple, and the Esharra Temple, (which is) the *topmost stage* of the temple-tower of the god Anu. From the first day of the month Nisannu through the thirtieth day of the month Adaru, (they shall be offered) for the main meal of the morning.

For the main meal of the morning, throughout the year: seven first-class, fat, clean rams which have been fed barley for two years; one fat, milk-fed *kalū*-ram, of the regular offering—totalling eight rams for the regular offerings. (Furthermore,) one large bull, one milk-fed bullock, and ten fat rams which, unlike the others, have not been fed barley. Grand total for the main meal of the morning throughout the year: eighteen rams, of which one is a milk-fed *kalū*-ram of the regular offering, one large bull, (and) one milk-fed bullock. While slaughtering the bull(s) and the ram(s), the slaughterer shall recite the (composition beginning with the words?) "*Mār Šamaš bēlu būli ina ṣēri ušabšā ri'īti.*"

Similarly, while slaughtering the bull(s) and ram(s), the chief slaughterer shall speak (a prayer for?) life to the deities Anu, Antu, the Great Star, and the planet Venus; he shall recite (it) to no other god.

(For) the second meal of the morning, the regular offering to the deities Anu and Antu and the household gods of the Resh Temple, the Irigal Temple, and the *topmost stage* of the temple-tower, throughout the year: six fat, clean rams which have been fed barley for two years; one fat, milk-fed ram, of the regular offering; and five fat rams which, unlike the others, have not been fed barley; one large bull; eight lambs; five ducks which have been fed . . .-grain; two ducks, of a lower quality than those just mentioned; three *cranes* which have been fed . . .-flour; four *wild boars*; thirty *marratu*-birds; twenty . . .-birds; three ostrich eggs; (and) three duck eggs.

(For) the main meal of the evening, the regular offering to the deities Anu (and) Antu and the household gods (of the temples), throughout the year: four fat, clean rams which have been fed barley for two years; one fat, milk-fed *kalū*-ram of the regular offering; five other rams which, unlike the previously mentioned, have not been fed barley; and ten . . .-birds.

(For) the second meal of the evening, the regular offering to the deities Anu (and) Antu and the household gods (of the temples), throughout the year: four fat, clean rams which have been fed barley for two years; one fat, milk-fed *kalū*-ram of the regular offering; and five other rams which, unlike those just mentioned, have not been fed barley.

The daily total, throughout the year, for the four meals per day: twenty-one first-class, fat, clean rams which have been fed barley for two years; two large bulls; one milk-fed bullock; eight lambs; thirty *marratu*-birds; thirty . . .-birds; three *cranes* which have been fed . . .-grain; five ducks which have been fed . . .-flour; two ducks of a lower quality than those just mentioned; four *wild boars*; three ostrich eggs; three duck eggs.

Every day throughout the year, ten fat, clean rams, whose horns and hooves are whole, shall be sacrificed in the . . . to the deities Anu and Antu of heaven, to the planets Jupiter, Venus, Mercury, Saturn, and Mars, to the sunrise, and to the appearance of the moon.

On the sixteenth day of each month, ten first-class, fat, clean rams, whose horns and hooves are whole, shall—after (the sacrificer's) hands have been cleaned—be offered boiled to the deities Anu and Antu of heaven and to the seven planets[1] on the *topmost stage* of the temple-tower of the god Anu—exactly as on the sixteenth day of the month Tebetu.

(All these are) in addition to the rams of the regular offerings throughout the year, in the Eanna Temple and the (other) temples of the city of Uruk; and (they are also) in addition to the bulls and rams which shall be offered for the *guqqānū*-sacrifices, for the *eššešu*-festivals, for (the ceremonies of) the Opening of the Gate, for the (ceremony) of the Clothing, for the *egubbū*-vessel (ceremonies?), for the brazier (ceremonies?), for the ritual of the (divine) marriage, for the "blessers," and for the sacrifices of the king, which are written down in the ritual instructions for the whole year, in the Resh Temple, the Irigal Temple, the Eanna Temple, and the (other) temples of the city of Uruk, to the deities Anu and Antu and all the (other) gods.

In the temple of the god Shamash, ram's meat shall never be offered to the deity Shakkan. In the temple of the god Sin, bull's meat shall never be offered to the god Harru. Fowl flesh shall never be offered to the goddess Beletseri. Neither bull's meat nor fowl flesh shall ever be offered to the goddess Ereshkigal.

(Colophon:) Tablet written by the hand of Shamashetir, son of Inaqibitanu, son of *Shipkat*anu. Tablet (containing) instructions for the worship of Anu; for the holy ritual; for the ceremonies of kingship, together with the rituals of the divinities of the Resh Temple, the Irigal Temple, the Eanna Temple, and the (other) temples of the city of Uruk. (Also)

[1] Mercury, Venus, Mars, Jupiter, Saturn, the sun, and the moon.

the procedures (to be followed) by the *mašmašu*-priests, the *kalû*-priests, the singers, and all the artisans behind the . . . , not to mention all things having to do with the novices of the *bārû*-priesthood. (This tablet was copied) from tablets which Nabuaplausur, king of the Sea Land, carried off as plunder from the city of Uruk; but *now* Kidinanu, a citizen of Uruk, a *mašmašu*-priest of Anu and Antu, a descendant of Ekurzakir, an *urigallu*-priest of the Resh Temple, looked at these tablets in the land of Elam, copied them in the reign of the kings Seleucus and Antiochus, and brought (his copies) back to the city of Uruk.

Hittite Rituals, Incantations, and Description of Festivals

TRANSLATOR: ALBRECHT GOETZE

Ritual for the Purification of God and Man

Text: *KUB*, XXIX, 7. Only the better-preserved parts, beginning with reverse 12, are translated here.

At nightfall they [. . .] and they . . . [. . .] the god. F[or the sake of the king] they treat him[1] with herbs against words of *blasphemy* (and) curse. Also [for the sake] of the queen's implements [they treat him with herbs]. She[2] hands a soda-plant to the one who holds the queen's implements during the ceremony and while doing so she speaks as follows: "If in the pr[esence of the god anyone, king or queen, has said in mal]ice: 'Let *blasphemy* and uncleanliness enter that temple (and) grow there like a soda-plant! Let it thrive (there) [like] a soda-[plant] so that it becomes abundant! Let no one be able [to uproot] the soda-plant!'

"Now look, [this is what has happ]ened: The god has [. . .] cut down that thriving (and) abundant soda-plant like a harvester, and then reduced it to ashes. Like that soda-plant let him also reduce to ashes and make into soap evil word, oath, cu[rse] (and) uncleanliness! So let it then no longer exist for my god; neither let it exist for the sacrificer's person! Let god and sacrificer be free (of them)! Just as he has re[duced] this soda-plant [to ashes] and made it into soap, even so let evil word, oath, curse and uncl[eanliness] be made into soap! Let god and sacrificer be free of that matter!"

Afterward they hand to him an o[nion], and while this is being done, she speaks as follows: "If in the presence of the god anyone sp[eaks] as follows: 'Just as this onion consists of skins which are wrapped together, one being [un]able to get loose from another—as (in) an on[ion] let evil, oath, curse (and) uncleanliness be wrapped around that temple!' See now, I have picked this onion apart and have [no]w left only one *wretched stem*. Even so let him[3] pick apart evil word, oath, curse (and) uncleanliness from the god's [temple]! Let god and sacrificer be free of that matter!"

After that they hand him a co[rd] which is twisted together toward the left. While this is being done, she speaks as follows: "If anyone has afflicted th[is] god with evil word, oath, curse and uncleanliness and has twisted them together like a cord, (if) it was . . . [. . .] twisted toward the left, I have it now untwisted toward the right. Let evil word, oa[th], curse and uncleanliness no longer exist for my god; neither let it exist for the sacrificer's person! Let god and sacrificer be free of that matter!"

After that they make a basin in front of [the . . .], and from the basin they build a [sma]ll ditch leading to the river. Into it they put a boat lined with a little silver (and) gold. They also make small "oaths" and "curses" of silver (and) gold and place them into the boat. Then the ditch which empties the basin carries the ship from the basin into the river. When it disappears, she pours out a little fine oil and honey and while doing so speaks as follows: "Just as the river has carried away the ship and no trace of it can be found any more—whoever has committed evil word, oath, curse and uncleanliness in the presence of the god—even so let the river carry them away! And just as no trace of the ship can be found any more, let evil word no longer exist for my god; neither let it exist for the sacrificer's person! Let god and sacrificer be free of that matter!"

"See! I have poured out fine oil and honey after them. The trail behind them is anointed with fine oil and honey. Let the evil word be turned away (to places) beyond! Just as the river does not flow backward, even so let it carry away these evil words! Let them not come back!" After that the sacrificer lifts up a piece of silver three shekels in weight, and from a pitcher he pours water over that piece of silver three shekels in weight. While this is being done, she[4] speaks as follows: "Whoever has spoken evil in the presence of the god, just as the dark earth has swallowed up this water, even so let the earth swallow up that evil word! Let these words be free and *unattached*! Let god and sacrificer be free of that matter!"

As a substitute for the king he hands over one ox, and as a substitute for the queen's implements he hands over one cow, one ewe and one goat. While this is being done, she speaks as follows: "With whatever evil word, oath, curse (and) uncleanliness the god was afflicted, let the substitutes carry them away from the god! Let god and sacrificer be free of that matter!" Afterward the sacrificer recites a hymn, (accompanying it) with (an offering consisting of) a small sacrificial loaf and a small cheese.

1 The sacrificer, i.e. the one who ordered the ritual.
2 The priestess, called Old Woman, who usually performs these rituals.
3 The sacrificer.

4 The priestess.

Ritual to Counteract Sorcery

Text: *KUB*, xvii, 27. This is a fragment which comprises less than half of the original composition.

(beginning lost)

(ii) [She[1] takes clay from the pit and ties it to the sacrificer. Thereafter we release it. She throws it into the hole which has been dug in the ground[2] and speaks as follows: "Just as . . . brought up this clay] from the pit [and] is presenting [it to the sacrificer, even so let . . . bring up] this man's recovery [(and) vigor!]"

She takes mud from the spring and ties [it] to [the sacrificer]. Thereafter [we] release it. She throws it [into the hole] which has been dug in the ground and speaks as follows: "Just as [the spring brought] up this mud from the nether world, [and] people are presenting [it to the sacrificer], even so let it bring up this man's [recovery] (and) vigor!"

Then she takes wine-*dregs* and ties them [to the sacrificer]. Then she goes to the vineyard, takes a [. . .] loaf, breaks it, scatters (the crumbs) about and [says as foll]ows: "Eat ye, gods of the trees! [Just as] ye, gods, let vanish every [trace of the dregs], even so let this man's evil [vanish]!"

She . . . takes branches from all (of them)—but . . . she does not take—, makes a *float* and puts [it into the river]. She returns to the clay pit, deposits a broken loaf for the demons of the clay pit and speaks as follows:

"Eat ye, demons of the clay pit! If the wicked sorcerer made over this man's form either to the clay pit or to the current of the river, give it back to him!"

Whatever she had taken to the open country, she carries back to the city and deposits it in the city within the inner chamber at a secret spot. The Old Woman goes forth and assembles in front of the Sun three pieces of bitumen, ⟨holds⟩ a bronze dagger ⟨in readiness⟩, and also kindles a fire. She throws the water[3] and the broken loaf into it and speaks as follows:

"Whatever words the sorcerer spoke, whatever he twined together, whatever he *wove*, whatever he made in whatever place, those (things) he did not (properly) know, the sorcerer. He built up sorcery like a pillar, twined it together like a string. I am thwarting him. I have *pushed over* these words of sorcery like a pillar, I have untwined them like a string."

The Old Woman *pushes* the pieces of bitumen *over*, breaks them and puts them into the fire. The Old Woman takes the cord, untwines it the left-hand way and untwines it the right-hand way and speaks as follows: "If the sorcerer twined it from the right, I am now untwining it [the right-hand way]. If he twined it from the left, I am now un[twining] it the left-hand way."

(iii) [The Old Woman throws the threads into the fire and says as follows: ". . .] Just as I have [bu]rned [these threads] and they will not [come back], [even so] let also these words of the sorcerer [be burned] up!" [She then] ext[inguishes] the fire with water.

[She say]s: "I have vanquished them, the words of sorcery. The spell [that was superi]or, my spell-binding has vanquished (it). [Since] I cast a double counterspell—I spat upon them and I trampled them under [foot]—let the ass bloody them and let the ox muck [them]! Let man [not] (even) walk over them, let him [sp]it on them! Let them be spat upon, the words of sorcery and the sorcerer (himself)!"

Afterward the [Old] Woman spits once and [speak]s as fo[llows]: "Let the thousand gods [cur]se him, the sorcerer! Let [hea]ven and earth curse him! . . ."

(The rest of the text is hopelessly mutilated or completely lost.)

[1] The priestess called Old Woman.

[2] The hole has been dug in order to dispose of the materials used in the ritual, materials which are now contaminated and dangerous.

[3] This must have been mentioned in the lost beginning of the text.

Ritual Against Pestilence

Text: *KUB*, ix, 31 ii, 43-iii 14 and its duplicate *HT*, 1, ii 17-47. Literature: J. Friedrich, *Aus dem hethitischen Schrifttum*, 2 (*AO*, xxv/2 [1925]), 10.

These are the words of Uhha-muwas, the Arzawa man. If people are dying in the country and if some enemy god has caused that, I act as follows:

They drive up one ram. They twine together blue wool, red wool, yellow wool, black wool and white wool, make it into a crown and crown the ram with it. They drive the ram on to the road leading to the enemy and while doing so they speak as follows: "Whatever god of the enemy land has caused this plague—see! We have now driven up this crowned ram to pacify thee, O god! Just as the herd is strong, but keeps peace with the ram, do thou, the god who has caused this plague, keep peace with the Hatti land! In favor turn again toward the Hatti land!" They drive that one crowned ram toward the enemy.

Afterward they bring fodder for the god's horses and mutton tallow, and while doing so they speak as follows: (iii) "Thou hast harnessed (thy) horses; let them eat this fodder and let their hunger be satisfied! Let also thy chariot be greased with this mutton tallow! Turn toward thy land, O Storm-god! In favor turn toward the Hatti land!"

Afterward they drive up one full-grown goat and two sheep. He sacrifices the goat to the Seven;[1] he sacrifices one sheep to the Sun-god. The other sheep they kill and cook. Then they bring 1 cheese, 1 curd, 1 *pulla* (vessel), leavened bread, 1 amphora of wine, 1 amphora of beer, (and) fruit. With these they make provision for the god's journey.

[1] The Pleiades.

Purification Ritual Engaging the Help of Protective Demons

Text: *KUB*, XXVII, 67. This ritual consists of four parts. The first three of them run mainly parallel with one another except that they are addressed to different demons. In the first section (i) Tarpatassis is invoked, in the second (ii) Alauwaimis, and in the third (most of iii) "he[1] who turns in front of the Tarpatassis demons." The fourth part (iii 67-iv 43) again invokes Tarpatassis. Only the second and the fourth parts are translated here.

(ii 2) [Aft]erward she[2] pours out a libation for Alauwaimis. She places pine cones upon a large pan and thereupon she strews grains of KAR;[3] these they roast. She then extinguishes the cones with water and says: "Just as I have quenched these, even so let evil also be quenched for the sacrificers!"

Balls of kneaded dough, (10) a bow of . . . (with the string taut), three arrows of . . . (with the balls of dough in front of them), a bolt, a *tarzu* (with a piece of *fur* fastened to it)—all this she places upon a tray of reeds.

(15) She takes a cord and strings it from the sacrificers' feet to their heads on either side. She also strings it down their backs. She takes it off them and places it on the tray of reeds (saying):

(20) "Loosen the evil tension of [his] head, his hands (and) his [feet]. Give it to (their) wicked adversaries! But to the sacrificers give [li]fe, vigor (and) long years!" She treats the bowstring in the same manner, and speaks in the same way.

(25) [The]n she treats the piece of (fur-)cloth in the same manner and says: "Just as the dressers scrape the cloth[4] and clear the tufts [away] so that it becomes white, even so let the gods clear away [this] man's evil sickness (30) from his [bo]dy!

"[Ala]uwaimis! Fight them no longer! [Go!] Fight this *tarzu*! Drive the evil away from them!"

She wraps up a small piece of tin in the bowstring (35) and attaches it to the sacrificers' right hands (and) feet.

She takes it off them (again) and attaches it to a mouse (with the words): "I have taken the evil off you and attached it to this mouse. Let this mouse carry it on a long journey to the high mountains, (40) hills and dales!"

She turns the mouse loose (saying): "Alauwaimis! This one pursue! I shall give thee a goat to eat!"

She sets up an *altar* of wood and breaks one long sacrificial loaf for the Alauwaimis gods, she breaks one sacrificial loaf for Alauwaimis, she breaks one sacrificial loaf for Mammas and she puts them upon the *altars*.

She then sacrifices a goat for Alauwaimis (saying): "Eat thou!" In front of the loaves she cuts it up and takes off the right shoulder. She cooks it on a fire (50) and puts [it] in a place apart from the loaves. The liver she offers in the same manner.

They cook [the left] shoulder also and she places the shank (upon the altar) for the (Alauwaimis) gods. She places the upper shoulder (upon the altar) for Alauwaimis. She places the . . . (upon the altar) for Mammas. Then she pours out a libation.

[Afterward] she offers the *heart* in the same way. She places one leg (55) [(and) one-half of the hea]d(?) (upon the altar) for the (Alauwaimis) gods. [She places] the other half of the head (upon the altar) [for Alauwaimis] (and) the womb (upon the altar) [for Mammas]; furthermore she pours out a libation.

[Then] they cook [the goat] in a cauldron and [eat] (and) drink. Then she scatters silver (and) gold, (60) [lapis], Babylon stone, *lulluri* stone, "life" stone, [Barahshi stone], iron, tin, copper (and) bronze—a little [of everything] (saying):

"[Alauwa]imis! Here [I have given] thee silver, gold, (and) lapis. Go! Say a good word for me before the gods!

"Grant [me . . .] . . . ; grant me to appear before thy face! Should someone else speak unfavorably of [me],—since thou art strong, [go] (and) speak a good word for me [before] all the gods!"

(iii 67) When she[5] comes home, she takes a *fir* tree—at the top it is in its natural state, at the bottom it is *trimmed*—and rams it (into the ground) at the right-hand side of the first gate. (70) Under the tree she places a pot.

(gap of about 15 lines)

(A tree is apparently set up at the left-hand side too.)

(iv 3) She goes away [and while *walking off*] she does not turn around [or . . .], (5) or curse. [In another place] she sets up [an *alta*]r and breaks three sacrificial loaves. Of these she breaks [one long sacrificial loaf] for the (Alauwaimis) gods, one sacrificial loaf for [Alauwai]mis (and) one sacrificial loaf for Ma[mmas] (saying):

"Tarpatassis! Accept [this] *fir* tree from me (10) and set me free! Let not [evil] sickness get to me! Stand by the side of my [wif]e, my children, (and) my children's children! Thou, who art a strong god—thou, Tarpatassis, [who] . . .[6], say a [favorable word] before all the gods!"

(15) She sacrifices a buck to Tar[patassis] and [cuts] it up before the god. She lets the blood run into a bronze cup [and empties it] into the pots on either side of [the ga]te.

[She takes off the right shoulder and] cooks [it on a fire]. (20) [. . . the left] shoulder she [cooks likewise. She puts the shank (upon the altar) for the (Alauwaimis) gods]; she puts [the upper sh]oulder (upon the altar) [for Alauwaimis]; [she puts the . . .

[1] Or: she. [2] The priestess called Old Woman. [3] A cereal.
[4] This should be the piece of fur mentioned above.

[5] It is not quite clear whether "she" or "he" be translated. In the first case the Old Woman is referred to, in the second the sacrificer.
[6] Literally: [who] turnest in front of [. . .].

(upon the altar)] for Mammas. Furthermore she pours out a libation.

She offers *heart* (and) liver [in the same way]. [She puts one-half of the hea]d(?) [(upon the altar) for the (Alauwaimis) gods; she puts the other half] of the head (and) the breast [(upon the altar) for . . .] . . . .[7] [Then they cook the buck] in a cauldron and ea[t (and) drin]k.

[When they] *clean up*, [the fir tree] is removed from the gate. On either side [of the gate] he d[rives] seven copper pegs . . . into the ground (saying): "Tarpatassis! Let neither [death], evil [fever] nor sickness enter my hou[se]! Drive [them] off into the land of the [. . .] . . . enemy!"

He scatters [silver] (and) gold, lapis, carneol, Babylon stone, Barahshi stone, *lulluri* stone, iron, tin, copper (and) bronze—[a little] (of everything). He [spreads] these (materials) here and there (saying):

"[See, I have given thee silver (and) gol]d, lapis, carneol (and) 'life' stone. [Speak thou, Tarp]atassis, [a good word for me] before all the gods! [Grant] me[8] life, vigor [(and) long years]! Stand by my house [(and) my *children*]!"

[Then] they consume the [goat which they have cooked].

Ritual Against Impotence

Text: *KUB*, VII, 5 + *KUB*, VII, 8 + *KUB*, IX, 27. Literature: J. Friedrich, *Aus dem hethitischen Schrifttum*, 2 (*AO*, XXV/2 [1925]), 16.

[1]These are the words of Pissuwattis, the Arzawa woman who lives in Parassa: If a man possesses no reproductive power or has no desire for women,

I bring sacrifices to Uliliyassis on his behalf and entreat him for three days. On the first day I prepare as follows: Rations for one man are assembled and to it the following is added: 3 sacrificial loaves of flour, water (and) . . . weighing one *tarnaš*, figs, grapes, chaff, grain, the god's meal, a little of everything; the fleece of an unblemished sheep, a pitcher of wine, [the headdress] or the shirt of the male sacrificer (in question)—they are put upon the rations.

A virgin takes up [these materials], and the sacrificer —having taken [a ba]th—walks behind them; [then] he bathes again. We shall take the materials to another place in the open country. We shall remain standing while [the . . .]. holds the rations up. I shall build a gate of reeds.

I shall twine together [a cord] of red wool (and) of white wool. I shall place a mirror (and) a distaff[2] in the sacrificer's [hand]. He will pass under the gate. When he comes [for]th through the gate, I shall take the mirror (and) the distaff away from him. I shall [gi]ve him a bow [and arrows] and while doing so I shall speak as follows: "See! I have taken womanliness away from thee and given thee manliness. Thou hast cast off the ways of a woman, now [show] the ways of a man!"

[3] Later we [present a *eun*]*uch* (as) a defend[ant] and [. . . .] While doing so I shall speak as follows: "Here [we present a *eunuch*. He has made his nature] the subject of an oracle; (whether) by . . . [the ways] of a man were indicated, or (those) of a girl were indicated for him. For his part he went down to her *bedchamber*, but all this fellow could produce was excrement (and) urine. Such ⟨will⟩ not be found to be the case with thee!

"Now see, he has gone down on his knees and is seeking thee for the sake of thy divine power. Whether thou art in the mountain, whether thou art in the meadow, whether thou art in the valley, or wherever else thou mayest be, in favor come to this man! Let driving wind and rain not hold thee back!

"He will go and worship thee, O god! He will provide a place for thee, he will give thee a house. He will give thee slaves (and) slave-girls. He will give thee cattle (and) sheep. He will have thee praised in hymns.

"See! I am entreating (and) alluring thee. So come! Bring with thee the moon, the star of the nether world, (and) the sun! Let slave-girls (and) slaves run before thee! Let gods [(and) goddesses] (ii)[4] run before thee! Come down to this man! Make his wife conceive a child, look after her! Turn to him and speak to him! Let him have thy maid, and let her bear his yoke! Let him take his wife and beget sons (and) daughters for himself! They will be thy servants and thy handmaids; they will always be giving thee offerings, sacrificial loaves, meal (and) libations.

"See! This man knew thee not. See! Now he has sought after thee. Since then this (man) has sought after thee. So stand by him, in favor, O god! In this matter in which he has come to thee, O god, show thy divine power and set all aright! Let him experience thy divine power, and he will come [and worship] thee. . . . ."

[5]I[6] shall take [the materials] from upon the rations and we shall go back into the house. In the house in which I make offerings a new table is set up and I shall put the rations upon that table; in front of it I shall put a pitcher.

The broken sacrificial loaves which are lying on the rations, I shall take a little of them and give it to the male sacrificer. He will put it into his mouth, and he will drink (for) Uliliyassis three times. When night falls, the sacrificer will lie down in front of the table; they will set up a bed for him in front of the table.

[7] It is again not clear whether the sacrificer or the Old Woman is meant.
[8] To the sacrificer.

[1] The beginning of column i is published as *KUB*, IX, 27.
[2] These two implements are considered as symbolic for womanhood.

[3] *KUB*, IX, 27 i 30 = *KUB*, VII, 5 i 3.
[4] The beginning of the second column is found on *KUB*, VII, 8.
[5] From here on the text follows *KUB*, VII, 5 ii.
[6] The priestess who is the author of the ritual is speaking.

The headdress or the shirt that is lying upon the rations, he will spread (it) out at night time. (20) I shall do that for three days. But daily I shall entreat three times, once at dawn, once at midday (and) once at nightfall. While doing so I shall speak the same words.

(25) One set of loaves I shall break at dawn, another set at noon, and another set at nightfall. I shall also strew another portion of meal. (iii) Then I shall sacrifice one sheep to Uliliyassis, and they will conjure him down in front of the table. They will finally remove the sheep (5) [cut] it up and then [cook] it. From the meat [they will select . . .]. breast (and) shoulder and place it upon the table [. . .]. Liver [(and) heart . . .] they will cook [on a fire . . .], two sacrificial loaves [they will break and put them] on the table for him.

(The following 15-20 lines are badly mutilated. The remnants point to a ceremony similar to that described in the earlier parts of the text, probably belonging to a second ritual. The preserved end of the text[7] contains the incantation which goes with that ritual:)

". . . (5) Let him have [thy maid], and let her bear his yoke! Let him take his wife and beget children for himself! Let him beget sons (and) daughters for himself. (10) Thou, O god, prove thy divine power!

"Let him experience thy might! and he will make thee his personal god. He will make thee praised in hymns." They will spread out a bed for him (15) in front of the table and they will also spread out the headdress or the shirt that had been lying on the rations. (iv) The sacrificer will lie down, (to see) whether he will experience the bodily presence of the deity in his dream, coming to him and sleeping with him. (5) During the three days on which he is entreating the deity he tells all the dreams which he has, whether the deity appears to him and whether the deity (10) sleeps with him.

He will go (and) worship the god. Furthermore, if sacrificial vessels are in order, he will set up sacrificial vessels; if not, (15) he will set up a stone pillar or erect a statue. But the new table which stood throughout the entreaty, becomes the property of the deity.

(After three mutilated lines, the text is completely destroyed and thus the end of the composition is missing.)

Ritual Against Domestic Quarrel

Text: *KBo*, II, 3 and its duplicates *KUB*, X, 76 + *KUB*, XII, 34 + *KUB*, XII, 59 + *KUB*, XV, 39 + *IBoT*, II, 109; *IBoT*, II, 110, 111. Literature: F. Hrozný, *Hethitische Keilschrifttexte aus Boghazköi* (1919), 60-89.

These are the words of Mastiggas, the woman from Kizzuwatna: If a father and (his) son, or a husband and his wife, or a brother and (his) sister quarrel, when I reconcile them, I treat them as follows:

[7] *KUB*, VII, 8 iii followed by *KUB*, VII, 5 iv.

(5) She[1] takes black wool and wraps it in mutton fat; *tiššatwa* they call it.[2] She presents it to the sacrificer and speaks as follows: "Whatever thou spokest with (thy) mouth (and) tongue[3]—see, here is *tiššatwa*! Let it be cut out (10) of your body these days!" She throws the tongues into the hearth.

Afterward the Old Woman takes salt, bl[ood, *fat*] and wax. She makes the wax into tongues and waves [them over the two] sacrificers. She also waves the salt and the [. . .] blood over them, [present]s it to them and they [flatten it] with (their) left (15) hands.

The Old Woman speaks as follows: "In whatever curses you indulged, let now the Sun-god turn those curses (and) tongues toward the left!"[4] And she throws them into the hearth.

The red wool (and) the blue wool that (20) had been placed upon the bodies of the two sacrificers,[5] the two figures of dough that had been placed before them, and the hands and tongues of dough that had been placed upon their heads, those the Old Woman removes. She cuts the strings off them, the Old Woman breaks the two hands and the tongues of dough to pieces.

(25) She then waves them over them and speaks as follows: "Let the tongues of these [days] be cut off! Let the words of these days be cut off!" And she throws them [into the hearth].

Afterward the Old Woman takes [a tray] and [places] (30) seven tongues [and seven hands . . .] upon it. She waves it over the two sacrificers and [speaks] as follows: "Here are the tongues and the hands [of that day] which is a source of disgust. Let the Sun-god [turn] them toward [the left] for thee!" And she puts them into the hearth.

The Old Woman takes the [. . .] dough. She sprinkles water upon them[6] (35) and [*purifies* them]. Then she waves the dough over them and speaks as follows: "Be ye cleansed of your evil tongue!" And she puts the dough into the hearth.

They drive up a ⟨white⟩ sheep. The Old Woman presents it to the two sacrificers and speaks as follows: "Here is a substitute for you, (40) a substitute for your persons. Let that tongue and that curse stay in (its) mouth!" They spit into its mouth.

She speaks as follows: "Atone ye for those evil curses!" They dig a hole in the ground, slaughter the sheep over it, and then put it into it.

(45) They put 1 fine sacrificial loaf down with it, she also pours out a libation of wine and they level the ground.

They drive up a black sheep, the Old Woman presents it to them[6] and speaks as follows: "For your heads and

[1] The priestess; the text changes abruptly into the third person.

[2] Probably in the Hurrian language.

[3] The text ends a section here, dividing the same sentence over two sections.

[4] i.e. destroy them.

[5] The persons who ordered the ritual performed.

[6] i.e. the sacrificers.

all parts of your bodies the black sheep is a substitute. In its mouth (and its) tongue (50) is the tongue of curses." She waves it over them.

The two sacrificers [spi]t into its mouth. They slaughter the sheep and cut it up. They [kindle] the hearth and [burn] it.

They pour honey (and) olive oil over it. She [brea]ks a sacrificial loaf (55) and throws it into the hearth. She also pours out a libation of wine.

The Old Woman takes a small pig, she presents it to them[6] and speaks as follows: "See! It has been fattened with grass (and) grain. Just as this one shall not see the sky and shall not see the (other) small pigs again, (ii) even so let the evil curses not see these sacrificers either!"

She waves the small pig over them, and then they kill it. They dig a hole in the ground (5) and put it down into it. They put a sacrificial loaf down with it, she also pours out a libation of wine and they level the ground.

The Old Woman makes a kneading-pan of clay. She puts into it a little dough into which she throws a little black *cumin*. She waves it over the two sacrificers (10) and speaks as follows:

"Just as this clay does not return to the clay pit and this *cumin* does not turn white and cannot be used for seed a second time;

"(as) this dough does not get into a sacrificial loaf for the gods, even so let the evil tongue not get to the body of the two sacrificers!"

(The following sections[7] are not intelligible as yet.)

The Old Woman [waves] water over the two sacrificers and purifies them. She also [waves] the dough over them.

(30) Afterward she again makes a kneading-pan of clay and pours oil into it. She severs the blue wool and throws the severed end in. The Old Woman hides it under the coat of the two sacrificers,

and she speaks as follows: "[Thou art] the kneading-pan of Ishtar.[8] Make [good] persist for them, and evil hide away from them likewise!"

Afterward [the Old Woman] takes [a *ḫupuwai* vessel] and fills it with honey, olive oil [(and) . . .]; she adds fruit, fig (and) . . . [. . .]; she puts in blood, salt (and) mutton-fat.

(40) [Before she throws the *ḫu*]*puwai* into the hearth, she breaks the *ḫupuwai* to pieces [and speaks as follows]: "Let him break it and with it the [evil] mouth (and the evil) tongue!"

[After the Old Woman] breaks the *ḫupuwai*, (45) she walks [*backward*] and [throws] it [into] the hearth.

They [drive up a black sheep] and call it "the substitute." The Old Woman holds 1 thin sacrificial loaf (and) 1 jug of wine (in readiness).

While offering the *black* sheep the Old Woman speaks as follows: (50) "O Sun-god! Here is a substitute in their place, for mouth and tongue." She sacrifices the sheep, breaks the loaf and pours out the wine. A white sheep they do not kill again; the Old Woman gets it.

(The next section is mutilated and therefore omitted here.)

(iii 10) They light fires on the right and on the left; in between they set seven stone pillars in the ground. The Old Woman presents one sacrificial loaf weighing 1 *tarnaš* and a cheese to the two sacrificers and they touch it with their hands.

(15) The Old Woman breaks the sacrificial loaf, pours out a libation of wine and speaks as follows:

"Whoever erected these stone pillars in this one place—see, now they totter. Whatever issued from the mouths (and) the tongues of the two sacrificers on that day—let those words totter in the same way!"

The two sacrificers overturn the stone pillars with (their) feet and throw them into the fire. (25) The fine garments which they are wearing they cast off and the Old Woman gets them.

She waves a pot over them, takes the DUG.LIŠ.GAL[9] off their heads and sp[eaks] as follows: "See! [I have taken the DUG.LIŠ.GAL] off your heads. [Let the evil] words [be taken off in the same way]!" (35) [. . .] the two sacrificers break the pot with their feet and [she says as follows: "Let them break] all the words [of mouth (and) tongue in the same way]!"

The Old Woman takes *hay*,[10] calls it *tiwariya*[11] and rubs down the limbs of the two sacrificers.

She speaks as follows: "Let the evil words of mouth (and) tongue be rubbed away from you!"

(iv) The Old Woman takes water from a cup or an amphora and presents it to the two sacrificers; salt is also put in. The two sacrificers pour the water over their heads, (5) they also rinse their hands (and) their eyes.

Then they pour it into the horn of an ox. The two sacrificers seal it up and the Old Woman speaks as follows:

(10) "On the day when the olden kings return and examine the state of the land,—then, and then only, shall this seal be broken."

Evocatio

Text: *KUB*, xv, 34 and its duplicates *KUB*, xv, 33a, 33b and 38. Literature: L. Zuntz, *Un testo ittita di scongiuri* (= *Atti del Reale Istituto Veneto di Science Lettere ed Arti*, xcvi/2 [1937]).

When the diviners attract the gods by means of nine trails from the meadows, the mountains (and) the rivers, from the sea, from the springs, from fire, from heaven and from the earth, they take the following things: He takes a basket and in the basket (materials)

[7] *KUB*, xv, 39 + *IBoT*, ii, 109 ii 21 ff.

[8] The allusion which may have a mythological background is unintelligible.

[9] This is usually considered as a kind of vessel; this apparently does not fit here.

[10] Reading in doubt.

[11] Again in Hurrian?

are made ready as follows: (5) there lies (in it) one *ḫupparaš*, upon it lies one sacrificial loaf made of fine flour, upon the loaf a (piece of) cedar is fastened and to the front (of the piece) of cedar red wool is tied.

It (the wool) is led down (to the ground). Fine oil . . . is poured into a *bitumen cup* and he soaks it (the wool) in it; (10) fine flour is strewn over it. Upon it 30 thin loaves of fine flour are placed. An ear of the gods' grain (and) the chaff of an ear (of grain), the wing of an eagle (and) the fleece of an unblemished sheep, are (also) placed there all wrapped together.

Apart (from these) are (kept) one wine jug (and) one pitcher filled with wine, (10) honey (and) fine oil mixed together, one jar of fine oil, one jar of honey; also fruit, figs, grapes, olives, barley, a broken leavened loaf, one pot filled with fat cake.

They go down from the Tawinia gate and set up a wickerwork table for the "cedar" gods on the road. (20) Upon it they place the prepared basket and in front of it they construct a fireplace for (burning) wood. They draw a length of cloth down from the wickerwork table and make it into a trail. Then they draw a trail in fine flour in front of the cloth; on the one side of the flour trail they draw a trail in honey, but on the other side they draw a trail in wine (25) (and) fine oil mixed together.

He then breaks one thin loaf, puts fat cake upon it and places it on the ends of the trails. He breaks one thin loaf, strews it upon the trail and pours out a libation of wine. He breaks one thin loaf, puts fat cake upon it, and places it upon the path, he also pours out a libation of wine. (30) One diviner takes the red wool that had been tied to the (piece of) cedarwood from the [. . .]. *bitumen cup*, out of the fine oil, and sprinkles [the *trails*] with fine oil. One diviner lifts up the wing of the eagle on which the chaff is lying and squeals; the diviner speaks the . . . [. . .]. prayer. (35) He places a length of cloth over the wickerwork table, takes pebbles from the trail and the path and places them upon the table. He strews out leavened bread (and) cheese, also fruit and barley, for the god, pours out a libation of wine (and) speaks as follows:

(40) "O Cedar-gods! See! I have covered your ways with the scarf that goes with the long gown and have spread for you fine flour (and) fine oil. So walk ye over it to this place! Let no fallen tree impede your feet, let no stones inconvenience your feet! (45) The mountains shall be leveled before you, [the rivers] shall be bridged before you!" He breaks thin loaves, strews out fat cake, also pours out a libation and says:

"Let the vigorous Cedar-gods eat and drink the trails! Let them satisfy their hunger and quench their thirst! O gods, (50) in favor turn ye toward the king and the queen! Wherever ye may be, O Cedar-gods, whether in heaven or on earth, whether on mountains or in rivers, whether in the Mitanni country[1] or in the country of Kinza,[2] the country of Tunip, the country of Ugarit,[3] the country of Zinzira, the country of Dunanapa, the country of Idarukatta, the country of Gatanna, the country of Alalha,[4] (55) the country of Kinahhi,[5] the country of Amurru, the country of Sidon, the country of Tyre, the country of Nuhassi, the country of Ugulzit, the country of Arrapha,[6] the country of Zunzurhi;

"Whether ye are in the country of Ashur, the country of Babylon, the country of Shanhara, the country of Egypt, the country of Alashiya,[7] the country of Alziya,[8] the country of Papahhi, the country of Kumma, the country of Hayasha, the country of Lulluwa,[9] the country of Arzawa, the country [of . . .], (60) [the country of . . .] . . . , the country of Talawa, the country of Masa, the country of Galkisa, the country of Kuntara, the country of Iyalanta, the country of Wilusa,[10] the country of Uraya, the country of Suhma, the country of Sappuwa, [the country of . . .], the country of Partahuina, the country of Kasula, the country of Himuwa, the country of Lalha, in the Kashkean country[11] or in whatever other countries—(65) come ye now back to the Hatti land!

"If anyone, either [a foreigner] or a Hittite, [either a common man] or a member of the nobility, has drawn you away, entreated you, lured you away [. . .] (70) into his house [. . .], see, here we are [drawing you back] . . . (and) we are squealing.

(small gap if any)

(ii) "Turn your backs on the enemy country and on the wicked p[eople]; turn your eyes toward the king and the queen! They will give you holy offerings. So [come here] in favor and receive your offerings with both hands [and . . .]! (5) Come ye forth from the enemy country and from evil uncleanliness!

"Come ye to the blessed, holy, fine (and) wonderful Hatti land! Bring with you life, good health, long years, *power of procreation*, sons (and) daughters, grandchildren (and) great-grandchildren, the gods' love, the gods' kindliness, (10) valor (and) . . . obedience! Lift ye from [the king (and) the queen] (their) thousand *shortcomings*! Look ye upon the king (and) the qu[een] with favor!

"Come ye back to your fine and wonderful sanctuaries! Sit ye down again on your thrones and chairs! Sit ye down again on your holy, fine (and) wonderful seats!

"Provide ye for the king (and) the queen life, good health, long years, *power of procreation*, sons (and) daughters, grandchildren (and) great-grandchildren! For the man manliness (and) valor, for the woman womanliness (and) *motherhood*!

[1] The region between the Euphrates and Assyria in the east.

[2] Qadesh on the Orontes, today Tell Nebi Mendo.

[3] Today Ras Shamra.

[4] The capital of Mukis(hi) excavated at Atchana (Tell Açana).

[5] The Hurrian form of Canaan.

[6] Today Kirkuk in Iraq.

[7] The island of Cyprus.

[8] The region on the upper Tigris.

[9] The three last mentioned countries are situated in the region where Turkey, Iran and Iraq meet today.

[10] This group comprises the main countries of southern and western Anatolia.

[11] The region along the Black Sea in Pontus.

"Throughout the land give ye love and loyalty, the gods' love, the gods' kindliness, high spirits in god (and) high spirits in man, valor, its victorious arms, fertility (and) prosperity in the country, fertility of man, cattle, sheep, grain (and) wine! Grant ye to him (the king) the loyalty (and) obedience of his charioteers (and) foot soldiers!"

He sprinkles fine oil (about) with the red wool and says: "Just as brightness has been imparted to this wool, even so let brightness be imparted to the persons of the Cedar-gods!

"Just as this fine oil is soothing, (as) it is agreeable to gods and agreeable to men, even so let the king and the queen of the Hatti land be agreeable to the gods! Let the soothing effect of the cedar, the *music* of the *lyres* (and) the words of the diviner be such an [alluring] inducement to the gods that they will get them called here! Wherever else ye may be, come (ye) here! If ye do not hear the first time, hear the second time! If ye do not hear the second time, hear the third, the fourth, the fifth, the sixth, the seventh time! So come ye! Come back to your holy, fine (and) wonderful temples, thrones (and) chairs!

"Turn with favor toward the king and the queen! Give them life, good health, long years (and) d[ays]!" At the feet of the gods they strew out a leavened loaf (and) cheese, fruit [and figs]; they pour out wine, honey and fine oil mixed together, and he speaks as follows:

"See! At your feet I have placed for you, Cedar-gods, [a leavened loaf] (and) a cheese. So abandon ye the enemy country and come back to the blessed, fine (and) wonderful Hatti land! Let not evil, evil [fever], . . . [. . .] (and) plague accompany you! *B[reak]* it! Wipe [it out fr]om the Hatti land and give it [to al]l [the enemy]! Those who do not perform [the proper rites], those who are [not rev]erent [to the gods], [let] those [suffer! . . .]"

(considerable gap)

(The reverse of the tablet describes ceremonies designed to attract the gods from the rivers [iii 1-20], the sea [iii 21-22], the springs [iii 23-47], the mountains [iii 48-58], gap, the nether world [iv 1-26], the heaven [iv 27-40]. The tablet closes with "the bringing up of the gods," presumably to their permanent dwelling places.)

The Soldiers' Oath

Text: *KBo*, vi, 34 and its duplicate *KUB*, vii, 59. Literature: J. Friedrich, *ZA*, NF i (1924), 161-192, reprinted with additions in the same author's *Hethitische Studien* (1924). Excerpts are also found in Zimmern's contribution to Lehmann-Haas, *Textbuch zur Religionsgeschichte*, 2nd ed. (1922), 335 f. and in J. Friedrich, *Aus dem hethitischen Schrifttum*, 2 (*AO*, xxv/2 [1925]), 16 ff. The tablet in question is marked as the second of a series entitled "When they lead the troops to the (ceremony of taking the) oath." At the beginning about 17 lines are missing.

[He[1] . . .]s and says: "[Just as this . . . cou]ld [see] and was able to find [(its) food], and (as) they have now blinded it at the place of the oath,—whoever breaks these oaths, betrays the king of the Hatti land, and turns his eyes in hostile fashion upon the Hatti land, let these oaths seize him! Let them blind this man's army and make it deaf! Let them not see each other, let them not hear each other! Let them make a cruel fate their lot! Below let them paralyze their feet, and above let them bind their hands! Just as the gods of the oath bound the hands and feet of the army of the Arzawa country[2] and made them unable to move, even so let them bind that man's army and make them unable to move!"

He places yeast in their hands, they *squeeze* it and he says: "Is not this that you have here yeast? Just as they take this little piece of yeast, mix it (into the dough) in the kneading bowl and let the bowl stand for a day (so that) it can ferment—whoever breaks these oaths, shows disrespect to the king of the Hatti land, and turns his eyes in hostile fashion upon the Hatti land, let these oaths seize him! Let him be ridden with disease! Make a cruel fate their lot!" The men declare: "So be it!"

Then he places wax and mutton fat in their hands. He throws them *on a pan* and says: "Just as this wax melts, and just as the mutton fat dissolves,—whoever breaks these oaths, (ii) [shows disrespect to the king] of the Hatti [land], let [him] melt lik[e wax], let him dissolve like [mutton fat]!" [The me]n declare: "So be it!"

He places sinews (and) salt in their hands. He throws them on a pan and speaks as follows: "Just as these sinews split into fragments on the hearth, and just as the salt is scattered on the hearth—whoever breaks these oaths, shows disrespect to the king of the Hatti land, and turns his eyes in hostile fashion upon the Hatti land, let these oaths seize him! Let him split into fragments like the sinews, let him be scattered like the salt! Just as salt has no seed, even so let that man's name, seed, house, cattle (and) sheep perish!"

He places malt (and) malt loaf in their hands, they *crush* them and he speaks as follows: "Just as they grind this malt loaf between mill stones, mix it with water, bake it and break it up—whoever breaks these oaths and does evil to the king (and) the queen, the princes (and) to the Hatti land, let these oaths seize him! Let them grind their bones in the same way! Let him *soak* in the same way! Let him be broken up in the same way! Let a cruel fate be his lot!" The men declare: "So be it!"

"Just as this malt no (longer) has the power of growth, (as) one cannot take it to a field and use it as

[1] The officiating priest.

[2] The most important group of countries in the southern part of Anatolia bordering on the Mediterranean Sea.

seed, (as) one cannot use it as bread or store it in the storehouse—whoever (35) breaks these oaths and does evil to the king (and) the queen and the princes, even so let the gods of the oath also destroy that man's future! Let not his wife bear sons and daughters! Let his land (and) his fields have no crop, (40) and his pastures no grass! Let not his cattle (and) sheep bear calves (and) lambs!"

They bring the garments of a woman, a distaff and a mirror, they break an arrow and you speak as follows: "Is not this that you see here (45) garments of a woman? We have them here for (the ceremony of taking) the oath. Whoever breaks these oaths and does evil to the king (and) the queen (and) the princes, let these oaths change him from a man into a woman! Let them change his troops into women, (50) let them dress them in the fashion of women and cover their heads with a length of cloth! Let them break the bows, arrows (and) clubs in their hands and (iii) [let them put] in their hands distaff and mirror!"

They parade in front of them a [blind woman] and a deaf man and [you speak] as follows: "See! here is a blind woman (5) and a deaf man. Whoever does evil to the king (and) the queen, let the oaths seize him! Let them make him blind! Let them [ma]ke him [deaf]! Let them [blind] him like a blind man! Let them [deafen] him like a deaf man! Let them [annihilate him], the man (himself) (10) together with his wife, [his children] (and) his kin!"

He places an *old* stone image [of a man] in their hands and speaks as follows: "Did not this man whom you see here take the oath? (15) [At some other time] he was sworn in before the gods and then broke his oath. The oaths seized him and his inner parts are sagging out in front, he has to hold his entrails in his hands. Whoever (20) breaks these oaths, let these oaths seize him! Let his inner parts sag out in front! Let 'Ishara sons'[3] [live] in his inner parts and eat him up!"

He presents to them [a . . .]. Before their eyes (25) he [throws] it on the ground; they trample it under foot and he speaks as follows: "Whoever breaks these oaths, even so let the Hatti people come and trample that man's town under foot! Let them make it bare of people!"

(30) They light [a *fire*]*brand* and trample it under foot so that it scatters here and there and he says: "Just as this one flies apart—whoever breaks these oaths, even so let this man's house be robbed of men, (35) cattle (and) sheep!"

You will place before them an oven. Also a plow, a cart (and) a chariot you will place before the congregation. These things they break and he speaks as follows: "Whoever breaks these oaths, let the Storm-god break his plow! Just as grass does not come [out of] the oven, let not spelt (and) barley (45) [come out] of his field, let *saḫlû*[4] come forth!"

[3] Apparently some kind of worms.
[4] A weed commonly found on ruins.

(iv) He pours water on the fire (5) and speaks to them as follows: "Just as this burning fire is snuffed out—whoever breaks these oaths, even so let these oaths seize him! Let this man's vitality, vigor (10) and future happiness be snuffed out together with (that of) his wife and his children! Let the oaths put an evil curse upon him! Let no offspring thrive in his corral, his fold (15) (and) his barnyard! From his field let grass not come forth, not even from (one) furrow!"

Ritual before Battle

Text: *KUB*, IV, 1. Literature: M. Witzel, *Hethitische Keilschrift-Urkunden* (*Keilinschriftliche Studien*, 4 [1924], 60-65).

When they perform the ritual at the boundary of the enemy country he sacrifices one sheep to the Sun-goddess of Arinna and to the Storm-god, the Patron-god (and) all the gods, to Telepinus (and) the gods and goddesses of Turmitta, (5) to all . . . gods (and) the . . . gods, to all the mountains (and) rivers.

But one sheep they sacrifice to Zithariyas.

(10) They speak as follows: "See! Zithariyas is appealing to all the gods. The sanctuaries which had long been assigned to Zithariyas' worship, the countries which have fallen into turmoil—in all of them they would celebrate great festivals for him.

(16) "But now the Kashkeans[1] have taken them. The Kashkeans have begun war. They boast of their power (and) strength. They have made light of you, O gods!

"See! Zithariyas (20) is appealing to all the gods; he brings his complaints before you. So pass judgment on his case, all ye gods! Let it be of great concern to the gods!

"In fact they (the sanctuaries) have been taken away by these people not from Zithariyas alone, (25) they have been taken away from all you gods, all of you; from the Sun-goddess of Arinna, from the Storm-god of Nerik, from the Storm-god (and) from the Patron-god, from Telepinus (and) from all the (other) gods. From you (also) have his cities been taken.

(30) "See! Zithariyas is bringing his case before all of you, gods. Take your own case to heart! Pass judgment on your own case in passing judgment on the case of Zithariyas!

(35) "Blot out the Kashkean country, O gods! Let every single god take thought for his place of worship and win it back!

"Let Zithariyas win back his place of worship! Let him again roam those countries (40) at will! Let people again celebrate [his] great festivals! . . ."

(Gap that must have contained a ritual in which the enemy gods are summoned.)

(ii) And he speaks as follows: "O gods of the Kashkean country! We have summoned you before this assembly.

[1] A group of wild tribes living in the mountains along the shore of the Black Sea who incessantly raid and plunder on Hittite territory.

Come ye, eat (and) drink! Hear ye the accusation (5) which we bring against you!

"The gods of the Hatti land have done nothing against you, the gods of the Kashkean country. (10) They have not put you under constraint.

"But ye, the gods of the Kashkean country, began war. Ye drove the gods of the Hatti land out of their realm and took over their realm for yourselves.

(15) "The Kashkean people also began war. From the Hittites ye took away their cities and ye drove them out of their field (and) fallow and out of their vineyards.

"The gods of the Hatti land and the (Hittite) people (20) call for bloody vengeance. The [vengeance] of the Hatti gods and the vengeance of the (Hittite) people [will be wrought] on you, the gods [of the Kashkean country] and the [Kashkean people]."

(Gap that must have contained, beside the end of the preceding, a ritual of purification which intends to enable the army again to vanquish the enemy.)

(iii) "Let him eat (and) d[rink! . . . Let him] re[turn to the army] and battle the enemy!"

(5) When he has finished he goes again before the Hatti gods, and they eat up the meat and the bread. He brings sacrifices to the Hatti gods, the Storm-god of the army (and) the Warrior-god.[2] They give them to drink (10) as much as they think fitting. The "master of the gods"[3] receives the implements used at the feast (and) the sheepskins. They return to the army, and go to battle in this condition.

Removal of the Threat Implied in an Evil Omen

Text: *KUB*, IX, 13 + *KUB*, XXIV, 5. Literature: M. Vieyra, *RHR*, CXIX (1939), 121-153. The upper third of the obverse and the corresponding part of the reverse are lost. The missing beginning must have stated the main theme of the text: a threat to the king implied in an evil omen. It must also have contained part of the treatment. It consists in the attempt at deflecting the predicted misfortune to persons who substitute for the king. The first preserved lines seem to finish the treatment of a first group of such substitutes. The better preserved part (beginning with obverse 6) deals already with a second group.

[During the night[1] the king] takes the . . . [substitu]tes and goes to the *sanctuary* of the Moon-god. [He presents them to the Moon-god and] says: "In the matter about which [I prayed] to you, listen to me, Moon-god, my lord! [That omen which thou] gavest—if thou foundest fault with me, (10) (witness) that I have given [thee] straightaway [these substitu]tes. These take, [but let me go fr]ee!" They drive up to the *sanctuary* a live steer [and sacri]fice it [. . .].

[2] His Hittite name is not known; in Hattian it was Wurunkatte "king of the country."

[3] Apparently the officiating priest.

[1] Restored because of the beginning of the second following section.

The king goes up to the *sanctuary* [and speaks as follows: "That] omen which thou gavest, O Moon-god—if thou foundest fault with me [and] wishedst to behold with thine own eyes [the sinner's] *abasement*, (15) [see, I, the king,] have come in person [to thy *sanctuary*] and have [given] thee these substitutes. Consider [the substitu]tion! Let these die! But, let me not die!" They hand [the substitutes over to the . . .] and he takes them away. [When] he has finished . . .ing [them], he[2] casts (spells of) deliverance (over him).[3]

He [brings a healthy prisoner to the *sanctuary*]. They anoint the prisoner with the fine oil of kingship, (20) and [he[4] speaks] as follows: "This man (is) the king. To him [have I given] a royal name. Him have I clad [in the vestments] of kingship. Him have I crowned with the diadem. Remember ye this: That evil omen [signifies] short years (and) short days. Pursue ye this substitute!" The one shekel of silver, the one shekel of gold, the one mina of copper, (25) the one mina of tin, the one mina of iron, the one mina of *lead*, all this is removed from his [body].[5] The one healthy prisoner is released, and he has him taken back to his country. The king submits to the waving ceremony, and afterward the king goes to bathe.

When it dawns, the king submits to the waving ceremony and afterward he performs the "Ritual of the House" (and) the "Pure Ritual." When it is light, the king performs the "[. . .] Sacrifice." (30) When he returns he takes a bath and sacrifices one . . . sheep to the Sun-god under the open sky.

Words [of . . .] he speaks as follows: "Sun-god of Heaven, my lord! That omen which the Moon-god gave—if he found fault with me, accept ye, Sun-god of Heaven and (all) ye gods, these substitutes that I have given (35) and let me go free! To (appearing before) thee, I might prefer appearing before the Sun-goddess of Arinna." (reverse) [Afterward] he goes into [. . .] and [sacrific]es [one . . . sheep] to Eresh-kigal.[6] He prays as follows: "Eresh-kigal, my lady! That omen which the Moon-god gave,—if (5) he found fault with me, (remember) that the Gods of Heaven have delivered me into thy hands. Take these substitutes that I have handed over to thee and let me go free! I want to see the Sun-god of Heaven with mine eyes!" They offer pieces of raw and cooked meat, (10) and the king arranges for cups at his own expense.

When night comes, he sacrifices one . . . sheep for the Moon-god under the open sky and speaks as follows: "Moon-god, my lord! That omen which thou gavest—if thou foundest fault with me, (remember that) thou didst deliver me (15) into the hands of the gods of the nether world and Eresh-kigal. I made my peace with the gods of the nether world (and) handed over substitutes (to them). Take those, but let me go free! To (appearing before) thee I might prefer (appearing

[2] The officiating priest. [3] The king. [4] The officiating priest.

[5] These pieces of metal must have been mentioned in the lost beginning of the text.

[6] The Sumero-Akkadian goddess of the nether world.

before) the Sun-god of Heaven." The king offers pieces of raw and cooked meat (20) and arranges for cups.

(end of text lost)

Ritual for the Erection of a House

Text: *KBo*, IV, 1 and its duplicates *KUB*, II, 2 and *KUB*, IX, 33. Literature: M. Witzel, *Hethitische Keilschrift-Urkunden* (=*Keilinschriftliche Studien*, 4 [1924]), 76-87.

(obverse)

When they rebuild a house that had been destroyed or (build) a new house in a different place and they lay the foundations, they deposit under the foundations as follows: 1 mina of *refined* copper, 4 bronze pegs, 1 small iron hammer. In the center, at the place of the *kurakki* (5) he digs up the ground. He deposits the copper therein, fixes it down on all sides with the pegs and afterward hits it with the hammer. While doing so he speaks as follows:

"Just as this copper is secured, (as) moreover it is firm, even so let this temple be secure! (10) Let it be firm upon the dark earth!"

He mentions the name of the sacrificer: "He who built this temple, let him be firm before the gods likewise! Graciously let him draw upon himself before the gods (the potency of) this temple for enduring life!

"Just as the four corner(stones) of the house are firm on the ground (15) and as they will not be overturned, even so let the sacrificer's well-being not overturn in future before the gods! Graciously, O god, let him draw upon himself before the gods (the potency of) this house for life, good health (and) vigor on the part of the lordship over the Hatti land (and) on the part of the throne of kingship!"

Beneath the four corner(stones), each one of them, (25) he deposits as follows: 1 foundation stone of silver, 1 foundation stone of gold, 1 foundation stone of lapis, 1 foundation stone of jasper, 1 foundation stone of marble, 1 foundation stone of iron, 1 foundation stone of copper, 1 foundation stone of bronze, 1 foundation stone of diorite. The four corner(stones) are (each) provided with these in the same way.

Beneath the four *kurakki*, each one of them, (25) he deposits as follows: he deposits 1 *kurakki* of silver, 1 *kurakki* of gold, 1 *kurakki* of lapis, 1 *kurakki* of jasper, 1 *kurakki* of iron, 1 *kurakki* of diorite, 1 *kurakki* of copper, 1 *kurakki* of bronze. While doing so he speaks as follows:

"See! This temple which we have built for thee, the god (he mentions the name of the god for whom they build it)—it is not we (30) who have (really) built it, all the gods have built it.

"The gods—those (who are) craftsmen—have built it. Telepinus has laid the foundations. The walls above them, Ea, the king of wisdom, has built (them). Timber and stones, all the mountains have brought (them). But the mortar, the goddesses have brought (it).

(35) "They have laid foundations of silver and gold; the gold they brought from Birunduma,[1] the silver they brought from. . . . The lapis they brought from Mount Takniyara.[1] The marble they brought from the country of Kanisha.[1] The jasper they brought from the country of Elam.[2] The diorite they brought from the earth. The black iron of heaven they brought from heaven. Copper (and) bronze (40) they brought from Mount Taggata in Alasiya.[3]

"See! beneath the foundations they have deposited gold for (firm) founding. Just as the gold is firm, (as) moreover it is clean (and) strong, (as) the mind of the gods is set on it, and (as) it is dear to god and man, even so let the gods be set on this temple (and) let it be dear (to them)!

(45) "Let the sacrificer, and (his) children and children's children likewise be dear to the gods (and gain) enduring life by their grace!"

9 *props* of silver, each one 1 shekel of weight; 9 *props* of gold, each one 1 shekel in weight; 9 *props* of iron; 9 *props* of bronze. (reverse) Beneath the altar he deposits 4 *props*, among them one of silver, one of gold, one of iron (and) one of bronze. At the front *kurakki* in the center he deposits 4 *props* in the same manner. Also against the *kurakki*, on the right (and) the left sides, on either he deposits 4 *props* in the same manner.

(5) Also at the four corner(stones), at each corner(stone), he deposits 4 *props* in the same manner.

A lion of gold weighing 1 shekel, 2 pairs of oxen of iron, yoked under a yoke of silver, every ox weighing 1 shekel,—beneath them are plates, and two oxen stand on one plate, (10) (while) the two other oxen stand on (the other) plate.

The weight of the plate is of no significance, nor is the weight of the yoke by which the oxen are yoked of significance. He deposits them under the front *kurakki* in the center.

Beneath the cult stand he deposits 1 cult stand of silver, 1 cult stand of gold, (15) 1 cult stand of lapis, 1 cult stand of jasper, 1 cult stand of iron, 1 cult stand of copper, 1 cult stand of bronze, 1 cult stand of marble, 1 cult stand of diorite.

Beneath the hearth (he deposits) 1 hearth of silver weighing 1 shekel, 1 hearth of gold weighing 1 shekel, 1 hearth of lapis, 1 hearth of jasper, 1 hearth of marble, 1 hearth of iron, 1 hearth of bronze, 1 hearth of diorite. (20) 4 *props*, among them one of silver, one of gold, one of iron (and) one of bronze, each one weighing 1 shekel (are also deposited there). The hearths made of stone, each one also weighs 1 shekel.

Beneath the door (he deposits) 1 door of silver weighing 1 shekel, 1 door of gold weighing 1 shekel, 1 door of lapis weighing 1 shekel, 1 door of jasper weighing 1 shekel, (25) 1 door of iron weighing 1

[1] Not otherwise known.
[2] The country toward the east of Babylonia.
[3] The island of Cyprus.

shekel, 1 door of bronze weighing 1 shekel, 1 door of marble weighing 1 shekel, 1 door of diorite also weighing 1 shekel.

2 . . . of bronze he deposits in the gate; their weight is of no significance.

16 . . . , among them 4 of gold, 4 of silver, (30) 4 of iron (and) 4 of bronze (are also deposited); their weight is of no significance.

Ritual for the Erection of a New Palace

Text: *KUB*, XXIX, 1 and its duplicates *KUB*, XXIX, 2 and 3. Literature: B. Schwartz, *Orientalia*, NS XVI (1947), 23-55; the lines i 26-41 and ii 39-54 are dealt with by H. G. Güterbock, *RHA*, VI (1942-43), 102-9.

[When the king] builds [a new palace and when the time comes for roofing it] with timber, [they speak as follows:] "By consulting [the Sun-god] and the Storm-god they have found out [that it is the right time for roofing the palace which] you are building."

A. ERECTION OF THE PALACE

Plastering the Walls

(5) When you have finished [building the palace, and [When you plaster (it)] on the outside, plaster (it) with long years [(and) plast]er (it) [with well-being]! [When you plaster (it)] on the outside, plaster (it) with awe, plaster (it) [with lordlin]ess!

Procuring Timber for the Roof

(It comes from the Mountain where the Throne rules.)

(10) The king says to the Throne: "Come! Let us go! But stay thou behind the mountains! Thou must not become my *rival*, thou must not become my in-law! Remain my [equal] (and) my friend!

"Come! Let us go to the Mountain! I, the king, will give thee glassware. Let us eat from glassware! Rule thou over the Mountain!

"To me, the king, have the gods—Sun-god and Storm-god—entrusted the land and my house. I, the king, shall rule over my land and my house. Thou shouldst not come to my house, (20) and I shall not come to your house.

"To me, the king, have the gods granted long years; to these years there is no limit.

"To me, the king, has the Throne brought from the Sea the (insignia of) authority (and) the coach;[1] thereupon have they opened to me the land of my mother[2] and called me (25) Labarnas, the King.

"From then on I have been directing my request to the Storm-god, my father. The king has been asking the Storm-god for the timber which the rains have made strong (and) tall.

[1] Apparently considered as characteristic for a king.
[2] The meaning of this phrase is not at all clear.

"Under the heavens ye[3] *grew*. The lion would rest beneath you, the panther would rest beneath you, the *snake* (30) would *coil up* in you. The Storm-god, my father, kept evil away from you.

"Cattle pastured beneath you, sheep pastured beneath you. Now I, the Labarnas, the King, have claimed my share of you. I hailed the Throne, my friend (and said):

(35) " 'Art thou not a friend of me, the king? Let me have that tree (that) I may cut it down!' " And the Throne answers the King: "Cut it down, cut (it) down! The Sun-god and the Storm-god have placed it at thy disposal."

Charm Spoken over the Trees

"Now come ye up from that country of yours! The Storm-god has placed you (40) at the King's disposal. They will assign work to you. He will *procure* (*experts*) for you and they will pronounce charms over you.

"Whatever is in your heart, cast it out! If (it is) a *flaw*, remove it! If (it is) an evil (45) . . . , cast it out! If (it is) a *curse*, cast it out!

"If weakness is in your heart, or (if) the ailment of the sun is in your heart, sweep it out! I, the Labarnas, the King, will come (and) put steel[4] and iron in your heart."

B. ENTRY INTO THE NEW PALACE

(50) When the king makes his entry into the house, the Throne hails the Eagle: "Go! I am sending thee to the Sea. When thou gettest there, drive out of field and woods those who still remain there!"

(ii) That one (i.e. the Eagle) answers: "I have driven (them) out. Only Isdustaya (and) Papaya who are the eternal gods of the nether world still remain there crouching."

(5) The Throne says: "What are they doing?" That one (i.e. the Eagle) answers him: "She[5] is holding a distaff; they are holding mirrors (and) *combs*.

"They are *spinning* the king's years. There is no limit to these years, no number (10) holds good for them."

The Throne says to the king: "Now bring all the king's sons to the palace window!"

The skilled weaver women are divided into two parties. Before (one of) them he[6] places glassware and strews figs thereon. (15) Before the (other) he places crockery and strews grapes and fruit thereon (saying): "Soothe ye the king!

"Soothe his eyes! Keep sickness from him! Keep *terror* from him! Keep the head-sickness from him! (20) Keep man's evil word from him! Keep the knee-sickness (from him)! Keep the heart-sickness (from him)!"

"Stay, great star!"[7] (he says) and halts the mountains in their place. "Mount Pentaya, stay in thy place! (25) Thou shalt not raise the great one![8] Mount Harga,

[3] The trees are addressed.
[4] Literally: tin.
[5] The feminine is chosen because of the feminine implement.
[6] The officiating priest?
[7] The sun is meant.
[8] Again the sun.

stay in thy place! Thou shalt not raise the great one! Mount Tudhaliya, stay in thy place! Thou shalt not raise the great one!

"Mount [Sid]duweni[9] (and) Mount Piskurunuwa, stay ye in your places! Ye shall not raise the great one!"

(30) [When] the king goes to the mountain to raise the great Sun, he[10] performs various charms (and) incantations (all of the general kind): "Such (and) such a one has taken an ailment away from the king."

"Affliction this one has taken away. Depression this one has taken away. Awe this one has taken away. Fear (35) this one has taken away. Heart-sickness this one has taken away. Sickness this one has taken away. Old age this one has taken away. Vigor this one has given back to him. Prowess this one has given back to him."

"Come thou, Eagle! Go forth! One of my charms (40) has failed. Go to the ghats[11] and bring a piece of crockery!

"Upon it *put together* a lion's *tail* (and) a panther's *tail*! Keep hold of them!

"Twine them together and make them one. Place them at man's heart. (45) Let the king's heart and soul be reunited!

"Let the Sun-god and the Storm-god enter into accord with the king! Let their word become one! Entrust ye, Sun-god and Storm-god, the land to the king! (50) They have restored his years, they have restored his awesomeness.

"They have made his frame of steel.[12] They have made his head of iron. They have made his eyes those of an eagle. They have made his teeth those of a lion.

(iii) "Let Telepinus come and open [the store]house, take out wine, nine casks, and bring (it) to the Mountain, all gods being assembled on the Mountain! They will make the king welcome (5) and give him their approval.

"The Sun-god and the Storm-god have taken care of the king. They have renewed his strength and set no limits to his years.

"They have strewn *šeppit* and *euwan* and crushed it (saying): 'He who plots evil against the king, let the gods abandon him to an evil fate! Let them crush him!'"

C. PROVISIONS FOR THE WORKMEN

In whatever town he[13] builds a palace, the carpenter who goes to the mountain to cut the beams (15) receives from the palace one full-grown ox, three sheep, three jugs of wine, one jug of *marnuwan*,[14] ten *wageššar* loaves, thirty "tooth loaves," and fifty "ration loaves."

When the carpenter goes to cut the ridgepole (and) the rafters, he receives from the palace (20) twenty-five "tooth loaves" and fifty "ration loaves."

[9] The restoration of the name is quite uncertain.
[10] The officiating priest, or perhaps the king.
[11] The place where the dead are cremated.
[12] Literally: tin.
[13] The king.
[14] An alcoholic beverage.

When they lay the foundations, they receive from the palace one full-grown ox, one cow, and ten sheep. They sacrifice the ox to the Storm-god, and the one cow to the Sun-goddess of Arinna.

(25) They sacrifice the sheep, everyone for another deity. Loaves and wine they receive from the palace.

When they stretch the beams across, they act in the same way.

The Festival of the Warrior-God[1]

Text: *KBo*, IV, 9. From V 9 on *KUB*, XXV, 1 is a duplicate, beginning with VI 30, also *KUB*, II, 5. Literature: J. Friedrich, *Aus dem hethitischen Schrifttum*, 2 (= *AO*, XXV/2 [1925]), 5 ff.; A. Goetze, *Kulturgeschichte Kleinasiens* (1933), 155.

(The preserved text begins in the middle of a day.)

The king remains seated. "*waganna*"[2] is called, but he does not perform any sacrifice. Then the king leaves the temple of the War-god.

(5) Two palace servants (and) one major-domo march before him. The king goes to the *ḫalentuwa* house. And if the king is so inclined, he makes a circumambulation. Just as he pleases, so (10) he does; nothing definite is laid down (about it).

Afterward they sweep the temple of the War-god. They place the raw meat of a bull, of cows, of sheep and of goats in front of the cult stand (15) before the god (all) in one and the same place.

Two silver basins for libations filled with wine they place on the right-hand side and the left-hand side of the meat.

(20) They announce: "*tališa*." The cult servants set out the *bread basḳets*.

The cooks put cooked meat upon the *bread basḳets*.

(25) The staff-men set up "long chairs." The king (and) the queen put on their ritual dress in the *ḫalentuwa* house. The forecourt of the guardsmen has previously been opened and all the noblemen, (30) palace servants and guardsmen are waiting there.

Then the king (and) the queen come forth from the *ḫalentuwa* house. (35) Two palace servants (and) one guardsman march before the king.

The noblemen, the palace servants and the guardsmen walk behind the king.

The worshipers of statues play the *arḳammi*, (40) the *ḫuḫupal* (and) the *galgalturi*[3] before (and) behind the king.

Entertainers stand beside the king; they dance and play *tambourines*.

(45) Other worshipers of statues are clad in red garments. They stand beside the king, hold their hands

[1] His name in Hittite is unknown; if the Hattic name is to be substituted as is likely it would be Wurunkatte, i.e. "king of the land."
[2] The meaning of this and the following cultic calls—probably in the Hattic language—is not known.
[3] Three musical instruments.

up and whirl around on the spot; (50) they also *recite psalmodies.*

(ii) Before the king (and) the queen enter the temple of the War-god, worshipers of statues, *psalmodists* (and) *ḳitaš*-priests (5) have come in and taken their places.

Then the king (and) the queen enter the temple of the War-god. The king arrives at the gateway and the dancers (10) whirl around once.

The king (and) the queen halt in the forecourt of the temple of the War-god.

The major-domo (and) the priest of the Patron-god—he holds a coat and the priest of the Patron-god (15) holds some *tuḫḫueššar.*[4] Two palace servants bring to the king (and) the queen water for their hands. The king (and) the queen rinse their hands. The chief of the palace servants hands them a linen and they wipe their hands.

(20) The priest of the Patron-god presents [the *tuḫḫueššar*][4] to the king. The king. . . .[5]

The chief of the palace servants presents to the king the pennant of a gold lance (25) and he wipes his hands.

A palace servant takes the *tuḫḫueššar*[4] from the priest of the Patron-god. The priest of the Patron-god pays homage to the king.

The palace servant (30) presents the *tuḫḫueššar*[4] to the queen. The queen. . . .[5]

Then the palace servant hands the *tuḫḫueššar*[4] back to the priest of the Patron-god. The chief of the palace servants (35) hands to the queen the pennant of a gold lance and the queen wipes her hands.

Then the king (and) the queen enter the temple of the War-god. They prostrate themselves once before the god. (40) The worshiper of statues recites hymns, the *ḳitaš* calls.

The king takes his stand at the throne, but the queen enters the inner temple.

The foreman of the cooks brings *ḳattapalaš* cuts. (45) He puts down one portion before the throne and before the War-god; he puts down one at the hearth, one at the throne, one at the window, one at the bolt of the door, furthermore (50) he puts down one by the side of the hearth.

The foreman of the cooks presents a libation vessel with wine to the king. The king touches it with the hand. (iii) The foreman of the cooks pours out three libations before the throne and three for the War-god.

The foreman of the cooks and the foreman of the table-men (5) sanctify themselves.

The foreman of the cooks pours out one libation for the hearth, one for the throne, one for the window, one for the bolt of the door. Furthermore (10) he pours out one libation by the side of the hearth.

Also for the statue of Hattusilis[6] he pours out one libation.

The king prostrates himself; the worshiper of statues recites hymns, the *ḳitaš* calls.

Then they drive out the worshiper of statues, the liturgists, the psalmodists (25) and the *ḳitaš.*

The king (and) the queen sit down on the throne. Then a palace servant brings in the pennant of a gold lance and the *ḳalmuš.*[7] He hands the pennant of the gold lance (30) to the king, but the *ḳalmuš* he places on the throne at the king's right.

This (palace servant) also leaves. He takes his stand before the *taršanzipaš* holding a gold lance (35) and calls "*ḳašmešša.*"[8]

Then the great major-domo enters holding a gold lance and also holding a staff of *šuruḫḫa* wood. (40) He takes his place opposite the king.

Two palace servants bring to the king (and) the queen water for (washing their) hands in a basin. The chief [of the palace] servants [holds a linen in readiness] behind them.

(one section destroyed)

(iv) The palace servants give [the king (and) the queen water] and the king (and) the queen rinse [their hands]. The chief of the [palace servants] hands [them a linen] and the king (and) the queen wipe [their] hands.

(5) They leave and the great major-domo also leaves.

A palace servant brings a gold lance and a *muḳar.*[9] He proceeds to place (it) on the throne (10) beneath the . . . at the king's right, and he leaves (again). He takes his stand over the *bread basḳets* (set out) for the palace servants.

The great major-domo comes forward (15) and takes his stand opposite the king. Two palace servants put two pieces of linen cloth upon the knees of the king (and) the queen.

The palace servants leave again and take their stand (20) over the *bread basḳets* (set out) for palace servants.

The great major-domo gives a sign with (his) gold lance, and calls "*mišša.*"[10] He then brings the gold lance and puts it at the king's left (25) against the wall.

Then the foreman of the table-men brings in a clean table. Three guardsmen walk at the right side of the table; they hold gold lances (30) and three staffs of *šuruḫḫa* -wood.

The great major-domo comes forth to face the table and stands behind the foreman of the table-men. He marches before him and gets hold of the table from underneath (35) and lifts it, he the foreman of the table-men.

The chief of the palace servants and all the palace servants walk at the right-hand side of the table. The foreman of the table-men (40) sets up the table for the king. The chief of the palace servants leaves (again)

[4] A material used in a purification rite.

[5] The missing verb related to the preceding noun signifies the purifying action for which it serves.

[6] An early king, probably Hattusilis I, a contemporary of the late Hammurabi Dynasty of Babylon.

[7] According to one view this is the Hittite word for the "lituus" which is so often seen in the hand of the king on contemporary monuments.

[8] A cultic call of unknown meaning.

[9] Probably a musical instrument, either a lyre or a drum.

[10] Another cultic call of unknown meaning.

and takes his stand over the *bread basḳets*. All the palace servants squat down.

(45) The great major-domo and the chief of the palace servants leave. The great major-domo stands behind the hearth and takes his place over the *bread basḳets* (set out) for the great major-domo. But the foreman of the table-men (50) leaves.

The three guardsmen who had marched at the right of the table, leave (again). (v) They squat down over their *bread basḳets*.

A single guardsman takes from them the lances and the staffs which they hold (5) and proceeds to put them with the gold lance of the great major-domo against the wall. That (guardsman) squats down over his *bread basḳet*.

A herald comes forward (10) and the table-men of first rank take their stand.

The sweeper brings one . . . loaf. He hands it to a palace servant. The palace servant hands it to the chief of the palace servants. But the chief of the palace servants breaks it *on* a gold lance for the Patron-god.

(15) The chief of the palace servants hands it back to the palace servant. The palace servant hands it back to the sweeper.

But in the forecourt *zeriyalli* covered with linen cloths have been standing ready beforehand.

(20) A herald goes in front of the princes and seats them.

Then the herald leaves (again) and marches in front of the cooks of higher rank. The cooks of higher rank take their stand.

Then the herald leaves (again) for another time (25) and marches before the holy priests, the Hittite EN (and) the mother-of-god of (god) Halkis[11] and seats them.

Then the great major-domo enters and announces to the king: (30) "Shall they carry forth the Ishtar instruments?" and the king says: "Let them carry them forth!"

But the herald goes before the gate (35) and says to the musicians; "They are ready. They are ready." Then the musicians lift the Ishtar instruments.

The herald goes in front of the musicians who carry the Ishtar instruments in.

(40) They take their place in front of the *taršanzipaš*.

The liturgists, the worshipers of statues, the psalmodists and the *ḳitaš*-priests walk with the same Ishtar instruments. (45) They go and take their seats.

The cooks serve "pot," water (and) meat. They distribute cold fat.

The herald marches before the citizens, the master of the *zaḫartiš* of the inner temple, and the dignitaries and seats them.

(vi) When the "pots" are distributed, the great major-domo announces the *marnuwan*[12] to the king: "Shall they serve the *marnuwan*?" and they serve the *marnuwan* to the congregation.

[11] The goddess of grain.
[12] An alcoholic beverage.

(5) The king throws the linen away. If he throws it toward the side where the palace servants have squatted down, the palace servants take it. But if (10) he throws it toward the side where the guardsmen have squatted down, the guardsmen take it. They hand it to the table-men.

The king gives a sign with his eyes. The sweepers (15) sweep the floor.

The great major-domo calls to the palace servants: "*mišša*."[13] Two palace servants bring to the king (and) the queen water for (washing) the hands in a golden basin. (20) The chief of the palace servants holds a linen ready behind them. The king (and) the queen rinse their hands. The chief of the palace servants hands them the linen and they wipe their hands. They leave (again).

(25) Then the cupbearer of squatting comes forth. The great cupbearer and a palace servant (acting as) cupbearer give to the king (and) the queen (the amount of) *marnuwan*[12] (necessary) for (the) drinking (ceremony).

(30) The king (and) the queen drink in standing position (god) Tauri. The great Ishtar instruments play, but they do not sing and there are no sacrificial loaves.[14]

(In the following, king and queen "drink" various gods in slightly varying ways.)

Then the cupbearer of squatting comes forth.[15]

The great major-domo enters and announces to the king that the "dog-men" will clad themselves with their proper vestments and deliver . . . , silver (and) gold.

The table-man ⟨selects⟩ two *tunnaptaš* loaves weighing 2 seah, (50) one of them white, the other red, and brings them from the table. Upon them lies an open cheese. He places them before the window.

The herald marches before the smiths. (60) Then the smiths (iv) bring in two silver heads of bulls. In front of them marches the cupbearer in his (ritual) dress.

(4 mutilated sections[16])

(21) The cupbearer seizes [the . . . (and)] the horns of the two silver bull heads and pours out a libation by the side of the hearth. They carry them (25) out (again).

The table-man takes the *tunnaptaš* loaves [from the table] and they carry those out (again).

Then he fills the two silver bull heads with wine. (30) [The . . . (and) the . . .] distribute the *tunnaptaš* loaves.

(In the following, the king and the queen "drink" more gods.)

(v 17) When the psalmodist says so, the citizens and the congregation pay homage to the king once.

(20) The cupbearer presents once an *išgaruḫ* vessel with wine.

The cupbearer brings from outside one sacrificial loaf

[13] The same cultic call as above; see n.10.
[14] *KBo*, IV, 9 ends here.
[15] *KUB*, XXV, 1 iii 41 ff.
[16] *KUB*, XXV, 1 iv 4-20.

(made) of *šeppit* weighing 3 seah. (25) The king breaks it, takes a bite and then they take it out (again).

The citizens pay homage to the king three times and sit down.

(30) Then the cupbearer of squatting comes forth.

The great major-domo (and) the cupbearer—he holds his coat in his hands, but the cupbearer (35) holds a silver cup with wine. He offers that to the king.

The cupbearer hands the silver cup with wine to the king. The great major-domo (40) walks out backwards, while his eyes are directed toward the king.

He takes his stand beside the hearth.

(45) The great major-domo (and) the cupbearer—he discards his coat, and the cupbearer pays homage to the king. Then the great major-domo takes his coat up again.

(50) He then brings it to the king. Then the cupbearer sets up the cup for the king. The great major-domo seizes it (and the coat) with his left.

(55) Then they go back and take their stand beside the hearth. The cupbearer squats down by the side of the hearth. (vi) The great major-domo leaves. Then the ZABBAR.DIB enters to squat down (*with*) the cupbearer. He takes the silver cup with wine away, (5) and they take it out (again).

Then the cult servants bring in a *bread basḳet*, . . . (and) cooked meat. (10) They offer it to the king.

The cupbearer who has been squatting beside the hearth gets up and pays homage to the king. (15) He takes the *bread basḳet* and he carries it out (again).

The herald makes the citizens and the congregation rise (21) and they stand.

Two palace servants take the linen from the knees of the king (and) the queen.

(25) The king (and) the queen drink in standing position the . . . Sun-god. The liturgists sing. They play the *arḳammi*, the *galgalturi* and the *ḫuḫupal* (30) and sing psalmodies.

The cupbearer brings one sacrificial loaf of flour weighing a *pārisu* and 3 *upnu* from the outside. He gives them to the king and the king breaks them. Then he takes them out (again).

. . . .

V. Hymns and Prayers

Egyptian Hymns and Prayers

TRANSLATOR: JOHN A. WILSON

A Hymn to Amon-Re

Egypt's world position under her Empire produced strong tendencies toward centralization and unification of Egyptian religion, with universalism and with syncretism of the gods. The following hymn antedates the Amarna Revolution. The imperial god Amon-Re is here viewed as supreme and as the force which creates and sustains life.

Papyrus Boulaq 17 in the Cairo Museum dates from the Eighteenth Dynasty (1550-1350 B.C.). It was published by A. Mariette, *Les Papyrus égyptiens du Musée de Boulaq* (Paris, 1871-76), II, Pls. XI-XIII. A facsimile of six columns is in G. Möller, *Hieratische Lesestücke*, II (Leipzig, 1927), 33-34. The text was studied by E. Grébaut, *Hymne à Ammon-Ra* (Paris, 1874). The manuscript is divided by marks of pause into four stanzas. Selim Hassan, *Hymnes religieux du moyen empire* (Cairo, 1928), 157-93, pointed out that British Museum statue 40959, which has been dated to the Thirteenth to Seventeenth Dynasties (1775-1575 B.C.), carries this hymn in broken context. Translated by Erman, *LAE*, 282-88.

ADORATION of Amon-Re, the Bull Residing in Heliopolis, chief of all gods, the good god, the beloved, who gives life to all that is warm and to all good cattle.

Hail to thee, Amon-Re,
Lord of the Thrones of the Two Lands, Presiding over Karnak,
Bull of His Mother,[1] Presiding over His Fields!
Far-reaching of stride, presiding over Upper Egypt,
Lord of the Madjoi and ruler of Punt,[2]
Eldest of heaven, first-born of earth,
Lord of what is, enduring in all things, enduring in all things.
UNIQUE IN HIS NATURE LIKE THE *FLUID* of the gods,
The goodly bull of the Ennead, chief of all gods,
The lord of truth and father of the gods.
Who made mankind and created the beasts,
Lord of what is, who created the fruit tree,
Made herbage, and gave life to cattle.
The goodly daemon whom Ptah made,

(ii)

The goodly beloved youth to whom the gods give praise,
Who made what is below and what is above,
Who illuminates the Two Lands
And crosses the heavens in peace:
The King of Upper and Lower Egypt: Re, the triumphant,[3]
Chief of the Two Lands,
Great of strength, lord of reverence,
The chief one, who made the entire earth.
MORE DISTINGUISHED IN NATURE THAN any (other) god,
In whose beauty the gods rejoice,
To whom is given jubilation in the Per-wer,
Who is given ceremonial appearance in the Per-nezer.[4]
Whose fragrance the gods love, when he comes from Punt,
Rich in perfume, when he comes down (from) Madjoi,
The Beautiful of Face who comes (from) God's Land.[5]
The gods FAWN (at) his feet,
According as they recognize his majesty as their lord,
The lord of fear, great of dread,
Rich in might, terrible of appearances,
Flourishing in offerings and making provisions.
Jubilation to thee who made the gods,
Raised the heavens and laid down the ground!

(iii)

THE END.

He who awakes in health, Min-Amon,[6]
Lord of eternity, who made everlastingness,
Lord of praise, presiding over [the Ennead],
Firm of horns, beautiful of face,
Lord of the uraeus-serpent, lofty of plumes,
Beautiful of diadem, and lofty of White Crown.
The serpent-coil and the Double Crown, *these are before him*,
The aromatic gum which is in the palace,
The Double Crown, the head-cloth, and the Blue Crown.
Beautiful of face, when he receives the *atef*-crown,
He whom the crowns of Upper and Lower Egypt love,
Lord of the Double Crown, when he receives the *ames*-staff,
Lord of the *mekes*-scepter, holding the flail.[7]
THE GOODLY ruler, CROWNED WITH THE WHITE CROWN,
The lord of rays, who makes brilliance,
To whom the gods give thanksgiving,
Who extends his arms to him whom he loves,
(But) his enemy is consumed by a flame.
It is his Eye that overthrows the rebels,
That sends its spear into him that sucks up Nun,

[1] As sun-god, Amon-Re recreated himself every day.
[2] Regions to the south and southeast of Egypt.
[3] Written as though Amon-Re were a former pharaoh.
[4] The *Per-wer*, "Great House," was the religious capital of Upper Egypt at el-Kab; the *Per-nezer* was the counterpart for Lower Egypt at Buto.
[5] "God's Land" was the east generally, the land of the rising sun. The countries south and east of Egypt were the incense-bearing lands.
[6] Amon had strong derivative ties with the old god of procreation Min of Koptos.
[7] The text describes Amon-Re with the various accoutrements of an Egyptian pharaoh.

(iv)

And makes the fiend disgorge what he has swallowed.[8]
HAIL TO THEE, O Re, lord of truth!
Whose shrine is hidden,[9] the lord of the gods,
Khepri in the midst of his barque,
Who gave commands, and the gods came into being.[10]
Atum, who made the people,
Distinguished their nature, made their life,
And separated colors, one from another.
Who hears the prayer of him who is in captivity,
Gracious of heart in the face of an appeal to him.
SAVING THE FEARFUL FROM THE TERRIBLE OF HEART,
Judging the weak and the injured.
Lord of Perception, in whose mouth Command is placed,[11]
For love of whom the Nile has come,
Possessor of sweetness, greatly beloved;
When he comes, the people live.
He who gives scope to every eye that may be made in Nun,[12]
Whose loveliness has created the light,

(v)

In whose beauty the gods rejoice;
Their hearts live when they see him.
THE END.

O Re, ADORED IN KARNAK,
Great of appearances in the House of the *Benben*,[13]
The Heliopolitan, lord of the New Moon Feast,
For whom the Sixth-Day and Quarter Month feasts are celebrated.[14]
The Sovereign—life, prosperity, health!—lord of all gods;
[They] behold him in the midst of the horizon,
The overlord of men *of the silent land*,[15]
Whose name is hidden from his children,
In this his name of Amon.[16]
HAIL TO THEE, WHO ART IN PEACE!
Lord of joy, terrible of appearances,
Lord of the uraeus-serpent, lofty of plumes,
Beautiful of diadem, and lofty of White Crown.
The gods love to see thee
With the Double Crown fixed upon thy brow.
The love of thee is spread throughout the Two Lands,
When thy rays shine forth in the eyes.
The good of the people is thy arising;
The cattle grow languid when thou shinest.
The love of thee is in the southern sky;

(vi)

The sweetness of thee is in the northern sky.
The beauty of thee carries away hearts;
The love of thee makes arms languid;
Thy beautiful form relaxes the hands;
And hearts are forgetful at the sight of thee.
THOU ART the sole one, WHO MADE [ALL] THAT IS,
[The] solitary sole [one], who made what exists,
From whose eyes mankind came forth,
And upon whose mouth the gods came into being.[17]
He who made herbage [for] the cattle,
And the fruit tree for mankind,
Who made that (on which) the fish in the river may live,
And the birds *soaring in* the sky.
He who gives breath to that which is in the egg,
Gives life to the son of the slug,
And makes that on which gnats may live,
And worms and flies in like manner;
Who supplies the needs of the mice in their holes,
And gives life to flying things in every tree.
HAIL TO THEE, WHO DID ALL THIS!
Solitary sole one, with many hands,[18]

(vii)

Who spends the night wakeful, while all men are asleep,
Seeking benefit for his creatures.
Amon, enduring in all things, Atum and Har-akhti—
Praises are thine, when they all say:
"Jubilation to thee, because thou weariest thyself with us!
Salaams to thee, because thou didst create us!"
HAIL TO THEE FOR ALL BEASTS!
Jubilation to thee for every foreign country—
To the height of heaven, to the width of earth,
To the depth of the Great Green Sea!
The gods are bowing down to thy majesty
And exalting the might of him who created them,
Rejoicing at the approach of him who begot them.
They say to thee: "Welcome in peace!
Father of the fathers of all the gods,
Who raised the heavens and laid down the ground,
WHO MADE WHAT IS AND CREATED WHAT EXISTS;
Sovereign—life, prosperity, health!—and chief of the gods!

(viii)

We praise thy might, according as thou didst make us.
Let (us) act for thee, because thou brought us forth.
We give thee thanksgiving because thou hast wearied thyself with us!"
HAIL TO THEE, WHO MADE ALL THAT IS!
Lord of truth and father of the gods,
Who made mortals and created beasts,

[8] The Eye of the sun repulsed the Apophis-dragon, which tried to check the journey of the sun. cf. pp. 11-12 above.
[9] A play on Amon and *amen* "hidden, secret."
[10] A play on Khepri and *kheper* "come into being."
[11] *Sia* "Perception," and *Hu* "Authoritative Command," were personified forces of creative rule.
[12] Nun was the primeval waters out of which life came. "Every eye" is figurative for "everybody."
[13] The sacred pyramidion stone in Heliopolis.
[14] The relation of the sun-god to these moon festivals is not very clear.
[15] The necropolis. Or, "men who are silent," i.e. submissive?
[16] See n.9 above.
[17] A reference to the myth that mortals came into being as the tears of the creator-god, gods as his spittle. cf. p. 6 above.
[18] Since he was alone at creation, he needed many hands for his work.

Lord of the grain,
Who made (also) the living of the beasts of the desert.
Amon, the bull beautiful of countenance,
The beloved in Karnak,
Great of appearances in the House of the *Benben*,
Taking again the diadem in Heliopolis,
Who judges the Two in the great broad hall,[19]
The chief of the Great Ennead.
THE SOLITARY SOLE ONE, WITHOUT HIS PEER,
Presiding over Karnak,
The Heliopolitan, presiding over his Ennead,
And living on truth every day.
The horizon-dweller, Horus of the east,
From whom the desert creates silver and gold,
Genuine lapis lazuli for love of him,

(ix)

Benzoin and various incenses from Madjoi,
And fresh myrrh for thy nostrils—
Beautiful of face when coming (from) Madjoi!
Amon-Re, Lord of the Thrones of the Two Lands,
Presiding over Karnak,
The Heliopolitan, presiding over his harem!
THE END.

The sole king, like the *fluid* of the gods,
With many names, unknown in number,[20]
Rising in the eastern horizon,
And going to rest in the western horizon;
Who overthrows his enemies,
(RE)BORN EARLY EVERY DAY.
Thoth lifts up his two eyes,[21]
And satisfies him with his effective deeds.
The gods rejoice in his beauty,
He whom his apes exalt.[22]
Lord of the evening barque and the morning barque;
They cross Nun in peace for thee.
Thy CREW IS IN JOY,
When they see the overthrow of the rebel,[23]
His body licked up by the knife.

(x)

Fire has devoured him;
His soul is more consumed than his body.
That dragon, his (power of) motion is taken away.
The gods are in joy,
The crew of Re is in satisfaction,
Heliopolis is in joy,
For the enemies of Atum are overthrown.
Karnak is in satisfaction, Heliopolis is in joy,
The heart of the Lady of Life is glad,[24]
For the enemy of her lord is overthrown.

[19] As supreme god, he presided over the trial between Horus and Seth. cf. pp. 14-17 above.
[20] cf. the myth of the names of Re, pp. 12-14 above.
[21] Sun and moon.
[22] At dawn apes warm themselves in the sun's rays.
[23] cf. n.8 above.
[24] Epithet of a goddess, here probably the Eye of the Sun.

The gods of Babylon are in jubilation,[25]
They who are in the shrines are salaaming,
WHEN THEY SEE HIM RICH IN HIS MIGHT.
The daemon of the gods,
The righteous one, Lord of Karnak,
In this thy name of Maker of Righteousness;
The lord of provisions, bull of *offerings*,
In this thy name of Amon, Bull of His Mother;
Maker of all mankind,
Creator and maker of all that is,

(xi)

In this thy name of Atum-Khepri.[26]
Great falcon, festive of bosom,
Beautiful of face, festive of breast,
Pleasing of form, lofty of plume,
On whose brow the two uraei *flutter*.
To whom the hearts of mankind make approach,
To whom the people turn about;
Who makes festive the Two Lands with his comings forth.
Hail to thee, Amon-Re, Lord of the Thrones of the Two Lands,
Whose city loves his rising!
IT HAS COME (TO ITS END) . . .

A Universalist Hymn to the Sun

The forces of empire and of international contacts were moving Egypt toward universalism and a partial approach to monotheism, even before the Amarna Revolution. One of the clearest expressions of the new spirit comes from a hymn to the sun-god on behalf of two brothers named Seth and Horus.

The date and provenience of the text are given in the facts that Seth and Horus were architects at Thebes under Amen-hotep III (about 1413-1377 B.C.). The hymn occurs on two stelae, British Museum 826 and Cairo Museum 34051 (the latter badly mutilated). The basic publication is by A. Varille in *BIFAO*, XLI (1942), 25-30, with two photographic plates, transcription, translation, and antecedent publications, of which J. H. Breasted, *The Dawn of Conscience* (New York, 1933), 275-77, might be mentioned.[1]

Praising Amon, when he rises as Har-akhti, by the Overseer of the Works of Amon, Seth, and the Overseer of the Works of Amon, Horus. They say:

Hail to thee, beautiful Re of every day, who rises at dawn without ceasing, Khepri wearying (himself) with labor! Thy rays are in (one's) face, without one knowing it. Fine gold is not like the radiance of thee. Thou who hast constructed thyself,[2] thou didst fashion

[25] Egyptian Babylon was a city near modern Cairo.
[26] *Ta-tem* "all mankind," provides a pun for Atum, *sekheper* "creator," a pun for Khepri.

[1] Amon Re Har-akhti, himself a syncretic deity, is greeted as the "sole lord" of universal sway, but this does not preclude the worship of other deities. In the scenes and texts surrounding the main inscription, the brothers give service to Osiris, Anubis, Amon-Re, Mut, Khonsu, Hat-Hor in two forms, Re Har-akhti, Sokar, Isis, and the deified queen Ahmes Nefert-iri.
[2] "Thou who hast Ptah'ed thyself," a play on the name of Ptah, the fashioner-god. The passages from "Thy rays . . ." to ". . . not shaped" occur also in the hymn to the rising sun, the 15th chapter of the Book

thy body, a shaper who was (himself) not shaped; unique in his nature, passing eternity above, (so that) the ways by millions carry thy image, according as thy radiance is like the radiance of heaven and thy color glistens more than its surface.

When thou crossest the sky, all faces behold thee, (but) when thou departest, thou art hidden from their faces. (5) Thou presentest thyself daily at dawn. Steadfast is thy sailing which carries thy majesty. A brief day—and thou racest a course of millions and hundred-thousands of leagues. Every day under thee is an instant, and when it passes, thou settest. So also thou hast completed the hours of the night: thou hast regulated it without a pause coming in thy labors.[3]

All eyes see through thee, and they have no fulfillment when thy majesty sets. Thou bestirrest thyself early to rise at dawn. Thy rays open the wakeful eyes. When thou settest in *Manu*,[4] then they sleep in the manner of death.

Hail to thee, sun disc[5] of the daytime, creator of all and maker of their living! Great falcon, bright of plumage, who came into being to elevate himself, self-created, who was not born! Horus, the first-born in the midst of the sky-goddess, for whom they make jubilation (10) at rising, as well as at his setting! The fashioner of that which the soil produces, the Khnum and Amon of mankind.[6] He who seizes upon the Two Lands, (from) great to small. A mother of profit to gods and men; a patient craftsman, greatly wearying (himself) as their maker, without number; valiant herdsman, driving his cattle, their refuge and the maker of their living.

Runner, racer, courser! Khepri, whose birth was distinct, whose beauty was upraised in the body of the sky-goddess. He who illuminates the Two Lands with his disc, the primordial one of the Two Lands, who made himself and who beheld what he would make.

The sole lord, who reaches the ends of the lands every day, being (thus) one who sees them that tread thereon. He who rises in heaven, (his) form being the sun. He makes the seasons by months, heat when he wishes, and cold when he wishes. He makes the body lax, or he gathers it together. Every land chatters[7] at his rising every day, in order to praise him. . . .[8]

Amon as the Sole God

The following hymns have been characterized as monotheistic in spirit. They come from the Nineteenth Dynasty, subsequent to the Amarna Revolution. They are extracts from a long document in praise of the imperial god Amon-Re of Thebes and treat that deity as the sole god, or, perhaps, as the first principle and the sole god of immediate attention.

The bibliography for Leyden Papyrus I 350 was given on p. 8 above.[1]

HUNDREDTH STANZA.

The first to come into being in the earliest times, Amon, who came into being at the beginning, so that his mysterious nature is unknown. No god came into being before him; there was no other (iv 10) god with him, so that he might tell his form. He had no mother, after whom his name might have been made. He had no father who had begotten him and who might have said: "This is I!" Building his own egg, a daemon mysterious of birth, who created his (own) beauty, the divine god who came into being by himself. All (other) gods came into being after he began himself.

TWO-HUNDREDTH STANZA.

Mysterious of form, glistening of appearance, the marvelous god of many forms. All (other) gods boast of him, to magnify themselves through his beauty, according as he is divine.[2] Re himself is united with his body. He is the great one who is in Heliopolis.[3] He is called Ta-tenen,[4] and Amon who came forth from Nun, *for he leads the people*. Another of his forms is the Ogdoad.[5] The procreator of the (15) primeval gods, who brought Re to birth; he completed himself as Atum,[6] a single body with him. He is the All-Lord, the beginning of that which is. His soul, they say, is that which is in heaven. It is he who is in the underworld and presides over the East; his soul is in heaven, his body is in the West, and his statue is in Hermonthis, heralding his appearances.[7]

One is Amon, hiding himself from them,[8] concealing himself from the (other) gods, so that his (very) color is unknown. He is far from heaven, he is *absent from* the Underworld, (so that) no gods know his true form.[9] His image is not *displayed* in writings. No one bears witness to him . . . He is too mysterious that his majesty might be disclosed, he is too great that (men) should ask about him, too powerful that he might be known. (20) Instantly (one) falls in a death of violence at the utterance of his mysterious name, unwittingly or wittingly.[10] No (other) god knows how to *call him* by it, the Soul who hides his name, according as he is mysterious.

of the Dead; E. A. W. Budge, *The Book of the Dead* (London, 1898), Text Vol., 41-42.

[3] Most of this paragraph occurs also in the Book of the Dead hymn just noted.

[4] The western mountain.

[5] The word is Egyptian *Aton*.

[6] The gods' names carry a pun: "the hidden builder of mankind."

[7] The picture is that of the apes who greet the warmth of the morning sun with jabberings and gesticulations.

[8] The final 7 lines of the stela carry successive statements by the two brothers. Seth avows: "I am a just man, whose abomination is deceit, not content with any words of him who speaks equivocally—except for my brother, like unto me: I am content with his ideas, for he came forth from the womb together with me on that (same) day." Each twin emphasizes his good works for Amon, in asking benefits from that god.

[1] In the papyrus the 100th stanza is iv 9-11, the 200th is iv 12-21, the 300th iv 21-26, and the 600th v 16-vi 1.

[2] The other gods are proud to be subsumed into his being.

[3] Atum.

[4] The procreator-god of Memphis.

[5] The "Eight," the precreation gods, including the abysmal waters, Nun.

[6] Pun: *tem* "complete," and Atum.

[7] The statue was not the god himself, but gave opportunity for his appearances at a cult-seat of his.

[8] The name Amon may mean "hidden."

[9] Probably invisibility, rather than absence.

[10] His secret name carries the blight of awful holiness. cf. pp. 12-14 above.

THREE-HUNDREDTH STANZA.

All gods are three: Amon, Re, and Ptah, and there is no second to them.[11] "Hidden" is his name as Amon,[12] he is Re in face, and his body is Ptah. Their cities are on earth, abiding forever: Thebes, Heliopolis, and Memphis unto eternity.

A message is sent from heaven, is heard in Heliopolis, and is repeated in Memphis to the Fair of Face.[13] It is composed in a despatch by the writing of Thoth, with regard to the City of Amon *and their (right to) possess* their property. The matter is answered in Thebes, and a statement is issued: "It[14] belongs to the Ennead." Everything that issues from his mouth *is (itself)* Amon. The gods are established according to command *because of* him. (25) A message is sent: "It[15] shall slay or shall let live. Life and death are with it for everybody."

Only he (is): Amon, with Re, [and with Ptah]—together three. . . .

(SIX-HUNDREDTH STANZA).[16]

Perception is his heart, Command is his lips.[17] . . . When he enters the two caverns which are under his feet, the Nile comes forth from the grotto under his sandals.[18] His soul is Shu, his heart is [*Tef*]*nut*. He is Har-akhti who is in (v 20) the heaven; his right eye is day, his left eye is night.[19] (Thus) he is one who leads *people* to every way. His body is Nun, and he who is in it is the Nile, giving birth to whatever is and making to live what exists. The warmth of him is breath for every nostril.

Fate and Fortune are with him for everybody. His wife is the fertile field; he impregnates her, for his seed is the fruit tree, and his fluid is the grain. . . . (vi 1) . . . The faces of everybody are on him among men *and* gods. He is *Perception*.

The God Amon as Healer and Magician

A Nineteenth Dynasty manuscript contains poetical praise of the Theban god Amon-Re. In one stanza of this composition the god is treated as a divine physician and magical healer.

The bibliography for Leyden Papyrus I 350 was given on p. 8 above.[1]

[11] The text does not say: "There is no *fourth* to them." This is a statement of trinity, the three chief gods of Egypt subsumed into one of them, Amon.

[12] cf. n.8 above.

[13] Ptah. The two messages state the primacy of Thebes. As various commentators have pointed out, the text has probable relation to the resumption of power by Thebes after the Amarna Revolution.

[14] Probably Thebes, possibly the authority claimed by Thebes.

[15] Thebes.

[16] The rubricized heading is lacking in the papyrus.

[17] *Sia* "cognitive perception," and *Hu* "authoritative utterance," were deified as two attributes of rule, through the ability to comprehend a situation and the power to create by command.

[18] The Nile was supposed to flow forth from two subterranean caves, sometimes located at Elephantine. cf. p. 32, n.11.

[19] Sun and moon.

[1] From iii 14-22 of the papyrus.

SEVENTIETH STANZA.[2]

He who dissolves[2] evils and dispels ailments; a physician who heals the eye without having remedies, (iii 15) opening the eyes and driving away the squint; . . . Amon. Rescuing whom he desires, even though he be in the Underworld; who saves (a man) from Fate as his heart directs.[3] To him belong eyes as well as ears wherever he goes, for the benefit of him whom he loves. Hearing the prayers of him who summons him, coming from afar in the completion of a moment for him who calls to him. He makes a lifetime long or shortens it. He gives more than that which is fated to him whom he loves.

Amon is a water-charm when his name is (pronounced) over the flood. The crocodile has no power when his name is pronounced. The breeze *opposing* the rebellious wind *and* turning (*it*) back. The *sportive* (*wind*) ceases at the (mere) thought (20) of him. Beneficial of mouth at the time of the melee,[4] and a sweet breeze for him who calls to him. Rescuing the faint, the *mild* god, efficient of plans. He belongs to him who bends the back to him when he is in his vicinity. He is more effective than millions for him who sets him in his heart. One (man) is more valiant than hundred-thousands because of his name, the goodly protector in truth, successfully seizing upon his opportunity, without being opposed.

The Hymn to the Aton

The Pharaoh Amen-hotep IV broke with the established religion of Egypt and instituted the worship of the Aton, the sun disc as the source of life. "The Amarna Revolution" attempted a distinct break with Egypt's traditional and static ways of life in religion, politics, art, and literature. Pharaoh changed his name to Akh-en-Aton (perhaps "He Who Is Serviceable to the Aton") and moved his capital from Thebes to Tell el-Amarna. Pharaoh's own attitude to the god is expressed in the famous hymn which follows. Beyond doubt, the hymn shows the universality and beneficence of the creating and re-creating sun disc. A similarity of spirit and wording to the 104th Psalm has often been noted, and a direct relation between the two has been argued.[1] Because Akh-en-Aton was devoted to this god alone, the Amarna religion has been called monotheistic. This is a debatable question, and a reserved attitude would note that only Akh-en-Aton and his family worshiped the Aton, Akh-en-Aton's courtiers worshiped Akh-en-Aton himself, and the great majority of Egyptians was ignorant of or hostile to the new faith.

This is the "long hymn" to the Aton, from the tomb of Eye at Tell el-Amarna. Akh-en-Aton's reign was about 1380 to 1362 B.C. The best copy of the text is that of N. de G. Davies, *The Rock Tombs of El Amarna*, VI (London, 1908), Pl. XXVII. Translations will be found in Erman, *LAE*, 288-91, and in J. H. Breasted, *The Dawn of Conscience* (New York, 1933), 281-86.

[2] The number "seventy," which contained the sounds *safekh* is carried over in a pun to the beginning and end of the stanza, with the words *sefekh* "dissolve," and *khesef* "oppose."

[3] The role of Fate was powerful at this period, but not immutable if the god intervened.

[4] From the context, this continues the idea of Amon as a soothing breeze against more violent winds.

[1] As in Breasted, *op. cit.*, 366-70.

Praise of Re Har-akhti, Rejoicing on the Horizon, in His Name as Shu Who Is in the Aton-disc,[2] living forever and ever; the living great Aton who is in jubilee, lord of all that the Aton encircles, lord of heaven, lord of earth, lord of the House of Aton in Akhet-Aton;[3] (and praise of) the King of Upper and Lower Egypt, who lives on truth, the Lord of the Two Lands: Nefer-kheperu-Re Wa-en-Re; the Son of Re, who lives on truth, the Lord of Diadems: Akh-en-Aton, long in his lifetime; (and praise of) the Chief Wife of the King, his beloved, the Lady of the Two Lands: Nefer-neferu-Aton Nefert-iti, living, healthy, and youthful forever and ever; (by) the Fan-Bearer on the Right Hand of the King . . . Eye. He says:

Thou appearest beautifully on the horizon of heaven,
Thou living Aton, the beginning of life!
When thou art risen on the eastern horizon,
Thou hast filled every land with thy beauty.
Thou art gracious, great, glistening, and high over every land;
Thy rays encompass the lands to the limit of all that thou hast made:
As thou art Re, thou reachest to the end of them;[4]
(Thou) subduest them (for) thy beloved son.[5]
Though thou art far away, thy rays are on earth;
Though thou art in *their* faces, *no one knows thy* going.

When thou settest in the western horizon,
The land is in darkness, in the manner of death.
They sleep in a room, with heads wrapped up,
Nor sees one eye the other.
All their goods which are under their heads might be stolen,
(But) they would not perceive (it).
Every lion is come forth from his den;
All creeping things, they sting.
Darkness *is a shroud*, and the earth is in stillness,
For he who made them rests in his horizon.[6]

At daybreak, when thou arisest on the horizon,
When thou shinest as the Aton by day,
Thou drivest away the darkness and givest thy rays.
The Two Lands are in festivity *every day*,
Awake and standing upon (their) feet,
For thou hast raised them up.
Washing their bodies, taking (their) clothing, (5)
Their arms are (raised) in praise at thy appearance.
All the world, they do their work.[7]

All beasts are content with their pasturage;
Trees and plants are flourishing.
The birds which fly from their nests,
Their wings are (stretched out) in praise to thy *ka*.
All beasts spring upon (their) feet.
Whatever flies and alights,
They live when thou hast risen (for) them.[8]
The ships are sailing north and south as well,
For every way is open at thy appearance.
The fish in the river dart before thy face;
Thy rays are in the midst of the great green sea.[9]

Creator of seed in women,
Thou who makest fluid into man,
Who maintainest the son in the womb of his mother,
Who soothest him with that which stills his weeping,
Thou nurse (even) in the womb,
Who givest breath to sustain all that he has made!
When he descends from the womb to *breathe*
On the day when he is born,
Thou openest his mouth completely,
Thou suppliest his necessities.
When the chick in the egg speaks within the shell,
Thou givest him breath within it to maintain him.
When thou hast made him his fulfillment within the egg, to break it,
He comes forth from the egg to speak at his completed (time);
He walks upon his legs when he comes forth from it.

How manifold it is, what thou hast made!
They are hidden from the face (of man).
O sole god, like whom there is no other!
Thou didst create the world according to thy desire,
Whilst thou wert alone:[10]
All men, cattle, and wild beasts,
Whatever is on earth, going upon (its) feet,
And what is on high, flying with its wings.

The countries of Syria and Nubia, the *land* of Egypt,
Thou settest every man in his place,
Thou suppliest their necessities:
Everyone has his food, and his time of life is reckoned.[11]
Their tongues are separate in speech,
And their natures as well;
Their skins are distinguished,
As thou distinguishest the foreign peoples.
Thou makest a Nile in the underworld,
Thou bringest it forth as thou desirest
To maintain the people (of Egypt)[12]
According as thou madest them for thyself,
The lord of all of them, wearying (himself) with them,
The lord of every land, rising for them,
The Aton of the day, great of majesty.

[2] The Aton had a dogmatic name written within a royal cartouche and including the three old solar deities, Re, Har-of-the-Horizon, and Shu.

[3] Akhet-Aton was the name of the capital at Tell el-Amarna.

[4] Pun: *Ra* "Re," and *er-ra* "to the end."

[5] Akh-en-Aton.

[6] cf. Ps. 104:20-21.

[7] cf. Ps. 104:22-23.

[8] cf. Ps. 104:11-14.

[9] cf. Ps. 104:25-26.

[10] cf. Ps. 104:24.

[11] cf. Ps. 104:27.

[12] The Egyptians believed that their Nile came from the waters under the earth, called by them Nun.

All distant foreign countries, thou makest their life (also),
For thou hast set a Nile in heaven,
That it may descend for them and make waves upon the mountains,[13]
Like the great green sea,
To water their fields in their towns.[14]
How effective they are, thy plans, O lord of eternity!
The Nile in heaven, it is for the foreign peoples
And for the beasts of every desert that go upon (their) feet;
(While the true) Nile comes from the underworld for Egypt.

Thy rays suckle every meadow.
When thou risest, they live, they grow for thee.
Thou makest the seasons in order to rear all that thou hast made,
The winter to cool them,
And the heat that *they* may taste thee.
Thou hast made the distant sky in order to rise therein,
In order to see all that thou dost make.
Whilst thou wert alone,
Rising in thy form as the living Aton,
Appearing, shining, *withdrawing or approaching*,
Thou madest millions of forms of thyself alone.
Cities, towns, fields, road, and river—
Every eye beholds thee over against them,
For thou art the Aton of the day over *the earth*. . . .

Thou art in my heart,
And there is no other that knows thee
Save thy son Nefer-kheperu-Re Wa-en-Re,[15]
For thou hast made him well-versed in thy plans and in thy strength.[16]

The world came into being by thy hand,
According as thou hast made them.
When thou hast risen they live,
When thou settest they die.
Thou art lifetime thy own self,
For one lives (only) through thee.
Eyes are (fixed) on beauty until thou settest.
All work is laid aside when thou settest in the west.
(But) when (thou) risest (again),
[*Everything is*] made to flourish for the king, . . .
Since thou didst found the earth
And raise them up for thy son,
Who came forth from thy body:
the King of Upper and Lower Egypt, . . . Akh-en-Aton, . . . and the Chief Wife of the King . . . Nefert-iti, living and youthful forever and ever.

[13] cf. Ps. 104:6, 10.

[14] The rain of foreign countries is like the Nile of rainless Egypt.

[15] Even though the hymn was recited by the official Eye, he states that Akh-en-Aton alone knows the Aton.

[16] Pharaoh was the official intermediary between the Egyptians and their gods. The Amarna religion did not change this dogma.

Hymns to the Gods as a Single God

These hymns have been called monotheistic. Whether they are so or not will depend upon the definition of monotheism and whether tendencies toward syncretism and universalism may be sufficient explanations. The hymns present different Egyptian gods of universal or cosmic nature, treated as a conflate personality and addressed in the singular.

Papyrus Chester Beatty IV (now British Museum 10684), recto vii 2 ff. The hieratic manuscript is probably from Thebes and dates to somewhere around 1300 B.C., definitely after the Amarna Revolution. Published in *Hieratic Papyri in the British Museum. Third Series. Chester Beatty Gift*, ed. by A. H. Gardiner (London, 1935), I, 28 ff.; II, Pls. 15-17.

. . . the Outline Draftsman of Amon, Mer-Sekhmet. He says: I sing to thee, intoxicated with thy beauty, with hands upon the minstrel's harp. I cause the children of singers to know how to worship the beauty of thy face. Mayest thou reward (me) with a goodly burial for the singer who gives thee song, that he may go forth upon earth as a good spirit to see the Lord of the Gods![1]

PRAISE TO THEE, Amon-Re-Atum-Har-akhti, who spoke with his mouth and there came into existence all men, gods, large and small cattle in their entirety, and that which flies and lights totally.

THOU DIDST CREATE the regions of the Hau-nebut,[2] settled in the towns thereof, and the productive meadows, fertilized by Nun[3] and giving birth thereafter—good things without limit to their number, for the provision of the living.

THOU ART VALIANT as a herdsman tending them forever and ever. Bodies are filled with thy beauty; eyes see through (thee). The [fear] of thee is for everybody; their hearts turn about to thee, good at all times. Everybody lives through the sight of thee.

DO (NOT) WIDOWS say: (viii 1) "Our husband art thou," and little ones: "Our father and our mother"? The rich boast of thy beauty, and the poor (worship) thy face. He that is imprisoned turns about to thee, and he that has a sickness calls out to thee. . . . Everybody is turned back to thy presence, so that they may make prayers to thee.

THY EARS ARE open, hearing them and taking care of them, O our Ptah who loves his crafts,[4] herdsman who loves his herds. His reward is a goodly burial for the heart which is satisfied with truth.[5]

HIS LOVE is (to be) the moon, as a child to whom everybody dances. When petitioners are gathered before his face, then he will search out hearts. Green plants turn about in his direction, that they may be beautiful, and lotuses are gay because of him.

[1] These words are actually part of a colophon which belongs to preceding hymns, but seem also to apply to the hymns which follow.

[2] The northern lands, particularly the Mediterranean coast and islands. This states the universality of the conflate creator-god.

[3] The abysmal waters, out of which life came at the creation and still comes.

[4] The conflate god is also Ptah, the craftsman who fashioned men.

[5] The god rewards the faithful with a proper burial.

HIS LOVE is (to be) the King of the Gods Presiding over Karnak.[6] . . . (10) . . . To him belongs the shrine of the north wind, and a Nile is under his fingers and comes from the heavens, *according as* he has spoken, (even) onto the mountains.[7] . . .

(ix 1) . . . HIS LOVE is (to be) Har-akhti shining in the horizon of heaven. Everybody is in praise to him, and hearts exult for him. He is a remedy for every eye, a genuine one that takes effect immediately, an (eye) cosmetic without its peer, driving away rain and clouds.[8] . . .

(7) . . . THY MOTHER IS Truth, O Amon! To thee she belongs uniquely, and she came forth from thee (already) inclined to rage and burn up them that attack thee. Truth is more unique, O Amon, than anyone that exists.[9] . . .

(x 2) . . . HOW BEAUTIFUL ART THOU AS A GOD, O Amon, verily Har-akhti, a marvel sailing in the heavens and conducting the mysteries of the underworld! The gods are coming before thee, exalting the forms which thou hast assumed. Mayest thou appear (again) from the hands of Nun, thou being mysterious in the form of (5) Khepri, reaching the gates of Nut, beautiful in thy body.[10] Thy rays foretell thee in the eyes of the regions of the Hau-nebut.[11] . . .

(xi 8) . . . HOW BEAUTIFUL IS THY RISING on the horizon! (Thus) we are in a renewal of life. We had entered (into) Nun, and it has refreshed (us), as when one began youth. [*The old state*] has been taken off, another has been put on. We praise the beauty of thy face.[12] . . .

(xii 12) . . . Thou art *the light* of the moon in the eyes of Nun. . . .

Hymn to the Nile

The Egyptians recognized that life was possible in their land only because of the existence of the Nile. The following hymn celebrated their gratitude. The extant texts have been brutally corrupted by schoolboys, who had to copy the hymn as an exercise. Fortunately, some of the briefer fragments give a more sensible text.

The text is a Theban composition. The documents are numerous, and the majority of them are fragmentary. Perhaps all of them derive from the Nineteenth and Twentieth Dynasties (1350-1100 B.C.), but the original composition may have gone back to the Middle Kingdom (2100-1700 B.C.). The text occurs on 4 papyri (Papyrus Sallier II = British Museum 10182; Papyrus Anastasi VII = British Museum 10222; Papyrus Chester Beatty V = British Museum 10685; and a papyrus in Turin); 1 writing tablet (Louvre 693); and at least 13 ostraca. The present translation was made from as many of these documents as were available to the translator; the line numbers follow Sallier II.

An up-to-date study of the texts is needed. Published by G. Maspero, *Hymne au Nil* (*Bibliothèque d'étude*, v, Cairo, 1912). A translation in Erman, *LAE*, 146-49.

(xi 6) WORSHIP OF THE NILE.

Hail to thee, O Nile, that issues from the earth and comes to keep Egypt alive! Hidden in his form of appearance,[1] a darkness by day, *to whom minstrels have sung*. He that waters the meadows which Re created, in order to keep every kid[2] alive. He that makes to drink the desert and the place distant *from water: that is his dew* coming down (*from*) heaven.[3] The beloved of Geb,[4] the one who controls Nepri,[5] and the one who makes the craftsmanship of Ptah to flourish.

THE LORD OF FISHES, HE WHO MAKES the marsh-birds TO GO UPSTREAM.[6] There are no birds which come down *because of the hot winds*.[7] He who makes barley and brings emmer into being, that he may make the temples festive. If he is sluggish, (xii 1) then nostrils are stopped up,[8] and everybody is poor. If there be (thus) a cutting down in the food-offerings of the gods, then a million men perish among mortals, covetousness is practised, the entire land *is in a fury*, and great and small *are on the execution-block*. (*But*) people *are different when he approaches*. Khnum constructed him. When he rises, then the land is in jubilation, then every belly is in joy, every *backbone* takes on laughter, and every tooth is exposed.[9]

THE BRINGER OF FOOD, rich in provisions, creator of all good, lord of majesty, sweet of fragrance. *What is in him is satisfaction*. He who brings grass into being for the cattle and (thus) gives (5) sacrifice to every god, *whether he be* in the underworld, heaven, or earth, *him who is* under his authority. He who takes in possession the Two Lands, fills the magazines, makes the granaries wide, and gives things (to) the poor.

HE WHO MAKES *every beloved* TREE TO GROW, without *lack* of them. He who brings a ship into being by his strength, without hewing in stone. *The enduring image with* the White Crown.[10] He cannot be seen; (*he has*) no taxes; he has no *levies*; no one *can read of* the mystery; no one knows the place where he is; he cannot

[6] Amon-Re.

[7] For the concept of the real Nile coming from underground caverns and of the rain as a Nile in the sky and falling upon the mountain tops, see the hymn to the Aton, p. 370 above.

[8] Diseases of the eye were common in Egypt. As a god of the weather, the deity averts *hay* "rain," and *shenit* "clouds," as a curative eye cosmetic averts *haty* "dim sight," and *shenu* "pain."

[9] Commonly the goddess Ma'at, "Truth," is the daughter of Re. Thus she comes forth from him. Here he is so composite a being that she may also be his mother.

[10] Khepri is the youthful form of the sun as it emerges at dawn from Nun, the underwaters, and moves to Nut, the sky-goddess.

[11] The remainder of the text deals with various beneficial activities of the sun-god, called Re and "the herdsman." Two extracts are given.

[12] Like the sun, man entered into Nun, the underwaters, was refreshed, and emerged at dawn, renewed in life. For the relation of this to sleep, see A. de Buck, De Godsdienstige Opvatting van den Slaap . . . (*Mededelingen en Verhandelingen, No. 4 van het Vooraziatisch-Egyptisch Gezelschap "Ex Oriente Lux,"* Leyden, 1939, English summary pp. 28-30).

[1] The Nile had no regular cult or temple in which he might appear in an image.

[2] The extant texts *ib* "kid," but the original may have had *ibw* "thirsty one."

[3] Regions cut off from the waters of the Nile had his rain to sustain them.

[4] The earth-god.

[5] The grain-god.

[6] South from the marshes of the Delta.

[7] An unknown word, determined in one text with signs for heat and wind. If the translation is justified, it suggests that the Nile cools Upper Egypt sufficiently so that no birds need to go down to the Delta.

[8] So that men cannot breathe in the breath of life.

[9] When the Nile floods, all Egyptians laugh in delight.

[10] Probably corrupt, although the following context compares the Nile to a king.

be found *by the power* of writing. (HE HAS) NO SHRINES; HE HAS NO PORTION. *He has no service of (his) desire.*[11] (But) generations of thy children jubilate for thee, and men give thee greeting as a king, stable of laws, coming forth (at) his season and filling Upper and Lower Egypt. (xiii 1) (Whenever) water is drunk, every eye is in him, who gives an excess of his good.

HE WHO WAS SORROWFUL IS COME FORTH GAY. Every heart is gay. Sobek, the child of Neith, *laughs*,[12] and the Ennead, *in which thou art, is exalted*. Vomiting forth and making the field to drink. Anointing the whole land. Making one man rich and slaying another, (but) there is no *coming to trial* with him,[13] who makes satisfaction without *being thwarted*, for whom no boundaries are made.

A MAKER OF LIGHT when issuing from darkness, a fat for his cattle. His limits are all that is created. There is no district which can live without him. Men are clothed (5) with flax from his meadows, for (he) made Hedj-hotep[14] for his service. (He) made *anointing* with his unguents, being the *associate* of Ptah in his nature, bringing into being all service *in* him,[15] all writings and divine words, his *responsibility* in Lower Egypt.[16]

ENTERING INTO THE UNDERWORLD AND COMING FORTH ABOVE, loving to come forth as a mystery.[17] If thou art (too) heavy (to rise), the people are few, and one begs for the water *of the year*. (Then) the rich man looks like him who is worried, and every man is seen (to be) carrying his weapons. There is no companion *backing up* a companion. There are no garments for clothing; there are no ornaments for the children of nobles. There is no *listening at night, that one may answer with coolness*.[18] There is no anointing for anybody.

HE WHO ESTABLISHES TRUTH in the heart of men, for it is said: "Deceit *comes after* poverty."[19] *If one compares thee* with the great green sea, *which does not* (xiv 1) *control the Grain-God*, whom all the gods praise, there are no birds coming down from his desert.[20] His hand does not *beat with* gold, *with* making ingots of silver. No one can eat genuine lapis lazuli. (But) barley is foremost and lasting.[21]

MEN BEGAN to sing TO THEE with the harp, and men sing to thee with the hand.[22] The generations of thy children jubilate for thee. Men equip messengers for thee, who come (back) bearing treasures (to) ornament this land. He who makes a ship to prosper *before* mankind; he who sustains hearts in pregnant women; he who loves a multitude of all (kinds of) his cattle.

WHEN THOU RISEST IN THE CITY OF THE RULER,[23] then men are satisfied with the goodly produce of the meadows. (5) *Oh for* the little lotus-blossoms, everything that *pours forth* upon earth, all (kinds of) herbs *in the hands of* children! *They have (even)* forgotten *how to* eat.[24] Good things are strewn about the houses. The land comes down *frolicking*.

WHEN THE NILE FLOODS, offering is made to thee, oxen are sacrificed to thee, great oblations are made to thee, birds are fattened for thee, lions are hunted for thee in the desert, fire is provided for thee. And offering is made to every (other) god, as is done for the Nile, with *prime* incense, oxen, cattle, birds, and flame. The Nile has made his cavern in Thebes, and his name is no (longer) known in the underworld.[25] Not a god will come forth *in his form, if the plan is ignored*.

O ALL MEN who uphold the Ennead, (10) fear ye the majesty which his son, the All-Lord, *has* made, *(by) making verdant* the two banks. *So it is "Verdant art thou!" So it is "Verdant art thou!" So it is* "O Nile, *verdant art thou*, who makest man and cattle to live!"

IT HAS COME TO A GOOD AND SUCCESSFUL END.

[11] The Nile has no temples, no temple service or labor.
[12] The crocodile-god delights in the inundation.
[13] The actions of the Nile are not subject to legal appeal.
[14] The weaver-god.
[15] Creating all work in Ptah as the earth-god?
[16] Corrupt and probably mistranslated. It may say that the Nile has made Ptah his deputy in Lower Egypt.
[17] The Egyptians thought that the Nile poured forth from underground caverns.
[18] If this has any meaning at all in its present form, it may claim that the failure of the Nile to rise makes the nights too hot for conversation.
[19] The poverty consequent upon a low Nile brings lawlessness.
[20] The thought is clouded but seems to compare the sea unfavorably with the Nile.
[21] The produce coming by sea is inedible; the Nile's produce is edible and sustains life.
[22] Beating time to music by clapping with the hands.

The Hymn of Victory of Thut-mose III

This hymn celebrating the conquests of the great Egyptian empire-builder, Thut-mose III, carried a victorious theme which became popular with later pharaohs. Amen-hotep III, Seti I, and Ramses III borrowed freely from the triumphant stanzas.

The stela containing the hymn was found in the temple of Karnak and is now in the Cairo Museum (34010). The approximate dates of the pharaohs who used themes from the hymn are: Thut-mose III, 1490-1436 B.C.; Amen-hotep III, 1413-1377; Seti I, 1318-1301; and Ramses III, 1195-1164.

Published, with photograph, transcription, and bibliography, by P. Lacau, *Stèles du nouvel empire* (*Catalogue général des antiquités égyptiennes du Musée du Caire*, Cairo, 1904), 17 ff.; Pl. VII. A transcription in K. Sethe, *Urkunden der 18. Dynastie* (*Urk.*, IV), II (Leipzig, 1906), 610-19, with a Thut-mose III duplicate, 619-24. Translated by Breasted, *AR*, §§655-62, and by Erman, *LAE*, 254-58.

The Amen-hotep III adaption is given below on p. 376. The Seti I version in the Temple of Karnak is translated by Breasted, *op. cit.*, III, §§116-17. The Ramses III version at the Temple of Medinet Habu is translated by W. F. Edgerton and J. A. Wilson, *Historical Records of Ramses III* (*SAOC* 12; Chicago, 1936), 111-12.

Words spoken by Amon-Re, Lord of the Thrones of the Two Lands:

Welcome to me, as thou exultest at the sight of my

[23] Thebes.
[24] Or: "Eating *makes him* forgotten"? The abundance of good things from the inundation makes people forgetful of the Nile, as they give themselves up to flowers and food.
[25] He is so well feted at Thebes that he transfers his source caverns to that city.

beauty, my son and my avenger, Men-kheper-Re,[1] living forever! I shine forth for love of thee, and my heart is glad at thy good comings into my temple, while my hands endow thy body with protection and life. How sweet is thy graciousness toward my breast!

I establish thee in my dwelling place. I *work a* wonder for thee:[2] I give thee valor and victory over all foreign countries; I set the glory of thee and the fear of thee in all lands, the terror of thee as far as the four supports of heaven. I magnify the awe of thee in all bodies. I set the battle cry of thy majesty throughout the Nine Bows.[3]

The great ones of all foreign countries are gathered together in thy grasp. I stretch out my own arms, and I tie them up for thee; I bind the barbarians of Nubia by ten-thousands and thousands, the northerners by hundred-thousands as living captives. I cause thy opponents to fall beneath thy sandals, so that thou crushest the quarrelsome and the disaffected of heart, according as I have commended to thee the earth in its length and its breadth, so that westerners and easterners are under thy oversight.

Thou treadest all foreign countries, thy heart glad. There is none who can thrust himself into the vicinity of thy majesty, while I am thy guide, (but) thou reachest them (thyself). Thou hast crossed the waters of the Great Bend of Naharin[4] by the victory and by the power which I have decreed to thee. They hear thy battle cry, having entered into caves. I have cut their nostrils off from the breath of life, so that I might set the dread of thy majesty throughout their hearts. My serpent-diadem which is upon thy head, she consumes them; she makes a speedy prey among *those twisted of nature*; she devours those who are in their islands by her flame; she cuts off the heads of the Asiatics. There is none of them missing, (but they are) fallen and *in travail* because of her might.

I cause thy victories to circulate in all lands. The gleaming (serpent), she who is upon my brow, is thy servant, (so that) there shall arise none rebellious to thee as far as that which heaven encircles. They come, bearing tribute upon their backs, bowing down to thy majesty, as I decree. I have made the aggressors who come near thee grow weak, for their hearts are burned up and their bodies are trembling.

I have come,
That I may cause thee to trample down the great ones of Djahi;[5]
I spread them out under thy feet throughout their countries.
I cause them to see thy majesty as the lord of radiance,[6]
So that thou shinest into their faces as my likeness.
I have come,
That I may cause thee to trample down those who are in Asia;
Thou smitest the heads of the Asiatics of Retenu.[7]
I cause them to see thy majesty equipped with thy adornment,
As thou takest the weapons of war in the chariot.
I have come,
That I may cause thee to trample down the eastern land;
Thou treadest upon those who are in the regions of God's Land.[8]
I cause them to see thy majesty as a *shooting* star,
Sowing its fire in a flame, as it gives off its *steam*.
I have come,
That I may cause thee to trample down the western land;
Keftiu and Isy are under the awe (of thee).[9]
I cause them to see thy majesty as a young bull,
Firm of heart, sharp of horns, who cannot be *felled*.
I have come,
That I may cause thee to trample down those who are in their islands;
The lands of Mitanni are trembling under the fear of thee,[10]
I cause them to see thy majesty as a crocodile,
The lord of fear in the water, who cannot be approached.
I have come,
That I may cause thee to trample down those who are in the islands;
They who are in the midst of the Great Green Sea are under thy battle cry.
I cause them to see thy majesty as the Avenger
Appearing in glory on the back of his sacrifice.[11]
I have come,
That I may cause thee to trample down the Tehenu;
The Utentiu belong to the might of thy glory.[12]
I cause them to see thy majesty as a fierce lion,
As thou makest them corpses throughout their valleys.
I have come,
That I may cause thee to trample down the ends of the lands;
That which the Ocean encircles is enclosed within thy grasp.
I cause them to see thy majesty as a lord of the wing,
Taking possession of what he sees as he wishes.
I have come,

1 Thut-mose III.
2 Perhaps: "I wonder at thee," but the expression is usually followed by a boon conferred by the god.
3 The nine traditional enemies of Egypt.
4 Naharin, a reasonable Semitic approximation to the term Mesopotamia, was a land along the great bend of the Euphrates.
5 Approximately the Phoenician coast.
6 The sun.
7 The highland of Palestine-Syria.
8 The land of the rising sun.
9 Disputed, but probably Crete (Caphtor) and Cyprus.
10 Mitanni, the lands of Upper Mesopotamia and northern Syria, was a political equivalent of the geographical term Naharin.
11 Horus defeating Seth.
12 The Tehenu were Libyans. The land of Utent is elsewhere listed among the peoples to the south of Egypt.

That I may cause thee to trample down the front of the land;[13]
Thou bindest the Sand-Dwellers as living captives.
I cause them to see thy majesty like a jackal of the Southland,
The lord of speed, the runner coursing the Two Lands.
I have come,
That I may cause thee to trample down the barbarians of Nubia;
As far as *Shat-Djeba* is in thy grip.[14]
I cause them to see thy majesty like thy two brothers;[15]
I have joined their hands together for thee in victory.

Thy two sisters (also),[16] I have set them in protection behind thee, while the arms of my majesty are uplifting, warding off evil.[17] I give thy protection, my son, my beloved, Horus: Mighty Bull, Appearing in Thebes, whom I begot in the divine [body], Thutmose, living forever, who has done for me all that my *ka* desires.

Thou hast erected my dwelling place as the work of eternity, made longer and wider than that which had been before, and the very great gateway (named) "[*Men-kheper-Re*], (25) *whose Beauty Makes Festive the* [*House of*] *Amon*.[18] Thy monuments are greater than (those of) any king who has been. I commanded thee to make them, and I am satisfied with them. I have established thee upon the throne of Horus for millions of years, that thou mightest lead the living for eternity.

From Amen-hotep III's Building Inscription

The following inscription illustrates the reciprocal relation between pharaoh and god in ancient Egypt. At great length Amen-hotep III (about 1413-1377 B.C.) details his building activities on behalf of the god Amon-Re. The text closes with the grateful hymn of the god to the king.

The stela is now Cairo 34025. It was set up by Amen-hotep III in his temple which stood behind the Colossi of Memnon at Thebes. The text was thoroughly hacked up under the Amarna Revolution, but restored under Seti I. Then Mer-ne-Ptah appropriated the stela and used its back for the "Israel Stela" in his mortuary temple, where it was found by W. M. F. Petrie; see his *Six Temples at Thebes* (London, 1897), 10-11, 23-26; Pls. XI-XII. It was published by P. Lacau, *Stèles du nouvel empire* (*Catalogue général . . . du Musée du Caire*, Cairo, 1909), I, 47-52, Pls. XV-XVI. It was translated by Breasted, *AR*, II, §§878-92.

. . . (Amen-hotep III). He made, as (3) his monument for his father Amon, Lord of the Thrones of the Two Lands, the erecting for him of an august temple on the west side of Thebes, an everlasting fortress, a possesssor of eternity, of fine sandstone, worked with gold throughout.[1] Its pavement was washed with silver, all its doorways with fine gold. It was made very wide and great, embellished forever, made festive with this very great monument, and abounding in statues of the lord[2] in the granite of Elephantine, gritstone, and every (5) august costly stone, perfected with the work of eternity. Their height shines up to heaven; their rays are in (men's) faces like the sun disc,[3] when he shines at dawn. It is equipped with a Station of the Lord,[4] worked with gold and many costly stones. At its face flagstaffs have been set up, worked with fine gold. It is made like the horizon which is in heaven when Re shines forth therein. Its canal is filled with the high Nile, the lord of fish and fowl, pure in *bouquets*. Its workhouse is filled with male and female slaves, the children of the princes of every foreign country of his majesty's plundering. Its magazines enclose good things of which the count is not known. It is surrounded with Syrian towns, settled with the children of princes.[5] Its cattle are like the sands of the shore; they total millions. It has the prow-rope of the Southland and the stern-rope of the Northland.[6] . . .

I made another monument for him who begot me, Amon-Re, Lord of the Thrones of the Two Lands, who is established upon his throne, (in) making for him a great barque upon the river, "Amon-Re in User-het," of (17) new cedar which his majesty cut in the country of God's Land,[7] dragged from the mountains of Retenu by the princes of all foreign countries. It was made very wide and great. The like had never been made. Its hull is washed with silver and completely worked with gold. The great shrine is of fine gold. . . .[8]

I made other monuments for Amon, (24) of which the like has never occurred. I built for thee thy house of millions of years in the precinct of Amon-Re, Lord of the Thrones of the Two Lands, "Appearing in Truth," an august (place) of fine gold, a resting place for my father in all his feasts.[9] It is embellished with fine sandstone and worked with gold throughout. Its pavement is decorated with silver, and all its doorways

[13] In contrast to "the ends of the lands" just above, this term would apply to the countries near Egypt, including the "Sand-Dwellers" of the nearby Asiatic deserts.

[14] Shat-Djeba (the reading is uncertain) was in Nubia.

[15] Horus and Seth.

[16] Isis and Nephthys.

[17] As Erman has pointed out, there is deliberate alliteration in the passage "the arms . . . evil," sounding something like: *'awi hemi hir heru hir seheri djut*.

[18] The name of the gateway is doubtful. Under the Amarna Revolution, this stela was attacked to remove the name of the god Amon. A restoration of the hacked out portions under the 19th dynasty did not always restore the probable sense.

[1] This was the now destroyed mortuary temple, which stood behind the Colossi of Memnon.

[2] The pharaoh himself.

[3] "Like the Aton."

[4] The official post of the king in the temple; cf. pp. 248, 446.

[5] On the policy of bringing Syrian princelings to Egypt, see pp. 239, 248.

[6] It has the leadership of the two lands. The translation omits several lines dealing with the building of other temples.

[7] Eastern lands in general; here specifically the Lebanon.

[8] The translation omits the remainder of the description of Amon's sacred barge upon the river and a statement of the building of the Third Pylon at Karnak.

[9] A. Varille, *Karnak I* (Cairo, 1943), 14-15, believes that this refers to the Temple of Amon-Re Montu in the northern group at Karnak.

with gold. Two great obelisks have been erected, one on each side, so that my father may appear between them, while I am in his retinue. I have sacrificed to him thousands of oxen, *as well as* choice cuts.

Words spoken by Amon-Re, King of the Gods:[10]—

My son, of my body, my beloved, Neb-maat-Re,
My living image, whom my body created,
Whom Mut, Mistress of Ishru in Thebes, the Lady
  of the Nine Bows, bore to me,
And (she) nursed thee as the Sole Lord of the
  people—
My heart is very joyful when I see thy beauty;
I *work a* wonder for thy majesty,[11]
That thou mightest renew youth,
According as I made thee to be Re of the Two
  Banks.

When I turn my face to the south, I *work a* wonder
  for thee:—
I make the princes of the wretched Ethiopia bestir
  themselves for thee,
Bearing all their tribute upon their backs.

When I turn my face to the north, I *work a* wonder
  for thee:—
I make the countries of the ends of Asia come to
  thee,
Bearing all their tribute upon their backs.
They themselves present to thee their children,
Seeking that thou mightest give to them the breath
  of life.

When I turn my face to the west, I *work a* wonder
  for thee:—
I let thee take Libya—they cannot escape—
(*Shut*) *up* in this fortress bearing the name of (thy)
  majesty,
Surrounded with a great wall reaching to heaven,
And settled with the children of the princes of the
  Nubian barbarians.

When I turn my face to the orient, I *work a* wonder
  for thee:—
I make the countries of Punt[12] come to thee,
Bearing all the sweet plants of their countries,
To beg peace from (thee and to) breathe the breath
  of thy giving.
. . .

[10] On the ancestry of this hymn, see p. 373.
[11] Or: "I wonder at thy majesty," as in the Thut-mose III hymn.
[12] An incense-producing country on or near the Red Sea.

Hymn of Victory of Mer-ne-Ptah (The "Israel Stela")

The date of this commemorative hymn (or series of hymns) relates it to Mer-ne-Ptah's victory over the Libyans in the spring of his fifth year (about 1230 B.C.). However, the text is not historical in the same sense as two other records of that victory, but is rather a poetic eulogy of a universally victorious pharaoh. Thus it was not out of place to introduce his real or figurative triumph over Asiatic peoples in the last poem of the hymn. In that context we meet the only instance of the name "Israel" in ancient Egyptian writing.

The "Israel Stela," now Cairo 34025, was discovered by Petrie in the ruins of Mer-ne-Ptah's mortuary temple at Thebes. There is also a fragmentary duplicate in the Temple of Karnak.

First published by W. M. F. Petrie, *Six Temples at Thebes* (London, 1897), Pls. xiii-xiv, later by P. Lacau, *Stèles du nouvel empire* (*Catalogue général des antiquités égyptiennes du Musée du Caire*, Cairo, 1909), i, 52 ff. The Karnak duplicate published by Ch. Kuentz in *BIFAO*, xxi (1923), 113-17. W. Spiegelberg studied and translated the text in *ZAeS*, xxxiv (1896), 1-25. A later translation in Erman, *LAE*, 274-78.[1]

Year 5, 3rd month of the third season, day 3, under the majesty of the Horus: Mighty Bull, Rejoicing in Truth; the King of Upper and Lower Egypt: Ba-en-Re Meri-Amon; the Son of Re: Mer-ne-Ptah Hotep-hir-Maat. The magnification of the strength and the exaltation of the strong arm of the Horus: Mighty Bull, who smites the Nine Bows,[2] whose name is given to eternity forever. The relation of his victories in all lands, to cause that every land together know and to let the virtue in his deeds of valor be seen: the King of Upper and Lower Egypt: Ba-en-Re Meri-Amon; the Son of Re: Mer-ne-Ptah Hotep-hir-Maat; the Bull, lord of strength, slaying his foes, gracious on the field of valor when his conquest has been effected;

The sun, uncovering the cloud which had been over
    Egypt
  And letting Egypt see the rays of the sun disc;
Removing the mountain of metal from the neck of
    the people,
  So that he might give breath to the folk who had
    been shut in;
Appeasing the heart of Memphis over their enemies,
  And making Ta-tenen[3] rejoice over those rebellious
    to him;
Opening the doors of Memphis which had been
    barred

  And letting its temples receive their food (again);

the King of Upper and Lower Egypt: Ba-en-Re Meri-Amon; the Son of Re: Mer-ne-Ptah Hotep-hir-Maat;

The sole one, restoring the courage of hundred-
    thousands,
  For breath enters into their nostrils at the sight of
    him;
Penetrating the land of Temeh[4] in his lifetime,
  And setting the terror of eternity in the hearts of the
    Meshwesh.

[1] In two scenes above the inscription, the god Amon-Re extends a scimitar to Mer-ne-Ptah for Pharaoh's use against "every foreign country." Thus the god commissioned the Pharaoh to undertake a campaign. cf. n.12 below.
[2] The nine traditional enemies of Egypt.
[3] A god of Memphis.
[4] Temeh, Meshwesh, Rebu (=Libyans), and Tehenu were names for various groups of Libyans, originally distinct, now to some extent interchangeable.

He causes to turn back the Rebu, who had trodden Egypt,
Great dread being in their hearts because of Egypt.

Their advanced guard abandoned their rear. Their legs did not stop, except to run. Their archers abandoned their bows. The heart of their runners was weak from traveling. They untied their waterskins, thrown on the ground; their packs were loosed and cast aside.

The wretched enemy prince of Rebu was fled in the depth of the night, by himself. No feather was on his head;[5] his feet were unshod. His women were taken before his face. The loaves for his provision were seized; he had no water of the waterskin to keep him alive. The face of his brethren was fierce, to slay him; among his commanders one fought his companion. Their tents were burned up, made ashes. All his goods were food for the troops.[6]

He reached his (own) country, and he was in mourning. Every survivor in his land was (too) aggrieved (to) receive him. "The prince (whose) plume evil fortune opposed!" they all say to him, those belonging to his town.

"He is in the power of the gods, the lords of Memphis;
The Lord of Egypt makes a curse of his name:—
'Merey[7] is the abominated one of Memphis,
One and the son of one of his family to eternity.
Ba-en-Re Meri-Amon shall be in pursuit of his children;
Mer-ne-Ptah Hotep-hir-Maat is given him as a fate!' "
He is become a proverbial saying for Rebu;
Generation says to generation of his victories:—
"It was not done to us another time since (the days of) Re!"
So he says, every old man, speaking to his son.

Woe to Rebu! They have ceased to live(in) the pleasant fashion of one who goes about in the field. Their going *is checked* in a single day. The Tehenu *are consumed* in a single year, for Seth[8] has turned his back upon their chief; their settlements are abandoned *on his account.* There is no work of carrying *baskets* in these days. It is advantageous to hide, for one is safe in the cave. The great Lord of Egypt is powerful; victory belongs to him. Who can fight, knowing his unhindered stride? Foolish and witless is he who takes him on! He who transgresses his frontier knows not for himself the morrow.

"As for Egypt," they say, "since (the time of) the gods, (she has been) the sole daughter of Re, and his son is he who is on the throne of Shu.[9] No heart has made *a reputation for* attacking her people, for the eye of every god is in pursuit of him who covets her, and she it is who will carry off the end of her enemies." So they say, *those who watch* the stars and who know all their magic spells by looking at the winds.[10] "A great wonder has fallen to Egypt! He who attacked her has been given (into) her hand as a living captive, through the counsels of the divine king, righteous against his enemies in the presence of Re."

Merey is he who did evil and *subversive* things against every god who is in Memphis. He is the one with whom there was litigation in Heliopolis, and the Ennead[11] made him guilty because of his crimes. The All-Lord has said: "Give the strong arm[12] to my son, the exact of heart, the merciful and kindly, Ba-en-Re Meri-Amon, the one who is solicitous for Memphis, who answers (on behalf of) Heliopolis, opening the towns which had been shut up, that he might set free many who had been imprisoned in every district, that he might give offerings to the temples, that he might cause incense to be brought in before the god, that he might cause the great to possess their property (again), that he might cause the poor to *turn* (*again to*) their cities."

Thus speak the lords of Heliopolis about their son, Mer-ne-Ptah Hotep-hir-Maat: "Give him a lifetime like Re, that he may answer (on behalf of) him who is suffering because of any country. Egypt has been assigned to him *to be the portion* of him who represents her, for himself forever, so that he might *protect* his people. Behold, as one dwells in the time of the mighty one, the breath of life comes immediately. The valiant one, who causes goods to flow to the *righteous man*—there is no cheat who retains his plunder. He who gathers the *fat* of wickedness and the strength of others (*shall have*) no children." So they speak.

Merey, the wretched, *ignorant* enemy of Rebu, was come to attack the "Walls of *the Sovereign*,"[13] the son of whose lord has arisen in his place, the King of Upper and Lower Egypt: Ba-en-Re Meri-Amon; the Son of Re: Mer-ne-Ptah Hotep-hir-Maat. Ptah said about the enemy of Rebu:[14] "Gather together all his crimes, returned upon his (own) head. Give him into the hand of Mer-ne-Ptah Hotep-hir-Maat, that he may make him disgorge what he has swallowed, like a crocodile. Now behold, the swift carries off the swift; the Lord, conscious of his strength, will ensnare him. It is Amon who binds him with his hand, so that he may be delivered to his *ka* in Hermonthis; the King of Upper and Lower Egypt: Ba-en-Re Meri-Amon; the Son of Re: Mer-ne-Ptah Hotep-hir-Maat."

Great joy has arisen in Egypt;
Jubilation has gone forth in the towns of Egypt.

[5] Libyan warriors wore a feather in the headdress.
[6] Plunder for the Egyptian troops.
[7] The Libyan prince.
[8] The Egyptians used their god Seth as a god of foreign peoples.
[9] Egypt was thus the daughter of Re, and the pharaoh, who was by dogma the Son of Re, sat upon the throne of Shu, the air-god who was the direct divine son of Re.

[10] The diviners by stars and winds see the evil eye of the gods as being against any of Egypt's attackers.
[11] The Ennead, the nine gods of Heliopolis over whom Atum-Re presided, is here conceived to be judging Mer-ne-Ptah and the Libyan ruler Merey. In the following context, first Re, the All-Lord, gives his verdict and reward to the victorious pharaoh, and then the Ennead confirm this award.
[12] The word may mean "scimitar." cf. n.1 above.
[13] Or the "Walls of (the god) Ta-tenen"? In either case, Memphis.
[14] Karnak variant: "Amon said about this one of Rebu."

They talk about the victories
Which Mer-ne-Ptah Hotep-hir-Maat made in Tehenu:
"How amiable is he, the victorious ruler!
How exalted is the king among the gods!
How fortunate is he, the lord of command!
Ah, how pleasant it is to sit when there is gossip!"

One walks with unhindered stride on the way, for there is no fear at all in the heart of the people. The forts are left to themselves, the wells (lie) open, *accessible* to the messengers. The battlements of the wall are calm in the sun until their watchers may awake. The Madjoi are stretched out as they sleep; the Nau and Tekten are in the meadows as they wish.[15] The cattle of the field are left as free to roam without herdsman, (even) crossing the flood of the stream. There is no breaking out of a cry in the night: "*Halt! Behold, a comer comes with* the speech of strangers!," (but) one goes and comes (25) with singing. There is no cry of people as when there is mourning. Towns are settled anew again. He who plows his harvest will eat it. Re has turned himself around (again) to Egypt. He was born as the one destined to be her protector, the King of Upper and Lower Egypt: Ba-en-Re Meri-Amon; the Son of Re: Mer-ne-Ptah Hotep-hir-Maat.

The princes are prostrate, saying: "Mercy!"[16]
Not one raises his head among the Nine Bows.
Desolation is for Tehenu; Hatti is pacified;
Plundered is the Canaan with every evil;
Carried off is Ashkelon; seized upon is Gezer;
Yanoam is made as that which does not exist;[17]
Israel is laid waste, his seed is not;[18]
Hurru is become a widow for Egypt![19]
All lands together, they are pacified;
Everyone who was restless, he has been bound
by the King of Upper and Lower Egypt: Ba-en-Re Meri-Amon; the Son of Re: Mer-ne-Ptah Hotep-hir-Maat, given life like Re every day.

Joy at the Accession of Mer-ne-Ptah

In the dogma of Egyptian religion each pharaoh was a god who repeated the creation miracle of establishing order out of chaos. The following hymn, from a papyrus of miscellaneous texts for school instruction, celebrates the accession of Mer-ne-Ptah of the Nineteenth Dynasty (about 1234-1222 B.C.).

From Papyrus Sallier I (British Museum 10185), recto viii 7-ix 1. A photographic facsimile in *Egyptian Hieratic Papyri in the British Museum. Second Series* (ed. by E. A. W. Budge, London, 1923), Pls. LX-LXI. Transcription into hieroglyphic by A. H. Gardiner, *Late-Egyptian Miscellanies* (*Bibliotheca Aegyptiaca*, VII, Brussels, 1937), 86-87. Translated in Erman, *LAE*, 278-79.

The Chief Archivist of the Treasury of Pharaoh—life, prosperity, health!—Amen-em-Onet, addressing the Scribe Pen-ta-Uret, thus: This writing is brought to thee (to) say: Another matter:[1]

Be glad of heart, the entire land! The goodly times are come! A lord—life, prosperity, health!—is given in all lands, and *normality* has come down (again) into its place: the King of Upper and Lower Egypt, the lord of millions of years, great of kingship like Horus: Ba-en-Re Meri-Amon—life, prosperity, health!—he who *crushes* Egypt with *festivity*, the Son of Re, (most) serviceable of any king: Mer-ne-Ptah Hotep-hir-Maat—life, prosperity, health!

All ye righteous, come that ye may see! Right has banished wrong.[2] Evildoers have fallen (upon) their faces. All the rapacious are ignored.

The water stands and is not dried up; the Nile lifts high. Days are long, nights have hours, and the moon comes normally.[3] The gods are satisfied and content of heart. [One] lives *in* laughter and wonder. Mayest thou know it.

THE END.

Joy at the Accession of Ramses IV

It was normal in Egypt to affirm that the accession of any pharaoh was the restoration of the normal divine order. In the case of the accession of Ramses IV, there was an additional justification, in that the reign of Ramses III did end in palace disorder, including a conspiracy within the royal harem, see pp. 214-216.

An ostracon in the Turin Museum, probably of the reign of Ramses IV (about 1164-1157 B.C.), published by G. Maspero in *Recueil de travaux . . .*, II (1880), 116-17; translated by Erman, *LAE*, 279. The following rendering benefits by a translation by W. Spiegelberg in *OLZ*, XXX (1927), 73-76.

A happy day! Heaven and earth are in joy, for thou art the great lord of Egypt.

15 The Madjoi were Sudanese used as police in Egypt. The word then came to mean "police." The Nau and Tekten policed the desert frontier.

16 Or "Peace!" The Canaanite word *shalam* is used here.

17 Hatti was the land of the Hittites. Yanoam was an important town of northern Palestine.

18 Much has been made of the fact that the word Israel is the only one of the names in this context which is written with the determinative of people rather than land. Thus we should seem to have the Children of Israel in or near Palestine, but not yet as a settled people. This would have important bearing on the date of the Conquest. This is a valid argument. Determinatives should have meaning, and a contrast between determinatives in the same context should be significant. This stela does give the country determinatives to settled peoples like the Rebu, Temeh, Hatti, Ashkelon, etc., and the determinative of people to unlocated groups like the Madjoi, Nau, and Tekten. The argument is good, but not conclusive, because of the notorious carelessness of Late-Egyptian scribes and several blunders of writing in this stela.

The statement that the "seed," i.e. offspring, of Israel had been wiped out is a conventional boast of power at this period.

19 The land of the biblical Horites, or Greater Palestine.

1 The pupil, Pen-ta-Uret, copies a letter from his master, Amen-em-Onet. This has been preceded by another letter on a different subject. Hence the words: "Another matter." cf. p. 379.

2 "Truth drives out lying." The Egyptian concept of *ma'at* "truth, order, right," was of the essential order of the universe, given by the gods at the beginning and maintained and reconfirmed by the god-king.

3 Order is found in the regularity of times and seasons, restored by the new king.

They who were fled have come (back) to their towns; they who were hidden have come forth (again).

They who were hungry are sated and gay; they who were thirsty are drunken.

They who were naked are clothed in fine linen; they who were dirty are clad in white.

They who were in prison are set free; they who were fettered are in joy. The troublemakers in this land have become peaceful.

High Niles have come forth from their caverns, that they may refresh the hearts of the common people.

The homes of the widows are open (again), so that they may let wanderers come in. The womenfolk rejoice and repeat their songs of jubilation . . . , saying: "Male children are born (again) *for good times*, for he brings into being generation upon generation. Thou ruler—life, prosperity, health!—thou art for eternity!"

The ships, they rejoice upon the deep. *They have* no (*need of*) ropes, for they come to land with wind and oars.[1] They are sated with joy, when it is said:

"The King of Upper and Lower Egypt: Heqa-maat-Re Setep-en-Amon—life, prosperity, health!—wears the White Crown again; the Son of Re: Ramses *Heqa*-maat—life, prosperity, health!—has taken over the office of his father!"

All lands say to him: "Gracious is the Horus upon the throne of his father Amon-Re, the god who sent him forth, the protector of the prince who carries off every land!"[2]

Made by the Scribe of the Necropolis Amon-nakht in the year 4, 1st month of the first season, day 14.[3]

[1] In the difficult times, even navigation on the river had required exceptional means. Now current and breeze have become helpful.

[2] On this refrain of triumph, see J. A. Wilson in *JEA*, XVII (1931), 214-16.

[3] Not the accession day of Ramses IV, but the date on which this ostracon was written.

A Prayer to Thoth

This prayer to Thoth, the god of wisdom and thus the patron of scribes, comes from a collection of letters and exercises to be used as models for schoolboys. Characteristically for the late Empire, the prayer makes a virtue of "silence" or submissive conformity.

From Papyrus Sallier I (British Museum 10185), recto viii 2-7. The manuscript dates from the latter part of the 13th century B.C. A photographic facsimile in *Egyptian Hieratic Papyri in the British Museum. Second Series* (ed. by E. A. W. Budge, London, 1923), Pl. LX. Transcription into hieroglyphic by A. H. Gardiner, *Late-Egyptian Miscellanies* (*Bibliotheca Aegyptiaca*, VII, Brussels, 1937), 85-86. Translated in Erman, *LAE*, 305-06.

The Chief Archivist of the Treasury of Pharaoh—life, prosperity, health!—Amen-em-Onet, addressing the Scribe Pen-ta-Uret, thus: This writing is brought to thee (to) say: Another matter:[1]

O Thoth, set me in Hermopolis, thy city, where life is pleasant! Thou suppliest (my) needs with bread and beer; thou guardest my mouth (in) speech. Would that I had Thoth behind me on the morrow! Come (to me)—thus one speaks—when I enter into the presence of the lords, that I may come forth justified![2]

Thou great dom-palm of sixty cubits (height), on which there are fruits! *Stones* are inside the fruits, and water is inside the *stones*.[3] Thou that bringest water (even in) a distant place, come and rescue me, the silent one!

O Thoth, thou sweet well *for* a man thirsting (in) the desert! It is sealed up to him who has discovered his mouth, (but) it is open to the silent. When the silent comes, he finds the well, (but for) the heated (man) thou art *choked up*.

THE END.

[1] The pupil, Pen-ta-Uret, copies a letter from his master, Amen-em-Onet. This has been preceded by another letter on a different subject. Hence the words: "Another matter." cf. p. 378.

[2] The scribe would like the advocacy of Thoth in the judgment after death.

[3] For the thirsty there is water, even though it may not lie easily at the surface. The same thought lies in the following context, where the babbler or "heated" man cannot find the well of wisdom, but the "silent" man can.

A Prayer to Re-Har-akhti

This prayer to the sun-god Atum Re-Har-akhti is found in a manuscript of model texts for the instruction of schoolboys. It illustrates the humble and penitential spirit of the late Empire.

From Papyrus Anastasi II (British Museum 10243), recto x 1-xi 2. The manuscript dates from the late Nineteenth Dynasty (about 1230 B.C.) and probably comes from Memphis. Facsimiled in *Select Papyri in the Hieratic Character from the Collections of the British Museum*, II (London, 1842), Pls. LXXII-LXXIII. A transcription into hieroglyphic in A. H. Gardiner, *Late-Egyptian Miscellanies* (*Bibliotheca Aegyptiaca*, VII, Brussels, 1937), 18-19. A translation in Erman, *LAE*, 307.

Come to me, O Re-Har-akhti, that thou mayest look after me! Thou art he who does, and there is none who does without thee, unless it be thou that [actest with] him.

Come to me, Atum, every day! Thou art the august god. My heart advances to Heliopolis, while my . . . and my heart is gay and my breast is in joy. My prayers, my supplications of every day, and my adorations of the night are heard. My petitions will continue in my mouth, and they are heard today.

Thou one and only, O Re-Har-akhti! There is no other here like unto him, who protects millions while he rescues hundred-thousands! The protector of him who calls out to him, the Lord of Heliopolis.

Do not punish me for my numerous sins, (for) I am one who knows not his own self, I am a man without sense. I spend the day following after my (own) mouth,[1] like a cow after grass. If I spend the evening in . . . , I am one to whom calm comes. I spend the day going around *and around* in the *temple* and spend the night . . .

[1] That is, he is not "silent" or submissive to the god.

A Prayer for Help in the Law Court

A characteristic of the later Empire was the humble submissiveness of a worshiper to his god. Man could achieve a good life only with the help of his god. For example, the helpless client in the court of law is bewildered by the clamor of human injustice and turns to the god for justice.

The text comes from Papyrus Anastasi II (British Museum 10243), recto viii 5-ix 1. The manuscript dates from the late Nineteenth Dynasty (about 1230 B.C.) and probably comes from Memphis. The hieratic text was facsimiled in *Select Papyri in the Hieratic Character from the Collections of the British Museum*, II (London, 1842), Pls. LXX-LXXI, and in G. Möller, *Hieratische Lesestücke*, II (Leipzig, 1927), 36. A transcription into hieroglyphic is given in A. H. Gardiner, *Late-Egyptian Miscellanies* (*Bibliotheca Aegyptiaca*, VII, Brussels, 1937), 17. There is a translation in Erman, *LAE*, 308.

O Amon, give thy ear to one who is alone in the law court, who is poor; *he is* [*not*] rich. The court cheats him (of) silver and gold for the scribes of the mat[1] and clothing for the attendants. May it be found that Amon assumes his form as the vizier, in order to permit [the] poor man to get off. May it be found that the poor man is vindicated. May the poor man surpass the rich.

THE END.

[1] The magistrates and clerks of the court sat on reed mats. "The attendants" were probably the bailiffs.

Gratitude for a God's Mercy

An artisan of the Nineteenth Dynasty here expresses his humble gratitude for the recovery of his son from illness. Neb-Re and his son Nakht-Amon were outline draftsmen of the Theban necropolis. It seems that Nakht-Amon acted impiously in respect to a cow belonging to the god Amon-Re and was then taken with a serious illness. He recovered after supplication had been made to the god. His father Neb-Re here gives pious thanks to Amon-Re.

The inscription is carved on a memorial stela, now Berlin 20377.[1] The text is published by G. Roeder in *Aegyptische Inschriften aus den Staatlichen Museen zu Berlin*, II (Leipzig, 1924), 158 ff. A. Erman gave a photograph and translation in Denksteine aus der thebanischen Gräberstadt (*SBAW*, 1911, 1088 ff.). Additional translations are by B. Gunn in *JEA*, III (1916), 83-85, and by Erman, *LAE*, 310-12.

The Scene Above[2]

Amon-Re, Lord of the Thrones of the Two Lands, the Great God Presiding over Karnak, the august god, he who hears the prayer, who comes at the voice of the poor and distressed, who gives breath (to) him who is weak.

(5) Giving praise to Amon-Re, Lord of the Thrones of the Two Lands, Presiding over Karnak; kissing the ground to Amon of the City,[3] the Great God, the lord of the great forecourt, the gracious one. May he grant to me that my eyes look at his beauty. To the *ka* of the Outline Draftsman of Amon, Neb-Re, the justified.[4]

The Memorial Prayer

(11) Giving praises to Amon. I make him adorations in his name; I give him praises to the height of heaven and to the width of earth; [I] relate his power to him who travels downstream and to him who travels upstream. Beware ye of him! Repeat him to son and daughter, to great and small; relate him to generations of generations who have not yet come into being; relate him to fishes in the deep, to birds in the heaven; repeat him to him who knows him not and to him who knows him! Beware ye of him!

Thou art Amon, the lord of the silent man,[5] who comes at the voice of the poor man. If I call to thee when I am distressed, thou (15) comest and thou rescuest me. Thou givest breath (to) him who is weak; thou rescuest him who is imprisoned. Thou art Amon-Re, Lord of Thebes, who rescues him who is in the underworld, inasmuch as thou art he who is . . . when one calls to thee; thou art he who comes from afar.

Made by the Outline Draftsman of Amon in the Place of Truth,[6] Neb-Re, the justified, son of the Outline Draftsman in the Place of Truth, Pay, . . . in the name of his lord Amon, Lord of Thebes, who comes at the voice of the poor man. Adorations were made for him in his name, because of the greatness of his strength; supplications were made to him before his face and in the presence of the entire land, on behalf of the Outline Draftsman Nakht-Amon, the justified, when he was lying ill and in a state of death, when he was (under) the power of Amon because of his cow.[7] I found the Lord of the Gods coming as the north wind, with sweet breezes before him.[8] He rescued the Outline Draftsman of Amon, Nakht-Amon, the justified, the son of the Outline Draftsman of Amon in the Place of Truth, Neb-Re, the justified, and born (20) to the Lady of the House, Pa-shed, the justified.

He says: Though it may be that the servant is normal in doing wrong, still the Lord is normal in being merciful.[9] The Lord of Thebes does not spend an entire day angry. As for his anger—in the completion of a moment there is no remnant, and *the wind* is turned about in mercy for us, and Amon *has turned around*

[1] Not Berlin 23077, as often listed.

[2] The two paragraphs of the following translation apply to the two figures in the scene above the memorial prayer. On the left the god Amon-Re is depicted as seated before the pylon of a temple. On the right Neb-Re kneels in worship of the god.

[3] "The City" is *No* or Thebes, as in the biblical *No-Amon*.

[4] The former dedication "to the vital force of" So-and-so has come to mean a dedication by that man, as in the case of contemporary papyri.

[5] A common expression at this time for the submissive or humble.

[6] A section in the Theban necropolis.

[7] It is uncertain whether "his" really means Amon's cow, i.e. of the temple herds, or Nakht-Amon's cow. It is uncertain what the transgression was.

[8] The north wind is the cooling and healing breeze of Egypt.

[9] An expression . . . the instruction of Amen-em-Opet, Chapter XVIII (p. 423 below). The word translated "normal," or "regular, usual" may mean "is disposed to" (do wrong or be merciful), as Gunn and Erman.

with his breezes. As thy *ka* endures, thou wilt be merciful, and we shall not repeat what has been turned away!

By the Outline Draftsman in the Place of Truth, Neb-Re, the justified, he says: I shall make this stela in thy name, and I shall establish for thee *these* adorations in writing upon it, because thou hast rescued for me the Outline Draftsman Nakht-Amon. (25) So I spoke unto thee, and thou didst listen to me. Now, see, I shall do what I have said. Thou art the lord of him who calls unto him, satisfied with truth, the Lord of Thebes.

Made by the Outline Draftsman Neb-Re (*and his*) son, the Scribe Khay.

A Penitential Hymn to a Goddess

The end of the Egyptian Empire produced a number of expressions of humble piety, unquestioning faith in a god, and penitence for wrongdoing. The following inscription was dedicated by a man of humble rank to a goddess, "Meres-ger, Lady of Heaven, Mistress of the Two Lands, whose good name is Peak of the West." Meres-ger means "She Loves Silence," that is, pious submissiveness. The Peak of the West was probably her location on a mountain-head of western Thebes. We do not know what the transgression of the workman Nefer-abet was.

This stela comes from Thebes and is now Turin Museum 102. It was published by G. Maspero in *Recueil de travaux . . .* , II (1880), 109, and studied by A. Erman, Denksteine aus der thebanischen Gräberstadt (*SBAW*, 1911, 1086-1110). It was translated by B. Gunn in *JEA*, III (1916), 86-87.

Giving praise to the Peak of the West; kissing the ground to her *ka*. I give praise; hear (my) call. I was a righteous man upon earth. Made by the Servant in the Place of Truth,[1] Nefer-abet, the triumphant, an ignorant and witless man.

I knew not good or evil. When I did the deed of transgression against the Peak, she punished me, and I was in her hand by night as well as day. I sat upon the brick(s) like the pregnant woman.[2] I called out to the wind, (but) it did not come to me. I was *tormented* by the Peak of the West, great in strength, and by every god and every goddess.

See, I shall say to great and small who are in the gang:[3] "Beware of the Peak! For a lion is in the Peak; she smites with the smiting of a savage lion. She pursues him who transgresses against her."

(But) when I called to my mistress, I found her coming to me with sweet breezes. She showed mercy unto me, after she had let me see her hand. She turned about to me in mercy; she made me forget the sickness which had been (upon) me. Lo, the Peak of the West is merciful, when one calls to her.

What Nefer-abet, the triumphant, says. He says:

"See, and let every ear of him who lives upon earth hearken:—Beware of the Peak of the West!"

For a possible admission of error, much earlier than these penitential prayers, cf. the Instruction for King Meri-ka-Re, p. 416, n.17; p. 417 n.44.

For other hymns among these translations, see pp. 33-34, 431.

For other prayers among these translations, see pp. 3, 35-36, 253, 257, 448.

[1] A part of the Theban necropolis.

[2] The Egyptian women in childbirth sat upon a support of bricks, the "birth-stones" of Exod. 1:16.

[3] Of necropolis workmen.

Sumerian Petition

TRANSLATOR: S. N. KRAMER

Petition to a King

The following text represents an epistolary composition highly prized by the Babylonian scribes who developed it into a special literary genre. Quite a number of these "petitions" are now extant. They take the form of a letter addressed to a king or deity; in the latter case the writer of the petition may be the king himself.[1] In the text before us, an individual from Ur by the name of Urshagga probably addresses the petition letter to the king of Ur, whose name he unfortunately fails to mention. Three copies of this text have been found to date: two were excavated in the city of Erech, and one may come from Nippur. The latter was published by S. Langdon, *Babylonian Liturgies* (1913), No. 5; a transliteration and translation were published by the same author in *BE*, XXXI (1914), p. 25. Photographs of the two Erech tablets were published by A. Falkenstein together with an excellent transliteration, translation, and commentary, in *ZA*, XLIV (1936), 1-25. All three texts date from the first half of the second millennium B.C.

To my king with varicolored eyes who wears a lapis lazuli beard,[2]
Speak;
To[3] the golden statue fashioned on a good day,[4]
The . . .[5] raised in a pure sheepfold, called *to* the pure *womb*[6] of Inanna,
The lord, hero of Inanna, say:
"Thou (*in*) thy judgment[7] thou art the son of Anu,
Thy commands, like the word of a god, cannot be *turned back*,
Thy words like *rain* pouring down from heaven, are without number,[8]
Thus says Urshagga, thy servant:
'My king has cared for me, who am a "son" of Ur.
If now my king is (truly) of Anu,[9]
Let not my father's house be carried off,[10]
Let not the *foundations* of my father's house be torn away.
Let my king know.' "[11]

[1] In spite of their epistolary formulae, these "petitions" are, of course, not to be thought of as real letters forwarded by an individual who expects a letter in reply; they seem to be but another form of the "prayer" type of composition developed by the scribes in imitation of real letters with urgent appeal for help. As our text shows, in spite of their typical letter headings, these petitions are not written in prose; they have all the earmarks of Sumerian poetry.

[2] As Falkenstein, *loc. cit.*, p. 8, n.2, states, representations of the bearded ox may be found illustrated in Leonard Woolley's *Royal Tombs*, Pls. 107, 109, and 110.

[3] Falkenstein takes this "to" to refer to line 5 only (the Sumerian construction is unfortunately ambiguous) and treats lines 3 and 4 as a parenthetical passage addressed to the king.

[4] Perhaps, then, this petition is addressed to a dead, deified king of Ur whose statue was placed in the temple for veneration and worship.

[5] The Sumerian word left untranslated here is *áb-za-za*; its usual meanings are "monkey" and "sphinx."

[6] The Sumerian word is ambiguous; it usually means "heart" but may also be rendered "womb," cf. now particularly Jacobsen, *JNES*, II (1943), 119-121.

[7] For this rendering of the Sumerian word *dím*, cf. *AS* 12, p. 12, line 31. The sense of the line seems to be that this king's judgment is as trustworthy as that of a heavenly deity.

[8] Note that the present translation differs to some extent from that of Falkenstein; the implications of the line are not too clear.

[9] The implication of the words "of Anu" is not too clear; Falkenstein renders the line as: "As surely as my king is (the king) of Anu."

[10] To judge from this and the next line, Urshagga seems to be pleading for the safety of his family in the most general terms. For the passive renderings in this passage, cf. *BASOR*, 79 (1940), p. 21, n.5.

[11] Presumably a phrase such as "this my plea" is to be understood.

Sumero-Akkadian Hymns and Prayers

TRANSLATOR: FERRIS J. STEPHENS

Hymn to Ishtar

After extolling the charms and virtues of the goddess, the hymn concludes by enumerating the blessings which she has bestowed upon the king, Ammiditana. While these are represented as accomplished facts, the statements should be taken as indications of the hope of the king for their eventual realization. The text publication does not indicate the provenience of the tablet. It was written in the latter part of the First Dynasty of Babylon, approximately 1600 B.C. Text: *RA*, XXII, 170-1; translation: *RA*, XXII, 174-7; metrical transcription: *ZA*, XXXVIII, 19-22.

Praise the goddess, the most awesome of the goddesses.
Let one revere the mistress of the peoples, the greatest of the Igigi.[1]
Praise Ishtar, the most awesome of the goddesses.
Let one revere the queen of women, the greatest of the Igigi.

She is clothed with pleasure and love.
She is laden with vitality, charm, and voluptuousness.
Ishtar is clothed with pleasure and love.
She is laden with vitality, charm, and voluptuousness.

In lips she is sweet; life is in her mouth.
At her appearance rejoicing becomes full.
She is glorious; veils are thrown over her head.
Her figure is beautiful; her eyes are brilliant.

The goddess—with her there is counsel.
The fate of everything she holds in her hand.
At her glance there is created joy,
Power, magnificence, the protecting deity and guardian spirit.

She dwells in, she pays heed to compassion and friendliness.
Besides, agreeableness she truly possesses.
Be it slave, unattached girl, or mother, she preserves (her).
One calls on her; among women one names her name.

Who—to her greatness who can be equal?
Strong, exalted, splendid are her decrees.
Ishtar—to her greatness who can be equal?
Strong, exalted, splendid are her decrees.

She is sought after among the gods; extraordinary is her station.
Respected is her word; it is *supreme* over them.
Ishtar among the gods, extraordinary is her station.
Respected is her word; it is *supreme* over them.

She is their queen; they continually cause her commands to be executed.
All of them bow down before her.
They receive her light before her.
Women and men indeed revere her.

In their assembly her word is powerful; it is dominating.
Before Anum their king she fully supports them.
She rests in intelligence, cleverness, (and) wisdom.
They take counsel together, she and her lord.

Indeed they occupy the throne room together.
In the divine chamber, the dwelling of joy,
Before them the gods take their places.
To their utterances their attention is turned.

The king their favorite, beloved of their hearts,
Magnificently offers to them his pure sacrifices.
Ammiditana, as the pure offering of his hands,
Brings before them fat oxen and gazelles.

From Anum, her consort, she has been pleased to ask for him
An enduring, a long life.
Many years of living, to Ammiditana
She has granted, Ishtar has decided to give.

By her orders she has subjected to him
The four world regions at his feet;
And the total of all peoples
She has decided to attach them to his yoke.

[1] A collective name for the great gods of heaven.

Prayer of Lamentation to Ishtar

A prayer to be accompanied by a ritual of incantation. Ishtar, in her aspect as goddess of valor and of war, is addressed as the greatest of goddesses. The supplicant describes his bitter affliction and prays for a restoration of his prosperity, so that he and all who see him may praise and glorify the goddess. A colophon of the text indicates that it was the property of the temple Esagila in Babylon; and that it was copied from an older version at Borsippa. The extant text was written in the Neo-Babylonian period as, in all probability, was the older text from which it was copied. Text: L. W. King, *STC*, II, Pls. 75-84. Translations: *ibid.*, I, 222-37; A. Ungnad, *Die Religion der Babylonier und Assyrer* (Jena, 1921), 217-22; E. Ebeling, in *AOT*, 257-60.

I pray to thee, O Lady of ladies, goddess of goddesses.
O Ishtar, queen of all peoples, who guides mankind aright,
O Irnini,[1] ever exalted, greatest of the Igigi,[2]
O most mighty of princesses, exalted is thy name.
Thou indeed art the light of heaven and earth, O valiant daughter of Sin.
O supporter of arms, who determines battle,
O possessor of all divine power, who wears the crown of dominion,
O Lady, glorious is thy greatness; over all the gods it is exalted.
O star of lamentation, who causes peaceable brothers to fight,
Yet who constantly gives friendship,
O mighty one, Lady of battle, who suppresses the mountains,
O Gushea,[3] the one covered with fighting and clothed with terror
Thou dost make complete judgment and decision, the ordinances of heaven and earth.
Chapels, holy places, sacred sites, and shrines pay heed to thee.
Where is not thy name, where is not thy divine power?
Where are thy likenesses not fashioned, where are thy shrines not founded?
Where art thou not great, where art thou not exalted?
Anu, Enlil, and Ea have made thee high; among the gods they have caused thy dominion to be great.
They have made thee high among all the Igigi; they have made thy position pre-eminent.
At the thought of thy name heaven and earth tremble.
The gods tremble; the Anunnaki[4] stand in awe.
To thine awesome name mankind must pay heed.
For thou art great and thou art exalted.
All the black-headed (people and) the masses of mankind pay homage to thy might.
The judgment of the people in truth and righteousness thou indeed dost decide.
Thou regardest the oppressed and mistreated; daily thou causest them to prosper.
Thy mercy! O Lady of heaven and earth, shepherdess of the weary people.
Thy mercy! O Lady of holy Eanna[5] the pure storehouse.
Thy mercy! O Lady; unwearied are thy feet; swift are thy knees.
Thy mercy! O Lady of conflict (and) of all battles.
O shining one, lioness of the Igigi, subduer of angry gods,
O most powerful of all princes, who holdest the reins (over) kings,
(But) who dost release the *bridles* of all maidservants,
Who art exalted and firmly fixed, O valiant Ishtar, great is thy might.
O brilliant one, torch of heaven and earth, light of all peoples,
O unequaled angry one of the fight, strong one of the battle,
O firebrand which is kindled against the enemy, which brings about the destruction of the furious,
O gleaming one, Ishtar, assembler of the host,
O deity of men, goddess of women, whose designs no one can conceive,
Where thou dost look, one who is dead lives; one who is sick rises up;
The erring one who sees thy face goes aright.
I have cried to thee, suffering, wearied, and distressed, as thy servant.
See me O my Lady; accept my prayers.
Faithfully look upon me and hear my supplication.
Promise my forgiveness and let thy spirit be appeased.
Pity! For my wretched body which is full of confusion and trouble.
Pity! For my sickened heart which is full of tears and suffering.
Pity! For my wretched intestines (which are full of) confusion and trouble.
Pity! For my afflicted house which *mourns bitterly*.
Pity! For my feelings which are satiated with tears and suffering.
O *exalted* Irnini, fierce lion,[6] let thy heart be at rest.
O angry wild ox,[6] let thy spirit be appeased.
Let the favor of thine eyes be upon me.
With thy bright features look faithfully upon me.
Drive away the evil spells of my body (and) let me see thy bright light.
How long, O my Lady, shall my adversaries be looking upon me,
In lying and untruth shall they plan evil against me,
Shall my pursuers and those who exult over me rage against me?
How long, O my Lady, shall the crippled and weak seek me out?
One has made for me long sackcloth; thus I have appeared before thee.
The weak have become strong; but I am weak.
I toss about like flood-water, which an evil wind makes violent.
My heart is flying; it keeps fluttering like a bird of heaven.
I mourn like a dove night and day.
I am beaten down, and so I weep bitterly.
With "Oh" and "Alas" my spirit is distressed.
I—what have I done, O my god and my goddess?
Like one who does not fear my god and my goddess I am treated;

[1] Another name of the goddess Ishtar, probably derived ultimately from Inanna, her Sumerian counterpart.

[2] A collective name for the great gods of heaven.

[3] Another name for the goddess Ishtar, sometimes appearing as Agushea, or Agushaya.

[4] A collective name for the gods, not always used in the same sense. Sometimes it appears to mean all the gods of heaven and earth, sometimes the gods of the earth and the nether world, and again only the gods of the nether world.

[5] Name of the temple of Inanna-Ishtar in Uruk, biblical Erech.

[6] In line 31 Ishtar is called a lioness, but here in her aspect of the fighting deity she is designated even as male ferocious animals.

While sickness, headache, loss, and destruction are provided for me;
So are fixed upon me terror, disdain, and fullness of wrath,
Anger, choler, and indignation of gods and men.
I have to expect, O my Lady, dark days, gloomy months, and years of trouble.
I have to expect, O my Lady, judgment of confusion and violence.
Death and trouble are bringing me to an end.
Silent is my chapel; silent is my holy place;
Over my house, my gate, and my fields silence is poured out.
As for my god, his face is turned to the sanctuary of another.
My family is scattered; my roof is broken up.
(But) I have paid heed to thee, my Lady; my attention has been turned to thee.
To thee have I prayed; forgive my debt.
Forgive my sin, my iniquity, my shameful deeds, and my offence.
Overlook my shameful deeds; accept my prayer;
Loosen my fetters; secure my deliverance;
Guide my steps aright; radiantly like a hero let me enter the streets with the living.
Speak so that at thy command the angry god may be favorable;
(And) the goddess who has been angry with me may turn again.
(Now) dark and smoky, may my brazier glow;
(Now) extinguished, may my torch be lighted.
Let my scattered family be assembled;
May my fold be wide; may my stable be enlarged.
Accept the abasement of my countenance; hear my prayers.
Faithfully look upon me and accept my supplication.
How long, O my Lady, wilt thou be angered so that thy face is turned away?
How long, O my Lady, wilt thou be infuriated so that thy spirit is enraged?
Turn thy neck which thou hast set against me; set thy face [toward] good favor.
Like the water of the opening up of a canal let thy emotions be released.
My foes like the ground let me trample;
Subdue my haters and cause them to crouch down under me.
Let my prayers and my supplications come to thee.
Let thy great mercy be upon me.
Let those who see me in the street magnify thy name.
As for me, let me glorify thy divinity and thy might before the black-headed (people), [saying,]
Ishtar indeed is exalted; Ishtar indeed is queen;
The Lady indeed is exalted; the Lady indeed is queen.
Irnini, the valorous daughter of Sin, has no rival.

Hymn to the Moon-God

A bilingual, Sumerian and Akkadian, text portraying the attributes and aspects of Sin, the god of the moon. Following the part of the text here translated there was a prayer; but this part of the text is so poorly preserved that it has not been thought worth-while to give the fragmentary translation. The tablet was found at the site of ancient Nineveh. The writing of the text may be dated to the reign of Ashurbanipal, king of Assyria, 668-633 B.C. The tablet states that it was copied from an older tablet; but the date of the original composition of the text cannot be determined. Text: Rawlinson (2d ed.), IV, 9. Translations: S. Langdon, *Babylonian Penitential Psalms* (*OECT*, VI), 6-11; E. Ebeling in *AOT*, 241-2; Landsberger in E. Lehmann and H. Haas, *Textbuch zur Religionsgeschichte* (Leipzig, 1922), 301-3.

(obverse)

O Lord, hero of the gods, who in heaven and earth is exalted in his uniqueness,
Father Nanna, lord Anshar, hero of the gods,[1]
Father Nanna, great lord Anu, hero of the gods,
Father Nanna, lord Sin, hero of the gods,
Father Nanna, lord of Ur, hero of the gods,
Father Nanna, lord of Egishshirgal,[2] hero of the gods,
Father Nanna, lord of the shining crown, hero of the gods,
Father Nanna, who is grandly perfected in kingship, hero of the gods,
Father Nanna, who solemnly advances in garments of princeliness, hero of the gods,
Ferocious bull, whose horn is thick, whose legs are perfected, who is bearded in lapis, and filled with luxury and abundance,
Offspring which is self-created, fullgrown in form, pleasant to the sight, whose exuberance is unrestrained,
Womb that gives birth to everything, which dwells in a holy habitation with living creatures,
Begetter, merciful in his disposing,[3] who holds in his hand the life of the whole land,
O Lord, thy divinity fills the wide sea with awe, as well as the distant heavens.
O progenitor of the land, who has founded temples, thou likewise dost give them their names.
O father begetter of gods and men, who founds shrines and establishes offerings,
Namer of kingships, giver of the scepter, thou dost determine destiny unto distant days.
O mighty prince whose deep heart no one of the gods comprehends,
Swift colt whose knees do not tire, who opens the way for his brother gods,

[1] The words "who in heaven and earth is exalted in his uniqueness," though not written at the ends of lines 2-9, are intended to be repeated after each of these lines as part of the refrain. Of the four proper names with which the god is addressed in lines 2-4, Nanna is the Sumerian name of the moon-god, Sin is his Akkadian counterpart, Anshar is a primitive father of the gods mentioned in the Babylonian Creation Epic, and Anu is the god of heaven and chief of all the gods.

[2] Egishshirgal is the name of the temple of the moon-god in Ur.

[3] So apparently the Sumerian; the Akkadian has "merciful and forgiving."

Whose light goes from the base of heaven to the zenith, who opens the door of heaven and gives light to all people,
Father begetter, who looks favorably upon all living creatures....
O Lord, decider of the destinies of heaven and earth, whose word no one alters,
Who controls water and fire, leader of living creatures, what god is like thee?
In heaven who is exalted? Thou! Thou alone art exalted.
On earth who is exalted? Thou! Thou alone art exalted.
Thou! When thy word is pronounced in heaven the Igigi prostrate themselves.
Thou! When thy word is pronounced on earth the Anunnaki kiss the ground.
Thou! When thy word drifts along in heaven like the wind it makes rich the feeding and drinking of the land.

(reverse)

Thou! When thy word settles down on the earth green vegetation is produced.
Thou! Thy word makes fat the sheepfold and the stall; it makes living creatures widespread.
Thou! Thy word causes truth and justice to be, so that the people speak the truth.
Thou! Thy word which is far away in heaven, which is hidden in the earth is something no one sees.
Thou! Who can comprehend thy word, who can equal it?
O Lord, in heaven as to dominion, on earth as to valor, among the gods thy brothers, thou hast not a rival.

Prayer to the Moon-God

A prayer to accompany an offering made on the thirtieth day of the month, a festival of the Moon-god. This prayer belongs to the common type of prayers used with the ritual of *šu íl-la* "raising of the hand." After a lengthy invocation of hymnic character, the supplicant prays for general well-being as well as for forgiveness of his sins. The text from which the translation is made comes from tablets found in the library of Ashurbanipal, king of Assyria, 668-633 B.C. For duplicates see Walter G. Kunstmann, *Die babylonische Gebetsbeschwörung* (Leipzig, 1932), 103. Text: L. W. King, *Babylonian Magic and Sorcery* (London, 1896), No. 1, lines 1-27. Translations: E. G. Perry, *Hymnen und Gebete an Sin* (Leipzig, 1907), 12-16; H. Zimmern, *AO*, XIII/1 (1911), 4-5.

O Sin, O Nannar, glorified one . . . ,
Sin, unique one, who makes bright . . . ,
Who furnishes light for the people . . . ,
To guide the dark-headed people aright . . . ,
Bright is thy light in heaven. . . .
Brilliant is thy torch like fire. . . .
Thy brightness has filled the broad land.
The people are radiant; they take courage at seeing thee.
O Anu[1] of heaven whose designs no one can conceive,
Surpassing is thy light like Shamash thy first-born.
Bowed down in thy presence are the great gods; the decisions of the land are laid before thee;
When the great gods inquire of thee thou dost give counsel.
They sit (in) their assembly (and) debate under thee;
O Sin, shining one of Ekur,[2] when they ask thee thou dost give the oracle of the gods.
On account of the evil of an eclipse of the moon which took place in such and such a month, on such and such a day,[3]
On account of the evil of bad and unfavorable portents and signs which have happened in my palace and my country,[3]
In the dark of the moon, the time of thy oracle, the mystery of the great gods,
On the thirtieth day, thy festival, the day of delight of thy divinity,
O Namrasit,[4] unequaled in power, whose designs no one can conceive,
I have spread out for thee a pure incense-offering of the night; I have poured out for thee the best sweet drink.
I am kneeling; I tarry (thus); I seek after thee.
Bring upon me wishes for well-being and justice.
May my god and my goddess, who for many days have been angry with me,
In truth and justice be favorable to me; may my road be propitious; may my path be straight.[5]
After he[6] has sent Zaqar, the god of dreams,
During the night may I hear the undoing of my sins; let my guilt be poured out;
(And) forever let me devotedly serve thee.

Prayer of Ashurbanipal to the Sun-God

This text is in reality a hymn of praise to the god Shamash, to which has been appended a prayer for the well-being of Ashurbanipal, king of Assyria, 668-633 B.C. This composition has a feature in its final lines which is unusual for hymns and prayers, but which is reminiscent of numerous royal inscriptions from very early times in Mesopotamia; a blessing is pronounced on whoever makes proper use of the piece, and a corresponding curse is added for its misuse. Duplicate copies of the text are preserved on two tablets found in the German excavations at Ashur. Text: E. Ebeling, *KAR*, Nos. 105, 361. Translations: E. Ebeling, Quellen zur Kenntnis der babylonischen Religion, *MVAG*, XXIII (1918), 1, 25-7; E. Ebeling in *AOT*, 247-8.

[1] Thus the moon-god is identified with the chief god of the pantheon.
[2] The name of the principal temple in Nippur.
[3] These two lines stand after line 11 in the original text. They represent a later insertion in the text, which interrupts the sense awkwardly. I have ventured to transpose them to the present place in the translation, where I believe the interpolator intended them to stand.
[4] A name of the moon-god meaning "bright rising."
[5] The text has a mark of division in the midst of this line, at a point corresponding to the first semicolon in the translation. The probable meaning of this is that the line formed two separate lines in an earlier tablet from which our copy was made.
[6] The personal deity mentioned two lines above.

O light of the great gods, light of the earth, illuminator of the world-regions,
. . . exalted judge, the honored one of the upper and lower regions,
. . .[1] Thou dost look into all the lands with thy light.
As one who does not cease from revelation, daily thou dost determine the decisions of heaven and earth.
Thy [rising] is a flaming fire; all the stars of heaven are covered over.
Thou art uniquely brilliant; no one among the gods is equal with thee.
With Sin, thy father, thou dost hold court; thou dost deliver ordinances.
Anu and Enlil without thy *consent* establish no decision.
Ea, the determiner of judgment in the midst of the Deep, depends upon thee.[2]
The attention of all the gods is turned to thy bright rising.
They *inhale* incense; they receive pure bread-offerings.
The incantation priests [bow down] under thee in order to cause signs of evil to pass away.
The oracle priests [stand before] thee in order to make the hands worthy to bring oracles.
[I am] thy [servant], Ashurbanipal, the exercising of whose kingship thou didst command in a vision,
[The worshiper of] thy bright divinity, who makes glorious the appurtenances of thy divinity,
[The proclaimer of] thy greatness, who glorifies thy praise to widespread peoples.
Judge his case; turn his fate to prosperity.
[Keep] him in splendor; daily let him walk safely.
[Forever] may he rule over thy people whom thou hast given him in righteousness.
[In the house] which he made, and within which he caused thee to dwell in joy,
May he rejoice in his heart, in his disposition may he be happy, may he be satisfied in living.
Whoever shall sing this psalm, (and) name the name of Ashurbanipal,
In abundance and righteousness may he rule over the people of Enlil.
Whoever shall learn this text (and) glorify the judge of the gods,
May Shamash enrich his . . . ; may he make pleasing his command over the people.
Whoever shall cause this song to cease, (and) shall not glorify Shamash, the light of the great gods,
Or shall change the name of Ashurbanipal, the exercise of whose kingship Shamash in a vision commanded, and then shall name another royal name,
May his playing on the harp be displeasing to the people; may his song of rejoicing be a thorn and a thistle.

[1] Two words, *tikip satakki,* which appear in the text at this point, are not included in the translation because they appear not to have formed part of the original composition. They probably constitute a note inserted by the scribe when he was copying the text from another tablet. Von Soden in *ZDMG* XCI (1937), 193, and Thureau-Dangin in *Textes mathématiques babyloniens* (Leyden, 1938), xvii, have pointed out that *satakku* is a loan word from Sumerian meaning a single "wedge" of cuneiform writing. The word *tikpu* means "layer," "section," or "row." The phrase here probably means, "a line of cuneiform writing." The most probable explanation is that the phrase was inserted here by the scribe to represent a line on his original which was damaged or for some reason was too obscure to be copied.

[2] Literally, "looks upon thy face."

Hymn to the Sun-God

Shamash is praised as a universal god. He shines on all the earth and even on the nether world. He enjoys the worship and devotion of all types of mankind even those in foreign lands. Appearing alternately with this thought throughout the hymn is the proclamation of the sun-god's interest in justice and righteousness. He punishes the wicked and rewards the righteous. The text is made up out of many fragments, all found in the library of Ashurbanipal, 668-633 B.C. The best edition of the text is that of C. D. Gray, *The Šamaš Religious Texts* (Chicago, 1901), Pls. I-II, to which must be added, R. E. Brünnow, Assyrian Hymns, *ZA*, IV (1889), 25-35. Translations: P. A. Schollmeyer, *Sumerisch-babylonische Hymnen und Gebete an Šamaš* (Paderborn, 1912), 80-94; E. Ebeling, in *AOT*, 244-47; F. M. Th. Böhl, De zonnegod als de beschermer der nooddruftigen, *JEOL* (1942), 665-80.

(i)

O illuminator of [darkness . . .],
Destroyer of [evil . . .] above and below,
O Shamash, illuminator of [darkness . . .],
Destroyer of [evil . . .] above and below,
Cast down like a net [over the land] are thy rays;
Over the mighty mountains . . . of the sea.
At thy appearance [all] princes are glad;
All the Igigi[1] rejoice over thee.
They are always kept hidden [in] thy . . . ;
In the brilliance of thy light their path [is obscured].
. . . constantly look at thy radiance.
The four world regions like fire. . . .
Opened wide is the gate which entirely. . . .
The bread-offerings of all the Igigi. . . .
O Shamash, at thy rising . . . are bowed down.
. . . O Shamash . . . ,
O shining one, who opens the darkness, who . . . ,
Who intensifies the noonday heat . . . the grain fields.
The mighty mountains are covered with thy brightness.
Thy brilliance fills the extent of the land.
(When) thou art risen over the mountains thou dost scan the earth.
Thou art holding the ends of the earth suspended from the midst of heaven.
The people of the world, all of them, thou dost watch over.
Whatever Ea, the counselor-king, has willed to create, thou art guarding altogether.
Those endowed with life, thou likewise dost tend;
Thou indeed art their shepherd both above and below.
Faithfully thou dost continue to pass through the heavens;

[1] A collective name for the great gods of heaven.

The broad earth thou dost visit daily.
. . . the sea, the mountains, the earth, and the heavens.
Like a . . . steadfastly thou goest every day.
The lower region, belonging to the prince Kubu[2] (and) the Anunnaki,[3] thou dost guard;
The upper world, consisting of all inhabited places, thou dost lead aright.
Shepherd of the lower world, guardian of the upper,
Guide, light of everything, O Shamash, art thou.
Thou dost constantly pass over the vast wide seas,
Whose innermost depths even the Igigi do not know.
. . . thy gleaming rays go down into the Deep;
The monsters of the sea look upon thy light.
. . . when thou art bound with a cord, when thou art clothed with a storm-cloud,
. . . thy protection is cast down on the lands.
As thou art [not] troubled in the daytime, and thy face is not darkened,
So thou art satiated at night; thou causest [thy light] to burn.
Over stretches of unknown distance and for countless hours,
O Shamash, thou dost keep awake; by day thou dost go and by night thou dost [return].
There is not among all the Igigi one who wearies (himself) except thee;
(Yet) none among the gods of all the world who is exuberant like thee.
At thy rising the gods of the land assemble;
By thy frightful brilliance the land is overwhelmed.
Of all countries (even) those different in language,
Thou knowest their plans; thou art observant of their course.
All mankind rejoices in thee;
O Shamash, all the world longs for thy light.
By the cup of the diviner, by the bundle of cedarwood,
Thou dost instruct the oracle priest and the interpreter of dreams.
. . . of spells are bowed down before thee;
[Before] thee are bowed down both the wicked and the just.

(ii)

[Who] penetrates into the sea except thee?
For the good and the wicked (alike) thou dost set up judgment.
(line 3 is too incomplete for translation)
Pours over him, and sleep . . .
Thou dost hold back the evildoer, who is not . . .
Thou dost bring up . . . which holds judgments.
By the true judgment, O Shamash, which thou hast spoken . . .
Glorious are thy pronouncements; they are not changed . . .
Thou dost stand by the traveler whose road is difficult;
To the seafarer who fears the waters thou dost give [courage].
(Over) roads which are not proven thou dost [guide] the hunter;
He follows along the high places just like the sun.
[The merchant with his] pouch thou dost save from the flood.
(seventeen broken lines omitted)
Spread out is thy wide net [to catch the man]
Who has coveted the wife of his comrade . . .
On an unlucky day . . .
(line omitted)
When thy weapon *is turned on him* [he has] no saviors.
In his trial his father will not stand by him;
To the word of the judge even his brothers do not answer;
By a *bronze trap* he will be caught unawares.
The horn of the perpetrator of abomination thou dost destroy.
He who manipulates the calculating of an account[4]—his foundation will be changed.
The unrighteous judge thou dost make to see imprisonment.
The receiver of a bribe who perverts (justice) thou dost make to bear punishment.
He who does not accept a bribe (but) intercedes for the weak,
Is well-pleasing to Shamash (and) enriches (his) life.
The solicitous judge who pronounces a judgment of righteousness,
Shall prepare a palace; the abode of princes (shall be) his dwelling.
He who invests money at an exorbitant rate of reckoning—what does he gain?
He will make himself lie for the profit and then lose (his) bag of weights.[5]
He who invests his money at liberal rates of reckoning, yielding one shekel for *three*,[6]
Is well-pleasing to Shamash, (and) enriches his life.
He who handles the scales in falsehood,
He who deliberately changes the stone weights (and) lowers [their weight,]
Will make himself lie for the profit and then lose [his bag of weights.]
He who handles the scales in truth, much . . .
As much as possible . . .
He who handles the measure . . .

(iii)

(six broken lines omitted)
He is well-pleasing to Shamash (and) enriches his life.

[2] The reading of the name of this deity is not certain; other readings, which have been proposed and which may be correct, are Kusud, or Kusig.

[3] See above, the Prayer of Lamentation to Ishtar, n.4.

[4] The word *šiddu* appears to be borrowed from Sumerian šid "reckoning," although it has not been recognized as such in the previous translations of this text, nor in the existing Akkadian dictionaries. The phrase *epeš šiddi* is an exact translation of Sumerian šid ag "to render an account."

[5] The word for "bag of weights" may also be translated "capital."

[6] The translation is based on a restoration which is uncertain but probable. Such an interest rate is very common in Babylonian contracts; higher rates are also frequent.

He will expand (his) family; he will acquire wealth.
Like the water of eternal springs, there shall be enduring seed
For the doer of good deeds, who is not crafty in accounts.
He who changes the least (thing) in an offering of . . .[7]
Those who do evil—their seed shall not endure.
Those who make appeal[8]—it is put before thee;
Quickly thou dost interpret their statements.[9]
Thou dost hearken; thou dost support them; thou dost reinstate the right of him who has been badly treated.
Each and every one is kept by thy hand;
Thou dost guide all their omens aright; what is bound thou dost loosen.
Thou hearkenest, O Shamash, to prayer, supplication, and adoration;
To devotion (and) kneeling, to reciting of prayers and prostration.
In his hollow voice the feeble man calls out to thee;
The miserable, the weak, the mistreated, the poor man
Comes before thee faithfully with psalms (and) offerings.
When his family is distant, his city is far away,
From the fear of the (open) field, the shepherd comes before thee.
The shepherd boy in confusion, the shepherd among enemies
O Shamash, comes before thee. The *caravan* which marches in fear,
The traveling trader, the peddler carrying the bag of weights,
O Shamash, comes before thee. The net-fisherman,
The hunter, the fighter and guard against animals
In the hiding place, the bird-catcher comes before thee.
The burglar, the thief, the enemy of the king,[10]
The vagabond in the roads of the desert, comes before thee.
The wandering dead, the fleeting ghosts
Came before thee, O Shamash . . .
Thou didst not exclude; they came before thee . . .
(three broken lines omitted)
[To guide] their omens [aright] thou art sitting on *a throne.*
In all directions thou dost investigate their past.

[7] The Akkadian for "in an offering of . . ." is *ina maš-da-ri šá. . . .* This might also be read: *ina maš-ṭa-ri šá-[ṭa-ri]* "in writing an inscription," The same word *maš-da-ri*, however, appears in line 22 below, where it seems certain that it means "offering."

[8] Literally: "those who make their mouth high."

[9] Literally: "Thou dost hasten; thou dost loosen the issue of their mouth."

[10] The word translated "king" means literally "sun" and is fundamentally the same word as the name of the sun-god. In this case the scribe has indicated by a phonetic complement that the word is to be read *šamši*; elsewhere in the text he writes the name of the sun-god consistently without a phonetic complement even when it is grammatically in the genitive case. It is probable, then, that the sun-god is not meant here. Frankfort has pointed out in *Kingship and the Gods*, 307-8, that in Mesopotamia as well as in Egypt the king often bore the epithet "the sun." Such an interpretation of the text fits in well here with the general context.

Thou dost open the ears of the whole world.
For the wings of the glance of thine eyes the heavens are not sufficient;
For a divination bowl all the countries are not enough.
On the twentieth day thou dost rejoice; in joy and gladness
Thou dost eat and drink. Their pure wine (and) beer of the quay tavern-keeper
They pour out for thee. Beer of the quay tavern-keeper thou dost receive.
Those whom . . . and flood surround thou indeed dost spare;
Their bright, pure outpourings thou dost accept.
Thou dost drink their mixture, the wine;
The wishes which they conceive thou indeed dost cause to be realized.
Those who are submissive—thou dost release their bans;
Those who do homage—thou dost accept their prayers.
They then fear thee; they honor thy name;
They praise thy greatness forever.
The foolish of tongue who speak evil,
Who, like clouds, have no face or *countenance,*

(iv)

Those who traverse the wide earth,
Those who tread upon the high mountains,
The monsters of the sea which are full of terror,
The product of the sea (and) what belongs in the Deep,
The spawn of the river which it produces from itself, (all) O Shamash, are in thy presence.
Which are the mountains that have not clothed themselves with thy brilliance?
Which are the world regions that do not warm themselves by the glow of thy light?
O brightener of gloom, who makes darkness to shine,
O opener of darkness, who makes the broad earth to shine,
Who makes the day bright (and) sends down burning heat on the earth in the midday,
Who like a fire heats the broad earth,
Who makes days short, who makes nights long,
. . . cold (and) frost, rain (and) snow,
(twenty more fragmentary lines)

Psalm to Marduk

The one purpose of this composition is to establish a quiet and favorable mood in the god Marduk, when he is returned to his temple, after a long ceremony known as the Akîtu, or New Year's Festival. To this end the principal temples where he is worshiped, and all the main gods are invoked, and asked to say to him, "Be appeased." This word is common to three slightly different refrains which run throughout the composition, at the ends of the lines. The most complete copy of the text is from a tablet found at Babylon. Other copies existed at Nineveh, and fragments of two of them are known from the time of Ashurbanipal, 668-633 B.C. The Babylonian text is said to have been copied from an older tablet. To judge from the name of the scribe, Bel-ahhim-iribam, this was done in Neo-Babylonian times. The date of the original composition can not be determined. It appears to have been written in Sumerian.

The extant copies are in the Emesal dialect of Sumerian with interlinear translation in Akkadian. Text: F. H. Weissbach, *Babylonische Miscellen* (Leipzig, 1903), Pls. xiii-xiv; Rawlinson, iv (2d ed.), 18, No. 2; *ibid.*, Additions and Corrections, p. 3. Translations: P. Jensen, *Texte zur assyrisch-babylonischen Religion* (*Keilinschriftliche Bibliothek*, vi, 2 [Berlin, 1915]), 36-41; A. Ungnad, *Die Religion der Babylonier und Assyrer* (Jena, 1921), 169-172; E. Ebeling, *AOT*, 256-7.

O Lord, at thy going into the temple [may thy house say to thee, "Be appeased."][1]
O Prince, Lord Marduk, at thy going into the temple, may thy house . . . .[2]
O great hero, Lord Enbilulu[3] at thy going into the temple, may thy house . . . .
Be appeased, O Lord; be appeased, O Lord; may thy house . . . .
Be appeased, O Lord of Babylon; may thy house . . . .
Be appeased, O Lord of Esagila;[4] may thy house . . . .
Be appeased, O Lord of Ezida;[5] may thy house . . . .
Be appeased, O Lord of Emachtila;[6] may thy house . . . .
(In) Esagila the house of thy lordship, may thy house . . . .
May thy city say to thee, "Be appeased"; may thy house . . . .
May Babylon say to thee, "Be appeased"; may thy house . . . .
May Anu the great, father of the gods, say to thee, "How long," (and) "Be appeased."[7]
May the great mountain, father Enlil, (say to thee) "How long," . . . .
May the princess of city and house, the great mother, Ninlil, (say to thee) "How long," . . . .
May Ninurta, the chief son of Enlil, the exalted arm of Anu, (say to thee) "How long," . . . .
May Sin, the lamp of heaven and earth, (say to thee) "How long," . . . .
May the hero Shamash, the bearded one, son of Ningal (say to thee) "How long," . . . .
May Ea, king of the Deep, (say to thee) "How long," . . . .
May Damkina, queen of the Deep, (say to thee) "How long," . . . .
May Sarpanitum, daughter-in-law of the Deep (say to thee), "How long," . . . .
May . . . Nabu (say to thee) "How long," . . . .
May . . . first born of Urash (say to thee) "How long," . . . .
May . . . Tashmetum say to thee, "How long," (and) "Be appeased."[8]
May the great princess, the lady Nana, (say to thee), "How long," . . . .
May the Lord Madana, director of the Anunnaki, (say to thee), "How long," . . . .
May Baba, the gracious lady, (say to thee), "How long," . . . .
May Adad, the son beloved of Anu, (say to thee), "How long," . . . .
May Shala, the great wife, (say to thee), "How long," . . . .
O Lord, mighty one who dwells in Ekur[9] let thine own divine spirit bring thee rest.
O thou who art the hero of the gods—may the gods of heaven and earth cause thine anger to be appeased.
Do not neglect thy city, Nippur; "O Lord, be appeased," may they say to thee.[10]
Do not neglect thy city, Sippar; "O Lord, be appeased," . . . .
Do not neglect Babylon, the city of thy rejoicing; "O Lord, be appeased," . . . .
Look favorably on thy house; look favorably on thy city; "O Lord, be appeased," . . . .
Look favorably on Babylon and Esagila; "O Lord, be appeased," . . . .
The bolt of Babylon, the lock of Esagila, the bricks of Ezida restore thou to their places; "O Lord, be appeased," may the gods of heaven and earth say to thee.[11]

1 The restoration is made on the basis of the following lines and in particular lines 31 and 36, following also Langdon, *Babylonian Penitential Psalms*, ix.

2 It is intended that the first eleven lines should all end with the same refrain as line 1, although the text actually gives only the first word of the refrain in 2-11.

3 One of the "Fifty Names" of Marduk listed in the seventh tablet of the Babylonian Creation Epic.

4 The name of the chief temple of Marduk, located in Babylon and known from Old Babylonian times until the Hellenistic period.

5 Although there was a chapel in the temple of Esagila known as Ezida, it is not probable that it is meant here; more likely the reference is to the great temple in Borsippa. It is true that Ezida of Borsippa was a temple of Nabu, but it is not inappropriate to call Marduk, the chief of the gods in Neo-Babylonian times, the "Lord of Ezida," especially since he seems to have been associated with this temple even as early as the time of Hammurabi.

6 A principal sanctuary in the temple of Ezida at Borsippa.

7 The refrain is now augmented by the words, "How long?" and continues in this form through line 28, although in its written form it appears only represented by the first word. "How long?" is an abbreviated exclamation, meaning, "How long will you remain in your present state? Is it not time for a change?"

8 The refrain is written out in full in this line because it is the first line on the reverse of the tablet.

9 The historic temple of Enlil in the city of Nippur. Since Marduk in Neo-Babylonian theology had been assigned the position that Enlil once held it is quite in order to say that he dwells in Ekur.

10 After two lines (29-30) without a refrain, the response now assumes its third form and continues so to the end.

11 The original composition seems to have ended here; but the Assyrian copy adds the following prayer: "Make Ashurbanipal, the shepherd, thy sustainer, to live; hear his prayer; lay well the foundation of the seat of his royalty; the control of the people let him hold unto distant days."

Prayer to the Gods of the Night

The occasion for this prayer is a divination ceremony carried on at night. The great gods who ordinarily control the affairs of the world are regarded as resting in sleep; and therefore the gods represented by several of the constellations of fixed stars are asked to witness the performance and to guarantee that truth will be revealed. The place from which this text comes is not known, but it was written in the Old Babylonian period, in the first half of the second millennium B.C. It is written in the Akkadian language and the Babylonian cursive script. Two slightly variant copies of the text are known, one of which is on a tablet giving two additional prayers of similar nature. These latter are not given here because they are somewhat fragmentary. Text A: V. K. Shileiko, *Izvestija Rossijskoj*

Akademii istorii material'noj kul'tury, III (Leningrad, 1924), 147; photograph, *ibid.*, Pl. VIII. Text B: G. Dossin, *RA*, XXXII (1935), 182-3. Translations: G. Dossin, *RA*, XXXII (1935), 179-187; W. von Soden, *ZA*, XLIII (1936), 305-8.

They are lying down, the great ones.[1]
The bolts are fallen; the fastenings are placed.
The crowds and people are quiet.
The open gates are (now) closed.
The gods of the land and the goddesses of the land,
Shamash, Sin, Adad, and Ishtar,[2]
Have betaken themselves to sleep in heaven.
They are not pronouncing judgment;
They are not deciding things.
Veiled is the night;[3]
The temple and the most holy places are quiet and dark.
The traveler calls on (his) god;[4]
And the litigant is tarrying in sleep.[5]
The judge of truth, the father of the fatherless,[6]
Shamash, has betaken himself to his chamber.
O great ones, gods of the night,[7]
O bright one, Gibil,[8] O warrior, Irra,[9]
O bow (star) and yoke (star),[10]
O Pleiades, Orion, and the dragon,[11]
O Ursa major, goat (star), and the bison,
Stand by, and then,
In the divination which I am making,
In the lamb which I am offering,[12]
Put truth for me.

[1] The word literally means "princes" and is an epithet of the gods.
[2] B has: "Adad and Ea, Shamash and Ishtar."
[3] The meaning is, "the night has put on its veil and hence the world has become dark."
[4] Instead of "calls on his god" B has, "prays to the god Nergal." The cuneiform signs involved are enough alike that one may have been mistakenly copied for the other.
[5] The litigant is contrasted with the traveler of the previous line. The reference in both cases is probably to tradespeople. When a trader entered a town he was frequently haled into court to settle some legal matter connected with his transactions.
[6] B has "truth" instead of "fatherless."
[7] This line in B is transposed to stand after line 20.
[8] The fire-god.
[9] A god of the nether world.
[10] B mentions only one constellation in this line, "the Elamite bow."
[11] A omits the Pleiades.
[12] A has "prayer" instead of "lamb."

Prayer to Every God

This prayer is addressed to no particular god, but to all gods in general, even those who may be unknown. The purpose of the prayer is to claim relief from suffering, which the writer understands is the result of some infraction of divine law. He bases his claim on the fact that his transgressions have been committed unwittingly, and that he does not even know what god he may have offended. Moreover, he claims, the whole human race is by nature ignorant of the divine will, and consequently is constantly committing sin. He therefore ought not to be singled out for punishment. The text is written in the Emesal dialect of Sumerian, furnished with an interlinear Akkadian translation. The colophon of the tablet indicates that it was part of a series of prayers, the next tablet of which began with the line "By his word he has commanded my well-being." The tablet comes from the library of Ashurbanipal, 668-633 B.C., and was copied from an older original. There are, however, numerous features of the Sumerian text which are characteristic of the late period, and it is probable that the original composition of the text is not much older than Ashurbanipal. Text: Rawlinson, IV (2d ed.), 10. Translations: A. Ungnad, *Die Religion der Babylonier und Assyrer* (Jena, 1921), 224-7; E. Ebeling, in *AOT*, 261-2; S. Langdon, *Babylonian Penitential Psalms* (Paris, 1927), 39-44.

May the fury of my lord's heart be quieted toward me.[1]
May the god who is not known be quieted toward me;
May the goddess who is not known be quieted toward me.
May the god whom I know or do not know be quieted toward me;
May the goddess whom I know or do not know be quieted toward me.
May the heart of my god be quieted toward me;
May the heart of my goddess be quieted toward me.
May my god and goddess be quieted toward me.
May the god [who has become angry with me][2] be quieted toward me;
May the goddess [who has become angry with me] be quieted toward me.
(lines 11-18 cannot be restored with certainty)
In ignorance I have eaten that forbidden of my god;
In ignorance I have set foot on that prohibited by my goddess.
O Lord, my transgressions are many; great are my sins.
O my god, (my) transgressions are many; great are (my) sins.
O my goddess, (my) transgressions are many; great are (my) sins.
O god whom I know or do not know, (my) transgressions are many; great are (my) sins;
O goddess whom I know or do not know, (my) transgressions are many; great are (my) sins.
The transgression which I have committed, indeed I do not know;
The sin which I have done, indeed I do not know.
The forbidden thing which I have eaten, indeed I do not know;
The prohibited (place) on which I have set foot, indeed I do not know.
The lord in the anger of his heart looked at me;
The god in the rage of his heart confronted me;
When the goddess was angry with me, she made me become ill.
The god whom I know or do not know has oppressed me;
The goddess whom I know or do not know has placed suffering upon me.
Although I am constantly looking for help, no one takes me by the hand;
When I weep they do not come to my side.

[1] Literally the Sumerian says, "Of my lord, may his angry heart return to its place for me." The phrase "return to its place" is figurative language meaning "to settle down"; the imagery may be that of a raging storm or of the contents of a boiling kettle. The scribe indicates that each of the next nine lines ends with the same phrase, although he actually writes only the first word of the phrase after having written it once fully.
[2] The restoration is based on line 32, after Langdon.

I utter laments, but no one hears me;
I am troubled; I am overwhelmed; I can not see.
O my god, merciful one, I address to thee the prayer, "Ever incline to me";
I kiss the feet of my goddess; I crawl before thee.
(lines 41-49 are mostly broken and cannot be restored with certainty)
How long, O my goddess, whom I know or do not know, ere thy hostile heart will be quieted?
Man is dumb; he knows nothing;
Mankind, everyone that exists,—what does he know?
Whether he is committing sin or doing good, he does not even know.
O my lord, do not cast thy servant down;
He is plunged into the waters of a swamp; take him by the hand.
The sin which I have done, turn into goodness;
The transgression which I have committed, let the wind carry away;
My many misdeeds strip off like a garment.
O my god, (my) transgressions are seven times seven; remove my transgressions;
O my goddess, (my) transgressions are seven times seven; remove my transgressions;
O god whom I know or do not know, (my) transgressions are seven times seven; remove my transgressions;
O goddess whom I know or do not know, (my) transgressions are seven times seven; remove my transgressions.
Remove my transgressions (and) I will sing thy praise.
May thy heart, like the heart of a real mother, be quieted toward me;
Like a real mother (and) a real father may it be quieted toward me.

Hittite Prayers

TRANSLATOR: ALBRECHT GOETZE

Prayer of Pudu-hepas[1] to the Sun-Goddess of Arinna and her Circle

Text: *KUB*, XXI, 27. Literature: Short quotations were given by E. Forrer, *Reallexikon der Assyriologie*, I (1929), 150 and by A. Götze, *Kulturgeschichte Kleinasiens* (1933), 129.

A. PRAYER TO THE SUN-GODDESS HERSELF

To the Sun-goddess of Arinna, my lady, the mistress of the Hatti lands, the queen of heaven and earth.

O Sun-goddess of Arinna, queen of all the countries! In the Hatti country thou bearest the name of the Sun-goddess of Arinna; but in the land which thou madest the cedar land thou bearest the name Hebat. I, Pudu-hepas, am a servant of thine from of old, a heifer from thy stable, a foundation stone (upon which) thou (canst rest). Thou, my lady, rearedst me and Hattusilis, thy servant, to whom thou espousedst me, was *closely* associated with the Storm-god of Nerik, thy beloved son. The place in which thou, Sun-goddess of Arinna, my lady, didst establish us was the residence of the Storm-god of Nerik, thy beloved son. How the earlier kings had neglected it, that thou knowest, Sun-goddess of Arinna, my lady. The earlier kings let [fall into ruins] even those countries which thou, Sun-goddess of Arinna, my lady, hadst given them.

(Small gap in which Hattusilis' achievements during the reign of his brother Muwatallis were related.)

[When he was king in] the country of Nerik and in the country of [Hakpis], he himself and his [soldiery kept in the field] while he (Muwatallis) waged war against [Egypt].

But when Muwatallis, [thy servant,] became god,[2] he (Hattusilis) took his [son] Urhi-Tessub and established him as king. How [Urhi-Tessub limited] Hattusilis, thy servant, to Nerik, that thou knowest, Sun-goddess of Arinna, my lady. How he harried his lord, and (how) they rallied the princes (with the call): "Come! To Nerik!" [that thou kno]west [Sun-goddess of Arinna, my lady]. That man[3] counted its ruin and its doom as naught: "Let there be death in Nerik! Let us throw Nerik into ruin!"

(small gap)

[In the way in which it is right to perform purifications, in the way in which ye want to be worshiped, in the way in which it is right to attend to your festivals] (ii) [thus] we shall perform the purifications, thus we shall worship you the gods, thus we shall attend to the ordinances (and) celebrations due to you, the gods. The festivals of you, the gods, which they had stopped, the old festivals, the yearly ones and the monthly ones, they shall celebrate for you, the gods. Your festivals, O gods, my lords, shall never be stopped again! For all our days will we, your servant (and) your handmaid, worship you.

This is what I, Pudu-hepas, thy handmaid, lay in prayer before the Sun-goddess of Arinna, my lady, the lady of the Hatti lands, the queen of heaven and earth. Sun-goddess of Arinna, my lady, yield to me, hearken to me! Among men there is a saying: "To a woman in travail the god yields her wish." [Since] I, Pudu-hepas, am a woman in travail (and since) I have devoted myself to thy son, yield to me, Sun-goddess of Arinna, my lady! Grant to me what [I ask]! Grant life to [Hattusilis, thy serv]ant! Through [the Good-women] (and) the Mother-goddesses [long (and) enduring] years (and) days shall be [gi]ven to him. [Since] thou, an exalted deity, holdest [a place set apart among the gods], all the gods are [subservient to thee], and no one appeals [to thee in vain]. In [the assembly] of all the gods request thou the life [of Hattusilis]! May [thy] request be received with favor! Because thou, [Sun-goddess] of Arinna, my [lady], hast shown favor to me and (because) the [g]ood of [the land] and of its realm [is close to thy heart], thou shalt enjoy the reverent [worship] of [my fam]ily. Where[as I have now pacified] thy soul, Sun-goddess of Arinna, my lady, hearken to whatever I lay before thee in prayer on [this] day! [Do something] for this cause! Let not the gods re[ject my] request!

(gap)

B. PRAYER TO LELWANIS[4]

. . . (iii) Hattusilis, that servant of thine, who [is ill]. In the presence of Sum[. . .], the physician, they spoke charms over him [. . .]. If [Hattusilis is accur]sed, and if Hattusilis, [my husband], has become [hateful] in the eyes of you, the gods; or (if) anyone of the gods above or below has taken offence at him; or (if) anyone has made an offering to the gods to bring evil upon Hattusilis—accept not those evil words, O goddess, my lady! Let evil not touch Hattusilis, thy servant! O gods, prefer not [our] advers[aries],

[1] Hittite queen and consort of Hattusilis, the son of Mursilis.
[2] i.e. died.
[3] Urhi-Tessub is meant; the expression is derogatory.

[4] This is probably the Hittite pronunciation of the name which is otherwise spelled "Ishtar" of Samuha; she was Hattusilis' special patroness.

(our) enviers (and our) . . . [. . .]. to us! If thou, goddess, my lady, wilt grant him life and relay to the gods, thy peers, the good (word), and (if) thou wilt tread under foot the evil words and shut them out—O Lelwanis, my lady, may the life of Hattusilis, thy servant, and of Pudu-hepas, thy handmaid, come forth from thy mouth in the presence of the gods! To Hattusilis, thy servant, and to Pudu-hepas, thy handmaid, give long years, months and days!

And if thou, Lelwanis, my lady, relayest the good (word) to the gods, grantest life to thy servant Hattusilis, (and) givest him long years, months (and) days, I will go (and) make for Lelwanis, my lady, a silver statue of Hattusilis—as tall as Hattusilis himself, with its head, its hands (and) his feet of gold—moreover I will hang it (with ornaments).

C. PRAYER TO ZINTUHIS

O Zintuhis, my lady, beloved granddaughter of the Storm-god and of the Sun-goddess of Arinna! Thou art the pectoral of the Storm-god and of the Sun-goddess of Arinna; they continually look at thee.

(small gap)

(iv) [In this matter], Zintuhis, my lady, [prove] thy divine power! Before the Storm-god, thy grandfather, [and before] the Sun-goddess of Arinna, thy grandmother, bring (the request) [of Ha]ttusilis, thy servant, for life and long years! Let that come forth from their mouth!

[And] if thou, Zintuhis, my lady, wilt [hear]ken to these words and relay them to the Storm-god, thy grandfather, [and] to the Sun-goddess of Arinna, thy grandmother, [then] I will make a [grea]t ornament for thee, Zintuhis, my lady.

D. PRAYER TO MEZZULLAS

O Mezzullas, my lady! Thou art the beloved daughter of the Storm-god [and] of the Sun-goddess of Arinna. Whatever thou, Mezzullas, my lady, sayest [to] the Storm-god, thy father, and to the Sun-goddess of Arinna, thy mother, [to that] they will hearken; they will not reject it. These words which [I], Pudu-hepas, thy handmaid, have laid in [pray]er before the Storm-god, thy father, and the Sun-goddess of Arinna, thy mother, announce them, Mezzullas, my lady, and convey them to the Storm-god, thy father, [and to the Sun-goddess of Arinn]a, thy mother!

[And if thou, Mezzullas, my lady, wilt hearken to these] words [and convey them to the Storm-god, thy father, and to the Sun-goddess of Arinna, thy mother], [then I will make . . .] and present (it) to Mezzullas, my lady, [. . .].

E. PRAYER TO THE STORM-GOD OF ZIPPALANDA

[O Storm-god of Zippalan]da, my lord! Thou art the beloved son [of the Storm-god and of the Sun-]goddess of Arinna. Announce [my words to the Storm-god, thy father,] and to the Sun-goddess of Arinna, thy mother! The Storm-god, thy father, (and) the Sun-goddess of Arinna, thy mother, will [not re]ject thy word, they will hearken to thee. This [word], which I, Pudu-hepas, thy handmaid, have sp[oken] in prayer, announce and relay thou (to thy parents), Storm-god of Zippalanda, my lord! O god, my lord, yield to this word of mine! Because as a woman in travail I have in my own person made reparation to the god, my lord, intercede for me, god, my lord, with the Storm-god, thy father, and the Sun-goddess of Arinna, thy mother! Hattusilis, thy servant, wore himself out in the god's service; he gave himself body and soul to the restoration of Nerik, the beloved city of the god, my lord. So be thou, O god, my lord, favorably inclined toward Hattusilis, thy servant! These words, which I lay in prayer before the Storm-god, thy father, and the Sun-goddess of Arinna, thy mother—convey them (to thy parents) for me, O Storm-god of Zippalanda, my lord!

And if thou, Storm-god of Zippalanda, my lord, wilt convey these words to the Storm-god, thy father, and to the Sun-goddess of Arinna, thy mother, and thereby wilt [deliver] Hattusilis from evil, (edge) then I will make [for thee . . .] (and) a golden shield weighing x minas; I will make [for thee . . .] and the . . . for the god [. . .]. . . .

Plague Prayers of Mursilis[1]

a

Text: *KUB*, xiv, 8 and its duplicates *KUB*, xiv, 10 + *KUB*, xxvi, 86 and *KUB*, xiv, 11. Literature: E. Forrer, *Forschungen*, ii/1 (1926), 12-18; A. Götze, *Kleinasiatische Forschungen*, i (1929), 204-35.

1. Hattian Storm-god, my lord, and ye, Hattian gods, my lords! Mursilis, the great king, your servant, has sent me (with the order:) Go! To the Hattian Storm-god, my lord, and to the gods, my lords, speak as follows:

What is this that ye have done? A plague ye have let into the land. The Hatti land has been cruelly afflicted by the plague. For twenty years now men have been dying in my father's days, in my brother's days, and in mine own since I have become the priest of the gods. When men are dying in the Hatti land like this, the plague is in no wise over. As for me, the agony of my heart and the anguish of my soul I cannot endure any more.

2. When I celebrated festivals, I worshiped all the gods, I never preferred one temple to another. The matter of the plague I have laid in prayer before all the gods making vows to them (and saying): "Hearken to me, ye gods, my lords! Drive ye forth the plague from the Hatti land! The reason for which people are dying in the Hatti land—either let it be established by

[1] Hittite king, son of Suppiluliumas; about third quarter of the 14th century B.C.

an omen, or let me see it in a dream, or let a prophet declare it!" But the gods did not hearken to me and the plague got no better in the Hatti land. The Hatti land was cruelly afflicted.

3. The few people who were left to give sacrificial loaves and libations were dying too. Matters again got too much for me. So I made the anger of the gods the subject of an oracle. I learnt of two ancient tablets. The first tablet dealt with the offerings to the river Mala.[2] The old kings had regularly presented offerings to the river Mala. But now a plague has been rampant in the Hatti land since the days of my father, and we have never performed the offerings to the river Mala.

4. The second tablet concerned Kurustama. When the Hattian Storm-god had brought people of Kurustama[3] to the country of Egypt and had made an agreement concerning them with the Hattians so that they were under oath to the Hattian Storm-god—although the Hattians as well as the Egyptians were under oath to the Hattian Storm-god, the Hattians ignored their obligations; the Hattians promptly broke the oath of the gods. My father sent foot soldiers and charioteers who attacked the country of Amka,[4] Egyptian territory. Again he sent troops, and again they attacked it. When the Egyptians became frightened, they asked outright for one of his sons to (take over) the kingship. But when my father gave them one of his sons, they killed him as they led him there. My father let his anger run away with him, he went to war against Egypt and attacked Egypt. He smote the foot soldiers and the charioteers of the country of Egypt. The Hattian Storm-god, my lord, by his decision even then let my father prevail; he vanquished and smote the foot soldiers and the charioteers of the country of Egypt. But when they brought back to the Hatti land the prisoners which they had taken a plague broke out among the prisoners and they began to die.

5. When they moved the prisoners to the Hatti land, these prisoners carried the plague into the Hatti land. From that day on people have been dying in the Hatti land. Now, when I found that tablet dealing with the country of Egypt, I made the matter the subject of an oracle of the god (and asked): "Those arrangements which were made by the Hattian Storm-god—namely that the Egyptians and the Hattians as well were put under oath by the Hattian Storm-god, that the Damnassaras deities were present in the temple of the Hattian Storm-god, and that the Hattians promptly broke their word—has this perhaps become the cause of the anger of the Hattian Storm-god, my lord?" And (so) it was established.

6. Because of the plague, I made the offerings to the river Mala the subject of an oracle also. And in that matter too it was established that I should have to account for myself before the Hattian Storm-god. See now! I have admitted my guilt before the Storm-god (and said): "It is so. We have done it." I know for certain that the offence was not committed in my days, that it was committed in the days of my father. . . . But, since the Hattian Storm-god is angry for that reason and people are dying in the Hatti land, I am (nevertheless) making the offerings to the Hattian Storm-god, my lord, on that account.

7. [5]Because I humble myself and cry for mercy, hearken to me, Hattian Storm-god, my lord! Let the plague stop in the Hatti land!

8. The reasons for the plague that were established when I made the matter the subject of a series of oracles, these have I removed. I have made [ample] restitution. The matter of the (broken) oath which was established (as a cause) in connection with the plague, offerings for those oaths I have made to the Hattian Storm-god, my lord. I have also made (offerings) [to the other gods]. The offerings have been presented to thee, Hattian Storm-god, my lord; the offerings have been presented to them too. (As for) the offerings to the river Mala that were established (as a cause) in connection with the plague—since I am now on my way to the river Mala, acquit me of that offering to the river Mala, O Hattian Storm-god my lord, and ye gods, my lords! The offering to the river Mala I promise to make, I promise to complete it properly. The reason for which I make it—namely the plague—O gods, my lords, take pity on me and let that plague abate in the Hatti land!

9. Hattian Storm-god, my lord, (and) ye gods, my lords! It is only too true that man is sinful. My father sinned and transgressed against the word of the Hattian Storm-god, my lord. But I have not sinned in any respect. It is only too true, however, that the father's sin falls upon the son. So, my father's sin has fallen upon me. Now, I have confessed before the Hattian Storm-god, my lord, and before the gods, my lords (admitting): "It is true, we have done it." And because I have confessed my father's sin, let the soul of the Hattian Storm-god, my lord, and (those) of the gods, my lords, be again pacified! Suffer not to die the few who are still left to offer sacrificial loaves and libations!

10. See! I lay the matter of the plague before the Hattian Storm-god, my lord. Hearken to me, Hattian Storm-god, and save my life! This is of what I [have to remind] thee: The bird takes refuge in (its) nest, and the nest saves its life. Again: if anything becomes too much for a servant, he appeals to his lord. His lord hears him and takes pity on him. Whatever had become too much for him, he sets right for him. Again: if the servant has incurred a guilt, but confesses his guilt to his lord, his lord may do with him whatever he pleases. But, because (the servant) has confessed his guilt to his lord, his lord's soul is pacified, and his lord will not punish that servant. I have now confessed

[2] A river marking the eastern frontier of Hittite dominated territory and separating it from the Hurri kingdom; perhaps the Bitlis Su.

[3] A city in the Kashkean country of northern Anatolia. The purpose for which these people were sent to Egypt is not known to us.

[4] The region between Lebanon and Antilibanus.

[5] The gap indicated in my previous treatment is now bridged by *KUB*, XXVI, 86.

my father's sin. It is only too true, I have done it. If there is to be restitution, it seems clear that with all the gifts that have already been given because of this plague, with all the prisoners that have been brought home, in short with all the restitution that Hattusa has made because of the plague, it has already made restitution twentyfold. But, if ye demand from me additional restitution, tell me of it in a dream and I will give it to you.

11. See! I am praying to thee, Hattian Storm-god, my lord. So save my life! If indeed it is for those reasons which I have mentioned that people are dying,—as soon as I set them right, let those that are still able to give sacrificial loaves and libations die no longer! If, on the other hand, people are dying for some other reason, either let me see it in a dream, or let it be found out by an oracle, or let a prophet declare it, or let all the priests find out by incubation whatever I suggest to them. Hattian Storm-god, my lord, save my life! Let the gods, my lords, prove their divine power! Let someone see it in a dream! For whatever reason people are dying, let that be found out! . . . Hattian Storm-god, my lord, save my life! Let this plague abate again in the Hatti land!

b

Text: *KUB*, xxiv, 3 and its duplicates *KUB*, xxiv, 4 + *KUB*, xxx, 12 and *KUB*, xxx, 13. Literature: O. R. Gurney, *AAA*, xxvii (1940), 24 ff.

What is this, O gods, that ye have done? A plague ye have let into the land. The Hatti land, all of it, is dying; so no one prepares sacrificial loaves and libations for you. The plowmen who used to work the fields of the god are dead; so no one works or reaps the fields of the god at all. The grinding women who used to make the sacrificial loaves for the gods are dead; so they do not make the sacrificial loaves any longer. From whatever corral (or) sheepfold they used to select the sacrifices of sheep and cattle, the cowherds and the shepherds are dead and the corral [and the sheepfold are empty]. So it comes to pass that the sacrificial loaves (and) libations, and the offerings of animals have stopped. And ye, O gods, come on this day and hold us responsible. Man has lost his wits, and there is nothing that we do aright. O gods, whatever sin you behold, either let a prophet rise and declare it, or let the sibyls or the priests learn about it by incubation, or let man see it in a dream! . . . O gods, take ye pity again on the Hatti land! On the one hand it is afflicted with a plague, on the other hand it is afflicted with hostility. The protectorates beyond the frontier, (namely) the Mitanni land (and) the Arzawa land, each one has rebelled; they do not acknowledge the gods and have broken the oaths of the gods. They persist in acting maliciously against the Hatti land, and the temples(?) of the gods they seek to despoil. Let the gods take an interest therein again! Send ye the plague, hostility, famine (and) evil fever into the Mitanni land and the Arzawa land! Rested are the rebellious countries, but the Hatti land is a weary land. Unhitch the weary, but the rested harness!

Moreover, those countries which belong to the Hatti land, (namely) the Kashkean country (they are swineherds and weavers of linen), also the country of Arawanna, the country of Kalasma, the Lukka country, the country of Pitassa—these lands have also renounced the Sun-goddess of Arinna. They cast off their tributes and began to attack the Hatti land in their turn. In olden days the Hatti land with the help of the Sun-goddess of Arinna used to take on the surrounding countries like a lion. Moreover, cities like Halba (and) Babylon that it would destroy—from all such countries they took goods, silver (and) gold, and their gods and placed them before the Sun-goddess of Arinna.

But now all the surrounding countries have begun to attack the Hatti land. Let it again become a matter of concern to the Sun-goddess of Arinna! O god, bring not thy name into disrepute!

Whatever rage (or) anger the gods may feel, and whosoever may not have been reverent toward the gods, —let not the good perish with the wicked! If it is one town, or one [house], or one man, O gods, let that one perish alone! Look ye upon the Hatti land with favorable eyes, but the evil plague give to [those other] countries!

Daily Prayer of the King

Texts: *KUB*, xxiv, 1-4 and the additional pieces *KUB*, xxx, 12 and 13. Literature: The hymn of section b. is translated in the following places: H. Ehelolf, *Berichte aus den preussischen Kunstsammlungen*, xlix (1928), 32-34; E. Forrer, *Reallexikon der Assyriologie*, i (1929), 149 f.; A. Götze, *Kulturgeschichte Kleinasiens* (1933), 128. The whole composition was treated by O. R. Gurney in *AAA*, xxvii (1940), 3-163. In part of the texts the addressed deity is the Sun-goddess of Arinna, in another part Telepinus. The latter version has been adopted here.

Entreaty

The scribe reads this tablet addressing the deity daily; he praises the deity (saying):

Telepinus, a mighty (and) noble deity art thou. Mursilis, the king, thy servant, and the queen, thy handmaid, have sent me (with the request): "Go! entreat Telepinus, our lord, the guardian of our persons!"

Whether thou art in heaven above among the gods, noble Telepinus; whether gone to the sea or to the mountains to roam; whether gone to war to the country of the enemy—

now let the sweet and soothing cedar essence lure thee! Come home into thy temple! Here I am entreating thee with sacrificial loaves and libations. Let me speak to thee alone and whatever I say unto thee—lend me thine ear, O god, and hearken to it!

Thou, Telepinus, art a noble god; thy godhead and the gods' temples are firmly established in the Hatti land. But in no other land anywhere are they so.

Festivals (and) sacrifices pure (and) holy they present to thee in the Hatti land. But in no other country anywhere do they present them so.

Lofty temples adorned with silver and gold thou hast in the Hatti land. But in no other country anywhere hast thou their like. (ii) Cups (and) rhyta, silver, gold and (precious) stones thou hast in the Hatti land. But in no other country hast thou their like.

Festivals too—the festival of the month, the festivals of the year and of the *decade*, the ceremonies of winter and spring, and of the summer, the festivals of entreaty—men celebrate for thee in the Hatti land. But in no other country anywhere do they celebrate their like. Thy divinity, O Telepinus, is honored in the Hatti land, and Mursilis, the king, thy servant, and the queen, thy handmaid, and also the princes, thy servants, are reverent toward thee in the Hatti land. They undertake the celebration of communion feasts, sacrifices and festivals for thee, Telepinus. Everything they present to thee holy (and) pure. Moreover, reverence is paid to thy temple, thy rhyta, [thy cups] (and) thy utensils and they are cared for scrupulously. To the utensils [of thy worship] no one draws near.

Hymn[1]

Thou, Telepinus, art a noble god; thy name is noble among names. Thy godhead is noble among the gods; among the gods art thou noble, O Telepinus. Great art thou, O Telepinus; there is no other deity more noble and mighty than thou. Of sure judgment thou art lord; thou watchest over kingship in heaven and on earth. Thou settest the bounds of the lands; thou hearkenest to entreaties. Thou, Telepinus, art a merciful god; thou art forever showing thy mercy. The godly man is dear to thee, O Telepinus, and thou, Telepinus, dost exalt him. In the orbit of heaven and earth thou, Telepinus, art the (source of) light; throughout the lands art thou a god who is celebrated. Of every land thou art father (and) mother; the inspired lord of judgment art thou. In the place of judgment thou art untiring; among the Olden Gods thou art the one who is celebrated. For the gods thou, Telepinus, assignest the rites; to the Olden Gods thou assignest their portions. For thee they open the door of heaven; thou, the celebrated Telepinus, art allowed to pass through the gate of heaven.[2] The gods of heaven are obedient to thee, O Telepinus; the gods of the earth are obedient to thee, O Telepinus. Whatever thou sayest, O Telepinus, the gods bow down to thee. Of the oppressed, the lowly . . . thou art father (and) mother; the cause of the lowly, the oppressed thou, Telepinus, dost take to heart.

[1] The following text is taken chiefly from *KUB*, xxiv, 3.

[2] The text, which is incomplete here in all copies, can be restored with the help of the closely related prayer *KUB*, xxxi, 127 + *ABoT*, 44 (there i 28 ff.) and its duplicates.

Blessings and Curses[3]

. . . Turn with favor [toward the king and the queen], and toward the princes [and the Hatti land!] Take thy stand, O Telepinus, strong god, [beside the king (and) the queen and the] princes! Grant them enduring life, health, long years [(and) strength]! Into their souls place [ligh]t and joy!

Grant them sons (and) daughters, grandsons (and) great-grandsons! Grant them . . . ! Grant them fertility of grain (and) vine, of sheep, cattle (and) people! Grant them a man's valiant (and) victorious weapon! Set the countries of the enemy beneath their feet and let [them die by the sword]!

From the Hatti land drive forth the evil fever, plague, famine and *misery*!

And (as for) the enemy countries that are in revolt and turmoil—some refuse the due respect to thee, Telepinus, and to the Hattian gods; others are out to burn your temples; (iv) others seek to obtain the rhyta, the cups (and) the utensils of silver (and) gold; others seek to lay waste your plowland and pasture, vineyards, gardens (and) groves; others seek to capture your plowmen, vinedressers, gardeners (and) millwomen—give evil fever, plague, famine (and) *misery* to these enemy countries.

But to the king (and) the queen, to the princes and to the Hatti land grant life, health, strength, long and enduring years and joy! Grant everlasting fertility to their crops, vines, fruit-bearing *trees*, cattle, sheep, goats, pigs, mules (and) asses together with the beasts of the fields, and to (their) people! Let them flourish! Let the rains [come]! Let the winds of prosperity pass over! Let all thrive (and) prosper in the Hatti land!

And the congregation shouts: "Let it be so!"

[3] The following text is taken chiefly from *KUB*, xxiv, 1.

Prayer to be Spoken in an Emergency

Text: *KUB*, vi, 45 + *KUB*, xxx, 14 (with the duplicates *KUB*, vi, 44 and *KUB*, xii, 35). Literature: F. M. Th. Boehl, *Theologisch Tijdschrift*, l (1916), 306 ff.; M. Witzel, *Hethitische Keilschrift-Urkunden* (= *Keilschriftliche Studien*, iv [1924]) 86-98.

(i) Thus speaks the Tabarnas[1] Muwatallis, the Great King, the king of the Hatti country, the son of Mursilis, the Great King, the king of the Hatti country, the valiant: When things get too much for a man and he approaches his gods in prayer, he sets up two offering-tables of wickerwork covered (with a cloth) on the roof under the open sky. He sets up one table for the Sun-goddess of Arinna, and one table for [all the (other)] gods. Upon them (there are deposited) 35 sacrificial loaves weighing one *tarnaš* made of barley meal, [x] thin loaves(?) with honey and fine oil inside,

[1] Title of the Hittite king.

mutton-fat cake, a full stewpot, meal, a full cup, 30 pitchers of wine. When this is all made ready, the king ascends to the roof and offers it to the Sun-god of Heaven.

(10) He speaks as follows: "Sun-god of Heaven and Sun-goddess of Arinna, my lady, queen of the Hatti land! Storm-god, king of heaven, my lord! Hebat, queen, my lady! Hattian Storm-god, king of heaven, master of the Hatti land, my lord! Storm-god of Zippalanda, my lord, beloved son of the Storm-god, lord of the Hatti land! (15) All ye gods and goddesses! All ye mountains (and) rivers of the Hatti land! (My) lords, lordly gods! Sun-goddess of Arinna, my lady, and all ye gods of the Hatti land, lords whose priest I am and who have accorded me unlimited kingship over the Hatti land!

(20) "Now, hearken ye, gods, to the prayer of me, your priest and your servant! I shall speak in prayer first of you, the lordly gods, of your temples (and) of your images; how the gods of the Hatti land are worshiped, and how they are abused.

(25) "Thereafter I shall speak in prayer of my own affairs. Lend me your ears, O gods, my lords! Listen to these my prayers! And whatever matters I lay before the gods in prayer, receive those matters, O gods, my lords, and listen to them! I may lay before you, (30) gods, matters which ye do not wish to hear; they rise from my mortal mouth. Those words, O gods, my lords, refrain from hearing!

"Seris, my lord, thou bull who standest in the presence of the Storm-god of the Hatti-land! These matters that I present in my prayer, (35) announce them to the gods! Let the lord gods listen to those matters that I present in my prayer, the lord gods of heaven and earth!"

(There follows a full list of the Hatti gods.)

(iii) "Storm-god of the house of the Tawannannas,[2] Storm-god *ḫulaššaššiš*! Gods and goddesses of king and queen, ye who have been invoked (and) ye who have not been invoked; ye in whose temples king and queen worship officiating as priests, (and) ye in whose temples they do not! Gods (and) goddesses, (10) . . . , dark nether world, heaven (and) earth, clouds (and) winds, thunder (and) lightning, place of assembly where the gods meet in assembly!

"Sun-god of Heaven, my lord, shepherd of mankind! Thou risest, O Sun-god of Heaven, from the Sea. Thou takest thy place in heaven, (15) Sun-god of Heaven, my lord. Over man, dog, swine (and) the beasts of the field dost thou, Sun-god, pronounce judgment daily.

"Here then am I, Muwatallis, the king, the priest of the Sun-goddess of Arinna and of all the gods, praying to the Sun-god of Heaven. (20) On this day, O Sun-god of Heaven, my lord, arouse the (other) gods! Whatever gods I invoked with (the word of) my mouth on this day, and with whatever request,

[2] Title of the Hittite queen.

"those gods, O Sun-god of Heaven, summon from heaven (and) from earth, from the mountains (and) from the rivers, from their temples (and) their thrones!"

(25) Thereafter the king speaks as follows: "Storm-god *piḫaššaššiš*, my lord! I was but a mortal. Yet my father was priest of the Sun-goddess of Arinna and of all the gods. My father begat me, but thou, Storm-god *piḫaššaššiš*, tookest me from my mother and rearedst me. Thou madest me priest of the Sun-goddess of Arinna (30) and of all the gods. In the Hatti land thou madest me king.

"So, I, Muwatallis, the king, reared by thee, Storm-god *piḫaššaššiš*, am now praying. The gods whom I invoked with (the word of) my tongue (35) the gods to whom I prayed,—intercede for me with all those gods! Take the words of my tongue, the words of me, Muwatallis, thy servant, and pass them on in full to the gods! In the matters that I lay before the gods in prayer let them not forsake me!

(40) "The bird takes refuge in (its) nest and lives. I have taken refuge with the Storm-god *piḫaššaššiš*, my lord; so save my life! The matters which I lay before the gods in prayer, pass them on in full to the gods! Let them hearken to me! Therefore too shall I praise the Storm-god *piḫaššaššiš*.

(45) "No sooner will the gods have heard my words, than they will put right (and) remove the evil that is in my soul. To whom is praise due, if praise is not due to the Storm-god *piḫaššaššiš*, my lord? Then, whenever a man looks upon god and mortal, (50) he will say: 'Surely, the Storm-god *piḫaššaššiš*, my lord, the king of heaven, has favored (that) man and *rescued* him; he has put him right and advanced him.' In the future my children (and) children's children, kings (and) queens (55) of Hatti, princes (and) noblemen will always show reverence to the Storm-god *piḫaššaššiš*, my lord. Thus they will speak: 'Surely, that god is a strong, valiant (and) glorious god!' And the gods of heaven, the mountains (and) the rivers will praise thee.

(60) "I, Muwatallis, thy servant,—my innermost soul rejoices, and I praise the Storm-god *piḫaššaššiš*. Thou, Storm-god *piḫaššaššiš*, shalt rejoice over the temples that I shall build for thee, over the decrees I shall issue for thee. The sacrificial loaves and the libations (65) which I am accustomed to present to the Storm-god *piḫaššaššiš*, my lord—I would give them to thee gladly; I would not give them to thee grudgingly. So, Sun-god *piḫaššaššiš*, my lord, beam upon me like the full moon, (70) and shine above me like the sun in the sky!

"Walk on my right hand! Team up with me as (with) a bull to draw (the wagon)! Walk by my side in true Storm-god fashion! Truly I wish to speak thus: 'He who is favored by the Storm-god *piḫaššaššiš*, he who is reared by him, [*prospers. . . .*']"

(There follow offerings to the gods.)

(iv[3]) When the Sun[4] has finished breaking the sacrificial loaves, he presents in prayer the (special) matters which are in his mind.

(Upon completion of that prayer new offerings to the gods are given. Finally the broken loaves are burned.)

Prayer of Arnuwandas and Asmu-Nikkal Concerning the Ravages Inflicted on Hittite Cult-Centers

Texts: *KUB*, xvii, 21 with its duplicates *KUB*, xxxi, 117 and *KUB*, xxxi, 124 (+) *KUB*, xxiii, 115. The text is still incomplete.

(beginning lost)

(1) The land of the Hittites is a land [that is devoted] to you, the gods. In the land of the Hittites we are accustomed to present to you pure and really [holy] sacrifices. In the land of the Hittites we are accustomed to show you, the gods, reverence.

(6) Ye should know, O gods, by your divine insight that no one has ever before taken care of your temples as we have;

that no one has ever paid more reverent attention to your implements; (11) that no one has ever taken care of the goods, silver (and) gold, of the rhyta (and) garments of you, the gods, as we have;

furthermore, that (in the case of) the images of silver (and) gold that exist of you, the gods,—(15) when anything had grown old on any god's body, when any implements of the gods had grown old—that no one has ever renewed them as we have;

furthermore, (20) that no one has ever paid more reverent attention to matters of cleanliness connected with your sacrifices; that no one has ever made more careful provisions for your daily, monthly, yearly (and) *ten-yearly* sacrifices (and) festivals;

furthermore, (as for) the slaves, slave-girls (and) villages of you, the gods,—they used to oppress them with imposts (25) (and) feudal services; the slaves (and) slave-girls of you, the gods, they would take and make them their own slaves and slave-girls. [We, Arnuwa]ndas the Great King,[1] [and Asmu-Nikkal, the Great Queen, shall free them] for you in every particular.

Ye should know by your divine insight what offerings of sacrificial loaves and libations they used to present.

[We], Arnuwandas, the Great King, and Asmu-Nikkal, the Great Queen, shall again give fat sheep (and) fine [oxen], fine sacrificial loaves and libations.

(small gap)

3 45 ff.

4 i.e. the king.

1 A predecessor of Suppiluliumas.

(ii) So stand ye by us!

(5) The territory which the enemies[2] plundered and kept for themselves when they invaded the Hatti country, that (territory) we promise to restore to you, the gods, and to make them account for it.

The territories which were under obligation to present to you, the gods of heaven, sacrificial loaves, libations (and) tribute—in some the priests, the mothers-of-god, the holy priests, (10) the anointed, the musicians (and) the singers had to leave, in others the gods' tributes and treasures were carried off;

in others there were carried off the Sun-goddess' of Arinna sun discs and lunulae (15) made of silver (and) gold, bronze (and) copper, the fine cloth, the *adupli* garments, the tunics (and) the gowns, the sacrificial loaves (and) the libation bowls;

in others they drove away the herds, the fattened oxen (and) the fattened cows, the fattened sheep (and) the fattened goats.

(20) In the country of Nerik, in Hursama, in the country of Kalasma, in the country of Serisa, in the country of Himuwa, in the country of Taggasta, in the country of Kammama, in the country of Zalpuwa, in the country of Katahha, in the country of Hurna, in the country of Dankusna, in the country of Tapa[panu]wa, in the country of Tarugga, in the country of Ilaluha, in the country of Zihana, in the country (25) of Sipidduwa, in the country of Washaya, in the country of Parituya[3]—

the temples[4] which ye, the gods, possessed in these countries, the Kashkeans sacked them. They smashed the images of you, the gods. (iii) They plundered silver (and) gold, rhyta (and) cups of silver (and) gold, (and) of copper, your implements of bronze (and) your garments; they shared out these things among themselves.

They scattered the priests and the holy priests, the mothers-of-god, the anointed, (5) the musicians, the singers, the cooks, the bakers, the plowmen (and) the gardeners and made them their slaves.

They also scattered your cattle (and) your sheep. They shared out among themselves your fields (and) lands, (the source) of the sacrificial loaves (and) the vineyards, (10) (the source) of the libations. Those the Kashkeans took for themselves.

Thus it has come about that in those countries no one invokes the names of you, the gods, any more; no one presents your daily, monthly, yearly (or) *ten-yearly* (15) sacrifices; no one celebrates your festivals (and) pageants.

Here, to the Hatti land, no one brings tribute (and) treasures for you anymore. No longer do priests, holy priests, mothers-of-god, musicians, (or) singers come to you from any[place].

2 The Kashkeans are meant, unruly tribes who live in the mountains of northern Anatolia and incessantly harass Hittite territory.

3 All these countries must be located along the Kashkean frontier.

4 The text is taken from *KUB*, xxxi, 124 ii 10 ff.

[Furthermore] no one brings sun discs and lunulae made of silver (and) gold, bronze (and) copper, fine cloth, *adupli* garments, tunics (and) gowns for you, the gods, (and for) the Sun-goddess of Arinna. No one presents sacrificial loaves (and) libations to you, the gods. No one drives up herds of fattened oxen (and) fattened cows, fattened sheep (and) fattened goats.

(small gap[5])

(iv) They (i.e. the Kashkeans) came here to the Hittite [land (and) they . . .]. They terrorized Tuhasuna. [. . .] . . . They terrorized Tahatariya. They came down to the gates [of . . .] and terrorized Hum[. . .].

Since, however, we are reverent toward the gods and hold ourselves responsible for the festivals of the gods, (and) since the Kashkeans have taken Nerik for themselves, we will send offerings from Hattusa to Hakmis for the Storm-god of Nerik and for the gods of Nerik, [. . .] . . . , sacrificial loaves (and) libations, cattle (and) sheep.

We will summon the Kashkeans; we will give them presents and then make them swear an oath: "Keep your hands off the offerings which we send to the Storm-god of Nerik! Let no one attack them on their way!"

They will come and accept the presents and then take the oath. But should they rise again and transgress the oath, make light of the words of you, the gods, and violate the seal of the oath they have sworn by the Storm-god;

should they seize the [present]s (sent) from the [Hittite] land, [withhold] from the Storm-god [of Nerik . . .] the offerings, sacrificial loaves (and) libations, [cattle (and) sheep, *they shall not escape unpunished*!]

(end lost)

[5] Perhaps bridged by *KUB*, XXIII, 115.

Prayer of Kantuzilis for Relief from his Sufferings

Text: *KUB*, XXX, 10. Literature: A few lines are translated by J. Friedrich *AfO*, XIII (1940), 154.

(beginning lost)

O Sun-god, when thou goest down to the nether world (to be) with him, forget not to tell that patron-god of mine: [". . . !"] Announce to him the word of Kantuzilis![1]

O god, ever since my mother gave birth to me, thou, my god, hast reared me. Thou, my god, (art) my [*refuge*] and my anchor.[2] Thou, [my god], broughtest me together with good men. Thou, my god, didst show me what to do in time of distress. [Thou], my god, didst call [me], Kantuzilis, thy favorite servant. The superior power of my god that I have not known since childhood [*must I experience*] it [*in my old age?*]

Even when I fared well, I always acknowledged the superior power (and) the wisdom of my god. Never have I sworn in thy name, my god, and then broken the oath afterward. That which is holy to my god and hence not fit for me to eat, never have I eaten it. I have not brought impurity upon my body.

Never have I withheld from thy stable an ox; never have I withheld from thy fold a sheep. Whenever I came upon food, I never ate it indiscriminately; whenever I came upon water, I never drank it indiscriminately. Were I now to recover, would I not have recovered at the word of thee, my god? Were I to regain my strength, would I not have regained it at the word of thee, my god?

Life is bound up with death, and death is bound up with life. Man cannot live for ever; the days of his life are numbered. Were man to live for ever, it would not concern him greatly even if he had to endure grievous sickness.

Would that my god might now freely open his heart (and) soul to me and [tell] me my fault so that I might learn about it! Either let my god speak to me in a dream! Would that my god would open his heart to me and tell [me] my [fau]lt so that I might learn about it! Or let the sibyl tell me, [or] let the Sun-god's seer tell [me] from the liver (of a sheep). Would that my god might freely open [his heart (and) his soul] to me and tell me my fault so that I might learn about it!

O my god! Let me know again [thy will] and [thy deci]sion! (reverse) [. . .] art thou. It has always been said about thee that thou [. . .]st [. . .] . . . Thou shouldst [. . .] me! Would that my god, who for[sook] me, [might take] pity on me! [Much as] I wearied myself with pleading before my god, it is yet of no avail. No sooner didst thou scrape [one thing evi]l off [me], than thou broughtest back [another] in its stead.

Would that [the Sun-god] might calm down again and that peace might return to his heart! Would that he might raise me up again out of my affliction. [O Sun-god], vigorous *scion*, [the favorite son of] Sin and Ningal[3] art thou. See! I, Kantuzilis, thy servant, have asked for [mercy] and humbled myself. [See!] I am beseeching thee.

To the Sun-god I sing. See! I, Kantuzilis, implore my god incessantly. Would that my god might hearken [to me]! Whenever in times past I, Kantuzilis, performed the oil rite for my god, whenever I . . . [. . .]ed to my god, thou *gavest* me *abundance*, thou *gavest* me *strength*. But now when I, Kantuzilis, performed the oil rites for thee with the merchant, a mortal, holding the balance for the Sun-god and upsetting the balance—what [wrong] did I do to my god?

[1] Kantuzilis is not otherwise identified in the text. He is probably the high official and member of the royal family who is mentioned in 2 *BoTU*, 24 among children of Suppiluliumas.

[2] Literally: my rope.

[3] The Sumero-Akkadian Moon-god and his wife who in Mesopotamian mythology are the parents of the Sun-god.

Through sickness my house has become a house of misery. Through misery my soul *longs* for another place. As (one who has been) sick for a year, for a *decade*,—thus have I become. Sickness and misery have now become oppressive to me; that I must declare to thee, my god.

At night sweet slumber does not overtake me on my bed. While I lie there, good tidings do not come to me. Now, my god, join thy strength to that of (my) patron-god! How thou couldst have ordained this sickness for me from (my) mother's womb on, that I have never asked thy sibyl.

Now I cry for mercy in the presence of my god. Hearken to me, my god! O my god, do not make me a man who is unwelcome at the king's court! Do not make my condition an offence to mankind! Those to whom I did good, none of them wishes [me] (long) life. [Thou], my god, [(art) father and mother] to me; [beside thee there is no fa]ther or mother for me. [. . .]

(end lost)

VI. Didactic and Wisdom Literature

Fables and Didactic Tales

Egyptian Didactic Tales

(Translator: John A. Wilson)

A DISPUTE OVER SUICIDE

This remarkable text carries the argument between a man who is weary of this life and his own soul. Since he finds life unbearable, the man contemplates suicide. His soul vacillates, first agrees, then fears that suicide will entail the danger that the man will have no mortuary service from his survivors, then proposes an abandonment to a life of careless pleasures, and finally agrees to remain with the man in any case.

The text dates from the Middle Kingdom, or, more probably, from the disturbed times between the Old and Middle Kingdoms (end of the third millennium B.C.), when the established order of life had broken down and men were groping for new values.

Berlin Papyrus 3024 was published by A. Erman, *Gespräch eines Lebensmüden mit seiner Seele* (*APAW*, 1896, 2). A transcription of much of the text into hieroglyphic appears in K. Sethe, *Aegyptische Lesestücke* (2nd ed., Leipzig, 1928), 43-46. It has been studied by A. Scharff, in German in *SBAW*, 1937, 9, by R. Weill, in French in *BIFAO*, XLV (1946), 89-154, and in Dutch by A. de Buck in *Kernmomenten. "Ex Oriente Lux"—Mededeelingen en Verhandelingen*, No. 7, (Leyden, 1947), 19-32. It was translated in Erman, *LAE*, 86-92. The beginning of the manuscript is lost. The translation starts with the man's answer to a previous argument by his soul.

I opened my mouth to my soul, that I might answer what it had said: "This is too much for me today, that my soul no (longer) talks with me.[1] It is really too great to be exaggerated. It is like *abandoning* me. Let [*not*] my soul go away; it should wait for me because of . . . There is no (10) competent person who deserts on the day of misfortune. Behold, my soul wrongs me, (but) I do not listen to it, dragging myself toward death before I come to it and casting (myself) upon the fire to burn myself up. . . . (15) May it be near to me on the day of misfortune and wait on that side . . . My soul is stupid to (try to) *win over* one wretched over life and *delay* me from death before I come to it. Make (20) the West pleasant for me! Is that (so) bad? Life is a circumscribed period: (even) the trees must fall. Trample down wrongs—(yet) my wretchedness endures. Let Thoth, who propitiates the gods, judge me. Let Khonsu, the scribe in truth, defend me. (25) Let Re, who *pilots* the sun barque, hear my speech. Let Isdes . . . defend me. My wretchedness is heavy . . . Pleasant would be the defense (30) of a god for the secrets of my body."[2]

What my soul said to me: "Art thou not a man? Art thou . . . whilst thou livest? What is thy goal? Thou art concerned with [*burial*] like a possessor of wealth!"[3]

I said: "I have not departed as long as these things *are neglected*. He who *carries (men) off forcibly* will take, without (35) caring about thee, (like) any *criminal* saying: 'I shall carry thee off, for thy (fate) is still death, (though) thy name may live.'[4] (But) yonder is a place for settling down, the *guide* of the heart; the West is home . . . If my soul will listen to me, an (40) *in*[*noc*]*ent* man, and its heart agrees with me, it will be fortunate. (Then) I shall make it reach the West like one who is in his pyramid, at whose burial a survivor has stood.[5] I shall make a *shelter* [*over*] thy corpse, (so that) thou mayest *scorn* another soul (45) as inert. I shall make a *shelter*—now it must not be (too) cool—(so that) thou mayest *scorn* another soul which is (too) hot. I shall drink at the watering place and shall . . . , (so that) thou mayest *scorn* another soul which is hungry.[6] If thou delayest (50) me from a death of this fashion, thou wilt not find a place where thou canst settle down in the West. (So) be [patient], my soul and my brother, until my heir has appeared, he who will make offerings and will stand at the grave on the day of burial, so that he may *prepare* the bed (55) of the cemetery."[7]

My soul opened its mouth to me, that it might answer what I had said: "If thou art thinking of burial, that is heart's distress. It is a bringing of tears, making a man sad. It is taking a man out of his house, (so that) he is left on the hillside, (whence) thou shalt never go up above that thou mightest see (60) the suns. They who build in granite and who hew out *chambers* in a pyramid, good men in good work, as soon as the builders have become gods,[8] their offering-stones are as bare, for lack of a survivor, as (those of) the weary ones, the dead on the dyke—(65) the waters take hold of an end of him, and the sunlight as well, and the fish of the water-banks talk to them.[9] Listen to me. Behold, it is good for men to listen. Pursue the happy day and forget care!

"The poor man plows his plot of ground and loads his harvest (70) into a ship's hold. He makes the journey by towing (the boat), (because) his feast day is ap-

1 This sounds as though the soul had refused to continue the argument.

2 The man wishes to seek death by fire, but his soul refuses to support him in this escape. He then longs for the advocacy of the gods and conceives of himself as pleading his case before a divine tribunal.

3 The soul makes the sharp retort that the man seems to be concerned with the proprieties of funerary observance, as though he were a man of means and position.

4 Death takes any man, whether he has prepared for it or not.

5 If the soul will only agree, then the death will effectively be like a normal death.

6 The argument seems to be that even a poor man can contrive a burial of adequate dignity, so that the soul need not fear its standing among other souls.

7 The man is not entirely without relatives or friends who will do what is necessary for his funerary care.

8 That is, are dead.

9 Ultimately the kings and nobles who were able to build themselves pyramids were no better off than the poor men abandoned as dead on the dykes and half immersed in the water. For a similar thought of the same period, see the Song of the Harper (p. 467 below). In the same way, the Song of the Harper urges that, because of the uncertainties of death, one should give himself up to pleasure.

proaching.[10] When he sees the forthcoming of an evening of *high water*, he is vigilant in the ship when Re retires, (and so) comes out (safely), with his wife. (But) his children are lost on the lake, *treacherous* with crocodiles in the night.[11] At last he sits down, when he *can take part* in speech, saying: 'I am not weeping for that girl, (although) there is no coming forth from the West for her, for another (*time*) on earth.[12] (But) I am concerned about her (unborn) children, broken in the egg, who saw the face of the crocodile-god before they had (even) lived!"[13]

"The poor man asks for an afternoon meal, (but) his wife says to him: 'It's for supper!' He goes out-of-doors to *grumble* for a while. If he comes back into the house and is like another man, his wife is (still) experienced in him: that he does not listen to her (but) *grumbles*, unresponsive to communications."[14]

I opened my mouth to my soul, that I might answer what it had said:[15]

Behold, my name will reek through thee[16]
More than the stench of bird-droppings
On summer days, when the sky is hot.
Behold, my name will reek through thee
(More than) a fish-*handler*
On the day of the catch, when the sky is hot.
Behold, my name will reek through thee
More than the stench of bird-droppings,
More than a *covert* of reeds with waterfowl.
Behold, my name will reek through thee
More than the stench of fishermen,
More than the *stagnant pools* which they have fished.
Behold, my name will reek through thee
More than the stench of crocodiles,
More than sitting *in the assembly among* the crocodiles.
Behold, my name will reek through thee
More than a (married) woman
Against whom a lie has been told because of a man.
Behold, my name will reek through thee
More than a sturdy boy of whom it is said:
"He belongs to his *rival*!"[17]
Behold, my name will reek through thee
(More than) a *treacherous* town, which plots rebellion,
Of which *(only) the outside* can be seen.[18]

To whom can I speak today?[19]
(One's) fellows are evil;
The friends of today do not love.
To whom can I speak today?
Hearts are rapacious:
Every man seizes his fellow's goods.
(To whom can I speak today?)
The gentle man has perished,
(But) the violent man has access to everybody.
To whom can I speak today?
(*Even*) the calm *of face is* wicked;
Goodness is rejected everywhere.
To whom can I speak today?
(Though) a man should arouse wrath by his evil character,
He (only) stirs everyone to laughter, (so) wicked is his sin.
To whom can I speak today?
Men are plundering;
Every man seizes his fellow's (goods).
To whom can I speak today?
The foul fiend is an intimate,
(But) a brother, with whom one worked, has become an enemy.
To whom can I speak today?
No one thinks of yesterday;
No one at this time acts for him who has acted.[20]
To whom can I speak today?
(One's) fellows are evil;
One has recourse to strangers for uprightness of heart.
To whom can I speak today?
Faces have disappeared:
Every man has a downcast face toward his fellows.
To whom can I speak today?
Hearts are rapacious;
No man has a heart upon which one may rely.
To whom can I speak today?
There are no righteous;
The land is left to those who do wrong.
To whom can I speak today?
There is lack of an intimate (friend);
One has recourse to an unknown to complain to him.
To whom can I speak today?
There is no one contented of heart;

[10] Because he is in a hurry to reach home for his feast, he tows his boat for greater speed.

[11] Before he reaches home a storm comes up, and his children are lost overboard, a prey to the crocodiles.

[12] His daughter, dying in this way, cannot "come forth by day" to enjoy continued contacts with this life, as do those who die normally and are given normal funerary service.

[13] This parable of the poor man who loses his children by accident is probably meant to persuade the man that the only proper death is the normal death.

[14] This parable is not clear. It seems to say that a poor man cannot expect to eat in the late afternoon and also in the evening. The soul's implication would then be that a poor man cannot ask for the luxury of an abnormal escape from life.

[15] The man's argument, by which he finally wins over his soul, is presented in four poems consisting of tristichs of uniform theme and structure: (a) the man's name will be in evil odor, if he follows the advice of his soul; (b) the people of his day are wholly hostile and unscrupulous; (c) death is a release from such miseries; (d) the dead have access to the gods.

[16] "Behold, my name is overflooded (with bad odor) from thee"—followed by a series of comparisons, most of which have to do with fetid smells.

[17] "To his hated one." It is whispered of the boy that he is the child of his father's rival.

[18] Uncertain. Perhaps the rebellious town shows a peaceful exterior while it is plotting within.

[19] "I speak to whom today?"—with whom can I have any friendly and satisfactory contact in times like these?

[20] There is disregard for the lessons of the past, including grateful response for good services.

That man with whom one went, he no (longer) exists.
To whom can I speak today?
I am laden with wretchedness
For lack of an intimate (friend).
To whom can I speak today?
The sin which treads the earth,
It has no end.

Death is in my sight today[21]
(Like) the recovery of a sick man,
Like going out into the open after a *confinement*.
Death is in my sight today
Like the odor of myrrh
Like sitting under an awning on a breezy day.
Death is in my sight today
Like the odor of lotus blossoms,
Like sitting on the bank of drunkenness.[22]
Death is in my sight today
Like the *passing away* of rain,
Like the return of men to their houses from an expedition.
Death is in my sight today
Like the clearing of the sky,
Like a man *fowling thereby* for what he knew not.[23]
Death is in my sight today
Like the longing of a man to see his house (again),
After he has spent many years held in captivity.

Why surely, he who is yonder[24]
Will be a living god,
Punishing a sin of him who commits it.[25]
Why surely, he who is yonder
Will stand in the barque of the sun,
Causing that the choicest (offerings) therein be given to the temples.
Why surely, he who is yonder
Will be a man of wisdom,
Not hindered from appealing to Re when he speaks.

What my soul said to me: "Set mourning *aside*, thou who belongest to me, my brother! (Although) thou be offered up on the brazier,[26] (150) (still) thou shalt cling to life, as thou sayest. Whether it be desirable that I (remain) here (because) thou hast rejected the West, or whether it be desirable that thou reach the West and thy body join the earth, I shall come to rest after thou hast relaxed (in death). Thus we shall make a home together."[27]

21 "Death is in my face today"—in such times, I look upon death as—.
22 There would be no more obloquy to this than to its modern counterpart: going on a picnic to the beach.
23 Obscure. Perhaps unexpectedly good weather permits a man to go fowling.
24 "Verily, he who is there will be"—he who is over there in the realm of the dead.
25 They who live on in the realm of the dead will share in the privileges of the gods.
26 Death by fire is likened to a burnt offering.
27 The soul is successfully won over to the idea of suicide and will share the man's fate, whatever it may be.

It has come (to its end), (155) its beginning to its end, as found in writing.

THE PROTESTS OF THE ELOQUENT PEASANT

The duty of social justice was an insistent theme of the Middle Kingdom. At that time the man of power and position was asked to deal impartially with all men—or even to be partial in seeking out and meeting need. In the following text, this theme is given a story setting and is emphasized by the mechanism of letting a poor man insist upon his rights.

The story is laid in the reign of Neb-kau-Re Khety III, king at Herakleopolis and one of the competing pharaohs of the early 21st century B.C. Almost all of the manuscript material derives from the Middle Kingdom (20th-18th centuries). These are three papyri in Berlin (10499-"R"; 3023-"B1"; and 3025-"B2") and a papyrus in the British Museum (10274), with other, smaller fragments.

The facsimile publication was *Hieratische Papyrus aus den königlichen Museen zu Berlin*, IV, I. *Die Klagen des Bauern*, bearbeitet von F. Vogelsang und A. H. Gardiner (Leipzig, 1908). The texts were then studied by Vogelsang, *Kommentar zu den Klagen des Bauern* (*Untersuch.*, VI, Leipzig, 1913). See also E. Suys, *Étude sur le conte du fellah plaideur* (Rome, 1933). There are translations by A. H. Gardiner, in *JEA*, IX (1923), 5-25, and by Erman, *LAE*, 116-31.

(R1) THERE WAS A MAN whose name was Khun-Anup, and he was a peasant of the Field of Salt.[1] Now he had a wife, whose name was [Me]rit. THEN THIS PEASANT SAID TO THIS HIS WIFE: "Behold, I am going down to Egypt to [fetch] food thence for my children. Now go and measure for me the grain which is in the barn, the grain remaining *from* [*last year*]." Thereupon he measured for her [*six*] *hekat* of grain.[2] (5) THEN THIS PEASANT SAID TO THIS HIS WIFE: "Behold, [*there are*] twenty *hekat* of grain for thee and thy children for food. But thou shouldst make for me these six *hekat* of grain into bread and beer for every day *in which* [*I may be traveling*]."

So this peasant went down into Egypt, after he had loaded his donkeys with *iaa*-plants, *rermet*-plants, (10) natron, salt, . . . staves of the Farafra Oasis, leopard skins, (15) wolf hides, . . . pebbles, . . . doves, . . .[3] earth's hair, and *anis*, (35) full (measure) of all the good produce of the Field of Salt. So this peasant went south toward Herakleopolis, and he reached the region of Per-Fefi, to the north of Medenit.[4] He met there a man standing on the riverbank, whose name was Thut-nakht. He was the son of a man (40) whose name was Isri, and he was a vassal of the Chief Steward, Meru's son Rensi.

THEN THIS THUT-NAKHT SAID, when he saw this peasant's donkeys, which were tempting to his heart: "Would that I had some effective idol, (so that) I might steal away the goods of this peasant with it!" Now the house of this Thut-nakht was on a riverbank (45) pathway. It was narrow; it was not at all wide: it

1 The modern Wadi Natrun, northwest of Herakleopolis.
2 A *hekat* was a little over four dry quarts.
3 The uncertain elements in a long list are here omitted.
4 The locations of Per-Fefi and of Medenit are unknown.

may have exceeded the width of a loincloth. One side of it was under the water, and the other side of it was under grain. Then this Thut-nakht said to his attendant: "Go and fetch me a sheet from my house." It was brought to him immediately. Then he spread it on the riverbank pathway. Thereupon (50) its *fringe* came to rest on the water and its *hem* on the grain. Then this peasant came along the public road.[5]

(B1,1) Then this Thut-nakht said: "Be accommodating, peasant! Wouldst thou tread upon my garments?" Then this peasant said: "I shall do thy pleasure. My course is good." So he went up higher. Then this Thut-nakht said: (5) "Wilt thou have my grain for a path?" Then this peasant said: "My course is good. The embankment is high, and the (only other) way is under grain, (but still) thou providest our road with thy garments. Now wilt thou not let us pass by on the road?"

Now he had (scarcely) finished saying [this] word, when one of the donkeys filled (10) his mouth with a wisp of grain. Then this Thut-nakht said: "Behold, I will take away thy donkey, peasant, because he is eating my grain. Behold, he will (have to) *thresh* because of his *boldness*." Then this peasant said: "My course is good. (Only) one (wisp) has been damaged. I brought my donkey because of . . . ; wilt thou take him (15) for filling his mouth with a wisp of grain? Moreover, I know the lord of this district. It belongs to the Chief Steward, Meru's son Rensi. Moreover, he is the one who punishes every robber in this entire land. Shall I be robbed in his district?" Then this Thut-nakht said: "Is this the proverb which men say: (20) 'The name of the poor man is pronounced (only) for his master's sake'?[6] I am the one who is speaking to thee, (but) it is the Chief Steward whom thou mentionest!"

Then he took a stick of green tamarisk against him. Then he belabored all his limbs with it, and his donkeys were taken away and driven into his estate. Thereupon this peasant (25) wept very greatly because of the pain of what had been done to him. Then this Thut-nakht said: "Do not be (so) noisy, peasant! Behold, thou art at the home of the Lord of Silence."[7] Then this peasant said: "Thou beatest me, thou stealest my goods, and now thou (even) takest away the complaint from my mouth! O Lord of Silence, mayest thou give me back (30) my property! Then I shall not cry out (so that) thou art alarmed!"[8]

Then this peasant spent the time up to ten days appealing to this Thut-nakht, (but) he would not pay attention to it. So this peasant went to Herakleopolis to appeal to the Chief Steward, Meru's son Rensi. He met him going out of the door (35) of his house to embark on his official barge.

[5] "On the way of all people."

[6] Thut-nakht quotes, somewhat inaptly, a proverb against the peasant's attempt to invoke higher authority.

[7] Osiris, god of the dead, had a sanctuary near Herakleopolis.

[8] By appealing to the god for justice, the peasant turns to his own account Thut-nakht's attempt to silence him.

Then this peasant said: "Would that I might be permitted to make a communication to thee about this recital of fact! It is (only) a matter of letting an attendant of thine of thy choice come to me, (so that) I might send him back to thee about it."[9] So the Chief Steward, Meru's son Rensi, had (40) an attendant of his choice go in front of him,[10] and this peasant sent him back about this affair in every aspect of it.

Then the Chief Steward, Meru's son Rensi, laid a charge against this Thut-nakht before the officials who were at his side. Then they said to him: "Probably it is a peasant of his who has gone to someone else beside him. (45) Behold, that is what they do to peasants of theirs who go to others beside them.[11] It is (only) a matter of having this Thut-nakht punished for a little natron and a little salt. Let him be ordered to replace it, and he will replace it." Then (50) the Chief Steward, Meru's son Rensi, was silent; he did not reply to these officials, nor did he reply to this peasant.

Then this peasant came to appeal to the Chief Steward, Meru's son Rensi. He said:

"O Chief Steward, my lord, greatest of the great, undertaker of that which is not and of that which is![12] If thou embarkest on the lake of (55) justice, mayest thou sail on it with a fair breeze! A *squall* shall not tear away thy sail, thy boat shall not lag, no misfortune shall overtake thy mast, thy *yards* shall not break, . . . the current shall not carry thee away, thou shalt not taste the evils (60) of the river, thou shalt not see a frightened face! (Even) the *timid* fish shall come to thee, and thou shalt attain (some) of the fattest fowl. Because thou art the father of the orphan, the husband of the widow, the brother of the divorcee, and the apron of him that is motherless. Let me make thy name in (65) this land according to every good law: a leader free from covetousness, a great man free from wrongdoing, one who destroys falsehood and brings justice into being, and who comes at the cry of him who gives voice. When I speak, mayest thou hear. Do justice, thou favored one whom the favored ones favor! Dispose of (70) my burdens. Behold me, (how) burdened I am! Count me: behold, I am lacking!"[13]

Now this peasant made this speech in the time of the majesty of the King of Upper and Lower Egypt: Neb-kau-Re, the triumphant. So the Chief Steward, Meru's son Rensi, went before his majesty and said: "My lord, (75) I have found one of these peasants who is really eloquent. His goods have been stolen, and, behold, he has come to appeal to me about it."

Then his majesty said: "As truly as thou wishest to see me in health, thou shalt make him linger here,

[9] A typically oriental proposal to treat the matter through an intermediary instead of by direct appeal.

[10] On their way to the official barge.

[11] The magistrates take the attitude that Thut-nakht's guilt is slight and may be expiated by repayment, whereas custom condones rough treatment of a peasant who has left his normal patron and has sought action elsewhere.

[12] i.e. of everything.

[13] In his first appeal the peasant is still courteous and takes justice for granted. Later he becomes more indignant in his appeals, daring to charge the Chief Steward with injustice.

without replying to anything which he may say. For the purpose of keeping him (80) talking, be thou silent. Then have his speech brought to us in writing, (that) we may hear it. But provide that on which his wife and children may live. Behold, one of these peasants may come before his house is empty down to the ground.[14] Further, keep this peasant himself alive. Thou shalt cause that provisions be given to him, without letting him know that thou art the one who has given them to him."

So they gave him ten loaves of bread and two jars of beer (85) every day. The Chief Steward, Meru's son Rensi, used to give them. He used to give them to a friend of his, and he was the one who gave them to him. Then the Chief Steward, Meru's son Rensi, sent to the Mayor of the Field of Salt about providing food for this peasant's wife: *thirty heḳat* of grain every day.

THEN THIS PEASANT CAME TO APPEAL TO HIM A SECOND TIME. . . . (100) . . .[15]

THEN THE CHIEF STEWARD, MERU'S SON RENSI, SAID: "Is what belongs to thee more important to thy heart than (the fact) that my attendant may carry thee off?"[16] Then this peasant said: "The measurer of (105) piles (of grain) cheats for himself. He who should fill up for another trims his share. He who should lead according to the laws orders robbery. Who then will punish meanness? He who should drive out *decay* (himself) makes distortions. One man is straightforward in crookedness, another *assents to* mischance. Dost thou thyself find (*a lesson*) for thee? *Punishment is short*, (but) mischance is long. A (good) example comes back to its place of yesterday.[17] Now this is the command: 'Do to the doer (110) to cause that he do.' That is thanking him[18] for what he may do. That is parrying something before (it is) shot. That is ordering something from him who (already) has business."[19] . . . (145) . . .

"Desire to live long, as it is said: 'Doing justice is the (very) breath of the nose.'[20] Carry out punishment against him who should be punished, and none shall equal thy scrupulousness. Does the hand-scales err? Does the stand-balance incline to the side? Is even Thoth (150) indulgent?[21] Then thou (also) mayest work mischief. When thou makest thyself the second[22] of these three, if the three are indulgent, then thou (also) mayest be indulgent. . . . Take not, (for) thou shouldst act against a taker. (165) That great one who is covetous is not really great. Thy tongue is the plummet (of the balance), thy heart is the weight, and thy two lips are its arms. If thou veilest thy face against violence, who then will punish meanness?

"Behold, thou art a wretch of a washerman, covetous in injuring (170) a friend, *abandoning his partner* for the sake of his client. He who comes *that he may buy* is his brother.[23] Behold, thou art a ferryman who ferries over (only) him that has a fare, a straight-dealer whose straight-dealing is clipped short. . . . Behold, thou art a butler whose delight is butchering, (177) the mutilation of which (does) not (fall) upon him. . . . Prepare not for the morrow before it arrives; one knows not what mischance may be in it."

Now when this peasant made this speech, (185) the Chief Steward, Meru's son Rensi, was at the entrance of the administration building. Then he had two guardsmen attend to him with whips. Then they belabored all his limbs therewith.

Then this peasant said: "So the son of Meru goes on erring! His face is blind to what he sees and deaf to what he hears, misguided of heart because of what has been related to him. Behold, thou art a town (190) which has no mayor, like a company which has no chief, like a ship in which there is no pilot, a confederacy which has no leader. Behold, thou art a *constable* who steals, a mayor who accepts (bribes), a district overseer who should punish robbery, (but) who has become the precedent for him that does (it)." . . .[24]

"Do not plunder of his property a poor man, a weakling as thou knowest him. His property is the (very) breath of a suffering man, and he who takes it away is one who stops up his nose. Thou wert appointed to conduct hearings, to judge between two men, (235) and to punish the brigand, (but) behold, it is the upholder of the thief which thou wouldst be. One trusts in thee, whereas thou art become a transgressor. Thou wert appointed to be a dam for the sufferer, guarding lest he drown, (but) behold, thou art his flowing lake."

Now then this peasant came (240) to appeal to him a sixth time, and he said: ". . . (250) . . . Cheating diminishes justice. (But) good full (measure)—justice neither falls short nor overflows. . . ."

Now then (290) this peasant came to appeal to him an eighth time, and he said: "O Chief Steward, my lord! One may fall a long way because of greed. The covetous man is void of success; (any) success of his belongs to failure. Though thy heart is covetous, it is not (of avail) for thee. Though thou robbest, it does not profit thee, who should still permit a man to attend to his (own) proper business. Thy (own) needs are in thy house; thy belly is full; the grain-measure overflows—(but) when it *is jostled* (295) its surplus is lost on the ground. Takers, robbers, appropriators, magistrates—(and yet) made to punish evil! Magistrates are a refuge for the violent—(and yet) made to punish deceit! . . .

[14] One of the peasants of the Wadi Natrun is to come to Egypt to get food for the peasant's family.

[15] In his second appeal the peasant boldly suggests that the expected dispenser of justice is becoming an abuser of justice.

[16] The Chief Steward interrupts with a threat of punishment if the peasant insists upon his property claims.

[17] A good deed is normative of the good times of the past.

[18] "That is praising god for him."

[19] Doing unto others, in order to induce them to do for oneself, produces in advance the desired results.

[20] The Egyptians inhaled the "breath of life."

[21] Thoth was the patron of just measure.

[22] *Sic*, in the sense of "companion."

[23] In these passages the Chief Steward is likened to a business man without charity, his sole interest being profit.

[24] The above is from the third appeal. The following extract is from the fifth.

"Do justice for the sake of the Lord of Justice,[25] the justice of whose justice exists! (305) Thou reed-pen, papyrus, and palette of Thoth,[26] keep apart from doing evil! It is good if thou art good—good indeed. Now justice lasts unto eternity; it goes down into the necropolis with him who does it. When he is buried and interred, (310) his name is not wiped out upon earth, (but) he is remembered for goodness. That is a principle of the word of god.[27] Is it the hand-scales—(then) it does not tilt. Is it the stand-balance—(then) it does not incline to the side. Whether I shall come or whether another may come, thou shouldst address (us) (315) with an answer. Do not address (us) silently. Do not attack him who cannot attack. . . ."

(B2,91) Now THEN this peasant CAME to appeal to him a ninth time, and he said: "O Chief Steward, my lord! The balance of men is their tongue. It is the scales which seeks out deficiencies (in weight). Carry out punishment against him who should be punished, (or some) one will equal thy scrupulousness. . . . If falsehood walks about, it goes astray. It cannot cross over in the ferry; [it] does not *advance.* (100) As for him who grows rich thereby, he has no children, he has no heirs upon earth. As for him who sails with it, he cannot reach land, his boat cannot moor at its town.

"Be not heavy; thou art not light. Do not delay; thou art not swift. Be not partial. Do not listen to (105) the heart. Do not veil thy face against him whom thou knowest. Do not blind thy face against him whom thou hast beheld. Do not rebuff him who petitions thee. Mayest thou *step down* from this sluggishness, (in order that) thy saying may be reported: 'Act for him who acts for thee.' Do not listen to everybody, (but) summon a man to his (own) rightful interests. There is no yesterday for the slothful,[28] (110) no friend for him deaf to truth, no holiday for the covetous. He who is (*now*) *esteemed may* become a sufferer, and the sufferer a petitioner, (*if*) the enemy becomes a killer.[29] Behold, I have been appealing to thee, (but) thou dost not hear it. I shall go that I may appeal (115) about thee to Anubis."

Then the Chief Steward, Meru's son Rensi, sent two guardsmen to bring him back. Then this peasant was afraid, for he thought that (it) was done in order to punish him for this speech which he had made. Then this peasant said: "The approach of a thirsty man to water, the tasting (120) of milk by the nursing child—*this* [*is*] *death, for* the coming *of which one* has longed to see, (*when*) his death comes for him delayed."[30]

Then the Chief Steward, Meru's son Rensi, said: "Do not be afraid, peasant! Behold, thou shalt *arrange to live* with me. Then this peasant *took* (125) *an oath*: "I will surely eat of thy bread, and I will surely drink [of] thy [beer] to eternity!" The Chief Steward, Meru's son Rensi, said: "Now tarry here, that thou mayest hear thy appeals." Then he caused to be read from a new roll of papyrus every appeal according to [its] content. (130) Then the Chief Steward, Meru's son Rensi, sent it in to the majesty of the King of Upper and Lower Egypt: Neb-kau-Re, the triumphant. Then it was more pleasing to [his] heart than anything which was in this entire land. Then [his majesty] said: "Give thou judgment thyself, O son of Meru!"

Then [the Chief Steward], Meru's son Rensi, sent two guardsmen to [*fetch Thut-nakht*]. (135) Then he was brought, and a report was made of [*all his property*]: . . . , his . . . , six persons, apart [from] . . . , his Upper Egyptian barley, his emmer, [his] donkeys, . . . , his pigs, and [his small] cattle. [*So the property of*] this Thut-nakht [*was given*] to [this peasant], . . .

For examples of myths explicative of origins, cf. pp. 8-9 and 10 above. For examples of legends conferring sanction upon Egyptian documents, cf. p. 495 below.

[25] In different contexts various gods carried this epithet. Perhaps no one god is meant here, but the appeal to the justice of the gods is still explicit.

[26] The writing instruments with which Thoth recorded justice.

[27] The divine order, as known in the sacred writings.

[28] A high past was a prized heritage of the Egyptians.

[29] Perhaps the peasant is here emboldened to threaten the Chief Steward, since his nine appeals have apparently been fruitless. If this threat carries on into the following sentences, it means that the peasant will petition the god of the dead to take action against the Chief Steward.

[30] Despite his fear of the maximum punishment, the peasant puts the best face on the prospect of death.

Akkadian Fable

(Translator: Robert H. Pfeiffer)

DISPUTE BETWEEN THE DATE PALM AND THE TAMARISK

A

Text: E. Ebeling, *KAR*, Vol. I, No. 1245. Translation: E. Ebeling, *Die babylonische Fabel*, pp. 6-8. (*MAOG*, II/3 [1927].) Ebeling, in *AOT*, pp. 294-5. For other fragmentary fables see Chr. Johnston, Assyrian and Babylonian Beast Fables, *AJSL*, XXVIII (1911-12), 81 ff.

(obverse)

. . . . (3) The tamarisk [opened] its mouth and [said,] "My flesh for the flesh of . . . . (5) You have destroyed the precious, beautiful one,[1] *you have cast* . . . like a maid-servant who has [raised her hand] against her mistress."

(7) The date palm's mouth became very large and it answered saying, "They have broken off your blossom with a stick! . . . For whom are they closed up? For sin! The flesh . . . (10) The tamarisk does not know the beauty of the gods, the beauty of [the goddesses]."

(11) Ditto.[2] "I am higher than you, O father of the wise, in every respect; the farmer has [made it known]. The farmer cuts all he has from my sprout. From my bosom he brings forth his hoe; [the earth] he opens up with my hoe. The irrigation ditch waters the field, and

[1] Perhaps Tammuz (Adonis) is meant.

[2] "Ditto" here and below (lines 17, 21, 28, 32, 37, 40, 45) means the repetition of line 7, except that in lines 11, 21, 32, and 40 the tamarisk is speaking and should be substituted for the date palm in this introductory formula.

I close it. (15) And in spite of the dampness of the earth, the grain . . . I thresh. So I bring in (the goddess of grain) Nisaba, the people's joy."

(17) Ditto. "I am higher than you, O father of the wise, in every respect; the farmer [has made it known]. All that he has, the bridle, the whip, the team's cover, . . . , the rope, the ox cloth, the cloth for the box, the net, the wagon, . . . , (20) . . . , the utensils of the farmer, as many as there are: [I am] higher [than you]."

(21) Ditto. "Pay attention, O lunatic.[3] What of mine [is set up] in the king's palace? In the king's house the king eats off my table, [the queen drinks] from my cup, with my *fork* the warriors eat, out of my basket the baker takes the flour; I am a weaver [and I weave] my threads; (25) I clothe the troops . . . . I am the chief exorcist of the god, I renew the house of god, [I am the] master. Let there be no rival of mine!"

(reverse)

(28) Ditto. "In *the shrine*, when sacrifices are offered to the great gods, where I am not standing the king does not sacrifice with a wise heart. (30) In (ritual) sprinkling they pour out my libation, they scatter my branches on the ground. [I am the master.] On the same day the date palm is the perfumer. A big mouth [pronounces] your replies."

(32) Ditto. "Come, let us go, I and you, to the city of Kish . . . where my work is. To wit, are not [the temples] filled with my omens, [are not the vessels] filled with my incense? The temple prostitute pours out water, . . . (35) she takes. They purify themselves (thereby) and perform rites with it. On the same day [the tamarisk] is available to the hand of the sacrificer and its container is in the place [*of the gods*]."

(37) Ditto. "Come, let us go, I and you, to the city of . . . . Where there are sins, there is your activity, O tamarisk. A carpenter . . . , and him they fear, and every day they dread [him]."

(40) Ditto. "Who is like . . . ? My cluster is luxuriant; (though) I lift it high, shepherd boys make out of it big sticks. But they cut up your face like a basketmaker who . . . . Terrible is my strength, let me gloat about my fury! I have placed you in the underworld. My work is might . . . ."

(45) Ditto. "I am taller than you, six times greater, seven times greater. I am a comrade of the goddess Nisaba, three months . . . . The orphan girl, the widow, the wretched man . . . eat the sweet dates which are not scarce . . . . (50) (Text) destroyed.[4] My ropes . . . (51-52 fragments; 53 ff. lost.)

[3] The restorations in lines 21-26 are based on the parallels in B, 31-36 (see below).

B

Text: E. Ebeling, *KAR*, Fascicule viii, No. 324. Translation: E. Ebeling, *Die babylonische Fabel*, pp. 11-2.

(1) In the holy (primeval) days,—in those days the people dug canals, the (gods of the) destinies assembled —they appointed (as) gods in the countries Anu, Enlil, Ea. Enlil and the people *came*, (5) the god Shamash sat between them. Ditto sat the mistress of the gods, the great (Ishtar). To them[5] the dominion of the countries did not belong, for the lordship was granted to the gods. Gishganmesh the gods appointed as king. (10) They ordered him (to accomplish) the image of the finest things. The king in his palace plants date palms, in addition, *ditto, just as many* tamarisks. In the shade of the tamarisk *a banquet* (15) *was arranged*. In the shade of the date palm decision concerning crime . . . opening . . . the path of the king. The trees . . . *compared* themselves one with the other. The tamarisk and the date palms became restless. (20) The tamarisk spoke, greatly [praising] himself; when the date palm (spoke), surpassing (in boastfulness) was (its) word. "As for you, O tamarisk, you are useless wood. What are your branches? Wood without fruit. Mine is the fruit of a big tree: (25) *fully grown* it is food; in the second place the gardener speaks well (of me) as a profit for slave and governor. The nourishment of my fruit makes the infant grow, adults eat my fruit. (30) Am I not well thought of in the king's presence? O lunatic,[6] in the king's palace what is set up of mine? In the king's palace the king eats off my table, the queen drinks out of my cup. (35) I am a weaver and I weave my threads. A god I purify as an exorcist . . . ." "My mouth is not a weapon; in the second place . . ." (said the tamarisk). "Its mouth is not a weapon," [*the king*] answered; he planted at its side the date palm (saying), "If (you stand) at the city gate, calm the strife; if in the wilderness, calm the heat."

[4] "Destroyed" is a scribal note.

[5] i.e. presumably the people.

[6] Lines 31-36 are substantially identical with parts of A, 21-26 (see above).

Proverbs and Precepts

Egyptian Instructions

(Translator: John A. Wilson)

THE INSTRUCTION OF THE VIZIER PTAH-HOTEP

The Egyptians delighted in compilations of wise sayings, which were directive for a successful life. To them, this was "wisdom." One of the earliest of these compilations purports to come from Ptah-hotep, the vizier of King Izezi of the Fifth Dynasty (about 2450 B.C.). The old councilor is supposed to be instructing his son and designated successor on the actions and attitudes which make a successful official of the state.

The chief manuscript is the Papyrus Prisse of the Bibliothèque Nationale in Paris (No. 183-194), written in the Middle Kingdom. Later documents, running into the Eighteenth Dynasty, are British Museum Papyri 10371, 10435, and 10509, and the reverse of Carnarvon Tablet I, now in the Cairo Museum (cf. pp. 232-233 above). Facsimiles of the hieratic texts were published by G. Jéquier, *Le Papyrus Prisse et ses variantes* (Paris, 1911). Extracts in facsimile are given in G. Möller, *Hieratische Lesestücke* (2nd ed., Leipzig, 1927), I, 2-3. The texts are transcribed into hieroglyphic in E. Dévaud, *Les maximes de Ptahhotep* (Fribourg, 1916). The following translation uses Dévaud's numbering for the texts. There are translations by B. Gunn, *The Instruction of Ptah-hotep and the Instruction of Ke'gemni* (*Wisdom of the East Series*; London, 1909), and by Erman, *LAE*, 54-66. On the general subject of Egyptian wisdom literature in successive periods, see R. Anthes, *Lebensregeln und Lebensweisheit der alten Aegypter* (*AO*, 32,2, Leipzig, 1933).

THE INSTRUCTION[1] OF THE MAYOR AND VIZIER PTAH-HOTEP,[2] UNDER the majesty of the King of Upper and Lower Egypt: Izezi, living forever and ever. The Mayor and Vizier Ptah-hotep says:

O sovereign, my lord! Oldness has come; old age has descended. Feebleness has arrived; dotage is coming anew. The heart sleeps wearily every day. The eyes are weak, the ears are deaf, the strength is disappearing because of weariness of heart, and the mouth is silent and cannot speak. The heart is forgetful and cannot recall yesterday. The bone suffers old age. Good is become evil. All taste is gone. What old age does to men is evil in every respect. The nose is stopped up and cannot breathe. (Simply) to stand up or to sit down is difficult.

Let a command be issued to this servant to make a staff of old age,[3] that my son may be made to stand in my place. Then may I speak to him the words of them that listen and the ideas of the ancestors, of them that hearkened to the gods.[4] Then shall the like be done for thee, that strife may be banished from the people and the Two Banks may serve thee.

Then the majesty of this god[5] said:

Teach thou him first about speaking. Then he may set an example for the children of officials. May obedience enter into him, and all heart's poise. Speak to him. There is no one born wise.

THE BEGINNING OF THE EXPRESSION OF GOOD SPEECH, SPOKEN BY the Hereditary Prince and Count, God's Father and God's Beloved, eldest son of the king, of his body, the Mayor and Vizier, Ptah-hotep, in instructing the ignorant about wisdom and about the rules for good speech, as of advantage to him who will hearken and of disadvantage to him who may neglect them.

Then he said to his son:

Let not thy heart be puffed-up because of thy knowledge; be not confident because thou art a wise man. Take counsel with the ignorant as well as the wise. The (full) limits of skill cannot be attained, and there is no skilled man equipped to his (full) advantage.[6] Good speech is more hidden than the emerald, but it may be found with maidservants at the grindstones. . . .[7]

IF THOU ART A LEADER commanding the affairs of the multitude, seek out for thyself every beneficial deed, until it may be that thy (own) affairs are without wrong. Justice is great, and its appropriateness is lasting; it has not been disturbed since the time of him who made it, (whereas) there is punishment for him who passes over its laws. It is the (right) path before him who knows nothing. Wrongdoing has never brought its undertaking into port. (It may be that) it is fraud that gains riches, (but) the strength of justice is that it lasts, and a man may say: "It is the property of my father."[8] . . .

IF THOU ART ONE OF THOSE SITTING at the table of one greater than thyself, take what he may give, when it is set before thy nose. Thou shouldst gaze at what is before thee. Do not pierce him with many stares, (for such) an aggression against him is an abomination to the *ka*.[9] Let thy face be cast down until he addresses thee, and thou shouldst speak (only) when he addresses thee. Laugh after he laughs, and it will be very pleasing to his heart and what thou mayest do will be pleasing to the heart. No one can know what is in the heart.

As for the great man when he is at meals, his purposes

[1] The word *sebayit* "teaching," came to be used by the Egyptians for "wisdom," because of their orientation toward the models of the past.

[2] There was more than one vizier named Ptah-hotep around the time of the pharaoh Izezi. The best known of them left a tomb at Sakkarah: M. Murray, *Saqqara Mastabas*, I (London, 1905).

[3] The son as the support of his father. "This servant," literally "the servant there," is polite for "me."

[4] Variant: "of them that served the forebears," i.e. previous government officials.

[5] The king.

[6] "Limits of craftsmanship," or "artistry," and "no skilled craftsman," or "artist"—here in eloquent speech.

[7] This translation omits many sections which are obscure.

[8] *Ma'at* "justice" or "truth," was an inheritable value.

[9] The *ka* was the protecting and guiding vital force of a man, and thus his social mentor.

conform to the dictates of his *ḳa*. He will give to the one whom he favors. The great man gives to *the man whom he can reach*, (but) it is the *ḳa* that lengthens out his arms. The eating of bread is under the planning of god[10]—it is (only) a fool who would *complain of* it.

If thou art a man of intimacy, whom one great man sends to another, be thoroughly reliable when he sends thee. Carry out the errand for him as he has spoken. Do not be reserved about what is said to thee, and beware of (any) act of forgetfulness. Grasp hold of truth, and do not exceed it. *(Mere) gratification is by no means to be repeated.* Struggle against making words worse, (thus) *making* one great man *hostile* to another *through vulgar speech*.[11] A great man, a little man—it is the *ḳa*'s abomination.[12] . . .

If thou art a poor fellow, following a man of distinction, one of good standing with the god, know thou not his former insignificance. Thou shouldst not be puffed-up against him because of what thou didst know of him formerly. Show regard[13] for him in conformance with what has accrued to him—property does not come of itself. It is their law for him who wishes them. *As for him who oversteps, he is feared.* It is god who makes (a man's) quality, and he defends him (even) while he is asleep. . . .

If thou art a man of standing and foundest a household and producest a son who is pleasing to god,[14] if he is correct and inclines toward thy ways and listens to thy instruction, while his manners in thy house are fitting, and if he takes care of thy property as it should be, seek out for him every useful action. He is thy son, whom thy *ḳa* engendered for thee. Thou shouldst not cut thy heart off from him.

(But a man's) seed (often) creates enmity.[15] If he goes astray and transgresses thy plans and does not carry out thy instruction, (so that) his manners in thy household are wretched, and he rebels against all that thou sayest, while his mouth *runs on* in the (most) wretched talk, *(quite) apart from his experience*, while he possesses nothing,[16] Thou shouldst cast him off: he is not thy son at all. He was not really born to thee. (Thus) thou enslavest him entirely according to his (own) speech. . . . He is one whom god has condemned in the (very) womb. . . .

If thou art one to whom petition is made, be calm as thou listenest to the petitioner's speech. Do not rebuff him before he has swept out his body or before he has said that for which he came. A petitioner likes attention to his words better than the fulfilling of that for which he came.[17] He is rejoicing thereat more than any (other) petitioner, (even) before that which has been heard has come to pass. As for him who plays the rebuffer of a petitioner, men say: "Now why is he doing it?" It is not *(necessary)* that everything about which he has petitioned *should* come to pass, (but) a good hearing is a soothing of the heart.

If thou desirest to make friendship last in a home to which thou hast access as master,[18] as a brother, or as a friend, into any place where thou mightest enter, beware of approaching the women. It does not go well with the place where that is done. *The face has no alertness by splitting it.*[19] A thousand men *may be distracted from* their (own) advantage. One is made a fool by limbs of fayence, as she stands (there), become (all) carnelian. A mere trifle, the likeness of a dream—and one attains death through knowing her. . . . Do not do it—it is really an abomination—and thou shalt be free from sickness of heart every day. As for him who escapes from gluttony for it, all affairs will prosper with him. . . .

Do not be covetous at a division. Do not be greedy, unless (it be) for thy (own) portion. Do not be covetous against thy (own) kindred. Greater is the respect for the mild than (for) the strong. He is a mean person who *exposes* his kinsfolk; he is empty of *the fruits of conversation*.[20] It is (only) a little of that for which one is covetous that turns a calm man into a contentious man.

If thou art a man of standing, thou shouldst found thy household and love thy wife at home as is fitting. Fill her belly; clothe her back. Ointment is the prescription for her body. Make her heart glad as long as thou livest. She is a profitable field for her lord.[21] Thou shouldst not contend with her at law, and keep her far from gaining control. . . . Her eye is her stormwind. Let her heart be soothed through what may accrue to thee; it means keeping her long in thy house. . . .

Satisfy thy clients with what has accrued to thee,[22] what accrues to one whom god favors. As for him who evades satisfying his clients, men say: "He is a *ḳa* of *robbery*. A proper *ḳa* is a *ḳa* with which one is satisfied."[23] One does not know what may happen, so that he may understand the morrow. If misfortunes occur among those (now) favored, it is the clients who (still) say: "Welcome!" One does not secure satisfaction from a stranger; one has recourse to a client when there is trouble. . . .

[10] "God" in these wisdom texts sometimes means the king, sometimes the supreme or creator god, and sometimes the force which demands proper behavior—a force not clearly defined, but perhaps the local god.

[11] "By the speaking of everybody"? Perhaps: "Do not talk (to) everybody."

[12] Do not draw invidious distinctions?

[13] "Fear."

[14] "God"—probably the king in this context.

[15] This sentence may be understood on the basis that the Egyptian words for "semen" and "poison" are the same word.

[16] "There is not, in his hands." It is characteristic of the period that moral qualities, filial piety, and the possession of property should be linked as virtues.

[17] Variant: "One who has woes likes the assuaging of his heart better than the doing of that for which he came."

[18] Variant: "as a son."

[19] Perhaps: He who has a wandering eye for the women cannot be keen.

[20] "A mean person is he who goes out (from?) under his kinsfolk; (he is) void of the bringing of speech."

[21] The desire for children—particularly male children—was perennial in the orient.

[22] The word "satisfy" sometimes means "pay off." The word "clients," literally "those who enter," may here apply to the entourage of a high official.

[23] Probably: He is the very spirit of rapacity; the right kind of a spirit is one which gratifies others.

If thou art a man of standing, one sitting in the counsels of his lord, summon thy resources[24] for good. If thou art silent, it is better than *teftef*-plants. If thou speakest, thou shouldst know how thou canst explain (difficulties). It is a (real) craftsman who can speak in counsel, (for) speaking is more difficult than any labor. It is explaining *it that puts it to the stick*.[25] . . .

If thou art (now) important after thy (former) unimportance, so that thou mayest do things after a neediness formerly in the town which thou knowest, in contrast to what was thy lot before, do not be miserly with thy wealth, which has accrued to thee as the gift of god. Thou art not behind[26] some other equal of thine to whom the same has happened.

Bow thy back to thy superior, thy overseer from the palace. (Then) thy household will be established in its property, and thy recompense will be as it should be. Opposition to a superior is a painful thing, (for) one lives as long as he is mild. . . .

If thou art seeking out the nature of a friend, one whom thou questionest, draw near to him and deal with him alone, until thou art no (longer) troubled about his condition. Reason with him after a while. *Test* his heart with a bit of talk. If what he may have seen should come out of him or he should do something with which thou art displeased, behold, he is still a friend. . . . . . . Do not answer in a *state* of turmoil; do not *remove* thyself from him; do not trample him down. His time has never failed to come; he cannot escape from him who predetermined him. . . .

If thou hearest this which I have said to thee, thy every project will be (*better*) than (*those of*) *the ancestors*. As for what is left over of their truth, it is their treasure—(*though*) the memory of them *may* escape from the mouth of men—because of the goodness of their sayings. Every word is carried on, without perishing in this land forever. It makes *for expressing well*, the speech of the *very* officials. It is what teaches a man to speak to the future, so that it may hear it, what produces a craftsman, who has heard what is good and who speaks to the future—and it hears it.[27] . . .

To hear is of advantage for a son who hearkens. If hearing enters into a hearkener, the hearkener becomes a hearer.[28] (When) hearing is good, speaking is good. Every hearkener (is) an advantage, and hearing is of advantage to the hearkener. To hear is better than anything that is, (and thus) comes the goodly love (of a man). How good it is when a son accepts what his father says! Thereby *maturity* comes to him. He whom god loves is a hearkener, (but) he whom god hates cannot hear. It is the heart which brings up its lord as one who hears or as one who does not hear. The life, prosperity, and health of a man is his heart.[29] . . .

If a son accepts what his father says, no project of his miscarries. He whom thou instructest as thy obedient son, who will stand well in the heart of the official, his speech is guided with respect to what has been said to him, one regarded as obedient. . . . (But) the *induction*[30] of him who does not hearken miscarries. The wise man rises early in the morning to establish himself, (but) the fool rises early in the morning (only) to *agitate* himself.

As for the fool who does not hearken, he cannot do anything. He regards knowledge as ignorance and profit as loss. He does everything blameworthy, so that one finds fault with him every day. He lives on that through which he should die, and guilt is his food. His character therefrom *is told* as something known to the officials: dying while alive every day. . . .

An obedient son is a follower of Horus.[31] It goes well with him when he hears. When he becomes old and reaches a venerable state, he converses in the same way to his children, by renewing the instruction of his father. Every man is *as (well) instructed as he acts*. If he converses with (his) children, then they will speak (to) their children. . . .

Mayest thou reach me,[32] with thy body sound, and with the king satisfied with all that has taken place. Mayest thou attain (my) years of life. What I have done on earth is not inconsiderable. I attained one hundred and ten years of life which the king gave me,[33] with favor foremost among the ancestors, through doing right for the king up to the point of veneration.[34]

It has come (to its end, from) its beginning to its end, like that which was found in writing.

THE INSTRUCTION FOR KING MERI-KA-RE

The confused period between the Old and Middle Kingdoms was a time of changing values. The overturn of the old sanctions of power and property exerted a sobering influence. New values were increasingly expressed in spiritual and social terms, as the following text from that period shows. It presents the advice which one of the several competing rulers of that time (end of the 22nd century B.C.) gave to his son and successor.

The text is on the verso of the Papyrus Leningrad 1116A, a manuscript copied in the Eighteenth Dynasty, in the latter half of the 15th century B.C.; published by W. Golénischeff, *Les papyrus hiératiques no. 1115, 1116A, et 1116B de l'Ermitage Impérial à St. Pétersbourg* (St. Petersburg, 1913), Pls. IX-XIV. Two other very fragmentary papyrus copies of the text are known. Translated by A. H. Gardiner in *JEA*, I (1914), 20-36, and by Erman, *LAE*, 75-84. An excellent special study is A. Scharff, *Der historische Abschnitt der Lehre für König Merikarê* (*SBAW*, 1936, Heft 8).

(1) [The beginning of the instruction which the

24 "Gather thy heart."

25 The ability to expound puts speech to the test?

26 Not behind or ahead of, but the same as?

27 Glorification of the verbal wisdom of the past. For a glorification of the written wisdom of the past, cf. pp. 431-432 below.

28 This section gives itself up to a literary play on the word "to hear." Its purpose is to prescribe "hearkening" or obedience upon the youth, so that he may become a "hearer" or magistrate who hears cases.

29 The seat of his mind and emotion.

30 Induction into the official service?

31 Elsewhere this term applies to the deified kings of past ages. Here it was probably a servant of the existing king, who was a Horus.

32 Join me in the next world.

33 The Egyptians considered 110 the ideal age limit. cf. Gen., 50:26.

34 Until death.

King of Upper and Lower Egypt: . . . made] for his son, King Meri-ka-Re, . . .[1]

(21) . . . [IF] THOU [FINDEST A MAN who] . . . , whose adherents are many in total, . . . and he is gracious in the sight of his partisans, . . . and he is *excitable*, a talker —remove him, kill [him], wipe out his name, [*destroy*] his faction, banish the memory of him and of his adherents who love him.

(25) THE CONTENTIOUS MAN IS A DISTURBANCE TO CITIZENS: he produces two factions among the youth. If thou findest that the citizens adhere to him . . . , denounce him in the presence of the court, and remove [him]. He also is a traitor. A talker is *an exciter* of a city. *Divert* the multitude and supress its heat. . . .

(30) . . . Thou shouldst be justified in the presence of the god. Then people will say, (*even*) [*in*] thy *ab*[*sence*], that thou punishest in conformance with . . . A good demeanor is a man's heaven, (but) cursing the *stormy* of heart is wrong.

BE A CRAFTSMAN IN SPEECH, (SO THAT) THOU MAYEST BE STRONG, (for) the tongue is a sword to [*a man*], and speech is more valorous than any fighting. No one can circumvent the skillful of heart. . . . They who know his wisdom do not attack him, and no [*misfortune*] occurs where he is. Truth comes to him (fully) brewed, in accordance with the sayings of the ancestors.

(35) COPY THY FATHERS AND THY ANCESTORS. . . . Behold, their words remain in writing. Open, that thou mayest read and copy (their) wisdom. (Thus) the skilled man becomes *learned*.

Be not evil: patience is good. Make thy memorial to last through the love of thee. . . . God will be praised as (thy) reward, . . . praises because of thy goodness and prayers for thy health . . .

RESPECT THE NOBLES AND MAKE THY PEOPLE TO PROSPER. Establish thy boundaries and thy *frontier-patrol*. It is good to act for the future. Respect a life of attentiveness,[2] for (*mere*) *credulity*[3] will (lead) to wretchedness. . . . (40) . . . He who is covetous when other men possess is a fool, (because) [life] upon earth passes by, it has no length. Happy is he who [*is without*] sin in it. (Even) a million men may be of no avail to the Lord of the Two Lands. . . .

ADVANCE THY GREAT MEN, SO THAT THEY MAY CARRY OUT THY LAWS. He who is rich does not show partiality in his (own) house. He is a possessor of property who has no wants. (But) the poor man does not speak according to what is right for him. It is of no avail to say: "Would that I had!" He is partial to him who possesses rewards for him.[4] Great is a great man when his great men are great. Valiant (45) is the king possessed of courtiers; august is he who is rich in his nobles.

Mayest thou speak justice in thy (own) house, (that) the great ones who are on earth may fear thee. Uprightness of heart is fitting for the lord. It is the forepart of the house that inspires respect in the back.[5]

DO JUSTICE WHILST THOU ENDUREST UPON EARTH. Quiet the weeper; do not oppress the widow; supplant no man in the property of his father; and impair no officials at their *posts*. Be on thy guard against punishing wrongfully. Do not slaughter: it is not of advantage to thee. (But) thou shouldst punish with beatings and with arrests; this land will be (firmly) grounded thereby—except (for) the rebel, when his plans are discovered, for the god knows the treacherous of heart, (50) and the god condemns his sins in blood.[6] . . . Do not kill a man when thou knowest his good qualities, one with whom thou once didst sing the writings.[7] He who reads in the *sipu*-book[8] . . . god, free-moving of foot in difficult places, (his) soul comes to the place which it knows. It does not miss the ways of yesterday. No magic can oppose it, (but) it reaches those who will give it water.[9]

THE COUNCIL WHICH JUDGES THE DEFICIENT, thou knowest that they are not lenient on that day of judging the miserable, the hour of doing (their) duty.[10] It is woe when the accuser is one of knowledge. Do not trust in length of years, (55) for they regard a lifetime as (but) an hour.[11] A man remains over after death, and his deeds are placed beside him in heaps.[12] However, existence yonder is for eternity, and he who *complains of* it is a fool. (But) as for him who reaches it without wrongdoing, he shall exist yonder like a god, stepping out freely like the lords of eternity.

FOSTER THY YOUNGER GENERATION, THAT THE RESIDENCE CITY MAY LOVE THEE, and increase thy adherents with *recruits*. Behold, thy citizenry is full of new growing (boys). It is twenty years that the younger generation is happy following its heart, (and then) *recruits* [*come*] *forth anew*.[13] . . . (60) . . . Make thy officials great, advance thy [*soldiers*], increase the younger generation of thy [follow]ing, provided with *property*, endowed with fields, and rewarded with cattle.

DO NOT DISTINGUISH THE SON OF A MAN[14] FROM A POOR MAN, (but) take to thyself a man because of the work of his hands. Every skilled work should be practised according to the . . . of the lord of a strong arm. Protect

[1] Scharff, *op.cit.*, 7-8, suggests that the author of these instructions was Wah-ka-Re Khety II, pharaoh at Herakleopolis in the Faiyum, the father and predecessor of Meri-ka-Re and a contemporary of Tef-ib of Siut and of Wah-ankh Intef I of Thebes. The first 20 lines of the manuscript are too broken for consecutive translation. They seem to deal with the treatment of rebellion, which was epidemic at the time.

[2] "Open(ness) of face."

[3] "Filling the heart."

[4] The poorly recompensed official inclines toward those who bribe him.

[5] The front part of an Egyptian house was the quarters of the master, the servants were in the rear. cf. n.56 below.

[6] Treason against the state was the one capital crime. Yet the Egyptian did not wish to lay the responsibility for capital punishment upon the pharaoh and stated that the sentence was a divine vengeance.

[7] A former schoolmate, with whom you chanted the lessons in school.

[8] An otherwise unknown book, perhaps an "inventory," helpful in attaining the eternal happiness of the next world.

[9] The soul of the rightly instructed will attain eternal happiness.

[10] The reference is to a judgment after death by a tribunal of gods, at this time under the presidency of the sun-god, later with Osiris as the judge.

[11] The judges of the dead remember all sins no matter now long the time may be.

[12] As legal exhibits.

[13] Might Egyptians be conscripted for duty at twenty?

[14] The son of a man of birth and position.

thy frontier and build thy *fortresses*, (for) troops are of advantage to their lord.

Make monuments . . . for the god. That is what makes to live the name of him who does it. A man should do what is of advantage to his soul: the monthly service of the priest, putting on the white sandals, visiting the temple, revealing the mysteries,[15] having access (65) to the shrine, and eating bread in the temple. Make the offering-table flourish, increase the loaves, and add to the daily offerings. It is an advantage to him who does it. Make thy monuments to endure according as thou art able. A single day gives for eternity, and an hour effects accomplishment for the future. The god is aware of him who works for him. Let thy statues be transported into a distant country, *without their giving the total thereof*, for (only) a sick man *is free (from) some hostility*, and the foe within Egypt is never calm.[16]

Generation will oppress generation, as the ancestors prophesied about it. Egypt fights (70) (even) in the necropolis, by hacking up graves, by . . . I did the same, and the same happened as is done to one who transgresses *the way of* the god.[17]

Do not (deal) evilly with the southern region, for thou knowest the prophecy of the Residence City concerning it.[18] That may come to pass as this came to pass. They do not transgress (our frontier), as they said . . . I should praise (also) This *over against* its southern frontier *at Taut*.[19] I took it like a cloudburst. King Mer[*y-ib*]-Re, the triumphant, had not (been able to) do it.[20] Be lenient because of it. . . . (75) . . . It is good to work for the future.

It goes well for thee with the southern region. The bearers of burdens come to thee with gifts. I did the same as the ancestors:—(though) he has no grain, (that) he might give it (to thee), may it (still) be pleasing to thee because they are compliant to thee; satisfy thyself with thy (own) bread and beer.[21] Granite comes to thee without hindrance.[22] Do not injure the monument of another; thou shouldst quarry stone in Troia.[23] Do not build thy tomb out of the ruins, what had been made (going) into what is to be made. Behold, O King, O lord of joy, (80) thou canst be lax and sleep in thy strength, following thy desire, through what I have done. There is no enemy within the compass of thy frontier.

He who arose (as) lord in a city arose with his heart troubled because of the Northland, Het-shenu *to Sebaqa*, with its southern boundary *up to the . . . Canal*.[24] I pacified the entire west, as far as the coast of the sea. It works for itself, as it gives *meru*-wood, and one may see juniper. They give it to us.[25] (But) the east is rich in bowmen,[26] and their work . . . Turned about are the islands in the midst and every man within it.[27] The *administrative districts say: "Thou art more honored* (85) *than I."*[28] Behold, [*the area*] which they injured is (now) made into nomes and all large cities.[29] The domain of one man is (now) in the hands of ten men. . . . lists with every (kind of) tax that exists. The priest is presented with fields, working for thee like a single troop.[30] It will not come to pass thereby that they be treacherous of heart. The Nile will not fail for thee, so that it does not come. The dues of the Northland are in thy hand. Behold, the mooring-stake is driven in *the region* which I have made on the east, up to the limits of Hebenu and as far as the Ways-of-Horus,[31] settled with citizens and filled with people, the picked men of the entire land, in order to oppose (90) *their arms thereby*. I should (like to) see a valiant man who could copy it, one who could do for himself more than I have done. . . .

But this further should be said because of the bowman. Lo, the wretched Asiatic—it goes ill with the place where he is, afflicted with water, difficult from many trees, the ways thereof painful because of the mountains. He does not dwell in a single place, (but) his legs *are made to go astray*. He has been fighting (ever) since the time of Horus, (but) he does not conquer, nor yet can he be conquered. He does not announce a day in fighting, like *a thief* who . . . for a gang.[32]

But as I live! (95) I am while I am! The bowmen, however, are a locked wall, opened . . .[33] I made the Northland smite them, I captured their inhabitants, and I took their cattle, to the disgust of the Asiatics against Egypt. Do not trouble thyself about him: he is (only) an Asiatic, *one despised* on his (own) coast. He may rob a single *person*, (but) he does not lead against a town of many citizens.

15 Perhaps only in the sense of carrying out the rites.

16 The sentence is not clear, but may urge upon the king that he should not shrink from hostility incurred if he advances himself abroad. If he feared hostility he would have enough fears right at home.

17 It is not clear what the king's failure and the resultant retribution were. Confession of error was very exceptional for any Egyptian, particularly for the pharaoh. cf. n.44 below.

18 A rival dynasty to that of Herakleopolis had been set up at Thebes at this time. Apparently on the basis of some "prophecy," there was a truce in force at the time of these instructions. Within a generation or two Thebes was to put an end to the Herakleopolitan rule.

19 This was the chief city of the Thinite (Abydos) nome and the frontier between the realms of Herakleopolis and Thebes. Taut(?) is unknown.

20 If the restoration is correct, this would be Mery-ib-Re Khety I, a ruler at Herakleopolis perhaps a century before the time of these instructions.

21 I followed the principles laid down by my predecessors: do not exact tribute from a friendly neighbor.

22 From the quarries at Assuan.

23 The limestone quarries across the River from Memphis. The preceding and succeeding sentences urge that it is wrong to take stone from the monuments of the ancestors, since granite and limestone are available from the quarries.

24 As every local ruler knew, the current peaceful relations with the south were not duplicated by those with the Delta. Het-shenu was near Heliopolis; the other two sites are unknown.

25 The western Delta was friendly to Herakleopolis and transmitted the timber of Asia.

26 Foreign warriors.

27 The "islands" cut off by waterways within the Delta were disaffected from Herakleopolis?

28 Internal local jealousy?

29 The land which has been delivered from the foreigners has been made into small administrative units—perhaps on the principle of *divide et impera*.

30 Even the priest must work out his taxes.

31 From somewhere near modern Minieh in Middle Egypt to the Suez frontier (on the "Ways-of-Horus" cf. pp. 21, 478). Thus the east Delta was anchored along a newly established frontier line.

32 The characterization is that of the nomad Bedouin, who raid but fight no campaigns.

33 Uncertain, but perhaps a contrast between the pharaoh and the (inscrutable?) foreigners.

Dig a dyke against [half] of it, and flood half of it as far as the Bitter Lakes. Behold, it is the (very) navel-cord of foreigners.[34] Its walls are warlike, and its soldiers are many. The subjects in it know (how) to take up *weapons—apart from the priest of the home.*[35] The region of Djed-sut[36] totals ten thousand men as commoners, free and without taxes. Officials have been in it since the time of the Residence City.[37] The boundaries are fixed, its garrisons are valiant. Many northerners water it as far as the Northland, tax-free in grain.[38] . . . They have made a dyke as far as Herakleopolis. Abundant citizens are the heart's *support.* Guard against *encirclement by* the retainers of an enemy. . . .

When thy frontier is endangered toward the [southern] region, it means that the [northern] bowmen will take on the girdle.[39] Build structures in the Northland. The name of a man will not be smaller through what he has done, and a (well-) founded city cannot be harmed. Build structures . . . The foe desires qualms of heart, his nature being miserable. King Khety, the triumphant, laid (it) down in [his] instructions:[40] "He who is silent with regard to violence of heart injures . . . The god will attack the rebel against the temple."[41]

. . . Revere the god. Do not say that he is weak of heart. Let not thy arms be slack, *yet create thy (own) joy. Satisfaction* is that which harms heaven, (*whereas*) *imprisonment* is a monument in the knowledge of the foe.[42] He cannot harm it through a desire that what he has done may be maintained by someone else coming after him. There is no one free from a foe. The (Lord of) the Two Banks is a wise man. The king and lord of courtiers cannot be a fool. He is (already) wise when he comes forth from the womb. (*The god*) has distinguished him ahead of a million lands.

It is a goodly office, the kingship. It has no son and no brother, made to endure on its monuments. (But) it is one (king) who promotes another. A man works for him [who] was before him, through a desire that what (he) has done may be maintained by someone else coming after him.[43]

Behold, a misfortune happened in my time. The Thinite regions were hacked up. It really happened through what I had done,[44] and I knew of it (only) after (it) was done. Behold, my recompense (came) out of what I had done. However, he is a wretch and one who has no advantage, who reconsolidates what he has brought to naught, who demolishes what he has built, or who improves what he has *damaged.*[45] Be on thy guard against it. A blow is to be repaid with its (own) like. That is the *application* of all that has been done.

Generation passes generation among men, and the god, who knows (men's) characters, has hidden himself. (But) there is none who can withstand the Lord of the Hand: he is the one who attacks what the eyes can see.[46] Revere the god upon his way, made of costly stones and fashioned [of] metal, like a flood replaced by (another) flood. There is no river that permits itself to be concealed; that is, it breaks the [*dam*] by which it was hidden.[47] (So) also the soul goes to the place which it knows, and deviates not from its way of yesterday. Enrich thy house of the West; embellish thy place of the necropolis, as an upright man and as one who executes the justice upon which (men's) hearts rely. More acceptable is the character of one upright of heart than the ox of the evildoer.[48] Act for the god, that he may act similarly for thee, with oblations which make the offering-table flourish and with a carved inscription—that is what bears witness to thy name. The god is aware of him who acts for him.

Well directed are men, the cattle of the god. He made heaven and earth according to their desire, and he repelled the water-monster.[49] He made the breath of life (for) their nostrils. They who have issued from his body are his images. He arises in heaven according to their desire. He made for them plants, animals, fowl, and fish to feed them. He slew his enemies and injured (even) his (own) children because they thought of making rebellion.[50] He makes the light of day according to their desire, and he *sails by* in order to see them. He has erected a shrine around about them, and when they weep he hears.[51] He made for them rulers (even) in the egg, a supporter to support the back of the disabled. He made for them magic as weapons to ward off what might happen or dreams *by* night as well as day. He has slain the treacherous of heart among them, as a man beats his son for his brother's sake.[52] For the god knows every name.

Thou shouldst do nothing harmful *with regard to me, who have given* all the laws concerning the

34 The east Delta region must be protected because it is the center of gravity for the Asiatics.

35 If the translation is correct, all citizens were available for military duty except the domestic priest.

36 Apparently used for Memphis.

37 Since the time of Memphis rule (the 6th dynasty)?

38 "Taxed with grain in a free condition."

39 Civil war toward the south would give the Asiatics to the north the chance to gird themselves for raids.

40 Apparently King Khety I (n.20) had composed a book of wisdom, distinct from the present book and which has not survived to us. cf. also p. 432 below.

41 Although ultimate vengeance may belong to the god, man must not be passive.

42 The enemy can understand firmness, but slackness encourages his attack?

43 This phrase is in place here—each king acts for his predecessor—but perhaps was in anticipatory error in the preceding paragraph.

44 For this abnormal confession of shortcoming and perhaps for the misfortune referred to, cf. n.17 above.

45 Perhaps: do not try to plug holes; be bold enough to meet damage with aggressive force.

46 God, the "Lord of the (creative) Hand," remains unseen from age to age, but he must be respected. Invisible, he controls the visible.

47 The creator god, a sun disc of stone and metal, goes his daily way like the annual, irresistible inundation.

48 cf. I Sam. 15:22; Prov. 15:17. A variant text begins: "More profitable is . . ."

49 "The submerger (determined with a crocodile) of the water." Scharff, *op.cit.*, 60, n.6, thinks of the Babylonian Tiâmat and suggests a monster which the creator god defeated at creation.

50 For the allusion see "The Deliverance of Mankind from Destruction" (pp. 10-11 above).

51 The unseen god is still close to men through his shrine in the temple.

52 God's punishments are for man's good, like a father's discipline.

king. *Open* thy face, that thou mayest be raised as a man. Thou shalt reach me, without having an accuser.[53] Do not kill a single one that comes close to thee, when thou hast shown him favor: the god knows him.[54] He who prospers on earth is one of them, and they who follow the king are gods.[55] Give the love of thee to the whole world; a good character is a remembrance . . . *It has been* said (*to*) thee: "May the time of the sufferer be destroyed!" by those who are in the back of the house of King Khety, in contrast to its *situation* today.[56]

Behold, I have spoken to thee the profitable matters of my (very) belly. Mayest thou act on what is established before thy face.

IT HAS COME SUCCESSFULLY (to an end), according to what was found in writing, in the writing of the scribe [Kha-]em-Waset for himself alone, the truly silent one, . . . experienced in the work of Thoth, the scribe Kha-em-Waset, for his brother, the beloved of his affections, the truly silent one, goodly of character, experienced in the work of Thoth, the scribe Meh, son of . . .

THE INSTRUCTION OF KING AMEN-EM-HET

This text purports to give the advice which Amen-em-het I, the first pharaoh of the Twelfth Dynasty, offered to his son and successor. As the reaction of an old and experienced ruler, it has some of the somber pessimism and some of the social idealism of the period. The specific historicity of the text has been challenged, on the grounds that *a dead king* is offering the advice. This argument is probably valid, but the text is historical in its applicability to the times.

Amen-em-het I died about 1960 B.C. However, all the extant documents of this text come from the Eighteenth to Twentieth Dynasties (1500-1100 B.C.), when the inscription was very popular as an exercise for schoolboys. The text was copied, in whole or in part, in 4 papyri (especially Papyrus Millingen = Berlin 3019 and Papyrus Sallier II = British Museum 10182); 1 leather roll; 3 writing tablets; and at least 35 ostraca. The present translation was made from as many of these documents as were available to the translator; the line numbers follow Sallier II.

The text was presented by F. Ll. Griffith in *ZAeS*, XXXIV (1896), 35 ff., and by G. Maspero, *Les enseignements d'Amenemhait Ier à son fils Sanouasrit Ier* (Cairo, 1914). A translation is given by Erman, *LAE*, 72-74. Two points of view on the historicity of the text will be found in *Mélanges Maspero*, I (Cairo, 1935-38), A. H. Gardiner arguing that Amen-em-het I was responsible for these words when he made Sen-Usert I his coregent (p. 495 f.), and A. de Buck arguing that the Instruction was composed in the name of Amen-em-het I after his death (pp. 847 ff.).[1]

THE BEGINNING OF THE INSTRUCTION WHICH the majesty of the King of Upper and Lower Egypt: Sehetep-ib-Re; the Son of Re: Amen-em-het, the triumphant,[2] made, when he spoke in a message of truth[3] to his son, the All-Lord.[4] He said:

Thou that hast appeared as a god, hearken to what I have to say to thee, that thou mayest be king of the land and ruler of the regions, that thou mayest achieve an overabundance of good.

HOLD THYSELF APART FROM THOSE SUBORDINATE TO (THEE), lest that should happen to whose terrors no attention has been given. Approach them not in thy loneliness. Fill not thy heart with a brother, nor know a friend. Create not for thyself intimates—there is no fulfillment thereby. (EVEN) WHEN THOU SLEEPEST, GUARD THY HEART THYSELF, because no man has adherents on the day of distress. I gave to the destitute and brought up the orphan. I caused him who was nothing to reach (his goal), like him who was (somebody).

(BUT) IT WAS HE WHO ATE MY FOOD THAT RAISED TROOPS (against me) and he to whom I had given my hands that created terror thereby. They who were clothed in my fine linen looked upon me as *(did) those who lacked (it)*. They who were perfumed with my myrrh poured out water *while having* (*it*).[5]

MY LIVING COUNTERPARTS, YE WHO SHARE WITH ME AMONG MORTALS,[6] make *lamentations* for me as something which cannot be heard, for a great *piece* of fighting cannot be seen. Indeed, one fights on the arena forgetful of yesterday. (But) there is no fulfillment of happiness for him who does not know what he should know.[7]

IT WAS AFTER SUPPER, WHEN EVENING HAD COME. I had taken an hour of *rest*, lying upon my bed, for I had become weary. My heart began to follow after slumber for me. Then the weapons *which should have been solicitous* for me were *brandished*, and I was like one crumbled, crumbled to *dust*, a snake of the desert.[8] I AWOKE AT THE FIGHTING, BEING BY MYSELF, and I found that it was a hand-to-hand conflict of *the guard*. If I had made haste with weapons in my hand, I should have made the cowards retreat *helter-skelter*. However, there

[53] Unblemished, he will join his father in the world of the dead.

[54] Leave to god the punishment of those close to you.

[55] Apparently the wildest exaggeration of majesty: serving the pharaoh is like being one of the gods. Or: the king's followers will become gods after death?

[56] The servants' quarters were in the rear of a house; cf. n.5 above. Scharff, *op.cit.*, 8, takes this passage as indicating that Khety is the king who is speaking. Meri-ka-Re is charged to bring times better than the present.

---

[1] Both commentators take into account a passage in a nineteenth dynasty manuscript, Papyrus Chester Beatty, IV, verso vi 12-vii 2 (*Hieratic Papyri in the British Museum. Third Series. Chester Beatty Gift*, ed. by A. H. Gardiner [London, 1935], I, 43 f.; II, Pls. 20-21), in which there is an appeal on behalf of the deceased scribe Khety (cf. p. 432), "that excellent one, choice of utterances! *I* give his name to eternity. He it was who made a book *which was* the Instruction of the King of Upper [and Lower Egypt: Se]hetep-ib-[Re]—life, prosperity, health!—when he had gone to rest, when he joined heaven and entered among the lords of the necropolis." This passage must be treated as a valid or as a misapplied tradition that a scribe Khety composed the present text.

[2] That is, the deceased. The applicability of this epithet and the question whether it might have been added in a later copy are critical to the problem whether the king spoke in life or posthumously.

[3] For the argument that "message of truth" means a "dream" or a "revelation" from the dead king to the living king, see B. Gunn in *JEA*, XXVII (1941), 2-5.

[4] Sen-Usert I, who was coregent in the last ten years of the reign of his father, Amen-em-het I.

[5] Corrupt, or perhaps figurative for a covert obscenity of disrespect.

[6] Future pharaohs. cf. Gardiner, in *Mélanges Maspero*, I, 484 f.

[7] Although he cannot transmit his own experience fully to his successors, and they must learn chiefly by their own struggles, still the ignorant cannot achieve anything.

[8] The old king illustrates his disillusionment by telling about a treacherous attack upon him by night. Apparently his own bodyguard was involved.

is no one valiant at night, and there is no fighting alone. No success may occur without *a protector*.[9]

Behold, *bloodshed* occurred while I was without thee, before the courtiers had heard that I was handing over to thee, before I had sat together with thee. Pray, *let me order thy affairs*, inasmuch as I had not prepared for it, I had not (even) thought of it, my heart had not accepted (the idea of) the slackness of servants.[10]

Had women ever marshaled (5) the battle array? Had contentious people been bred within the house? Had the water *which cuts the soil* (ever) been opened up, *so that* poor men were frustrated at their work?[11] No mischance had come up behind me since my birth. Never had there been the like of my reputation as a doer of valiant deeds.

I trod as far as Elephantine; I attained to the marshes of the Delta.[12] I stood upon the margins of the land and saw its enclosure. I reached the limits of *the armed territory*,[13] by my (own) strong arm and in my (own) form of being. I was the one who made barley, the beloved of the grain-god. The Nile honored me on every broad expanse. No one hungered in my years; no one thirsted therein. (But) men sat (quietly), because of what I had done, talking about me. Everything which I had commanded was in the proper place.

I overcame lions; I caught crocodiles. I subjugated them of Wawat;[14] I carried off the Madjoi;[14] (iii 1) I made the Asiatics do the dog-walk.[15]

I made for myself a house adorned with gold, its ceiling of lapis lazuli, the floors of . . . , the doors of copper, and the bolts of bronze, made for eternity, prepared *for everlastingness*. I know *all the limits thereof; I am the All-Lord*.[16]

Much idle cant is in the streets. The wise man says "Yes," *making search for his* "No," because he does not know it, *when deprived of thy countenance*,[17] a man of King Sen-Usert, my son, *as my (own) legs depart*. Thou art my own heart; my eyes behold thee. *The children have an hour of rest beside the people*, as they give (5) thee praise.[18]

Behold, I made the beginning, and I *will fix* for thee the end. I am he who comes to port *for the sake of* him who is in (*my*) heart.[19] *It is seemly* to lay aside the White Crown *for the sake of* the seed of a god, *so that things sealed should be* in their proper place through that which I began for thee. *Jubilation* is in the barque of Re, *because* the kingship, which came into being formerly, *(still) stands, through him who acts lovingly, through him who acts valiantly*. Erect thy monuments *perfected and enduring*. Fight on behalf of *the man who is wise*, because he *will not love himself* beside *thy* majesty—life, prosperity, health![20]

[9] This seems to say that the attack on Amen-em-het was successful. In conflict with that impression, the following context would suggest that his long coregency with his son had not yet begun. In the latter case, the attack could not have been fatal.

[10] The old king feels constrained to offer his son advice because his own misplaced confidence in his servants had been so costly.

[11] Following Gardiner, *op.cit.*, 489 ff., the first two questions may carry chagrin at the actual situation, a conspiracy within the king's own harem, while the third question would be a metaphorical bridge to the king's benevolences which are to be listed. He was the beneficent channel of irrigation for the soil of Egypt, and the treason was an injurious breach in that channel.

[12] The southern and northern limits of Egypt.

[13] Perhaps "the regions be-armed," as a designation of Egypt within its frontier protection.

[14] Peoples to the south of Egypt.

[15] As submissive as a cur in one's own home.

[16] Corrupt in the extant texts, but perhaps: I know the time limits of my palace, since I am the Lord-to-the-Limit.

[17] This is an example of our difficulties in translating a corrupt text without aid. The passages from "Much" to "countenance" are rendered as they are visible in the best of four broken and currupt texts. It is assumed that the initial sentence means: "Much (insincere) 'Oh surely, surely!' is in the streets." If the sentences have any meaning at all, they deal with the sincere loyalty of men to Sen-Usert I, the successor. However, our passage is a quotation from the Admonitions of Ipu-wer (p. 442 below), to the effect that there is distress in the land, of which the wise man is aware, but of which the fool is ignorant: "Why, surely, the children of nobles are *cast out* in the streets. The wise man says: 'Yes, (it is so).' The ignorant man says: 'No, (it is not)'; and it is fair in the sight of him who knows it not." How this quotation fits in the present context is obscure.

[18] Quite obscure, unless the intention is to deny that children will be abandoned in the streets under Sen-Usert I. See the preceding note.

[19] Texts: "thy heart." The tentative translation assumes that Amen-em-het states here that, through death, he is turning over rule to his son.

[20] The last paragraph is so corrupt that translation is very shaky and any commentary would be futile.

THE INSTRUCTION OF PRINCE HOR-DEDEF

The only excuse for introducing the miserable remains of the following text is that the composer to whom it is ascribed was so frequently mentioned as one of the traditional wise men of Egypt.[1] Ii-em-hotep, a high official of the pharaoh Djoser, and Hor-dedef, a son of the pharaoh Khufu (or Cheops, about 27th century B.C.), became legendary for their wisdom. It is unfortunate that the sole surviving elements of their ascribed lore should be in such miserable physical condition, uncertain of translation, and rather trite in content.

Munich Ostracon 3400, published by E. Brunner-Traut in *ZAeS*, LXXVI (1940), 3-9, Pl. 1, and Oriental Institute Ostracon 17003 (unpublished). Both come from Thebes and are to be dated, on the basis of handwriting to the late Nineteenth or early Twentieth Dynasty (1250-1150 B.C.). However, the language indicates a date of composition somewhat earlier.

Beginning of the instruction which the Hereditary Prince and Count, the King's Son Hor-dedef, made for his son, . . .

[*Be not*] *boastful* before (*my very*) eyes, and beware of the boasting *of* another. If thou art a man of standing and foundest [a household, *take*] thou a wife as *a man of feeling*,[2] and a male child will be born to thee.

Thou shouldst build thy house for thy son (*in*) the place where thou art. Embellish thy [*house*] of the necropolis, and enrich thy place of the West.[3] *A lowly reception is for him who is dead, (but) a high reception for him who is living, and thy house of death is (destined) for life*.[4]

[1] cf. pp. 432, n.4; 467, n.4; 476, n.16, and the Westcar Papyrus: Erman, *LAE*, 36 ff. In the "Satirical Letter" (p. 476 below), there is an allusion to a written treatise of Hor-dedef. This translation continues the customary rendering of his name as Hor-dedef, despite equally good reasons to adopt the form Djedef-Hor.

[2] Apparently, "as the master of a heart."

[3] For the passage beginning "If thou art a man of standing," cf. the Instruction of Ptah-hotep (p. 413 above), and for the passage beginning "Embellish thy," cf. the Instruction for Meri-ka-Re (p. 417 above).

[4] Apparent corruptions and differences between the two texts make any translation uncertain. The meaning may be that a deceased Egyptian is living and not dead if the needful rites have been observed.

Seek thou the . . . for the fields which *should be* inundated. . . .

THE INSTRUCTION OF ANI

The following extracts are from a set of instructions given by a father to his son toward the end of the Egyptian Empire. They exist only in later copies, so that there has been abundant opportunity for corruption to enter the copies. However, they do reflect the later emphases of quietude, personal piety, and ritual activity. The final sections, not translated here, give the respectful answer of Ani's son, fearing that he cannot measure up to his father's high standards.

The main manuscript is a papyrus of the Twenty-first or Twenty-second Dynasty (11th-8th centuries B.C.), now in the Cairo Museum, "Boulaq no. 4." It was published by F. Chabas, *Les maximes du scribe Ani* (Châlon-sur-Saône, 1876-78). There is also a fragmentary papyrus of a somewhat earlier period, No. 16959 in the Musée Guimet in Paris; a writing tablet of the Twenty-second Dynasty, No. 8934 in Berlin; and two extracts elsewhere. There is a transcription into hieroglyphic in E. Suys, *La sagesse d'Ani* (Rome, 1935), and there are several extracts in A. Volten, *Studien zum Weisheitsbuch des Anii* (Copenhagen, 1937). The Berlin tablet begins: "The beginning of the instruction and teaching which the Scribe Ani of the Temple of King Nefer-. . .-Re-teri made." This king cannot be identified.

(iii 1) . . . Take to thyself a wife while thou art (still) a youth,[1] that she may produce a son for thee. Beget [him] for thyself while thou art (still) young. Teach him to be a man. A man whose people are many is happy; *he is* saluted (respectfully) with regard to his children.

Celebrate the feast of thy god and repeat it at its season. God is angry at them who disregard him. Have witnesses attending (5) when thou makest offering *at* the first time *of doing it*. If someone comes to *require thy examination*, have them set on papyrus thy goings-down at this time.[2] . . . Singing, dancing, and incense are his[3] food, and to receive prostrations is his property (right). The god will magnify the name of him who *does it*. . . .

(13) . . . Be on thy guard against a woman from abroad, who is not known in her (own) town. Do not *stare at* her when she passes by. Do not know her carnally: a deep water, whose windings one knows not, a woman who is far away from her husband. "I am sleek," she says to thee every day. She has no witnesses when she waits to ensnare thee. It is a great crime (worthy) of death, when one hears of it. . . .

(iv 1) Do not talk a lot. Be silent, and thou wilt be happy. Do not be garrulous. The dwelling of god, its abomination is clamor. Pray thou with a loving heart, all the words of which are hidden, and he will do what thou needest, he will hear what thou sayest, and he will accept thy offering. . . .

(14) Embellish thy place which is in the desert-valley, the pit which will hide thy corpse. Set it before thee as thy business, which is of account in thy eyes, like unto the great elders, *who* rest in their *store-chambers*. No blame attaches to him who does it, (but) he is happy. Prepare thou likewise, and when thy (v 1) messenger[4] comes to thee to take thee, he will find thee prepared *to come* (*to*) the place where thou hast rest, saying: "Behold, he who prepared himself before thee is coming." Do not say: "I am (too) young for thee to take," for thou knowest not thy death. When death comes, he steals away the infant which is on its mother's lap like him who has reached old age. . . .

(vi 1) . . . I shall let thee know upon earth about the man who seeks to found his household.[5] Make thou a garden-plot. Enclose thou (a bed of) cucumbers in front of[6] thy plow-land. Plant thou trees *inside*, (so that) they may be *a shelter* in every section of thy home. And fill thy hand (with) every flower which thy eye may behold. One *feels the need of* them all, and it is good fortune not to lose them. . . .

Thou shouldst not sit (11) when another who is older than thou is standing, or one who has been raised higher in his rank. . . . Go every day according to the prescribed way, that thou mayest walk (with regard to) precedence. . . .

(vii 7) . . . Thou shouldst not express thy (whole) heart to the stranger, to let him discover thy speech against thee. If a *passing* remark issuing from thy mouth is hasty and *it is* repeated, thou wilt make enemies. A man may fall to ruin because of his tongue. . . . THE BELLY OF A MAN IS WIDER THAN A STOREHOUSE, AND IT IS FULL OF EVERY (KIND OF) RESPONSE. Thou shouldst choose the good and say them, while the bad are shut up in thy belly. . . .

(12) . . . Make offering to thy god, and beware of sins against him. Thou shouldst not inquire about his *affairs*.[7] Be not (too) free with him during his procession. Do not approach him (too closely) to carry him. Thou shouldst not *disturb the veil*; beware of *exposing what it shelters*.[8] Let thy eye have regard to the nature of his anger, and prostrate thyself in his name. He shows (his) power in a million forms. (Only) they are magnified whom he magnifies. The god of this land is the sun which is on the horizon, and (only) his images are upon earth.[9] If incense be given (17) as their daily food, the Lord of Appearances will be established.

Double the food which thou givest to thy mother, and carry her as she carried (thee). She had a heavy load in thee, but she did not leave it to me. Thou wert born after thy months, (but) she was still yoked (with thee, for) her breast was in thy mouth for three years, *continuously*. Though thy filth was *disgusting*, (her)

[1] This section appears also in Papyrus Chester Beatty V, verso ii 6-8 (of the late 19th dynasty), where the clause "and teach her about that which men do" is inserted at this point—*Hieratic Papyri in the British Museum. Third Series. Chester Beatty Gift*, ed. by A. H. Gardiner (London, 1935), I, 50, II, Pl. 27.

[2] If the translation is correct, the worshiper's temple activity should be attested in writing.

[3] The god's.

[4] Death.

[5] Also in Papyrus Beatty V, verso ii 8-11; reference in n.1 above.

[6] Beatty: "in addition to."

[7] Or "about his form of appearance," the cult image.

[8] The images of some gods were enshrouded during their public appearances.

[9] Some of that approach to monotheism which appeared in later Egypt. The sun is the god, appearing in a myriad of forms, including his images.

heart was not *disgusted*, saying: "What can I do?" She put thee into school when thou wert taught to write, and she continued *on thy behalf* every day, with bread (viii 1) and beer in her house.

When thou art a young man and takest to thyself a wife and art settled in thy house, set thy eye on how thy mother gave birth to thee and all (her) bringing thee up as well. Do not let her blame thee, nor may she (have to) raise her hands to the god, nor may he (have to) hear her cries.

Thou shouldst not eat bread when another is waiting and thou dost not stretch forth thy hand to the food *for him. It is here* forever. A man is nothing. The one is rich; another is poor, while bread continues—*can he pass it by*? The man rich in the time of last year is a vagabond this year. Be not greedy to fill thy belly. . . . The course of the water of last year is gone, and it is in a different area this year. Great seas have become dry places, and sandbanks have become abysses. . . .

(ix 1) . . . Thou shouldst not supervise (too closely) thy wife in her (own) house, when thou knowest that she is efficient. Do not say to her: "Where is it? Fetch (it) for us!" when she has put (it) in the (most) useful place. Let thy eye have regard, while thou art silent, that thou mayest recognize her abilities. How happy it is when thy hand is with her! Many are here who do not know what a man should do to stop dissension in his house. . . . Every *man* who is settled in a house should hold the hasty heart firm. Thou shouldst not pursue after a woman; do not let her steal away thy heart. . . .

THE INSTRUCTION OF AMEN-EM-OPET

A general parallelism of thought or structure between Egyptian and Hebrew literature is common. It is, however, more difficult to establish a case of direct literary relation. For this reason, special attention is directed to the Instruction of Amen-em-Opet, son of Ka-nakht, and its very close relation to the Book of Proverbs, particularly Prov. 22:17-24:22. Amen-em-Opet differs from earlier Egyptian books of wisdom in its humbler, more resigned, and less materialistic outlook.[1]

The hieratic text is found in British Museum Papyrus 10474 and (a portion only) on a writing tablet in Turin. The papyrus is said to have come from Thebes. The date of the papyrus manuscript is debated. It is certainly subsequent to the Egyptian Empire. A date anywhere between the 10th and 6th centuries B.C. is possible, with some weight of evidence for the 7th-6th centuries.

Only a selection of items from an extensive bibliography will be noted. The papyrus was reproduced in *Facsimiles of Egyptian Hieratic Papyri in the British Museum. Second Series*, ed. by E. A. W. Budge (London, 1923), Pls. I-XIV; followed by Budge, *The Teaching of Amen-em-apt, Son of Kanakht* (London, 1924). A. Erman established the specific relation of Amen-em-Opet and Proverbs in Eine ägyptische Quelle der "Sprüche Salomos" (*SPAW*, May, 1924, 86-93). H. Gressmann advanced the study of the relationship in *ZAW*, XLII (1924), 273-96. The standard study of the texts is now H. O. Lange, *Das Weisheitsbuch des Amenemope* (Copenhagen, 1925). The best translation and commentary in English are those of F. Ll. Griffith, in *JEA*, XII (1926), 191-231, which is followed (pp. 232-39) by D. C. Simpson, The Hebrew Book of Proverbs and the Teaching of Amenophis. Although most commentators have inclined toward the view of a direct or indirect dependence of the Hebrew upon the Egyptian, a counteropinion was expressed by R. O. Kevin, *The Wisdom of Amen-em-apt and its Possible Dependence upon the Hebrew Book of Proverbs* (Philadelphia, 1931).

Introductory

THE BEGINNING OF THE TEACHING OF LIFE, the testimony for prosperity, all precepts for intercourse with elders, the rules for courtiers, to know how to return an answer to him who said it, and to direct a report to one who has sent him, in order to direct him to the ways of life, to make him prosper upon earth, let his heart go down into its shrine, steer him away from evil, and to rescue him from the mouth of the rabble, revered in the mouth of the people;

made by the Overseer of the Soil, one experienced in his office, the seed of a scribe of Egypt, THE OVERSEER OF GRAINS WHO REGULATES THE MEASURE and manages the *yield of grain* for his lord, who registers islands and newly appearing lands in the Great Name of his majesty,[2] [who] establishes landmarks at the boundaries of the arable land, (ii 1) who protects the king by his records, and who makes the land-register of Egypt; the scribe who sets up the divine offerings for all the gods and gives land-titles to the common people; THE OVERSEER OF GRAINS [AND *PROVIDER*] OF FOODS, who *transports magazines with* grain, the truly silent one[3] in Abydos of the Thinite Nome, the triumphant one of Akhmim, possessor of a tomb on the west of Panopolis, possessor of a grave in Abydos, AMEN-EM-OPET, THE SON OF KA-NAKHT, the triumphant one of Abydos;

(for) his son, the smallest of his children, the littlest of his adherents, the Privy Councillor of Min Ka-mutef, the Water Pourer of Wen-nofer, who installs Horus upon the throne of his father, . . . , (iii 1) *Examiner* of the God's Mother, Inspector of the Black Cattle of the Terrace of Min, who protects Min in his shrine, Hor-em-maa-kheru being his right name, the child of a notable of Akhmim and son of the Sistrum-Player of Shu and Tefnut and Chief Choir-Leader of Horus, Ta-Usert.[4]

HE SAYS: FIRST CHAPTER:

Give thy ears, hear what is said,
Give thy heart to understand them.
To put them in thy heart is worth while,[5]
(But) it is damaging to him who neglects them.
Let them rest in the casket of thy belly,
That they may be a *key* in thy heart.

[1] On the characteristics of older and later Egyptian books of wisdom, see R. Anthes, *Lebensregeln und Lebensweisheit der alten Aegypter* (*AO*, 32, Leipzig, 1933).

[2] The shifting of the course of the Nile brought new lands into being. Apparently these were crown domains.

[3] Properly submissive or conformist.

[4] The mother's titles and name. The members of the family enjoyed no high offices.

[5] For these first 3 lines, cf. the first 3 lines of the corresponding section of Prov. 22:17-18a.

At a time when there is a whirlwind of words, (15)
They shall be a mooring-stake *for* thy tongue.
If thou spendest thy time while this is in thy heart,
Thou wilt find it a success;
Thou wilt find my words a treasury of life, (iv 1)
And thy body will prosper upon earth.[6]

SECOND CHAPTER:
Guard thyself against robbing the oppressed
And against overbearing the disabled. (5)
Stretch not forth thy hand against the approach of an old man,
Nor *steal away* the speech of the *aged*.
Let not thyself be sent on a dangerous errand,
Nor love him who carries it out.
Do not cry out against him whom thou hast attacked, (10)
Nor return him answer on thy own behalf.
He who does evil, the (very) river-bank abandons him,
And his *floodwaters* carry him off.
The north wind comes down that it may end his hour;
It is joined to the tempest; (15)
The thunder is loud, and the crocodiles are wicked.
Thou heated man,[7] how art thou (now)?
He is crying out, and his voice (reaches) to heaven.
O moon,[8] establish his crime (against him)!
So steer that we may bring the wicked man across, (v 1)
For we shall not act like him—
Lift him up, give him thy hand;
Leave him (in) the arms of the god;
Fill his belly with bread of thine, (5)
So that he may be sated and may *be ashamed*.[9]
Another good deed in the heart of the god
Is to pause before speaking. . . .[10]

FOURTH CHAPTER:[11]
As for the heated man of a temple, (vi 1)
He is like a tree growing in the open.
In the completion of a moment (comes) its loss of foliage,
And its end is reached in the shipyards;
(Or) it is floated far from its place, (5)
And the flame is its burial shroud.
(But) the truly silent man holds himself apart.
He is like a tree growing in a *garden*.
It flourishes and doubles its yield;
It (stands) before its lord. (10)
Its fruit is sweet; its shade is pleasant;
And its end is reached in the garden. . . .[12]

SIXTH CHAPTER:
Do not carry off the landmark at the boundaries of the arable land,
Nor disturb the position of the measuring-cord;
Be not greedy after a cubit of land,
Nor encroach upon the boundaries of a widow.[13] . . . (vii 15)
Guard against encroaching upon the boundaries of the fields,
Lest a terror carry thee off. (viii 10)
One satisfies god with the will of the Lord,
Who determines the boundaries of the arable land.[14] . . .
Plow in the fields, that thou mayest find thy needs, (17)
That thou mayest receive bread of thy own threshing floor.
Better is a measure that the god gives thee
Than five thousand (taken) illegally.
They do not spend a day (in) the granary or barn; (ix 1)
They make no provisions for the beer-jar.
The completion of a moment is their lifetime in the storehouse;
At daybreak they are sunk (from sight).
Better is poverty in the hand of the god (5)
Than riches in a storehouse;
Better is bread, when the heart is happy,
Than riches with sorrow.[15]

SEVENTH CHAPTER:
Cast not thy heart in pursuit of riches, (10)
(For) there is no ignoring Fate and Fortune.[16]
Place not thy heart upon externals,
(For) every man belongs to his (appointed) hour.
Do not strain to seek an excess,
When thy needs are safe for thee. (15)
If riches are brought to thee by robbery,
They will not spend the night with thee;
At daybreak they are not in thy house:
Their places may be seen, but they are not.
The ground has opened its mouth . . . that it might swallow them up,
And might sink them into the underworld. (x 1)
(Or) they have made themselves a great breach of their (own) size
And are sunken down in the storehouse.
(Or) they have made themselves wings like geese
And are flown away to the heavens.[17] (5)

[6] It is obvious that each chapter (Egyptian: "house") is divided into stanzas. For example, the first chapter divides 4-4-4. However, the division is not always clear. Does the second chapter divide 4-4-2-4-4-4-2 or 4-4-8-6-2? Does the fourth chapter divide 4-2-4-2 or 6-6? Therefore, this translation does not attempt such divisions.

[7] The "hot" man is the passionate or impulsive man, in contrast to the "silent" or humbly pious man.

[8] The moon-god Thoth was the barrister of the gods.

[9] The thought of this section is akin to the "coals of fire" passage in Prov. 25:21-22 or 24:29.

[10] The third chapter, here omitted, advises restraint in debate. "Sleep before speaking." Avoid arguing with "the heated man," because "the god knows how to answer him."

[11] This chapter has general similarity to Ps. 1 or Jer. 17:5-8.

[12] The fifth chapter urges honesty in relations with the temple, because today's dispositions may be upset by tomorrow's changes.

[13] cf. Prov. 22:28; 23:10. The omitted following portion gives god's penalties against the encroacher.

[14] The thought is generally that of Prov. 23:11.

[15] cf. Prov. 15:16-17.

[16] The god *Shay* and the goddess *Renenut* were two deified concepts, whose governing role was particularly strong at this time.

[17] cf. Prov. 23:4-5.

Rejoice not thyself (over) riches (gained) by robbery,
Nor mourn because of poverty.
If an archer *in the van* advances (too far),
Then his *squad* abandons him.
The ship of the covetous is left (in) the mud, (10)
While the boat of the silent man (has) a fair breeze.
Thou shouldst make prayer to the Aton when he rises,
Saying: "Give me prosperity and health."
He will give thee thy needs for this life,
And thou wilt be safe from terror.[18] . . .

NINTH CHAPTER:
Do not associate to thyself the heated man,
Nor visit him for conversation.[19]
Preserve thy tongue from answering thy superior, (xi 15)
And guard thyself against reviling him.
Do not make him cast his speech to lasso thee,
Nor make (too) free with thy answer.
Thou shouldst discuss an answer (*only*) *with* a man of thy (own) size,
And guard thyself against plunging headlong into it.
Swifter is speech when the heart is hurt (xii 1)
Than wind *of the head-waters*.[20] . . .
Do not leap to hold to such a one,
Lest a terror carry thee off.

TENTH CHAPTER: (xiii 10)
Do not greet thy heated (opponent) in thy violence,[21]
Nor hurt thy own heart (thereby).
Do not say to him: "Hail to thee!" falsely,
When a terror is in thy belly.
Do not talk with a man falsely— (15)
The abomination of the god.
Do not cut off thy heart from thy tongue,
That all thy affairs may be successful.
Be sincere[22] in the presence of the common people,
For one is safe in the hand of the god. (xiv 1)
God hates him who falsifies words;
His great abomination is the contentious of belly.

ELEVENTH CHAPTER:
Be not greedy for the property of a poor man, (5)
Nor hunger for his bread.
As for the property of a poor man, it (is) a blocking to the throat,
It makes a *vomiting* to the gullet.
If he has *obtained* it by false oaths,
His heart is perverted by his belly.[23] . . . (xiv 10)
The mouthful of bread (too) great thou swallowest and vomitest up, (xiv 17)
And art emptied of thy good.[24] . . .

THIRTEENTH CHAPTER:
Do not confuse a man with a pen upon papyrus— (xv 20)
The abomination of the god.
Do not bear witness with false words, (xvi 1)
Nor *support* another person (*thus*) with thy tongue.
Do not take an accounting of him who has nothing,
Nor falsify thy pen.
If thou findest a large debt against a poor man, (5)
Make it into three parts,
Forgive two, and let one stand.
Thou wilt find it like the ways of life;
Thou wilt lie down and sleep (soundly); in the morning
Thou wilt find it (again) like good news. (10)
Better is praise as one who loves men
Than riches in a storehouse;
Better is bread, when the heart is happy,
Than riches with sorrow.[25] . . .

SIXTEENTH CHAPTER:
Do not *lean on* the scales nor falsify the weights,
Nor damage the fractions of the measure.[26]
Do not wish for a (common) country measure, (xvii 20)
And neglect those of the treasury.
The ape[27] sits beside the balance,
And his heart is the plummet. (xviii 1)
Which god is as great as Thoth,
He that discovered these things, to make them?
Make not for thyself weights which are deficient;
They *abound in grief* through the will of god.[28] . . .

EIGHTEENTH CHAPTER: (xix 10)
Do not spend the night fearful of the morrow.
At daybreak what is the morrow like?
Man knows not what the morrow is like.[29]
God is (always) in his success,
Whereas man is in his failure; (15)
One thing are the words which men say,
Another is that which the god does.[30]
Say not: "I have no wrongdoing,"
Nor (yet) strain to seek quarreling.
As for wrongdoing, it belongs to the god; (20)
It is sealed with his finger.
There is no success in the hand of the god,
But there is no failure before him.
If he[31] pushes himself to seek success, (xx 1)
In the completion of a moment he damages it.
Be steadfast in thy heart, make firm thy breast.
Steer not with thy tongue (alone).

18 The omitted eighth chapter tells the effects of evil speech.

19 cf. Prov. 22:24. For the last two lines of this chapter, cf. *ibid.* 22:25.

20 A long omitted passage sets forth the miseries of "the heated man."

21 Perhaps: You will suffer if you treat an excited opponent with arbitrary abruptness. Prov. 27:14 has been cited as a parallel, with the alteration of Hebrew *re'e(hu)* "his friend," to *ra'* "an evil (man)."

22 "Heavy."

23 cf. Prov. 23:6-7.

24 cf. *ibid.*, 23:8. The omitted twelfth chapter advises honesty in the trusted factor of a noble.

25 cf. *ibid.*, 16:8. The fourteenth chapter asks honest relations with a client, the fifteenth honest recording by the secretary.

26 cf. *ibid.*, 20:23.

27 The animal sacred to Thoth, god of just measure.

28 cf. Prov. 16:11. The seventeenth chapter continues the theme of false measures.

29 Meaning and the probable strophic structure call for a line following this, to the effect that tomorrow is in the hand of god.

30 cf. Prov. 19:21 and 16:9 and the *Homo proposuit sed Deus disponit* of Thomas à Kempis.

31 A man.

If the tongue of a man (be) the rudder of a boat,
The All-Lord is its pilot.[32] . . .

TWENTIETH CHAPTER:
Do not confuse a man in the law court,
Nor *divert* the righteous man.
Give not thy attention (only) to him clothed in white, (xxi 1)
Nor give consideration to him that is unkempt.[33]
Do not accept the bribe of a powerful man,
Nor oppress for him the disabled.
As for justice, the great reward of god,
He gives it to whom he will. . . .
Do not falsify the *income* on the records,
Nor damage the plans of god.
Do not discover for thy own self the will of god,
Without (reference to) Fate and Fortune.[34] . . .

TWENTY-FIRST CHAPTER:
Do not say: "I have found a strong superior, (xxii 1)
For a man in thy city has injured me."
Do not say: "I have found a *patron*,
For one who hates me has injured me."
For surely thou knowest not the plans of god,
Lest thou *be ashamed* on the morrow.
Sit thou down at the hands of the god,
And thy silence will cast them down.[35] . . .
Empty not thy belly to everybody,
Nor damage (thus) the regard for thee.
Spread not thy words to the common people,
Nor associate to thyself one (too) outgoing of heart.[36]
Better is a man whose talk (remains) in his belly
Than he who speaks it out injuriously.[37]
One does not run to reach success,
One does not *throw* to his (own) damage.[38] . . .

TWENTY-THIRD CHAPTER:
Do not eat bread before a noble,
Nor lay on thy mouth at first.
If thou art satisfied with false chewings, (xxiii 15)
They are a pastime for thy spittle.
Look at the cup which is before thee,
And let it serve thy needs.[39]
As a noble is great in his office,
He is as a well abounds (in) the drawing (of water).[40] . . .

TWENTY-FIFTH CHAPTER:
Do not laugh at a blind man nor tease a dwarf
Nor injure the affairs of the lame. (xxiv 10)
Do not tease a man who is in the hand of the god,[41]
Nor be fierce of face against him if he errs.
For man is clay and straw,
And the god is his builder.
He is tearing down and building up every day.
He makes a thousand poor men as he wishes,
(Or) he makes a thousand men *as overseers*,
When he is in his hour of life.
How joyful is he who reaches the West,
When he is safe in the hand of the god.[42] . . .

TWENTY-EIGHTH CHAPTER:
Do not *recognize* a widow if thou catchest her in the fields,[43]
Nor fail to be *indulgent* to her reply. (xxvi 10)
Do not neglect a stranger (with) thy oil-jar,
That it be doubled before thy brethren.
God desires respect for the poor
More than the honoring of the exalted.[44] . . .

THIRTIETH CHAPTER:
See thou these thirty chapters:
They entertain; they instruct;[45]
They are the foremost of all books;
They make the ignorant to know. (xxvii 10)
If they are read out before the ignorant,
Then he will be cleansed by them.
Fill thyself with them; put them in thy heart,
And be a man who can interpret them,
Who will interpret them as a teacher.
As for the scribe who is experienced in his office,
He will find himself worthy (to be) a courtier.[46]
(colophon:)
It has come to its end
In the writing of Senu, son of the God's Father Pa-miu.[47] (xxviii 1)

[32] The nineteenth chapter concerns honest statement in the court of law.
[33] *Sic*, although the negative seems out of place.
[34] cf. n.16 above.
[35] cf. Prov. 20:22 and 27:1.
[36] cf. *ibid.*, 23:9 and 20:19.
[37] cf. *ibid.*, 12:23.
[38] The twenty-second chapter again advises restraint in debate.
[39] cf. Prov. 23:1-3.
[40] The twenty-fourth chapter advises the secretary to keep the affairs of his master in confidence.
[41] The insane.
[42] Death releases a man from the helplessness of this world. The twenty-sixth chapter deals with respect toward elders or superiors, with the twenty-seventh continuing this theme.
[43] Literally: "Do not find a widow." The reference is to the poor gleaning in the fields.
[44] The twenty-ninth chapter recommends appropriate etiquette for the ferryboat across the river.
[45] In Prov. 22:20, the Hebrew is to be read: "Have I not written unto thee thirty (sayings)?"
[46] cf. Prov. 22:29. The special relation of "the Words of the Wise," Prov. 22:17-24:22, to the Wisdom of Amen-em-Opet may best be shown by Simpson's comparison of passages.

Prov.	Amen-em-Opet
22:17-18	3:9-11; 3:16 (Chapter I)
22:19	1:7 (Introductory)
22:20	27:7-8 (Chap. XXX)
22:21	1:5-6 (Introductory)
22:22	4:4-5 (Chap. II)
22:23	no parallel
22:24	11:13-14 (Chap. IX)
22:25	13:8-9 (Chap. IX)
22:26-27	no parallel
22:28	7:12-13 (Chap. VI)
22:29	27:16-17 (Chap. XXX)
23:1-3	23:13-18 (Chap. XXIII)
23:4-5	9:14-10:5 (Chap. VII)
23:6-7	14:5-10 (Chap. XI)
23:8	14:17-18 (Chap. XI)
23:9	22:11-12 (Chap. XXI)
23:10-11	7:12-15; 8:9-10 (Chap. VI)
23:12-24:10	no parallels
24:11	11:6-7 (Chap. VIII)
24:12-22	no parallels

[47] Senu was the scribe who made this copy, as distinct from Amen-em-Opet, the author of the Instruction.

Two others texts to which the Egyptians applied the term "Instruction" are that on the divine attributes of the pharaoh (p. 431 below) and the Satire on the Trades (pp. 432-434 below).

For a listing of the sages of Egypt who composed "instructions," cf. p. 432 below. For a recurring proverbial saying, cf. p. 233, n.2.

Akkadian Proverbs and Counsels

(Translator: Robert H. Pfeiffer)

PROVERBS

I

Text: E. F. Weidner, *KUB*, IV, Nos. 40 and 97. Translation: E. Ebeling, in *Altorientalische Studien Bruno Meissner zum sechzigsten Geburtstag . . . gewidmet*, pp. 21-25 (*MAOG*, IV).

(40:4) My cistern has not gone dry, so my thirst is not excessive.[1] (5) The net is loosened, but the fetters were not remiss.[2] (6) I have obtained a pawn, but the loss does not stop.[3] (9) If I myself had not gone, who would have gone at my side?[4] (10a) He consecrated the temple before he started it.[5] (10b-11) If indeed he had not stood up, when would he sit high up, like gentlemen, on a chair?[6] (12b-13) My mouth had not spoken as gentlemen (do), (consequently) when have I sat and eaten high up on a chair?[7] (14-15) My friend, my secret knowledge is not safeguarded by an enemy: on the contrary, by a son or a daughter, my friend, is my secret knowledge safeguarded.[8]

(97:7-8) Fruit in the spring (of the year)—fruit of mourning.[9] (9) A canal in the direction of the wind brings water in abundance.[10]

II

Text: L. Legrain, *Historical Texts* (*PBS*, Vol. XIII [1922]) No. 11, lines 7 ff. Translation: B. Meissner, *Babylonien und Assyrien*, Vol. II, p. 424. Date: about 1800-1600 B.C.

As long as a man does not exert himself, he will gain nothing.[11]

Whoso has neither king nor queen, who is then his lord?

III

Text: Rawlinson, Vol. II, No. 16. S. Langdon, *AJSL*, XXVIII (1912), 234-43. Translation: Langdon, *ibid.*, pp. 219-33. B. Meissner, *Die babylonische-assyrische Literatur* (Wildpark-Potsdam, 1928), p. 82; same, *Babylonien und Assyrien*, Vol. II, pp. 424-6. Date: about 1800-1600 B.C. The proverbs are numbered here according to Langdon.

A. K 4347

(20) Deal not badly with a matter, then [no sor]row [will fa]ll into your heart. (21) Do [no] evil, then you will [not] clutch a lasting [sorr]ow. (27) Without copulation she conceived, without eating she became plump![12] (28) Copulation causes the breast to give suck.[13] (29) When I labor they take away (my reward): when I increase my efforts, who will give me anything?[14] (34) The strong man is fed through the price of his hire, the weak man through the price (or: the wages) of his child. (37) He is fortunate in everything, since he wears a (fine) garment.[15] (38) Do you strike the face of a walking ox with a strap?[16] (39) My knees keep walking, my feet are tireless, yet a man devoid of understanding pursues me with sorrow.[17] (40) Am I (not) a thoroughbred steed? Yet I am harnessed with a mule and must draw a wagon loaded with reeds.[18] (44) I dwell in a house of asphalt and bricks, yet some clay . . . pours over me.[19] (50) The life of the day before yesterday is that of any day.[20] (53) You are placed into a river and your water becomes at once stinking; you are placed in an orchard and your date-fruit becomes bitter.[21] (55) If the shoot is not right it will not produce the stalk, nor create seed.[22] (56) Will ripe grain grow? How do we know? Will dried grain grow? How do we know?[23] (57) Very soon he will be dead; (so he says), "Let me eat up (all I have)!" Soon he will be well; (so he says), "Let me economize!"[24] (60) From before the gate of the city whose armament is not powerful the enemy cannot be repulsed.[25] (64) You go and take the field of the enemy; the enemy comes and takes your field.[26]

B. Sm 61

(3) The gift of the king (produces) the good work of the cupbearer. (5) Friendship is of a day, slavery is perpetual. (6) Where servants are there is quarrel, where

1 cf. "We never know the worth of water till the well is dry."

2 cf. Amos 5:19; and "Out of the frying-pan into the fire."

3 Eccles. 9:11; and "One fair day assureth not a good summer"; "No fence against ill fortune."

4 "If you want a thing done, go; if not, send"; "Fortune helps those who help themselves"; "Every man for himself."

5 I Kings 20:11; and "Catch the bear before you sell his skin."

6 cf. "A good beginning makes a good ending."

7 cf. "First creep, then go"; and "Step by step the ladder is ascended."

8 cf. Prov. 25:9. In English, "Tell it not in Gath!" (II Sam. 1:20) has become proverbial.

9 cf. "Soon ripe, soon rotten."

10 cf. "It pays to sail with the wind and tide."

11 cf. Prov. 10:4; 12:11a; 13:4; etc.; and "No gains without pains."

12 To indicate something impossible; cf. Amos 6:12a. The Sumerian original reads: "Without his cohabiting with you, can you be pregnant? Without his feeding you, can you be fat?"

13 i.e. cause and effect; cf. Amos 3:3-6.

14 cf. Matt. 6:34. The Sumerian has: "If I save, he has taken it away from you; as for that which I have increased, who will give it to you?"

15 cf. "Fine feathers make fine birds"; "Apparel makes the man."

16 cf. "Do not spur a free horse."

17 cf. Eccles. 9:11.

18 The text is fragmentary and obscure; the translation is tentative.

19 cf. Eccles. 9:12. The Sumerian seems to mean: "In the house the asphalt was removed from the brick; . . . last year the roof drain was dripping on me."

20 The text has been restored at the end, and the translation is in part conjectural. For the meaning, cf. Eccles. 1:9-10; 3:15a. The Sumerian reads: "Out of the victuals of yesterday is what is also of today."

21 Said of a man afflicted with persistent bad luck, or of one bringing misfortune to others through the evil eye.

22 cf. "Of evil grain no good seed can come." Dr. R. J. Williams translates: "May a crooked furrow not produce a stalk! May it not yield seed!"

23 cf. Eccles. 1:15; 3:11; 7:13-14.

24 cf. Isa. 22:13.

25 This is the perennial argument adduced against pacifists.

26 cf. "Tit for tat"; "Turn about is fair play." In contrast with the preceding, this is the argument of the pacifists.

cosmeticians are there is slander.[27] (7) A (plain) citizen in another city becomes its chief.[28]

C. Bu 80-7-19, 130

An alien ox eats grass, one's own ox lies down in the pasture.[29]

IV

Text: C. Bezold and E. A. W. Budge, *The Tell el-Amarna Tablets in the British Museum* (London, 1892), No. 12, lines 17-19. Translation: J. A. Knudtzon, *Die el-Amarna-Tafeln* (*VAB*, II), No. 74 (cf. Vol. II, pp. 1159-60). S. A. B. Mercer, *The Tell el-Amarna Tablets* (Toronto, 1939). The original form of the proverb (attested in 1400-1360 in the letter of Rib-Addi of Byblos just quoted) may have been, "A woman without a husband is like a field without cultivation."

My field is like a woman without a husband, on account of its lack of cultivation.

Text: Bezold and Budge, *The Tell el-Amarna Tablets*, No. 61, (lines 16-19). Translation: Knudtzon, *Die el-Amarna Tafeln*, No. 252. W. F. Albright, An Archaic Hebrew Proverb in an Amarna Letter from Central Palestine, *BASOR*, No. 89 (February, 1943), pp. 29-32. On ants, cf. Prov. 6:6; 30:25. This proverb may be seen in its context in the translation of the Amarna letter No. 252, p. 486.

When ants are struck, they do not accept (it passively), but bite the hand of the man who smites them.

V

Text: R. F. Harper, *ABL*, No. 403, lines 5-7; 14-15; No. 652, lines 10-13. Translation: L. Waterman, *Royal Correspondence of the Assyrian Empire*, Vol. I (Ann Arbor, 1930). R. H. Pfeiffer, *State Letters of Assyria* (*American Oriental Series*, Vol. 6, New Haven, 1935). On the third of these proverbs cf. A. L. Oppenheim in *BASOR*, No. 107 (October, 1947), p. 9, n.6. The first and second proverbs are quoted by Ashurbanipal, king of Assyria (668-633 B.C.) in a sarcastic letter to the Babylonians. In a fuller and clearer form the first proverb occurs in Ahiqar 8:17 (Syriac) and 8:14 (Arabic). "My son, you have been to me like the dog that came to the potters' oven to warm himself, and after he was warm rose up to bark at them" (Syriac). "O my son! You have been to me like the dog that was cold and went into the potters' house to get warm. And when it had got warm, it began to bark at them, and they chased it out and beat it, that it might not bite them" (Arabic). See: R. H. Charles, *The Apocrypha and Pseudepigrapha of the Old Testament* (Oxford, 1913), Vol. II, p. 771. The third proverb is dated to the reign of Esarhaddon (680-669 B.C.).

(1) When the potter's dog went into the oven, the potter blew on the fire inside of it.[30]

(2) A sinful woman at the gate of a judge's house—her word prevails over that of her husband.

(3) Man is the shadow of a god, a slave is the shadow of a man; but the king is like the (very) image of a god.

COUNSELS OF WISDOM

Text and translations: Kerr Duncan Macmillan, *Some Cuneiform Tablets Bearing on the Religion of Babylonia and Assyria* (*BA*, V [1906]), 5, pp. 557-62, 622 f. H. Zimmern, in *ZA*, XXIII (1908), 367 ff.; and in *AO*, XIII/1 (1911), pp. 27-9. S. Langdon, A Tablet of Babylonian Wisdom, *PSBA*, XXXVIII (1916), 105-16, 131-37; see also his *Babylonian Wisdom* (London, 1923), pp. 88-92. E. Ebeling, *AOT*, pp. 291-93. B. Meissner, *Babylonien und Assyrien*, Vol. II, pp. 421 f.; *Die babylonisch-assyrische Literatur* (Wildpark-Potsdam, 1928), p. 81 f. We do not know how long before 700 B.C. this text was written. The lines are numbered as in Langdon's edition of the text. *KAR* 27 is regarded as the beginning of this work.

As a wise man, let your understanding shine modestly,
Let your mouth be restrained, guarded your speech.
Like a man's wealth, let your lips be precious.[1]
Let affront, hostility, be an abomination unto you.
Speak nothing impertinent, (give no) unreliable advice.
Whoever does something ugly—his head is despised.
Hasten not to stand in a public assembly,
Seek not the place of quarrel;
For in a quarrel you must give a decision,
And you will be forced to be their witness.
They will fetch you to testify in a lawsuit that does not concern you.
When you see a quarrel, go away without noticing it.[2]
But if it is really your own quarrel, extinguish the flame;
For a quarrel is *a neglect* of what is right,
A protecting wall . . . (for) the nakedness of one's adversary:
Whoever stops it is thinking about the interests of a friend.
Unto your opponent do no evil;
Your evildoer recompense with good;
Unto your enemy let justice [be done].
Unto your oppressor . . . .
Let him rejoice over you, . . . return to him.[3]
Let not your heart be induced to do evil.
(some lines lost)
Give food to eat, give date wine to drink; (ii 12)
The one begging for alms honor, clothe:
Over this his god rejoices,
This is pleasing unto the god Shamash, he rewards it with good.
Be helpful, do good.
A maid in the house do not . . . .[4]
. . . .

[27] Barbershop gossip and the loquacity of barbers were proverbial long before their attestation in Hellenistic and Roman times. This proverb illustrates commonplace, ordinary, regular happenings (cf. Eccles. 1:5-10).

[28] cf. John 4:44.

[29] cf. the Italian saying, "Paese che vai, usanza che trovi" (if you go into [another] country you will find [other] customs).

[30] Another possible translation is, "When the potter's dog went into the oven, he even growled at the potter" (B. Meissner, *Babylonien und Assyrien*, Vol. II, p. 423).

[1] cf. Prov. 13:3 and the Ahiqar text from Elephantine, col. vii, lines 96-98 (dating from about 430 B.C.): "My son, chatter not overmuch. . . . More than all watchfulness watch your mouth . . ." (H. L. Ginsberg's translation, p. 428 of this volume).

[2] cf. the Arabic version of Ahiqar ii 54 (R. H. Charles, *The Apocrypha and Pseudepigrapha of the Old Testament*, Vol. II, p. 736): "And stand not between persons quarreling, because from a bad word there comes a quarrel, and from a quarrel there comes war, and from war there comes fighting, and you will be forced to bear witness; but run from thence and rest yourself."

[3] Lines 35-40, about rendering good for evil, are on the level of the Sermon on the Mount (Matt. 5:38-45). The closest parallels in the Old Testament are Ex. 23:4-5; Prov. 24:17-18; 25:21-22; Job 31:29-30; cf. Lev. 19:18; Prov. 24:29; Ecclus. 28:2; Tobit 4:15. In Ahiqar, Syriac *A* version, we read (2:20), "My son, if your enemy meet you with evil, meet him with wisdom" (R. H. Charles, *Apocrypha and Pseudepigrapha*, II, 730).

[4] On col. ii, lines 12-17, cf. Job 31:13-20.

Do not marry a harlot whose husbands are six
thousand. (obverse 23)
An Ishtar-woman vowed to a god,
A sacred prostitute whose favors are unlimited,
Will not lift you out of your trouble:
In your quarrel she will slander you.[5]
Reverence and submissiveness are not with her.
Truly, if she takes possession of the house, lead her out.
Toward the path of a stranger she turns her mind.
Or the house which she enters will be destroyed, her
husband will not prosper.[6] (reverse i)
My son, if it be his will, you belong to the prince:
Guard his seal, bind it to your *person*;
Open his treasury, enter therein,
For before you no stranger was ever there.
Wealth without measure you will see therein;
(But) to any such thing do not turn your eye,
Do not let your mind consider doing something stealthy,
For eventually the matter will be investigated.
And whatever stealthy action you have done will become
manifest;
The prince will hear of it, [will punish you].
. . . . (42-47)

(reverse A)

Do not slander, speak what is fine.
Speak no evil, tell what is good.
Whoever slanders (or) speaks evil,
As a retribution the god Shamash will pursue after his
head.
Open not wide your mouth, guard your lips;
The words of your inner self do not speak (even) when
alone.
What you now speak hastily you will later take back,
And you should cause your mind to refrain by its efforts
from speech.[7]
Pay homage daily to your god
With sacrifice, prayer, and appropriate incense-offering.
Towards your god you should feel solicitude of heart:
That is what is appropriate to the deity.
Prayer, supplication, and prostration to the ground
Shall you offer in the morning: then your might will be
great,
And in abundance, through god's help, you will prosper.[8]
In your learning examine the tablet.

(reverse B)

Reverence (for the deity) produces well-being, (1)
Sacrifice prolongs life,
And prayer atones for sin.
A god-fearing man is not despised by [his god];
A worshiper of the Anunnaki lengthens his days.
With a friend and a comrade speak not [evil];
Speak nothing base, [relate] what is favorable.
If you have promised, give . . . .

[5] On harlots, see Lev. 21:7; Prov. 2:16-19; 5:1-23; 6:24-29; Ecclus. 9:2-9; I Cor. 6:13-19; Ahiqar in R. H. Charles, *Apocrypha and Pseudepigrapha*, II, 728-9. On sacred prostitutes, see Deut. 23:18-19; Hos. 4:14; and probably Amos 2:7.

[6] See Prov. 7:5-27.

[7] See above, n.1.

[8] On the duties of ritual worship (lines 35-41) see: Prov. 3:9-10; Eccles. 5:1-7 (Hebr. 4:17-5:6); Ecclus. 7:29-31; Tobit 1:6-8.

If you have encouraged, [help].
. . . . (10-33)

(colophon):

Written according to the prototype and collated.

Aramaic Proverbs and Precepts

(Translator: H. L. Ginsberg)

THE WORDS OF AHIQAR

The text is preserved as the more recent writing on eleven sheets of palimpsest papyrus of the late fifth century B.C. recovered by German excavators from the debris of Elephantine, Upper Egypt, in the years 1906-7. The first four papyri, with a total of five columns, contain the story of Ahiqar, which is in the first person; the remaining seven, with a total of nine columns, contain Ahiqar's sayings. The composition of the work may antedate the preserved copy by as much as a century.

The action of the narrative centers about the court of the Assyrian kings Sennacherib (704-681) and Esarhaddon (680-669). Of other persons named therein, Nabusumiskun actually was a high official of Sennacherib, and Ahiqar himself may be a reflex of Adadsumuṣur, a priest who officiated in the reigns of Sennacherib and Esarhaddon and exerted a certain amount of influence over them. All of the proper names fit well into an Assyrian milieu. For the sayings, too, a Mesopotamian origin is indicated by repeated references to Shamash as god of justice.

Prior to the recovery of the old Aramaic text, several post-Christian recensions of the book of Ahiqar were known, the Syriac one being the oldest. The man Ahiqar is mentioned in the book of Tobit (1:22; 14:10; etc.).

Text and translation: Sachau, Pls. 40-50 (translation, pp. 147-182). Editions: Ungnad, 50-63 (pp. 62-82); Cowley, pp. 204-248. Studies: H. Baneth, Zu den Achikarpapyri, *OLZ*, 1914, 248-251, 295-299, 348-354. J. N. Epstein, *ZAW*, 1912, 132-135; 1913, 224-233, 310-312; *OLZ*, 1916, 204. Th. Nöldeke, *Untersuchungen zum Achiqar-Roman* (Berlin, 1914). F. Stummer, *Der kritische Wert der altaramäischen Aḥiḳartexte aus Elephantine* (Münster i. W., 1914). W. von Soden, *ZA*, XLIII (1936), 9-13.

Columns i-ii (lines 1-31) are too defective for smooth translation. In them Ahiqar (*'ḥyqr*) relates how, having grown old piloting the Assyrian ship of state throughout the reign of Sennacherib, and being without a son of his own, he adopted and instructed his sister's son Nadin and then persuaded Esarhaddon to make him his (Ahiqar's) successor; whereupon Nadin requited his foster-father's kindness with calumny.

(iii 32-48) Then [Esa]rhaddon, the king of Assyria, [answered] and said: "[*Do you, Nabusumiskun on*]e of my father's officers, who [ate] of my father's bread, seek [the old man Ahiqar] wherever you may find [and kill him]. Otherwise this old man [Ah]iq[ar] is a wise scribe [and counselor of all Assy]ria, and is liable to corrupt the land against us." Then, when [the king of As]syria [had spoken thus], he appointed with him 2 other men to see how [it would turn out]. So this officer [Nab]usumiskun [went away] riding on a swif[t h]orse, [and those men] with him. Then, after three more d[a]ys, [he and the o]thers who were with him s[ighted me] as I was walking among the vineyards. [Now when this] officer [Nab]usumiskun [beheld me] he [straig]htway rent his mantle and moaned, "[Are you] the wise scribe and man of good counsel, who [was a righteous] man [and b]y whose counsel and words all of Assyria was guided? *Extinguished be* [the lamp[1] of your son whom you brought] up, whom you set up at the gate of the palace. He has ruined you, and an [evil] return [is it." Th]en I, Ahiqar, was afraid. I answered and said to [that officer] Nabusum[iskun, "Am] I [not] the same Ahiqar who once saved you from an undeserved death? [When Sennacherib], the father of this King Esarhaddon, sought to [kill you, th]en I brought you to my house. There I sustained you (iv 49-63) as a man deals with his brother, having hidden you from him and having said 'I killed him,' until at a la[ter] tim[e] and after many days I brought you before King Sennacherib and cleared you of offenses before him and he did you no evi[l]. Moreover, Sennacherib was well pleased with me for having kept you alive and not having killed you. Now do you do to me even as I did to you. Don't kill me. Take me to your house until other times. King Esarhaddon is merciful as any man(?). In the end he will remember me and wish for my advice. Th[e]n you will [prese]nt me to him and he will spare me alive." Then the officer Nabusumiskun [answered] and said, "Fear not, my [lord] Ahiqar, father of all Assyria, by whose counsel King Sennacherib and (all) the host of Assyria (were guided)!" Then the officer Nabusumiskun said to his companions, those two men that were with him, "[Do you lis]ten [and pay attention] to me while I tell you [my] plan, and a [very] good plan it is." S[o] those [men answered] and said *t[o him.* "Te]ll us, O officer Nabusumiskun, what[ever you will, and we shall listen to] you." The [of]ficer Nabusumiskun then spoke and said to them, "Listen to me. This is [Ahi]qar. He [is] a great man [and a bearer of the se]al of [King] Esarhaddon, and the whole army of [Assy]ria was guided by his counsel and words. Let us not kill him [*undeservedly*]. I will give you [a] eunuch [slave] of mine. Let him be slain bet[ween these] two mountains instead of this Ahiqar. Whe[n it is reported, and] the king [se]nds other [m]en [af]ter us to see the body of this Ahiqar, then [they'll see the bod]y of [th]is eunuch slave of mine. (v 64-78) In the end [King] Esarhaddon [will remember Ahiqar and desire his advice] and he will [regret etc.]."

(Since only the right half—or less than half—of col. v is preserved, its translation involves too much conjecture. It is, however, certain that Nabusumiskun's companions agree to his plan, and Nabusumiskun secretly maintains Ahiqar in his house as Ahiqar once maintained Nabusumiskun. The latter and his two companions report to Esarhaddon that they have slain Ahiqar. The rest of the story is missing altogether. We know from the later recensions that eventually the king did, in fact, miss Ahiqar's advice sorely and was overjoyed to learn that he was still alive, and that Ahiqar was rehabilitated while Nadin got his deserts.)

(vi 79-94) [Wh]at is stronger than a braying ass? The *l[o]ad*. The son who is trained and taught and on [whose] feet the fetter[2] is put [*shall prosper*]. Withhold not thy son from the rod, else thou wilt not be able to save [him from *wickedness*]. If I smite thee, my son, thou wilt not die, but if I leave thee to thine own heart [thou wilt not live]. A blow for a bondman, *a reb[uke]* for a bondwoman, and for all thy slaves dis[cipline. One who] buys a run[away] slave [or] a thievish handmaid *squanders his fortune* and disgraces] the name of his father and his offspring with the reputation of his wantonness.—The scorpion [finds] bread but is not *p[leased, and something b]ad* and is more pleased than if one fe[eds it . . .] The lion will *lie in wait* for the stag in the concealment of the . . . and he [. . .] and will shed its blood and eat its flesh. Even so is the meeting of [*me*]*n*.— . . . a lion. . . . An ass which leaves [*its load*] and *does not carry it* shall take a *load* from its companion and take the b[urde]n which is not its [own with its own] and shall be made to bear a camel's load.—The ass *bend*[*s down*] to the she-ass [from lo]ve of her, and the birds [. . .]. Two things [which] are meet, and the third pleasing to Shamash: one who dr[inks] wine and gives it to drink, one who guards wisdom, and one who hears a word and does not tell.—Behold that is dear [to] Shamash. But he who drinks wine and does not [give it to drink], and one whose wisdom goes astray, [and . . .] is seen.—[. . . Wisdom . . .].

(vii 95-110) To gods also she is dear. F[or all time] the kingdom is [hers]. In he[av]en is she established, for the lord of holy ones has exalted [her.—My s]on, ch[at]ter not overmuch so that thou speak out [every w]ord [that] comes to thy mind; for men's (eyes) and ears are everywhere (trained) u[pon] thy mouth. Beware lest it be [thy] *undoing*. More than all watchfulness watch thy mouth,[3] and [over] what [*thou*] *h*[*earest*] harden thy heart. For a word is a bird: once released no man *can re*[*capture it*].[4] First *co*[*un*]*t the secrets of* thy mouth; then bring out thy [words] by *number*.[5] For the *instruction*[6] of a mouth is stronger than the *instruction* of war. Treat not lightly the word of a king: let it be healing for thy [flesh].[7] Soft is the utterance of a king; (yet) it is sharper and stronger than a [two]-edged knife. Look before thee: a hard look[8] [on the f]ace of a k[ing] (means) "Delay not!"[9] His wrath is swift as lightning: do thou take heed unto thyself that he disp[lay i]t not against thine ut[tera]nces and thou perish [be]fore thy time.[10] [The wr]ath of a king, if thou be commanded, is a burning fire. Obey [it] at once. Let it not be kindled against thee and cover (read: *burn*) thy hands. [Cov]er up the word of a king

[1] If reading and restoration are correct, cf. Prov. 13:9; 20:20; etc.

[2] cf. line 196 and Isa. 41:3b, which render "no fetter is put to his feet."

[3] cf. Prov. 4:23.

[4] Or, "who releases it is a man of no *un*[*derstanding*]."

[5] Reading *b'ddh* and interpreting according to the Arabic.

[6] Reading *'db* and again interpreting according to the Arabic.

[7] cf. Prov. 4:22; 16:24; and 3:8 LXX.

[8] Literally "thing (word)."

[9] Literally "stand not."

[10] cf. for the whole saying Eccles. 8:2-3; where the verse division of the LXX must be followed, and *'npy* and *bpny mlk* are perhaps to be read at the beginnings of vv. 2 and 3 respectively.

with the veil of the heart.—Why should wood strive with fire, flesh with a knife, a man with [*a king*]?[11] I have tasted even the bitter medlar, and [*I have eaten*] endives;[12] but there is naught which is more [bi]tter than poverty. Soft is the tongue of *a k*[*ing*], but it breaks a dragon's ribs;[13] like a plague, which is not seen.—Let not thy heart rejoice over the multitude of children [nor grieve] over their fewness. A king is like *the Merciful*; his voice also is loud: who is there that can stand before him, except one with whom is God? Beautiful is a king to behold, and noble is his majesty to them that walk the earth *as* [*free*]*men.* A good vessel cove[rs] a word in its heart, and a broken one lets it out. The lion approached to [greet the ass]: "Peace be unto thee." The ass answered and said to the lion: . . .

(viii 111-125) I have lifted sand, and I have carried salt; but there is naught which is heavier than [*rage*].[13a] I have lifted bruised straw, and I have taken up bran; but there is naught which is lighter than a sojourner.[14] War troubles calm waters between good *friends.*[15] If a man be small and grow great, his words *soar* above him. For the opening of his mouth is an *utte*[*ra*]*nce* of gods,[16] and if he be beloved of gods they will put something good in his mouth to say. Many are [the st]ar[s of heaven, and] no man knows their names.[17] There is (n)o lion in the sea, therefore they call a flood a *lb'*.[18] The leopard met the goat when she was cold. The leopard answered and said to the goat, "Come, I will cover thee with my hide." The goat [answered] and said to the leopard, "What need have I for it, *my lord*? Take not my skin from me." For he does not greet the gazelle[19] except to suck its blood.—The bear went to the lam[bs. "Give me one of you and I] will be content." The lam[bs] answered and said to him, "Take whichever thou wilt of us. We are [thy] la[mbs]." Truly, 'tis not in the power of m[e]n to li[ft u]p their feet or to put them down with[out the gods]. Truly, 'tis not in thy power to li[ft u]p thy foot [o]r to put it down.—If a good thing come forth from the mouths of m[en, it is well for them], and if an evil thing come [forth] from their mouths, the gods will do evil unto them.—If God's eyes are on men, a man may chop wood in the dark without seeing, like a thief, who demolishes a house and . . . (ix 123-141) [Bend not] thy [b]ow and shoot not thine arrow at a righteous man, lest God come to his help and turn it back upon thee. . . . thou, O my son, *take every trouble* and do every labor, then wilt thou eat and be satisfied and give to thy children. [If thou be]nd thy bow and shoot thine arrow at a righteous man, from thee is the arrow but from God the *guidance.* [. . .] thou, O my son, borrow corn and wheat that thou mayest eat and be sated and give to thy children with thee. Take not a heavy loan, from an evil man. More[over, if] thou take a loan, give no rest to thyself until [thou repay the l]oan. [A loa]n is sweet as [. . .] but its repayment is trouble for the house. [Whatsoever thou hearest, test] with thine ears. For a man's charm is his truthfulness; his repulsiveness, the lies of his lips. [At fi]rst a throne [is set up] for the liar, but in the e[nd they fi]nd out his lies and spit in his face. A liar's neck is cut [i.e. he speaks very softly?] like a . . . virgin that [is hidden] from sight, like a man who causes misfortune which does not proceed from God.—[Despise not] that which is in thy lot, nor covet a wealth which is denied thee. [Multiply not] riches and make not great thy heart. [Whosoever] *takes no pride* in the names of his father and mother, may the s[un] not shine [upon him];[20] for he is a wicked man. [From myself] has my misfortune proceeded: with whom shall I be justified?—The son of my body has spied out my house: [wh]at can I say to strangers? [*My son* has] been a false witness against me: who, then, has justified me?—From my house has gone forth wrath: with whom shall I strive? Reveal not thy [*secrets*] before thy [fri]ends, lest thy name become despised of them.[21] (x 142-158) With him who is more exalted than thou, *quarrel not.* With him who is . . . and stronger than thou, [*contend not; for he will take*] of thy portion and [*add it to*] his. Behold even so is a small man (who strives) with [a great one]. Remove not wisdom from thee [. . .]. Gaze not overmuch [les]t thy vi[sion] be dimmed. Be not (too) sweet, lest they [swallow] thee: be not (too) bitter [*lest they spit thee out*]. If thou wouldst be [exalted], my son, [humble thyself before God], who humbles an [exalted] man and [exalts a lowly man]. What me[n's] l[i]ps curse, God does n[ot] curse. (lines 152-5 badly damaged and omitted here) God shall twist the twister's mouth and tear out [his] tongue. Let not good [ey]es be darkened, nor [good] ears [be stopped, and let a good mouth love] the truth and speak it. (xi 159-172) A man of [beco]ming conduct whose heart is good is like a mighty c[it]y which is *si*[*tuated*] upon a *m*[*ountain*]. There is [*none that can bring him down. Except*] a man *dwell* with God, what shall he be by his own refuge? . . ., but he with whom God is, who can cast him down? (line 162 difficult and omitted here) A man [knows not] what is in his fellow's heart. So when a good man [se]es a wi[cked] man [let him beware of him]. Let him [not] join with him on a journey or be a *neighbor* to him—a good man [wi]th a ba[d] m[an]. The [bram]ble sent to [the] pomegranate tree [saying], "The bramble to the pomegranate: Wherefore the mul(titude) of (thy) thorns [to him that to]uches thy [fru]it?" . . . The [pomegranate tree]

11 cf. Eccles. 6:10b.
12 Possibly *ḥsyn*=Ugar. *ḥswn*, rather than the plural of *ḥs* "lettuce."
13 cf. Prov. 25:15b.
13a Prov. 27:3; Job 6:2-3.
14 i.e. there is nothing less respected. Despised (especially dependent) classes of people are similarly said to be "lighter than bran" in TB, Baba Batra, 98b.
15 Or "shepherds"?
16 cf. Prov. 16:1.
17 cf. Isa. 40:26; Ps. 147:4.
18 Which resembles a word meaning "lion"; the flood, according to our saying, being so designated on the principle of *lucus a non lucendo et canis a non canendo.*
19 The kid seems to have become a gazelle through inadvertence.
20 cf. Prov. 20:20.
21 cf. Prov. 25:9-10.

answered and said to the bramble, "Thou art al[l] thorns to him that touches thee." All that come in contact with a righteous man are on his side. [*A city*] of wicked men shall on a gusty day be pulled apart, and in . . . its gates be brought low; for the spoil [of the righteous are they].—Mine eyes which I lifted up unto thee and my heart which I gave thee in wisdom [hast thou scorned, and thou ha]st brought my name into disg[race]. If the wicked man seize the corner of thy garment, leave it in his hand. Then approach Shamash: he will [t]ake his and give it to thee.

(xii 173-190) (Ends of all lines and beginnings of some missing. Only the point of line 188 is entirely clear: "Hunger makes bitterness sweet, and thirst [sourness]."[22] In column xiii 191-207, only of a few sayings is enough preserved for making out the point.)

. . . If thy master entrust to thee water to keep [*and thou do it faithfully, he may*] leave gold with thee. . . . [A man] one [day said] to the wild ass, "[Let me ride] upon thee, and I will maintain thee [. . . ." Said the wild ass, "Keep] thy maintenance and thy fodder, and let me not see thy riding."—Let not the rich man say, "In my riches I am glorious."[23]

(Column xiv 208-223 has only shreds preserved; the point of the first one can be guessed: "[*Do not sh*]*ow* an Arab the sea nor a Sidonian the *de*[*sert*]; for their work is *different*.")

[22] cf. Prov. 27:7.

[23] cf. Jer. 9:22.

Observations on Life and the World Order

Egyptian Observations

(Translator: John A. Wilson)

THE DIVINE ATTRIBUTES OF PHARAOH

The king of Egypt ruled the land as a god, as the Son of Re, or as the Horus, or as the incorporation of the deities of Upper and Lower Egypt. He was also a synthesis of other gods who represented forces of proper rule, a blend of force and intelligence, of terror and nurture, or of sustenance and punishment. The following poem sets forth some of the divine elements which went into the composition of a pharaoh. It is framed as a father's instruction to his children on right living: if they faithfully serve so great a god, they will prosper.

The stela of Sehetep-ib-Re, Chief Treasurer under pharaoh Ni-maat-Re (Amen-em-het III, about 1840-1790 B.C.) of the Twelfth Dynasty, was found at Abydos, and is now Cairo Museum 20538. It was published by H. O. Lange and H. Schäfer, *Grab- und Denksteine des mittleren Reichs (Catalogue général . . . du Musée du Caire*, Berlin, 1902-08), II, 145-49, Pl. XL, and by K. Sethe, *Aegyptische Lesestücke* (2nd ed., Leipzig, 1928), 68-70. Ch. Kuentz's study in *Studies Presented to F. Ll. Griffith* (London, 1932), 97-110, brought forth a parallel perhaps six centuries later. Translated in Erman, *LAE*, 84-85.

The beginning of the instruction which he made for his children.

I tell something important
And cause that ye hear (it).
I cause that ye know a counsel of eternity
And a manner of living aright[1]
And for passing a lifetime in peace.
Worship King Ni-maat-Re, living forever, within your bodies
And associate with his majesty in your hearts.
He is Perception which is in (men's) hearts,[2]
And his eyes search out every body.
He is Re, by whose beams one sees,
He is one who illumines the Two Lands more than the sun disc.
He is one who makes the land greener than (does) a high Nile,
For he has filled the Two Lands with strength and life.
The nostrils are chilled when he inclines toward rage,
(But) when he is merciful, (they) will breathe the air.[3]
He gives food to them who are in his service,
And he supplies them who tread his path.
The king is a *ka*,[4]
And his mouth is increase.[5]
He who is to be is his creation,
(For) he is the Khnum of all bodies,[6]
The begetter who creates the people.
He is the Bastet who protects the Two Lands;[7]
He who worships him will be one whom his arm shelters.
He is Sekhmet against him who transgresses his command;
He whom he hates will bear woes.[8]
Fight on behalf of his name,
And be scrupulous in the oath to him,
(That) ye may be free from a taint of *disloyalty*.
He whom the king has loved will be a revered one,
(But) there is no tomb for a rebel against his majesty,
And his corpse is cast into the water.
If ye do this, your persons shall be unblemished—
Ye will find it (so) forever.

IN PRAISE OF LEARNED SCRIBES

The Egyptian Empire built up a large bureaucracy. A constant theme of the writings for schoolboys in that period deals with the high standing and privileges of the secretarial profession. The following extract sets forth the advantages of learning in terms of the immortality of great writings. In that respect it stands in contrast to the Song of the Harper (p. 467), where the theme was the powerlessness of the ancient sages to leave a standing memorial. The Song of the Harper was addressed to an occasion of entertainment, whereas the present text was a call to more diligent application to studies.

Papyrus Chester Beatty IV (now British Museum 10684), verso ii 5-iii 11. Probably from Thebes and about 1300 B.C. *Hieratic Papyri in the British Museum. Third Series. Chester Beatty Gift*, ed. by A. H. Gardiner (London, 1935), I, 38-41; II, Pls. 18-19.

NOW THEN, IF THOU DOST THESE THINGS, THOU ART skilled in the writings. As for those learned scribes from the time of those who lived after the gods, they who could foretell what was to come, their names have become everlasting, (even though) they are gone, they completed their lives, and all their relatives are forgotten.

THEY DID NOT MAKE FOR THEMSELVES pyramids of metal, with the tombstones thereof of iron. They were not able to leave heirs in children, . . . pronouncing their names, but they made heirs for themselves in the writings and in the (books of) wisdom which they composed. THEY GAVE THEMSELVES [*the papyrus-roll* as a

1 "Aright," *ni ma'au*, is a play on the name of the pharaoh, Ni-ma'at-Re.

2 "Cognitive intelligence" or "Perception" was an attribute of personality deified as the god *Sia*. It was particularly an attribute of good rule.

3 A favorite device was to set terror and kindliness in juxtaposition as components of rule.

4 *Ka* "vital force," or protecting and sustaining "soul," or "fortune," etc. —the other self which supported a man. cf. p. 3, n.4 above. Here the pharaoh is the *ka* of his people.

5 His command created surplus of provisions.

6 Khnum was a god who fashioned mortals, as on a potter's wheel.

7 Bastet was a kindly cat-goddess.

8 The gentle Bastet is contrasted with the terrible Sekhmet, a lioness-goddess. Sekhmet had also to do with disease, and the word rendered "woes" might be read "sickness."

lector] priest, the writing-board as a son-he-loves,[1] (books of) wisdom (as) their (ii 10) pyramids, the reed-pen (âs) their child, and the back of a stone for a wife.[2] From great to small were made into his children.[3] (As) for the scribe, he is the foremost of them. If there were made for (them) doors and buildings, they are crumbled. Their mortuary service is [*gone*]; their tombstones are covered with dirt; and their graves are forgotten. (But) their names are (still) pronounced because of their books which they made, since they were good and the memory of him who made them (lasts) to the limits of eternity.

Be a scribe, put it in thy heart, that thy name may fare (iii 1) similarly. More effective is a book than a decorated tombstone or an established *tomb-wall.* Such things make buildings and pyramids for the sake of pronouncing their names. Without doubt a name in the mouth of men is of benefit in the necropolis. A man is perished, his corpse is dust, all his relatives are come to the ground—(but) it is writing that makes him remembered in the mouth of a reciter. More effective is a book than the house of the builder or tombs in the West. It is better than a (well-) founded castle or a stela (5) in a temple.

Is there (anyone) here like Hor-dedef? Is there another like Ii-em-hotep? None has appeared among our relatives like Nofry or Khety, the foremost (one) of them. I cause thee to know the names of Ptah-em-Djedhuti and Kha-kheper-(Re)-seneb. Is there another like Ptah-hotep, or Ka-iris as well?[4] These learned men who foretold what was to come, that which issued from their mouths happened, being found as a statement written in his[5] books. (Thus) the children of other people are given to them to be heirs, as though (they were) their own children. Though they concealed their magic (10) from everybody (else), it may be read in a (book of) wisdom. Though they are gone and their names are forgotten, it is writing that makes them remembered.

[1] The lector priest and the "son-he-loves" performed the funerary rites which beatified and maintained the deceased.

[2] A stone ostracon?

[3] Because they were dependent upon the scribe's writings.

[4] We know a surprising number of these famed sages. Hor-dedef and Ii-em-hotep are the traditional wise men (pp. 31, n.6 above; 467, n.4; 476, n.16 below). Khety, the son of Duauf, is credited with the much-copied Satire on the Trades (pp. 432-434 below). A lament by Kha-kheper-Re-seneb is on a writing board now in the British Museum (A. H. Gardiner, *The Admonitions of an Egyptian Sage* [Leipzig, 1909], 95 ff.). The Vizier Ptah-hotep was the author credited with one of the earliest books of wisdom (pp. 412-414). Nofry, Ptah-em-Djedhuti, and Ka-iris are unknown, although it is tempting to emend Nofry into Nefer-rohu (pp. 444-446 below) and Ptah-em Djedhuti into a Djed-Djehuti invoked in a literary controversy (cf. Gardiner's comment following his translation of the present text).

[5] *Sic*, read "their."

THE SATIRE ON THE TRADES

Egyptian schoolboys who were learning to write frequently had to copy the classics which extolled the profession of the scribe, to the disparagement of other vocations. One of the popular models under the Empire was the Satire on the Trades, which details the wretchedness of nonscribal activities. The unhappy schoolboys who made the extant copies mangled the text so thoroughly that translation is often uncertain.

The documents are numerous, most of them from the Nineteenth Dynasty (1350-1200 B.C.) and most of them fragmentary. There are clear indications that the lost original derived from the Middle Kingdom or earlier (2150-1750 B.C.). In whole or in part, the text occurs on 3 papyri (Papyrus Sallier II = British Museum 10182; Papyrus Anastasi VII = British Museum 10222; Papyrus Chester Beatty XIX = British Museum 10699); 1 writing tablet (Louvre 693); and more than 60 ostraca. The present translation was made from as many of these documents as were available to the translator; the line numbers follow Sallier II. The text has commonly been called the "Instruction of Duauf," but the author was apparently a Khety, as Gardiner pointed out in *Hieratic Papyri in the British Museum. Third Series. Chester Beatty Gift*, 1, 40, n.1.

The hieratic texts have not recently been worked over in publication. An old study which still has some value is G. Maspero, *Du genre épistolaire chez les Égyptiens de l'époque pharaonique* (Paris, 1872), 48 ff. There is a translation in Erman, *LAE*, 67-72.

Other Egyptian texts which might have been included under this heading are the statement of a creation in terms of equal opportunity for all men (pp. 7-8 above); the two didactic tales of pp. 405-410 above; the Song of the Harper (p. 467 below); and the song on the happiness of the dead (pp. 33-34 above).

(iii 9) The beginning of the instruction which a man of the ship's cabin, whose name was Duauf's son Khety, made for his son, (whose) name was Pepy, as he was journeying upstream (iv 1) (to) the Residence City, to put him into the Writing School *among* the children of officials, *in the lower part of* the Residence City.[1] Then he said to him:

I have seen *how the belabored man is belabored*—thou shouldst set thy heart in pursuit of writing. And I have observed *how one may be rescued from* his duties—behold, there is nothing which surpasses writing. . . . Read thou at the end of the *Conclusion.*[2] Thou wilt find this statement in it, to wit: "As for the scribe, every place of his is at the Residence City, and he will not be poor in it. (But) *if he uses the wisdom of someone else*, he will not come out successfully." Thus have I seen the professions: they are in *the meaning* of this statement (5) *on* it.

I shall make thee love writing more than thy (own) mother; (thus) I shall make beauty enter before thy face. Moreover, it is greater than any (other) office; there is not its like in the land. If he[3] began to prosper when he was (only) a child, men greet him (respectfully). If some one sends him to carry out an errand, he does not return (*only*) *that he may clothe himself in the (workman's) apron.*

I have never seen a sculptor on an errand nor a goldsmith when he was sent out. (But) I have seen

[1] Khety imparted the advice during the journey south to the Capital, where he was putting his son into the government's secretarial training school. Khety and his son Pepy are apparently of no high degree. It is not clear whether "man of the ship's cabin" is the father's title or his location as he gave the advice.

[2] Either the title of a well-known book of advice, or the conclusion of this text in its general purport. The word occurs again in Papyrus Beatty IV, verso vi 11 (*Hieratic Papyri in the British Museum. Third Series. Chester Beatty Gift*, 1, 43; 11, Pl. 20):—(Readers) "have all beatified my name (when coming) near the conclusion."

[3] The scribe.

the metalworker at his work at the mouth of his furnace. His fingers were somewhat like crocodiles;[4] he stank more than fish-roe.

Every craftsman that wields the adze, he is wearier than a hoeman. His field is the wood, and his *job* is the metal. At night, though he is released, he does more (v 1) than his arms can (really) do. At night *he has to strike* a light.

The fashioner of costly stones seeks for skill in every (kind of) hard stone. When he has *fully* completed things, his arms are destroyed, and he is weary. When he sits down at the going in of Re,[5] his thighs and his back are cramped.

The barber is (still) shaving at the end of dusk. When he gives himself *up to chins*, he puts himself upon his (own) shoulder.[6] He gives himself from street to street, to seek out those whom he may shave. *Thus* if he is valiant his arms will fill his belly, (5) like a bee eating for its work.

The *itinerant merchant* sails downstream to the Delta to get trade for himself. When he has done more than his arms can (really) do, the gnats have slain him, the sand flies have made him *miserably miserable*. Then there is *inflammation*.

The small building contractor carries mud.[7] . . . He is *dirtier* than vines or pigs, *from treading* under his mud. His clothes are stiff with clay; his *leather belt is going to ruin*. Entering into the wind, he is miserable. His *lamp goes out*, though (still) in good condition. He *pounds* with his feet; he *crushes* with his own self, *muddying* the court of every house, when the water *of the streets has flooded*.

(vi 1) Let me tell thee also of the builder of walls. His *sides* ache, since he must be outside *in a treacherous* wind. He builds in an apron, while he is girt with lotuses of the workshop, at a distance *from* his rear.[8] His arms are destroyed with technical work; every calculation of his is different.[9] What he eats is the bread of his fingers,[10] and he washes himself (*only*) *once a season*. He is simply wretched through and through. . . . As for (5) food, he must give it to his house, for his children are *very many*.

The gardener brings *vegetables*, both his shoulders being under . . . upon his neck. Early in the morning he must water the vegetables and in the evening the vines. . . . "The sand fly of his mother" is his name, "the *sheikh* of every profession."[11]

The tenant-farmer, his reckonings (go on) forever.[12] His voice is louder (than) the *abu*-bird. . . . Wearier is he than a *wayfarer* of the Delta. Yet he is (vii 1) a picked man: his safety is a safety from lions.[13] His *sides* ache, *as if heaven* and earth were in them. When he goes forth *thence from* the meadows and he reaches his home in the evening, *he is one cut down by traveling*.

The weaver in the workshops, he is worse than a woman, with his thighs against his belly. He cannot breathe the (open) air. If he cuts short the day of weaving, he is beaten with fifty thongs. He must give food to the doorkeeper to let him see the light of day.

The arrow-maker, he is very miserable as he goes out (5) into the desert.[14] Greater is that which he gives to his donkey than its work thereafter (is worth). Great is that which he gives to him who is in the meadows, who sets him on the way. When he reaches his home in the evening, the traveling has cut him down.

The *courier* goes out to a foreign country, after he has made over his property to his children, being afraid of lions and Asiatics. *And what of him*, when he is in Egypt? When he arrives thence from the meadows and he reaches his home in the evening, the traveling has cut him down. His *house is* (*only*) an apron of brick.[15] He does not return happy of heart.

The *embalmer*, his fingers are foul, for the odor thereof is (that of) corpses. His eyes *burn from the greatness of the heat*. (viii 1) He could not oppose his (own) daughter.[16] He spends the day cutting up old rags,[17] so that clothing is an abomination to him.

The cobbler, he is very badly off, *carrying his equipment* forever. His safety is a safety from corpses, as he bites into the leather.[18]

The laundryman launders on the (river) bank, a neighbor of the crocodile. When a father comes out of the greasy waters, he could not oppose his (own) daughter. There are no satisfying jobs *in thy sight, O sheikh* of every profession![19] He is mixed up by the differences in his accounts. . . . When he puts (5) on the apron of a woman, then he is in *woe*. I weep for him, spending the day under the rod. . . .

The bird-catcher, he is very miserable, when he looks at the denizens of the sky. If marsh-fowl pass by in the heavens, then he says: "Would that (I had) a net!", (but) god does not let (it) happen to him, being neglectful of his affairs.

Let me tell thee also of the fish-catcher. He is more miserable than any (other) profession. Behold, *there is nothing in* his work on the river, mingled with the crocodiles. If there is a cutting down in the total *of the official register*,[20] then there is complaint. He

4 "His fingers were like a thing of crocodiles"; they were tough and wrinkled.

5 At sunset?

6 Has to carry his own heavy responsibility to earn a living?

7 To make mud-bricks.

8 Since we do not know the meaning of "lotuses of the workshops," we cannot say how his costume was absurd.

9 He loses count of his bricks or his measurements.

10 For lack of food, he gnaws his fingers?

11 Sarcastic designations, which have a general similarity of phrasing to those of the modern Arab world.

12 He must always render account to his landlord.

13 A heavy-handed jibe at the peaceful farmer.

14 To get flint points.

15 The text may be corrupt. If the translation is approximately correct, it means that his house has become a mere shell in his absence.

16 Is too weak from weariness to stand up to a girl?

17 For strips with which to wrap mummies.

18 May he have only animal hides to bite on.

19 cf. n.11 above.

20 Of fish due the government.

cannot (even) say: "A crocodile is (ix 1) waiting (there)," for fear has made him blind.[21] ...

Behold, there is no profession free of a boss—except for the scribe: he is the boss.

But if thou knowest writing, then it will go better with thee than (in) these professions which I have set before thee. . . . Behold, it is done in journeying upstream to the Residence City; behold, it is done for love of thee. A day in school is of advantage to thee. The eternity of its work is (like that of) the mountains. It is: "*Quick* (5) *quick*!"—(so) I let thee know....

Let me tell thee also other matters, to teach thee what thou shouldst know. . . . If thou goest to the rear of officials, approach (only) at a distance *after a* (*decent interval*). If thou enterest in, while a householder is in his house and his *activity* is for some one else before thee, as thou sittest with thy hand to thy mouth, do not ask for something beside him. *Thou shouldst act according to what he says to thee*, by guarding (thy) speech at the dining table.

Be dignified, (yet) be not under awe when speaking (x 1) words of reserve—he who hides his belly (is) one who makes a shield for himself—or when speaking words of boldness when one sits with thee *in hostility*.

If thou goest forth from the school, after midday is announced to thee, and goest *rollicking* in the street, men dispute with thee *in the end. It is not for thee.*

If an official sends thee on an errand, say it (just) as he said it; do not take away or add to it. He who leaves (*things alone*) creates jubilation.... (One) trusts in every good characteristic of his. There is nothing hidden from him; there is no *separating him from* any place of his.... (5) . . . How wretched it is, the belly which thou heedest! If three loaves should satisfy thee, and the swallowing of two *hin* of beer, (but) there is (still) no *limit* [to] the belly, fight against it....

Behold, it is good that thou send away the multitude and hear the words of officials (only).... When the scribe has been seen to listen, listening becomes a heroic quality. Thou shouldst combat words *which may be* against it.[22] Let thy legs hasten as thou goest, (or) it *cannot* (xi 1) *be attained*. Associate with him *who leads the way* to it, and make friends with a man of thy (own) generation.

Behold, I have set thee on the way of god.[23] The Renenut of a scribe is on his shoulder on the day of his birth.[24] He reaches the halls of the magistrates, when he *has become a man*. Behold, there is no scribe who lacks food, from the property of the House of the King—life, prosperity, health! Meskhenet is (the source of) the scribe's welfare,[25] he being set before the magistrates. His father and his mother praise god, he being set upon the way of the living.

Behold these things—I (*have set them*) before thee and thy children's children.

(5) It has come to a happy ending in success....

[21] He is so blinded by fear of crocodiles that no one will believe his excuses for not delivering a full quota of fish.

[22] In this context "it" means "hearing," the respectful obedience of the scribe to higher authority.

[23] Only one text so, whereas three texts have: "Behold, Renenut is on the way of god," which we take to be a corruption affected by the following sentence.

[24] Slaves were branded with the master's name. Renenut, the harvest-goddess, was a goddess of fortune. Thus, the good fortune of a scribe was fixed for him from birth.

[25] Meskhenet was a goddess of birth and destiny.

Akkadian Observations on Life and the World Order

(Translator: Robert H. Pfeiffer)

"I WILL PRAISE THE LORD OF WISDOM"

Text: Rawlinson, IV, 2nd ed., No. 60. V. Scheil, *Une saison de fouilles à Sippar* (Cairo, 1902), No. 37. R. C. Thompson, *PSBA*, XXXII (1910), 18 ff. E. Ebeling, *KAR*, Nos. 10, 11, 108, 175, 326. S. Langdon, *Babylonian Wisdom* (London, 1923), Plates I-V.

Transcriptions and translations: H. Zimmern, *Hymnen und Gebete* (*AO*, VII/3), pp. 28 ff. M. Jastrow, *JBL*, XXV (1906), 135-191. R. W. Rogers, *Cuneiform Parallels to the Old Testament*, pp. 164-169. B. Landsberger, in Lehmann-Haas, *Textbuch zur Religionsgeschichte*, 2nd ed. (Leipzig, 1923), pp. 311 ff. S. Langdon, *Babylonian Wisdom*, pp. 35-66. E. Ebeling, *AOT*, pp. 273-81. See also, for some parts, Th. Jacobsen, in H. and H. A. Frankfort and others, *The Intellectual Adventure of Ancient Man* (Chicago, 1946), pp. 212-16.

... I have become like a deaf man. (I 11)
. . . Once I behaved like a lord, now I have become a slave.... (13)
The fury of my companions destroys me.
. . .
The day is sighing, the night is weeping; (20)
The month is silence, mourning is the year.
. . .
I have arrived, I have passed beyond life's span. (II 1)
I look about me: evil upon evil!
My affliction increases, right I cannot find.
I implored the god, but he did not turn his countenance;
I prayed to my goddess, but she did not raise her head.
The diviner through divination did not discern the situation.
Through incense-offering the dream-interpreter did not explain my right.
I turned to the necromancer, but he did not enlighten me.
The conjurer through magic did not dispel the wrath against me.
Whence come the evil things everywhere? (10)
I looked backwards: persecution, woe!
Like one who did not offer a libation to a god,
And at meal-time did not invoke a goddess,
Who did not bow his face and did not know reverence,
In whose mouth prayer and supplication ceased,
For whom the holiday had been eliminated, the *eššešu*[1] festival has been curtailed,
Who became negligent, despised their images,

[1] The *eššešu* festival was celebrated on the 4th, 8th and 17th day of the month.

Who did not teach his people religion and reverence,
Who did not remember his god, although eating his food,
Who forsook his goddess and did not offer her *a libation*;
Nay, worse than one *who became proud* and forgot his (divine) lord,
Who swore frivolously in the name of his honorable deity—like such a one have I become!
Yet I myself was thinking only of prayer and supplication:
Supplication was my concern, sacrifice my rule;
The day of the worship of the gods was my delight,
The day of my goddess' procession was my profit and wealth.
Veneration of the king was my joy,
And I enjoyed music in his honor.
I taught my land to observe the divine ordinances,
To honor the name of the goddess I instructed my people.
The king's majesty I equated to that of a god,
And reverence for the (royal) palace I inculcated in the troops.
Oh that I only knew that these things are well pleasing to a god!
What is good in one's sight is evil for a god.
What is bad in one's own mind is good for his god.
Who can understand the counsel of the gods in the midst of heaven?
The plan of a god is deep waters, who can comprehend it?
Where has befuddled mankind ever learned what a god's conduct is?
He who was living yesterday has died today:
Instantly he is made gloomy, suddenly is he crushed.
One moment he sings a happy song,
And in an instant he will moan like a mourner.
Like day and night their mood changes.
When they are hungry they resemble corpses,
When they are sated they rival their god;
In good luck they speak of ascending to heaven,
When they are afflicted they grumble about going down to the underworld.

. . . .

An evil ghost has come from its abyss, (53)
. . . a headache has come out from Ekur.[2]
The . . . [demon] has descended from the (underworld) mountain.
[My] . . . . shook [with] a chill,
Like the grass of the earth the disease turns one pale . . .
all these together drew near unto me.
(fragmentary description of pathological symptoms) (59-65)

. . . . (II reverse)

The tall [body] they destroyed like a wall, (3)
My broad figure they brought low like a reed.
Like a *sungirtu* (water plant) I was torn away and cast on my belly.
The *alû* (disease demon) has clothed himself with my body as with a garment.
Like a net, sleep has covered me.
My eyes stare without seeing.
My ears are open without hearing.
Faintness has seized my whole body.
A stroke has fallen upon my flesh.
Weakness has taken hold of my hand.
Weariness has fallen upon my knees.

. . . .

Death [pursued me] and covered my whole body.
If someone asking for me calls me, I do not answer.
My people weep, I myself no longer exist.
In my mouth a gag is placed,
I hold back the word of my lips.

. . . .

Wheat, even though putrid, I eat.
Beer—life divine!—I have eliminated from me.
Extremely long has lasted the distress.
Through starving my appearance . . . .
My flesh is flaccid, my blood is [going].
My bones are *smashed* . . . .
My muscles are inflamed . . . .
I took the bed to the jail, they have blocked (my) exit.
My prison—that is what my house has become.
My hands have been cast into fetters—(i.e.) my flesh;
Into my own chains have my feet been thrown.
My *wheals* are sore, the wound is serious.
The lash striking me is filled with *terror*.
They have pierced me with a goad, the sting was fierce.
All day a pursuer pursues me.
At night he does not let me draw my breath for a moment.
Through straining my sinews have been loosened,
My limbs are wrecked, hit aside.
I spend the night in my dung, like an ox.
I was soaked like a sheep in my excrements.
My arthritis baffled the conjurer,
And my omens confused the diviner.
The enchanter has not determined the condition of my illness,
And the time (of the end) of my malady the diviner did not give (me).
No god helped, (none) seized my hand;
My goddess showed no mercy, she did not come to my side.
While the grave was still open they took possession of my jewels,
Before I was dead the weeping (for me) was ended.
All my land said, "How sad!"[3]
My ill-wisher heard it, and his countenance shone (with joy);

[2] Ekur (meaning "mountain house") the great temple of Enlil at Nippur, is used here in the sense of the underworld.

[3] Another possible translation, instead of "How sad!" is "How has he been mistreated!"

They brought the good news to the woman who was my ill-wisher, and her spirit[4] was delighted.
But I know the day on which my tears will cease,
On which in the midst of the protecting deities their divinity will show mercy.
Heavy was his hand, I could not bear it; (III 1)
Mighty was his frightfulness.
(fragments) (3-7)
A dream in the morning *appeared* twice with the same meaning. (8)
A certain man, immense in stature, . . .
He removed their obstruction, he opened my hearing.
. . . .
My nose, whose [breathing] was hindered by *the oppression* of the heat, (20)
Its injury he healed so that I could breathe . . . .
My lips, that were constricted and [trembled],
He dispelled their fear and loosed their bonds.
My mouth that was covered and with which I spoke in whispers,
He cleansed like copper and *made to shine.*
My teeth that were locked together and . . . ,
He opened the space between them and their roots he . . . .
The tongue that was bound, was unable to function,—
He [removed] *its dumbness* and its speech became [distinct].
The windpipe that was tightened and *stiff* as in a corpse, (30)
Its songs he made glad, so that *they sounded* like a flute.
The lungs that are constricted and do not receive [breath],
Their . . . was made right, their stoppage he opened.
. . . .
The large intestine that had become empty through hunger and was entwined like a basket, (51)
Receives food, takes drink.
The neck that had become flabby and bent,
Rose mountainlike, stood up high like a cedar.
Similar to (that of) one having full might became my strength.
(obscure) (56-57)
The knees that were stiff like a falcon . . . .
. . . .
He rubbed off the rust, made it shiningly clean.
Gigantic in size, clad in new raiment . . . . (III A 10)
. . . .
. . . . he came to me. (13)
. . . . my flesh became *numb.*
. . . "The lady sent me.
. . . .
. . . . saying, '. . . sent me.' (18)
They shouted . . .
Shamash . . . ." (20)
A second time [I saw a dream],
In a dream I saw . . .
A certain man . . .
A tamarisk (branch), a purification vessel he held in his hand.
"Tab-utul-Enlil,[5] the dweller of Nippur,
Has sent me to purify you."
Lifting water, he poured it over me.
The incantation of life he recited, he anointed me [with . . .].
I saw a third dream.
. . . the dream which I saw in the night. (30)
After the manner of humans, a [beautiful] maiden, with nice features.
The queen of life, saying,
"Declare mercy [for him] . . . ."
"Fear not!" he (or, she) said . . . .
"Whatever happened in the dream . . . ."
He (or, she) declared for me mercy—me, the sorely afflicted.
Someone, who in the night saw a vision,
Saw in the dream Ur-Nin-tin-ug-ga,[6]
A mighty man, wearing his crown; a conjurer carrying a [tablet]. (40)
"Marduk has sent me."
Unto Šubshi-mešre-Nergal he brought . . . ,
In his clean hands he brought . . . .
To my attendant he entrusted (it).
Early in the morning he sent a message,
His (Marduk's) omen caused my people to see benevolence (done unto me).
In malady the patient . . . .
He quickly ended my illness, broken was . . . .
After my lord's heart had found rest,
The spirit of Marduk the merciful was quieted.[7] (50)
(fragments) (51-58)
He caused the wind to carry away my trespasses.
. . . . (III reverse)
He sent the storm wind to the foundations of heaven, (5)
Unto the bosom of the earth . . . . (5b)
To his abyss he caused the evil ghost to descend.
The countless demons he sent back to Ekur (i.e. the underworld).
The demon Labartu he knocked down, he drove her straight to the mountain (of the underworld).
Into the waves of the sea he sank the fever heat.
The root of the sickness he pulled out like a plant. (10)
The unhealthy sleep, the spell of slumber,
As when the heavens are filled with smoke . . . ,
They were driven away, with the woe and pain . . . .
He caused them to withdraw like a hurricane, causing the earth to . . . . (13b)
The torturing headache . . . .
He removed the running of my eyes and drove it from me.

[4] The word translated "spirit" means literally "liver"; cf. Morris Jastrow, Jr., The Liver as the Seat of the Soul, in *Studies in the History of Religion Presented to Crawford Howell Toy,* edited by D. G. Lyon and G. F. Moore (New York, 1912), pp. 143-68.

[5] This name is written ideographically in Sumerian LAL-UR-^{d}ALIM-MA, meaning "good is the bosom of Enlil."

[6] This Sumerian name means, "Servant of the divine mistress of the revivification of the dead."

[7] On "spirit" cf. n.4; "merciful" could be rendered "shepherd."

The blur of my eyes, over which had spread the curtain of night,
A mighty wind blew it off and cleared their sight.
My ears, stopped and closed as in a deaf man,
The faded appearance became brilliant.
On the holy river shore (in the underworld) where the (last) judgment of men is manifested,
(My) forehead was rubbed clean, my slavery mark was obliterated.[8]
. . . . (64-65)
Out of *trouble*, through deliverance, I came.
The waters of Esagila[9] though weary, I set forth in my hands.
Into the mouth of the lion who was devouring me Marduk placed *a bit.*
Marduk removed *the incantation* of the one hounding me, turned back his lumps.
. . . . (70-74)
. . . . (IV 1[10])
. . . .
. . . he took me.
. . . he opened for me.
. . . he revived me.
[From *distress*] he saved me.
[Out of the river] Hubur (in the underworld) he drew me.
Marduk seized my hand.
. . . smote me.
[Marduk] lifted high my head,
He smote my smiter's hand;
His weapon Marduk shattered.
. . . .
With lowly countenance I entered Esagila[11]:
I, who had gone down into the grave, returned to Babylon.
In the "Gate of Abundance" abundance was given to me.[12]
In the "Gate of the Great Lamassu" my Lamassu approached me.
In the "Welfare Gate" I beheld welfare.
In the "Gate of Life" I met life.
In the "Gate of Sunrise" I was reckoned with the living.
In the "Radiant Omen Gate" my omens became radiant.
In the "Release from Guilt Gate" my guilt was released.
In the "Gate of the Mouth's Inquiry" my mouth inquired.
In the "Release from Sighing Gate" my sighing was appeased.
In the "Gate of the Purifying Waters" I was sprinkled with purifying waters.
In the "Welfare Gate" I appeared before Marduk.
In the "Gate of Full Opulence" I kissed the foot of the goddess Sarpanit.[13]
In supplication and imploration I persisted before them.
Sweet-smelling incense smoke I offered to them.
I presented (to them my) produce, gifts, *angub-te*-offerings.
I slew fat oxen, I sacrificed *lambs.*
I offered a libation of sweet date wine, . . . wine.
I . . . the divine Shedu, to the divine protectors of the walls of Esagila;
With libations I made happy their mood,
[With] abundant . . . I gladdened their heart.
. . . , bolt, lock of the doors
With pure [oil], *butter*, . . . grain
. . . . [*according to*] the temple ritual.
. . . .
Bread . . . .
The product of the *hašurru* tree [*pleased him*].
(At) a banquet the Babylonians . . . .
They had made his grave, at a banquet . . . .
The Babylonians saw that (Marduk) had restored [his] life.
All mouths praise [his] greatness.
"Who commanded it, who accomplished the vision of the deity?
In whose mind is the going (freely) on one's way realized?
Apart from Marduk, who revived his lifeless state?
Besides Sarpanit, what goddess conferred life unto him?"
Marduk is able to revive in the grave.
Sarpanit knows how to deliver from destruction.
Wherever the earth reaches, the heavens are spread out,
The sun shines, fire glows,
Water flows, the wind blows,
(Wherever the beings) whose clay the goddess Aruru has nipped off,[14]
Creatures endowed with breath, stride rapidly,
. . . as many as there are, *glorify* Marduk!
(fragments) (64-68)

[8] Here ends the Sippar No. 55 text. The following lines (64-74) are translated from a commentary to our text published in the original in H. C. Rawlinson, *A Selection from the Miscellaneous Inscriptions of Assyria and Babylonia*, Vol. v (London, 1884), Plate 47, rev. 14-15. See also S. Langdon, *Babylonian Wisdom*, Plate II, lines 14-25; Plate III, lines 26-45.

[9] Esagila ("The house of the lofty head") was the temple of Marduk in Babylon.

[10] Tablet IV has been translated from the Ashur text published in E. Ebeling, *KAR*, Nos. 10 and 11.

[11] cf. n.9 above.

[12] The patient whose health has been restored now goes through the twelve gates of Esagila (cf. above, n.9).

[13] Sarpanit was Marduk's consort.

[14] Aruru's clay-beings are humanity.

A PESSIMISTIC DIALOGUE BETWEEN MASTER AND SERVANT

Text: G. Reisner, *Sumerisch-babylonische Hymnen*, (*Mitteilungen aus den orientalischen Sammlungen der königl. Museen zu Berlin,* Vol. x [Berlin, 1896]), No. 6. E. Ebeling, *KAR*, I, No. 96. E. Ebeling, *Quellen zur Kenntnis der babylonischen Religion*, Vol. II (*MVAG*, XXIII/2 [1919]), p. 85.

Translations: Ebeling, *Quellen* (see above), pp. 50 ff. S. Langdon, *Babylonian Wisdom* (London, 1923), pp. 67-81. Ebeling, *AOT*, pp. 284-7. See also: G. B. Gray, Job, Ecclesiastes, and a New Babylonian Literary Fragment, *Expository Times*, XXXI (1920), 440-3. Th. Jacobsen, in *The Intellectual Adventure of Ancient Man*, by H. and H. A. Frankfort, and others (Chicago, 1946), pp. 216-18.

(I) ["Servant,] obey me." Yes, my lord, yes. ["Bring me at once the] chariot, hitch it up. I will ride to the palace." [Ride, my lord, ride] . . . he will appoint you and they will be yours. . . . he will be gracious to you. ["No, servant,] I shall not ride [to] the palace." [Do not ride], my lord, do not ride. [To a place . . .] he will send you. [*In a land which*] you know [not] he will let you be captured. [Day and] night he will let you see trouble.

(II) "Servant, obey me." Yes, my lord, yes. ["Bring me at] once water for my hands, and give it to me: I wish to dine." [Dine,] my lord, dine. To dine regularly is the opening of the heart (i.e. brings joy). [To a dinner] eaten in happiness and with washed hands (the sun-god) Shamash comes. "No, [servant,] I shall not dine." Do not dine, my lord, do not dine. To be hungry and eat, to be thirsty and drink, comes upon (every) man.

(III) "Servant, obey me." Yes, my lord, yes. "Bring me at once the chariot, hitch it up. I will ride to the wilderness." Ride, my lord, ride. The fugitive's stomach is full. The hunting dog will break a bone; the fugitive *ḫaḫur* bird will build its nest; the wild ass running to and fro will . . . . "No, servant, to the wilderness I will not ride." Do not ride, my lord, do not ride. The fugitive's mind is variable. The hunting dog's teeth will break; the house of the fugitive *ḫaḫur* bird is in [*a hole*] of the wall; and the abode of the wild ass running to and fro is the desert.

(IV) "Servant, [obey me." Yes, my lord, yes.] (20-31) (fragments). . . . the silence of the evil one make complete. ["My enemy] I shall capture and *quickly* shackle. I shall lie in wait for my adversary." Lie (in wait), my lord, lie (in wait). "I will build a house." A house you will not build. He who goes . . . destroys his father's house.

(V) ["Servant, obey me." Yes, my lord, yes.] "At the [word of my adversary I shall remain silent."] Remain silent, my lord, remain [silent. Silence is better than speech.] "No, servant, at the [word of my adversary I shall not remain silent."] Do not remain silent, my lord, [do not remain silent.] If you do not speak with your mouth . . . . Your adversary will be angry with you . . . .

(VI) "Servant, obey me." Yes, my lord, yes. "I intend to start a rebellion." Do (it), my lord, [do (it)]. If you do not start a rebellion what becomes of your clay?[1] Who will give you (something) to fill your stomach? "No, servant, I shall not do something violent." [Do (it) not, my lord, do (it) not.] The man doing something violent is killed or [*ill-treated*], or he is maimed, or captured and cast into prison.

(VII) "Servant, obey me." Yes, my lord, yes. "A woman will I love." Yes, love, my lord, love. The man who loves a woman forgets pain and trouble. "No, servant, a woman I shall not love." [Do not love,] my lord, do not [love]. Woman is a well,[2] woman is an iron dagger—a sharp one!—which cuts a man's neck.

(VIII) "Servant, obey me." Yes, my lord, yes. "Bring me at once water for my hands, and give it to me: I will offer a sacrifice to my god." Offer, my lord, offer. A man offering sacrifice to his god is happy, loan upon loan he makes. "No, servant, a sacrifice to my god will I not offer." Do not offer (it), my lord, do not offer (it). You may teach a god to trot after you like a dog when he requires of you, (saying), "(Celebrate) my ritual" or "do not inquire (by requesting an oracle)" or anything else.

(IX) ["Servant,] obey me." Yes, my lord, yes. "I shall give food to our country." Give it, my lord, give it! [The man who] gives food [to his country]—his barley (remains) his own but his receipts from interest (payments) become immense.[3] ["No, servant,] food to my country I shall not give." [Do not give, my lord,] do not give. Giving is like *lov*[*ing*]. . . . giving birth to a son. . . . they will curse you. [They will eat] your barley and destroy you.[4]

(X) "Servant, obey me." Yes, my lord, yes. "I will do something helpful for my country." Do (it), my lord, do (it). The man who does something helpful for his country,—his helpful deed is placed in the bowl of Marduk.[5] "No, servant, I will not do something helpful for my country." Do it not, my lord, do it not. Climb the mounds of ancient ruins and walk about: look at the skulls of late and early (men); who (among them) is an evildoer, who a public benefactor?[6]

(XI) "Servant, obey me." Yes, my lord, yes. "Now, what is good? To break my neck, your neck, throw (both) into the river—(that) is good." Who is tall enough to ascend to heaven? Who is broad enough to embrace the earth? "No, servant, I shall kill you and send you ahead of me." (Then) would my lord (wish to) live even three days after me? (Colophon) Written according to the original and collated.

A DIALOGUE ABOUT HUMAN MISERY[1]

Cuneiform text: J. A. Craig, *Babylonian and Assyrian Religious Texts*, Vol. I (*Assyriologische Bibliothek*, XIII [Leipzig,

[1] "Your clay" means of course "your body" (cf. Gen. 2:7).

[2] The following gloss has been added in the cuneiform text: "well—pitfall, ditch." Woman (and more specifically the wife) is compared to a well (Hebrew, *bĕ'ēr*) and to a cistern (Hebrew, *bôr*) in Prov. 5:15, cf. 5:16-18; Cant. 4:15. H. Graetz and others after him propose to read, "Remember thy cistern (*bôrĕkhā*)" or "thy well (Hebrew, *bĕ'ērêkhā*)" instead of "thy creator" (Hebrew, *bôr' äkhā*) in Eccles. 12:1, interpreting, "remember thy wife." The Akkadian *bûrtu* (used here) means well and cistern, and is a cognate of the two Hebrew words in Prov. 5:15 mentioned above.

[3] A variant text reads: "His barley is barley immense (in quantity)."

[4] The variant of lines 73b-76 reads, "He eats your barley, they will diminish the interest on your barley, and besides they will curse you."

[5] The tablets listing men's deeds were stored in Marduk's bowl.

[6] cf. Eccles. 1:11; 2:14-16; 6:8; 9:1-6; etc.; Ps. 49:10 (Hebr. 49:11); Job 21:26.

[1] This poem is sometimes called "The Babylonian Ecclesiastes." The cuneiform text is an acrostic poem. Each of the eleven verses, comprising one of the 27 partially extant stanzas, begins with the same syllable, as in Ps. 119 each of the eight distichs of each stanza begins with the same letter of the alphabet. The acrostic reads: *a-na-ku* [*ša*]*-ag-gi-il-ki-*[*i-na-am*]*-ub-bi-ib ma-aš-ma-šu ka-ri-*[*bu*] *ša i-li u šar-ri*, "I, Shaggil-kinam-ubbib, the conjurer, bless god and king." The poet's name preserved in this acrostic means, "O Esagil (i.e. the temple of Marduk in Babylon), pronounce the righteous pure!" The extant tablets on which the poem is written are

1895]), Plates 44-52. S. A. Strong, On Some Babylonian and Assyrian Alliterative Texts, I, *PSBA*, XVII (1895), pp. 142-7. H. Zimmern in *ZA*, x (1896), pp. 17 ff. Translations: E. Ebeling, *Ein Babylonischer Kohelet* (*Berliner Beiträge zur Keilschriftkunde*, I:1 [1923]); also in *AOT*, pp. 287-91; and in *Festschrift Max von Oppenheim gewidmet* (1933), pp. 27-34. B. Meissner, *Babylonien und Assyrien*, Vol. II (Leipzig, 1925), p. 432; and *Die babylonisch-assyrische Literatur* (Wildpark-Potsdam, 1928), p. 80. B. Landsberger, Die babylonische Theodizee, *ZA*, XLIII (NF IX [1936]), pp. 32-76.

... [*my woes*] let me tell you,
... let me relate to you.
... [a companion *I seek*] ...
[*Comfort*] (me), a sufferer, (then) ... shall I praise you.
Where is *your brother*, comparable to you?
Where a wise man such as you are?
[To whom] may I flee and relate my torment?
[I was finished] and mental evil came straightway.
I was left behind, fate snatched away (my) begetter;
The mother who begat me *was murdered* by Hades.
My father and my mother forsook me, and I had no guardian.

My respected friend, what you said is grief! (II)
What you caused your beloved heart to meditate is evil!
Your clever understanding you made similar to that of an imbecile;
Your radiant features you turned into darkness.
(The humans) are given up, may they go the way of death.
"You shall cross the (underworld) river Hubur," they were told long ago.
If you look, people are uniformly *dull*.
The wealthy man ... they have glorified eagerly,
(But) who ever favored the radiant just man?
The one who beholds the countenance of a god has a (protecting) Lamassu,
The one who reverently worships a goddess heaps up abundance.

Is your heart, my friend, a *spring of water* which gathers all [wisdom]? (III)
Is [your] know[ledge] ... the surge of the sea *rushing forth*?
Accurately will I search you; learn my word.
Pay attention a moment, and listen to my speech.
My ... is finished, *I am forgotten* ....
My good luck *I allowed to slip away*, I passed (it) by ....
My strength has vanished, ... has ceased.
Trouble and despair have ....
... for the satiety ....
The date wine, vivifier of men, in (my) case [*fails*].
....

Does the fierce lion, who eats the best of the meat, (V)
Present his dough-and-incense burnt offering to appease his goddess' displeasure?
Does [really] the upstart, whose affluence has increased,
Weigh [precious metal] to the goddess Mami?[2]
Have I withheld the meal-oblation? (No), I have prayed to the gods,
I have presented the prescribed sacrifices to the goddess ....

(O) palm, tree of wealth, precious brother, (VI)
Endowed with the totality of wisdom, jewel of *choice gold*!
You are firmly established like the earth, but [divine] counsel is remote.
Consider the noble onager in ... ;
He has trampled on *the produce* of the fields, the arrow turns against him.
The enemy of the herds, the lion, which you mentioned, please consider:
(For) the brutality which the lion has committed, a pit was opened against him.
The upstart endowed with wealth, whose property is heaped up,
In the fire, before his appointed time, the ruler burns him.
Do you wish to follow the paths these have trod?
Seek (instead) incessantly the gracious favor of a god.

Your opinion is a north-wind, a [good] breeze for the people; (VII)
Pure, choice, is your ... counsel.
But a single word [let me add] in your presence:
"They walk on a lucky path those who do not seek [a god],
Those who devoutly pray to [a goddess] become poor and weak."
In my childhood I [investigated] the mind of the god,
In humility and piety have I searched for the goddess:
(And yet) a corvée without profit I bear like a yoke;
The god brought me scarcity instead of wealth;
A cripple above, a fool in front,
Have stolen my necklace, and I have been brought low.

In reality, (O) sharp-witted one, what you have in mind is not proper: (VIII)
You have rejected the truth, you have despised the decree of the god.
Not to observe the ordinances of the god was the wish of your soul,
The correct purifications of the goddess you have [*neglected*].
Like the center of the heavens, so the divine counsel [is remote].
The utterance of the god (and) goddess is not taken [*to heart*].
True understanding [*is excluded*] for mankind,
(While) to plan evil [*is unavoidable*] for men.
To teach [*people*] an *evil* path ...
....

Let me forsake the house .... (XIII)

---

not earlier than the seventh century B.C., but the poem may have originated a few centuries before then. The sufferer speaks in the stanzas with uneven numbers, his friend in the others.

[2] Mama (variant, Mami) is the mother goddess.

Let me not crave property....
Let me forget the votive gifts of the god, trample upon ritual prescriptions.
Let me *slaughter the bullock*, ... eat.
Let me go to a fortress, reach distant places.
Let me open a spring, free the flow (of water),
A spring of the steppe, ... let me wander about,
Let me enter house after house, control my hunger,
Let me camp in the fields, hunt along the highways,
Let me [enter] in like a beggar....
The necklace, the beauty of which you craved, (XXII)
... his legs, quickly he was lost.
The godless, the scoundrel, who has acquired wealth,
The murderer (with) his weapon pursues him.
You, who do not seek the counsel of the god, what is your success?
Whoever draws the yoke of the god, verily ... his food (supply) is constant.
Seek (then) the good breath of the gods,
And what you have lost this year you will recover at once.
Among men I have made observations, (but) the signs were variable. (XXIII)
The god does not stop the advance of the *šarrabu*-demon.
In the canals the begetter draws the ship,
(While) his first-born lies in bed;
The oldest brother moves about on his way like a lion,
(While) the second son delights in driving a mule.
In the street the senior son hunts disgracefully (for plunder),
(While) the second son distributes food to the needy.
In the presence of a leader I, who *humble myself*, what do I gain?
I must submit (even) to my *slave*:
The wealthy and thriving man despises me,—the last (of all).
(O) wise (and) strong one, endowed with insight, (XXIV)
Your heart *is eating itself* (when) you treat God unjustly.
The mind of the god, like the center of the heavens, is remote;
His knowledge is difficult, men cannot understand it.
The product of the hand of the goddess Aruru is life in general.
The *premature* offspring is always *thin*:
A cow's first heifer is inferior,
Her second offspring is *twice as large*.
The fool gives birth to an outstanding son,
The mighty hero to one whose designation is quite different.
Let him know (that) people cannot understand what the *counsel* of a god is.
Give heed, my friend! Understand my *meaning*, (XXV)
Guard the choice expression of my speech.
(People) extol the word of a prominent man, expert in murder,
(But) they abase the humble, who has committed no violence.
They justify the evildoer, whose iniquity is ...,
(But) they drive away the righteous, who gives [heed] to the god's counsel.
They fill with precious metal the ... of the bandit,
(But) they empty of food *the larder* of the helpless man.
They strengthen the mighty man, whose *retinue* is [*wicked*],
(But) they ruin the weakling, they cast down the feeble.
Even me, helpless (as I am), the upstart persecutes.
The primeval king, the god Naru,[3] creator of mankind, (XXVI)
The glorious god Zulummaru,[4] who nipped off their clay,
The queen who formed them, the divine lady Mama,[2]
They bestowed upon humanity ingenious speech:
Falsehood and untruth they conferred upon them forever.
Enthusiastically they speak of the rich man's graciousness,
"He is a king! His tutelary deities go at his side!"
As if he were a thief, they mistreat a wretched man,
They bestow slander on him, they plot murder against him,
Disloyally they bring every evil upon him because he lacks *protection*;
Dreadfully they destroy him, they extinguish him like a flame.
Be merciful, my friend: listen to my woe! (XXVII)
Help me! See (my) misery, and you will truly understand.
A wise and imploring slave am I.
Help and encouragement I have not experienced for an instant.
I walked quietly through the squares of my city,
My voice was never loud, my speech was low;
I did not raise my head, I looked (down) at the ground.
Like a slave I was not glorified in the assembly of [*my peers*].
May the god Ninurta, who ..., supply help!
May the goddess Ishtar, who ..., have mercy upon me!
May the shepherd,[5] the sun of the people,[5] [*have mercy*].

[3] A cuneiform commentary identifies Nâru or Narru with the god Enlil.

[4] Zulummaru is the god Ea, according to the commentary.

[5] i.e. the king.

Oracles and Prophecies

Egyptian Oracles and Prophecies

(Translator: John A. Wilson)

THE ADMONITIONS OF IPU-WER

The following text is "prophetic" in a biblical sense. The "prophet" is not foretelling the future but is standing before a pharaoh and condemning the past and present administration of Egypt. The manuscript is too fragmentary for a full, connected sense. It seems clear, however, that Egypt had suffered a breakdown of government, accompanied by social and economic chaos. These calamities met with indifference in the palace. A certain Ipu-wer, about whom nothing is known apart from the surviving text, appeared at the palace and reported to the pharaoh the anarchy in the land. Ipu-wer first was inclined to absolve the pharaoh of guilt for these woes, but grew more bold and ended with a denunciation of the king who evaded his responsibilities.

Although our manuscript was written in the Nineteenth or Twentieth Dynasty (1350-1100 B.C.), the original belonged to an earlier time, perhaps to the period between the Old and Middle Kingdoms (2300-2050 B.C.). The language and orthography are "Middle Egyptian." The situation described conforms to that which followed the breakdown of the central government at the end of the Old Kingdom. The pharaoh who is denounced is not named, but may have been one of the last rulers of the Sixth Dynasty or one of the kings of the weak dynasties following.

The beginning and end of the manuscript are missing, and the body of the text is full of lacunae. Only extracts may be given here. The lost beginning of the text probably gave the narrative setting of Ipu-wer's arrival in court and the reasons for his speeches.

Leyden Papyrus I 344, recto, was facsimiled in C. Leemans, *Monumens égyptiens du Musée d'antiquités des Pays-Bas à Leide* (Leyden, 1841-82), II, Pls. CV-CXIII. The significance of the text was first presented by H. O. Lange, Prophezeiungen eines ägyptischen Weisen (*SPAW*, 1903, 601-10). The definitive study of the text is still that of A. H. Gardiner, *The Admonitions of an Egyptian Sage* (Leipzig, 1909). The text is translated in Erman, *LAE*, 92-108. The significance of the text was studied by J. H. Breasted, *The Dawn of Conscience* (New York, 1933), 193-200.

(i 1) . . . Door[keepers] say: "Let us go and plunder." . . . The laundryman refuses to carry his load. . . . Bird-[catchers] have marshaled the battle array. . . . [*Men of*] the Delta marshes carry shields.[1] . . . (5) . . . A man regards his son as his enemy. . . . A man of character goes in mourning[2] because of what has happened in the land. . . . Foreigners have become people[3] everywhere. . . .

(ii 2) . . . [4]Why really, the [face] is pale. The bowman is ready. Robbery is everywhere. There is no man of yesterday.[5] . . .

Why really, the Nile is in flood, (but) no one plows for himself, (because) every man says: "We do not know what may happen throughout the land!"

Why really, women are dried up, and none can conceive. Khnum cannot fashion (mortals) because of the state of the land.[6]

Why really, poor men have become the possessors of treasures. He who could not make himself (5) a pair of sandals is (now) the possessor of riches. . . .

Why really, many dead are buried in the river. The stream is a tomb, and the embalming-place has really become the stream.

Why really, nobles are in lamentation, while poor men have joy. Every town says: "Let us banish many from us."

Why really, . . . dirt is throughout the land. There are really none (whose) clothes are white in these times.

Why really, the land spins around as a potter's wheel does. The robber is (now) the possessor of riches. . . .

(10) Why really, the River is blood. If one drinks of it, one rejects (it) as human and thirsts for water.

Why really, doors, columns, and *floor planks* are burned up,[7] (but) the *flooring* of the palace—life, prosperity, health!—(still) remains firm.[8] . . .

Why really, crocodiles [*sink*] *down because of* what they have carried off, (for) men go to them of their own accord.[9] . . .

(iii 1) [Why] really, the desert is (spread) throughout the land. The nomes are destroyed. Barbarians from outside have come *to* Egypt. . . . There are really no people anywhere.[10] . . . (5) . . .

Why really, they who built [*pyramids* have become] farmers. They who were in the ship of the god are *charged with forced* [*labor*]. No one really sails north to [Byb]los today. What shall we do for cedar for our mummies? Priests were buried *with* their[11] produce, and [nobles] were embalmed with the oil thereof as far away as Keftiu,[12] (but) they come no (longer). Gold is lacking. . . . How important it (now) seems when the oasis-people come carrying their festival

[1] Men formerly in peaceful pursuits have become violent.

[2] "In blue," the color of mourning garments.

[3] The term "men, humans, people," was used by the Egyptians to designate themselves, in contrast to their foreign neighbors, who were not conceded to be real people.

[4] A number of parallel stanzas, in general poetic form, begin with words of surprise or protest, rubricized in the text, and here translated: "Why really!"

[5] To the Egyptian the past was the good time given by the gods. Here the sudden breakdown of order gives specific point to this statement.

[6] The potter god shaped infants on his wheel.

[7] Probably those parts of private houses which were made of wood.

[8] Either this is said out of respect for the king, or it sets an invidious contrast between the fate of the people and the indifference of the pharaoh.

[9] Suicide in the River.

[10] cf. n.3 above. In a breakdown of government, restless foreigners infiltrated into the fertile land of Egypt.

[11] The produce of foreign trade. Byblos in Phoenicia was an Egyptian shipping point for coniferous wood and resinous oil.

[12] Probably Crete.

provisions: reed-mats, . . . fresh *redmet*-plants, (10) . . . of birds, and . . .[13]

Why really, Elephantine, the Thinite nome, and the [*shrine*] of Upper Egypt do not pay taxes because of [civil] war. . . . What is a treasury without its revenues for? The heart of the king (must) indeed be glad when truth comes to him![14] But really, every foreign country [*comes*]! Such is our water! Such is our welfare! What can we do about it? Going to ruin!

Why really, laughter has disappeared, and is [no longer] made. It is wailing that pervades the land, mixed with lamentation. . . . (iv 1) . . .

Why really, the children of nobles are dashed against the walls. The (once) prayed-for children are (now) laid out on the high ground. . . . (5) . . .

Why really, the entire Delta marshland will no (longer) be hidden: the confidence of the Northland is (now) a beaten path.[15] What is it that one could do? . . . Behold, it is in the hands of those who did not know it, as well as those who knew it; foreigners are (now) skilled *in* the work of the Delta. . . . (10) . . .

Why really, all maid-servants make free with their tongues.[16] When their mistresses speak, it is burdensome to the servants. . . . (v 10) . . .

Why really, the ways [*are not*] guarded roads. Men sit in the bushes until the benighted (traveler) comes, to take away his burden and steal *what is* on him. He is presented with the blows of a stick and slain wrongfully. . . . Ah, would that it were the end of men, no conception, no (vi 1) birth! Then the earth would cease from noise, without wrangling! . . .

Why really, grain has perished on every side. . . . Everybody says: "There is nothing!" The storehouse is stripped bare; its keeper is stretched out on the ground. . . . (5) . . . Ah, would that I had raised my voice at that time—it might save me from the suffering in which I am!

Why really, the writings of the august enclosure are read.[17] The place of secrets which was (so formerly) is (now) laid bare.

Why really, magic is exposed. *Go-spells* and *enfold-spells* are made ineffectual because they are repeated by (ordinary) people.[18]

Why really, (public) offices are open, and their reports are read.[19] Serfs have become the owners of *serfs*. . . .

Why really, the writings of the scribes of the mat have been removed.[20] The grain-sustenance of Egypt is (now) a come-and-get-it.[21]

Why really, the laws (10) of the enclosure are put out-of-doors. Men actually walk on them *in* the highways. Poor men *tear them up* in the streets. . . .

Why really, the children of nobles are *abandoned* in the streets. He who knows says: "Yes, (it is so)!" The fool says: "No, (it is not)!" It is fair in the sight of him who knows it not.[22] . . .

(vii 1) [23]Behold now, the fire has mounted up on high. Its flame goes forth against the enemies of the land.

Behold now, something has been done which never happened for a long time: the king has been taken away by poor men.[24]

Behold, he who was buried as a falcon (*now lies*) on a (*mere*) bier. What the pyramid hid has become empty.

Behold now, it has come to a point where the land is despoiled of the kingship by a few irresponsible men.[25]

Behold now, it has come to a point where (men) rebel against the uraeus,[26] the . . . of Re, which makes the Two Lands peaceful.

Behold, the secret of the land, whose limits are unknow(able), is laid bare.[27] The Residence (may) be razed within an hour. . . . (5) . . .

Behold, the (guardian-)serpent is taken from her hole.[28] The secrets of the Kings of Upper and Lower Egypt are laid bare. . . . (10) . . .

Behold, nobles' ladies are (now) *gleaners*, and nobles are in the workhouse. (But) he who never (even) slept on a *plank* is (now) the owner of a bed. . . .

Behold, the owners of robes are (now) in rags. (But) he who never wove for himself is (now) the owner of fine linen. . . .

Behold, he who knew not the lyre is (now) the owner of a harp. He who never sang for himself (now) praises the goddess of music. . . . (viii 1) . . .

Behold, the bald-headed man who had no oil has become the owner of jars of sweet myrrh.

(5) Behold, she who had not (even) a box is (now) the owner of a *trunk*. She who looked at her face in the water is (now) the owner of a mirror. . . . (10) . . .

Behold, the king's men *thrash around among* the cattle of the destitute.[29] . . .

13 The paltry trade from the nearby oases is contrasted with the former foreign commerce.

14 This may be ironical. But it may also mean that Ipu-wer was the first to tell the pharaoh about the sad state of the land.

15 With the frontier policing ineffective, the security of the Delta was broken by invaders.

16 "Have power-rights over their mouths."

17 Or "are taken away." The restricted area of the administration had civil and religious writings which were not open to the ordinary public. cf. the following stanzas.

18 Magic known to everybody was no longer magic. The tentative translation assumes that there were two kinds of magic charms, one beginning with the word "go," the other with the word "enfold."

19 Or "are taken away."

20 Scribes seated on mats kept the records of Egypt's grain produce.

21 A compound and perhaps colloquial phrase, "when-I-go-down-it-is-brought-to-me."

22 Those who are blissfully unaware of the troubles are fools. The statement may have been intended to implicate the pharaoh indirectly. The passage is in place here. It is an inapt quotation in the Instruction of King Amen-em-het (p. 419 above).

23 A section in which the stanzas are introduced by a different rubricized word, "Behold." In place of an attitude of surprised protest, Ipu-wer now brings his charges closer home to the palace.

24 The next stanza makes this explicit as the robbing of royal tombs. But there is an implicit attack here on the king who heard the words for his failure to preserve former order.

25 "Men who know not plans."

26 The serpent on the brow of the king, and thus the symbol of kingship.

27 The "secret" was the awful mystery and inviolability of the god who was pharaoh of Egypt. cf. the following stanza.

28 The deified snake which was the guardian of a temple or a palace.

29 The sense seems to be that those directly responsible to the king are

BEHOLD, the king's men *thrash around among* geese, which are presented (to) the gods instead of oxen.[30] . . . (ix 1) . . .

BEHOLD, nobles' ladies are growing hungry, (but) the king's men are sated with what they have done.

BEHOLD, not an office is in its (proper) place, like a stampeded herd which has no herdsman.

BEHOLD, cattle are (left) free-wandering, (for) there is no one to take care of them. Every man takes for himself and brands (them) with his name. . . .

BEHOLD, he who had no grain is (now) the owner of granaries. (5) He who had to get a loan for himself (now) issues it. . . . (x 1) . . .[31]

So Lower Egypt WEEPS. The storehouse of the king is a (mere) come-and-get-it for everybody,[32] and the entire palace is without its taxes. To it (should belong) barley, emmer, birds, and fish. To it (should belong) white cloth, fine linen, metal, and (5) ointment. To it (should belong) rug, mat, [*flowers*], palanquin, and every good revenue. . . .[33]

Remember (xi 1) . . . how fumigation is made with incense, how water is offered from a jar in the early morning.

Remember fattened *ro*-geese, *terep*-geese, and *sat*-geese, how the divine offerings are made to the gods.

Remember how natron is chewed and how white bread is prepared by a man on the day of moistening the head.[34]

Remember how flagstaffs are set up and a stela is carved, while a priest purifies the temples and the house of god is whitewashed like milk; how the fragrance of the horizon[35] is made sweet, and how offering-bread is established.

Remember how (ritual) regulations are adhered to, how (religious) dates are distributed, how (5) one who has been inducted into priestly service may be removed for *personal* weakness—that is, it was carried out wrongfully. . . .[36]

. . . It shall come that he brings coolness upon the heart. (xii 1) Men shall say: "He is the herdsman of all men. Evil is not in his heart. Though his herds may be small, still he has spent the day caring for them." . . . Would that he might perceive their character from the (very) first generation![37] Then he would smite down evil; he would stretch forth the arm against it; he would destroy the *seed* thereof and their inheritance. . . . (5) . . . (But) there is no pilot in their hour. Where is he today? Is he then sleeping? Behold, the glory thereof cannot be seen. . . . (10) . . .[38]

. . . Authority, Perception, and Justice are with thee,[39] (but) it is confusion which thou wouldst set throughout the land, together with the noise of contention. Behold, one thrusts against another. Men conform to that which thou hast commanded. If three men go along a road, they are found to be two men: it is the greater number that kills the lesser. Does then the herdsman love death?[40] So then thou wilt command that (xiii 1) a reply be made: "It is *because* one man *loves* and another hates. *That is, their forms* are few everywhere."[41] *This really means that thou hast acted* to bring such (a situation) into being, and thou hast spoken lies.[42] . . . All these years are civil strife. A man may be slain on his (own) roof, while he is on the watch in his boundary house. Is he brave and saves himself?—that means that he will live. . . . (5) . . . Would that thou mightest taste of some of the oppressions thereof! Then thou wouldst say: . . .[43]

. . . (10) . . .[44] But it is still good when the hands of men construct pyramids, when canals are dug, and when groves of trees are made for the gods.

But it is still good when men are drunken, when they drink *miyet* and their hearts are happy.

But it is still good when rejoicing is in the mouths (of men), when the notables of the districts are standing and watching the rejoicing (xiv 1) from their *houses*, clothed in finest linen, and *already* purified. . . . (10) . . .

". . . None can be found who will stand *in their places*. . . . Every man fights for his sister, and he protects his own person. Is (it) the Nubians? Then we shall make our (own) *protection. Fighting police* will hold off the barbarians. Is it the Libyans? Then we shall *act again*. The Madjoi *fortunately* are with Egypt.[45] How is it that every man kills his brother? The military classes (xv 1) which we marshal for ourselves have become *barbari-*

---

running wild in appropriating the property of ordinary citizens. Ipu-wer is now directing his criticism closer to the person of the king.

[30] Probably thereby making a profit on a contracted obligation.

[31] Another series of stanzas, each beginning with the word "destroyed," describes further chaos. This section is too damaged for connected translation.

[32] cf. n.21 above.

[33] In the section which follows, each stanza begins with the word "remember," recalling the pious observations of the past as the necessary norm for the future.

[34] Moistening the head, like cleansing the mouth with natron-water, was probably some kind of purificatory rite.

[35] "The horizon" was the temple.

[36] In context full of lacunae there is a transition to a new theme. Unfortunately we cannot be sure about the argument. Ipu-wer is certainly describing the ideal ruler. The alternatives are (a) that this ruler is a pattern from the past, perhaps the sun-god Re, or (b) that the passage is truly messianic and that Ipu-wer is looking forward to the god-king who will deliver Egypt from her woes. This translation takes the latter alternative.

[37] The ideal king should know the perennial nature of man. Grammatically, the sentence is not an unreal condition, "Would that he had perceived," referring to Re's punishment of mankind (pp. 10-11 above), but a condition of wish, probably referring to the future.

[38] In an unintelligible section, here omitted, Ipu-wer uses the second person singular. As Nathan said to David: "Thou art the man," so Ipu-wer must finally be addressing the pharaoh, pinning the responsibility for Egypt's woes directly on the king, as indicated in the following context.

[39] *Hu* "authoritative utterance" or "creative command," and *Sia* "intellectual perception" or "cognition," were a pair of related attributes, often deified. As attributes of kingship, they were sometimes linked to *ma'at* "justice" or "truth." Kingship thus needed the ability to comprehend a situation, the authority to meet the situation by command, and the balance of equitable justice.

[40] The slain people belong to the herd of pharaoh, the herdsman.

[41] It is impossible to understand the statement which Ipu-wer attributes to the pharaoh as an excuse for weakness. Perhaps he is saying that there is more than one side to a question.

[42] In milder form, this might be translated: "Lies are told thee."

[43] In combatting the pharaoh's obscure argument, Ipu-wer again recites some of the anarchy in Egypt. Seemingly he states that personal experience in such troubles would make the king talk differently.

[44] A series of stanzas now begins with the formula: "It is still, however, good," introducing a nostalgic recollection of former days, which would still be happy in the future.

[45] The Madjoi, people from lands south of Egypt, were used as police in Egypt.

ans, beginning to destroy that from which they took their being and to show the Asiatics the state of the land.[46] And yet all the foreigners are afraid of *them.* . . . (10) . . ."[47]

THAT WHICH Ipu-wer SAID, when he answered the majesty of the All-Lord: ". . . To be ignorant of it is something pleasant to the heart. Thou hast done what is good in their hearts, (for) thou hast kept people alive *thereby.* (But still) they cover up (xvi 1) their faces for fear of the morrow.

"Once upon a time there was a man who was old *and in the presence of* his salvation,[48] while his son was (still) a child, without understanding. . . ."[49]

THE PROPHECY OF NEFER-ROHU

The Middle Kingdom delivered Egypt from the civil war and anarchy which had followed the Old Kingdom. These troubles and their ultimate resolution produced a sense of messianic salvation, a feeling which the early pharaohs of the Middle Kingdom probably fostered in their own interests. The following text was apparently composed at that time of happy deliverance, although the earliest extant copies happen to date from the Eighteenth Dynasty, about five centuries later. The text purports to relate how King Snefru of the Fourth Dynasty sought entertainment and how a prophet foretold the downfall of the Old Kingdom and the reestablishment of order by Amen-em-het I, the first king of the Twelfth Dynasty.

Papyrus Leningrad 1116B was published by W. Golénischeff, *Les papyrus hiératiques no. 1115, 1116A, et 1116B de l'Ermitage Impérial à St. Pétersbourg* (St. Petersburg, 1913). The text was studied and translated by A. H. Gardiner in *JEA*, I (1914), 100-06, and translated by Erman, *LAE*, 110-15. The text was used for school purposes in the Eighteenth and Nineteenth Dynasties and portions appear on two ostraca and two writing tablets.

NOW IT HAPPENED THAT the majesty of the King of Upper and Lower Egypt: Snefru, the triumphant, was the beneficent king in this entire land. On one of these days it happened that the official council of the Residence City entered into the Great House—life, [prosperity], health!—to offer greeting.[1] Then they went out, that they might offer greetings (elsewhere), according to their daily procedure. Then his majesty—life, prosperity, health!—said to the seal-bearer who was at his side: "Go and bring me (back) the official council of the Residence City, which has gone forth hence to offer greetings on this [day]." (Thereupon they) were ushered in to him (5) immediately. Then they were on their bellies in the presence of his majesty a second time.

Then his majesty—life, prosperity, health!—said to them: "(My) people, behold, I have caused you to be called to have you seek out for me a son of yours who is wise, or a brother of yours who is competent, or a friend of yours who has performed a good deed, one who may say to me a few fine words or choice speeches, at the hearing of which my [majesty] may be entertained."

Then they put (themselves) upon their bellies in the presence of his majesty—life, prosperity, health!—once more. THEN THEY SAID BEFORE his majesty—life, prosperity, health!: "A great lector-priest of Bastet,[2] O sovereign, our lord, (10) whose name is Nefer-rohu—he is a commoner valiant [with] his arm, a scribe competent with his fingers; he is a man of rank, who has more property than any peer of his. Would that he [*might be permitted*] to see his majesty!" Then his majesty—life, prosperity, health!—said: "Go and [bring] him to me!"

Then he was ushered in to him immediately. Then he was on his belly in the presence of his majesty—life, prosperity, health! Then his majesty—life, prosperity, health!—said: "Come, pray, Nefer-rohu, my friend, that thou mayest say to me a few fine words or choice speeches, at the hearing of which my majesty may be entertained!" Then the lector-priest Nefer-rohu said: "Of what has (already) happened or of what is going to happen, O Sovereign—life, prosperity, health!—[my] lord?" (15) Then his majesty—life, prosperity, health!—said: "Rather of what is going to happen. *If it has* taken place *by* today, *pass it* [*by*]."[3] Then he stretched forth his hand for the box of writing equipment; then he drew forth a scroll of papyrus and a palette; thereupon he put (it) into writing.[4]

What the lector-[priest] Nefer-rohu said, that wise man of the east, he who belonged to Bastet at her appearances, that child of the Heliopolitan nome,[5] AS HE BROODED over what (was to) happen in the land, as he called to mind the state of the east, when the Asiatics would move about with their strong arms, would disturb the hearts [of] those who are at the harvest, and would take away the spans of cattle at the plowing. (20) He said:

Reconstruct, O my heart, (*how*) thou bewailest this land in which thou didst begin! To be silent is *repression.* Behold, there is something about which men speak as *terrifying,* for, behold, the great man is a thing passed away (in the land) where thou didst begin. BE

46 It would seem that Egypt's own troops were disloyal.

47 Since the following words contain an "answer" of Ipu-wer, this paragraph, much of which is omitted as unintelligible, contains the pharaoh's disturbed comment, trying to assay Egypt's strength.

48 "His salvation" means death. The formula at the beginning of this paragraph is the storytelling formula, "There was a man, who was," and we certainly have the beginning of a narrative here. Either it is told by Ipu-wer as a parable, or it does not belong to the Admonitions of Ipu-wer, which would then end on the ominous note of "fear of the morrow."

49 The story defies consecutive translation. It apparently deals with violence to the tomb and to the corpses and funerary furniture. The last two columns of the papyrus are in lamentable destruction.

1 "To ask after the state," i.e. to offer respectful greetings, undoubtedly here a polite circumlocution for the daily report, first to the pharaoh and then to the other highest officials. "The Great House" (*per-aa*) was at this time the palace and did not designate the king as "pharaoh" until the 18th dynasty.

2 The lector-priest (literally, "he who carries the ritual") was initiated into the sacred writings and thus was priest, seer, and magician. Bastet was the cat-goddess of Bubastis in the eastern half of the Delta.

3 This must be the general sense, although the wording is obscure. An Egyptian interest in the future, rather than the past, was not normal, but a prophecy which promised that the future would restore the past would be acceptable.

4 The pharaoh himself wrote down the prophecy. The Egyptian texts treat Snefru as a friendly and approachable ruler; see B. Gunn in *JEA*, XII (1926), 250-51. Here, instead of calling upon a scribe, he does his own writing; he addresses his courtiers as "my people" and Nefer-rohu as "my friend."

5 Although now serving in Bubastis, he had been born in the Heliopolitan nome.

NOT LAX; BEHOLD, IT is before thy face! Mayest thou rise up against what is before thee, for, behold, although great men are concerned with the land, what has been done is as what is not done. *Re must begin the foundation* (*of the earth over again*). The land is completely perished, (so that) no remainder exists, (so that) not (even) the black of the nail survives from what was fated.[6]

THIS LAND IS (SO) DAMAGED (that) there is no one who is concerned with it, no one who speaks, no eye that weeps. How is this land? The sun disc is covered over. It will not shine (so that) people may see. No one can live when clouds cover over (the sun). Then everybody is deaf for lack of it.[7]

I shall speak of what is before my face; I cannot foretell what has not (yet) come.[8]

THE RIVERS of Egypt are empty, (so that) the water is crossed on foot. Men seek for water for the ships to sail on it. Its course is [become] a sandbank. The sandbank *is against* the flood; the place of water *is against* the [flood]—(*both*) the place of water *and* the sandbank.[9] The south wind will oppose the north wind; the skies are no (longer) in a single wind.[10] A foreign bird will be born in the marshes of the Northland. It has made a nest beside men, and people have let it approach through want of it.[11] DAMAGED INDEED ARE THOSE good things, those fish-ponds, (where there were) those who clean fish, overflowing with fish and fowl. Everything good is disappeared, and the land is prostrate because of woes from that *food*,[12] the Asiatics who are throughout the land.

Foes have arisen in the east, and Asiatics have come down into Egypt. . . . No protector will listen. . . . Men will enter into the *fortresses*. Sleep will *be banished* from my eyes, as I spend the night wakeful. THE WILD BEASTS OF THE DESERT WILL drink at the rivers of Egypt and be at their ease on their banks for lack of *some one to scare them away*.

This land is helter-skelter,[13] and no one knows the result which will come about, which is hidden from speech, sight, or hearing. The face is deaf, for silence *confronts*. I show thee the land topsy-turvy.[14] That which never happened has happened. Men will take up weapons of warfare, (so that) the land lives in confusion. MEN WILL MAKE ARROWS of metal,[15] beg for the bread of blood, and laugh with the laughter of sickness.[16] There is no one who weeps because of death; there is no one who spends the night fasting[17] because of death; (but) a man's heart pursues himself (alone). (Dishevelled) mourning is no (longer) carried out today, (for) the heart is completely *separated from* it. A man sits *in his corner*, (*turning*) his back while one man kills another. I show thee the son as a foe, the brother as an enemy, and a man killing his (own) father.

EVERY MOUTH IS FULL OF "LOVE ME!", AND everything GOOD has disappeared. The land is perished, (*as though*) laws *were* destined *for it*: the damaging of what had been done, the emptiness of what had been found,[18] and the doing of what had not been done. Men take a man's property away from him, and it is given to him who is from outside. I show thee the possessor in need and the outsider satisfied. He who never filled for himself (*now*) *empties*.[19] Men will [*treat*] (fellow) citizens as hateful, in order to silence the mouth that speaks. If a statement is answered, an arm goes out with a stick, and men speak with: "Kill him!" THE UTTERANCE OF SPEECH IN THE HEART is like a fire. Men cannot suffer what issues from *a man's* mouth.

The land is diminished, (but) its administrators are many; bare, (but) its taxes are great; little in grain, (but) the measure is large, and it is measured to overflowing.[20]

Re separates himself (from) mankind. If he shines forth, it is (but) an hour. No one knows when midday falls, for his shadow cannot be distinguished.[21] There is no one bright of face when seeing [him]; the eyes are not moist with water, when he is in the sky like the moon. His prescribed time does not fail. His rays are indeed in (men's) faces in his former way.[22]

I SHOW THEE THE LAND TOPSY-TURVY. The weak of arm is (now) the possessor of an arm. Men salute (respectfully) him who (formerly) saluted. I show thee the undermost on top, turned about *in proportion to* the turning about *of my belly*. Men live in the necropolis. The poor man will make wealth. . . . It is the paupers who eat the offering-bread, while the servants *jubilate*. The Heliopolitan nome, the birthplace of every god, will no (*longer*) *be on earth*.

(THEN) IT IS THAT a king WILL COME, BELONGING TO THE SOUTH, Ameni, the triumphant, his name. He is the son of a woman of the land of Nubia; he is one born

[6] Not so much of the "Black Land" of Egypt survives as might be under a fingernail.

[7] "Deaf" is unexpected where one awaits "blinded" by the lack of sunlight. The sense may be stunned or inert.

[8] A curious statement, since the point of the story is that he will prophesy the future. The psychology is apparently that he is projecting himself into a present which extends only to the time of Amen-em-het I—which is an exposure of the actual time of this "prophecy." Note also the significant fluctuation of tenses throughout the "prophecy."

[9] Perhaps mistranslated, but attempting to hold the idea that neither the banks nor the bed of the stream would receive the life-giving inundation.

[10] The pleasant north wind is the normal wind of Egypt.

[11] A strange passage, which either emphasizes the unnaturalness of nature in the distressed times or else is an oblique reference to Asiatics infiltrating into the Delta.

[12] The Asiatics are a bitter diet for the Egyptians?

[13] A compound expression, "is brought-and-taken."

[14] A compound expression, *seni-meni* "is passed-by-and-sick."

[15] W. Wolf, *Die Bewaffnung des altägyptischen Heeres* (Leipzig, 1926), 50, notes that metal arrow-points were first used in Egypt in the 11th dynasty (about 2100 B.C.).

[16] Hysteria.

[17] "Hungry."

[18] A pious obligation resting upon the Egyptians was to restore the inscriptions of the ancestors which were "found empty," i.e. damaged or containing lacunae. Under the present unsettled conditions what was found empty was left empty.

[19] Perhaps: he who never had to insist on full measure for himself now scrapes the bottom.

[20] A land smaller and poorer has more bureaucrats and higher and more exacting taxes.

[21] The sun's shadow on the shadow-clock determined the hour of noon.

[22] The last sentence accords poorly with the idea that the sun is dimmed and is like the moon. A negative may have fallen away.

in Upper Egypt.[23] He will take the [White] Crown; he will wear the Red Crown; (60) he will unite the Two Mighty Ones;[24] he will satisfy the Two Lords[25] with what they desire. The encircler-of-the-fields (will be) in his grasp, the oar . . .[26]

Rejoice, ye people of his time! The son of a man[27] will make his name forever and ever. They who incline toward evil and who plot rebellion have subdued their speech for fear of him. The Asiatics will fall to his sword, and the Libyans will fall to his flame. The rebels belong to his wrath, and the treacherous of heart to (65) the awe of him. The uraeus-serpent which is on his brow stills for him the treacherous of heart.

There will be built the Wall of the Ruler—life, prosperity, health![28]—and the Asiatics will not be permitted to come down into Egypt that they might beg for water in the customary manner, in order to let their beasts drink. And justice will come into its place, while wrongdoing is *driven* out.[29] Rejoice, he who may behold (this) (70) and who may be in the service of the king!

The learned man will pour out water for me,[30] when he sees what I have spoken come to pass.

It has come (to its end) in [success], by the *Scribe* . . .

THE DIVINE NOMINATION OF THUT-MOSE III

Although the pharaoh Thut-mose III became the great conqueror and empire builder, his origins seem to have been comparatively humble. He was one of the sons of a pharaoh, but his mother was probably not of the royal line. Powerful forces—perhaps the priesthood of Amon of Karnak, to whom he always was particularly generous—made him their choice for the throne when he was a young and modest priest. This was stated as being the oracular choice of the god himself. In the later years of Thut-mose's reign, he gave the following account of his miraculous nomination to the kingship and his indebtedness to the god Amon.

The inscription is carved on the walls of the Temple of Amon at Karnak. The text was published by K. Sethe, *Urkunden der 18. Dynastie* (*Urk.*, IV, Leipzig, 1905), II, 155-76, with antecedent bibliography. In a companion volume (Leipzig, 1914), Sethe gave a translation into German. The significance of the text was brought out by J. H. Breasted, *A New Chapter in the Life of Thutmose III* (*Untersuch.*, II, ii, Leipzig, 1900). Translation by Breasted, *AR*, II, §§131-66. Sethe guesses at a date in Thut-mose's 42nd year (close to 1450 B.C.). The beginning of the inscription is lost, but the pharaoh seems to be acquainting his court with the basis of his divine title to rule.

(1) . . . (The god Amon)—he is my father, and I am his son. He commanded to me that I should be upon his throne, while I was (still) a nestling. He begot me from the (*very*) *middle* of [his] heart [*and chose me for the kingship* . . . There is no lie], there is no equivocation therein—when my majesty was (only) a puppy, when I was (only a newly) weaned child who was in his temple, before my installation as prophet had taken place.[1] . . .

While I was in the guise and role of the "Pillar-of-His-Mother" priest, like the youth of Horus in Khemmis,[2] and I was standing in the north colonnaded hall,[3] [*Amon-Re came forth from*] the glory of his horizon.[4] He made heaven and earth festive with his beauty, and he began a great marvel, with his rays in the eyes of men like the rising of Har-akhti. The people gave him (5) [*praise, when he halted at the* . . .] of his temple. Then his majesty[5] offered him incense upon the flame and presented to him a great oblation of oxen, cattle, and wild beasts of the desert . . . [*The procession*] made the circuit of the colonnaded hall on its two sides, but (it) was not in the heart of those who were present to his actions,[6] in seeking out my majesty everywhere. (Then he)[7] really recognized me, and he halted . . . [*I touched*] the ground; I bowed myself down in his presence. He set me before his majesty, I being posted at the Station [of] the Lord.[8] Then he *worked a marvel* over me.[9] . . . [*These things really happened*, without] equivocation, though they were remote from the faces of mankind and mysterious in the hearts of the gods . . . There is no one who knows them; there is no one who can judge them . . .

[He opened for] me the doors of heaven; he spread open for me the portals of its horizon.[10] I flew up to the sky as a divine falcon, that I might see his mysterious form which is in heaven, that I might adore his majesty. (10) . . . I saw the forms of being of the Horizon God on his mysterious ways in heaven.

Re himself established me, and I was endowed with [his] crowns [which] were upon his head, his uraeus-serpent was fixed upon [my brow] . . . I [*was equipped*] with all his states of glory; I was made satisfied with the understanding of the gods, like Horus when he took account of himself[11] at the house of his father Amon-Re. I was [*perfected*] with the dignities of a god . . . [He established] my crowns, and drew up for me my titulary himself.[12]

23 Ameni was an abbreviated name for Amen-em-het (I). Nothing is known of his mother's race.

24 The two tutelary goddesses of Upper and Lower Egypt, who united as the Double Crown.

25 Horus and Seth.

26 As one act of the coronation ceremonies, the pharaoh, grasping an oar and some other object, dedicated a field by running around it four times.

27 A man of birth and standing.

28 A series of fortresses along the eastern frontier, as in the story of Si-nuhe, p. 19 above.

29 The coronation of each pharaoh reinstituted the old order of *ma'at* "justice," and expelled "deceit" or "wrongdoing."

30 As a libation at the tomb.

1 The rank of the *hem-netjer* "servant of the god," conventionally translated as "prophet," was that of a high temple officiant.

2 The priestly role, "Pillar-of-His-Mother," goes back to the myth of Horus and his mother Isis in the Delta swamps of Khemmis, the mythical birthplace of Horus.

3 This should have been located between the 4th and 5th pylons of the Temple of Amon at Karnak.

4 The image of the god was carried out of his shrine.

5 The then reigning king, Thut-mose I or II.

6 Those who witnessed the movements of the god's portable shrine could not understand why he was circling the hall.

7 The omission of the pronoun is troublesome, but the sense demands its restoration.

8 The place where the king stood in the temple. cf. pp. 248, 375.

9 Or: "Then he marvelled over me."

10 Poetical terms are used for the entry of the king-designate into the holy of holies of the temple.

11 "Counted his body," in the sense of recognizing his mature powers, after Horus had been awarded the kingship by Re.

12 Sethe points out that the fivefold titulary which follows has a form which characterizes the latter part of Thut-mose's reign (after his 30th year), which would set a *terminus a quo* for this inscription.

(I) He fixed my falcon upon the facade; he made me mighty as a mighty bull; he made me appear in the midst of Thebes, [in this my name of "Horus: the Mighty Bull, Appearing in Thebes."][13]

(II) [*He made me wear the Two Goddesses; he made my kingship to endure like Re in heaven,* in] this my [name] of "the Two Goddesses: Enduring in Kingship like Re in Heaven."[14]

(III) He fashioned me as a falcon of gold; he gave me his power and his strength; I was august in these his appearances, in this my name [of "Horus of Gold: Powerful of Strength, August of Appearances."]

(IV) [*He caused that I appear as King of Upper and Lower Egypt in the Two Lands; he established my forms like Re,* in this my name of] "King of Upper and Lower Egypt, Lord of the Two Lands: Men-kheper-Re."[15]

(V) I am his son, who came forth out of him, perfect of birth like Him Who Presides over Hesret;[16] he united all my beings, in this my name of "the Son of Re: Thut-mose-United-of-Being, living forever and ever."

(15) . . . He made all foreign countries [come] bowing down to the fame of my majesty. Terror of me is in the hearts of the Nine Bows;[17] all lands are under [my] sandals. He has given victory through the work of my hands, to extend [the frontiers of Egypt] . . . He is rejoicing in me more than (in) any (other) king who has been in the land since it was (first) set apart.

I am his son, the beloved of his majesty. What I shall do is what his *ka* may desire. I bring forward this land to the place where he is. I cause that [*his temple*] encompass . . . effecting for him the construction of enduring monuments in Karnak. I repay his good with (good) greater than it, by making him greater than the (other) gods. The recompense for him who carries out benefactions is a repayment to him of even greater benefactions. I have built his house with the work of eternity, . . . my [*father*], who made me divine. I have extended the places of him who made me. I have provisioned his altars upon earth. I have made the god's slaughtering-block to flourish for him with great sacrifices in his temple: oxen and cattle without limit. . . . I have enriched for him his two granaries with barley and emmer without limit. I have increased for him the divine offerings, and I have given him more (20) [than there was before] . . . for this temple of my father Amon, in every feast [of his] every day, and he is satisfied with that which he wished might be.

I know for a fact that Thebes is eternity, that Amon is everlastingness, Re (is) the Lord of Karnak, and his glorious Eye which is in this land (is) Hermonthis.[18] . . . [*I*] *have* [*provided his temple workshop with*] . . . , settled with serfs. I have filled it with my cap[turings] in the countries of the north and south, with the children (40) of the princes of Retenu and with the children [of the princes] of Nubia, as my father, [Amon-Re, Lord of the Thrones of the Two Lands], decreed. . . .

[13] The first, or "Horus," name was characteristically written within a palace facade surmounted by a falcon.

[14] The second, or "Two Goddesses," name made the pharaoh the embodiment of his two crowns.

[15] The prenomen of this pharaoh, Men-kheper-Re, meant something like: "Established is the Form of Re."

[16] The god Thoth. The nomen, Thut-mose, meant "Thoth Has Given Birth."

[17] The nine traditional enemies of Egypt.

[18] The Eye of the sun-god was a force of great and complex nature. It is here identified with the old cult-site of Hermonthis, the original seat of the Theban district. The inscription continues with a detailed statement of Thut-mose's good works, of which only the passage about foreign captives is here translated.

THE DIVINE NOMINATION OF AN ETHIOPIAN KING

The diffusion and persistence of custom are shown by the following inscription, which is to be dated shortly after 600 B.C. and comes from the Ethiopian kingdom which had its capital at Napata near the Fourth Cataract. Despite differences in time and distance, the essential situation is the same as in the nomination of Thut-mose III: it is the god of Karnak, Amon-Re, here resident at Napata, who makes the choice. The situation conforms generally to the account of the selection of Ethiopian kings as given by Diodorus (III, 5,1).

Stela 939 in the Cairo Museum was found at Gebel Barkal near the Fourth Cataract. The text is published in H. Schäfer, *Urkunden der älteren Aethiopienkönige* (*Urk.*, III, Leipzig, 1905), 81-100. All the royal names in the inscription have been hacked out and are here supplied with probability but not with certainty.

Year 1, 2nd month of the second season, day 15,[1] under the majesty of the Horus: Beautiful of Appearances; the Two Goddesses: Beautiful of Appearances; the Horus of Gold: Mighty of Heart; the King of Upper and Lower Egypt, Lord of the Two Lands: [Mer-ka-Re]; the Son of Re, Lord of Diadems: [Aspalta], beloved of Amon-Re, Lord of the Thrones of the Two Lands, Resident in the Pure Mountain.[2]

Now the entire army of his majesty was in the town named Pure Mountain, in which Dedwen, Who Presides over Nubia, is the god—he is (also) the god of Cush[3]—after the death of the Falcon upon his throne.[4] Now then, the trusted commanders from the midst of the army of his majesty were six men, while the trusted commanders and overseers of fortresses were six men. Now then, the trusted chief secretaries were six men, while the officials and chief treasurers of the palace were seven men.[5] Then they said to the entire army: "Come, let us cause (5) our lord to appear, (for we are) like a herd which has no herdsman!" Thereupon this army was very greatly concerned, saying: "Our lord is here with us, (but) we do not know him! Would that we might know him, that we might enter in under him and work for him, as the Two Lands work for Horus, the son of Isis, after he sits upon the throne of his

[1] Or "day 13." Around 600 B.C., this date would fall early in July.

[2] "Lord of the Thrones of the Two Lands" was the title of Amon-Re at Karnak in Egypt. "The Pure Mountain" was Gebel Barkal, dominating the town of Napata. Here Amon-Re was an honored and effective guest god.

[3] Ethiopia. It is interesting that Dedwen does not effect the oracular nomination, but Amon-Re does, just as he did in Egypt.

[4] The previous Ethiopian king, G. A. Reisner, in *JEA*, IX (1923), 75, gives Inle-Amon (Anlaman) as the predecessor of Aspalta.

[5] *Sic*, but read probably "six men," as the nominating college would presumably have equal numbers from the various branches of the government.

father Osiris![6] Let us give praise to his two crowns." ... (10) ...[7]

Then the army of his majesty all said with one voice: "Still there is this god Amon-Re, Lord of the Thrones of the Two Lands, Resident in the Pure Mountain. He is (also) a god of Cush. Come, let us go to him. We cannot do a thing without him; nothing is good which is done without him, (but) a good fortune (comes) from the god. He is the god of the kings of Cush since the time of Re. It is he who will guide us. In his hands is the kingship of Cush, which he has given to the son whom he loves. . . ."

So the commanders of his majesty (15) and the courtiers of the palace went to the Temple of Amon. They found the prophets and the major priests waiting outside the temple. They said to them: "Pray, may this god, Amon-Re, Resident in the Pure Mountain, come, to permit that he give us our lord, to revive us, to build the temples of all the gods and goddesses [of] Upper and Lower Egypt,[8] and to present their divine offerings! We cannot do a thing without this god. It is he who guides us."

Then the prophets and the major priests entered into the temple, that they might perform every rite of his purification and his censing. Then the commanders of his majesty and the officials of the palace entered into the temple and put themselves upon their bellies before this god. They said: "We have come to thee, O Amon-Re, Lord of the Thrones of the Two Lands, Resident in the Pure Mountain, that thou might give (to) us a lord, to revive us, to build the temples of the gods of Upper and Lower Egypt, and to present divine offerings. That beneficent office is in thy hands—mayest thou give it to thy son whom thou lovest!"

Then they offered[9] the King's Brothers before this god, (but) he did not take one of them. For a second time there was offered the King's Brother, Son of Amon, and Child of Mut, Lady of Heaven, the Son of Re: [Aspalta], living forever. Then this god, Amon-Re, Lord of the Thrones of the Two Lands, said: "He is your king. It is he who will revive you. It is he who will build every temple of Upper and Lower Egypt. It is he who will present their divine offerings. His father was my son, the Son of Re: [*Inle-Amon*], the triumphant. His mother is the King's Sister, King's Mother, Mistress of Cush, (20) and Daughter of Re: [Nenselsa], living forever.[10] ... He is your lord."

[6] Ethiopia adhered scrupulously to the hallowed tradition of Egypt, where the dead king was an Osiris and the new king a Horus. Ethiopia even had two crowns to correspond to the two parts of the land of Egypt.

[7] Four different members of the nominating college next voice opinions, but without a satisfactory solution.

[8] An unconscious or a propagandistically deliberate extension of the power of the Ethiopian king to Egypt proper.

[9] "Laid."

[10] At the top of the stela a scene shows this queen mother pleading with "Amon of Napata" for the nomination of her son [Aspalta]. Here her epithet "living forever"—not "the triumphant"—shows that she is still alive. In the main inscription there follow the names of six maternal ancestors of [Nenselsa].

(The Ethiopian officials accept this nomination gratefully. Aspalta enters into the presence of Amon, receives the crown and sceptre, asks for divine guidance, and receives the god's assurances.)

A DIVINE ORACLE THROUGH VISIBLE SIGN

The gods of Egypt gave visible indications to answer questions which were put to them at appropriate times and in appropriate ways. Examples of the divine nomination of rulers are given on pp. 446-448. A case of simpler nature is given below, in which the deified pharaoh Neb-pehti-Re (Ah-mose I), who was being carried in procession by priests, halted to give answer to questions submitted to him. In the presence of witnesses, the god accepted one of two alternatives laid before him with regard to the ownership of a certain field.

The scene above the inscription shows the ceremonial barque of "the good god, the Lord of the Two Lands: Neb-pehti-Re Ah-mose," carried on the shoulders of four pairs of priests and attended by the "Prophet Pa-iry, the triumphant." Facing this barque in an attitude of worship or appeal is the "Priest of Osiris, Pa-ser."

The inscription is dated in the fourteenth year of Ramses II (about 1287 B.C.). Ah-mose I, who had reigned about 1570-1545 B.C., presumably had a mortuary chapel at Abydos, where he was worshiped as a god and from which he might emerge in procession. The stela was found at Abydos and is in the Cairo Museum (*Journal d'entrée* No. 43649). It was published by G. Legrain in *ASAE*, XVI (1916), 161-70, with a photographic plate.

Year 14, 2nd month of the first season, day 25, under the majesty of the King of Upper and Lower Egypt: User-maat-Re Setep-en-[Re; the] Son [of Re: Ra]mses [Meri-Amon], given life.[1] The day of the appeal[2] which the Priest Pa-ser and the Priest Tjay made, to *lay a* [*charge before the good god*] Neb-pehti-Re. The Priest Pa-ser appealed: "As for this field, it belongs to *Pai, the son of* Sedjemenef,[3] *and* (*to*) the children of Hayu." And the god remained still.[4] [*Then* he] appealed to the god with the words: "It belongs to the Priest Pa-ser, son of Mose." [*Then*] the god nodded very much,[5] in the presence of the priests of [*the good god*] Neb-pehti-Re: the Prophet Pa-iry, the Priest of the Front Yanzab, the Priest [of the Front] Tja-nofer, the Priest of the Rear Nakht, and the Priest of the Rear Thut-mose.[6]

Done by the Outline Draftsman of the House-of-Ramses-Meri-Amon-in-the-House-of-Osiris, Neb-mehit.[7]

[1] About 1287, this date would fall close to the beginning of September.

[2] Here and below, literally "approach (with a petition)."

[3] It is possible to read "my son Sedjemenef," but the translation given is equally possible, and it seems less likely that Pa-ser would be disputing the possession of a field with his own son.

[4] The portable image of the god in his shrouded shrine gave no visible response to the first alternative. In other oracular texts, a word is used for a visible negative response, probably to be translated "recoil," that is, to lean backward.

[5] That is, leaned forward repeatedly or very markedly.

[6] The five witnesses to the oracle, which established legal ownership of the field in question, were the "prophet" (a conventional rendering of a priestly title) who attended the portable barque, two priests of the front carrying-poles, and two priests of the rear carrying-poles.

[7] The inscription was made by an artist of a temple of Ramses II at Abydos.

A DIVINE ORACLE THROUGH A DREAM

One way in which the gods might make their wishes known was through dreams.[1] The "Sphinx Stela" relates how the god who was in the Sphinx, Harmakhis, asked Thut-mose IV, before he had ascended the throne, to clear that great image of its encumbering sand.

Thut-mose IV reigned about 1421-1413 B.C. The present text is a pious restoration from somewhere between the 11th and 7th centuries B.C. The general similarity of the inscription to the "Sports Stela" of Amen-hotep II (pp. 244-245 above) shows that it faithfully restores a known psychology of the Eighteenth Dynasty.

The stela was discovered between the paws of the Sphinx and still stands there. The text was presented in C. R. Lepsius, *Denkmäler aus Aegypten und Aethiopien* (Berlin, 1849-59), III, 68. Its best publication was by A. Erman, *Die Sphinxstele* (*SPAW*, 1904, 428-44). Translated by Breasted, *AR*, II, §§810-15.

(1) Year 1, 3rd month of the first season, day 19, under the majesty of (Thut-mose IV).[2] . . .

(5) . . . Now he used to occupy himself with sport on the desert highland of Memphis, on its southern and northern sides, shooting at a target of copper, hunting lions and beasts of the desert, making excursions in his chariot, (for) his horses were swifter than the wind, together with one or another of his retinue, and nobody at all knew of it.[3]

Now when his hour came for giving a rest to his retinue, (he paused) at the *ruins* of Harmakhis,[4] beside Sokar in Gizeh; Renenut in Tjamut in the heavens; Mut *of* the northern . . . , Lady of the Southern *Wall*; Sekhmet, Presiding Over *Khas*; and Hike,[5] the first-born of the holy place of primeval times; near the lords of Babylon,[6] the divine way of the gods to the horizon west of Heliopolis. Now the very great statue of Khepri[7] rests in this place, great of fame, majestic of awe, upon which the shadow of Re rests. The villages of Memphis and of every town which is beside it come to it, with their arms (outstretched) in praise before it, bearing great oblations to its *ka*.

One of these days it happened that the King's Son Thut-mose[8] came on an excursion at noon time. Then he rested in the shadow of this great god. Sleep took hold of him, slumbering at the time when the sun was at (its) peak. He found the majesty of this august god speaking with his own mouth, as a father speaks to his son, saying: "See me, look at me, my son, Thut-mose! I am thy father, Harmakhis-Khepri-Re-Atum. I shall give thee my kingdom (10) upon earth at the head of the living. Thou shalt wear the southern crown and the northern crown on the throne of Geb, the crown prince (of the gods). Thine is the land in its length and its breadth, that which the Eye of the All-Lord illumines. Provisions are thine from the midst of the Two Lands and the great tribute of every foreign country. The time is long in years that my face has been toward thee and my heart has been toward thee and thou hast been mine. Behold, my state was like (that of) one who is in *need,* and my whole body was going to pieces. The sands of the desert, that upon which I had been, were encroaching upon me; (but) I waited to let thee do what was in my heart, (for) I knew that thou art my son and my protector. *Approach* thou! Behold, I am with thee; I am thy guide."

When he had finished these words, then this king's son *awoke*, because he had heard these [*words*] . . . and he understood the speech of this god. (But) he set silence in his heart, (for) [he] said: ". . . Come, let us go to our house in the city. They shall protect the offerings to this god which ye will bring to him: cattle, . . . , and all green things. We shall give praise [to] Wen-nofer[9] . . . , Khaf-[Re], the image made for Atum-Harmakhis,[10] . . . Khepri in the horizon west of Heliopolis. . . ."[11]

For an example of a prophetic frenzy, see the passage in the story of Wen-Amon (p. 26 above). Another example of an oracle through visible sign is in the Legend of the Possessed Princess (p. 30 above). Other examples of divine guidance through dreams will be found on pp. 30; 32; 246; and 418; n.3.

[1] cf. the encouragement given to Amen-hotep II by the god Amon in the text of p. 246 above and perhaps the appearance of Amen-em-het I to his son (n.3 on p. 418). See also B. Gunn in *JEA,* XXVII (1941), 4, n.1.

[2] Around 1420 B.C. this date would have fallen in October. The present translation omits some lines of general praise of the king.

[3] The setting is similar to that in the "Sports Stela," pp. 244-245.

[4] The Sphinx. Other gods and goddesses of the Gizeh necropolis are listed in the following context.

[5] The god "Magic."

[6] Egyptian Babylon, on the east bank opposite Gizeh.

[7] The Sphinx.

[8] Thus, before he had become king.

[9] Osiris.

[10] Thus relating Khaf-Re (Chephren) to the Sphinx, as does the "Sports Stela," p. 244.

[11] The end of the text is lost, but it is clear that Thut-mose must have cleared the Sphinx from sand for the story to have point.

Akkadian Oracles and Prophecies

(Translator: Robert H. Pfeiffer)

ORACLES CONCERNING ESARHADDON

Text: Rawlinson, Vol. IV, Plate 68 (2nd ed., Plate 61). Translations: M. Jastrow, Jr., *Die Religion Babyloniens und Assyriens* (Giessen, 1912), Vol. II, pp. 158-65; for earlier translations see *ibid.* p. 158, note 2. Fr. Schmidke, *Asarhaddons Stadthalterschaft in Babylonien und seine Thronbesteigung in Assyrien* (*Altorientalische Texte und Untersuchungen,* I, 2 [Leyden, 1916]). E. Ebeling, *AOT*, pp. 281-3. Luckenbill, *AR*, Vol. II, pp. 238-241. The text is dated during the reign of Esarhaddon (680-669 B.C.).

(i 5) [Esarhad]don, king of the countries, fear not! [No]tice the wind which blows over you; I speak of it without. . . . Your enemies, (10) like a wild boar in the month of Sivan, from before your feet will flee away. I am the great divine lady, I am the goddess Ishtar of Arbela, who (15) will destroy your enemies from before your feet. What are the words of mine, which I spoke to you, that you did not rely upon? I am Ishtar of Arbela. (20) I shall lie in wait for your enemies, I shall give them to you. I, Ishtar of Arbela, will go before you and behind you: (25) fear not! You are in a state of rebirth: I am in a state of woe, (whether) I stand (or) I sit down.

(Oracle) from the lips of the woman Ishtar-latashiat (30) of Arbela.

(31) King of Assyria, fear not! The enemy of the king of Assyria I deliver to slaughter! (i 34-40 and ii 1-8 are fragmentary)

(ii 9) (Oracle) from the lips of the woman Sinqisha-amur (10) of Arbela.

(11) I rejoice over Esarhaddon, my king; Arbela rejoices!

(13) (Oracle) of the woman Rimute-allate of the city Darahuya (15) which is in the midst of the mountains.

(16) Fear not, Esarhaddon! I, the god Bel, speak to you. The beams of your heart (20) I strengthen, like your mother, who caused you to exist. Sixty great gods are standing together with me and protect you. The god Sin is at your right, the god Shamash at your left; (25) sixty great gods stand round about you, ranged for battle. Do not trust men! Turn your eyes to me, look at me! (30) I am Ishtar of Arbela; I have turned Ashur's favor unto you. When you were small, I sustained you. Fear not, praise me! Where is that enemy (35) which blew over you when *I did not notice*? The future is like the past! I am the god Nabu, lord of the tablet stylus, praise me!

(40) (Oracle) from the lips of the woman Baia of Arbela.

(iii 15) I am Ishtar of Arbela, O Esarhaddon king of Assyria. In the cities of Ashur, Nineveh, Calah, Arbela, protracted days, (20) everlasting years, unto Esarhaddon my king shall I grant. I am your great *protector*. (25) Your gracious leader am I, who unto protracted days, everlasting years (30) have fixed your throne under the wide heavens; with golden *nails*, in the midst of the heavens I *make it firm*. The light of the *diamond* before Esarhaddon king of Assyria (35) I cause to shine. Like the crown of my head *I guard* him. "Fear not, O king," I said to you, (40) "I have not abandoned you." (iv 1) I have given you confidence, I shall not let you be disgraced. With assurance I have made you cross the river. (5) O Esarhaddon, legitimate son, offspring of the goddess Ninlil, *hero*! For you, with my own hands, your foes (10) shall I crush. Esarhaddon, king of Assyria . . . (lines 11 and 12 are obscure). Esarhaddon in the city Ashur (15) protracted days, everlasting years shall I grant you. Esarhaddon, in Arbela my mercy is your shield. (20) Esarhaddon, [legitimate] son, offspring of the goddess Nin[lil], [your] mind is sagacious. I love you (25) greatly . . . (lines 26-39 are fragmentary).

(v 1-3, obscure) (4-5) Those who speak (deceitfully) soothing (words), from before his feet I shall cut to pieces. You, you indeed, O king, are my king!

(10) (Oracle) from the mouth of the woman Ishtar-bel-daini, *oracle-priestess* of the king.

(12) I, Belit of Arbela, (say) to the king's mother, "Because you have complained with me (saying), (15) 'What is to the right, what is to the left you place in your bosom; but where is the offspring of my heart? (20) You let him be chased through the open country.'—Now, O king, fear not! The royalty is in you, the might is in you indeed!"

(24-25) (Oracle) from the lips of the woman Belit-abisha of Arbela.

(26) Peace to Esarhaddon king of Assyria! Ishtar of Arbela has gone forth into the open country. Peace unto her child (the king)! (30) You will send into the midst of the city. . . .

(vi 1) . . . good. [Ishtar] of Arbela his . . . (5) will fill. (Why) did you not trust the former oracle which I spoke to you? Now (10-11) you may trust the later one. Praise me! Like the day (14-15) (when) the storm *shrieked* (line 16 is obscure) before me; praise me! (line 18 is obscure) from my palace (20) shall I drive. Excellent food you will eat, excellent water you will drink; in your palace (25) you will be comfortable. Your son, your grandson will exercise the royal power on the knees of the god Ninurta.

(30) (Oracle) from the lips of Ladagil-ilu, of Arbela.

A LETTER TO ASHURBANIPAL

Text: *ABL*, Vol. IX, No. 923. Translation: E. G. Klauber, *Assyrisches Beamtentum nach den Briefen der Sargonidenzeit* (*LSS*, v, 3), p. 20. A. T. Olmstead, *History of Assyria* (New York, 1923), pp. 380, 415 f. L. Waterman, *Royal Correspondence of the Assyrian Empire* (1930), Vol. II, pp. 140-3. R. H. Pfeiffer, *State Letters of Assyria* (*American Oriental Series*, Vol. 6 [New Haven, 1935]), pp. 173 f. The text is a letter of Marduk-shum-usur to Ashurbanipal (668-633 B.C.).

(obverse 7)

In a dream the god Ashur said to (Sennacherib) the grandfather of the king my lord, "O sage!" You, the king, lord of kings, are the offspring of the sage and of Adapa. . . . You surpass in knowledge Apsu (the abyss) and all craftsmen. . . . (10) When (Esarhaddon) the father of the king my lord went to Egypt, he saw in the region of Harran a temple of cedarwood. Therein the god Sin was leaning on a staff, with two crowns on his head. The god Nusku was standing before him. The father of the king my lord entered. (The god) placed [*a crown*] upon his head, saying, "You will go to countries, therein you will conquer!" (15) He departed and conquered Egypt. The remaining countries, not yet subjected to the gods Ashur (and) Sin, the king, lord of kings, will conquer.

ORACLE OF NINLIL CONCERNING ASHURBANIPAL

Text: S. Arthur Strong, On Some Oracles to Esarhaddon and Ashurbanipal, *BA*, II (1894), 645. J. A. Craig, *Assyrian and Babylonian Religious Texts*, Vol. I (*Assyriologische Bibliothek*, XIII [Leipzig, 1895]), Plates 26-7. Translations: M. Jastrow, Jr., *Die Religion Babyloniens und Assyriens* (Giessen, 1912), Vol. II, pp. 170-4; for earlier translations and for other oracles, see *ibid.* p. 170, note 1, and M. Streck, *Assurbanipal* (*VAB*, VII, [Leipzig, 1916]), Vol. I, p. clxxiii. Dated presumably in 667 B.C., at the beginning of Ashurbanipal's reign.

(1) The goddess Ninlil is highly regarded (as a) sibyl. This is the word of Ninlil herself for the king, "Fear not, O Ashurbanipal! Now, as I have spoken, it will come to pass: I shall grant (it) to you. Over the people of the four languages (and) over *the armament* of the princes (5) you will exercise sovereignty....

(8) [The kings] of the countries confer together (saying), "Come, (let us rise) against Ashurbanipal.... (10) The fate of our fathers and our grandfathers (the Assyrians) have fixed: [let not his might] cause divisions among us.

(12) [Nin]lil answered saying, "[The kings] of the lands [I shall *over*]*throw*, place under the yoke, bind their feet in [strong fetters]. For the second time I proclaim to you that as with the land of Elam and the Cimmerians [I shall proceed]. (15) I shall arise, break the thorns, open up widely my way through *the briers.* With *blood* shall I turn the land into a rain shower, (fill it with) lamentation and *wailing*. You ask, "What lamentation and *wailing*?" Lamentation enters Egypt, *wailing* comes out (from there).

(20) Ninlil is his mother. Fear not! The mistress of Arbela bore him. Fear not! As she that bears for *her child*, (so) I care for you. I have placed you like an *amulet* on my breast. At night I place a spread over you, all day I keep a cover on you. In the early morning heed your supplication, heed your conduct. (25) Fear not, my son, whom I have raised.

AN ORACULAR DREAM CONCERNING ASHURBANIPAL

Text: Rawlinson, Vol. III, Plate 32. G. Smith, *History of Assurbanipal* (London, 1871), pp. 117 ff. H. Winckler, *Sammlung von Keilschrifttexte* (Leipzig, 1895), Vol. III, pp. 38-48. Translations: Smith, *op. cit.* P. Jensen, in E. Schrader's *Keilinschriftliche Bibliothek* (Berlin, 1890), Vol. II, pp. 250-3. M. Streck, *Assurbanipal* (Leipzig, 1916), Vol. II, pp. 114-19. Luckenbill, *AR*, Vol. II, pp. 332-3. For other examples of oracular dreams in cuneiform texts, see M. Jastrow, Jr., *Die Religion Babyloniens und Assyriens* (Giessen, 1912), Vol. II, pp. 955-8. This text (cylinder B of Ashurbanipal) is dated in 648 B.C.

(v 46) The goddess Ishtar heard my anxious sighs and, "Fear not!" she said, and filled my heart with confidence. "Inasmuch as you have lifted your hands in prayer (and) your eyes are filled with tears, I have mercy." During the night in which I appeared before her, (50) a seer reclined and saw a dream. When he awoke Ishtar showed him a night vision. He reported to me as follows: "Ishtar who dwells in Arbela came in. Right and left quivers were hanging from her. She held the bow in her hand (55) (and) a sharp sword was drawn to do battle. You were standing in front of her and she spoke to you like the mother who bore you. Ishtar called unto you, she who is exalted among the gods, giving you the following instructions: 'You will contemplate fulfilling my orders. (60) Whither your face is turned, I shall go forth. You told me: Wherever you go, let me go with you, O Lady of Ladies!' She informed you as follows: 'You shall stay here, where the dwelling of Nabu is. (65) Eat food, drink wine, supply music, praise my divinity, while I go and do that work in order that you attain your heart's desire. Your face (need) not become pale, nor your feet become exhausted, (70) nor your strength come to nought in the onslaught of battle.' In her loving bosom she embraced you and protected your whole figure. Before her a fire was then burning. To the conquest of [your] enemies [she will march forth] at (your) side. (75) Against Teumman, king of Elam, with whom she is wroth, she has set her face."

PROPHECIES

Text: E. Ebeling, *KAR*, Fascicule IX, No. 421. Translation: E. Ebeling, *AOT*, pp. 283-4.

(obverse i)

A prince will arise and [exercise sover]eignty eighteen years.
The country will live safely, the heart of the country will be glad, men will [enjoy abun]dance.
The gods will make beneficial decision for the country, good rainfalls [will come].
... (obscure)
The deity of cattle and the deity of grain will produce *abundance* in the land.
Rainfalls (*sic*!) and high water will prevail, the people of the land will observe a festival.
But the ruler will be slain with a weapon during an uprising.

A prince will arise, thirteen years will he exercise sovereignty.
There will be a rebellion of Elam against Akkad.
Akkad's booty will be plundered.
(Elam) will destroy the temples of the great gods, the downfall of Akkad will be decided.
Revolution, chaos, and calamity will occur in the country.
A dreadful (man), son of a nobody, whose name is not mentioned, will arise.
As king he will seize the throne, he will destroy his lords with weapons.
Half the troops of Akkad will fall, in the gorges of Tupliash
They will fill plain and hills.
The people of the land will experience great scarcity.

A prince will arise, his days will be few, the land (will have) no lord.

A prince will arise, three years will he exercise sovereignty.
[The canals] and the rivers will fill up with sand.
....

(obverse iii)

[A prince will arise, . . . years will he exercise sovereignty.] (1)
This same king [will rule] the world.
His people will [produce] abundance. . . .
The regular sacrifice *for the gods,* which had been discontinued will come (again), the gods. . . .
Good rainfalls will come, there will be abundance in [the land].
Cattle [will lie down] safely on the plain. . . .
. . . .
The procreation of cattle [will thrive].

A prince will arise, eight years will he exercise the sovereignty.

(the rest is lost)

(reverse i)

A prince will arise, three years [will he exercise the sovereignty]. (2)
The rest of mankind [*will descend*] into the earth.
Cities will decay, houses [will be desolate].
Revolution, destruction will occur, ...
Unto Akkad *from* the enemy's country. . . .
The sacred object of Ekur and of Nippur will [be brought] into the [enemy] country.
. . . to Nippur. . . .
The same ruler [will defeat] with weapons the land of Amurru.

A prince will arise, eight years will he [exercise] the sovereign[ty]. (10)
The temples of the gods [*will rise*] from the dust.
The sanctuaries of the great gods (*sic*!) [will be restored] on their sites.
Rain showers and high water [will come].
People, who have *seen* evil. . . .
Wealth will come on the street, . . . wealth. . . .
. . . will prostrate himself before the child, stretch out *his hand.*
. . . the mother will speak what is right with her daughter. . . .

(the rest is fragmentary and obscure)

VII. Lamentations

A Sumerian Lamentation

TRANSLATOR: S. N. KRAMER

Lamentation over the Destruction of Ur

The composition bewails the destruction of Ur at the hands of the Elamites and Subarians.[1] It consists of 436 lines divided into 11 "songs"[2] or stanzas of uneven length; they are separated from one another by an "antiphon"[3] of one or two lines. The text has been reconstructed from 22 tablets and fragments; except for one tablet which probably comes from Ur,[4] they were all excavated at Nippur. The tablets on which the poem is inscribed all date from the Early Post-Sumerian period, that is, the period between the fall of the Third Dynasty of Ur and the beginning of Kassite rule in Babylonia: roughly speaking therefore, sometime in the first half of the second millennium B.C. Its actual composition, too, must of course postdate the fall of Ur III; just how long after, however, it is impossible to say.[5] A scientific edition of the poem including a transliteration, translation, and commentary, as well as a complete list of variants, will be found in *AS* 12 (1940). One of the most significant discussions of the text is that of Jacobsen in *AJSL*, LVIII (1941), 219-224;[6] Jacobsen has also translated several passages from the poem in *The Intellectual Adventure of Ancient Man* (1946), where Mrs. H. A. G. Frankfort is responsible for the poetical renderings.[7] A new translation of the entire composition based on the text as reconstructed in *AS* 12, has been published by M. Witzel in *Orientalia* NS, XIV (1945), 185-234 and *ibid.*, XV (1946), 46-63.

[8]He has abandoned hi[s] stable, his sheepfold (*has been delivered*) *to*[9] the wind;
The wi[ld o]x has abandoned his stable, his sheepfold (*has been delivered*) *to* the wind.
The lord of all the lands has abandoned (his stable), his sheepfold (*has been delivered*) *to* the wind;
Enlil has abandoned ... Nippur, his sheepfold (*has been delivered*) *to* the wind.
His wife Ninlil has abandoned (her stable), her sheepfold (*has been delivered*) *to* the wind;
Ninlil has abandoned their house Ki[ur], her sheepfold (*has been delivered*) *to* the wind.
The qu[ee]n of Kesh has [ab]andoned (her stable), her sheepfold (*has been delivered*) *to* the wind;
Ninmah has [aba]ndoned their house Kesh, her sheepfold (*has been delivered*) *to* the wind.
She who is[10] of Isin has abandoned (her stable), her sheepfold (*has been delivered*) *to* the wind;
Ninisinna has a[ban]doned the shrine Egalmah, her sh[ee]pfold (*has been delivered*) *to* the wind.
The queen of Erech[11] has abandoned (her stable), her [sheepfold] (*has been delivered*) *to* the wind;
Inanna has abandoned their house Erech, her sheepfold (*has been delivered*) *to* the [wind].
Nanna has abandoned Ur, his sheepfold (*has been delivered*) *to* the [wind];
Sin has abandoned Ekishnugal,[12] [his] sheep[fold] (*has been delivered*) *to* the wind.
His wife Ningal has aban[doned] (her stable), her [sheepfold] (*has been delivered*) *to* the wind.
Ningal has aban[doned] her Enunkug, her [sheepfold] (*has been delivered*) *to* the wind.
The wild ox[13] of Eridu has abandoned (his stable), his sheepfold (*has been delivered*) *to* the wind;
Enki has abandoned their house Eridu, his sheepfold (*has been delivered*) *to* the wind.
Nin ... has abandoned their house Larak, her sheepfold (*has been delivered*) *to* the wind.
Shara has abandoned the Emah, his sheepfold (*has been delivered*) *to* the wind;
Usaharra has abandoned their house Umma, her sheepfold (*has been delivered*) *to* the wind.

[1] cf. Jacobsen, *AJSL*, LVIII (1941), 220, n.4.

[2] The word "song" or "stanza" is an approximate rendering for a Sumerian complex whose more exact meaning is still uncertain.

[3] The word "antiphon" is an approximate rendering of a Sumerian complex whose more exact meaning is still uncertain.

[4] cf. *AS* 12, 77, n.716a; and *ibid.*, 96, n.800a.

[5] Jacobsen, *loc. cit.*, 219-221, comes to the very definite conclusion that the lamentation was written no more than seventy or eighty years after the destruction, but, unless I am very much mistaken, he has considerably oversimplified the problems involved.

[6] Especially valuable is the last paragraph entitled "Details," where he makes some excellent suggestions for the translation of a number of passages.

[7] cf. pp. 141-142 for lines 173-189, 203-204, and 208-218 of the lamentation, and pp. 196-197 for lines 152-164.

[8] The first song begins with the line "He has abandoned his stable, his sheepfold (*has been delivered*) *to* the wind," and repeats the second half of this line as a sort of refrain in each of the remaining lines which list the more important temples of Sumer together with the deities who have abandoned them. This list runs as follows: Enlil has abandoned Nippur, while his wife Ninlil has abandoned the Kiur, a part of great Ekur temple in Nippur; the mother-goddess Ninmah has abandoned Kesh; the goddess Ninisinna, "the lady of Isin," has abandoned the shrine Egalmah in Isin; Inanna has abandoned Erech; Nanna, the moon-god, has abandoned Ur and its temple Ekishnugal, while his wife Ningal has abandoned her shrine the Enunkug; Enki, the water-god and god of wisdom, has abandoned Eridu; the goddess Nin . . . has abandoned Larak; Shara, the tutelary deity of Umma, has abandoned his temple the Emah, while his wife Usaharra has abandoned Umma; the remaining deities and place names all belong to the city of Lagash and its environs, thus: Bau, the wife of Ningirsu, the tutelary deity of Lagash has abandoned the city Urukug and the temple *Bagara*, while her son Abbau has abandoned the shrine Maguenna; The *lamassu*, a protecting genie, has abandoned the temple Etarsirsir; the mother of Lagash, Gatumdug, has abandoned Lagash; Ningula of Nina has abandoned Sirara; Dumuziabzu, "Tammuz of the Apsu," has abandoned Kinirshag; the goddess Ninmar has abandoned the shrine Guabba. For some reason as yet uncertain, the first "song" is written not in the main Sumerian dialect but in the Emesal dialect, which is usually reserved for speeches by female deities or recitations by certain classes of priests.

[9] The words "has been delivered to" in this and the following lines should have been treated as uncertain in the translation in *AS* 12 because of the grammatical uncertainty in the preceding Sumerian complexes.

[10] The Sumerian word rendered "the lady" in *AS* 12 should have been translated "she who is."

[11] In *AS* 12 the name of this city is written throughout as Uruk; however in my following publications I have used the biblical form Erech, and for the sake of consistency this form will be used in the present translation.

[12] For the reading Ekishnugal instead of Ekishshirgal, cf. Shuster, *ZA*, XLIV (1938), 263, n.10, and particularly the phonetic writing of the name in Gadd and Legrain, *UET*, I, No. 169, line 9, where it is written as Ekeshnu(n)gal.

[13] "The wild ox" should not have been rendered as uncertain in *AS* 12.

Bau[14] has abandoned Urukug, her sheepfold (*has been delivered*) *to* the wind;
The holy *Bagara*, her chamber, she has abandoned, her sheepfold (*has been delivered*) *to* the wind.
Her son Abbau has abandoned (his stable), his sheepfold (*has been delivered*) *to* the wind;
Abbau has abandoned the Maguenna, his sheepfold (*has been delivered*) *to* the wind.
The *lamassu of the holy house*[15] has abandoned (his stable), his sheepfold (*has been delivered*) *to* the wind;
The *lamassu* has abandoned Etarsirsir,[16] his sheepfold (*has been delivered*) *to* the wind.
The mother of Lagash has abandoned (her stable), her sheepfold (*has been delivered*) *to* the wind;
Gatumdug[17] has abandoned their house Lagash, her sheepfold (*has been delivered*) *to* the wind.
She who is[18] of Nina has abandoned (her stable), her sheepfold (*has been delivered*) *to* the wind;
Ningula has abandoned their house Sirara, her sheepfold (*has been delivered*) *to* the wind.
The lord of Kinirshag has abandoned (his stable), his sheepfold *has been delivered to* the wind;
Dumuziabzu has abandoned their house Kinirshag, his sheepfold *has been delivered to* the wind.
She who is[18] of Guabba has abandoned (her stable), her sheepfold (*has been delivered*) *to* the wind.
Ninmar has abandoned the shrine Guabba, her sheepfold (*has been delivered*) *to* the wind.
The first song.
His sheepfold *has been delivered to* the wind, he makes [grie]vous its wail;
The cow of . . . without a stable . . . ;
Its antiphon.
O city, a bitter lament set up as thy lament;[19]
Thy lament which is bitter—O city, set up thy lament.
His righteous city which has been destroyed—bitter is its lament;
His Ur which has been destroyed—bitter is its lament.
Thy lament which is bitter—O city, set up thy lament;
His Ur which has been destroyed—bitter is its lament.
Thy lament which is bitter—how long will it grieve thy weeping lord?
Thy lament which is bitter—how long will grieve the weeping Nanna?
O thou brickwork of Ur, a bitter lament set up as thy lament;
O Ekishnugal, a bitter lament set up as thy lament;
O thou shrine Enunkug, a bitter lament set up as thy lament.
O thou Kiur, thou *ḳigallu*,[20] a bitter lament set up as thy lament;
O thou shrine of Nippur . . . , a bitter lament set up as thy lament;
O thou brickwork of the Ekur, a bitter lament set up as thy lament.
O Magishshua, a bitter lament set up as thy lament.
O Ubshukinnakku, a bitter lament set up as thy lament.
O thou brickwork of Urukug, a bitter lament set up as thy lament;
O Etarsirsir, a bitter lament set up as thy lament;
O Maguenna, a bitter lament set up as thy lament.
O thou brickwork of Isin, a bitter lament set up as thy lament;
O thou shrine Egalmah, a bitter lament set up as thy lament.
O thou brickwork of Erech, a bitter lament set up as thy lament.
O thou brickwork of Erid[u], a bitter lament set up as thy lament.[21]
Thy lament which is bitter—how long will it grieve thy weeping lord?
Thy lament which is bitter—how long will it grieve the weeping Nanna?
O thou city *of name*, thou hast been destroyed;[22]
O thou city *of high walls*, thy land has perished.
O my city, like an innocent ewe thy lamb has been torn away from thee;
O Ur, like an innocent goat thy kid has perished.
O city thy rites *unto inimical dread and awe*,[23]
Thy ordinances[24]—unto inimical ordinances, have been transformed.
Thy lament which is bitter—how long will it grieve thy weeping lord?
Thy lament which is bitter—how long will it grieve the weeping Nanna?
The second song.

14 The names Bau and Abbau are also read Baba and Abbaba, but probably the two readings represent slightly variant pronunciations of the same word.

15 "House" instead of "temple" in *AS* 12.

16 For the reading Etarsirsir, cf. Nougayrol, *JCS*, I (1947), 332, n.18.

17 In *AS* 12 this name was read in its Emesal form Masisib; this was inconsistent since all the other names were read as they appear in the main dialect, and not in the Emesal.

18 "She who is" instead of "the lady" in *AS* 12.

19 Like the first "song," the second too is written in the Emesal dialect (cf. end of n.8). Beginning with a cry directed to Ur to "set up a bitter lament," the first part of the "song" continues with several variations on the theme of Ur and her lament. The cry to "set up a bitter lament" is then directed to other centers of Sumer, namely to Nippur and its main temple, the Ekur, as well as the shrines Magishshua, Ubshukinnakku, and perhaps Kiur; to Lagash, particularly its district Urukug, the temple Etarsirsir, and the shrine Maguenna; to Isin and its temple Egalmah; to Erech and Eridu. Toward the end of the "song" however, it returns once more to Ur and in words spoken directly to the city, bewails its destruction, the loss of its people, and the transformation of its ordinances into inimical ordinances.

20 For one meaning of the word *ḳigal* (*ḳigallu* is the Akkadian loan word), cf. *PAPS*, LXXXV (1942), 312; its meaning when used alongside of the Kiur is uncertain.

21 Lines 48-62 have quite a different arrangement in one of the texts; cf. *AS* 12, p. 22, n.41a.

22 For another possible rendering of this and the following line, cf. Jacobsen, *loc. cit.*, p. 223.

23 Note the new rendering of this difficult line; it is based on the assumption that it parallels the first part of line 70. Actually the last part of the line might have been expected "unto inimical rites" rather than "unto inimical dread and awe"; perhaps "dread and awe" are intended as a descriptive substitute for "rites."

24 The word "ordinances" attempts to render the Sumerian word *me* which designates a theological concept developed by the Sumerian thinkers to answer the problem as to what keeps the cosmic entities and phenomena, once created, operating continuously and harmoniously, without conflict and confusion. To judge from the various contexts, the word *me* seems to denote a set of rules and regulations assigned to each cosmic deity and phenomenon for the purpose of keeping it operating forever in accordance with the plans laid down by the creating deities.

His [righteous city] which has been destroyed—bitter is its lament;
His Ur which has been destroyed—bitter is its lament;
Its antiphon.
Together with the lord, whose house has been attacked, his city was given over to tears;[25]
Together with Nanna, whose land had perished,
Ur joined (its) lament.
The righteous woman,[26] because of his city to grieve the lord,
Ningal, because of his [*land*] to give no rest to [*the lord*]
Unto h[im] for the sake of his city approached—bitterly she weeps,
Unto the lord for the sake of his house which had been attacked approached—bitterly she weeps;
[*For the sake*] of his [*city which had been attacked*] she approached him—bitterly she weeps.
[*For the sake*] of his [*house*] which had been attacked she approached him—its bitter lament *she sets before him.*
The woman, *after* her . . . *had set the lamentation down upon the ground,*[27]
Herself utters *softly* the wail *of the smitten house.*
"The storm *ever breaking forth*—its wail has filled me full.[28]
Raging about because of the storm,
Me, a woman, the storm *ever breaking forth*—its wail has filled me full.
The storm *ever breaking forth*—its wail has filled me full.
During the day a bitter *storm* having been raised unto me,
I, *although*, for that day I tremble,
Fled not before that day's violence.
Because of its affliction I saw not one good day during my rule, one good day during my rule.
At night a bitter lament having been *raised unto me*,
I, *although*, for that night I tremble,
Fled not before that night's violence.
The storm's cyclonelike destruction—verily its terror has filled me full.
Because of its [affliction] in my nightly sleeping place, in my nightly sleeping place verily there is no *peace* for me;
Nor, verily, *because of its affliction*, has the quiet of my sleeping place, the quiet of my sleeping place been allowed me.
Although, because in my land there was bitter [distress],
I, like a cow for (its) calf, *trudge the earth*,
My land was not *delivered of fear.*
Although, because in my city there was bitter [distress],
I, like a bird of heaven, flap (my) wings,
(And) to my city I fly,
My city on its foundation verily was destroyed;
Ur where it lay verily perishes.
Although because the *hand of the storm appeared above*,
I screamed and cried to it, 'Return, O storm, to the plain,'
The storm's breast verily rose not to depart,
Me, the woman,[26] in the Enunkug, my house of ladyship,
For whose rule long days had not been granted me,
Verily weeping and lamentation follow.
As for the house which used to be the place where was soothed the spirit of the black-headed people,
Instead of its feasts wrath (and) distress verily *multiply.*[29]
Because of its affliction, in my house, the favorable place,[30]
My attacked righteous house upon which no eye *had* been cast,
With heavy spirit, laments that are bitter,
Laments that are bitter, have been brought.
My house founded by the righteous,[31]
Like a garden hut, verily on its side has caved in.
The Ekishnugal, my royal house,
The righteous house, my house which has been given over to tears,
Whose building, falsely, *whose* perishing, truly,
Had been set for me *as* its lot and share,[32]
Like a tent, the house where the crops have been . . . ,
Like the house where the crops have been . . . , to wind and rain verily has been exposed.
Ur, my *all-surpassing chamber*,[33]
My *smitten* house (*and*) city which have been *torn down*,
Like the sheepfold of a shepherd verily has been torn down;
My possessions which had accumulated in the city verily have been dissipated."

[25] The third "song" informs us that Ningal, the wife of the moon-god Nanna, moved by Ur's bitter plight, approached her husband and, determined to give him no rest and to arouse him to the fate of her city and house, wept bitterly before him: Day and night she is pursued by the wailing and lamenting resulting from a destructive storm; not even in her sleeping place is there any peace and rest. To be sure, she makes numerous attempts to halt the suffering and destruction of her city and land, but she fails to save Ur from its cruel fate. The Ekishnugal has caved in like a garden hut; it is exposed to wind and rain like a tent. Her house and city have been torn down like a sheepfold; her possessions are dissipated. As for the renderings of lines 77-79, the modifications follow Jacobsen, *loc. cit.*, 221, n.11, where most of the points are well taken.

[26] "Woman" instead of "lady" in *AS* 12.

[27] Note the new, though still doubtful, translations for lines 86-7; they are based primarily on Jacobsen's suggestions (*loc. cit.*, 223, n.18); cf. also Witzel's excellent suggestion that the third sign in line 86 is AD (*Orientalia* NS, xv [1946], 47) its meaning in our line, however, remains uncertain.

[28] For lines 88-112, cf. the excellent rendering by Jacobsen-Frankfort in *The Intellectual Adventure of Ancient Man*, pp. 196-197; much of its effectiveness is due to a not overly literal approach in the translation of the Sumerian words and phrases and to a flexible treatment of the Sumerian line order. However, for our present purpose, and under present conditions—not a few of the renderings in the Jacobsen-Frankfort translation of this passage are far from assured—it is advisable to follow the more literal translations in *AS* 12. Note, however, the modifications in the translations of lines 94, 98, 99, 100, 102, 103, 104, and 109; some of these were suggested by the renderings in *The Intellectual Adventure of Ancient Man*; others are due to several excellent suggestions made by Witzel, *loc. cit.*, pp. 48-49, to lines 99, 102, 103, and 108.

[29] Note the modified rendering of this line; cf. Witzel's comment to *ḫé-en-ga, loc. cit.*, p. 50; Witzel also suggests a variant rendering of this line which is well worth noting.

[30] Note the modifications in the renderings of lines 118-121; cf., too, Witzel, *loc. cit.*, p. 50. The implications of the phrase "upon which no eye *had* been cast," are uncertain.

[31] "The righteous" instead of "a righteous man" in *AS* 12.

[32] "Had" and "set" for "has" and "established" in *AS* 12.

[33] "All-surpassing" instead of "extra large" in *AS* 12; note, too, Witzel's suggestion to the line in *loc. cit.*, p. 50.

The third song.
Ur has been given over to tears;
Its antiphon.
"On that day, after *the lord had been overcome by the storm*,[34]
After, *in spite of the 'lady,'* her city had been destroyed;
On that day, *after the lord had been overwhelmed by the storm*,
After they had *pronounced*[35] the utter destruction of my city;
After they had *pronounced* the utter destruction of Ur,
After they had directed[36] that its people be killed—
On that day verily I abandoned not my city;
My land verily I forsake not.
To Anu the water of my eye verily I poured;
To Enlil I in person verily made supplication.
'Let not my city be destroyed,' verily I said unto them;
'Let not Ur be destroyed,' verily I said unto them;
'Let not its people perish,' verily I said unto them.
Verily Anu changed not[37] this word;
Verily Enlil with its 'It is good; so be it' soothed not my heart.
For the second time, when the council had . . . ed[38]
(And) the Anunnaki . . . *had seated themselves*,
The legs verily I . . . ed, the arms verily I *stretched out*,
To Anu the water of my eye verily I poured;
To Enlil I in person verily made supplication.
'Let not my city be destroyed,' verily I said unto them;
'Let not Ur be destroyed,' verily I said unto them;
'Let not its people perish,' verily I said unto them.
Verily Anu changed not this work;
Verily Enlil with its 'It is good; so be it' soothed not my heart.
The utter destruction of my city verily they directed,
The utter destruction of Ur verily they directed;
That its people be killed, as its fate verily they decreed.
Me like one who has given them my. . . .—
Me of my city verily they *deprived*;[39]
My Ur of me verily they *deprived*.
Anu changes not his command;
Enlil alters not the command which he had issued."
The fourth song.
Her city has been destroyed; her ordinances have become inimical;
Its antiphon.

Enlil called the storm;[40] the people groan.[41]
The storm of overflow he carried off from the land; the people groan.
The good storm he carried off from Sumer; the people groan.
To the evil storm he issued directions;[42] the people groan.
To Kingaluda, the tender of the storm, he entrusted it.[43]
The[44] storm that annihilates the land he called; the people groan.
The evil winds he called; the people groan.
Enlil brings Gibil to his aid.[45]
The great storm of heaven he called; the people groan.
The great storm howls above; the people groan.
The land-annihilating storm roars below; the people groan.
The evil wind, like the rushing torrent, cannot be restrained;
The boats of the city it attacks (and) devours,[46]
At the base of heaven *it made the . . . whirl*; the people groan.
In front of the storm *fires burned*;[47] the people groan.
To the battling storms was joined the scorching heat;[48]
. . . fires burned.[49]
The day *was deprived* of the rising of the bright sun, *of* the good *light*,[50]
In the land the bright sun rose not, like the evening star it shone.
The night *was deprived by* the South Wind of *its customary feasts and banquets*;

[34] In the fourth "song" Ningal continues her lament before Nanna, describing her efforts in behalf of her city and bemoaning their futility: It was Anu and Enlil who had ordered Ur to be destroyed and its people to be killed. And when she, Ningal, wept before them and pleaded that Ur should not be destroyed and that its people should not perish, they denied her plea. Anu and Enlil have ordered the destruction of Ur and the death of its people, and they are not wont to change their commands.

[35] "Pronounced" in this and the following line instead of "commanded" in *AS* 12.

[36] "Directed" in this line and in lines 162-163 instead of "ordered" in *AS* 12.

[37] "Changed not" for "turned not to"; cf. Witzel's constructive comment in *loc. cit.*, p. 51.

[38] For lines 152-164, cf. Jacobsen, *JNES*, II (1943), 172, and Jacobsen-Frankfort, *The Intellectual Adventure of Ancient Man*, p. 197; the suggestions there made for the rendering of the words and phrases here left untranslated in the first three lines of this passage do not seem to me to hit the mark.

[39] The new renderings of this line and the next follow Witzel's suggestion, *loc. cit.*, p. 52.

[40] In the fifth "song" which is written entirely in the main Sumerian dialect, the poet describes in detail an overwhelming affliction which overtook Ur in the form of a devastating storm. Beginning with a statement that after he had carried off from Sumer the "good storm," the "storm of overflow," Enlil called against the land the "evil storm," much of the remainder of the "song" concerns itself with a description of this evil storm and with other destructive elemental forces which aid and abet it.

[41] There is some possibility that the rendering "groan" should be changed to "mourn"; cf. Jacobsen, *loc. cit.*, p. 223. For lines 173-189, cf. now the Jacobsen-Frankfort translation in *The Intellectual Adventure of Ancient Man*, pp. 141-142; it reads excellently indeed, but its renderings are perhaps too free for reference works. Thus e.g. the same Sumerian word is translated as "storm" in one line and "wind" in another; the same Sumerian complex is rendered as "disastrous wind" in one line and as "tempest" in another. Moreover, starting with the line "All these he gathered at the base of heaven" (the last line on p. 141 of the book; it corresponds to our line 186) some of the renderings should be treated as doubtful; particularly is it uncertain that the subject of these lines is Enlil. For although it is to be admitted that the assumption that Enlil is the subject gives excellent sense to the passage, the text as it stands hardly justifies it.

[42] "Issued directions" instead of "gave (his) order" in *AS* 12.

[43] For the rendering of this line cf. Jacobsen's excellent comment in *loc. cit.*, p. 223. Note that the refrain is omitted here since the line is really a continuation of the preceding line.

[44] "The" in this line and the next and in line 181, for "to the" in *AS* 12.

[45] Note the omission of the refrain; perhaps this line is closely connected with the preceding, cf. n.43 (note, too, the period at the end of this line instead of the semicolon in *AS* 12).

[46] Lines 185-187 seem to go together (the subject is "the evil wind" in all three lines), hence perhaps the refrain is found only in the last of the three lines; note, too, that the refrain is missing in lines 188-192, perhaps for no better reason in some cases than for lack of space.

[47] Note that in this line and those following the present rendering differs from that in *AS* 12 in not treating "the evil wind" (line 184) as the subject of the verbal forms.

[48] For the new rendering, cf. particularly Jacobsen, *loc. cit.*, p. 223.

[49] The first half of the line seems to me too doubtful at present for any fruitful attempt at its translation.

[50] Note the new renderings for lines 190-192; cf. Witzel, *Orientalia* NS, XIV, 209.

At the side of their[51] *cups* dust was piled high; the people groan.
Over the black-headed people, the winds swept; the people groan.
Sumer *is broken up by the gišburru*;[52] the people groan.
It *attacks* the land and devours it.[53]
The afflicting storm by tears is not adjured;
The destructive storm makes the land tremble and quake;[54]
Like the flood storm it destroys the cities.
The land-annihilating storm set up (*its*) *ordinances*[55] in the city;
The all-destroying storm *came doing evil*;[56]
Like a . . . -storm it *placed* the . . . upon the people.
The storm ordered by Enlil in hate, the storm which wears away the land,[57]
Covered Ur like a garment, *enveloped* it like linen.
The fifth song.
The raging storm has attacked unceasingly; the people groan;
Its antiphon.
On that day the (good) storm was carried off from the city;[58] that city into ruins,[59]
O Father Nanna, that city into ruins was made; the people groan.
On that day the (good) storm was carried off from the land; the people groan.
Its people, not potsherds, filled its sides;[60]
Its walls were breached; the people groan.[61]
In its lofty gates, where they were wont to promenade, dead bodies were lying about;
In its boulevards, where the feasts were celebrated, *scattered they lay*.[62]
In all its streets, where they were wont to promenade, dead bodies were lying about;
In its places, where the festivities of the land took place, the people lay in heaps.[63]
The blood of the land, like bronze and lead . . . ;
Its dead bodies, like fat placed in the sun,[64] of themselves melted away.
Its men who were brought to an end by the axe were not covered with *head-bandages*;[65]
Like a gazelle held fast by the *gišburru*,[66] (their) mouths bit the dust.
Its men who were struck down by the *spear* were not bandaged;
Lo (as) in the place where their mother labored they lay stricken in their blood.
Its men who were brought to an end by the *battle-mace* were not . . . d;
(Although) they were not drinkers of strong drink, they drooped neck over shoulder.
Who kept standing[67] near the weapons, by the weapons was killed; the people groan.
Who escaped them, *by the storm was prostrated*;[68] the people groan.
Ur—its weak and (its) strong perished through hunger;
Mothers and fathers who did not leave their houses, were overcome by fire;
The young lying on their mothers' laps,[69] like fish were carried off by the waters;
Of the nursemaids, *pried open were their strong kirimmu-garments*;[70]
The judgment of the land perished; the people groan.
The counsel of the land *was dissipated*; the people groan.
The mother left her daughter; the people groan.
The father turned away from his son; the people groan.
In the city the wife was abandoned, the child was abandoned, the possessions were scattered about;
The black-headed people *into their family places*[71] . . . were carried off.
Its lady like a flying bird departed from her city;
Ningal like a flying bird departed from her city;
On all its possessions which had been accumulated in the land, a defiling hand was placed.
In all its *storehouses* which abounded in the land, fires were kindled;
At its rivers Gibil,[72] the purified, relentlessly did (his) work.
The lofty unapproachable mountain, the Ekishnugal—
Its righteous house by large axes is devoured;

[51] "Their" refers perhaps to the "black-headed people" in the next line.
[52] The *gišburru* is a weapon used in hunting gazelles; cf. line 220.
[53] Note the new rendering of the line. Note, that in this and the following lines, the refrain is omitted.
[54] More literally, "makes the land tremble again and again."
[55] "Decrees" (here rendered "*ordinances*") should have been treated as doubtful in *AS* 12; cf. Jacobsen, *loc. cit.*, p. 223.
[56] "Came doing evil" should have been treated as doubtful in *AS* 12; note, too, the slightly different rendering in the next line.
[57] Note the new rendering; cf. particularly Jacobsen, *loc. cit.*, p. 223.
[58] The sixth "song" too is written in the main Sumerian dialect. The first three lines speak of a "storm" which had been directed against Ur and Sumer and had turned them into ruins; practically the entire remainder of the "song," however, treats of the calamities that befell Ur as a result of her defeat in battle: The walls of Ur were breached, and the dead bodies of its people filled the gates. In their streets and boulevards they were ruthlessly attacked and laid low. Those who had been killed by the enemies' weapons lay unburied and untended; those who escaped were prostrated by the "storm." In Ur weak and strong alike perished through famine. Parents who did not leave their houses were overcome by fire, suckling babes were carried off by the waters. Judgment and counsel perished in the land. Parents abandoned their children, husbands their wives; all their possessions were scattered about. Gone is Ningal, its lady; she has departed like a flying bird. Lofty Ekishnugal is devoured by the axe; the Subarians and the Elamites break it up with the pickaxe and turn it into ruins. Ningal cries "Alas for my city, alas for my house." Ur is destroyed and its people are dispersed.
[59] Note that the refrain is only used intermittently throughout this "song." For lines 208-218, cf. the Jacobsen-Frankfort translation in *The Intellectual Adventure of Ancient Man*, p. 142.
[60] cf. Jacobsen's suggestion in *loc. cit.*, p. 223.
[61] For the new rendering, cf. Jacobsen, *loc. cit.*, p. 223, and Witzel, *Orientalia* NS, xv, 53.
[62] For the new rendering, cf. Jacobsen-Frankfort, *loc. cit.*, p. 142.
[63] For the new rendering, cf. Falkenstein, *ZA*, XLVII (1942), 190 and Jacobsen-Frankfort, *loc. cit.*, p. 142.
[64] cf. Jacobsen-Frankfort, *loc. cit.*, p. 142, and Witzel, *Orientalia* NS, XIV, 211.
[65] Note the new renderings of this line, line 221, and lines 223-224, and cf. several excellent suggestions made by Witzel, *Orientalia* NS, xv, 53-54.
[66] cf. n.52.
[67] "Kept standing" instead of "was stationed" in *AS* 12.
[68] The rendering of this phrase should have been indicated as doubtful in *AS* 12.
[69] "Laps" instead of "bosoms," cf. Jacobsen, *loc. cit.*, p. 224, and Witzel, *Orientalia* NS, XIV, 213.
[70] Note the new and still doubtful rendering of this line; cf. Jacobsen, *loc. cit.*, p. 224.
[71] For the new rendering of this phrase, cf. Jacobsen, *JNES*, II, 171, n.70.
[72] The god of fire.

The Subarians and the Elamites, the destroyers, *made of it* thirty shekels.[73]
The righteous house they break up with the pickaxe; the people groan.
The city they make into ruins; the people groan.
Its lady cries: "Alas for my city," cries: "Alas for my house";
Ningal cries: "Alas for my city," cries: "Alas for my house.
As for me, the woman,[74] my city has been destroyed, my house too has been destroyed;
O Nanna, Ur has been destroyed, its people have been dispersed."
The sixth song.
In her stable, in her sheepfold the lady utters bitter words:
"The city is being destroyed by the storm"; (252a)
Its antiphon.
Mother Ningal in her city like an enemy stood aside.[75]
The woman[76] loudly utters the wail for her attacked house;
The princess in Ur, her attacked shrine, bitterly cries:
"Verily Anu has cursed my city, my city verily has been destroyed;
Verily Enlil has turned inimical to my house, by the pickaxe verily it has been *torn up*.
Upon him who comes from below verily he hurled fire—alas my city verily has been destroyed;
Enlil upon him who comes from above verily hurled the flame.
Outside the city, the outer city[77] verily has been destroyed —'alas for my city' I will say.
Inside the city, the inner city verily has been destroyed —'alas for my house' I will say.
My houses of the outer city verily have been destroyed— 'alas for my city' I will say;
My houses of the inner city verily have been destroyed —'alas for my house' I will say.
My city like an innocent ewe has not been . . . ed, gone is its trustworthy shepherd;
Ur like an innocent ewe has not been . . . ed, gone is its shepherd boy.
My ox in its stable has not been . . . ed, gone is its herdsman;
My sheep in its fold has not been . . . ed, gone is its shepherd boy.
In the rivers of my city dust has gathered, into *fox-dens*[78] verily they have been made;
In their midst no sparkling waters flow, gone is its *riverworker*.
In the fields of the city there is no grain, gone is its fieldworker;
My fields verily like fields torn up by the pickaxe have brought forth. . . .
My palm groves and vineyards that abounded with honey and wine verily have brought forth the mountain thorn.
My plain where the *kazallu*[79] and *strong drink were prepared* verily like an oven has become *parched*.
My possessions like *heavy locusts* on the move verily . . . *have been carried* off—'O my possessions' I will say.
My possessions verily he who came from the (lands) below,[80] to the (lands) below has carried off—'O my possessions' I will say.
My possessions verily he who came from the (lands) above, to the (lands) above has carried off—'O my possessions' I will say.
Verily my (precious) metal, stone, and lapis lazuli have been scattered about—'O my possessions' I will say.
My treasure verily *has been dissipated*[81]—'O my possessions' I will say.
My (precious) metal, verily they who know not (precious) metal have fastened about their hands.
My (precious) stones verily they who know not (precious) stones have fastened about their necks.
Verily all my birds and winged creatures have flown away—'alas for my city' I will say.
My daughters and sons verily . . . have been carried off— 'alas for my men' I will say.
Woe is me, my daughters verily in a strange city carry strange banners;
With . . . verily *the young men and young women have been fastened*.
[*Woe is me*, my city] which no longer exists—I am not its queen;
[O Nanna], Ur which no longer exists—I am not its mistress.

[73] That is, perhaps, treated it with the utmost contempt; note the amount "thirty shekels."

[74] "Woman" instead of "lady" in *AS* 12.

[75] In the first three lines the poet introduces "mother" Ningal on the point of uttering a bitter wail for the terrible fate that overtook her city and shrine; the contents of this rather long lament are then given in the form of a soliloquy by the embittered goddess (lines 257-298): Anu has cursed her city, and Enlil has turned inimical to her house. The inner city as well as the outer city have been destroyed. In the rivers of Ur the dust has gathered; there is no fresh water. There is no grain in the fields; gone is the field worker. Her palm groves and vineyards have brought forth the mountain thorn. Her possessions have been carried off to the lower lands and the upper lands; her precious metal, stone, and lapis lazuli lie scattered about. Her ornaments of precious metal and stone adorn the bodies of those who "know" not precious metal and stone. Her sons and daughters have been carried off into captivity; she is no longer queen of Ur. Her city and house have been destroyed; a strange city and a strange house have been erected in their place. Woe is her; Ur is destroyed, and its people are dead. Where then shall she sit down, where shall she stand up? Here follows an interruption of the goddess's words in which the poet describes the violence of her lament (lines 299-301); the deity's bitter soliloquy then continues: Woe is her; her house is a stable torn down, her cows are dispersed, the weapon has fallen on her ewes. She has gone forth from the city and found no rest; she has gone forth from the house and found no dwelling place. She is a stranger in a strange city; curses and abuse are heaped upon her. She approached her lord Nanna for the sake of his house and city which have been destroyed and weeps bitterly before him. Woe is her; "O my 'city-fate,'" she will say, "bitter is my 'city-fate.'" "O my house which has been destroyed," she will say, "bitter is my 'house-fate.'" Like a fallen ox she will lie down beside the ruins of her city and her house, and will not rise up. Bitter is the destruction of her house and city attacked without cause.

[76] "Woman" instead of "lady" in *AS* 12.

[77] For "outer city" and "inner city," cf. Witzel, *Orientalia* NS, XIV, 215, 217.

[78] cf. Jacobsen, *loc. cit.*, p. 224.

[79] Perhaps some kind of drug.

[80] "(Lands) below" and "(lands) above" in this and the next line instead of "lower lands" and "upper lands" in *AS* 12.

[81] The four dots in *AS* 12 are superfluous.

[82] "Woman" instead of "lady" in *AS* 12.

I whose house verily has been made *into ruins*, whose city verily has been destroyed,
I, the righteous woman, in place of whose city verily a strange city has been built,[83]
I whose city verily has been made *into ruins*, whose house verily has been destroyed,
I, Ningal, in place of whose house verily a strange house has been built—
Woe is me, the city has been destroyed, the house too has been destroyed;
O Nanna, the shrine Ur has been destroyed, its people are dead.
Woe is me, where shall I sit me down, where shall I stand up?
Woe is me, in place of my city a strange city is being built;
I, Ningal—in place of my house a strange house is being erected.
Upon its removal *from its place*, from the plain, 'alas for my city' I will say;
Upon its removal from my city, Ur, 'alas for my house' I will say."
The woman tore her hair like the . . . reed;[84]
Her chest, the pure . . . , she strikes, "alas for my city" she cries.
Her eyes are flooded with tears; bitterly she weeps.
"*Woe is me*, in place of my city a strange city is being built;
I, Ningal—in place of my house a strange house is being erected.
Woe is me, I am one whose house is a stable torn down, I am one whose cows have been dispersed;
I, Ningal—like an unworthy shepherd the weapon has fallen on (my) ewes.
Woe is me, I am one who has been exiled[85] from the city, I am one who has found no rest;
I, Ningal—I am one who has been exiled from the house, I am one who has found no dwelling place.
Lo, I am a stranger sitting *with raised head* in a strange city;
Curses and abuses press upon me, head and limb;
(Against) the curse of those who inhabit its dwelling places, I (dare) not speak out.
In that place for the sake of his city I approached him—bitterly I weep;
To the lord for the sake of his house which had been attacked I approached—bitterly I weep.
For the sake of his house which had been attacked I approached him—bitterly I weep.
Woe is me, 'O my city-fate'[86] I will say, 'bitter is my city-fate';
I, the queen—'O my house which has been destroyed,' I will say, 'bitter is my house-fate.'
O my brickwork of Ur which has been torn down, which has been wrecked,
O my righteous house, my city which has been made into ruins,
In the *debris* of thy righteous house which has been destroyed, I lay me down alongside of thee;
Like a fallen ox, from thy wall I do not rise up.
Woe is me, untrustworthy was *thy* building, bitter is thy destruction.
O Ur, my, the woman's shrine[87] whose offerings have been cut off,
O Enunkug, my house of *burnt offerings* whose bounty is no longer satisfying,
O my city which *exists no longer*, my (city) attacked without cause,
O my (city) attacked and destroyed, my (city) attacked without cause,
Behold the storm ordered in hate—its violence has not *abated*;[88]
O my house of Sin in Ur, bitter is thy destruction."
The seventh song.
"Alas for my house, alas for my house."
Its antiphon.
O queen, *make* thy heart *like water*; thou, how dost thou live![89]
O Ningal, *make* thy heart *like water*, thou, how dost thou live!
O thou righteous woman[90] whose city has been destroyed, now *how dost thou exist*!
O thou Ningal whose land has perished, *make* thy heart *like water*!
After thy city had been destroyed, now *how dost thou exist*!
After thy house had been destroyed, *make* thy heart *like water*!
Thy city *has become* a strange city; now *how dost thou exist*!
Thy house *has become* a house of tears, *make* thy heart *like water*!

[83] For a somewhat different interpretation of lines 289, 291, 295-296, cf. Jacobsen, *loc. cit.*, p. 221 and n.7. In line 289, note "city" instead of "cities" in *AS* 12.

[84] The subject in lines 299-301 is Ningal; for the new rendering of the passage, cf. Jacobsen, *loc. cit.*, p. 222, n.12, and Witzel, *Orientalia* NS, xv, 56.

[85] For "been exiled" in this and the next lines, cf. the excellent suggestion by Witzel, *loc. cit.*, p. 56.

[86] For the new renderings in this and the next line, cf. Witzel, *loc. cit.*, p. 57.

[87] "Woman's" for "lady's" in *AS* 12.

[88] Note the new rendering of this line; it follows in part the suggestions made by Jacobsen, *loc. cit.*, p. 224.

[89] In the eighth "song," our poet once again addresses the goddess Ningal. Beginning with the words "O queen, *make* thy heart *like water*; thou, how dost thou live!" and repeating this and parallel phrases as a persistent refrain, the "song" dwells on the misfortunes that have befallen her city and temple, but concludes with words of comfort and consolation. Her city has been destroyed and her house has perished. Her city has become a strange city; her house has become a house of tears and has been given over to the pickaxe. She is no longer queen of her people; these have been led to slaughter. Her city has been made into ruins, her house has been laid bare. Ur, the shrine, has been given over to the wind. Its priests are gone; its rites are no longer performed. The black-headed people celebrate not her (Ningal's) feasts, play no music, pour no libations. Her song has turned to weeping and her music to lamentation. The fat of the ox is not prepared for her, nor the milk of her sheep; the fisherman brings not her fish, nor the bird-hunter her birds. Her rivers and roads are overgrown with weeds. Her city weeps before her; her house cries her "Where, pray?" May she, Ningal, return like an ox to her stable, like a sheep to her fold, like a young child to her chamber. May Anu utter her *ahulappu*, her "*'tis enough*" (of suffering); may Enlil decree her favorable fate, may he return Ur to its place for Ningal to exercise her queenship.

[90] "Woman" instead of "lady" in *AS* 12.

Thy city which has been made into ruins—thou art not its *mistress*;[91]
Thy righteous house which has been given over to the pickaxe—thou dost not dwell as its dweller.
Thy people who have been led to slaughter—thou enterest not as their queen.
Thy tears *have become* strange tears, thy land weeps not;
Without "tears of supplication" it inhabits foreign lands;[92]
Thy land like one who has *multiplied . . . shuts tight its mouth.*[93]
Thy city has been made into ruins; now *how dost thou exist!*
Thy house has been laid bare;[94] *make* thy heart *like water!*
Ur, the shrine, has been given over to the wind; now *how dost thou exist!*
Its *pašišu* verily *has not been brought into the*[95] . . . make thy heart *like water!*
Its *ênu* verily dwells not in the *giparru*; now *how dost thou exist!*
Its . . . who cherishes lustrations makes no lustrations for thee;
Father Nanna has not perfected thy decrees in the holy . . .[96]
Thy *maḫḫu* in thy holy *gigunû* dressed not in linen;
Thy righteous *ênu* chosen . . . ,[97] *in* the Ekishnugal,
From the shrine to the *giparru* proceeds not joyfully.
In the *aḫu*, thy house of feasts, they[98] celebrated not the feasts;
On the *uppu* and *alû*[99] they played not for thee that which brings joy to the heart, the . . . -music.[100]
The[101] black-headed people do not wash themselves *during* thy feasts,
Like . . . verily dirt has been decreed for them; verily their appearance has changed.
Thy song has been turned into weeping . . . ;
Thy . . . -music has been turned into lamentation. . . .
Thy ox verily has not been brought into its stable, its fat has not been prepared for thee;
Thy sheep verily stays not in its fold, its milk is not *presented to* thee.[102]
Thy . . . fat from the stable has not been brought for thee . . . ;
Thy . . . milk from the sheepfold has not been brought for thee. . . .
Thy fisherman *and* . . . fish were *overtaken* by misfortune . . . ;
Thy bird-hunter *and* . . . birds. . . .
Thy river which had been made fit for the *makurru*-boats—in its midst the . . . -plant grows;
On thy road which had been prepared for the chariots the mountain thorn grows.
O my queen, thy city weeps before thee *as its mother*;[103]
Ur, like the child of a street which has been destroyed *seeks a place* before thee.
The house, like a man who has lost *everything stretches out* the hands to thee;
Thy brickwork of the righteous house, like a human being cries thy "Where, pray?"
O my queen, verily thou art one who has departed from the house; thou art one who has departed from the city.
How long, pray, wilt thou stand aside in the city like an enemy?
O Mother Ningal, (how long) wilt thou hurl challenges in the city like an enemy?
Although thou art a queen beloved of her city, thy city . . . thou hast abandoned;
[Although] thou art [a queen[104] beloved of her people], thy people . . . thou hast abandoned.
O Mother Ningal, like an ox to thy stable, like a sheep to thy fold!
Like an ox to thy stable of former days, like a sheep to thy fold!
Like a young child to thy chamber, O maid, to thy house!
May Anu, the king of the gods, utter thy "*'tis enough*";
May Enlil, the king of all the lands, decree thy (favorable) fate.
May *he* return thy city to its place for thee; exercise its queenship![105]
May *he* return Ur to its place for thee; exercise its queenship!
The eighth song.
My ordinances have become inimical;
Its antiphon.
Alas, all the storms together have flooded the land.[106]
The great storm of heaven, the ever roaring storm,

[91] The four dots at the end of this line in *AS* 12, are superfluous.

[92] Perhaps the rendering of this line should read: "Without 'tears of supplication' foreigners inhabit it." cf. Witzel, *loc. cit.*, p. 58.

[93] In *AS* 12, p. 59, n.551 should read: More literally perhaps: "*pressed* the hand on the mouth."

[94] "Laid bare" instead of "made into a pasture" in *AS* 12.

[95] Note the new rendering of the line; the word following "into the" might be expected to parallel the *giparru* in line 349 and the *gigunû* in line 352 and thus be the name of a part of the temple complex; cf. also *JCS*, I (1947), 43, n.250. The *pašišu*, the *ênu* (line 349), and the *maḫḫu* (line 352) are important priestly classes in the service of the temple.

[96] Note the new rendering of the line.

[97] Note the new rendering; it is doubtful if the suggested restoration *ḫi-li* in *AS* 12 is correct.

[98] "They" in this and the next line presumably refer to "the black-headed people" of line 357.

[99] The *uppu* and the *alû* are two musical instruments.

[100] Note the different word order in the translation in *AS* 12.

[101] "The" for "thy" in *AS* 12. Note, too, the new rendering of the remainder of the line, cf. Witzel, *Orientalia* NS, XIV, 227.

[102] "Presented to" instead of "prepared for" in *AS* 12.

[103] Note the new rendering; cf. Witzel, *loc. cit.*, p. 227.

[104] Note restoration of "a queen" instead of Mother Ningal, and cf. Witzel, *Orientalia* NS, XV, 59.

[105] Two variant texts have two lines preceding this line; they read: "May *he* return Nippur to its place for thee; exercise its queenship! May he return Isin to its place for thee; exercise its queenship!" In these two texts, therefore, Nippur and Isin are treated more or less as equals of Ur.

[106] The ninth and tenth "songs" together—from the point of view of their contents there seems to be no reason for the division into two songs—contain the poet's plea to Nanna not to permit the "storm" to overwhelm Ur and its inhabitants. Beginning with the statement: "*Alas*, all the storms together have flooded the land," they continue with a description of the "storms" and their destructive deeds, and conclude with a number of curses against it.

The afflicting storm which sated the land,[107]
The storm which destroyed cities, the storm which destroyed houses;
The storm which destroyed stables, the storm which destroyed sheepfolds;
Which stretched out (its) hand over the holy *rites*,[108]
Which placed a defiling hand on the weighty counsel,
The storm which cut off all that is good from the land,
The storm which held the black-headed people in its ban—[109]
The ninth song.
The storm which . . . ;
Its antiphon.
The storm which knows not the mother, the storm which knows not the father,
The storm which knows not the wife, the storm which knows not the child,[110]
The storm which knows not the sister, the storm which knows not the brother,
The storm which knows not the weak, the storm which knows not the strong,
The storm *on whose account* the wife *is forsaken, on whose account* the child *is forsaken*;
The . . . -storm, the storm which caused the land to perish,[111]
The storm ordered in hate which sated the land—
O Father Nanna, let not that storm establish itself *near* thy city!
Look not (unfavorably) upon thy black-headed people!
Let not the storm, like rain pouring down from heaven, *turn* . . . !
(*The storm*) which *overwhelmed* the living creatures of heaven and earth, the black-headed people—
May that storm be entirely destroyed!
Like the great gate of night may the door be closed on it!
Let not that storm be given a place in the *numbering*
May its record *hang by a (clay) nail outside* the house of Enlil!
The tenth song.
Unto distant days, other days, future days;
Its antiphon.
From distant days, when the land was founded,[112]
O Nanna, the *humble*[113] *who have taken thy path*,
Have brought unto thee *their* tears *of the smitten* house; before thee *is their cry*!
Verily[114] thy black-headed people who have been cast away, prostrate themselves unto thee!
Verily thy city which has been made into ruins set up a wail unto thee!
O Nanna, may thy city which has been returned to its place, step forth gloriously before thee!
Like a bright star let it not be destroyed; may it proceed before thee!
. . . man shall . . . ;
[The man] of [offer]ings shall utter prayers unto thee.
. . . who art . . . of the [lan]d,
. . . ,
Undo the sins of its . . . !
Soothe the heart *of*. . . .[115]
Upon that which the man of offerings has brought, gaze with steadfast eye!
O Nanna, thou whose penetrating gaze *searches* the bowels,[116]
May every evil heart of its people be pure before thee!
May the heart of those who dwell in the land be *good* before thee![117]
O Nanna, thy city which has been returned to its place exalts thee.
The eleventh song.[118]

107 Note the new renderings of lines 390, and 395-396; they are based on the assumption that the first Sumerian word has the meaning "storm"; cf. also Witzel, *Orientalia* NS, XIV, 229, 231. Note, too, that lines 390, 393-396, 398, 400-406, and 410, end in a Sumerian sign which may indicate that line 388 is to be repeated after each of them as a refrain.

108 "Destroyed" instead of "destroy" in *AS* 12; so quite correctly Witzel, *loc. cit.*, 229.

109 Note that line 396 should not be followed by a period; the description of the storm is continued after lines 397-399 which, for reasons that are far from obvious, have been interposed here to separate the two "songs."

110 As Witzel, *Orientalia* NS, XV, 60, has pointed out, the Sumerian transliteration to this line in *AS* 12 erroneously read *šeš* for *dumu*.

111 Note the new renderings to lines 405-406 and cf. the comparable text in lines 202-203; indeed one of the texts has a variant to line 406 whose contents are identical with line 203, that is: "The storm ordered by Enlil in hate, the storm which wears away the land."

112 The last "song" contains a prayer addressed by the poet to Nanna to restore Ur and its people to their original and favored position. While the first five lines seem to describe the abjectness and humility of the black-headed people, the remaining lines contain a plea to Nanna to look steadfastly and kindly upon the prayers, offerings, and "hearts" of the dwellers of Ur.

113 cf. Jacobsen's excellent suggestion in *loc. cit.*, p. 224.

114 "*Verily*" in this and the next line for "may" in *AS* 12.

115 Note the modified renderings in this and the next line.

116 For "searches the bowels" cf. Jacobsen's suggestion in *loc. cit.*, p. 224.

117 For a possible variant rendering, cf. Jacobsen, *loc. cit.*, p. 224.

118 The colophon of the best preserved tablet contains the statement that it is the work of "the hand of Apil-Sumugan; the month of Tishrê, the sixteenth day." The line giving the date-formula for the year is destroyed, but there is some reason to believe that it belonged to the reign of Samsu-iluna, the son of Hammurabi.

VIII. Secular Songs and Poems

Egyptian Secular Songs and Poems

TRANSLATOR: JOHN A. WILSON

A Song of the Harper

A common scene in the tombs of ancient Egypt shows a harper entertaining guests at a feast. More than once he calls upon them to surrender themselves to pleasure, because they can have no certainty that earthly diligence will lead to eternal bliss.

The present translation is made from Papyrus Harris 500 (now British Museum 10060), recto vi 2-vii 3, a manuscript of about 1300 B.C. A closely similar version was in the Sakkarah tomb of Pa-Aton-em-heb, of the Amarna period (about 1375-1360 B.C.), now in Leyden. The version in the tomb of Nefer-hotep at Thebes (Tomb No. 50, about 1350-1320 B.C.) was somewhat different. The title given below shows that the original was ascribed to the reign of one of the Intef kings before or after the Twelfth Dynasty. The theme may have been characteristic of the groping for value which followed the collapse of the Old Kingdom. However, the use of the text in the Eighteenth and Nineteenth Dynasties shows that this hedonism was an acceptable literary expression for some centuries.

M. Lichtheim studied this and other harper's songs in *JNES*, IV (1945), 178 ff., translation on pp. 192 f., bibliography on pp. 211 f. The present translation is made from W. M. Müller, *Die Liebespoesie der alten Aegypter* (2nd printing, Leipzig, 1932), Pls. 13-15.

The song which is in the House of King Intef, the triumphant, and which is before the singer with the harp.

Prosperous is he, this good prince,
Even though good fortune may suffer harm![1]
Generations pass away, and others remain
Since the time of the ancestors.[2]
The gods who lived formerly rest in their pyramids,
The beatified dead also, buried in their pyramids.[3]
And they who built houses—their places are not.
See what has been made of them!
I have heard the words of Ii-em-hotep and Hor-dedef,
With whose discourses men speak so much.[4]
What are their places (now)?
Their walls are broken apart, and their places are not—
As though they had never been!
There is none who comes back from (over) there,
That he may tell their state,
That he may tell their needs,
That he may still our hearts,
Until we (too) may travel to the place where they have gone.

Let thy desire flourish,
In order to let thy heart forget the beatifications for thee.[5]
Follow thy desire, as long as thou shalt live.
Put myrrh upon thy head and clothing of fine linen upon thee,
Being anointed with genuine marvels of the god's property.
Set an increase to thy good things;
Let not thy heart flag.
Follow thy desire and thy good.
Fulfill thy needs upon earth, after the command of thy heart,
Until there come for thee that day of mourning.
The Weary [of Heart] hears not their [mourn]ing,[6] (vii 1)
And wailing saves not the heart of a man from the underworld.

REFRAIN: Make holiday, and weary not therein!
Behold, it is not given to a man to take his property with him.
Behold, there is not one who departs who comes back again!

Love Songs

The later Egyptian Empire (1300-1100 B.C.) has provided us with several collections of love songs. They were apparently intended to be sung to the accompaniment of some musical instrument. They express an enjoyment of nature and the out-of-doors. As in the Song of Songs, the lovers are called "my brother" and "my sister."

a

Papyrus Harris 500, now British Museum 10060, recto iv 1-7, of the Nineteenth Dynasty. Photograph in *Facsimiles of Egyptian Hieratic Papyri in the British Museum. Second Series*, ed. by E. A. W. Budge (London, 1923), Pl. XLIII. Hieratic text, transcription into hieroglyphic, translation, and commentary in W. M. Müller, *Die Liebespoesie der alten Aegypter*, Pls. 8-9, pp. 20-22. Translation in Erman, *LAE*, 246-47.

THE BEGINNING OF THE beautiful SONGS OF ENTERTAINMENT of thy sister, the beloved of thy heart, as she comes from the meadow.

My brother, my beloved,
My heart pursues the love of thee,
All that thou hast brought into being.

[1] The fate of death may not be happy, but this prince need not fear. The version in the tomb of Nefer-hotep, "How weary is this righteous prince; the goodly fortune has come to pass," makes death a kindly release.

[2] The Nefer-hotep version, "Generations pass away since the time of the god, (but) young people come in their place," shows that the meaning is the transition from one generation to another.

[3] The dead kings and nobles of older times.

[4] Ii-em-hotep, the famous vizier of Djoser, and Hor-dedef, the son of Khufu, were traditional sages of Egypt. See p. 432, n.4.

[5] An important part of the funerary services was "beatification" or "making (the deceased) an effective personality."

[6] Osiris, the god of the dead, is not concerned with the earthly mourning for the dead.

I say to thee: "See what I am doing!"
I have come from setting my trap with my (own) hand;
In my hand are my bait and my snare.
All the birds of Punt, they alight in Egypt,
Anointed with myrrh.[1]
The first one comes and takes my worm.
Its fragrance is brought from Punt,
And its talons are full of resin.
My wish for thee is that we loose them together,
When I am alone with thee,
That I might let thee hear the cry
Of the one anointed with myrrh.
How good *it would be*
If thou wert there with me
When I set the trap!
The best is to go to the fields,
To the one who is beloved!
THE END.

b

Also from Papyrus Harris 500, recto v 6-8. Facsimiled on Pl. XLIV of the British Museum publication noted above. Müller, *op. cit.*, Pls. 10-11, p. 24. Erman, *op. cit.*, 247-48.

The voice of the swallow speaks and says:
"The land has brightened—What is thy road?"[2]
Thou shalt not, O bird, *disturb* me!
I have found my brother in his bed,
And my heart is still more glad,
(*When he*) said to me:
"I shall not go afar off.
My hand is in thy hand,
I shall stroll about,
And I shall be with thee in every pleasant place."
He makes me the foremost of maidens.
He injures not my heart.
THE END.

c

From Cairo Ostracon 25218, lines 6-10. Photographs of the potsherd carrying the text in G. Daressy, *Ostraca* (*Catalogue général des antiquités égyptiennes du Musée du Caire*, Cairo, 1901), Pls. XLIII-XLV. Transcript of the hieratic in G. Möller, *Hieratische Lesestücke*, II (Leipzig, 1927), 39. Müller, *op. cit.*, Pl. 17, p. 42. Erman, *op. cit.*, 243. Nineteenth Dynasty.

The love of my sister is on yonder side,[3]
A stream lies between us,
And a crocodile waits in the shallows.
But when I go down into the water,
I wade the current,
My heart is great upon the stream,
And the waves are like land unto my feet.
It is the love of her that makes me steady,
For it makes a water-charm for me!
When I see my sister coming,
My heart dances,
And my arms open wide to embrace her, . . .
When *the mistress* comes to me.
THE END.

d

From Papyrus Chester Beatty I, verso C ii 4-9, of the Twentieth Dynasty and from Thebes. Published by A. H. Gardiner, *The Library of A. Chester Beatty* (London, 1931), Pl. XXIII, pp. 31-32.

THIRD STANZA.[4]
My heart intended to see *Nefrus*,[5]
That I might sit in her home.
But I found *Mehy* driving on the road,
Together with his gallants.
I know not how to take me from his presence,
That I might pass him freely by.
See, river is like road,
And I know not the place of my feet.
Very foolish art thou, my heart—
Wherefore wouldst thou make free with *Mehy*?
Behold, if I pass by before him,
I shall tell him of my waverings;
"Behold, I am thine!" I shall say to him;
And he will boast of my name
And assign me to the foremost harem
Of those who are in his retinue.

e

Also from Papyrus Beatty I, verso C iv 6-v 2. Gardiner, *op. cit.*, Pls. XXV-XXVI, p. 34.

SEVENTH STANZA.[6]
Seven (days) to yesterday I have not seen the sister,
And a sickness has invaded me.
My body has become heavy,
Forgetful of my own self.[7]
If the chief of physicians come to me,
My heart is not content (with) their remedies;
The lector priests,[8] no way (out) is in them:—
My sickness will not be probed.

[1] Punt, a land on the Arabian Sea, was famous for gums and perfumes. The theme of this song is that the maiden has been catching birds from the lands of fragrant gums, and she wishes that her "brother" might join her in this pastime, with its implications of rich perfumes and merry-making. cf. the frequent references to myrrh and spices in the Song of Songs, chap. 4 and 5.

[2] Where are you walking in the early morning? The swallow invites the maiden to the pleasures of the open fields. She, however, seeks out the company of her "brother." cf. Song of Songs 2:12-13, with "the voice of the turtle-dove."

[3] Though a flowing stream with lurking crocodiles lies between the youth and his "sister," the love of her is a magic charm to carry him successfully across to her. cf. Song of Songs 8:7.

[4] Papyrus Beatty I, C, contains "THE BEGINNING OF THE SPEECHES OF GREAT ENTERTAINMENT," with seven numbered stanzas, of which this is the third. By a characteristic Egyptian literary device, there is a pun on the word "third" at the beginning and end of the stanza: *khemet* "three," *khemet* "intended," and *imiu-khetef* "who are in his retinue."

[5] The translation depends for good sense on treating two words as proper names, even though they are not properly determined as names: *nefrus* "her beauty," and *mehy* "flax." Possibly there was some colloquially known implication in these two terms. It would then seem that the maiden went out to visit a girl friend and unexpectedly met her "brother" riding with other lusty youths. She was covered with confusion and feared that her emotions might be so obvious that he would scorn her and turn her over to one of his group.

[6] cf. n.4 above. Here the word "seven" is employed in place of a pun. The theme of the song is that of Song of Songs 2:5 or 5:8: "I am sick from love." Physicians and magicians cannot diagnose or cure the youth's ailment, but the mere sight of his "sister" will make him well.

[7] Often in the sense of losing consciousness.

[8] Who read magic spells for the cure of disease.

To say to me: "Here she is!" is what will revive me;
Her name is what will lift me up;
The going in and out of her messengers
Is what will revive my heart.
More beneficial to me is the sister than any remedies;
She is more to me than the collected writings.
My health is her coming in from outside:
When (I) see her, then (I) am well.
If she opens her eye, my body is young (again);
If she speaks, then I am strong (again);
When I embrace her, she drives evil away from me—
But she has gone forth from me for seven days!

f

Also from Papyrus Beatty I, verso G i 5-ii 1. Gardiner, *op. cit.*, Pls. XXIX-XXX, p. 35.

Would that thou wouldst come (to the sister speedily),[9]
Like a horse of the king,
Picked from a thousand of all steeds,
The foremost of the stables!
It is distinguished in its food,
And its master knows its paces.
If it hears the sound of the whip,
It knows no delay,
And there is no foremost of the chasseurs[10]
Who can stay before it (to hold it).
How well the sister's heart knows
That he is not far from the sister!
THE END.

Songs of the Common People

WORKERS IN THE FIELD

Many of the working songs in the modern Near East are antiphonal, with a leader and a chorus. Scenes and legends suggest that the same was true in antiquity, although it is difficult to present a single clear case. The following two songs are separated in the scene in which they occur: the first is attached to a group of plowmen and the second to a near-by group of reapers. The general similarity of words and the "answering refrain" justify their juxtaposition here.

The texts are in an agricultural scene in an Eighteenth Dynasty (16th-14th centuries B.C.) tomb at el Kab, published by J. J. Tylor, *The Tomb of Paheri* (*Wall Drawings and Monuments of El Kab*, London, 1895), Pls. IV-V.

Over the Plowmen

A good day—it is cool.
The cattle are pulling,
And the sky does according to our desire—
Let us work for the noble!

Over the Reapers

The answering refrain which they say:
This good day is come forth in the land;
The north wind is come forth,
And the sky does according to our desire—
Let us work as our hearts may be bound!

A Threshing Song

In the same scene, a herdsman is shown driving his cattle around and around to thresh out the grain. He urges them that their monotonous labor is easy and profitable.

Thresh ye for yourselves, thresh ye for yourselves, O cattle!
Thresh ye for yourselves, thresh ye for yourselves!
Straw to eat, and barley for your masters—
Let not your hearts be weary, for it is cool.

A SONG OF THE HERDSMAN

In scenes of earlier times, as the herdsman drives his sheep to tread out the grain, he sings a song which, in humorous allusion, implies that he is out of his usual place. The text occurs in the same setting in two Sakkarah tombs of the Old Kingdom (25th-24th centuries B.C.). It is given in A. Erman, *Reden, Rufe und Lieder des alten Reiches* (*APAW*, 1919), 19-20, and translated in Erman, *LAE*, 131.

The herdsman is in the water among the fish:
He talks with the shad
And greets the oxyrhynchus fish.
O west, where is the herdsman (now),
The herdsman of the west?

A SONG OF THE CARRIERS OF A PALANQUIN

Three Old Kingdom scenes which depict a noble traveling in a palanquin give the words of the porters. The recurring words, "It is pleasanter full than when it is empty," link these three together in the recognized refrain of a song. The longest of these texts is the most difficult, and only the concluding words can be translated with certainty. It comes from the Dahshur tomb of Ipi, and is now Cairo Museum 1536, published by L. Borchardt, *Denkmäler des alten Reiches I* (*Catalogue général . . . du Musée du Caire*, Berlin 1937), 240. The following translation follows the imaginative rendering of W. Wreszinski in *OLZ*, XXVI (1923), 309-12, which has the merit of giving the feeling of the song, even though some of the words remain uncertain.

Go down into *the palanquin*, and it is sound!
Go down into *the palanquin*, and it is well!
The carrying-poles are on the support of the carriers.
O palanquin of Ipi, be as *heavy* as I wish—
It is pleasanter full than when it is empty!

SONGS AT A FEAST

An annual feast at Luxor had as its central feature the journey of the god Amon and of the pharaoh by boat between Karnak and Luxor. In scenes of the time of Tut-ankh-Amon (about 1361-1352 B.C.) in the Temple of Luxor, this ceremonial

[9] This is one of three stanzas. Since the other two stanzas begin: "Would that thou wouldst come to the sister quickly," it is clear that the text here should be so completed. The first stanza expresses the maiden's hope that her "brother" will come to her as swiftly as a royal courier, the third stanza that he would come as swiftly as a gazelle bounding over the desert. Here we have the second stanza, longing that he come as swiftly as the fastest horse of the royal stables. cf. Song of Songs 1:9: "I have compared thee, O my love, to a steed in Pharaoh's chariots." For the gazelle as a figure of swift arrival, cf. Song of Songs 2:8-9; 8:14.

[10] *Teher*, a foreign word (perhaps Hittite) for a chariot-warrior; cf. p. 239, n.3.

procession is shown, and there are two brief songs about a drinking place set up for the entertainment of the sailors of the god's boat. Each song is credited to the goddess Neith. One of them follows, as published by W. Wolf, *Das schöne Fest von Opet* (Leipzig, 1931), 56-57, (No. 15 a,b), and by K. Sethe in *ZAeS*, LXIV (1929), 1-5.

A drinking place has been built for the menials who
are in the ship of ships.
The ways of the earth god have been hacked open
for (thee), O Nile, great and high!
Mayest thou satisfy thy Two Goddesses
For Horus, the strong of arm,
When the god is rowed, carrying the beauty of the
god.[1]
Hat-Hor has effected the beauty of good things
For King (Tut-ankh-Amon), beloved of Amon and
favored of the gods.
So says Neith.

Close by this song there are depicted eight women with sistrum-rattles and eight priests clapping their hands in measure. The text (Wolf, *op. cit.*, 57 [No. 15, c]) relates them to the songs of the entire scene.

The chorus which sets the measure while the journey takes place upon the river:

O Amon, Lord of the Thrones of the Two Lands, thou livest forever!

In the same large scene units of soldiers swing along in gay and vigorous movement, with some of the Negro troops breaking out in jubilant dance. Over the heads of the soldiers their songs of festivity are written (Wolf, *op. cit.*, 63-64 [No. 34]).

[*The leaders* of] the army. They rejoice in front of his majesty: "How happy is the good ruler when he has conveyed Amon, for He decreed to him valor against the south and victory against [the north]! Amon [is the god who decreed] the victory to the ruler!"[2]

[*The soldiers*] who are following his majesty. The chorus of jubilation which they utter: "King (Tut-ankh-Amon) is conveying Him who begot him! Decreed for him was kingship from the beginning of the lifetime of Re in heaven. He is rewarded with valor and victory over every foreign country that attacks him. Amon decreed the victory to King (Tut-ankh-Amon)! Amon is the god who decreed the victory to the ruler!"

Another song of military triumph, presumably sung by returning soldiers, will be found on p. 228 above.

In Praise of the City Ramses

The pharaohs of the Nineteenth Dynasty established their residence city, the biblical Ramses or Raamses, in the northeastern Delta.[1] The glories of this new capital were celebrated in poetical compositions like the following.

(*a*) From Papyrus Anastasi II (British Museum 10243), recto i 1-ii 5, with a parallel text in Papyrus Anastasi IV (British Museum 10249), recto vi 1-10. Both manuscripts are school compositions dated to the end of the 13th century B.C. and ascribed to Memphis. Facsimiled in *Select Papyri in the Hieratic Character from the Collections of the British Museum*, II (London, 1842), Pls. LXIII-LXIV, LXXXVII, with the Anastasi II text also in G. Möller, *Hieratische Lesestücke*, II (Leipzig, 1927), Pls. 37-38. Transcription into hieroglyphic by A. H. Gardiner, *Late-Egyptian Miscellanies* (*Bibliotheca Aegyptiaca*, VII, Brussels, 1937), 12-13, 40-41. Translations by A. H. Gardiner in *JEA*, V (1918), 187-88, and by Erman, *LAE*, 270-71.

(*b*) From Papyrus Anastasi III (British Museum 10246), recto i 11-iii 9, of the same characteristics as the above. Parallels from a papyrus in Vienna (Papyrus Rainer 53) and from an ostracon in Queen's College, Oxford. Facsimiled in *Select Papyri*, etc., Pls. LXXIV-LXXVI. Transcription into hieroglyphic by Gardiner, *Late-Egyptian Miscellanies*, 21-23, 137-38. Translations by Gardiner in *JEA*, V, 184-86, and by Erman, *LAE*, 206-07. The present translation omits many of the good products listed as available at Ramses.

a

THE BEGINNING OF THE RECITAL of the might of the Lord of Egypt.

His majesty—life, prosperity, health!—has built himself a castle, the name of which is "Great of Victories." It is between Djahi[2] and Egypt, and is full of food and provisions. It is like unto Hermonthis,[3] and its lifetime is like (that of) Memphis. The sun rises in its horizon, and sets within it. All men have left their towns and are settled in its territory. Its west is the House of Amon, its south the House of Seth. Astarte appears in its orient, and Uto in its north.[4] The castle which is in it is like the horizon of heaven. Ramses Meri-Amon is in it as a god, Montu-in-the-Two-Lands as a herald, Sun-of-Rulers as a vizier, and Joy-of-Egypt (ii 1) Beloved-of-Atum as a mayor.[5] (Thus) the land comes down into its (proper) place.

The Great Prince of Hatti sent (a message) to the Prince of Kode:[6] "Prepare thyself, that we may hasten to Egypt and say: 'The will of the god is come to pass,'[7] that we may make words of blandishment to User-maat-Re[8]—life, prosperity, health! He gives breath to whom he will, and every foreign country exists (only)

[1] The divine pharaoh is rowed, transporting the image of the god Amon.

[2] The triumphant words, "Amon is the god who decreed the victory to the ruler!" may be followed from the texts of Hat-shepsut (about 1486-1469 B.C.) to Ramses IV (about 1164-1157 B.C.), with at least fifteen occurrences and perhaps a partial recurrence under Pi-ankhi (about 720 B.C.). Its setting is always some scene or text of triumphant return. See J. A. Wilson in *JEA*, XVII (1931), 214-16.

[1] The location of Ramses has been much disputed, and scholars are not yet in agreement. For its location at Tanis, modern San el-Hagar in the northeastern Delta, see A. H. Gardiner in *JEA*, XIX (1933), 122 ff.; XXX (1944), 60; and R. Weill in *JEA*, XXI (1935), 17 ff. For a view that Ramses may have been at modern Qantir, about 15 miles south of San el-Hagar, cf. W. C. Hayes, *Glazed Tiles from a Palace of Ramesses at Ḳantir* (*Metropolitan Museum of Art Papers*, No. 3, New York, 1937), 8.

[2] Centrally the Phoenician coast, but carrying down into Palestine.

[3] An old cult-center south of Thebes.

[4] Temples of the gods mark the four quarters of the city. The Semitic goddess Astarte is appropriately in the east. The Egyptian goddess Uto is sometimes called Buto modernly.

[5] Ramses II is a god of the city, and, through his epithets, is all the important administrators.

[6] Kode or Qedi was the north Phoenician coast, carrying into Cilicia. The present section does not deal with the city Ramses, but with a projected visit by the Hittite king to Egypt. This may have fallen shortly before Ramses II's 21st year, in which he signed a treaty with Hatti. cf. pp. 199-201 and 256-258 above, ad Breasted, *AR*, III,§§425-26; E. Cavaignac, *L'Égypte et le Hatti vers 1302*, in *Mélanges Maspero* (Cairo, 1934), I, 357-60.

[7] The god would be Ramses II, and the statement would be an expression of submission by Hatti and Kode to Egypt.

[8] Ramses II.

through the love of him. Hatti is in his power alone. If the god receives not its offering, it does not see the water of heaven, for it is in the power of User-maat-Re—life, prosperity, health!—the bull that loves valor!"[9]

THE END.

b

The Scribe Pai-Bes communicating to his lord, the Scribe Amen-em-Opet: In life, prosperity, health! It is a letter to let [my] lord know. Another communication to my lord, to wit:[10]

I have reached Per-Ramses,[11] and have found (ii 1) it in [very, very] good condition, a beautiful district, without its like, after the pattern of Thebes. It was [Re] himself [who founded it.]

The Residence is pleasant in life; its field is full of everything good; it is (full) of supplies and food every day, its *ponds* with fish, and its lakes with birds. Its meadows are verdant with grass; its banks bear dates; its melons are abundant on the sands. . . . Its granaries are (so) full of barley and emmer (that) they come near to the sky. Onions and leeks (5) are *for food*, and lettuce of the *garden*, pomegranates, apples, and olives, figs of the orchard, sweet wine of *Ka*-of-Egypt,[12] surpassing honey, red *wedj*-fish of the canal of the Residence City, *which* live on lotus-flowers, *bedin*-fish of the *Hari*-waters, . . .[13]

The Shi-Hor[14] has salt, and *the Her canal* has natron. Its ships go out and come (back) to mooring, (so that) supplies (10) and food are in it every day. One rejoices to dwell within it, and there is none who says: "Would that!" to it.[15] The small in it are like the great.

Come, let us celebrate for it its feasts of the sky, as well as its feasts at the beginning of the seasons.[16]

The reed-thicket[17] comes to it with papyrus; the Shi-Hor with rushes. . . . (iii 1) . . . The young men of "Great of Victories" are dressed up every day, with sweet oil upon their heads and newly dressed hair. They stand beside their doors, their hands bowed down with flowers, with greenery of the House of Hat-Hor and flax of *the Her canal*, on the day when User-maat-Re Setep-en-Re—life, prosperity, health!—Montu-in-the-Two-Lands enters in, on the morning of the Feast of Khoiakh.[18] (5) Every man is like his fellow in uttering their petitions.

The ale of "Great of Victories" is sweet; . . .[19] beer of Kode[20] from the harbor, and wine of the vineyards. The ointment of the *Segbeyen* waters is sweet, and the garlands of the *garden*. The singers of "Great of Victories" are sweet, being instructed in Memphis.

(So) dwell content of heart and free, without stirring from it, O User-maat-Re Setep-en-Re—life, prosperity, health!—Montu-in-the-Two-Lands, Ramses Meri-Amon—life, prosperity, health!—thou god!

THE END.

[9] If Ramses does not receive Hatti's offer of submission, Ramses is able to withhold rain from Hatti. cf. p. 257 above.

[10] Pai-Bes, the pupil, is writing to Amen-em-Opet, his master.

[11] "The House of Ramses," in full, "the House of Ramses Meri-Amon—life, prosperity, health!" to which the Vienna papyrus adds "the great *ḳa* of the Re-Har-akhti" as an epithet. Our text uses another epithet of Per-Ramses, "Great of Victories," as a designation for the city.

[12] A well-known vineyard of the Delta.

[13] Other varieties of fish follow.

[14] The biblical "the Shihor (which is before Egypt)," literally, "the Waters of Horus." Presumably the Tanite branch of the Nile, with its salt-flats.

[15] No one feels a lack in the city Ramses.

[16] The "feasts of the sky" were those astronomically set, such as those of the phases of the moon. The seasonal feasts included the Coronation Feast, the Rising of the Dog-Star, the Feast of Opet, etc., which recurred with regularity.

[17] The word used appears also in Hebrew in "the Sea of Reeds" (conventionally translated "Red Sea"). See Gardiner, *Ancient Egyptian Onomastica*, II, 201* f.

[18] The relation of this feast to the king's entry into the city is not clear.

[19] Other drinks are listed.

[20] See n.6 above.

IX. Letters

An Egyptian Letter

TRANSLATOR: JOHN A. WILSON

A Satirical Letter

This text was one of the admired literary compositions of the late Empire and was used for the instruction of apprentice scribes. A royal official Hori received a letter from a scribe Amen-em-Opet. Hori responded in lofty and sarcastic vein, attempting to expose the weaknesses in his correspondent's qualifications for office. A particular value for our purposes is the summary catalogue of places in the Egyptian empire in Asia.

Papyrus Anastasi I (British Museum 10247) is of the late Nineteenth Dynasty (end of the 13th century B.C.) and probably comes from Memphis. In addition, from the Nineteenth and Twentieth Dynasties, there are three fragmentary papyri and about forty ostraca, schoolboy exercises. Facsimiled in *Select Papyri in the Hieratic Character from the Collections of the British Museum*, II (London, 1842), Pls. XXXV-LXII. The standard study of the text was made by A. H. Gardiner, *Egyptian Hieratic Texts. Series I. Part I. The Papyrus Anastasi I and the Papyrus Koller Together with the Parallel Texts* (Leipzig, 1911). The most significant fragments appearing since Gardiner's publication have been presented by G. Farina, in *RSO*, XIII (1932), 313 ff., by G. Posener, *Catalogue des ostraca hiératiques littéraires de Deir el Médineh (Documents de fouilles . . . I*, Cairo, 1934-38), I, cf. Index on pp. 29-30, by G. Posener, in *Mélanges Maspero*, I (Cairo, 1934), 327 ff., by J. Černý, *Ostraca hiératiques (Catalogue général . . . du Musée de Caire* (Cairo, 1930-35), No. 25773, and by A. H. Gardiner, ed., *Hieratic Papyri in the British Museum. Third Series. Chester Beatty Gift* (London, 1935), 130, Pl. 72. A translation in Erman, *LAE*, 214-34.

The Writer

THE SCRIBE, CHOICE OF HEART, persevering of counsel, for whose utterances there is rejoicing when they are heard, skilled in the Word of God,[1] (for) there is nothing which he does not know. He is a hero valiant in the work of Seshat,[2] a servant of the Lord of Hermopolis[3] in his bureau of writing, the teacher of apprentices in the Office of Writings, the first of his fellows, foremost of his colleagues, prince of his generation, without any like unto him. . . . (5) . . . Swift is he in inscribing empty scrolls, a youth distinguished of appearance and pleasing of charm, who can explain the difficulties of the annals like him who composed them. All that issues from his mouth is steeped in honey, and the heart is treated therewith as if (with) medicines. The groom of his majesty—life, prosperity, health!—the attendant of the Lord—life, prosperity, health!—who trains the steeds of the Sovereign. He is an energetic digger (ii 1) for the stable. . . . Hori, son of Wen-nofer, of Abydos, the Island of the Righteous, born of Ta-Usert in the district of Bilbeis, the Singer of Bastet in the Field of the God.[4]

[1] The divine order as revealed in the sacred writings. Hence, skilled at writing.

[2] The goddess of writing.

[3] Thoth, god of wisdom and patron of scribes.

[4] His mother was a singer for the goddess Bastet in the Bubastis region.

The Salutation

HE GREETS his friend, his excellent brother, the royal scribe of orders to the victorious army, choice of heart, goodly of character, wise of understanding, whose like does not exist in any scribe, . . . (5) . . . the Scribe of . . . , Amen-em-Opet, son of the Steward Mose, the possessor of reverence:

MAYEST THOU LIVE, MAYEST THOU PROSPER, MAYEST THOU BE HEALTHY, MY excellent BROTHER, equipped and steadfast, without having a wish. . . .[5]

Criticism of Amen-em-Opet's Letter

ANOTHER MATTER, to wit: Thy letter (iv 6) reached me in an hour of relaxing for a while. I found thy message as I was sitting beside the horse which is in my charge. I rejoiced and was glad and ready to answer. When I went into thy[6] stall to look at thy letter, I found that it was neither praises nor insults. Thy statements mix up this with that; all thy words are upside-down; they are not connected. . . . (v 1) . . . (So) I write to thee to instruct thee, like a friend teaching one greater than himself to be an excellent scribe. Now as for me, when thou speakest, I shall answer it. Lo, thy speeches are (*only*) *idle*[7] talk. Thou makest thyself like one *agitated* to scare me. (5) But I am not in dread before thee, (for) I know thy nature. So I thought that thou wouldst answer it all by thyself. (But) lo, thy supporters stand behind thee.[8] Thou hast gathered many *fowlers*[9] as helpers, like those who would be (gathered) for a law court. Thy face is wild, as thou standest wheedling the *backers*, saying: "Come with me, that ye may give me a hand!" Thou presentest them with gifts for each man, and they say [to] thee: "Let thy heart be steadfast. We shall attack him." Thou standest in *agitation* . . . , and they sit deliberating, (vi 1) the six scribes.[10] . . . (vii 1) . . . Thy letter is (too) inferior to permit that one listen to it. . . . If thou hadst known beforehand that it was no good, thou wouldst not have sent it. . . .

Hori's Reply

I REPLY TO THEE IN LIKE MANNER in a letter (5) which is original from the first page to the *colophon*. It is filled with utterances of my lips, which I created all by myself, no other being with me. By the *ka* of Thoth,[11]

[5] The text continues at length with good wishes.

[6] *Sic*, read "my."

[7] "Cool," perhaps in the sense of spiritless or vain.

[8] Hori intimates that Amen-em-Opet cannot write a letter without help.

[9] The word may be corrupt. If correct, the sense would be that common persons like catchers of birds were helping Amen-em-Opet, gathered as he might gather witnesses for a law court.

[10] "Scribes" is of course sarcastic. The text goes on to detail how each of six assistants contributes to Amen-em-Opet's own confusion.

[11] cf. n.3 above.

I did (it) by myself! I did not call to a scribe to have him witness (it). I shall give thee more in twenty parts; I shall repeat for thee what thou hast said, (each) part in its place, the fourteen *sections* (of) thy letter. Fill my hand with papyrus, and I shall tell thee many things and pour out for thee choice things. (viii 1) . . . All my words are sweet and pleasant; that is, I do not act like thee, when . . . thou beginnest to me with insults in the first part and dost not greet me at the beginning of thy letter. Far from me is what thou hast said; it does not come near, for my god Thoth is a shield about me. . . . (5) . . . Why am I evil in thy heart, so that thou shouldst slander me? To whom have I mentioned thee with evil words? I (only) composed for thee a volume like a (work of) entertainment, at hearing which men are amused as (at) a sport.[12]

Again thou hast said of me: "Crippled of arm and without strength." Thou dost minimize me as a scribe when thou sayest: "He does not know (anything)." I shall not spend a moment (ix 1) beside thee, wheedling thee and saying: "Be my supporter: another man is troubling me!" . . . I know many men without strength, crippled of arm, feeble, and without their force, but they are rich in houses, in supplies and food, and they speak no wish [about] anything. Come, let me tell thee the nature of the scribe Rey, (5) who was called the *firebrand* of the granary. He did not stir nor run since his birth. His abomination was energetic work, and he would not know it. (Yet) he is resting in the West, with his body whole, and terror of the good god has not carried him off.[13] . . . (x 1) . . . Let me tell thee of Pa-hery-pedjet, who is in Heliopolis. [He is an] old man [of] the Palace—life, prosperity, health! He is smaller than a tomcat (but) bigger than an ape, and he is in good state in his (own) house. . . . Thou hast heard the name of *Ki-sep*, . . . who goes on the ground without being noticed, unkempt of clothing and firmly wrapped up. If thou shouldst see him in the evening in the dark, then thou wouldst say of him: "A bird that is passing by." Put him in the scale that thou mayest see (5) how heavy he is. He will come out for thee at twenty *deben*,[14] not counting *old clothes*. If thou blowest beside him as he is passing by, he will fall far down like a leaf of foliage. . . . O Who-is-it,[15] my friend who knows not what he says, see, I solve thy grievous difficulties and make them easy!

Thou art come (xi 1) provided with great mysteries, and thou tellest me a saying of Hor-dedef,[16] (although) thou knowest not [whether it is] good or bad. What chapter is before it, what after it? Now thou art a scribe of experience at the head of his colleagues. The teaching of every book is engraved upon thy heart. How felicitous is thy tongue, corresponding to thy words! A saying comes out from thy mouth at more than three *deben* (weight).[17] . . . My eyes are dazzled by what thou doest, and I am astonished when thou sayest: "I am more profound (5) as a scribe than heaven or earth or the underworld. I know the mountains in *deben* and *hin*!"[18] (But) the House of Books is hidden; it is not visible; its Ennead is concealed and far from [*thy sight*]. Tell me what thou knowest; then I shall answer thee: "Beware lest thy fingers approach the Word of God!"[19] . . .

(In the context not translated here, Hori sets Amen-em-Opet a number of tests of calculation or administration, to demonstrate that Amen-em-Opet is incapable as a responsible government official.)

The Problem of a Military Mission

O alert scribe, understanding of heart, who is not ignorant at all, (xvii 3) torch in the darkness at the head of the troops—and it gives light to them! Thou art sent on a mission to *Djahan*[20] at the head of the victorious army, to crush those rebels called *Nearin*.[21] The bowmen of the army which is before thee amount to 1,900, the Sherden 520, the Qeheq 1,600, the Meshwesh (*100*), and the Negroes 880—total 5,000 in (5) all, not counting their officers.[22] There is brought thee a peace offering before thee: bread, cattle, and wine. The number of men is too great for thee, whereas the provisions are too small for them. . . . Thou receivest them, placed in the camp. The troops are ready and prepared. Make them quickly into portions, that of each man at his hand. The Bedouin look on furtively, (saying): "*Sopher yodea*!"[23] Midday is come, the camp is hot. "Time to start! Don't let the troop commander be angry! Much marching is ahead of us. *What* bread *have we* at all? (xviii 1) Our night-quarters are far away. O Who-is-it,[24] what does it mean, this beating of us?" So thou art an experienced scribe, if thou (canst) approach to give the provisions, (but) an hour *comes into* a day for lack of a scribe from the Ruler—life, prosperity, health![25] "This (business of) bringing thee to beat us—it's no good, *my boy*! He[26] will hear and will send to destroy thee!"

The Problem of Asiatic Geography

Thy letter abounds in *cutting speeches*, is loaded with big words. See, thou art rewarded with that which was sought—a greater load for thee than thou hast

[12] Amen-em-Opet took offense at Hori's previous letter, which had been intended as playful rather than malicious.

[13] Despite his laziness, Rey rests content in death. Hori now follows with accounts of three other officials who were successful despite handicaps.

[14] Not quite four pounds.

[15] What's-Your-Name, a lofty pretended forgetfulness of Amen-em-Opet's name.

[16] One of the traditional wise men of Egypt. cf. p. 432, n.4. For his "wisdom," cf. pp. 419-420.

[17] All this is of course ironical.

[18] In weight and measure.

[19] See n.1 above. Hori is arguing that real learning is not as simple as Amen-em-Opet airily claims.

[20] Probably to be emended to Djahi, "Phoenicia" and adjacent territory.

[21] Hebrew *ne'ârîm* "boys, young men," also used of warriors, e.g. I Kings 20:14 ff. cf. p. 256, n.12.

[22] We know too little about the sizes of armies at this time to state whether this is a large expedition or a small punitive force. Of the 5,000, 1,900 were Egyptian. The Sherden were of the "Peoples of the Sea," like the Philistines, cf. p. 255b, n.2. The Qeheq and Meshwesh were Libyans.

[23] Semitic: "O wise scribe!"

[24] See n.15 above.

[25] With his troops aggrieved about their rations, he waits endlessly for help from the king.

[26] The king.

wished. "I am a scribe, a *mahir*!"[27] thou sayest again. If there be truth in what thou sayest, come out (5) that thou mayest be tested! A horse is harnessed for thee, swift as a jackal . . . It is like a whirlwind when it goes forth. Thou loosest the reins and takest the bow. Let us see what thy hand can do. I shall explain for thee the nature of a *mahir* and let thee see what he has done.

Thou hast not gone to the land of Hatti,[28] thou hast not seen the land of Upi.[29] Khedem, thou knowest [not] its nature, nor Yegdy either. What is it like, the Simyra of Sessi[30]—life, prosperity, health!? On which side of it is the city of Aleppo? (xix 1) What is its stream like? Thou hast not gone forth to Kadesh and Tubikhi.[31] Thou hast not gone to the region of the Bedouin with the bowmen of the army. Thou hast [not] trodden the road to *the Magur*, where the sky is darkened by day and it is overgrown with *cypresses* and oaks and cedars which reach the heavens. Lions are more numerous than leopards or *hyenas*, (and it is) surrounded by Bedouin on (every) side of it. Thou hast not climbed the mountain of Shawe, *barefoot*, thy hands (5) laid upon [*thy bow*], thy chariot *laced* with ropes, thy horse in tow. Pray let [me tell thee of] . . . -beret. Thou art dismayed (at) climbing it and crossest its stream *above* it. (Thus) thou seest the taste of (being) a *mahir*, with thy chariot laid upon thy [*shoulder*] and thy [*assistant*] tired out. Thou reachest a halt in the evening, with thy whole body crushed and battered, thy [members] belabored, . . . thyself in sleep.

Thou awakest, (xx 1) for it is the hour of starting in the *sickly* night. Thou art alone for the harnessing; no brother comes for a brother. The *sneak-thieves*[32] have entered into [the] camp, the horse is untied, the . . . has been lost in the night, and thy clothes have been stolen. Thy groom awoke in the night, saw what he[33] had done, and took what was left. He has entered among those who are wicked, he has mingled with the Bedouin tribes, and he has made himself into the likeness of an Asiatic. (5) The foe had come to *raid* furtively and found thee inert. When thou awakest, thou findest no trace of them, and they have carried off thy property. (Thus) thou art become a fully equipped *mahir*, as thou fillest thy ear.[34]

LET ME TELL THEE OF another strange city, named Byblos. What is it like? And its goddess? Once again—[thou] hast not trodden it. Pray, instruct me about Beirut, about Sidon and Sarepta. Where is the stream (xxi 1) of the Litani? What is Uzu like?[35] They say another town is in the sea, named Tyre-the-Port. Water is taken (to) it by the boats, and it is richer in fish than the sands.

LET ME TELL THEE another difficult case—the crossing of Seram.[36] Thou wilt say: "It burns more than a sting!" Very sick is the *mahir*. Come, set (me) on the way southward to the region of Acre. Where does the Achshaph road come? (5) *At* what town? Pray, teach me about the mountain of User. What is its head[37] like? Where does the mountain of Shechem come? . . . Where does the *mahir* make the journey to Hazor? What is its stream like? Put me (on) the track to Hamath, Deger, and Deger-El, the promenade ground of every *mahir*. (xxii 1) Pray, teach me about its road and show me *Yan*. If one is traveling to *Adummim*, which way is the face? Do not *shrink from* thy teaching! Guide *us* (*to*) know them!

COME, that I may tell thee other towns which lie above them. Thou hast not gone to the land of Takhshi,[38] Kur-mereren, Timnat, Kadesh, Deper, Azai, or Harnaim. Thou hast not seen Kiriath-Anab and (5) Beth-Sepher. Thou dost not know Adurun or Zedpet either. Thou dost not know the name of Khenrez, which is in the land of Upi,[39] the bull upon its boundary, the place where the battle array of every hero may have been seen. Pray, teach me about the *appearance* of Qiyen, let me know Rehob, explain Beth-Shan and Tirqa-El. The stream of (xxiii 1) Jordan, how is it crossed? Let me know the way to pass Megiddo, which is *above* it.

Thou art a *mahir*, experienced in deeds of heroism. A *mahir* such as thou art should be found (able) to *stride* at the head of an army! O *maryanu*,[40] forward to shoot! Behold, the *ambuscade* is in a *ravine* two thousand cubits deep, filled with boulders and pebbles. Thou makest a *detour*, as thou graspest the bow. Thou makest a *feint* to thy left, that thou mightest make the chiefs to see, (but) (5) their eyes are good and thy hand *falters*. "*Abata kama ir, mahir ne'am*!"[41] (Thus) thou makest a name for every *mahir*, officers of Egypt! Thy name becomes like (that of) Qazardi, the Chief of Aser,[42] when the *bear* found him in the balsam tree.

The narrow valley is dangerous with Bedouin, hidden under the bushes. Some of them are of four or five cubits[43] (*from*) *their noses to the heel*, and fierce of face. Their hearts are not mild, and they do not listen to wheedling. Thou art alone; there is no *messenger* with thee, no army host behind thee. Thou findest no

[27] Semitic "swift, skillful," here used of the Egyptian courier to foreign lands.

[28] The Hittite territory of Anatolia and north Syria.

[29] Or Ube, the Damascus area. Some of the following place names cannot be identified.

[30] Simyra was a north Phoenician town. Sessi was a nickname of Ramses II, who must have had some special interest in that town.

[31] Since Tubikhi was in Syria and the other towns here identifiable are northern, this Kadesh is probably that on the Orontes.

[32] Apparently from the Semitic root *nahar* "to flow," here in a feminine noun, perhaps collective, "the band of gliders"?

[33] *Sic*, but read "they."

[34] With this experience.

[35] Old Tyre on the mainland.

[36] Written *D̲-r-ʿ-m*. If the geographic progress south along the Phoenician coast applies here, this should be Ras Naqura, the "Ladder of Tyre." It has been pointed out that there is here a pun on the Hebrew word *sirʿah* "hornet," with the crossing of Seram stinging like a hornet.

[37] The Semitic word *ras* is used for "head."

[38] Near Damascus.

[39] See n.29 above.

[40] From the Vedic *márya* "man, noble." cf. p. 22, n.2.

[41] Hori is showing off his knowledge of Semitic with this sentence. The first and third words cannot be translated with certainty. Gardiner, following M. Burchardt, *Die altkanaanäischen Fremdworte* . . . (Leipzig, 1909), II, 2-3, renders: "Thou slayest like a lion, O pleasant Maher." W. F. Albright, *The Vocalization of the Egyptian Syllabic Orthography* (New Haven, 1934), 33, renders: "I perish like a lamb, O good mahar!"

[42] Possibly Asher. The episode referred to is unknown. See A. H. Gardiner, *Ancient Egyptian Onomastica*, I, 193*; II, 265*.

[43] Around seven to nine feet tall.

scout, that he might make thee a way of (xxiv 1) crossing. Thou comest to a decision by going forward, although thou knowest not the road. *Shuddering* seizes thee, (*the hair of*) thy head *stands up*, and thy soul lies in thy hand. Thy path is filled with boulders and pebbles, without a *toe hold* for passing by, overgrown with reeds, thorns, *brambles*, and "wolf's-paw." The ravine is on one side of thee, and the mountain rises on the other. Thou goest on *jolting*, with thy chariot on its side, afraid to press (5) thy horse (too) hard. If it should be thrown toward the abyss, thy *collar-piece* would be left uncovered and thy *girth* would fall. Thou unfastenest the yoke in order to *repair the collar-piece* in the middle of the narrow valley. Thou art not competent in the way to bind it; thou knowest not how to *lash* it. The . . . is left where it is; the harness is (already) too heavy to carry its weight. Thy heart is disgusted. Thou startest to trot. The sky is opened.[44] Then thou thinkest that the foe is behind thee. Trembling seizes thee. (xxv 1) If only thou hadst a hedge of *shrubs*, that thou mightest put it on the other side! The horse is *played out* by the time thou findest a night-quarters. Thou seest the taste of pain!

Thou art come into Joppa, and thou findest the meadow blossoming in its season. Thou breakest in *to the inside* and findest the fair maiden who is watching over the gardens. She takes thee to herself as a companion and gives thee the color of (5) her lap. (But) thou art perceived and makest a *confession*. Judgment is passed on a *mahir*: thou must sell thy shirt of good Upper Egyptian linen. Tell (me) *how* thou sleepest every evening with a piece of *wool* over thee. Thou dost sleep, for thou art worn out. A *coward* steals thy bow, thy *sheath*-knife, and thy quiver. Thy reins are cut in the darkness. Thy horse is gone and *starts a runaway* over the slippery ground, as the road stretches out before him. He (xxvi 1) smashes thy chariot. . . . Thy weapons have fallen to the ground and are buried in the sand; [they] are become *dry land*. Thy *assistant* begs *food for thee*: "May ye give food and water, for I have arrived safely." (But) they act deaf of face, they do not listen, they pay no attention to thy talk.

Thou art introduced into the armory, and workshops surround thee. Craftsmen and leatherworkers are close by thee, and they do (5) all that thou hast desired. They take care of thy chariot, so that it ceases to be loose. Thy pole is newly *trimmed*, its *attachments* are applied. They put *bindings* on thy *collar-piece* and the . . . They fix up thy yoke. They apply thy *ensign*, engraved (with) the chisel, to the . . . They put a *knob* on thy whip and fasten a *lash* to it. Thou goest forth quickly to fight at the pass, to accomplish deeds of heroism.

O WHO-IS-IT,[45] thou choice scribe, *mahir* (xxvii 1) who knows (how to use) his hand, foremost of the *nearin*,[46] first of the army host, [let me relate to] thee the [foreign countries] of the end of the land of the Canaan. Thou answerest me neither good nor evil; thou returnest me no report. Come, let [me] tell thee *many things as far as* the Fortress of the "Ways [of Horus]."[47] I begin for thee with the "Dwelling of Sessi—life, prosperity, health!"[48] Thou hast not trodden it at all. Thou hast not eaten the fish of . . . ; thou hast not bathed in it. Pray, let me recall to thee Husayin—where is its fortress?[49] (5) Come now to the region of Uto of Sessi—life, prosperity, health![50]—*in his stronghold of* User-maat-Re—life, prosperity, health!—and Seba-El, and Ibsaqab.[51] Let me tell thee the nature of Aiyanin. Thou knowest not its rules.[52] Nekhes and Hebret,[53] thou hast not seen them since thy birth. O *mahir*, where are they? Raphia—what is its wall like? How many *iters* march is it as far as Gaza?[54] Answer quickly! Make me a report, that I may call thee *mahir* and boast to (xxviii 1) others of thy name *maryanu*[55]—so shall I speak to them.

Conclusion

Thou art angry at what [I] say to thee. (But) I am competent of heart in every office. My father taught me what he knew and instructed me a million times. I know how to take the reins—even beyond thy experience! There is no hero who can compare himself to myself. I am initiated in the *service* of Montu.[56]

How damaged is everything which comes forth over thy tongue! How futile are thy speeches! Thou comest to me wrapped up in confusions, loaded down with mistakes. Thou splittest words apart in charging ahead, and thou dost not weary of *fumbling*. Be strong! Forward! *Make haste*! Thou wilt not fall. What is it like, not to know what one has attained?

Now how will this end? Should I withdraw? Behold, I have arrived! Submit thou! If (5) thy heart is heavy, (still) thy heart is composed. Do not be angry. . . . I have shorn for thee the end of thy letter, that I might answer for thee what thou hast said. Thy speeches are gathered together on my tongue and remain upon my lips. They are confused when heard, and there is no interpreter who can explain them. They are like the words of a man of the Delta marshes with a man of Elephantine.[57]

Now thou art a scribe of the Great Double Door,

44 He comes out of the wooded valley into the open.

45 See n.15 above. In the listing of Asiatic places, there has been some rough and inconsistent itinerary, working from north Syria to Joppa. The final section deals with the road between Egypt and Palestine, working east from the Egyptian frontier to Gaza. See A. H. Gardiner in *JEA*, VI (1920), 99-116, for a parallel to the material of Seti I (which is on p. 254 above).

46 See n.21 above.

47 The "Ways of Horus" was applied to the frontier station for the main road across Sinai. Here it is probably the frontier post of Sile, near modern Kantarah. cf. pp. 21, 416.

48 cf. n.30 above on "Sessi." Gardiner tentatively locates this place at Tell Habweh, a few miles northeast of Kantarah.

49 Despite some difficulties, this might be located at Tell el-Her, about a dozen miles northeast of Kantarah.

50 Uto was a goddess. The name "Uto of Sessi" corresponds to a Sinai oasis known at the time of Seti I.

51 "The Well Ibsaqab" under Seti I.

52 Perhaps the rules governing the use of water at "Two Springs."

53 These two occur as stations having water under Seti I.

54 Raphia (Rafa) is the first frontier town of Palestine, about 20 mi. southwest of Gaza. The length of an *iter* is not absolutely certain, but may have been a mile and a third.

55 See n.40 above.

56 God of war.

57 At the two extremities of Egypt dialectical differences were marked.

reporting the affairs of the lands, good and fair, [to him] who may see it. Thou shouldst not say: "Thou hast made my name to stink before the rabble and everybody!" See, I have told thee the nature of the *mahir*. I have traversed for thee the *roads of foreign countries.*[58]

[58] Papyrus Anastasi I gives *tenu,* probably to be emended to *Retenu* "Syria-Palestine," but a Turin parallel text gives *metenu* . . . , perhaps "roads . . ."

I have marshaled for thee the foreign countries all together and the towns according to their *order*. Pray, *let thyself* look at them calmly, that thou mayest find thyself (able) to recount them, that thou mayest become with us a . . .[59]

[59] Here Papyrus Anastasi I breaks off. The Turin parallel continues with a few disconnected phrases.

A Sumerian Letter

TRANSLATOR: S. N. KRAMER

Letter of King Ibbi-Sin

This document is of considerable importance to the modern historian; it provides us with a lively and probably contemporary account of the troubled conditions of the last years of the Third Dynasty of Ur.[1] It purports to be a letter addressed by Ibbi-Sin, the last ruler of the Third Dynasty of Ur,[2] to Puzur-Numushda, the governor of Kazallu,[3] and it refers primarily to events involving Ishbi-Irra, Ibbi-Sin's mortal enemy and founder of the Dynasty of Isin.[4] Its contents run approximately as follows:[5] Following the conventional letter heading (lines 1-3) and two lines whose meaning is at present obscure (lines 4-5), we find Ibbi-Sin complaining to Puzur-Numushda that he (i.e. the latter) and a fellow governor by the name of Qirbubu had failed to come to his support at a crucial moment in the struggle with Ishbi-Irra (lines 6-14). Ibbi-Sin then continues with an admission that Enlil, the leading deity of the Sumerian pantheon, had indeed bestowed the kingship on Ishbi-Irra, the man of Mari,[6] who is not a Sumerian, and that the latter seems to be on the verge of subjecting all Sumer to his rule (lines 15-31).[7] Nevertheless he ends the letter on a note of optimism; with the help of the Martu,[8] Ishbi-Irra and the Elamites[9] will be defeated and once again Sumer's might will become known throughout the foreign lands (lines 32-38).[10]

The text of this document is restored from three tablets excavated at Nippur and dating from the first half of the second millennium B.C.; all three are now located in the University Museum.[11] One of these tablets was published by G. A. Barton as No. 9 of his *Miscellaneous Babylonian Inscriptions* (1918); there, too, will be found a transliteration and translation of the text, pp. 57-59.[12] The other two were published by Leon Legrain as Nos. 3 and 6 of *PBS*, XIII (1922); a transliteration and translation of their contents will be found there on pp. 28-32. The first to recognize that all three tablets contain copies of the same document was Stephen Langdon who published a partial transliteration and translation of the letter in *RA*, XX (1923), 49-51. But it is Adam Falkenstein who has prepared the first scientific edition of the text, including a complete transliteration, translation, and detailed commentary. Falkenstein's study, which is to appear in the near future, represents by all odds the most trustworthy effort to get at the meaning of the text, and the present translation is based primarily upon it.[13]

To Puzur-Numushda, the governor[14] of Kazallu speak; thus says your king Ibbi-Sin. (4). ... since *I have selected* for you ... troops (and) have put them at your disposal *as* the governor of Kazallu, are not, *as in my case*,[15] your troops *your renown*?[16] (6). Why did you send me thus: "Ishbi-Irra has[17] his eyes on me, and (only) after he has *left* me will I come." (10) How is it that you did not know *when* Ishbi-Irra *will* return to (his) land?[18] (11) Why did not you together with Qirbubu, the governor of Girkal,[19] march forth the troops which had been placed in your hand before

[1] Unfortunately the authenticity of the contents of the document, at least as it now lies before us, is open to question. On the surface, to be sure, it seems to be a bona fide copy of a letter addressed by the king Ibbi-Sin to his governor Puzur-Numushda; the heading is that in common use for letters from one individual to another. But there are several factors which tend to indicate that, at least in part, it was a literary fabrication of the Sumerian scribes who lived quite some time after the struggle between Ibbi-Sin and Ishbi-Irra which resulted in the end of the Third Dynasty of Ur. In the first place it is important to bear in mind that the present text, as we have it, can be only a copy of the original letter, if one ever existed; the script dates from a time considerably later than the Ur III period. Secondly, we now have three copies of the letter, and in the course of time, several more may be uncovered. Obviously, therefore, this letter—and there are also examples of letters purported to be written by Ibbi-Sin and a well-known Isin ruler, Lipit-Ishtar—was treated by the teachers of the Nippur scribal schools as a kind of practice composition for the use of their students. Moreover, the contents of the letter, particularly the passage describing Enlil's harsh decisions against Sumer and Ur (lines 15-24), have a literary flavor which seems rather incongruous in a prosaic letter written for an immediate and practical end. Finally, in the matter of grammar, the text before us follows principles current in post Ur III days; that is, if there was an original letter from Ibbi-Sin to Puzur-Numushda, its text was tampered with and "modernized." But no matter how and why the later scribes modified the original text of the letter, its historical portions are no doubt authentic. Indeed, even if we assume that the document before us is a literary fiction of the later scribes, and that no such letter was ever written by Ibbi-Sin, it is still reasonable to assume that its historical details were not invented, but were based on actual data available to the scribes.

[2] The Third Dynasty of Ur ruled from approximately the middle of the twenty-first century to the middle of the twentieth century B.C.

[3] The exact location of Kazallu is still unknown; it is generally assumed to be east of the Tigris.

[4] After the fall of the Third Dynasty of Ur, the control of Babylonia was in the hands of two dynasties who ruled simultaneously for many years; the one was established by Ishbi-Irra at Isin, about 30 kilometers south of Nippur, and the other at Larsa, not far from Ur.

[5] As the all too frequent italics show, the text is at times difficult to translate, and the context is not infrequently obscure; the interpretation here presented and based largely on Falkenstein's study, seems to be the most probable on the available data, but is far from assured.

[6] Mari is situated on the Euphrates more than three hundred kilometers northwest of Nippur; in spite of its distance from the center of Sumer, the city played at times an important role in Sumerian affairs, and a Mari Dynasty ruled over Sumer as early as the middle of the third millennium B.C.

[7] Note, however, that the meaning of lines 25-31 is very uncertain.

[8] The Martu are the nomadic people who lived west of Sumer and are generally known by their Akkadian name Amurru.

[9] According to the present rendering of the relevant passage (lines 35-36), the Elamites were the enemies of Ibbi-Sin and the allies of Ishbi-Irra; this agrees with the later tradition that Ibbi-Sin was carried off to Elam as a captive, as well as with the "Lamentation over the Destruction of Ur" (cf. p. 460 of this volume), where it is stated that it was the Elamites who were largely responsible for the destruction of Ur. However the meaning of the crucial verb in line 36 is quite uncertain, and Falkenstein's rendering assumes that the Elamites were the allies, not the enemies, of Ibbi-Sin.

[10] As later events proved, Ibbi-Sin's optimism was quite unjustified. Following his defeat and the destruction of Ur, the Sumerians gradually disappeared from the military and political scene.

[11] One of these tablets originally contained the entire text of the letter, while the other two contained only extracts, one being inscribed with lines 1-21 and the other with lines 21-38.

[12] Barton was under the impression that the text was an oracle of Ishbi-Irra.

[13] Important variations from Falkenstein's renderings will be indicated in the notes. The present writer has also had the opportunity of collating the three tablets, and the results of this collation will be noted in their place.

[14] "Governor" renders the Sumerian word *ensi(k)*, more commonly known in its Akkadian form *ishakku*.

[15] Literally, "like me."

[16] Presumably the implication of this difficult sentence is that Puzur-Numushda should have proceeded with his troops against Ishbi-Irra instead of procrastinating. Falkenstein's rendering, which is grammatically quite as justifiable as the present translation, reads: Since I have (sent) you selected . . . troops, they stood at your disposal as governor of Kazallu. But while I was all for (you), not so your troops (and) your levies.

[17] The last sign in this line is miscopied; it is probably GAR.

[18] As Falkenstein correctly surmised, the end of line 10 reads *a-gim*(!) *nu-e*(!)*-zu*.

[19] Reading of last part of name is uncertain.

him?[20] (13) How is it that you *delay* to *turn back* the . . . ? (15). . . . Enlil has sent[21] evil upon Sumer. (16) Its *enemy* descending from the land . . . ,[22] he has raised unto the shepherdship of the land.[23] (18) Now did Enlil give the kingship to a worthless man, to Ishbi-Irra who is not of Sumerian seed. *Lo, in* the assembly of the gods Sumer has been prostrated.[24] (21) Father Enlil whose commands are . . . , verily commanded thus: "*As long as evil doers exist* in Ur,[25] Ishbi-Irra, the man of Mari, will tear down its foundations, will measure out[26] Sumer." (25) And (*so*) *when* you have been appointed governors of the several cities, they[27] have gone over to Ishbi-Irra in accordance with Enlil's word.[28] (27) (*Even*) after you, like a . . . , hand over the city to the enemy[29] and *have become*[30] a faithful servant, Ishbi-Irra does not know (*you*).[31] (29) Now *bring you (help) hither*[32] in order to restore the good word *and to put an end to the false; let them*[33] *perform . . . among its people*. (32) Do not turn away; do not *go against* me. (33) His[34] hand will not *reach over* the city; the man of Mari will not exercise lordship *in accordance with* (*his*) inimical plan. (35) (For) now Enlil has stirred up the Martu from out of their land; *they* will *strike down*[35] the Elamites and capture Ishbi-Irra. With the restoration of the land to its (former) place, (its) might will become known throughout all the lands. It is urgent, do not. . . .

20 Line 12, according to the original reads: *a-na-aš-àm erín(!) šu(!)-zu-šè ì-gál-la igi(!)-zu(!)-šè la-ba-an-súg-gi-za(!)-na*(!). Falkenstein correctly surmised the reading of several of the miscopied signs.

21 The verb read *mu-un-gi*₄; the sign A following *-un-* is a miscopy.

22 The three dots stand for a destroyed sign which may have given the name of the land.

23 "Land" here refers to Sumer.

24 In *PBS*, XIII, No. 3, the sign U following *ki-en-gi* is a miscopy for PA.

25 Falkenstein renders this line as: Until the enemy *plunders* (everything) in Ur.

26 To judge from the context "will measure out" should denote some destructive action.

27 That is presumably the inhabitants of the cities.

28 Falkenstein translates lines 25 f. as: If he (Ishbi-Irra) sets you up (now) as governors of the several cities, they (really "you") will go over to Ishbi-Irra in accordance with the word of Enlil.

29 That is perhaps Ishbi-Irra.

30 Rendering assumes that the end of line 14 of Barton, *Miscellaneous Babylonian Inscriptions*, No. 9 reads *mu(!)-dím* instead of *še-ni*-DÍM.

31 That is, perhaps it means to say that Ishbi-Irra will not recognize his services to him.

32 That is, perhaps to Ur.

33 "Them" may perhaps refer to those whom he brought as help.

34 "His" refers to Ishbi-Irra.

35 The meaning of the Sumerian verb rendered as "strike down" is quite uncertain. Falkenstein, who assumes that the Elamites were allies of Ibbi-Sin, renders this same verb by "will stand at my side" and concludes that it is the Elamites who will capture Ishbi-Irra.

Akkadian Letters

TRANSLATOR: W. F. ALBRIGHT*

The Mari Letters

In 1935-38 André Parrot excavated the palace of king Zimri-Lim (about 1730-1700 B.C.) at Tell el-Hariri, ancient Mari on the Middle Euphrates. Among nearly 20,000 cuneiform tablets found in this palace were some 5,000 letters, mostly written by native Amorites (Northwestern Semites) in a Babylonian full of West-Semitic words and grammatical usages. Personal names, language and customs reflect the culture of the Patriarchal Age in Genesis. There is already a very extensive literature on the letters, only a few of the more important items of which can be listed here. The principal edition of them is in Volumes XXII ff. of *Musée du Louvre: textes cunéiformes* (1941-); *Archives royales de Mari* by G. Dossin, Charles-F. Jean and J. R. Kupper. Many letters have been published and translated elsewhere by MM. Jean and Dossin. For a general survey of their content see Dossin, *Syria*, XIX (1938), pp. 105-126; W. F. Albright, *BASOR*, No. 77, pp. 30 ff., 78, pp. 23 ff.; W. von Soden, *Welt des Orients*, I, pp. 187-204 (where a good bibliography and map will also be found). For historical orientation see also F. M. Th. Böhl, *King Hammurabi of Babylon in the Setting of His Time* (Amsterdam, 1946), and Dossin, *Samsi-Addu Ier roi d'Assyrie* (Brussels, 1948). J. R. Kupper's monograph, Un gouvernement provincial dans le royaume de Mari (*RA*, XLI, 1947), pp. 149-183, provides an excellent survey of the administrative system of Mari. A very good popular account of the results of the excavations of Mari, with particular attention to the letters, will be found in George E. Mendenhall's Mari, in the *Biblical Archaeologist*, XI (1948), pp. 1-19.

a

Published and translated by G. Dossin in *RA*, XXXV (1938), pp. 178 f.

To my lord say: Thus Bannum, thy servant. Yesterday, I departed from Mari, and spent the night at Zuruban. All the Benjaminites[1] raised fire-signals.[2] From Samanum to Ilum-Muluk, from Ilum-Muluk to Mishlan, all the cities of the Benjaminites of the Terqa district raised fire signals in response, and so far I have not ascertained the meaning of those signals. Now, I shall determine the meaning, and I shall write to my lord whether it is thus or not. Let the guard of the city of Mari be strengthened, and let my lord not go outside the gate.

b

Published by C. F. Jean in *Archives royales de Mari*, II, No. 22. For his preliminary translation see *RA*, XXIX, pp. 64 f.; the following is fully revised.

To my lord say: Thus Ibal-pi-Il, thy servant. Hammurabi spoke to me as follows: "A heavily armed force had gone out to raid the enemy column, but there was no suitable base to be found, so that force has returned empty-handed and the column of the enemy is proceeding in good order without panic. Now let a light armed force go to raid the enemy column and capture informers."

Thus Hammurabi spoke to me. I am sending Sakirum with three hundred troops to Shabazum, and the troops which I have sent are one hundred fifty [Hanu], fifty Suhu, and one hundred troops from the bank of the Euphrates River; and there are three hundred troops of Babylon. In the van of the troops of my lord there goes Ilu-nasir, the seer,[3] the subject of my lord, and one Babylonian seer goes with the troops of Babylon. These six hundred troops are based in Shabazum, and the seer assembles the omens. When the appearance of their omens is favorable, one hundred fifty go out and one hundred fifty come in. May my lord know this. The troops of my lord are well.

c

Published by C. F. Jean in *Archives royales de Mari*, II, No. 37, and translated in *Revue des études sémitiques*, 1944, pp. 10 f.; the following is fully revised.

To my lord say: Thus Ibal-Il, thy servant. The tablet of Ibal-Adad from Aslakka reached me and I went to Aslakka to "kill an ass"[4] between the Hanu and Idamaras. A "*puppy* and *lettuce*"[5] they brought, but I obeyed my lord and I did not give the "*puppy* and *lettuce*." I caused the foal of an ass[6] to be slaughtered. I established peace between the Hanu and Idamaras. In Hurra, in all of Idamaras, the Hanu are victorious, as a victor who has no enemy.[7] May my lord be pleased. This tablet of mine I will have delivered to my lord in Rataspatum. I will reach my lord by the third day after this tablet of mine. The camp and the Banu-Sim'al[8] are well.

* In collaboration with George E. Mendenhall.

[1] The cuneiform text has the singular *Bin-yamina'a*, but the name is generally written *Banu-yamina*, literally "Children of the South (Right)." On this nomadic group, opposed to the *Banu Sim'al*, "Children of the North (Left)," see G. Dossin, *Mélanges Dussaud*, II, pp. 981-996. There is no reason to suppose that these Benjaminites are the same as the later biblical tribe.

[2] On fire signals in the Mari Letters, with parallels from other ancient literature, including the Bible and the Lachish ostraca, see Dossin, *RA*, XXXV, pp. 174-186. With their aid the ancients were able to communicate with great rapidity over considerable distances.

[3] Cuneiform *barum*. In later times Balaam was just such a *baru*; cf. *JBL*, LXIII (1944), p. 231 and n.141.

[4] This expression is always in Amorite, transcribed in cuneiform *ḥayaram qatalum* (Heb. *qatol 'air*); it means simply "make a treaty," which was solemnized by the sacrifice of a young ass, much as the later Saracens of St. Nilus' time sacrificed a camel.

[5] This enigmatic expression evidently reflects some Amorite practice of quasi-magical character which might involve the official of Mari too deeply. The words *meranum* and *ḫassum* are translated with their ordinary Akkadian meanings; they may, of course, have some special sense here.

[6] The expression is "young ass, son of a she-ass." Exactly the same Hebrew words are employed in the passage Zech. 9:9=Matthew 21:5.

[7] The cuneiform text must be read *šabi'um gerem ul išu*, obviously referring to the bloodless victory of the Hanu (the most important tribe of Mari) over their former foes in the southeastern marches.

[8] See above, n.1.

d

Published by C. F. Jean in *Archives royales de Mari*, II, No. 131, and translated in *Revue des études sémitiques*, 1944, pp. 26 f.; the following is fully revised.

To my lord say: Thus Mashum, thy servant. (5) Sintiri wrote to me for help, and I reached him with troops at Shubat-Shamash. The next day word of the enemy (10) came as follows: "Yapah-Adad has made ready the settlement Zallul on this side on the bank of the Euphrates River, and with two thousand troops of the Hapiru of the land (15),[9] is dwelling in that city." This word came to me, and from Shubat-Shamash, with troops of my command and with troops of the command of (20) Sintiri, I hurried, and made ready the town of Himush over against the town of Zallul. Between the two (25) cities (there is a distance of) thirty "fields." When I had made ready the city of Himush over against him, and he saw that the land was hastening to (my) aid, (30) he raised a fire signal, and all the cities of the land of Ursum on the other side acknowledged it. The *security* forces which are stationed within the brick-*enclosure* are numerous, and, lest they (35) wipe out the troops, I did not draw near the city. This tablet of mine I send to my lord from the bank of the Euphrates River. The troops and *cattle* are well.

The Amarna Letters

In 1887 an Egyptian peasant woman discovered a collection of cuneiform tablets at Tell el-Amarna in Middle Egypt, the site of Akh-en-Aton's capital in the early fourteenth century B.C. These tablets were sold to European museums and private dealers; some of them escaped attention for nearly thirty years. Subsequently excavation disclosed enough additional tablets to bring the total collection up to about 377 numbers. Almost all of them are letters belonging to the royal archives of Amen-hotep III and his son Akh-en-Aton. Nearly 300 letters were written by Canaanite (or rarely Egyptian) scribes in Palestine, Phoenicia, and southern Syria, about half of them in Palestine proper. These letters are written in a conventional vulgar Akkadian, full of canaanitisms in grammar and vocabulary. Occasionally we find a letter written mostly in Canaanite with scattered Akkadian formulas and ideograms. They date from the last years of Amen-hotep III and the reign of his successor; a very few may date from the ephemeral reign of Akh-en-Aton's son-in-law and successor, Smenkhkere.

The original publications, though antiquated, are important for the cuneiform texts: note especially H. Winckler and L. Abel, *Der Thontafelfund von El Amarna*, Berlin, 1889-90; C. Bezold and E. A. W. Budge, *The Tell El-Amarna Tablets in the British Museum*, London, 1892. All the older material was reexamined and collated with the greatest care by the Norwegian Assyriologist, J. A. Knudtzon, in his invaluable transcription and translation, to which O. Weber added a detailed commentary and E. Ebeling a valuable glossary: *Die El-Amarna-Tafeln* (*VAB*, Vol. II), Leipzig, 1907-15. Since then the Berlin tablets were reedited admirably by O. Schroeder, *Die Tontafeln von El-Amarna* (Leipzig, 1915). S. A. B. Mercer's two-volume work, *The Tell el-Amarna Tablets* (Toronto, 1939), has no independent value and is full of errors not found in Knudtzon's edition.

[9] On the Hapiru (Habiru) or 'Apiru in the Mari texts see especially E. Dhorme, *RHR*, CXVIII, pp. 170-187.

Among minor publications the following will be found of particular significance: F. Thureau-Dangin, Nouvelles lettres d'el-Amarna, *RA*, XIX, pp. 91-108; C. H. Gordon, The New Amarna Tablets, *Orientalia*, XVI, pp. 1-21; W. F. Albright, The Egyptian Correspondence of Abimilki, Prince of Tyre, *JEA*, XXIII, pp. 190-203; Albright, Cuneiform Material for Egyptian Prosopography, 1500-1200 B.C., *JNES*, v, pp. 7-25; Albright, The Letters of 'Abdu-Kheba, Prince of Jerusalem, *BASOR SS*, 1950; Albright, various papers, mainly in *BASOR*, No. 86 ff. J. De Koning's monograph, *Studiën over de El-Amarnabrieven en het Oude-Testament, inzonderheid uit historisch oogpunkt* (Delft, 1940), contains much material, but must be used with the greatest caution.

The translations offered below represent the combined work of W. F. Albright and George E. Mendenhall.—Ed.

EA, No. 137[1]

Rib-Ad[di spoke] to the king, [his] lor[d, the Sun-god of the lands.] Beneath the feet [of the king, my lord,] seven times, and seven times [I fall.] (5) I have written repeatedly for [garrison troops], but they were not given, [and] the king did [not] listen to the word[s of his servant.] And I sent my courier to the palace, but [he returned] (10) empty-handed—he had no garrison troops. And when the peop[le of] my [house] saw that silver was not given, they ridiculed me like the governors, my brethren, and they despised me.

Further, I (15) went to Hamuniri, and my younger brother is estranging Byblos in order to give the city to the sons of 'Abdu-Ashirta. (20) When my brother saw that my courier came out (from Egypt) empty-handed, (that) there were no garrison troops with him, he despised me, and so he committed a crime and drove me (25) from the city. Let the king not restrain (himself) at the deed of this dog!

Behold, I cannot enter the land of Egypt. I am an old man, there is grievous illness (30) in my body, and the king, my lord, knows that the gods of Byblos are holy, and the illness is severe; and my sin I have redeemed (by a vow) from the gods, so I have not entered (35) the presence of the king, my lord.

But behold, my son, the servant of the king, my lord, I have sent before the king, my lord. Let the king hear the words of his servant, and let the king, my lord, give (40) archers, and let them take Byblos, lest rebellious troops and the sons of 'Abdu-Ashirta enter it, and the archers of the king, my lord, (then) need (46) to capture it (*by force*). Behold, many are the people who love me in the city; few are the rebels in it. When an army of archers goes out and they hear (50) about the day of its arrival, then the city will return to the king, my lord. Let my lord know that I would die for him. When I am in the city, I will protect it for my lord, and my heart is fixed (55) on the king, my lord; I will not give the city to the sons of 'Abdu-Ashirta. So my brother has estranged the city in order

[1] This letter was dictated by Rib-Addi, prince of Byblos, to Akh-en-Aton (Amen-hotep IV) about 1370 B.C. or a little later. The old enemy of Rib-Addi, 'Abdu-Ashirta of Amurru (land of the Amorites), was now dead, but his son, 'Aziru, and the latter's brothers continued to menace the territory of Byblos. At this time Rib-Addi had actually been forced to retire from his own city to the comparative safety of Berytus (Beirut), whose prince 'Ammuniri was related to him by marriage.

to give it to the sons of 'Abdu-Ashirta. Let the king, my lord, not hold back from (60) the city. Verily, there is very much silver and gold within it; in its temple there is much wealth. If they take it (the city), let the king my lord do as he please with his servant, but let him give the city Buruzilim (65) for my dwelling place,—behold, I am now with Hamuniri—since *there is left but one city*, namely, Buruzilim. The sons of 'Abdu-Ashirta were hostile, and I was afraid. When I went to Hamuniri (70) because of the sons of 'Abdu-Ashirta when they were powerful against me and there was no breath of the mouth of the king to me, then I said to my lord: "Behold our city Byblos! There is much wealth of the king in it, the property (75) of our forefathers. If the king does not intervene for the city, all the cities of the land of Canaan will (no longer) be his. Let the king not ignore this deed!"

Now I have sent thy servant, my son, to the king, my lord; let the king quickly send him back (80) with troops to take the city. If the king, my lord, be gracious to me and return me to the city, then I will guard it *as before* for the king, my lord. If the king, my lord, does not bring me back into it, then [. . .] (85) the city from ⌜*Buruzilim*⌝ [. . . may he do] as he please [to his servant(?). . . .] Forsa[ke . . .] Hamu[niri . . .] until when [shall I remain with him(?)].

(90) May [the king, my lord,] hear [the words of] his servant q[uickly(?)] [and send] troops quickly to take the city. Let the king not ignore (95) this grievous deed which was done to the lands of the king, my lord; but let the king rush archers to take the city immediately. (100) If it is said to the king concerning the city: "The city is strong," it is not strong against the warriors of the king, my lord.

EA, No. 147[2]

To the king, my lord, my pantheon, my Sun-god say: Thus Abimilki, thy servant. Seven and seven times I fall at the feet of the king, my lord. I am the dirt under (5) the feet of the king, my lord. My lord is the Sun-god who rises over the lands day by day, as ordained by the Sun-god, his gracious father; who gives life by his sweet breath, (10) and who lessens when he is hidden; who sets the whole land at peace by his might, who utters his battle-cry in heaven like Baal, so that the whole land quakes at his cry.

Behold, the servant has written to his lord because he has heard the gracious messenger of the king who comes to his servant, and the sweet breath which went forth (20) from the mouth of the king, my lord, to his servant (he has received); and his breath was feeble before the arrival of the messenger of the king, my lord, (but now his) breath is not feeble. I remember the words of my father: "Behold, now (25) that the breath of the king has come forth to me, I rejoice greatly, and I am happy day by day. Because I rejoice, the earth does not . . . (30) that I have heard the gracious messenger who (came) from my lord, and all the earth is reverent before the face of my lord, for I have heard the sweet breath, and the gracious messenger (35) who came to me. When the king, my lord, says: "*Be valiant*!" before the great army, then the servant says, "*Aye, Aye*!" to his lord. On my belly, on my back (40) I bear the word of the king, my lord. As for him who hearkens to the king, his lord, and serves him in his place, the Sun-god shall rise over him, and the sweet breath from the mouth of his lord *shall give him life*(!); (45) but as for him who hearkens not to the word of the king, his lord, his city shall perish, his dynasty shall perish, his name shall not exist in the whole land forever. Behold, the servant who hearkens to his lord—(50) it shall be well with his city, it shall be well with his house; his name shall exist forever. Thou art the Sun-god who rises over me, and a brazen wall which is reared for me, and because of the mighty power of the king my lord (56), I am tranquil.

Behold, I have said to the Sun-god, the father of the king, my lord, "When shall I see (60) the face of the king, my lord?" But behold, I am guarding Tyre, the great city, for the king, my lord, until the mighty power of the king come out unto me, (65) to give water for me to drink, and wood to warm me.

Further: Zimreda, the king of Sidon, has written day by day to the criminal 'Aziru, the son of 'Abdu-Ashirta, concerning everything that he heard from Egypt. (70) Behold, I have written to my lord, (for) it is good that you should know.

RA, XIX, p. 100[3]

To Indaruta, prince of Achshaph say: Thus the king. Behold, this tablet I have sent to you, saying to you: Be on guard! Verily thou shalt guard (5) the place of the king which is with you. Behold, the king is sending you Hanni, son of Mairea, the commissioner of the king for the land of Canaan, and what he says to you, hear thou (10) very attentively, lest the king find thee at fault. Every word which he speaks to thee, hear thou very willingly, and do it very willingly. And watch, watch, do not be negligent, (15) and thou shalt prepare for the archers of the king much food, much wine of every sort. Behold, he will come to thee quickly, quickly, (20) and will cut off the head of the enemies of the king!

EA, No. 234[4]

To the king, my lord, the Sun-god from heaven: Thus Zatatna, prince of Accho, thy servant, the servant

[2] This letter was dictated by Abimilki (Abimelech) of Tyre to Akh-en-Aton about the same time as the previous letter, or perhaps a little later. We know from the peculiar spelling and grammar, as well as from a great many Egyptian words and expressions translated literally from Egyptian, that the scribe who wrote the Abimilki letters was himself a native Egyptian, a fact which is not surprising, since the Amarna letters from the Egyptian court to Asiatic kings and chieftains were all written by Egyptian scribes who had learned cuneiform in the palace schools.

[3] This is a characteristic letter from pharaoh to a Palestinian chieftain. Indaruta (who bears the same Indo-Aryan name as his contemporary Indrota or Indrauta of the Rig Veda) was prince of Achshaph, probably Tell Kisan in the Plain of Acre in southwestern Galilee.

[4] This letter comes from the time of Akh-en-Aton. Shuta (pronounce *Suta*) was an Egyptian officer, probably the great-grandfather of Ramses II;

of the king, and (5) the dirt (under) his two feet, the ground which he treads. At the two feet of the king, my lord, the Sun-god from heaven, seven times, seven times I fall, both prone and supine. (10) Let the king, my lord, hear the word of his servant! [Zir]damyashda has withdrawn from Biryawaza. [He was] with Shuta, the s[ervant] of the (15) king in the city of [. . . .] He did not say anything to him. The army of the king, my lord, has departed. He was with it in Megiddo. (20) I said nothing to him, but he deserted to me, and now Shuta has written to me: "Give (25) Zirdamyashda to Biryawaza!" But I did not consent to give him up. Behold, Accho is (as Egyptian) as Magdal (30) in Egypt, but the king, my lord, has not heard that [Shut]a has turned against me. Now let the king, my lord, send (35) his commissioner and fetch him.

EA, No. 244[5]

To the king, my lord, and my Sun-god, say: Thus Biridiya, the faithful servant of the (5) king. At the two feet of the king, my lord, and my Sun-god, seven and seven times I fall. Let the king know that (10) ever since the archers returned (to Egypt?), Lab'ayu has carried on hostilities against me, and we are not able to pluck the wool, and we are not able to go outside the gate in the presence of Lab'ayu, since he learned that thou hast not given (20) archers; and now his face is set to take Megiddo, (25) but let the king protect his city, lest Lab'ayu seize it. (30) Verily, the city is destroyed by death from pestilence and *disease*. Let the king give (35) one hundred garrison troops to guard the city lest Lab'ayu seize it. Verily, there is no other purpose in (41) Lab'ayu. He seeks to destroy Megiddo.

EA, No. 245[6]

Further, I said to my brethren, "If the gods of the king, our lord, grant (5) that we capture Lab'ayu, then we will bring him alive to the king, our lord"; but my mare was felled by an arrow, and I alighted (10) afterwards and rode with Yashdata, but before my arrival, they had slain him. (15) Verily, Yashdata is thy servant, and he entered the battle with me. And verily, [. . .] (20) the life of the king, m[y lord] [and] [. . .] all in [. . .] of the king, [my] lord, [. . .], and Zurata (25) removed Lab'ayu from Megiddo, saying to me: "I will send him by ship (30) to the king," and Zurata took him and sent him home from Hannathon, for Zurata had received his ransom money (35) in his hand.

Further, what have I done to the king, my lord, that he should despise me and honor (40) my younger brothers? Zurata has sent Lab'ayu, and Zurata has sent Ba'lu-mihir to their homes, and let the king, my lord, be informed!

RA, XIX, p. 97[7]

To the king, my lord, and my Sun-god say: Thus Biridiya, the true servant of the king. (5) At the feet of the king, my lord, and my Sun-god, seven times and seven times I fall. Let the king be informed concerning his servant and concerning his city. (10) Behold, I am working in the town of Shunama, and I bring men of the corvée, (15) but behold, the governors who are with me do not as I (do): they do not (20) work in the town of Shunama, and they do not bring men for the corvée, but I alone (25) bring men for the corvée from the town of Yapu. They come from Shu[nama], and likewise from the town of Nuribda. (30) So let the king be informed concerning his city!

EA, No. 250[8]

⌜To⌝ the king, my lord, say: Thus Ba'lu-UR.SAG, thy servant. At the feet of the king, my lord, seven times, seven times, I fall. Let the king, my lord, know that (5) the two sons of a rebel against the king my lord, the two sons of Lab'ayu, have determined to destroy the land of the king, my lord, after their father's death. And let the king, my lord, know that (10) many days the two sons of Lab'ayu have *accused* me (saying): "Why hast thou given the town of Giti-padalla into the hand of the king, thy lord—the city which Lab'ayu, our father, captured?" (15) So thus the two sons of Lab'ayu spoke to me: "Declare war against the people of the land of Qena, because they slew our father; and if you do not declare war, then we are hostile to you."

But I answered them: (20) "May the god of the king, my lord, preserve me from making war against the people of the land of Qena, the servants of the king, my lord!" Now may it be agreeable to the king, my lord, to send one of his officers to Biryawaza (25) and let him say to him: "Wilt thou march against the two sons of Lab'ayu, or art thou a rebel against the king?" And after him, let the king, my lord, send to me [. . .] the deed (30) ⌜of the king,⌝ thy ⌜lord⌝, against the two sons of Lab'ayu [. . .] Milkilu *has gone in to them*[? . . .] (35) . . . ⌜land of the king, my lord, with them after Milkilu and Lab'ayu died.⌝ (40) And thus the two sons of Lab'ayu spoke: "Be hostile to the king, thy lord, like our father, when he attacked Shunama and Burquna and Harabu, and (45) destroyed them/

Biryawaza (whose name was formerly read erroneously *Namyawaza*) was prince of Damascus under Egyptian suzerainty. All personal names (except Shuta) are Indo-Aryan. Magdal is the Migdol of Exod. 14:2, etc.

[5] Biridiya was prince of Megiddo at the end of the reign of Amen-hotep III and the beginning of the reign of Akh-en-Aton; his name is Indo-Aryan like most other princely names of northern Palestine at that time. Lab'ayu (whose name meant approximately "lion-like" in Canaanite) was prince of Shechem in the central hill-country and was constantly raiding the territory and caravans of his neighbors on all sides.

[6] This is the latter part (all that is preserved) of a continued letter from Biridiya of Megiddo. Zurata, whom Biridiya accuses of treachery, was prince of Acre (biblical Accho).

[7] This letter from the prince of Megiddo is very instructive because of the light it throws on forced labor for the king in the Plain of Esdraelon, several of whose towns and villages are mentioned. The word for "corvée" is the Hebrew *mas*, which is employed a little later of the tribe of Issachar in this very region (Gen. 49:15).

[8] The prince from whom this letter comes was in control of a district in the northern coastal plain of Palestine, south of Carmel. The death of Lab'ayu is described in *EA*, No. 245 (cf. n.6). Here his sons are described as continuing their father's activities. Biryawaza, whose help is wanted to subdue the recalcitrants, was prince of Damascus (cf. n.4). Milkilu was prince of Gezer, whose territory adjoined the territory of Ba'lu-UR.SAG ("Baal is a warrior") on the south.

smote them. And he took Giti-rimuni, and he betrayed the helpers of the king, thy lord."

But I answered them: "The god of the king, my lord, preserve me from making (50) war against the king, my lord. The king, my lord, I serve, and my brothers who hearken to me." But the courier of Milkilu does not move from the two sons of Lab'ayu (55) a (*single*) day. Behold, Milkilu seeks to destroy the land of the king, my lord. But there is no other intention with me—I serve the king, my lord, and the word which the king, my lord, speaks do I hear.

EA, No. 252[9]

To the king, my lord, say: Thus Lab'ayu, thy servant. At the feet of my lord I fall. (5) As for what thou hast written, "Are the people strong who have captured the town? How can the men be arrested?" (I reply) "By fighting was the town captured, (10) in spite of the fact that I had taken an oath of conciliation and that, when I took the oath, an (Egyptian) officer took the oath with me! The city as well as my god are captured. I am slandered/blamed (15) before the king, my lord."

Further, when (even) ants are smitten, they do not accept it (passively), but they bite the hand of the man who smites them. (20) How could I hesitate this day when two of my towns are taken?

Further, even if thou shouldst say: "(25) Fall beneath them, and let them smite thee," I should still repel my foe, the men who seized the town and (30) my god, the despoilers of my father, (yea) I would repel them.

EA, No. 254[10]

To the king, my lord and my Sun-god: Thus Lab'ayu, thy servant, and the dirt on which thou dost tread. At the feet of the king, my lord, (5) and my Sun-god, seven times and seven times I fall.

I have heard the words which the king wrote to me, and who am I that the king should lose his land (10) because of me? Behold, I am a faithful servant of the king, and I have not rebelled and I have not sinned, and I do not withhold my tribute, and I do not refuse (15) the requests of my commissioner. Now they wickedly slander me, but let the king, my lord, not impute rebellion to me!

Further, (20) my crime is namely that I entered Gezer and said publicly: (25) "Shall the king take my property, and not likewise the property of Milkilu?" I know the deeds which Milkilu has done against me.

(30) Further, the king wrote concerning my son. I did not know that my son associates with the 'Apiru (36), and I have verily delivered him into the hand of Addaya.

Further, if the king should write for my wife, (40) how could I withhold her? If the king should write to me, "Plunge a bronze dagger into thy heart and (45) die!", how could I refuse to carry out the command of the king?

EA, No. 256[11]

To Yanhamu, my lord say: Thus Mut-ba'lu, thy servant. At the two feet of my lord I fall. How is it said (5) before thee, "Mut-ba'lu has fled, Ayab has hidden himself?" How can the prince of Pella flee from the face of the commissioner (10) of the king, his lord? As the king my lord lives, as the king my lord lives, Ayab is not in Pella. Behold, he has not been (here) for two months(?). (15) Indeed, ask Ben-ilima, ask Taduwa, ask Yashuya. Again, *at the instance of* (20) the house of Shulum-Marduk, the city of Ashtartu came to (my) help, when all the cities of the land of Garu were hostile, (namely) Udumu, Aduru, (25) Araru, Meshqu, Magdalu, Eni-anabu and Zarqu, and when Hayanu and Yabilima were captured.

Further, behold—after (30) thy writing a tablet to me, I wrote to him. Before thou dost arrive with thy caravan, behold, he will have reached Pella, and he will hear (thy) words.

EA, No. 270[12]

To the king, my lord, my pantheon, my Sun-god, say: Thus Milkilu, thy servant, (5) the dirt (under) thy feet. At the feet of the king, my lord, my pantheon, my Sun-god, seven times, seven times I fall. Let the king, my lord, know (10) the deed which Yanhamu did to me after I left the presence of the king, my lord. Now he seeks (15) two thousand (shekels) of silver from my hand, saying to me: "Give me thy wife and (20) thy children, or I will smite!" Let the king know this deed, and let my lord send to me (26) chariots, and let him take me to himself lest I perish!

EA, No. 271[13]

To the king, my lord, my pantheon, my Sun-god, say: Thus Milkilu, thy servant, (5) the dirt (under) thy feet. At the feet of the king, my lord, my pantheon, my Sun-god, seven times, seven times, I fall. Let the king know (10) that powerful is the hostility against me and against Shuwardata. Let the king, my lord, protect his land (15) from the hand of the 'Apiru. If

[9] This letter is written in almost pure Canaanite and was not understood until very recently; for a detailed commentary on it see *BASOR*, No. 89, pp. 29-32. Lab'ayu virtuously protests that he was only repelling aggressors who had attacked his native town (not Shechem, which was his capital) in spite of a previous treaty sworn in the presence of an Egyptian official.

[10] In this letter Lab'ayu protests his innocence of all charges against him and assures the king (Amen-hotep III) that he is more loyal than the neighbors who complain against him.

[11] For a detailed interpretation of this letter see *BASOR*, No. 89, pp. 7-15. Mut-ba'lu (literally "Man of Baal") was prince of Pella in the northern Jordan Valley, opposite Beth-Shan; Ayab (Ayyab, Hebrew Job) was prince of Ashtartu (biblical Ashtaroth) in Bashan. The land of Garu lay in southern Golan between Pella and Ashtartu. Yanhamu, to whom the letter is addressed, was a high Egyptian official of Canaanite (possibly of Hebrew) origin, who seems to have been the Egyptian governor of Palestine at the beginning of the reign of Akh-en-Aton.

[12] Milkilu (Heb. Malchiel) was prince of Gezer. For Yanhamu see the previous letter.

[13] For Milkilu see the previous letter. Shuwardata (with an Indo-Aryan name) was prince of the Hebron region in the southern hill-country, and frequently appears in association with Milkilu. The 'Apiru (formerly called Habiru) were a strong semi-nomadic people, or rather class of population in Syria and Palestine. While there is much reason to identify them with the Hebrews of the Patriarchal Age, the combination still remains uncertain and cannot be made the basis for any historical inferences.

not, (then) let the king, my lord, send chariots (20) to fetch us, lest our servants smite us.

Further, let the king, my lord, ask (25) Yanhamu, his servant, concerning that which is done in his land.

RA, xxxi, pp. 125-136[14]

To Milkilu, prince of Gezer. Thus the king. Now I have sent thee this tablet to say to thee: Behold, (5) I am sending to thee Hanya, the commissioner of the archers, together with goods, in order to procure fine concubines (i.e.) *weaving women*: silver, gold, (linen) garments, (10) *turquoise*, all (sorts of) precious stones, chairs of *ebony*, as well as every good thing, totalling 160 deben. Total: 40 concubines: the price of each concubine is 40 (shekels) of silver. (15) So send very fine concubines in whom there is no blemish. (19) And let the king, thy lord, say to thee, "This is good. To thee life has been *decreed*." And mayest thou know that (25) the king is well, like the Sun-god. His troops, his chariots, his horses are very well. Behold, the god Amon has placed the upper land, (30) the lower land, the rising of the sun, and the setting of the sun under the two feet of the king.

EA, No. 280[15]

To the king, my lord, my pantheon, my Sun-god, say: Thus Shuwardata, (5) thy servant, the dirt (under) thy feet! At the feet of the king, my lord, my pantheon, my Sun-god, seven times, seven times, I fall! (9) The king, my lord, sent me to make war against Keilah. I have made war (and) I was successful; my town has been restored (15) to me. Why did 'Abdu-Heba write to the people of Keilah (saying): "Take (my) silver and (20) follow me!" And let the king, my lord, know that 'Abdu-Heba had taken the town from my hand.

Further, (25) let the king, my lord, investigate; if I have taken a man or a single ox or an ass from him, then he is in the right! (30)

Further, Lab'ayu is dead, who seized our towns; but behold, 'Abdu-Heba is another Lab'ayu, and (35) he (also) seizes our towns! So let the king take thought for his servant because of this deed! And I will not do anything until the king sends back a message to his servant.

RA, xix, p. 106[16]

To the king, my lord, my Sun-god, my pantheon, say: Thus Shuwardata, thy servant, servant of the king (5) and the dirt (under) his two feet, the ground (on) which thou dost tread! At the feet of the king, my lord, the Sun-god from heaven, seven times, seven times I fall, both (10) prone and supine.

Let the king, my lord, learn that the chief of the 'Apiru has risen (in arms) against the lands which the god of the king, my lord, gave me; (16) but I have smitten him. Also let the king, my lord, know that all my brethren have abandoned me, and (20) it is I and 'Abdu-Heba (who) fight against the chief of the 'Apiru. And Zurata, prince of Accho, and Indaruta, prince of Achshaph, it was they (who) hastened (25)—for fifty chariots, *(of which) I have (now) been robbed*—to my help; but behold, they are fighting against me, so let it be agreeable to the king, my lord, and (30) let him send Yanhamu, and let us make war in earnest, and let the lands of the king, my lord, be restored to their (former) limits!

EA, No. 286[17]

To the king, my lord, say: Thus 'Abdu-Heba, thy servant. At the two feet of my lord, the king, seven times and seven times I fall. (5) What have I done to the king, my lord? They blame me before the king, my lord (saying): "'Abdu-Heba has rebelled against the king, his lord." Behold, as for me, (it was) not my father (10) and not my mother (who) set me in this place; the arm of the mighty king brought me into the house of my father! Why should I commit (15) transgression against the king, my lord? As long as the king, my lord, lives, I will say to the commissioner of the king, my lord, "Why do ye like the 'Apiru and dislike the governors?"—And thus (21) I am blamed in the presence of the king, my lord. Because it is said, "Lost are the lands of the king, my lord," thus am I blamed to the king, my lord! (25) But let the king, my lord, know that (when) the king had established a garrison, Yanhamu took ⌜it all⌝ away, [and . . .] ⌜the troops⌝ (30) [of archers(?) . . .] the land of Egypt [. . .] O king, my lord, there are no garrison troops (here)! [So] let the king take care of his land! (35) Let the king take care of his land! [The land]s of the king have all rebelled; Ilimilku is causing the loss of all the king's land. So let the king take care of his land! I keep saying, "Let me enter (40) into the presence of the king, my lord, and let me see the two eyes of the king, my lord." But the hostility against me is strong, so I cannot enter into the presence of the king, my lord. So may it please the king (45) to send me garrison troops in order that I may enter and see the

14 This letter from pharaoh to Milkilu of Gezer throws an interesting light on the rôle of the Canaanite princes in organizing royal commerce in Asia; Egyptian products and manufactured articles are to be exchanged for the best quality of slave-girls.

15 Shuwardata, prince of the Hebron district (cf. n.13) here protests to pharaoh (Akh-en-Aton) that 'Abdu-Heba, prince of Jerusalem, is just as aggressive as the unlamented Lab'ayu (see the previous letters).

16 This letter, from the beginning of Akh-en-Aton's reign, is an extraordinarily illuminating illustration of the situation in Palestine at that time. Just who this redoubtable 'Apiru chieftain was we do not learn, since the proud feudal princes disdained even to mention names of the semi-nomadic 'Apiru. However, he was sufficiently dangerous to unite the arch-foes, 'Abdu-Heba and Shuwardata, and to induce them to offer fifty chariots (a very considerable offer for Palestinian chieftains) to the princes of Accho and Achshaph (for whom see notes 3 and 6) in the Plain of Acre, far to the north. One suspects that Milkilu of Gezer and Lab'ayu of Shechem, who are not mentioned at all, were—either or both—involved with the 'Apiru.

17 This lettter is characteristic of the continuous requests of 'Abdu-Heba, prince of Jerusalem, for Egyptian assistance in his chronic struggle with the 'Apiru. However, it seems certain from other letters that he was inclined to lump his enemies among the "governors" (i.e. the native princes) with the 'Apiru. It is uncertain whether the Ilimilku (Elimelech) of lines 35 ff. was an 'Apiru chieftain, was one of the sons of Lab'ayu, or was even Milkilu of Gezer (whose name might have been transposed accidentally by the scribe).

two eyes of the king, my lord. As truly as the king, my lord, lives, when the commis[sioners] go forth I will say, "Lost are the lands of the king! (50) Do you not hearken unto me? All the governors are lost; the king, my lord, does not have a (single) governor (left)!" Let the king turn his attention to the archers, and let the king, my lord, send out (55) troops of archers, (for) the king has no lands (left)! The 'Apiru plunder all the lands of the king. If there are archers (here) in this year, the lands of the king, my lord, will remain (intact); but if there are no archers (here) (60) the lands of the king, my lord, will be lost!

To the scribe of the king, my lord: Thus 'Abdu-Heba, thy servant. Present eloquent words to the king, my lord.—All the lands of the king, my lord, are lost!

EA, No. 287[18]

[To the kin]g, my lord, [say:] [Thus] 'Abdu-Heba, thy servant. [At the feet] of my lord seven t[imes and seven times I fall.] [Let my king] [know (?) this] matter! [Milkili and Tagu (?)] (5) have caused [their troops (?)] to enter [the town of Rubutu (?)] [Behold] the deed which [Milkilu (?)] has done; [bows] (and) copper arrows [. . . he has given (?) . . .] word [. . . (10) . . .] into the town of [Rubutu (?)] they brought in. Let my king know that all the lands are at peace (but that) there is war against me. So let my king take care of his land!

Behold the land of Gezer, the land of Ashkelon, (15) and ⸢Lachish,⸣ they can give them grain, oil, and all their requirements; and let the king (thus) take care of his archers! Let him send archers against the men who transgress against the king, my lord. (20) If there are archers (here) in this year, then the lands and the governor⟨s⟩ will (still) belong to the king, my lord; [but] if there are no archers, the lands and the governors will (no longer) belong to the king! (25) Behold this land of Jerusalem: (It was) not my father (and) not my mother (who) gave (it) to me, (but) the arm of the mighty king (which) gave (it) to me.

Behold, this deed is the deed of Milkilu (30) and the deed of the sons of Lab'ayu who have given the land of the king to the 'Apiru. Behold, O king, my lord, I am right!

With reference to the Nubians, let my king ask the commissioners whether my house is (not) very strong! (35) Yet they attempted a very great crime; they took their implements and breached the roof-residence. [If] they send into the land [of Jerusalem] ⸢troops⸣, let them come up with [an (Egyptian) officer (40) for] (regular) service. Let [my king] take heed for them; let the lands provide food for them from their stores, [and] let my king requisition for them much grain, much oil, (and) much clothing, (45) until Pawure, the royal commissioner, comes up to the land of Jerusalem.

Addaya has left, together with the garrison (and) the (Egyptian) officer which my king had given (me). Let the king know! Addaya spoke to me, (saying,) (50) [Loo]k, let me go, (but) do not thou leave it (the city)! So send me a garrison this [year], and send me a commissioner *hither*, O my king. I have sent [gifts (?)] to the king, my lord: [. . .] captives, five thousand [silver (shekels)] (55) and eight porters for the caravans of the king, *my lord*; (but) they were captured in the plain of Ajalon. Let the king, my lord, know that I cannot send a caravan to the king, my lord. For thy information!

(60) Behold, the king has set his name in the land of Jerusalem for ever; so I cannot abandon the lands of Jerusalem!

To the scribe of the king, my lord, (65) say: Thus 'Abdu-Heba, thy servant. At thy two feet I fall—thy servant am I! Present eloquent words to the king, my lord. I am (only) a petty officer of the king; (70) I am more insignificant (?) than thou!

But the men of the land of Nubia have committed an evil deed against ⟨me⟩; I was almost killed by the men of the land of Nubia (75) in my own house. Let the king [call] them to (account). Seven times and seven times let the [king,] my lord, [avenge (?)] me!

EA, No. 288[19]

To the king, my lord, my Sun-god, say: Thus 'Abdu-Heba, thy servant. At the two feet of the king, my lord, seven times and seven times I fall. (5) Behold the king my lord, has set his name at the rising of the sun, and at the setting of the sun! (It is) vile what they have done against me. Behold, I am not a governor (10) (nor even a) petty officer of the king, my lord; behold, I am a shepherd of the king, and a bearer of the royal tribute am I. It was not my father (and) not my mother, (but) the arm of the mighty king (15) (which) placed me in the house of my father. [. . .] came to me [. . .] I delivered ten slaves [into his] hand. Shuta, the royal commissioner, came (20) to me. Twenty-one maidens (and) eighty captives I delivered into the hand of Shuta as a gift for the king, my lord. Let my king take thought for his land! The land of the king is lost; in its entirety (25) it is taken from me; there is war against me, as far as the lands of Seir (and) as far as Gath-carmel! All the governors are at peace, but there is war against me. I have become like an

[18] In this letter the prince of Jerusalem complains about a number of events which recur in other letters. In the first place he excoriates Milkilu of Gezer and Tagu of the northern Coastal Plain of Palestine for their aggression against Rubutu, which lay somewhere in the region southwest of Megiddo and Taanach. In the second place he urges the king to instruct his officers to supply the Egyptian archers from the towns of the Philistine Plain and Sharon (in order to avert heavy drain on the scanty supplies of Jerusalem). He goes on to complain that the Nubian (biblical Cushite) slave-troops (or mercenaries) of Egypt, stationed as garrison in Jerusalem, had burglarized the residence of 'Abdu-Heba himself, nearly killing the prince in his own house. He finally complains that his last caravan containing tribute and captives for the king was attacked and robbed near Ajalon, presumably by the men of Milkilu of Gezer and the sons of Lab'ayu.

[19] This letter continues the complaints of the previous letter, and incidentally paints a vivid picture of the anarchic condition of the country early in the reign of Akh-en-Aton. The references to "the very gate of Sile (Zilu)" mean that the outrages against the *pax Aegyptiaca* extend to the frontiers of Egypt itself, near modern Qantarah.

'Apiru (30) and do not see the two eyes of the king, my lord, for there is war against me. I have become like a ship in the midst of the sea! The arm of the mighty king (35) conquers the land of Naharaim and the land of Cush, but now the 'Apiru capture the cities of the king. There is not a single governor (remaining) (40) to the king, my lord—all have perished! Behold, *Turbazu* has been slain in the (very) gate of Sile, (yet) the king holds his peace. Behold Zimreda, the townsmen of Lachish have smitten him, slaves who had become 'Apiru. (45) Yaptih-Hadad has been slain [in] the (very) gate of Sile, (yet) the king holds his peace. [Wherefore] does not [the king] call them to account? [So] let the king take care of his land; [and l]et the king decide, and let the king send (50) archers to his land! [But] if there are no archers (here) this year, all the lands of the king, my lord, will be lost. They shall not say to the king, my lord, (55) that the land of the king, my lord, has been lost, and (that) all of the governors have perished! If there are no archers (here) this year, let the king send a commissioner, and let him take me (60) to himself (!) together with ⟨my⟩ brothers, and we shall die near the king, our lord!

[To] the scribe of the king, my lord: [Thus] 'Abdu-Heba, ⟨thy⟩ servant. At [thy (?)] two feet I fall. Present eloquent words (65) [. . .] to the king, [my lord! Thy] servant [and] thy son am I.

EA, No. 289[20]

To the king, my lord, [say]: Thus 'Abdu-Heba, thy servant. At the two feet of my lord, the king, seven times and seven times I [fall.] (5) Behold, Milkilu does not break (his alliance) with the sons of Lab'ayu and with the sons of Arzayu in order to acquire the land of the king for themselves. As for a governor who does (such a) deed (as) this, (10) why does not my king call him to account? Behold Milkilu and Tagu! The deed which they have done is this, that they(!) have taken it, the town of Rubutu. And now as for Jerusalem—(15) if this land does belong to the king!—why like the town of Gaza is it loyal to the king? Behold the land of the town of Gath-carmel, it belongs to Tagu, and the men of Gath (20) have a garrison in Beth-Shan. Or shall we do like Lab'ayu, who gave the land of Shechem to the 'Apiru? (25) Milkilu has written to Tagu and the sons of ⟨Lab'ayu⟩, (saying) "Ye are (members of) my house. Yield all of their demands to the men of Keilah, and let us break our alliance ⟨with⟩ Jerusalem!" (30) The garrison which thou didst send through Haya, son of Miyare, Addaya has taken (and) has put into his residence in Gaza, [and] twenty men to Egypt (35) he has sent. Let my king know (that) there is no royal garrison with me. So now, as my king lives, truly the master of the stable, Puwure, has taken leave of me (40) and is in Gaza; and let my king look out for him! And let the king send fifty men as a garrison to guard the land! The entire land of the king has revolted. (45) Send me Yanhamu and let him take care of the land of the king!

To the scribe of the king, [my lord]: Thus 'Abdu-Heba, [thy] servant. Present eloquent words (50) to the king. I am much more insignificant than thou; I am thy servant.

EA, No. 290[21]

[To] the king, my lord, say: Thus ['Abdu]-Heba, thy servant. At the two feet of the [king,] my lord, seven times and seven times I fall. (5) Behold the deed which Milkilu and Shuwardata did to the land of the king, my lord! They rushed troops of Gezer, troops of Gath (10) and troops of Keilah; they took the land of Rubutu; the land of the king went over to the 'Apiru people. But now even (15) a town of the land of Jerusalem, Bit-*Lahmi* by name, a town belonging to the king, has gone over to the side of the people of Keilah. Let my king hearken to 'Abdu-Heba, thy servant, (20) and let him send archers to recover the royal land for the king! But if there are no archers, the land of the king will pass over to the 'Apiru people. (25) This deed [is the deed] of the son of Milkilu. [So now] (this) is what [the people (?)] [of the land (?) of Keilah (?) have done to me.] So let my king (30) take care of [his] land!

EA, No. 292[22]

To the king, my lord, my pantheon, my Sun-god say: Thus Ba'lu-shipti, thy servant, the dirt (under) thy two feet. (5) At the feet of the king, my lord, my pantheon, my Sun-god, seven times, seven times I fall. I have looked this way, and I have looked that way, (10) but it was not bright. I looked toward the king, my lord, and it was bright. A brick may move from beneath its companions, (15) but I will not move from beneath the two feet of the king, my lord. I have heard the words, which the king, my lord, wrote to his servant: (20) "Guard thy commissioner, and guard the cities of the king, thy lord." Behold, I guard, and behold, I hearken day (25) and night to the words of the king, my lord. But let the king, my lord, *learn* concerning his servant, (that) there is hostility against me from the mountains, so I have built (30) a house—Manhatu is its name—in order to make ready before the archers of the king, my lord; but Maya took it from my hands, and installed (35) his commissioner within it. So command Reanap, my commissioner, to restore the city to my hands, that I may make ready for (40) the archers of the king, my lord.

Further, behold the deed of Peya, the son of Gulate, against Gezer, the maidservant of the king, my lord,

[20] Addaya was the Egyptian resident governor of Palestine, with his seat at Gaza.

[21] In lines 15 ff. there is an almost certain reference to the town of Bethlehem, which thus appears for the first time in history. Keilah may have been the home of Shuwardata, prince of the Hebron district.

[22] Ba'lu-shipti was prince of Gezer in the period following the death of Milkilu, and this letter comes from the middle of the reign of Akh-en-Aton. Maya was a high Egyptian official at the court of the latter, then acting as commander of the Egyptian forces in Palestine. Peya bears an Egyptian name, in spite of the Canaanite name of his mother(?), and he was probably a minor Egyptian officer.

how many days he plundered it, so that it has become an empty cauldron because of him. From the mountains (50) people are ransomed for thirty (shekels) of silver, but from Peya for one hundred (shekels) of silver; so know these words of thy servant!

EA, No. 297[23]

To the king, my lord, my pantheon, my Sun-god, say: Thus Yapahu, thy servant, the dirt (under) thy two feet. (5) At the feet of the king, my lord, my pantheon, my Sun-god, seven times, seven times, I fall. Everything which the king, my lord, said to me (10) I have heard most attentively.

Further: I have become like an empty bronze cauldron (because of) the debt (15) at the hands of the Sutu, but now I have heard the sweet breath of the king, and it goes out (20) to me, and my heart is very serene.

EA, No. 298[24]

To the king, my lord, my pantheon, my Sun-god, the Sun-god of heaven. Thus Yapahu, the prince of (5) Gezer, the dirt (under) thy two feet, the groom of thy horse. At the two feet of the king, my lord (10) the Sun-god of heaven, seven times and seven times I fall, both prone and supine; and everything (15) which the king, my lord, commands me I hear very attentively. A servant of the king am I, and the dirt of thy two feet. (20) Let the king my lord know that my youngest brother is estranged from me, and has entered (25) Muhhazu, and has given his two hands to the chief of the ʿApiru. And now the [land of . . .]anna is hostile to me. (30) Have concern for thy land! Let my lord write to his commissioner concerning this deed.

EA, No. 320[25]

To the king, my lord, my pantheon, my Sun-god, the Sun-god of heaven: Thus (5) Widia, the prince of Ashkelon, thy servant, the dirt (under) thy feet, the groom of thy horse. (10) At the feet of the king, my lord, seven times and seven times verily I fall, both prone and (15) supine.

Now I am guarding the place of the king which is with me, and whatever the king, my lord, has sent to me (20) I have heard very attentively. Who is the dog that does not hearken to the words of the king, his lord, (25) the son of the Sun-god?

[23] Yapakhu was prince of Gezer after the death of Milkilu. By *Sutu* is meant the nomadic tribesmen of Semitic origin who were in Egyptian service, as we know from other documents.

[24] cf. the preceding note.

[25] Note the Indo-Aryan name of the prince of Ashkelon, whose servile words illustrate the impotence to which he was condemned by his nearness to the Egyptian residence at Gaza, as well as by the smallness of his territory.

Letter from Tell el-Hesi[26]

[To] the (Egyptian) officer say: [Thus P]aʾpu. At thy feet I fall. Thou shouldst know that (5) Shipti-baʿlu and Zimreda have plotted publicly and Shipti-baʿlu said to Zimreda: ["The pr]ince of Yaramu wrote to me: 'Give me ⌜six⌝ bows, and three daggers, and three swords. (15) Verily I am going out against the land of the king, and thou art my ally!'" And yet he returns (the charge of) (20) lèse-majesté (saying): "The one who plots against the king is Paʾpu! And send him to (confront) me!" And [now] I have sent Rabi-ilu (25) to bring him (to thee) [because of] this matter.

Shechem Letter[27]

To Birashshena say: Thus Baniti-[. . .]. From three years ago until now (5) thou hast caused me to be paid. Is there no grain nor oil nor wine which thou canst send? What is my offense that thou hast not paid me? (10) The children who are with me continue to learn. I am their father and their mother every day alike [. . . (15) . . . .] Now [behold] whatever [there is] beneath the feet [of my lord] let him [send] to me (20) and let him infor[m me].

Taanach, No. 1[28]

To Rewashsha say: Thus Guli-Adad. Live well! (5) May the gods take note of thy welfare, the welfare of thy house, of thy children! Thou hast written to me concerning silver (10) and behold I will give fifty (shekels) of silver, truly I will do (so)!

Further, and if (20) there is a wizard of Asherah, let him *tell our fortunes* and let me hear *quickly*, and the omen and the interpretation send to me. (25)

As for thy daughter who is in the town of Rubutu, let me know concerning her welfare; and if she grows up thou shalt give her to become *a singer*, (30) or to a husband.

[26] For this letter and its interpretation see *BASOR*, No. 87, pp. 32-38. It vividly characterizes the atmosphere of mutual suspicion and treachery which prevailed in Palestine in the early part of Akh-en-Aton's reign. Zimreda was prince of Lachish (Tell ed-Duweir) and Shipti-Baʿlu was to succeed him in that capacity. As shown by his name, Paʾpu was an Egyptian official, perhaps the local commissioner at Lachish.

[27] For the interpretation of this letter see *BASOR*, No. 86, pp. 28-31. The letter was published by F. M. Th. Böhl, *ZDPV*, XLIX, pp. 321-27. The name *Birashshena* is Indo-Aryan.

[28] For a detailed study of this letter and the other letters found by Ernst Sellin at Taanach, five miles southeast of Megiddo in northern Palestine, see W. F. Albright, *BASOR*, No. 94, pp. 12-27. The tablets were first published, with some photographs, by F. Hrozný in *Tell Taʿannek (Denkschriften der Kaiserlichen Akademie der Wissenschaften, Phil.-hist. Klasse*, L, Vienna, 1904, Part IV), pp. 113 ff., and in *Eine Nachlese auf dem Tell Taʿannek in Palästina* (*Denkschriften*, LII, 1906, Part III), pp. 36 ff. They unquestionably belong to the fifteenth century B.C., and they may be dated roughly about three generations before the bulk of the Amarna Tablets. Rewashsha was prince of Taanach; his Egyptian name illustrates the extent of Egyptian penetration about a century after the initial conquest. The word here rendered "wizard" is Akkadian *ummanu*, which passed into Hebrew as *omman* and into later Phoenician as *ammun*, always with the general sense of "learned, skilled man, expert." The diviners of Asherah appear in the time of Elijah (I Kings 18:19 ff.) as "prophets of Asherah": they also figure in the Baal Epic of Ugarit.

Aramaic Letters

TRANSLATOR: H. L. GINSBERG

Letters of the Jews in Elephantine

"THE PASSOVER PAPYRUS"

A very defective strip of papyrus with writing on both sides. Text: Sachau, 6; Ungnad, 6; Cowley, 21. Date: 419 B.C.

[To] my [brethren Yedo]niah[1] and his colleagues the [J]ewish gar[rison], your brother Hanan[iah].[2] The welfare of my brothers may God[3] [seek at all times]. Now, this year, the fifth year of King Darius, word was sent from the king to Arsa[mes[4] saying, "*Authorize a festival of unleavened bread for the* Jew]ish [garrison]." So do you count fou[rteen days of the month of Nisan and] obs[erve *the passover*],[5] and from the 15th to the 21st day of [Nisan observe the festival of unleavened bread]. Be (ritually) clean and take heed. [Do n]o work [on the 15th or the 21st day, no]r drink [beer,[6] nor eat] anything [in] which the[re is] leaven [from the 14th at] sundown until the 21st of Nis[an. For seven days it shall not be seen among you. Do not br]ing it into your dwellings but seal (it) up between these date[s. *By order of King Darius.* To] my brethren Yedoniah and the Jewish garrison, your brother Hanani[ah].

CONTRIBUTIONS TO THE CULT OF YAHO

A very broad sheet of papyrus with 7 columns of Aramaic; traces of palimpsest. Text: Sachau, 17-19; Ungnad, 19; Cowley, 22. Date: 419 or 400 B.C.[7] See the special study of U. Cassuto in *Kedem*, I, pp. 47-52.

On the 3rd of Phamenoth,[8] year 5. This is (*sic*!) the names of the Jewish garrison which (*sic*!) gave money to the God Yaho, [2 shekels] each.

(Lines 2-119, 126-135 name 123 contributors of both sexes.)

(120-125) Cash on hand with Yedoniah the son of Gemariah on the said day of the month of Phamenoth: 31 *ḳarash*, 8 shekels. Comprising: for Yaho 12 *ḳ*., 6 sh.;[9] for Ishumbethel[9a] 7 *ḳ*.; for Anathbethel[10] 12 *ḳ*.

1 A priest and head of the Jewish community (military colony) of Elephantine.

2 Apparently a secretary for Jewish affairs to Arsames. See n.4.

3 Literally "the gods," but with Hananiah this is obviously nothing but a fossilized formula.

4 Satrap of Egypt from 455/4 to at least 407.

5 The word *psḥ'* in two ostraca from Elephantine may mean "passover (offering)." See Sukenik and Kutsher, *Kedem*, I (1942), 53-56.

6 This restoration is only correct if Hananiah's tradition, like rabbinic law, included under "leaven" fermented corn but not fermented fruit (wine). The Samaritans take a more rigorous view.

7 Depending on whether the fifth year is that of Darius II or of the native Egyptian king Amyrtaeus (cf. Cowley, 35).

8 A month in the Egyptian calendar.

9 Since 1 *ḳarash* = 20 (light) shekels, this is the correct total for 123 contributions of 2 shekels each. The monies for the other two deities were doubtless contributed by non-Jews, Yedoniah (see n.1) acting as treasurer or banker for all the Arameans of Elephantine.

9a Male divinity.

10 Probably female divinity.

SETTLEMENT OF CLAIM BY OATH

Text: Sayce-Cowley, F; Cowley, 14. Date: 440 B.C.

The Jewess Mibtahiah (*Mbṭḥyh*) had apparently married the Egyptian Pi' and then the marriage had been dissolved. The marriage had meant Mibtahiah's exit from the Jewish community and adoption into the Egyptian. Even its liquidation necessitated her swearing by an Egyptian deity. The witnesses to this document are neither Jewish nor Egyptian.

On the 14th of Ab, being the 19th day of Pahons, in the year 25 of King Artaxerxes, Pi' the son of Pahi (*Pḥy*), builder, of the fortress of Syene, said to Mibtahiah, daughter of Mahseiah the son of Yedoniah, an Aramean of Syene of the detachment of Varizata (as follows): In accordance with the action which we took at Syene, *let us make a division* of the silver, grain, raiment, bronze, iron, and all goods and possessions and marriage contract. Then an oath was imposed upon you, and you swore to me concerning them by the goddess Sati. I was satisfied with the oath which you took to me concerning your goods, and I renounce all claim on you from this day for ever.

GREETING FROM A PAGAN TO A JEW

Ostracon. Published by A. Dupont-Sommer, *RHR*, CXXVIII (1944), 28-39. The sender's name, *Yrḥw*, resembles the Palmyrene personal name *Yrḥy*, which in turn is connected with that of the Palmyrene god *Yrḥbwl*. His Aramean nationality is also betrayed by the gods he invokes, Mesopotamian deities favored by Arameans.

To my brother Haggai, your brother Yarho. The welfare of my brother (may) Bel and Nabu, Shamash and Nergal (seek at all times).

LETTER FROM ONE JEW TO ANOTHER OF SUPERIOR STATION

Ostracon. Published by A. Dupont-Sommer, *RHR*, CXXX (1945), 17-28.

To my lord Micaiah, your servant Giddel. I send you welfare and life. I bless you by Yaho and Khn[ub].[11] Now, send me the garment that is on you and they will mend it. I send the note for your welfare.

PETITION FOR AUTHORIZATION TO REBUILD THE TEMPLE OF YAHO

A well-preserved papyrus with writing on both sides, apparently a copy of one sent to Jerusalem. Text: Sachau, 1-2;

11 A famous male deity of Elephantine. If the completion is erroneous, the writer in any case invokes another deity besides Yaho.

Ungnad, 1; Cowley 30. Date: 407 B.C. (Another, defective copy, with some variants: Sachau, 3; Ungnad, 2; Cowley 31.)

To our lord Bagoas, governor of Judah, your servants Yedoniah and his colleagues, the priests who are in the fortress of Elephantine. May the God of Heaven seek after the welfare of our lord exceedingly at all times and give you favor before King Darius and the nobles a thousand times more than now. May you be happy and healthy at all times. Now, your servant Yedoniah and his colleagues depose as follows: In the month of Tammuz in the 14th year of King Darius,[12] when Arsames (5) departed and went to the king, the priests of the god Khnub, who is in the fortress of Elephantine, conspired with Vidaranag, who was commander-in-chief here, to wipe out the temple of the god Yaho from the fortress of Elephantine. So that wretch Vidaranag sent to his son Nefayan, who was in command of the garrison of the fortress of Syene, this order, "The temple of the god Yaho in the fortress of Yeb is to be destroyed." Nefayan thereupon led the Egyptians with the other troops. Coming with their weapons to the fortress of Elephantine, they entered that temple and razed it to the ground. The stone pillars that were there they smashed. Five (10) "great"[13] gateways built with hewn blocks of stone which were in that temple they demolished, but their doors *are standing*, and the hinges of those doors are of bronze; and *their* roof of cedarwood, all of it, with the . . . and whatever else was there, everything they burnt with fire. As for the basins of gold and silver and other articles that were in that temple, they carried all of them off and made them their own.—Now, our forefathers built this temple in the fortress of Elephantine back in the days of the kingdom of Egypt, and when Cambyses came to Egypt he found it built. They knocked down all the temples of the gods of Egypt, but no one did any damage to this temple. (15) But when this happened, we and our wives and our children wore sackcloth, and fasted, and prayed to Yaho the Lord of Heaven, who has let us see our desire upon that Vidaranag. The dogs took the fetter out of his feet,[14] and any property he had gained was lost; and any men who have sought to do evil to this temple have all been killed and we have seen our desire upon them.—We have also sent a letter before now, when this evil was done to us, ⟨to⟩ our lord and to the high priest Johanan[15] and his colleagues the priests in Jerusalem and to Ostanes the brother of Anani[16] and the nobles of the Jews. Never a letter have they sent to us. Also, from the month of Tammuz, year 14 of King Darius, (20) to this day, we have been wearing sackcloth and fasting, making our wives as widows, not anointing ourselves with oil or drinking wine. Also, from then to now, in the year 17 of King Darius,[17] no meal-offering, in(cen)se, nor burnt offering have been offered in this temple. Now your servants Yedoniah, and his colleagues, and the Jews, the citizens of Elephantine, all say thus: If it please our lord, take thought of this temple to rebuild it, since they do not let us rebuild it. Look to your well-wishers and friends here in Egypt. Let a letter be sent from you to them concerning the temple of the god Yaho (25) to build it in the fortress of Elephantine as it was built before; and the meal-offering, incense, and burnt offering will be offered in your name, and we shall pray for you at all times, we, and our wives, and our children, and the Jews who are here, all of them, if you do thus, so that that temple is rebuilt. And you shall have a merit before Yaho the God of Heaven more than a man who offers to him burnt offering and sacrifices worth a thousand talents of silver and (because of)[18] gold. Because of this we have written to inform you. We have also set the whole matter forth in a letter in our name to Delaiah and Shelemiah, the sons of Sanballat the governor of Samaria.[19] (30) Also, Arsames knew nothing of all that was done to us. On the 20th of Marheshwan, year 17 of King Darius.

[12] 410 B.C.

[13] So emend according to Cowley, 31:9.

[14] Perhaps a mistake for "his feet out of the fetter."

[15] No doubt the Johanan of Neh. 12:22, 23.

[16] Perhaps the Anani of I Chron. 3:24; if Ostanes is an alternative name of one of the brothers mentioned there, or if "brother" here means merely "kinsman."

[17] 407 B.C.

ADVICE OF THE GOVERNORS OF JUDAH AND SAMARIA TO THE JEWS OF ELEPHANTINE

Text: Sachau, 4; Ungnad, 3; Cowley, 32.

Memorandum of what Bagoas and Delaiah said to me: Let this be an instruction to you in Egypt to say before Arsames about the house of offering of the God of Heaven which had been in existence in the fortress of Elephantine (5) since ancient times, before Cambyses, and was destroyed by that wretch Vidaranag in the year 14 of King Darius: to rebuild it on its site as it was before, and the meal-offering and incense[20] to be made on (10) that altar as it used to be.

PETITION BY ELEPHANTINE JEWS, PERHAPS TO ARSAMES

Text: Sachau, 4; Ungnad, 4; Cowley, 33.

Your servants Yedoniah the son of Ge[mariah] by name 1, Ma'uzi the son of Nathan by name [1], Shemaiah the son of Haggai by name 1, Hosea the son of Yatom by name 1, (5) Hosea the son of Nathun by name 1, 5 men in all, Syenians who [ho]ld proper[ty] in the fortress of Elephantine, say as follows: If your lordship is [favo]rable, and the temple of ou[r] God Yaho [is rebuilt] in the fortress of Elephantine as it was for[merly buil]t, (10) and n[o] *sheep*, ox, or goat are offered there as burnt offering,[21] but (only) incense, meal-offering, [and drink-offering], and (if) your lordship giv[es] orders [to that effect, then] we shall pay into your lordship's house the s[um of . . . and] a thous[and] *ardabs* of barley.

[18] Erroneous anticipation of the following "because of." cf. also M. Vogelstein, *JQR*, XXXIII (1942), 89-92.

[19] The well-known contemporary of Nehemiah.

[20] The Mazdean Arsames was likely to react more favorably if no mention was made of burnt offering, since it involved the profaning of fire by contact with dead bodies.

[21] See preceding note.

X. Miscellaneous Texts

Egyptian Texts

TRANSLATOR: JOHN A. WILSON

The Authority of Ancient Documents

The Egyptians had a strong sense of past dignity and accomplishment, so that they constantly invoked the authority of previous times in order to give sanction to the present. In literature of various kinds, a frequent statement emphasized the fidelity of the present copy to an older model.[1] A common case lay in the medical papyri, in which the prescriptions were given authority through the claim that there had been discovered an old document which went back to the days of Egypt's first dynasties, and which was also related to the gods or the temples. Thus an anatomical treatise in the Ebers medical papyrus was emphasized as:

BEING WHAT WAS FOUND IN WRITING UNDER THE FEET of Anubis IN LETOPOLIS. IT WAS BROUGHT TO THE MAJESTY OF THE KING OF UPPER AND LOWER EGYPT: Usaphais, the triumphant.[2]

Similarly a section in the Berlin Medical Papyrus:

which was found among old writings in a box containing documents under the feet of Anubis in Letopolis in the time of (King) Usaphais... It was brought to the majesty of (King) Senedj, because of its efficacy.[3]

It was comforting to a man suffering from the itch to know that the prescription for his ailment had been "found during an inventory in the Temple of Wen-nofer," that is, Osiris.[4] That has a matter-of-fact sound, but sometimes the claim bore a miraculous character, as in a remedy credited to the goddess Isis:

This remedy was found in the night, fallen into the court of the temple in *Koptos*, as a mystery of this goddess, by a lector-priest of this temple, when this land was in darkness, and it was the moon *which shone* upon every side of this scroll. It was brought as a marvel to the majesty of the King of Upper and Lower Egypt: Khufu, the triumphant.[5]

For praise of the sages of the past, see the text of pp. 431-432 above. For advice to copy the ancestors, as shown in their writings, see the passage on p. 415 above.

For the recopying of an older text, see the Memphite Theology on p. 4 above. For pious forgeries, cast back into the past, see the discussions of the two legends on pp. 29 and 31.

1 For example, pp. 22, 414, 418.

2 G. Ebers, *Papyros Ebers* (Leipzig, 1875), II, ciii 1-2. This papyrus has been rendered into English by B. Ebbell, *The Papyrus Ebers* (Copenhagen and London, 1937). The manuscript dates from the early 18th dynasty (16th century B.C.), while Usaphais was a king of the 1st dynasty (perhaps 31st-29th century B.C.). The phrase "under his feet" puts the original document in the direct charge of an image of a god in his temple.

3 Berlin Pap. 3038, xv 1-4; W. Wreszinski, *Der grosse medizinische Papyrus des Berliner Museums* (Leipzig, 1909), 33. Senedj was of the 2nd dynasty (perhaps 29th-27th century B.C.).

4 Papyrus Ebers, lxxv 12-13.

5 British Museum Papyrus 10059, viii 11-13; W. Wreszinski, *Der Londoner medizinischer Papyrus . . . und der Papyrus Hearst in Transkription* (Leipzig, 1912), 149. This papyrus is perhaps of the 21st dynasty (11th-10th century B.C.), Khufu of the 4th dynasty (27th-26th century B.C.).

The Interpretation of Dreams

A recently discovered hieratic papyrus gives a reference book for the interpretation of dreams. A few examples—out of more than two hundred—will show the nature of these interpretations. Very commonly the principle of similars is used, either similars of sound, that is, puns, or similars of situation, like the dreams which Joseph interpreted.

The physical arrangement of the text is distinctive. The words, "if a man see himself in a dream," are written once for each column of various dreams. Set in a column over against each dream is the word "good" or the word "BAD" (written in red), followed by the meaning of the dream.

The manuscript presumably comes from Thebes, and is dated to the Nineteenth Dynasty (about 1300 B.C.), although the editor cites evidence that its material may derive from the Twelfth Dynasty (2000-1800 B.C.). Papyrus Chester Beatty III, now British Museum 10683, extracts from recto, i-xi. Published in *Hieratic Papyri in the British Museum. Third Series. Chester Beatty Gift*, ed. by A. H. Gardiner (London, 1935), I, 9-23; II, Pls. 5-8.

If a man see himself in a dream:

(iii 4) white bread being given to him—	good: it means things at which his face will light up.[1]
(iv 3) seeing a large cat—	good: it means a large harvest will come [to him.][2]
(v 19) plunging into the river—	good: it means cleansing from all evils.
(22) [seeing the] moon as it shines—	good: forgiveness to him by his god.
(vii 11) seeing his face in a mirror—	BAD: it means another wife.[3]
(13) seeing himself with a pain in his side—	BAD: taking something away from him.
(28) seeing the catching of birds—	BAD: it means taking away his property.[4]
(viii 5) looking into a deep well—	BAD: putting him into prison.

For an indication that the Egyptians divined through an observation of the stars and the winds, see p. 377 above.

1 Pun: *hedj* "white," and *hedj* "light up."

2 Pun: *miu 'aa* "large cat," and *shemu 'aa* "large harvest."

3 Gardiner, the editor of the text, explains: "to see one's face in a mirror is to discover a second self, which second self must naturally have a wife." Why this is "bad" is not clear.

4 Pun: *ham* "catching," and *nehem* "taking away."

Sumerian Love-Song

TRANSLATOR: S. N. KRAMER

Love-Song to a King

This little poem seems to be a love-song dedicated to Shu-Sin, the fourth ruler of the Third Dynasty of Ur, who reigned sometime about 2000 B.C. It was probably composed by a woman[1] who belonged to the priestly order known as *lukur* by the Sumerians and *naṭitu*[2] by the Akkadians. Only one tablet inscribed with the poem has as yet been found; it was excavated in Nippur and dates from the first half of the second millennium B.C. Its text was copied and published by Edward Chiera as No. 23 of his *Sumerian Religious Texts* (1924). Only recently a scientific edition of the composition, including transliteration, translation, and commentary, was published by A. Falkenstein in *Die Welt Des Orients* (1947), 43-50.

[3]She gave birth to him who is pure, she gave birth to him who is pure,
The queen gave birth to him who is pure,
Abisimti[4] gave birth to him who is pure,
The queen gave birth to him who is pure.
O my (queen) who is favored of limb,
O my (queen) who is . . . d *of head*, my queen Dabbatum,[5]
O my (lord) who is . . . d *of hair*, my lord Shu-Sin,[6]
O my (lord) who is . . . of word, my son of Shulgi![7]
Because I *uttered it*, because I *uttered it*, the lord gave me a gift,
Because I *uttered a cry of joy*, the lord gave me a gift,
A *pendant* of gold, a seal of lapis lazuli, the lord gave me as a gift,
A ring of gold, a ring of silver, the lord gave me as a gift.
O lord, thy gift is brimful of . . . , [lift] thy face[8] [unto me],
O Shu-Sin, thy gift is brimful of . . . , [lift] thy face unto me.[9]
. . . [l]ord . . . [l]ord . . . ,
. . . like *a weapon* . . . ,
Thy city [lift]s its hand like a cripple, O my lord Shu-Sin,
It lies at thy feet like a *lion-cub*, O son of Shulgi.[10]
O my god, of the wine-maid,[11] sweet is her date wine,
Like her date wine sweet is her vulva, sweet is her date wine,
Like her . . .[12] sweet is her vulva, sweet is her date wine,
Sweet is her *diluted drink*, her date wine.
O my Shu-Sin who hast favored me,
O my (Shu-Sin) who hast favored me, who hast *fondled* me,
O my Shu-Sin who hast favored me,
O my beloved of Enlil, (my) Shu-Sin,
O my king, the god of his[13] land!
It is a *balbale* of Bau.[14]

[1] The poem is written in the Emesal dialect of Sumerian, which is known to have been reserved for female deities, and no doubt also for priestesses.

[2] Practically nothing is known of the specific duties of this priestly class, but cf. n.4 below.

[3] By and large our poem seems to consist of a number of four-line strophes, thus: lines 1-4, 5-8, 9-12, 15(?)-18(?), 19-22, and 23-26(?); difficult to fit in are lines 13-14 and line 27. The logical relationship between the various strophes, however, is not too clear. Thus the first strophe sings of the birth of Shu-Sin by Abisimti; the second strophe seems to contain exclamatory lines exalting Shu-Sin, his mother Abisimti, and perhaps his wife Dabbatum; in the third strophe the poet-priestess sings of the gifts presented her by Shu-Sin. The six partially destroyed lines which follow seem to contain a two-line plea to Shu-Sin and four exclamatory lines exalting the king. In the next four-line strophe the poetess probably sings temptingly of strong drink and sexual love. The last lines again seem to be exclamatory in character and leave one with the feeling that the poem is incomplete, unless perhaps we are to understand that the strophe contained in lines 19-22 was intended to be repeated after line 27.

[4] Since "him who is pure" refers to Shu-Sin, our poem provides us with the name of King Shu-Sin's mother and of King Shulgi's wife (or, rather one of his wives); cf. n.7 below.

[5] Dabbatum who is addressed in this line by the poetess as "my queen," is probably the name of a *lukur*-priestess who may have become one of Shu-Sin's wives. In the excavations carried on in Erech before the war, there was found a precious necklace one of whose beads was inscribed with the words "Dabbatum, the *lukur*-priestess of Shu-Sin"; cf. Falkenstein's interesting comment, and particularly his suggestion that one of the duties of the *lukur*-priestess was to participate in a hieros-gamos with the divine king, as representative of the goddess whom she served (*loc. cit.*, pp. 46 and 50).

[6] The king's name is preceded by the god-determinative throughout the poem.

[7] The poem provides us with the significant information that, in spite of the Sumerian King List, Shu-Sin, the fourth king of the Third Dynasty of Ur, is not the son of Bur-Sin, his immediate predecessor, but his brother, and that both Bur-Sin and Shu-Sin are the sons of Shulgi; cf. Falkenstein, *loc. cit.*, p. 45.

[8] Perhaps "eye" instead of "face" in this and the next line.

[9] The punctuation assumes that lines 13-14 form a couplet and that lines 15-18 contain another four-line strophe; cf. n.3 above.

[10] The text does not have the expected "my" before "son of Shulgi."

[11] Falkenstein may be right in suggesting that the "wine-maid" refers to the priestess herself.

[12] The first two signs are hardly to be read (with Falkenstein) $du_{10}(g)$-$du_{10}(g)$, since the third sign would then in all likelihood have been GA, not A; for a similar reason they are hardly to be read *inim-inim* "words." Perhaps they are to be read su_{11}-su_{11} "teeth," though the context seems to ask for a word such as "lips."

[13] "His" instead of the expected "thy."

[14] For *balbale* as a technical term for a specific type of Sumerian composition, cf. p. 42 of this volume. As for the phrase "of Bau," it may imply that the priestess who composed this poem was in the service of the goddess Bau (also pronounced Baba, cf. p. 456 of this volume); for additional details, cf. Falkenstein, *loc. cit.*, pp. 48-50.

Hittite Omen

TRANSLATOR: ALBRECHT GOETZE

Investigating the Anger of the Gods

Text: *KUB*, v, 7.

(2) In the temple of (god) Kismaras. (blank space),[1] unfavorable. [We asked the temple officials and they said: "The] *ḫaršiyalli* vessel has not been poured out [for] 9 days, and the wine portion has been omitted." Bird omina, un[favorable. If it is only this, ditto.[2]] We asked them again and they said: "They omitted the fresh loaves." Bird omina, unfavorable. If it is only this, [ditto[3]]. We [asked them again] and they said: "The daily (ration of) sacrificial loaves spoiled." Bird omina, unfavorable. If it is [only this, ditto[3]]. We [asked them again] and they said: "They continually omit the monthly festival of the third day (and) of the fourth day and [. . . .]" Bird omina, unfavorable. If it is only this, ditto.[3] So [we have] not yet [found the solution].

(7) In the Ea temple (god) Ea held the good symbol in his hand. It is (no longer) there. [. . .], unfavorable.

If it is only this, bird omina, unfavorable.

We asked the temple officials and they said: "The foot of the Sun[4] is broken." Bird omina, unfavorable. If it is only this, unfavorable.

Ditto:[5] "The mountain on which (god) Kallis stands, that mountain was silver plated; the silver on that mountain is chipped off." Bird omina, unfavorable. If it is only this, ditto. The first bird omen was favorable, but afterward it was unfavorable. The monthly festival which they omitted, he will celebrate (it) as it should be. As a penalty they will give 1 sheep, bread (and) beer. The [. . .] festival which they omitted, they will make up for it to the double amount. Favorable.

. . . .

(17) If (god) Huriyanzipas [is angry] in the temple, let [the omina] be favorable. Unfavorable.

We asked the temple officials and they said: "The house [. . . and] it is shaky." Is the god angry for that reason? Let the omina be favorable [. . . . If it is only this, di]tto, let the omina be favorable. Unfavorable.

(20) We asked the temple officials again and they said: "The [. . .] festival has been omitted; the cult stand is not adorned with stars." Is the god angry for that reason? Unfavorable. If it is only this, let the omina be favorable. Unfavorable.

With regard to what was unfavorably answered again—because they sacrificed to the god belatedly, is the god angry for that reason? Let the omina be unfavorable. Unfavorable. If it is only this, let the omina be favorable. Unfavorable.

(24) We asked the temple officials again and they said: "A dog came into the temple, he shook the table and the sacrificial loaves fell down. The daily ration of sacrificial loaves they cut considerably down." Is the god angry for that reason? Unfavorable.

If the god is angry only about the offences that have so far been ascertained by us, ditto, let the omina be favorable. Unfavorable.

We asked the temple officials and they said: "Two deficient people came into the temple. Bird omina, unfavorable.

If it is only this, ditto. Bird omina, unfavorable. We asked them again and they said: "Mutilated people walked about the temple." Bird omina, unfavorable. If it is only this, ditto. The first bird omen was favorable, but afterward it was unfavorable.

(30) The four pairs of monthly festivals which had been omitted—if the god did not feel revengeful because they had made the sacrifices already, ⟨ . . . . ⟩ Bird omina, unfavorable.

They have already celebrated the four pairs of festivals. But as a penalty they will give 1 sheep, bread (and) beer and. . . . Favorable. It has already been given. Because they had omitted the daily (ration of) sacrificial loaves, they will give 30 sacrificial loaves. Bird omina, favorable.

Since a dog reached the table and ate the daily (ration of) sacrificial loaves, they will *discard* the table. For the daily (ration of) sacrificial loaves they will make up twofold and as a penalty they will give 1 sheep, bread (and) beer and. . . . Bird omina, favorable.

Since deficient and mutilated people walked about (the temple), the Hittite Old Woman will perform a rite for the god in the manner to which she is accustomed. Bird omina, favorable.

. . . . (reverse) . . . .

If (god) Ziparwas is not at all [angry in the temple . . . .]

We asked the temple officials and they said: "Three rhyta have been stripped of their precious stones, one rhyton is mutilated; 2 pairs of 'fruit' festivals . . . have not been celebrated." We asked the bird omina: Is the god angry for that reason? [. . . .]

(10) If it is only this, ditto, let the bird omina be favorable. Unfavorable.

We asked them again and they said: "When the entreaty [was due], from 3 palaces they did not give

[1] Apparently the scribe was unable to decipher this passage on the tablet from which he was copying.

[2] i.e. there was an unfavorable answer for the second time.

[3] There was another unfavorable omen.

[4] i.e. of a statue of the Hittite king.

[5] Substitute here: We asked the temple officials and they said.

it, ..." Is the god angry for that reason? Bird omina, unfavorable.

We asked them again and they said: "The daily (ration of) sacrificial loaves, [for x days] they did [not] give it. When they brought up the gods from Dattassa [and . . .], individual cult stands became separated." Is the god angry for that reason? Bird omina, unfavorable.

If it is only this, ditto, let the bird omina be favorable. Unfavorable.

If the Hattian Halkis[6] is not at all angry in the temple, let the omina be favorable. Unfavorable.

⟨We asked⟩ the temple officials ⟨and they said:⟩: "The implements of the god which . . . they have stripped of the silver, he has stripped of the silver. Two *ḫarišanaš*—one of gold and ⟨one⟩ of silver—they brought to Marassantiya, but did not bring (them) back. The festival of the mother-of-god has not been celebrated. For three days the daily (ration of) sacrificial loaves has been omitted. He has stripped the *baldachin* which the god had of its *covering*. The god had a quiver and there were 20 arrows in it; they are gone. The two iron handles of the shield are gone." If the god ditto, favorable.

If (god) SUMUKAN[7] is not at all angry in the temple, let the omina be favorable. Unfavorable.

We asked the temple officials and they said: "One eyebrow of the god is fallen off. The bucks which he had harnessed—of one buck the horns have fallen off. The rhyta (set) with pearls are broken. The alabaster cup is broken. They have stripped the rhyta of their (precious) stones."

(The text stops here, although obviously its end had not yet been reached.)

[6] The Hattic name is Kait; it is probably to be used here.

[7] A god of fertility and patron of the animal life.

Indexes

Contents Listed by Language

I. Egyptian Texts

JOHN A. WILSON

MYTHS, TALES, AND MORTUARY TEXTS

LEGAL TEXTS

HISTORICAL TEXTS

RITUALS AND INCANTATIONS

HYMNS AND PRAYERS

DIDACTIC AND WISDOM LITERATURE

SECULAR SONGS AND POEMS

II. Sumerian Texts

S. N. KRAMER[1]

III. Akkadian Texts

[1] Except when otherwise indicated.

IV. Hittite Texts

ALBRECHT GOETZE

V. Northwest Semitic Texts

Index of Biblical References

The purpose of the following index is to suggest to the student of the Old Testament some significant points of interest in the translations of the texts from the ancient Near Eastern world. The index includes two types of references: first, there are those references to the books of the Old Testament which are listed in the introductions and footnotes to the translations; secondly, there is a listing of biblical analogues suggested by the various contributors to the volume. By the listings of the latter category neither the translators nor the editor venture any scientific opinion with regard to the relationship between the biblical reference and the text cited. Since the noting of these possible biblical parallels was a by-product of the main work of attempting to render accurately the principal texts into English, it is not to be expected that the list be comprehensive. It is intended to be suggestive rather than exhaustive. Scholars who approach this work from a primary concern for the biblical material, it is to be hoped, will be able in subsequent years to enlarge greatly upon this list. This index should be used along with the index of names: many biblical names of persons and places will be found in the alphabetical listing there, rather than according to the chapter and verse of the Bible.

According to the system of reference used here each column of the page of this book is divided into two halves: the first column of the page, into *a* and *b*; the second column, into *c* and *d*. When the biblical reference does not actually appear printed in a footnote or in an introduction to a translation, the reader must read the entire quarter of the page of text or annotation in order to judge what portion of it is intended as a possible parallel to the biblical citation. The biblical references are listed according to the order and numbering of the Hebrew Bible. Numberings used in the English Bible have been given in parentheses.

GENESIS

EXODUS

LEVITICUS

NUMBERS

DEUTERONOMY

PROVERBS

JOB

SONG OF SONGS

RUTH

LAMENTATIONS

ECCLESIASTES

Index of Names

INCLUDED in this index are the names of deities, demons, persons, places, and other proper names which appear in the translations of the texts. In addition this listing includes the names of importance in the introductions and in the footnotes. In choosing the names from the footnotes and introductions some discretion has been exercised in excluding the more general geographical designations which, if included, would have made the index unnecessarily cumbersome.

The simpler forms of the names (the spellings without diacritics) have been used in the index, even though the reference is to a more technical spelling in the footnotes, in the introductions, or within parentheses in the text proper. In most cases the preferences of individual translators in the spelling of proper names have been preserved in the alphabetical listings; the one exception to this rule is in cases where the variant spellings appear in adjacent positions in the index.

Identification of ancient place names should be sought in the footnotes or within the parentheses following the occurrence of the name in the translations, rather than in the index itself. This procedure will enable the reader to be more fully aware of the problems involved in some of the proposed identifications.

In the alphabetical arrangement of the list the *'aleph* (') and the *'ayn* (') have been disregarded for purposes of classification. Likewise the Arabic article, *el-*, either in this form, or when assimilated with the following consonant, does not generally figure in the arrangement of the names. In the transliteration of some names the Semitic *'ayn* is transliterated by the *'aleph* if the name is from a cuneiform text.